'This *Handbook* not only re-thinks and re-conceptualizes the dimensions of global cultural policy studies, but also documents up-to-date policy cases from global north to global south.'

—*Anthony Fung,* Professor, The Chinese University of Hong Kong
and Beijing Normal University, China

'Research and scholarship in cultural policy has grown in recent years alongside a continuing expansion in the interpretation of the concept at a practical policy-making level. How do these developments play out in an increasingly globalised world? This volume brings together a wide range of original essays that consider the political, economic, sociological and cultural dimensions of cultural policy in a context of globalisation and international cultural relations. The contributors are drawn from a variety of disciplines, intellectual traditions and geographical origins. Based on a thoughtful division of the subject matter into coherent sections, and edited by acknowledged leaders in the field, the book will appeal to scholars, researchers and policy-makers concerned about culture and policy in international affairs today.'

—*David Throsby*, Distinguished Professor of Economics, Macquarie University, Australia

'A must-have for any arts and culture scholar, this book provides a walkthrough of the "weird, wired world" of cultural policies around the globe, plus a foundational survey of their roots, theories and practices, from the field's chief protagonists.'

—*Abigail Gilmore*, Senior Lecturer, Arts Management and
Cultural Policy, University of Manchester, UK

The Routledge Handbook of Global Cultural Policy

Cultural policy intersects with political, economic, and socio-cultural dynamics at all levels of society, placing high and often contradictory expectations on the capabilities and capacities of the media, the fine, performing, and folk arts, and cultural heritage. These expectations are articulated, mobilised and contested at – and across – a global scale. As a result, the study of cultural policy has firmly established itself as a field that cuts across a range of academic disciplines, including sociology, cultural and media studies, economics, anthropology, area studies, languages, geography, and law. This *Routledge Handbook of Global Cultural Policy* sets out to broaden the field's consideration to recognise the necessity for international and global perspectives.

The book explores how cultural policy has become a global phenomenon. It brings together a diverse range of researchers whose work reveals how cultural policy expresses and realises common global concerns, dominant narratives, and geopolitical economic and social inequalities. The sections of the book address cultural policy's relation to core academic disciplines and core questions, of regulations, rights, development, practice, and global issues.

With a cross-section of country-by-country case studies, this comprehensive volume is a map for academics and students seeking to become more globally orientated cultural policy scholars.

Victoria Durrer is Lecturer in Arts Management and Cultural Policy at Queen's University Belfast, Northern Ireland, UK.

Toby Miller is Director of the Institute for Media and Creative Industries, Loughborough University London, UK.

Dave O'Brien is Chancellor's Fellow in Cultural and Creative Industries at the University of Edinburgh, UK.

The Routledge International Handbook Series

A full list of titles in the series is available at www.routledge.com.

The Routledge Handbook of Global Cultural Policy

*Edited by Victoria Durrer, Toby Miller
and Dave O'Brien*

LONDON AND NEW YORK

First published 2018
by Routledge

2 Park Square, Milton Park, Abingdon, Oxfordshire OX14 4RN
52 Vanderbilt Avenue, New York, NY 10017

Routledge is an imprint of the Taylor & Francis Group, an informa business

First issued in paperback 2019

British Library Cataloguing-in-Publication Data
A catalogue record for this book is available from the British Library

Library of Congress Cataloging-in-Publication Data
Names: Durrer, Victoria, editor. | Miller, Toby, editor. | O'Brien, Dave, editor.
Title: The Routledge handbook of global cultural policy / edited by Victoria Durrer, Toby Miller, and Dave O'Brien.
Description: New York: Routledge, 2018. | Includes index.
Identifiers: LCCN 2017011463 | ISBN 9781138857827 (hardback) | ISBN 9781315718408 (ebook)
Subjects: LCSH: Cultural policy. | Globalization—Social aspects.
Classification: LCC HM621 .R686 2018 | DDC 303.48/2—dc23
LC record available at https://lccn.loc.gov/2017011463

ISBN: 978-1-138-85782-7 (hbk)
ISBN: 978-0-367-24416-3 (pbk)

Typeset in Bembo
by codeMantra

Contents

Contents

Figures

Tables

Contributors

Devin Beauregard is Doctor of Public Administration from the School of Political Studies of the University of Ottawa in Canada. His postdoctoral work includes cultural policy in a digital age and cultural policy and minorities.

Tony Bennett is Research Professor in Social and Cultural Theory in the Institute for Culture and Society at the University of Western Sydney. He is a member of the Australian Academy of the Humanities and of the Academy of the Social Sciences in the UK. His main books include *Formalism and Marxism* (1979), *Bond and Beyond: The Political Career of a Popular Hero* (1987, with Janet Woollacott), *Outside Literature* (1991), *The Birth of the Museum* (1995), *Culture: A Reformer's Science* (1998), *Pasts beyond Memory: Evolution, Museums, Colonialism* (2004), and *Making Culture, Changing Society* (2013).

Anne-Marie Callus is Senior Lecturer at the Department of Disability Studies, Faculty for Social Wellbeing, University of Malta. She obtained her PhD at the Centre for Disability Studies, University of Leeds in 2011. Her research subject was the self-advocacy movement of people with intellectual disability in Malta. Among other subjects, she lectures and researches on the cultural representations of disabled people, and issues of rights and empowerment especially for persons with intellectual disability. She has worked in the disability sectors in Wales and in Malta since 1994. Prior to her appointment as a lecturer, she worked in special and inclusive education, community-based services, development of disability policy and research about disability issues. From 2010 to 2013 she was the Executive Director of the National Commission Persons with Disability, Malta's disability anti-discrimination body.

Peter Campbell is Lecturer in Sociology and Social Policy at the University of Liverpool. His research to date has focused upon cultural policy and on attempts to align culture and creativity with processes of socioeconomic urban regeneration. In addition to doctoral research studying political discourse and activity regarding the 'creative industries' and their broader social role, he has worked on evaluation of the European Capital of Culture research programme and the London 2012 Cultural Olympiad.

Eun-Kyoung Choi is Lecturer and Executive Researcher of Institute for East Asian Studies at Sungkonghoe University, Seoul, Republic of Korea. Her MA and PhD degrees in the communication and media departments are from Goldsmiths University of London and Loughborough University, UK. Her research interests include political economy of communications, new media studies and Asian broadcasting.

Roberta Comunian is Lecturer in Creative and Cultural Industries at the Department of Culture, Media and Creative Industries, King's College London. She recently published an edited collection on *Higher Education and the Creative Economy* (Routledge, 2016) and numerous papers on creative graduate careers in the UK. She is interested in the relationship between public and private investments in the arts, art and cultural regeneration projects, creativity and competitiveness.

Bridget Conor is Senior Lecturer in Culture, Media and Creative Industries at King's College London. Most recently, she edited and contributed to *Gender and Creative Labour* (with Professor Rosalind Gill and Dr Stephanie Taylor, 2015). Her research interests include cultural labour, screen production policymaking and inequalities in the cultural industries.

Tamsin Cox is Head of Policy and Research at DHA and an Honorary Research Fellow in the School of Sociology, Social Policy and Criminology at the University of Liverpool. She has undertaken a range of work with funding bodies, local authorities, organisations, networks, and events.

Mafalda Dâmaso is a PhD candidate in Visual Culture at Goldsmiths, University of London. Her thesis analyses the visual rhetoric of the United Nations. Her research interests also include contemporary art and international relations and, increasingly, culture and development.

Victoria Durrer is Lecturer in Arts Management and Cultural Policy at Queen's University Belfast. She is Co-founder of the Cultural Policy Observatory Ireland and an Arts and Humanities Research Council, UK – funded research network, Brokering Intercultural Exchange: Interrogating the Role of Arts and Cultural Management. Her research focuses on cultural policy design and delivery, the social processes of cultural production and engagement within institutional settings, the socialisation of arts managers and cultural policy makers and issues of inclusion within the arts and cultural sector.

Maura Edmond is a Research Fellow in the School of Media, Film and Journalism, Monash University, Australia. She has written about arts and culture for a range of Australian publications and cultural organisations. Her research has been published in *New Media and Society, TV and New Media, Screening the Past, Media International Australia, Senses of Cinema* and elsewhere.

Carla Figueira is the Director of the MA in Cultural Policy, Relations and Diplomacy and of the MA in Tourism and Cultural Policy at the Institute for Creative and Cultural Entrepreneurship, Goldsmiths, University of London. Carla is an International Relations graduate of the Instituto Superior de Ciências Sociais e Políticas, Universidade Técnica de Lisboa (Portugal), she moved to London after a career in arts management. In the UK, she went on to gain an MA in Arts Management (City University, UK, Chevening Scholar) and a PhD in Cultural Policy and Management (City University, UK, Praxis XXI Scholar). Her research interests include international cultural relations, cultural diplomacy, cultural policy, language policy, and *lusofonia*.

Beatriz Garcia is Head of Research at the Institute of Cultural Capital, University of Liverpool. She has led international research on the cultural impact and legacy of large-scale urban interventions since 1998, specialising on the local and global cultural policy implications of Olympic Games and the European Capital of Culture Programme. She is the author of *The Olympic Games and Cultural Policy* (Routledge, 2012), chartering 100 years of Games cultural programming, and *European Capitals of Culture: Success Factors and Long-term Effects* (European Parliament, 2013), documenting the programme's first 30 years in operation.

Mark Gibson is Associate Professor of Communications and Media Studies in the School of Media, Film and Journalism at Monash University, Australia. He is author of *Culture and Power – A History of Cultural Studies* (Berg, 2007) and has published widely on cultural and creative industries, media practices and cultural geography. His research interests include cultural economies, the history of communication and cultural studies and suburban cultures.

Rebecca Gordon-Nesbitt is based at King's College London, UK. She is Researcher for an Inquiry instigated by the All-Party Parliamentary Group on Arts, Health and Wellbeing. She obtained her PhD in Sociology from the University of Strathclyde in 2012 and published a study of the cultural policy of the Cuban Revolution in 2015. Her research interests include the social value of the arts and culture and the underlying politics and economics.

Laurie Hanquinet is Senior Lecturer in Sociology at the University of York. Her work has focused on tastes, art museum visitors, cultural participation and inequalities. She is the author of *Du musée aux pratiques culturelles. Enquête sur les publics de musée d'art moderne et contemporain* (2014-Editions de l'Université de Bruxelles) and the editor of *The Routledge International Handbook of the Sociology of Culture and Art* (2016) with Mike Savage.

Javier J. Hernández Acosta is Director of the Business Administration Department and Assistant Professor on Entrepreneurship and Marketing at Universidad del Sagrado Corazón in Puerto Rico. He earned a PhD in Entrepreneurship and Managerial Development at the Interamerican University of Puerto Rico; he has published in several books and journals on topics such as cultural policy and creative entrepreneurship. He is also an advisor for creative industries policies in Puerto Rico.

Louis Ho is Research Assistant Professor at the Department of Humanities and Creative Writing, Hong Kong Baptist University. He was previously Programme Leader of Cultural Studies and Communication Programme and Visual Arts Programme at the Community College at Lingnan University. He received his PhD in Humanities and Creative Writing from Hong Kong Baptist University. Beyond the university, he has continued to participate in various arts and cultural organisations by serving as board member of 1a Space, a local influential art organisation, and Renaissance Foundation Hong Kong. His research interests include cultural policy studies, cultural and creative industries, creative labour, museum and museology, and visual arts.

Shane Homan is Associate Professor of media and cultural studies at the School of Media, Film and Journalism at Monash University, Australia and is currently leading the Australian Research Council project 'Interrogating the Music City: pop and the cultural economy of Melbourne'. He has commissioned reports on the Australian music industries; in 2015 he was involved in reviewing the Victorian Government's *Music Works* program of popular music infrastructure and funding. His most recent book is *Popular Music Industries and the State: Policy Notes* (Routledge, 2016) with Martin Cloonan and Jen Cattermole.

Yudhishthir Raj Isar is Professor of Cultural Policy Studies at The American University of Paris, founder-editor of the 'Cultures and Globalization Series' (SAGE) and author of many scholarly articles and edited volumes on a wide range of cultural policy issues across the world. He is also currently Education Director of the Aga Khan Trust for Culture. Between 2011 and 2016 he was Eminent Research Visitor and Adjunct Professor at the Institute for Culture and Society, Western Sydney University.

Kristina Karvelyte is a Visiting Researcher at the Research Institute for the Humanities and Social Sciences, National Taiwan University. She recently completed her PhD at the School of Media and Communication, University of Leeds, UK. Her work looked at mobility and transformation of the 'creative city' policies – particularly at large-scale cultural events – in Shanghai, Hong Kong and Taipei. Kristina's research interests revolve around Chinese cities, creative cities, large-scale cultural events, urban cultural policies in East Asia and policy transfer/mobility.

Gooyong Kim is an Assistant Professor of Communication Arts at the Department of English, Languages, and Communication Arts in Cheyney University of Pennsylvania, Cheyney, PA, USA. He obtained his PhD in Cultural/Media Studies from the University of California, Los Angeles (UCLA), in 2010. His research interests include Critical/Cultural Studies, Media Studies, Media Aesthetics/ Criticism, Media Literacy, Political Economy of the Media, Philosophy of Technology, Cultural Politics of Neoliberalism, and Social Movements. He is finalising a book manuscript, *From Factory Girls to K-Pop Idol Girls: Cultural Politics of Developmentalism, Confucianism, and Neoliberalism in Korean Popular Music Industry*, which examines how Korean popular music has become a dominant socio-cultural phenomenon since the late 1990.

Yu-Peng Lin is a PhD Candidate in Film and Television studies, the University of Nottingham, UK; he is a member of Campaign for Media Reform [CMR] in Taiwan. His research interest includes informal distribution of media, cultural policy and film industry.

Tony Tai-Ting Liu is Associate Research Fellow at the Center for Contemporary China Studies, National Chung Hsing University, Taiwan. He was a visiting researcher at the Institute for Social Justice, Australian Catholic University. He is the author of a dozen journal articles and book chapters in English and Chinese. His research interests include International Relations Theory, International Political Economy, and East Asia international relations with a focus on China, Japan and Taiwan.

Susan Luckman is Professor of Cultural Studies and Associate Director of the Hawke EU Centre, University of South Australia. She is the author of *Craft and the Creative Economy* (2015) and *Locating Cultural Work* (2012), and co-editor of *The New Normal of Working Lives: Critical Studies in Contemporary Work and Employment* (2018), *Craft Economies* (2018), and *Sonic Synergies: Music, Identity, Technology and Community* (2008).

Kate Mattocks is a teaching fellow in the Department of History & Politics at Liverpool Hope University. She completed her doctoral research, which examined cultural policy coordination in the European Union, at City, University of London. She has held previous teaching posts at City and Richmond University. Kate is interested in many aspects of the politics of cultural policy-making.

Jade L. Miller is Assistant Professor of Communication Studies, Wilfrid Laurier University, Waterloo, ON, Canada. She works on media industries from a global networked and geographic perspective. Her first book, *Nollywood Central*, on the industrial structure and global connections of the Southern Nigerian movie industry, was published in 2016 by BFI Press. Besides her work on the Nigerian movie industry, Dr Miller researches the geographies and implications of film tax credits and the culture of quantification that global Hollywood uses to make sense of new markets for investment and distribution.

Toby Miller is Emeritus Distinguished Professor, University of California, Riverside; Sir Walter Murdoch Professor of Cultural Policy Studies, Murdoch University; Profesor Invitado, Escuela de Comunicación Social, Universidad del Norte; Professor of Journalism, Media and Cultural Studies, Cardiff University/Prifysgol Caerdydd; and Director of the Institute for Media and Creative Industries, Loughborough University London.

Tony Moore is an Associate Professor in Media Studies at Monash University and author of *Dancing with Empty Pockets: Australia's Bohemians* and *Death or Liberty: Rebels and Radicals Transported to Australia 1788–1868*, recently adapted as a major documentary. A former ABC TV documentary-maker and commissioning editor at Pluto Press and Cambridge University Press, Tony heads up a major Australian Research Council project examining the connection between emerging creative arts and popular culture, entitled *Fringe to Famous*.

Graham Murdock is Professor of Culture and Economy at Loughborough University, UK. He has held visiting professorships in Belgium, New Zealand, Norway, Sweden and the United States and taught widely across China. His distinctive writings on culture and communications combine insights and methods from political economy, sociology and cultural studies and have been translated into 21 languages. His recent books include, as co-editor, *Digital Dynamics, The Idea of the Public Sphere, The Handbook of Political Economy of Communication* and *Money Talks: Media, Markets, Crisis*. He is currently working on the transformation of public culture.

Jennifer L. Novak-Leonard, PhD, specializes in the development and use of novel measurement systems to understand cultural participation, and the personal and public values derived from those experiences. Her research considers the role of cultural and creative expression within public policy and enterprise. She is a faculty member at Northwestern University, USA.

Dave O'Brien is the Chancellor's Fellow in Cultural and Creative Industries at the University of Edinburgh. He is the author and editor of several books on cultural policy and writes widely on a range of social science and humanities issues, including cultural work, urban regeneration and public policy.

Seamus O'Hanlon teaches urban and cultural history at Monash University in Melbourne. His research focuses on the impacts of economic, demographic and social change on the architecture and culture of the contemporary city. He has written extensively on the history and culture of Melbourne, with his most recent books *Melbourne Remade: The Inner City since the Seventies* (2010) and *Melbourne's Federation Square: The First Ten Years* (2012). His current research focuses on the history of pop and rock music in Melbourne since the 1960s and a history of the impacts of globalisation on the Australian city since the 1970s.

Jonathan Paquette is Professor of Public Administration at the School of Political Studies of the University of Ottawa in Canada. He is also executive editor of the *Journal of Arts Management, Law and Society*. His research interest includes heritage and cultural policies and arts management.

Phil Ramsey is Lecturer in the School of Communication, and Member of the Centre for Media Research, Ulster University, UK. He obtained his PhD in Media Studies at Ulster in 2011, and his research focuses on cultural policy, media governance and public service media. His work has been published in international journals that include *Media, Culture & Society, International Journal of Cultural Policy, Cultural Trends, Convergence* and *Television & New Media.*

Mareia Quintero Rivera is Associate Professor at the Interdisciplinary Studies Program and the Masters in Cultural Agency and Administration of the University of Puerto Rico, Rio Piedras Campus. She obtained her PhD in Social History from the University of São Paulo, Brazil, in 2002. Her research and publications focus on cultural criticism in the Hispanic Caribbean and Brazil; cultural practices, policies, and social agency. She served as president of the Puerto Rican Commission for Cultural Development, and board member of the Institute of Puerto Rican Culture.

Abiodun Salawu is Professor of Journalism, Communication and Media Studies and Director of the research entity Indigenous Language Media in Africa at the North-West University, South Africa. His major areas of research interest include indigenous language media, development communication, critical studies and new media. He has to his credit numerous journal articles and book chapters. He edited the seminal book, *Indigenous Language Media in Africa*. He was also the lead editor of the book *Indigenous Language Media, Language Politics and Democracy in Africa*. He is rated as an established researcher by the National Research Foundation of South Africa.

Nicola C. Searle is an economist specialising in intellectual property (IP) at the Institute for Cultural & Creative Entrepreneurship, Goldsmiths, University of London, United Kingdom. She obtained her PhD in the economics of trade secrets at the School of Economics & Finance, University of St Andrews in 2010. Nicola is a prominent blogger in the IP community. Her book *Economic Approaches to Intellectual Property* was published by Oxford University Press in 2016.

J.P. Singh is Chair and Professor of Culture and Political Economy and Director of the Centre for Cultural Relations at the University of Edinburgh. His latest book is *Sweet Talk: Paternalism and Collective Action in North-South Trade Negotiations* (Stanford, 2017). His book *Globalized Arts: The Entertainment Economy and Cultural Identity* (Columbia, 2011) won the American Political Science Association's award for best book in information technology and politics in 2012. His current book project is *Development 2.0: How Technologies Can Foster Inclusivity in the Developing World* (Oxford, forthcoming). He has advised international organisations such as UNESCO, the World Bank and the World Trade Organization and played a leadership role in several professional organizations.

Rike Sitas is Researcher at the African Centre for Cities at the University of Cape Town. She received her PhD from the University of Cape Town in Architecture, Planning and Geomatics, focusing on the role of public art in urban knowledge production. Her research interests revolve around the intersection of art, culture and heritage and cities, particularly in the global South. Implicit in this is a fascination with cultural and urban policy coalitions and recasting creative economies and creative cities in Africa. She currently coordinates the Mistra Urban Futures project in Cape Town, manages Public Art and the Power of Place, UrbanAfrica.Net and the Academic Seminar Series at ACC.

Catherine Strong is Senior Lecturer in Music Industry at RMIT University in Australia. She has published on popular music and collective memory, gender and heritage; she is the author of

Grunge: Music and Memory (Routledge, 2011) and co-editor (with Barbara Lebrun) of *Death and the Rock Star* (Ashgate, 2015). She is the reviews editor for *Perfect Beat* journal and Chair of the International Association for the Study of Popular Music, Australia-New Zealand branch.

Ali Akbar Tajmazinani is currently the Dean of Social Science Faculty at Allameh Tabataba'i University (Tehran, Iran) and Deputy President of the Iranian Social Welfare Association. Prior to completing his PhD in Social Policy (Youth Studies) in the UK (holding an ORS Award) he was attached to the National Youth Organization of Iran as Director General of Youth Research Office and Head of International Affairs Department. Tajmazinani has undertaken several research projects and published extensively on youth and social policy with various national and international institutions including the National Youth Organization, UNICEF Representative in Iran, Council of Europe's Youth Directorate, Secretariat of the Cultural Revolution Council, Social Security Research Institute and Tehran Municipality.

Tomoko Tamari is a lecturer in the Institute for Creative and Cultural Entrepreneurship and member of the Centre for Urban and Community Research, Goldsmiths, University of London. She is managing editor of Body & Society (SAGE). Her long standing research interests focus on consumer culture in Japan and Japanese new women, which will be discussed in her forthcoming book entitled, *Women and Consumer Culture: the Department Store, Modernity and Everyday Life in Early Twentieth Century Japan* (Routledge). She has recently published 'Metabolism: Utopian Urbanism and the Japanese Modern Architecture Movement' in *Theory Culture & Society*, (2016) Vol.31 (7–8) and 'Body Image and Prosthetic Aesthetics' in *Body & Society* (2017) Vol.23 (1). She is currently working following areas: Body image and disability; human perception and the moving image; probiotics and immunity; Olympic culture and cities.

John Tebbutt is a Senior Lecturer in the School of Media, Film and Journalism at Monash University. John is a managing editor for 'Continuum' and on the board of *The Radio Journal; international studies broadcast and audio media*. He is a coordinator for the Australian Audio Radio Researcher's Association (ARARA) and researches transnational media cultures with a focus on community and public media.

Hui-Ju Tsai is a PhD Candidate in Social Sciences at Loughborough University, UK and a member of Campaign for Media Reform [CMR] in Taiwan. Her recent published articles include *Fighting the Neoliberalised Media Market & State Interference: The Interdependency of Taiwan PTS and Civil Society Organisation* (2016). Her research orientation is a critical political economy approach to studying culture and communication policies. Tsai is especially interested in creative industries, public service media and the democratisation of mass culture.

Enrique Uribe-Jongbloed is Full Professor at Universidad de Bogotá Jorge Tadeo since January 2017, formerly Professor and Researcher at the Department of Social Communication in Universidad del Norte, Barranquilla, Colombia. He obtained his PhD from the Department of Theatre, Film and Television Studies at Aberystwyth University, Wales, in 2013. His research interests include identity, language and media production. He edited the book *Social Media and Minority Languages*.

Siva Vaidhyanathan is the Robertson Professor of Media Studies and the Director of the Center for Media and Citizenship at the University of Virginia. He is the author of

Intellectual Property: A Very Short Introduction (Oxford University Press, 2017), *The Googlization of Everything—and Why We Should Worry* (University of California Press, 2011), *Copyrights and Copywrongs: The Rise of Intellectual Property and How it Threatens Creativity* (New York University Press, 2001), *The Anarchist in the Library: How the Clash between Freedom and Control is Hacking the Real World and Crashing the System* (Basic Books, 2004). He also co-edited (with Carolyn Thomas) the collection, *Rewiring the Nation: The Place of Technology in American Studies* (Johns Hopkins University Press, 2007).

Jeremy Valentine is Reader in Media, Culture and Politics in the Media, Culture and Performing Arts Division, Queen Margaret University, Edinburgh. He got a PhD in Political Theory at Essex University in 1993. He is a founding editor of the monograph series Taking on the Political. His research interests include political economies of culture, contemporary political thought and critical theory.

Antonios Vlassis is a FNRS (Fonds national de la recherché scientifique-Belgium) Researcher and Lecturer in the Center for International Relations Studies (CEFIR) at the Department of Political Science, Liege University. He obtained his PhD in International Relations from Bordeaux University (France) in 2010, and his scientific contributions have appeared, among others, in the *European Journal of Communication, International Journal of Cultural Policy, Third World Quarterly, Politique européenne, Études Internationales,* and *Cuadernos de Información y Comunicación*. His research and teaching fields focus on international and regional cultural policy, cultural diplomacy and cultural globalisation.

Bethany Waterhouse-Bradley is Research Associate in the Psychology Research Institute at Ulster University, UK. She obtained her PhD in Social Policy at Ulster in 2012 and taught in Social Policy, Sociology and at the Transitional Justice Institute. She worked in migration policy between Northern Ireland and Westminster before returning to take up an academic post in 2015. Her research explores social movements, claims-making and agency in traditionally excluded groups.

David Wright teaches in the Centre for Cultural and Media Policy Studies at the University of Warwick. His research interests are in cultural consumption, popular culture and the politics of cultural participation. He is the author of *Understanding Cultural Taste* (Palgrave, 2015).

George Yúdice is at the University of Miami, FL, USA. He is the author of *The Expediency of Culture: Uses of Culture in the Global Era* (Duke University Press, 2003), *Cultural Policy*, with Toby Miller, (Sage, 2002), *Música, nuevas tecnologías y experiencia* (Gedisa, 2007). He is on the editorial board of the *International Journal of Cultural Policy*.

Amy Camilleri-Zahra is an Assistant Lecturer at the Department of Disability Studies, Faculty for Social Wellbeing, University of Malta. She graduated from the University of Malta with a Bachelor of Psychology degree (First Class Honours) in 2011 and then went on to obtain a Master of Arts degree in Disability Studies (Distinction) at the University of Leeds, United Kingdom. She is currently a Master of Philosophy candidate at the University of Malta with the possibility of transferring to a Doctor of Philosophy degree at a later stage. Her main research interests are gender and disability issues, implementation of the UNCRPD and social representations of disabled people.

1

Towards global cultural policy studies

Victoria Durrer, Toby Miller and Dave O'Brien

- Bulgarian: Единство в многообразието
- Croatian: Ujedinjeni u različitosti
- Czech: Jednotná v rozmanitosti
- Danish: Forenet i mangfoldighed
- Dutch: In verscheidenheid verenigd
- English: United in Diversity
- Estonian: Ühinenud mitmekesisuses
- Finnish: Moninaisuudessaan yhtenäinen
- French: Unie dans la diversité
- German: In Vielfalt geeint
- Greek: Ενωμένοι στην πολυμορφία
- Hungarian: Egység a sokféleségben
- Irish: Aontaithe san éagsúlacht
- Italian: Uniti nella diversità
- Latvian: Vienoti daudzveidībā
- Lithuanian: Suvienijusi įvairovę
- Maltese: Magħquda fid-diversità
- Polish: Zjednoczeni w różnorodności
- Portuguese: Unidade na diversidade
- Romanian: Unitate în diversitate
- Slovak: Zjednotení v rozmanitosti
- Slovene: Združeni v različnosti
- Spanish: Unida en la diversidad
- Swedish: Förenade i mångfalden

European Union Motto, adopted 2000—https://europa.eu/european-union/about-eu/symbols/motto_en

For 40 years cultural policy has had close connections with the complex interaction of political, economic, and socio-cultural dynamics at all levels of society. This relationship has placed high and, at times, contradictory expectations on the capabilities and capacities of the media, the fine, performing, and folk arts, and on cultural heritage.

These expectations are well illustrated by the European Union's motto, quoted above in its official languages. 'United in Diversity' represents the ways in which culture is assigned the role of fostering cooperation whilst symbolising and celebrating individuality and difference. However, this motto, like much of culture and cultural policy, has to do with power, distinction, and protectionism as well as common citizenship, alliances, and bonds. This is due to the global context confronting cultural policies: regional unions, nation-states, and citizens. Consideration, then, of a global sense of cultural policy has much potential to illuminate the social and political world, and has been our goal with this *Handbook*.

The *Handbook of Global Cultural Policy* sets out to explore numerous traditions and histories of culture, policy, politics, and globalization, along with their relationship to one another. This introduction sets out our position in relation to the endeavour to articulate a 'global' cultural policy. We begin by considering the core terms 'culture,' 'policy,' and 'globalization,' giving them some history, theory, and contour. We then reflect on the hybrid that is cultural policy studies. The introduction subsequently turns to an explication of the chapters that make up this collection and the hopes we have for fostering a wider, more global conversation on cultural policy.

Culture

Culture has a weird and wired heritage. It derives from the Latin *colere*, which describes subsistence and slave agriculture. Under capitalism, this understanding of culture bifurcated, as farming and forms of taste took different directions (Adorno 2009: 146; Benhabib 2002: 2). With the spread of literacy and printing, customs gave way to the written word, and cultural texts became important guarantors of authority. Anxieties about cultural imperialism also appeared, via debates over Western domination that occupied intellectuals, politicians, and moral guardians, particularly in what is often referred to as 'the Muslim world' (Mowlana 2000; Briggs and Burke 2003; Kraidy 2010).

The work of Immanuel Kant explains and indexes these changes. He argued that culture ensured 'conformity to laws without the law' and that aesthetics could generate 'morally practical precepts,' schooling people to transcend particular interests via the development of a '*public* sense, *i.e.* a critical faculty which in its reflective act takes account (*a priori*) of the mode of representation ... to weight its judgement with the collective reason of mankind' (1987; also see Hunter 2008). Kant envisaged an '*emergence from ... self-incurred immaturity*,' independent of religion, government, and commerce (1991: 54).

In other words, if readers could interpret art, literature, and drama in logical, emotional, and social ways—and comprehend the difference between them—they could be relied upon to govern themselves. Hence Kant's renowned blend of anthropology and aesthetics. This blend has coloured the social-science and humanities dualities of understanding culture: simultaneously and coevally as custom and text, population and interpretation, number and *noumen*, organization and language, laboratory and library.

By the time of an emergent consumer society, culture became valuable as a means of binding together the social order through custom and keeping people happy through entertainment. However, it was not read or framed as being significant economically, at least not as directly as it is today. Positive discourses about culture saw it elevating people above ordinary life, transcending body, time, and place, or settling us into society through the wellsprings of community, as part of daily existence (Frith 1991).

A further transformation has occurred in the past three decades: from social cohesion to economic contribution. These days, it is close to the *heart* of that economy, thanks to the replicable and hence marketable nature of culture via analogue and then digital techniques of capture and transmission. Nations recognize that a prosperous economic future lies in selling pleasure and ideology rather than agriculture and manufacturing—seeking revenue from innovation and intellectual property, not minerals or masses. This is a moment at which the Global North uses culture as a selling point for deindustrialized societies, and the Global South does so for never-industrialized ones. Here, governmental and corporate manoeuvres alike have internationalized the sale of culture as part of the growing trend towards globalization, as we explain below.

Thus, culture is now more than textual signs or everyday practices, more than objects of subcultural appropriation and re-signification. It offers important resources to markets and nations. Crucial to advanced and developing economies alike, culture can also provide the legitimizing ground on which particular groups claim resources and seek inclusion in national and international narratives (see Yúdice 2002 on Latin America; Kraidy 2010; Pahwa and Winegar 2012 on the Arab world; Yang 2009 on China). This struggle over legitimising ground and economic value, accelerated by technological change, is a crucial animating force for policy associated with culture.

Policy

Policy refers to a regularized set of actions based on overarching principles. All entities, not just governments, make policies, in the sense of regularized plans of actions and norms that they follow. The authority of a policy is founded in transparent rationality rather than in ancestral tradition or individual charisma (Weber 1978). Yet, how culture is articulated and operationalised within policy is historically loaded with socio-political and economic meanings, beliefs, traditions, and values that find both similarity and difference when considered on a global scale. This section thus explores the meaning of cultural 'policy' in this wider context.

Because culture's organic law and lore, and their textual manifestations, represent each 'epoch's consciousness of itself' (Althusser 1969: 108), audiences, artists, cultural producers, governments, and corporations make extraordinary investments in cultural policy. Across the globe, states function through two modes of control: an indirect one, which operates through regulation, taxation, and incentives, particularly of business and markets; and more formal, direct cultural production.

Cultural policy therefore applies to both private and public concerns. Although a strict private-public distinction may be problematic, policies are developed and implemented by businesses as often—if less publicly—as by governments. The same applies to the third sector. Thus, culture lives a hybrid life as a creature of the state, commerce, and civil society. In cultural policy scholarship, this has manifested itself as an implicit/explicit division in characterising cultural policy (Ahearne 2009).

Because culture increasingly transcends both state boundaries and commercial rents, it is often managed by international organizations. This phenomenon is neither new nor entirely dissociated from national citizenship. Away from the utopic hopes of world government on a grand scale, international organizations have been working for a long time, sometimes quietly and sometimes noisily, to manage trans-territorial, cultural, and culturally related, issues from postage to religion to sports. Their business is sometimes conducted at the state level, sometimes through civil society, and sometimes both. This configuration is a core concern for many authors in the collection.

Cultural policy and 'the global'

Cultural policies have informed imperial rapaciousness for a very long time. Spain's *conquista de América*, Portugal's *missão civilizadora*, and France and Britain's *mission civilisatrice* created global anxieties about foreign cultural domination. That has never subsided, and it has been exacerbated by the entertainment dominance of the US over the last century, the co-option of culture for 'soft power' purposes within foreign relations (Nye 2002), and the continued hegemony of post-colonial powers in their former possessions (Mowlana 2000).

Conversely, and indeed for many authors in our collection, culture still holds the promise of transformation for citizens, places, nations, and the world. That promise has been an ongoing feature of the policy discourse on culture—that what may appear to be grounded in particular spaces can transcend them and make for universal understanding, as per Kant's notion of shared critical principles. Despite the equal ability to do the exact opposite, cultural objects, symbols, and processes have thus been imbued with faith that they may foster greater equality on a global scale.

Between the 1950s and 1970s, this tension found expression in public-policy debates through such sources as the Non-Aligned Movement and then the United Nations Educational, Scientific and Cultural Organization (UNESCO). The Global South (known then as the Group of 77, after the number of post-colonial states at the time) lobbied for a New World Information and Communication Order (NWICO) to match the wider search for a New International Economic Order. UNESCO set up an International Commission for the Study of Communication Problems to investigate North-South flows and power (1981). It reported on the need for equal distribution of the electronic spectrum, reduced postal rates for international texts, protection against satellites crossing borders, and media systems that would serve social justice rather than capitalist commerce (Mattelart and Mattelart 1998: 94–97). However, UNESCO soon assumed a more problematic status, confronted with US power, Cold-War stereotypes of freedom, and the contradictions of balancing a universalist idea of cultural pluralism with the Organization's basis in nation-states.

The other site for cultural policy and 'the global' has been trade. There has been a remarkable evolution of global cultural trade since the Second World War. The General Agreement on Tariffs and Trade and its successor, the World Trade Organization, sought to reduce tariff and non-tariff barriers to free trade. This was in the context of differing versions of culture, whether as just one more set of tradable commodities or a *sui generis* human activity. This latter narrative was associated with a defence of public broadcasting and national cinemas to express national identity. This position has continued even in the context of *laissez-faire* evangelism, because sovereign-states continue to include culture as a vital part of belonging, for example, relating citizenship to language skills, knowledge of culture and history, or the embrace of a particular national way of life.

This moment of cultural policy as national identity gestures towards the question of citizenship in a globalised world. The idea of loyalties split through hybrid cultural identifications has long been difficult for citizenship theory and practice, which tends to require unity rather than diversity. Multiple citizenships institutionalize split subjectivity. The impact goes further than querying voting, military service, and diplomatic assistance. It gets to the heart of an affective relation to the sovereign-state and provides a clue to the fragility of citizenship.

Liberal philosophy long held that the integration of migrants would follow from the acquisition of citizenship and a non-discriminatory, culture-blind application of the law, once successive generations mastered the dominant language and entered the labour market as equals with the majority. But, the patent failure to achieve this outcome has seen governments recognizing cultural difference, intervening to counter discrimination in the private sector, and imposing quotas for minority hiring. Migration, and more substantively the challenges of the refugee crisis, shows the limits of cultural policy, citizenship, and globalization.

Cultural policy studies

So how can this weird, wired world be understood? How might we theorise and analyse global cultural policy, if it is both the source of exploitation and the promise of liberation? Cultural policy studies had a marginal, if safe, life within the arts management side of political science, represented by the *Journal of Arts Management, Law, and Society* and an associated annual conference, and in economics, as per the Association for Cultural Economics (now known as 'International') and its *Journal of Cultural Economics*. Then, cultural policy gained status within the humanities. This was a natural, if problematic, location, thanks to a tendency within the hitherto anti-statist, social-movement-oriented field of cultural studies.

Stuart Cunningham suggested 25 years ago that:

> Many people trained in cultural studies would see their primary role as being critical of the dominant political, economic and social order. When cultural theorists do turn to questions of policy, our command metaphors of resistance and opposition predispose us to view the policy making process as inevitably compromised, incomplete and inadequate, peopled with those inexpert and ungrounded in theory and history or those wielding gross forms of political power for short-term ends.
>
> *(1992: 9)*

He called for cultural studies to displace its 'revolutionary rhetoric' with a 'reformist vocation' that would draw energy and direction from 'a social democratic view of citizenship and the trainings necessary to activate and motivate it' (1992: 11). This engagement with policy could avoid a politics of the status quo because cultural studies' ongoing concern with power would ground it in radicalism. Angela McRobbie responded that cultural policy might offer a 'missing agenda' for cultural studies, a pathway to change (1996: 335), and Jim McGuigan made the case for a counter-public sphere and citizenship rights as core values (2004: 21).

This trend within cultural studies, seeking to propel the field into cultural policy, took off at various sites. In late-1980s Australia, it involved both locals and scholars who had departed Thatcher's Britain.[1] In Latin America, similar engagements materialized in the work of Néstor García Canclini (2004) along with many others.[2] In Britain, cognate practice was underway at the Greater London Council (Lewis 1991). In Canada, policy was never far from the concerns of people who are uniquely placed to value and criticize cultural imperialism and its nationalistic counters and who inherit a rich blend of economic and textual analysis.[3] Numerous prominent figures in US cultural studies were similarly dubious about safely side-lined critique. They were either supportive of critical developments or autonomously involved in equivalent tendencies and operated across anthropology, law, sociology, education, political science, feminism, and literary, area, and communication studies.[4]

Cultural policy studies gave rise to the more problematic creative-industries discourse, which differed radically from cultural studies' initial theorisation of policy. This discourse offered those who had been involved in cultural policy a place at the central table of economic policy-making. Although most governments regarded the arts as outside inner-cabinet discussions and quite marginal, communications had always been central. This is due to the vast amounts of money involved in infrastructure and the *gravitas* of those populating it (engineers versus the sociologists and literary critics of cultural policy). Creative industries magically blended these elements and appeared to guarantee a place at the top table. With the business nous of its intellectual founder, Richard Florida, and the imperialistic export of its sponsors in the Australian and British governments, creative-industries discourse became economistic in its claims (Florida 2002; Hartley 2005).

It is perhaps here that one sense of global cultural policy emerges. That is to say, as an area of cultural policy, the development of creative-industries discourse is a key example of how policy rhetoric has come to travel and be interpreted, translated, and transplanted across different nations, languages, cultures, and societies.

Contents

From cultural studies to creative industries is one possible narrative of a series of often-fraught transformations. We have seen culture blend and transcend its early life in anthropological and artistic discourse to become a site of international contestation, even as it succumbs to a wholesale, and far from wholesome, commodification.

The essays that follow offer much greater depth and variety in their account of this environment, and the eight individual parts housing them explore various research questions in cultural policy. Not all of them agree, and in selecting them, we have set common themes alongside longstanding theoretical and political enmities. Indeed, even the most central term, culture, is contested.

The borders between parts are not exact, and we have endeavoured to approach each theme in a variety of ways. This is both to reflect the range of possible takes on issues such as regulation or development and to gesture towards the extension of themes beyond the current academic frames. Obviously, this is open to the criticism that we have been too loose in our associations. However, we hope that the strength of the collection justifies the approach. The approach is an ethos that results in debates, most obviously in our section on regulation, but also in oblique strategies, for example, on rights and regional responses. The scope of cultural policy as a field, along with the range of globalised challenges the world faces, does not fit neatly under one specific theme or idea. We hope to address these challenges through this eclectic and open approach.

Part I: Situating cultural policy

Part I situates cultural policy in relation to other academic disciplines. Its chapters give us cause to review not only the history of theoretical developments in cultural policy-making and cultural policy studies but also how those theories have travelled. Whilst we have emphasized the lineage of cultural studies in this introduction, we look at politics, economics, sociology, and arts management in the opening part, thus reflecting the diversity of cultural policy studies. This range has allowed cultural policy research to grapple with central questions about the role of research *vis-à-vis* policy, practice, and the public. Moreover, it has allowed cross-, multi-, and inter-disciplinary approaches to emerge, which have synthesised the debates and insights of disciplines grappling with both cultural policy as public policy and cultural policy much more broadly, and anthropologically, defined. This eclecticism has seen cultural policy struggle to establish and define itself as a discipline, as opposed to a field of study.

Each chapter traces the ways in which cultural policy mingles with other disciplines. For instance, whilst the relationship between cultural policy research and governments animated cultural studies' initial vision of the field, this has not been the case in political science, as demonstrated by Paquette and Beauregard. They differentiate its engagement with cultural policy from that of cultural studies in several ways by explaining the place of cultural policy research in political science, identifying traces of cultural policy research within political science, and specifying the contributions of political science to studying cultural policy. Searle's understanding of the history of cultural economics, as well as the case study of the economist's understanding of IP (contrasted with a media-studies understanding offered by Vaidhyanathan in Chapter 8), gives a sense of both the disciplinary boundaries and the research possibilities of cultural economics for cultural policy. Moreover, the chapter's case study demonstrates how policy interpretations of IP have global implications in terms of the economic power of particular communities, cultures, and nation-states—a common theme across several parts and chapters.

A much less fractious relationship is found in the final two entries in this opening part, Wright on sociology and Durrer on arts management. For Wright, the relationship between nation-state and cultural policy runs in parallel to the relationship between nation-state and sociology. Indeed, in thinking through the porous boundaries between sociology and cultural policy, particularly in examples from French scholarship associated with Pierre Bourdieu, Wright shows the potential, but also the limits, of cultural policy's relationship to sociology and to policy-making itself. This relationship is also one bound up with the reconstruction, or otherwise, of sociology's attempt to explain the consumption and production of culture in modernity.

In addition to tracing the contours of cultural policy and arts management, Durrer offers a first step in empirically assessing the boundaries and bridges between the two, particularly via the socialisation of arts managers into their profession, which is an increasingly international process. In this context, cultural policy may be viewed as the operational and regulatory context for arts management, thus leaving the practice and scholarship of the arts manager open to political and utilitarian influence. At the same time, mutual benefits between cultural policy and arts management practice do arise, which provide opportunities for policy influence by the practice and scholarship of the arts manager. Durrer's exploration of these issues implicitly calls for greater recognition within cultural policy discourse of the viewpoints, positions, and experiences of individuals (practitioners and policy-makers) who traverse policy.

Part II: Regulating cultural policy

Regulation both concerns the rule-making activities of nations and cross-national bodies and is the site for the emergence and discovery of cultural policy. Part II considers cultural policy and regulation, most notably in the form of cross-, trans-, and international trade. The theme provides a useful route into thinking about cultural policy in two ways. In the first instance, it is the most obvious point for state and culture relations, particularly in settings that have non-institutional, informal, or implicit cultural policies. Second, by thinking about regulation and cultural policy, we immediately draw attention to a way of understanding cultural policy that goes beyond state-funded or state-sponsored arts.

Moving beyond viewing cultural policy within those set parameters is important when conceiving of cultural policy in global terms. We see this immediately in Singh's contribution, which focuses on the international trade and exchange of cultural and creative goods. Whilst much has been done to conceive of culture in international terms, the nation-state is still crucial, as Wright identifies in Chapter 4, to both the meaning and the regulation of culture. In this context, regulation is offered in both defence and prosecution of cultural forms, artefacts, practices, and ultimately identities. Regulation can thus respond to or enable perceived threats from global competition in cultural production. For Singh, there is much potential in trade, particularly if it can be allied to regulation that is deliberative and participatory. However, this form of regulation, perhaps enabled by emerging forms of digital technology, is something that, in his analysis of institutions such as UNESCO and WTO, has yet to emerge.

Murdock and Choi are much less hopeful than Singh about the role of trade and its regulation. In examining the relationship between the US and South Korea, they see it as a vehicle for US interests, rather than for transnational dialogue. They suggest that the regulation of trade in culture needs a remodelled theory of cultural imperialism to understand properly the dynamics of the US-Korea relationship. Critical to their examination is the issue of intellectual property, its protection, and its 'free' trade. Intellectual property, according to Vaidhyanathan, is itself cultural policy and represents a hidden cultural policy regime, particularly in places like the US, which, for Vaidhyanathan, has often marginalised, ignored, or denied the very idea of cultural policy within trade, industrial, educational, tourism, and economic policy. He adopts a comparative approach to IP regulation, situating IP-as-cultural policy in terms of the differing regulatory regimes across the world. In doing so, he develops Singh's and Wright's interests in the nation-state as an important, but potentially frustrating, actor in cultural policy, especially when confronted with traditional cultural expressions or electronic developments.

Through the lens of cultural diplomacy, Figueira provides much thought regarding the potential of cultural policy collaboration on a global scale, outside of the formal regulatory regimes represented by organisations such as UNESCO or WTO. Her analysis of the politico-linguistic Lusophone bloc introduces the literature on cultural diplomacy as a form of cultural policy and considers the Community of Portuguese Language Countries (CPLP) as a manifestation of multilateral cooperation and intervention. The study demonstrates how groups like CPLP may cooperate in ways, however small, that 'mediate global policy agendas' with international policy influence. It is also a case study in the increasing salience of culture to a range of governmental objectives, a theme taken up in the critical reading of cultural governance offered by Valentine.

Governance itself is bound up with the neo-liberal project, a hegemonic discourse for picturing and acting upon social, economic, and political problems. Cultural policy, especially in its globally transferred iterations as creative industries or creative economy, is a manifestation of this set of practices. This raises questions not only about the politics of cultural policy, particularly when enacted in authoritarian settings, but also about the possibility or potential of culture as a site or source of alternatives and oppositions. This issue is particularly acute in rights-based discourses and their relationship to cultural policy.

Part III: Rights and cultural policy

Issues of identity—its recognition and marginalisation—are bound up in explorations of the relationship of rights to cultural policy, and these issues extend beyond the bounds of nation-states. We take three case studies, of disability rights, language rights, and rights in post-conflict societies, to explore the role, or otherwise, of cultural policy. We are left with more questions than answers regarding the promise of, alongside the neglect of rights within, cultural policies.

Recognition of disabled people's rights *in* culture and *as* culture, emphasised by Callus and Camilleri-Zahra, is often absent in the literature on cultural policy. Here, rights are the source of a transformed, and transformative, cultural policy. A similar line of thought, framed through the paradigm of cultural sustainability, runs through Uribe-Jongbloed and Salawu's comparison of minority language media in Colombia and South Africa. They present a dilemma for cultural policy, of how to balance the demands of nation-states seeking cohesive, often linguistically unified, cultures whilst giving recognition to linguistic, and thus cultural, difference. Again, cultural policy provides the source of possibility, albeit from the very same starting point that seems to limit linguistic and cultural autonomy within the project of the nation-state. What is necessary is an intercultural approach to the state. However, as Uribe-Jongbloed and Salawu observe, there is much to be done in order to make sure that cultural policy does not stay only at the policy level but engages with cultural sustainability practices of exchange and interaction, beyond just awareness and promotion of minority languages.

In Northern Ireland, Ramsey and Waterhouse-Bradley's case study, cultural citizenship has proven to be a mode of oppositional and binary divisions, rather than the exchanges and interactions identified by Uribe-Jongbloed and Salawu's consideration. Indeed, the question of the rights of communities is superseded by economic development as the core focus for cultural policy in Northern Ireland, perhaps because the economy is a site around which political consensus may most easily be garnered. Still, this situation represents both a missed opportunity and a fundamental misreading of the purpose and potential of cultural policy itself.

Part IV: Practice and cultural policy

Rights are, of course, grounded in practices. This part on practice is intended to reflect a diverse understanding of cultural policy as enacted in a range of national and international settings. These eclectic chapters were commissioned with the aim of illustrating the vast range of practices that can be associated with the idea of cultural policy. The practices are intended to bridge questions of disciplinary boundaries, regulation and rights, as well as the issues, development, and national case studies offered in later parts. They bring to life the importance of global perspectives on cultural policy that can be the basis of a positive academic contribution and practical intervention.

The chapters presented here show how cultural policies can be representations of global power. For instance, the practices of gifting and curating the UN's art collection or the work of the Confucius Institute promote a particular desired view on the part of the nation-states participating: one can see that the promise of genuine and equal international cooperation outlined earlier by Figueira remains unfulfilled. Yet, cultural policies themselves can wield power—with the notion of the 'creative city' being one of the most travelled. Whatever the differences in local contexts, though, the zero-sum game of competition between cities will be replicated, as Karvelyte shows in relation to Shanghai and Hong Kong.

The mobility of neoliberal cultural policies has had great impact on (and exploitation of) cultural work, despite its limited investigation in cultural policy studies until recently. Cultural work becomes visible in cultural policy, as education, skills, or labour. In stressing these connections and moments of visibility, Comunian and Conor unpack the broader cultural- and creative-industries discourse that dominates much cultural policy, whilst returning to a narrative of potential in cultural policy. The 'invisibility' of cultural work is not a natural product of the business models of cultural and creative industries. Rather, cultural policy must be open about the problems of cultural work, to challenge explanation and foreground workers too often left out of celebratory policy discourses.

Case studies from Australian cultural production and cultural audiences develop this area of practice. Gibson, Moore, and Edmond think through the relationships and transitions between fringe activities, such as post-punk music, comedy, and film, and commercial or popular audiences. Traditionally, the opposition between the business facing creative economy and the more 'culturalist' narratives of value has framed that relationship. Rather than straightforwardly solving this tension by arguing that the fringe provides innovation for the famous, they engage the seemingly rigid boundaries between culture and commerce, as well as questioning the linear narrative of innovation. This approach tells us of a much more complex position for cultural policy, where ideas of 'excellence' may produce a static version of culture, and 'innovation' may be equally reductionist.

Novak-Leonard articulates audience research as an important part of cultural policy in the US, where there is an absence of the more formal traditions of Arts Councils or ministries of culture found in other nations' cultural policy systems. This chapter explains the struggle for a broader definition of 'the arts' in academic, state, organizational, and foundation-based research, presenting US cultural policy with the question of 'how, or whether, the current deeply rooted infrastructure surrounding non-profit arts organizations can serve as bridges to achieving real equity/diversity of art forms and means of engagement?'

Gordon-Nesbitt's essay addresses an area that may become an important form of cultural policy over the next decade, as both medical practice and the cultural sector search for new ways to deal with the consequences of an ageing population in certain parts of the world. The chapter is part of a larger debate over the ability of the arts to fit into the current taste for evidence-based forms of policy-making, which allows Gordon-Nesbitt to reflect on the underlying trends shaping how research is done in this area of cultural policy. Health outcomes are, of course, related to a range of wider social and economic issues grounded in inequality. This concept, which demonstrates culture's inextricable link to socio-economic and political dynamics, segues into the following part on issues and responses.

Part V: Global issues, regional cultural policy

Part V attempts to connect the global issues confronting cultural policy with various regional responses. It begins with a consideration of inequality, perhaps the defining issue of our age, encompassing economic, social, and cultural issues, and giving rise to a vast array of complex policy problems.

Hanquinet addresses inequality and cultural policy through a detailed engagement with Bourdieu. In assessing the implications of cultural capital, Hanquinet thinks through debates over forms of cultural consumption, such as omnivorous and 'emerging' cultural capital, that frame the relationship between cultural policy and inequality. Indeed, it is only by knowing how cultural capital is formed, maintained, and replicates social inequality that cultural policy can address this pressing issue through cultural diplomacy, transnational cultural cooperation, and the commercial market.

Creative-industries discourse offered to unify the commercial imperatives of mass culture with the elite aesthetics favoured by state support. However, this has not proven to be the case, particularly as commercial cultural forms did not achieve state recognition in the form of institutions and funding, and neither did cultural elements associated with state legitimacy become foci of creative activity. Luckman's and Ho's chapters offer two perspectives on this narrative within creative industries' influence on cultural policy. They illustrate the constructed nature of creative industries as a problem for cultural policy, rather than simply an economic opportunity. These perspectives from Hong Kong and Australia are cognisant of the global nature of creative-industries discourse and its impact on specific parts of the world. Luckman gives a broad overview of creative industries, charting the lines of flight that this concept has taken across the globe and outlining questions of space, place, gender, and even the idea of culture itself. This poses a challenge and opportunity for cultural policy: how to develop new ways to articulate the value of culture to a wider public.[5]

Ho uses Hong Kong to argue in defence of arts and cultural policies in the face of a global, perhaps hegemonic, policy framework. He defends culture in the face of a creative-industries policy that has done much to transform Hong Kong at the cost of marginalising cultural practitioners. This defence of cultural policy echoes the articulation of values that ends Luckman's contribution. It is taken up in the practices analysed by Garcia.

Mega-events are perhaps the highest profile and most visible form of cultural policy, and often come with a global audience. They are seductive to policy-makers, promising that the urban transformations that Ho shows are associated with creative-industries discourses, whilst at the same time seeming to play a role in cultural diplomacy, arts, and health, alongside more diffuse, but no less significant, cultural impacts. Garcia uses the Olympics to bring out some of these tensions, notably in the importance of cultural policy to local organisers of a mega-event versus its lack of significance to global stakeholders and audiences. This is most notably due to the mediatized nature of the mega-event, a moment of important intersection between cultural and media policy. Here, cultural policy 'becomes a tool to condense time and place into spectacular images and phrases' to rebrand or reimagine the host city and host nation. However, this reduces the potential of cultural policy contributing to brand or image construction and management, which are often at odds with local interests and expectations. It is only through action by international bodies, regional organisations, and national governments, in conjunction with local stakeholders, that the undoubted potential, which is often left aside in the reductionist form of image-based mega-events, can be realised.

The phenomenon of mega-events transitions the part to two concrete regional examples, which, in turn, open the discussion of development in Part VI. The first example is a new translation of a recent piece by Yúdice, focused on Latin America. His chapter sketches a predominant global challenge—the problem of who will provide the essential public service of digital connectivity. This is read through the lens of changes in cultural enjoyment, the bio-politics of those changes, and the political economy of this new media scenario. The regional issues are framed by the boom in the use of information and communications technology (ICT) by younger parts of the Latin American population. At the same time, the embedding of ICT as an essential part of the human experience within an internet of things, points towards the increasing marginalization of governmental actors in this area of culture and thus cultural policy. Google and Facebook, core platforms of contemporary capitalism, demand regional responses as they supplant traditional media and physical infrastructure to dominate cultural life. However, the demand for a regional response often produces complex manifestations, as in the case of the EU.

The EU is a pre-eminent example of regional cooperation across a range of economic, social, and political activities. Yet, as made implicit at the start of our introduction, the question of culture has often been marginal to the formal operations of the EU, whilst being essential to the broader project of European integration. The latter is obvious in event-led activity such as the European Capital of Culture, or creative and knowledge economy discourses, but less apparent if one looks for a formal EU cultural policy. Mattocks grapples with this question from the perspective of governance, seeking to understand how decisions over culture are made, as well as offering a cultural understanding of the EU itself. This dual approach presents a complex task, given the fragmented nature of EU decision-making, and perhaps the Union itself, and the disputed meaning and nature of the term culture. Mattocks' able route through this complex and fragmented regional assemblage provides an historical analysis of the EU and cultural policy, examples of specific policy programmes, such as the 2007 Agenda for Culture, and a map of key actors, including the European Commission and European Parliament. In the course of describing both the institutions and actions of EU cultural policy, Mattocks demonstrates the need for more attentiveness to regional cultural policy, its impact at the cross-national level, and the potential of scholarship to shed light on contested institutions and political programmes. The lack of connection between policy and practice is made clear.

Part VI: Development and cultural policy

Development has become an important part of both cultural policy practice and research. In part, this is driven by the assumption that culture can have positive impacts at social, urban, and national levels that are akin to those on individuals. It is also bound up with the role of culture in the Enlightenment's project of colonisation. The contested space of cultural policy and development thus deserves proper attention in any discussion of global cultural policy.

The part begins with Vlassis' overview of the politics of culture and development, addressing four crucial questions: 'Who seeks to set an international policy agenda on the 'culture-development' nexus, for what reasons, under which conditions, and with which outcomes?' These four questions are related to four policy agendas, from free trade, through diversity of cultural expressions and the creative economy, to intangible cultural heritage. Vlassis shares the concerns of Singh, Murdock, Damaso, and Liu, as to the practices and ideologies of cross-national institutions. By presenting the history of these four agendas for development, Vlassis draws attention to the impact of the digital age on the assumptions underpinning previous cultural policy and development concepts.

A practical manifestation of Vlassis' reflections comes from Quintero Rivera and Hernández Acosta. They discuss the Puerto Rican Commission for Cultural Development, which is centred on a proposed, if not consistently actual, devolution of decision-making power to citizens. They detail the process of academic engagement in formulating new cultural policies in a development context. The dilemma posed by their narrative concerns the struggle to implement recommendations that have emerged from a participative policy-making process that might have reframed the social purpose of culture in Puerto Rico. They emphasize the potential for cultural policy, through participatory methodologies, to re-imagine development strategies away from the application of cultural policy for linear, externally imposed, development agendas that emphasise economic gains, towards ones that see culture as a 'transversal and fundamental dimension of public policy.'

The part closes with two pieces in which the promise of cultural policy is much more uncertain and contested. Tsai and Lin offer an explicitly critical position on the role of cultural policy in promulgating creative-economy discourses in Taiwan. The import of British creative-economy discourses, via a new National Development Fund focused on the profitability of films, failed to develop the domestic film industry. This shows the limits of market-oriented forms of cultural policy, whether for development or more general goals. They assert the need for longer-term policy engagement and planning, and the role of a cultural exception for films, if cultural policy is to develop Taiwanese film.

The problematic relationship between cultural policy and economic development continues in the case of Melbourne, Australia, as a 'music city.' Strong, Homan, O'Hanlon, and Tebbutt juxtapose the objectives of the contemporary city and state with community production and consumption of music. The question for cultural policy is how to read the distance between the two sides—whether as a question of balancing competing claims, integrating oppositional agendas, or, as Quintero Rivera and Hernandez Acosta have demonstrated in Puerto Rico, transforming cultural policy itself. The remaining question is how to ensure diverse voices in a context where, as Strong, Homan, O'Hanlon, and Tebbutt comment, 'music is increasingly framed as an economic good rather than as a fundamental aspect of social life.'

Part VII: The nation-state and cultural policy

Our final substantive part addresses the various themes analysed in previous parts at the national level. Notwithstanding the global focus of the book, and the attempt by many individual chapters to apply a cross-national lens to their case studies and theoretical insights, the nation-state remains central to many of the essays. As such, it is appropriate to draw on individual contributions that look at particular nation-states, both as examples of wider trends, such as the use of mega-events for cultural policy in Japan, or because those states have been under-represented in mainstream cultural policy research; Iran and India provide useful examples of this line of thought. Here, we have chosen to combine nations that have previously been peripheral to some cultural policy discussions, such as Iran, India, and South Africa, with countries that have been important to understanding the need for a global understanding of cultural policy, such as Japan and South Korea. These case studies open up the possibility of understanding a rich and complex cultural policy landscape.

We set these chapters alongside the UK, a nation that has been important to shared *clichés* of cultural policy practice, such as mega-events and the creative industries. It is obviously difficult to draw together different national experiences of cultural policy. Key themes can be found in the tensions created by cultural policy's relationship with projects of nationalism and state-building. Isar begins the section, looking at the oxymoron of cultural policy in India. This frame results from the implicit status of much of cultural policy in India. Whilst this situation results in the fragmentary settlement described by Isar, it also opens the possibility of understanding a rich and complex cultural policy landscape. This is the backdrop for the rise of a contested cultural politics, focused on religious cultural policing, allied to a changing political context in which appointments to cultural institutions are shaped by a counterattack against secularist and pluralist voices.

Tajmazinani's chapter on Iran serves to extend Isar's analysis into a setting where explicit cultural policy has been vital to national transformation. Indeed, the Iranian situation is best captured through the concept of 'Cultural Engineering,' aligning economic, social, and political policy with the overall cultural orientation of the Islamic Revolution. This is a striking contrast to many other cultural policy examples, whereby the dominance of economic conceptions of culture is inverted to serve the state's primarily cultural, revolutionary ends.

Kim offers a very different example from South Korea, using K-pop to demonstrate the impact of a more general neo-liberal turn in Korean cultural and social policy. K-pop has been a central part of the reimagining of Korea in the democratic era, but it is intertwined with the gendered exploitation of those seeking commercial and cultural success. There is an over-determination of the role of cultural policy in the Korean case, resulting in the need for a more nuanced reading of the national context, the broader political economy of cultural production, and the neo-liberal discourses of individualisation animating the supposed success of the Korean national brand.

The remaining chapters, by Campbell and Cox, Tamari, and Sitas, locate their national engagements at the urban level. Campbell and Cox offer a commentary on the rise to dominance of a British model for doing urban regeneration with culture, by analysing the production of evidence of impact. The use of culture for urban regeneration, and the rise of specific forms of evidence and evidential practice, is one dominant form of cultural policy shared across all of Britain's nations. The British case study, we should note, is a warning as to the limits of evaluations and evidence-based policy-making for culture.

Tamari's case study of Japan draws together the thinking of several other chapters that have engaged with the use of mega-events for city and nation branding. Ultimately, Tamari narrates the promise of cultural policy as an act of consensus making around citizen participation in culture. She does so by situating the forthcoming Tokyo Olympics in the broader sweep of Japanese cultural policy, through initiatives such as Cool Japan, to the emergence of creative city discourses for Tokyo 2020. In this focus, the chapter reveals historic, colonial, and geopolitically informed influences shaping how cultural policies travel across the globe.

This movement is a focus of the chapter by Sitas, who situates South Africa cultural policy within a context of what she describes as 'global policy mobilities'. In the South African context, the inequalities associated with cultural-economy practices have a racialised character, with disproportionate benefits accruing to those who are white. Sitas uses the Public Art and the Power of Place project, based in Cape Town, as a way of illustrating global and local cultural policy relationships, alongside the potentially unequal impact of current South African approaches. The urban setting illustrates the limits of global forms of cultural policy externally imposed upon communities, whilst gesturing towards a more attentive, place-based, cultural policy.

Conclusions

The collection concludes with two essays that address fundamental challenges for cultural policy. On the one hand, we are confronted with the issue of what is successful cultural policy, in a context that seems to eschew formal cultural policy; on the other, the meaning of culture itself. These contributions offer an unsettling question for cultural policy, as to the limits of success and the need for its existence.

Miller's essay on 'Nollywood' concentrates on the development of the alternative, populist Nigerian film industry as an example of cultural production in the absence of cultural policy, notably intellectual property protection and formal arts funding, two important pillars of the discussions of cultural policy throughout this collection. Transformations in the technological basis for cultural production suggest that there will be much to learn from the Nigerian experience if we are to answer the question of what is a successful cultural policy.

Bennett, who has done much to shape cultural policy research, returns us to the question at the heart of cultural policy studies and practice, which is the meaning of culture itself, who determines that meaning, and in what context it is interpreted and promulgated. He offers a powerful critique of the idea of culture in contemporary cultural policy through analysing what he describes as 'a distinctive episode in the political career of the cultural concept.' This episode is a theoretical period in time, if you will, that ranges from Franz Boas' impact on American anthropology, through British cultural studies. He demonstrates how aesthetics may reflect global issues of power and, particularly, racial exclusion. This argument presents a challenge to those of us, as researchers, authors, and editors, who seek to defend the potential of cultural policy. Bennett demands a new agenda for an emancipatory cultural policy that considers culture's relationship to 'questions of power, history and value' (Hesmondhalgh and Saha 2013: 179).

As editors, we write from particular standpoints, reflecting our location within the British, Colombian, and Australian academic systems. Taking a global perspective on cultural policy studies has been a humbling and incomplete task. Absences and blind spots are inevitable, but we trust that it will help to build a picture of how—to borrow a term from Bennett's chapter that closes the collection—cultural policy has been 'patterned' across the globe, whether in international or global versions. With this *Handbook*, we aim then to develop a conversation about the need for *global* scholarship. This scholarship will emerge from political, social, and environmental contexts in which understanding the interconnectedness, alongside the difference, of cultural perspectives is essential.

The chapters presented here show the inter- and transnational mobility of cultural policies; instances in which policies have been normalised, but also altered, through their global mobility. As a result, cross-cultural policy movement and influence are not just about the application or transplantation of a particular policy—with creative industries being the most obvious example—to a new location. Differences are recognisable. One instance is the theoretical approaches underpinning how cultural policies are varyingly and individually articulated and formed within and between different nations. Language and meaning are part of the story of a global cultural policy—one that is continually forming. What emerges from the collection is that many cultural policy concerns are shared across the globe. These include issues related to rights: identity, diversity, heritage, and belonging, as well as marginalisation and inequality—social, cultural, spatial, and economic. The potential of regional and cultural collaboration and cooperation is made evident alongside historically based geopolitical domination. Overall, however, the chapters reveal a sense of optimism for the potential of cultural policy studies itself.

Notes

1 Apart from Cunningham, key figures included Tom O'Regan, Tony Bennett, David Saunders, Ian Hunter, and Colin Mercer.
2 We'd mention Rosalía Winocur Iparraguirre, Ana Rosas Mantecón, Daniel Mato, Ana Maria Ochoa Gautier, Bianca Freire, Alejandro Grimson, João Freire Filho, and Eduardo Nivón.
3 They include Will Straw, Rebecca Sullivan, Jody Berland, Ric Gruneau, Charles Acland, the late Paul Attalah, Michael Dorland, Clive Robertson, Bart Beaty, Ron Burnett, David Taras, Ira Wagman, Vincent Mosco, Serra Tinic, Yuezhi Zhao, and Catherine McKercher.
4 A quick list would feature the late James Carey, Manju Pendakur, Larry Grossberg, Andrew Ross, Bill Grantham, Paula Chakravartty, Jennifer Holt, Fred Myers, George Marcus, Lisa Parks, Ellen Seiter, Cameron McCarthy, Paula Treichler, David Kennedy, Rob Nixon, Arvind Rajagopal, Cristina Venegas, George Yúdice, Tom Streeter, Larry Gross, Kelly Gates, Herman Gray, Rick Maxwell, Faye Ginsburg, Michael Hanchard, James Hay, and Michael Curtin.
5 We note that this is a typical anxiety of the Global North. This value is pretty much taken for granted, for example, across Latin America.

References

Adorno, Theodor W. (2009). "*Kultur* and Culture." Trans. M. Kalbus. *Social Text* 99: 145–58.
Ahearne, Jeremy. (2009). "Cultural Policy Explicit and Implicit: A Distinction and Some Uses." *International Journal of Cultural Policy* 15(2): 141–53.
Althusser, Louis. (1969). *For Marx*. Trans. Ben Brewster. Harmondsworth: Penguin.
Benhabib, Seyla. (2002). *The Claims of Culture: Equality and Diversity in the Global Era*. Princeton: Princeton University Press
Briggs, Asa and Peter Burke. (2003). *A Social History of the Media: From Gutenberg to the Internet*. Cambridge: Polity Press.

Cunningham, Stuart. (1992). *Framing Culture: Criticism and Policy in Australia*. Sydney: Allen and Unwin.

Florida, Richard. (2002). *The Rise of the Creative Class and How It's Transforming Work, Leisure and Everyday Life*. New York: Basic Books.

Frith, Simon. (1991). "The Good, the Bad, and the Indifferent: Defending Popular Culture from the Populists." *Diacritics* 21(4): 102–15.

García Canclini, Néstor. (2004). *Diferentes, desiguales y desconectados: Mapas de interculturalidad*. Barcelona: Editorial Gedisa.

Hartley, John, ed. (2005). *Creative Industries*. Malden: Blackwell.

Hesmondhalgh, D. and Saha, A. (2013). "Race, Ethnicity, and Cultural Production." *Popular Communication* 11(3): 179–95.

Hunter, Ian. (2008). "Critical Response II: Talking about My Generation." *Critical Inquiry* 34(3): 583–600.

International Commission for the Study of Communication Problems. (1981). *Many Voices One World: Towards a New, More Just, and Efficient World Information and Communication Order*. London: Kogan Page; New York: Unipob; Paris: UNESCO.

Kant, Immanuel. (1987). *Critique of Judgment*. Trans. Werner S. Pluhar. New York: Hackett Publishing.

Kant, Immanuel. (1991). *Metaphysics of Morals*. Trans. M. Gregor. Ed. R. Guess. Cambridge: Cambridge University Press.

Kraidy, Marwan M. (2010). *Reality Television and Arab Politics: Contention in Public Life*. Cambridge: Cambridge University Press.

Lewis, Justin. (1991). *Art, Culture, and Enterprise: The Politics of Art and the Cultural Industries*. London: Routledge.

Mattelart, Armand and Michèle Mattelart. (1998). *Theories of Communication: A Short Introduction*. Trans. S. G. Taponier and J. A. Cohen. London: Sage.

McGuigan, Jim. (2004). *Rethinking Cultural Policy*. Maidenhead: Open University Press.

McRobbie, Angela. (1996). "All the World's a Stage, Screen or Magazine: When Culture is the Logic of Late Capitalism." *Media, Culture & Society* 18(3): 335–42.

Mowlana, Hamid. (2000). "The Renewal of the Global Media Debate: Implications for the Relationship between the West and the Islamic World." *Islam and the West in the Mass Media: Fragmented Images in a Globalizing World*. Ed. Kai Hafez. Cresskill: Hampton Press. 105–18.

Nye, Joseph S. (2002). "Limits of American Power." *Political Science Quarterly* 117(4): 545–59.

Pahwa, Sonali and Jessica Winegar. (2012). "Culture, State and Revolution." *Middle East Report* 42: 263.

Weber, Max. (1978). *Economy and Society: An Outline of Interpretive Sociology*. Ed. Guenther Roth and Claus Wittich. Berkeley: University of California Press.

Yang, Guobin. (2009). *The Power of the Internet in China: Citizen Activism*. New York: Columbia University Press.

Yúdice, George. (2002). *El recurso de la cultura: Usos de la cultura en la era global*. Barcelona: Editorial Gedisa.

Part I
Situating cultural policy

2

Cultural policy in political science research

Jonathan Paquette and Devin Beauregard

Introduction

Academic disciplines are, for better or worse, characterised by a certain sense of unity. They often share a common core of literature and – if only minimally – definition(s) of their object(s) of study. When students join a field, they subject themselves to a number of activities aimed at giving them the basic knowledge and essential references to that field. The socialisation process at play in a student's education also conveys a number of competencies and dispositions that are seen as essential for progression in the field. When reflecting upon academic disciplines, the narrative of unity is important; it is a belief we entertain about the social world – especially when we approach the world through the lenses of education, training, and socialisation. When we introduce the narrative of research into the equation, academic disciplines – as social worlds – appear less homogeneous: less consensual and more competitive. A sociological look at academia reveals a paradoxical juxtaposition of unity and diversity, of divisions or fractures. These divisions can serve to shape the identity of a discipline; they act as both topography and map. In economic sciences, for instance, the divide between orthodox and heterodox economists is a key element to understanding the structure of theory development. In sociology, similar theoretical and methodological divides can be observed, though divisions in sociology can also come in the form of new objects and specialisations (e.g. a sociology of family, a sociology of labour, a sociology of art and culture, etc.), that reveal the proteiform nature of the discipline.

When it comes to divisions in academic research, it is striking how political science has institutionalised some of its divisions as a way of organising its discipline. Political science has been structured by many subfields or subdivisions, wherein students and researchers specialise based on personal preferences. These subdivisions often require or make use of methods and basic theoretical literature that can vary significantly from one subdivision to the next. While these subdivisions may vary depending on one's national context, they remain, in most cases, a federation comprised of, at the very least: political philosophy, political sociology and electoral behaviours, comparative politics, international relations, and public administration. These subdivisions evolve in different institutional contexts and, historically, have even been the subject of secessionist ambitions in some cases. In North America, public administration is often thought of as a political science – this, despite the fact that, since the 1920s, public administration programs have developed separately, with disciplinary ambitions of their own. A similar evolution has occurred for international relations, which is now increasingly thought of and taught as separate programs (i.e. international relations or public affairs). Additionally, the fact that disciplines are influenced and defined by national cultures is reflected in the shape and orientations of their subdivisions. In Anglo-Saxon traditions of political science, for instance, it is common to specialise in a country's politics (e.g. British politics, United States (US) politics, Canadian politics, etc.); while in many other traditions, such forms of specialisation are seen as part of the field of comparative politics. This is just a sample of the myriad of institutionalised divisions that characterise political science.

In this context, how can we understand the place of cultural policy research in political science? Where can we find cultural policy research's traces in political science? How do we identify or recognise the contributions of political science to the study of cultural policy? Are these contributions distinctive? The aim of this chapter is to provide answers to these important questions. Of course, we could simply answer, right from the start, that for political scientists today, the study of cultural policy is a subfield of public policy research, and, when compared to other subfields – such as environment policy, health policy, or educational policy, to name but a few – is not an extremely important one. That being said, by offering greater nuance, not to mention a little bit of historical background, this chapter intends to provide answers that offer a greater account of cultural policy research in relation to political science – answers that are a great deal less pessimistic than what one might expect from a political scientist.

Moreover, this chapter reflects upon the greater political implications of studying culture: while this chapter aims to chart the contributions of political science to cultural policy research, it is done with the understanding that this presentation is debatable. As a result, what we are presenting is a discipline whose contribution to the study of cultural policy is far less critical and much more politically liberal than what is offered by other traditions such as cultural studies. For its part, the field of cultural studies has evolved contextually, in a similar fashion to other political science fields: in its narrowest of scopes, cultural studies can be said to be British in both origin and tradition. This tradition has been decidedly critical in nature, in large part as a response to sociologists who saw the field of cultural studies as "too soft" and too reliant on quantitative interpretations (Gray & McGuigan, 1993, pp. vii–viii). As a result, this criticalness has often taken on a political dimension, with many cultural researchers feeling the need to critique dominant political, economic, and social orders (Miller & Yúdice, 2002, p. 29). In this respect, one might conclude that cultural studies and cultural policy studies go relatively hand-in-hand given that policy studies invariably involve political, economic, and social considerations. Yet, cultural studies researchers have often questioned the need and importance of studying policy, let alone cultural policy (O'Brien, 2014, p. 1). The prevailing assumption has been that cultural policy – regardless of its intent – has, in some way, been compromised by political and commercial agendas. The logic follows a relatively Marxist critique that if one can answer the question of who controls the production of mass media and culture, then one can invariably understand the process of cultural policymaking (Cunningham, 2003, p. 17). Despite this critical appraisal of cultural policy – or perhaps because of it – cultural policy studies have sought to strike a balance between critical and practical policy studies, in the process exploring the relationship between government and culture (Bennett, 1998, p. 285). By contrast, political science has been more liberal in its treatment of culture and far less critical as it is primarily focused on institutions and their functions.

Culture and political science

Culture and political science intersect in three different ways. In a first intersection, political scientists often approach culture from either aesthetic or anthropological registers. With the aesthetic register, culture is understood in the context of artistic output and is used to qualify or mark "differences and similarities in taste and status within social groups" (Miller & Yúdice, 2002, p. 1). The anthropological register takes culture a step further and articulates it as a way of life, grounded "by language, religion, custom, time, and space" (p. 1). Much in the same way that culture in the aesthetic register is understood as a question of taste, so do the elements of culture-as-a-way-of-life – that is to say the language, customs, etc., that go into a culture – represent tastes and choices – albeit "unconscious canons of choice" that have gradually evolved and come into being, sometimes over spans of hundreds and even thousands of years (Benedict, 1934 [2005], pp. 47–48). The common trait of both these registers is the notion that culture can and does serve as a foundation in the development of identity and/or a sense of community. Both provide elements around which people come to identify – both personally and collectively. A country and its citizens, for instance, will identify under the banner of that country's name and symbols; those same citizens will often express a sense of comradery and community – a sense of nationalism and national pride – towards each other in recognition of their shared nationality. Yet this sense of community that comes from culture is often superficial in nature; the community is imagined because the bonds that hold it together are, more often than not, built on arbitrary and often circumstantial factors (i.e. the fact that two people were simply born in the same country or geographic region or were raised in the same religion) and not on the basis of personal relations or familiarity (Anderson, 1991, pp. 6–7). In this respect, culture takes on a more substantive form and can refer to a national culture, a regional culture, or local culture for that matter; it is a signifier used to identify and distinguish people based on any number of factors (e.g. race, ethnicity, language, class, religion, sexual orientation, gender, age, status, and distinctive life experiences) (Rosaldo, 1993).

The second understanding of culture in political science has to do with "political culture." This notion is crucial for the field and refers to different types of political behaviours. A political culture, in a nutshell, is a "conceptual umbrella" that covers a "wide and apparently homogenous range" of political issues and areas and sits in the proverbial "vanguard of the behavioural revolution in political science" (Dittmer, 1977, pp. 552–553). Emerging from the literature on nationalism – and strongly influenced by the "psychocultural approach" to studying politics – political culture is used to describe the ways in which a political system has been "internalized in the cognitions, feelings, and evaluations of its population" (Almond & Verba, 1966, pp. 13–14). The focus, with political culture, is largely on the sets of values, attitudes, and beliefs that give a political system meaning and structure; it is the political orientation of a political system (p. 13). Broadly, the famous work of Almond and Verba (1966) outlines three political cultures based around the degree to which citizens have a say in the inputs and outputs of government: parochial, subject, and participant. In a parochial culture, there are "no specialized political roles" and little expectation of change from the political system. In many respects, a parochial culture is emblematic of pre-democratic and tribal societies where citizens have no input and receive no output (pp. 17–18). In a subject culture, there is an awareness of a specialised governmental authority, but there is little impetus from the general public to evoke change at any given point; there is an awareness of the output of government, but there is no input. The subject culture is likened to a French royalist who "is aware of democratic institutions" but chooses not to "accord legitimacy to them" (p. 19). Finally, in a participant culture, citizens are active both in the input and output of government: they have a say in what the government does and how it does it. Where the concept of political culture has been most salient is in comparisons between existing and emerging democracies (Denk et al., 2015, p. 359). While this second understanding of culture in relation to political science has little to do with what many cultural policy researchers look for or have in mind when researching art and cultural policy, it nevertheless touches on the overall malleability of culture as a concept – particularly in the broader context of political science.

Thus far, we have insisted on presenting these two notions of culture in an effort to demonstrate the diversity of meanings of culture in political science. More importantly, however, what we have tried to evidence is how the discipline's most important notions of culture are, in fact, unrelated to the definition of culture that has been most salient to the study of cultural policy. This brings us to the third understanding of culture: as both art and heritage. When it comes to historically situating the first fundamental contributions of political science to the study of cultural policy in the context of art and heritage, it would be difficult not to start with the contributions of political philosophy and its philosophers. The linkages between arts and politics are as ancient as Western philosophy, and Plato's *Republic* is one of the innumerable works[1] in which such links (and the questions they raise) are offered in analytical reflection. While the boundaries of philosophy, aesthetics, and political philosophy (in political science) are fluid in nature and open to debate, it remains that political scientists have incorporated these considerations – these works and authors – into their academic landscape. Today, political philosophy remains actively concerned with the political dimensions of the arts, with contributions such as Jacques Rancière's (2001, 2008, 2011), for instance, showing how political philosophy can address cultural (policy) issues with a much-needed critical eye.

In sum, apart from political philosophy, the vast majority of work done by political scientists with respect to cultural policy rests on definitions of culture that have more to do with identity (national, regional culture) or behaviour (political culture) than with arts or heritage. While this may have little if nothing to do with cultural policy's relevance, it should be stated that cultural policy research – as the study of governmental action in arts, culture, and heritage – is relatively marginal in political science in comparison to other research agendas. To better characterise cultural policy research, we should also state that – within the tradition of political science – it is mostly rooted in two subfields: it is an object of interest for international relations and for public policy and public administration researchers. With this in mind, the following subsections present the evolution of cultural policy research in political science from disciplinary, historical, and global perspectives. While this chapter has endeavoured to be as comprehensive as possible, we must acknowledge that there is a prominent Euro-American bias in our references to political science. Consequently, while there are obvious and unavoidable asymmetries, this chapter, nevertheless, sheds some light on how cultural policy research has evolved through time and from different significant turning points.

Political science and the arts (1930s–1960s)

Political philosophy has engaged with questions related to arts and culture for millenniums; unfortunately, the same cannot be said for the rest of political science's subfields, nor can it be said for the discipline in general. In other subfields, interest for cultural policy developed timidly in the 1930s. Over a period of roughly three decades (1930s–1960s), political science's interest in cultural policy gradually developed around four main themes: the study of political regimes and totalitarianism; international relations and cultural diplomacy; the development and regulation of mass communication; and the rationalisation and bureaucratisation of the relationship between state and culture through the development of agencies and ministries of culture across the globe.

Interest for cultural policy in political science first grew through the study of political regimes. As with many other interests in political science, the influence of Max Weber undoubtedly played a part in political scientists' first engagements with cultural policy. In particular, Weber's (1895–1919) political essays on the German State and on cultural imperialism in Europe (Beetham, 1985) inspired a number of scholars, in the 1930s, to further his work by exploring the evolution of the German State (Salomon, 1935). This work emphasised the importance of culture as a tool for power in service to the State's aspirations. Cultural policy, in turn, was defined as an instrument that fashioned many social and political aspects – from citizenship to foreign policy (Schuman, 1934; Hartshorne, 1938). Since then, the incorporation of cultural policy in comparative politics and in the study of political regimes has become relatively common. In the 1950s and 1960s, cultural policy became one of the many dimensions studied in relation to understanding the consolidation of the totalitarian Soviet regime and the cultural imperialism employed in its sphere of influence. Many of the works that came out in this period were concerned with either the (Soviet Union's) political influence on the Arts (Slusser, 1956; Gömöri, 1958; Johnson & Labedz, 1965) (what was valued, permitted by political elites) or by the use of culture as a tool for social regulation (Byrnes, 1958). The advent of the Cultural Revolution in China also contributed interest in the mobilisation of culture by political regimes (Gupta, 1970).

Not only did arts and cultural policy research inspire the political science's interest in political regimes, it also provided insights into the inner-life of European political parties. The work of Jean Touchard (1967) on the cultural and intellectual life of the French Communist Party is a good case in point; it illustrates how the study of arts, the cultural aspirations of a party's members, and their engagement with culture can provide insightful material for the study of political parties. A collected edition by Ralph Croizier (1970) on the Communist party's cultural policy also points to the importance of studying culture in the inner-life and history of political parties.

Perhaps the second most important contribution to cultural policy research in this era also stemmed from the era's social and political conditions. Cultural diplomacy, as an object of study – which has, in recent years, reconquered its place in academic research (e.g. Singh, 2010) – is, first and foremost, a product of academia originating from the Cold War. Cultural diplomacy broadly refers to the different programs and methods used by states to conduct their politics on a cultural front. In other words, cultural diplomacy is seen as an additional tool in the conduct of foreign affairs. In the 1950s and 1960s, political scientists developed a keen interest in "cultural exchanges" and "cultural relations" as they were seen as tools for enhancing a state's global sphere of influence (Barghoorn, 1958; 1967; Malik, 1961; Merritt, 1965; Spiller, 1966; Frankel, 1969). Frankel's (1965) book on cultural diplomacy – *A Neglected Aspect of Foreign Affairs* – was one of the first major works on the topic, and his views were welcomed by academics and practitioners alike. This is to say, this research was not only seen as policy-relevant for foreign affairs, it also attracted interest from an audience well beyond academic circles. Interest in cultural diplomacy, however, was not unique to US academics; Italian, French, and Canadian academic journals all published in abundance on the cultural dimension of foreign affairs – though, with a strong emphasis on bilateral relations and the role of cultural institutes (Magistrati, 1958; Schroeder-Gudehus, 1970).

A third stream of academic contributions that characterises this era's cultural policy research in political science concerns the development of mass communication. The freedom of the press, censorship, and the development of radio and television (Harris, 1955) attracted the attention of political scientists who tried to chart the political issues and intricacies that were relevant to these channels of artistic and cultural expression. On the one hand, these researchers were planting the seeds for a deeper subsectoral (e.g. radio, television, publication, performing arts, etc.) understanding and paving the way for the kind of subsector research that we are accustomed to today. On the other hand, political science was also heavily under the interdisciplinary influence of communication sciences. In Canada, for instance, following the Canadian tradition of political economy, the works of Harold Innis (1946, 1950) emphasised the inter-relations of power and communications as a means of exploring culture as a space where power could be expressed and performed. This style of research – with its strong emphasis on communications – had an enduring and definitive effect on Canadian cultural policy research orientations up until the end of the 1990s; it gave Canadian cultural policy research its strong emphasis on subsector issues as they relate to publishing and (radio and television) broadcasting.

Finally, the development of governmental institutions (arts councils and departments and ministries of culture) devoted to supporting, promoting, and funding cultural initiatives has created conditions in which the question of cultural policy has become evidently more salient. The foundation of the British Arts Council in 1946, the Canada Council for the Arts in 1957, France's Ministry of Culture in 1959, Québec's Ministry of Cultural Affairs in 1961, and the United States' National Endowment for the Arts in 1965 all attracted the attention of political scientists (Harris, 1969; Morin, 1969) interested in the political intricacies and inner-functionings of these new public sector institutions.

Thus, with respect to political science, we can conclude that this era of cultural policy research was characterised by a quantitatively limited, albeit diverse, range of works focused on specific cultural issues – though works that do not necessarily recognise cultural policy as their research object. Apart from some notable works and essays that sought to raise awareness of the importance of cultural policy – such as Ralph Purcell's (1956) *Government and Art*, André H. Mesnard's (1969) *action culturelle*[2] in France, Arthur Schlesinger's (1960) essay on National Cultural Policy, or even Alvin Toffler's (1967) conceptual piece that laid the grounds for a systemic style of cultural intervention – there were relatively few published works in political science that substantively addressed broader cultural issues (or cultural policy, for that matter). Simply put, political science's contributions to the study of cultural policy were not nearly as ground-breaking or rich as those made by researchers in the fields of sociology or cultural studies – though that should not discourage scholars from exploring the limited offerings of political science from this era.

Cultural policy: the definition of an object of study (1970s–1990s)

One of the first attempts to define the field of cultural policy research by a political scientist came from Canadian researcher John Meisel (1974). Elements of Meisel's views with respect to culture and cultural policy can be found in his 1974 presidential address at the Annual meeting of the Canadian Association of Political Science. For Meisel, political science had, for too long, neglected the importance of "leisure culture" as he called it, because ultimately this leisure culture has an effect on "political culture":

> In urging political scientists to lift the darkness which surrounds the political aspect of leisure culture, I admit to starting out with something close to an act of faith. Underlying my comments is the unproven assumption that certain relationships between culture

and politics in fact exists. But I find inconceivable that the programs children and adults see on television and at the cinema or hear on the radio, the games they play and watch, the comics, books, magazines they read, the town and architecture which surround them, do not exercise a strong influence on their political culture. (p. 604)

In other words, Meisel tried to articulate the importance of cultural policy research for political science by defending the idea that culture was not an end in itself, but its research could further important disciplinary themes such as "political culture." In doing so, Meisel presented the idea that cultural policy can cultivate good citizenship – an idea that has since taken root in academia and in the ideologies of many policymakers and activists. Moreover, from Meisel's perspective, we can conclude that cultural policy was beginning to be seen as a broad area of governmental action that includes many subsectors.

The conceptual developments and influence of public administration and public policy research in the 1970s and 1980s had seminal effects on the development of cultural policy research in political science. The basic definition of policy that most political scientists will refer to, as a last resort, takes root in notions developed in public policy research: it is defined as what a government "chooses to do or not to do" (Dye, 1995, p. 2) – a government's action or inaction. For others, the importance in researching policy comes from its outcome; it is about uncovering the pressures, resource mobilisation, and strategies for obtaining rare resources that have shaped or influenced the policy itself. In other words, and in the classical definition of policy offered by Lasswell (1936), policy is about "who gets what, when and how." How political scientists engage with cultural policies is often a product of one or both of these basic definitions of public policy.

In a plea for the development of cultural policy research in political science, Paul DiMaggio (1983) offers a poetic definition of cultural policy as the policies that regulate "the market place of ideas" (p. 242). However, in plainer terms, DiMaggio suggests that, in this instance, he is using "the term 'policy' loosely to include unintended but systematic consequences of government actions as well as action towards identified [cultural] ends" (p. 242). More recently, Clive Gray (2010) has offered a definition of cultural policies as "[...] the range of activities that governments undertake-or do not undertake – in the arena of culture" (p. 222). In this context, cultural policy refers to government action (or inaction) in and as it relates to the cultural sector – which broadly includes the arts, communications, and heritage, though it is often defined in more restrictive terms and applied to specific areas of cultural practice (publishing, performing arts, visual arts, etc.).

Over the years, attempts have been made to add or expand on these definitions of cultural policy as a means of encompassing new elements of culture and/or to delineate cultural policy's territory vis-à-vis other policy fields. One such example would be the definition of cultural policy developed by Margaret J. Wyszomirski (2002), which suggests that cultural policies are "[...] a large, heterogeneous set of individuals and organizations engaged in the production, presentation, distribution, preservation, and education about aesthetic, heritage, and entertainment activities, products and artifacts" (p. 186). This definition emphasises the diffused nature of cultural policy development and echoes the division of labour that is commonly seen as part of cultural production. Perhaps one of the most helpful definitions of cultural policy comes from Kevin Mulcahy (2006), who posits that cultural policy should not be restricted to the confines of arts policy, but should also include areas of activity such as heritage and the humanities (p. 321). Ultimately, however, in all of these cases, the underlying elements of Dye and Lasswell's classic definitions of policy are evident – albeit in a distinctively cultural vernacular.

To say, however, that a definitional awareness of cultural policy led to a greater appreciation of the policy field in the 1980s and 1990s would be misleading. For sure, cultural policy is – alongside environmental policy, tax policy, health policy, and transportation policy (etc.) – a public policy sector like any other. Political scientists, however, will often and unapologetically suggest that, compared to other fields, the cultural policy sector is not considered important – whether that is from the perspective of government interventions (Gray & Wingfield, 2011) or from the perspective of the discipline itself (Eling, 1999).

Despite this dismissal, the 1970s and 1980s had more to offer cultural policy research than simply to define its object of study – though defining an object, it should be noted, is of fundamental importance. The first kind of cultural policy research contributions this era of political science saw relate to detailed analysis, with an emphasis on institutional elements, of national cultural policies – in places such as Great Britain (Green & Wilding, 1970), France (Mesnard, 1974; Wengermée & Gournay, 1988), Canada (Fortier & Schafer, 1989), the US (Mulcahy, 1987), Nicaragua (Ross, 1990), and Norway (Dahl, 1984). This era also saw academics engage more thoroughly in policy analysis and program reviews as they related to cultural policy (e.g. McCormack, 1984; Handler, 1985). In French-speaking countries and areas, studying cultural policy also meant analysing the effects or capacities of the state in terms of "cultural development" (Dumont, 1979; Girard & Gentil, 1982; Pascallon, 1983) – a logic of governmental action in culture that finds its origins in the creation of the French ministry of culture.

Finally, some of the works from political scientists of this period took the shape of essays, wherein academics assumed the role (and voice) of public intellectual more than that of technician – though most of these writings pertain to the orientation of cultural policies rather than their applications. In North America, the notion of "public culture" (Mulcahy, 1981; Joyce, 1984) and the role of the government in the arts was a dominant theme; while in France, cultural policy debates materialised as critiques of the national cultural policy (Giordan, 1982; Ritaine, 1983) – especially its allegedly failed (forced) attempts to democratise culture. Acting as social critics and public intellectuals, many political scientists favoured an alternative logic of cultural policy that was more inclusive and respectful of the diversity of tastes. Despite their structural commonalities, both of these debates – North American and French – evolved in parallel on their respective sides of the Atlantic, never meeting though raising a number of the same questions, albeit in largely different contexts (Mulcahy, 2006).

Policy theories and new fieldworks (1990s–2000s)

The 1990s marked a turn for political scientists and public administration scholars engaged in cultural policy research. Cultural policy research had gained currency because it could circulate in academic journals that were (and remain still) largely interdisciplinary. The *Journal of Arts Management, Law and Society* attracted its fair share of cultural policy analysis – mostly comparative work – while other journals – such as the *European Journal of Cultural Policy* (eventually the *International Journal of Cultural Policy*), and *Cultural Trends* – offered new platforms for debates where political scientists were welcomed to contribute. While disciplinary journals of political science and public administration were also seen as viable outlets for research, these new cultural policy-driven journals opened platforms for creative interdisciplinary discussions that had hitherto been unavailable to cultural policy scholars. Given how political scientists approach cultural policy, and their (at least minimal) agreement on the nature of the object, debates on issues such as the instrumentality of cultural policy or the implicit or explicit (e.g. Ahearne, 2009; Throsby, 2009) nature of cultural policy – reminding us of the direct or indirect effects of governments (or their influence) through their actions or inactions – opened avenues for rich intellectual encounters where political scientist could step in and contribute to the discussion. More importantly, this period saw the full influence of the intellectual tradition of public policy research ("policy sciences") – that had developed in political science throughout the 1950s and 1960s – take hold; it consolidated the texture of what political science contributes to cultural policy today: namely, the policy cycle and comparative research.

From a theoretical perspective, the policy cycle results from the influence of systems theory on political science and public policy research; it is an adaptation of the basic principles of these models to the world of public policy; and it is, for good or ill, the backbone of policy research (Lerner & Lasswell, 1951; Brewer & DeLeon, 1983). The role of political science in policy studies often resides in attempting to explain policy change and policy transformation – and this is usually approached through a study of the policy cycle. The policy cycle is typically approached through four (sometimes five) basic – often overlapping – steps: the emergence or recognition of an issue/problem; the formulation of a policy(ies) to address the issue; the implementation of the policy(ies); and, finally, the evaluation of the policy(ies). While political scientists studying cultural policy have been interested in the interaction among these different steps, the tendency has generally been to focus, specialise, and/or provide an in-depth analysis of one individual step. In the context of cultural policy, the first step of the cycle, issue-emergence, often begins with (various social and political) actors expressing a social or cultural demand that, in turn, is recognised and placed on the government's agenda. Researches focusing on this stage will typically emphasise the configuration(s) of actors and their capacity to mobilise and exert pressures on government (e.g. Barbieri, 2012). The second step of the cycle, policy formulation, involves the development and selection of policy option(s). While the line between the emergence of an issue and the formulation of a policy may be thin at times, the formulation process is often a more formal stage of the cycle, where the issues are discussed and often (re)defined in political arenas (e.g. Stevenson, 2013), and research of this stage tends to focus on the contributions of the various actors involved.

The third stage, policy implementation, involves the study of strategies and means put in place (i.e. administration, plans, and funds) and their mobilisation for the delivery of (cultural) policy. Implementation research is the poor cousin of cultural policy studies and, as such, is no different from other fields (health, environment, etc.) or applications of public policy theory. That being said, beyond the strict confines of the discipline, researchers in cognate fields – such as urban studies, urban planning, or regional development – who have researched cultural policy often rely on public policy concepts and have carried out significant research on policy implementation, with an emphasis, of course, on local cultural policy implementation involving themes such as the creative city (e.g. Kovacs, 2010). Finally, political scientists are also interested in cultural policy evaluation – and by evaluation, we mean the practice of evaluation and its technical aspects – but without being restricted to the technical aspects alone. With policy evaluation, researchers are also interested in the social reception of the policy; they are interested in what the communities (i.e. artists, professionals, advocates, users, amateurs) and media have to say about the policy(ies). The notion of policy evaluation in policy research should not to be mistaken for analysing the policy itself, or serving as evidence-based policy; it refers simply to a conceptual part of the policy process that is both technical and social.

While these stages have been defined and used for a long time in public policy research, it is only in the 1990s that they truly became analytical categories commonly used in cultural policy research. Thus, the cycle provides a useful, yet minimalistic, cartography of political science's main contribution to cultural policy studies. Beyond these broad categories, researchers often apply or test some conceptual frameworks (i.e. institutional theory, advocacy-coalition framework, rational choice theories, narrative theories, referentials, etc.) or focus on a distinct phenomenon that adds an additional level of analysis – such as policy instruments, path dependencies, policy diffusion, or policy transfer. Like other political scientists, those who seek explanations of cultural policy formulation, implementation, or evaluation often base their analysis on theoretical frameworks that privilege interest-based, ideas-based, or institutional-based explanations (Palier & Surel, 2005) to make sense of cultural policies.

The other main legacy of political science in cultural policy research has to do with comparative research, a core intellectual tradition in political science that seeks to understand the evolution of political regimes and institutions through a comparative focus on the administrative structures, institutional features, and functioning of political systems or policy subsystems such as cultural policy. This kind of research tends to be either descriptive or typological in nature. Different national, regional, or local cultural policies are compared and juxtaposed with the goal of distilling patterns and, eventually (or potentially), types. With that being said, it should be noted that the comparative tradition in political science does not always involve systematic comparisons. This may sound confusing, but researchers specialising in understanding the structures of a single country or region over time – engaging in what some may label as "area studies" – commonly belong to a comparative tradition of research from the point of view of a political scientist.

Belonging to this research tradition, the vast majority of cultural policy research conducted by French political scientists since the 1990s has focused on the study of local cultural policy. Issues of system development and cultural decentralisation have occupied a central role in academic production. The works of Guy Saez or Emmanuel Négrier (Négrier et al., 2007) are representative of the comparative orientations of French cultural policy research. In Belgium, the work of Genard (2010) also focuses on local and regional cultural policies in relation to the country's linguistic communities. In Canada, the work of Saint-Pierre and Gattinger (2010) surveyed the development and variation in subnational (provincial) cultural policies. Another important theme of comparative research concerns the development and evolution of cultural agencies around the world. The works of Gray (2000) on Great Britain or Bordat (2012) on the evolution of cultural policy in Mexico and Argentina offer a good sample of this outlook from a political science perspective. While the number of comparative cultural policy works is much greater than what has been presented here, research of this nature remains relatively limited compared to works that focus on (a step or steps of) the policy cycle.

Cultural policy research in political science: today and new orientations

From this historical survey, it becomes clear that political science has made a contribution to the study of cultural policy – albeit relatively limited by comparison to its contributions to other issues (e.g. the study of political regimes, democratic transitions, or political ideologies) or policy subsectors (e.g. health policy, education policy, or social policy). Nevertheless, while political science's impact on the cultural policy sector – as a whole – is smaller, its reach via global and interdisciplinary communities of cultural policy researchers remains significant. Recently, some of the notions stemming from the conceptual apparatus of public policy research seem to have had a direct or indirect influence on how the object of research is approached by researchers in cognate fields. The policy stages can also be said to be implicitly contributing to the organisation of cultural policy research in disciplines such as urban studies, regional development, or, in some cases, communications.

From the outside, then, the relationship between political science and cultural policy research would seem somewhat tacit: the relationship exists, most definitely, but is often left unspoken in political science discourse. In recent years, even with a seeming surge in cultural policy research's popularity in political science literature, cultural policy is often contextualised as an element of another policy sector's strategy or as a piece of a much broader policy program. An emphasis on the instrumentality of art and culture – that is to say, an emphasis on its usefulness in non-traditionally cultural sectors or fields, such as the aforementioned urban studies and regional development, for more than just aestheticism (e.g. Belfiore, 2002) – has allowed for a more tangential use of cultural policy research in political science studies, though it arguably does so in a diluted fashion. Questions of culture and cultural policy are being broadly applied in political science disciplines but often only in conjunction with other policy fields – and often only in the context of their potential for fostering socio-economic growth or as an element of arts management (most notably in US cultural policy literature, re: Paquette & Redaelli, 2015). In other words, while significant strides have been made in political science towards the development and understanding of cultural policy and cultural policy research, there remains an inherent stigmatism towards using it as the primary thrust of a political science research program. Rather, the default has seemingly been to "pepper" cultural policy into a larger narrative as a means of adding a new or unique flavour to an otherwise well-treaded discourse. Thus, to a certain degree, cultural policy research has become political science's moped: everyone enjoys riding them, but no one wants to be seen on one.

Looking back at the evolution of cultural policy research in political science – considering its current state, and contemplating its future orientations – a number of questions emerge regarding cultural policy research, in general, and for political scientists, in particular. A first observation has to do with the contributions of US scholars to cultural policy research. Apart from their constant contributions to subthemes such as cultural diplomacy and local cultural planning, the US political scientists' presence on broader debates of cultural policy has become far less important than it was in the 1980s, in comparison to British, Canadian, Australian, and French scholars. Consequently, has arts management become the new home for cultural policy research in the US, with the broader field of political science serving as only an occasional backdrop for cultural considerations? There are obvious structural and contextual issues at play in the US – most notably the structure of government support for the arts – that might explain the managerial turn in cultural policy research. Nevertheless, the question of whether US cultural policy research remains the purview of arts management is salient – especially considering that most of political science's public policy vocabulary has been inspired by the US policy discourse. Similarly, will the current fascination with French policy theories (e.g. policy referentials, cognitive approaches, or French conception of policy instruments) over the last decade in English-speaking and global academic spaces eventually have an effect on how we approach cultural policy theories and cultural policy research? Finally, how will the relationship between political science and cultural policy research continue to evolve? Are political scientists simply conducting cultural (policy) research in "passing," before moving on to another field or policy subfield – to the new "flavour" of the day? While it is unlikely that cultural policy research is entirely a "passing fad" for political scientists – as they seem to exhibit less of a desire to reorient or mobilise around other policy objects compared to researchers in different fields – this concern does raise obvious questions about the structure of political science collaborations – especially with other researchers who more broadly work in the global community of cultural policy research. Are political scientists working on cultural policy more attached to culture? Or are they contributing to a trans-disciplinary space, with its own issues, objectives, debates and its own symbolic capital?

While it would be simple to conclude that cultural policy research will almost invariably hold a place of ambivalence in the minds of many political scientists, the truth is that as our world has become progressively more globalised, the role of culture and cultural policy, in turn, has become progressively more politicised. The place of cultural policy is changing, and so too is its appreciation by scholars from political science fields who might otherwise have snuffed their noses it at. Does this mean that cultural policy research will assume a place of prestige and reverence in the annals of political science research and discourse? Unlikely. But given its ubiquitous nature, it is relatively safe to say that culture (and cultural policy research) will always be omnipresent in political science research.

Notes

1 Cultural policy researchers interested in these issues can access a comprehensive survey of political philosophy's contribution to the field in Eleonora Belfiore and Oliver Bennett's remarkable work, *The Social Impact of the Arts: An Intellectual History,* published by Palgrave in 2008.
2 In French, cultural policy is commonly referred to using "*politiques culturelles*" and even "*action culturelle.*"

References

Ahearne, J. (2009). Cultural policy explicit and implicit: a distinction and some uses. *International Journal of Cultural Policy*, 15(2): 141–153.

Almond, G. A. & S. Verda. (1966). *The Civic Culture: Political Attitudes and Democracy in Five Nations.* Princeton: Princeton University Press

Anderson, B. (1991). *Imagined Communities: Reflections on the Origin and Spread of Nationalism.* London: Verso.

Barbieri, Nicola. (2012). Why does cultural policy change? Policy discourse and policy subsystem a case study of the evolution of cultural policy in Catalonia. *International Journal of Cultural Policy*, 18(1): 13–30.

Barghoorn, F. C. (1958). Conditions of East-West peace. *The Annals of the American Academy of Political and Social Science* 318: 122–131.

Barghoorn, F. C. (1967). Cultural exchanges between communist countries and the United States. *The Annals of the American Academy of Political and Social Science,* 372: 113–123.

Beetham, D. (1985). *Max Weber and the Theory of Modern Politics.* Cambridge: Polity Press.

Belfiore, E. (2002). Arts as a means of alleviating social exclusion: does it really work? A critique of instrumental cultural policies and social impact studies in the UK. *International Journal of Cultural Policy*, 8(1): 91–106.

Belfiore, E. & O. Bennett. (2008). *The Social Impact of the Arts: An Intellectual History.* London: Palgrave.

Benedict, R. (1934, [2005]). *Patterns of Culture.* New York: Mariner Books.

Bennett, T. (1998). Culture and policy – Acting on the social. *International Journal of Cultural Policy*, 4(2): 271–289.

Bordat, E. (2012). De la mobilisation à l'institutionnalisation: Une analyse comparative historique des politiques culturelles au Mexique et en Argentine. *Pôle Sud*, 41(2): 49–64.

Brewer, G. D. & P. DeLeon. (1983). *The Foundations of Policy Analysis.* Pacific Grove: Brooks and Cole.

Byrnes, R. F. (1958). The climax of Stalinism, 1950–1953. *The Annals of the American Academy of Political and Social Science*, 317: 8–11.

Croizier, R. C. (1970). *China's Cultural Legacy and Communism.* New York: Praeger.

Cunningham, S. (2003). Cultural studies from the viewpoint of cultural policy. In J. Lewis & T. Miller (eds.), *Critical Cultural Policy Studies: A Reader.* Malden: Blackwell, pp. 13–22.

Dahl, H. F. (1984). In the market's place: cultural policy in Norway. *The Annals of the American Academy of Political and Social Science*, 471(1): 123–131.

Denk, T., H. Christensen & D. Bergh. (2015). The composition of political culture—A study of 25 European democracies. *Studies in Comparative International Development*, 50(3): 358–377.

Dittmer, L. (1977). Political culture and political symbolism: toward a theoretical synthesis. *World Politics*, 29(4): 552–583.

Dumont, F. (1979). L'idée de développement culturel: esquisse pour une psychanalyse. *Sociologie et sociétés*, 11(1): 7–31.

Dye, T. (1995). *Understanding Public Policy 8th edition*. New York: Prentice Hall.

Eling, K. (1999). *The Politics of Cultural Policy in France*. New York: St. Martin's Press.

Fortier, A. & P. Schafer. (1989). *Historique des politiques dans le domaine des arts au Canada (1944–1988)*. Ottawa: Conférence Canadienne des arts.

Frankel, C. (1965). *The Neglected Aspect of Foreign Affairs: American Educational and Cultural Policy Abroad*. Washington, DC: The Brookings Institution.

Frankel, C. (1969). The "cultural contest". *Proceedings of the Academy of Political Science*, 29(3): 139–155.

Genard, Jean-Louis. (2010). Les politiques culturelles de la Communauté française de Belgique: fondements, enjeux et défis. In D. Saint-Pierre and C. Audet (eds.), *Tendances et défis des politiques culturelles – Cas nationaux*. Québec: Les Presses de l'Université Laval.

Giordan, H. (1982). *Démocratie culturelle et droit à la différence: Rapport présenté à Jack Lang, ministre de la culture*. Paris: La documentation française.

Girard, A. & G. Gentil. (1982). *Le développement culturel: Expériences et politiques*. Paris: Dalloz.

Gray, C. (2000). *The Politics of the Arts in Britain*. London: Palgrave.

Gray, C. (2010). Analysing cultural policy: Incorrigibly plural or ontologically incompatible? *International Journal of Cultural Policy*, 16(2): 215–230.

Gray, A. & J. McGuigan. (1993). Introduction. In Authors (ed.), *Studying Culture: An Introductory Reader*. London: Edward Arnold, pp. vii–xi.

Gray, C. & M. Wingfield. (2011). Are governmental culture departments important? An empirical investigation. *International Journal of Cultural Policy*, 17(5): 590–604.

Green, M. & M. Wilding. (1970). *La politique culturelle en Grande-Bretagne*. Paris: Éditions de l'Unesco.

Gömöri, G. (1958). Cultural and literary developments: Poland and Hungary. *The Annals of the American Academy of Political and Social Science*, 317: 71–78.

Gupta, K. P. (1970). Culture and politics in China. *China Report*, 6(4): 41–45.

Handler, R. (1985). Canadian content and the nationalism of Applebaum-Hebert. *Canadian Public Policy*, 11(4): 677–683.

Harris, J. S. (1955). The television as a political issue in Britain. *The Canadian Journal of Economics and Political Science*, 21(3): 328–338.

Harris, J. S. (1969). Decision-makers in government programs for arts *patronage*: The Arts Council of Great-Britain. *The Western Political Quarterly*, 22(2): 253–264.

Hartshorne, E. Y. (1938). German universities and the government. *The Annals of the American Academy of Political and Social Science*, 200: 210–234.

Innis, H. (1946). On the economic significance of culture. *The Journal of Economic History*, 4: 80–97.

Innis, H. (1950). *Empire and Communications*. Oxford: Clarendon Press.

Johnson, P. & L. Labedz (1965). *Kruschev and the Arts*. Cambridge, MA: MIT Press.

Joyce, M. S. (1984). Government funding of culture: What price the Arts? *The Annals of the American Academy of Political and Social Science*, 471(1): 27–33.

Kovacs, J. F. (2010). Cultural plan implementation and outcomes in Ontario, Canada. *International Journal of Cultural Policy*, 19(3): 209–224.

Lasswell, H. (1936). *Politics. Who Gets What, When and How?* New York: McGraw-Hill.

Lerner, D. & H. Lasswell. (1951). *The Policy Sciences: Recent Developments in Scope and Methods*. Stanford: University of California Press.

Magistrati, M. (1958). Dieci anni di cooperazione internazionale. *Rivista di Studi Politici Internazionali*, 25(1): 7–18.

Malik, C. H. (1961). The world looks at the American program. *The Annals of the American Academy of Political and Social Science*, 335: 132–140.

McCormack, T. (1984). Culture and the state. *Canadian Public Policy*, 10(3): 267–277.

Meisel, J. (1974). Political culture and the politics of culture. *Canadian Journal of Political Science*, 7(4): 601–615.

Merritt, R. L. (1965). Politics, theater, and the East-West struggle: The theater as a cultural bridge in West Berlin1948–1961. *Political Science Quarterly*, 80(2): 186–215.

Mesnard, A-H. (1969). *L'action culturelle des pouvoirs publics.* Paris: Librairie générale de droit et de jurisprudence.

Mesnard, A-H. (1974). *La politique culturelle de l'État.* Paris: Presses universitaires de France.

Miller, T. & G. Yúdice. (2002). *Cultural Policy.* London: Sage Publications.

Morin, E. (1969). De la culturanalyse à la politique culturelle. *Communications,* 14: 5–38.

Mulcahy, K. V. (1981). Public culture and the public: A review article. *The Western Political Quarterly,* 34(3): 461–470.

Mulcahy, K. V. (1987). Cultural policy and administration in the United States. In Milton C. Cummings and Richard S. Katz (eds.), *The Patron State: Government and the Arts in Industrialized Democracies.* Oxford: Oxford University Press, pp. 311–331.

Mulcahy, K. V. (2006). Cultural policy: Definitions and theoretical approaches. *Journal of Arts Management, Law and Society,* 35(4): 319–330.

Négrier, E., J. P. Colin & S. Breux. (2007). Political rescaling and municipal cultural public policies: A comparison France and Québec. *International Journal of Urban and Regional Research,* 31(1): 128–145.

O'Brien, D. (2014). Cultural policy: Management, value and modernity in the creative industries. London: Routledge.

Palier, B. & Y. Surel. (2005). Les trois "I" et l'analyse de l'État en action, *Revue française de science politique,* 55(1): 7–32.

Pascallon, P. (1983). *Le développement culturel et les pays du Tiers-Monde,* 24(95): 497–512.

Purcell, R. (1956). *Government and Art.* Washington, DC: Public Affairs Press.

Rancière, J. (2001). *L'inconscient esthétique.* Paris: La Fabrique.

Rancière, J. (2008). *Le spectateur émancipé.* Paris: La Fabrique.

Rancière, J. (2011). *Aisthesis. Scène du régime esthétique de l'art.* Paris: Galilée.

Ritaine, E. (1983). *Les stratèges de la culture.* Paris: Les éditions de SciencePo.

Rosaldo, R. (1993). *Culture & Truth: The Remaking of Social Analysis.* Boston: Beacon Press.

Ross, P. (1990). Cultural policy in a transitional society: Nicaragua 1979–1989. *Third World Quarterly,* 12(2): 110–129.

Saint-Pierre, D. & M. Gattinger (eds.) (2010). *Les politiques culturelles provinciales et territoriales du Canada. Origines, évolutions et mises en œuvre.* Québec: Les Presses de l'Université Laval.

Salomon, A. (1935). Max Weber's sociology. *Social Research,* 2(1): 60–73.

Schlesinger, A. (1960). Notes on a national cultural policy. *Daedalus,* 89(2): 394–400.

Schroeder-Gudehus, B. (1970). Problèmes de politique culturelle extérieure: Aspects culturels des relations Canada-Europe. *Études Internationales,* 1(3): 45–60.

Schuman, F. L. (1934). The conduct of German foreign affairs. *The Annals of the American Academy of Political and Social Science,* 176: 187–221.

Singh, J. (2010). *International Cultural Policies and Power.* New York: Palgrave.

Slusser, R. M. (1956). Soviet music since the death of Stalin. *The Annals of the American Academy of Political and Social Science,* 303: 116–125.

Spiller, R. E. (1966). American Studies abroad: Culture and foreign policy. *The Annals of the American Academy of Political and Social Science,* 366: 1–16.

Stevenson, D. (2013). What's the problem again? The problematisation of cultural participation in Scottish cultural policy. *Cultural Trends,* 22(2): 77–85.

Throsby, D. (2009). Explicit and implicit cultural policy: some economic aspects. *International Journal of Cultural Policy,* 15(2): 179–185.

Toffler, A. (1967). The art of measuring the arts. *The Annals of the American Academy of Political and Social Science,* 373(2): 141–155.

Touchard, J. (1967). Le Parti Communiste Français et les intellectuels (1920–1939). *Revue Française de Science Politique,* 17(3): 468–483.

Weber, M. (1895–1919), [2004]. *Oeuvres politiques.* Paris: Albin Michel.

Wengermée, R. & B. Gournay. (1988). *La politique culturelle de la France.* Paris: La documentation française.

Wyszomirski, M. J. (2002). Arts and culture. In L. M. Salamon (ed.), *The State of Nonprofit in America.* Washington, DC: Brookings Institution.

3

Cultural economics, innovation and intellectual property

Nicola C. Searle

Introduction

The combination of economics and the cultural and creative industries is complicated. The intangible nature of the cultural and creative industries does not lend itself to standard economic analysis deploying the utility and profit-maximising emphasis of neoclassical economics. Despite this awkward matching, the economic analysis of the cultural and creative industries, and the role of creativity, is a vibrant and growing area.

This chapter examines themes in what is known as *cultural economics*, with a particular focus on innovation, creativity and intellectual property (IP). It details emerging trends in the economic analysis of the cultural and creative industries and highlights challenges that mainstream, neoclassical economic analysis faces when confronting characteristics of the creative industries.

Terminology

A great deal of energy in academic studies of the creative industries (CI), and related terms,[1] is spent on their definition. These are important discussions as the classification of industries, primarily through Standard Industrial Classifications, reflects political and social constructs of industry. While these nuances are important to wider debates, for the purposes of the chapter, this chapter focuses on five key terms: *the creative industries, creativity, innovation, cultural economics* and *cultural policy* and largely adopts the terminology as detailed in Towse (2014) and Towse (2010).

Creative industries indicates the UK government's Department for Media, Culture and Sport 1998[2] definition consisting of advertising, antiques, architecture, crafts, design, fashion, film, leisure software, music, performing arts, publishing, software, and TV and radio (antiques has since been removed, DCMS (2015)).

Creativity, discussed in Towse (2010), refers to 'artistic creativity,' described by UNCTAD (2008) thus, "artistic creativity involves imagination and a capacity to generate original ideas and novel ways of interpreting the world, expressed in text, sound and image (Economy, 2008, p. 9)." This chapter focuses on creativity as related to the creative industries. Towse (2010) notes, "Creativity has thus come to be seen as the contemporary equivalent of innovation in the industrial age" (Towse, 2010:105). This chapter adopts a Shumpeterian approach to *innovation* as a wider concept than creativity. Schumpeter (1942:83) approaches innovation as 'creative destruction' in a, "process of industrial mutation–if I may use that biological term–that incessantly revolutionizes the economic structure from within, incessantly destroying the old one, incessantly creating a new one." Schumpeter further describes examples of innovation as the launch of new products, opening of new markets, application of new methods, acquiring of new supply sources and new industry structures. In the singular as opposed to the general process, an innovation is typically described in economics as an applied invention. The emphasis, like with creativity, is on the idea of 'new.'

Finally, this chapter will use *cultural economics* as the branch of economics concerned with the application of economic principles to the study of the cultural and creative industries. This is in line with the Towse (2010) definition, but excludes the cultural economics sub-disciplines as defined by the Journal of Economic Literature (JEL) codes of the economics of religion, economic ideologies and social economy. Likewise, the use of the term *cultural policy* is broadly in line with the Towse (2010, 2014) definition of cultural policy to include policies related to the creative industries, including funding, taxation, measurement, regulations, and, to explicitly reflect recent trends in scholarship, IP.

This approach is not without its critics as Garnham (2005:16) notes. He adopts "arts and media policy" instead of "cultural policy," as the latter is not neutral. Indeed, "arts and media policy" may be a better descriptor of the economic definition, but one that has not been adopted by the literature. Hesmondhalgh (2005) also argues for including media policy as part of policy; tensions between these policy definitions are detailed in Hesmondhalgh and Pratt (2005). In short, an economic approach to cultural policy examines government policy related to the cultural and creative industries.

To summarise, this chapter focuses on the creative industries as part of cultural policy, the economic study of the creative industries, and relates these analyses to innovation and creativity.

Cultural economics: evolution and critiques

> Whenever economists study areas outside their traditional field, the economy, they run the danger of misperceiving what contribution they are able to make. Only if the choice of which aspects to study is carried out carefully can a useful and novel contribution on the part of economics be expected.
>
> *(Frey 1994:3)*

Cultural economics as a discipline, in its current form,[3] gained currency in the 1960s with the works of William Baumol and William Bowen and their analysis of cost structure in the arts (Throsby, 1994). Despite the half century that has passed since Baumol, many economists still argue that economics continues to neglect, or fails to adapt to, the creative industries. Arguments of this sort can be found in Howkins (2002); Throsby and Throsby (2001) argue the outputs and structures of the creative industries do not fit into the neo-classical economic classification of goods and services; Caves (2000) argues economics has largely neglected the creative industries; and, finally, Stoneman (2010) argues economics has largely excluded creativity and 'soft' innovation in studies of innovation, amongst others.

The category of "Cultural Economics" was introduced under the "Miscellaneous" classification of JEL codes in 1991, following a move amongst economists to, "claim an independent category for their field" (Cherrier, 2014:35). JEL codes reflect mainstream economic disciplines and are in keeping with their North American origins. The structure of JEL, like with Standard Industrial Classification (SIC), deliminates intradisciplinary boundaries. The bulk of what would be considered cultural policy or creative industries by the literature discussed in this chapter, falls under the JEL Z11, "Economics of the Arts and Literature" which is described as, "studies about economic issues related to the arts and literature, including demand, supply and pricing analysis." AEA (2016) and Z18 "Cultural Economics; Public Policy," described as, "studies concerning public policy on art, religion and other matters in Z1 [the top level classification for Cultural Economics]." This, however, is an awkward fit for some of the definitions of cultural policy and creative industries discussed earlier, which are perhaps better encompassed when including codes from other areas, such as L82 "Industry Studies: Services: Entertainment; Media (Performing Arts, Visual Arts, Broadcasting, Publishing, etc.)," O3 "Innovation; Research and Development; Technological Change; Intellectual Property Rights" and other codes addressing trade, international agreements, production and industrial organisation.

Written soon after the 1991 inclusion of cultural economics in JEL codes, Throsby (1994:1) describes, in JEL, the *cultural* industries to mean, "the arts, motion pictures, radio and television, and printing and publishing," which, very loosely, could be interpreted to include publicly funded arts organisations. He identifies the key focuses of cultural economics at the time as markets and public funding for art.

Since the formal recognition of cultural economics, there remains significant scope for the expansion of cultural economics. Blaug (2001) and Caves (2000) suggest that the areas of publishing and contracts, respectively, are under-addressed. Both areas are now garnering further attention as in Ghose et al. (2006) and Baker and Evans (2013). More recent arguments, Throsby (2012), Müller et al. (2009), and Towse (2010, 2014), suggest that cultural economics is coming into its own.

In the last decades of cultural economics, key themes of economic analysis have emerged. Both Rushton (2003) and Throsby (2012) suggest that the starting premise of cultural economics is that the creative industries are a case of market failure. Frey (1994) suggests that analytical approaches progress in two main categories: the first being the relationship between sectors of spheres of society, and the second type being the rational choice approach to characterise the economic framework. He notes that cultural economic analysis typically combines the two approaches and uses the rational choice approach to analyse the effect of economic factors on the arts.

The application of these approaches is often concerned with cultural policy, industrial organisation, welfare economics, economic geography, economic growth and development, amongst others. In 1994, Throsby details the development of cultural economics from the 1960s and its adoption of neoclassical interpretations of taste, markets, demand, supply and labour markets to inform public policy. He predicted cultural economics would develop empirical insights to solve 'nontrivial theoretical and empirical problems' (Throsby 1994:26) both in cultural policy and in economic methodologies in general, which, more than two decades later, continues to be thwarted by poor data. Towse (2010) describes a brief history of cultural economics as starting with subsidies for the arts, then moving through art markets, the development of theoretical models, the economics of museums, the introduction of the concept of the creative industries in the late 1900s, contractual and labour approaches, and a more recent focus on IP.

IP has recently become a more dominant theme in cultural economics, and economics in general, as interest in innovation and creativity lends itself to analysis of IP. In the

1990s, economists largely used IP to define the creative industries. As noted by Throsby and Throsby (2001), IP as an industry's output was so central to meeting the definition, to the point that the 'copyright industries' and 'cultural industries' were virtually synonymous. In 1996, the *Journal of Cultural Economics* devoted an edition to IP. Since then, cultural economics is turning its attention further to IP. Of four key books published by cultural economists in 2000 and 2001, Caves (2000), Frey (2000), Throsby (2011) and Howkins (2001), Frey and Throsby have only cursory mentions of IP, Caves offers one chapter, of 22, and Howkins's text is devoted to the topic. As Towse (2006) notes, there is a wealth of areas to be explored in the application of cultural economics to IP. These themes are developed later in the chapter and highlight the insights that may be gleaned from combining economics, culture and IP.

Audiences for economic analysis

> Several reviewers of the progress of cultural economics over the years have observed that many writers have begun their books or papers with an apology for presuming that economics might have anything useful to say about art.
>
> *(Throsby 1994:26)*

The demand for economic analysis of cultural policy varies. In the Baumol days of the 1960s, arts funding changes provided a ready audience. However, the interaction between economics and cultural policy has not enjoyed a smooth ride. Peacock (2004), reflecting on three decades as an economist in arts and arts policy, details the challenges of economic analysis[4] in creative industries and their use in policy. He notes the reluctance of vested interests, and special pleading by stakeholders, to admit that, "government support for the arts involves an opportunity cost" (Peacock, 2004:177). In particular, he argues that economics is widely accepted in policy for broadcasting, but that in preservation of works of art, buildings and the like, "there appears to be implacable opposition to the application of economic analysis designed to produce a rational system of pricing and investment which takes account of consumer interests" (Peacock, 2004:175). He notes that institutions in publicly-funded parts of the cultural industries (e.g. museums) view themselves as 'guardians of public interest' and consider themselves to know better, or be more likely to know, what is in the interests of future generations. However, Hesmondhalgh (2005) suggests that economics enjoys a favoured position in UK politics starting in the late 1990s. Instead, he argues economic analysis had a ready audience in being a malleable tool to legitimise political stances. However, he repeats Peacock's argument and notes that, "Cultural policy has usually been strongly associated with the subsidised arts sector, whereas media and communications policy has tended to be analysed in terms of economics and politics" (2005:95). Whereas media and communications policy has traditionally been amenable to economic analysis, cultural policy has largely not. This again speaks to an on-going debate on the economics of the creative industries as part of cultural policy analysis.

Similar developments are to be found in the growing interaction between management and media studies. As with economics, the literature addressing the interaction of cultural and management perspectives has noted the general reluctance of traditional media studies to the use of market or industrial terminology (McDonald, 2013). Media studies are also expanding into interdisciplinary work under the term "media industries studies" (Schatz, 2014). Pick et al. (2015) also note a tension between creative industries and management studies, and suggest that 'creative industries management' is both an oxymoron and an opportunity. This points to a general frustration over on-going tensions between media economics and political economy approaches to the study of media industries and cultural products (Wasko and Meehn 2013).

A concerted attempt to persuade reluctant audiences of the importance and potential of economic analysis can be found in Bahkshi et al. (2007). The authors seek to persuade stakeholders in cultural policy that economics can, and should, bolster the case for the arts. The authors, along with O'Brien (2010), provide critiques of economic methodologies and note the measurement challenges the intangible nature of culture creates. Bahkshi et al. make their case on the basis that the special pleading of the arts/cultural policy implies that, "arts funding choices should be made independent of their effects on society" (2007:19). Economics, instead, offers a means to avoid this 'arts exemption' and strengthen the case for the arts.

Tensions with neoclassical economics

The reluctance of policy audiences for cultural economics speaks to a wider critique of neo-classical economics. Neoclassical economics has long been criticised; this criticism experi-enced a sharp uptick in the 1990s as detailed in Thompson (1997). Noted critic McCloskey (1998) condemns 'the rhetoric of economics' and the utility maximising approaches influ-enced by Ayn Rand's objectivism. McCloskey's critiques are directed at the discipline as a whole, and cultural economics and neoclassical economics are not mutually exclusive. The McCloskey school of thought, when combined with the policy scepticism noted by Peacock, means that cultural economics is prone to external and internal criticism. Rational choice theory is a particular target of condemnation and, as noted by Throsby (2001), leads to the expectation that all behaviours can be fully accounted for in economic models, without re-gard to social, cultural or historical factors. O'Brien (2014), using the tensions between the humanities and economics as an analytical framework, largely confirms this view and details oppositions to economic constructs of individual rationality in UK cultural policy. Throsby (2001, 2012) also notes this tension, which he suggests stems from economics' emphasis on the individual in contrast to the, by definition, collective emphasis of culture. He also argues (1994) that neoclassical views of tastes (the utility function) accommodate taste for the arts, but that this may fail to account for the irrationality of demand for art. However, he also notes that, "the aggregate behaviour of consumers and of artists can be modelled in ways that are mostly consistent with economic theory" (1994:4). To summarise, scepticism and criti-cism of the neoclassical economic approach abounds and is particularly sharp in the creative industries and in cultural policy as a whole.

IP, innovation and creativity

Creativity and innovation

While cultural policy has struggled to hold the attention of its intended audience, analysis of innovation has an eager audience. In developed economies, politicians, policy makers and economists have a collective obsession with innovation in the hopes that it contrib-utes to economic growth. These obsessions, and the associated economics of innovation, benefit from neoclassical, mainstream economic roots. While critics of the approach exist (e.g. feminist critiques as detailed later), the innovation-development-growth narrative is firmly entrenched in the political economy. A long-term trend of developed economies moving away from manufacturing-based to service-based economies has led to a greater emphasis on knowledge and the emergence of the "knowledge economy" as discussed in

Garnham (2005). The focus on this new knowledge-based paradigm has promoted further analysis of innovation, which has led innovation-focused economists to look at creativity. Examples are, Lee and Rodríguez-Pose (2014), who examine the 'innovativeness' of the creative industries and creative occupations, and The Work Foundation's 2007 report that argues, "creativity and innovation are overlapping concepts. In the main, creativity ... is about the origination of new ideas ... while innovation is about the successful exploitation of new ideas." Similarly, Doyle (2016) notes a growing emphasis on innovation in the creative economy and media studies. This innovation approach follows a path dependency from the neoclassical understanding of innovation, particularly from an industrial organisation or economic development foundation. As cultural economics also begins to look further at innovation and creativity arguments, with a focus on the creative industries, analyses from both neoclassical and cultural perspectives are meeting. This section discusses these perspectives, and their reflection in IP debates.

Economists link innovation to the creative industries – often done with the intent of proving the economic value of the creative industries – and implicitly discuss creativity. For example, Bakhshi and McVittie (2009) detail how the creative industries enable other industries to be more innovative. Müller et al. (2009) note three innovation impacts from the creative industries: creative industries contribute to the innovative potential of an economy; they may create inputs for innovation elsewhere in the economy; and may serve a pull function as consumers of innovation. Howkins (2001:x) argues that creativity is not an economic activity but can become so when transformed into an "idea with economic implications or a tradable product." This goes part way to fitting the classic definition of an innovation as an applied invention.

Concepts of creativity, as detailed in Towse (2006), became more popular within cultural economics with Frey (1997). Howkins (2001) devotes his entire book to the role of creativity and the concept of the creative economy. Previously, economics flirted with the concept of creativity by combining psychological research on creativity with economics. This approach often took the form of the examination of creativity in the marketplace in the form of entrepreneurship and management (e.g. works in the *Journal of Creative Behaviour* such as the 1988 Volume 22 Number 3 special edition including Fernald (1988) "The Underlying Relationship between Creativity, Innovation and Entrepreneurship," or the *Creativity and Innovation Management Journal* for example Jeffcut and Pratt (2003) "Managing Creativity in the Cultural Industries") or in the analysis of human capital (e.g. Rubenson and Runco, 1992, whose theories were taken up more by psychologists than economists). Recent years have seen, as discussed earlier, creativity to be associated more with innovation and the creative industries.

However, Garnham (2005) argues that the addition of creativity, rather than a critique or extension of the economics of innovation, is instead an attempt by cultural policy to capture the prestige of innovation. Like Hesmondhalgh and Pratt (2005), Garnham notes the cultural policy tensions between creators (the purveyors of creativity) and rightsholders (typically large corporations), arising from innovation/creativity approaches. These tensions can be seen in intellectual property policy, as discussed in the next section.

This relationship between creativity and innovation is an evolving one and highlights the challenges faced by cultural economics. The economics of innovation, particularly as related to economic growth and development, are well established and reflect a distinctly scientific focus. This focus on science, and the narrow definition of innovation, is sometimes construed as a bias and challenged by proponents of the creative or knowledge economy (e.g. Rushton (2003) and feminist critiques of innovation and measurements of economic growth).

Intellectual property

The interaction of creativity, the creative industries and innovation has become more obvious in recent years with the rise of interest in IP policy. Major changes in the legal structure of IP have been marked by a step change introduced by the World Trade Organisation's 1995 Trade-Related Aspects of IP (TRIPS) agreement, which harmonised and strengthened IP across the world. This, along with changes in markets and technology, dominated by the advent of the Internet and the digital era, have challenged existing IP structures, in particular that of the right most relevant to the creative industries, copyright. The relationship of the creative industries and copyright is so strong, that at various times the term 'the copyright industries' has served as a synonym for creative industries. Towse (2006) makes the case for copyright as falling within the realm of cultural economics. IP, which by definition only protects original contributions, also reflects the infinite variety of Caves (2000) and "extreme case of a heterogeneous commodity" of Throsby (1994:4), by which each unit of the creative industries output is unique. As a result, IP policy has become a string in the cultural economist's bow.

The predominance of IP is not without its critics. Potts (2009) notes that the DCMS definition of the creative industries rests on a connection between creativity and IP that emphasises, "creativity as an input and IP as an output, a view that implicitly presumes that the value of the creative industries is ultimately in consumption of these creative outputs." Müller et al. (2009:39) also note that IP is considered the main output of the creative industries, as opposed to goods and services. Potts is critical of this approach, as he argues that the outputs of the creative industries play an important role in innovation as a whole, rather than being defined by the production and consumption of end outputs.

Feminist interpretations of IP provide a further critique of IP and neoclassical economics. Bawra and Rai (2002, 2004) argue that IP denies the contribution of women to knowledge by taking a narrow approach to knowledge and assigning it to realms that have traditionally excluded women. Halbert (2006) notes the lack of IP protection for the outputs of female knowledge. Halbert in particular relates this discussion to the creative industries by providing case studies on quilting and knitting, two creative practices dominated by women, as lying predominately outside the IP framework. Santhosh and Sengupta (2011) argue that IP undervalues the 'gendered science' of traditional knowledge. Collectively, the development of 'creativity' in the cultural economics sense, along with the feminist perspective, suggests that the definition of innovation, as protected by IP, is too narrow. This plays into wider critiques of neoclassical economics' core assumption of rationality and utility; however, as Bakhshi et al. (2007) note, this critique is often directed at bad economics rather than at a systematic failure of economic approaches.

Economics' love of innovation and subsequent focus on IP pre-dates the cultural economic analysis of IP. As a result, discussions on creativity follow a path dependency into innovation and specific constructs of IP. The next section highlights this by detailing the evolution of the economic analysis of trade marks, in contrast to the analysis of the relatively newer rights of Traditional Knowledge (TK) and related rights.

Creative industries and IP

Having established the relevance of IP policy to cultural economics, this section of the chapter uses examples of IP to further illustrate the challenges facing cultural economics as a critique of neoclassical economics.

Approaches to IP

IP policy and the laws that create it generally exist to solve the problem of intangibility. The intangible nature of creativity and innovation means that ideas can easily be appropriated, and, in contrast to physical property, this appropriation is difficult to control. This can undermine creators' ability to recoup their investments or profit from their creations. For simplicity, I shall use the term 'creator' as being more inclusive to the creative industries than the more common 'innovator' used in general economics. IP policy seeks to create property rights over the intangible to bolster ownership and control of innovation and creativity.

Justifications for why societies should have property rights over the intangible are dominated by two[5] main approaches. These are, IP rights as intrinsic rights and IP as an incentive to innovate. Granstrand (2000) refers to these, respectively, as deontological approaches based on the intrinsic, moral rights and arguments that fall outside the economic perspective; and consequentialist approaches founded in the economic implications (e.g. incentive to innovate) of the legal structure of IP. These two approaches are often incompatible, with the incentive-to-innovate theory gaining traction in recent decades.

Approaching IP rights as intrinsic comes from a Lockean perspective in which individuals own the fruit of their own labour (Hettinger 1989; Granstrand 2000). Using this framework, the creativity and innovation stemming from an individual's application of his or her labour should be owned by said individual. IP rights allow individuals rights over their outputs. This approach is also known as labour-dessert theory and is an approach popular with lawyers and existing owners of IP rights. The focus rests on the benefits to the individual creator.

In contrast, the traditional economic approach to IP is to construe it as an incentive to innovate (Scotchmer 2004; Lemley 2005). In this model, often referred to as the social contract theory, the creator is rewarded with property rights in the form of IP. These rights allow the creator to appropriate the returns to their efforts and serve as an incentive to innovate. While society may incur higher costs and lower quantities because of the monopoly conditions generated by IP rights, society is rewarded with long-term innovation. This approach, crucially, also requires the expiration of IP rights so that, on expiration, the knowledge contained falls into the public domain where it will spur further innovation. The incentive-to-innovate theory is focused ultimately on economic growth and the benefits to society, and assumes innovation leads to economic growth and development.

The incentives-to-innovate theory of IP has served economics well in analysing the IP rights of patents and copyright. Economics is largely comfortable with viewing patents and copyright as economic policies. The same cannot be said, however, for trade marks, traditional knowledge (TK), and Geographical Indications (GI), all three of which are relevant intellectual assets for the creative industries. These rights are heavily linked to the creative industries by way of branding, arts, textiles, design and advertising. Economics tends to be wholly uncomfortable with these rights as serving economic purposes as they do not fit the social contract. This tension between the neoclassical, incentive-to-innovate theory and these noncompliant rights highlights the challenges cultural economics continues to face.

Incompatible IP: the cases of trade marks, TK and GI

Patents have dominated economists' analysis of IP, which is likely due to the relative wealth of data in this area and patents as fitting the science bias of constructs of innovation. Recent decades have seen an expansion of economic analysis to copyright, trade marks and design rights. In the case of the former, because of the dramatic changes in technology and its market consequences, and in the case of the latter two, likely due to the trend in national IP offices publishing data in these areas. However, trade marks, along with TK and GI, do not easily fit the social contract theory and remain an awkward fit as an economic policy.

Trade marks

Trade marks[6] are an important intellectual asset for most firms, in particular as a means of protecting the creative outputs of the advertising and graphic design sectors. However, trade marks lack two key characteristics of the social contract theory: they do not expire as long as renewal fees are paid, and they do not necessarily qualify as innovation. Assuming the owner of a trade mark pays his or her renewal fees, a trade mark can potentially last forever. Trade marks are traditionally not considered a form of innovation, a topic discussed further below.

Two foundational papers on the economics of trade marks are those of Landes and Posner (1987) and Economides (1998). Both of these papers argue that trade marks exist primarily to promote economic efficiency rather than innovation. Landes and Posner further posit that trade marks serve to incentivise linguistic innovation. Economides (1988), however, is critical of the role of trade marks in distorting competition and market equilibria. The bulk of subsequent analysis has taken a neoclassical approach, and the economic scholars here do not self-identify as cultural economists.

A standard economic interpretation of trade marks is their role in promoting efficiency by reducing information gathering costs via signalling consumers. A trade mark is an exclusive mark that signals a brand's reputation (or lack thereof). This reputation will consist of a variety of factors influencing consumer decision-making. The mark is an efficient way of signalling quality, an important factor to the consumer. This signal reduces search costs as, at a glance, the consumer will have information about the quality of a good, such as taste, provenance, etc. Thus, trade marks reduce the information asymmetries between consumers and producers and promote efficiency.

Initially, economic analysis suggested that branding was useful for a brand owner to increase market share, but at the expense of another's (discussed in Putsis 1998). Using this approach, the branding protected by trade marks operates in a zero-sum game. Following this line of thought, trade marks do not promote innovation because they operate in a zero-sum game. Lemley (2004a:143) is particularly scathing on justification of trade marks:

> Unlike patents and copyrights, trademark law and the right of publicity do not exist to encourage the creation of new brand names, personal names, or likenesses. There is no affirmative social interest in encouraging their proliferation, and, in any event, the fixed costs invested in creating a new name are so minimal that it is hard to imagine that creating one would require incentive.

However, starting in the mid-90s (Putsis 1998), economists explored the relationship of branding, promotions (temporary discounts or details) and sales of a particular category of goods, particularly in Fast Moving Consumer Goods (FMCG). This research, and further discussions (Corrado and Hao 2013), suggests that the branding incentivised by trade marks can result in innovation. Additionally, there are discussions on trade marks and branding as a good indicator of innovative activities[7] and branding as facilitating the introductions of innovations to markets. Greenhalgh and Rogers (2007:24), adopting a Schumpeterian approach to innovation, examine the relationship between trade mark and innovation activities in firms and find that, "applications for trade marks are suggestive of product innovation." Thus, if trade marks can promote or embody innovation, there is room for them to fit in an incentive-to-innovate interpretation of IP.

Other economic analysis of trade marks extends to their role in facilitating the firm's appropriation of the returns to their investments in reputation. The leads to the conclusion that brands are often a firm's most valuable asset (discussed and critiqued by Klein (2010)). Other analysis examines the role of trade marks in conspicuous consumption, a la Veblen. The use of trade marks and trade mark policy have also been examined in competition discussions and policy-specific analysis such as the optimal structure of trade mark registration processes and registries (e.g. Von Graevenitz 2013). A rare explicitly cultural economic analysis by Cuccia et al. (2008:1) looks at the role of collective trade marks in the San Gregorio Armenio district of Naples. Known for its hand carved nativity scenes, the authors examine, from a creative cluster and regional government perspective, the potential use of trade marks to, "promote market incentives sustaining local development and preserving or enhancing the common knowledge." The authors conclude a collective trade mark would increase prices of the nativity scenes by 10%. Generally, economics finds trade marks to be an important intangible asset for firms and collectives.

Trade marks illustrate the evolution of the economic analysis of IP. Whereas early focus of analysis focused on the signalling and efficiency aspects of trade marks, more recent analysis has incorporated creativity and innovation aspects of branding. These contemporary arguments are not incompatible with neoclassical economics and suggest that development of cultural economics does not necessarily require departure from the mainstream, neoclassical perspective that is so often the subject of critique. The same cannot be said of the current state of economic analysis of TK and GI.

Traditional knowledge (TK) and geographical indications (GI)

Both TK and GI are relatively new types of IP as they have only existed in law and policy in the last century. Zappalaglio (2013) describes the origins of TK in international policy debates as starting in 1948. Montén (2005) notes that GI was largely unrecognised until the mid 1990s in TRIPs. TK, however, exists legally in predominately nonbinding agreements, whereas GI is enshrined in law in many jurisdictions (e.g. the EU.) The relative youth of these types of IP goes in part to explain their absence from cultural economics. However, in both cases, these IP are based on cultural and creative goods and services.

Yudice (2009) notes tensions between IP regimes and anthropological approaches to culture. He argues that uses of culture cluster around two main poles: *anthropological* approaches that focus on values and symbolic uses and a *creative* element that focuses on innovation. IP falls under the latter and leads to discordant cultural policies where IP impinges on cultural policies, such as those promoting access to cultural goods. Akin to this anthropological descriptor, Doyle (2016) explains policy interventions in indigenous content media production as acting on 'socio-cultural grounds.' Garnham (2005) argues that the creative approach and its policies, under the knowledge economy focus, are now inseparable from Information and Communications Technology (ICT) policy. However, ICT, which is a relatively new phenomenon, clearly does not interact with the bulk of issues regarding TK, which is long established. The tension between these anthropological and creative approaches can be seen in TK and GI policy.

Traditional knowledge (TK)

TK, which covers all manners of intangible assets of a community, speaks to the collective emphasis of culture. At present, economic analysis, with its individual, innovation focus, is at odds with the collective, traditional focus on TK.

The World IP Organisation defines TK as,

> Knowledge, know-how, skills and practices that are developed, sustained and passed on from generation to generation within a community, often forming part of its cultural or spiritual identity. … TK in a general sense embraces the content of knowledge itself as well as traditional cultural expressions, including distinctive signs and symbols associated with TK. TK in the narrow sense refers to knowledge as such, in particular the knowledge resulting from intellectual activity in a traditional context, and includes know-how, practices, skills, and innovations.
>
> *(WIPO 2015)*

A subset of TK is Traditional Cultural Expressions (TCE),

> Also called "expressions of folklore", [TCE] may include music, dance, art, designs, names, signs and symbols, performances, ceremonies, architectural forms, handicrafts and narratives, or many other artistic or cultural expressions. … Their protection is related to the promotion of creativity, enhanced cultural diversity and the preservation of cultural heritage.
>
> *(WIPO 2015)*

TK is a very awkward fit for a neoclassical, incentive-to-innovate analysis of IP. To start, the rights are poorly defined, as TK itself lacks a clear definition. Further, TK is most often not expressed in any fixed way, and its ownership is unclear, both of which make identifying the protected knowledge difficult. TK itself is unlikely to be traded in a monetary fashion, and thus arguments in favour of recouping rewards to innovation are thin. Additionally, by definition, TK is *traditional,* and any rights may actively discourage innovation. However, the codification of the knowledge contained in TK may promote its diffusion and subsequent innovation; thus, TK may encourage further innovation.

A common economic argument in favour of innovation is the economic growth and development of indigenous communities. These communities are often rural and economically poor. Protection of TK 'owned' by these communities could foster local development. However, the development of a thriving market is dependent on many factors other than IP protection. The introduction of an IP right merely provides the right to *exclude* others from using the IP. The capabilities to translate TK into economic success may require skills (absorptive capacity) not present in the community, and the community could license to a third party. In this case, the TK may function as the equivalent of a natural resource with no long-term development impact. Dutfield (2005) is less pessimistic than this analysis but notes that the development of goods and services incorporating TK exposes communities to the vagaries of the dominant economic system surrounding them. Yudice's concept of the 'anthropological' approach to culture, by focusing on a social, value-driven side of culture, neither introduces nor addresses this economic doom, which the 'creative' approach does. In short, TK fails to fit the social contract, incentive-to-innovate economic interpretation of IP.

Stronger arguments in favour of TK lie outside the domain of neoclassical economics in the social, cultural and historical context described by Throsby (2001). As noted in a WIPO fact-finding mission report, the value of TK is in the community's cultural benefits. Discussions on IP frameworks in the Caribbean suggest that communities view their TK, "as an economic asset and as cultural patrimony.... [and] did not separate "artistic" from "useful" aspects of their intellectual creations and innovations" (WIPO 2008:6).

Economics is ill-equipped to incorporate measurements of TK or cultural patrimony into its analysis. Financial valuations are difficult in any form of intangible asset such as IP, but cultural patrimony is even more ethereal. One possible angle for inclusion would be to consider cultural patrimony part of the community's utility function. This might capture some of the value and decision-making but would be subject to the same market failures that form the basis of many approaches to cultural economics. This points to a contingent value methodology and choice modelling as potential solutions (O'Brien 2010). It may also be that the costs of creating such empirical, quantitative measurements are disproportionate to the benefits. This combination of methodological challenges and practical costs suggests that a theoretical or qualitative, rather than empirical or quantitative, analysis may be better deployed to inform TK policy.

Current economic thinking does not allow for TK to fit into an innovation approach to IP. The same could be said for trade marks; however, recent analysis, adopting a wider definition of innovation, suggests trade marks can fit. The analysis of TK may follow a similar path. As a cultural policy, TK suffers from this lack of positive economic interpretation, in addition to its already tenuous position in international policy debates. This suggests Yudice's anthropological approach is at the core of justifications for TK and that attempts to fit TK into an overarching creativity and innovation approach are inappropriate. This is not to say that economic analysis cannot inform cultural policy, but that a standard social contract/incentives-to-innovate approach is incomplete in its current form. Revisiting the scope of economic analysis of the benefits of creativity and innovation to capture social values may introduce needed flexibility into social contract theory. This might benefit from beginning economic analysis of IP for a cultural economics perspective rather than an industrial organisation/growth perspective. In short, adopting an intradisciplinary economic approach. Further analysis is required.

Geographical indications (GI)

GI, which overlaps with TK, suffers from similar challenges in fitting social contract theory and innovation arguments. Unlike other rights, they confer no freedom to contract or freedom to license. Instead of incentivising innovation, GIs can actively discourage innovation. A GI provides legal structure to the branding and quality of a product associated with a particular geographical region. The neoclassical economic justification for GI is additionally undermined by the overlapping coverage of other rights (for example, collectively owned trade marks serve a similar purpose).

A geographical indication (GI) is a sign used on products that have a specific geographical origin and possess qualities or a reputation that are due to that origin. In order to function as a GI, a sign must identify a product as originating in a given place. In addition, the qualities, characteristics or reputation of the product should be essentially due to the place of origin. Since the qualities depend on the geographical place of production, there is a clear link between the product and its original place of production.

(WIPO 2015)

Like trade marks, an economic argument for GI is to protect producers from free riding by competitors. However, the long-term economic benefits conferred on producers and these regions remain unproven. The introduction of a GI may benefit producers through legal protection, economic development and environmental concerns, but, like TK, these impacts are unclear. Furthermore, the GI may distort incentives and affect both the quality and quantity of the product.

The economic rhetoric focuses heavily on GI's role in economic development of rural areas (Bramley 2011). However, these arguments are weaker if individual producers are owned by larger businesses where profits may not develop the local economy. Indeed, the production of wines and spirits has undergone significant consolidation[8,9] in past years and, in these markets, the majority of production of GI goods is owned by large multi-nationals. This stands in contrast to the local, rural rationale for GI.

As with the impact on indigenous peoples with respective to TK, the long-term impact of GI on producers is uncertain. Existing producers may initially benefit from the price premium and reduced competition from products outside GI protection, but cost inputs and distorted incentives may mean that the economic distribution of these benefits changes over time. Thus, the original economic goals of the introduction of a GI may not be realised.

GI have become more contentious as some countries seek to expand GI to non-agricultural products. These products are typically textiles such as pottery or woollens that still are strongly influenced by the environment in which they are produced. As a relatively new right,[10] non-agricultural GI are still developing; further refinement of both the right and the economic understanding may occur. Yet to be fully considered by the literature is the appropriateness of government resources to protect rights not available to the general public.

While neoclassical economic analysis of trade marks has evolved to incorporate a wider understanding of the economic contribution of branding, the same cannot be said for TK and GI. However, cultural economics, with its well-developed understanding of cultural policy and creative industries, can contribute to this development and highlight the shortcomings of an incentive-to-innovate social contract approach to IP.

Conclusions

Cultural economics continues to evolve as analysis of the creative industries, intellectual property policy and economics, both in economic literature and policy development, merge. As this chapter has detailed, discussions on innovation and creativity have led both innovation-focused and cultural economists to examine IP as a cultural and innovation policy. However, analysis of IP highlights the restrictions that traditional economics faces when examining the realm of cultural policy and creative industries. While long-standing IP such as patents and copyright fit a neoclassical, incentive-to-innovate approach and are satisfied with rational choice theory and the maximisation of profits and utility, emerging IP rights are not. Economics' focus on the individual falters when faced with the collective approach of rights such as TK and GI. However, the evolution of economic analysis of trade marks suggests that economic tools and analysis have the potential to adapt.

Given the progression of IP as a topic of international negotiations, cultural economics' interest in IP is likely to continue. IP as a cultural policy merits further examination. Areas to consider for future research are examination of the impact on economic development stemming from IP such as TK and GI. Progression of the understanding of innovation, to include 'soft' innovation and creativity, will likely reformulate innovation policy. Copyright, only mentioned in passing in this chapter, is very poorly understood empirically; it may benefit from the growth in data availability stemming from the digital era. Ultimately, these investigations may lead to a departure from, or further developments of, incentive-to-innovate approaches to IP.

Notes

1 Including, but not limited to, the creative economy, the copyright industries, the creative industries, the cultural industries, cultural-political economy and the creative classes.
2 The list of these industries, shown in "Creative Industries Mapping Documents 1998," is available at www.gov.uk/government/publications/creative-industries-mapping-documents-1998.
3 Thorstein Veblen's seminal work, "Theory of Leisure Class" in 1898, could be classified as cultural economics. Works by Adam Smith (1700s) also consider the market for arts.
4 He also notes, unfortunately for your author, the challenges of a career as a cultural economist are many. He argues that foundations favour funding research building on well-established areas of economic analysis, one-off funding is rare, the opportunity costs of such careers are high, and the audience for economic research in the arts is limited.
5 There is an emerging third nexus, which involves a near or total rejection of IP, which is not discussed here.
6 Defined by WIPO (2015), as "A trademark is a distinctive sign which identifies certain goods or services as those produced or provided by a specific person or enterprise." Available at www.wipo.int/trademarks/en/.
7 Further information on the use of trade marks as a complementary measurement in industrial and innovation analysis can be found in Mendoca et al. (2004).
8 Emler, R. (June 13, 2012), "Spirits Firms Poised for Further Consolidation," The Drinks Business, available at www.thedrinksbusiness.com/2012/06/spirits-firms-poised-for-further-consolidation/.
9 Morss, E. (January 14, 2012), "The Future of the Global Wine Industry," Morss Global Finance, available at www.morssglobalfinance.com/the-future-of-the-global-wine-industry/.
10 The first formalized system of GI is that of France which was put into law in the early 1900s. The European Commission began a consultation on NAGI in 2014.

References

Baker, D. & Evans, W. 2013. A handbook of digital library economics: operations, collections and services. Oxford: Chandos Publishing. http://public.eblib.com/choice/publicfullrecord.aspx?p=1574975.

Bakhshi, H., Freeman, A. & Hitchen, G. 2009. Measuring Intrinsic Value. *How to Stop Worrying and Love Economics* www.missionmodelsmoney.org.uk/papers/measuring-intrinsic-value/ (accessed on 1 October 2011).

Bakhshi, H. & Mcvittie, E. 2009. Creative supply-chain linkages and innovation: Do the creative industries stimulate business innovation in the wider economy? *Innovation,* 11, 169–189.

Bawra, S. & Rai, S. M. 2003. Knowledge and/as power: a feminist critique of trade related intellectual property rights. *Gender, Technology and Development,* 7(1), 91–113.

Blaug, M. 2001. Where are we now on cultural economics. *Journal of Economic Surveys,* 15, 123–143.

Bramley, C. and June, I. 2011. 'A Review of the Socio-economic Impact of Geographical Indications: Considerations for the Developing World' WIPO Worldwide Symposium on Geographical Indications, Lima, Peru.

Caves, R. 2000. *Creative industries: contracts between art and commerce.* Cambridge, MA: Harvard University Press.

Cherrier, B. 2015. Classifying economics: a history of the JEL Codes. *Journal of Economic Literature.* Available at SSRN: https://ssrn.com/abstract=2537382.

Corrado, C. A. & Hao, J. 2013. *Brands as Productive Assets: Concepts, Measurement, and Global Trends* Economic Research Working Paper No. 13. Available at http://world-intellectual-property-organization.com/publications/en/details.jsp?id=3957&plang=EN (accessed on August 15 2017).

Cuccia, T., Marrelli, M. & Santagata, W. 2008. Collective trademarks and cultural districts: the case of San Gregorio Armero, Naples. In Cooke, P. & Lazzeretti, L. (eds.), *Creative Cities, Cultural Clusters and Local Economic Development.* Cheltenham: Edward Elgar, 121–135.

DCMS (UK Department for Cultural, Media and Sport). 2015. 'Creative Industries Economic Estimates January 2015 - Key Findings'. Available at www.gov.uk/government/publications/creative-industries-economic-estimates-january-2015/creative-industries-economic-estimates-january-2015-key-findings.

Doyle, G. 2016. Creative economy and policy. *European Journal of Communication,* 31, 33–45.

Dutfield, G. Harnessing traditional knowledge and genetic resources for local development and trade. International seminar on intellectual property and development. WIP–UNCTAD–UNIDO–WHO–WTO, Geneva, 2005.

Economides, N. 1988. The economics of trademarks. *Trademark Reporter,* 78, 523.

Economy, C. 2008. Report 2008: The Challenge of Assessing the Creative Economy: towards Informed Policymaking, UNDP-UNCTAD.

Emler, R. 2012. 'Spirits Firms Posed for Further Consolidation'. The Drinks Business, 13 June 2012. Available at www.thedrinksbusiness.com/2012/06/spirits-firms-poised-for-further-consolidation/.

Fernald, L. W. 1988. The underlying relationship between creativity, innovation and entrepreneurship. *The Journal of Creative Behavior,* 22, 196–202. doi:10.1002/j.2162-6057.1988.tb00497.

Frey, B. 1994. Art: the economic point of view. *In:* Peacock, A. & Rizzo, I. (eds.) *Cultural Economics and Cultural Policies.* Springer Netherlands.

Frey, B. S. 1997. *Not just for the money: an economic theory of personal motivation.* Cheltenham: Elgar.

Frey, B. S. 2000. *Arts & economics: analysis & cultural policy.* Berlin: Springer.

Garnham, N. 2005. From cultural to creative industries: An analysis of the implications of the "creative industries" approach to arts and media policy making in the United Kingdom. *International Journal of Cultural Policy,* 11, 15–29.

Ghose, A., Smith, M. D. & Telang, R. 2006. Internet exchanges for used books: An empirical analysis of product cannibalization and welfare impact. *Information Systems Research,* 17, 3–19.

Granstrand, O. 2000. *The Economics and Management of Intellectual Property: Towards Intellectual Capitalism.* Cheltenham: Edward Elgar.

Greenhalgh, C. & Rogers, M. 2007. *Trade Marks and Performance in UK Firms: Evidence of Schumpeterian Competition through Innovation.* Oxford: University of Oxford.

Halbert, D. 2006. Feminist interpretations of intellectual property. *American University Journal of Gender, Social Policy & the Law,* 14(3), 431–460.

Hesmondhalgh, D. 2005. Media and cultural policy as public policy: the case of the British Labour government. *International Journal of Cultural Policy,* 11, 95–109.

Hesmondhalgh, D. & Pratt, A. C. 2005. Cultural industries and cultural policy. *International Journal of Cultural Policy,* 11, 1–13.

Hettinger, E. C. 1989. Justifying intellectual property. *Philosophy & Public Affairs,* 18, 31–52.

Howkins, J. 2002. *The Creative Economy: How People Make Money from Ideas,* Penguin.

Jeffcutt, P. and Pratt, A. C. 2002. Managing creativity in the cultural industries. *Creativity and Innovation Management,* 11(4), 225–233.

Klein, N. 2010. *No Space, No Choice, No Jobs, No Logo.* London: Flamingo.

Landes, W. M. & Posner, R. A. 1989. An economic analysis of copyright law. *The Journal of Legal Studies,* 18(2), 325–363.

Lee, N. & Rodríguez-Pose, A. 2014. Creativity, cities, and innovation. *Environment and Planning A,* 46, 1139–1159.

Lemley, M. A. 2004a. Ex ante versus ex post justifications for intellectual property. *The University of Chicago Law Review*, 129–149.

Lemley, M. A. 2004b. Property, intellectual property, and free riding. *Tex L. Rev.*, 83, 1031.

McCloskey, D. N. 1998. *The Rhetoric of Economics*. Madison: University of Wisconsin Press.

McDonald, P. 2013. Introduction. *Cinema Journal*, 52, 145–149.

Mendonça, S., Pereira, T. S. & Godinho, M. M. 2004. Trademarks as an indicator of innovation and industrial change. *Research Policy*, 33, 1385–1404.

Montén, L. 2005. Geographical indications of origin: should they be protected and why-an analysis of the issue from the US and EU perspectives. *Santa Clara Computer & High Tech. LJ*, 22, 315.

Morss, E. 2012. 'The Future of the Global Wine Industry' Elliot R. Morss blog. Available at www.morssglobalfinance.com/the-future-of-the-global-wine-industry/.

Müller, K., Rammer, C. & Trüby, J. 2009. The role of creative industries in industrial innovation. *Innovation*, 11, 148–168.

Nesta, T. W. F. A. 2007. *Staying Ahead: The Economic Performance of the UK's Creative Industries – Creative Blueprint*. Available at http://creative-blueprint.co.uk/library/item/staying-ahead-the-economic-performance-of-the-uks-creative-industries [Accessed].

O'Brien, D. 2010. *Measuring the Value of Culture: A Report to the Department for Culture Media and Sport*, Department for Culture, Media and Sport.

O'Brien, D. 2014. Cultural value, measurement and policy making. *Arts and Humanities in Higher Education*, 14(1), 79–94.

Peacock, A. 2004. The credibility of cultural economists' advice to governments. *Contributions to Economic Analysis*, 260, 165–178.

Pick, D., Weber, P., Connell, J. & Geneste, L. A. 2015. Theorising creative industry management: rebooting the woolly mammoth. *Management Decision*, 53, 754–762.

Potts, J. 2009. Introduction: creative industries & innovation policy. *Innovation*, 11, 138–147.

Putsis Jr, W. P. 1998. Are brand promotions just a zero–sum game–or can they increase the size of the pie? *Business Strategy Review*, 9, 21–32.

Rubenson, D. L. & Runco, M. A. 1992. The psychoeconomic approach to creativity. *New ideas in Psychology*, 10, 131–147.

Rushton, M. 2003. Cultural diversity and public funding of the arts: a view from cultural economics. *The Journal of Arts Management, Law, and Society*, 33, 85–97.

Santhosh, M. R. & Sengupta, R., 2011. Trade, Intellectual Property Rights (IPRs) and Gender Issues in India. *Trade and Gender Briefs' Series*. India. InditeGlobal, New Delhi: Third World Network (TWN) and Heinrich Boell Foundation (HBF).

Schatz, T. 2014. Film studies, cultural studies, and media industries studies. *Media Industries*, 1.

Schumpeter, J. A. 1942. *Capitalism, socialism, and democracy*. New York: Harper.

Scotchmer, S. 2006. *Innovation and Incentives*, Cambridge, MA: MIT Press.

Stoneman, P. 2010. *Soft Innovation: Economics, Product Aesthetics, and the Creative Industries*. Oxford: Oxford University Press.

Thompson, H. 1997. Ignorance and ideological hegemony: a critique of neoclassical economics. *Journal of Interdisciplinary Economics*, 8, 291–305.

Throsby, D. 1994. The production and consumption of the arts: a view of cultural economics. *Journal of Economic Literature*, 32, 1–29.

Throsby, D. 2012. Why should economists be interested in cultural policy? *Economic Record*, 88, 106–109.

Throsby, D. & Throsby, C. 2001. *Economics and Culture*. Cambridge: Cambridge University Press.

Towse, R. 2006. Copyright and artists: a view from cultural economics. *Journal of Economic Surveys*, 20, 567–585.

Towse, R. 2010. *A Textbook of Cultural Economics*. Cambridge: Cambridge University Press.

Towse, R. 2014. *Advanced Introduction to Cultural Economics*. Cheltenham: Edward Elgar Publishing.

UNCTAD. 2008. 'The Challenge of Assessing the Creative Economy: towards Informed Policy-making. Available at http://unctad.org/en/docs/ditc20082cer_en.pdf.

Von Graevenitz, G. 2013. Trade mark cluttering–evidence from EU enlargement. *Oxford Economic Papers*, 65, 721–745.

Weldon, W. 1972. Why creativity? An analogy to the economics of supply and demand. *The Journal of Creative Behavior*, 6, 55–60.

WIPO. 2008. WIPO Regional Expert Meeting on the Establishment of a Caribbean Framework for the Protection of Traditional Knowledge, Folklore and Genetic Resources.

WIPO. 2015. 'Traditional Knowledge' WIPO website. Available at www.wipo.int/tk/en/tk/.

Work Foundation. 2007. *Staying Ahead. The Economic Performance of the UK's Creative Industries*. London: The Work Foundation.

Yúdice, G. 2009. Cultural diversity and cultural rights. *Hispanic Issues Online*.

Zappalaglio, A. 2013. Traditional knowledge: emergence and history of the concept at international level. Available at SSRN: http://dx.doi.org/10.2139/ssrn.2554132.

4

Sociology and cultural policy

David Wright

Introduction

In this chapter, I examine the relations between sociology and cultural policy. Such an exercise requires some careful de-lineation, not least because, at a distance, these objects might both appear to be more 'solid' than they actually are close up. The chapter proceeds first with some brief working definitions of these terms. The story sketched here reflects the shared historical processes, from the nineteenth century onwards, and a shared geography, of Western Europe and North America, in which the discipline of sociology and the problem of culture for the modern state have been formed. While sociological analysis is increasingly post-national in its orientations, the problems of policy are almost inevitably located in specific territories. In exploring the relations between sociology and cultural policy below, I focus on the UK, where the development of the discipline of sociology was bound up, in the early twentieth century, with a changing conception of the role of academic knowledge and of culture in the practice of government. The discussion then moves to France, where the work of Pierre Bourdieu in the mid-twentieth century helps to bring a particular version of the problem of culture, produced through the techniques of social science, under the lens of 'modernising' governments in Europe. We return to the UK, via a brief sojourn to the United States, as the research infrastructure that might underpin sociological analysis of patterns of cultural participation continues to be refined and integrated into the practices of policymakers. Any attempt to identify the relations between these objects of analysis is likely to be partial and strategic. Accepting that other stories can be told from other national and regional perspectives, these examples are chosen to highlight particular moments of intersection between sociology and cultural policy that continue to resonate, rather than because of their universal applicability. The chapter concludes with some reflection on why, despite a brief flowering of the empirical techniques of gathering evidence about the cultural lives and practices of populations, if not the theoretical mode of analysing such evidence, sociological perspectives on culture might have become less useful to cultural policymakers in these places than they once were.

Defining the terms of debate

Both sociology and cultural policy have histories that reveal much about the shifting intellectual landscape of the 'advanced' democracies of the global North, in which the development of academic disciplines and their institutional location on university teaching curricula are bound up with the development of the state itself. A working definition of *sociology* might emphasise a genealogy that incorporates specific, foundational, theoretical accounts and combines them with a set of methodological techniques that can be applied to help understand social life. The theoretical accounts would most likely include the range of eighteenth-, nineteenth- and twentieth-century European and North American thinkers (Max Weber, Emile Durkheim, Mary Wollstonecraft, W. E. B. Du Bois, Georg Simmel, Auguste Comte, Gabriel Tarde, Karl Marx, Thorstein Veblen, Beatrice Webb) who are credited, sometimes retrospectively, with defining and giving some shape to the concept of 'the social' through work that engaged with the emerging problems of modern, urban, industrial, patriarchal, market-oriented democracies. As Michael Burawoy describes it, the early manifestations of what we now call sociological modes of thinking were bound up with narratives of social reform and struggles for civil rights, such that sociology could imagine itself as an 'angel of history, searching for order in the broken fragments of modernity, seeking to salvage the promise of progress' (Burawoy, 2005: 5).

The methodological techniques applied to this significant task include the identification and production of social statistics of various forms, often in this formative period produced in direct relation to, and on behalf of, the emerging modern state and through such mechanisms as population censuses and, later, the sample survey. These techniques are shared with other social sciences developing in the same period, such as economics and psychology, and they can also be contrasted with and complemented by other methods, including ethnography, participant observation and interviewing, which also overlap with anthropology. Like these other social sciences, sociology privileges the observable, empirical world in making its claims to knowledge, and it is from some combination of these empirical ways of capturing the social world and the theoretical lenses through which it is examined that a disciplinary identity of sociology – the 'sociological imagination' of C. Wright Mills' (1959) definitive statement of professional intent – begins to emerge.

A working definition of *cultural policy* for this purpose might identify an intriguingly similar geographic and historical period in which civic and national institutions associated with various forms of cultural and artistic production begin to be established and in which the organisation and management of such institutions become a concern for the modern state, in regard to which forms of cultural expression should be displayed or preserved, whether a given population should or should not access them and how, if at all, such institutions are to be supported and financed. A more recent history, from the early to mid-twentieth century concerns the formation of specific ministries of culture, or equivalents, which are given responsibility for the strategic management of the various forms of cultural production within a particular national territory, e.g. through the re-distribution of some proportion of public funding or taxation. This more recent phenomenon is the culmination of older inter-relations between the ideals, and indeed anxieties, that governments have about artistic and symbolic forms of expression, democracy and self-realisation and their spread within and across the developing public spheres of modern nation states.

This working definition of cultural policy itself depends on a working definition of *culture*. In the developing history of cultural policy, such a definition can be initially associated with those cultural forms that are becoming institutionalised in the civic spaces of eighteenth- and nineteenth-century Europe and North America, such as fine art, sculpture, orchestral forms of music, opera, theatre, literature and poetry. The establishment of these forms and the venues in which they are cultivated, performed and exhibited can be seen as part of a process of the formation of distinctive *national* identities, which have been of interest to sociologists (e.g. Anderson, 1991). The creation and management of such identities through the circulation of national cultural forms is one imperative of developing cultural policies to establish the legitimacy of modern states over their territories (Alasuutari, 2001; Parkhusrt Clarke, 1987), to sustain national identities in the context of supra-national pressures (Robins, 2007) and, more recently, to promote the nation on a global cultural stage (Kwon and Kim, 2014; Minnaert, 2014). In their more recent iterations, questions of cultural policy also variously take account of a widened conception of culture, including commercial culture; they have come to incorporate concern with all aspects of the symbolic life of a nation. This includes national and international debates about film, broadcasting, the regulation and management of intellectual property, the strategic definition of and public support for 'the creative industries'. In early-twenty-first-century UK, the field even incorporates a concern with questions of national technical infrastructure inasmuch as the British Department of Culture, Media and Sport (DCMS) is responsible for the implementation of government policies relating to the maintenance of the UK's broadband Internet network. In this latter version, cultural policy perhaps completes a journey from being a distinct set of concerns about a relatively discrete set of special cultural 'things', towards being implicated in a far more dispersed set of social and economic processes.

If sociology's early project was to explain and moderate the forces of modernity and the shifting relations among people in new urban contexts, new forms of workplace and new forms of family life, then questions of 'culture' can be understood as part of this project, too. Durkheim's *The Elementary Form of Religious Life* (2001[1912]) and Simmel's reflections on fashion (1997 [1905]), for example, both emphasise the symbolic aspects of social life and the importance of meaning-making to the maintenance of social relations in modernity. A more specific sociological concern with the restricted definition of culture as associated with cultural policy – meaning initially 'the arts' and latterly the cultural and media industries – is a more recent development. The elisions and collisions created by the general 'cultural turn' within the social sciences create, by the end of the twentieth century and early twenty-first, a variegated set of research territories including a distinct sociology of artistic forms (e.g. Wolff, 1993; Zolberg, 1990) and a somewhat antagonistic distinction between a 'sociology of culture' – in which cultural forms and practices are the focus of analysis – and 'cultural sociology' – where 'cultural' describes an approach privileging the symbolic in analysing a wider range of social phenomena (see Inglis (2016) for useful summary discussion of what is at stake in these territorial battles). A more restricted focus on culture as an object of analysis itself also became difficult to sustain in the light of the rise of Cultural Studies towards the end of the twentieth century, itself an accommodation between sociology and literary studies. This approach's influential insistence on the relations between culture and everyday life drew concerted attention to forms of cultural production and consumption that went beyond the legitimated, institutionalised forms that had been the preserve of the state or its variously constituted elites. The project to identify and explore the ideologies of popular cultural forms as sites of domination, resistance and symbolic expression of identity, especially for previously marginalised groups, plays a significant role in re-shaping the sociological imagination for the late twentieth century (e.g. Hall and Jefferson, 1975; Hebdige, 1979).

This brief historical story at least indicates that the barriers around sociology and cultural policy are rather porous. With this proviso in mind, the chapter now goes on to discuss in more detail how and why questions of culture have been important to the development of the discipline of sociology, first with a particular focus on the UK and then with some discussion of how sociology has helped to bring the problem of culture into being for cultural policy, with a focus on France.

The sociology of culture and cultural policy in the twentieth century

If questions of 'culture' were always implicit in the development of the discipline of sociology and its commitment to explaining modernity, the emergence of more identifiable 'sociology of culture' was bound up with specific anxieties about mass society and mass culture and their consequences. Such anxieties begin in the late nineteenth century as adult suffrage, universal models of education and the possibility of industrially produced symbolic forms became increasingly cemented. They are deepened in post-war Europe and the US, when sociological work emerges focussing on the products of the cultural industries (Adorno and Horkheimer, 1944) and the potential influence of 'mass' forms of broadcasting and entertainment on social life (Lazarsfeld and Merton, 1948). In the UK, in this period, these concerns were part of a general re-alignment in which the rise of the social sciences, as a specific aid to the workings of the modern state, was itself a direct challenge to the primacy of the kinds of knowledge that emerged from the arts and humanities, i.e. from those forms of academic knowledge that had previously held the primary responsibility for understanding 'culture' in its more restricted sense. In his account of the *cultural* significance of the rise and spread of social scientific forms of knowledge across the twentieth century, Savage (2010) identifies a fissure within the British elites of the post-war years between a more traditional 'aristocratic' intellectual for whom authority was a product of family and social networks, but legitimised through humanistic forms of education, and a more technically oriented intellectual concerned with the gathering and analysis of evidence to identify and address social problems. The difference between these two 'sides' is perhaps felt most acutely in relation to questions of culture where the relative value or worth of cultural artefacts was assumed to rest with established artists, writers and their largely elite scholars and audiences who had neither reason nor inclination to test or question their judgement about such matters or to recognise that forms of cultural life outside this purview had anything substantive or valuable to contribute to national life, beyond keeping 'the masses' entertained or distracted. It is a difference that is evident in higher education at the time in the relative presence of chairs in social sciences and the arts in British universities in 1939, as revealed by the Clapham report. Only five percent were in the still nascent social sciences (covering sociology, economics, psychology and a range of cognate disciplines) compared to 42 percent in the arts and humanities – and 27 percent in the natural sciences (Savage, 2010: 120).

The story of British intellectual life in the post-war period is arguably of a slow shift in dominance from the former kind of intellectual to the latter, at least in terms of their relative influence over the workings of the modern state. The tensions between the positions can be neatly embodied, in the story of British cultural policy at least, by the figure of the economist John Maynard Keynes who was both a co-architect of the post-World War II global economic order and a major proponent of the value of public investment in the arts and culture, culminating in his role in the establishment of the British Arts Council (Upchurch, 2004, 2011). Keynes represents both the rise of the technocratic social scientist at the heart of government, and, through his association with the influential Bloomsbury group of writers and intellectuals, retains an association with a more gentlemanly and 'aristocratic' conception of culture as a set of things of intrinsic value. Keynes's own interest was arguably to *preserve* this conception of culture in the light of the rise of mass forms of society, with the modernist intellectuals of the Bloomsbury group more usually exhibiting deep ambivalence towards, and occasional outright loathing of, the masses themselves (Carey, 1992) and deep scepticism of their ability to appreciate culture.

As well as the kinds of theoretical perspectives and methodological tools outlined in sketching a distinct sociological approach, disciplines also need places, institutions and people in order to establish themselves. In Savage's account, the growing influence of the social sciences in the UK – including sociology – is nurtured and sustained away from the traditional centres of humanistic, aristocratic forms of knowledge (the universities of Oxford and Cambridge) in newer institutions, including the LSE, Kent and Manchester, with expansionist ambitions that reflected the widening access to higher education in the mid-twentieth century and in which new forms of technical, social science knowledge could be encouraged in people from a wider range of backgrounds. These forms of knowledge were self-consciously promoted as an explicit challenge to the legitimacy of inherited forms of authority, and possessors of these 'progressive technical identities' (Savage, 2010: 85) conceptualised themselves as an alternative to the aristocratic modernist establishment, able to apply the tools of social science to the problems of national life. This included attention to the lived experience of the population and the collection of evidence of various kinds, through censuses, surveys and initiatives such as the Mass Observation program of diary-keeping, in which the everyday lives and cultural practices of the broader population could be captured and analysed. This principle of attention to empirically identifying the thoughts, behaviours and activities of a population, rather than assuming to know what is best for them – the call to 'make things transparent, to refuse myth, to tell it how it really is and to understand ordinary lives' (Savage, 2010: 90) – is central to the cultural influence of the rise of the social sciences in general. The particular contribution of sociology, which becomes more formally established as an academic discipline in the UK in the 1950s, and reaches particular prominence in the 1960s, is to conceptualise the population as more than 'just' economic agents, knowledge of whom could be valuable in shaping a new kind of government and a new kind of inclusive national story. In this period sociology became, as Steve Fuller describes it, 'the science of and for the welfare state, the political rubric under which society travelled' (2006: 17), and we can perhaps see how sociologically inspired research into urban life, family life, the workplace or understanding patterns of health and illness could be directly useful to policymakers concerned with managing complex societies. Sociologists in this period could have imagined themselves as part of a progressive, democratising project in which the evidence emerging from the identification and measurement of the life experiences of the population was brought directly into the process of governing.

In the UK, the apparently fading aristocratic mode of governing was perhaps most stubbornly attached to questions of culture – even though such questions are precisely defined by the rather opaque, taken-for-granted and unexamined forms of authority that were the target of the technical-democratising project of the social sciences. In his short history of the rise of community art – itself a movement that attempted to challenge elite notions of art and culture –Owen Kelly describes the disquiet expressed, as late as 1976, by Lord Gibson, chair of the Arts Council, at the notion that, because the finer arts had traditionally been enjoyed by a select group of the population, public funding entailed a pressure to make artistic producers more accountable to or accessible by the wider public. He expresses scepticism that there is a '"cultural dynamism" in the people that will emerge if only they can be liberated from the cultural values hitherto accepted by an elite' and outright hostility to 'one European "cultural expert"', who referred to such values as 'the "cultural colonialism of the middle-classes"' (Gibson, quoted in Kelly, 1984: 21). Neither Kelly nor Gibson reveals precisely who this parenthesised expert is, but it is a notion that resonates most strongly with the work of Pierre Bourdieu, whose contribution provides a key moment in the relations between sociology and cultural policy as it was emerging in the same period in France.

A useful sociology?

Bourdieu's sociological analysis of European museum attendance, conducted with Alain Darbel, was published in France in 1969. This study, *The Love of Art*, employed the established empirical techniques of sociology, based around survey-interviews, with audiences at a range of art museums across Europe (including France, Greece, the Netherlands, Poland and Spain) and used the statistical analysis, and other forms of observation and measurement (including length of time of visit and qualitative analysis of the language used to describe the visit) to examine how the experiences of museum visitors were socially patterned. With the application of these techniques to this subject, the study provides a significant set of methodological and theoretical templates for subsequent relations between sociology and cultural policy, focussed upon the policy 'problem' of cultural inequality, i.e. the differential engagement of the populace of a particular country or territory with its public cultural resources. Laurie Haniquet (this volume) gives a fuller discussion of the theoretical and empirical construction of this problem in Bourdieu's work. For my purposes here, Bourdieu embodies a particular moment in the overlapping histories of sociology and cultural policymaking in that his emergence as the predominant sociologist of culture of the late twentieth century began in the 1960s and was given momentum and impetus through a research programme directly connected with the apparatus of the French state.

As Ahearne (2004) and Dubois (2011) relate, the late 1950s and early 1960s, i.e. the same period in which sociology was establishing itself as an influential social science discipline in the UK, was a key period in the formation of modern cultural policy in France, culminating in the formation of the Ministry of Cultural Affairs under the leadership of the novelist Andre Malraux in 1959. As in the UK, this is a period characterised by an increased concern with *modernisation*, and the possibility of corralling and applying various emerging forms of technical and scientific expertise to achieve that modernisation. While in the UK the field of culture remained rather insulated from these imperatives, in France, the aspiration to modernise extended to questions of culture and meant that, according to a key civil servant in the Ministry of Culture, 'Cultural policy must no longer be commanded by aesthetic and moral motives but must be conceived on the basis of objective data and be scientifically based on social needs' (quoted in Dubois, 2011: 496). The Ministry's funding of the project that eventually becomes *The Love of Art* reflects this impetus.

There was, then, a mutually reinforcing rationale for a relationship between sociology and matters of cultural policy in this period in France. On the one hand was a state, similar to that previously identified in the UK, increasingly influenced by technocratic concerns with evidence, and on the other was a discipline's attempt to cement its status as a science through the application of its techniques and technologies of data gathering and analysis. Social scientific forms of knowledge were used as a 'mode of legitimation' (Dubois, 2011: 496) for policy initiatives, while, 'state commissioned research was a means to promote a renewed sociology which, having gained social and scientific legitimacy thanks to support outside academia, could subsequently assert its position in the academic field' (Dubois,

2011: 495). These conditions also proved especially fertile for Pierre Bourdieu in his own attempts to mark a distinct place for himself in the French intellectual field. The use and application of the methods of social science were important in this task. While his early work is more closely associated with the techniques of ethnography, based on fieldwork in Algeria, and most usually identified as anthropological in its orientation, upon his return to France in the late 1950s, Bourdieu embarked on a series of works that drew explicitly on survey questionnaires, beginning with *The Inheritors* (1979), but including *The Love of Art* (1991) and culminating in his most enduring work, *Distinction* (1984). As Robbins describes it, in this formative period, 'he was opting for self-presentation in terms of social and cultural anthropology or sociology so as to present himself as a scientist rather than a speculative philosopher.' (Robbins, 2005: 22) The use of these forms of empirical quantitative methods was not without controversy, given that this was also a period in which such evidence, with its strong associations with the mechanisms of the state, was beginning to be critiqued. For Bourdieu, though, these methods were precisely the basis upon which he could construct his sociology in contrast to the abstract philosophical theorising that dominated French intellectual life and build up the discipline's self-belief that it was rigorous in its claim-making. One consequence of a commitment to such forms of evidence, as described by Lebaron (2009), was the use of its 'scientific' authority, more usually attached to economistic explanations for social life, to generate convincing counter-explanations, which could be taken equally seriously.

The combination of these impulses – from policymakers for evidence, from social scientists for official recognition and from Bourdieu himself for a place in the intellectual landscape – perhaps explains the on-going significance of *The Love of Art* in setting the terms of the relations between sociology and cultural policy. It also gives some indication as to why, at least for Bourdieu, such relations proved untenable. If the aim of applying the technologies of contemporary social science to the operation of cultural policy through the support of empirical research like *The Love of Art* was to re-shape cultural policy towards a more modern, accountable, democratic mode and away from an aesthetic, moral one, then the evidence presented by Bourdieu could indeed have been useful. The establishment of statistical relationships between social groups and the extent and nature of their attendance of museums seems likely to be a productive basis for initiatives that alter or shape the nature of exhibits or venues to make them more attractive to broadened audiences – and indeed this approach proves remarkably resilient, as we shall see. Bourdieu's interpretation of this evidence, though, and his more nuanced engagement with the nature of the museum audience generated a different set of solutions.

For Dubois, Bourdieu's interpretation of the 'problem' of accessing culture comes down to four interlocking points. First, the ability to choose whether to visit a museum or not is determined by previously acquired dispositions; second, the appreciation of art in the museum depends on codes that, again, are acquired elsewhere; third, the meanings of works of art are not always self-evident or obvious; fourth, the cultural institutions themselves are potentially intimidating spaces for a significant portion of the population. The last two points reflect what Bourdieu later refers to as the 'cult of the work of art' (Bourdieu, 1984: 53) and the belief in its charismatic power. The former two points imply that solutions to the problems of cultural institutions do not lie with the institutions themselves but in other spheres such as the family or school. Both positions challenged the very legitimacy of the Ministry of Culture itself. Moreover they 'de-sacralised' legitimate culture, making Bourdieu's intervention problematic for those individuals, institutions and policymakers most invested in maintaining the special place ascribed to culture in social life.

While under Malraux cultural policy was explicitly evoked as a means of using the arts to re-invigorate the kind of social ties and bonds associated with religious life for a modern, secular society, the Ministry and the cultural institutions themselves were to remain guardians of the faith and therefore complicit in maintaining art's charismatic ideology. For Bourdieu, a democratic cultural policy really demanded that this ideology be revealed, subverted and even over-turned. More pragmatically, but no less damning, was the implication that the cultural institutions, and the Ministry, were actually rather marginal to the problem of cultural inequality, at least compared to the equivalent department for education with responsibility for the position of various forms of culture on curricula and for how the codes of appreciation were taught and learned. This made Bourdieu's findings something of anathema to a new Ministry at a time in which it was trying to establish and legitimise its role within government.

Although this experience raised questions for Bourdieu about the potential relations between an objective 'science' of sociology and the pragmatic demands of policymakers, Swartz (2004) reveals it did not end these relations, as Bourdieu was involved in producing two reports on the role and future of education in France under the socialist Mitterand government of the 1980s. Bourdieu's interventions can be seen, in retrospect, to have done much to help define the field of the sociology of culture and to have set the terms of the problem of cultural policy inasmuch as it is focussed on questions of cultural 'inequality'. The coincidence of forces (the forming of a ministry, the development of a discipline, the pressures of the academy) which underpins these interventions, though, also reflects a high water mark in direct relationships between sociology and cultural policy that has prefaced a more general parting of the ways. In the years since the *Love of Art* and especially *Distinction* sociology, certainly in Europe and North America, became *more* interested in culture, especially as informed by the popularity and influence of Cultural Studies. Direct dialogue between sociologists and policymakers though has become relatively rare.

Notable exceptions to this include the role of Richard A. Peterson and in the US and Tak Wing Chan and John Goldthorpe in the UK, contributions that both engage directly and critically with Bourdieu's applicability beyond France. A key figure in the development of the sociology of culture in the US, especially in relation to the 'production of culture perspective' (Peterson, 1976), and one of the co-founders of the ASA's sociology of culture section in 1986, Peterson joined the research division of the National Endowment for the Arts (NEA), the primary policy body with responsibility for federal funding of the arts, in 1979. There he was directly involved in the production of a national survey instrument on cultural participation, the Survey of Public Participation in the Arts (SPPA). He undertook this work in the light of abiding caution over research enterprises that 'focus on the manipulation of people's tastes, attitudes and behaviour' (quoted in Santoro, 2008: 50), and with a specific aim of helping those who were interested in increasing participation in the arts, as opposed to aiding market researchers. The analysis of findings from this instrument was used as the basis for Peterson, together with a range of collaborators (Peterson, 1992; Peterson and Kern, 1996; Peterson and Simkus, 1992), to develop the concept of the 'cultural omnivore' based on the empirical discovery of the relatively wide-ranging musical taste preferences of educated professionals, contrasted with the less varied 'univorous' tastes of the relatively less affluent with fewer educational qualifications. This concept – conceptualised as something of a challenge to the kinds of relationships identified by Bourdieu in the France of the 1960s and 1970s – emerges as one of the most significant in the sociology of culture in the early twenty-first century. Its growth and spread (see Peterson, 2005; Wright, 2016) also reflects the bringing of culture under the lens of modern government, inasmuch as that can be seen in the development of equivalent forms of survey to the SPPA in other territories as measurements of cultural participation are seen as worthwhile indicators of national policy success.

A similar relationship occurs in the UK with the work of John Goldthorpe (himself a key figure in the establishment of the technical identity of the sociologist in Savage's account) and his work with Tak Wing Chan examining the UK Arts Council's *Taking Part* survey and its predecessors (Chan and Goldthorpe, 2005, 2007a,b). This work, undertaken in a significant period in the recent history of UK cultural policy to be discussed below, used findings from surveys about participation in arts and cultural activities to engage directly with policy debates about cultural participation but also to contribute to the scholarly debates instigated by Richard Peterson about the omnivore. In relation to the latter, Chan and Goldthorpe's analysis points to some tentative support for the omnivore thesis, in that, as they describe, 'higher status, higher educational qualifications and a higher income all increase individuals' chances of being an omnivore rather than a univore' (Chan and Goldthorpe, 2005: 208). Work from this project (Chan and Goldthorpe, 2007a) also raised direct challenges for policy in questioning the extent, given that non-participation in the arts was common across social strata, that such 'self-exclusion' from the arts should be conceptualised as a policy concern at all. Later work emerging from the direct collaboration with policymakers includes the 2008 report *From Indifference to Enthusiasm* (Bunting et al., 2008), which found some 84 percent of the surveyed population of the UK engaged with little or no publicly funded arts activity and that education and social status were strong influences on the likelihood of participation. Qualitative work integrated into this analysis also identified strong barriers to participation, including those that were practical (relating to caring responsibilities for potential participants' children and to geographical proximity to the UK's cultural offer, concentrated in cities, especially London) but also 'psychological', relating to discomfort or unfamiliarity with the spaces and settings in which the arts were exhibited and performed. If these latter points contain echoes of the kinds of findings that emerge from *The Love of Art*, then the conclusion that, 'there does not appear to be any evidence of a cultural elite that engages with 'high art' rather than popular culture' (Bunting et al., 2008: 62) resonates more with the omnivore thesis. Such findings also suggest that the 'problem' of access to culture is one that is solvable by cultural organisations themselves through, for example, improved marketing messages or information about 'dress codes or etiquette' (Bunting et al., 2008: 12). This latter point offers the starkest contrast with the insights of Bourdieu – although one that is in keeping with Goldthorpe's established and clearly articulated suspicion of the conceptual and empirical basis of this position (Goldthorpe, 2007).

These differing intersections between sociologists and policymakers reflect recurrent tensions in relations between academic forms of research with apparent commitments to disinterested 'discovery' or 'truth' and those forms of research that are more instrumental in nature and directly oriented towards and sympathetic with the pragmatic problems of policymakers. In the specific field of cultural policy studies, this was a debate played out productively in the 1990s between McGuigan (1996) and Bennett (1998) about the possibility of a pure, critical Cultural Studies. For McGuigan, suspicious of any direct engagement between the state and scholarship,

> knowledge that is produced solely for official use and funded accordingly rarely questions the fundamental aims and objectives of the client organization. Under such conditions, it is very difficult for a policy-oriented research programme to observe the critical aims and responsibilities that have characterised a 'disinterested' cultural studies.
>
> *(McGuigan, 1996: 14)*

Such a position, for Bennett, is unsustainable in a context in which culture itself is a site of government, and in which universities, and intellectuals working within them, are part of the state's own infrastructure. Recognition of this belies a distinction between critical and 'practical' or 'technically' oriented intellectuals and suggests that the former should directly engage with the latter rather than preserve their—somewhat mythical—status as 'disinterested'.

This division maps nicely onto a general divergence in the field of sociology identified by Michael Burawoy for whom early twenty-first-century sociology exists in public, policy, critical and professional forms. A policy-oriented sociology can 'provide solutions to problems that are presented to us, or to legitimate solutions that have already been reached' (Burawoy, 2004: 9). A critical sociology, by contrast, has to 'supply moral visions' (Burawoy, 2004: 16). Both are united by the principles of 'professional sociology' underpinned by commitments to the set of methods, epistemological assumptions and the inherited theoretical perspectives that define the discipline. The relative usefulness of sociological knowledge for cultural policy, or any policy for that matter, is always likely, in this light, to reflect the varying priorities of both sociologists and policymakers.

Sociology, reflexivity and the 'creative industries'

The last decades of the twentieth century were a period in which the discipline of sociology and the technocratic states of the global North were both re-imagining the nature of social life. The oft-quoted assertion from former UK Prime Minister Margaret Thatcher that, 'there is no such thing as society. There are individual men and women and there are families' (quoted in Fuller, 2006: 12) was likely to cause greater problems for those social scientists more invested in the 'social' bit of that label than economists or psychologists, for example, whose epistemological assumptions worked outwards from the level of individual actors or agents. At least the economic and political context of the 1970s, 1980s and 1990s, in which successive governments in the UK, Europe and the US attempted to re-draw the terms of the social contract and re-evaluate the role of government in managing it, meant that the 'science of the welfare state' became a less influential voice. The dominant economic and political philosophies of the day no longer looked to the kinds of solutions that sociology provided because the problems of policy had, so the story goes, moved beyond the provision of basic needs and services, the management of the economy and the construction of a coherent national cultural space in which these other goals could be located and achieved. Instead the body politic could be re-conceptualised as being made of individuals (and families) concerned with the creation of self-directed lifestyles in a consumer-led economy and a globalised world.

Sociology was complicit in this shift, given that influential sociological thinkers of this period, such as Anthony Giddens (1991) – himself a key figure in the development of the intellectual rationale for the Tony Blair-led Labour governments post 1997 – Ulrich Beck (1992) and Zygmunt Bauman (1990), were also concerned with re-imagining the texture of the social life, emphasising, in different ways, the relative decline of traditional social structures such as class and nation with the resulting possibility of new forms of 'reflexive' freedom in which individuals could potentially take control of and shape their own lives, rather than accept the roles that were assumed to be inevitable to earlier generations. Cultural Studies arrived at a similar point from a different direction, emphasising, in its re-appraisals of popular youth subcultures and inspired by an emancipatory identity politics, the ability of individuals to craft meaningful identities for themselves in spite of the conditions with which they were faced. Both the rise of the notion of 'reflexivity' and the attention to the everyday forms of creative expression evident in Cultural Studies' accounts of the cultural world served to de-privilege – or to de-sacralise, to revisit Bourdieu's terminology – the position of the sociologist. In its place were empowered, self-aware individuals with less immediate need of the authority of experts to interpret their own life experiences.

If questions of culture came late to sociology, the selective application of sociological concepts and techniques also had a late flowering in UK policymaking – in ways that perhaps reflected the incorporation of these broader changes to the 'social' and their application to the 'problem' of cultural policy. The New Labour government post 1997 placed considerable emphasis on 'the creative industries' as potential drivers of economic growth in the emerging symbolic economy (Hewison, 2014). It also emphasised the importance of evidence in underpinning cultural policies, whether in terms of mapping the extent and measuring the success of these industries or in providing legitimation to the funding of its flagship policy of free admission to museums and galleries (see Hesmondhalgh et al. (2015) for a critical reappraisal of this direction in policymaking). This latter strand of cultural policy was strengthened by a new belief that culture – and especially 'the arts' could contribute to the resolution of a range of abiding social problems (from the integration of migrant communities, to improving health, to tackling crime) and indeed that the cultural sector *should* make such contributions in return for funding.

Sociological techniques and theories can be detected in relation to this strand of policymaking. First the empirical methods that sociology helped refine – including the survey and various forms of qualitative data-gathering – formed a major part of the infrastructure of 'evaluation' that underpinned work in the cultural sector, assessing the relative success of projects or events against criteria established by policymakers or funders (including diversity of the audience, as in the Chan and Goldthorpe/Arts Council research referred to above). Theoretically, the catch-all New Labour policy concept of 'social exclusion' draws on conceptual language that emerges from influential sociological studies of the multi-dimensional nature of late-twentieth-century poverty (Townshend, 1979), incorporating understanding of the roles of gender, ethnicity and disability in compounding the experience of poverty, even in contexts of what appeared to be, from a historical perspective, relative material comfort. The career of this problem in New Labour discourse, though, as Levitas (2005) explains, re-imagines it as one that can be solved through supporting individuals in their aspirations to make better choices –including the choice to participate in publicly funded forms of culture – rather than one that requires attention to the 'social' and its structures and arrangements in a more fundamental sense.

In relation to the more diffuse conception of the creative industries, the place of sociology is rather more ambiguous. While rhetorically at least this aspect of cultural policy has become more significant as these industries, widely defined, are conceptualised as strategically significant to economic success, sociological accounts are less welcome than other academic contributors to the formation of policy. This might reflect the dispersion of the profession of sociology itself, which has seen researchers trained in sociological ways of knowing and researching finding institutional locations away from dedicated departments. These might be in more generic applied social science or law or business schools or portmanteau research centres with specific interests in aspects of policy, such as urban regeneration, all of which exist in a more variegated inter-disciplinary academic field with significant competition for research funding. It might also reflect that despite – or perhaps because of – the critical reflexivity of the re-imagined social landscape, sociological accounts sound old-fashioned in the apparently dynamic world of the cultural and media industries. For McRobbie this reflects the broader, entrenched political climate and its

> successful discrediting of the political vocabulary associated with the left and with feminism including equal opportunities, anti-discrimination, workplace democracy, trade union representation etc. The only site for the dissemination of these values is actually the academy, the place of training or education of the creatives.
>
> *(McRobbie, 2016: 24)*

Sociology itself, though, is a less welcome presence 'on the guest list' of official conversations within the creative industries and between these industries and policymakers.

Here, in conclusion, we hear an echo of the 'moral' mission of Burawoy's critical sociology and indeed of the foundational aspiration to reform a 'broken' modernity that underpinned the early establishment of the discipline. We can also hear something of an admission of defeat, or at least a potential retreat, from the aspiration of a progressive sociology providing the evidence base for policy as an integral part of a democratising empirical mission such as that underpinning the discipline's rise to prominence in the 1960s. Culture and cultural policy may have been quite marginal to that rise, but the specific tension between social scientific forms of knowledge and the kinds of authority they produce, and the forms of authority that, in Savage's account, had previously attached to forms of aesthetic or literary knowledge, means the historical relationships between the development of the discipline and the development of the problem of cultural policy are revealing.

The experience of Bourdieu in France suggests sociology could be influential, at least in identifying the nature of policy problems if not in determining their solutions. Sociology does not speak with one voice, politically, but it can, as in the case of Bourdieu, come up with answers that are challenging and complex, albeit immediately impractical, for institutions concerned with the pragmatic process of governing. At the heart of this tension is sociology's status as one of a range of academic disciplines – but also as one of a range of voices beyond the academy – that attempt the ambitious and frustrating task of identifying, explaining and reflecting on human experience itself. Other, sometimes louder, voices emerge from other social sciences, politics and the policymaking machinery of the modern state but also, significantly in term of this discussion, from artists, writers, film makers and other cultural producers themselves. There is, then, something of a complex matrix of perspectives and priorities in which sociology and the objects and makers of cultural policy are best seen as occasional collaborators and equally likely as competitors or even antagonists in understanding the role of culture in the social world.

References

Adorno, T. and Horkheimer, M. (1944) 'The culture industry: enlightenment as mass deception', in J.B Schor and D.B. Holt (eds.) (2000) *The Consumer Society Reader*. New York: The New Press, pp. 3–19.

Ahearne, J. (2004) 'Between Cultural Theory and Policy: The Cultural Policy Thinking of Pierre Bourdieu, Michel de Certeau and Regis Debray', *Centre for Cultural Policy Studies Research Papers*, No.7: University of Warwick.

Alasuutari, P. (2001) 'Arts, entertainment, culture and nation', *Cultural Studies/Critical Methodologies*, 1 (2): 157–184.

Anderson, B. (1991) *Imagined Communities*. London: Verso.

Bauman, Z. (1990) *The Individualised Society*. Cambridge: Polity.

Beck, U. (1992) *Risk Society*. London: Sage.

Bennett, T. (1998) *Culture: A Reformer's Science*. London: Sage.

Bourdieu, P and Darbel, A. (1991) *The Love of Art*. Cambridge: Polity Press.

Bourdieu, P. and Passeron, J. (1979) *The Inheritors*. Chicago: University of Chicago Press.

Bourdieu, P. (1984) *Distinction: A Social Critique of the Judgment of Taste*. London: Routledge.

Bunting, C., Chan, T.W., Goldthorpe, J., Keaney, E., Oskala, A. (2008) *From Indifference to Enthusiasm: Patterns of Arts Attendance in England*. London: Arts Council England.

Burawoy, M. (2005) 'For public sociology', *American Sociological Review*, 70: 4–28.

Carey, J. (1992) *The Intellectuals and the Masses: Pride and Prejudice among the Literary Intelligentsia*. London: Faber.

Chan, T.W. and Goldthorpe, J. (2005) 'The social stratification of theatre, dance and cinema attendance', *Cultural Trends*, 14 (3): 193–212.

Chan, T. W. and Goldthorpe, J. (2007a) 'The social stratification of cultural consumption: some policy implications of a research project', *Cultural Trends*, 16 (4): 373–384.

Chan, T.W. and Goldthorpe, J. (2007b) 'Social stratification and cultural consumption: music in England', *European Sociological Review*, 23 (1): 1–19.

Dubois, V. (2011) 'Cultural capital theory vs. cultural policy beliefs: how Pierre Bourdieu could have become a cultural policy advisor and why he did not', *Poetics*, 39 (6): 491–506.

Durkheim, E. (2001 [1912]) *The Elementary Forms of Religious Life*. Oxford: Oxford University Press.

Fuller, S. (2006) *The New Sociological Imagination*. London: Sage.

Giddens, A. (1991) *Modernity and Self-Identity*. Cambridge: Polity Press.

Goldthorpe, J. (2007) 'Cultural capital: some critical observations', *Sociologica*, 2. doi:10.2383/24755.

Hall, S. and Jefferson, T. (1975) *Resistance through Rituals*. London: Hutchinson.

Hebdige, D. (1979) *Subculture: The Meaning of Style*. London: Routledge.

Hesmondhalgh, D., Oakley, K., Lee, D. and Nisbett, M. (2015) *Culture, Economy and Politics: The Case of New Labour*. London: Palgrave.

Hewison, R. (2014) *Cultural Capital: The Rise and Fall of Creative Britain*. London: Verso.

Inglis, D. (2016) 'Culture/sociology/sociology of culture/cultural sociology', in D. Inglis and A. Almila (eds.) *The Sage Handbook of Cultural Sociology*. London: Sage, pp. 1–7.

Kelly, O. (1984) *Storming the Citadels*. London: Comedia.

Kwon, S.H and Kim, J. (2014) 'The cultural industry policies of the Korean Government and the Korean wave', *International Journal of Cultural Policy*, 20 (4): 422–439.

Lazarsfeld, P. and Merton, R. (1948) 'Mass communication, popular taste and organised social action', in L. Bryson (ed.) *The Communication of Ideas*. New York: The Institute for Religious and Social Studies, pp. 95–118.

Lebaron, F. (2009) 'How Bourdieu "quantified Bourdieu": the geometric modelling of data', in K. Robson and C. Sanders (eds.) *Quantifying Theory: Pierre Bourdieu*. Berlin: Springer, pp. 11–29.

Levitas, R. (2005) *The Inclusive Society; Social Inclusion and New Labour*, 2nd ed. London: Palgrave.

McGuigan, J. (1996) *Culture and the Public Sphere*. London: Routledge.

McRobbie, A. (2016) *Be Creative: Making a Living in the New Cultural Industries*. Cambridge: Polity.

Minnaert, T. (2014) 'Footprint or fingerprint: international cultural policy as identity policy', *International Journal of Cultural Policy*, 20 (1): 99–113.

Parkhurst Clarke, P. (1987) *Literary France: The Making of a Culture*. Berkeley and Los Angeles: University of California Press.

Peterson, R. (1976) 'The production of culture: a prolegomenon', *American Behavioural Scientist*, 19: 669–684.

Peterson, R.A. (1992) 'Understanding audience segmentation: from elite and mass to omnivore and univore', *Poetics*, 21: 243–258.

Peterson, R. A. (2005) 'Problems in comparative research: the example of omnivorousness', *Poetics*, 33: 257–282.

Peterson, R. A. and Simkus, A. (1992) 'How musical tastes mark occupational status groups', in M. Lamont and M. Fournier (eds.) *Cultivating Differences*. Chicago: University of Chicago Press, pp. 152–186.

Peterson, R. A. and Kern, R. M. (1996) 'Changing highbrow taste: from snob to omnivore', *American Sociological Review*, 61: 900–909.

Robbins, D. (2005) 'The origins, early development and status of Bourdieu's concept of "cultural capital"', *British Journal of Sociology*, 56 (1): 13–30.

Robins, K. (2007) 'Transational cultural policy and European cosmopolitanism', *Cultural Politics*, 3 (2): 147–174

Savage, M. (2010) *Identities and Social Change in Britain since 1940: The Politics of Method*. Oxford: Oxford University Press.

Santoro, M. (2008) 'Producing cultural sociology: an interview with Richard A. Peterson', *Cultural Sociology*, 2 (1): 33–55.

Simmel, G. (1997) 'The philosophy of fashion', in D. Frisby and M. Featherstone (eds.) *Simmel on Culture*. London: Sage, pp. 187–205.

Swartz, D. (2004) 'From critical sociology to public intellectual', in Swartz, D. and Zolber, V. (eds.) *After Bourdieu: Influence, Critique, Elaboration*. Dordrecht: Kluwer, pp. 333–363.

Townshend, P. (1979) *Poverty in the United Kingdom*. Harmondsworth: Penguin.

Upchurch, A. (2004) 'John Maynard Keynes, the Bloomsbury group and the origins of the arts council movement', *International Journal of Cultural Policy*, 10 (2): 203–217.

Upchurch, A. (2011) 'Keynes's legacy: an intellectual's influence reflected in arts policy', *International Journal of Cultural Policy*, 17 (1): 69–80.

Wolff, J. (1993) *The Social Production of Art*, 2nd ed. London: Macmillan.

Wright, D. (2016) 'Cultural consumption and cultural omnivorousness', in D. Inglis and A. Almila (eds.) *The Sage Handbook of Cultural Sociology*. London: Sage, pp. 567–577.

Wright-Mills, C. (1959) *The Sociological Imagination*. Oxford: Oxford University Press.

Zolberg, V. (1990) *Constructing a Sociology of the Arts*. Cambridge: Cambridge University Press.

5

The relationship between cultural policy and arts management[1]

Victoria Durrer

For some scholars within cultural policy and arts management studies, the relationship between the field of cultural policy and arts management practice seems an obvious one. Whilst there is some academic work that makes this connection explicit or even visible, there is little scholarship that develops our understanding of how these two areas interact, how ideas are exchanged and implemented, and where the power is located within this relationship. This chapter is a start at building such understanding.

The chapter explores how the relationship between arts management and cultural policy is articulated within two main sites where arts managers are socialised into the assumptions, traditions and norms of their profession. These are the realms of education/academic study and vocational practice, both highly interconnected, epistemological domains for the discipline. Drawing from a review of academic and practice-based, or vocational, research literature within Europe and the UK and interviews with UK-based arts managers and arts management educators, the chapter shows that the relationship between arts management and cultural policy is both symbiotic and fragmented. The relationship is in one way transactional, with cultural policy viewed as a heavily influential and sometimes constraining structure in which arts management practice operates. This interpretation places valuations of art and culture as utilitarian to political issues and raises questions about the arms' length principle upon which the relationship between the state and arts and cultural bodies have been founded. At the same time, this connection is perceived as providing opportunities for mutual benefit. This interpretation places agency in the hands of arts managers to drive, influence and uphold policy objectives. These findings have implications for how we understand what individuals, networks and institutions structure the governance of cultural policy as well as how and why. Such knowledge would enhance our understanding of what, and how, value becomes attached to particular forms of arts and culture, as well as how those forms are legitimated as types of goods, services, practices and/or symbols in society.

The chapter focuses on arts management and cultural policy in relation to publicly funded arts and culture in the UK. Within the UK, public – or State, funding – of arts and culture follows an arm's length principle. The principle is argued, in theory, to keep Arts Councils at a distance from government in order to minimise state intervention into the arts and foster artistic autonomy. In practice, it means that bodies in the UK regional executives

(Creative Scotland in Scotland and the Arts Councils of England, Northern Ireland and Wales respectively), are intended to make funding and policy decisions in relation to arts and cultural practice (and management) that are independent from government influence upon receiving their own annual grants from the (devolved) state. As a result and as will be discussed further in the chapter, this principle directly impacts how arts management and cultural policy interact in the UK.

Typically, 'arts management' relates to the working practices of a profession comprising the protection, preservation, distribution, marketing, mediation and financial organisation of arts and cultural objects and experiences. Here, arts management is interpreted as encompassing both arts and cultural management with a particular focus on the fine and performing arts and heritage, including museums. While it is acknowledged that individual arts organisations have their own policies, this chapter focuses on state, government or public policy. In doing so, the chapter defines 'cultural policy' as "whatever governments choose to do or not to do" (Dye 2005, p. 1 cited in Mulcahy 2006, p. 320) in relation to art and culture.

The chapter begins with an analysis of how the relationship between arts management and cultural policy is described in academic and practice-based, or vocational, research literature within Europe and the UK specifically. Followed by a more detailed explication of the research method and rationale, the chapter presents findings from an initial audit of arts management programmes at the postgraduate level within UK universities and qualitative interviews with UK arts managers. As this is a collection of work with a global inflection, the chapter concludes with a broader discussion of questions raised and what lessons can be learnt about the relationship of arts management to cultural policy at an international level.

Academia and practice: what relationship does the literature reflect?

As the sites in which arts managers are socialised into the profession, 'practice' and 'education' are where the historical, institutional and social assumptions and traditions of arts management and cultural policy are exchanged, enacted and reproduced. As a result, this chapter begins by investigating how the relationship between arts management and cultural policy is expressed in vocational and academic literature. Paquette and Redaelli (2015) have provided a thorough and most up-to-date analysis of the interrelations of the research from both fields. While focused on the North American situation, their findings are relevant to the UK. They argue that numerous agents, institutions and groups, including academic institutions, arts organisations, government bodies, quangos and private foundations as well as specific practitioners, consultants and researchers, shape knowledge in and about both disciplines. All have differing levels and varieties of interest, knowledge and stake in the economic, social, political and aesthetic dimensions of arts and culture ranging from, for example, international tourism to local community development (Chong 2009; Vuyk 2010; O'Brien 2013). What results are epistemological viewpoints that are currently not equally valued or mutually recognised in either academia or professional practice. This disjoint contributes to a perception that the two fields are fractured parts of a whole. It also impacts the perceived and actual level of agency arts managers have, in shaping not only their own practice but also policy decisions.

This section further explores this imbalance. It is argued that the multi-discipline nature of both fields and the variety of actors and agencies involved in knowledge production has precipitated studies from multiple theoretical frameworks and fostered varying views on what forms of knowledge should be privileged over others. Cultural policy is often viewed as a space for critical discourse on the role of arts and culture in society and arts management as an applied discipline. The involvement of state bodies in the establishment of arts and cultural management courses and educational networks in the UK and Europe has helped facilitate this view. This positioning has led to thinking, which confines arts management as an instrument for public policy. Yet, it could equally be argued to position the cultural practice of arts managers within potentially influential roles in social, economic and political spheres. This dissimilitude is not argued here to be a – or rather 'the' – problem, per se. Instead, in restricting our study of each as an individual field, we have limited our understanding of their relationship. In actual fact there is much interaction between the two, particularly in the arena of education and professional practice. The disparity in how the two fields are perceived to interact, has stunted our understanding of who makes policy, how and for what ends.

Multiple voices and viewpoints

First, as realms of both academic and vocational knowledge, arts management and cultural policy are complex. A number of scholars have demonstrated how their interdisciplinary, trans-disciplinary and/or cross-disciplinary nature – depending on one's viewpoint – has presented challenges to the legitimacy of both as professional practices, study and research areas (for example, Scullion and Garcia 2005; Paquette and Redaelli 2015). For instance, research is produced by both academic and practitioner-based circles, involving a range of actors from higher education institutes to consultancies who have different perceptions of the validity of one another's findings and approaches (Paquette and Redaelli 2015). Furthermore, as disciplines of practice and study, neither is wholly focused on, for example, the arts and culture, aesthetics, management, social interaction, public policy or political and economic processes, but draw on all of these in varying ways (Brkić 2009; Chong 2009). In fact, arts management and cultural policy courses in universities are housed in a variety of different departments (Sternal 2007).

Arts management and cultural policy are thus influenced by epistemological approaches from, for instance, political science, cultural studies, sociology, economics, management and the arts and humanities. Each discipline frames arts management and/or cultural policy differently, presenting unique vantage points from which to critically investigate the fields (see preceding chapters in this collection, which illustrate this point). At the same time, their relationship to multiple disciplines means that neither arts management nor cultural policy rests solely within any particular boundaries of knowledge formation (Scullion and Garcia 2005). What can result is the disparaging of different theoretical frameworks from one discipline to another. This disfavour is evidenced in some discussions within both arts management and cultural policy research where approaches to 'management' studies are described as 'out of touch' with approaches in the arts and humanities (Belfiore and Bennett 2008; Brkić 2009). So, even though arts management and cultural policy share disciplines of interest and common stakeholders and agents involved in building knowledge, their flexibility in scope presents challenges to their perceived validity as areas of practice and study. With these blurred distinctions, it has been difficult to fully appreciate and articulate their relationship to one another.

Different forms of knowledge

Differences in emphasis between the two are also evident in the literature. Cultural policy is often articulated as a space for critical discourse on the values society places on (or espouses with) arts and culture. Arts management, on the other hand, is often articulated as a space for exploring applied management approaches to arts and cultural practice. This division, which has undoubtedly impacted the ways in which the relationship to one another may be perceived within academic and education circles, will be explored further here. Much arts management research and education has tended to privilege what are often seen as 'transferrable', "utilitarian" and/or toolkit approaches for 'how to' fund, manage and share the arts with audiences and participants (Bennett 2001; Devereaux 2009, p. 65; Ebewo and Sirayi 2009, p. 282; Paquette and Redaelli 2015). As a result, arts management education in European third-level institutions has tended to value applied skills in business management and entrepreneurialism as well as the more technical aspects of producing artwork (Brkić 2009, p. 270, see also Dewey and Wyszomirski 2004; Suteu 2006).

The rationale for this emphasis has not been greatly researched, but some reasons will be advanced here. For one, arts management as a field of study developed from practical training needs that emerged in Europe in the 1960s when an increase in arts and cultural infrastructure there required professionals with new expertise to staff them (Suteu 2006; Paquette and Redaelli 2015). In addition, the development of the Bologna Process, which has allowed the transfer of qualifications from higher education institutes between European countries, has likely influenced a weighting of 'transferrable' skills within arts management degrees (for more discussion see Sternal 2007). Since that time, there has been a breadth of development of third-level and professional development courses outside of Europe (Boylan 2000; Dragićević Šešić 2015). Many of these programmes in arts management and cultural policy have involved the engagement of practitioners in design and teaching (Suteu 2006; Paquette and Redaelli 2015). These are individuals who:

> have developed their expertise 'on the job' …[For them,] learning through experience, be it by trial and error or with and from colleagues, has been the norm.
>
> *(Summerton 2009, p. 115)*

It is thus not surprising that 'real world', practical experience is highly valued in educational programme content. As a result, such programmes tend to position the relevance of cultural policy to arts management as the context (political and spatial) for actions and behaviours within arts management practice (Suteu 2006).

In this vein, educational study of cultural policy in relation to arts management has been shown to "highlight the role of public governance as a higher principle" against which arts management practice is situated (quote from Brkić 2009: 270, see also Bennett 2001, Schuster 2003, Dragićević Šešić and Dragojević 2005). Sternal (2007, p. 69) explains:

> Many [arts management and cultural policy] programmes, even if they do not mention cultural policy in their names, devote substantial space to issues concerning this topic, with courses such as European/national/regional cultural policy; local and regional cultural development policies, cultural policy instruments, historical development of cultural policies in Europe; and cultural policy: study, analysis, action.

This assessment has implications for how the relationship between arts management and cultural policy is reviewed, critiqued and understood within arts management research. In fact, cultural policy is still relatively absent in much published work presented in academic journals and conference proceedings dedicated to arts management. Topics instead focus on operative, professional issues; those related to marketing, audiences, consumer behaviour, institutional governance, strategic management and planning (Evrard and Colbert 2000;

Pérez-Cabañero and Cuadrado-García 2011). Though networks like ENCATC (European network on cultural management and policy) have been addressing this gap. As a result, Paquette and Redaelli (2015, p. 10) argue that the "research discourse around arts management is still relatively weak", while Devereaux (2009, p. 68) has found that the discipline lacks critical discourse around the "assumptions" and "traditions" from which the field operates. So, when viewed as the frame in which arts management practice exists, examination of cultural policy is often held as the purview of theoretical, critical and "intellectual" reflection, with study and research in arts management appearing to serve more functional or technical purposes (Suteu 2006; Devereaux 2009, p. 68). This delineation has tended to position cultural policy as a more legitimated field of academic study to that of arts management.

Perspectives on agency

These perspectives further imply that cultural policy has an inherent power over arts management practice. They place the arts manager as a passive delivery agent of specific and fixed approaches to practice that serve policy goals. Such an interpretation may not be surprising when considering the strong involvement of state bureaucrats and policymakers in the development of many European arts management and cultural policy training programmes. In fact, Dubois (2016) has pointed out the correlation in changes in cultural policy and the professionalisation of arts management. Suteu (2006), Sternal (2007) and Dragićević Šešić (2015) remind us of the influential roles both UNESCO and the Council of Europe have played in the development of arts, cultural policy and cultural management training worldwide. The UNESCO Chairs Programme has led to the evolution of a number of higher education programmes in places such as Serbia, Lithuania and Spain. Work by the Council of Europe helped initiate the establishment of the European Network of Cultural Administration Training Centres in 1992 as well as a number of networks for professional development and training (Suteu 1999, 2006). Dragićević Šešić (2015, p. 102) details the many networks at play today, including, but not limited to, Trans Europe Halles, Culture Action Europe and the Soros Art and Culture Network Programme. With regards to cultural policy, there is the International Federation of Arts Councils and Culture Agencies (IFACCA), which connects a global network of arts councils and ministries of culture in over 80 countries.

The involvement of policymakers in establishing higher education training of arts managers is also seen in the UK, particularly England, where the Arts Council partnered with City University in establishing what is largely regarded as the first arts administration training programme in the late 1960s/early1970s (Sternal 2007).[2] This relationship, in particular, is an example of how changing requirements for efficiency and effectiveness in public sector accountability for state funding had a direct impact on the training and development of arts managers in Europe. These developments have likely fostered the perspective that the areas of arts management and cultural policy interact as delivery agent and context, respectively.

In fact, this development of arts management as a discipline of study and research in Europe since the 1960s/70s was also a result of changing impressions of the role of arts and culture as a resource for addressing social, political and economic challenges in public policy (Suteu 2006). Since the 1970s, US and European cultural policy has associated publicly funded arts and culture with urban regeneration and tourism through, for instance, flagship cultural projects and the Capital of Culture programme as well as international cultural exchange projects (Bianchini and Parkinson 1993, Garcia 2005). Dragićević Šešić (2015) explains the increasing social, political and cultural importance of arts managers in parts of Western and Eastern Europe at local, national and international levels at the fall of the

Berlin Wall. This focus has been particularly visible in the UK since New Labour came to government in 1997. While long recognised in community art circles, this period saw the practice of cultural institutions and in turn, arts managers, in the UK officially 'attached' to public policies regarding major societal concerns such as social inclusion, job creation, education, diplomacy, equality and social justice (Matarasso 1997; Gray 2007). In 2000, the UK's Department for Culture, Media & Sport, which focuses much of its work on England, declared that museums (and presumably other cultural organisations) were now 'centres of social change' (Department for Culture, Media & Sport 2000). Similar policies can still be found in Northern Ireland's former Department of Culture, Arts and Leisure (subsumed into the Department for Communities in 2016) (Department of Culture, Arts and Leisure 2015), with strategies in Wales and Scotland making similar intimations (CyMAL 2010; Creative Scotland 2014). On an international level, UNESCO policies have argued for the role of culture in peace and reconciliation, protection of cultural diversity and promotion of sustainable development (UNESCO 2005, 2013, 2014). It can be argued that this evolution not only makes the role of policy significant to the work of practice, but also the work of arts managers significant in shaping policymaking. While still servicing public policy goals, arts managers are not mere instruments, but, as articulated in the UN's *Declaration of Arc-et-Senans* in 1972, active "operators and mediators at different levels of action and decision" (United Nations 1972 quoted in Suteu 2006, p. 21).

Following studies on 'cultural intermediaries' (Bourdieu 2000; Maguire and Matthews 2014), reading arts managers as mediators reveals their potential agency in the policymaking process as shapers of the "use values and exchange values" of arts and culture (Negus 2002, p. 504) in the political arena. Doing so also highlights the possibility of a more reciprocal relationship between cultural policy and arts management practice. In fact, some support for public policies from managers within the cultural sector has been evidenced (see Durrer and O'Brien 2014; Nisbett 2013; Newsinger and Green 2016). Dragićević Šešić (2015) sees arts managers as participants in the cultural policymaking process alongside funders, donors and politicians. Woddis (2014) argues similarly in her study on theatre practitioners. Applying public policy research, she contends that arts practitioners, including managers, contribute to cultural policymaking in two ways. For one, they are key actors in state agencies, quangos, arts development agencies, councils and national cultural institutions that participate in the design and development of cultural policy directives and strategies (Schuster 2003). They also influence policy development in their involvement in consultation processes or advocacy activities and campaigns. This role can take place locally, nationally and internationally. It is evidenced in both professional and third-level education-based networking groups, which stress ways to influence policy through advocacy actions and international knowledge exchange activities and projects (see the work of ENCATC for third-level education net-working at EU level and Trans Europe Halles for arts and cultural organisations, Suteu 1999; Dragićević Šešić and Dragojević 2005; Rowntree *et al.* 2010).

Socialisation processes are critical here, as the opportunity to actually influence policy may depend upon an arts manager's disposition, professional status and position, manage-ment (especially advocacy) skills and network (Woddis 2014). Still, the role, perceptions and practices of arts managers are often neglected in arts management and cultural policy research (Woddis 2014; Newsinger and Green 2016). In fact, there appears to be a lack of understanding of arts management practices and their relationship to cultural policy and artistic production (see McCall 2012 for some discussion on this). For instance, Gray (2009), a political scientist by training, has demonstrated that in the six leading political and pub-lic administration journals, there were only four articles on museums and galleries in a collective 347 years of publication. Others researching in the UK have tended to focus on the impact of policy on practice (such as Kawashima 2000; Belfiore 2004) or have called for a rethinking of cultural policy agendas for practice (for example, Miles and Sullivan 2012). Only recently have researchers, educators and practitioners started to consider the power and agency of arts managers in the policymaking process (see, for example, Newsinger and Green 2016; Dragićević Šešić 2015; Bell and Oakley 2014; McCall 2012; Rowntree *et al.* 2010; Nisbett 2013). These studies reveal a need for greater understanding of the institutional and social dynamics underlying exchanges between arts management and cultural policy. How the relationship of arts management to cultural policy is perceived and experienced in the realms of arts management education and practice will shed light on the habits and assumptions involved in these interactions.

Methodology and data

The literature reviewed demonstrates that the hybrid nature of arts management and cultural policy as both academic and vocational disciplines makes defining each field, and the precise relationship of one to the other, difficult. Still, two main perceptions regarding how these areas interact do emerge from the literature. The first describes cultural policy as an authoritative context in which arts management operates. This stance positions arts managers as passive receivers of funding and thus delivery agents for policy directives. Another interpretation emphasises a different degree of interaction between arts management and cultural policy, one in which arts managers have greater agency in the policymaking process. This perspective sees arts management practice and individual arts managers as having active roles in influencing and shaping policy. Such activity tends to occur through the exchange that takes place in the management of artistic projects, advocacy work and networks.

Inherent in these perspectives are assumptions regarding where power is located in the relationship between arts management and cultural policy. The frames of arts management *practice* and *education* provide an effective foundation from which to explore these assumptions and how they manifest and develop in the socialisation of arts managers. These two areas are of particular interest because, as the discussion above demonstrates, they are deeply interlinked with practitioners (policymakers and arts managers) often involved in the formation and teaching of higher educational courses in arts management as well as cultural policy. More significantly, these realms are where the historical, institutional and social traditions, principles, habits and values of arts management and cultural policy are exchanged, challenged, cemented and/or reproduced (Paquette and Redaelli 2015). Gathering an understanding of the perspectives of the individuals (arts managers, educators, students and cultural policymakers) involved in these fields of practice will develop a fuller picture of how the two fields do, and may, relate on institutional and social levels. As such, this study takes an interpretive approach (Taylor 1971; Geertz 1973; Denzin 2007) to investigate individuals' interpretations and their experiences of the interaction between arts management and cultural policy. While discussions with arts managers focused on their understanding and experience of policy, those with educators/academics focused on course content and the placement of cultural policy in relation to arts management within course structure.

Arts management and cultural policy practice and study within the UK provide a good basis for examining this relationship more closely. O'Brien (2013) has previously illustrated the position of UK cultural policy research as a valuable international case study. With respect to arts management, the region has a strong tradition of state funding for the arts, heritage and culture with a well-developed cultural infrastructure and a highly professionalised management practice that has international influence (Pick 1980; Dragićević Šešić 2003; Tchouikina 2010). This influence is underpinned by an established framework for training those who want to enter the field, including everything from university degree courses to professional development, such as the Clore Leadership Programme. Furthermore, the dynamic between arts management practice and cultural policy has changed much as a result of cultural policy since the New Labour government but in ways still in need of study (Hesmondhalgh *et al.* 2015).

This chapter draws upon early insights from two data sets, still in formation. At this stage in the study, these data sets focus on two 'types' of participants: arts managers (identified as AM) and educators (identified as E). Qualitative approaches, employed here, allow research participants to describe the meanings, beliefs and values they attach to their experiences, which form the assumptions and traditions of the field (Geertz 1973; Delanty 1997). First is an audit of seven arts management and cultural policy programmes within UK universities. These courses are taught by a combination of arts management practitioners and cultural policy scholars, and all produce research within both areas. All of the institutions offer courses in either cultural policy or arts management, or both. Some of these were explicitly labelled as such, for example, 'MA Cultural Policy and Arts Management', and others had more specific titles yet were essentially based on these fields, such as 'Festival Management'. As Masters level programmes are more common and longer established within Europe (Brkić 2009), postgraduate rather than undergraduate degrees are the focus here. There are fewer opportunities and options to study cultural policy or arts management as an undergraduate degree, which straightforwardly reflects the level of specialisation required and the professionalisation of the sector (Paquette and Redaelli 2015).

The initial audit and scoping was then followed by email interviews (Mann and Stewart 2000) with academic staff members, where further enquiries about the structures of their degree programmes and their understanding of the relationship between arts management and cultural policy were made. These participants are teaching staff, module convenors and course directors. They were selected on the basis of their involvement in the structure, design and delivery of their degree programmes. Whilst recognising the key influence of directors in terms of course design (Suteu 2006, p. 52), it is also understood that individual staff members shape the content of courses and make key decisions about what materials to include within their modules and individual lectures and seminars. Some of the educators participating in the study would have previously worked as arts managers themselves, having shifted into academic careers.

The second set involves qualitative interviews with arts managers (N = 6) with experience working in England, Scotland and Northern Ireland. These individuals are involved in all or some of the following activities: leading, programming, planning, organising and/or marketing publicly funded arts and cultural services and goods for a public audience. Interviews seek to ascertain their understanding of the relationship between arts management and cultural policy, how they comprehend cultural policy and how political shifts impact on their daily practice. In order to ensure some exposure to cultural policy, arts managers selected for study have mid- to higher-level managerial positions. Their status means that they may manage a number of staff members or volunteers to deliver their programme of work, and/or they oversee a programme, e.g. education, artistic, curatorial, director and therefore lead in liaising with social and/or cultural policymakers in a particular area of practice (e.g. arts and health, youth arts, etc...). Most of the research participants, both practicing arts managers and educators, would have learned arts management practice 'on-the-job', with a few having received formal training. Thematic analysis (Braun and Clarke 2006), a systematic technique within the social sciences that aims to identify prominent themes and provides a complex analysis of their meaning in context, was applied to both data sets.

Before sharing this data, it is important to put it into context. At the time of collection in early to mid 2015, austerity culture as part of the global banking crisis and ensuing recession had fully hit the publicly funded sector. Funding cuts affected all the arm's length bodies for arts and culture in the UK with Northern Ireland being the most severe. Arts Council Northern Ireland passed an 11.2% cut from the Northern Ireland Executive's 2015–6 budget on to the sector. This cut was coupled with the announcement that Northern Ireland's Department of Culture, Arts and Leisure would be subsumed into a Department for Communities in 2016. Within England, recognition and debate about the geographic imbalance of arts funding between London and the regions was growing alongside blows suffered by the arts due to major changes in provision from local authorities. These difficulties have emerged aside greater recognition as to the lack of equality of opportunity and thus diversity reflected in the sector's labour force, including artists (O'Brien and Oakley 2015). These circumstances would undoubtedly impact on research participants' perceptions and articulations of cultural policy.

Discussion

Emerging findings from the data thus far support both interpretations found in the literature: 1) that cultural policy is viewed as the operational context for arts management practice, in which 2) individual or organisational influence is possible. Both educators and arts managers interviewed reveal that while power seems to reside in the policy arena, arts management and cultural policy have a symbiotic relationship that is at times compatible and at times fragmented or oppositional. Cultural policy frames the conditions in which arts management activity takes place. However, the extent to which such conditions are viewed as malleable, guiding, directing or restricting differs amongst respondents. The socialisation of arts managers into the field of practice appears to have a strong bearing on this perception and an arts manager's potential role or agency in the cultural policymaking process. Individual dispositions and beliefs as well as the like-mindedness shared among managers, policymakers and public service bureaucrats, such as political, social and aesthetic values, are factors that may influence the dynamics of policymaking as well as arts management practice.

These issues are further explored below. The first section, *Framing Arts Management Practice*, explores how cultural policy can be seen to structure arts management practice. Section two details how this approach may infringe upon the arm's length principle upon which UK cultural policy is founded. What can result is an arts and cultural sector that is responsive to the social, political and economic needs of the state with little recourse to be otherwise. Sections three, four and five highlight how this alignment between policy and practice is both a social and an institutional process, subject to the professional standing of, and social relationships between, individuals and organisations within both fields of policymaking and arts management.

Framing arts management practice

Both educators and arts managers describe cultural policy as the context or "framework" (AM2) in which arts management practice occurs. At one side of the scale, cultural policy is viewed as a set of guidelines for arts management practice; on the other, it is perceived as a set of strict requirements that legitimise arts (management) practice. Two arts managers explain:

> [Cultural policy is where] …a body of people would have collective opinion on what they would fund [or endorse in some way]… I suppose that's usually government isn't it, who make money available? Or someone like the [national] Arts Council or [the]… city council. That, I'm assuming they have a policy that they don't just look at each individual project in relation to nothing. There's some sort of guidelines.…
>
> *(AM1)*

> Do you pander to the cultural policy or the… [strategy] of the Arts Council in order to get funding or do you not do that and continue to do the work that you want to do and not get funding?
>
> *(AM4)*

So, for arts managers interviewed, cultural policy is an articulation of 'why' government funds artistic activity (Mulcahy 2006). It can feel "confining" and impact on artistic programming:

> There's an awareness of how cultural policy affects the kind of work that you do and can affect how venues programme what they programme and when it comes to teaching and developing projects in education and community context. It's shaped by that, maybe because the funding is shaped by that and has been I think really since I started working.
>
> *(AM2)*

The operational authority of cultural policy is wielded on arts management practice financially. As a result, the relationship between the two is typically perceived as a transactional one. An arts manager explains how negotiating policy requirements impacts finances: "We know that if we resist those [cultural policy] agendas, it is very likely that funding will be removed." (AM6). It thus becomes necessary to engage, or "fit in" (AM4) with policy in order to survive financially with some arts managers perceiving it has little relevance to the everyday realities of practice.

While educators acknowledge these realities, they tend to place conceptual emphasis on the contextual connection between arts management and cultural policy. Though not exclusively, many of the MA programmes examined here seem to stress the applied and technical aspects of management in modules on marketing, business planning, governance and fundraising. Teaching and learning involves lectures with professionals and what Devereaux (2009, p. 67) refers to as "pragmatic, action-oriented issues" – project based activity and work placements along with written assessments where students apply knowledge to essays as well as practically, in making their own fundraising and marketing strategies, for example. While theories of management, leadership, and entrepreneurship are explored there, cultural policy module descriptions more overtly emphasise "theoretical perspectives" and from diverse disciplines, including political science, cultural studies and sociology.

In cultural policy modules, arts management is but one "part of the focus of cultural policy" (E1). In being the context for arts management practice, cultural policy is typically, though not wholly, described as a wider set of circumstances in which that practice occurs. From the educators' perspective it appears that the transactional monetary exchange between the two is how that context is realised, though it is but one aspect of their relationship. It also includes consideration of the historical, political, spatial and socio-economic conditions surrounding arts and cultural production and consumption as well as their "impact" on arts management in real terms (E1, E2, E5, E6). Lessons and assessments appear to be less focused on the technical aspects of developing a state policy and more on "intellectual reflection" where students explore the implicit and explicit "traditions", norms and "principles" for artistic and cultural activity in society (Devereaux 2009, p. 67), as embedded in state policy.

As a result, learning about cultural policy provides opportunity for arts managers to, "evaluate", "analyse" (E3) and think critically about power relationships and value choices inherent in the relationship between arts/culture and society and policy rhetoric (regarding, e.g. cultural participation, creative labour, international practices). Though how this relationship may play out in practice does not overtly appear to be addressed in modules, except, perhaps, so far as guest speakers may address the subject. Nevertheless, such engagement may, as Suteu (2006) implies, foster greater reflective arts management practice for those having undergone training. Specifically, "critical capacities and empowering competencies" that can promote one's adaptability to different political and spatial contexts. Suteu (2006) indicates that by doing so, arts managers will be enabled to take a more (and perhaps realise their existing) agentic role in influencing cultural policymaking at local, national and even international level. What impact this training has in developing agency in the policymaking process is, however, unclear.

'Directing the arm' of arts management

Interviews with both educators and arts managers show that understanding the relationship between cultural policy and arts management as a transactional one means that cultural policy operationalises arts management activity – as both 'goods' and 'services – in exchange for financial support. Within a public policy context these goods and services are recognised as socio-economic resources for the State. Gray (2007, p. 210) has explained that the low-priority set for arts and culture as a dedicated area of public policy by the UK government has cultivated an "attachment... of arts and cultural policies to other sets of policy concerns" in order to garner and maintain political and financial support. One arts manager explains, "A lot of cultural policy is driven by ideas about funding, so very often those policies grow out of a need to defend cultural spending" (AM6).

As a result, cultural policy has come to address not only creative and artistic expression, but also wider social, economic and political issues, such as promoting democracy, celebrating national image, creating jobs, and fostering social cohesion. The manipulation of the arts for tackling other public policy areas was acknowledged by arts managers interviewed. One illustrates, "You're aware of certain reasons why you're doing things either socially, economically, um, to develop certain things in certain areas" (AM2). In this regard, it appears as if cultural policy can be interpreted as a 'utilitarian' arts policy (Mulcahy 2006; Gray 2007), which one arts manager describes as being "inflicted upon artists" (AM4).

Such remarks by arts managers raise questions about the 'arm's length' principle at the heart of UK cultural policy. In actual fact, valuing the arts and culture in ways relevant to other public policy areas appears to have fostered a greater level of "intimacy" between cultural policy and arts management (Quinn 1997, p. 128); a relationship by which cultural policy can be understood as directing or influencing arts managers in their work:

"Often where you work is dictated by cultural policy because that funding is targeted towards those areas. You know you might be asked to work with a certain group of people..."

(AM2)

The same arts manager continues: "I have been told by local authority staff to have projects up and ready, so that they fit in [with funding requirements as they arise]" (AM2).

This intimacy is "politically determined" (Mulcahy 2006, p. 320). Two respondents explain,

"... I keep abreast of political debate, it's a specialist political debate ... and if you do that and you're paying attention to what politicians say and the kind of things they respond to ... you get a better sense of what [policies] might come next"

(AM6)

"The 'need to know' about policy is more urgent because of the pernicious things [funding cuts] that are now going on ... if you were working in the arts pre-2008 in a period of growth and investment and your reality has been that economic bubble, you might not have engaged with cultural policy in the way that you'll need to now [during this time of austerity]"

(AM5)

Arts managers interviewed share Schuster's (2003, p. 45) perspective from his research on cultural policy in the United States; specifically that policies respond "to the politics of the moment." In other words, the political climate and which party holds government office has impact on how cultural policy is interpreted and experienced by arts managers (see also Chaney 2014). These circumstances leave the sector in a state of structural "impermanence" (AM5), with policies subject to the values and beliefs of changing political parties, politicians and public administrators (see also Belfiore and Bennett 2010). Without a perceived "coherent narrative" (AM5) for State support for the arts, the sector is left to determine what types of political alignment might foster their survival. One educator indicated that viewing policy in such a deterministic way gives it too great a "status" (E1). Both educators and arts managers reflected on how engaging with and learning about policy, then, becomes about "crisis management" (E1, AM5) rather than about "self-sufficiency" (E1).

As a result, the arm's length principle allows bodies like the Arts Council to yield significant authority over the arts in practice. Agendas can be set without clear accountability to, or recourse by, the sector (Quinn 1997, p. 154). One arts manager explains:

"...If you feel a policy is not appropriate, you can have that conversation and you can resist to an extent but if you take it to an extreme or you don't win that argument then your funding will be removed so it's something you have to be constantly aware of and you can't let the ball drop"

(AM6)

This perception indicates that informal dialogue and negotiation rather than any formalised process is how recourse is achieved. Such an approach means that individual beliefs, personalities and mutual affinity between arts managers, public service bureaucrats and cultural policy makers may play a large part in shaping policy and funding decisions as well as practice.

Alignment between practice and policy

Arts managers appear to recognise and/or accept a relationship between cultural policy and arts management that is based on social and economic return for investment in the arts. Where arts management activity must be aligned with policy goals, arts managers appear to look for mechanisms, which are perceived to be mutually beneficial to the aims of both policy and practice. One arts manager demonstrates the importance of finding alignment:

> "…[Cultural policy goals have] to be really aligned with our artistic vision and it has to go together… I think probably, it's about trying to match those two things together over the next period and see where there's common ground…. "
>
> *(AM2)*

Political alignment is perceived to both protect and challenge artistic and creative autonomy. In describing how policy can hamper arts management practice, one arts manager positions cultural policy as oppositional to arts management:

> "I worry from my organisation's perspective that it [cultural policy] confines you. Then I worry about how that affects the work that people are making. You're trying to fit into strands [policy dictates] that have come down from…[ministerial department] policies into the Arts Council's policy down to the arts organisations. Sometimes I wish there were no restrictions…I think being aware of it [cultural policy] might be restrictive…"
>
> *(AM4)*

Another highlights the tensions that result from alignment:

> "Of course there is a wonderful impact in terms of developing confidence and skill sets and citizenship etc… But you can't lead by the utilitarian argument. The poetry has got to be there and the imagination and the space for the unexplored and unthinkable. You cant be too prescriptive… that's always hovering around as a backlash… I think that's something to be really wary of"
>
> *(AM3)*

However, politics can also be perceived to help arts managers advance artistic agendas, an idea that will be explored further in the next section. This support was most widely perceived to take place at the local level. Arts managers reflected positive relationships with their local authority funders, both historically and currently. It appears that the shared territorial space fosters opportunities to find commonalities for two-way dialogue, engagement and learning through practice, and partnerships through which individuals feel they are being heard and in ways that may "inform…cultural policy" (AM4). Similarly, local authority arts services provide opportunities for educators to give students direct, 'real-world' perspectives and experiences of cultural policymaking not necessarily available at Arts Council or ministerial level. Further research is needed to explore the extent of this impression.

Practice driving policy

The intimacy perceived between policy and practice, particularly the operationalisation of the arts as resources for social and economic policy concerns, indicates that there is the potential for arts management to yield influence on cultural policy. Arts managers and educators reflected on the potential role of arts managers in innovating and directing change in the sector. For instance, one arts manager described how her organisation's practice in the 1980s and 1990s "ultimately did lead to a shift in cultural policy" (AM3) in the way that it challenged the expectations of funders and policymakers. She continues:

> "We decided [to develop a programme outside our usual activity]... ...And the Arts Council said to us, 'why are you doing that? We don't fund you to do that. You don't have to do that.'
>
> "...We sort of looked at them and it was like, 'Do you think we do the work that we do just because you give us the money to do it?'...
>
> "So ... in that sense, cultural policy was lagging behind [arts management practice] again. People couldn't really understand what we were doing...
>
> "...[As a result], the practice was a catalyst, which ultimately feeds into cultural policy. And what is new and different, and there is resistance to adopting at one point [what] will soon become common"
>
> *(AM3)*

Examples where arts managers interviewed described they have made an impact on policy are in areas of public health, international exchange, youth arts, and the establishment of arts and business partnerships. Whether or not this impact on policy was actual or perceived is a question.

How the tacit knowledge developed from arts management practice might integrate, or translate, into cultural policies also requires further understanding. The structure of UK public policymaking is based on a culture of evidence-based policy-making, which has become more prevalent since New Labour government (Sanderson 2002). In this process, policy sets arguably measurable targets for public service performance based on equally arguable 'objective' evidence. Research in the UK has long contended that this linear, deterministic and reductionist approach is inappropriately applied within cultural policymaking, where arts and cultural activities rely on risk-taking, flexibility and experimentation rather than predictability (Selwood 2002; Belfiore 2004; Geyer 2012). Both academia and the professional arts and cultural sector have produced studies and evaluations that both legitimise and challenge this method (Newsinger and Green 2016).

Still, policymakers draw on more than these assets for making decisions. Writing in 1978 (p. 304), LJ Sharpe explained the significance of practice, or "accumulated experience" in shaping the British policymaking tradition. Other sources can include academic research, consultancy reports, professional publications and activities by interest groups and professional associations (Jennings and Hall 2012). Weiss (1995) and Jennings and Hall (2012) have found that the types of information policymakers consult vary considerably, as does the value they place on these different sources. In fact, social interaction and personal value systems have a strong bearing on policymaking and analysis (Bevir *et al.* 2003). Information can be communicated formally, via written submission or meeting or informally, in conversations over lunches and at conferences, for instance.

Within the arts, Suteu (2006) and Woddis (2014) identify network memberships and activities aimed at specific advocacy and lobbying goals as ways to impact on policy. While this work is not necessarily solicited by cultural policymakers as part of any consultation process, the financial and intellectual resources evident in the collective group make arts managers part of legitimised "networks and circles [of policy] influence" (AM2). This influence increases when arts networks join into larger coalitions (Beyers and Braun 2014). Nisbett's

(2013) research on cultural diplomacy activities carried out by museum professionals goes a step further in exploring arts managers' potential involvement in policymaking. Her work demonstrates how specific arts management activities may foster support for and the development of new cultural policies that are mutually beneficial to policymakers and practitioners. The study sets out a cause to look more closely at the "positive and symbiotic" (Nisbett 2013, p. 562) nature of the relationship between arts management and cultural policy.

Sites of access

The capacity to influence policy, however, is dependent upon having direct access to policymakers and civil servants. Access points to cultural policymaking bodies, individual policymakers and public service bureaucrats may be established in various ways. Policy studies, including cultural policy specifically, demonstrate that the policymaking process typically involves the interaction of a network of different types of governmental and non-governmental actors that have professional and/or social relationships with one another (Hogwood and Gunn 1984; Beyers 2004; Woddis 2014). Education in arts management has become a way in which to make connections to policymakers. In fact, studying arts management in itself is an opportunity to build one's professional network (Suteu 2006). For instance, all of the programmes reviewed so far have policymakers from local authority and Arts Council levels as guest speakers. Within the profession itself, access (or not) to cultural policymakers is established based on the following: 1) the art form in which an arts manager specialises, 2) the arts manager's position or status within the organisation in which he or she is based and/or 3) the focus of the work that person does, for instance, as a marketing or community outreach professional or artistic director. Each contributes to a perceived level of legitimacy for involvement in a given policymaking venture.

Beyond the obligatory funding application process, an organisation's position within the arts and cultural sector, artistically, politically, geographically, spatially and financially can correlate with the level of access to, engagement in and influence on cultural policymaking at local and national levels. As mentioned above, the resources available to an organisation or group play a large part in influencing the access individual practitioners have to cultural policymakers. These resources include budget, number of staff and status within the art world (Woddis 2014; Beyers and Braun 2014).

Financial resources, or more specifically the monetary exchange that takes place between policy body and arts organisation can influence not only awareness of policy, but also access to policy makers:

> If you are a regularly funded organisation, you're going to understand a lot more [about cultural policy] but if you are a freelance producer, you're maybe not going to know... I do think that when you're in a small arts organisation, it's not high on people's agendas.
> *(AM5)*

Beyers (2004, p. 5) explains that in order to have access to policymakers, "credible and valid expertise" is required. A "regularly funded organisation" in the UK is one that receives funding for core operational costs from the regional Arts Council. This award is an acknowledgement that the organisation is conducting itself in a way that matches the regional Arts Council's own mission. It is thus a financial validation of expertise within the arts and cultural sector of a given region, area of practice (e.g. community arts, arts in education) and/or artform. The research also indicates that the position of the arts manager within the cultural organisation is crucial to determining access. Those in leadership positions appear to have little choice but to engage with cultural policy:

> I'm much more aware [of policy], as a director, as I'm having direct conversations with the funders and in order to be able to do my job well, I need to be on top of those agendas.
>
> *(AM6)*

For others, engagement appears to be on a 'need to know basis', which suggests that there is little desire to learn about policy for its own sake. Another arts manager reflected on how during her previous experience working in larger arts organisations she had no engagement with, or awareness of, cultural policy. Now, working in a smaller arts organisation with less staff she is acutely aware of the influence cultural policy holds on the arts:

> Previously ... I suppose I was working with such large organistions, that I, or being a freelance, I would have had no, nothing to do... but having [now] worked at ... a small organisation and having to deal with all of the funders and things....
>
> *(AM5)*

Art world status also appears to be a determinant of access to policymakers and decision-making processes. Status is typically determined by the commercial exchange, audience figures and/or critical reception of creative/artistic output (Harris 2004). One arts manager indicates that the art form in which she works influences her personal and professional access to cultural policymakers:

> I work in the dance sector ... where it's quite a small world, so I would meet people who work for [the] Arts Council—both people who do the research and the policy development there.
>
> *(AM1)*

Her experience resonates with research from political science, which indicates that smaller territories of practice provide individuals with social and spatial 'nearness' to centres of power and elite decision makers (Bray 1992; Olaffson 1998). Territories of practice could constitute a geographical area, an art form or a funding relationship, for instance. Regarding geography, the same respondent continues,

> We're also a regional organisation, so we would have sat on different...[art form specific] networks which work with Arts Council to develop policy around arts development.
>
> *(AM1)*

Additionally and as previously explored, direct contact and exchange with local government arts officers or public servants and local level politicians also appears to be an important access point:

> Relationships and trust further down the chain [at local government level] are definitely strong. But um, why is that, because I think with the council we're engaged in our local community more on the ground... We're not far away sitting [or meeting] in an office in [national government] or in the [national] Arts Council's head office.
>
> *(AM3)*

As these examples show, access to policymaking is predicated on perceptions of power, prestige and mutual interest. These perceptions are based on economic circumstances, party politics and administrative, institutional and art form structures and cultures. As a result, alignment of beliefs and values, as well as mutual trust, is necessary to develop mutually beneficial policy objectives (Bevir *et al.* 2003). Arts managers clearly have a role to play here. Their ability and capacity to do so is likely related to how they are socialised into and within the profession. Yet, the extent is not yet fully understood.

Conclusion

This chapter has explored how the fields of arts management and cultural policy interact through the experiences and interpretations of individuals involved in practicing arts management and teaching arts management and cultural policy courses in the UK. In doing so, the chapter investigates the manifestation of the relationship in both training and practice. These areas not only constitute important epistemological foundations for both arts management and cultural policy but are also significant sites of socialisation for arts managers. This section will summarise the findings emerging from this study thus far. It will also point to new areas of research that could promote better understanding of the institutional and social dynamics involved in how the value of arts and culture is defined in society and by whom. While this study has focused on the UK specifically, attention will be paid to what may be learnt about the relationship of arts management to cultural policy at an international level.

The emergent findings reflect a fragmented yet allied relationship between arts management and cultural policy. Access to the processes of exchange that take place between cultural policy and arts management is largely based on financial authority, professional standing and/or mutual interest. Due to the transactional nature of state funding for the arts in the UK, cultural policy can no doubt be seen as the framework in which arts management practice takes place. Yet, this influence is erratic, dependent upon changing political interests, individuals' personal beliefs, dispositions and skills and social relationships. Some arts managers appear to respond adeptly to the transitory nature of cultural policy directives, finding ways and means to align their goals to the political interests of the day and beliefs held by individual actors. Such an approach may simultaneously be a form of "crisis management" in the face of adverse funding conditions as well as initiative and "self-sufficiency" (E1).

Mutual interests do exist between the two fields. They share too many common stakeholders for it to be otherwise. In fact, arts managers have been found to match their practice quite comfortably with public policy objectives and in ways that can be perceived to lead rather than follow. Still, while there is acknowledgement of the resourceful nature of the arts for other public policy areas, there is tension around being "too prescriptive" with a sector that requires flexibility and experimentation. So, while alignment between policy and practice is not always forced, it can be contentious. Recognising the role and relationship of arts managers as actors in the cultural policy process locates them as actors in the *business of governance*, rather than as passive recipients of funding merely deployed to implement and deliver the state's vision for culture. Yet, how and why they may do so, and what impact these decisions make, remain unclear (Newsinger and Green 2016).

As a result, a number of new areas of research emerge from this initial analysis. Policy and public administration studies have demonstrated that individuals and institutional cultures and practices play an important part in public policymaking. Yet there are very few studies that unpick the roles arts managers and arts organisations play in the cultural policymaking process. Greater consideration of this role is needed, particularly how specific arts management activities may justify existing and/or develop new cultural policies. Furthermore, study of the impressions of cultural policymakers themselves is an important area not yet explored by this study.

Policymaking is dependent upon a number of variables as yet not fully explored in the study of arts management practice and cultural policymaking. These include, for instance, the personal beliefs and preferences of individual policymakers for particular issues or practices; the perceived or actual reputation of the arts management practitioner and/ or organisation within the arts and cultural sector; personal and professional relationships between policymakers and arts managers and the autonomy and discretionary authority of policymakers and public sector bureaucrats involved (Bevir et al. 2003; Schuster 2003; Lipsky 2010; Jennings and Hall 2012). Such investigation would help develop understanding of how tacit knowledge, institutional dynamics and social interaction may influence policy decisions and thus the legitimation and privileging of particular forms of arts and cultural practice and expression.

This study has indicated there may be different impressions and experiences of influence and alignment between spheres of policy influence at national and local levels. The social interaction that occurs between arts managers and cultural policymakers through network activity and the development of funding bids and projects may contribute to shaping new initiatives in cultural policy at local and regional levels in the UK.

As a result, further study of the interrelation between policy and practice is needed on different regional scales. For instance, comparative examination across different UK executives (i.e. Northern Ireland, Scotland, Wales and England) may yield new insights regarding the specific role that politics and personalities play in cultural policymaking and funding decisions. At an international scale, globalisation and internationalisation have influenced the variety and number of international exchanges taking place in the arts and cultural sector, both commercial and publicly funded. Within the publicly funded sector, exchanges have increased through European networks and cultural-cooperation funding (see Suteu 1999 for the history) and also through international artist residences, festivals and arts management education. These exchanges, which happen at personal levels, have broader political implications as they have been shown to facilitate learning and policy mobility at both organisational and public policy levels (Rowntree et al. 2010; Bell and Oakely 2014). Yet, very little is understood about the role of individual practitioners and institutions in this global process (Durrer et al. 2016).

Finally, the field of arts management education is vastly under-researched. The research presented here shows that studying cultural policy is thought to build arts managers' capacity for critical and reflective thinking. Suteu (2006, p. 62) goes as far as to say that studying international models of cultural policy can inspire and "internationalise" the perspectives of (future) arts managers. Yet, what impact these courses have on promoting greater "intellectual reflection" and "analysis" of policy or of practice in reality is not fully known. Further comparative research on arts management and cultural policy education at both national and international levels is needed. Such research requires moving beyond an audit of courses to exploring how students apply learning.

In summary, it is certain that arts management and cultural policy are deeply interdependent fields of practice and study. Yet very little research has progressed our understanding of how the two fields interrelate. Further scholarship would develop our understanding of the epistemological foundations – the beliefs, values, assumptions and traditions – on which both fields are based. While focusing on the impressions and experiences of UK arts managers and arts management and cultural policy educators in academia has furthered such understanding, greater knowledge of the complex network of actors involved, how they interact and where the power is located among them at personal, institutional and spatial/geographic levels is needed. In their work with creative and aesthetic expressions, which are inherently reflective of cultural ideas, knowledge and values, arts managers and cultural policymakers have a critical role directing, administering and mediating "who gets to 'consume' and who gets to 'make' and what is at any time considered legitimate culture" (O'Brien and Oakley, 2015, p. 3). More study would build critical discourse regarding the institutional and social dynamics underpinning the power structures that determine how and what value becomes attached to particular forms of arts and culture in society.

Notes

1 The author would like to thank Dr. Melissa Nisbett for her contribution to the development of the study as well as early stages of the writing process.
2 See also Paquette and Redaelli, 2015, p. 20, who talk about the courses as being separate and Suteu, 2006, who refers to the original situation of the course at the Polytechnic of Central London and the transfer to City University.

References

Belfiore, E., 2004. Auditing culture: The subsidised cultural sector and the New Public Management. *International Journal of Cultural Policy*, 10 (2), 183–202.

Belfiore, E., and Bennett, O., 2008. *The social impact of the arts: An intellectual history*. Basingstoke: Palgrave Macmillan.

Belfiore, E., and Bennett, O. 2010. Beyond the "Toolkit Approach": Arts impact evaluation research and the realities of cultural policy–making. *Journal for Cultural Research*, 14 (2), 121–142.

Bell, D., and Oakley, K. 2014. *Cultural policy*. London: Routledge.

Bennett, T. 2001. *Differing diversities: Transversal study on the theme of cultural policy and cultural diversity*. Brussels: Council of Europe. Available from: www.coe.int/t/dg4/cultureheritage/culture/completed/diversity/EN_Diversity_Bennett.pdf [Accessed 20 May 2015].

Bevir, M., Rhodes, R., and Weller, P., 2003. Traditions of governance: Interpreting the changing role of the public sector. *Public Administration*, 81 (1), 1–17.

Beyers, J., 2004. Voice and access: The political practices of European interest associations. *European Union Politics*, 5(2), 211–240.

Beyers, J., and Braun, C., 2014. Ties that count: Explaining interest group access to policymakers. *Journal of Public Policy*, 34 (1), 93–121.

Bianchini, F., and Parkinson, M., eds., 1993. *Cultural policy and urban regeneration: The West European experience*. Manchester: Manchester University Press.

Bourdieu, P., 2000. *Distinction: A social critique of the judgement of taste*. R. Nice, trans. Cambridge: Harvard University Press.

Boylan, P., 2000. *Resources for training in the management and administration of cultural institutions, a pilot study for UNESCO*. London: City University London.

Braun, V., and Clarke, V., 2006. Using thematic analysis in psychology. *Qualitative Research in Psychology*, 3 (2), 77–101.

Bray, M., 1992. *Educational planning in small countries*. Paris: UNESCO.

Brkić, A., 2009. Teaching arts management: Where did we lose the core ideas? *The Journal of Arts Management, Law, and Society*, 38 (4), 270–280.

Chaney, P., 2014. Parties, promises and politics: Exploring manifesto discourse on arts policy in Westminster, Scottish, Welsh and Northern Irish elections, 1945–2011. *International Journal of Cultural Policy*, 21 (5), 611–630.

Chong, D., 2009. *Arts management*. London: Routledge.

Creative Scotland, 2014. *Unlocking potential embracing ambition: A shared plan for the arts, screen and creative industries 2014–2024*. Edinburgh: Creative Scotland. Available from: www.creativescotland.com/__data/assets/pdf_file/0012/25500/Creative-Scotland-10-Year-Plan-2014-2024-v1-2.pdf [Accessed 6 April 2016].

CyMAL: Museums, Libraries and Archives, 2010. *A museums strategy for wales, 2010–2015.* Cardiff: CyMAL Museums Archives and Libraries Wales. Available from: http://gov.wales/docs/drah/publications/100615museumstrategyen.pdf [Accessed 6 April 2016].

Delanty, G. 1997. *Social science: Beyond constructivism and realism.* Minneapolis, MN: University of Minnesota Press.

Denzin, N. 2007. *Symbolic interactionism and cultural studies: The politics of interpretation.* Oxford: Blackwell Publishing Ltd.

Department of Culture, Arts and Leisure, 2015. *Strategy for culture and arts, 2016–2026, consultation document.* Belfast: Department of Culture, Arts and Leisure.

Department for Culture, Media & Sport, 2000. *Centres for social change: Museums, galleries and archives for all.* London: Department for Culture, Media & Sport.

DeVereaux, C., 2009. Practice versus a discourse of practice in cultural management. *The Journal of Arts Management, Law, and Society,* 39 (1), 65–72.

Dewey, P., and Wyszomirski, M., 2004. International issues in cultural policy and administration: A conceptual framework for higher education. In: *Third International Conference on Cultural Policy Research International Conference on Cultural Policy Research,* Montreal, Quebec. Available from: http://neumann.hec.ca/iccpr/PDF_Texts/Dewey_Wyszomirski.pdf [Accessed 22 April 2015].

Dragićević Šešić, M., 2003. Survey on institutions and centres providing training for cultural development professionals in Eastern Europe, Central Asia and the Caucus Region. In: *Training in Cultural Policy and Management, International Directory of Training Centres,* Brussels: UNESCO/ENCATC, 6–14. Available from: http://unesdoc.unesco.org/images/0013/001305/130572e.pdf [Accessed 7 April 2016].

Dragićević Šešić, M., 2015. Capacity-building programmes: Keeping institutional memory and regional collective consciousness alive. In: P. Dietachmair, and M. Ilić, eds. *Another Europe: 15 Years of Capacity Building with Cultural Initiatives in the EU Neighbourhood,* Amsterdam: EU Cultural Foundation, 101–117. Available from: www.culturalfoundation.eu/library/another_europe [Accessed 18 May 2016].

Dragićević Šešić, M., and Dragojević, S. 2005. *Arts management in turbulent times: Adaptable quality management—Navigating the arts through the winds of change.* Amsterdam: European Cultural Foundation/Boekmanstudies.

Dubois, V., 2016. *Culture as vocation: sociology of career choices in cultural management.* Trans. Jean-Yves Bart, Abingdon: Routledge.

Durrer, V., Henze, R., and Ross, I. 2016. Approaching an understanding of arts and cultural managers as intercultural brokers. *Arts Management Quarterly [online],* 124, 25–30. Available from: http://artsmanagement.net/images/file/newsletter/AMN_Quarterly_124.pdf[Accessed 26 October 2016].

Durrer, V., and O'Brien, D., 2014. Arts promotion. In: J. Maguire and J. Matthews, eds. *The Cultural Intermediaries Reader,* London: Sage.

Dye, T., 2005. *Understanding public policy.* 11th ed. Upper Saddle River, NJ: Pearson Prentice Hall.

Ebewo, P., and Sirayi, M., 2009. The concept of arts/cultural management: A critical reflection. *The Journal of Arts Management, Law, and Society,* 38 (4), 281–295.

Evrard, Y. and Colbert, F., 2000. Arts management: a new discipline entering the millennium? *International Journal of Arts Management,* 2 (2), 4–13.

Garcia, B., 2005. Deconstructing the city of culture: The long-term cultural legacies of Glasgow 1990. *Urban Studies,* 42 (5–6), 841–868.

Geertz, C. 1973. *The interpretation of culture: Selected essays.* New York: Basic Books.

Geyer, R., 2012. Can complexity move UK policy beyond 'evidence-based policy making'and the 'audit culture'? Applying a 'complexity cascade' to education and health policy. *Political Studies,* 60 (1), 20–43.

Gray, C., 2000. *The politics of the arts in Britain.* New York: St. Martin's Press.

Gray, C., 2007. Commodification and instrumentality in cultural policy. *International Journal of Cultural Policy,* 13 (2), 203–15.

Gray, C., 2009. *Museums, galleries, politics and management.* In: Proceedings of the Public Administration Committee Annual Conference, 7–9 September 2009 held at the University of Glamorgan, Wales.

Harris, J., ed., 2004. *Art, money, parties: New institutions in the political economy of contemporary art.* Liverpool: Liverpool University Press.

Hesmondhalgh, D., Oakley, K., Lee, D., and Nisbett, M., 2015. *Cultural policy under new labour.* Basingstoke: Palgrave Macmillan.

Hogwood, B., and Gunn, L., 1984. *Policy analysis for the real world*. Oxford: Oxford University Press.

Jennings, E., and Hall, J., 2012. Evidence-based practice and the use of information in state agency decision making. *Journal of Public Administration Research and Theory*, 22 (2), 245–266.

Kawashima, N., 2000. *Beyond the division of attenders vs. non-attenders: A study into audience development in policy and practice*, vol. 6. Coventry: Centre for Cultural Policy Studies, University of Warwick, Research Papers.

Lipsky, M., 2010. *Street-level bureaucracy, 30th anniversary ed.: Dilemmas of the individual in public service*. New York: Russell Sage Foundation.

Maguire, J., and Matthews, J., eds., 2014. *The cultural intermediaries reader*. London: Sage.

Mann, C., and Stewart, F., 2000. *Internet communication and qualitative research: A handbook for researching online*. London: Sage.

Matarasso, F., 1997. *Use or ornament: The social impact of participation in the arts*. Stroud: Comedia.

McCall, V., 2012. The 'chalkface' of cultural services: Exploring museum workers' perspectives on policy. Thesis (PhD). University of Stirling.

Miles, A., and Sullivan, A., 2012.Understanding participation in culture and sport: Mixing methods, reordering knowledges. *Cultural Trends,* 21 (4), 311–324.

Mulcahy, K., 2006. Cultural policy: Definitions and theoretical approaches. *The Journal of Arts Management, Law, and Society*, 35 (4), 319–330.

Negus, K., 2002. The work of cultural intermediaries and the enduring distance between production and consumption. *Cultural Studies*, 16 (4), 501–515.

Newsinger, J., and Green, W., 2016. The infrapolitics of cultural value: Cultural policy, evaluation and the marginalisation of practitioner perspectives. *Journal of Cultural Economy*, 9 (4), 382–395.

Nisbett, M., 2013. New perspectives on instrumentalism: An empirical study of cultural diplomacy, *International Journal of Cultural Policy*, 19 (5), 555–575.

O'Brien, D., 2013. *Cultural policy: Management, value and modernity in the creative industries*. London: Routledge.

O'Brien, D., and Oakley, K., 2015. *Cultural value and inequality: A critical literature review*. London: AHRC. Available from: www.ahrc.ac.uk/documents/project-reports-and-reviews/cultural-value-and-inequality-a-critical-literature-review/ [Accessed 31 August 2016].

Olaffson, B., 1998. *Small states in the global system: Analysis and illustrations from Iceland*. Farnham: Ashgate.

Paquette, J., and Redaelli, E., 2015. *Arts management and cultural policy research*. Basingstoke: Palgrave Macmillan.

Pérez-Cabañero, C., and Cuadrado-García, M., 2011. Management of cultural organisations: Evolution of arts and cultural management research over the first ten AIMAC Conferences (1991–2009). *International Journal of Arts Management*, 13 (3), 56–68, 83.

Pick, J., 1980. *Arts administration*. London: Spon Press.

Quinn, R., 1997. Distance or intimacy?—The arm's length principle, the British government and the arts council of Great Britain 1. *International Journal of Cultural Policy*, 4 (1), 127–159.

Rowntree, J., Fenton, R., and Neal, L., 2010. *International cultural leadership: Reflections, competencies and interviews*. London: British Council. Available from: http://creativeconomy.britishcouncil.org/media/uploads/files/International_Cultural_Leadership_report.pdf [Accessed 30 October 2016].

Sanderson, I., 2002. Evaluation, policy learning and evidence-based policy making. *Public Administration*, 80 (1), 1–22.

Schuster, J., 2003. *Mapping state cultural policy: The state of Washington*. Chicago: University of Chicago, Cultural Policy Center.

Scullion, A., and García, B., 2005. What is cultural policy research? *International Journal of Cultural Policy*, 11 (2), 113–127.

Selwood, S., 2002. The politics of data collection. *Cultural Trends*, 12 (4), 13–32.

Sharpe, L. 1978. The social scientist and policy making in Britain and America: A comparison. In: M. Bulmer, ed. *Social Policy Research*. London: MacMillan, 303–312.

Sternal, M., 2007. Cultural policy and cultural management related training: Challenges for higher education in Europe. *The Journal of Arts Management, Law, and Society*, 37 (1), 65–78.

Summerton, J., 2009. The place of practical wisdom in cultural leadership development. In: S. Kay, and K. Venner, eds. *Cultural leadership reader: Cultural leadership programme*, London: Cultural Leadership Programme, Creative Choices, 16–22.

Suteu, C., 1999. *Networking culture: The role of European cultural networks*. Strasbourg: Council of Europe Publishing.

Suteu, C., 2006. *Another brick in the wall: A critical review of cultural management education in Europe.* Amsterdam: Boekmanstudies.

Taylor, C., 1971. Interpretation and the sciences of man. *Review of Metaphysics*, 25 (1), 3–51.

Tchouikina, S., 2010. The crisis in Russian cultural management: Western influences and the formation of new professional identities in the 1990s–2000s. *The Journal of Arts Management, Law, and Society*, 40 (1), 76–91.

United Nations, 1972. *Declaration of Arc-et-Senans, The Future of Cultural Development.* Available from: www.coe.int/t/dg4/cultureheritage/culture/resources/CDCC(80)7-F_AeS.pdf [Accessed 12 May 2016].

UNESCO, 2005. *Convention on the Protection and Promotion of the Diversity of Cultural Expressions.* 20 October, Paris: UNESCO. Available from: http://en.unesco.org/creativity/ [Accessed 2 May 2015].

UNESCO, 2013. *Culture: A Key to Sustainable Development.* Hangzhou International Congress, China, 17 May. Hangzhou: UNESCO. Available from: www.unesco.org/new/fileadmin/MULTIMEDIA/HQ/CLT/pdf/final_hangzhou_declaration_english.pdf [Accessed 2 May 2015].

UNESCO, 2014. *Action Plan for the International Decade for the Rapprochement of Cultures (2013–2022).* 194/EX10 3 March 2015. Available from: http://unesdoc.unesco.org/images/0022/002266/226664e.pdf [Accessed 13 April 2015].

Vuyk, K., 2010. The arts as an instrument? Notes on the controversy surrounding the value of art. *International Journal of Cultural Policy*, 16 (2) 173–183.

Weiss, C. 1995. The haphazard connection: Social science and public policy. *International Journal of Education Research,* 23 (2), 137–150.

Woddis, J., 2014. Arts practitioners in the cultural policy process: Spear-carriers or speaking parts? *International Journal of Cultural Policy*, 20 (4), 496–512.

Part II
Regulating cultural policy

6

Regulating cultural goods and identities across borders

J.P. Singh

Puzzle

Nation-states often cite safeguarding cultural identity as their chief motive for regulating international trade in creative products. This essay analyses this motivation in the context of theories of regulation and international trade. I argue that the shift from naming creative products as cultural products implicates cultural anxiety, which makes such politics especially vulnerable to influence from powerful groups. In doing so, cultural identity often becomes synonymous with national identity and marginalises other cultural voices. Creative products in this essay mostly refer to those from fine and performing arts and entertainment industries in broadcasting, film, and music. The term cultural product implies a sense of group identity and, therefore, the co-option of creative products as symbols of cultural identity.

The efforts to enhance or preserve national cultural identity seem to run counter to the logic of the information age in which cultural meanings circulate at 'hyper-speeds' across national and other borders. Furthermore, culture – as a way of life or a representation of this way of life through art – is the most malleable of human formations, forever subject to syncretism and adaptability. However, we live in an age of cultural anxiety: the fears of the loss of an identity seem to be almost as ubiquitous as the social media networks over which cultural politics are discussed. At the end of 2015, there were nearly 1.5 billion active Facebook users, over one billion unique viewers on YouTube, and 646 million Twitter users.[1] While these and other social networks proliferate, or perhaps because of them, the politics of cultural representation are rife with the idea that identities are becoming homogenised or worse, dominated with powerful representations circulated through global corporations (Pieterse 2004; Miller and Yúdice 2002). Add to this the fear of other 'foreign' influences and the anxiety deepens with a diverse list that includes, depending on the context, migrants, refugees, terrorists, Chinese or Indian capital and products, and religious ideas.[2] Until recently, though, the chief culprit named in international cultural debates was 'Hollywood' or the United States media with its global reach. The U.S. entertainment industry exports, collectively the country's biggest trade item – average above $100 billion dollars when royalty payments are taken into consideration. Released in December 2015, the global box office receipts for "Star Wars: The Force Awakens" were over $1 billion within a month, and the film was set to break all previous records after garnering more than \$2 billion within six months of its release. Seemingly, viewers vote with their feet while at the same time fearing the loss of identity.

This essay shows that regulation of cultural identity often parallels pressures from powerful political-economic interests to define 'culture' in accordance with their needs. In doing so, the politics of cultural identity often posit the strong against the weak both domestically and internationally. However, the political economy of cultural expressions does not always marginalise the voice of the weak. The first section below describes the rise of the politics of both national and cultural identity, before describing the regulation of cultural content. Thereafter, the essay describes the interplay of both the politics of national and cultural identities at the global level. I examine the cultural politics of the global South, often marginalised from the corridors of international regulation, and then turn to the commerce versus culture debate in international trade. Regulation in this essay is understood as explicit rule making through national or international institutions, which shapes the production and exchange of creative products.

National and cultural identities: a macro picture

The path from everyday cultural anxieties to international regulation of creative products, in two historical twists, led to the rise of the regulation of cultural products in the first half of the 20th century and, subsequently, co-joined their fate with social and cultural identity movements in the century's second half. What comes through in the cultural identity debates of the last century is a great uptick around the 1980s of the notion of a national culture along with an awareness of the notion of a group or cultural identity. A rough illustration of this twin trend can be seen in Figure 6.1, which follows the terms 'national identity' and 'cultural identity' through Google Books' n-grams viewer, tracking the use of these terms, in this case for the 1970 to 2010 period. The two decades of the cultural uptick between 1985 and 2005 are the chief subject of this essay.

'National identity' continues to triumph through the current institutional logic of regulation, but the more interesting logic of the future may rest in the second line of 'cultural identity' in the n-gram figure. While the two lines of uptick run almost parallel, the logic governing them might be different. The dominant line of national identity is that of the powerful voices mentioned above, while cultural identity also includes those without a voice or a representation in a story, song, or dramatization that gets circulated globally. From the great decolonising movements of the early 20th century to those of anti-racism raging across the world today, the chief struggle in cultural identity has been the ability of people to tell their own story and earn a just reward for their labours.

Another empirical suggestion in this essay acknowledges the role of market production and exchange, at local and global levels, which encourage the parallel cultural movements of our times: those fostering national cultures and those encouraging cultural diversity and voice. Most broadcast media, until the 1980s in most countries in the West, were primarily government owned, and here the link to the 'national interest' was already quite direct. Thus, the era of market liberalisation since the 1980s produced fears about the fate of 'national identity' championed through such media, while at the same time, even if only marginally providing an impetus to alternative cultural voices. The two politics of cultural production, that of cultural voices and of their market forms, are as apparent in the great debates on the creation and circulation of these images as they are in the emergent property rights, or chiefly economic incentives, that define who will profit from them.

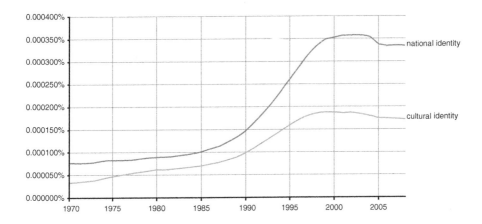

Figure 6.1 Frequency of terms 'national identity' and 'cultural identity' in Google Ngrams
Source: books.google.com/ngrams.
Note: n-grams measured on the Y axis provide relative frequencies of word counts in Google Books. For methodology, see: http://books.google.com/ngrams/datasets.

The regulatory politics of cultural products link back directly to the rise of cultural anxieties of our times, but favor those with access to the political processes. From the right and the left, regulation has always been understood as the recourse of the powerful to get what they want (Lipietz 1986; Stigler 1971). Those with power in global cultural politics are nation-states, public or private corporations, and elite international bureaucracies including intellectual ones. Those contesting the meaning of these politics are groups at local and transnational levels who seek a cultural voice or, as the educator Paulo Freire put it, the ability to name their world (Freire 1970).

Rise of cultural regulation

The regulation of creative products offers a unique instance of the elevation of moral and social reasons, often termed public interest in liberal theories of regulation, along parallel terms to the political economy of comparative advantage that has regulated international trade.[3] Historically, the logic of regulation of such products within nation-states was informed with an entirely different rationale than one for their trade across national frontiers.

Royal patronage, historically, defined the terms of regulation of art in Europe. Art occupied a dubious position in politics, either positioned as antithetical to reason and the rational art of governance following Platonic thought, or marginalised to being a luxury for the extremely prosperous but ultimately for the benefit of the crown (Goodwin 2006). An opera house signified power: the most ornate opera houses, such as those in Paris and Vienna, were constructed in absolutist monarchies to project power (Cummings and Katz 1987). With growing urbanisation and the rise of the bourgeoisie, art collections expanded, and art moved from being a luxury dependent on patronage to a commodity that could now be afforded by a rising middle class as well. Therefore, art became unhinged from patronage and the prerogatives of the crown in the 19th century, in turn encouraging a class of creative workers that by the 20th century could earn full-time wages in artistic production (Goodwin 2006; Throsby 2001). In other words, art moved from a part-time activity of the privileged few, and many a starving artist, to full-time employment for many.[4] Art has several types of value, and price is one of them: the movement of art from patronage to markets has also shifted price fixings of royal commissions to those of art auctions and royalty payments from copyright (Frey 2000; Singh 2011). The rise of the market system also allowed a greater number of artists to fetch returns that were available only to a few through royal patronage (Cowen 1998). This new political economy altered traditional patrimonies of art even if institutions such as a national museum remain defenders of patrimonial practices. Most of the London Tate Modern museum's work since 2000 has been acquired from the Global South, including Asia, Africa, and Latin America: "The 21st century museum is evolving into a place of encounter, social nexus, a contemporary agora" (Wullschlager 2016).

Along with shifting patterns of patronage and patrimony, the technological basis of creative industries has also changed. With the rise of the creative class and associated industries, especially in entertainment, a new basis for regulation had to be invented. This became imperative in the 20th century with the ability to record sounds and to broadcast or convey them over long distances through telephones, radio, and television. Creative products could earn market returns for sustenance, but entertainment industries also possessed some public goods aspects: congestion of airwaves or argument about a natural monopoly in telephones, which necessitated state intervention to ensure that the state and the people had access. Early universal service regulation in telephony, for example, was meant to ensure that telephones reached the rural areas (Mueller 1996). This necessitated regulation especially in industries that were monopolistic (telecommunications) or oligopolistic (broadcasting), in order to make incumbent providers not just "cream-skim" in urban areas, but also provide access to less-privileged demographics in the population, for example in rural areas.

The theory of regulation is surprisingly consensual among conservative economists and radical Marxists, albeit with different policy implications (Horwitz 1991). Economist George Stigler (1971) notes that regulation is provided on behest of those who are regulated, while Karl Marx wrote of the state as the committee for the management of the interests of the bourgeoisie (Poulantzas 1969). Based on this view, public choice economics believes in a minimalist role for the state, while radical political economy prescribes either the state's overthrow or a maximalist role to thwart the capitalist class. The liberal welfare alternative is an in-between position, prescribing regulation on behalf of public interest. The state ownership of media in the Eastern bloc and many parts of the developing world was an extension of this notion of public interest; the media served the state, which served citizens. In post-war Western Europe, the state owned most of the means of broadcasting in the name of national interest.

In the United States, 'public interest' guided the regulation of the media industries through the Federal Communication Commission, which applied historically to telecommunication and broadcasting, and in the last two decades to digital content transmission. Regulation of airwaves was necessary to ensure that a TV or radio station represented all political opinions and social stratifications. In practice, this became a question of access to the airwaves: the famous precedent-setting case of WLBT in Jackson, Mississippi, started with petitions and lawsuits from the black community in Mississippi to have its voice represented; the case began in 1955 and settled in favour of the Black community in 1966 (Rabin 1975–6).

While the U.S. notion of public interest historically seemed different from national ownership of broadcasting in Western Europe, public interest coincided with a somewhat ill-defined notion of public welfare based on utilitarian calculations. In practical terms, therefore, public interest was often conflated with notions of national interest.

Public interest regulation in the U.S., mandating access, or national interest regulation in other parts of the world now continues to decrease in importance as multiple access channels proliferate and cost-effective satellite technologies reach rural or far-flung areas. These developments along with increasing flows of global digital content have contributed to the rise of both the politics of cultural anxiety and identity. The old regulatory model catered to a middle ground of national interest. However, just as public interest lawsuits challenged the old media in the United States, the proliferation of TV and radio channels globally has directed people toward dedicated media. This has increased rather than decreased the politics of cultural anxiety. One of the unfortunate results is the proliferation of media homophily effects, with broadcast media viewers or social media users drawn to only those sources and networks that share their values (Axelrod 1997; Lazarsfeld and Merton 1954). With de facto universal access for all values and users, the unfortunate side effect has been the inability of homophilous networks to communicate with each other, further resulting in the degradation of the public sphere (Centola et al. 2007; Singh 2013).

Enter two great global debates starting in the 1970s that elevated existing national concerns about the creation of cultural content to the international level, and interestingly both cases featured the United Nations Educational Scientific and Cultural Organization as a central player. The broader legacies of these debates will be discussed in the next two subsections, but a summary is necessary to discuss the broad implications for international regulation. In both cases, countries pushed back against global information flows, which sought to represent them, often calling these flows either inaccurate and prejudiced, or destructive toward local ways of life understood mostly in national ways. The first phase began in the post-colonial era when developing countries began to consider the role of communication 'modernisation' in their societies, which soon led to questioning the role of global media firms, mostly Western, in their territories. It culminated in the calls for New World Information and Communication Order (NWICO) in 1976 in the UN General Assembly and the publication of The MacBride Commission (1980) report that articulated the importance of communication and information in the developing world. NWICO sought to correct the imbalance of information flows between the North and the South and sought to make the developing world self-reliant with its own communication infrastructures. Nordenstrung (1983) traced NWICO concerns back to the nationalist movement of the colonies and wrote of the four D's of NWICO: decolonization, democratization, demonopolization, and development. Unfortunately, UNESCO was unable to prevent NWICO becoming mired in the Cold War/East-West confrontation, and the developing world leaned heavily on the resources and rhetoric of the Soviet bloc for support in the UN and UNESCO. The NWICO controversies contributed to the departure of the U.S., U.K., and Singapore from UNESCO in the 1980s. After the departure of these three countries and budget cuts, NWICO died in UNESCO. The second great debate on global content flows dealt with the dominant position of the United States versus the rest of the world. It came to a head in the 1980s as the U.S. pushed for further liberalisation of trade flows governing entertainment industries. The liberalisation push started in the General Agreement for Tariffs and Trade and then moved to UNESCO. In 2005, in a vote of 148 countries for and two against (U.S and Israel), UNESCO voted for the Convention on the Protection and Promotion of the Diversity of Cultural Expressions. After ratification by 33 percent of the countries, as required in international law, the Convention became effective in 2008.

The implications for international regulatory theory can be summarized now. The basis for international trade has been the comparative advantage of nations in the production of commodities. The first great debate, namely NWICO, was often portrayed in the West, a sub-section of the Global North, as the inability of the resource-poor Global South to represent itself and therefore beholden to global conglomerates and their advantages in producing cultural and media content (Boyd-Barrett 1977). In conservative parts of the West, especially in Thatcher's Britain and Reagan's United States, NWICO was understood in official circles as efforts to curtail free speech in the Global South. For its part, the South called attention to the power of global conglomerates to gather, produce, and disseminate news and entertainment content. In hindsight, both sides were making a partially cultural argument: the West in citing press freedoms and the South in questioning the representations and cultural dominance of the West.

In the second debate, the European Community waged a 'cultural war' against the United States, in trying to institute exceptions from free flows of entertainment content. While most West European states had not supported the Global South in the NWICO advocacy, in the 1980s, the EC states cited preservation of cultural diversity as a rationale for derogating from international trade in entertainment industries. The United States merely saw the moves as protectionist in a trade sense, designed to safeguard entertainment industries in EC that were highly subsidized or state-owned.

Two important elements of cultural regulation can be shifted from the historical discussion above. First, international and domestic policy makers regularly acknowledged issues of cultural identity and access to technologies of representation as important issues in regulating international trade. Second, international regulation privileged national identity. The last point is consistent with theories of regulation covered earlier. Those opposing and abetting cultural identity issues at GATT's successor World Trade Organization or UNESCO generally named their representation in terms of national interest and identity. In fact, national elites employed debates on cultural identity to further endow meaning to national borders (Goff 2000). This essay now discusses the history of North-South regulatory issues during NWICO and thereafter, and then turns to efforts that led up to the 2005 UNESCO convention on cultural diversity.

Post-colonial cultural politics

The communication and cultural aspirations of the post-colonial world found expression through the NWICO debates. The influential MacBride Commission report (1980: 254–255), that outlined the historical and epistemic rationales for NWICO, articulated the aspirations as follows: "The object must be to utilize the unique capacities of each form of communication, from interpersonal and traditional to the most modern, to make men and societies aware of their rights, harmonize unity and diversity, and foster the growth of individuals and communities within the wider frame of national development in an interdependent world."

While NWICO debates were broader than those of cultural identities and rights, nevertheless the precedence is important for both articulating post-colonial aspirations and ran parallel to UNESCO's universalism, which often rested on Eurocentric conceptions of national identity (Singh 2011). Although called by different names, notions of cultural or group identities and respect for cultural diversity run parallel to UNESCO's universal ideals, which often rested on Eurocentric humanistic conceptions. UNESCO's Eight-Volume *General History of Africa* begun in the 1950s challenged canonical interpretations of Eurocentric views, even if couched in universal terms. Political controversies in the 1960s and 1970s provide further evidence. The 1966 International Covenant on Economic, Social, and Cultural Rights (ICESCR) came at the behest of the Eastern bloc and many post-colonial countries that viewed the individualistic focus of the Universal Declaration of Human Rights in Western terms.

In the 1980s, UNESCO began considering the role of culture in development. Here, too, it reflected broader ideational and transnational movements that spoke to culture. Examples include the Mayan Rights movements in Latin America (Davis 2004) or the push back from the developing world on development objectives and instruments framed in the global North (Escobar 1995). The 1982 World Conference on Cultural Policies, or Mondiacult, in Mexico forwarded an anthropological view of culture. But underlying it were broad political and cultural pressures. Group of 77 (G-77) developing countries were behind the move in 1987 to declare 1988–97 the Decade for Culture and Development. In 1993, UN Secretary-General Boutros Boutros-Ghali and UNESCO's Director-General Federico Mayor created the World Commission on Culture and Development. The first sentence of the Commission's 1995 report, Our Creative Diversity, notes: "Development divorced from its human and cultural context is growth without a soul" (Perez de Cuellar 1995: 15).

The most relevant example of international regulation for this essay may be UNESCO's efforts to recognise non-Western ideas of cultural heritage. Just as indigenous rights movements began to circulate in the world, UNESCO adopted this cause. In the 1970s, the Smithsonian Institution in Washington, DC, and UNESCO organised a series of symposia on folklore and cultural life that are now regarded as the beginnings of the moves that eventually led in 2003 to the Convention on the Safeguarding of the Intangible Cultural Heritage (Aikawa 2004; Mason and de la Torre 2000). In the United States, the impetus came from acknowledging the role of folklore and oral cultures in African-American and Native-American groups. The 2003 UNESCO convention on intangible cultural heritage, therefore, safeguards historical processes rather than products and monuments. East Asia and Sub-Saharan Africa, in particular, championed the discussions as conforming to their notions of heritage. There was also a link to the 2005 convention discussed later: the 2003 convention, in its politics of negotiation, is also regarded as the price these regions extracted for supporting the 2005 convention. The 2003 convention was a counterpart to the 'tangible' heritage convention of 1972, while the 2005 convention dealt mostly with cultural industries, conceived in terms of diversity.

The soul of cultural diversity in the developing world may be in the notion of cultural voice, which Freire (1970) described as the ability of the people to name their world. Despite UNESCO's de facto need to work with national-states, the post-colonial state (or any state really), an evolving architecture, is far too incomplete a project to speak to all cultural voices and aspirations in the developing world. It would also be simplistic to note that the space is completely filled in by Western cultural representations. While detailing the political economy of creative and cultural productions from the Global South is beyond the scope of this essay, it is useful to consider that the cultural spaces in the developing world may also showcase transnational linkages rather than only Western corporate domination. Post-apartheid South African cinema has relied on links with Hollywood networks for marketing and circulation. In general, Browne (2009: 95) notes that "The African film producer has not copied the American producer although he may have been influenced by the Western world in making films in the first place." While religious conservatives bemoan the rise of sexy female singers in the Arab world, these singers have relied on music industry networks to destabilise patriarchal roles (Mellor 2005). Nestor García Canclini (1995) notes that cultural hybridity in the developing world is understood as much through the mix of the modern and the traditional as the intermixing of nations, ethnic groups, and classes.

Commerce versus cultural rules and regulations

The case analysed here involves initially the United States and the European Community, in particular France during the Uruguay Round (1986–94) of the GATT, and, in recent years, the entire world in the framing of the Universal Convention on Protection and Promotion of Cultural Expressions at UNESCO in 2005. From the late-1940s onwards, Western Europe successfully argued that creative industries, especially films, needed special protections such as quotas to protect its war-ravaged 'infant-industry' in films. During the Uruguay Round of trade talks, the language of 'cultural exception' supplemented that of quotas. As a result, the European Union took the now-famous Most Favored Nation or MFN exemption, which allowed it to preserve its cultural industry policies.

The main issue of concern was the European Commission's Television without Frontiers Directive that came into force in 1992 just as the Uruguay Round headed into its final hours of negotiations. The Directive sought to reserve 51 percent of the total program broadcast on any European channel to home-grown programs. The EU wanted the 51 percent restriction institutionalised through the evolving General Agreement on Trade in Services (GATS).

A related issue was the EU position that content restrictions apply to all of 300-plus channels that were coming about as a result of satellite and cable technologies. The U.S. wanted content restrictions applied to only 50–70 percent of the channels. Presumably, through this measure, U.S. networks such as CNN or Discovery could operate in Europe without using local content. Furthermore, the Motion Picture Association of America also argued that inasmuch as U.S. films and television programs dominate in Europe, its members were subsidising European television and thus objected to the agreement sought by the Europeans at the Uruguay Round.[5] With the EU and U.S. squaring off on opposite sides, these negotiations came to be called *guerres des images* or "war of the images" in France. Transnational cultural industry coalitions among the Europeans led the way toward the MFN exemption that allowed the EU not to make any commitments toward liberalising its audio-visual sectors as they are known in the GATT/WTO jargon. In the EU, this provision came to be known as the 'cultural exception' underscoring the firm belief that cultural industries were non-negotiable.[6]

In the decade following the Uruguay Round, there was a progressive hardening of the European position on creative industries. Europeans framed the issue in cultural identity terms but shifted the focus from cultural exception to cultural diversity. Canada and France led an international coalition to switch the cultural industry issue over to UNESCO from the WTO.[7] This resulted in the introduction at UNESCO of a Universal Declaration on Cultural Diversity in 2001 and Universal Convention on the Protection and Promotion of Cultural Expressions in 2005. The Preamble to the 2005 convention starts by "affirming that cultural diversity is a defining characteristic of humanity." Its 35 articles affirm the rights of nations to formulate cultural policies that promote cultural diversity and protect indigenous cultures. Taken collectively, these articles outline a legal rationale against liberalisation. One of the articles states that if there were a trade versus cultural protection issue in the future, it would have to be resolved in a spirit of "mutual supportiveness" that does not subordinate the UNESCO convention.

At its core, the convention upholds a notion of cultural identity as national identity. The convention preamble affirms that "cultural diversity is a defining characteristic of humanity." However, the task of defining what constitutes diversity and the implementation of the policies and regulations thereof is left to nation-states. For example, Article 2 recognises "the sovereign right to adopt measures and policies to protect and promote the diversity of cultural expression within their territory." Article 6 recognises the rights of states to adopt "regulatory measures aimed at protecting and promoting diversity of cultural expression." For countries such as France, this has meant promoting a conception of Frenchness in French language to the non-recognition of any other cultural identity in France. UNESCO (2013) statistics show, for example, that only one language is represented in French films while in Finland there are 11 and in the UK 12 languages.

There are other contradictions. While the force of the international coalition rested upon the feared onslaught of cultural exports from the United States, those seeking cultural protections were themselves top cultural exporters or seeking to become so. In the statistics released by UNESCO (2005), Canada and France rank among the top ten countries in terms of international trade in cultural products. Second, while the share of trade for the United States and European Union has declined, that for East Asia has doubled; it is increasing for other parts of the developing world as well (UNESCO 2005). UNESCO statistics might underestimate the scope of U.S. exports by counting customs data and not royalty receipts, yet the undercounting issue might go beyond the United States in significant ways. For example, these statistics do not count related activities such as information technology, advertising, and architectural services. Many of these activities are now outsourced to developing countries. Similarly, emerging centres of film and television production in the developing world – Argentina, Brazil, Mexico, Egypt, West Africa, South Africa, India and China – are also underestimated here. Last, if cultural tourism receipts were to be included, the total 'exports' of those seeking cultural protections would rise even further. According to the World Tourism Organization annual reports, France tops the list of international tourist arrivals, accounting for 84 million of the total 1.13 billion international tourist arrivals in 2014 (World Tourism Organization 2015: 6).

In 2015, UNESCO celebrated the 10th anniversary of the cultural diversity convention: the convention is widely viewed as an important policy instrument addressing debates on cultural diversity, but one that is limited in scope in terms of issues of cultural identity and rights and the new technologies of cultural representation (De Beukelaer et al. 2015). A look at the convention's articles show that although it is supposed to be framed for the broader purpose of ensuring cultural diversity, its main focus seems to be preserving and protecting (from trade) a few cultural industries in national terms. Thus, cultural industry seems to be coterminous with national identity. The case of France is especially ironic because, like many other European states, its government does not collect any data on any identity but national identity. Its ethnic minorities often see themselves as excluded from socio-political-economic life. Just as the ink was drying on the 2005 convention, a few days later riots broke out in several French cities over police brutality leading President Jacques Chirac to declare a state of emergency on 8 November 2005 that lasted until 4 January 2006. On the other hand, France's partner in leading the moves for the 2005 Convention is Canada, which is a de jure two-nation bi-lingual state (de facto, it has many languages) and well known for recognising its indigenous groups (first nation) and their cultures.

At an organisational level, UNESCO can point to several intra-organisational measures that attest to the smooth functioning of the organisation.[8] The Convention was ratified on 18 March 2007. According to the provision of article 18, an International Fund for Cultural Diversity was set up with voluntary contributions; it has spent $5.8 million since its inception on 84 projects in 49 developing countries. The parties to the Convention submit quadriennial reports to UNESCO, and several offices have contributed to the work of the Convention. The UNESCO Institute for Statistics (UIS) issued a new Framework for Cultural Statistics (UNESCO 2009), which took into account the work of the Convention. UIS also set up an Expert Group on Measuring the Diversity of Cultural Expressions.[9]

At the level of global norm formation, four other issues provide some context for evaluating the implementation record of the conference. First, legally the Convention lacks force.

The Vienna Convention on the Law of Treaties allows for later Conventions to supersede earlier ones on the same topic. Article 20 language, as noted earlier, sets a new legal precedent of 'mutual supportiveness,' which means that the Convention does not subordinate instruments at the WTO. Second, the re-entry of the United States to UNESCO changed not just the wording of specific articles as mentioned above, but also the trajectory of the implementation. The Convention was not a priority for the United States, and it wanted to direct resources of the organisation elsewhere. While UNESCO's budgetary processes are arcane and complex, great powers do carry clout (Hoggart 1978; Singh 2011). In a further twist, the United States stopped paying its dues in 2011 after UNESCO voted to admit Palestine as a member. Just when the organisation could have hoped to allocate resources to the measures, the United States cut off funding. The U.S. engagement with UNESCO can then be summarised in two phases: dilute the convention (2004–5) and then drop funding for the organisation altogether (2011). Third, the Convention is premised on an analogue model of product flows in cultural industries. In such a world, member-states ship cultural products to each other in metal containers, which can be regulated at national borders, while governments encourage their own creative industries in a variety of ways. In a world of digital technologies, the analogue model falls apart.

The workings of the convention in the last ten years, therefore, can also be examined within the broad context of overlapping issue-areas in other international organisations that attend to issues such as trade, intellectual property, or economic development. The 2005 Convention sought to address the economic aspects of cultural globalisation. However, the lack of movement on further liberalisation on culture (or any other issue) from the World Trade Organization has, in an ironic twist, put a damper on UNESCO's efforts to thwart such moves because the original impetus is now removed. Furthermore, the increasing salience of intellectual property concerns has changed the geo-strategic dimension of the cultural globalisation debate from the United States versus EU/Canada parameter to a Global North-South axis. Global economic rule-making in culture now concentrates on intellectual property issues rather than cultural production.

The trade versus culture debate has settled in favour of trade in another way on the issue of intellectual property. In the last decade, the chief debate on cultural content has been on global North's attempts to develop a digital trade agenda, which includes copyright issues. In fact, digital trade may be one of the most important trade issues for the United States at present (Aaronson 2016). Proponents of strong copyright protection have argued that its enforcement results in further innovation, appropriate rewards for the artists, and further creativity. Digitisation has also altered the major battle in cultural productions from Hollywood versus the rest to once again a global North-South battle on international intellectual property regulation and enforcement. Countries such as Canada and France have formed a formidable global coalition with their cultural adversaries such as the United States to enact and enforce restrictive intellectual property rights. Examples include the many preferential trade agreements that the U.S. and EU have signed with countries in Latin America and Sub-Saharan Africa. A particularly restrictive measure is the most recent Anti-Counterfeiting Trade Agreement (ACTA) signed in 2011 but not yet ratified mostly due to civil society protests worldwide (Sell 2013). ACTA went far beyond the existing WTO agreements in intellectual property protection and enforcement, which are now the most important cultural industry issues for both the rich-country signatories and the non-signatories to the 2005 Convention. The 2015 TransPacific Partnership agreement among 13 trade partners including the U.S., Canada, Japan, and Australia has included comprehensive provisions for online protection.

Conclusion

International cultural regulation is sometimes analysed as the ability of the nation-states to regulate an international cultural division of labour in production and exchange of creative artefacts. Certainly, a debate such as NWICO can be analysed as a struggle against cultural domination by Western conglomerates. The UNESCO Convention can similarly be viewed as a moderation within dominant cultural producers. However, such a view is incomplete at best and empirically incorrect at worst. In the former case, it does not explain the struggle between cultural and national identities and the non-material anxieties in which they are embedded. In the latter case, it privileges material production (and labour or class) as an antecedent condition or an article of faith.

This essay has presented a somewhat non-linear and multi-causal argument about international cultural regulation especially in the two decades of what this essay called the cultural uptick from 1985–2005. The argument starts with technologies of representation and cultural anxieties that provide the context for understanding the struggle between national and cultural identities. It also distinguishes between creative expressions and cultural expressions. National identity is one among many types of cultural identities but one that makes the nation-state salient in its politics. The imprint of the nation-state is expansive in current international regulatory instruments at the WTO and UNESCO. However, in the case of the WTO the state seems beholden to commercial factors while at UNESCO the state has tried to reinforce its own paternal powers to regulate cultural production within its borders in the name of national identity. The imprint of commercial production of creative products and their relationship is, therefore, ambiguous.

Future research will need to confront two interlinked issues. First, it must move beyond a tenuous regulatory binary between culture and trade. As this essay shows, this debate itself reflects powerful interests within nation-states who either want to protect and regulate domestic creative industries in the name of (national) cultural identity or promote exports as creative products that are either not cultural or do not threaten cultural identity. Trade can promote, restrict, or transform cultural identities. Positioning trade as a threat or a thrust toward maintaining cultural identities is misleading. Second, regulation obeys the dictums of the powerful, but this essay shows that cultural voices from the meek and the marginalised are not always absent. New technologies establish affordances for these new cultural voices. Research needs to explore both the empirical and the normative possibilities for these cultural voices and the regulatory provisions that can enhance these affordances.

International cultural regulation that is deliberative, in the sense of being inclusive and informed with public reasoning, must result from participatory processes that go beyond the elite in international organisations, nation-states, and commercial enterprises. More and more, artists, creative producers, and civil society are involved in shaping the commerce and politics of cultural regulation. Their voices are incipient but increasingly important to understanding international cultural politics. The emerging international cultural regulation will result from the interstialities and intersections among national and cultural identities, commercial and creative products, and the aspirations among people to name and present their world.

Notes

1 Zephoria (2016), YouTube (2016) and Twitter Statistics (2016).
2 See, for example, Benhabib (2002); Esposito (1992), Evrigenis (2008); Kang (2009).
3 Notion of public interest is derived from welfare economics, which sanctions state regulation and redistribution to ensure the greatest satisfaction of citizens. Comparative advantage relies on the

relative abundance of resources or factors of production within an economy. Intuitively understood, it rests upon a division of labor across countries.

4 Indirectly, the elite continued to shape the type of art would be produced through their influence on educational and other institutions that defined taste, in this case in cultural terms (Becker 2000; Miller and Yúdice 2002).

5 Television programs in France, and in many other European states, are subsidised by film box office receipts, the majority of which are generated by American films and levies on blank video-tapes used to record these programs.

6 The European Union negotiates as a single entity at the WTO. However, its single position often reveals fissures. UK, the biggest cultural products exporter in the EU, and countries such as Denmark and Netherlands are reluctant to go along with protectionist measures.

7 The EU does not does not negotiate as a single entity at UNESCO. However, most EU states took the same position on the 2005 UNESCO Convention discussed in this essay.

8 Many of these measures are listed on the Convention's website. http://www.unesco.org/new/en/culture/themes/cultural-diversity/diversity-of-cultural-expressions/the-convention/.

9 The author served on both the Taskforce and the Working Group.

References

Aaronson, Susan Ariel. February 2016. The Digital Trade Imbalance and Its Implications for Internet Governance. Global Commission of Internet Governance. Paper Series: No. 25. Available at: https://www.cigionline.org/publications/digital-trade-imbalance-and-its-implications-internet-governance.

Aikawa, Noriko. 2004. "An historical overview of the preparation of the UNESCO International Convention for the Safeguarding of the Intangible Cultural Heritage." Museum International 56(1–2): 137–149.

Axelrod, Robert. 1997. "The dissemination of culture a model with local convergence and global polarization." *Journal of Conflict Resolution* 41(2): 203–226.

Becker, Howard S. 2000/1986. Art Worlds. 25th Anniversary Edition. Berkeley, CA: University of California Press.

Benhabib, Seyla. 2002. *The Claims of Culture: Equality and Diversity in the Global Era*. Princeton, NJ: Princeton University Press.

Boyd-Barrett, Oliver. 1977. "Media imperialism: Towards an international framework for the analysis of media systems." *Mass Communication and Society* 116–135.

Browne, Sandra. 2009. "Film industry in Nigeria." In Helmut Anheier and Yudhister Raj Isar. Eds. *The Cultural Economy* 95–96. London: Sage.

Centola, Damon, Juan Carlos Gonzalez-Avella, Victor M. Eguiluz, and Maxi San Miguel. 2007. "Homophily, cultural drift, and the co-evolution of cultural groups." *Journal of Conflict Resolution* 51(6): 905–929.

Davis, Shelton H. 2004. "The Mayan movement and national culture in Guatemala." In Vijayendra Rao and Michael Walton. Eds. *Culture and Public Action*. 328–358. Stanford, CA: Stanford University Press.

De Beukelaer, Christiaan, Miikka Pyykkönen, and J. P. Singh, eds. *Globalization, Culture, and Development: The UNESCO Convention on Cultural Diversity*. Houndmills: Palgrave Macmillan, 2015.

Escobar, Arturo. 1995. *Encountering Development: The Making and Unmaking of the Third World*. Princeton, NJ: Princeton University Press.

Esposito, John L. 1992. *The Islamic Threat: Myth or Reality?* New York: Oxford University Press.

Evrigenis, Ioannis D. 2008. Fear of Enemies and Collective Action. Cambridge: Cambridge University Press.

Freire, Paulo. 1970. *Pedagogy of the Oppressed*. New York: Continuum.

Frey, Bruno S. 2000. *Arts and Economics: Analysis & Cultural Policy*. Berlin: Springer.

García Canclini, Nestor. 1995. *Hybrid Cultures: Strategies for Entering and Leaving Modernity*. Minneapolis, MN: University of Minnesota Press.

Goff, Patricia M. 2000. "Invisible Borders: Economic Liberalization and National Identity."*International Studies Quarterly* 44: 533–62.

Goodwin, Craufurd. 2006. "Art and culture in the history of economic thought." In Victor A. Ginsburgh and David Throsby. Eds. *Handbook of the Economics of Art and Culture*. Handbooks in Economics 25. Amsterdam: North-Holland.

Hoggart, Richard. 1978. *An Idea and Its Servants: UNESCO from Within*. New York: Oxford University Press.

Horwitz, Robert Britt. 1991. *The Irony of Regulatory Reform: The Deregulation of American Telecommunications*. New York: Oxford University Press on Demand.

Kang, David C. 2009. *China Rising: Peace, Power, and Order in East Asia*. New York: Columbia University Press.

Lazarsfeld, Paul F., and Robert K. Merton. 1954. "Friendship as a social process: A substantive and methodological analysis." Freedom and Control in Modern Society 18(1): 18–66.

The MacBride Commission. 1980. *Many Voices, One World: Towards a New, More Just, and More Efficient World Information Many and Communication Order*. Lanham, MD: Rowman & Littlefield, 1980, 254–255.

Mason, Randall, and Marta De La Torre. 2000. "Heritage conservation and values in globalizing societies." In UNESCO, Ed. *World Culture Report: Cultural Diversity and Pluralism*. 164–179. Paris: UNESCO.Mellor, N. November 11, 2005. "Girl Power." Financial Times.

Miller, Toby, and George Yúdice. 2002. *Cultural Policy*. London: Sage.

Mueller, Milton. 1996. Universal service: Interconnection, competition, and monopoly in the making of the American telephone system. Washington, DC: American Enterprise Institute.

Nordenstrung, Kaarle. 1983. The Mass Media Declaration of UNESCO. Norwood, NJ: Ablex Publishing.

Peréz de Cuéllar, Javier. 1995. *Our Creative Diveristy: Report of the World Commission on Culture and Development*. Paris: UNESCO Publishing.

Pieterse, Jan Nederveen. 2004. *Globalization & Culture: Global Mélange*. Lanham, MD: Rowman & Littlefield.

Poulantzas, Nicos. 1969. "The problem of the capitalist state." *New Left Review* 58: 67.

Rabin, Robert L. 1975–1976. "Lawyers for social change: Perspectives on public interest law." *Stanford Law Review* 28: 207–261.

Sell, Susan K. 2013. "Revenge of the "Nerds": Collective action against intellectual property maximalism in the global information age." *International Studies Review* 15 (1): 67–85.

Singh, J. P. 2010. *United Nations Educational, Scientific, and Cultural Organization (UNESCO): Creating Norms for a Complex World*. London: Routledge.

Singh, J. P. 2011. *Globalized Arts: The Entertainment Economy and Cultural Identity*. New York: Columbia University Press.

Singh, J. P. 2013. "Information technologies, meta-power, and transformations in global politics." *International Studies Review* 15(1): 5–29.

Stigler, George J. 1971. "The theory of economic regulation." *The Bell Journal of Economics and Management Science* 2(1): 3–21.

Throsby, David. 2001. *Economics and Culture*. Cambridge: Cambridge University Press.

Twitter Statistics. January 2016. Available at: http://www.statisticbrain.com/twitter-statistics/ Accessed 16 January 2016.UNESCO Institute for Statistics. 2005. International Flows of Selected Cultural Goods and Services, 1994–2003. Montreal, Quebec: UNESCO Institute for Statistics. Accessed from www.uis.unesco.org/ev_en.php?ID=6372_201&ID2=DO_TOPIC.

UNESCO Institute for Statistics. 2013. Feature Film Diversity. UIS Fact Sheet. No. 24. Montreal: UNIESCO Institute for Statistics. Available at: http://www.uis.unesco.org/culture/Documents/fs24-feature-film-diversity-en.pdf.

UNESCO. *2009 UNESCO Framework for Cultural Statistics*. Montreal: UNESCO Institute for Statistics.

World Tourism Organization. 2015. Tourism Highlights 2015 Edition. Madrid: WTO. Accessed from www.world-tourism.org.

Wullschlager, Jackie. 27 May 2016. "How Tate Modern Transformed the Way We See Art." *Financial Times*. Available at: http://www.ft.com/intl/cms/s/2/8c961a2c-2192-11e6-9d4d-c11776a5124d.html.

You Tube, January 2016. Statistics. Available at http://www.youtube.com/yt/press/statistics.html Accessed 16 January 2016.

Zephoria, 16 January 2016. The Top 20 Valuable Facebook Statistics – Updated December 2015. Available at https://zephoria.com/top-15-valuable-facebook-statistics/ Accessed 16 January 2016.

7

No exceptions

Cultural policy in the era of free trade agreements

Graham Murdock and Eun-Kyoung Choi

> We are free traders. I guess next to John Wayne ....Adam Smith is one of our favourite people, at least insofar as a free market is concerned...The minute anybody tries to erect trade barriers, there is a viral contagion effect which spreads all over the world.
>
> *Jack Valenti, President of the Motion Picture Association of America, speaking in 1977 (quoted in Yecies 2007:4)*

Style and substance

Most commentary on cultural policy focuses on developments within nation states, analysing the genesis, career and impact of selected central and local government initiatives. There are secondary literatures comparing countries and examining policy processes within the European Union and other regional blocs, but studies exploring the interplay between national polices and global trade regimes remain few and far between. Taking the changing relations between the United States and South Korea (hereafter simply Korea), from immediately after World War II through to the present, as an illustration, this paper aims to show how placing developments in cultural policy within the wider frame of trade relations helps to illuminate them in new ways.

In July 2012 the South Korean entertainer Psy released a song, *Gangnam Style,* mocking the residents of Gangnam, an affluent suburb of Seoul, accompanied by a promotional video based around a dance routine featuring a parody of horse riding. Within weeks it was a world-wide phenomenon and by the year's end the first video to achieve one billion views on You Tube.

In May 2013, Park Geun-hye, the newly installed President of South Korea, selected the United States for the first state visit of her tenure. The daughter of Park Chung-hee who had headed the country's military government for almost two decades, until his assassination in 1979, she symbolised the country's double transition, from authoritarianism to electoral democracy and from strong state direction of the economy to a market-centred approach to growth. In his speech welcoming her to the White House President Obama joked, "my daughters have taught me a pretty good Gangnam Style" before turning to the Korea-US free trade agreement, KORUS, finalised in 2007 but only ratified by the legislatures of both countries in the autumn of 2011.

Hailing the Agreement as "historic", Obama seized the opportunity to underline its advantages to the United States pointing out that "On our side…it will boost US exports by some $10 billion and support tens of thousands of American jobs", noting that car industry "exports are up nearly 50% and our Big Three – Ford, Chrysler and GM – are selling more to Korea", adding, almost as an afterthought, that "obviously it will be creating jobs in Korea" (White House Office of Press Secretary 2013). Given that the crisis in the US automobile industry required an $80 billion government bail-out and became emblematic of America's decline as an industrial power, it was a politic choice, but KORUS was also strongly informed by the push to further open export markets for the information and cultural goods that a growing consensus of analysts and commentators saw as the primary engine of future economic growth.

A reading anchored in models of globalisation would be tempted to see Psy's symbolic presence in the White House as strong evidence of a new pattern of cultural flows and confirmation of Korea's successful transition from one of the world's poorest nations immediately after World War II to a major economic power whose information and cultural industries are achieving global reach. Critical analysis however needs to move from style to substance and detail how Korea's cultural industries have been progressively captured by ideologies and conditions of practice promoted by the major US communications companies. To unpack this process we need to return to a revised model of cultural imperialism.

Cultural imperialism revisited

The argument that cultural goods play a key role in sustaining America's global economic ascendency is not new. In a 1926 essay entitled "When the movies go abroad" written for *Harper's* magazine, the journalist Charles Merz, who later edited the *New York Times*, saw the lavish displays of consumer goods in Hollywood films as persuasive ambassadors, stoking international demand for American brands. "Trade", he argued, "no longer follows the flag, it follows the film":

> Automobiles manufactured here are ordered abroad after screen shadows have been observed to ride in them. China wants sewing machines; rich Peruvians buy piano players; orders come from Japanese who have admired mission armchairs in the films.
>
> *(Merz 1926:159/165)*

Cultural artefacts are not only promotional vehicles for other goods or commodities to be traded in their own right. They also provide the major imaginative spaces in which individual nations and social groups explore and project their sense of themselves and affirm their way of life and core values. This makes them both unique and ambiguous. They persistently escape the confines of particular policy domains and stoke rival claims from competing interests intent on recapturing them.

The argument that cultural goods are not like other commodities was forcefully restated in 2005 by Jacques Chirac in a speech opposing their inclusion in the areas covered by the newly launched World Trade Organisation (WTO). "What is at stake", he argued,

> is our vision of what it means to be human. The cultural exception is based on a political and moral affirmation of the utmost importance: that there are human activities that cannot be reduced to their status as merchandise.
>
> *(quoted in Littoz-Monnet 2007:21–22)*

This view was summarily dismissed by Jack Valenti, the long-serving head of the Motion Picture Association of America (MPAA), the leading US entertainment industry group lobbying for the removal of all barriers to open trade. Before moving to the MPAA, a post he held for almost four decades, from 1966 to 2004, Valenti had been an advisor to Lyndon Johnson and retained a network of influential political contacts. He was adamant that counting popular film and television as exceptions "had nothing to do with culture, unless European soap operas and game shows are the equivalent of Moliere [it] is all about the hard business of money" (quoted in Grant and Wood 2004:359). Discounting the role of popular cultural forms as valid spaces of expression was a necessary rhetorical move in defence of his Association's primary "mission", which, as he candidly admitted elsewhere, was "to make sure that American film [and] television can move freely and unhobbled around the world in marketplaces that are competitive" (quoted in Wasko 1994:225–226). What is being exported however is not simply an array of cultural commodities but a cumulative vision of a way of life.

In his path-breaking 1969 analysis, *Mass Communication and American Empire,* Herbert Schiller argued that commercialised American popular culture promotes an enveloping "vision" organised around "a mountain of artefacts, privately furnished and individually acquired and consumed" (Schiller 1969:3), adding in a later work, that this "American life style, from its most minor details and deeply felt practices reflects an exclusively self-centred outlook" (Schiller 1973:10). By insistently addressing people in their role as consumers, making personal choices, this vision of plenty and its pleasures pushes the collective identities of citizen and worker to the margins, elevates corporate interests over the public interest and confirms markets as the preferred form of economic organisation.

The present era of Free Trade Agreements, of which KORUS is a leading example, is the latest phase in an unfolding history of shifting relations between national cultural polices and a global trading regime in which the United States has taken a leading role in promoting this consumerist ideology by pressing for perceived blockages to 'free trade' in cultural goods to be abolished.

Over and above the tariffs (customs duties) charged on imports governments may introduce a range of 'non-tariff barriers' designed to secure space and resources for local cultural production. Restrictions typically take the form of quotas limiting the amount of overseas material that can be imported and ceilings on foreign ownership or investment in domestic communications and media companies. Active support for local production is advanced through public funding or tax exemptions for selected cultural initiatives and projects. All these interventions are roundly condemned by militant advocates of 'free' markets, as granting unfair preferences to domestic institutions and companies and placing unwarranted restrictions on open-market entry and competition. They accept no exceptions.

Companies wishing to realise the full value of their entry into overseas markets also require their goods be protected from use and copying without payment, a demand that has led in recent decades to intellectual property provisions being incorporated into trade agreements for the first time. On the face of it "inserting intellectual property into the multilateral trade regime makes no sense" since the aim of trade liberalisation is to "increase consumer access to goods and services, intellectual property policy cuts across this by constructing scarcity and rationing access " (Sell 2010:763). Its integration into debates on trade is the result of concerted pressure from major US rights holders intent on maximising returns, in conjunction with policy agencies concerned about international competitiveness.

Copyright rules have traditionally sought to strike a balance between originators' claims to a reasonable return on their labour and the open circulation of the full range of cultural resources required to support current and future creative activity and innovation. The US-led drive to extend the scale and scope of intellectual property provisions has been a major point of contention in recent debates on global trade, with audio visual products and services emerging as a flash point.

We can usefully think of the promotion of Free Trade Agreements as the pursuit of cultural imperialism by other means. This may seem a surprising, even foolhardy, assertion since for the last three decades dominant approaches to understanding cultural flows have been organised around theories of globalisation animated by sharp criticisms of cultural imperialism as a drastically oversimplified account operating with an outdated centre-periphery model that casts the US as a dominant power able to impose its interests with only weak opposition. This, it is argued, fails on three counts. Firstly, it ignores the rise and significance of alternative centres of cultural production, in India, Latin America, and Asia. Secondly, it underestimates the growing strength of counter flows and regional markets. Thirdly, it plays down the consistent evidence that given an effective choice between equivalents, audiences prefer local productions or imports that resonate with their values and sense of self.

An attentive reading of Herbert Schiller's formulation, however, suggests a more layered conception than many critics allow. Schiller defines cultural imperialism as:

> the sum of processes through which a society is brought into the modern world system and how its dominating stratus is attracted, pressured, forced and sometimes bribed into shaping social institutions to correspond to, or even, promote, the values and structures of the dominating centre of power.
>
> *(Schiller 1976:9)*

Three aspects of this conception are central to the present argument:

Firstly, by insisting that cultural imperialism is a process, it underlines the need to examine how the strategies and points of pressure employed shift over time in response to changes in the economic and political operating environment.

Secondly, by placing class centre stage and focusing on relations between the 'dominating centre of power' and the 'dominating stratum' in the target nation, it draws attention to the ways that the deals struck between elites consistently privilege corporate interests and exclude the general public from full participation. Negotiations around Free Trade Agreements, which take place behind closed doors, away from parliamentary scrutiny and accord privileged access and participation to leading corporations, are a clear instance of this process in action and have been met by mounting public suspicion and anger.

The third key point in Schiller's definition of cultural imperialism is his insistence on the central role played by conceptions of modernity and the deployment of 'attraction' alongside 'force' and 'pressure' in securing compliance.

Over the post-war period Korean economic policy has moved from the drive for reconstruction and growth organised around manufacturing and heavy industry to a vision of a new modernity that takes full advantage of innovations in communication technologies and the expanded markets for information and cultural goods opened up by the global embrace of commercial enterprise and competition. External pressure has certainly played an important role in Korea's transition to a market-centred economy, but this movement has also been fuelled by Korean corporate and governmental ambitions, which have been shaped in turn by shifts in the wider global economic and political order.

Economically the post-war period has been dominated by the retreat from comprehensive state management and the ascendancy of neo-liberalism's promotion of marketization.

Originating in the UK and the US in the early 1980s, its militant advocacy of selling state assets, opening monopoly or protected markets to new entrants and loosening regulations on corporate activity has been widely adopted in emerging economies as a necessary precondition of the next phase of economic expansion. Dominant conceptions of future prosperity have also been strongly influenced by the growing academic and policy consensus that information, cultural, and service industries are displacing manufacturing as the major engines of capitalist growth and that nations wishing not be left behind need to modernise their infrastructures and develop their cultural and service sectors. As a consequence, the emphasis in the term 'cultural industries' has shifted from 'culture' to 'industries' and symbolic goods have increasingly come to be evaluated for their potential economic returns rather than as symbolic spaces for exploring the state of the nation and its complexities and contradictions. Korea exemplifies these shifts.

The sections that follow examine in more detail how this transition has been shaped firstly by US moves to incorporate cultural goods into the global trading system while extending protections for the intellectual properties controlled by the major US media corporations and secondly by the strategies developed by successive Korean government in response to these pressures and in pursuit of their own ambitions.

Consolidating corporate interests: US strategies

The initial US push to secure the free movement of cultural goods was pursued through the General Agreement on Tariffs and Trade (GATT), one of a cluster of institutions designed to regulate global capitalism that the Allied powers put in place in the immediate aftermath of World War II. They also included the International Monetary Fund (IMF), which came to play a significant role in advancing the liberalisation of markets through the 'structural adjustment' requirements attached to the loans made to struggling emerging economies, including, in 1987–8, Korea.

Launched in January 1948, the GATT agreement was aimed at securing substantial reductions in tariffs and other trade barriers by requiring imported goods to be treated in the same way as equivalent domestically produced goods. This gave the United States, which had boomed economically during the War, a significant competitive advantage over economies that had been disrupted and damaged in the conflict. At the same time, the cultural industries' pivotal role as spaces for the construction and repair of national identities placed them at the centre of contention. Initial disputes centred on film, the major popular entertainment medium of the time. Fearing that the global ascendency of Hollywood would derail attempts to revive domestic film production and undermine the vitality of the national language, France pressed for an 'exclusion' clause to be added to the GATT agreement, setting cultural industries apart from its general provisions (Grant and Wood 2004).

The American delegation was adamantly opposed. As Jack Valenti insisted in an interview with *Le Monde*: "The United States will not sign a GATT agreement which makes culture an exception. There would be commercial war about it if we don't set competition and free access to market" (quoted in Magder 2004). Talks ended in stalemate but the French did win a concession allowing countries to reserve screen time for "films of national origin". It was a conditional victory, however, since Article IV(d) of the Agreement specified that questions around screen quotas remained open for later negotiations over their "limitation, liberalisation or elimination".

Having failed to secure a multilateral agreement on quotas, the United States increasingly turned to unilateral channels of pressure and strengthening protections for the intellectual property rights of major corporate rights holders. One of the principle agencies employed was the Office of the United States Trade Representative (USTR) established to advise the President on trade policy. Deliberations were conducted in closed meetings that excluded both the press and the public but relied heavily on the analysis and advice provided by the major copyright holders, opening the process to comprehensive corporate capture (Kaminski 2014). The 1974 US Trade Expansion Act contained a provision that instructed the USTR to compile a special annual report under Section 301 identifying "those foreign countries that deny adequate and effective protection of intellectual property rights, or deny fair and equitable markets access to United States persons that rely upon intellectual property protection". Countries failing to meet these requirements could be subjected to sanctions. As we will see, this provision was deployed against Korea.

By then, however, mounting US frustration with the overall failure to advance the commercialisation of cultural exchange through the GATT system, had fed into growing pressure for a major reorganisation of the international trade regime. The final round of talks began in 1986 and ended in 1994 at a meeting in Marrakesh at which it was decided to replace GATT with a new body, the World Trade Organisation (WTO). Launched in January 1995, the WTO incorporated the GATT provisions, while adding two new areas of oversight and control that directly addressed the perceived problems posed by the audio-visual industries: the General Agreement on Trade in Services (GATS) and the Agreement on Trade-Related Aspects of Intellectual Property (TRIPS).

The GATT regime had been built around a model that identified trade primarily with flows of physical goods, with services occupying an uncertain status. GATS resolved this and extended the WTO's reach unambiguously to key areas defined as 'services', including broadcasting and telecommunications. At the same time, TRIPS responded to mounting concerns over unauthorized copying and loss of revenues on the part of major rights holders by incorporating protections for intellectual property into the international trading regime for the first time, a move that one influential commentator has described as "one of the most dramatic instances of international market regulation in the twentieth century" (Sell 2010:762). Taken together, these innovations opened a second phase in the push to fully incorporate cultural goods into the global trading regime. This initiative did not go unopposed, however, as advocates of cultural exception regrouped and sought to work through the United Nations Education, Scientific and Cultural Organisation (UNESCO), founded in 1945 to protect cultural heritage and promote international understanding through cultural exchange.

In 1980, UNESCO had issued the McBride Commission report on the global communications system, *Many Voices, One World*. The subtitle announced it as work towards a "more just and more efficient" order. The Report's guiding conception of cultural justice however sat very uneasily alongside dominant market driven definitions of 'efficiency', a tension highlighted in the passage pointing to the "grave danger of the distorting power" arising "on an international level" from structures of communication that "reflect the life-styles, values and models of a few societies, spreading to the rest of the world certain types of consumption and certain development patterns" (UNESCO 1980:24) Supporters of free markets perceived this stance as openly antagonistic towards commercial cultural trade and the US withdrew from the organisation in 1984, re-joining in 2003 to find that the issue had once again moved to the centre of UNESCO's agenda under the banner of promoting cultural diversity.

The argument that cultural diversity was a public good essential to the full realisation of democracy had been formally stated in *Our Creative Diversity,* a report produced by the World Commission on Culture and Development for the UN General Assembly (Graber 2006).

Two later reports on 'World Culture', in 1998 and 2000, expressly identified the rise of integrated media conglomerates, led by the US majors, as the principal threat to diversity.

The rhetoric of diversity moved the locus of debate from the predominantly defensive stance underpinning the argument for exception to a positive advocacy of citizens' access to the full range of available experiences and views as a cultural right. Diversity of provision was presented as a necessary guarantor of diversity of expression and representation, an argument that lent added weight to the case for publicly owned media, including public service broadcasting, operating outside the commercial system.

In 1998 Ministers of Culture from a range of countries supported by an association of creative workers and civic groups met to discuss how to advance the case for diversity (Acheson and Maule 2004). Coinciding with the launch of the WTO, this new coalition set out to insulate cultural products from the new trade provisions (Hahn 2006). In October 2003, the UNESCO General Conference responded to this initiative and asked the Director General to draft a legally binding convention protecting diversity of cultural expression.

The resulting *Convention on the Protection and Promotion of the Diversity of Cultural Expression* announced itself as the first international "instrument of its kind to recognize the very specific nature of cultural goods and services, having both an economic and cultural dimension" (UNESCO 2013:Foreword v). This restatement of the unique nature of cultural activity was followed by a strong commitment to creating "an enabling environment in which artists, cultural professionals, practitioners and citizens worldwide can create, produce, distribute, disseminate and enjoy a broad range of cultural goods, services and activities" (UNESCO 2013:op cit). This elevation of the cultural rights of creators and citizens over the economic requirements of corporations was widely interpreted as undermining arguments for extending market driven trade in cultural goods and intellectual property provisions.

The US, which had only just re-joined the organisation, saw this as an unwarranted erosion of the WTO's remit, but when the draft Convention was put to the vote at the General Conference in 2005, they found themselves isolated in opposition with only Israel supporting their position.

The Convention's comprehensive definition of diversity as all "the manifold ways in which the cultures of groups and societies find expression" covered all established and emerging media and gave signatories unlimited discretion to decide which policies they saw as necessary to ensure diversity (Graber 2006). At the same time, signatories who were also members of the WTO remained bound by their endorsement of the organisation's general agreement to progressive liberalisation. With no clear guidance of how this circle might be squared, fractious disputes within the WTO were inevitable.

In this changed context, it became increasingly clear that the WTO would be unable to resolve this issue and remove perceived blockages to trade in cultural goods or enforce copyright rules that fully met US requirements. As more members joined, including emerging economies with significant bargaining weight, led by India, Brazil and China, the scope for conflicts of interest grew. Under the old GATT provisions, agreements could be amended by a simple majority vote. WTO rules required that any changes that applied to all members be endorsed by three-quarters of the membership of the Ministerial Conference (Dunkley 2001). Added to which resolving disputes was a long drawn-out process with adjudication taking an average of 18 months and compliance a further 15 months, and even then there was no absolute guarantee that countries would act on decisions in a timely manner (Choi 2009). In contrast, disputes between parties within the US-led North American Trade Agreement (NFTA), the first major FTA the US had brokered, were fully resolved within four to five months.

The US had signalled its intention making audio-visual services a major focus of the talks launched in Doha in 2001. By 2005, however, discussion had reached deadlock and major decisions concerning market access put on hold, leading to predictions that the era of multilateralism was at an end. The US responded by increasingly seeking to extend the NAFTA model and secure Free Trade Agreements with single partners or a restricted range of carefully chosen participants, on the assumption that a favourable deal was more likely to be arrived at when the sharp clashes of interest characteristic of the WTO's broad membership were replaced by a clear recognition by all parties of the advantages of privileged relationships. The US has seized the opportunity offered by these more hospitable bargaining spaces to press for settlements in the areas of culture and copyright that go beyond those tabled in WTO discussions, including so-called TRIPS-Plus provisions in the field of intellectual property.

This move was a response to two developments Firstly, the copyright on some of the most valuable intellectual properties owned by the major US entertainment corporations was about to expire under prevailing copyright regimes. Secondly, the rapid rise of digital technologies was not only expanding revenue-generating opportunities by creating new distribution platforms, it was undermining them by making unauthorised copying easier.

The first attempt to secure an international agreement on intellectual property came in 1883 with the signing of the Paris Convention for the Protection of Intellectual Property. Designed to safeguard patents, trademarks and industrial designs, it was matched in 1886 by the Berne Convention for the Protection of Literary and Artistic Works. This covered all forms of artistic expression but only applied to original 'work', excluding the ideas it contained and performances. It offered protection for the life of the author plus 50 years after his or her death and required signatories to treat domestic and foreign works equally. The US did not endorse the Berne Convention, but faced with the changing global arena that emerged after World War II it launched a rival system, the Universal Copyright Convention (UCC). Although it was firmly rooted in US national copyright law, the word 'universal' in the title announced a clear ambition to install US provisions as the de facto global standard. This perception was widespread and led to the UCC's attracting fewer signatories than the Berne Convention.

In 1967, the administrations of the Berne and Paris Conventions were merged to form the World Intellectual Property Organisation (WIPO). The fact that most signatories were drawn from emerging economies positioned it as an important new arena in which the US could pursue its aim of 'harmonizing' the global intellectual property regime around its nationally determined provisions. In 1996, in response to pressure to address concerns around piracy on the Internet, WIPO adopted two new treaties, the Copyright Treaty and the Performances and Phonograms Treaty. Taken together they had potentially far-reaching implications for copying and distributing digitised material. In implementing the provisions, however, signatories were free to determine whether their existing national regulations already met the terms of the treaties, opening the way for an uneven implementation that cut directly across the US drive to generalise its national intellectual property laws. The TRIPS provisions of the WTO were also seen as falling some way short in advancing this aim.

TRIPS followed the Berne convention in guaranteeing copyright protection for literary and artistic works for the life of the author plus 50 years, but extended the principle to computer software, databases and rental rights for sound and visual recordings. This imposed significant new burdens of compliance on signatories, particularly in emerging economies, since it required them to establish and fund new oversight agencies, diverting public funds away from other areas. But it failed to match the far-reaching provisions of the two major revisions to US law introduced in 1998: the Copyright Term Extension Act and the Digital Millennium Copyright Act.

In 1993, the European Union extended copyright protection for authors' works from 50 to 70 years after their death, as a temporary measure to compensate cultural producers for the interruptions to income caused by the disruption of two World Wars on the continent. Spared from invasion and saturation bombing US cultural industries boomed both during and after both wars allowing them to strengthen their international reach, but major interests in the entertainment industries seized the opportunity to argue that US law needed to match European provisions in order to maintain international competitiveness. The Walt Disney Company, whose exclusive rights to the character of Mickey Mouse were about to run out, was particularly vocal and found a forceful advocate in the person of Sonny Bono, a popular singer who had become a Republican politician. The term for collective productions was set at 120 years after creation or 95 years after publication, whichever endpoint was the earliest.

In response, other US politicians rallied to defend the principle that authors' rights needed to be weighed against the need to ensure that resources for new intellectual and creative work circulated without undue restrictions. As Senator Herb Kohl argued, copyright provisions should be deployed in the public interest and not "for the sole purpose of improving the balance of trade [or] ensuring that the heirs of copyrighted works can enjoy an unfettered income stream... yet [the Act] is justified upon precisely these bases" (US Senate 1995–6). The argument that by adding 20 years to the term of copyright, Congress was failing in its constitutional duty to advance progress in the "useful arts" was tested in the Supreme Court, which ruled in the Act's favour.

Lengthening the term of copyright was accompanied by an extension of its principles to the new arenas created by emerging technologies of digital copying and distribution. The Digital Millennium Copyright Act made it illegal to disable or evade devices designed to prevent unauthorised copying or to distribute information that would allow users to do so. By criminalising any and all attempts to circumvent copy protection, these provisions ran counter to widely accepted understandings of fair use that legitimated copying as a resource for personal education and creativity.

This issue was at the centre of popular opposition to a major revision to the country's copyright provisions that the Korean government introduced in 2005, under pressure from the US. The protests coincided with the US administration's decision to draw up a list of priority countries with which to initiate Free Trade Agreements. There were several reasons Korea was on that list. Firstly, the balance of trade between the two countries was worsening as Korean exports gained ground. Secondly, China had risen to become Korea's largest trading partner and was exercising increasing economic influence in the Asia-Pacific challenging US power in the region. A Free Trade Agreement with Korea was expected to strengthen US influence by encouraging other Asian countries to seek similar arrangements.

As a precondition for commencing talks, however, the US demanded concessions in a range of areas. They included ending the ban on imports of US Beef, imposed in the wake of an outbreak of 'mad cow' disease, the elimination of import tariffs and domestic taxes on American cars and a relaxation of screen quotas on film (Lee 2009). The Korean government acceded to these demands but entered into negotiations with ambitions to advance their own global position as an economic power and cultural force, shaped by the country's double transition from authoritarian rule to democratic process and from a managed economy centred on heavy industry to a marketized economy organised around information technology and cultural production.

From national reconstruction to cultural industrialisation: Korean ambitions

The early post-war years were defined politically by the ideological Cold War between the US and the Soviet Union and successive wars of decolonisation. Korea was caught in the crosshairs of both conflicts. Over three decades of military rule (between 1961 and 1992) it pursued a strategy of economic and cultural nation building, supported by comprehensive state direction and control. Industrial regeneration was built around a select group of large companies, the *Chaebols,* whose size and scope enabled them to act as 'national champions', competing effectively in export markets. Despite recurrent scandals around corrupt business practises and bribes to politicians and persistent calls for reform, these family owned conglomerates continue to dominate the Korean economy. Samsung, founded in 1938, remains the country's largest company followed by three concerns launched in the immediate post-war years: Hyundai in 1947, LG in 1947 and SK Group in 1953.

Industrial policy was accompanied by an ideological policy of defending national cultural markets and imposing strong limits on public speech and expression. With Japan's wartime defeat in 1945, Korea, which had been part of the Japanese empire since 1910, became an independent nation but was partitioned along the 38th parallel. Following the failure of attempts to create a unified national government in 1948, Syngman Rhee was elected as the first president of South Korea. In 1950, North Korean communist troops, supported by China, crossed the demarcation line precipitating a three-year-long civil war that ended with the North's defeat and the reestablishment of partition, creating a de facto Asian 'Iron Curtain'. Although US troops played a leading role in the UN force that defended the South, the ideology of the Korean government was organised around the drive to foster a distinctive and durable sense of national identity coupled with militant anti-communism. These aims were reinforced when a coup in 1961 installed a military government led by Park Chung-hee. The country remained under military rule for three decades until 1992 (three years before the launch of the WTO) when the election of Kim Young-sam restored civilian government on a permanent basis. Building the nation, both economically and ideologically, dominated the years of military rule with major consequences for cultural policy.

As the leading audio-visual medium, film was seen as central to the construction of national identity. Japanese films, which had dominated Korea screen under imperial rule, were banned and not readmitted until 1988. Koreans however had already acquired a taste for Hollywood movies, which under the US Army Military Government, which had administered the country between 1945 and 1948, were distributed directly to cinemas. The seductive visions of affluence and individualism they offered sat uneasily alongside the appeals to sacrifice and collective effort at the heart of the drive for national reconstruction.

Efforts to ensure a flow of film production that supported national objectives were pursued through a combination of financial support and the imposition of export quotas. Following the 1953 armistice the film industry was exempted from taxation, an intervention that saw locally made productions increase from 8 to 108 between 1954 and 1959 (Song 2012:4). Direct subsidies to the film industry were introduced in the 1963 Motion Picture Law.

Support for domestic production was accompanied in 1958 by the imposition of limits on the number of foreign films that could be imported. Licenses were given to local companies that had been successful in exporting films as reward for generating overseas revenues that could be ploughed back into local production. Only companies making a minimum of 15 commercial films a year were admitted to the scheme. The result was a rapid move towards consolidation with the number of small film companies falling from 71 to 6 between 1959 and 1963. This highly concentrated market structure offered little incentive to diversity or competition, and in 1966 the minimum annual production requirement was cut from 15 to 2, opening opportunities for small and medium-sized enterprises.

Support for local production was accompanied by limits on the volume and visibility of overseas films. Import quotas were established at the beginning of each year. In 1965, only 53 were imported, and in 1966 cinemas were required to screen domestic productions for a minimum of 90 days a year.

This led to a marked increase in cheap local productions, 'quota quickies', produced solely to retain the right to import movies from overseas. This had two negative impacts. It reduced the foreign earnings returned to domestic production and boosted the popularity of imported movies, which had much higher production values, almost all of which originated in the US. The first priority for the military regime was to limit American influence.

In 1973 the number of days allocated to domestic films was increased to 121, and imports were reduced. In 1974 only 39 films from overseas were screened, down from 60 the year before. In the 1980s, under the presidency of General Chun Doo-hwan, efforts to promote a distinctively Korean cultural identity were intensified (Yim 2002:40), and in 1981 the number of domestic screening days was increased to 165.

The US, however, kept pushing and successfully brokered Korea-US Film Agreements in 1985 and 1988. These produced two major gains. The import quota system was abolished, and US film companies were allowed to establish local branch offices to distribute their productions directly, rather than employing Korean intermediaries (Shim 2006). The impact was immediate. In 1985 only 30 films were imported. By 1988 that figure rose to 176. In contrast, 1985 saw only two films exported overseas, earning a paltry total of $20,000. In 1970, exports stood at 253. This situation provoked a strong reaction with protesting film industry workers, supported by academics and opposition politicians, demonstrating outside Seoul cinemas screening *Fatal Attraction* in full view of the overseas film crews in the city for the Seoul Olympics.

Domestic films continued to lose market share steadily and by 1993 were accounting for only 16% of cinema admissions (Song 2012:5). By 1994 Hollywood movies were enjoying an 80% share, up from 53% in 1987 (Shim 2006). As one observer noted, the "domestic film business barely survived, while foreign players extended their dominance" (Kim 2006:9).

In an effort to protect the newly emerging television system, a quota system was introduced in the 1987 Broadcasting Law specifying that stations could allocate a maximum of 20% of their total screen time to entertainment programming, the area where US imports enjoyed the greatest competitive advantage. Alongside continuing battles over quotas, there was escalating pressure from the US to increase protection for intellectual property.

The original Korean Copyright Act of 1957 established a copyright term of 30 years from the death of the author. In 1968, under pressure from the US, as a condition of renegotiated general trade relations, the term was extended to 50 years. The US continued to press for further measures, and in 2004 the USTR 310 Report placed Korea on the Priority Watch List of countries, not providing an adequate level of intellectual property protection.

That same year the Korean government addressed the issue of digital copying with a twelfth revision to the Copyright Act. This gave copyright owners a monopoly right to transmit material over the Internet or on mobile devices and criminalised "the uploading or sharing of copyrighted music files, visual images, and video clips on individual blog sites, online fan club cafes, and personal web sites" (Lee 2009:2). Many users saw the ban on non-commercial sharing as an unwarranted expansion of "citizen's liability for copyright infringement" and an unacceptable restriction on free cultural expression. Pushed through parliament without public consultation, the Act's implementation in 2005 was met by protests outside parliament, the mobilisation of a broadly based coalition of opposition, and the construction of an alternative licencing model (Lee 2009:2–3).

It is over simple to see the Korean government's adoption of increasingly restrictive copyright regimes solely as a response to US pressure. This was certainly a factor, but later decisions were also informed by the perceived need to provide greater protection for the intellectual properties owned by major domestic entertainment, corporations that were driving an increasingly successful export push. The resulting subordination of citizens' cultural rights to the interests of corporate rights holders is a further indication of the ascendency of an officially promoted economistic view of culture that had been gathering momentum for some time.

The final years of authoritarian rule saw government policy take a neo-liberal turn towards deregulation and reduced state intervention. In 1990, in the expectation that competition would generate more value-added services, monopoly control over the two major telecommunication sectors, Korea Telecom and Korea Mobile Telecommunications, was relaxed and new entrants admitted. 1991 saw the public broadcasting monopoly end with the launch of the first terrestrial commercial channel, SBS, and the foundations of the cable television laid by the Composite Cable Broadcasting Act (Kwak 2010).

This embrace of neo-liberalism intensified with Kim Young-sam's election in 1992, as the first civilian president since the military coup of 1961. The new government initiated two major shifts in policy. Firstly, there was a concerted drive to rebalance the economy away from labour-intensive manufacturing industries to cultural and knowledge-based sectors (Lee 2006). Secondly, international policies moved from a fortress mentality to positive evaluation of the opportunities presented by globalisation.

The internal realignment was reinforced in 1997 when the International Monetary Fund required the Kim Young-sam government to implement a program of comprehensive economic restructuring, financial and corporate-sector reform and trade liberalisation as conditions attached to the bailout addressed Korea's severe economic crisis, which had been initiated by shortages of overseas currencies the financial difficulties and bankruptcies of leading Chaebols.

There was a strong sense that the Chaebols had overreached themselves, acquiring interests in too many unrelated areas. Companies still operating were instructed to divest themselves of their peripheral holdings and refocus on core businesses. CJ, one of the major forces that emerged in the media sector, had spun off from Samsung in 1993, before the crisis, and quickly moved to capitalise on the shift towards a more positive evaluation of globalisation. In 1995 it entered into a strategic alliance with Steven Spielberg's Dreamworks studio, taking an 11% stake, and in 1998 it opened Korea's first multiplex cinema in partnership with Golden Harvest of Hong Kong and Village Roadshow of Australia. Another leading media company, Lotte Entertainment, was launched in 2003 as a subsidiary of Lotte (a major food company with a portfolio of interests spanning hotels, financial services, and heavy industry). As one recent analysis concludes, the economic crisis combined with the acceleration of marketization increasingly concentrated control over key media markets in the hands of chaebol groups with access to overseas partners or foreign capital generating an increasing polarization between the major players and the smaller independents (Kim 2014).

There was a parallel restructuring of the labour market with a growing divergence between employees on continuing contracts, with their associated company supported benefits, and the growing ranks of irregular and insecure workers. By 2011, over a third (34.2%) of the labour force was in this second group, earning on average only 60% of a regular worker's wage (Keo 2014). As a result, while "the Korean economy recovered from the crisis as swiftly as it had succumbed … income inequality sharply worsened" (Cheong 2011). In the years between 1990 and 1995, the Gini coefficient measure of income inequality (where 0 equals perfect equality) averaged 0.258. By 2010, it had risen to 0.315 with the top ten per cent of earners seeing their share of income rising from 29% in 1995 to 46% in 2016.

Alongside these structural realignments, the 1997 crisis and its aftermath had a major impact on popular attitudes, which "dramatically shifted toward individualism from cooperativism /collectivism, moving much closer to western culture" reinforcing the appeal of the consumerist culture being promoted by the new media majors. (Lee and McNulty 2003:54).

The shift from a defensive to a proactive stance towards external pressures was announced in 1994 with the launch of "an official globalization drive known as *segyehwa*" (Jin 2006:9). Domestic and international ambitions came together in 1999 in the Cyber Korea 21 project aimed at improving "national competitiveness" and "raising the quality of life to the level of the more advanced nations" by creating nationwide broadband Internet networks that would provide the backbone of "knowledge based society". In 2003, these aims were extended in the E-Korea Vision 2006 programme designed to promote a national "information society" and develop strong "international cooperation" in pursuit of a global information society. Two years later, in 2005, the Ministry of Culture and Tourism published its C-Korea 2010 vision for a new creative economy in which increased exports of film, popular music and television dramas would play a central role.

In these projections for the nation's economic future building state-of-the-art digital infrastructures and developing the country's cultural industries assumed a central position in policy thinking. Government would play a facilitating and enabling role, but innovation would be driven primarily by market competition.

The huge success of *Jurassic Park* in 1993 famously prompted President Kim to remark that "this movie is worth sales of 1.5 million Hyundai Sonata sedans". In an effort to boost the industry, film was reclassified as a manufacturing sector allowing filmmakers to claim tax exemptions and encouraging banks to lend to them (Kim 2007). There were government subsidies but they remained modest. In 2011 the highest estimate for the total amount of subsidy going to the Korean film industry was USD 106 million, which was less than 12% of the total received by the French film industry that year (Parc 2014:18). Here, as elsewhere, growth was primarily driven by commercial interests.

By outperforming *Titanic* to become Korea's highest grossing film of all time, with box office returns of $25 million earning its backers, KBB Capital a 300% return on their original investment, Kang Je-gyu's blockbuster *Shiri* in 1999 seemed to offer incontrovertible proof of the effectiveness of the market-oriented policies announced in the 1995 Motion Picture Promotion Law and promoted under the banner of 'Learning from Hollywood'. The success of *Shiri* reinforced two lessons: the need to have large integrated corporations in order to compete effectively and the value of tapping into audience tastes for narrative styles formed by American films.

The film industry was given an additional boost in October 1996 when the Constitutional Court ruled that the system of pre-censorship that had been in place since 1948 was unconstitutional and should be abandoned. Its replacement, a system of ratings classification, gave filmmakers much more flexibility, although it could still be used to impose restrictions.

In the years between 1999 and 2006, the Korean film industry enjoyed what one leading commentator has characterised as a "never-before-seen success both at home and abroad" (Shim 2011:214). From 2001 domestic productions achieved an average 50% share of box office receipts, and the number of titles exported rose from 14 in 1993 to 202 in 2005 (op cit:2014).

In the broadcasting sector, the rapid growth of commercial and cable television Korea experienced was being repeated in other Asian nations, significantly expanding the export markets for Korean broadcast productions. In the competition for sales Korea could capitalise on the 'cultural proximity', which attracts audiences to productions featuring people like themselves, in situations they can relate to, underpinned by values they endorse.

The growing force and reach of Korea's popular cultural exports, collectively dubbed, *Hallyu*, translated as the Korean Wave, was confirmed in 2003 when the popular television drama, *Winter Sonata*, recounting the careers and romances of four young people, was aired on Japan's national public broadcaster, NHK, and received a spectacular 20.6% programme rating (Jung 2009). It marked a highly resonant symbolic reversal of the historical relations of domination and subordination and confirmed Korea's arrival as a regional cultural force. By the end of 2003 Korean television productions were generating export earnings triple the sum for 1999, almost all from markets in Asia (Shim 2006). The distinctive Korean hybrid style of pop music, K-Pop, was also becoming a major regional phenomenon. This success, and the desire to establish a greater presence in major western markets, fed into the economic roadmap the Korean government drew up in 2003. It included the possibility of entering into a free trade agreement with the United States, but it was not until two years later, in 2005, that bilateral talks were officially launched.

Contested visions, conflicting interests: KORUS and after

In 2002, the US was running an overall trade deficit with Korea of 13.0 billion US dollars (Tong and Tung 2012). Against this background, government projections of the gains from KORUS were unremittingly positive. Their optimism was strongly endorsed by the business community.

Through the public relations activities of their lobby group, The Federation of Korean Industry, established in 1963, the chaebols had tirelessly promoted themselves as indispensable engines of economic growth and pushed aggressively for market-oriented policies that allowed them maximum freedom of operations. They consistently "deployed their significant economic resources to strategically dominate both public media and state-generated policy debate about the economy" (Lee 2016:2) squeezing out "the voices of labour, reform civil society groups and small and medium companies" (op cit:6). They played a pivotal role in promoting the case for KORUS and co-ordinating the pro Agreement lobby (Kim 2011). They were supported by leading mainstream economists who predicted gains for the key export sectors of automobiles and electronics goods of core concern to leading chaebols but saw significant adverse impacts on agriculture. This proved to be a flash point.

In early 2008, while negotiations on KORUS were continuing, the Korean government announced that they were revoking the ban on imports of US beef imposed in 2003. The decision sparked widespread popular protests fuelled by immediate fears of 'mad cow' disease and wider anxieties that KORUS was a 'Trojan Horse' for the further advance of US interests. Peaceful candlelit rallies in the centre of Seoul were met with water cannons, a response that generalised popular discontent with overall support for KORUS falling sharply, from 75.4% to 45.4% and objections increasing from 22.3% to 43.7% (Kim 2011).

Opposition was particularly strong among young people where perceptions of the government's heavy-handed response to legitimate protest were widely seen as a return to the authoritarian past and combined with a tide of anti-Americanism that had been steadily rising since two Korean middle school girls had been accidently killed by a US army vehicle in 2002 and the soldiers involved acquitted by a US military court. In an opinion poll conducted in 2003, over a third (35.4%) of those in their 20s nominated the United States as their "least favoured country", compared to only 5.3% of those in their 50s who had grown up with the extensive US military and economic support granted in the wake of the Korean War (Lee 2006).

Opposition intensified after the public broadcaster, *Munhwa Broadcasting Company* (MBC) carried a current affairs program analysing the decision and was immediately attacked by the three leading conservative newspaper, all owned by families supportive of the government. In a move widely seen as an attempt to dampen dissent, President Lee appointed a personal friend as head of the public 24-hour news channel, *YTN*. The subsequent protests by journalists against government interference attracted widespread popular support. The government later moved to discipline MBC by appointing a member of President Lee's inner circle, Kim Jea Chul, as president. Once in post, Kim cancelled the flagship current affairs programme *News Who* and dispersed dissenting employees to local branches. Those involved in the critical coverage of the 'mad cow' decision were a particular target. These moves were met by the longest strike of staff in the organisation's history. Called by the union, it lasted six months, from January to July 2012, until eventually being discontinued.

In 2009, new legislation was introduced relaxing the restrictions on media cross-ownership, allowing press companies to take stakes in broadcasting companies from 2013 onwards, prompting concern that the leading conservative titles would see an opportunity to extend their ideological remit.

Concerns around restrictions over the range of views and positions represented in programming were also evident in cinema. In 2005, Im Sang-soo, one of Korea's leading directors, released *The President's Last Bang,* recounting President Park's final hours before his assassination by the Director of Korea's Central Intelligence Agency. Its black comedy and mixture of political archive footage and attention to Park's sexual peccadillos ensured that it attracted controversy. Im was required to delete documentary inserts after a court ruling supported the case brought by Park's son, but the major blow came when CJ Entertainment cancelled its agreement to distribute the film. As a result it was only shown in 190 screens, half the number allocated to the top five domestic films released that year (Yecies 2008:54).

Concerns over the resurgence of political conservatism were accompanied by mounting anxieties over the economic impact of KORUS on public broadcasting and the audio-visual industries more generally. The Agreement extended the opportunities for US companies to invest in Korean broadcasting, reduced quotas on foreign content and allowed more of that content to come from a single country.

Two years after KORUS was implemented, US controlled companies were free to invest up to 100% in Korean channel operators and from three years after to hold up to a 100% equity interest in programme providers not engaged in multi-genre programming or home shopping. Quotas for domestic films on non-terrestrial channels were reduced from 25% to 20% and from 35% to 30% for animation. The quotas for terrestrial networks remained unchanged at 25% and 45%.The percentage of quarterly broadcasting hours allocated to imported programs that can come from providers from a single country was increased to 80%.

Taken together, these provisions were widely seen within the industry as likely to significantly increase the amount of US programming on Korean screens while placing domestic broadcasters under additional pressure, making it difficult to sustain a national production system that spoke to the full diversity of contemporary Korean life and opinions. Surveys of broadcast professionals revealed increasing pessimism. Between 2005 and 2008 the percentage expecting KORUS to have more positive than negative impacts on the broadcast sector dropped from 62% to 24% (Choi 2013:155–56).When asked, in the aftermath of the mad cow protests, if public service broadcasting was likely to come under increasing challenge in the coming years, three quarters (74.6%) answered 'yes'. The figure for older professionals, who had experienced the cumulative impact of marketization, was even higher at 86.7% (Choi 2013:171).

The terms of the KORUS agreement also required significant changes to the intellectual property regime to reinforce protections for digital content, including temporary copies held on hard drives. These were introduced in a 2008 bill that required websites hosting illegal content to be shut down, the suspension of users' accounts found to be actively duplicating or transmitting such material and the interception of the networks of online service providers involved in distributing illegal content. The side letter within the Agreement specified only that "Korea will strengthen enforcement" with no provision for reciprocal guarantees on the US side. Responsibility for overseeing compliance within Korea lay with the Korean Communication Commission, established in 2008 to oversee both the telecommunication and broadcasting industries. Critics complained that this potentially gave the government the ability to monitor and control both users and Internet service providers.

In 2004, the year before KORUS talks began, the US dollar value of Korean film imports from the US stood at 51.82 million. In contrast, film exports to the US only generated 2.36 million. This highly asymmetrical pattern of exchange was repeated for broadcast programming, with US imports valued at 24.14 million as against only 1.4 million in Korean exports to the US (Choi 2013:122). By 2010, Korean exports of terrestrial broadcast programs were booming, but three-quarters (74.3%) of the returns were coming from three Asian markets led by Japan (38.4%), followed by Taiwan (23.2%) and mainland China (12.7). The US accounted for only 1.7%, the same percentage as in 2001. (Song 2012: Table 10: 13). In December 2011, a month after the implementation of KORUS, the Lee Myung-Back Government licenced four new general service broadcasting companies opening more spaces for overseas programs and putting additional pressure on local production.

The success of the genres and style associated with the Korean Wave in Asian markets has generated economic returns that go well beyond program sales and the promotion of goods featured in the shows to provide a major boost to the tourist industry as fans visit the locations featured in the most popular productions. At the same time, it has created a barrier to effective entry into the US market where until the beginning of 2016 no attempts to produce a remake of a successful Korean production had progressed past the pilot program stage.

At first sight, Korean film is thriving. The number of multiplex screens since 2000 has tripled, from 720 to 2184, opening more potential exhibition windows for Korean films, and by 2011 domestic productions were achieving a market share of 51.1% by box office receipts with US imports taking 45.5% (Song 2012:6/9). This pattern has been sustained with Korean films accounting for 52% of ticket sales in 2015, and six of the top ten box office hits, with two releases, *Veteran* and *Ode to* My Father, becoming the second and third most successful releases of all time (Kil 2016). As one observer noted approvingly "The Korean film industry is flourishing because, unlike Europe, it has an industry with an increasing portion of big commercial films" (Kim 2004:208). The fusion of *Hallyu* and Hollywood has produced an economic complex widely dubbed 'Planet Hallyuwood' (Yecies 2008:39).

This industrial success, however, conceals the increasing closure of production around established blockbuster formulas and the marginalisation of alternatives. As one industry analyst noted, box-office records "have come at the cost of intense polarization with huge-budget blockbusters dominating screen counts and leaving increasingly low budget indies to pick up the scraps" (Lee 2016). In 2015, only 1.37% of the total titles released were shown on 50 or more screens and on an average weekend three-quarters of available screens were showing the top three box office hits (Lee 2016). Access to those screens is largely controlled by the vertically integrated entertainment conglomerates led by C J Entertainment, which accounted for 40% of distribution in 2011, followed by Lotte with 18.9% and Showbox with 13.3% (Shim 2011:221) This effective oligopoly exercises decisive control over which films gain wide public circulation. In 2010, Han Sang-soo's *Oki's Movie* won the prestigious critics' award, Un Certain regard, at the Cannes Film Festival but was only shown on 20 screens in Korea (Shim 2011:215), pointing to restricted diversity and increasing closure of production around established stars and already popular genres, led by thrillers. That same year the thriller *The Man from Nowhere* sold 6.22 million tickets.

Recent years have also seen a significant increase in product placement in films and television dramas as companies seek to promote their commodities as indispensable to the desirable styles of life and self-presentation shown on screen. Activity has been particularly intense in broadcasting since popular drama episodes are shown uninterrupted by spot advertising and a significant share of viewing is moving from scheduled transmission to on demand. The main beneficiaries of these shifts are the leading chaebols who use placements to cement positive associations around their familiar brands. One of the most successful Korean soap operas of recent years, *My Love from the Star,* screened in 2013–14, offered prominent windows to CJ's mini snacks and Samsung's smart phones. Industry insiders estimate that Samsung is involved in around two-thirds of all domestically produced popular dramas and aims for "a full package, meaning all visible consumer electronics like smartphones, computers, cameras, air conditioners, TVs and refrigerators are Samsung products, from beginning to end," (quoted in *The Japan Times* 2014). This production economy has two major consequences. Firstly, it favours narratives set in glamorous settings that generate a positive aura around the products displayed and militates against depictions that engage with poverty and deprivation. Secondly, it reinforces the individualised address to audiences as consumers to the exclusion of identities built around social solidarities.

With more and more program making being allocated to independent producers, with the attendant insecurities of employment, an ethos of individuality is also becoming more prevalent among broadcast professionals eroding "their willingness to band together for bargaining power to defend their rights" (Kim 2014b: 576) and reinforcing the control exercised by the major corporate players.

In recent years the *chaebols'* close relations to successive governments have been tainted by repeated instances of bribery and corruption. Soon after leaving office, former President Roh Moo-hyun (2003–2008) committed suicide when faced with allegations of accepting $6 million in bribes. The brother of his successor, Lee Myung-bak (2008–2013) was sentenced to two years in prison for accepting payments from business in return for exerting political influence. The persistence of these collusive relations was dramatically confirmed in May 2017 when former President Park Geun-hye was brought before a criminal court charged with collaborating with her long term confidant , Choi Soon-sil, to pressure leading corporate heads into paying massive sums in return for business favours. Those charged with paying bribes included central figures in concerns with a significant presence in the cultural industries. Lee Jae-yong, the acting head of Samsung, was alleged to have paid £20.5 million in return for government help in facilitating the contested merger of two of the company's subsidiaries smoothing the way for him to assume control of the family business empire from his father. Prosecutions were also brought against the chair of Lotte Group and Cha Eun-taek, one of the best known K-pop video entrepreneurs who had worked with Psy. In May 2017 Moon Jae-in, a former human rights lawyer, was elected President by a landslide promising to end the collusion between government and big business.

Conclusion

Some observers have celebrated the resurgence of Korean cinema and the success of the Korean Wave in television production as exemplary case studies in resistance to American cultural domination. Against this, the argument presented here offers strong support for Herbert Schiller's conception of cultural imperialism as the sum of the processes through which a society's dominating strata are both pressured and attracted to reorganise its core cultural institutions around the values of the dominant centre of power. We have traced the way that relentless US pressure for open cultural markets has combined with shifts in internal policy to construct a cultural system characterised by increasing corporate concentration, geared to capitalizing on already established styles, saturated with product promotion and reinforcing the centrality of consumer identities. The result is a system unable to address the full range of social experiences and political debate in the core sites of public culture.

In 1995 the top 10% of the population accounted for 29% of earned income. By 2016 that figure had risen to 45% making Korea the most unequal society of 20 nations surveyed by the IMF (Kim 2016). The 'structural adjustments' demanded in 1997 laid the basis for an economic recovery that has progressively widened gender and generational inequalities and marginalised the poor. These lives and voices find it increasingly difficult to secure a sustained hearing in a media system where the space not occupied by imported material is increasingly commanded by a small number of vertically integrated domestic conglomerates.

President Obama may have learned to dance Gangnam style, but critical observers in Korea are more inclined to note that Gangnam is the area of Seoul where a number of chaebols have their headquarters and to see "the Korean Wave [as] the embodiment of the West penetrating our bodies" (Hae-Joang 2005).

References

Acheson, K & Maule, C (2004) 'Convention on Cultural Diversity', *Cultural Economics,* Vol 28, No 4, pp. 243–256.

Cheong, K S (2011) 'Economic Crisis and Income Inequality in Korea', *Asian Economic Journal,* Vol 15, No 1, pp. 39–60.

Choi, W-M (2009) 'Aggressive Regionalism in Korea-US FTA: The Present and Future of Korea's FTA Policy', *Journal of International Economic Law,* Vol 12, No 3, pp. 595–615.

Choi, E-K (2013) *Digitalising Korea-Transformations and Tensions: The Case of Audiovisual Service Trade and Intellectual Property Rights.* Loughborough University. Department of Social Sciences. Unpublished Doctoral Thesis.

Dunkley, G (2001) *The Free Trade Adventure: The WTO, the Uruguay Round and Globalism-A Critique.* London. Zed Books.

Graber, C B (2006) 'The New UNESCO Convention on Cultural Diversity: a Counterbalance to the WTO?, *Journal of International Economic Law,* Vol 9, No 3, pp. 553–574.

Grant, P S and Wood, C (2004) *Blockbusters and Trade Wars: Popular Culture in a Globalised World.* Vancouver. Douglas and McIntyre.

Hae-Joang, C (2005) 'Reading the "Korean wave" as a sign of global shift', *Korean Journal,* Winter, Vol 45, No 4, pp. 147–182.

Hahn, M (2006) 'A Clash of Cultures? The UNESCO Diversity Convention and International Trade Law', *Journal of International Economic Law,* Vol 9, No 3, pp. 515–552.

Han, S L (2010) 'A Study of the Role of Ideology in the Film Supporting Policy: The Case of the Korean Film Council', *Korean Journal of Public Administration,* Vol 48, No 2, pp. 309–337. [in Korean].

The Japan Times (2014) 'Product placement puts South Korean TV Dramas on map" www.japantimes. co.jp/news/2014/06/12/world/product-placement-puts-s-korean-soaps-map/.

Jin, D Y (2006) 'Cultural Politics in Korea's Contemporary Film Under Neoliberal Globalization', *Media, Culture and Society,* Vol 28, No 1, pp. 5–23.

Jung, E Y (2009) 'Transnational Korea: A critical assessment of the Korean Wave in Asia and the United States', *Southeast Review of Asian Studies,* Vol 31, pp. 69–80.

Kaminski, M E (2014) 'The Capture of International Intellectual Property Law Through the US Trade Regime' *Southern California Law Review* [forthcoming]. Available at http://ssrn.com/abstract=2354324.

Kil, S (2016) 'Korea Cinema Sets Box Office and Admissions Record in 2015', *Variety,* January 4th.

Kim, E-M (2004) 'Market Competition and Cultural Tensions Between Hollywood and the Korean Film Industry', *The International Journal of Media Management,* Vol 6, Nos 3&4, pp. 207–216.

Kim, J Y (2007) *Rethinking Media Flow Under Globalisation: Rising Korean Wave and Korean TV and Film Policy Since 1980s.* University of Warwick. Unpublished Phd Thesis. Available from http://wrap.warwick.ac.uk/1153/1/WRAP_THESIS-Kim_2007.pdf.

Kim, C-W (2011) *South Korea's Business Section and the Transformation of the ROK-US Alliance: A Case Study of the KORUS FTA.* Seoul. East Asia Institute. Asia Security Initiative Working Paper 16.

Kim, C (2014) *A Family Affair: The Political Economy of Media Ownership in the Republic of Korea (1998–2012).* Southern Illinois University. Department of Mass Communication and Media Arts. Unpublished PhD Thesis.

Kim, C (2014b) 'Labour and the Limits of Seduction in Korea's Creative Economy', *Television and New Media,* Vol 15, No 6, pp. 526–576.

Kim, K-R (2016) 'Income inequality in South Korea the most severe in Asia', *The hankyoreh,* March 17th http://English.hani.co.kr/arti/English_edition/e_national/735462.html.

Koo, H (2014) 'Inequality in Korea' *East Asia Forum,* Ist July. www.eastasiaforum.org/2014/07/01/inequality-in-south-korea/ [accessed May 30th 2017]

Kwak, K-S (2010) 'Broadcast Deregulation in South Korea', *Academic Paper Series on Korea,* Volume, 3. Seoul. Korea Economic Institute, pp. 81–93.

Lee, K-S (2009) *The Electronic Fabric of Resistance: A Constructive Network of Online Users and Activists Challenging a Rigid Copyright Regime in Korea.* University of Woolongong. Faculty of Arts. Research Papers.

Lee, B-H (2016) *The Corporate Takeover of Economic Discourse in Korea.* London. Goldsmiths London University. Political Economy Research Centre. PERC Paper Series No14.

Lee, H C & McNulty, P (2003) *Korea's Economic Crisis and Cultural Transition Toward Individualism.* Tokyo. Cabinet Office Economic and Social Research Institute. ESRI Discussion Paper Series. No 71.

Lee, H-W (2016) 'South Korea's Polarizing Film Market: Can Mid-Budget Genre Movies Survive?', *The Hollywood Reporter,* February 13th.

Littoz-Monnet, A (2007) *The European Union and Culture: Between Economic Regulation and European Cultural Policy.* Manchester. Manchester University Press.

Magder, T (2004) 'Transnational Medai, Interantional Trade and the Idea of Cultural Diversity', *Continuum: Journal of Media and Cultural Studies,* Vol 18, No 3, pp. 380–397.

Merz, C (1926) 'When movies go abroad', *Harper's,* January, pp. 159–163.

Parc, J (2014) *A Retrospective on the Korean Film Polices: Return of the Jedi. http://gem.sciences-po.fr/content/publications/pdf/audiovisual/Parc_KoreanFilmPolicies102014.pdf* [accessed May 30th 2017]

Sell, S K (2010) 'The Rise and Rule of Trade Based Strategy: Historical Institutionalism and the International Regulation of Intellectual Property', *Review of International Political Economy,* Vol 17, No 4, pp. 762–790.

Schiller, H (1969) *Mass Communication and American Empire.* Boston. MA. Beacon Press.

Schiller, H (1973) *The Mind Managers.* Boston. MA. Beacon Pres.

Schiller, H (1976) *Communication and Cultural Domination.* New York. White Plains. M.E.Sharpe.

Shim, D (2006) 'Hybridization and the Rise of Korean Popular Culture in Asia', *Media Culture and Society,* Vol 28, No 1, pp. 25–42.

Shim, D (2011) 'Whither the Korean Film Industry?', *Acta Korana,* Vol 14, No 1, pp. 213–227.

Song, Y (2012) *Audio Visual Services in Korea: Market Development and Policies.* ADBI Working Paper No 354. Tokyo. Asian Development Bank Institute.

Tong, L-I & Tung, C (2012) 'The US and South Korea: Building a Win-Win Trade Relationship', *Competition Forum,* Vol 10, No 2, pp. 136–140.

UNESCO (1980) *Many Voice, One World: Towards a New More Just and More Efficient World Information and Communication Order.* Paris. UNESCO.

UNESCO (2013) *Basic Texts of the 2005 Convention on the Protection and Promotion of the Diversity of Cultural Expressions* [2013 Edition]. Paris. UNESCO.

US Senate (1995–6) 2nd Session 104-315 Copyright Term Extension Act July 10th 1996 'Minority views of Mr Kohl' www.congress.gov/congressional-report/104th-congress/senate-report/315/1?q= %7B%22search%22%3A%5B%22copyright%22%5D%7D

Wasko, J (1994) *Hollywood in the Information Age: Beyond the Silver Screen.* Cambridge. Polity Press.

White House Office of Press Secretary (2013) 'Remarks by President Obama and President Park of South Korea in a Joint Press Conference' www.whitehouse.gov/the-press-office/2016/09/06/remarks-president-obama-and-president-park-republic-korea-after [Accessed September 27th 2016].

Yecies, B (2007) 'Parleying Culture Against Trade: Hollywood's Affairs With Korean Screen Quotas', *Korea Observer,* Vol 38, No 1, pp. 1–32.

Yecies, B (2008) 'Planet Hallyuwood's Political Vulnerabilities: Censuring the Expression of Satire in *The President's Last Bang',* *International Review of Korean Studies,* Vol 5, No 1, pp. 37–64.

Yim, H (2002) 'Cultural Identity and Cultural Policy in South Korea', *The International Journal of Cultural Policy,* Vol 8, No 1, pp. 37–48.

8

Intellectual property as cultural policy

Siva Vaidhyanathan

Intellectual property is the most pervasive form of cultural policy. It affects almost every good, service, and product distributed globally, nationally, and locally. The major areas of intellectual property – copyright, patents, and trademarks – enable much of this commerce, but they also tax producers and consumers of products, goods, and services. Because of their pervasiveness, intellectual property rights have emerged as major tools of international trade policy as well as cultural policy. Therefore, nations that have strong regimes of copyright protection, patent filings, and trademark protection are at a distinct advantage in world trade and the exercise of cultural, political, and economic power.

Many regimes of intellectual property rights are the result of colonial legacies. Others have been imposed or generated under the duress or influence of global trade negotiations. Many of the issues surrounding intellectual property rights globally reflect the contours of power differences across the globe.

While pervasive and growing in scope and strength, intellectual property is a hidden cultural policy regime. Many nations, including the United States of America, do not acknowledge intellectual property as an element of cultural policy. In fact it's difficult to discuss something called cultural policy within the United States at all. Even though many areas of policy affect how American culture operates, cultural policy is almost never a subject of conversation in the American polis. Instead, the United States masks cultural policy within trade, industrial, educational, tourism, and economic policy (Miller and Yúdice 2002). As a result, intellectual property is rarely debated within the United States in terms of its effects on culture. Instead, intellectual property is justified or criticized based on its perceived effects on "innovation," rather than on "creativity" (Vaidhyanathan 2005b).

There are several major differences among how different parts of the world handle intellectual property. The United States considers intellectual property rights to be expressions of purely market function, separate from any moral or cultural value claims. However, the major traditions on the European continent consider the cultural needs of the nation-states in their intellectual property policy choices (Ginsburg 1990; Goldstein 2001). Postcolonial nations, such as Ghana, consider both the needs of cultural preservation and assertions of pride along with the strong desire to protect some traditional forms of cultural expression from exploitation by powerful multinational corporations often based in Europe or North America (Boateng 2011).

The dominant debates about intellectual property over the past 20 years have emanated loudly from North America and Western Europe. These debates have been framed between polls of extreme intellectual property protection and arguments for free, weaker, or even no intellectual property rights. These conflicts have pitted claims of economic efficiency against claims of intellectual freedom. However, much of the world does not consider these two loopholes of debates to be particularly relevant to its conditions. The north-south cultural policy debates since the 1990s have included considerations of the value of copyright, patent, trademark, the public domain, and the possibility of generating a new form of intellectual property to protect traditional cultural expression (Brown 2003).

How we got here

In the 19th century the United States was a pirate nation. American readers took advantage of the fact that the United States did not respect copyrights issued by other countries to purchase cheap versions of novels by Thomas Hardy and Charles Dickens. Many of the legendary American publishing houses such as Harper Brothers and Henry Holt started as pirate firms. Even as late as the 1920s the early American film industry was a pirate operation (Vaidhyanathan 2001; Decherney 2012). Directors lifted plots and characters from copyrighted plays and novels. The value of weak copyright laws was not lost on the pioneers of the software industry much later, despite many changes in American political economy by the late 20th century. On one side of the battle over controlling software were upstart "hobbyists" and academics who believed that software should flow freely among users. On the other were entrepreneurs like Bill Gates who hoped to build a fortune from using strong intellectual property to create artificial scarcity for Microsoft products. And there was a fervent debate in the early years of the software industry over whether software should be protected by copyright, patent, both, or neither (Cohen and Lemley 2001). Every country, and every industry, goes through periods of preferring weak or no intellectual property because they are more interested in cheap goods and low-cost creativity. Then, as countries grow wealthier and certain industries become powerful exporters of goods, they flip their positions on intellectual property and fight for maximum protection. Now the United States is the leading force behind global standardization and maximization of intellectual property protection. Not coincidentally, the export of film, software, and the spread of brands like Starbucks around the world followed a period of deindustrialization. If the United States could not sell as many Chevrolets to the rest of the world, at least it could get people to sit through Spider-Man movies.

By the late 20th century major economic powers such as Germany, Australia, Japan, and the United States had shifted investment from heavy machinery to semiconductors, software, and cinema. Thus the entire rhetorical (and regulatory) sphere of intellectual property grew in importance. The "copyright industries," for instance (film, music, software, publishing) constitute the second-leading sector of U.S. exports after agriculture. That does not even take into account patent licensing, pharmaceuticals, computer hardware such as mobile phones, and other technology transfer transactions that are more often covered by patent law. For this reason, the most powerful economies in the world have a strong interest in embedding strong methods of control and enforcement over emerging economies. The fight over the global standardization of intellectual property has become one of the most important sites of tension and conflict in North-South global relations.

Patents, trademarks, and copyrights

There are three major branches of "intellectual property": patent, trademark, and copyright law. In recent years, a fourth area, trade secret law, has grown in importance as a way of rewarding commercial innovations outside the public licensing schemes that patent and copyright law employ. In addition, most industries that deal in "intellectual property" contractually constrain their participants such that contract law becomes de facto "intellectual property" law. Lately, there have been some efforts to create new types of "intellectual property" law to handle new practices and technologies such as architecture, semiconductor design, and database production. Each of these branches of what has become known as "intellectual property law" has distinct forms and functions, but many people blend their terms and purposes when discussing "intellectual property."

Copyright encourages the dissemination of creative and informative work. Patent law encourages invention by granting a temporary monopoly to an inventor of a tangible, useful, and "nonobvious" device or process. Patents cover inventions and processes, not words, texts, or phrases. Trademark law lets a company protect and enjoy its "goodwill" in the marketplace. A trademark is some specific signifier – such as a logo, design, colour scheme, smell, sound, or container shape – that points to the product's origin. Beyond these, there are other, less-often-invoked modes of intellectual property such as the right to publicity. That right governs how celebrities may control their names, images, and likenesses. Of these areas of law, copyrights and patents are most frequently conflated in public discourse.

Copyrights and patents share a foundational idea. They are both intended to establish incentives to create and bring to market otherwise expensive things. Both systems allow the state to create temporary, limited monopolies over expressions (under copyright) or ideas and plans (under patent). Both systems grew out of British statute and common law and spread throughout the British Empire. Yet in both structure and practice these two areas of law are very different. There is one major area of creativity and commerce in which discreet creations are covered by both patent and copyright law: computer software. This double-coverage has been controversial since the dawn of the commercial software industry in the 1970s, and it remains an area of hot debate.

Of these three major branches of intellectual property law, copyright has the most expansive and obvious effect on culture, and thus it is the major site of the exercise of cultural policy. But it is a peculiar type of cultural policy. It is generally directed to favour certain modes of creation and distribution over others, rather than favouring one type of content over another. Copyright is designed to be what speech lawyers would call "content neutral." It protects a song written by Madonna as well as it protects a song written by Jay-Z. However, copyright operates in such a way that it promotes the system of commerce that favours Jay-Z over that of artists who work collaboratively and collectively within local communities and traditions across the globe. So copyright is far from neutral. It favours works and their creators if they are produced through established channels and companies. It generally favours works created by companies that have deep roots and thus political influence over the nature of copyright in Europe and North America. And it offers little to habits of cultural creativity that work in ways beyond the linear modes of distribution that have grown so dominant over the past century.

Trademarks, location designations, and wine and cheese

Other forms of intellectual property have significant influences on culture and thus should be considered within the realm of cultural policy. Trademarks grant a strong privilege to the products originating with a specific firm. Often, as in the case of Coca-Cola, Starbucks, or McDonalds, the firms and its products play a role in more than consumption. They can play a role in signalling meaning on a streetscape, at an airport, or through the generation of quasi-public standardized spaces in which an aura of cosmopolitanism flows.

Perhaps more significantly, many nation-states protect geographic designations for the foods and beverages they produce, granting more than exclusivity to a region's cheese or wine. Geographic designations can carry cultural meaning as well as simple information about origin. Champagne is not just a sparkling wine from Champagne, after all (Hughes 2006). A designation of place can also invoke assumptions of "terroir," the notion that a food or wine carries with it the essences of the soil from which it comes (Trubek 2008).

There is no dominant firm in Parma, Italy, that makes and sells Parmigiano cheese. There is no major international corporation based in Champagne, France, that has pushed that region's carbonated wines and that term into bars and restaurants around the world. Yet cheese makers in Parma and winemakers in Champagne collectively have rights that they exercise over the use of "Parmigiano" and "Champagne" in their respective markets. These are not trademarks. They are not tied to a particular brand or company. They represent the work of a region. Since the early 20th century France has protected regions from which cheese, wine, truffles, and other foods originate through a system called *appellation d'origine contrôlée* (AOC). With the establishment of the European Union in the 1990s all of Europe now issues strong protections to regional sources of both agricultural and processed products like beer. The relationship between geographic indicators and trademarks is weak, although the justification is similar. Consumers should not be fooled into purchasing cheese from Wisconsin that looks like it comes from Switzerland, especially if they are paying a premium for a luxury good. And just as – if not more – importantly, the farmers, cheese makers, and wine producers around the world who produce their goods with traditional methods should be protected from the economies of scale and political power of large multinational food conglomerates like Kraft or Anheuser-Busch InBev.

In India geographic indicators have risen to protect growers of products such as Basmati rice (as opposed to Texmati brand rice from Texas) or the leaves of the neem tree, which is alleged to have many healing properties. So geographic indictor protection serves both as trade protection (and thus works against the general trend toward greater global integration of markets) and as cultural policy, preserving something of the traditions of local craft and foodways (Wolfgang 1995; Shiva 2001).

Of course, like trademarks, geographic indicators can "go generic." So while "Parmigiano" enjoys protection, "parmesan" long ago became associated with the stale, flavourless flakes of cheese product that Kraft encases in plastic tubes. Thus "parmesan" is generic and cheese makers in Parma have no control over its distribution. And if a trademark application comes too close to resembling a registered geographic indicator in Europe then the registration will be denied.

In the United States, which does not have a strong tradition of *sui generis* protection of geographic origins, traditional trademarks often work on behalf of onions from Vidalia, Georgia, or oranges from Florida. As a party to the Trade-Related Aspects of Intellectual Property Rights (TRIPs) treaty, the United States is obligated to protect other countries' geographic indicators if another product causes confusion in the marketplace and falsely represents its origin. But the United States itself has a much lighter tradition of enforcing geographic indications, largely because it does not have a tradition of respecting "terroir" or the "sense of place" that many who produce wine and cheese assert exists in a discernible form when a product comes from a place with distinctive soil or, in the case of cheese, bacteria.

Traditional culture and the public domain

The opposite of copyright is the public domain. Expressions that are not protected by copyright law are available for anybody who wants to create a new expressive work to take and use. The material in the public domain is vast. It includes all facts, ancient myths, data, books published before the 20th century, works that were never protected by copyright at all, most fashion designs, and expressions that have never been fixed in a medium. The public domain is a "commons," is owned by no one. Therefore, it is owned by everyone (Hyde 1983).

The idea of the commons is as romantic as authorship (Sunder 2012). It conjures ideas of vast parks, of clean air, and of the collective resource that can be used by all for the benefit of all. Of course many economists have warned against the "tragedy of the commons." A commons can become "tragic" if its finite resources are abused in the interest of each individual user of the commons. An uncoordinated group of users would tax the resource to its limit (Hardin 1968), but commons of facts, ideas, and expressions are not susceptible to such tragic ends. The subject matter of intellectual property, after all, is non-rivalrous. If someone takes and uses part of the commons, no one else is left with less. All substance within an intellectual or cultural commons is easily reused because it can never be exhausted (Lessig 2004). Rock and roll artists used elements of Delta blues music from its public domain; Walt Disney made his fortune and his company dominant by exploiting and revising public domain works such as Cinderella and Snow White. Without a rich and plentiful public domain, new creators would have high transaction costs and other barriers to entry if they wished to converse using the elements of a common culture. When the public domain fails to grow as copyrights fail to expire – as has been happening as legislators around the world have extended copyright terms – historians, poets, journalists, and songwriters find it harder to refer to stories and images that make up collective memory (Vaidhyanathan 2001).

But there is a problem with the public domain. Those who create and wish to market goods that reflect created traditions that are older than the 20th century tend to find no help in the standard and established modes of intellectual property protection. Their work, no matter how creative or labour-intensive or important to their cultural identity, is considered part of the grand global cultural commons. As several scholars of indigenous or traditional cultural production have argued in recent years, the cultural production of local communities is "delegitimized as knowledge through the hegemony of Western systems of knowledge production" (Boateng 2011, 14).

Intellectual property does not treat all cultural expression equally. In her exploration of the politics of regulation of traditional weaving techniques in Ghana, Boateng argues that in a global political economy in which Ghana trades with India, China, the rest of Africa, Europe, and North America, protecting the interests of traditional weavers is more complex than merely defending their arts against corporate poachers from the "developed" world. The weavers of Adinkra and Kente cloth face competition from weavers who wish to mimic their patterns working in Korea, China, India, and other parts of the world that host members of the Ghanaian diaspora. So the examination of the policies and politics of traditional weaving in Ghana is not just a case study of a poor fit between a traditional African mode of cultural production and a system of intellectual property that was imposed by a colonial master and enforced by global trade agreements. Boateng explores the place of nation-states like Ghana within a dynamic and fluid order of global trade and regulation. "To the extent that the copyright saying doesn't work in Ghana, it is because intellectual property law is part of the normative modernization framework that leaves very little space for alternative modes of social, economic, political, and legal organization," she writes (166).

To accept that only the "new" shall be protected by intellectual property accepts the modernist view that new is better than old. To mark Kente and Adinkra cloth as "traditional" is hegemonic. It must reside permanently in the past and must be inferior to the "innovations" of the present and future. Importantly, the government of Ghana deftly markets the past. It distinguishes its "traditional" cloth as "authentic." It is hand-woven and not mass-produced. Global market logic demands that Ghana invest value in protecting its weavers' work as "traditional" because that is what differentiates it from the hundreds of other similar expressive goods flowing across trade channels. Boeteng concludes that efforts to create new forms of intellectual property law to protect "traditional knowledge" would only reaffirm the permanent inferiority of creative works that have older origins and deeper modes of production. These works would be stuck just outside of modernity in an effort to fully exploit the modern market.

The free culture movement vs. the traditional cultural expression movement

Since 2002 a loose but growing set of law professors, librarians, artists, hackers, and free speech activists have been pushing back against what they consider overly strong copyright protections. Lawrence Lessig, among others, has dubbed this phenomenon the "Free Culture movement" (2004). This movement has been successful at exposing efforts of the copyright industries to insert stronger protections into international trade treaties and has launched political campaigns to raise awareness and concern about intellectual property around the world. This movement has found a strong following in northern Europe and Brazil, and it is growing in India and Latin America (Vaidhyanathan 2005c).

The Free Culture movement exposes the frustrations and limitations of efforts to generate a global public sphere that can wrestle with any issue of global importance: cultural, trade, health, or environmental questions. First, it's not always clear what the global public sphere is. The local (or national) public sphere in Habermas' model mediates between the private and the state. There is rarely a clear state-like supranational body that has effective sovereignty over any particular global issue. Sometimes it seems to be the World Trade Organization, but that might just be a mask for the interests of a particular nation-state. Other times it seems to be UNESCO or the World Intellectual Property Organization. But such organizations might just be acting as an instrument of policy execution at the behest of a nation-state that demands the illusion of multilateral cover for its will. Second, public spheres imply (perhaps require) real spaces for deliberation and debate. The Free Culture movement has proliferated not merely through the use of e-mail lists and web sites. It has generated energy and strategy through a long series of face-to-face meetings sponsored by foundations, universities, and small groups of activists. These meetings might have been organized through digital information communication technologies, but free culture activists still feel the need to meet face-to-face to forge consensus and agendas for action. This privileges activists in wealthier places in the world or those privileged by institutional affiliation. Frequent fliers become agenda-setters.

The very marginality of the Traditional Cultural Expression movement – its reason for being – renders it peripheral to global discussions of cultural policy. Only when represented by a friendly and supportive nation-state such as Canada or Australia do Traditional Cultural Expression movement members find their claims considered by policy-making officials, but this is state-driven action.

The role of the state in the potential protection of traditional cultural expression presents many problems. How shall the state determine who is and is not a member of a group trying to protect such expressions? What if the group is in opposition to the state? What if the group is split among factions? Who will determine the terms of licensing for songs, styles, and designs? The potential for censorship is daunting. So efforts toward a *sui generis* traditional cultural expression regime have been halting and have faced strong criticism (Brown 2003).

Global electronic cultural policy

There is a global battle raging over the terms of access, use, re-use, combination, re-combination, execution, and distribution of cultural materials. It is not necessarily aligned along a north–south axis; it is more often a struggle between individuals and communities reaching out and puncturing the fragile, permeable membranes of state-set cultural limits. While inexpensive digital technology has exponentially expanded the power of individuals to master their own media spaces and manipulate texts and images in ways that seem to signal an age of "semiotic democracy" (Coombe 1998) centralized corporate power struggles to lock down the flows of re-used commercial cultural production through otherwise potentially liberating and empowering technological systems. The battle between forces of cultural anarchy and cultural oligarchy continues to rage more than 20 years after it was declared in the late 20th century at the height of the romance of globalization and the seeming dominance of what was once known as the "Washington Consensus."

The nexus of such "re-imagineering" is electronic cultural policy. It is a particular flavour of cultural policy that guides the architecture of interfaces, networks, standards, protocols, and formats that house and deliver cultural products. Cultural policy is itself an understudied factor in global cultural change (and stasis). Only recently have scholars taken seriously the systematic interactions between states and cultural practices, between the bureaucratic and the creative. Although it is common in the United States to assume that culture is in general subject to minimal state influence (with the obvious counterexamples of lightly funded yet oddly controversial national endowments), much of the mechanics and economics of culture are subject to heavy levels of governance from the state. Trade policies, defence policies, and educational policies all have cultural elements and depend on complementary cultural policies to generate consensuses and mobilize support.

"Cultural imperialism" has become a cliché. The academic "cultural imperialism thesis," dominant among leftist critics in the 1970s and 1980s, is in severe need of revision (Schiller 1976). While those who complain about cultural imperialism cite the ubiquity of KFC in Cairo and McDonalds in Manila, anxious cultural protectionists in the United States quiver at the sound of Spanish spoken in public or Mosques opening in Ohio. Some American nationalists argue that cultural imperialism would be good for the world, as we Americans have so much figured out (Rothkopf 1997). Others dodge its complications by celebrating "Creolization" at all costs, while ignoring real and serious imbalances in the political economy of culture. While the evidence for cultural imperialism is only powerful when selectively examined, the evidence for infrastructural imperialism is much stronger. There are imbalances of power in global flows of culture, but they are not what traditional cultural imperialism theorists claim.

Instead, it seems that if there is a dominant form of "cultural imperialism," it concerns the pipelines, not the products – the formats of distribution and the terms of access and use. It is not exactly "content neutral," but it is less necessarily "content specific" than cultural imperialism theorists assume. The texts, signs, and messages that flow through global communications networks do not carry a clear and unambiguous celebration of ideas and ideologies we might lazily label "Western" – consumerism, individualism, and secularism. These commercial pipelines may carry texts that overtly hope to threaten the tenets of global capitalism. What flows from North to South does not matter as much as how it flows, how much revenue the flows generate, and who may re-use the elements of such flows.

By the end of the 20th century, major cultural industries in the United States decided that copyright was obsolete and insufficient to protect their interests and expand their markets. Copyright, as it had emerged in much of the world, granted strong public interest safeguards such as "fair use" or "fair dealing," non-protection of facts and ideas, and eventual expiration and entry into the public domain (Vaidhyanathan 2003). Frustrated with the longevity and strength of these democratic safeguards, the leaders of copyright-producing industries started a steady movement to shift the site of regulation from civil courts to machines themselves. Understanding that multilateral policy-making bodies had the power to impose policies on sovereign states without deliberation or compromise within them, industry leaders and representatives from the United States Patent and Trademark Office and Department of Commerce employed forums like the World Intellectual Property Organization (WIPO), the World Trade Organization (WTO), and regional organs such as the European Union (EU) and the Free Trade Area of the Americas (FTAA) to gain leverage and avoid public interest non-governmental organizations (Sell 2003). They sought to standardize intellectual property across the globe as more nations joined the ranks of the industrialized and con-sumptive. American and European companies seeking new markets did not want to see their products copied in countries with weak or no intellectual property protections. So the de-veloped world pushed for the establishment of the World Intellectual Property Organization (WIPO) and the Trade Related Aspects of Intellectual Property Rights (TRIPS) accord. WIPO members generate treaties and agreements about global intellectual property stan-dards. Signatories of the TRIPS accord may, through the World Trade Organization, enforce mechanisms or seek retribution for a violation of intellectual property standards.

In the 1980s the United States tried to use WIPO, under the auspices of the United Nations, to negotiate the first round of global electronic cultural policy treaties. After en-countering resistance, and realizing that such a forum allows developing nations the ability to form blocs and act in concert to protect their interests, the United States moved its intellec-tual property efforts into the mainstream trade negotiations through the General Agreement on Tariffs and Trade (GATT). As GATT morphed into a permanent resolution body, the World Trade Organization (WTO) in the 1990s, the United States used it to force nations that sought favourable trade in other areas to sign the Agreement on Trade Related Aspects of Intellectual Property (TRIPs), a set of global minimal standards for copyright, patent, trade secret, trademark, semiconductor, and geographic marker regulations (Sell 2003).

By 2001 the United States found that its leverage at the WTO was weakening, most significantly because of failures to standardize intellectual property regimes. In this case, however, it was the patent instead of the copyright system that stifled the global reach of American policy. Such globalization and standardization efforts have generated much con-sternation among developing nations, where farmers do not always appreciate being told they must respect limits on the use and replantation of patented seeds and plants, and gesta-tional publishing and media companies must play by rules written by their more powerful and established global competitors. Yet northern concerns that developing nations serve as havens for software and video pirates (and huge potential markets for everything) has kept the pressure on their governments to adopt and enforce laws that resemble those of the United States and Western Europe.

As a result of the 1997 WIPO Treaty, many countries, including the United States, have passed laws forbidding the distribution of any technologies – even simple mathematical algorithms – that might evade or crack access or copy control mechanisms that surround digital materials. Such digital rights management technologies protect not only copyrighted material but also material that is already in the public domain and facts and data not covered by copyright law. Digital "lockdown" grants far greater control over works than traditional copyright law ever did. Through such laws as the U.S. Digital Millennium Copyright Act (DMCA), information regulation is leaving the realm of human judgement and entering a technocratic regime (Gillespie 2007).

Where once users could assume wide latitude in their private, non-commercial use, now a layer of code stands in the way of access to the work itself, preventing a variety of harmless uses. Because the DMCA allows content providers to regulate access, they can set all the terms of use. The de facto duration of protection under the DMCA is infinite. While copyright law in 2001 protects any work created today for the life of the author plus 70 years, 95 years in the case of corporate "works for hire," electronic gates do not expire. This allows producers to "recapture" works in the public domain. This also violates the constitutional mandate that Congress copyright laws that protect "for limited times." The DMCA works over and above real copyright law (Lessig 2004).

Most dangerously, such measures enable producers to exercise editorial control over the uses of their materials. They can extract contractual promises that the use will not parody or criticize the work in exchange for access – many web sites already do this. Despite its failures to protect music and video, some have found a use for the DMCA. It's more important than ever in garages, offices, and living rooms. Increasingly hardware industries (industries outside what we generally consider "software" or copyright industries like film, music, text, and computer code) are using the DMCA to lock in monopoly control over secondary goods. These are goods that have nothing to do with copyright, nothing to do with creativity, knowledge, or art. Because it is possible to put a computer chip into almost anything, companies are. If a company puts software on a chip that sits on a removable part of a machine and puts some other software on a complementary chip in the larger device, the DMCA prevents another company from developing a replacement for that part (Vaidhyanathan 2004).

Resistance

Since 2000 awareness of the cultural implications of intellectual property has risen. But both the tangle of laws and the modes of resistance remain incoherent, contradictory, and too complex for standard political action. Nonetheless, there is hope that movements and states across the globe will confront the fact that intellectual property regimes have profound effects on how humans make meaning, make connections, and make societies function. A world-wide "Access to Knowledge" movement has grown. It is a loose confederation of local-knowledge and indigenous-rights activists, hackers, librarians, legal scholars, and global public health experts. The movement at various times advocates for sui generis rights for local culture protection from the torrent of global corporate culture industries, against state censorship, for technological access for underprivileged communities, and global policies that aim to allow for maximal expression and creativity from below. Perhaps most importantly, the movement strives to keep pharmaceutical prices low and access high. Overall, the movement strives to preserve and extend dignity to peoples who do not have the advantages of capital or state power working on their behalf. Toward these ends, the Access to Knowledge movement has made clear that cultural policy choices have profound implications for the future of many peoples and communities across the planet. (Sunder 2007, Kapczynski 2010)

References

Boateng, Boatema. *The Copyright Thing Doesn't Work Here Adinkra and Kente Cloth and Intellectual Property in Ghana.* Minneapolis: University of Minnesota Press, 2011. http://public.eblib.com/choice/publicfullrecord.aspx?p=718868.

Brown, Michael F. *Who Owns Native Culture?* Cambridge, MA: Harvard University Press, 2003.

Chen, Jim. There's No Such Thing as Biopiracy... And It's a Good Thing Too. *SSRN eLibrary.* Accessed September 20, 2011. http://papers.ssrn.com/sol3/papers.cfm?abstract_id=781824.

Cohen, Julie E., and Mark A. Lemley. Patent Scope and Innovation in the Software Industry. *California Law Review* 89, no. 1 (2001): 1–57. doi:10.2307/3481172.

Coombe, Rosemary J. *The Cultural Life of Intellectual Properties: Authorship, Appropriation, and the Law.* Durham, NC: Duke University Press, 1998.

Cowan, Jane K, Marie-Bénédicte Dembour, and Richard Wilson. *Culture and Rights: Anthropological Perspectives.* Cambridge; New York: Cambridge University Press, 2001.

Decherney, Peter. *Hollywood's Copyright Wars from Edison to the Internet.* New York: Columbia University Press, 2012. http://public.eblib.com/choice/publicfullrecord.aspx?p=895258.

Gillespie, Tarleton. *Wired Shut Copyright and the Shape of Digital Culture.* Cambridge, MA: MIT Press, 2007. http://search.ebscohost.com/login.aspx?direct=true&scope=site&db=nlebk&db=nlabk&AN=190972.

Ginsburg, Jane C. A Tale of Two Copyrights: Literary Property in Revolutionary France and America. *Tulane Law Review* 64, no. 5 (1990): 991–1032.

Goldstein, Paul. *International Copyright: Principles, Law, and Practice.* Oxford, UK: Oxford University Press, 2001.

Hardin, Garrett. "The Tragedy of the Commons." *Science* 162, no. 3859 (December 13, 1968): 1243–48. doi:10.1126/science.162.3859.1243.

Hughes, Justin. Champagne, Feta, and Bourbon-the Spirited Debate about Geographical Indications. SSRN Scholarly Paper. Rochester, NY: Social Science Research Network, October 11, 2006. http://papers.ssrn.com/abstract=936362. Accessed 25 May, 2017.

Hyde, Lewis. *The Gift: Imagination and the Erotic Life of Property.* New York: Vintage Books, 1983.

Kapczynski, Amy. *Access to Knowledge in the Age of Intellectual Property.* New York: Zone Books, 2010.

Lessig, Lawrence. *Free Culture: The Nature and Future of Creativity.* New York: Penguin Press, 2004.

Miller, Toby, and George Yúdice. *Cultural Policy.* London; Thousand Oaks, CA: Sage, 2002.

Rothkopf, David J. "In Praise of Cultural Imperialism?" *Foreign Policy,* 1997, 38–53.

Schiller, Herbert I. *Communication and Cultural Domination.* White Plains, N.Y., 1976.

Sell, Susan. *Private Power, Public Law: The Globalization of Intellectual Property Rights.* Cambridge, UK; New York: Cambridge University Press, 2003.

Shiva, Vandana. Special Report: Golden Rice and Neem: Biopatents and the Appropriation of Women's Environmental Knowledge. *Women's Studies Quarterly* 29, no. 1/2 (2001): 12–23. www.jstor.org/stable/40004606.

Sunder, Madhavi. "The Invention of Traditional Knowledge." *Law and Contemporary Problems* 70, no. 2 (2007): 97–124. www.jstor.org/stable/27592181.

Sunder, Madhavi. *From Goods to a Good Life Intellectual Property and Global Justice.* New Haven, CT: Yale University Press, 2012. http://site.ebrary.com/id/10568939.

Trubek, Amy B. *The Taste of Place: A Cultural Journey into Terroir.* Berkeley, CA: University of California Press, 2008.

Vaidhyanathan, Siva. *Copyrights and Copywrongs: The Rise of Intellectual Property and How It Threatens Creativity.* New York: New York University Press, 2001.

Vaidhyanathan, Siva. *The Anarchist in the Library: How the Clash between Freedom and Control Is Hacking the Real World and Crashing the System.* New York: Basic Books, 2004.

Vaidhyanathan, Siva. *Open Source as Culture-Culture as Open Source. SSRN eLibrary.* OPEN SOURCE ANNUAL 2005, Clemens Brandt, ed., Berlin: Technische University, 2005. http://papers.ssrn.com/sol3/papers.cfm?abstract_id=713044. Accessed 25 May, 2017.

Vaidhyanathan, Siva. Remote Control: The Rise of Electronic Cultural Policy. *SSRN eLibrary*, Vol. 597, January 2005a. http://papers.ssrn.com/sol3/papers.cfm?abstract_id=713022. Accessed 25 May, 2017.

Vaidhyanathan, Siva. Critical Information Studies: A Bibliographic Manifesto. *SSRN eLibrary*, August 23, 2005b. http://papers.ssrn.com/sol3/papers.cfm?abstract_id=788984. Accessed 25 May, 2017.

Vaidhyanathan, Siva. Between Pragmatism and Anarchism: The American Copyright Revolt since 1998. 31 October 2005c. *SSRN eLibrary*. Accessed May 25, 2017. http://papers.ssrn.com/sol3/papers.cfm?abstract_id=827824.

Wolfgang, Lori. Patents on Native Technology Challenged. *Science* 269, no. 5230 (1995): 1506–7. www.jstor.org/stable/2889089.

9

Cultural policy between and beyond nation-states

The case of *lusofonia* and the *Comunidade dos Países de Língua Portuguesa*

Carla Figueira

Introduction

This chapter analyses a particular case of cultural policy-making beyond and between nation-states, that of *lusofonia*, a postcolonial politico-linguistic bloc of Portuguese-language countries and peoples, in one of its institutional forms, the Community of Portuguese Language Countries (in Portuguese, *Comunidade dos Países de Língua Portuguesa*, CPLP). The purpose is to demonstrate how cultural policy can be conceptualised and practised outside of the usual framework of a single state and developed multilaterally to potentially impact different national public spheres, by connecting cultural policy and cultural diplomacy. The countries that are part of *lusofonia* –Portugal, Brazil, five African countries (Angola, Cape Verde, Guinea Bissau, Mozambique, and São Tomé and Príncipe) and Timor-Leste (all former colonies of Portugal) – institutionalised their relationship in 1996 through the Community of Portuguese Language Countries and have as recently as 2014 welcomed into this organisation Equatorial Guinea.

Lusofonia, similar to other linguistic-cultural-political realities, can be seen as a new site for the development of cultural policies for collective identity building by an association of states, which in a traditional cultural diplomacy reading also allows for a particular representation of their unity in the international society. The sharing of language and culture between countries has been an important factor in the creation of political organisations geared towards their defence and promotion, such as *la francophonie* or the Arab League. A situation easily understood as "(t)hose who speak the same language not only can make themselves understood to each other; the capacity of being able to make oneself understood also founds a feeling of belonging and belonging together" (Weiβ and Schwietring 2006, p. 3). However, language is only one of the aggregate elements of culture, and we must look, among other factors, at the importance of the political engineering of culture through public policies to understand the building of collective identities, as well as other increasingly important instrumental uses of culture particularly appreciated in our neo-liberal world, such as the development of the cultural and creative industries. This analysis shows the Community of Portuguese Language Countries as developing within *lusofonia* a (tentative) multilateral cultural policy, which can impact in the ways of imagining, narrating and enacting belonging to that particular transnational social/cultural space.

The chapter includes a background discussion on the links between cultural policy and cultural relations/diplomacy, which attempts to establish a framework for the understanding of the internal/external boundaries of cultural policy as public policy and its connection with foreign policy. The bulk of the chapter critically analyses why and how cultural policies are developed between and beyond the nation-states engaged in building *lusofonia*, looking specifically at the implicit and explicit cultural policies and activity of its most important governmental institution, the *Comunidade dos Países de Língua Portuguesa* (hereafter CPLP). The setting up of CPLP in 1996 marked the constitution of this 'geocultural' area or space as a political actor in international relations, becoming thus a sphere of responsibility, inter-action and coexistence (Tardif 2004). The other major political organisation of *lusofonia* is the International Institute of Portuguese Language (*Instituto Internacional da Língua Portuguesa*, IILP), which will not be a focus for this chapter. The research for this chapter is based on the critical analysis of documentary sources and interviews, within a theoretical framework combining elements from cultural policy and international relations.

Cultural policy beyond and between nation-states

Most often the research and study of cultural policy focuses on the arts and related public policy processes and practices within the domestic realm of the state: national/internal cultural policy. However, international cultural policy is a growing field encompassing global issues such as the trade and regulation of cultural products and labour, involving a multiplicity of actors at international, supranational, subnational levels (e.g. UNESCO, EU, regions and cities), and venturing into cultural diplomacy and exchange, as for example recently sketched in Bell and Oakley (2015). It is this last aspect, the links between cultural policy, cultural diplomacy and foreign policy, that I would like to further analyse to establish a clear theoretical basis for the analysis of transnational cultural policies within CPLP.

Despite the lack of an uncontested definition, cultural diplomacy is often understood as the use of culture by governments to achieve their foreign policy goals and a prime activity for achieving 'soft power' (Nye 2004) as a relational outcome. This thinking clearly positions cultural diplomacy in the discipline of international relations, highlighting the main role of state actors, and resting on the assumption that "art, language, and education are among the most significant entry points into a culture" (Goff 2013, pp. 419–420), which links it directly to cultural policy. Here the author must reiterate her positioning: like others, she does not conceive of cultural diplomacy in the absence of state involvement (*ibid.* explores well the nuances of the debate surrounding what can be cultural diplomacy), preferring to use for those situations the label cultural relations (Mitchell 1986, Arndt 2005).

The analysis of cultural policies and practices beyond the national framework is a necessary consequence of cultural globalisation. This broader space of analysis, to include the global, international, transnational, regional and local, allows for a more complex understanding of cultural policy and practice. As DeVereaux and Griffin (2006, p. 3) highlight:

> What is clear, then, is that the flow of culture into, out of, and even within countries has a lot to do with how we understand these terms. Because global, international, transnational, and the underlying framework of "nation" itself define the territory on which cultural activity can take place, the very meaning of "culture" and the identities we construct both individually and collectively depend acutely on the territory-and the possibilities – these terms delimit and define.

It is no longer possible to frame a national cultural policy within methodological nationalism, the pervasive assumption that the nation-state is the natural unit of analysis in modernity (according to the 1974 original concept of Herminio Martins and A. D. Smith's 1979 interpretation in Chernillo 2006). However, as noted by MacNeill and Reynolds (2013, p. 19), "when a government is framing a 'national' cultural policy, the impact of this explicit framing is that the opportunity to think transnationally is mediated, and ... constrained by the imperative to think nationally". To overcome this implicit boundary and think transnationally beyond the nation-state and transcend nationalism is a difficult task. This is an opportunity and a challenge for *lusofonia* as it develops a layer of identity uniting peoples of different countries, potentially set in transnationalism, here viewed ideally as emphasising the value of increased openness or fluidity of barriers to facilitate cultural exchanges within the cultural community (DeVeraux and Griffin 2006, p. 5).

The concept of transnational cultural policy connects with cultural relations/diplomacy and foreign policy. For example, Ahearne (2009) understands that, although under different denominations, both cultural policy and cultural/public diplomacy – which we can define as the use of culture in the relations between governments and foreign publics – deal with the same reality. Thus in his view cultural/public diplomacy can qualify as implicit cultural policy – i.e. government policy not labelled as such. Other cultural policy authors acknowledge this same connection but add caveats. Bell and Oakley (2015, p. 162) link cultural diplomacy (which they choose to frame in the discourse of exchange and understanding) and cultural policy more cautiously: "The degree to which it [cultural diplomacy] is a cultural policy *per se* – a chance to develop artistic reputations, ideas and new markets – or an element of foreign policy is disputed ...; the answer is probably both". However, in his book *International Cultural Relations*, Mitchell (1986, p. 9) clearly brings together the different elements of the cultural policy and cultural diplomacy puzzle:

> The motive force behind *international cultural relations* work, whether of the responsible ministry or of non-governmental organisations, is expressed in *external cultural policy*. ... Clearly, external cultural policy cannot be practised in abstraction: its validity will depend on the vitality of the domestic scene, on *internal cultural policy*. The two should ideally interlock.
>
> *(emphasis added)*

He (*ibid.*, p. 82 and 84) notes that the connections between external and internal cultural policy are often obscured by the traditional division of powers between foreign ministries overseeing the former and ministries with domestic remit (often ministries of culture) overseeing the latter, which also works in detriment of collaboration. The integration between the two areas is also affected by the fact that external cultural policy is often seen as an intrinsic aspect of foreign policy, which results in the reinforcement of one-way, outward concepts connected with national self-projection (*ibid.*, p. 67/8 and 120). However, Mitchell (*ibid.*, p. 120) notes the development of the principle of mutual benefit in bilateral relations and questions: "If the principle of mutual benefit were to be fully developed, might it not be considered more appropriate to broaden the scope of mutuality more extensively into the multilateral dimension?" Interestingly, Ang, Isar and Mar (2015) try to reconcile the tension between national interest and common interest in cultural diplomacy concluding that going beyond the national interest, by developing processes of dialogue and collaboration (i.e. focusing on cultural relations), "*is* in the national interest" (*ibid.*, p. 378). This is the case of CPLP.

Globalisation has created new spaces for policy formation where different levels of agency coexist – multilateral spaces in which nation-states cooperate according to mutually beneficial principles are one of those levels. CPLP embodies such a particular instance of agency: it is an international actor participating in complex policy networks, which can be defined as "clusters of policy actors, agencies, institutions and organisations whose work is aimed at generating and implementing policies via transnational agreements, policy advisory, philanthropy and conditionality" (Ozga 2005 in Fimyar 2010, p. 12).

In the next section, the author argues that CPLP, as an international actor and space, is a potential agent and site for the development of mutually beneficial cultural policy at transnational level – often articulated in CPLP's official discourse as cultural cooperation, although explicit mentions to a common cultural policy have also been identified. The chapter is developed on the assumption that cultural policy-making is "a dynamic process in which the nation state exerts power and deploys resources in conjunction with regional, local and even institutional agencies" in the area of culture (the wording is borrowed from Bell and Stevenson's 2006, p. 4, clear definition of educational policy). In the case of CPLP, albeit with different degrees of investment and involvement, different countries pool resources to consensually implement agreed-upon projects to reach common and mutually beneficial aims and objectives pertaining to culture and the arts.

CPLP as a an agent and site for *lusofonia's* multilateral cultural policy

The discourse of *lusofonia* and its political incarnation, the CPLP, can be seen as an embodiment of a complex web of experienced and fabricated feelings and intellectual constructions of belonging, where the imagination is key – both in Appadurai's (1996, p. 48) sense of an organised field of social practice contributing to the interactive construction of the ethnoscapes of group identity and Anderson's (1991) conception of building narratives of the 'national' community.

Lusofonia, a compound word combining the Latin term *luso*, the inhabitant of *Lusitânia*, an area roughly corresponding to modern Portugal, and *fonia* from the Ancient Greek meaning voice (in English *Lusophone*) permanently refers this postcolonial notion to the former colonial master's language. This stress on Portuguese language as a symbol of a 'community' of countries and peoples is often the target of critique. Mainly because not all the inhabitants of the countries that are part of *lusofonia*/CPLP speak the Portuguese language and those who do speak it have different levels of fluency – although the countries will have Portuguese language as their implicit or explicit official language. Also problematic is presenting *lusofonia* as a cultural community, which may often be no more than wishful thinking (as the author explored elsewhere, Figueira 2013). Language builds particular solidarities (Anderson 1991) that, along with other elements – in the case of *lusofonia*, a shared colonial past that has fostered people and cultural exchanges as well as fed similarities in administrative structures and other connections/dependencies too complex to examine here-can be politically used to foster alliances, from which the different members can extract political, social, economic and cultural benefits (Figueira 2013).

The creation of the CPLP in 1996 was a major step in the institutionalisation of *lusofonia*. However, the organisation, more than representing an actual community, has been a political and ideological strategic plan that has been rather slow in being implemented by its member states. At the time of writing, February 2016, CPLP prepares to celebrate in July its 20th anniversary and has been perceived for most of its life as not very active, focused more on institutional matters than promoting a closeness with and among its peoples. A lack of resources (financial and human) and divergences regarding objectives (and their implementation) between its member states are at the source of CPLP's problems (for detailed examination and a range of views on *lusofonia* and the CPLP see for example Lourenço 1999, Chacon 2002, Santos 2003, Cristóvão 2008, Pinto 2009, Maciel 2015).

Culture has not been a priority for CPLP, although culture and language are posited as the community's building blocks, and the organisation has worked more as a political and diplomatic forum. The dissemination and promotion of Portuguese language undertaken by CPLP has not been matched by a similar level of activities in the broad area of culture, or specifically the arts. However, from being not much more than a talking shop for politically correct discourse around political, economic, social and cultural cooperation, the still young organisation (and less financially endowed than for example the International Organisation of *La Francophonie* created in 1970 and the modern Commonwealth of Nations created in 1949) has recently shown signs of having a strategic vision for culture – as examined later – that may be the key for it to represent an actual site for cultural affiliation respectfully and actively fostering the diversity of expressions of its peoples.

It should be noted that many of the countries that are part of *lusofonia* possess affiliations with other international politico linguistic blocs, such as the ones named above, which denotes a practical approach from the countries to using these as opportunities to make their voices heard and participate more actively in international society. *Lusofonia* as a collective identity cannot (should not) obscure the individual and group multiple identities, which result in multiple diverse arrangements (Figueira 2013). CPLP countries also demonstrate different levels of engagement with the organisation. This is a situation far too complex to examine here, so I will simply highlight two of the challenges in this area and make a brief critical comment to the policy context. Firstly, the member states have different levels of development and different financial capacity to contribute to the organisation, which, to an extent, is a limitation to the possibility of taking part and shaping the direction of the organisation – even if decisions are consensual (Art. 23 of the CPLP Statutes) and there are common funds for projects. Secondly, the political priority countries place on their active participation in the organisation may be influenced by regional affiliations and commitments that take precedence over those of the territorially discontinued *lusofonia* (e.g. Mozambique with the Southern African Development Community). Finally, in terms of context for the development of a multilateral cultural policy, Brazil and Portugal are the two countries with greater interest and capacity to act in this area. Brazil has an interest in the export of its cultural products, and Portugal can use language as a symbolic and 'harmless' continuation of empire. It is, thus, not surprising, for example, to find that Portugal's external cultural strategy aligns so well with that of the CPLP: some of the measures indicated in the Portuguese Government programme for 2015–2019 (Governo de Portugal 2015, p. 254) mirror perfectly some of the CPLP's projects in the area of culture (which I examine later), and it is telling that CPLP's headquarters are in Lisbon.

CPLP operates in a complex context, and the development of policy and practice in the area of culture presents significant challenges but also important opportunities. Cooperation in the domain of culture is one of the objectives of CPLP. In the 1996 CPLP Constitutional Declaration (CPLP 1996), the Heads of State and Government stated as one of the objectives of the organisation the fostering of cultural exchange within a framework of international cooperation; this is also being explicitly mentioned under article 4 of the CPLP Statutes. The general CPLP cooperation agreement[1] of 1999 encapsulates the wish of the member states to develop a mutually advantageous cooperation anchored in shared linguistic, cultural, political and historic communalities. However, if the different member states have significant different development levels and if some countries, as suggested above, have particular vested interests, would this mean that a mutually advantageous cultural co-operation/policy within CPLP is by definition not possible? I propose to view the activities developed within CPLP as a kind of asymmetrical cooperation (assuming a certain hegemonic leadership by Portugal, as previously mentioned), thus linking cooperation to (a certain degree of) hegemony – under the assumption that they are not antithetical as suggested by Keohane (1984, p. 49). He defines cooperation by the requirement that "the actions of separate individuals or organizations-which are not in pre-existent harmony – be brought into conformity with one another through a process of negotiation, which is often referred to as 'policy coordination'" (Keohane 1984, p. 51). So, I would say that CPLP can be viewed as a setting for processes of policy coordination, in the case we are interested in, resulting in a multilateral cultural policy.

This analysis of CPLP as a potential site for cultural policy starts by looking at texts contained in three documents that marked important anniversaries of the organisation: the first celebrating the 10th anniversary of the organisation entitled *Pensar, comunicar, actuar em língua portuguesa/Thinking, communicating and acting in Portuguese* (CPLP 2006); a second published on the occasion of the 12th anniversary entitled *Construindo a Comunidade/Building the Community* (CPLP 2008) and a third marking the 18th anniversary: *Os Desafios do Futuro/The Challenges of the Future* (CPLP 2014b).

In the 2006 publication *Pensar, comunicar, actuar em língua portuguesa,* it is acknowledged that the CPLP objectives remain unfulfilled. The then Executive Secretary, Ambassador Luis Fonseca, advances as justification for the situation the lack of resources and the lack of consensus between the member states regarding strategic plans (CPLP 2006, p. 13). 'Cultural cooperation' is reiterated in the document as a main objective of CPLP and its substance consists of projects with governmental institutions and civil societies of the member states as well as international organisations and the development of several agreements (CPLP 2006, p. 113). Mention is made to projects of relevance privileging film, audio-visual and museums (*ibid.*) – these still remain key areas. The executive secretary's efforts to facilitate the contact between cultural institutions are highlighted as a way to foster intercultural (institutional) dialogue (*ibid.*, p. 114).

In 2008, in the 12th anniversary publication *Construindo a Comunidade/Building the Community* (CPLP 2008), the 2004–2008 Executive Secretary Ambassador Luis de Matos Monteiro da Fonseca argues that CPLP has reached the end of a cycle and is now ready to develop as a community (CPLP 2008, p. 11). In this document, cultural activities are framed as promoting cultural diversity and as efforts for the development of the mutual knowledge of the different cultures within CPLP (*ibid.*, p. 105). The first CPLP Cultural Week that took place between 3 and 11 May 2008 in Lisbon is also mentioned and presented as a reflection space on aims and themes of common agendas (*ibid.*, p. 118). In this document the then Director General of CPLP, Helder Vaz Lopes, presents a vision for the future of CPLP, advancing ten key areas, of which only one pertains directly to culture: "Reinforcement, promotion and conservation of the common cultural heritage" (ibid., p. 141). Heritage is a consistent focus for CPLP.

The 2014 publication celebrating the 18th anniversary of the organisation refers to 'cultural action', and under this heading a diversity of initiatives is mentioned: the Day of Portuguese Language and of Culture in the CPLP (*Dia da Língua Portuguesa e da Cultura na CPLP*) celebrated for the first time on 5 May 2010; the DOCTV CPLP programme, which encourages audio-visual production and dissemination, took place in 2009, sponsored by Brazil and Portugal, and was inspired by a similar Brazilian and South American programme; the strengthening/revitalisation of the CPLP museums network that met in 2012 after an interruption of 11 years; the CPLP Games; and the film festival *Festival de Cinema Itinerante da Língua Portuguesa* (FESTin) taking place since 2010, with the objective of celebrating and strengthening lusophone culture. There is also a general mention to promoting the diversity of cultural expressions through exhibitions, seminars and other events (CPLP 2014b, p. 112).

Most importantly, the above documents include explicit mentions of a cultural policy of the CPLP in relation to the contribution of the CPLP Groups/*Grupos CPLP* to "the promotion of a common cultural policy of the Community"[2] (CPLP 2014b, p. 116, but also in CPLP 2008 and CPLP 2006). Created in 2005, these groups, of at least three representatives of CPLP countries, accredited with foreign governments or international organisations represent the community and work together to promote it. An example of good practice provided by the organisation is the coordination of cultural events for the commemoration of the Day of Portuguese Language and of Culture in the CPLP, celebrated on 5 May (*ibid.*). This event attempts to display to the world a united front in terms of narrative and action.

The three documents above indicate a concern with heritage/museums and with film/audiovisual. Thus we could say that CPLP's cultural policy tries to balance its commitments between traditional and contemporary cultural policy frameworks. The author believes contemporary frameworks of cultural policy, namely, those related to creative and cultural industries and the creative economy, are the way forward in what should be CPLP's focus. Bissau-Guinean development economist Carlos Lopes (CPLP 2006, p. 141) suggests that the advancement of CPLP rests in the development and support of cultural policies in close consultation with civil societies and stresses the importance of the cultural and creative industries. He says:

> You can feel the CPLP when a group of citizens of the lusophone countries find common reference points. Not when you organise a formal meeting of politico-diplomatic concertation. To strengthen the basis of the relation we have to translate the friendship in a set of concrete actions. In my view **it is mostly in the area of culture and of the creative industries that new possibilities reside**. Without that lever the Community will be no different from other groupings which we only remember when it's convenient'.[3] [My emphasis]

So, what is currently the policy and practice of CPLP in relation to culture? Since 2000 the CPLP ministers of culture have been meeting and issuing common declarations that constitute a loose basis of the organisation's cultural policy. This body of texts substantiates common concerns and projects that in 2014 finally came together under a strategy and plan of action – this has been described by the CPLP Secretariat as a way to highlight the importance of culture for the consolidation of CPLP's objectives (CPLP 2014d).

In 2014 the *Strategic Plan for Multilateral Cultural Cooperation of the CPLP and respective Action Plan (2014–2020)* was approved by the IX Meeting of the Ministers of Culture in Maputo, Mozambique. The development of this strategy and action plan was prompted by a 2009 resolution, *Cooperation in the CPLP – A Strategic Vision for Cooperation post Bissau*, that recommended the draft of sectorial cooperation strategies with the aim of improving the performance of the organisation in terms of cooperation for development guided by a results-based strategy (CPLP 2009, p. 2). CPLP's 2014 multilateral cultural cooperation strategy and action plan is an important turning point for the organisation that can be read as a multilateral cultural policy document, representing a common cultural policy, albeit one that it is still in its very early stages. As we shall see, the rationales are not always well developed, and because resources for implementation are an issue, one can question whether this exercise is simply a tidier framework in which to develop cooperation that will remain punctual and haphazard.

The preamble of the CPLP's 2014 strategy and action plan sets as its foundational basis for action the need to protect, promote and disseminate the historical, cultural and linguistic legacy composed of tangible and intangible heritage built through the shared history of the peoples of the CPLP (2014c, p. 3). Heritage, in both its communality and diversity, is seen as a factor for the deepening of the relationships of the CPLP peoples and also for increasing CPLP's international visibility ("*afirmação da CPLP no mundo*" in the Portuguese original, *ibid.*). This reveals a strong concern with the use of culture, and particularly heritage, for prestige and international visibility. This emphasises heritage as a value in itself, although there are remarks in the preamble to the enrichment of cultural life and to the strengthening of the development of the member states through culture.

In the 2014 strategy and action plan, we can also see how CPLP relates to particular meta-narratives in cultural policy. The document presents the development of multilateral cultural cooperation as based around a series of judgements regarding culture's conceptualisation (human rights, diversity of cultural expressions), functions (mutual knowledge and understanding, building of collective identities, knowledge transfer, economic and social development), and enactment (harmonious cooperation, accessibility and participation of all) (2014c, p. 2). This represents a mediation of global policy agendas to the level of this community of countries. Policy transfer is an area in which the organisation could have an important role. CPLP Groups can be very active within the international organisations in which they exist; they follow, for example, policy developments at UNESCO for the protection of cultural heritage in the CPLP countries.

The stated aim of the strategy and action plan is the reinforcement of cultural cooperation between its member states, under the principle of multilateralism, with the following general objectives: strengthening their development through culture; contributing to closer relations among the peoples; and increasing the visibility of CPLP in the world (2014c, p. 4 and 5). These high-level objectives are further unpacked in a series of specific objectives, a few of which are very focused (facilitate knowledge exchange between cultural operators by ensuring conditions for their mobility and for the circulation of cultural products; provide tools to support cultural professionals in the development and safeguard of their creations; promote artistic and cultural education activities targeting a range of audiences), but most, one could say, remain quite fuzzy and/or general (undertaking joint activities benefitting the populations; establish mechanisms for the communication and transmission of information; encourage the internationalisation of CPLP through culture; structure and strengthen cultural heritage cooperation) (2014c, p. 5). The author sees these specific objectives as constituting basic tenets of the multilateral cultural policy being developed by CPLP.

The objectives, and the priority axes of their implementation, implicitly position the organisation in relation to certain cultural policy frameworks (Matarasso and Landry 1999) – although one cannot interpret these frameworks as either/or poles as we shall see, for example, in relation to CPLP's focus on heritage and also on the contemporary through film and the audio-visual. The multilateral cultural cooperation strategy and action plan outlines five strategic axes: cultural industries and creative economy in CPLP; diversity of cultural expressions in the CPLP; internationalisation of the CPLP in the domain of culture; cultural heritage and historical memory of the CPLP; and human resources development (2014c).

The first axis, cultural industries and creative economy in CPLP, covers three main objectives. Firstly, encouraging the production, distribution and circulation of cultural goods and services within the CPLP area as well as its internationalisation – the priority action identified in this area is the development of a mechanism for the temporary export/import of goods. Secondly, supporting the mobility of cultural agents, by disseminating information on and creating opportunities for mobility (such as artistic residencies), as well as drafting a status of the artist, based on UNESCO's guidelines. Thirdly, to foster exchange of information regarding cultural policies and activities and the cultural economy, as well as collate and consolidate cultural information and statistics, (e.g. copyright laws).

Within the second axis, diversity of cultural expressions in the CPLP, three areas are sketched. One is promoting culture for sustainable development, by subscribing to the UN 2015 resolution on this matter and promoting traditional knowledge. Another area is promoting Portuguese language and the cultural and linguistic diversity of the peoples of the CPLP, for example through the celebration on the 5th of May of the Day of Portuguese Language and of Culture in the CPLP (*Dia da Língua Portuguesa e da Cultura na CPLP*). And a final area is promoting cultural and arts education, focusing particularly on primary/secondary age children.

The third axis, internationalisation of the CPLP in the domain of culture, includes three main dimensions: the development of relations with international and regional organisations – e.g. UN, UNESCO, WIPO, OEI, AU, EU – with the objective of raising CPLP's profile and promoting the culture of its members, accessing funding and development opportunities, participating in international debates/projects and being part of related agreements; fostering politico-diplomatic consultations for concerted action in the area of culture between the CPLP member states; developing the international visibility of culture in the CPLP though the creation of an e-Portal (*Portal da Cultura da CPLP*).

As part of the fourth axis, cultural heritage and historical memory of the CPLP, there are three areas of intervention: conservation, digitisation and development of the accessibility of the heritage of the member states; here a lot of emphasis is given to historical archives and museums; capacity-building of professionals and organisations; and promoting the visibility of the cultural heritage of the CPLP's members.

The fifth and final axis, human resources development, is aimed at capacity building of governmental and civil society cultural operators. The foreseen activities include training of professionals and trainers in cultural management and other relevant areas.

Priority actions have been identified for each of the areas of the five axes outlined above. From different projects matching the diverse priority actions, seven projects were prioritised by the CPLP ministers of Culture meeting in Maputo (CPLP 2014a) and of these, five were developed by CPLP Secretariat and by the Focal Points for Culture/*Pontos Focais de Cultura* (which ensure the permanent coordination of cultural cooperation between the member states and CPLP), for implementation in the first two years of the 2014–2020 action plan, no doubt having in mind the limited human and financial capacity of the organisation to implement them.

The first action proposed by the ministers of culture was the submission of the UN proposed resolution on "Culture and sustainable development in the post-2015 development agenda" for consideration to the *XIX Reunião Ordinária do Conselho de Ministros da CPLP*. This meeting took place three months later, in July 2014, and it recommended the Secretariat to follow the debates and promote a concerted position for the CPLP members, as well as encourage the member states to integrate culture and the creative economy in development (2014e). The ministers also commissioned the CPLP Executive Secretariat to develop a status of the artist for CPLP in line with the UNESCO's recommendations (CPLP 2014a) – this second action, a policy transfer activity, was not selected for immediate development. These two first actions both reveal a concern of CPLP, aligning its policy with dominant political meta-narratives, namely with the UN agencies.

A third action selected by CPLP's ministers of culture consisted of mandating the organisation's Secretariat to prepare a comparative study of their countries' legislation regarding copyright and related rights as an information gathering exercise and in preparation for negotiations with the World Intellectual Property Organization (Secreatariado Executivo da CPLP 2014b). In August 2015 the Secretariat was about to launch the commissioning of the study, which is part of strategic axis one *Creative Industries and Creative Economy*. This demonstrates an alignment and a concern with this important current policy area, particularly with the thematic of intellectual rights, and it is a step forward in raising awareness and creating an ambitioned network and database on copyright and related rights within the CPLP.

Reinforcing the visibility of the culture in the CPLP seems to be a driver for the ministers of culture, as they propose that the presiding member state hosts simultaneously the CPLP's Capital of Culture and Book Fair. The author interprets this as an economy of scales and an attempt to accumulate synergies from the different events to enable a maximisation of impact with some decrease of investment. Both activities, which are part of strategic axis two *Diversity of Cultural Expressions in the CPLP*, have had detailed proposals developed by the Secretariat during 2014/5 (Secretariado Executivo da CPLP 2014a and 2014d). The CPLP Book Fair is not a new activity; the first *CPLP Feira do Livro* took place in Luanda, Angola, in 2013 and the second took place in Díli, Timor-Leste, in July 2015. Book fairs fall under a very traditional way of engaging in international cultural relations, in this way quite different from the proposal of a CPLP Capital of Culture, situated in more contemporary modes of developing cultural engagement, where urban cultural policy and place branding meet. The project *Capital da Cultura da CPLP* has yet to come to life and the Secretariat has instead developed a less ambitious project for axis two, that of a CPLP Children's Song Festival (Secretariado Executivo da CPLP 2014c).

A concern with visibility and the building of a common narrative for identity is also associated with the proposal of the ministers of culture for the development of a Common CPLP Historical Collections Platform. Concerns with conservation and access are no doubt included, but a few of the proposals under strategic axis four *Cultural Heritage and Historical Memory of CPLP*, which incidentally have not been developed in a first phase by the Secretariat – are geared towards creating a sense of communality (note for example also the proposal for a Common Historical Archive for the Colonial and Liberation Period of the African Countries having Portuguese as Official Language, CPLP 2014c, p. 23).

The choice of projects by the CPLP ministers of culture in Maputo (2014a) reveals some concern with the development of the cultural milieu of the different countries, although this seems to be restricted to official, or at least institutional, stakeholders – thus leaving out of scope civil society/culture at the grass roots level. This interpretation is based on the fact that – although there is an increasing number of civil society activities related to *lusofonia* and that CPLP itself has civil society organisations as consulting observer members (in Portuguese *Observador Consultivo*) – the initiatives proposed within the remit of CPLP are quite limited, only including: regular training seminars for senior officials (*Altos Quadros* in the Portuguese original) in the area of cultural policies and creative industries of CPLP; and the organisation of an event gathering the member states Film and Audio-visual Authorities (Secretariado Executivo da CPLP 2014e). The positive note for axis five *Human Resources*

Development activities is that an activity has actually happened: the CPLP Forum of Film and Audio-Visual Authorities took place in Lisbon in November 2014.

The above limited and relatively safe choice of activities reveals an organisation taking little steps. More than strategic choices backed up by strong rationales and substantial resources by committed member states, CPLP (or more precisely its Executive Secretary and the Secretariat) continue to do what is possible to move the organisation forward in the area of culture according to a diversified range of commitments by the different member states.

CPLP, and specifically its cultural policy and practice, is weakened by being under resourced and under staffed. The Cultural Action Directorate/*Direção de Ação Cultural*, created in 2011, was an answer to increasing demands in this area allowing for more strategic planning and an increase in staffing (albeit limited from 1 person to 2), replacing a modus operandi in which member states would work on different areas according to their own interests (Vieira, personal interview 2015). Meagre funds to implement the projects are an endemic concern for CPLP, and the global economic crisis is acknowledged to have had a negative impact in the organisation. In 2012, the then director for CPLP Cultural Action and Portuguese Language/*Acção Cultural e Língua Portuguesa*, Luís Kandjimbo, stated that, during the 16-year existence of the organisation, the multilateral cooperation in the cultural sector had not been as productive as anticipated due to the inexistence of a structure within the Secretariat to ensure and monitor the implementation of the deliberations of the ministries of culture (ANGOP 2012). Having a strategy and an action plan as well as an organisation structure (the *Direção de Ação Cultural* and the *Pontos Focais de Cultura*) is a step forward to be able to construct and develop a multilateral cultural policy that can benefit each individual country and the collective identity represented by CPLP.

The above developments indicating support for culture within CPLP must take into account other less-supportive signs that the arts component may not be a priority for CPLP. Executive Secretary Murade Murargy, interviewed in 2015 (CEO Lusófono 2015, p. 17), stated that mobility was fundamental for the development of the community and that governments needed to develop the necessary conditions and mechanisms for the freedom of movement. The secretary said CPLP was approaching the matter by groups: i.e. business people, students, teachers and researchers were the priority group and then, if this were successful, the second group would include artists and journalists. Surely mutual understanding and circulation of information would be most advanced if priority were given to the arts and media: you would want to learn and do business with those that arouse your curiosity and interest you. Trade no longer follows the flag, as advocated by the 19th century imperialist maxim; it is more likely that it follows cultural interactions.

These contradictory signs are not surprising. CPLP countries and their agents operate in complex and dynamic environments, where conflicting priorities shape policies. Nevertheless, the recent developments have confirmed that CPLP has become an agent and a site for policy formation and coordination resulting – in the case we are concerned with – in the development, within lusofonia, of a multilateral cultural policy. The CPLP groups, created in 2005, contributing to the promotion of an (implicit) common cultural policy, are good examples of this new level of agency. However, the turning point for CPLP's cultural policy is the 2014 multilateral cultural cooperation strategy and action plan. Here the common interests in cultural policy are made explicit and developed through cultural relations/diplomacy processes of dialogue and collaboration (ministers of culture meetings, CPLP Secretariat and Focal Points for Culture) and implemented utilising (albeit meagre) common resources.

The challenges and limits of interstitial cultural policy in the CPLP

Our globalised societies need to be able to link with different levels and approaches to cultural policy. UNESCO, considering "[t]he new socio-cultural fabric of our societies combined with global interconnectedness necessitates new governance systems" (2011, p. 11) proposes a new cultural policy vision requiring "thinking outside the box, reinforcing and inventing reliable inter-ministerial approaches, and embracing the broad range of actors playing a role in taking the culture and development agenda forward" (2011, p. 20). CPLP is a site for cultural policy development, but how much that role will be developed is still uncertain and ultimately depends on the will (and resources) of the member states.

CPLP is developing (transnational, multilateral) cultural policy, within its territorial definition, insofar as its activities (including policy discourse and sponsoring of activities) influence/impact the conditions of the cultural producers and operators, the production of cultural goods and services and their distribution to users/participants, as well as the management of cultural resources (Bennett and Mercer 1998). One has observed that the activities developed are still limited and their impact probably, in many cases, negligible – but this is something that has not been ascertained in context, and one imagines that in the case of the 'less developed' member states even a small impact can be very important for development. CPLP should better articulate this connection between culture and development, which is played out at different levels: development of the cultural milieu in each member state; development of a 'lusophone' identity; cultural industries development; development of cultural diversity.

Indeed, the development of a common/multilateral cultural policy and practice poses opportunities and challenges, which recent developments are only starting to explore. For example, besides the challenge of deciding where to prioritise investment in the development of a common cultural policy, another important challenge is the articulation of this common policy with the different national cultural policies of the Member States – an area outside the scope of this chapter. Carefully curated nodes of interaction between the national and transnational spheres of cultural policy and practice can represent major opportunities by bringing added value and creating spill-over effects for cultural agents and operators.

One of these nodes could be the cultural economy. The cultural and creative industries could be a successful way to link culture and development, for the profit of states and peoples, securing the sustainable diversity of cultural expressions and enabling a recognisable role for the organisation. If, as defended by Executive Secretary Murade Murargy (Exame 2014), the organisation should focus on economic diplomacy, perhaps the focus on the creative economy is not far fetched.

The further development and recognition of a common transnational cultural policy could be seen as a sign of maturity of this community project, leaving behind years of debate of what it means to be part of *lusofonia*. And although the CPLP structure is created top-down, the author sees it as an encouragement of bottom-up initiatives, resulting in mutually structuring influences, as in a symbiotic relation (Maciel 2015, p. 388).

This chapter analysed a conceptualisation and practice of cultural policy at multilateral levels seeking to reinforce the study of cultural policy beyond the domestic realm of a state (the often default level of analysis of cultural policy research) and thus challenging methodological nationalism and also the conceptual divide between cultural diplomacy and cultural policy. The CPLP case study demonstrated that it is relevant to the understanding of contemporary cultural policy to examine units of analysis beyond the nation-state and that the concept of a transnational cultural policy bridges the concepts of cultural relations/diplomacy and foreign policy.

This chapter needs to be complemented by further research. At a general level by the examination of transnational cultural policy through multiple disciplinary analysis that include cultural diplomacy/foreign policy (and the implicit reverse: cultural diplomacy being analysed with the input of cultural policy thinking), and at a specific level, through further research on the operation of transnational levels of policy (examination of the role of particular individuals, bureaucracies and networks) and its connections with both the national level (in this case researching the links with the national cultural policies, practices and agents/operators of each CPLP member state) and other international spheres (for example regarding the adoption and transfer of meta-narratives from UNESCO).

By restricting this chapter to the analysis of the CPLP, the author missed other important strands of the construction of the lusophone community, such as the bilateral relations between the countries, the work of important organisations operating at other levels of governments (e.g. UCCLA at the local level) or the Camoes Institute at the national level. Also not covered are the important networks of cultural professionals, i.e. museum networks, and other fundamental links of civil society, such as those embodied and practiced by artists and cultural professionals: curators, writers, musicians and visual artists. The focus on CPLP, an intergovernmental institutional structure, was intended to investigate how important that structuring role is for the cultural construction of the community and its display. There is still a lot of work to be done, and thus the author is in agreement with Carlos Lopes' words written 10 years ago and still valid: "Even with buckets of friendship, the reality of the discontinuity will impose itself dramatically and with no escape. Unless one seriously invests in a set of singular factors"[4] (CPLP 2006, p. 140). The future will tell what singular factors the member states choose to develop.

In July 2016, Brazil assumed CPLP's presidency for two years, and the Brazilian minister of culture, Juca Ferreira, has already voiced his interest in increasing the organisation's activity in the area of culture, even advancing some specific projects such as a conference on Portuguese language having culture as a reference point or the potential for policy/practice transfer of the Brazilian cultural policy initiative *Pontos de Cultura* (Ministério da Cultura do Brasil, 2015). Perhaps 2016, the year the organisation commemorated 20 years, will be seen as the start of a new impetus in CPLP's multilateral cultural policy.

Notes

1 For convenience, the author refers to the text of this agreement as well as other CPLP agreements, unless otherwise stated, as published in Barreiras Duarte (2014).

2 In the Portuguese original: "*a promoção de uma política cultural comum da Comunidade*".

3 In the Portuguese original: "*A CPLP sente-se quando um grupo de cidadãos de países lusófonos encontram pontos de referência comuns. Não quando se organiza uma reunião formal de concertação político-diplomática. Para fortalecer a base do relacionamento pode-se traduzir amizade num conjunto de ações concretas. A meu ver **são sobretudo na área cultural e nas indústrias criativas que se abrem novas potencialidades**. Sem essa alavanca a Comunidade não será muito diferente de outros agrupamentos que nos lembramos apenas 'quando dá jeito'.*"

4 In the Portuguese original: "*Mesmo com carradas de amizade a realidade da descontinuidade acabará por impôr-se de forma dramática e sem hesitações. A não ser que se invista seriamente num conjunto de factores que sejam singulares*".

References

Ahearne, J. (2009) Cultural policy explicit and implicit: a distinction and some uses. *International Journal of Cultural Policy*, 15(2), 141–153.

Anderson, B. (1991) *Imagined Communities: Reflection on the Origins and Spread of Nationalism*. Revised Edition. London: Verso.

ANGOP Agencia Angola Press (2012) Responsável considera pouco produtiva cooperação multilateral cultural na CPLP – 03 Abril de 2012 15h16. Available at: www.angop.ao/angola/pt_pt/noticias/lazer-e-cultura/2012/3/14/Responsavel-considera-pouco-produtiva-cooperacao-multilateral-cultural-CPLP,adb6e718-b348-42c6-8d88-3281e26624b1.html (Accessed 20 February 2016).

Ang, I., Isar, Y.R., and Mar, P. (2015) Cultural diplomacy: beyond the national interest? *International Journal of Cultural Policy*, 21(4), 365–381. doi:10.1080/10286632.2015.1042474.

Appadurai, A. (1996) *Modernity at Large: Cultural Dimensions of Globalization.* Minneapolis, MN: University of Minnesota Press.

Arndt, R.T. (2005) *The First Resort of Kings: American Cultural Diplomacy in the Twentieth Century.* Washington, DC: Potomac Books.

Barreiras Duarte, F. (2014) *Os Acordos Internacionais da CPLP.* Lisboa: Âncora Editora.

Bell, D. and Oakley, K. (2015) *Cultural Policy.* London; New York: Routledge.

Bell, L. and Stevenson, H. (2006) *Language Policy: Process, Themes and Impact.* London: Routledge.

Bennett, T. and Mercer, C. (1998) Improving research and international cooperation for cultural policy. UNESCO. Available at: www.culturalpolicies.net/web/files/137/en/bennet-mercer.pdf (Accessed 20 February 2016).

CEO Lusófono (2015) Murade Murargy: Dar mais energia as pontes lusófonas in CEO Lusófono: Decisores da Lusofonia em Diálogo para a Ação, N.61, Abr/Mai/Jun 2015, pp. 14–18.

Chacon, V. (2002) *O Futuro Político da Lusofonia.* Lisbon: Verbo.

Chernillo, D. (2006) Social theory's methodological nationalism: myth and reality. *European Journal of social Theory*, 9(1), 5–22.

CPLP (1996) Declaração Constitutiva da CPLP. Available at: www.cplp.org/Files/Filer/Documentos%20Essenciais/DeclaraoConstitutivaCPLP.pdf (Accessed 12 January 2016).

CPLP (2006) Pensar, comunicar, actuar em língua portuguesa: 10 anos da CPLP. Comunidade dos Países de Língua Portuguesa.

CPLP (2008) Construindo a Comunidade: 12 Anos de Vitalidade e Dinamismo. Comunidade dos Países de Língua Portuguesa.

CPLP (2009) XIV Reunião Ordinária do Conselho de Ministros da CPLP, Cidade da Praia, 20 de julho de 2009: Resolução sobre a "Cooperação na CPLP-Uma visão Estratégica de Cooperação pós Bissau". Available at: www.cplp.org (Accessed 12 January 2016).

CPLP (2014a) Declaração de Maputo. Declaração Final da IX Reunião de Ministros da Cultura da Comunidade dos Países de Língua Portuguesa (CPLP), na cidade de Maputo, Moçambique, nos dias 10 e 11 de Abril de 2014. Available at: www.cplp.org/Files/Billeder/cplp/Declarao-Final-IX-Reunio-CPLP.pdf (Accessed 12 January 2016).

CPLP (2014b) Os Desafios do Futuro: 18 Anos CPLP. Comunidade dos Países de Língua Portuguesa.

CPLP (2014c) Plano Estratégico de Cooperação Cultural Multilateral da CPLP e respetivo Plano de Ação (2014–2020), 11 de Abril de 2014. (VIII Reunião de Ministros da Cultura da CPLP, 2 e 3 de abril de 2012, e Declaração de Maputo, IX Conferencia de Chefes de Estado e de Governo da CPLP, 20 de Julho de 2012).

CPLP (2014d) Nota Informativa: CPLP reforça cooperação na Cultura. Available at: www.cplp.org/id-4447.aspx?Action=1&NewsId=3425&M=NewsV2&PID=10872 (Accessed 12 January 2016).

CPLP (2014e) XIXa Reuniao do Conselho de Ministros – Dili, Timor-Leste, 22 de Julho de 2014 link entitled Resolução sobre a Cultura na Agenda para o Desenvolvimento Pós 2015. Available at: www.cplp.org/id-4447.aspx?Action=1&NewsId=3463&M=NewsV2&PID=10872 (Accessed 12 January 2016).

Cristovão, F. (2008) *Da Lusitanidade à Lusofonia.* Coimbra: Almedina.

DeVereaux, C. and Griffin, M. (2006) International, global, transnational: Just a matter of words? In Eurozine, published 11 October 2006. The article was originally presented in Vienna at the 4th International Conference on Cultural Policy Research, iccpr 2006. Available at www.eurozine.com/articles/2006-10-11-devereauxgriffin-en.html.

Exame (2014) CPLP: Um Sonho Sempre Adiado in Revista Exame, N.20, March 2014, Mozambique Edition, pp. 20–30.

Figueira, C. (2013) *Languages at War: External Language Spread Policies in Lusophone Africa: Mozambique and Guinea-Bissau at the Turn of the 21st Century.* Frankfurt am Main: Peter Lang. ISBN: 978-3-631-64436-2 hb.

Goff, P.M. (2013) *Cultural Diplomacy. The Oxford Handbook of Modern Diplomacy.* Oxford, UK: Oxford University Press, pp. 419–435.

Governo de Portugal (2015) Programa do XXI Governo de Portugal 2015–2019. Available at www. portugal.gov.pt/media/18268168/programa-do-xxi-governo.pdf (Accessed 12 January 2016).

Keohane, R.O. (1984) *After Hegemony: Cooperation and Discord in the World Political Economy*. Princeton, NJ: Princeton University Press.

Lourenço, E. (1999) *A Nau de Ícaro e Imagem e Miragem da Lusofonia*. Lisboa: Gradiva.

Maciel, C. (2015) *A Construção da Comunidade Lusófona a partir do antigo centro: Micro-comunidades e praticas da lusofonia*. Lisbon: Camões – Instituto da Cooperação e da Língua.

MacNeill, K. and Reynolds, S. (2013) Imagining transnational cultural policy. *Asia Pacific Journal of Arts and Cultural Management*, 10(1), 15–24.

Matarasso, F. and Landry, C. (1999) *Balancing Act: Twenty-One Strategic Dilemmas in Cultural Policy*. Strasbourg: Council of Europe.

Ministério da Cultura do Brasil (2015) Brasil e CPLP vão intensificar cooperação na área da cultura – Notícias em destaque 7.7.2015 18:38. Available at: www.cultura.gov.br/noticias-destaques/-/asset_publisher/OiKX3xlR9iTn/content/brasil-e-cplp-vao-intensificar-cooperacao-na-area-de-cultura/10883 (Accessed 20 February 2016).

Mitchell, J.M. (1986) *International Cultural Relations*. London: Allen and Unwin.

Nye, J.S. (2004) *Soft Power: The Means to Success in World Politics*. New York: Public Affairs.

Pinto, J.F. (2009) *Estrategias da ou para a Lusofonia: O Futuro da Lingua Portuguesa*. Lisbon: Prefacio.

Santos, L.A. (2003) Portugal and the CPLP: heightened expectations, unfounded disillusions. Universidade do Minho. Available at: http://repositorium.sdum.uminho.pt/bitstream/1822/3079/1/lantos_CPLP_2003.pdf (Accessed 12 January 2016).

Secretariado Executivo da CPLP (2014a) Documento de Projeto: Capital da Cultura da CPLP, proposto pela Direção para Ação Cultural e Língua Portuguesa (Cultura) da CPLP em 18/11/2014. Lisbon: CPLP.

Secretariado Executivo da CPLP (2014b) Documento de Projeto: Estudo Comparado da Legislação dos Países de Língua Portuguesa sobre Direitos Autorais e Direitos Conexos, proposto pela Direção para Ação Cultural e Língua Portuguesa (Cultura) da CPLP em 18/11/2014. Lisbon: CPLP.

Secretariado Executivo da CPLP (2014c) Documento de Projeto: Festival da Canção Infantil da CPLP, proposto pela Direção para Ação Cultural e Língua Portuguesa (Cultura) da CPLP em 18/11/2014. Lisbon: CPLP.

Secretariado Executivo da CPLP (2014d) Documento de Projeto: II Feira do Livro da CPLP, proposto pela Direção para Ação Cultural e Língua Portuguesa (Cultura) da CPLP em 18/11/2014. Lisbon: CPLP.

Secretariado Executivo da CPLP (2014e) Documento de Projeto: Seminário sobre Politicas Culturais e Indústrias Criativas da CPLP destinado a Altos Quadros ao Nível Institucional e Estratégico, proposto pela Direção para Ação Cultural e Língua Portuguesa (Cultura) da CPLP em 18/11/2014. Lisbon: CPLP.

Tardif, J. (2004) Globalization and Culture. Permanent Forum on Cultural Pluralism. Available at: www.other-news.info/2004/12/globalization-and-culture/ (Accessed 12 January 2016).

UNESCO (2011) *A New Cultural Policy Agenda for Development and Mutual Understanding: Key Arguments for a Strong Commitment to Cultural Diversity and Intercultural Dialogue*. Paris: UNESCO.

Vieira, V. (2015) Personal Interview. Senior Official at Direção para Ação Cultural e Língua Portuguesa, CPLP, Lisbon, August 2015.

Weiβ, J. and Schwietring, T. (2006) The Power of Language: A Philosophical-Sociological Reflection. Available at: www.goethe.de/lhr/prj/mac/msp/en1253450.htm (Accessed 12 January 2016).

10

Cultural governance and cultural policy

Hegemonic myth and political logics

Jeremy Valentine

To govern, one could say, is to be condemned to seek an authority for one's authority.

(Rose, 1999: 27)

Introduction: 'Welcome aboard the Black Pearl, Miss Turner'

The phrase 'cultural governance' does not enjoy a rigid designation. In semiotic terms, it is a syntagm that comprehends a variety of ways in and through which the paradigms of culture and governance can be combined. Culture is notoriously ambivalent. It can mean both sensation and meaning, experience or symbol, a way of life or its artefacts. Governance appears to be relatively straightforward. It means the conduct or process of governing, in the sense of ordering, commanding or directing. So cultural governance can mean the conduct or process of governing in or by culture, and it can also mean the cultural characteristics of governance or an aspect of governance particularly concerned with culture. Those and other possible combinations can overlap, and any strict denotation is always fixed within specific pragmatic contexts. Even then, it is not possible to completely eliminate all residual connotations through action alone. A context is never completely closed. So instead of attempting to list all possible uses of the phrase, this chapter will attempt to demonstrate that cultural governance has a relatively fixed and determined value as a component of hegemonic discourse in a specific historical conjuncture roughly co-extensive with the emergence of neoliberalism in the 1980s and its consolidation and dominance in post-industrial capitalist social formations since the 1990s. Despite its economic connotations, neoliberalism is not reducible to an economic base. It is primarily a political project seeking to extract value from economic processes by acting on political systems and structures to transform them to its advantage. Part of that hegemonic project is the extension of economic processes insofar as they are reducible to market institutions. In that way value becomes calculable, but neoliberalism is not simply a matter of establishing market mechanisms. It is also a matter of protecting itself from their negative effects. Neoliberalism is rule through rather than by markets. In economic terms, neoliberalism is most accurately categorised as a rentier regime as it is not value creating because it relies on extra-economic political power. One only has to reflect on the growth of bureaucracy and administration to grasp that point. The argument of this chapter is that contemporary cultural policy emerges from that context. It does not resolve the ambivalence of culture but mobilises it.

The argument acknowledges the extensive theoretically and methodologically diverse field of research that demonstrates some of the relations between culture, both as way of life and artefact, and neoliberalism. These include things like attempts to shape subjectivity in order to comply with codes of strategic personal responsibility, the normalisation of precarity, the instrumentalisation of culture as a self-policing solution to problems of social cohesion and the promotion of intellectual property monopolies as a means to deflect chronic problems of accumulation in economic formations that remain tied to capitalism. This chapter is positioned in relation to that research by focussing on culture in the context of the relation between governance and neoliberalism. It does that in order to show that the neoliberal determination of governance is not exactly straightforward. It is ambiguous because it means both the process of governing and action on that process. In that respect, the ambiguity of governance acquires something like the Barthesian status of myth (Barthes, 1973). In semiotic terms, the general signifier 'governance' is transferred from its conventional signified to become at the same time a signified within a particular mode of power that is characterised by acting on governance in order to make that which is to be governed governable. The additional, particular sense, is parasitic on a prior general sense such that the latter appears as an alibi for the former and the power of governance is naturalised. Consequently, as Enroth points out in a similar Barthesian observation on governance, reality is emptied of history and filled with nature, the way things are independently of human action (2013: 69). The mythological sense has enabled governance to become a hegemonic sense-making project. According to Davies (2011), 'governance' has become hegemonic because of the persistence of the general meaning of the term through which power hierarchies persist in the structures represented as unmotivated processes to erase conflicts and contestations. Neoliberal cultural policy is mobilised by the ambiguity of governance.

The myth of governance does not just make sense of things. It changes the relations between things that are made sense of, not least with respect to structures of political power in capitalist post-industrial state formations. Thus, Jessop goes so far as to reformulate Gramsci's notion of the integral state defined as 'political society + civil society' in terms of 'government + governance in the shadow of hierarchy' (2015: 480) where 'shadow' refers to the concealment of power. However, concealment does not entail elimination. Governance creates particular political logics of command, obedience, contestation and subversion as a consequence that stems from its ambiguity. As Best points out, the ambiguity of governance is an 'interpretive lubricant in an uncertain world' (2012: 101). Ambiguity creates the slack in the system in which a balance between coercion and consent can be established. At the same time, it prevents the constitution of governance as an antagonistic frontier on the old power bloc versus the people model. The point of the myth of governance is the prevention of a War of Manoeuvre and the maintenance of conflicts as multiple Wars of Position. The argument of this chapter is that insofar as governance as myth is hegemonic, it conditions power relations and the cultural policy that is formed within them and its actions on culture in whatever sense. That is to say, cultural policy is agnostic with regard to the ambivalence of culture, which in many cases is a resource. In that respect, it's useful to recall Hall's observation of the emergence of 'governing by culture' (1997: 231) which became possible on the basis that as a descriptive category culture had expanded beyond a narrowly conceived cultural sphere to become a terrain on which to act. Its political significance could no longer be reduced to an opposition between domination and resistance, and its authority, or belief in it, had evaporated (Valentine, 2002). However the significance of culture is measured its political conditions and its existence as an object of policy are determined by the political logics of governance. Cultural policy is action on the governance of culture.

An example from a famous scene within a justifiably popular film might serve to illustrate how power operates within neoliberal governance. It occurs in Walt Disney Pictures' 2003 blockbuster comedy 'Pirates of the Caribbean: The Curse of The Black Pearl' when, without simplifying the complexities of the plot too much, Elizabeth Swann, daughter of Weatherby Swann, the governor of the Caribbean island of Port Royal, is captured by Pirate Captain Barbossa of the Black Pearl, which has besieged the island in search of a gold medallion that will lift a curse on the ship and its crew. To deceive Barbossa about her true identity in order to increase her chances of escape, Elizabeth gives her family name as Turner, which happens to be the surname of Will, a young blacksmith's apprentice whom she had encountered as a survivor floating amongst the wreckage of a shipwreck rescued by the HMS *Dauntless*, the ship on which she and her father had travelled to arrive at the island eight years earlier when she was 12 years old. In order to obtain her release, Elizabeth appeals to the Pirate's code, which she assumes governs Barbossa's conduct, in order to constrain his actions by the force of normative consistency. In this brief exchange, the presuppositions of Elizabeth's tactic are erased by Barbossa:

ELIZABETH: Wait! You have to take me to shore. According to the Code of the Order of the Brethren...
BARBOSSA: First, your return to shore was not part of our negotiations nor our agreement so I must do nothing. And secondly, you must be a pirate for the pirate's code to apply and you're not. And thirdly, the code is more what you'd call "guidelines" than actual rules. Welcome aboard the Black Pearl, Miss Turner.

(Pirates of the Caribbean: The Curse of The Black Pearl: 2003)

Pirates of the Caribbean probably does not have the direct ideological-critical power of the Bill and Ted and Wayne's World films' lampoons of the hegemonic Total Quality Management notion of 'excellence' in the late 1980s/early 1990s. Nevertheless, the brief dialogue neatly condenses a movement through three main types of rule and their corresponding forms of organisation: contract, solidarity and governance, which in this scene trumps and appears through the reference to 'guidelines'. The significance of the notion of 'guidelines' is explained by Brown's recent critique of governance as the dominant neoliberal political rationality in which: 'Centralized authority, law, policing, rules and quotas are replaced by networked, team-based, practice-oriented techniques emphasizing incentivization, guidelines, and benchmarks' (2015: 34). For Brown the emergence of governance is decisive for understanding the contemporary exercise of power as it has 'become neoliberalism's primary administrative form, the political modality through which it creates environments, structures constraints and incentives, and hence conducts subjects' (122). Although the substitution may not be as complete and uniform as Brown suggests, 'guidelines' are a ubiquitous component of governance and condense normative values and material practices of rule while appearing unmotivated and allowing for the flexibility of self-determined action.

For Barbossa, the advantage of 'guidelines' is that they are vague, indeterminate and elastic. Their binding and obligatory force is temporary and derives from an ability to interpret them within a strategic and pragmatic power relation, which, in this context, is asymmetrical to Barbossa's advantage. At the same time, 'guidelines' are flexible enough to persist through any possible reversal of power. Several comic moments in the film feature the pirates trying to interpret the code that they presume governs their own actions. 'Guidelines' are not opposed as they are too indefinite to target. Instead, they are continually revised to take account of the situation in which they are applied. They thus constitute a ground of consensus that has become hegemonic within neoliberalism. The consensual basis of 'guidelines' allows social agents to avoid being governed by strict rules, even, and especially, when those social agents are in positions of governing. Hence, governance conditions a political logic of flexible or 'pop-up' sovereignty where advantage is obtained by the capacity to limit the range of possible contextual interpretations. In that sense the political logic of neoliberal governance operates in the undecidable gap between a rule and its application, which Wittgenstein opened in Philosophical Investigations: 'This was our paradox: no course of action could be determined by a rule, because any course of action can be made out to accord with the rule'. Consequently, a course of action is governed not by a rule but by the context of action, which is never completely closed. If necessary, it can be 'made out to accord with the rule' afterwards.

To establish the context of cultural policy, the chapter begins with an account of the emergence and consolidation of the discourse of governance. To avoid any misunderstanding, it is important to emphasise that discourse is not just a matter of organised communication or meaning. It is also the context wherein the communication makes sense and the actions are consistent with it, which is in no sense guaranteed. If it were, it wouldn't be political. It would be a fantasy of rational technocratic administration. On that basis, the chapter will attempt to explain the discourse of governance as a hegemonic project (which does not entail that it is successful). From that the chapter discusses how cultural policy emerges from governance and its characteristic political logics have become codified, which is followed by a discussion of some examples drawn from recent research. The chapter concludes with some brief remarks about future problems that research on cultural governance may encounter.

Governance as hegemonic discourse

Brown's critique of governance is based on the claim that it depoliticises through the erasure of agency and its replacement with processes as a consequence of what Lemke refers to as 'the eclipse or erosion of state sovereignty' (124: Lemke, 2007: no page reference given). However, it would be more accurate to say that through governance as myth the political is displaced. This is illustrated by Offe's irritated critique of governance and in particular its 'inherent vagueness' (2009). For Offe governance is an 'empty signifier' that oscillates between an institutional sense of a structure of rules, the general sense, and a political sense of steering, the particular sense. The force of the general sense occludes the particular such that, as Offe observes, the subjectless character of governance as structure of rules makes steering look like price formation in markets. It is as if 'something happens, but nobody has done it and would thus be responsible for the result' (550). The notion of subjectless action is reinforced by the common political science technocratic fantasy definition of governance as 'self-organizing, interorganizational networks' (Rhodes, 1996: 660). But the subject does not disappear. Collective action is displaced through the weakening of binding decisions in order to encourage 'enlightened self-binding' (Offe: 559), and principal-agent relations become political outcomes rather than causes. To eliminate that sort of thing Offe proposes that 'a boundary must be set around the core sphere of state institutions, for which one should retain the concept of *government*' (552) by eliminating 'the unresolved polysemy of the concept' (557). Doing so would draw a clear distinction between state and civil society in order to reinscribe an old school functional structure of modern political authority within which political actors would compete over the possession of power and the distribution of rights, responsibilities and resources, either democratically or by other means.

Whether or not Offe's proposals for disambiguation are realistic, practical or even desirable, this chapter takes a different approach. The discourse of 'governance' may be 'gibberish', in Brown's judgement, (140) but nevertheless its ambiguity works as a hegemonic sense-making activity and produces specific political logics. The focus is on the conditions in which the discourse is formed and the characteristics that enable its hegemonic project. Governance emerges in the context of the crisis of capitalist social democracies in which the structure of governing had, for various reasons, become problematic. In the early 1970s political scientists explained this phenomenon through notions such as 'the crisis of governability', the 'fiscal crisis of the state' and 'legitimation crisis'. Phenomena like general irreverence, the popular rejection of deference, the decline of assumptions about the authority and value of a unified culture and punk in general were represented as symptoms of decline in media and elite discourses. In fact these developments are more accurately understood as consequences of the success of the post WWII consensus, and in particular the rise of the citizen as consumer who placed demands on the state that created problems of overload that could not be solved without unpopular and expensive state expansion. Phenomena like that became understood in terms of the 'contradictions of the welfare state' (Offe, 1984). As well as such endogenous shocks, Western European and North American polities were increasingly confronted with exogenous unpredictability and contingency beyond their control, not least with respect to world commodity prices and the development of industrial productive capacity in the non-West, which served to 'disorganise capitalism' (Lash and Urry, 1987).

In response to those circumstances states have in general 'hollowed out' and 'reinvented' themselves as a consequence of their reduced capacity to act within environments over which they have decreasing control as the increased cost of doing so is prohibitive, both financially, as no one wants to pay for it, and politically, as the presence of state intervention serves to create a target at which opponents can aim. In other words, hierarchical structures of modern political authority, where linear command corresponds to serial cause, can no longer cope with the stress of governing contingency. At best, governments remain legitimate only insofar as they offer citizen-subjects the possibility of acting on other citizen-subjects to their comparative advantage. Authority and decision making are pushed up to para and international organisations, some formal and accountable, others not so much, which can take the flak for unpopular decisions precisely because of their distance, and pushed down to the local and molecular organisations of pressure groups, special interest groups and communities in general, which become contained by the conflicting pressures of maintaining authentic popular support and conforming to rules in order to gain resource. Hence, states reconfigure the vertical and horizontal distribution of power as both a resource and an object of action. Governance is a reflexive process that seeks to maintain the conduct of governing under conditions in which the governability of that which is to be governed is no longer taken for granted. So governance is about acting on governing so that government can continue.

These developments have significant practical consequences. Firstly, the creation of quasi-markets by states in order to distance themselves from welfare provision by making users responsible for it, reconfigured as consumers within the neoliberal project of capital. Here states govern through regulation, strategically limiting or expanding the effects of markets, which in turn becomes the object of political gaming. Secondly, the networkification of political society in order to establish lines of inclusion and exclusion, which build consensus through the figure of the 'stakeholder' and other weasel word terms developed within neoliberal governance. These activities are supported by actions such as the agen-tification of state administration, for example through the UK government's New Public Management programmes introduced in the 1980s to incentivise innovation through 'policy entrepreneurs' who would introduce market efficiencies (Clarke and Newman, 1997; Hood and Dixon, 2015; O'Brien, 2014). More generally, political action becomes an epistemolog-ical tactic of 'problematisation', in Foucault's sense, through which something enters into 'the play of true and false' and becomes an object for thought and action (Foucault, 1997). The main mechanism for doing that is the rather banal practice of counting things or, more specifically, making things countable and thus the invention of procedures and processes to do that, or 'audit' (Power, 1997; Valentine 2004). By making things and actions auditable they become organisable and controllable. Subjects are included on the condition that they act as if they are assets or resources, 'human capital', and thus prepared to bear risk and re-sponsibility for their actions. Such a strategy incentivises subjects to conform to courses of action that are likely to create least risk and cost to themselves.

However, this is not a straightforward matter of calculation because cost and risk are not necessarily known and change in relation to the objectification of the subject. Consequently, in a cruel irony, subjection is not simply a matter of obedience or discipline. Rather, subjection entails what Deleuze called 'modulation' with respect to changing regulatory codes (1995). Deleuze's observation is part of a broader argument about the decline of what Foucault had called 'disciplinary societies'. For Deleuze, these no longer work in the context of 'a general breakdown of all sites of confinement – prisons, hospi-tals, factories, schools, the family' (1995: 178). State agency has become characterised by continual 'reform' such that nothing is ever finished. Control is exercised through admin-istration and their allies in management and marketing, 'the arrogant breed who are our masters' (181). Agamben, in a lecture at the Nicos Poulantzas Institute in Athens in 2013, developed the political consequences of Deleuze's observations through improvising on his own Schimittian notion of the 'state of exception'. For Agamben 'destituent power' explains the character of contemporary state agency as it follows the embryonic political logic of Quesnay's proposition that: 'Since governing the causes is difficult and expensive, it is more safe and useful to try and govern the effects'. In this way, the distinction between the rule and the exception is weakened through flexible casuistry, which in turn becomes the vehicle of internal and external power struggles and a means for expanding or con-tracting the scope of policies.

Governance discourse is a way of making sense of these conditions in order to act on them. Although there is probably no single point of origin, the emergence of its mythic sense can be traced in its development by institutions and organisations that responded to the situation that had emerged in the 1970s. One source is private sector corporate reform in the USA. The notion of 'corporate governance', which emerged in conjunction with similar phrases such as 'corporate social responsibility', tried to do two things: solve corpo-rate legitimacy problems and maintain autonomy through self-monitoring against juridical and media attacks from the non-corporate sector. These projects were given an intellectual framework by such remarkably influential theoretical models as Williamson's Transaction Cost Analysis (TCA), which following institutional economics and the Coaseian theory of the firm, defines governance in the general sense of 'the institutional framework within which the integrity of a transaction is decided' (Williamson, 1979: 238) and 'the institutional matrix within which transactions are negotiated and executed' (239), but which, at the same time, identifies governance in the particular sense as an object of action with the observation that: 'Governance structures which attenuate opportunism and otherwise infuse confidence are evidently needed' (242). Williamson's theory is grounded in a rational functionalist approach that aims to minimise transaction costs through standardisation and the elimination of idiosyncrasy. However, the context in which it was taken up was very different, as the weakness of authority structures encouraged idiosyncrasy and difference. Mediated by management consultants and lobbyists through 'regulatory capture' TCA and similar ideas were adopted by business facing states through 're-inventing government' projects in the 1980s that allowed their formation as solutions to problems of rule in post-disciplinary societies (e.g. Osborne and Gaebler, 1992). Governance obtained a wider dominium than nation-states when, possibly as early as 1989, it was adopted by the World Bank through the development of Worldwide Governance Indicators in order to manage its relations with national economies in the non-West and subsequently the West (Best, 2012; Buduru and Pal, 2010; Offe, 2009). Thus, governance exercises leadership by hegemonising institutions in order to transform them. The institutions remain to all outward appearances the same. As even the anarcho-situationist graffitism of The Invisible Committee recognises, the targets of change are the infrastructures where power is now located (2015: 83).

Not only does governance make sense, governance also acts on sense-making itself. A peculiarity of governance discourse is that it develops a particular vocabulary, grammar and syntax in which subjectless action becomes imaginable. In addition to guidelines, as Eagleton–Pierce points out, governance is part of a particular vocabulary and conceptual organising grid that makes sense in relation to other terms such as 'partnership', 'empowerment' and 'network' (2014: 10). Best (2012) draws attention to the circulation of notions such as 'best practice', which require judgements to verify conformity that can only be established in opposition to worst practice. At the same time, governance discourse develops an enunciative logic that Moretti and Pestre demonstrate through a statistical analysis of a corpus of World Bank documents (2015). Words are modulated syntactically and grammatically in order to erase the World Bank's representation of itself and its world as a linear and causal sequence of knowledge, agents, actions, procedures, objects, facts and effects linked by a temporal structure of verbs. The main linguistic mechanism that achieves this is nominalisation, the derivation of abstract nouns from verbs. Thus, for example, co-operating, which implies the existence of agents who co-operate, is replaced by cooperation, in which agents are subject to an abstract process in which temporality is abolished and no one is responsible. Because nominalisations appear to lack agency in order to appear as a process that conditions action they are difficult to oppose, and they are equally difficult to define as they are trapped in the circle of gerundification, which functions to leave an action's completion undefined and suspended in a continuous progression without actual movement. Sequence is replaced by listing, a succession of 'ands' or even, one might add, bullet points and other para-discursive marks. In this way governance discourse transcends all determinants of place and time, and to prove it Moretti and Pestre provide a graph that shows a 50% reduction in temporal adverbs between 1948 and 2008 in World Bank documents. Even though Bankspeak is a 'tortuous form of expression' (Moretti and Pestre, 2015: 96) it is always good, phrased as euphoric, progressive, compassionate and empathetic and achieved through dialogue and partnership. Importantly, as Mulderrig points out in a detailed analysis of a corpus of UK education policy documents circulated during the period of the New Labour government, the grammar of governance discourse presupposes the conformity of actors rather than seeking to secure their volition (2011). Obedience is simply unmarked. In this way actions are 'enabled', autonomy is 'regulated', compliance is 'ensured' and obligation and responsibility are distributed.

The cultural governance imaginary

In general, the initial motivations that established relations between culture and governance understood culture in an anthropological 'way of life' sense and aimed to unify it as a solution to a situation that Habermas recognised with the proposition that: 'Modern societies no longer have at their disposal an authoritative center for self-reflection and steering' (1987: 553). Even though Habermas's rational-functionalist notion of an absent centre begs the question of its former presence, in conditions in which 'binding decisions' don't really bind the anthropological properties of culture become thinkable as a solution to governing. In part, this is because given modern individual freedom 'regulatory norms cannot motivate behaviour that depends on personal initiative, innovation and positive engagement' (Mayntz, 1994: 14). It is on that basis that action on subjectivity through culture as a form of governing appears as a solution. This approach is explicit in some of the more ham-fisted instrumental proposals for scaling up corporate 'cultural change' projects to the level of state and nation, for example, 6's suggestion that the state should act to provide a coherent framework of meanings in which social relations can be based making it possible for a society to organise itself through the shared understandings of a common culture. A reinvented government 'must be about nothing less than changing the whole culture' (1997, 283). Of course, such a suggestion presupposes the existence of what it is designed to remedy, namely, the absence of a centred cultural authority and the presence of a shared culture, let alone a whole one. Nevertheless, instrumental approaches to the alleged problems of 'social cohesion' do trickle down into projects for managing the problems of so-called multiculturalism.

A similar but more sophisticated rational-functionalist approach understands cultural governance as the outcome of the functional differentiation of the reflexive complexity of modern liberal democratic political systems. For Bang, cultural governance is the solution to the problem of the absence of command and control for commanders and controllers to adopt (2004). On this basis, leaders and managers seek to incorporate as many different types of actor into the 'systematic articulation, organizing, programming and implementing of collective decisions and actions'. Expert systems 'must invent new modes of indirect steering for empowering their members and environments and in such a way that they freely, willingly and self-reflexively can help them solve their problems and deliver desired outcomes in an effective manner'. This is because systems cannot afford to seal themselves off from the 'conventional practices of its ordinary members or environments' (165). In this way citizens are responsibilised and compelled to recognise 'that in an authority relationship, if citizens fall into confusion and disorder, then not only the political system but also the whole of society will do so as well' (186). Obviously, such a technocratic approach relies on the existence of strong communitarian bonds through which the threat of shaming can be implemented, and Bang admits that this instrumental and programmed approach compromises citizen capacity for autonomous reason. Bang developed this approach out of ethnographic work on Danish local government initiatives to include citizens in the process of governing as, effectively, self-governing. As it turned out, the sorts of re-structuring cultural governance required were rejected by Danish citizens. Nevertheless, Bang makes explicit some of the assumptions of commanders and controllers in search of a disinterested rational function to legitimate their position.

A more amusing interpretation of governance rejects rational-functionalism in favour of the wisdom of the organic unity of tradition inscribed in the specific culture of the UK state. Jointly and separately, the work of Bevir and Rhodes has established this approach (e.g. Bevir and Rhodes, 2005). The state is a cultural entity that 'consists of all kinds of practices from everyday polite exchanges over cups of tea, through symbolic displays of authority and status, to decisions about policy and its implementation. Yet, each of these practices is anything but monolithic. Polite exchanges over tea do not have a fixed form' (Bevir, 2011: 463) or, one may suppose, impolite exchanges. Governance works through ad hoc networks and muddled interactions with all sorts of individuals and organisations inside and outside the state as formally understood, and in a pragmatic higgledy-piggledy way without underlying laws and overarching steering institutions. Political actors are primarily interpreters, and governance is the process of working out shared meanings, often through conflict, which then become sedimented as common sense narratives. Everything is network, even markets and hierarchies, which evolves out of inherited historical traditions, which in turn explain actions and the formations of interests. Bevir and Rhodes are notoriously coy about the exercise of power. Instead, politics is about dealing with difficulties and dilemmas, in order to preserve business as usual. However, the nodding and winking system of rule is not impervious to exogenous shocks. For reasons that are never entirely clear, Bevir admits that 'a managerial narrative has clearly made headway in recent years' (438), which emerged from neoliberal reforms of the 1980s such as New Public Management. This development is explained through a disavowal in which the strategic emphasis on networks as a means of acting on governance is reconciled with governance as tradition such that 'community groups, private firms and new governmental agencies all had to be integrated into a coherent policy process. The result was the rise of all kinds of networks and partnerships based on common agendas' (467). In fact, Bevir's disavowal occludes a transition from one myth of governance, depicted in the famous warm and fuzzy BBC TV satirical situation comedies 'Yes, Minister' and 'Yes, Prime Minister' of the 1980s, to another depicted by the equally famous cold and prickly 2005–2012 BBC TV satirical situation comedy omnishambles 'The Thick of It' and spin-off film 'In The Loop'. Through that shift the relation between cultural governance and cultural policy emerges and becomes more clearly defined through an agnostic approach to the ambivalence of culture, or culture in whatever sense.

A good account of this process is Barnett's analysis of the development of cultural policy in The European Union (2001). One thing that the EU has never managed to achieve is cultural unity and identity despite the efforts of its elites to create a common reference point in Europe's cultural heritage as a basis for affective legitimacy and despite the notoriously fragmented or 'multi-level' character of EU governance across which cultural policy is distributed and within which policy actors compete.[1] In addition to the democratic deficit, one of the major obstacles to such a task remains the persistent popularity of American entertainment and its market logic. Such was the anxiety provoked by popular culture that dirigiste elite responses developed as an official form of Cultural Action, which was consolidated in the formal recognition of culture in the 1992 Treaty of the European Union. Barnett shows that despite an elite obsession with elite culture, the development of culture as an object that could be formed transformed its ontological status from symbol to practice of governing via its passage through EU governance processes. Culture is transformed from an anthropological symbolic object of ritual and ceremony to a governable object of policy. According to Barnett, the vehicle for that process is the development of an 'ethic of participation', designed to encourage active citizenship contributions to cultural development. However, the presupposition of a common unified culture is minimised in favour of the cultivation of affective participation or 'engagement' that legitimates governance pragmatically. Culture is no longer used as a means to establish a common European identity. Rather, it becomes a means by which to legitimise EU policies. In that respect Barnett confirms the relevance, if perhaps not the intent, of Bennett's Foucauldian approach that displaced questions of the essence of culture in favour of questions of its effects (Barnett, 2001: 27; Bennett, 1992). EU policy governmentalizes culture in order to shape 'discrete repertoires of conduct' in both cultural and non-cultural policy domains.

Barnett observes that 'the Commission has found a means by which to reconcile the discursive tensions between culture and economy in the field of cultural action in a way that respects the intrinsic qualities of 'the cultural' while enabling their instrumental deployment in the service of economic and political imperatives of integration' (28). Culture becomes whatever, for example through the weakening of the distinction between cultural action as a contribution to a European cultural identity and the legal and economic regulation of audio-visual policy, or as a means to encourage the acquisition of personal skills such as flexibility and self-confidence, as well as skills of participation (putting aside the question of how such attributes became categorised as skills). The limits of the uses of culture are set by the capacity to invent extensions of its ambivalence. At the same time, political logics emerge from the ambiguity of governance. Networks of interest-group collective actors develop and become attached to cultural policy at vertical and horizontal levels of governance and as different degrees of subsidiarity develop. The ambivalence of culture is deployed instrumentally to mark out territory within administrator-stakeholder networks from which to obtain and deploy position within the policy process. This development in turn stimulates a politics of interpretation with respect to definitions of culture and limits to legitimate action and with respect to competing policy agendas such as economics, law and welfare. Needless to say, all that stimulates free-riding 'gravy train' phenomena through the invention of bureaucratic devices such as committees, working groups and initiatives organised around the essentially conflicting demands of harmonisation and diversity that monitor, measure and evaluate culture to tie subjective will to objective effects in order to calibrate 'the transformation of the disposition of citizens in line with multiple objectives' (31). Insofar as these objectives change, this process and the strategies of objectification that support it are in principle unlimited. The tension between the transformative and the expressive cultural imaginaries is exploited in order to establish 'legitimate claims over cultural policy functions' where 'success depends upon finessing a complex set of questions regarding authority and accountability; questions of who represents diversity, when this has been primarily defined in terms of bounded communities bought together in forms of dialogue and exchange, and questions of who defines the core values around which diversity should be encouraged to flourish' (32).

In many respects the developments Barnett analyses are part of a wider, global development of the political logics of cultural policy within the hegemonic myth of governance characterised by the emergence of a material and subjective infrastructure that Yudice describes as 'an enormous network of arts administrators who mediate between funding sources and artists and/or communities. Like their counterparts in the university and business world, they must produce and distribute the producers of art and culture, who in turn deliver communities or consumers' (2003: 13). Yudice's critique is aimed at the 'NGO-fication' of cultural policy and the emergence of a 'UNESCO-racy'. In turn, these groups support, sponsor and fund numerous projects and firms, both subsidised and for profit, to support their activities, creating a vast consultocracy. On the one hand, outsourcing this work to external contractors allows their conclusions, often in the form of evaluations, to appear objective and disinterested. On the other, many of the subjects overlap in their group memberships, which are further complicated by the circulation and exchange of knowledge and people through close and often exclusive networks. As Prince has shown, through a study of UK DCMS and its regional networks, the consultocracy does not simply record but actively intervenes (2013, 2015). One of Prince's key points is that such interventions are mobilised through social relations and in doing so participate in the power games that in turn structure cultural policy. Hence, experts subject themselves to governance requirements in order to obtain recognition and accreditation, yet at the same time ironise those requirements in order to maintain subjective agency. The political logics of this process can be seen in the following examples, which illuminate attempts at cross-national and regional policy transfer.

Political logics of cultural policy

It would be inaccurate to conclude that cultural governance is a monolithic discourse that is simply 'rolled out', to use a teeth-grinding phrase loved by UK manager administrators in order to occult their own subjectivity, into an eternal future 'going forward', to use another. If the sense-making discourse of cultural governance is understood as a way of hegemonically coding phenomena, it does not follow that it is guaranteed simply by following and repeating its rules of enunciation. Instead, the codes through which cultural governance makes sense become the objects of political action, usually through interpretation in order to gain resource and occasionally through opposition in order to maintain or gain power. One code, common in governance discourse as Best (2012) pointed out, is the notion of 'best practice', which motivates shortening implementation chains through imitation, repetition and reproduction. If something is badged as 'best' then it stands a chance of being copied because it requires less effort and less risk because responsibility can be deflected to pre-constructed criteria, especially if these are not explicitly stated. In that way idiosyncrasy is marginalised, costs are reduced and action can appear subjectless. The policy is *transferred*. Yet the implications of this process are not always fully understood. Improvising on Peck's notion of 'fast policy' (Peck, 2005), Pratt discusses the diffusion and 'trickle down' of cultural policy 'best practice' across national borders in the institutional context of the EU and UNESCO through the critical notion of 'xerox policy', and in particular its effects on urban planning as an effect of the attractions of the 'magic dust' of culture and creativity to solve problems of regeneration and development (2009). Pratt objects to this approach because its 'rationalist and normative approach to policy' is blind to questions of variation of place and context. However, the reason for Pratt's criticism is that the fragmented and contradictory character of EU cultural policy is a hindrance to centrally directed implementation and the reason for that is the persistence of national and regional cultural policy development. According to Pratt: 'At best, the 'model' that emerges from Europe is idiosyncratic, subjective and contradictory' (19). Pratt's criticism erases the values of sensitivity to place and context it had relied on for moral justification, and the necessarily fragmented multi-level governance character of EU policy, its formalisation in elastic frameworks and subordination to principles of subsidiarity, and the turf wars and institutional rivalries that arise from that, are disavowed (Bach et al., 2016). So Pratt's replacement for xerox policy is, paradoxically, the expansion of an original that would homogenise difference through a top-down command and control structure based on 'a policy department which has the CCI [Culture and Creative Industries] as a core and high priority, and an agency which has real resources and power to implement policy' (20). In other words, Pratt proposes that the autonomy of place and context is eliminated through establishing a single model of authoritative governance.

Pratt claims that the UK DCMS is a model of best practice in that regard. It might be an aspiration but hardly describes the reality. Based on his own experience, as academic expert and policy advisor for a project that sought to transfer UK DCMS policy to St Petersburg, as part of the EU's Tacis programme of 'technical assistance' to Russia and the former Soviet Union in order to provide the city with a 'cultural industries' strategy, O'Connor (2005) reports a series of obstacles that undermined rather than directly opposed it. Firstly, 'culture industry' in the positive sense did not fit with the Russian Tolstoy style 'spiritual' cultural paradigm, which coded both official and Bohemian hipster independent cultural imaginaries. To weaken that solidarity the project attempted to divide the independents from the state by deciding to establish 'an independent intermediary agency that would give voice to the sector in the city' (53) and represent its interests to government in coherent policy language. However, independents rejected that as it would sever access to state subsidy and encourage the attention of state regulatory agencies and their informal tax extracting mechanisms. In general, the project could not provide alternative protection against 'theft of ideas, abuse of goodwill, arbitrary breaking of lease agreements and unpaid debts', which characterised the cash economy of the local business environment. Another strategy aimed to appeal to the values that united the state and the independents in opposition to the importation of the 'crassest popular culture' but unfortunately would have required direct government intervention, which would in turn require 'a fundamental shift in attitude to culture' as well as 'root and branch reform of the legal and regulatory frameworks' (57), in other words, action on governance from an external source.

It would be a mistake to read such obstacles as straightforward resistance, as they are elements of the negotiation process through which cultural policy is exchanged. Two factors in particular are important for shaping outcomes. Firstly, the extent to which neoliberal imaginaries are already normalised within governance discourse. Secondly, the extent to which conflicts over position and position-taking already structure the field of cultural policy. In the case of South Korea, for example, cultural policy adoption appears to have been relatively straightforward (Lee, 2016). The ambiguities of cultural policy enabled the attachment of a spectrum of different interests without creating conflict, even if these subsequently sought to out manoeuvre each other. The state had adopted the notion of a 'creative economy' as its economic master narrative and tied that to the organisation of the production of wealth through the development of human capital in flexible networks in order to establish continuities with the 'knowledge economy' that had otherwise been economically disappointing. Hence, the cultural sector enjoyed economic legitimacy as a way of avoiding the fate of cheap labour commodity production competition that had befallen so many of South Korea's regional rivals. Moreover, South Korea has been able to enjoy a degree of regional cultural hegemony and benefitted from revenues from intellectual property rents through the export of its own commercially successful culture industry products. By coding these products in terms of traditional culture any opposition between that and popular culture was avoided. However, by developing cultural policy in the direction of 'creative' economy the opportunity was created for science and technology interest groups and their manufacturing base to compete with 'content industries' for subsidy by appealing to the certainties of conventional economic thought based on familiar and easily calculable assumptions about the scalability of production and objective certainties of the market. Consequently cultural governance developed in South Korea as a War of Position, rather than, as in the case of St Petersburg, an external position around which conflicts are organised as a War of Manoeuvre. In South Korea, as Lee argues, cultural policy is, in Cunningham's terms, both 'Trojan Horse' and 'Rorschach blot', and hence ambivalent.

In their account of the development of cultural policy in Norway, Pinheiro and Hauge analogise the negotiation process to script editing (2014). The script is comprised of the mundane and commonplace statistical and diagrammatic images through which it is presented. The feedback on the presentation process at conferences, seminars, 'away days' and other rituals of governance provides the opportunity for editing. In the case of Norway, the process was assisted by the existence of mature multi-level governance structures that expanded the field of play while preventing direct competition for limited resource. Thus 'the policy process is a dynamic system or cycle rather than a unilateral one way route from origin (design) to target (implementation). Hence, in this context, it makes more sense to talk about 'nested scripts' – global, national and sub-national levels – that interact with, and influence one another, over time' (92). Such structures serve to prevent an experience of the imposition of policy as 'top-down' command and thus increase the chances of relatively frictionless adoption within the policy interest tier, if not necessarily within broader social, economic and cultural sections, because the governance policy process game is already being played. However, the fortune of scripts is by no means guaranteed, particularly if they are overcoded, repetitive and familiar. In their account of the development of cultural policy in Frankfurt, Dzudezek and Lindner (2013) note how presentation audiences would sometimes ironise and subvert the performance of scripts by, for example, responding to governance buzzwords such as 'flagship project' with exaggerated applause in order to call attention to their meaninglessness. The opposition partly arose from the fact that computer software and video game firms had been able to 'own' cultural policy at an early point in the process, thus restricting the ambiguity necessary to recruit as wide a spectrum of interest groups as possible. Culture was reduced to conventional economic notions giving the local Economic Development Agency the upper hand and isolating the Department for Arts and Culture. Consequently, similarly to South Korea, the script was instrumentalised in favour of narrow socio-economic interests that restricted its hegemonic reach.

Such cases point to the political logic of political actors taking advantage of different positions advocated by the global cultural policy consultocracy in order to compete with local rivals. Rindzeviciutte, Svenson and Tomson found something like that in the case of Lithuania (2015). The adoption process was 'used by local actors as resource for forging new actorial identities and practices' (3) enabling organisational and institutional entrepreneurs to rearrange the cultural policy field rather than seek consensus. Local actors used both the British Council and the Open Society Fund as resources to obtain revenue from the EU, establishing their own organisations in the process, such as the European Cultural Program Centre at the Lithuanian Cultural Contact Point. The authority of 'foreign actors' armed with 'graphs and lists' was used to weaken establishment resistance so that cultural policy terms became an accepted framework with which to propose solutions to local economic problems. Despite the British Council's promotion of the UK DCMS approach, the Lithuanian Ministry of Culture adopted what they believed to be a Swedish model of cultural economy, but which in fact was Throsby's 'concentric circles' or 'solar' model promoted by Tobias Nielsen, a Swedish consultant and entrepreneur. In response, rival organisations sought to verify the DCMS model by overlaying its maps on Lithuania in order to mobilise its optimistic growth predictions, despite accusations that this was just a means to advance narrow organisational interests to obtain funding. The DCMS emphasis on economic growth provoked some defensive responses from established cultural interests who recognised that an expectation of profitability would negate the justification for subsidy. In fact, some organisations were able to play both ends against the middle, using funds to stimulate economic growth to subsidise heritage, conservation and publishing. In this way, Lithuanian actors were able to subvert the linearity of implementation by complicating the translation process and by exploiting differences between competing scripts.

The Lithuanian case is an example of cultural policy stimulating tactical positioning around resource games. In such contexts, there is minimal capacity to govern the passion/reason balance through which strategic interests are formed at the subjective level. Matthews's detailed ethnographic account of the promotion of cultural policy in the Shetlands, a group of Norwegian islands annexed by Scotland in 1470 as part of a claim on a dowry debt for James III's daughter Margaret, describes a more openly hostile response to cultural policy (2015). In Scotland any threat to the elites that govern the cultural status quo creates a bit of a 'stooshie' (Stevenson, 2014). Indeed, a long-held position in the Scottish nationalist imaginary is the idea that its cultural elites are entitled to enjoy the role of a sort of bardic legislator (Moffat and Riach, 2014). However, the Shetlands enjoyed a long history of antagonism towards Edinburgh, the Scottish capital, with crofters liberated from the tyranny of the Scottish landowning class by British Prime Minister Gladstone's Crofter's Act in 1886. Thus, its relations to Edinburgh-driven nationalist discourse has always been complex and the reception of cultural policy is consistent with that pattern. It was implemented through the creation of *Mareel*, an arts centre based in Lerwick, the main town, which at the same time changed the status of Shetland Arts, the local cultural support organisation, to a commercial 'social enterprise' required to generate profits from the sale of popcorn and cinema tickets. For Matthews, these developments verified the observation that the main local political players were 'relatively indifferent or even defiant towards the 'creative economy' discourse' (154), a position that was widely shared, not least because it would undermine a comfortable dependence on revenues from fishing, oil and gas rents and subsidies to a recently invented tourist magnet 'traditional culture', which, Matthews notes, is 'defended and passed on in a much more authoritarian manner than one might imagine at first glance, often against whole segments of the population, and by the means of an unusual (and often vaguely threatening) institutional and political complex' (157). In fact, the reality of the Shetlands is a large service economy with a minority of inhabitants engaged in directly productive labour, with alcoholism, crack and heroin consumption and violence significantly higher than the traditionally high Scottish average. In that context self-destruction and self-conservation merge and cultural governance is neutralised by its absorption in the management of *Mareel*. Clearly, for some the costs of cultural inclusion do not outweigh the risks that cultural policy creates.

Anticipating problems of cultural governance

In conclusion, here are some critical issues that might benefit from further research, although the myth of governance may lose its hegemonic reach through the development of antagonisms from a spectrum of populisms and a general 'revolt against intermediary bodies' (Urbinati, 2015). By the same token, the conjuncture of cultural governance may have passed. So, for example, O'Connor refers to a 'cultural industries' moment in the past tense (2013: 379), suggesting that this may be because, in a cruel irony, cultural policy has been so successful in demonstrating the ubiquity of culture that its economic specificity has been lost in a broader 'creative economy' master narrative, although perhaps this claim underestimates the extent to which culture has always been subordinate to creative economy in order to obtain policy traction. In any event, as the GDP component of culture appears to be pretty uniform and stable globally, questions of how that is measured notwithstanding, has the economic boosterism of culture run out of steam? To what sort of problematisations in 'the play of true and false' will it be subject? Will it be able to maintain links with social policy questions of inclusion, diversity and equality in order to incentivise subsidy and regulation?

Secondly, given the reflexivity of 'policy learning' such that its codes are themselves modes of political gaming within cultural policy, has its discourse run out of sense-making capacity? Will the consultocracy develop strategies of institutional lock-in to gain security and mutual dependency? For example, a recent issue of Arts Professional reported the case of Arts Council England funding a consultancy on a non-competitive basis to the tune of £300k to develop an evaluation system for quality metrics that organisations in receipt of funding will be obliged to use at £2000 a pop (Hill 2015)[2] Or will new discursive strategies and enunciative positions emerge to overcome overcoding and stimulate 'policy learning'?

Thirdly, will cultural policy adapt to local conditions through greater sensitivity to local regimes? For example, in April 2016 Vince Cable, Liberal Party MP and former Secretary of State for Business, Innovation and Skills in the UK coalition government of 2010–2015, gave a talk at Polovcova House in St Petersburg with all the usual PowerPoint slides to explain 'how creative industries work in UK'. The title of the presentation was 'Creative Authority', presumably chosen in order to enhance compatibility with Russian style authoritarian democracy.[3] Or will the consultocracy adopt a universal moral prism with which to frame cultural advocacy, as, for example, in De Beukelaer's application of Sen and Nussbaum's 'capabilities approach' to culture industry development in Ghana and Burkina Faso (2012).

Fourthly, what challenges are emerging to the governability of culture? A critical aspect of that question is the processes understood as effects of globalisation. States and governments have invested considerable resources in protections against the flow of global culture industry but with very little success without the support of authoritarian violence, often under the sign of 'diversity'. But these processes are not restricted to the infrastructures of texts and symbols. They include people, often as a consequence of authoritarian violence. As Robins pointed out (2007), in these circumstances investment in a common shared culture is restricting and reactive. Culture increasingly frees itself from roots and attachment and defies 'the containing powers of nation states and national societies' (157). Consequently, Robins proposes extending the rights recognised through multiculturalism to transcultural diversity, but with less emphasis on integration and stability, more on mobility, porosity, fluidity, as a sort of right to impurity and hybridity, to nomadism. Such an approach privileges a poetics of becoming over a rhetoric of being. So a question for the politics of culture is what side of that opposition is it on?

Acknowledgements

I would like to thank Dave O'Brien for helpful comments and suggestions and editorial direction.

Notes

1 For an account of EU cultural policy that outlines the institutional structures that support these characteristics, see Chapter 26.
2 For criticisms of the tendering process, see Selwood (2015) and subsequent correspondence in cultural trends.
3 I am grateful to Tatiana Romashko of Herzen University, St Petersburg, for this information.

References

6, Perri (1997) 'Governing by Cultures' in Mulgan, G. (ed.) *Life After Politics: New Thinking for the Twenty-First Century.* London: Fontana, 260–273.

Agamben, Georgio (2013) 'For a theory of destituent power' Public Lecture, Nicos Poulantzas Institute, Athens, 16 November 2013.

Bach, Tobias, De Francesco, Fabrizo, Maggetti, Martino and Ruffing, Eva (2016) 'Transnational Bureaucratic Politics: An Institutional Rivalry Perspective on EU Network Governance' *Public Administration*, 94, 1, 9–24.

Bang, Henrik P. (2004) 'Culture Governance: Governing Self-Reflexive Modernity' *Public Administration*, 82, 1, 157–190.

Barnett, Clive (2001) 'Culture, Policy, and Subsidiarity in the European Union: From Symbolic Identity to the Governmentalisation of Culture' *Political Geography*, 20, 4, 405–426 (draft version at: oro.open.ac.uk).

Barthes, Roland (1973) *Mythologies*. St Albans: Granada Publishing Limited.

Bennett, Tony (1992) 'Putting Policy into Cultural Studies' in Grossberg, L., Nelson, C. and Treichler, P. (eds.) *Cultural Studies*. London: Routledge, 23–34.

Best, Jacqueline (2012) 'Bureaucratic Ambiguity' *Economy and Society*, 41, 1, 84–106.

Bevir, Mark (2011) 'Governance and Governmentality after Neoliberalism' *Policy and Politics*, 39, 4, 457–472.

Bevir, Mark and Rhodes, R.A. (2005) 'Interpretation and its Others' *Australian Journal of Political Science*, 40, 2, 169–187.

Brown, Wendy (2015) *Undoing the Demos: Neoliberalism's Stealth Revolution*. New York: Zone Books.

Buduru, Bogdan and Pal, Leslie A. (2010) 'The Globalized State: Measuring and Monitoring Governance' *European Journal of Cultural Studies*, 13, 4, 511–530.

Clarke, John and Newman, Janet (1997) *The Managerial State Power, Politics and Ideology in the Remaking of Social Welfare*. London: Sage.

Davies, Jonathan S. (2011) *Challenging governance theory: From Networks to Hegemony*. Bristol: The Policy Press.

Deleuze, Giles (1995) 'Postscript on Control Societies' in *Negotiations*. New York: Columbia University Press, 177–182.

De Beukelaer, C. (2012) *Developing Cultural Industries*. Amsterdam: The European Cultural Foundation.

Dzudezek, Iris and Lindner, Peter (2013) 'Performing the Creative Economies Script: Contradicting Urban Rationalities at Work' *Regional Studies*, 49, 3, 388–403.

Eagleton–Pierce, Matthew (2014) 'The Concept of Governance in the Spirit of Capitalism' *Critical Policy Studies*, 8, 1, 5–21.

Enroth, Henrik (2013) 'Governance: The art of Governing after Governmentality' *European Journal of Social Theory*, 17, 1, 60–76.

Foucault, Michel (1997) 'Polemics, Politics and Problematizations' in *Ethics: Essential Works of Foucault*, Vol. 1. New York: The New Press.

Habermas, Jürgen (1987) *The Philosophical Discourse of Modernity*. Cambridge: The Polity Press.

Hall, Stuart (1997) 'The Centrality of Culture: Notes on the Cultural Revolution of Our Time' in Thompson, K. (ed.) *Media and Cultural Regulation*. London: Sage.

Hill, Liz (2015) 'EXCLUSIVE: £300k grant sidesteps ACE procurement rules' Arts Professional

Hood, Christopher and Dixon, Ruth (2015) *A Government that Worked Better and Cost Less? Evaluating Three Decades of Reform and Change in UK Central Government*. Oxford: Oxford University Press.

Jessop, Bob (2015) 'Crises, Crises-Management and State Restructuring: What Future for the State?' *Policy & Politics*, 43, 4, 475–92.

Lee, Hye-Kyung (2016) 'Politics of the 'Creative Industries' Discourse and its Variants' *International Journal of Cultural Policy*, 22, 3, 438–455.

Lemke, Thomas (2007) 'An Indigestible Meal? Foucault, Governmentality and State Theory' *Distinktion: Scandinavian Journal of Social Theory*, 8, 2, 43–64.

Matthews, Jacob T. (2015) 'Like a Fraction of Some Bigger Place – The "Creative Industries" in a Peripheral Zone: Reflections from a Case Study' *Triple C*, 13, 1, 144–162.

Mattocks, Kate (2018) 'Uniting the nations of Europe? Exploring the European Union's cultural policy agenda' in Durrer, V., Miller, T. and O'Brien, D. (eds) *The Routledge Handbook of Global Cultural Policy*. Abingdon: Routledge.

Mayntz, Renate (1994) 'Governing Failures and the Problem of Governability: Some Comments on a Theoretical Paradigm' in Kooiman, J. (ed.) *Modern Governance: New Government – Society Interactions*. London: Sage.

Moffat, Alexander and Riach, Alan (2014) *Arts of Independence*. Edinburgh: Luarth Press.

Moretti, Franco and Pestre, Dominique (2015) 'Bankspeak: The Language of World Bank Reports' *New Left Review*, 92, 75–99.

Mulderrig, J. (2011) 'The Grammar of Governance' *Critical Discourse Studies*, 8, 1, 45–68.

O'Brien, Dave (2014) *Cultural Policy: Management, Value and Modernity in the Creative Industries*. London: Routledge.

O'Connor, Justin (2005) 'Creative Exports: Taking Cultural Industries to St Petersburg' *International Journal of Cultural Policy*, 11, 1, 45–60.

O'Connor, Justin (2013) 'Intermediaries and Imaginaries in the Cultural and Creative Industries' *Regional Studies*, 49, 3, 374–387.

Offe, Clauss (1984) *Contradictions of the Welfare State*. Cambridge, MA: The MIT Press.

Offe, Clauss (2009) 'Governance: An "Empty Signifier"?' *Constellations*, 16, 4, 550–562.

Osborne, David and Gaebler, Ted (1992) *Reinventing Government: How the Entrepreneurial Spirit Is Transforming the Public Sector*. Reading, MA: Addison-Wesley.

Peck, Jamie (2005) 'Struggling with the Creative Class' *International Journal of Urban and Regional Research*, 29, 4, 740–770.

Pinheiro, Rómulo and Hauge, Elisabet (2014) 'Global Scripts and Local Translations: The Case of Cultural and Creative Industries (CCIs) in Norway' *City, Culture and Society*, 5, 87–95.

Power, Mike (1997) *The Audit Society: Rituals of Verification*. Oxford: Oxford University Press.

Pratt, Andy C. (2009) 'Policy Transfer and the Field of the Cultural and Creative Industries: What Can Be Learned from Europe?' in Kong, L. and O'Connor, J. (eds.) *Creative Economies, Creative Cities: Asian – European Perspectives*. GeoJournal Library 98. London: Springer, 9–23..

Prince, Russell (2013) 'Calculative Cultural Expertise? Consultants and Politics in the UK Cultural Sector' *Sociology*, 48, 4, 747–762.

Prince, Russell (2015) 'Economies of Expertise: Consultants and the Assemblage of Culture' *Journal of Cultural Economy*, 8, 5, 582–596.

Rhodes, R.A. (1996) 'The New Governance: Governing Without Government' *Political Studies*, XLIV, 652–667.

Rindzeviciutte, Egle, Svenson, Jenny and Tomson, Klara (2015) 'The International Transfer of Creative Industries as a Policy Idea' *International Journal of Cultural Policy*, 22, 4, 594–610.

Robins, Kevin (2007) Transnational Cultural Policy and European Cosmopolitanism' *Cultural Politics*, 3, 2, 147–174.

Rose, Nicholas (1999) *Powers of Freedom: Reframing Political Thought*. Cambridge: Cambridge University Press.

Selwood, S. (2015) 'Measuring Quality in the Cultural Sector: The Manchester Metrics Pilot: Findings and Lessons Learned' *Cultural Trends*, 24, 3, 268–275.

Stevenson, D. (2014) 'Tartan and Tantrums: Critical Reflections on the Creative Scotland 'Stooshie'' *Cultural Trends*, 22, 2, 77–85.

The Invisible Committee (2015) *To Our Friends*. New York: semiotext(e).

Urbinati, Nadia (2015) 'A Revolt against Intermediary Bodies' *Constellations*, 22, 4, 477–486.

Valentine, Jeremy (2002) 'Governance and Cultural Authority' *Cultural Values*, 6, 1&2, 49–64.

Valentine, Jeremy (2004) 'Audit Society, Practical Deconstruction and Strategic Public Relations' *Parallax*, 10, 2, 20–37.

Walt Disney Pictures (2003) Pirates of the Caribbean: The Curse of The Black Pearl.

Williamson, Oliver E. (1979) 'Transaction Cost Economics: The Governance of Contractual Relations' *Journal of Law and Economics*, 22, 2, 233–261.

Yudice, George (2003) *The Expediency of Culture: Uses of Culture in the Global Era*. Durham, NC: Duke University Press.

Part III
Rights and cultural policy

11

Disabled people and culture
Creating inclusive global cultural policies

Anne-Marie Callus and Amy Camilleri-Zahra

Introduction

Cultural policy is inevitably shaped by dominant cultural assumptions. In many cultures, disability is largely viewed negatively, with disabled people seen either as tragic figures rendered bitter or helpless through their circumstances or as heroes bravely overcoming the odds created by their impairments. Such representations are oppressive for disabled people and continue to propagate a disabling culture. However, culture can be a source of liberation or emancipation (Brown 2003). In fact, the politicisation of disability has prompted a new disability culture, which challenges long-held stereotypes and traditional representations of disability. Through the disability arts movement, disabled people have sought to produce a culture aimed at exploring a positive identity of disability whilst combating the dominant disablist culture (Swain and French 2000, Arts Council England 2003). Disability culture can thus be an agent of change and a means of promoting and validating disabled people's own constructions of disability (Barnes and Mercer 2010).

Culture is a vast subject to deal with, has manifold manifestations and has developed in different ways around the world. In order to give this chapter a defined scope, we focus on five different cultural forms from a Western and mostly Anglophone cultural perspective, namely: narratives, poetry, visual arts, performing arts, and online media. The points raised are applicable to other forms of culture and to culture in different parts of the world. The relevance of the issues raised to cultural policy is highlighted throughout the chapter.

A note on terminology

In line with the social model of disability, as explained later in this chapter, a distinction is made between 'disability' and 'impairment'. Therefore, impairment is taken to mean 'the functional limitation within the individual caused by physical, mental or sensory impairment' (Disabled People's International 1982, p. 105), and disability to mean 'the loss or limitation of opportunities to take part in the normal life of the community on an equal level with others due to physical and social barriers' (Disabled People's International 1982, p. 105). Thus, the term 'disabled people' will be used throughout this chapter in order to refer to 'people with impairments who are disabled by socially constructed barriers' (Clark and Marsh 2003, p. 2) and to particularly emphasise the disabling barriers of stigma, prejudice and discrimination encountered by disabled people.

Disabled people's history: from rejects to rights holders

The year 2006 was a significant year for the disabled people's movement and for the one billion disabled people across the world. It was the year that the United Nations General Assembly adopted by general consensus the Convention on the Rights of Persons with Disabilities (CRPD). The adoption of the CRPD came after many years of relentless work by disabled people who were finally able to tackle discrimination and oppression through international legislation. One of the most significant aspects of the CRPD is that, for the first time, disabled people were directly involved in the drafting of a legislation that specifically targets them, in line with the disabled people's movement battle cry of 'Nothing about us, without us'. One of the eight general principles of the CRPD listed under Article 3 is: 'Full and effective participation and inclusion in society'. One way of ensuring the implementation of this particular principle is by securing the participation of disabled people in the arts and culture sector both as consumers and as producers. In addition, the right to participation in cultural life is also particularly enshrined in Article 30 of the CRPD, to which we return later.

In order to understand the need for enshrining disabled people's rights in international legislation, and the relevance of this legislation to cultural policy, it is important to be aware of the ways in which disability has historically been represented in culture. For its representation in Western culture, the focus of this chapter, it is interesting to note that the roots of the association between disability and weakness stem from the culture of ancient Greece. As Barnes (1996) points out, Greek city states were constantly warring with each other, and physical and mental prowess was therefore greatly valued. 'Inevitably in this type of society, physical and intellectual fitness was essential: there was little room for people with any form of flaw or imperfection', and severely deformed babies were left to die (Barnes 1996, p. 52).

The Judeo-Christian religious traditions are also considered to have exerted significant influence on cultural constructions of disability in Western Europe. Stiker (1999) explains, in his *History of Disability*, that in the Book of Leviticus (part of the Jewish Torah as well as of the Old Testament in the Christian Bible), disability is linked with uncleanliness, although the duty to care for disabled people is emphasised. Stiker (1999) argues that these attitudes – of exclusion on the one hand and benevolence on the other – are not contradictory. 'Sin and defect deny the disabled a religious role, but they introduce an ethical and social imperative' (p. 27).

Therefore, bodily impairments have long been viewed as a sign of weakness, and responses have varied from ostracism to charity. Industrialisation and the concomitant need for people to be able to work new machinery and the imperative to be economically productive created a clear demarcation between disabled and non-disabled people (Barnes 1997). Advances in medicine and science eventually moved disability into the medical sphere, especially with the rise of rehabilitation after the First World War (Stiker 1999). In all of these cases, physical impairments place the disabled person outside the bounds of what is considered to be human normality. The same can be said for impairments, which affect the functions of the mind, such as mental health issues or cognitive impairments. These run counter to the value placed on rationality in Western philosophy, especially since the Enlightenment 'which put its faith in the power of human reason to explain the universe and provide a basis for morality' (Bowie 2003, p. 274). Foucault (2001) links the receding of the threat of leprosy at the end of the Middle Ages with the identification of the mentally disturbed person as the new scapegoat, the outcast.

The disabled person, whatever his or her impairment, has thus historically been placed outside of society not only physically but also conceptually. In his seminal critique of residential institutions for persons with intellectual disability in the United States, Wolfensberger (1972) links the setting up of these institutions with the deleterious cultural perceptions of the roles persons with intellectual disability are deemed to play within society. He identifies perceptions of the 'retarded person', the terminology used at his time of writing, as sick; a sub-human organism; a menace; an object of pity; a burden of charity; a holy innocent; a developing individual; and an object of merriment and ridicule.

A common feature of the different concepts and representations of disability outlined above is that they have all been conceived by non-disabled people. The perspectives of disabled people themselves would not gain any voice until the twentieth century, especially after the Second World War when the disabled people's movement became more vocal and effective. In the United Kingdom and the United States, people with physical disabilities were the first to campaign for their right to be included in a society adapted for their needs (Shapiro 1994, Campbell and Oliver 1996). Meanwhile, in these as well as Scandinavian countries, parents of disabled children placed in institutions were campaigning for the right of their children (most of whom had an intellectual disability) to live in community-based residences (Mansell and Ericsson 1995).

The most significant outcome of the disabled people's movement was convincing legislators and policy and decision makers of the need to shift responsibility for adapting and changing from the disabled individual onto society. This shift is linked to the acknowledgement that the difficulties encountered by disabled people are not simply the inevitable effect of their impairments, but also the effect of socially constructed barriers, which can often be removed. This led to the formulation of the 'social model' of disability by Oliver (1990). It is the model on which the distinction between impairment and disability, set out in the note on terminology above, is based. It is also the model on which the CRPD, various disability discrimination laws and policies are based.

The social model is therefore important for cultural policy. Guidance in this regard is provided by the CPRD (United Nations 2006), especially Article 30 Participation in cultural life, recreation, leisure and sport. Meeting the requirements of this Article entails ensuring that, first of all, disabled people have the means to express themselves through different cultural forms; second, they have access to cultural activities and cultural products and third, they enjoy recognition and support of their own cultural identities. The first two of these points are considered further below in this chapter. Addressing the third point entails first analysing the perspectives that dominate in the cultural representations of disability. The next section deals with the representations of disability in different Western, and especially Anglophone, cultural forms and relates the analyses to the development of disability-aware cultural policy.

Cultural representations of disabled people

There is a rich, and ever growing, body of scholarship that analyses historic and cultural representations of disabled people, some of which is explored in this section. The analysis provided in this scholarship shows that, generally speaking, the effect of normative and therefore exclusionary views of disability can be seen in traditional and even contemporary representations of disability in various cultural forms. These representations are increasingly counterbalanced by more nuanced representations of disability. The study of cultural representations of disability is vast. For reasons of space, this section considers just four types of representations from high and popular culture: visual art, literature, film, and the use of disability in inspirational posters.

In his seminal work *Disability Aesthetics*, Siebers (2010) explores the role of disability in visual representations of the human body, especially in modern and contemporary art. Siebers states his position very clearly at the outset of his book:

> My claim is that the acceptance of disability enriches and complicates notions of the aesthetic, while the rejection of disability limits definitions of artistic ideas and objects. (p. 3)

Siebers (2010) argues that, far from rejecting disability, art embraces it even if not always in an explicit manner. He uses the Nazi's stance on art as the prime example of how the pursuit of human perfection leads to sterility in art. Siebers refers to the Nazi's rejection of modern art as degenerate and sick. He contrasts Nazi sculpture, such as that displayed in the Great German Art Exhibition of 1939, with the *Venus de Milo*. The loss or 'amputation' of her arms does not in any way detract from her beauty. And while this 'amputation' was undoubtedly unintentioned by the original sculptor, it is highlighted in Magritte's 1931 version in *Les Menottes de cuivre* with its flesh-coloured body and the blood-like pigment on the stump of its left shoulder. As Siebers argues:

> The figure of disability checks out of the asylum, the sick house, and the hospital to take up residence in the art gallery, the museum, and the public square. Disability is now and will be in the future an aesthetic value in itself.
>
> (2010, p. 139)

Whether the disabled figure in modern and contemporary art is articulated as such is another matter. In her discussion of our perceptions of anomalous bodies, Silvers (2000) contrasts the attraction held by representations of such bodies in works of art and the rejection of these bodies in real life. She describes her own experience of wanting to keep looking at a Picasso portrait, with his trademark depiction of deformed faces, but avoiding to look at the face of her friend, who was born with facial and bodily deformities, and asks why this should be so. Silvers contends that:

> we must conclude that ugliness is neither an objective property, nor is it an epiphenomenon of deformation or other objective anomalies, or else that ugliness pertains to being real, so that it is an objective property, but only of real things, and never of their artistic imitations or representations.
>
> (2000, p. 203)

Therefore, while representations of disability in visual art are used as reflections on the human condition, culturally dominant interpretations of that art do not extend to reflections on what it means to live with a disability and on disabled people's culture.

Mitchell and Snyder (2000) make a related observation regarding literary representations of disability. Disabled people's physical and mental differences have been used extensively as literary devices, what the authors call 'narrative prosthesis'. One of the most famous prosthesis, in both the literal and the figurative senses of the word, is Captain Ahab's. His monomaniacal pursuit of Moby Dick, the whale that bit off his leg, is symbolised by his impairment in a way that, as Mitchell and Snyder (2000, p. 121) write, 'yokes disability to insanity, obsessive revenge, and the alterity of bodily variation'. Examples of the link between disability and negative emotions abound in literature. They are symptomatic of the fact that disability is not seen as 'a natural part of the human condition. … it was understood as an "attachment", as something extra that, for whatever reason, happened to a person' (Michalko 2003, p. 5). The inclusion of disabled characters in narratives therefore ironically serves to further entrench the exclusion of disabled people from society (Mitchell and Snyder 2000).

Another problematic aspect of this attitude towards disability in literature is that many depictions of disabled characters are not realistic. Susan Nussbaum, the disabled American playwright and novelist, writes thus:

> I used to wonder where all the writers who have used disabled characters so liberally in their work were doing their research. When I became a wheelchair-user in the late seventies, all I knew about being disabled I learned from reading books and watching movies, and that scared the shit out of me. Tiny Tim was long-suffering and angelic and was cured at the end. Quasimodo was a monster who loved in vain and was killed at the end, but it was for the best. Lenny was a child who killed anything soft, and George had to shoot him. It was a mercy killing. Ahab was a bitter amputee and didn't care how many people died in his mad pursuit to avenge himself on a whale. Laura Wingfield had a limp, so no man would ever love her.
>
> (2014, p. 301)

The works of literature in this quotation all have filmic versions, and the problematic depictions of disabled characters in them are transposed to the screen, as can be seen in Longmore's (2003) seminal review of some films where the main character has a disability. One of these is *Whose Life Is It Anyway?* (1981), which tells the story of Ken, a young sculptor who becomes quadriplegic following a traffic accident. Longmore (2003) criticises the film for distorting the contemporary situation with regards to the opportunities for rehabilitation and the assistive equipment that could have helped Ken lead a more independent life. For example, Ken is pushed around in a manual wheelchair instead of being given a power wheelchair that he could operate himself. But, as Longmore argues, introducing these elements would have undermined the validity of the claim that Ken's wanting to die was justified. 'If he operated a power chair himself, that would further undermine the false impression of his utter helplessness' (2003, p. 120). Significantly, a film that was released 23 years after *Whose Life Is It Anyway?*, *Million Dollar Baby* (2004), picks up on the same theme of a quadriplegic wanting to die – this time with the story of Frankie, a female boxer who is also paralysed from the neck down during a boxing match.

As a counterbalance to these narratives, others present more rounded portrayals of disabled persons. One such film is *My Left Foot* (1989), based on the autobiography of Christy Brown, an Irishman born with severe cerebral palsy who could only manipulate his left foot. In his review, Longmore (2003) comments that in this film Brown is portrayed as an agent in his own life who, although he does contemplate suicide at one point, has much to live for. This is also the case for two biopics, based on memoirs, of persons with severe physical disabilities – *Untouchable* (2011) and *The Theory of Everything* (2014). But, as Longmore argues, this is not necessarily how film critics see these characters. For example, he criticises a film reviewer who spoke of Brown in *My Left Foot* as helpless.

The point made by Longmore (2003) in this criticism touches on a very important issue regarding the reception of portrayals of disability by non-disabled people: seeing Brown as a helpless victim of his condition is a reflection of stereotyped misconceptions of what it is like to live with a severe and lifelong disabling condition. Such stances ignore the viewpoints of disabled persons, especially those of disabled activists, and remain entrenched in the traditional equation of disability with tragedy and loss. This tendency can also be seen in the reactions to films portraying people with other types of impairments. One film whose reception by (presumably non-disabled) film reviewers and disabled activists provides sharp contrasts is *Tropic Thunder* (2008), a satire on Hollywood. Self-advocacy groups, led by people with intellectual disability, protested strongly against the film especially because of the repeated use of the word 'retard', which they find highly offensive, and the portrayal of the character Simple Jack (see for example Egle 2008). Jack (played by Ben Stiller) is presented as an ill-groomed, awkward and overgrown child and a grotesque embodiment of all the stereotypes associated with people with intellectual disability. Reviews of the film focus mostly on whether *Tropic Thunder*'s satire, and Stiller's own brand of humour, work or not. Those reviewers who do refer to the issues raised by disabled activists tend to be dismissive of them.

Many scholars within the humanities and reviewers and critics whose job it is to appraise different cultural expressions do not seem to have caught up with the work of disabled activists and that of Disability Studies scholars. The negative connotations of disability that have been inherited from antiquity still appear dominant, albeit sometimes in subtle ways. For instance the portrayal of the disabled person as superhero is not, *prima facie*, a negative one. It is nonetheless problematic. Possibly one of the best analyses of what is wrong with such representations is by Stella Young (2014). Young criticises the portrayal of ordinary activities – such as working, studying and pursuing personal interests – as extraordinary simply because they are carried out by disabled people.

Young is particularly critical of what she calls 'inspirational porn' – the use of images of disabled people accompanied by inspirational quotes. One such image is a poster of the paralympian athlete Oscar Pistorius (prior to his shooting of Reeva Steenkamp) running on his blades alongside a small girl who also has prosthetic legs with a quotation from disabled figure skater, Scott Hamilton, 'the only disability in life is a bad attitude'. This and similar posters often shared on social media sites are problematic because they entrench the idea of disability as an individual problem, with the onus remaining on the disabled person to strive to overcome the challenges presented by the impairment rather than responsibility being placed on society to adapt itself to the needs of disabled persons. Such quotations can also lead disabled people to feel ashamed of their lack of achievement in different areas of life. And they can easily lead to a dehumanised view of disabled people. As Young (2014, at 2.33 minutes) states, in this view, 'We are not real people. We are there to inspire'.

The views of disability activists and scholars on the cultural representations of disabled people often remain the sole concern of those directly involved in the disability sector. However, the push for the inclusion of disabled people in the mainstream of society needs to be complemented with the mainstreaming of their culture and cultural identity, not least in cultural policy. Such a move entails taking on board the views of disability activists and scholars on the representation of disability in various forms of culture produced by non-disabled as well as by disabled people.

The cultural expressions of disabled people themselves merit analyses in their own right since they often run counter to the representations of disability found in mainstream culture. It is to these expressions that we must now turn.

Disabled people's own cultural expressions

In response to a negative disabling culture and with the aim of arguing against social exclusion and marginalisation, disabled people have been, especially since the 1980s, generating cultural expressions to create meaning from their own experiences of disability. They have been using different forms of art to show the world that they are proud of who they are and that they claim their disability with pride as part of their identity (Brueggemann 2013). In fact, according to Swain and French (2000) and the Arts Council England (2003), one of the areas where a positive identity of disability is appreciably cultivated is definitely within the area of 'disability arts'. The philosophy of disability art is based on disabled people coming together and collectively identifying themselves as a group bound by experiences of oppression (Hargrave 2015). A focus on 'disability arts' is also made in Article 30 (2) of the CRPD, which highlights the need for State Parties to take all appropriate measures to give disabled people the opportunity to be producers of art themselves. In this section we shall be looking at some of disabled people's own expressions of culture within a Western and Anglophone context, namely theatre, poetry, art and music.

Britain saw the vigorous development of a disability arts culture in the mid-1980s. Disability arts culture is an integral product of the disability political movement of the 1970s and 1980s (Darke 2003). Disability cultural expression in Britain became mostly visible with the foundation of the London Disability Arts Forum, along with two influential magazines: *Disability Arts* and later *Disability Arts Magazine* (Darke 2003). The London Disability Arts Forum (LDAF) was founded in 1986 by a group of disabled artists and activists frustrated by the lack of provision for disabled people in the arts world and focused on promoting disability arts and the work of disabled artists (Darke 2003). LDAF used art as a means of identifying and revealing how cultural forms can have the power to establish a different world and not simply reflect an already given social world (Bowler 1994). LDAF aimed at putting forward cultural expressions that were inclusive, accessible, revolutionary and egalitarian in a social world that was exclusive and discriminatory towards disabled people (Darke 2003).

Similarly, the disability arts movement in America stemmed from disability activists who insisted on making their voices heard in all aspects of life through art and by affirming a positive identity of disability. Just as children of slavery came together to assert that: 'Black is beautiful', so, Owen (an American disability activist) claims that the disability arts culture in America is a product of disabled people coming together to mutually affirm a sense of pride and to express a desire to identify themselves with disability as a positive identity (Fleischer and Zames 2011). One of the areas where American disabled artists found space to express themselves was the magazine *The Disability Rag* (Nielson 2012).

Barnes and Mercer (2010) point out that disability arts have three aims: First, they are concerned with using the arts as a means of activism with the purpose of exposing discrimination and prejudice as well as challenging the stereotypes experienced by disabled people. Second, they are concerned with the exploration of the experience of living with an impairment and with giving positive value to disability. Third, through disability arts disabled people argue the case for mainstream access to artistic production and consumption.

Although through traditional paternalistic attitudes, art has often been regarded as an appropriate activity for special schools and day centres, or a form of individual therapy, 'disability arts' are politically influenced and take both a reflective and active orientation. Thus, as explained by Barnes and Mercer (2010, p. 207) there exists a very clear distinction between 'disability arts' and what they refer to as 'disabled people doing art'. 'Disability arts' is also different from the kind of art created by artists with impairments such as musicians Ray Charles and Def Leppard's drummer Rick Allen, who contrary to artists who produce 'disability arts', have reacted in a personal and private rather than in a political and overt way. The fundamental aim of disability arts is 'work of disabled artists, whose experiences with disability are recognised as an integral force underlying the artistic process' (Baglieri and Shapiro 2012, p. 100).

According to Vasey (1992), disability arts provides a space in which disabled people can come together to have a good time and also think about issues of common concern. One of the most popular expressions of art by disabled people for disabled people with the aim of '...speak[ing] the truth about the disability and experience' (Masefield 2006, p. 22) and of bringing disabled people together is Johnny Crescendo's song titled "Choices and Rights". Johnny Crescendo is considered one of the first disability artists from the first wave of the Disability Arts Movement in the United Kingdom. His songs are considered extremely political, and he is well known for not being afraid of expressing his views directly (Sutherland 2008). The song with the words:

> I don't want your sorrow, I don't want your fear, I want choices and rights in our lives,
> I don't need your guilt trip, I don't want your tears, I want choices and rights in our lives
> (www.disabilityartsonline.org.uk)

became known as the 'anthem' of the international disability rights movement (Campbell and Oliver 1996).

One of the aims of disability art is exposing negative images and stereotypes of disability as well as challenging the discrimination and oppression often encountered by disabled people (French and Swain 2012). One such cultural expression is Liz Crow's film project titled *Resistance: Which way the future?* (2008). The project outlines the Aktion-T4 Nazi mass murder programme, which targeted disabled people. Liz Crow, through the main character named Ellie Blick, showed the atrocities that disabled people suffered as an effect of this mass murder programme. Furthermore, she drew a parallel between the Nazi's oppression of disabled people during the Second World War and the discrimination that disabled people face today. Liz Crow later also accepted the request to participate in Anthony Gormley's Fourth Plinth Project *One and Other* at Trafalgar Square in 2009 with the aim of giving more people the opportunity to engage with the act (Hambrook 2014). Liz portrayed her project by sitting in her wheelchair in full Nazi regalia whilst lifting a flag and quoting Niemoeller, 'First they came for the sick, the so-called incurables and I did not speak out because I was not ill...' (www.roaring-girl.com).

Bedding Out (2012) is another striking performance by Liz Crow. In an interview for The Guardian, Crow describes this project as 'a sort of un-performance' (Adewunmi 2013). *Bedding Out* is about making her private life public, something that according to Liz herself, she had not divulged for over 30 years. For a period of 48 hours, on stage, Crow performs the other side of her 'fractured' self, that is, her bed-life. In another interview in 2013, with the organisation Disabled People's Against Cuts, Crow reveals how she wears a public self that is 'energetic, dynamic and happening' and has another, private, life she spends in bed due to her illness. According to Crow her private self is '...neither beautiful nor grown-up, it does not win friends or accolades and I conceal it carefully' (Disabled People Against Cuts, 2012).

Canadian disabled scholar and activist Catherine Frazee explains that the role of disability arts in shaping disability cultures is vital. According to her (as cited in Johnston 2012, p. 10): 'In Canada, the United States and around the world, [disabled] artists and performers...are contributing to one of the most radical and effective aspects of disability culture – challenging conventional notions of beauty, form and notion'. Riva Lehrer is a disabled artist who continuously challenges the conventional notions of beauty through her artwork. Lehrer actively campaigns for disability rights and disability pride through her art (Millett-Gallant 2010). Lehrer's artwork offers a strong visual image of the human-nonhuman relationship between a disabled person and the environment.

In the painting "In the Yellow Woods", Lehrer shows a woman kneeling on the ground in what looks like a forest, whilst peeling the bark off a tree branch with a knife. Surrounding the woman are human bones – a perfect pelvis, a rib cage and parts of the legs and spine, bones that look like they were carved from tree branches and tree trunks by the same woman. The bones look perfect and like they have not been marked by pain, surgery or breakage. The painting also shows the woman immensely concentrating on her task at hand, suggesting that these bones are a great necessity. Yet, the woman in the painting does not seem to be after creating wholeness or after a cure as has often been the role of narratives pertaining to disability (Anderson and O'Sullivan 2010). Rather, in this painting, the bones are scattered around her sinking into the ground and becoming part of the autumn landscape (Kafer 2013). According to Kafer (2013, p. 146), the painting is not about the triumph over disability, or an 'ableist story of bodies without limitation', but rather a story about a woman who is '...making a connection between caring for the body and caring for the earth'.

One particular characteristic of disability art is black humour, and this is clearly illustrated in one of the works of actor, playwright and poet Lynn Manning. His poem, "The Magic Wand", about an African-American man with a white cane, cynically compares two stereotypes, one of racism and one of disability:

> Quick-change artist extraordinaire,
> I whip out my folded cane
> and change from black man to blind man

Manning is well known for his autobiographical solo *Weights*. The play is about Manning's own personal journey of being a black man who, at the age of 27, also became a blind man after having been shot by a drunk driver (Piggott-McMillan 2005). Through *Weights*, Manning brings to the forefront a chronology of experiences from his childhood to his life after the shooting with a touch of funny episodes about his adjustment to blindness. *Weights* premiered in 2000 and went on to receive a Fringe Review Theatre Award at the 2008 Edinburgh Fringe Festival (www.lynnmanning.com).

As mentioned in the first section of this chapter, for many years, the definition of disability has been rooted in a medicalised understanding (Barnes 1997). According to Oliver (1990) the representation of disability as a pathology reduces its experience to a tragedy borne only by the individual and treatable only through the intervention of health. Furthermore, Oliver (1990) contends that the medicalisation of disability often affects the individual experience of disability. Disability art has been used as a powerful tool to question the medicalisation of disability and to challenge ableist assumptions (Darke 2004). Neil Marcus, a New York poet and playwright, uses his poem, "Disabled Country" to claim disability as an identity and to move out of the shadow of constant medicalisation:

> If there was a country called disabled,
> I would be from there.
> ...I came there at age 8. I tried to leave.
> Was encouraged by doctors to leave.

In addition, Marcus uses the poem to explain how through his life he has had to take on a project, that of making himself comfortable and "at home" in his country called "disabled", a process both personal and political (Hall 2015).

The final example of disability art brings to the fore the role of the non-disabled artist in disability arts. The statue of *Alison Lapper Pregnant,* referred to by many as a collaboration between Quinn and Lapper, received contrasting comments during its participation in the Fourth Plinth Project in London's Trafalgar Square (Millett 2008). Alison Lapper, a contemporary artist and photographer born without hands and feet, posed naked whilst pregnant for the sculptor Marc Quinn, who in Lapper's own words managed to capture her as "naked, pregnant and proud" (as cited in Smith 2015). Quinn wanted to draw attention to stereotypes and to include them in public debate with the aim of educating the public (Millett-Gallant 2010). As Millett (2008) points outs, *Alison Lapper Pregnant* makes a public statement about this disabled woman's right to be represented as a productive social subject and a reproductive sexual being and her right to represent others. The statue of Alison Lapper brings to the foreground two intertwining identities, that of a disabled identity and that of a gendered identity (Garland-Thomson 2010).

Notwithstanding the considerable amount of disability art created by disabled people with the aim of putting forward a positive identity of disability and the adoption of the CRPD by the United Nations, particularly Article 30 (2), most disabled people still encounter obstacles when trying to access mainstream culture both as producers and as consumers. Access to culture will be discussed in the next section.

Access to culture

We have so far explored how, on the whole, various forms of culture produced by non-disabled people do not acknowledge disabled people's cultural identities and how performances, writing and cultural expressions produced by disabled people run counter to dominant cultural representations of disability. As seen above, Article 30 of the CRPD (United Nations 2006) affirms the right of disabled people to these cultural expressions and to accessibility in the sphere of culture. It sets out arrangements that need to be in place for this right to be enjoyed. While it is important that on a conceptual level disabled people's own cultural expressions and their critique of mainstream representations of disability inform cultural policy, it is also essential for cultural policy makers to be aware of how to make these expressions and representations accessible to all.

One of the obligations included in Article 30 concerns the provision of 'access to cultural material in accessible formats', including by ensuring that 'laws protecting intellectual property rights do not constitute an unreasonable or discriminatory barrier to access by persons with disabilities to cultural materials' (United Nations 2006, p. 22). The reference point in this regard is the Marrakesh Treaty, adopted by the World Intellectual Property Organisation (2013). This Treaty covers the rights of persons who have difficulty accessing printed material, such as those with visual impairments, those who have other reading difficulties and those who cannot physically handle a book or move their eyes to be able to read. Countries ratifying this Treaty are obliged to ensure that intellectual copyright laws do not hinder persons with print disabilities from accessing printed material such as novels, poetry anthologies and scripts, in accessible formats, such as Braille, large print and electronic and audio formats. The latter two have become increasingly possible thanks to advances in information and communication technology.

Another aspect of access to information is the Internet, including social media. The World Wide Web Consortium (2015) provides guidelines for ensuring access to websites and web-based services. Yet another aspect is access to information for people with intellectual disability. Generally speaking, this requires the provision of easy-to-read material – both in terms of creating documents that are easy to read and providing easy-to-read versions of already existing documents such as the ones mentioned above. The Department of Health's (2010) guidelines as well as those published by Mencap (no date) are very useful in this regard.

Access, as set out in Article 30 of the CRPD, is also related to accessibility to audiovisual material, including sign language interpreting for deaf persons, captioning for hearing-impaired persons and audio description for visually impaired persons. Sign language interpreting is also possible for plays, musicals, dance and other performances. The usual practice is for specific performances to provide this service. Article 30 also specifies access to, among others, 'theatres, museums, cinemas, libraries and tourism services, and, as far as possible, … access to monuments and sites of national cultural importance' (United Nations 2006, p. 22). The Centre for Universal Design (2015) provides comprehensive guidelines regarding access to the built environment, outdoor environments and products. Museums offer a good example of how different aspects of accessibility can be brought together (Chimirri-Russell 2010, Sandell and Dodd 2010). The most obvious aspect is physical access to the museum and to the rooms and facilities within it. Then there is also access to information – including sub-titling of audiovisual information, Brailling of printed information and the provision of easy-to-read information sheets. Because museums are largely based on providing visual information through their various exhibits, they should also offer additional arrangements for people with visual impairments. These include audio descriptions, touch tours that are provided at set times and tactile zones where visitors are allowed to touch certain artefacts (for example reproductions of sculptures or scale models of buildings); for more on this topic see Strechay and Annis (2012).

Crucially, Article 30 also deals with disabled people's right 'to develop and utilise their creative, artistic and intellectual potential, not only for their own benefit, but also for the enrichment of society' (United Nations 2006, p. 22). This includes having access to 'appropriate instruction, training and resources' (p. 23). It also means, of course, giving disability arts their due importance and providing the spaces and resources for them to flourish.

Conclusion

In conclusion, it is vital for the makers of cultural policies, and those involved in their implementation, to take disabled people's issues into account. As seen in this chapter, they need to understand historical and contemporary influences on cultural representations of disabled people, especially through the insights afforded by Disability Studies scholars. They also need to appreciate the unique contribution made by disabled people to culture especially through disability arts, in which the experience of living with a disability is foregrounded in an affirmative manner. Finally, cultural policy makers and implementers need to recognise how they can and should set about ensuring disabled people's access to culture as consumers and producers of culture themselves. These three points are intimately linked, and by taking them into account we can help ensure that cultural policy and its implementation truly represent the variety of human experience and the meanings made out of that experience.

References

Adewunmi, B., 2013. Artist-Activist Liz Crow's 'bed-out' for disabled rights. *The Guardian*, 9 April. Available from: www.theguardian.com/artanddesign/2013/apr/09/liz-crow-bed-disabled-rights [Accessed 8 September 2015].

Anderson, J., and O'Sullivan, L., 2010. Histories of disability and medicine: Reconciling historical narratives and contemporary values. *In*: R. Sandell, J. Dodd and R. Garland-Thomson, eds. *Representing disability: Activism and agency in the museum*. New York: Routledge, 143–154.

Arts Council England, 2003. *Celebrating disability arts*. London: Arts Council England.

Baglieri, S. and Shapiro, A., 2012. *Disability studies and the inclusive classroom: Critical practices for creating least restrictive attitudes*. London: Routledge.

Barnes, C., 1996. Theories of disability and the origins of the oppression of disabled people in Western society. *In*: L. Barton, ed. *Disability and society: Emerging issues and insights*. Harlow, Essex: Pearson Education Limited, 41–60.

Barnes, C., 1997. A legacy of oppression: A history of disability in Western culture. *In*: L. Barton and M. Oliver, eds. *Disability studies: Past present and future*. Leeds: The Disability Press, 3–25.

Barnes, C. and Mercer, G., 2010. *Exploring disability*. Cambridge: Polity Press.

Bowie, A., 2003. *Introduction to German philosophy: From Kant to Habermas*. Cambridge: Polity.

Bowler, A., 1994. Methodological dilemmas in the sociology of art. *In*: D. Crane, ed. *The sociology of culture*. Oxford: Blackwell, 247–266.

Brown, S. E., 2003. *Movie stars and sensuous scars: Essays on the journey from disability shame to disability pride*. Lincoln, NE: Iuniverse, Inc.

Brueggemann, B. J., 2013. Disability studies/disability culture. *In*: M. L. Wehmeyer, ed. *The Oxford handbook of positive psychology and disability*. Oxford: Oxford University Press, 279–299.

Campbell, J. and Oliver, M., 1996. *Disability politics: Understanding our past, changing our future*. London: Routledge.

Centre for Universal Design, 2015. Welcome!. Available from: www.ncsu.edu/ncsu/design/cud/ [Accessed 17 September 2015].

Chimirri-Russell, G., 2010. The red wheelchair in the white snowdrift. *In*: R. Sandell, J. Dodd and R. Garland-Thomson, eds. *Representing disability: Activism and agency in the museum*. New York: Routledge, 168–178.

Clark, L. and Marsh, S., 2003. *Patriarchy in the UK: The language of disability*. Leeds: Disability Archive. Available from: www.leeds.ac.uk/disabilitystudies/archiveuk/Clark, %20Laurence/language.pdf [Accessed 9 September 2015].

Crow, L., 2008. Resistance: Which way the future?. Available from: www.roaring-girl.com/work/resistance/ [Accessed 16 September 2015].

Crow, L., 2012. Bedding out. Available from: www.roaring-girl.com/work/bedding-out/ [Accessed 16 September 2015].

Darke, P. A., 2003. Now I know why disability art is drowning in the river Lethe (with thanks to Pierre Bourdieu). *In*: S. Riddell and N. Watson, eds. *Disability, culture and identity*. New York: Routledge, 131–142.

Darke, P. A., 2004. The changing face of representations of disability in the media. *In*: J. Swain, S. French, C. Barnes and C. Thomas, eds. *Disabling barriers-enabling environments*, 2nd ed. London: Sage, 100–105.

Department of Health, 2010. Making written information easier to understand for people with learning disabilities. Available from: www.gov.uk/government/uploads/system/uploads/attachment_data/file/215923/dh_121927.pdf [Accessed 17 September 2015].

Disabled People Against Cuts, 2012. Bedside conversations. Available from: http://dpac.uk.net/2013/03/bedding-out-liz-crow-10-12-april-2013/ [Accessed 29 September 2015].

Disabled People's International (DPI), 1982. *Proceedings of the First World Congress*. Singapore: Disabled People's International.

Egle, J., 2008. Can we talk Ben Stiller?. Available from: www.youtube.com/watch?v=7eOBOAlQH54 [Accessed 3 September 2015].

Fleischer Zames, D. and Zames, F., 2011. *The disability rights movement: From charity to confrontation*. Philadelphia, PA: Temple University Press.

Foucault, M., 2001. *Madness and civilisation*. London: Routledge.

French, S. and Swain, J., 2012. *Working with disabled people in policy and practice*. New York: Palgrave Macmillan.

Garland-Thomson, R., 2010. Picturing people with disabilities. Classical portraiture as reconstructive narrative. *In*: R. Sandell, J. Dodd and R. Garland-Thomson, eds. *Re-presenting disability: Activism and agency in the museum*. New York: Routledge, 23–40.

Hall, A., 2015. *Literature and disability*. London: Routledge.

Hambrook, C., 2014. Disability arts. *In*: C. Cameron, ed. *Disability studies: A student's guide*. London: Sage, 30–33.

Hargrave, M., 2015. *Theatres of learning disability: Good, bad, or plain ugly?* Hampshire, UK: Palgrave Macmillan.

Inspiration porn and the objectification of disability: Stella Young at TEDxSydney, 2014. Video. Sydney: TEDx. Available from: www.youtube.com/watch?v=0iDmvAUokWk [Accessed 3 September 2015].

Johnston, K., 2012. *Stage turns: Canadian disability theatre.* Montreal, QC: McGill-Queen's University Press.

Kafer, A., 2013. *Feminist, queer, crip.* Bloomington, IN: Indiana University Press.

Longmore, P., 2003. *Why I burned my books and other essays.* Philadelphia, PA: Temple University Press.

Manning, L., 2005. *Weights* [Audio CD-ROM]. Bridge Multimedia.

Manning, L., 2009. A poem by Lynn Manning: The Magic Wand. *International Journal of Inclusive Education* 13(7), 785–785.

Manning L. (n.d.). About. Available from: www.lynnmanning.com/About.html [Accessed 12 September 2015].

Mansell, J. and Ericsson K., 1995. *Deinstitutionalisation and community living intellectual disability services in Scandinavia, Britain and the USA.* London: Chapman and Hall.

Masefield. P., 2006. *Strength: Broadsides from disability on the arts.* Stoke-on-Trent, UK: Trentham Books Limited.

Mencap, (n.d.). Make it clear: A guide to making easy read information. Available from: www.mencap. org.uk/sites/default/files/documents/2008-04/make%20it%20clear%20apr09.pdf [Accessed 17 September 2015].

Michalko, R., 2003. *The difference that disability makes.* Philadelphia, PA: Temple University Press.

Millett, A., 2008. Sculpting body ideals: Alison Lapper Pregnant and the public display of disability. *Disability Studies Quarterly,* 28 (3). Available from: http://dsq-sds.org/article/view/122/122 [Accessed 20 September 2015].

Millett-Gallant, A., 2010. *The disabled body in contemporary art.* London: Palgrave Macmillan.

Million Dollar Baby, 2004. Film. Directed by Clint Eastwood. USA: Warner Brothers.

Mitchell, D. T. and Snyder, S. L., 2000. *Narrative prosthesis: Disability and the dependence of discourse.* Ann Arbor, MI: University of Michigan Press.

My Left Foot, 1989. Film. Directed by Jim Sheridan. Ireland: Ferndale Films.

Nielson, K. E., 2012. *A disability history of the United States (Re-visioning American History).* Boston, MA: Beacon Press.

Nussbaum, S., 2014. *Good kings bad kings.* London: Oneworld Books.

Oliver, M., 1990. *The politics of disablement.* London: Macmillan. Available from: http://disability-studies.leeds.ac.uk/library/author/oliver.mike [Accessed 11 September 2015].

Piggott-McMillan, F., 2005. *The North Carolina black repertory company: 25 Marvtastic years.* Greensboro, NC: Open Hand Publishing.

Riva Lehrer – Self Portraits. Available from: www.rivalehrerart.com/#!self-portraits/cfq6 [Accessed 2 September 2015].

Sandell, R. and Dodd, J., 2010. Activist practice. *In*: R. Sandell, J. Dodd and R. Garland-Thomson, eds. *Re-presenting disability: Activism and agency in the museum.* New York: Routledge, 3–22.

Shapiro, J., 1994. *No pity: People with disabilities forging a new civil rights movement.* New York: Three Rivers Press.

Siebers, T., 2010. *Disability aesthetics.* Ann Arbor, MI: University of Michigan Press.

Silvers, A., 2000. From the crooked timber of humanity, beautiful things can be made. *In*: P. Zeglin Brand, ed. *Beauty matters.* Bloomington, IN: Indiana University Press, 197–221.

Smith, K., 2015. Victims and heroes: Exhibiting difference in Trafalgar Square. *In*: B. Tauke, K. Smith and C. Davis, eds. *Diversity and design: Understanding hidden consequences.* New York: Routledge, Chapter 12.

Stiker, H. J., 1999. *A history of disability.* Translated from French by W. Sayers. Ann Arbor, MI: University of Michigan Press.

Strechay, J. and Annis, T., 2012. Accessibility issues. *AFB Access World Magazine,* 13 (2). Available from: www.afb.org/afbpress/pub.asp?DocID=aw130206 [Accessed 17 September 2015].

Sutherland, A., 2008. Choices, rights and cabaret: Disability arts and collective identity. *In*: J. Swain and S. French, eds. *Disability on equal terms.* London: Sage, 79–89.

Swain, J. and French, S., 2000. Towards an affirmation model of disability. *Disability & Society,* 15 (4), 569–582.

The Theory of Everything, 2014. Film. Directed by James Marsh. UK: Working Title Films.

Tropic Thunder, 2008. Film. Directed by Ben Stiller. USA: Dreamworks SKG.

United Nations, 2006. Convention on the rights of persons with disabilities and optional protocol. Available from: www.un.org/disabilities/ documents/convention/convotprot-e/pdf [Accessed 11 September 2015].

Untouchable, 2011. Film. Directed by Olivier Nakache and Eric Toledano. France: Quad Productions.

Vasey, S., 1992. Disability arts and culture: An introduction to key issues and questions. *In*: S. Leeds, ed. *Disability arts and culture papers*. London: Shape, part 1.

Whose Life Is It Anyway? 1981. Film. Directed by John Badham. USA: Metro-Goldwyn-Mayer.

Wolfensberger, W., 1972. *The Origin and nature of our institutional models*. Syracuse, NY: Human Policy Press.

World Intellectual Property Organisation, 2013. Marrakesh Treaty to facilitate access to published works for persons who are blind, visually impaired or otherwise print disabled. Available from: www.wipo.int/wipolex/en/treaties/text.jsp?file_id=301019 [Accessed 17 September 2015].

World Wide Web Consortium, 2015. Web accessibility initiative. Available from: www.w3.org/WAI/ [Accessed 17 September 2015].

12

Minority languages, cultural policy and minority language media

The conflicting value of the 'one language–one nation' idea

Enrique Uribe-Jongbloed and Abiodun Salawu

On October 1st, 2015, the NGO Plataforma per la llengua published a news article on its web page complaining about the lack of Catalan subtitles vis-à-vis Spanish on the films exhibited at the Sitges Film Festival hosted in the Catalonian town south of Barcelona. Plataforma per la llengua argued that despite an investment by the regional culture department (Department de Cultura de la Generalitat) of €600.000, less than 15% of films originally produced in other languages were subtitled into Catalan compared to 99% of films that were subtitled in Spanish. Plataforma per la llengua created a small poster (see Figure 12.1) to express this position and encouraged people to go to the festival displaying it. On October 13th, Plataforma per la llengua issued a second statement claiming that, despite the Sitges Film Festival officials denying the situation, they continued to pursue their claim that less than 16% of films were available in Catalan.

The discussion about Catalan dubbing and subtitling at movie theaters in Catalonia is not new. Despite the passage of a law in 2010 by the Generalitat in Catalonia demanding that 50% of films to be exhibited in cinemas across Catalonia be dubbed or subtitled in Catalan (Cordonet & Forniès 2013), exemptions had to be made in 2014 regarding European films as demanded by the EU (ABC, 2014-02-04), and the 2015 case at Sitges has continued with the same linguistic critiques of cultural policies.

The situation described above highlights one of the conflicts between cultural subventions and cultural representation of minority, or even minoritised, languages within nation-states.

Not only is cultural policy aimed at the subvention or promotion of audiovisual products to broker the difference between the economic interests of those looking for larger markets and those in search of a national identity in production (Miller & Yúdice 2004, p. 74), but also within the nation, in terms of linguistic identity and ascription. Language is an important carrier of culture, and a general comparison between the number of languages in the world and the small number of established nation-states shows how the latter are likely to be multilingual, if not also multicultural in their make-up. This provides a very nuanced dilemma for cultural policy, because not only does it have to deal with the cultural perspectives promoted by the nation-state and national identity, but also with those various linguistic identities, whether indigenous or the product of old or recent migrations (Extra & Gorter 2008).

Figure 12.1 Campaign by Plataforma per la llengua

The following pages seek to illustrate the relevance of language in cultural policy development, in particular in the case of minority language media policy, regarding both media production and broadcasting. A cultural sustainability paradigm (Martín Barbero 2011) is presented as a form to place language in the cultural policy debate. To that effect, we present a discussion on language as part of cultural policy, followed by a discussion about language normalisation as a path to be achieved by languages within national borders, and finally addressing minority language media studies as an area of inquiry in its own right. Then we present two case studies of multilingual nations, Colombia in South America and South Africa on the African continent, to highlight the struggles, achievements and possible challenges of cultural policy in relation to minority language media development.

Although it may be erroneous to set languages and cultures as one and the same, a tight interdependent relationship between language and culture is true and evident. The grammar, the richness of vocabulary, the different forms to express a concept, the presence or absence of certain terms, simply to mention some aspects, may tell us a lot about that people. In order to fully enjoy a 'culture' you must know the associated language, and on the other side knowing a language you have the main entry point to the associated culture (Ronchi 2015, p. 73).

Language is an inextricable part of culture, yet cultural policy seldom reflects upon the language component, glossing over it. In fact, even international conventions promoting the protection of cultural expression, such as the Convention for Safeguarding Intangible Cultural Heritage, are at odds with this description because "in the process of drafting this Convention, some countries objected to including languages as such, presumably out of fear that this might fuel separatist tendencies of minorities" (Wintermans 2008, p. 232).

This exemplifies the fact that "the relationship between languages and language groups is inevitably a relationship of power, so it's not surprising that the terms we use to describe categories of language have political overtones and implications" (Thomas 2001, p. 44) and that "the language and identity link cannot be understood in isolation from other factors of identity, nor from the political conditions in which it is situated" (May 2001, p. 135), because "language, after all, is not only a means of communication, but it is also a marker of identity and, through its pragmatics, a cultural institution" (Laitin 2000, p. 144).

Language poses particular problems for policy makers because "frequently in Europe, though very much less frequently elsewhere, the nationalist perspective assumes that each nation has a clearly distinct national language, peculiar to that nation" (Barbour 2002, p. 11), creating a two-tier system between the language(s) of the nation-state, and those languages spoken only by a non-state represented minority. The myth of equating nation and language has been a tenet of conservative policies where:

> the emphasis on cultural and linguistic homogeneity associated with the rise of political nationalism is predicated on the notion of 'nation-state congruence'. Nation-state congruence holds that the boundaries of political and national identity should coincide. The view here is that people who are citizens of a particular state should also, ideally, be members of the same national collectivity.
>
> *(May 2000, p. 370)*

There are often discussions about the usefulness of having one single language for communication, either to simplify translation costs or to increase economic opportunities for those learning a prestigious language (Crystal 2003, p. 12). Capitalist and communist pressures alike seemed to favour the single language strategy to increase potential markets or to ensure that state bureaucracy was equally applicable to all citizens, with the added advantage of an intercommunicated working class that would need no translation, often seen as a privilege of the aristocrats. Even today there is constant pressure from government bodies to increase the knowledge of the global English language, sometimes at the expense of national minority languages, as the cases below will show.

In a multicultural view of the nation, such as the one espoused by countries in Latin America and Africa, as the cases of Colombia and South Africa will illustrate, there is an interest in reversing the shift to ensure that all languages have the possibility to carry with them their value and tradition. Similarly, linguistic minorities the world over seek to keep their languages alive and to gain access to the same spaces where dominant languages have found their footing. As the example from Catalonia illustrates, this is not an easy task and requires constant reminders to the homogenised and monolingual national majority that other languages are present and relevant within specific regions, if not throughout the nation. Indigenous and aboriginal languages, as well as other pre-colonial languages, can argue even further because of their historical presence in given territories prior to colonisation by other languages (Spencer 2008).

Language, then, also fits within the cultural sustainability paradigm, presented by Martin-Barbero (2011, p. 46) along three vectors: *awareness* that a community has its own cultural capital, capacity of the community to take decisions that enable its *cultural capital to be preserved and renewed* and capacity to open up culture itself to *exchange and interaction* with other cultures in the country and the world. When applied to linguistic diversity, the first vector would imply recognition both within and outside the linguistic community. The second vector implies empowerment in decision-making processes and governmental support in a variety of sectors, including education, media and industry. Finally, the third aspect would encourage and promote bilingualism, with majority languages seen as assets rather than requirements.

In general, the aim of cultural sustainability in terms of those languages is to allow them to remain the 'normal' form of communication for a linguistic community.

Linguistic normalisation

The idea behind linguistic normalisation is that of creating the social circumstances that enable a language to become the 'normal' element of exchange in everyday life (Cormack 2007). It has been used to define the linguistic process of incorporating language into every domain and every register (Leisen 2000, p. 43). This is done in such a way that its users are able to carry out their day-to-day routines without having to resort to any other language (Guardado Diez 2008). The process of linguistic normalisation has been relevant for the development of the media in Catalan (Corominas Piulats 2007), Basque (Amezaga & Arana 2012; Amezaga et al. 2000) and Asturian (Guardado Diez 2008) because the media are seen as necessary tools for making a language available for use in all aspects of everyday life in specific communities.

The concepts of functional and institutional completeness are similar to normalisation (Moring 2007; Moring & Dunbar 2008). Moring says that *functional completeness* "[occurs when] speakers of the language… can live their life in and through the language without having to resort to other languages, at least within the confines of everyday matters in their community" (2007, p. 18). He goes on to argue that a precondition for *functional completeness* is *institutional completeness*, defined as "media platforms available in the minority language for each type of media" (2007, p. 19). However, *institutional completeness*, even when fully achieved (assuming there are specific radio and television broadcasters, a printed newspaper and internet provisions) may not truly reach *functional completeness* until it covers pretty much the same areas and genres as the majority language media do. It could be argued, then, that a language is normalised when it achieves both institutional and functional completeness.

Although the specific use of the term 'normalisation' has not been widely applied outside the Iberian peninsula (Cormack 2007, p. 11), its usefulness rests in its definition of the ultimate goal each minority language struggles to attain: "its standardisation both from a structural and social perspective, namely, its corpus and its status" (Guardado Diez 2008, p. 85).[1] Since normalisation aims at enabling people to discuss all aspects of life through the language, it looks for the creation of a space of debate that overcomes the need to use any other language for communication practices.

Minority language media

One of the areas where minority languages have started to find space within nation states is in their media output. In Europe, for instance, there were many campaigns in the 1980s and 1990s, looking for greater televisual presence of national minority languages (Cormack 1998; Hourigan 2004). In the Americas, as well as other countries with a clear Western European colonial past, there have been different types of media development by indigenous minorities, particularly radio stations (Ramos Rodríguez 2005; Uribe-Jongbloed 2014b; see, for instance, Castells-Talens et al. 2009; Meadows & Molnar 2002; Rodríguez & El Gazi 2007) and video festivals (Salazar 2009; Salazar & Córdova 2008). Alongside this recent development of indigenous media, the concept of a New Media Nation (Alia 2010) has emerged to describe all these ways of distributing content, communicating local knowledge and fostering cultural traditions, including language maintenance. Similarly, immigrant groups have continued to maintain close ties to their home countries or ethnic identities, consuming or accessing locally produced ethnic or heritage media, or connecting to media from their home countries.

However, despite the symbolic value that media, created and developed by linguistic or indigenous minorities, may have, it is difficult to find a direct correlation between minority-language media output and linguistic maintenance. Functional completeness and normalisation certainly create an environment where the language is consistently available for all users, but the costs of achieving said normalisation, both in terms of infrastructure and capacity-building, have usually set them as goals seldom achieved in countries with various linguistic minorities. Europe, for instance, has low linguistic diversity in comparison to Latin America, Asia and Africa.[2] The question of resource allocation, as well as the variety of political issues at stake, has often had a bearing upon the choice of linguistic output by minority communities. In Colombia, for instance, political interest has prompted indigenous communities such as the Nasa to limit the use of their indigenous language, Nasa Yuwe, in order to gather more popular support from peasant farmers, Afro-Colombian settlers and other indigenous people alike, through the use of Spanish (Uribe-Jongbloed 2016). This situation is the opposite of Sami journalists in northern Scandinavia, who have accepted losing some ethnically identified audiences because they are committed to broadcasting in Sami (Pietikäinen 2008a,b). Hence, the likelihood of survival of certain endangered languages relies on the willingness of the community to bear the costs and trade-offs of supporting the language (Van Parijs 2008).

Despite the growth of minority language media, thanks to lowered costs of production, their situation is far from safe (Browne & Uribe-Jongbloed 2013; Wilson & Stewart 2008). Suspicion of the minority language being used in the media, be it because of the fear of potential secessionist nationalism or any form of rebellious or anti-establishment propaganda, tends to keep governmental support low. The notion of one single language as the language of the nation seems to remain a central part of the political neglect of minority languages.

What we aim to do now is present two case studies, one from Latin America and one from Africa, to highlight how cultural policy has been defined to include linguistic demands, absent from other areas of political debate. Despite the impact of language on economic, communication or education policy, linguistic issues in policy and research have been addressed from the angle of culture and heritage. But since language has bearing on education practices (i.e. language of instruction), economic and development goals (i.e. territorial disputes between linguistic groups) and communication (i.e. language of broadcast) policies, a discussion of language policy must therefore acknowledge some of the remits of other governmental bodies not directly connected to cultural policy development.

Colombian case: ethnolinguistic diversity policy as part of cultural policy

The Colombian constitution of 1991, stemming from a peace agreement with the M-19 Guerrilla,[3] changed the 'one nation, one language' idea to include articles that accept the multiethnic and multilingual reality of the state. Article 7, for instance, says that "The State recognizes and protects the ethnic and cultural diversity of the Colombian nation", and Article 10 recognises Castilian Spanish as the official language and the languages and dialects of ethnic groups as official in their territories (Anon 1991). As these articles attest, the Constitution regards Colombia as a multilingual and pluriethnic state. This fact has been central to the modification of educational, cultural and economic policies and particularly important for the recognition of cultural diversity (see also Cuesta Moreno 2012; Rodríguez & El Gazi 2007; Uribe-Jongbloed 2014a). Yet it can also be criticised for having co-opted the ethnic and other minority groups previously ignored and merely inserted them into the pre-existing Western liberal democracy (Zambrano 2006). The concept can be easily understood by the metaphor of a house employed by Zambrano (2006):

> The house is the State. Until 1991, in that house no Indian, Black or popular culture were to be found. By accepting their entry, the owner of the house did not put at their service the upkeep of the house, but rather he refurbished it keeping the structure and architecture intact. He built an extra room in the house, and to find the space he reduced other rooms and moved some walls... what was achieved was that all new citizens settled in that room and the owner had them fight over the organization of the room, but not the organization of the house.... (p. 197)[4]

The conceptual structure of the state was not modified but accommodated those who were previously excluded yet keeping them apart from the 'normal' population. Those new members of the Colombian society were the ethnic minorities, which made up roughly 14% of the total population of 41,468,384 Colombians in 2005, among them 1,392,623 (3.4%) indigenous peoples, 4,311,757 (10.6%) African-, or Black-Colombians, and 4, 858 (0.01) members of a Rom community (DANE 2007, p. 33).[5]

The Constitution of 1991 led to Law 397 of 1997, which created the Ministry of Culture (Bravo 2010, pp. 54–55), whose remit was to develop the country's cultural policy. More recently this role has taken into account that cultural policies are not "enclosed orientations but flexible proposals that seek to interpret creatively the cultural demands of the society" (Rey 2010, p. 38).

As part of its intended remit, Colombian cultural policy has included both intangible heritage and the social revitalisation of [South] American native tongues[6] (Rey 2010, p. 39). Because of the particular condition of the fields that are covered by cultural policy, the Ministry of Culture has had to pair up with other Ministries, particularly Education and Communication, to develop some of the programs aimed at the protection and maintenance of the minority languages. One such collaboration was the "Comunidad Señal de Cultura y Diversidad" program carried out between 2002 and 2006 in three phases, which sought to provide equipment and training to enable indigenous communities to establish and develop their own radio stations (Ministerio de Cultura 2010, p. 358). Despite an important strategy of consultation with the different indigenous groups (Rodríguez & El Gazi 2007), the program was cut short, and the 26 media outlets developed were soon left without support from the national government. For instance, the Wayuu radio station developed under the program, *Jujunula Makuira*, spent many years off the air because of lightning damages they could not claim under insurance because the insurance company required sending the equipment to Bogotá, and they could not afford it (Peña Sarmiento 2012; Uribe-Jongbloed & Peña Sarmiento 2014). Though for some other stations this lack of governmental support meant less government interference and meddling in their affairs (see Murillo 2008), it also explains why some of them experienced difficulties in the upkeep of their equipment and broadcast continuity. Furthermore, despite an interest in supporting language maintenance efforts through media output, little is known about the use of indigenous languages in broadcasting or if it is used at all (ONIC 2009; Uribe-Jongbloed 2016).

The lack of continuity of the "Comunidad" program is akin to the program covering sociolinguistic self-diagnosis of competence and knowledge among the linguistic minorities of Colombia. This program started in 2008, with two stages, seeking to reach 29 tongues that would account for 616,000 people, 71% of the linguistic minorities, leaving 250,000 speakers of the 39 remaining languages for later studies (Ministerio de Cultura 2010, p. 365). However, due to the change of government in 2010, the study was only partly completed, with just 16 self-diagnoses fully developed and five more in early stages of development (Bodnar 2013). Thus, there is a lack of information to really comprehend the situation of the 68 minority languages of Colombia, which leads to speculation and contradictory reports from most governmental agencies (Uribe-Jongbloed & Anderson 2014).

Even though 2010 saw Language Law 1381 enacted, and its various articles led the way to present issues as ethno-education and media development in minority languages as part of Colombia's cultural policy (Uribe-Jongbloed & Anderson 2014), lack of information concerning the situation of the languages remains the burden of any policies that seek to encourage and maintain minority languages in the country. Also, at the same time there is a cultural policy supporting indigenous and other ethnic languages, the national examinations to gain access to universities require knowledge of English as the second language, ignoring that for many indigenous Colombians, Spanish is already a second language (Truscott de Mejía 2006).

Minority languages are seen as integral to the nation's cultural policy, but a serious problem of continuing funding and dedication to linguistic, media and ethno-educational endeavours has made policy less effective. Although one cannot deny the advances made since the Constitution of 1991, the fact that it took 19 years for specific linguistic policy to be enacted, at the same time as crucial information gathering was discontinued due to administrative changes, makes it evident that cultural policy has yet to be a definitive tool for language maintenance. However, the advances should not be underestimated. To continue with Zambrano's (2006) metaphor quoted above, the new lodgers in the extra room have started to challenge the structure of the house. The house will soon be remodelled.

South Africa: an uneven picture of the multilingual reality

South Africa is a multilingual country, having 11 of its many languages officially recognised: Afrikaans, English, IsiNdebele, IsiXhosa, IsiZulu, Sepedi, Sesotho, Setswana, SiSwati, Tshivenda and Xitsonga. Besides the official languages, other languages in South Africa include Khoi, Nama and San languages, sign language, Arabic, German, Greek, Gujarati, Hebrew, Hindi, Portuguese, Sanskrit, Tamil, Telegu and Urdu (Lewis et al. 2015).

The 2011 Census in the country indicates isiZulu as the mother-tongue of 22.7% of South Africa's population, followed by isiXhosa (16.0%), Afrikaans (13.5%), English (9.6%), Sepedi (9.1%), Setswana (8.0%), Sesotho (7.6%), Xitsonga (4.5%), SiSwati (2.5%), Tshivenda (2.4%) and IsiNdebele (2.1%) (Statistics South Africa 2012).

IsiZulu, isiXhosa, siSwati and isiNdebele all belong to the Nguni group of languages. They are similar both in syntax and grammar. The Sotho languages – Setswana, Sepedi and Sesotho – also have much in common. All nine officially recognised original African languages in South Africa belong to the Bantu language family.

Using UNESCO's schema (Moseley 2010), African languages can be said to be at different levels of endangerment. These levels are 'safe', 'vulnerable' (not spoken by children outside the home), 'definitely endangered' (children not speaking), 'severely endangered' (only spoken by the oldest generations) and 'critically endangered' (spoken by few members of the oldest generation, often semi-speakers). Despite most South African languages being considered 'safe', there is a clear sense of risk, since a major cause of language endangerment is the shifting of speakers to another language. Coetzee-Van Rooy (2012) notes that there is a vibrant public and scholarly debate about the potential language shift of speakers of African languages to English. In particular because:

> the dominance of English and Afrikaans languages is not necessarily caused by a lack of political will to implement policies by government, but rather the power that English and Afrikaans speakers wield upon the South African economy.
>
> *(Moyo 2010, p. 433)*

Three camps in the academic debate are identified. There are scholars who predict that African languages will die in (South) Africa (de Klerk 2000; Kamwangamalu 2003). There are others who argue that there is a slow shift from the use of African languages as home languages to English (Deumert 2010; Meshtrie 2008); and there are those who maintain that African languages are not endangered as home languages but they are also not developing to be used in certain domains, such as the sciences (Coetzee-Van Rooy 2012, 2013, 2014; Prah 2010). The fact is that any language can be used in any domain if properly developed; that should be the target for African languages.

Prah (2003) speaks of the 'collective amnesia' that is occurring as a result of not using African languages as languages of education (see Roy-Campbell 2006, p. 3). Prah's concern is that when African languages are devalued in this manner, much of the indigenous knowledge contained in those languages becomes devalued. This must also have been part of the concern of the South African Ministry of Education when, on 27 November 2003, it set up a ministerial committee to advise on the development of African (indigenous) languages as mediums of instruction in higher education. The report noted that the "Minister (of Education) called to mind the challenge facing higher education to ensure the simultaneous development of a multilingual environment in which all South African languages would be developed to their full capacity while at the same time ensuring that the existing languages of instruction did not form a barrier to access and success" (DOE 2003, p. 3).

Furthermore, the Constitution of the Republic of South Africa Act 108 of 1996 recognises the historically diminished status of the indigenous languages of the people. Therefore, the state resolves to take practical and positive measures to elevate the status and advance the use of the languages. Similarly, the constitution provides for the recognition of the principle of multilingualism. "Provision is also made for measures designed to achieve respect, adequate protection and furtherance of the official South African languages and for the advancement of those official languages which in the past did not enjoy full recognition, in order to promote the full and equal enjoyment of the languages used for communication and religious purposes".

In order to promote indigenous languages recognised by the Constitution as historically diminished in use and status, the South African government is according a growing importance to the learning of these languages. Happily, in this regard, there are changes happening in some South African universities. The University of KwaZulu-Natal has made isiZulu a compulsory first-year subject. At Rhodes University, journalism students must pass an isiXhosa for journalism course at either mother tongue or second language level (Kaschula 2015).

A major institution established by the South African government for the purpose of facilitating media and information access among historically disadvantaged communities as well as historically diminished indigenous language and cultural groups is the Media Development and Diversity Agency (MDDA). The MDDA was established by an Act of Parliament (Act 14 of 2002) to enable historically disadvantaged communities and persons not adequately served by the media to gain access to the media. The major beneficiaries of the agency are the community media and small commercial media.

The objectives of the MDDA are to:

i   Encourage ownership and control of, and access to, media by historically disadvantaged communities as well as by historically diminished indigenous language and cultural groups;
ii Encourage the development of human resources and training, and capacity building, within the media industry, especially amongst historically disadvantaged groups;
iii Encourage the channelling of resources to the community media and small commercial media sectors;
iv Raise public awareness with regard to media development and diversity issues;
v   Support initiatives which promote literacy and a culture of reading;
vi Encourage research regarding media development and diversity; and
vii Liaise with statutory bodies such as the Independent Communications Authority of South Africa and the Universal Service Agency. (The Presidency 2002, pp. 4–5)

The agency is guided by a number of relevant and related legislations such as the MDDA Act No. 14 of 2002, The Public Finance Management Act No. 1 of 1996, The Electronic Communication Act No. 35 of 2005, The Constitution Act 108 of 1996, The Broad-Based Black Economic Empowerment Act No. 96 of 1995, The Employment Act of 2000, The Skills Development Act, and The Basic Conditions of Employment No. 75 of 1997. Other MDDA regulations include the White Paper on Broadcasting Policy, IBA Triple Inquiry Report, Review of 10 Year Broadcasting Regulation, Community Television Broadcasting Services Position Paper, ICASA – Independent Communication Authority of South Africa and General Licenses Fees Regulation.

The language diversity of South Africa is well observable in its broadcast media, particularly the community radios that have been fundamental for language maintenance (Moyo 2010). This, however, is not so much for the print media as the so-called community newspapers do not necessarily "speak" the language of the community they serve. Indigenous African languages do not occupy a central place in community newspaper publishing. This also is the situation with the use of the languages on digital media. The use of local African languages is not as extensive in the digital media as the use of English and Afrikaans. Policy apart, a major drive will be for the Africans to promote their languages through conscious and robust use in the various media. Implementation, rather than policy development, is required to ensure that multilingual policy does not stay at the policy level (Coetzee-Van Rooy 2014, p. 136).

Conclusions and discussion

The linguistic homogeneity paradigm that has led the idea of the state as a monolingual and monocultural society is still to be found in most countries the world over. Despite recent recognition in various nation states of the intercultural and multilingual nature of their existence, language hierarchisation remains constant in a variety of places world-wide, including Canada (Haque & Patrick 2015), Zimbabwe (Mpofu & Mutasa 2014), Kenya (Orao 2009), New Zealand (de Bres 2015) and Spain (Plataforma per la llengua 2015). As the two case studies presented also evidence, because of the nature of language as a conveyor of culture, the media are central to all debates about cultural representation, and media policies immediately become linguistic policies.

It is clear that:

> Cultural diversity has become a new goal of public policy. The uncertainty that surrounds its definition springs from the struggle for power (between different actors as well as between territorial levels) that views it as the prize. Its ambivalence and the dilemmas which it creates do not justify the radical critiques levied against it. On the contrary, they demand a deeper level of debate as to the implementation of policies of cultural diversity.
>
> *(Bonet & Négrier 2011, p. 587)*

At least from the standpoint of the nation state, the challenges are clear. Adopting the multilingual reality as part of the constitution of the state is one thing, but to really account for an intercultural approach to the state is a very different one. As the Colombian and South African cases highlight, governmental advances have been made in order to address the disadvantage experienced by minority languages, especially since they had been minoritised by the same state that now grants them recognition. The policy approach from the top-down seems to deal with a given sense of guilt based on previous negligence but does not really incorporate the multicultural aspect as an intercultural reality.

Following the cultural sustainability paradigm mentioned in the introduction, the first two steps seem to have been overcome. In both South Africa and Colombia, as in most countries now, there is recognition of multilingualism, an *awareness* of the cultural capital of linguistic diversity. The developments mentioned show there is a concerted effort to *promote and foster* those languages, even if the gap between policy and implementation remains ample. Thus, it is with the third part of the paradigm, *exchange and interaction*, where cultural policy in favour of minority languages is still just making the first steps forward. The campaign by Plataforma per la llengua illustrates this problem, because it shows how distant even a buoyant minority language, such as Catalan, is from the majority language of the nation state when it comes to normalisation of the language.

Further research steps

It is clear that there is considerable research required in order to find, quantify, assess and evaluate minority language media production, in particular to comprehend the dual role of ethnic media practitioners as both professionals and cultural identity advocates (Husband 2005). Research in those fields can further prompt debates and lead to structural media policy reforms that encompass linguistic and cultural aspects, often overlooked by the traditional broadcasting policies. Alongside audience research of minority language media, it would address the *exchange and interaction* part of the paradigm, providing the evidence required for cultural policy development. The two cases presented, both of the global South, highlight a situation dissimilar yet not all that different from the situation in First-World countries regarding minority language debates.

As pointed out by Le (2015), we could consider the research focus to follow a framework divided on two strands, one that looks at the status of media in minority contexts and a second that focuses on the participation of minorities in national, transnational and international debates with media in minority contexts. Within the latter, Le recommends pursuing research in three subfields: media access and use; identities; and media practices. Within those boundaries, further research could help evidence the true multicultural value of linguistic diversity and through research, pose challenges to national or international policy that sets up the goal of diversity as integral to broadcasting policy.

Notes

1 Original text in Asturian: "Por *normalización llingüística* entendemos la estratexa de caltenimientu o revitalización d'una llingua subordinada que tien como oxetivu la so estandarización tanto dende'l puntu de vista estructural como social, ye dicir, del so corpus y el so estatus".

2 Europe sports only 286 living languages, whereas the Americas account for 1,064, Africa 2,138 and Asia 2,301 (Lewis et al. 2015). Unless one includes the cosmopolitan situation of most European metropolises, Europe is clearly less diverse than other regions of the world.

3 M-19 (Movimiento 19 de abril) was a Guerrilla group founded in 1970 in Colombia as a reaction against the supposedly rigged presidential elections of that year. The group entered a peace process in 1989 and finally left armed insurgency becoming a political party for the 1990 presidential elections and won several seats at the constitutional assembly, which created the Constitution of 1991.

4 Translation by the authors of an original in Spanish.

5 Notice that the information is from 2005, and the new census has been scheduled for 2017 because of economic constraints.

6 It is important to note here that policy usually refers to *lenguas* or *dialectos* in Spanish, which could be translated into 'tongues' or 'dialects', rather than *idioma*, which translates into 'language'. It would seem, thus, that even on the description given of the languages of Colombia there is an evident hierarchisation between the majority language and the minority 'tongues'. It is because of this division that we have decided to use tongues instead of languages whenever the word *lenguas* appears in the text.

References

Alia, V., 2010. *The New Media Nation: Indigenous Peoples and Global Communications*. New York and Oxford: Berghahn Books.

Amezaga, J., Arana, E., Basterretxea, J.I. & Iturriotz, A., 2000. Politics, Language and Identity in the Basque Media. *Mercator Media Forum*, 4, pp. 16–40.

Amezaga, J. & Arana, E., 2012. Minority Language Television in Europe : Commonalities and Differences between Regional Minority Languages and Immigrant. *Zer*, 17(32), pp. 89–106.

Anon, 1991. Constitución Política de Colombia. Available at: www.banrepcultural.org/blaavirtual/derecho/constitucion-politica-de-colombia-1991

Barbour, S., 2002. Language, Nationalism and Globalism: Educational Consequences of Changing Patterns of Language Use. In P. Gubbins & M. Holt, eds. *Beyond Boundaries: Language and Identity in Contemporary Europe*. Clevedon: Multilingual Matters, pp. 11–18.

Bodnar, Y., 2013. Estudio comparativo de la vitalidad lingüística de 14 pueblos de Colombia realizado mediante una encuesta (autodiagnóstico sociolingüístico). *Notas de Población*, 40(97), pp. 249–293.

Bonet, L. & Négrier, E., 2011. The end(s) of National Cultures? Cultural Policy in the Face of Diversity. *International Journal of Cultural Policy*, 17(5), pp. 574–589.

Bravo, M.E., 2010. Políticas culturales en Colombia. In G. Rey, ed. *Compendio de Políticas Culturales*. Bogotá, DC: Ministerio de Cultura, pp. 49–78.

Browne, D.R. & Uribe-Jongbloed, E., 2013. Ethnic/Linguistic Minority Media: What Their History Reveals, How Scholars Have Studied Them, and What We Might Ask Next. In E.H. G. Jones & E. Uribe-Jongbloed, eds. *Social Media and Minority Languages: Convergence and the Creative Industries*. Bristol, Buffalo, and Tronto: Multilingual Matters, pp. 1–28.

Castells-Talens, A., Ramos Rodríguez, J.M. & Chan Concha, M., 2009. Radio, Control, and Indigenous Peoples: The Failure of State-Invented Citizens' Media in Mexico. *Development in Practice*, 19(4–5), pp. 525–537. Available at: www.scopus.com/inward/record.url?eid=2-s2.0-70449724358&partnerID=40&md5=1d5ebfc7b06f616f8a34de908629d113

Coetzee-Van Rooy, S., 2012. Flourishing Functional Multilingualism: Evidence from Language Repertoires in the Vaal Triangle Region. *International Journal of the Sociology of Language*, 2012(218), pp. 87–119. Available at: www.scopus.com/inward/record.url?eid=2-s2.0-84876858075&partnerID=tZOtx3y1 [Accessed 17 November 2015].

Coetzee-Van Rooy, S., 2013. Afrikaans in Contact with English: Endangered Language or Case of Exceptional Bilingualism? *International Journal of the Sociology of Language*, 2013(224), pp. 179–207. Available at: www.scopus.com/inward/record.url?eid=2-s2.0-84890259139&partnerID=tZOtx3y1 [Accessed 17 November 2015].

Coetzee-Van Rooy, S., 2014. Explaining the Ordinary Magic of Stable African Multilingualism in the Vaal Triangle Region in South Africa. *Journal of Multilingual and Multicultural Development*, 35(2), pp. 121–138. Available at: www.tandfonline.com/doi/abs/10.1080/01434632.2013.818678

Cordonet, J. & Forniès, D., 2013. Legislating the Language of Cinema: Developments in Catalonia. In E.H.G. Jones & E. Uribe-Jongbloed, eds. *Social Media and Minority Languages: Convergence and the Creative Industries*. Bristol: Multilingual Matters, pp. 202–211.

Cormack, M., 1998. Minority Language Media in Western Europe. *European Journal of Communication*, 13(1), pp. 33–52.

Cormack, M., 2007. Introduction: Studying Minority Language Media. In M. Cormack & N. Hourigan, eds. *Minority Language Media*. Clevedon: Multilingual Matters, pp. 1–16.

Corominas Piulats, M., 2007. Media Policy and Language Policy in Catalonia. In M. Cormack & N. Hourigan, eds. *Minority Language Media: Concepts, Critiques and Case Studies*. Clevedon: Multilingul Matters, pp. 168–187.

Crystal, D., 2003. *English as a Global Language*, Second edition, New York: Cambridge University Press.

Cuesta Moreno, O., 2012. Investigaciones radiofónicas : de la radio a la radio indígena. Una revisión en Colombia y Latinoamérica. *Anagramas*, 10(20), pp. 181–196.

DANE, 2007. *Colombia: Una Nación Multicultural*. Bogotá, DC: DANE. Available at: www.dane.gov.co/files/censo2005/etnia/sys/colombia_nacion.pdf.

de Bres, J., 2015. The Hierarchy of Minority Languages in New Zealand. *Journal of Multilingual and Multicultural Development*, 36(7), 677–693. Available at: www.tandfonline.com/doi/abs/10.1080/01434632.2015.1009465.

de Klerk, V., 2000. Language Shift in Grahamstown: A Case Study of Selected Xhosa-Speakers. *International Journal of the Sociology of Language*, 146, pp. 87–110. Available at: www.scopus.com/inward/record.url?eid=2-s2.0-15744379611&partnerID=tZOtx3y1

Deumert, A., 2010. Tracking the Demographics of (Urban) Language Shift—An Analysis of South African Census Data. *Journal of Multilingual and Multicultural Development*, 31(1), pp. 13–35.

DOE, 2003. *The Development of Indigenous African Languages as Mediums of Instruction in Higher Education: Report Compiled by the Ministerial Committee appointed by the Ministry of Education in September 2003*, Pretoria.

Extra, G. & Gorter, D., 2008. The Constellation of Languages in Europe: An Inclusive Approach. In G. Extra & D. Gorter, eds. *Multilingual Europe: Facts and Policies*. Berlin and New York: Mouton de Gruyter, pp. 3–60.

Guardado Diez, D., 2008. *Llingua Estándar y Normalización Llingüística: La Revitalización de les Llingües Subordinaes*. Gijón: Araz Llibros.

Haque, E. & Patrick, D., 2015. Indigenous Languages and the Racial Hierarchisation of Language Policy in Canada. *Journal of Multilingual and Multicultural Development*, 36(1), pp. 27–41. Available at: www.tandfonline.com/doi/abs/10.1080/01434632.2014.892499

Hourigan, N., 2004. *Escaping the Global Village: Media, Language and Protest*. Lanham, MD and Oxford: Lexington Books.

Husband, C., 2005. Minority Ethnic Media as Communities of Practice: Professionalism and Identity Politics in Interaction. *Ethnic and Migration Studies*, 31(3), pp. 461–479.

Kamwangamalu, N.M., 2003. Globalization of English, and Language Maintenance and Shift in South Africa. *International Journal of the Sociology of Language*, 164, pp. 65–81. Available at: https://doi.org/10.1515/ijsl.2003.056.

Kaschula, R.H., 2015. African Languages Have the Power to Transform Universities. *The Conversation*. Available at: http://theconversation.com/african-languages-have-the-power-to-transform-universities-40901 [Accessed 17 November 2015].

Laitin, D.D., 2000. What Is a Language Community? *American Journal of Political Science*, 44(1), pp. 142–155.

Le, E., 2015. Media in Minority Contexts: Towards a Research Framework. *Journal of Applied Journalism & Media Studies*, 4(1), pp. 3–24. Available at: https://doi.org/10.1386/ajms.4.1.3_1

Leisen, S., 2000. Die Printmedien in den Autonomen Gemeinschaften mit eigener Sprache Spaniens-Auf dem Weg der Normalisierung. *Mercator Media Forum*, 4(1), pp. 41–63.

Lewis, M.P., Simons, G.F. & Fenning, C.D. eds., 2015. *Ethnologue: Languages of the World*, Eighteenth edition. Dallas, TX: SIL International. Available at: www.ethnologue.com.

Martín Barbero, J., 2011. From Latin America: Diversity, Globalization and Convergence. *Westminster Papers in Communication and Culture*, 8(1), pp. 40–64. Available at: http://doi.org/10.16997/wpcc.160.

May, S., 2000. Uncommon Languages: The Challenges and Possibilities of Minority Language Rights. *Journal of Multilingual and Multicultural Development*, 21(5), pp. 366–385.

May, S., 2001. *Language and Minority Rights: Ethnicity, Nationalism and the Politics of Language*. Harlow: Pearson Education Limited.

Meadows, M.H. & Molnar, H., 2002. Bridging the Gaps: Towards a History of Indigenous Media in Australia. *Media History*, 8(1), pp. 9–20.

Meshtrie, R., 2008. "Death of the Mother-Tongue"—Is English a Glottophagic Language in South Africa? *English Today*, 24(2), pp. 13–19.

Miller, T. & Yúdice, G., 2004. *Política Cultural*. Barcelona: Gedisa.

Ministerio de Cultura, 2010. *Compendio de Políticas Culturales*. Bogotá, DC: Ministerio de Cultura.

Moring, T., 2007. Functional Completeness in Minority Language Media. In M. Cormack & N. Hourigan, eds. *Minority Language Media: Concepts, Critiques and Case Studies*. Clevedon: Multilingual Matters, pp. 17–33.

Moring, T. & Dunbar, R., 2008. *The European Charter for Regional or Minority Languages and the Media*. Strasbourg, France: Council of Europe Publishing.

Moseley, C. ed., 2010. *Atlas of the World's Languages in Danger*. Paris: UNESCO Publishing. Available at: www.unesco.org/languages-atlas/

Moyo, L., 2010. Language, Cultural and Communication Rights of Ethnic Minorities in South Africa: A Human Rights Approach. *International Communication Gazette*, 72(4–5), pp. 425–440. Available at: http://gaz.sagepub.com/cgi/doi/10.1177/1748048510362712

Mpofu, P. & Mutasa, D.E., 2014. Language Policy, Linguistic Hegemony and Exclusion in the Zimbabwean Print and Broadcasting Media. *South African Journal of African Languages*, 34(2), pp. 225–233. Available at: www.tandfonline.com/doi/abs/10.1080/02572117.2014.997059

Murillo, M., 2008. Weaving a Communication Quilt in Colombia: Civil Conflict, Indigenous Resistance and Community Radio in Northern Cauca. In P. Wilson & M. Stewart, eds. *Global Indigenous Media: Cultures, Poetics, and Politics*. Durham & London: Duke University Press, pp. 145–159.

ONIC, 2009. *Diagnóstico Integral de Emisoras y/o Radios Indígenas*, Bogotá, DC: ONIC.

Orao, J., 2009. The Kenyan Indigenous Languages and the Mass media : Challenges and Opportunities. *Stellenbosch Papers in Linguistics*, 38, pp. 77–86.

Peña Sarmiento, M.F., 2012. "Voces y Sonidos de la Madre Tierra": Jujunula Makuira, la Radio que Fortalece el Tejido Social en la Guajira Colombiana. *Anagramas*, 10(20), pp. 197–212.

Pietikäinen, S., 2008a. Broadcasting Indigenous Voices. *European Journal of Communication*, 23(2), pp. 173–191. Available at: http://doi.org/10.1177/0267323108089221

Pietikäinen, S., 2008b. "To Breathe Two Airs": Empowering Indigenous Sámi Media. In P. Wilson & M. Stewart, eds. *Global Indigenous Media: Cultures, Poetics and Politics*. Durham and London: Duke University Press, pp. 214–231.

Plataforma per la Llengua, 2015. *Informe Cat 2015: 50 dades sobre la llengua catalana*, Barcelona.

Prah, K.K., 2003. Going Native: Language of Instruction in Education, Development and African Emancipation. In B. Brock-Utne, Z. Desai, & M. Qorro, eds. *Language of Instruction in Tanzania and South Africa (LOITSA)*. Dar es Salaam: E & D Limited, pp. 14–34.

Prah, K.K., 2010. Multilingualism in Urban Africa: Bane or Blessing. *Journal of Multicultural Discourses*, 5(2), pp. 169–182.

Ramos Rodríguez, J.M., 2005. Indigenous Radio Stations on Mexico: A Catalyst for Social Cohesion and Cultural Strength. *The Radio Journal: International Studies in Broadcast and Audio Media*, 3(3), pp. 155–169.

Rey, G., 2010. Las políticas culturales en Colombia: La progresiva transformación de sus comprensiones. In G. Rey, ed. *Compendio de Políticas Culturales*. Bogotá, DC: Ministerio de Cultura, pp. 23–48.

Rodríguez, C. & El Gazi, J., 2007. The Poetics of Indigenous Radio in Colombia. *Media, Culture and Society*, 29(3), pp. 449–468.

Ronchi, A., 2015. Is the Internet a Melting Pot? In E. Kuzmin & A. Pashakova, eds. *Linguistic and Cultural Diversity in Cyberspace*. Moscow: Interregional Library Cooperation Center and UNESCO, pp. 71–81.

Roy-Campbell, Z.M., 2006. The State of African Languages and the Global Language Politics: Empowering African Languages in the Era of Globalisation. In O.F. Arasanyin & M.A. Pemberton, eds. *Selected Proceedings of the 36th Annual Conference on African Linguistics: Shifting the Center of Africanism in Language Politics and Economic Globalization*. Somerville, MA: Cascadilla Proceedings Project, pp. 150–160.

Salazar, J.F., 2009. Indigenous Video and Policy Contexts in Latin America. *International Journal of Media and Cultural Politics*, 5(1&2), pp. 125–130. Available at: www.ingentaconnect.com/content/intellect/mcp/2009/00000005/F0020001/art00010

Salazar, J.F. & Córdova, A., 2008. Imperfect Media and the Poetics of Indigenous Video in Latin America. In P. Wilson & M. Stewart, eds. *Global Indigenous Media: Cultures, Poetics, and Policies*. Durham and London: Duke University Press.

Spencer, V., 2008. Language, History and the Nation: An Historical Approach to the Evaluating Language and Cultural Claims. *Nations and Nationalism*, 14(2), pp. 241–259.

Statistics South Africa. 2012. *Census 2011: Key Results*. Pretoria, South Africa: Statistics South Africa.

Thomas, N., 2001. Speech Laws. *Index on Censorship*, 30, pp. 44–51.

Truscott de Mejía, A.-M., 2006. Bilingual Education in Colombia: Towards a Recognition of Languages, Cultures and Identities. *Colombian Applied Linguistics Journal*, 8(1), pp. 152–168.

Uribe-Jongbloed, E., 2014a. Minority Language Media Studies beyond Eurocentrism : Cormack's Seven Conditions Revisited. *Catalan Journal of Communication and Cultural Studies*, 6(1), pp. 35–54.

Uribe-Jongbloed, E., 2014b. Identity Negotiations on the Native and Ethnic Colombian Radio: Three Study Cases. *Anagramas*, 13(25), pp. 167–188.

Uribe-Jongbloed, E., 2016. Issues of Identity in Minority Language Media Production in Colombia and Wales. *Journal of Multilingual and Multicultural Development*, 37(6), pp. 615–627. Available at: www.tandfonline.com/doi/full/10.1080/01434632.2015.1111895.

Uribe-Jongbloed, E. & Anderson, C.E., 2014. Indigenous and Minority Languages in Colombia : The Current Situation. *Zeszyty Łużyckie*, 48, pp. 217–241.

Uribe-Jongbloed, E. & Peña Sarmiento, M.F., 2014. Negociaciones de identidad en la radio indígena y étnica colombiana: tres casos de estudio. *Anagramas*, 13(25), pp. 167–188.

Van Parijs, P., 2008. Linguistic Diversity as Curse and as By-Product. In X. Arzoz, ed. *Respecting Linguistic Diversity in the European Union*. Amsterdam and Philadelphia: John Benjamins Publishing Company, pp. 17–46.

Wilson, P. & Stewart, M., 2008. Indigeneity and Indigenous Media on the Global Stage. In P. Wilson & M. Stewart, eds. *Global Indigenous Media*. Durham and London: Duke University Press, pp. 1–35.

Wintermans, V., 2008. UNESCO and Endangered Languages. In T. De Graaf, N. Ostler & R. Salverda, eds. *Endangered Languages and Language Learning*. Leeuwarden, The Netherlands: Foundation for Endangered Languages, Fryske Akademy, pp. 231–233.

Zambrano, C.V., 2006. *Ejes políticos de la diversidad cultural*. Bogotá, DC: Siglo del Hombre Editores y Universidad Nacional de Colombia.

13

Cultural policy in Northern Ireland

Making cultural policy for a divided society

Phil Ramsey and Bethany Waterhouse-Bradley

Northern Ireland (NI) is a small region of the United Kingdom with a history of violent conflict associated with the national and religious identities of its inhabitants. Post-conflict societies face complex challenges in the development of cultural policy, particularly where some cultural markers have become associated with antagonism or political affiliation. This chapter will focus on how the social, spatial, educational, religious and political divisions in NI – coupled with deep socio-economic deprivation and a lack of political consensus – mean that many issues relating to cultural policy are neglected. We chart how the history of NI has left significant barriers to shared culture within NI, leading to inertia on policy in relation to community relations and social cohesion. That being the case, we show how the government Department of Culture, Arts and Leisure (DCAL) and the Arts Council of Northern Ireland (ACNI), the main arm's length body for funding, have clear policies relating to how arts and culture can alleviate socio-economic problems. This is shown in the context of how the wider political system gives a central role to cultural policy as a driver of economic development, seen through the work of the publicly funded body Northern Ireland Screen, responsible for attracting international film and television productions to NI through direct financial subsidisation of production costs. With this example, we show that there is much clearer consensus on the economic role for culture in NI than there is in relation to the more contentious cultural issues relating to historic divisions.

The historical context of Northern Ireland

NI is a small region with a population of 1.81 million under the jurisdiction of the United Kingdom (UK), sharing a border with the Republic of Ireland (ROI). Following the partitioning of Ireland in 1921, which led to the creation of NI, there has been ethnic conflict between the Protestant (largely identifying as British) majority and the Catholic (largely identifying as Irish) minority for several decades (although conflict and violence in the region dates back centuries). From the late 1960s, NI descended into a violent political struggle known as the 'Troubles', which lasted until the 1990s in its most intense phase and led to the deaths of more than 3500 people in the following 30 years. Attacks and murders that are sectarian in their nature, and attacks upon the police and armed forces, continue almost to the present day. The economic and social scars of the conflict remain, with NI rated as one of the most deprived regions of the UK. The divided nature of society in NI can be charted back across multiple centuries, although what Hennessy (1997, p. 1) calls the "deeper roots of conflict" can be traced to the Ulster Plantation in the Seventeenth Century, which involved the movement of (mainly) Protestants from England and Scotland into the province of Ulster (which maps largely onto the present-day NI). This situation led to hostility between the Planters and the already-existing Catholic population, especially in relation to land displacement, cultural and religious differences (Tonge, 2002, p. 5).

Following the 1921 establishment of NI, it was ruled by the Ulster Unionist Party (the then dominant political party aligned to maintaining NI's position within the UK) through the NI Parliament until 1972 (Bew et al., 2002). Because the border of NI was drawn with the specific intent of retaining a majority population who identified as British and as such wished to retain the union with the Great Britain, cultural identity, and thus expressions of culture, became fundamental issues in the jurisdiction. After decades of direct rule from Westminster and several attempts at a political solution to the Troubles, the Belfast Agreement (1998) led to the setting up of a Legislative Assembly at Stormont and a devolved Executive Government to NI. Despite that, the NI Assembly has for some time existed in a precarious state. Ongoing threats to political power-sharing include: dealing with continued political violence, the perpetuation of the main paramilitary groupings many years after their ceasefires, and a failure to reach and implement agreement over a raft of cultural issues that include flags and symbols (Bryan, 2015).

It is impossible to discuss conflict, culture and identity in NI without some generalisation and simplification of what are invariably complex and nuanced issues. The foundations of these are explored in depth in Ruane and Todd (1996) and Nic Craith (2003); a historical examination of the conflict in NI can be found in Hayes and McAllister (2013) and O'Dochartaigh (2016). Within NI entrenched division remains: schools, residential areas and to a certain extent sport and social pursuits remain largely segregated through most of the region, the social and economic costs of which will be discussed later in the chapter. The following sections will discuss the demographic, socio-economic and political backdrop against which cultural policy is developed in NI.

Demographic and socio-economic context of NI

The economy in NI is highly dependent on the public sector, and economic policy has been focused on emphasizing private growth, innovation and skills improvement and building a more appropriate economic infrastructure (NI Executive, 2012a). However, during a period of economic decline across Europe and the UK, NI continues to be one of the most affected regions economically, with a 10% drop in Gross Value Added (GVA) between 2008 and 2011 – the largest decrease in the UK (Nolan, 2014). The rate of child poverty in NI in 2012–2013 was 20.5%, one of the highest in the UK, and is predicted to rise to 29% in 2020–2021, a rate higher than in the rest of the country (Browne et al., 2014, pp. 19–21). Unemployment, underemployment and economic inactivity contribute to these problems. Nearly 15% of usual residents in NI aged 16–74 are economically inactive (excluding students and retired persons). Of the almost 5% of working age people who are unemployed (excluding students), 44.98% of them are long-term unemployed and 16.8% have never worked (NISRA, 2012). Poor health among those from lower socio-economic backgrounds is also a significant problem (Bell et al., 2016).

In addition, there are myriad socio-economic problems among young people in NI, especially in terms of educational achievement among Protestant boys (Nolan, 2014). Segregation in education continues to be the norm, with only 6.5% of children educated in integrated schools (as opposed to Protestant/Catholic schools) (Nolan, 2014). There is no sign of change in these figures, as rather than supporting the education of Protestant and Catholic children side by side with a uniform-curriculum, the Executive has opted for the encouragement of shared schools, where students share campus resources while retaining separate teaching and learning (OFMDFM, 2013). Finally, space and territory in NI remain substantially segregated, and while there has been a significant decrease in 'single identity wards' across the region from 55% to 37% (wards where more than 80% of residents identify with a single community), at a micro level in many areas segregation still persists (Shuttleworth and Lloyd, 2013). In spite of a period of sustained relative peace in the region and a clear shift towards moving away from self-identification as one side or the other, public attitudes reflect a pessimistic view of the future of good relations (McDermott, 2014). As we discuss below, opposing politicians more readily find consensus around economic issues than cultural issues, which often leads to policy inertia.

Northern Ireland and the politicization of culture

In this section we advance a discussion of the politicization of culture within NI and discuss how the notion of a national cultural policy frame of reference is instead undermined by a 'bipolar' notion of culture in NI (Graham and Nash, 2006). NI stands alongside a number of other countries and regions where "ethnic and cultural diversity" (Saukkonen and Pyykkönen, 2008) necessitates the management of cultural policy accordingly, such as France (Kiwan, 2007), the Netherlands (Delhaye and van de Ven, 2014) and Catalonia (Barbieri, 2012, p. 17). Outside of Europe, there is some relevance to NI of the case of cultural policy in Canada, which has long been required to balance linguistic diversity, in addition to ethnic diversity in its cultural policy (Rabinovitch, 2007). In NI culture is often defined within the public sphere, policy development and implementation in a narrow manner. While the reasons for this are myriad, the primary issues are political and historical in their origin (see Nic Craith, 2003).

One prominent issue within cultural policy in NI is the lack of a *national cultural policy* frame of reference (Ahearne, 2011, p. 155), the like of which can "provide a means of reconciling contending cultural identities by holding up the nation as an essence that transcends particular interests" (Miller and Yudice, 2002, p. 8). Were a policy official or politician attempting to invoke the nation within this approach, he or she would not have this as an available option or rather would not have it if attempting to achieve consensus within the political and cultural sphere. (Later, one of the first attempts by a government department to construct a national cultural policy for NI will be discussed.) Rather, as we have seen, with marked heterogeneous national identities being identified by NI's population, cultural policy that seeks to reflect a "distinctive cultural identity" (Mulcahy, 1998, p. 249) immediately alienates almost half of the population.

Moreover, viewing NI through what might be termed the 'two community straitjacket' (Feldman et al., 2005), a cultural paradigm reproduced by many politicians, major media outlets and public policy, suggests the majority of people in the region can be neatly divided into these classifications. This notion is challenged through the most recent census data, which points to a marked change in self-identification of nationality and ethnicity. When asked to identify nationality 29.44% of respondents chose the moniker of 'Northern Irish', eschewing more 'traditional' identification as either British, 48.41% or Irish, 28.35%

(NISRA, 2012). Also increasing is the number of respondents from national and ethnic backgrounds (4%) falling outside British, Irish and Northern Irish, as increasing migration and the associated increase in births to foreign-born mothers begin to be reflected in demographic figures (NISRA, 2012).

The so-called two-community straitjacket is particularly difficult for those from minority cultures, where race and ethnicity are seen as 'an extension' of sectarian divisions (Graham and Nash, 2006). The creation of cultural identity allied to citizenship, religion and/or nationality is already problematic within NI; it is further problematized when other groups are considered, leaving as it does very little space for layered perceptions of personal identity. Demographic changes, however, are visibly absent or disproportionately attended to by community cohesion and cultural policy. In the next section, we discuss the theory of cultural citizenship in relation to NI and discuss that culture that is consumed by the overall population that tends to be less politicized and shared. We then turn to a discussion of 'traditional' culture in NI, the culture often attached to contested practices and those that are often politicized as a means of identifying oneself as one group or differentiating from the 'other'. We focus here on sport, music and language.

Cultural citizenship and cultural practices

We can develop this theme by considering the concept of cultural citizenship (Stevenson, 2003). When considering the implications of this theory for NI, we first see that citizenship as a foundational process is disrupted. For example, O'Brien (2010, p. 600) argues that an understanding of citizenship "in the sense that citizens accept the right of other individuals to be citizens" has "never existed in Northern Ireland due to differences in allegiances". Thus, to take Stevenson's authoritative quotation on cultural citizenship, we see that such a concept travels very poorly to NI:

> Cultural citizenship therefore is the struggle for a democratic society that enables a diversity of citizens to lead relatively meaningful lives, that respects the formation of complex hybrid identities, offers them the protection of the social state and grants them the access to a critical education that seeks to explore the possibility of living in a future free from domination and oppression.
>
> *(Stevenson, 2010, p. 289)*

In some regards, Stevenson's conception can be seen to be realizable within NI society, where for example the social state is considered. However, for Stevenson "Only when public spaces become participatory and democratic spaces can we say that the project for an autonomous society has come to fruition" (2010, p. 276).

Far from that being the case in NI, physical markers of cultural identity are signifiers of territory and used as a way of creating internal cohesion while 'othering' outsiders. Many of NI's public spaces are contested and segregated (Shirlow and Murtagh, 2006), used for commemoration activities that divide (McDowell et al., 2015) and marked out by the flying of flags that evoke other conflict areas, such as Israeli and Palestinian flags (Hill and White, 2008). Moreover, this co-optation of cultural identity for the purpose of marking territory is extended to government departments, where placement of ministers in certain spaces to ensure dominance of a political perspective in that space is clear (Sinn Féin and DUP always look to the Departments of Culture, Arts and Leisure, and Education – areas where there is strong sense of using culture as a marker in the middle classes).

That said, much cultural consumption in NI, at the level of popular culture, is largely shared between the two main communities rather than divided. As such, much popular culture is globalized in nature (Drache and Froese, 2006), with an area such as film being akin to the picture across Europe and indeed much of the rest of the developed world. The broadcasting system in NI is dominated by that of the UK (Ofcom, 2015; Ramsey, 2015), leading to strong British cultural influences especially in terms of television drama, and in radio, in addition to that produced locally in NI (Moore, 2003). In many of these areas there are often no discernible differences between members of the two main religious-political communities, while culture broadly construed is being shaped by aspects of 'British culture' (see numerous entries on NI in Childs and Storry, 1999) and 'Irish culture'. However, as O'Malley (2011, p. 159) notes, "Irish culture is deeply entwined with that of Britain" and thus the two are more difficult to demarcate.

Sport

Culture becomes more divided along community lines when the areas of sport and cultural identity are concerned, with sport an area that is greatly divided along religious lines (Hassan, 2005). In NI, participation in playing and watching Rugby Union and Cricket is dominated by those identifying or brought up as Protestant; those identifying or brought up as Catholic almost exclusively participate in and watch the historic Gaelic Games, under the auspices of the Gaelic Athletic Association (Burgess, 2015a, p. 107). While these sports are mainly linked to their community, sporting apparel has caused tensions in the past, and wearing it is banned in certain public places; this is not exceptional to NI. Soccer is played by and has spectators from both Protestant and Catholic communities (Hassan, 2002), although the teams in the premier division of soccer in NI are supported almost exclusively by Protestants (e.g. Linfield F.C.) or Catholics (e.g. Cliftonville F.C.). It is the most contested sport in terms of clashes between fans of teams from opposing communities, and many sporting fixtures are heavily policed for this reason. In addition, support for the national soccer team – Northern Ireland – has been traditionally linked to Protestants, though there have been significant efforts in recent years by the governing body to make international matches more accessible (Hargie et al., 2015). In other areas of cultural identity and traditions, we can see strong demarcations along community lines (Nic Craith, 2003). Space does not allow for a full examination of a range of topics that could be usefully surveyed, and so we choose to focus on music – which "for several centuries … has been used as a primary means of encoding 'party' and religious affiliations" (Cooper, 2010, p. 94) – and language, as two key sites for cultural contestation.

Music

Music in NI has the potential to be evocative in nature by virtue of its relationship to historical conflict. Among Protestants, for example, there is a strong musical tradition that accompanies Orange Order events. The most notable example is that of the commemoration of the Battle of the Boyne – a significant historical marker for Unionists which is symbolic of victory over a Catholic monarch. Each 12 July, King William III's victory over King James II in 1690 (Tonge, 2002, p. 4–5) has been commemorated by those brought up as Protestants, especially in rural areas. Implicit in this is the tradition that members of the Orange Order parade with marching bands, replete with fifes and 'Lambeg' drums (Cooper, 2010, p. 94), which causes significant tensions in some areas (Bryan and Jarman, 1997; Bryan, 2015).

Accordingly, the Parades Commission, an independent public body set up in 1998 to reach determinations on which public parades can receive approval, can issue conditions for how they must be conducted.

In recent years, there have been attempts to open up Orangeism to a wider audience, and through the introduction of *Orangefest* to make it more culturally relevant (Kennaway, 2015). That said, such cultural expressions generally play quite poorly on the European and global cultural stage, no doubt contributing to a sense that Ulster loyalists, one group associated with Orangeism, have been called "the least fashionable community in Western Europe" (McDonald as cited in Burgess, 2015b, p. xii). Among those brought up Catholic, there are firm Gaelic traditions, especially in relation to Irish traditional music – itself with clear musical connections to Scottish traditional music (Cooper, 2009, p. 65). The annual traditional music festival *Fleadh Cheoil na hEireann* is a massive event that attracts over 400,000 people (McLaughlin, 2013), remarkable given that the all-island population of Ireland is just ~6.4 million people (CSO/NISRA, 2014).

Language

The use of the Irish language is linked mainly to the Catholic-Nationalist community, from which the vast majority of its speakers are located in terms of expressed national identity. McMonagle (2010, p. 255) argues that "Irish has come to be associated with nationalist/ republican identities"; for Pritchard (2004, p. 62), the language is "an important basis of Irish nationalism". Often, this had not just been the 'fault' of one side or the other but about how language – both Irish and Ulster-Scots – has been used as a political tool in the so-called 'culture wars' (Nolan, 2014, pp. 154–162). However, the politicization of the Irish language has occurred in a manner that is extremely reductionist when viewed historically. For example, Protestants "have made an important historical cultural contribution to the preservation and development of the Irish language" (Pritchard, 2004, p. 75), with Presbyterians in particular playing their part. Today, the Irish language has been 'rediscovered' among very small pockets among the Protestant-Unionist population. However, as we discuss below, issues in relation to language remain deeply contested at the policy level, with a continued failure among NI's politicians to find an agreeable role for Irish within Northern Irish public life.

The legal and political context for cultural policy in NI

Under the New Labour government (1997–2010), powers were initially devolved to Scotland, NI and Wales through the Scotland Act (1998), the Northern Ireland Act (1998) and the Government of Wales Act (1998), respectively. Each of these legislatures has a different set of responsibilities (in the case of Scotland, a Parliament and a Government), and different reserved and devolved matters (Trench, 2007). NI had a period of devolved government prior to this from 1922–1972, but the NI Parliament became untenable after increasing ethnic conflict between Protestant and Catholic communities in the region and NI underwent a lengthy period of direct rule from Westminster (McQuade and Fagan, 2002). When devolution was established as part of the Belfast Agreement in 1998, it was a means of establishing the institutions through which conflict resolution could be achieved (Holloway, 2005). Shortly after devolution was established in 1998, there was another suspension of the local Assembly due to disagreements between the main political parties (2002–2007). The most recent incarnation of devolution in NI is still in its early stages – at the time of writing the Assembly is in its third term of a mandatory coalition government – and the Executive is currently led by two diametrically opposed political parties: Sinn Féin, the major Irish Nationalist party, and the Democratic Unionist Party (DUP), the major British Unionist party.

The first NI Assembly after the Northern Ireland Act 1998 was elected in June 1998. Led by a First Minister and Deputy First Minister, it was supported by 10 ministries allocated proportionally across political parties (Knox, 1999). The Assembly was based on a consociational model of governance – a model particularly designed for the management of post-conflict governance, which seeks to find a balance between the two conflicting communities and preserve the different identities (Graham and Nash, 2006; McGarry and O'Leary, 2006). However, the manner in which the Executive is constructed entrenches sectarian division and normalizes it in the political sphere (Graham and Nash, 2006). This division has the potential to lead to inhibited decision-making and delays in the policy process, with the failure to progress the proposed Irish Language Act that we discuss below in a notable example. This delay in particular has resulted in international condemnation from the Council of Europe due to failure to comply with the European Charter for Regional and Minority Languages and is perceived to be a direct result of divisions between the DUP and Sinn Féin, as well as a result of the politicization of the Irish Language in the region (Meredith, 2014). This section will outline some of the key cultural frameworks in the devolved Assembly, as well as provide insight into how political differences play out in the development of cultural policy.

The proposed Irish Language Act

The statutory requirements to promote and protect the Irish language are embedded in regional legislation and international charters, and the commitment to the production of Irish Language legislation was a condition of the St. Andrews Agreement in 2006, which outlines the conditions for the main parties to re-enter power sharing at the local Assembly after a period of direct rule (NIHRC, 2010). The UK is a signatory to the Council of Europe Framework Convention for National Minorities and the European Charter for Regional and Minority Languages (1992), which came into force in 1998. Nation states choose what languages they register and under which jurisdiction to be accountable. The European Charter for Regional or Minority Languages outlines a commitment to positive, proactive duties on minority language rights and is legally binding under European Law (NIHRC, 2010). Irish and Ulster-Scots are both registered for the region of NI; however, the region has failed to produce evidence submissions to the monitoring reports in the past two rounds due to failure to reach consensus on the submission (Council of Europe, 2017).

The proposal for an Irish Language Act, under a Sinn Féin-led Department of Culture, Arts and Leisure, is the NI Assembly's attempt at developing the Irish language legislation promised by the St Andrews Agreement and calls for the following actions (among others): define Irish as an official language; the right to use Irish in courts, tribunals and other legal settings; parity for use of Irish in the NI Assembly; the promotion of Irish in public bodies, including affirmative action for Irish speakers; Irish language schemes in public bodies; parity of English and Irish on road signage and place names and a guaranteed right to education in Irish (DCAL, 2015a). However, there has been strong and consistent resistance from the DUP and other Unionist politicians, with claims ranging from economic wastefulness in times of austerity to Sinn Féin political posturing, to deliberate removal of 'Britishness' from NI (*The Newsletter*, 10 February 2015). The argument around the Irish language is another example of the application of zero-sum politics in the region, where rather than being treated like a minority language, Irish is instead treated as a political symbol or emblem and as such is a threat to the 'other side' of the political community (NIHRC, 2010).

Good relations and social cohesion

There is a legislative imperative set out by the Belfast Agreement which requires statutory agencies to address issues of equality and good relations. In spite of this imperative, there has been little documented long-term success of community relations. The *Harbison Review of Community Relations Policy* (2002) found that there had been no substantive change in decreasing division "as measured by greater integration of housing and education" (as cited in Graham and Nash, 2006). Measuring the success of community relations policy based on public attitudes, Morrow et al. (2013) found that while there are some reasons for optimism, segregation remains significant and individuals are still sceptical about the possibility of sustained peace and integration. Good relations policy in NI has very rarely been proactive in creating shared space (regardless of the implied language), but is rather focused on creating neutral space to share and maintaining the rights to separate but equal space elsewhere. The first attempt at social cohesion policy post-conflict, *A Shared Future* (OFMDFM, 2005), was imperfect in its response but attempted to address the issue of shared space. It placed some emphasis on putting integration in the foreground and fostering trust and interdependence. The document was not implemented and was ignored in the Programme for Government by the Sinn Féin- and DUP-led Assembly, which took over from the Direct Rule authors of the document. It was followed by the proposed *Cohesion Sharing and Integration,* which was again scrapped after a highly critical reception from both the public respondents to the consultation and other political leadership (Nolan, 2014).

Without public consultation, or the involvement of their partners in government – the Ulster Unionist Party, the Social Democratic and Labour Party, and Alliance – the Office of the First Minister and Deputy First Minister (in the NI Executive) produced *Together: Building a United Community* (TBUC) in 2013. The document, which focuses on children and young people, a shared community, a safe community and cultural expression (OFMDFM, 2013), provides little in the way of new developments in good relations and community cohesion and did not have overt support from government outside of the two main parties (Nolan, 2014). TBUC follows previous policies in the expression of what Dixon (2002) refers to as 'constructive ambiguity' of good relations policy, which allow for them to be interpreted however the audience sees fit. This is not restricted to post-conflict societies but is part of the wider notion of status quo policy making, where this ambiguity can be used to seemingly address relevant concerns without commitment to one or another ideological stance. There is a policy of avoidance in addition to the idea of ambiguity in cultural policy – where discussions of history are often excluded, as is the aspiration for a united Ireland, a regular criticism of Sinn Féin in other policies (Nolan, 2014). Constructive ambiguity therefore becomes both a contributor to and a product of consociational governance. To illustrate some of the policy inertia referred to throughout the chapter, we turn to a more-detailed examination of some current cultural policy in NI by addressing the work of the aforementioned DCAL (Department of Culture, Arts and Leisure) and ACNI (Arts Council of Northern Ireland).

The Department of Culture, Arts and Leisure and the Arts Council of Northern Ireland

The government department in the NI Executive with responsibility for many areas of cultural policy is DCAL, which has legislative powers for cultural policy issues such as museums, libraries, the arts and language issues. However, not all areas in relation to culture are devolved, with broadcasting policy reserved to Westminster (Ramsey, 2015)[1]. The current minister is Carál Ní Chuilín MLA of Sinn Féin, who has been in post since 2011. DCAL had a budget in 2015–2016 of £91.7 million, which had been reduced by 8% since the previous year (DCAL, 2015b). The largest budget item at the department is spending on libraries (£29.4m, 32% of its 2015–2016 spending) (DCAL, 2015b, p. 20). Much of the department's work – like its counterpart the Department for Culture, Media and Sport in Westminster – is carried out by a number of arm's length agencies that include the delivery of the aforementioned library spending through Libraries NI, National Museums Northern Ireland and Sport Northern Ireland (DCAL, 2011).

DCAL is focused on two main areas: economic development; and equality and social inclusion. This is clear in its *key objectives*:

1   To ensure that culture, arts and leisure activities positively impact on promoting equality, and tackling poverty and social exclusion
2   To ensure that culture, arts and leisure contribute to the growth of the economy and building a united community. (DCAL, 2015b, p. 7)

Taken collectively, we can first see the policy approach of DCAL is towards equality and social inclusion as underpinned by economic development. The first of five DCAL *strategic pillars* focuses on how the arts can help to 'rebalance' the economy, stemming from a long-held notion that the NI economy is too dependent on the public sector. This is followed by the fifth pillar, which is "social inclusion and equality" (DCAL, 2011, p. 16). In its corporate plan, the department identifies the results that it expects within the year 2015–2016 on these matters, through the utilisation of the Promoting Equality, Tackling Poverty and Social Exclusion framework. Here for example, the department's target is to "increase the proportion of people in the 20% most deprived areas who engage in the arts to 79%" and to "increase the proportion of people in the 20% most deprived areas participating in sport to increase to 50%" (DCAL, 2015b, p. 14). In terms of its targets for economic development, it focuses on ongoing and planned redevelopment at Windsor Park and Casement Park, NI's main stadia for soccer and GAA respectively.

The aforementioned lack of an overarching national cultural policy for NI has been tentatively addressed by a DCAL draft strategy (DCAL, 2015c), which had just completed its consultation period at the time of writing. The draft strategy maintains the themes of equality promotion and alleviation of poverty and social exclusion. As one of its five themes, Creativity and Skills places an emphasis on the contribution of arts and culture to the economy, a theme discussed in more detail below. The draft strategy attempts to fit within current government programmes under the NI Executive, with a cross-departmental approach. However, the draft strategy is very light on detail, particularly in terms of implementation. Indeed, for a policy that strives for innovation, it has a strikingly similar vision statement to the department's existing 'key objectives' discussed above. In this version, the vision is: "To promote, develop and support the crucial role of arts and culture in creating a cohesive community and delivering social change to our society on the basis of equality for everyone" (DCAL, 2015c, p. 11).

In an arts and cultural sector heavily dependent on public funding, major financial cuts have a substantial impact on many organisations important for the sustenance of diverse sector. To mitigate cuts across government departments in the Assembly, DCAL significantly reduced funding to ACNI, the main arm's length body working in the arts in 2015–2016

(ACNI, 2015, p. 18; Meredith, 2015a). These cuts were set to be passed on to many of the organizations in receipt of ACNI funding, such as the Grand Opera House Belfast, the MAC and the Ulster Orchestra (Meredith, 2015b). In terms of its direct funding of outside organisations, ACNI is responsible for distributing funds to community organisations, many of which are tied almost exclusively to one side of the ethno-politico-religious divide or the other, such as in the funding of marching bands that represent narrow community groupings (Nolan, 2012). At the time of writing, it is unclear what the long-term impacts of austerity will be on the arts sector, but one can infer that it will have knock-on effects for cultural policy and good relations, given the inextricable links between policy and society, as outlined in this chapter thus far.

ACNI's policy approach, like DCAL's, is marked by an emphasis on fostering social inclusion within the arts. For example, it reported that in the period 2010–2013 74% of its funding had "gone directly into the most deprived areas" (ACNI, 2013, p. 7). Moreover, through its *Arts and Older People Strategy* it conducted programmes with the aim of ensuring older people in NI were not cut off from the arts, a programme underpinned by principles that were recognisably social democratic (Ramsey, 2013). As part of its current five-year plan, the ACNI planned to "increase the proportion of arts activities delivered to the top 20% of the most deprived Super Output Areas" (ACNI, 2013, p. 14). Despite such an approach, the ACNI has reported during this five-year cycle that "Arts engagement rates for the least deprived group was 86%, falling to 70% for the most deprived group" (ACNI, 2014, p. 3), and thus much work remains to be done in this area.

ACNI's *Intercultural Arts Strategy 2011–2016* (ACNI, 2011) acknowledges that NI society had become more markedly ethnically diverse in the ten or so years leading up to that point. Accordingly, it set out that ACNI ought to "seek to foster the expression of cultural pluralism; build dialogue and promote understanding, through interchanges within and between communities and their cultures" (ACNI, 2011, p. 10). In the detail of the strategy, it set out six 'strategic themes' that included *Using the Arts to Develop Community Cohesion; Using the Arts to Develop Good Relations; Using the Arts as a Vehicle to Tackle Racism* (ACNI, 2011, p. 67). Finally, and akin to DCAL, ACNI is also concerned with economic growth, where it argues "Stimulating the growth and development of our creative sector will optimize our economic potential and increase our competitiveness" (ACNI, 2014, p. 7). The ACNI also has responsibility for the NI's Creative Industries Innovation Fund, which takes us to the second point, where cultural policy is seen in the service of economic development, a path that closely follows the wider UK model (e.g. DCMS, 2008).

Cultural policy as a driver of economic development

The creative industries (CIs) in NI have assumed a similar place in the political economy as is the case in the wider UK, where successive governments have sought to stimulate and measure the sectors (DCMS, 2001, 2011). Statistics for the CIs are measured in the same manner as in the rest of the UK and their contribution to the economy highlighted by government departments. The most recent figures available at the time of writing show that the CIs comprised 3.9% of NI's GVA in 2014, an 11.7% increase since the previous year (DCAL, 2015d, p. 5). Compared with a national GVA of 5.2%, the NI rating is remarkably high given the weak NI economy, highlighted above. At the forefront of this development has been NI Screen, which has a key economic role to play in the development of the film and television industries. In place since 1997, it was originally named the Northern Ireland Film and Television Commission (NI Screen, 2015a).

Northern Ireland Screen

The NI Screen approach to investing directly in productions, and seeing the economic bene-fits returned, correlates directly with that of its core funder Invest NI. Invest NI is a publicly funded body, which provides grants to international companies to locate in NI and for re-gional companies to invest and expand with the aim of stimulating a private sector that was greatly suppressed by the Troubles. Seen in its two most recent strategies, in *Driving Global Growth* (NI Screen, 2010) and *Opening Doors* (NI Screen, 2014), NI Screen argues for the value of economic return on investment, alongside a role in education and the development of a skills base with the television and film industries. The sector grew from being mainly involved with production for local television networks to an industry competing interna-tionally for major productions, the best known of which is HBO's *Game of Thrones* (GOT) (2011–present), which has filmed six series of the show predominantly in NI at the time of writing (NI Screen, 2015a).

NI Screen provides direct funding for productions, with a limit of £800,000, "up to a ceiling of 25% of the overall project budget" (NI Screen, 2015b). For those companies choosing to film in NI, the UK's tax relief schemes apply, where companies can claim a maximum of 25% relief on qualifying expenditure, either under the UK Film Tax Relief (BFI, 2015a) or under the UK High-end TV Tax Relief (BFI, 2015b), with various caveats. The Northern Ireland Screen Fund budgeted resources of £15.89m between 2010–2014, while NI Screen's *Opening Doors* strategy budgeted £36.3m between 2014–2018 (NI Screen, 2014, p. 84). Much of this spending has gone, and will continue to go, to GOT production (though NI Screen notes that it was able to reduce GOT funding from £3.2m to £1.6m when the UK tax relief was introduced) (NI Screen, 2014, p. 38) with an anticipated return of £136m by the end of 2018 with an 11.25 ratio between cost and return (NI Screen, 2014, p. 48). To date, NI Screen "has invested £12.45m in the series … For that investment, it is estimated that £110.7m has been spent on goods and services in the Northern Ireland econ-omy" (Meredith, 2015c).

The Irish Language Broadcast Fund and the Ulster-Scots Broadcast Fund

NI Screen also administers the Irish Language Broadcast Fund (£3m in 2015–2016) and the Ulster-Scots Broadcast Fund (£1m in 2015–2016). Both are available for application by produc-tion companies for the support of broadcasting in the Irish language and on Ulster-Scots themes and have aimed to support 55 hours of Irish programming and 12 hours of Ulster-Scots pro-gramming in 2015–2016 (NI Screen, 2015c). Broadcasters who have utilized content supported from these funds include the BBC, RTÉ, TG4 and UTV (Ofcom, 2014, p. 29), with a supposed direct relationship between the public funding and spending in the broadcasting sector.

The Belfast Agreement provided an impetus for such an initiative, though only in relation to Irish (NIO, 1998, Section 6, Paragraph 4), not to Ulster-Scots (Ulster-Scots was solely mentioned in the context of it being "part of the cultural wealth of the island of Ireland" (NIO, 1998, Section 6, Paragraph 3)). Little (2004) observes that Irish language was priori-tized over Ulster-Scots in the GFA and that the latter has always enjoyed a slightly tenuous position in NI. He argued that "making a special case for Irish language does not breach the general intentions of the Agreement given that Irish language is not, in itself, disrespectful towards the culture of other groups" (Little, 2004, p. 17). This differentiation is also marked in the UK's commitments to the European Charter for Regional or Minority Languages, where Ulster-Scots is listed only under category II, focused on the principle of protection in general, and Irish is listed under parts II and III, which dictate specific measures to be undertaken in statutory agencies (NIHRC, 2010).

Discussion

Following our previous discussion of cultural citizenship, we now return to this theme as a means of further exploring the contested nature of cultural policy in NI. Rather than cultural citizenship taking form – in the Stevenson mould that we discussed above – the equation of citizenship with cultural identity in NI (on both sides) in ways that are binary and oppositional, perpetuates the politicization of culture at every level (Graham and Nash, 2006). This brings us to some key cultural policy questions for NI: is it possible to implement a pluralist cultural policy, one where the concept of cultural citizenship might take root, when culture and territory are inextricably linked, and where territory remains entrenched and divided as contested space (Hughes and McCandless, 2006, Knox, 2011)? What would such a 'Northern Irish' cultural policy look like, taking account both of the past and of the changing nature of NI society with increased immigration? Such an endpoint is so distant under the current paradigm as to seem almost unimaginable, and as we have seen, the recent DCAL attempt falls somewhat short.

Whenever 'culture' is invoked in NI, in policy or in discourse, there is division to be found. Graham and Nash's (2006) point that the language of culture has been co-opted as a means to justify or classify division is relevant here, further underlining how much work would be required: "In Northern Ireland, the attempt to deal with sub-state patterns of ethno-sectarian antagonism though principles of parity of cultural respect and esteem has inadvertently created a legitimating vocabulary of 'culture' and 'cultural rights' for antagonistic expressions of separatist difference" (Graham and Nash, 2006, p. 258). That said, the work of DCAL under Sinn Féin has often been rather oddly non-political at the level of party politics, apart from the proposal for an Irish Language Act. While the emphasis on social exclusion and equality is stronger than may be the case from the main Right and Centre-Right Unionist parties, examples of where ire has been drawn from Unionist parties have sometimes been found elsewhere (e.g. the February 2016 publication of a book about the Republican Bobby Sands, part funded by ACNI (BBC, 2016)). Herein lies one particular issue in relation to the formation of cultural policy. Due to the consociational nature of the NI Assembly, as discussed above, and the nature of a power-sharing Executive, DCAL often fails to take on any real kind of political direction as shaped by the Party with that Ministerial responsibility.

While DCAL is now under the control of Sinn Féin, it was previously under DUP control. There are some differences in the discourse used by these Parties – e.g. "in this part of Ireland", used by DCAL under Sinn Féin in the department's mission statement (DCAL, 2015b), as opposed to using the term 'Northern Ireland' – however it is less of a politicized department than might be assumed given the myriad cultural issues we have considered here. Indeed political differences at DCAL, depending on which party controls it, are not discernible in the same way that they would be in relation to DCMS either under the control of Labour or the Conservative parties in the UK. As the parties in the NI Executive are tied into the *Programme for Government* (NI Executive, 2012b), the work of individual departments cannot deviate far from the collectively agreed policy positions. It is worth noting, however, that these priorities are inherently impacted by party divisions given that they must be approved by both Sinn Féin and DUP, who are the two main parties in the Executive and hold the current powers for the Office of the First Minister and Deputy First Minister.

Rather, the policy approach of DCAL has been more in keeping with Bonet and Négrier's (2011, p. 578) notion that the dominant cultural policy trend since 1980 has been one of "economic and cultural development". In addition to its work on socio-economic matters, the DCAL's approach here mirrors that of where the NI Executive has arguably found its clearest *shared ground,* that of economic development driven by inward investment and actualized in the built environment as the hegemonic political-economic vision for NI. This is shown in its work in supporting NI Screen and its apparent dedication to GOT as a driver of economic growth through jobs creation and tourism transcends the community divide. In some ways this is unsurprising, with consensus over job creation perhaps more easily reached as compared to some of the more contentious issues. However, the unquestioning nature of some of the economic assumptions relating to investment and growth exposes the depth at which the neoliberal paradigm has become engrained.

While government departments in NI are required to take delicate steps over territory and space when it comes to political and social issues, the economic imperative for NI Screen with the blessing of the NI Executive seemingly trumps all other concerns. In this understanding, NI's space is 'ripe' for development, with the attendant picturesque vistas ready to be exploited by global television businesses. Attracting HBO to NI has spurred growth in the tourism sector, with fans travelling to numerous filming locations around NI (e.g. Boland, 2014). Further attention was drawn to filming in NI through visits by Queen Elizabeth II in 2014 and the British Prime Minister David Cameron in 2015. Such examples are then used by the supporting politicians to further justify support for the film and television sector. However, the work that NI Screen does and the excitement generated by GOT's filming in NI means that the enterprise has escaped with almost no criticism or detailed scrutiny over its operation, either from journalistic or academic sources. A dearth of analysis has meant that very little has been said about the precarious nature of HBO's relationship with NI, the ethics of providing public funding to a global-national on the scale of HBO (ultimately owned by its parent company Time-Warner), the nature of the employment it creates – often employing workers on short-term contracts – or indeed on the impact on the environment.[2]

Conclusion

NI remains very much shaped by the events of its past in terms of cultural identity, in the division of society, and in terms of socio-economic conditions, which often lag considerably behind the rest of the UK. NI's political institutions, while they remain based on consociational principles, are often found to be inadequate to deal with key cultural policy questions due to a lack of consensus. The agreement between the main parties, that using publicly funded agencies to attract investment into NI, especially in the area of the creative industries, has led to NI becoming a somewhat unlikely leading site outside of London in film and television production. However, pointing to the cultural policy 'success stories' cannot mask what are deep-rooted problems, further underlined by wider divisions within NI society. Cultural policy could contribute to a more-shared future in NI, but what are at times seemingly intractable cultural problems remain as significant obstacles to be surmounted. Future research on the subject is required to develop a theory of cultural policy in NI – the current literature specific to the subject is limited – to further understand the role of culture in the context of political, economic and social progress in the region. To this end, more empirical work that deals with arts and cultural institutions is required, along with the further policy analysis that will be required when DCAL transitions into its new departmental context.

Notes

1 In January 2015 it was proposed that the work of DCAL could be amalgamated with that of two other government departments in a new department, the Department of Social Welfare, Communities and Sport (Gordon, 2015). The department was eventually named the Department for Communities.
2 Thanks to Steve Baker for drawing our attention to this point about the environmental impact.

References

ACNI, 2011. *Intercultural Arts Strategy. December 2011.* Belfast: Arts Council of Northern Ireland.
ACNI, 2013. *Ambitions for the Arts: A Five Year Strategic Plan for the Arts in Northern Ireland 2013–2018.* Belfast: Arts Council of Northern Ireland.
ACNI, 2014. *Arts and Culture in Northern Ireland 2014.* Belfast: Arts Council of Northern Ireland
ACNI, 2015. *Annual Report & Accounts for the Year Ended 31 March 2015.* Belfast: Arts Council of Northern Ireland.
Ahearne, J., 2011. Questions of religion and cultural policy in France. *International Journal of Cultural Policy*, 17 (2), 153–169.
Barbieri, N., 2012. Why does cultural policy change? Policy discourse and policy subsystem: a case study of the evolution of cultural policy in Catalonia. *International Journal of Cultural Policy*, 18 (1), 13–30.
BBC News, 2016. *Bobby Sands Comic Book: Unionists Criticise Arts Council over Funding.* London: BBC News. Available from: www.bbc.com/news/uk-northern-ireland-35650389 [Accessed 25 February 2016].
Bell, C., Robinson, A., and Laverty, C., 2016. *Health Inequalities: Regional Report 2016.* Belfast: Department of Health.
Bew, P., Gibbon, P., and Patterson, H., 2002. *Northern Ireland 1921/2001: Political Forces and Social Classes.* London: Serif.
BFI, 2015a. *UK Film Tax Relief.* London: British Film Institute. Available from: www.britishfilmcommission.org.uk/film-production/uk-film-tax-relief/ [Accessed 9 October 2015].
BFI, 2015b. *UK High-End TV Tax Relief.* London: British Film Institute. Available from: www.britishfilmcommission.org.uk/hetvtaxrelief/ [Accessed 9 October 2015].
Boland, V., 2014. 'Game of Thrones' Brings Fantastical Footfall to Northern Ireland. *Financial Times.* Available from: www.ft.com/cms/s/0/05688764-02cd-11e4-81b1-00144feab7de.html#axzz3o43 Q8uIs [Accessed 12 October 2015].
Bonet, L., and Négrier, E., 2010. Cultural policy in Spain: processes and dialectics. *Cultural Trends*, 19 (1–2), 41–52.
Browne, J., Hood, A., and Joyce, R., 2014. *Child Working Age Poverty in Northern Ireland over the Next Decade: An Update.* London: Institute for Fiscal Studies.
Bryan, D., 2015. Parades, flags, carnivals, and riots: public space, contestation, and transformation in Northern Ireland. *Peace and Conflict: Journal of Peace Psychology*, 21 (4), 565–573.
Bryan, D., and Jarman, N., 1997. Parading Tradition, Protesting Triumphalism: Utilising Anthropology in Public Policy. *In:* H. Donnan and G. McFarlane, eds. *Culture and Policy in Northern Ireland: anthropology in the public arena.* Belfast: Institute of Irish Studies, 211–230.
Burgess, T.P., 2015a. This Sporting Life: Anything to Declare? Community Allegiance, Sports and the National Question. *In:* T.P. Burgess and G. Mulvenna, eds. *The Contested Identities of Ulster Protestants.* Basingstoke: Palgrave Macmillan, 98–112.
Burgess, T.P., 2015b. Preface. *In:* T.P. Burgess and G. Mulvenna, eds. *The Contested Identities of Ulster Protestants.* Basingstoke: Palgrave Macmillan, x–xiii.Childs, P. and Storry, M., eds. 1999. *Encyclopedia of Contemporary British Culture.* London: Routledge.
Cooper, D., 2009. *The Musical Traditions of Northern Ireland and its Diaspora: Community and Conflict.* Farnham: Ashgate.
Cooper, D., 2010. Fife and Fiddle: Protestants and Traditional Music in Northern Ireland. *In:* J.M. O'Connell and S. El-Shawan Castelo-Branco, eds. *Music in Conflict: Ethnomusicological Perspectives.* Champaign, IL: University of Illinois Press, 89–106.
Council of Europe, 1992. *European Charter for Regional and Minority Languages.* Strasbourg: Council of Europe.

Council of Europe, 2017. *Advisory Committee on the Framework Convention for the Protection of National Minorities: Fourth Opinion on the United Kingdom*. Strasbourg: Council of Europe.

CSO/NISRA, 2014. *Census 2011 Ireland and Northern Ireland*. Dublin and Belfast: Central Statistics Office and Northern Ireland Statistics and Research Agency.

DCAL, 2011. *Corporate Plan and Balanced Scorecard 2011–15*: Belfast: Department of Culture, Arts and Leisure.

DCAL, 2015a. *Proposal for an Irish Language Bill*. Belfast: Department of Culture, Arts and Leisure.

DCAL, 2015b. *Business Plan 2015–16*. Belfast: Department of Culture, Arts and Leisure.

DCAL, 2015c. *Strategy for Culture & Arts 2016–2026*. Belfast: Department of Culture, Arts and Leisure.

DCAL, 2015d. *Creative Industries Economic Estimates Northern Ireland. Experimental Statistics 2014. DCAL Findings 3/2014–15*. Belfast: Department of Culture, Arts and Leisure.

DCMS, 2001. *Creative Industry Task Force: Mapping Document*. London: Department for Culture, Media and Sport.

DCMS, 2008. *Creative Britain: New Talents for the New Economy*. London: Department for Culture, Media and Sport.

DCMS, 2011. *Creative Industries Economic Estimates: Full Statistical Release: 8 December 2011*. London: Department for Culture, Media and Sport.

Delhaye, C., and van de Ven, V., 2014. 'A commitment to cultural pluralism'. Diversity practices in two Amsterdam venues: Paradiso and De Meervaart. *Identities*, 21 (1), 75–91.

Dixon, P., 2002. Political skills or lying and manipulation? The choreography of the Northern Ireland peace process. *Political Studies*, 50 (4), 725–741.

Drache, D., and Froese, M.D., 2006. Globalisation, world trade and the cultural commons: identity, citizenship and pluralism. *New Political Economy*, 11 (3) 361–382.

Feldman, A., Ndakengerwa, D., Nolan, A., and Frese, C., 2005. *Diversity, Civil Society and Social Change in Ireland: A North-South Comparison of the Role of Immigrant/'New' Minority Ethnic-Led Community and Voluntary Sector Organisations*. Dublin: Migration and Citizenship Research Initiative.

Gordon, G., 2015. *Stormont Shake-Up: Three Departments Likely to be Broken Up*. London: BBC News. Available from: www.bbc.co.uk/news/uk-northern-ireland-30922226 [Accessed 8 October 2015].

Graham, B., and Nash, C., 2006. A shared future? Territoriality, pluralism and public policy in Northern Ireland. *Political Geography*, 25 (3), 253–278.

Hargie, O., Somerville, I., and Mitchell, D., 2015. *Social Exclusion and Sport in Northern Ireland: Report on Research Funded by the Equality Directorate Research Branch, Office of the First Minister and Deputy First Minister*. Jordanstown: University of Ulster.

Hassan, D., 2002. A people apart: soccer, identity and Irish nationalists in Northern Ireland. *Soccer & Society*, 3 (3), 65–83.

Hassan, D., 2005. Sport, Identity and Irish Nationalism in Northern Ireland. *In:* A. Bairner, ed. *Sport and the Irish: Histories, Identities, Issues*. Dublin: UCD Press, 123–139.

Hayes, B., and McAllister, I., 2013. *Conflict to Peace: Politics and Society in Northern Ireland over Half a Century*. Manchester: Manchester University Press.

Hennessy, T., 1997. *A History of Northern Ireland: 1921–2006*. Basingstoke. Macmillan Press.

Hill, A., and White, A., 2008. The flying of Israeli flags in Northern Ireland. *Identities: Global Studies in Culture and Power*, 15 (1), 31–50.

Holloway, D., 2005. *Understanding the Northern Ireland Conflict: A Summary and Overview of the Conflict and Its Origins*. Belfast: Community Dialogue.

Hughes, J., and McCandless, F., 2006. A Shared Future: Policy and Strategic Framework for Good Relations in Northern Ireland: Recommendations for Action in Community Relations and Community Development. *In: Sharing Over Separation*. Belfast: Community Relations Council, 159–180.

Kennaway, B., 2015. The Re-invention of the Orange Order: Triumphalism or Orangefest? *In:* T.P. Burgess and G. Mulvenna, eds. *The Contested Identities of Ulster Protestants*. Basingstoke: Palgrave Macmillan, 70–82.

Kiwan, N., 2007. A critical perspective on socially embedded cultural policy in France. *International Journal of Cultural Policy*, 13 (2), 153–167.

Knox, C., 1999. Northern Ireland: at the crossroads of political and administrative reform. *Governance: An International Journal of Policy and Administration*, 2 (3), 311–328.

Knox, C., 2011. Cohesion, sharing and integration in Northern Ireland. *Environment and Planning C: Politics and Space*, 29(3), 548–566.

Little, A., 2004. *Democracy and Northern Ireland: Beyond the Liberal Paradigm?* Basingstoke: Palgrave Macmillan.

McDermott, P., 2014, *Intolerance of Minority Ethnic Communities: An Overview of Responses 2005–2015*. Belfast: ARK.

McDowell, S., Braniff, M., and Murphy, J., 2015. Spacing commemorative-related violence in Northern Ireland: assessing the implications for a society in transition. *Space and Polity*, 19 (3): 231–243.

McGarry, J., and O'Leary, B., 2006. Consociational theory, Northern Ireland's conflict and its agreement. Part 1: what consociationalists can learn from Northern Ireland. *Government and Opposition*, 41 (1), 43–63.

McLaughlin, D., 2013. *Derry Fleadh Week 'Biggest Ever' Say Organisers*. London: BBC News. Available from: www.bbc.co.uk/news/uk-northern-ireland-foyle-west-23752870 [Accessed 18 September 2015].

McMonagle, S., 2010. Deliberating the Irish language in Northern Ireland: from conflict to multiculturalism? *Journal of Multilingual and Multicultural Development*, 31 (3), 253–270.

McQuade, O., and Fagan, J., 2002. *The Governance of Northern Ireland*. Lexington, NC.: BMF Publishing.

Meredith, R., 2014. *Irish Language Policy of Northern Ireland Executive Criticised*. London: BBC News. Available from: www.bbc.co.uk/news/uk-northern-ireland-25750658 [Accessed 29 September 2015].

Meredith, R., 2015a. *Arts Council of Northern Ireland Facing Further Budget Cuts This Year*. London: BBC News. Available from: www.bbc.co.uk/news/uk-northern-ireland-34224303 [Accessed 8 October 2015].

Meredith, R., 2015b. *Northern Ireland Arts: 32 Leading Organisations Face Cuts of 7%*. London: BBC News. Available from: www.bbc.co.uk/news/uk-northern-ireland-34460938 [Accessed 8 October 2015].

Meredith, R., 2015c. *Game of Thrones: TV Drama 'Contributes £110m to NI Economy'*. London: BBC News. Available from: www.bbc.co.uk/news/uk-northern-ireland-33573492 [Accessed 9 October 2015].

Miller, T., and Yudice, G., 2002. *Cultural Policy*. London: Sage.

Moore, P., 2003. Legacy: fourth phase public service broadcasting in Northern Ireland. *The Radio Journal: International Studies in Broadcast and Audio Media*, 1 (2), 87–100.

Morrow, D., Robinson, G., and Dowds, L., 2013. *The Long View of Community Relations in Northern Ireland*. Belfast: ARK.

Mulcahy, K.V., 1998. Cultural patronage in comparative perspective: public support for the arts in France, Germany, Norway, and Canada. *The Journal of Arts Management, Law, and Society*, 27 (4), 247–263.

Nic Craith, M., 2003. *Culture and Identity Politics in Northern Ireland*. Basingstoke: Palgrave Macmillan.

NI Executive, 2012a. *Economic Strategy: Priorities for Sustainable Growth and Prosperity*. Belfast: Northern Ireland Executive.

NI Executive, 2012b. *Programme for Government 2011–2015*. Belfast: Office of the First Minister and Deputy First Minister.

NIHRC, 2010. *Minority Language Rights: The Irish Language and Ulster-Scots*. Belfast: Northern Ireland Human Rights Commission.

NIO, 1998. *The Agreement: Agreement Reached in the Multi-Party Negotiations*. Belfast, Northern Ireland Office. Available from: http://cain.ulst.ac.uk/events/peace/docs/agreement.pdf [Accessed 30 June 2014].

NI Screen, 2010. *Driving Global Growth: Celebrating our Culture, Enhancing Our Children's Education, Boosting Our Economy*. Belfast: Northern Ireland Screen.

NI Screen, 2014. *Opening Doors: A Strategy to Transform the Screen Industries in Northern Ireland: Phase 1 2014–18*. Northern Ireland Screen.

NI Screen, 2015a. *Northern Ireland Screen Commission. Strategic Report, Directors' Report and Financial Statements for the year ended 31 March 2015*. Belfast: Northern Ireland Screen.

NI Screen, 2015b. *Production Funding*. Belfast: NI Screen. Available from: www.northernirelandscreen.co.uk/filming/production/ [Accessed 18 May 2017].

NI Screen, 2015c. *Operating Plan 2015–16. Year 2 of the 4-year plan Opening Doors*. Belfast: Northern Ireland Screen.

NISRA, 2012. *Census 2011: Key Statistics for Northern Ireland*. Belfast: Department of Finance and Personnel.

Nolan, P., 2012. *Northern Ireland Peace Monitoring Report: Number One*. Belfast: Community Relations Council.

Nolan, P., 2014. *Northern Ireland Peace Monitoring Report: Number Three*. Belfast: Community Relations Council.

Northern Ireland Office, 1998. *The Agreement: Agreement Reached in the Multi-Party Negotiations*. Belfast: Northern Ireland Office.

O'Brien, K., 2010. A Weberian approach to citizenship in a divided community. *Citizenship Studies*, 14 (5), 589–604.

O'Dochartaigh, N., 2016. Northern Ireland since 1920. *In:* R. Burke, and I. McBride, eds. *The Princeton History of Modern Ireland*. Princeton, NJ: Princeton University Press, 141–167.

Ofcom, 2014. *Public Service Content in a Connected Society: Ofcom's Third Review of Public Service Broadcasting, December 2014*. London: Ofcom.

Ofcom, 2015. *Communications Market Report: Northern Ireland*. London: Ofcom.

OFMDFM, 2005. *A Shared Future: Improving Relations in Northern Ireland*. Belfast: Office of the First Minister and Deputy First Minister.

OFMDFM, 2013. *Together: Building a United Community*. Belfast: Office of the First Minister and Deputy First Minister.

O'Malley, E., 2011. Culture and Lifestyle. *In: Contemporary Ireland*. Basingstoke: Palgrave Macmillan, 159–182.

Pritchard, R.M.O., 2004. Protestants and the Irish Language: historical heritage and current attitudes in Northern Ireland. *Journal of Multilingual and Multicultural Development*, 25 (1), 62–82.

Rabinovitch, V., 2007. *Four 'Constants' in Canadian Cultural Policy*. Montreal, QC: Canadian Museum of History. Available from: www.historymuseum.ca/research-and-collections/research/resources-for-scholars/essays-1/cultures/victor-rabinovitch/four-constants-in-canadian-cultural-policy/ [Accessed 16 October 2015].

Ramsey, P., 2013. Arts and older people strategy 2010–2013, arts council of Northern Ireland. *Cultural Trends*, 22 (3–4), 270–277.

Ramsey, P., 2015. Broadcasting to reflect 'life and culture as we know it': media policy, devolution, and the case of Northern Ireland. *Media, Culture & Society*, 37 (8), 1193–1209.

Ruane, J., and Todd, J., 1996. *The dynamics of conflict in Northern Ireland: power, conflict and emancipation*. Cambridge: Cambridge University Press.

Saukkonen, P., and Pyykkönen, M., 2008. Cultural policy and cultural diversity in Finland. *International Journal of Cultural Policy*, 14 (1), 49–63.

Shirlow, P., and Murtagh, B., 2006. *Belfast: Segregation, Violence and the City*. London: Pluto Press.

Shuttleworth I., and Lloyd, C., 2013. Moving apart or moving together? A snapshot of residential segregation from the 2011 census. *Shared Space*, 16, 57–70.

Stevenson, N., 2003. *Cultural Citizenship: Cosmopolitan Questions*. Maidenhead: Open University Press.

Stevenson, N., 2010. Cultural citizenship, education and democracy: redefining the good society. *Citizenship Studies*, 14 (3), 275–291.

Tonge, J., 2002. *Northern Ireland: Conflict and Change*, 2nd edition. Harlow: Pearson.

Trench, A., 2007. *Devolution and Power in the United Kingdom*. Manchester: Manchester University Press.

The Newsletter, 2015. *Unionists Brand Irish Language Bill 'Pointless and Dictatorial'*. Belfast: News Letter. Available from: www.newsletter.co.uk/news/unionists-brand-irish-language-bill-pointless-and-dictatorial-1-6572058 [Accessed 10 October 2015].

Part IV
Practice and cultural policy

14

The art collection of the United Nations

Origins, institutional framework and ongoing tensions

Mafalda Dâmaso

Introduction

The United Nations Art Collection, exhibited in the United Nations (UN) Headquarters in New York and in other duty stations worldwide, is mostly composed of official gifts offered to the UN by its member states. This chapter will argue that the collection foregrounds the core contradiction of the UN, that is, between its international values and responsibilities and its modus operandi, which remains nation-centric. The chapter will describe the origins of the collection, analyse its current institutional framework, describe how it reflects the organisational contradictions of the UN and identify the audiences of the collections. Throughout this analysis, the art collection will emerge as a platform in which the member states and the UN deploy soft power – a notion that is briefly related to that of cultural diplomacy.

Uniting these sections is the argument that the collection reflects, in different ways, the institutional ambivalence of the UN itself (serving an international community in whose name it was created yet funded and organised according to the logic of the nation-state).[1] This tension reveals the limits of the use of art by political institutions to reinforce a specific message when the different parties do not agree with the transfer of certain powers to said institution – in this case, the ability of the UN to develop and communicate a position of its own in relation to ongoing international affairs debates (which would be reflected in the curation by the UN of its own exhibitions using its art collection, for example).

Origins and goals

It is difficult to find details of the origins of the collection of the UN. However, the existing evidence points to the collection originating from a combination of, on the one hand, the personal interest in the arts of the first UN Secretary General and, on the other hand, practical concerns regarding the need to decorate its New York headquarters:

> appropriate decoration of the Headquarters was an early concern of the architects who planned the buildings. The theme of peace was reflected in many of the first offerings.

Two huge murals representing "War" and "Peace", by the Brazilian artist Candido Portinari, dominate the Delegates' Lobby of the General Assembly building, along with Belgium's mural tapestry, "Triumph of Peace", one of the largest ever woven [...]. A mural by José Vela Zanetti of the Dominican Republic titled "Mankind's Struggle for a Lasting Peace" was the gift of the Guggenheim Foundation [...]. Iran, Iraq and Turkey have given interesting replicas of ancient peace treaties.

(Urquhart 1995, p. i)

Although I will focus on its artworks, the collection also includes historic objects, all of which have been donated as gifts to the UN by its member states, associations or individuals. Additionally, each UN headquarters (Geneva, Vienna and Nairobi) has its own collection. This said, the total number of objects included in the collection (let alone in each office) is unclear. Michael Adlerstein, Assistant Secretary-General and Executive Director of the Capital Master Plan (CMP), i.e. of the renovation plan of the New York headquarters, said in a 2014 interview that there were 311 gifts listed in the UN's inventory; however, there isn't a complete registry listing all the elements of the collection. This uncertainty is evident in another of Adlerstein's statements – who also belongs to the collection's committee:

We also continuously have loans from different museums or Member States [...]. There is more art in Geneva, Nairobi, Bangkok, and Vienna and in all of the regional offices. *I think* there is far more art than in the New York Headquarters but *I would assume* that we have the largest collection in the organisation.

(Adlerstein 2014, p. 152; emphasis my own)

The elements of the collection are exhibited not only in the New York headquarters but also in other duty stations worldwide (for example, The United Nations Office at Geneva inherited a considerable number of works of art from the League of Nations – see UNOG, no date and International Geneva 2012). Interestingly, the growth of the collection accompanied that of the UN.

The diverse permanent collection of art here has tripled in size [...]. The growth in the number of art objects has roughly paralleled the growth in membership – from 51 nations in 1946, when it was decided to build the headquarters here, to 157 today.

(Blair 1983)[2]

But this momentum has since slowed down, as has the number of donations. Moreover, one must note a recent change in the UN's position vis-à-vis said donations, even if that was due to practical constraints rather than to wider strategic or policy changes.

In the early days of the UN, some gifts were donated by foundations and by the city of New York and by others that were invited to gift. Since that time, the number of gifts has grown significantly. Wall space has become in high demand so that at this point in time, we prefer gifts from Member States, and this is the Member States' preference as well [...]. We have had a pause for the Capital Master Plan where we have not received gifts for the past six years, because there is too much construction going on [...]. Part of what the Arts Committee tries to do is to make sure we do not get overwhelmed with art.

(Adlerstein 2014, p. 152)

That is, today every member can only make one offer and is also responsible for the installation of the offered artefacts. Additionally, as Adlerstein mentions, the renovation of the headquarters (the Capital Master Plan) between 2008 and 2015 led to a pause in the growth of the collection – which is likely to continue due to space constraints.

Although I cannot discuss all the elements of the collection, it is important to mention some of its particularly well-known pieces. The first is Marc Chagall's 1964 stained-glass piece. This memorial to those who died in the plane crash that killed Dag Hammarskjöld, the Secretary General, in Africa during the Congo crisis in 1961, was gifted by the artist and by the United Nations staff in 1964.

> *Peace* is filled with symbolism of peace drawn from the New Testament and depicted in the artist's signature swirling, dreamlike style. Imagery includes a young boy representing the Biblical "Prince of Peace, " the Tree of Knowledge amid a pastoral setting from the Garden of Eden, Christ on the cross, and an angel bestowing the Ten Commandments to the residents of a walled city. References to Beethoven's Ninth Symphony (a favorite of Hammarskjold's) also figure throughout.
>
> *(Halcyon 2015)*

Barbara Hepworth's *Single Form* (1961–64), a stone sculpture surrounded by water and with a slightly off-center hole, was also donated in memory of the late Secretary General. Indeed, it was gifted 'on a grant from Jacob Blaustein, a former member of the United States delegation' (Blair 1983). Finally, a bronze statue of a reclining figure by the British sculptor Henry Moore (the eighth of nine castings of a plaster executed in 1979–80) and positioned at the entrance to the Secretariat building, is also a memorial to Hammarskjold – who wished that one work of the sculptor would be included in the collection. In fact,

> the second Secretary General of the United Nations, the Swede Dag Hammarskjold, had a special relationship with the arts. He saw in them important 'Ambassadors of Hope' after the Second World War. Hammarskjold […] laid the foundation for the great art collection of the United Nations […].
>
> *(Theill 2014, p. 168)*

Apart from artworks, as I mentioned earlier, the collection includes tapestries from countries such as China and Iran, sculptures from Nigeria, Mali and others, furniture, a peace bell from Japan, a third-century mosaic mural donated by Tunisia in 1961 and a 3000-year-old ceremonial mantle received in 1957 from Peru, among others. Finally, it also includes more unconventional elements.

> Hanging in a Secretariat building corridor is a small painting by an amateur presented by the artist in 1978. "Please accept this small painting as a gift of peace from me in this Year of the Child," said an accompanying letter, signed, Muhammad Ali.
>
> *(Blair 1983)*

This gift is interesting in that it highlights the gradual openness of the UN to celebrities and, most recently, to public relations (Cooper and Frechette 2015). But it also reveals that this is indeed an extremely varied collection. For example, in 1955 the Netherlands offered the UN a Foucault pendulum, which moves according to earth's rotation – a non-artistic work that supports the idea of the UN as representing the globe and hence the international community.

Indeed, in its whole, the collection is often described as representing the ideals and the values of the UN as an international organisation. Its former Secretary-General wrote that:

> the art displayed at the United Nations – at its Headquarters in New York, offices in Geneva and Vienna, regional commissions, and more than twenty agencies and programmes of the United Nations system – reflects the diversity of cultures and historical traditions of the Member States, and therefore of humanity itself.
>
> *(Boutros-Ghali 1995, p. 9)*

However, it is impossible to find any institutional evidence that this aim (representing humanity as well as addressing or representing the central values of the UN) is indeed the goal of the collection. Rather, the idea that it showcases the richness of the world's cultures seems to have emerged as a retrospective justification for its existence. The fact is that the collection doesn't

> have a single mission or purpose or selecting group. It is a collection which has been donated by the Member States and reflects their impression of what they would like the world to see of their culture or of the UN mission.
>
> *(Adlerstein 2014, p. 152)*

The next sections will reveal that this lack of clarity or ambivalence is also reflected, on the one hand, on the institutional framework of the collection (a committee with very limited independence and powers, which reflects a broader tension at the core of the UN regarding the nature of sovereignty) and, on the other hand, on the multiple audiences that are served by it (which is associated with its use as an instrument of soft power, as will be argued).

Institutional framework

First, when presenting an official gift to the UN, the member states must follow specific procedures, including giving speeches and attending ceremonies, which are coordinated by the Protocol and Liaison Service. Indeed, there 'are frequently gifts from member nations, often to commemorate an anniversary or the appointment of a new Secretary General' (Halcyon, 2015). The act of making a donation to the collection can be interpreted as either a public demonstration of agreement with the values of the UN or as a way to increase the visibility of a specific member state within the UN. In any case, such an act reveals an implicit agreement with the importance of the UN as an inter-governmental organisation. However, the fact that the donor remains the holder of the rights of the artwork also attests to the refusal to provide it a supranational status – which, as we will see later, further reinforces the ambivalence and the non-independence of the collection.

Second, the collection is managed by an art committee that meets when needed, composed of nine UN staff members.[3] Its functions are to establish policies to be followed by the Secretary-General regarding the gifts offered to the collection, to recommend their acceptance or rejection and to assist with their management. Interestingly, Adlerstein is very open regarding the fact that the elements of the committee aren't invited based on their knowledge of art but, rather,

> because we are in fields of endeavor that the Secretary-General needs to pay attention to, political affairs and facilities and public information [...]. We do not have the actual staff experienced in art curation.
>
> *(2014, p. 153)*

This said, the UN originally invited art specialists to join this board.

> The arts committee used to be composed of both Secretariat officials and outside experts. But, Mr. Urquhart said, the outsiders "dwindled away out of frustration" by the mid-1970's [sic]. "I don't remember we accomplished very much, and we sort of disbanded ourselves, "said Elizabeth Parkinson Cobb, a former president of the Museum of Modern Art, who left the committee in 1975. "We had to accept everything, whether we liked it or not".
>
> *(Blair 1983)*

The fact that the committee was (and still is) forced to accept all offers highlights the fact that the collection isn't built from the point of view of either experts or artists – i.e. as a curated section of objects representing the values of the UN. Rather, the collection 'represents the diversity of each member's art' (Williams 2014, p. 152). This absence of power to reject specific artworks also reiterates – again, implicitly – the sovereignty of each member state. This might also explain why the committee subsequently diminished in size, before expanding again with the arrival of political advisors. As the journalist Nicole Winfield wrote in a piece for the Los Angeles Times in 2000,

> the U.N. Arts Committee, which chooses what gifts from U.N. countries get placed where, consists of a single person – one of Secretary-General Kofi Annan's top political advisors who has no fine arts background. Indeed, the business of art at the United Nations is hardly artistic. It's politics and diplomacy at its most basic. Diplomats try to score subtle political points through their gifts to the organization, and U.N. officials try desperately to avoid insulting any country when the organization has to object to, reject or otherwise intervene over an offering. "I see my work more as being in the realm of diplomacy than in the realm of curatorship, "concedes arts committee chairman Alvaro de Soto, who on most days carries the title of U.N. assistant secretary-general for political affairs.

This committee is the main entity responsible for the conservation of the collection. However, restoration work, for example, requires returning the artworks to the member states that donated them. The absence of power of the UN is also evident in the fact that changes to the location of the artworks require its previous acceptance by the donors. This is one of the reasons why, in the report 'Managing Works of Art in the United Nations' (1992), the UN Joint Inspection Unit made several recommendations to the Security Council, including the reorganisation of the Arts Committee and stronger clarity regarding the responsibility for the artworks. Such recommendations included the following:

> Recommendation One: That the Secretary-General make proposals to the General Assembly at the earliest possible date for adoption by Member States of an arts policy for the United Nations.

> Recommendation Two: That the Secretary-General undertake the reorganization and strengthening of the arts committee, specifying its composition and terms of reference [...].

> Recommendation Three: That the Secretary-General inform Member States of the specific and details measures he [sic] plans to take to develop, preserve and safeguard the arts collection of the United Nations, including his [sic] proposed programmes for registry, evaluation, conservation, insurance and protection.

Recommendation Four: That the Secretary-General, in the interest of an effective arts policy over the long term, should engage a professional curator to assure the relevance, coherence and value of the United Nations collection.

(UN Joint Inspection Unit 1992, p. ii)

Although it was published 15 years ago, its recommendations are yet to be enacted. Nonetheless, Adlerstein recently affirmed that 'the terms of reference for the Arts Committee and the management of the gifts is presently in review again by the Arts Committee [...]. The donor is responsible for the maintenance of the art' (Adlerstein 2014, p. 155). This said, the UN does have some elements of responsibility for the collection. As he stated,

the budget for art is *sort of* under the umbrella of the Office of Central Support Services (OCSS), Department of Management. They manage the Art Collection. They manage it on a day-to-day basis; they clean it; they paint the walls; they move the art off the wall in order to do the maintenance of the building [...]. The curatorial work is done by the Member States, so there is not a significant work load [sic] for us. Most of the staff involved, including the Arts Committee, treats this part of their work as collateral duty.

(Adlerstein 2014, p. 155; emphasis my own)

The responsibility of the member states for the curatorial work is particularly interesting. Once again, this reiterates the fact that the UN (in this case, via the art committee) is unable to function as an authority responsible for establishing a narrative connecting the different artworks. This is important because doing so would require connecting the positions of individual states and relating them to ongoing discussions in the UN's fora. This absence of power is also evident in the committee's role (or lack thereof) in evaluating the appropriateness of gifts and, subsequently, in their rejection. According to Adlerstein,

there are no specific criteria for what makes a work of art unacceptable. The purpose of the Arts Committee is to give the Secretary-General its opinion to determine if a gift might be inappropriate. Generally speaking, the UN avoids gifts that might be offensive to Member States or to any particular group.

(2014, p. 154)

However, as Winfield notes in her piece, there is indeed evidence of previous rejections.

Urquhart [...] recalls having to politely decline a gift from an unnamed Pacific island ambassador to display a prized, stuffed coelacanth – a prehistoric fish. A decomposing animal, Urquhart remembers arguing, was perhaps not an appropriate addition.

(2000)

Williams also describes a further conflict between the committee and those who wanted to give yet another object to the collection. Reading the full quote suggests how politically charged such decisions are.

Mihail Simeonov, a Bulgarian sculptor, in 1980 had the idea of felling an African elephant with narcotic darts and making a mold in latex, to be cast later in bronze-five tons of it. The idea was taken up by Austrian former Secretary General of the Socialist

International Hans Janitschek who worked at the UN. He set up the "Cast the Elephant Trust" as a not-for-profit. The Secretariat breathed a sigh of relief—they were under no obligation to accept gifts from NGOs [...]. However, Janitschek enlisted three elephant-populated countries as sponsors, Nepal, Malawi and Namibia, so the UN had to give way

(2014, pp. 150–151)

Altogether, and despite their brevity, these stories reveal that the committee is very limited in its powers to evaluate the inappropriateness of the artworks that it receives, which it can only do in regard to conservation issues (as well as, potentially, other safety issues) and if there is reason to believe that other member states or groups might find such gifts offensive. The practical consequence of this situation is clear: gifts that do not explicitly oppose a specific member state or group must be accepted, leaving the door open to objects that do so implicitly, as I will discuss later.

Two central issues have emerged from this initial analysis: on the one hand, the absence of institutional autonomy of the committee; on the other hand, the role of political influence in the expansion of the collection. They reflect a broader institutional conflict, as I will now discuss.

Organisational contradictions

The management of the collection can be seen as reiterating the argument made by Seth Center, an historian in the American Department of State, in 'The United Nations Department of Public Information: Intractable Dilemmas and Fundamental Contradictions' (2009). Center proposes that the work of the communication and public relations department of the UN foregrounds the core contradictions of the institution, such as that between its international values and responsibilities and its modus operandi, which is nation-centric.

This tension is reflected in the art collection: despite being described as belonging to the UN, as we have seen the artworks belong to the nation states (which would have to give permission for the use of the former in support of any specific curatorial narrative). In light of this, and following Center, the strategic challenges faced by the UN collection emerge as inherent to the nature of the UN. Let us consider in detail his discussion of what he views as the contradictory aims served by the Department of Public Information (DPI), which is responsible for the communication of the UN.

> While the UN General Assembly is infamous as a forum for member states' propaganda, the United Nations bureaucracy maintains, at least in principle, an ethos of impartiality in global affairs, a culture of deference to its member states, and an adherence to the principle of state sovereignty. This situation has produced intractable dilemmas in the formulation and execution of UN information policy.
>
> *(2009, pp. 886–887)*

That is, Center proposes that despite the recent attempted reorganisation of the public relations of the UN, its mission and institutional nature oppose the possibility of a fully unified communication strategy. He illustrates this argument with an analysis of the history of the DPI, focusing both on earlier tensions and on the multiple reorganisations to which it has been subjected during the last 20 years. In particular, Center argues that, during the Cold War, and with regard to controversial issues such as assigning responsibility for the Korean War, too much "objective" information was sure to alienate one of the two superpowers and lead to charges of partiality [...]. In seeking to adhere to the ethos of impartiality, the DPI elided controversial issues [...]. The DPI consistently strove to avoid singling out individual states for approbation in its treatment of global issues because of the implicit challenge to state sovereignty and the exigency of impartiality.

(2009, p. 891)

Nonetheless, and crucially, Center argues that

the DPI has found a formula that produced an uneasy détente in the historical conflict over the means and ends of UN information policy. The DPI and wider UN information efforts embrace activism in the conduct of information policy, but abjure politicization in the content.

(2009, p. 896)

There are further complications in analysing the relationship between the UN and its member states. For instance, as Anne-Marie Slaughter demonstrates (2005), the term sovereignty is itself contested, and its scholarly understanding has gradually shifted away from a Westphalian, zero-sum understanding. Instead, authors such as Kal Raustiala (2003) and Abram Chayes and Antonia Handler Chayes (1995) propose to see it as flexible and expandable. In this view, when a state makes the decision to join an international organisation with supranational elements (hence partly limiting one's own powers), the result is an expansion of the autonomy of said state. This is because such membership allows it to participate in a wider pool of resources (economic, military, diplomatic and others).

However, this dualism – between the mission of the UN and the sovereignty of the individual member states – is not exclusive to the UN; rather, it could be seen as an example of a tension that is inherent to international or supranational organisations. This tension is clear when one reads Tuuli Lähdesmäki's (2012) discussion of the role played by the rhetoric of the European Union's (EU's) cultural policy in the context of its aim to strengthen the unification of its member states. Lähdesmäki notices a central contradiction in an analysis of four cases – the Treaty of Lisbon, the European Agenda for Culture, the EU's European Capital of Culture programme (ECC) and specifically the Pécs, Hungary ECC programme in 2010:

the fundamental aim of the cultural policy of the EU is to stress the obvious cultural diversity of Europe, and at the same time, find some underlying common elements which unify the diverse cultures of Europe. Through these common elements, the EU's policy produces an imagined cultural community of Europe (Sassatelli 2002, p. 436) which is 'united in diversity', as one of the slogans of the Union states.

(Lähdesmäki 2012, p. 59)

Further, cultural elements are critical in communicating the values of the European Union:

pan-Europeanists or cosmopolitans have thus stressed the role of the cosmopolitan aspects of culture in the creation of Europe – even on the administrative level in the EU – as is suggested, e.g., by the selection of Beethoven's Ode to Joy as the EU's anthem.

(Delanty 2000, p. 226; Lähdesmäki 2012, pp. 63–64)

To be more specific, Lähdesmäki is here referring to the fact that, when applying for the European Capital of Culture programme, interested cities must demonstrate that they have contributed significantly to European culture. At the same time, "the guide and the ECC decisions both emphasize the significance of important historical figures in the making of a 'European dimension' to the ECC events", a practice that the author sees as mirroring 'nationalist attempts to boost national self-esteem and create a national narration of history' (Lähdesmäki 2012, pp. 66–68). This is why, broadly joining the analysis developed by Vivien Fryd (1994), which I will mention later, Lähdesmäki suggests that the role played by

> common cultural heritage in the production of Europeanness can be interpreted as a reflection of the past colonialist ideology (see Palonen 2010) [...]. In a sense, the heritage is colonized by the EU for its identity political purposes [...]. The rhetoric tends to emphasize the heritage of 'original' Europeans [...] and draws attention [away] from the cultural and social problems of the present-day cultural diversity.
>
> *(2012, p. 72)*

Although I do agree that, in an analogous manner, the UN collection can undoubtedly be seen as unveiling the institutional complexity of the UN, I do not believe that the term colonisation and its logic apply to this case (and, before the conclusion, I question whether the logic of colonisation applies at all). Rather, the comparison between the art collection of the UN and the European City of Culture reveals exactly the opposite: the collection is a vehicle for multiple (and sometimes contradictory) 'national narration[s] of history', as is identified by Lähdesmäki (2012, p. 68). This possibility emerges from the broader ambivalence that the collection exemplifies, as I will be arguing throughout this chapter: that between the mission of the UN (to represent and work in the name of the international community – as a supranational organisation) and its implementation (which depends on the UN's individual nation states – and, hence, as an international organisation with some supranational elements).

This ambivalence is also reflected in the lack of clarity regarding who the intended audiences of the collection are. As we will see, it has several overlapping audiences: the visitors of the headquarters of the UN (as well as of other offices) taking official tours of the buildings (UNESCO 2010); the UN staff, national civil servants and other individuals who are able to visit parts of the headquarters of the UN (as well as other offices) that are closed to the general public; finally, the global public, who has access to the collection through media stories about the donations.

The audiences of the collection

As Edward Marks mentions in his piece in *A World of Art: The United Nations Collection* (1995), the only publication dedicated to the collection, the intended audience (or audiences) of the collection is (or are) not immediately clear. Elements of the collection are mentioned during tours of the headquarters in New York (see Gimlette 2012). UNESCO's headquarters (in Paris) also offer guided tours to the public (see UNESCO, no date).[4] However, there is a second audience that only partly overlaps with that of the participants in its tours. Indeed, Marks writes that:

> quite a number of these artworks, for security and other reasons, are not accessible to the public, even in those buildings where there are guided tours. They are seen only by UN staff, delegates of member nations and visitors on official business. Since they are not in museums or established galleries, their existence is relatively unknown, even to art connoisseurs.
>
> *(1995, p. 15)*

In a similar direction, in the interview that was quoted earlier, Adlerstein states that 'a lot of the collection is not visible to the public because it is in the delegates' areas. The delegates enjoy the collection, it is their art, and it is their house' (2014, p. 152). That is, the collection is seen as having a similar identity-building effect in these two audiences (those who visit the headquarters of the UN and other offices as either visitors or as members of staff), clearly communicating the values and the diversity of the institution. This experience, if it does indeed take place, has important consequences. To understand why, it is enough to read Carol Duncan's 'The Art Museum as Ritual' (1995), in which the art historian discusses the values associated with the buildings that house public art collections and argues that 'to control a museum means precisely to control the representation of a community and its highest values and truths' [...] (Duncan 1995, p. 8). Crucially, however, Duncan stresses not the role of collections but that of visitors:

> In art museums, it is the visitors who enact the ritual [...]. The museum's larger narrative structure stands as a frame and gives meaning to individual works [...]. A ritual experience is thought to have a purpose, an end. It is seen as transformative: it confers or renews identity or purifies or restores order in the self or to the world through sacrifice, ordeal, or enlightenment.
>
> *(1995, pp. 12–13)*

Nonetheless, such statements highlight the need for research aimed at understanding how visitors from different cultural, social and national backgrounds interpret the art collection of the UN and to test to what extent its visit might be associated with the enactment, to use Duncan's words (1995, p. 478), of a stronger sense of belonging to the international community, as suggested by Adlerstein. In a similar direction, Susan Pearce also discusses the role of museums in constructing or sustaining specific identities in *Interpreting Objects and Collections*, in which she analyses museums such as the Louvre. Pearce demonstrates that:

> museums can be powerful identity-defining machines. To control a museum is to control the representation of a community and some of its highest most authoritative truths [...]. What we see and do not see in our prestigious art museums [...] involves the much larger questions of who constitutes the community.
>
> *(1992, p. 286)*

Read in light of these comments, the UN art collection emerges as contributing to the definition of both its visitors and its professionals as part of a common group – the international community uniting peoples beyond borders and in the name of which the preamble of the Charter of the UN starts ('We the peoples of the United Nations', UN, 1945). Although this notion is discussed in the literature as legally complicated (Greenwood 2011), one can also interpret it rhetorically, i.e. as making the case for the relevance, and hence the legitimacy, of the UN itself.[5] The collection can be read in the same way: as strengthening the idea that the global mission of the UN (to represent and advocate for the global community) is worthy of support. This is significant in that it attests that the UN, even without having the power to curate the artworks in a way that would organise them according to a supranational narrative, can use the collection to support its mandate.

It is also interesting to consider the partial closeness of the collection vis-à-vis the wider public in view of a further comment made by Adlerstein:

the UN Headquarters is not a museum. The UN could not afford to open itself up in a way of a museum, to open up all its floors on a regular basis, because the UN Headquarters is the functioning office of an inter-governmental organisation.

(2014, p. 155)

This quote suggests that contrarily to most art museums, which have as their main goal to disseminate their collections to audiences that are as broad as possible, evaluating the art collection of the UN exclusively based on those two dimensions (i.e. on its elements and on its dissemination within a multifaceted audience) would be limiting. Rather, as I will discuss in the following section, the art collection of the UN could also be seen as a platform for soft power. This idea is connected with the third audience of the collection: the global viewers who read or watch news pertaining to specific items within the collection. Indeed, the decision by nation states to contribute to the art collection of the UN is often accompanied by strong media campaigns.

This analysis resonates with the argument of Simon Mark in 'A Greater Role for Cultural Diplomacy' (2009), which affirms the importance of cultural diplomacy within public diplomacy, particularly in terms of the broader audiences the former reaches both domestically and internationally. Mark follows the definition of Mark Leonard (1997), who organises it (i.e. public diplomacy) into three tiers:

The first tier, short term, reactive news management, takes hours and days. The next tier, medium term strategic communications, takes months. The third tier, cultural diplomacy, is about the development of long-term relationships, and can take years.

(Mark 2009, p. 13)

That is, in this definition the audiences of cultural diplomacy also differ from those of public diplomacy because the former includes, contrarily to the latter, 'politicians, diplomats and other government officials' – an idea that is confirmed in the partial availability of the art collection to the visitors. In this view, the motivation for giving to the UN art collection is more complex than a simple one-sided demonstration of support towards the UN. This complexity – both in terms of audiences and, potentially, in motivation for giving – demands that one revisit the notion of soft power.

Soft power within the collection

Let us then consider some of the artworks included in the collection from the point of view of this hypothesis, i.e. to test whether their donation to the UN art collection may function as a form of soft power. As is well known, this term was originally defined by Joseph S. Nye Jr. (1990) in opposition to hard power (i.e. military and economic resources). Writing after the fall of the Berlin Wall, Nye opposed the idea of geopolitical multipolarity and affirmed that the United States was the major global potency, stressing the changing nature of power.

The appropriate response to the changes occurring in world politics today is not to abandon the traditional concern for the military balance of power, but to accept its limitations and to supplement it with insights about interdependence [...]. Creating and resisting linkages between issues [...] becomes the art of the power game. Political leaders use international institutions to discourage or promote such linkages.

(1990, pp. 156–158)

As examples of soft power, Nye mentions American culture and lifestyle,[6] which allow the country 'to get its messages across and to affect the preferences of others' (1990, p. 169). By giving artworks to the art collection of the UN, member states are also 'getting their messages across', both within the UN and internationally. That is, they are potentially reinforcing their positions in regard to ongoing geopolitical disagreements or tensions as well as, in Nye's terminology, discouraging or promoting linkages (as we saw in the case of the elephant cast).

However, as Melissa Nisbett carefully demonstrates in 'Who Holds the Power in Soft Power?' (2016), Nye's discussion of the term has evolved and its definition remains unclear, particularly regarding its position within canonical discussions of power (not to mention the lack of evidence regarding the effectiveness of practices inspired by the term). Specifically, the author argues that Nye's concept of soft power can be understood according to Steven Lukes's 1974 third dimension of power, which regards the ways individual beliefs and preferences are influenced by the powerful.

> In the words of Joseph Nye (2004, p. 2), soft power is the ability "to influence the behavior of others to get the outcomes one wants". Soft power can therefore reside both in the realm of the imagination, as well as within some kind of operationalized action. Soft power involves the assimilation of thoughts, beliefs and values, through sometimes subtle and imperceptible means. This idea of the power to shape desires and beliefs maps very neatly onto the concept of soft power.
>
> *(Nisbett 2016, no page)*

Nonetheless, I do think that the concept is relevant for this discussion in that it hints at the nation-centric order of the UN. As Nisbett suggests when she discusses the British approach to soft power and cultural diplomacy during the last 10 years (2016), while the latter strategy combined the goals of cooperation and competition with other nations, the more recent focus on soft power has mostly abandoned the idea of collaboration. To put it differently, soft power suggests and is associated with the idea of competition between states – namely, as I will now argue, regarding the visibility or the control of a narrative.

A well-known piece of the UN art collection that confirms this analysis is Evgeniy Vuchetich's *Let Us Beat Swords into Plowshares* (1957), a bronze sculpture depicting a powerful man using a hammer to transform a sword, which was offered to the UN in 1959 by the former Soviet Union. Along the same ideological lines (albeit with a much more violent undertone, making the case for the continuous geopolitical relevance of the former Soviet potency), the Soviet Union also offered the UN Zurab Tsereteli's *Good Defeats Evil* (1990), another sculpture that depicts St. George slaying a dragon and that is composed of 'fragments of USS Pershing nuclear missiles and Soviet SS-20 missiles that were destroyed under the terms of the 1987 Intermediate-Range Nuclear Forces Treaty' (Halcyon 2015).

Although this artwork fulfils the definition of appropriateness of the committee, it would be impossible not to read in it a subtle critique of the American stance in the Cold War. This cunning way of making a political statement without targeting a specific nation state as responsible for the current state of affairs is evident throughout the collection. It is worth quoting the journalist Ian Williams at length:

> The visitor's hall to the General Assembly typifies the highs and lows of the collection. Going through doors with Ernest Cormier bas reliefs more reminiscent of the interwar art of the Palais des Nations in Geneva, visitors see a replica of Sputnik hanging in the air above a statue of Zeus, while visitors file past a moon rock in a glass case from the US […].

> Everyone seems too polite to point out the Chinese gift—the huge ivory carving celebrating the opening of the Chengtu-Kunming Railway, a period piece from 1974 representing a combination of Mao's proletarian triumphalism and traditional Chinese artistry, contains the ivory from no less than eight dead elephants.
>
> *(Williams 2014, pp. 148–149)*

All of these artworks have clear political undertones and reveal details about the particular geopolitical position of the nation states that gifted them. This is not only the case of the most evidently political pieces (such as those mentioned in Williams's quote), but is also manifest when one considers the story of Per Krohg's painting, which adorns the Security Council. In the essay 'The iconology a new world order: Per Krohg's paintings in the UN Security Nations' (2014), the art historian Maria Veie Sandvik argues that Krohg received his mandate from the Norwegian architect Arnstein Arneberg, who was commissioned to design the chamber and was a good friend of the first Secretary-General, Trygve Lie. Although there is no evidence that Arnsberg played a direct role in this selection, neither are there historical records of an open tender.

> Secretary-General Lie was apparently able to place the order completely to Norway, although the country paid only for the decoration of the hall [...]. Members of the Art Board at UN Headquarters, who had to evaluate proposals for works of art in boardrooms, expressed strong reservations about the use of figurative painting [...]. But then a Royal Norwegian Decree of 7 January 1950 tied the donation of dollars 15 000 to the condition that Krohg's work would be mounted in the hall of the Security Council.
>
> *(Sandvik 2014, p. 158)*

Clearly, this incident may be read as attesting to Norway's wish to take a central role within the UN even if it isn't one of the permanent members of the Security Council.

Another example that is relevant in this context is the tapestry reproduction of Pablo Picasso's *Guernica*. After being gifted by the Nelson Rockefeller Estate in 1985, it was placed in the corridor leading to the Security Council until 2009 and is now shown in Madrid's Reina Sofia Museum (Halcyon 2015). Interestingly, in what points to the awareness of politicians and diplomats regarding the political undertones of the collection and their potential in supporting or opposing a political narrative, and following Colin Powell's 2003 case in the Security Council for military intervention in Iraq (Dowd 2003), Picasso's tapestry was famously covered by a cloth in order to avoid appearing in the background of Powell's press conference.[7]

The idea that the artworks illustrate both the relations between the UN and those who gifted them and, at the same time, the political history of the latter goes in the direction of the analysis made by Vivien Fryd in 'The Politics of Public Art: Art in the United States Capitol' (1994), where the art historian analyses the art collection of the US Capitol building in Washington. Combining formal and iconographic art historical analysis with social and political history, Fryd discusses Thomas Crawford's *Statue of Freedom* (which decorates its dome) and two artworks decorating the

> central staircase of the Capitol's east facade – Luigi Persico's Discovery of America and Horatio Greenough's Rescue [...]. An examination into the meanings of these state-supported sculptures reveal political controversies that involve slavery, ethnic identities, and racism against African Americans and Native Americans.
>
> *(Fryd 1994, p. 327)*

Although a similar analysis of the potential controversies associated with the art collection of the UN would justify an even closer engagement with the collection, unfortunately it is impossible to do so within the constraints of this chapter. Nonetheless, to try to understand how the collection navigates similarly unresolved tensions, I can briefly consider a recently commissioned project by the UN resulting from an international competition: a memorial for the victims of slavery and the transatlantic slave trade.

Ark of Return (2015) by Haitian-American Rodney Leon is an abstract sculpture that is presented as a 'reminder of the bravery of those slaves, abolitionists and unsung heroes who managed to rise up against an oppressive system' (Ban Ki-moon quoted in Sanches 2013). The artist sees it as:

> a spiritual space of return [of the slave ships and slave trade routes], an 'Ark of Return, ' a vessel where we can begin to create a counter-narrative and undo some of that experience" [...]. Mr. Leon [...] hopes the monument can become both a pilgrimage for the public and a totem for dignitaries at the UN, reminding them [...] of mistakes made in the past. Highlighting some of the features of the monument, he notes the triangular marble panels [...]. "These three triangular patterns describe the slave routes from specific locations in West Africa and throughout Africa to South America, to the Caribbean and Central America, and to North America, " he says [...]. "It's about acknowledging that condition and thinking about future generations.
>
> *(UN 2015)*

Nonetheless, and interestingly, these maps aren't truly specific; they fail to identify the countries that were (or still are) responsible for such practices. This resonates with a point made by Winfield on the absence of maps in the collection: 'with borders on nearly every continent in dispute, maps are considered too politically sensitive to be displayed as part of the vast U.N. art collection' (2000).

Despite not naming the member states responsible for the history of slavery, the *Ark of Return* reiterates the importance of the values and mission of the UN in identifying this issue as a tragic past that must be acknowledged and whose repetition must be avoided. Additionally, the artwork serves a narrative that has two audiences – the global media consumers and the individual nation states – and, by supporting unquestionable principles, cannot be criticised by the latter. This allows the UN to attempt to influence its members without opposing any of them directly, which exemplifies Center's argument (2009) regarding the ways the institutional ambiguity of the UN is reflected in its communications work. As a result of this analysis, the collection emerges as a platform of soft power, suggesting the existence of competition (following Nisbett's discussion) not only between the nation states but also between the UN and the former (i.e. between the international/supranational and the national levels).

In this context, it is important to consider to what extent similar artistic practices would be compatible with the strengthening of the role of the UN, namely in terms of setting a curatorial narrative. In this context, it is helpful to return briefly to the notion of cultural diplomacy. Mark (2009, p. 15), whom I referred to earlier, also sees public and cultural diplomacy as 'elements of soft power'. However, he stresses the need for changes in the implementation of cultural diplomacy, especially in terms of limiting political control over the delivery of cultural content. Similarly, ambassador Cynthia Schneider (2006) agrees with the need for its increased independence from political entities. This is because:

cultural diplomacy when delivered through an independent entity is more likely to incorporate aspects of a state's culture opposed to, or critical of, a government, its policies or its performance [...]. [Hence, one should] establish an independent entity within a foreign service. It should be accountable to an independent board.

(2009, pp. 33–34)

Specifically, writing about the American case, the ambassador affirms that:

Cultural diplomacy succeeded during the cold war in part because it allowed and even fostered dissent [...]. That the United States permitted critical voices as part of government-sponsored performances and emissaries astonished audiences everywhere, particularly behind the Iron Curtain.

(2006, p. 193)

This quote, stressing the importance of independent cultural practices, also goes in the direction of the argument made by Roger Blomgren's in 'Autonomy or Democratic Cultural Policy: that is the question' (2012), which discusses the role autonomy plays in cultural policy debates. Such independence is evident in the arm's length principle, which – as is well known – refers to the institutional settings that guarantee independence for cultural institutions and artists. In this model, cultural policy emerges as neutral regarding artistic content. By comparison, the autonomy of the art collection of the UN is extremely weak.

This said, one must stress that these discussions are focused on national practices. It could be argued that, at an international level, increased artistic independence and dissent would risk originating or increasing diplomatic conflicts, hence making the resolution of said issues (particularly when they require international collaboration) more difficult. Following this logic, if its art collection were to be given increased independence, the UN would have to strike a difficult balance between using the collection to highlight ongoing issues requiring increased attention from the international community and being respectful towards the history and current foreign policy positions of its member states.

Nonetheless, a compromise is possible. One can envisage strengthening the art collection of the UN as a form of cultural diplomacy serving the international community without 'colonising' (to use the terminology employed by Lähdesmäki 2012) the gifts of the nation states – it suffices to reiterate that any international organisation with supranational elements originates from the decision of its member states to transfer part of their sovereignty, as argued by Kal Raustiala's (2003, 846–847). In this direction, the curatorial work of the collection could be organised around a set of topics agreed to by majority in the General Assembly while avoiding shaming specific member states publicly: i.e. in the words of Center (2009, pp. 896), to actively 'embrace activism in the conduct of [...] policy' without politicising the content of said policies or, in this case, curatorial practices.

That is, even within these constraints it is possible to strengthen the institutional framework of the art collection of the UN and its potential in its communication strategy. If one were to expand the role of the collection in representing the UN and the international community rather than only its member states, that would require, first, a clear reformulation of its aims, as well a clear redefinition of its framework and mission and, more broadly, of the strategy that it supports. This requirement is clear when one reads the four recommendations of the UN Joint Inspection Unit. Despite being from 1992, their urgency remains – particularly the need to strengthen the autonomy of the collection, professionalising the art committee and ensuring specific funding for the conservation of the collection and for dedicated staff.

Second, and more specifically, strengthening the autonomy of the art collection would require establishing new agreements between the donors and the UN (that is, making the donations gifts both de jure and de facto). Additionally, once there was a clear mission and dedicated staff, the UN could then curate the art collection and commission artists to engage with it. This said, it is important to reiterate that such curated exhibitions would have to strike a balance between communicating the values of the UN and respecting the principle of neutrality, i.e. to reveal the complexity associated with specific challenges facing the UN without assigning direct responsibilities for them. Doing so would finally allow the UN to use culture (through its art collection) strategically, joining some European member states who already do so (as evidenced in Fisher and Figueira, 2011). Indeed, although Rod Fisher and Carla Figueira argue that there isn't 'evidence of a paradigm shift in EU Member States cultural relations [...] to more strategically focused international cultural co-operation' (2011, p. 5), the report reveals nonetheless that 'cultural policy [has] become more strategically integrated into foreign policy objectives in some EU states' (2011, p. 14) – as is evident in the adoption by the European Council of the conclusions on the role of culture in the European Union's external relations (EU, 2017). Finally, it would also allow the art collection of the UN to be managed in a way that is consistent with the most recent discussions and definitions of sovereignty.

Conclusion

The analysis of the United Nations art collection foregrounded its lack of clarity in terms of its goals, the audiences that it serves and the motivation behind the donations. It was argued that this lack of clarity reflects the central tension between the sovereignty of the member states and the supranational order of the UN. However, the essay also highlighted the need for further research on this art collection, including a qualitative study of the experience of the audiences that see the collection dedicated to measuring its impact on their thoughts regarding their membership in the international community represented by the UN, as well as an analysis of the importance of the art collection in the organisation's communication strategy (and, particularly, within the work of the Department of Public Information). Two other studies emerge as crucial: a historical analysis of the process of commissioning of artworks for inclusion in the collection and a comparison of the national official communication strategies that accompany the donations by member states.

Such research would allow us to better understand to what extent the intentions of the UN, the nation states and the artists are reflected in the reception of these artworks. It would also confirm whether the collection plays a role in influencing ongoing political and/or intercultural relations. Finally, doing so would contribute to evaluating the effectiveness or lack thereof of strategies framed by the ideas of soft power and cultural diplomacy.

Notes

1 An argument that I apply to the modes of presentation of the UN in my doctoral thesis (*Unstable Mediation – Regarding the United Nations as a Visual Entity*, 2017).

2 In 2017, this number is 193.

3 The members were, at the time of Adlerstein's interview, 'Yukio Takasu, Under-Secretary-General for Management (Chairperson), Peter Launsky-Tieffenthal, Under-Secretary-General for Communications and Public Information, Zainab Hawa Bangura, Special Representative on Sexual Violence in Conflict, Joseph V. Reed, Special Adviser to the Secretary-General, Michael Adlerstein, Assistant Secretary-General, Capital Master Plan, Levent Bilman, Director of Policy and Mediation Division, Department of Political Affairs, Yeochol Yoon, Chief, Protocol Liasion

Service, Executive Office of the Secretary-General (EOSG), Victor Kisob, Director, EOSG, Claudio Santangelo, Secretary of the Arts Committee' (Adlerstein 2014, p. 153).

4 Indeed, according to UNESCO (2010), it holds "a collection of 600 works of art by Masters such as Picasso, Miro, Arp, Appel, Afro, Matta, Calder, Chillida, Giacometti, Moore, Tamayo, Soto, Vasarely, Cruz-Diez and many others". Interestingly, the website also notes that "UNESCO's Headquarters boasts the largest artistic heritage within the United Nations systemæ," which points to the lack of a clear listing (UNIS, no date).

5 An argument that I develop in my Ph.D. thesis, mentioned earlier.

6 The relation between soft power and neoliberalism is discussed in detail by Melissa Nisbett in 'Who Holds the Power in Soft Power?' (2016).

7 An incident that I discuss in detail in 'Images against Images – On Goshka Macuga's The Nature of the Beast', included in *Meta- and Inter-Images in Contemporary Art* (ed. by Carla Laban, Leuven University Press, 2013).

References

Adlerstein, M., 2014. We Are Not a Museum. *Vereinte Nationen: German Review of the United Nations*, 62 (4), 152–155.

Blair, W., 1983. The UN Art Collection, Like the UN, Keeps Growing. New York Times. Available from: www.nytimes.com/1983/03/13/world/un-art-collection-like-the-un-keeps-growing.html [Accessed 2 November 2015].

Blomgren, R. 2012. Autonomy or Democratic Cultural Policy: that is the question. *International Journal of Cultural Policy*, 18 (5), 519–529.

Boutros-Ghali, B., 1995. Foreword. In: Marks, E. ed. *A World of Art: The United Nations Collection*. Rome: Il Cigno Galileo Galilei, 9.

Center, S., 2009 The United Nations Department of Public Information: Intractable Dilemmas and Fundamental Contradictions. In: Sriramesh, K. and Verčič, D. eds, *The Global Public Relations Handbook, Revised and Expanded Edition: Theory, Research, and Practice*. London; New York: Routledge, 975–994.

Chayes, A. and Chayes, A. H. 1995. The New Sovereignty: Compliance with International Regulatory Agreements. Cambridge: Harvard University Press.

Cooper, A. and Frechette, L., 2015. *Celebrity Diplomacy*. London: Routledge.

Delanty, G. 2000. *Citizenship in a Global Age: Society, Culture, Politics*. Buckingham: Open University Press.

Dowd, M., 2003. Powell without Picasso. New York Times. Available from: www.nytimes.com/2003/02/05/opinion/powell-without-picasso.html [Accessed 6 November 2015].

Duncan, C. 1995. The Art Museum as Ritual. In: Duncan, C. Civilizing Rituals: Inside Public Art Museums. London; New York: Routledge, 7–20.

EU, 2017. "Culture is an essential part of the EU's international relations": Council adopts Conclusions. Available from: www.consilium.europa.eu/en/press/press-releases/2017/05/23-conclusions-culture/ [Accessed 24 May 2017].

Fisher, R. and Figueira, C., 2009. Revisiting EU Member States' International Cultural Relations. *A Report to the European Cultural Foundation*. London: International Intelligence on Culture. Available from: www.moreeurope.org/sites/default/files/EU%20International%20Cultural%20Relations%20Final%20Version%2006May2011.pdf [Accessed 18 March 2016].

Fryd, V., 1994. The Politics of Public Art: Art in the United States Capitol. *The Journal of Arts Management, Law, and Society*, 23 (4), 327–340.

Gimlette, J., 2012. New York Tour: Inside the UN Headquarters. Available from: www.telegraph.co.uk/travel/destinations/north-america/united-states/new-york/articles/New-York-tours-inside-the-UN-Headquarters/ [Accessed 12 March 2016].

Greenwood, C., 2011. The Role of the International Court of Justice in the Global Community. *Journal of International Law and Policy*, 233, 248–252.

Halcyon, 2015. The UN's World-Class Art Collection. Available from: www.halcyonny.com/news-press/the-uns-world-class-art-collection/ [Accessed 2 November 2015].

International Geneva, 2012. The Palais des Nations, A Vibrant City in the Heart of International Geneva. Available from: www.geneve-int.ch/en/palais-des-nations-vibrant-city-heart-international-geneva [Accessed 2 November 2015].

Laban, C., 2013. ed. *Meta- and Inter-Images in Contemporary Art*. Leuven: Leuven University Press.

Lähdesmäki, T., 2012. Rhetoric of unity and cultural diversity in the making of European cultural identity, *International Journal of Cultural Policy*, 18 (1), 59–75.

Leonard, M. 1997. *Britain TM: Renewing Our Identity*. London: Demos.

Lukes, S. 1974. *Power: A Radical View*. London: Macmillan.

Mark, S., 2009. A Greater Role for Cultural Diplomacy. *Discussion Papers in Diplomacy: Netherlands Institute of International Relations Clingendael*. Available from: www.clingendael.nl/sites/default/files/20090616_cdsp_discussion_paper_114_mark.pdf [Accessed 10 March 2016].

Marks, E., 1995. The UN's World of Art. In: Marks, E. ed. *A World of Art: The United Nations Collection*. Rome: Il Cigno Galileo Galilei.

Nisbett, M., 2016. Who Holds the Power in Soft Power? *Arts and International Affairs*. Available from: https://theartsjournal.net/2016/03/13/nisbett/ [Accessed 11 March 2016].

Nye, J. S., 1990. Soft Power, *Foreign Policy*, 80, 153–171.

Nye, J. S. 2004. *Soft Power: The Means to Success in World Politics*. New York: Public Affairs.

Palonen, E. 2010. Multi-Level Cultural Policy and Politics of European Capitals of Culture, *Nordisk Kulturpolitisk Tidskrift*, 13 (1), 87–108.

Pearce, S., 1992. *Interpreting Objects and Collections*. London: Routledge.

Raustiala, K., 2003. Rethinking the Sovereignty Debate in International Economic Law, *Journal of International Economic Law*, 6 (4), 841–878.

Sanches, P., 2013. Ark of Return: Telling the Stories of 15 Million Slaves in a UN Permanent Memorial. Available from: http://mofokoranti.nl/?paged=2 [Accessed 2 March 2016].

Sandvik, M., 2014. Die Ikonologie einer neuen Weltordnung: Per Krohgs Gemälde im Sicherheitsrat der Vereinten Nationen. *Vereinte Nationen: German Review of the United Nations*, 62 (4), 156–162. [my own translation].

Sassatelli, M. 2002. Imagined Europe: The Shaping of a European Cultural Identity through EU Cultural Policy, *European Journal of Social Theory*, 5 (4), 435–451.

Schneider, C., 2006. Cultural Diplomacy: Hard to Define, but You'd Know It If You Saw It, *Brown Journal of World Affairs*, 13 (1). Available from: www.culturaldiplomacy.org/academy/content/articles/e-learning/read/a1/Cultural_Diplomacy-_Hard_to_Define-_Schneider,_Cynthia.pdf [Accessed 10 March 2016].

Slaughter, A.-M. 2005. Security, Solidarity, and Sovereignty: The Grand Themes of UN Reform, *The American Journal of International Law*, 99 (3), 619–631.

Theill, S., 2014. United Nations Revisited. *Vereinte Nationen: German Review of the United Nations*. 62 (4), 167–168.

UN, 1945. *Charter of the United Nations*. Available from: www.un.org/en/documents/charter/preamble.shtml [Accessed 5 November 2015].

UN, 2015. Architect of UN Slavery Memorial Explains 'The Ark of Return'. Available from: www.un.org/apps/news/story.asp?NewsID=50424#.VwUg_z-fWHn [Accessed 10 March 2016].

UNESCO, 2010. UNESCO Offers Tours of Its Art Collection in Paris Headquarters for "European Night of Museums" on 15 May 2010. Available from: http://portal.unesco.org/culture/en/ev.php-URL_ID=40879&URL_DO=DO_TOPIC&URL_SECTION=201.html [Accessed 2 March 2016].

UNESCO, no date. Welcome to UNESCO Headquarters. Available from: www.unesco.org/new/en/unesco/about-us/where-we-are/visit-us/ [Accessed 2 March 2016].

UNIS, no date. *Visit the United Nations: The VIC Art Collection*. Available from: www.unis.unvienna.org/unis/en/visitors_service/art_tour.html [Accessed 10 March 2016].

UN Joint Inspection Unit, 1992. Managing Works of Art in the United Nations. Available from www.unjiu.org/en/reports-notes/JIU%20Products/JIU_REP_1992_7_English.pdf [Accessed 27 October 2015].

UNOG, no date. Art Collection and Donations. Available from: www.unog.ch/80256EE600594458/%28httpPages%29/24A9D61439DC0F8DC12576B90056F08F?OpenDocument [Accessed 3 November 2015].

Urquhart, B., 1995. Preface. In: Marks, E. ed. *A World of Art: The United Nations Collection*. Rome: Il Cigno Galileo Galilei.

Williams, I., 2014. Elephants, Fishes and Saint George. The UN's Art Collection Reflect the World "Warts and All". *Vereinte Nationen: German Review of the United Nations,* 62 (4), 147–151.

Winfield, N., 2000. At United Nations, Diplomacy Requires Some Artful Dodging. LA Times. Available from: http://articles.latimes.com/2000/jan/07/entertainment/ca-51554 [Accessed 2 November 2015].

15

Exporting culture
The Confucius Institute and China's smart power strategy

Tony Tai-Ting Liu

Introduction

Since the turn of the century, China has gradually taken on new roles in the international community. Supported by a fast-growing economy, China has not only developed into a regional power with expanded roles in Central and Southeast Asia, but the country also shows aspirations to become a great power through increased military capacities and political influences. While traditional power provides the mainstay for China's rise, political elites in Beijing have taken notice of the unintentional challenges China may bring to the world as it continues to grow. For Beijing, such anxieties must be eliminated if China seeks to improve its global status. Employing the concept of "smart power," this article examines the Confucius Institute, a language institution established by Beijing to serve as a channel for disseminating traditional Chinese culture to the world while shaping China's international image. The Confucius Institute is an important part of cultural policy exploited by China to complement its hard power strategies and achieve its interests in the world.

The discussion is carried out in four parts: part one examines China's rise and Beijing's gradual adoption of a soft power strategy in foreign policy; part two discusses the development of the Confucius Institute and its strategic functions; part three notes the definition of "smart power" and the success and challenge China has encountered through the Confucius Institute, most notably the Braga incident; part four concludes with some reflections on the benefits and limitations of using cultural attraction as a diplomatic strategy.

China's rise in the twenty-first century

China's economic rise is arguably one of the most important phenomena of the new century. *New York Times* reporter Nicholas Kristof (1993, pp. 62–63) recognized the phenomenon as early as 1993 and pointed out that China is growing at an approximate rate of 9% per annum. Table 15.1 shows the trend of China's economic growth since 2000, with growth accelerating in 2002 and recording double digits for five straight years from 2003 to 2007.

Table 15.1 China real GDP growth 2000–2013 (%)

Year	GDP growth	Year	GDP growth
2000	8.4	2007	14.2
2001	8.3	2008	9.6
2002	9.1	2009	9.2
2003	10.0	2010	10.4
2004	10.1	2011	9.3
2005	11.3	2012	7.7
2006	12.7	2013	7.7

Source: The World Bank, "GDP Growth," http://data.worldbank.org/indicator/ NY.GDP.MKTP.KD.ZG.

In 2010, China surpassed Japan to become the second largest economy in the world and the largest economy in Asia. Adjusted for purchasing power, China stands as the second largest economy in the world after the US with USD 9.872 trillion in GDP (2010) (WTO 2011). China's total export has grown from USD 1,400 million in 2005 to over USD 1,500 million in 2010 (WTO 2011). Regardless of debates, in 2014, according to statistics provided by the International Monetary Fund (IMF), the Chinese economy edged out the US (USD 17.4 trillion) to become the largest economy in the world at USD 17.6 trillion (Duncan and Martosko 2014).

Although long-term growth of China's economy remains unpredictable, the country's economic performance has already caused observers such as Noble Laureate Joseph Stiglitz (2015) to tout the twenty-first century as the Chinese century. Besides growth, China's economic power is reflected in other aspects. For example, in terms of foreign exchange reserves, or the holding of gold and other convertible foreign currencies, China leads the world with USD 3899 billion, a figure that reflects the country's surplus trade. In terms of foreign direct investment (FDI), in 2013, the Chinese market attracted USD 123,911 million, a figure topped only by the US (USD 187,528 million) and led the next largest market, Russia, by more than a margin (Arnett 2014; UNCTAD 2014). Another indicator of China's new wealth can be found in the amount of official development aid (ODA) Beijing provides to other countries. According to a comparative study by Kitano and Harada (2015), Chinese ODA was estimated to reach USD 7.1 billion in 2013, a figure that made China into one of the largest donors in the world.

As China's economic status advanced, skepticism from the world grew as well. Perhaps noting Beijing's hard hand against student demonstrations in the summer of 1989, instead of peace, Japanese scholar Tomohide Murai (村井友秀) (1990) noted the rise of an aggressive China intent on threatening and destabilizing regional peace and stability in the early 1990s. Kristof and Murai's position represents two contrasting images of China that continue to shape the debate on China today, a country that has yet to relax its pursuit of great power status. After China's test firing of missiles aimed at influencing Taiwan's first direct presidential election in 1996, outcries over the so-called "China threat" grew stronger. Pessimistic observers such as Richard Bernstein and Ross Munro (1997) pointed to the potential conflict scenario between China and the US, while political scientist John Mearsheimer (2004; 2010; 2014), based on the theory of offensive realism, hints at the inevitability that a rising power such as China will challenge the global status quo and provoke great power conflict.

In response to critics and so-called "China threat" theorists who saw China's increasing power as a danger to international peace and order, at the Boao Forum for Asia in 2003, former Vice Principal of the Central Party School, Zheng Bijian (郑必坚), introduced the concept of China's "peaceful rise" (和平崛起, hepingjueqi). As Zheng (2005) propounded in an article in *Foreign Affairs* in 2005, "China does not seek hegemony or predominance in world affairs. … China's development depends on world peace." Zheng's statement eventually set the grounds for the commencement of efforts by Beijing to defend and re-validate China's global status as a peaceful and benevolent power that seeks to integrate into the world and contribute to the international community. In the Asia-Africa Summit held in Jakarta in 2005, former President Hu Jintao (胡锦涛) stressed that countries from Asia and Africa should jointly "promote friendship, equal dialogue, prosperity among civilizations and jointly establish a harmonious world" (Tsai et al. 2011, p. 27). Hu's proposal later became the concept of a harmonious world (和协世界, hexie shijie), an idea that eventually served as the theoretical mainstay for China's promotion of good neighbor policies including the establishment of the Confucius Institute.

Returning to *kongfuzi* for guidance

Despite the sacred and revered status of Confucius or *kongfuzi* (孔夫子, literally "Master Kung") in China's long history, there was a time when the "most venerated mentor" (至圣先师, zhishengxianshi) did not have a place in contemporary China. Following the establishment of the Chinese Communist Party (CCP) regime in 1949, Mao Tse-tung set China on a path of reforms that sought to elevate the country to the ranks of strong states. For Mao, in order for China to "stand up on its feet," it must break with its feudal past, a past foremost grounded in the teachings of Confucius. Besides replacement of the *Analects* (四书, sishu) with the *Quotations of Mao Tse-tung* (毛主席语录, maozhuxi yulu, also known as the *Little Red Book*) as required curriculum in classrooms throughout China, the derision of China's Socrates included the abolishment of the "four olds" (四旧, sijiu) during the Cultural Revolution and the exploitation of the sage as a political tool in the "criticize Lin, criticize Confucius" movement (批林批孔运动, pilinpikong yundong). While the Cultural Revolution and the defilement of Confucius ended with the death of Mao Tse-tung in 1976, China's most revered mentor did not return to his traditional status until recent years.

Perhaps noting the world's growing anxiety over the future intentions of a rising China and its increasing interest in understanding China's language, culture and history (so-called "China fever" or zhongguore), in 2004, Beijing established the first Confucius Institute in South Korea (Wang 2009, p. 290). Headquartered in Beijing and overseen by the Chinese National Office for Teaching Chinese as a Foreign Language, a department usually known by the simple name of "Hanban" (汉办), the Confucius Institute was established as a formal channel for the world to learn about China. Through the establishment of Confucius Institutes in higher education institutions around the world, Beijing hopes the international community can gain a better understanding of China and recognize the rising power as a peaceful country that seeks no harm to the world.

It is interesting to note that from a cultural studies perspective that emphasizes the sharing of history, language, customs, beliefs, institutions and arts among a particular society as "culture," the Confucius Institute, though commonly regarded as an agency for the distribution of culture, is not in itself a conspicuous cultural entity. However, as Stuart Hall (1997, p. 2) argued, "culture is concerned with the production and the exchange of meanings – the 'giving and taking of meaning' – between members of a society or group." In such sense, the

Confucius Institute, as a unit with trained teachers that repetitively interpret the Chinese language and disseminate knowledge of China to pupils, hence becomes a cultural entity. As Cynthia Weber (2014, p. 3) points out, "culture has to do with how we make sense of the world and how we produce, reproduce and circulate that sense." While not comparable to language, customs, beliefs or a piece of art in their characteristic of being produced, re-produced and circulated, the fact that the Confucius Institute provides a particular view of China that can be produced, reproduced and circulated among teachers and students alike deems the institute a cultural entity that warrants examination.

According to the Constitution of the Confucius Institute released online, it is a non-profit educational institution devoted to enhancing the understanding of the Chinese language and culture to people from different countries and strengthening educational and cultural exchange and cooperation between China and the world (Confucius Institute 2016). Besides the provision of language teaching service and organization of cultural exchange activities with other countries, the Confucius Institute also carries out related tasks such as the training of language instructors, provision of language teaching resources and information on China's education and culture, as well as holding the Hanyu Shuiping Kaoshi (HSK) exam (汉语水平考试) and tests for the Certification of Chinese Language Teachers (Confucius Institute 2016). It is important to note that in addition to language service, the HSK exam, also known as the Chinese Proficiency Test, has become the standard examination for Chinese language ability across the world. The HSK exam is currently held and monitored in more than 120 countries.[1]

Currently (as of December 1, 2015), there are 500 Confucius Institutes established in 134 countries throughout the continents of Asia, Africa, America, Europe and Oceania. In addition, 1000 Confucius Classrooms (孔子课堂, *kongzi ketang*) are established in high schools and primary schools spread across 72 countries in the world. Table 15.2 shows the current distribution of Confucius Institutes and Classrooms in the world.

In contrast with Asian countries that are notable for soft power and the export of cultural products, China's investment in the Confucius Institute stands as one of a kind, as the strategy essentially follows a top-down instead of a bottom-up approach in terms of the dissemination of cultural influences. Compared with the Japan wave or Korean wave, developments founded on popular cultural forms such as cartoon (anime), music, television drama and food (Cho 2005; Kim and Ryoo 2007; Shim 2008; Lee 2009), or areas that did not catch the attention of officials until their evolution into regional and global subcultures, China chose to tackle the issue of soft power and cultural export from Beijing. By establishing language institutes across the world, China looks deeply into its culture and history first before letting subcultures such as movies, television dramas and martial arts or kung fu take over the task of

Table 15.2 Number of Confucius Institutes and Confucius Classrooms

Region	Confucius Institute	Confucius Classroom
Asia	110	90
Africa	46	23
Americas	157	544
Europe	169	257
Oceania	18	86

Source: Confucius Institute Headquarters (Hanban), "About Confucius Institutes/Classrooms," www.hanban.edu.cn/confuciousinstitutes/node_10961.htm.

constructing its outer image. Through such method, Beijing may in some sense oversee the Chinese image that is disseminated – benevolent, cordial and virtuous – and look forward to positive responses from the world. For such reasons, the selection of Confucius, an upright figure and a master of Chinese traditions, is appropriate to represent China. Despite the irony, the scholarly image of Confucius serves the purpose of dispelling claims and quelling anxieties to the China threat while promoting the status of China as a friend to the world – a function a rising power well needs.

In tangible terms, China has set out specific requirements for the establishment of Confucius Institutes. In other words, Beijing chooses its partners. As Article 19 of the Constitution of the Confucius Institute states, higher education institutes that seek the language centers must be legally registered with a demand for the learning of Chinese language and culture, accompanied by personnel, facilities, equipment and funds for collaboration (Confucius Institute 2016). In the initial start-up period of the Confucius Institute, the collaborating higher education institute will receive a set amount of sponsorship funding from Hanban; following the initial stage, annual funding for the Confucius Institute is generally split between Hanban and its partner institution on a one-to-one ratio (Confucius Institute 2016).

As stated in the Constitution, one of the main goals of the Confucius Institute is the aim of constructing a harmonious world (Confucius Institute 2016).[2] In a sense, such objective corresponds well with Beijing's strategic view of the world since the Hu Jintao era – a world in which China enjoys peaceful and friendly relations with other countries. China's motivations aside, higher education institutes across the world may have independent reasons for pursuing the establishment of the Confucius Institute. In general, the lack of government funding in humanities and social sciences programs in higher education institutes globally has encouraged many universities and colleges to look towards Hanban and the Confucius Institute as a potential source of support.[3] On the other hand, as China continues to rise economically, the increasing level of public interest in Chinese language and culture means that institutions with a Chinese program or the Confucius Institute may be more competitive and lucrative for students (Hill 2014).[4] In short, while one may safely make the claim that a certain symbiotic relationship may be developing between the Confucius Institute and higher education institutes – a relationship that sees China in pursuit of a more peaceful global environment through the Confucius Institute while universities and colleges seek more student enrollment – whether such relationship develops into a general phenomenon awaits further evidence and investigation.

China's smart power strategy and Confucius' secret ambitions

While China attempts to teach the world about its language, culture and history through the Confucius Institute, it does not remain idle on traditional issues pertaining to political and economic interests. In other words, besides a demonstration of soft power, China is willing to demonstrate its muscle and tougher side when the situation demands such moves. China's behavior in the South China Sea offers a clear example of Beijing putting its hard power to use. Meanwhile in Southeast Asia, China continues to expand on economic and cultural relations with countries in the region, hence giving rise to a smart power strategy at work – a strategy that seeks to strike a balance between hard and soft power. Nonetheless, beginning in 2014, expansion of the Confucius Institute seemed to have struck a reef in North America and Europe, which has since raised questions about the true face of the Chinese initiative. This section examines the case of China's growing smart power strategy in Southeast Asia and describes the potential challenges such a strategy may face in light of missteps in cultural policy.

Smart power: the case of China in Southeast Asia

The concept of "smart power" is generally believed to have been first introduced by Suzanne Nossel (2004). Observing the George W. Bush administration and its neo-conservative policies that emphasized unilateralism and the use of force, Nossel concluded that US policy under Bush was a mistake and called for Washington's return to liberal internationalism. Besides outright military force, trade, economic aid and the promotion of cultural and political values should also be considered important diplomatic means (Nossel 2004). In terms of foreign policy, smart power implies that a reliance on hard power is not necessarily the best choice; rather, states are encouraged to attract recognition of their values and promote their interests through a combination of allies, international institutions, foreign policy and moral attraction. Following Nossel's proposal, in 2006, Joseph Nye and Richard Armitage authored the report "A Smarter, More Secure America," in which the meaning of smart power and its application in foreign policy is elaborated. For Armitage and Nye (2007), smart power is "a combination of hard and soft power, a way to achieve America's goals through the integration of strategy, resource and foreign policy."

Despite its appearance, smart power has not enjoyed as much attention as the concepts of hard and soft power, a fact perhaps contributed by the limited number of states in the world that have enough capability to wield both the carrot and the stick. However, as China continues to grow, one may argue that to a certain extent, alongside the US, Beijing is beginning to demonstrate that it holds enough influence to be smart about the use of power. Among different regions in the world, Southeast Asia remains the site where China's smart power is most vividly played out. In the sense that China applies both hard and soft power strategies towards countries in Southeast Asia, the relationship between Beijing and countries such as Singapore, Vietnam and Thailand is complicated and difficult to define.

In terms of hard power, in recent years, China has not been shy to resort to the use of force or aggressive means to defend its interests in the South China Sea. As an important sea of transport that links Asia with the Middle East and Europe and an area that boasts rich petroleum and natural gas reserves, the South China Sea has long given itself to sovereign disputes among neighboring states. In March 2010, in response to the US strategy to rebalance towards Asia, Beijing claimed the South China Sea as its "core interest" (核心利益, *hexin liyi*) (Hung and Liu 2011, p. 100), a notion previously reserved for Tibet, Xinjiang and Taiwan. While no major conflicts have broken out in the South China Sea since 2010, a smattering of short maritime standoffs and skirmishes have strained the relations between China and the Philippines and Vietnam. Since 2014, Beijing began to reinforce its position on the South China Sea by commencing the building of islands in the region (McKirdy and Hunt 2015), an action deemed by many states, including the US and Japan, as a reckless act of aggression.

Interestingly, regardless of sovereign tensions, China and the Association of Southeast Asian Nations (ASEAN) continue to move forward economically. In terms of regional integration, China continues to vow its support for Southeast Asia and establishment of the Regional Comprehensive Economic Partnership (RCEP) as the center of free trade in Asia (Miller 2015). The RCEP serves as a counterweight to the US-led Transpacific Partnership (TPP), an initiative that advocates high-quality trade that challenges the survival of many economies in the Asia Pacific. In terms of trade, as Kent Harrington (2015) points out, since the turn of the new century, trade between China and ASEAN countries has expanded tenfold from 32 billion USD in 2000 to 350 billion USD in 2014, making China the largest trading partner of Southeast Asia at the moment. Beyond the numbers, China's Asia Infrastructure Investment Bank initiative is expected to take effect in Southeast Asia in the near future, while both Thailand and Indonesia have agreed to cooperate with China on railway construction projects.

While tensions in the South China Sea pushed China and Southeast Asia apart and economic cooperation draw the two neighbors together – a seemingly contradictory combination – as efforts to improve relations, China has initiated a series of cultural exchange policies towards ASEAN countries. For example, under the China-ASEAN Expo, an event first introduced by former Chinese Premier Wen Jiabao (温家宝) in 2004 for discussions on commercial and trade exchange between China and Southeast Asia, the China-ASEAN Cultural Forum was introduced. The China-ASEAN Cultural Forum currently serves as a channel for member countries to promote their respective artistic achievements each year. In 2015, the 9th China-ASEAN Cultural Forum was hosted in Nanning, Guangxi (China-ASEAN Expo Secretariat 2015). On the other hand, 2014 marked the China-ASEAN Cultural Exchange Year. At the opening ceremony, Chinese Premier Li Keqiang (李克强) noted that "[China] attaches great importance to developing friendly relations and strengthening mutually beneficial cooperation with ASEAN, hoping to take advantage of the Cultural Exchange Year to demonstrate the outcome of cultural cooperation of the two sides" (China Daily 2014a).

In terms of the Confucius Institute, ASEAN countries make up more than a quarter of all institutes established in Asia, with the Philippines (4), Malaysia (2), Thailand (14), Singapore (1), Indonesia (6), Cambodia (1), Laos (1) and Vietnam (1) contributing to 30 of 110 institutes established in the region.[5] Although conflicts in the South China Sea have not stopped as a result of the establishment of Confucius Institutes in Southeast Asia, the latter is ever becoming a foreign policy tool for advancing state relations. A recent example can be found in Chinese President Xi Jinping's (习近平) state visit to Vietnam in 2015, during which the mutual establishment of cultural centers and the success of the Confucius Institute in Hanoi were noted (People's Daily 2015). The event was significant in that both leaderships from China and Vietnam seemed to have ignored or deliberately forgotten bilateral tensions in the South China Sea that served as the reason for massive anti-Chinese protests in Vietnam in 2014. Xi's gesture followed his address at the 15th China-Vietnam Youth Friendship Meeting, in which the Chinese leader called for the prosperity of friendship among young people from both China and Vietnam (Nie 2015). It remains to be observed whether increased establishments of Confucius Institutes can indeed foster deeper cultural understandings that can potentially transform state relations.

In short, in Southeast Asia, China clearly adopts a dual handed or "smart" approach that seeks to strike a balance between the use of hard and soft power. Despite tensions in the South China Sea, China's relations with Southeast Asia have not broken down completely, an outcome perhaps contributed in part by Beijing's continued efforts to strengthen relations through the Confucius Institute and other cultural exchange activities. However, beyond Southeast Asia, the success of China's smart strategy is unclear, particularly in 2014, when an academic gathering in Portugal unexpectedly became the starting point of a series of questions and doubts against the Confucius Institute. The following section turns to the Braga Incident and its implications for the development of the Confucius Institute.

The Braga incident and challenges for the Confucius Institute[6]

Since its advent in Korea in 2004, the Confucius Institute has met little friction in its expansion abroad, a matter that was perhaps only slowed by the amount of time and funds Beijing could devote to the project at once. In terms of the impact of the Confucius Institute, housing 100 Confucius Institutes and 356 Confucius Classrooms – the highest total among all states – the US is a case in point. According to a *New York Times* report in 2010, as a result of Beijing's support for the Confucius Institute, the landscape for the study of foreign languages in the US has changed significantly. A survey carried out by the Washington-based research group Center for Applied Linguistics showed that in the decade from 1997 to 2008, among US middle and high schools that offer at least one foreign language, the offering of Chinese increased from 1% to 4% (Dillon 2010). Rough estimates in 2010 suggested as many as 1600 public and private schools were teaching Chinese, a large increase from 300 almost a decade ago (Dillon 2010). In September 25, 2015, after receiving Chinese President Xi Jinping at the White House, US President Barack Obama announced the "One Million Strong Initiative" that seeks to increase the number of students learning Chinese in America from 20,000 to 100,000 by 2020, a further sign that as a language, Chinese is taking root in the US (Klein 2015).

Nonetheless, elsewhere around and outside the US, different thoughts have emerged against China's language export. In 2012, after preliminary reviews of the Confucius Institute program in the US, the US Department of State claimed that a significant number of university-based Chinese language teachers sponsored by China violated visa regulations and had to pay the consequence of returning to China upon visa expiration (Fischer 2012). The incident alerted many observers, who speculated on Beijing's true face to carry out espionage or propaganda through the Confucius Institutes (Mattis 2012), some calling the language schools China's own Trojan Horse (Carlson 2012). Although the visa incident was quickly forgotten following leadership change in China, (political) "subversion" and "subterfuge" remained deep concerns that awaited opportunities to break out again following missteps by China.

2014 proved to be the break-out year for China in recent memory. Besides making international headlines with grand initiatives such as the One Belt One Road, the Silk Road Fund and the Asia Infrastructure Investment Bank (AIIB), China's expanding influence also began to make parts of the world uneasy, giving rise to the Sunflower Movement in Taiwan, the Umbrella Revolution in Hong Kong and anti-China protests in Vietnam.[7] While the Confucius Institute did not directly contribute to the anger of protesters in China's vicinities, connections with Beijing made the institute a target of constant scrutiny and attack. In the months before the start of summer in 2014, little did the world know that the Confucius Institute would generate controversies again, this time triggering fallouts that may have important consequences for China.

On July 22–26, 2014, the European Association for Chinese Studies (EACS) hosted its four-day annual conference at the cities of Braga and Coimbra, Portugal. As an important gathering for researchers on China, the event attracted more than 400 participants worldwide. Unfortunately, on the evening before the commencement of the event, an incident that would change the course of the conference occurred. Displeased with the conference program and abstracts, Xu Lin (许琳), Director General of the Hanban and Chief Executive of the Confucius Institute Headquarters, noted that a portion of the content in the abstracts violated China's sponsorship guidelines and demanded the EACS organizing team remove the title of the "Confucius China Studies Program" from the abstracts. In addition, Xu Lin was disgruntled by the EACS' description of the Chiang Ching-kuo (CCK) Foundation

(蒋经国基金会), a long-time sponsor of the annual conference from Taiwan, amidst the pages of the program. Xu later ordered the removal of the remaining copies of the program from the conference venue to prevent their distribution the following day.

Unsurprisingly, more than 300 participants were baffled by the lack of a conference program on July 22. While the EACS organizing team negotiated with Xu Lin prior to the morning of the conference, Hanban and the EACS failed to reach an agreement. Hanban demanded the removal of the descriptions of the CCK Foundation from the program, to be replaced by the logo of the foundation without any textual details. Although Carmen Mendes from Coimbra University – a main organizer of the EACS conference – rejected Xu's request, a settlement that saw the removal of four pages from the program, including descriptions on the CCK Foundation, was eventually reached later, out of consideration for the smooth functioning of the event.

On the second day of the conference, July 24, the tempered program was distributed to registered participants. By noon, President of the EACS Roger Greatrex, greatly annoyed by Hanban's demands, ordered the reprinting of 500 copies of the forcefully removed CCK Foundation descriptions and redistributed the print copies on the afternoon of July 24, when participants were to travel from Braga to Coimbra on the chartered bus arranged by the conference organizer. On July 25, in the speech given at the opening ceremony of the conference at Coimbra University, Greatrex publicly denounced Hanban's intervention in academic freedom and voiced his support for the suppressed CCK Foundation. Following the annual conference, the EACS released a formal statement criticizing Hanban's actions at Braga and emphasized that the association "cannot and will never tolerate the censorship of conference material" (Greatrex 2014).

In the aftermath of the Braga incident, observers around the world vowed their support for the EACS, a phenomenon that translated into a flurry of harsh critiques against the Confucius Institute and China's international image (EACS, 2014). In December 2014, the British Broadcasting Company (BBC) interviewed Xu Lin in Beijing and brought up the topic of Braga (Sudworth 2014). Xu not only refused to address the Braga incident but also demanded BBC to remove many portions for public broadcast. The latter refused. Regarding the interview, scholar Gary Rawnsley (2014) noted that "Xu Lin not only refused to answer difficult questions, she also politicised the Confucius Institutes and reinforced the idea that they are led by dogmatists."

In terms of real effects of the Braga incident, many higher education institutes in Europe and North America began to re-evaluate their cooperation with the Confucius Institute, with several institutes shutting down the China-sponsored programs altogether. For example, in the US, the University of Chicago and Pennsylvania State University subsequently terminated their contracts with the Confucius Institute in September and October 2014 (Penn State College of the Liberal Arts 2014; Redden 2014), while the Toronto District School Board decided to end its cooperation with the Confucius Institute in the same year (South China Morning Post 2014b), prior to Prime Minister Stephen Harper's scheduled visit to Beijing. In December 2014, confronted by a wave of public criticism against China domestically, Stockholm University, the first higher education institute in Europe to establish the Confucius Institute, decided to follow in the footsteps of its counterparts in the US as well (Fiskesjo 2015). Although the domino effect generated by Braga seems to have diminished since 2015, the retraction of renowned higher education institutes has already cast a heavy shadow over Beijing's international image and uncertainties on the future of the Confucius Institute.

The use of culture in foreign policy: benefits and limits

In short, China's effort to re-establish its image through the Confucius Institute has met with both success and challenges. To a large extent, the Confucius Institute can be considered a success in terms of its number of establishments and the level of interest it has generated in the study of Chinese language and culture around the world. As a harmless cultural policy intended to raise attention and awareness for China, Beijing's experiment with the Confucius Institute may have much to teach. However, in the case that cultural policy touches on and becomes a part of foreign policy, the crossing-over between realms entails that cross-fertilization of extended connotations and implications, both positive and negative, may be inevitable. In other words, when the Chinese leadership promotes the Confucius Institute abroad while making claims to territorial sovereignty in the South China Sea at the same time, one may find the true face of Beijing's policy hard to distinguish. While one may be drawn to what the Confucius Institute has to offer, China's strategic ambitions may raise doubts and questions about the underlying motive of China's language establishments. Noting China's experiment with the Confucius Institute, this section concludes with some considerations for the benefits and limits of exploiting culture in foreign policy.

In a sense, if the sheer number of institutes established, currently totaling 500, serves as evidence that China's Confucian venture is a success, the amount of positive claims that may be made based on such a fact becomes endless. For example, Beijing may point to the number of institutes as evidence that China is a peacefully rising state that is keen on realizing global harmony. The fact that Confucius Institutes are established across different countries suggests that China enjoys good relations with the international community regardless of disputes and conflicts. On the other hand, perhaps as a way to rebuff arguments against China's peaceful rise, Beijing may also make the claim that China is revealing its true nature through the Confucius Institute by allowing the international community a chance to see for itself. Such gesture speaks to the honesty and benign nature of the Chinese. Still further, the number of students enrolled in Chinese programs in the Confucius Institutes could only suggest that many individuals identify with Chinese values.

While part of the success may come from China's rising economy and large investments placed in the Confucius Institute project, distinguishing the driving force for expansion becomes difficult: is expansion driven by state investments by China or is expansion driven by higher student interest? In turn, coupled with the image of Confucius the sage, the foregoing question becomes almost irrelevant, as the provision of education itself is a virtuous deed that overshadows other priorities, including political and strategic objectives that may easily be considered as separate interests. Perhaps because policymakers delegated to make political or strategic decisions are generally expected to be pragmatic and self-interested, cultural projects such as the Confucius Institute thus become good ways to replace pragmatism and self-interest with charity and good will while pragmatism is not entirely lost. A touch of culture in such sense wins the benefit of the doubt for policies (for example, foreign policy) that are usually self-serving, a common phenomenon in the international political arena.

Yet a fine line exists between success and failure when culture is adopted as a foreign policy tool. In light of the controversies related to the Confucius Institute in recent years, limitations of how far such policy can be carried on as a charitable foreign policy warrant consideration. Three issues are particularly relevant: the potential for soft power strategies to accomplish tangible political goals, the "mismatch" problem between "soft" means and "hard" goals and the sustainability of culture based foreign policies. The three issues challenge the continued success of the Confucius Institute.

First, as a common definition of "power" states—power is the ability for A to get B to do something he would otherwise not do—regarding soft power, one must consider whether influencing others is possible without resorting to force. An extended consideration relates to the effect of soft power: what should one expect to accomplish through soft means? In terms of the Confucius Institute, while the project receives strong support from Beijing, achieving short-term political goals through the institute is difficult if not far-fetched. It is hard to imagine that through issue linkage, the de-establishment of Confucius Institutes from a state can be used as a bargaining chip towards high politics issues such as territorial sovereignty or military conflict. On the other hand, it is equally questionable how language education may be brought out in one's favor in trade negotiations. As with most culture-based strategies that harbor the characteristic of slowly transforming the heart and mind of peoples through attraction, the Confucius Institute can be expected to accomplish the minimal goal of generating popular interest in the study of the Chinese language, history and culture.[8] Beyond general interest, the Confucius Institute may remain limited in its outreach. Previous studies on comparable institutions such as the Goethe Institute, Alliance Francaise and the British Council suggest that the initiating countries have all kept to the objectives of promoting respective state values and cultural exchange (Wyszomirski et al. 2003; Ngamsang and Walsh 2013). One may be surprised if the Confucius Institute can achieve more.

For China, a further challenge that confronts the Confucius Institute is the mismatch between the priority of reducing claims to the perceived China threat and the means of language education. Two points are worth noting. First, through the Confucius Institute, China seems to be pursuing a long-term strategy that seeks to influence young Chinese learners who may play critical roles in changing China's relationship with the world in years to come. Yet current learners usually do not play any role in the decision-making process of a state; how much influence language instructors and students alike have on foreign policy is quite vague. Second, while education may potentially bring about the outcome of transforming the outlook of a generation of China watchers, its effects are negligible in the face of ongoing geopolitical conflicts and economic disputes. While some experts have recognized the continued importance of building trust with China through education and other channels for exchange,[9] such outcries are few and shy in the presence of those with misgivings on China's political system and ambitions (Sahlins 2013; Hughes 2014; Brady 2015). For skeptics, issues such as the South China Sea and the Senkaku/Diaoyu Islands provide ready evidences of China's threat. Education is a long process, while international affairs change constantly. As suggested by the Braga incident, a slight misstep may severely undermine Beijing's hard-won image while giving way to criticisms that pile up and spread quickly.

Finally, in contrast with subcultures such as music and movies that are flowing and constantly refreshed, perhaps more than fads and popular trends, the Confucius Institute faces the problem of sustaining mass interest in the learning of the Chinese language. In retrospect, besides individuals having a strong interest in China, an important reason that interest for Chinese increased rapidly in recent years relates directly to China's rise and its implications for international business and economy. If language learning correlates positively with a state's expansion in power, one may also suppose that as a state declines, interest in its language and culture may decline as well. Hence depending on China's economic performance, general interest in Chinese may wax and wane and challenge the functioning of the Confucius Institute. On the other hand, as mentioned above, the Confucius Institute uses a top-down strategy that should ideally connect with other subcultural forms that would, in a sense, sustain popular interest in China. In such case, the development of popular culture in China becomes a critical issue that bears on the maintenance of Beijing's foreign policy.

In the face of Japanese, Korean, Taiwanese and Western cultural exports into China, Beijing may need to ponder how the Chinese language can be given new life and how Chinese culture can maintain its foothold amidst competition in a globalized world.

Looking towards the future, the cultural turn in Chinese foreign policy has brought forth several issues that await further research. For example, the relationship between China's central government and Hanban remains under-explored despite doubts and criticisms against the Confucius Institute. While discussions on the Confucius Institute abound with individual experiences dealing with Chinese personnel, such stories may only start to scratch the surface of a complex system governing the works of language establishments. More revelations are needed to support the fact that individual stories are not random, independent incidents. On the other hand, more studies into the texts and materials used in Confucius Institutes are necessary in order to gain a better understanding of the image China is trying to construct on the international stage and its effects on the perception of others on China. How China establishes itself in the international community will inevitably decide how much space the country has in which to maneuver its foreign policy.

Notes

1 "hanyu kaoshi fuwuwang" (HSK service net), www.chinesetest.cn/goKdInfoOrPlan.do
2 See Article 1 of the Constitution of the Confucius Institute.
3 See: Ella Delany, "Humanities Studies Under Strain Around the Globe," The New York Times, December 1, 2013, available: www.nytimes.com/2013/12/02/us/humanities-studies-under-strain-around-the-globe.html?_r=0
4 See: Michael Hill, "The Debate Over Confucius Institutes Part II," www.chinafile.com/conversation/debate-over-confucius-institutes-part-ii
5 The number in the parentheses denotes the current number of Confucius Institutes in the country. Currently, Myanmar and Brunei do not host Confucius Institutes. Myanmar hosts three Confucius Classrooms, while Brunei hosts neither Institutes nor Classrooms.
6 This section's description of the Braga incident is based on the testimony provided in an open message by Roger Greatrex, President of the European Association for Chinese Studies (EACS). See: Roger Greatrex, "Report: The Deletion of Pages from EACS Conference Materials in Braga (July 2014)." www.chinesestudies.eu/index.php/432-report-the-deletion-of-pages-from-eacs-conference-materials-in-braga-july-2014
7 These events are all examples of reactions by neighboring communities against China's expansion in recent years. The spurt of demonstrations began with the Sunflower Movement in Taiwan. On March 18, 2014, infuriated by the ruling Nationalist (KMT) Party's attempt to forcefully pass the Cross-Strait Service Trade Agreement with China, student activists charged into the legislature and stagnated the functioning of government for three weeks. The movement provided a precedent for student activists in Hong Kong, who carried out street protests against China's decision to curtail proposed reforms to the electoral system in Hong Kong. The Umbrella Revolution lasted for almost three months from late September to mid-December 2014. Outside the greater Chinese community, anti-China protests broke out in Vietnam in May 2014. Demonstrations broke out across Vietnam as a result of China's move to deploy an oil rig in a contended area in the South China Sea.
8 As Thorsten Pattberg points out in an interview, "The CI first wins the hearts and minds of [people]... frankly, I don't think the CIs are very successful in promoting Chinese culture. The West brought western values to China – concepts like democracy, human rights... China, on the other hand, has nothing to offer in return." See Thorsten Pattberg interview with BRICS Business Magazine, available online at: http://bricsmagazine.com/en/articles/has-beijing-s-trojan-horse-developed-a-limp
9 See US-China Bi-National Commission on Trust-Building and Enhancing Relations, "Building US-China Trust through Next Generation People, Platforms and Programs," April 2014, available online at: http://uschinaexchange.usc.edu/sites/default/files/us-china-trust-2014.pdf

References

Anon., 2014a. China-ASEAN Cultural Exchange Year 2014 Kicks Off in Beijing, *China Daily*, 9 April.

Anon., 2014b. Toronto Schools Reject Tie-Up with China's Confucius Institute, *South China Morning Post*, 30 October.

Anon., 2015. chuancheng youyi jiwangkailai de hepingzhilu: xi jinping zhuxi fangwen yuenan xinjiapo chengguo fengshuo" (A Peaceful Journey that Inherits Friendship: Rich Results from Xi Jinping's Visits to Vietnam and Singapore), *People's Daily*, 9 November.

Armitage, R. and Nye, J., 2007. *CSIS Commission on Smart Power: A Smarter, More Secure America*. Washington, DC: The CSIS Press.

Arnett, G., 2014. Foreign Direct Investment: Which Countries Get the Most? *The Guardian*, 24 June 24.

Bernstein, R. and Munro, R., 1998. *The Coming Conflict with China*. New York: Vintage Books.

Brady, A-M., 2015. China's Foreign Propaganda Machine, *Journal of Democracy*, 26 (4), 51–59.

Carlson, B., 2012. Confucius Institute: Education Bonus or Wily Trojan Horse? *Global Post*, 3 June.

China-ASEAN Expo Secretariat. *The 9th China-ASEAN Cultural Forum Opens*. Available from: http://eng.caexpo.org/index.php?m=content&c=index&a=show&catid=10114&id=200428

Cho, H., 2005. Reading the 'Korean Wave' as a Sign of Global Shift. *Korea Journal*, 45 (4), 147–182.

Confucius Institute, 2016. *Constitution and By-Laws of the Confucius Institutes*. Available from: http://english.hanban.org/node_7880.htm

Dillon, S., 2010. Foreign Languages Fades in Class – Except Chinese, *New York Times*, 20 January.

Duncan, H. and Martosko, D., 2014. America Usurped: China Becomes World's Largest Economy – Putting USA in Second Place for the First Time in 142 years, *Daily Mail*, 9 October.

European Association for Chinese Studies, 2014. *The 'Braga Incident' – Timeline with Links to Articles and Comments*. Available from: http://chinesestudies.eu/?p=609

Fischer, K., 2012. State Department Directive Could Disrupt Teaching Activities of Campus-Based Confucius Institutes, *The Chronicle of Higher Education*, 21 May.

Fiskesjo, M., 2015. *Stockholm University Terminating Its Confucius Institute*. Available from: https://networks.h-net.org/node/22055/discussions/56521/stockholm-university-terminating-its-confucius-institute

Greatrex, R., 2014. *Report: The Deletion of Pages from EACS Conference Materials in Braga*. Available from: www.chinesestudies.eu/index.php/432-report-the-deletion-of-pages-from-eacs-conference-materials-in-braga-july-2014

Hall, S. ed., 1997. *Representation: Cultural Representations and Signifying Practices*. London: Sage Publication.

Harrington, K., 2015. How China is Winning Southeast Asia, *Project Syndicate*. Available from: www.project-syndicate.org/commentary/how-china-is-winning-southeast-asia-by-kent-harrington-2015-08

Hughes, C. R., 2014. Confucius Institutes and the University: Distinguishing the Political Mission from the Cultural, *Issues and Studies*, 50 (4), 45–83.

Hung, M. and Liu, T., 2011. Sino-US Strategic Competition in Southeast Asia: China Rise and US Foreign Policy Transformation Since 9/11, *Political Perspectives Graduate Journal*, 5 (3), 96–119.

Kim, E. and Ryoo, J., 2007. South Korean Culture Goes Global: K-Pop and the Korean Wave, *Korean Social Science Journal*, 34 (1), 117–152.

Kitano, N. and Harada, Y., 2015. Estimating China's Foreign Aid 2001–2013, *Journal of International Development*, 28 (7), 1050–1074.

Klein, R., 2015. Hundreds of Thousands More Students Will Be Learning Mandarin Soon. Here's How, *The Huffington Post*, 13 October.

Kristof, N., 1993. The Rise of China, *Foreign Affairs*, 72 (5), 59–74.

Lee, G., 2009. A Soft Power Approach to the 'Korean Wave', *The Review of Korean Studies*, 12 (2), 123–137.

Mattis, P., 2012. Reexamining the Confucius Institutes, *The Diplomat*. Available from: http://thediplomat.com/2012/08/reexamining-the-confucian-institutes/

McKirdy, E. and Hunt, K., 2015. Showdown in the South China Sea: How did we get here? *CNN*, 28 October.

Mearsheimer, J., 2014. Can China Rise Peacefully? *The National Interest* [online] (October 25). Available from: http://nationalinterest.org/commentary/can-china-rise-peacefully-10204

Mearsheimer, J., 2010. The Gathering Storm: China's Challenge to US Power in Asia, *Chinese Journal of International Politics*, 3 (4), 381–396.

Mearsheimer, J., 2004. *Why China's Rise Will Not Be Peaceful*. Available from: http://mearsheimer. uchicago.edu/pdfs/A0034b.pdf

Miller, M., 2015. *China's Relations with Southeast Asia*, Testimony for the US-China Economic and Security Review Commission, 13 May. Available from: www.uscc.gov/sites/default/files/Miller_ Written%20Testimony_5.13.2015%20Hearing.pdf

Murai, T., 1990. shin chugoku kyoi ron (New China Threat), *Shokun*, 22 (5), 186–197.

Ngamsang, S. and Walsh, J., 2013. Confucius Institutes as Instruments of Soft Power: Comparison with International Rivals, *Journal of Education and Vocational Research*, 4 (10), 302–310.

Nie, H., 2015. *xi jinping fang yuenan jiangou zhongyue mingyungongtongti puxie youyi xinpianzhang* (Xi Jinping Visits Vietnam Constructs China-Vietnam Community of Common Destiny Writes New Chapter in Friendship). Available from: http://big5.china.com.cn/gate/big5/news.china. com.cn/world/2015-11/05/content_36977874.htm

Nossel, S., 2004. Smart Power, *Foreign Affairs*, 83 (2), 131–142.Penn State College of the Liberal Arts, 2014. *Confucius Institute Update*. Available from: www.la.psu.edu/news/confucius-institute-update

Rawnsley, G., 2014. *BBC Interview with Xu Lin about Confucius Institutes*, 22 December. Available from: www.pdic.blogspot.co.uk/2014/12/bbc-interview-with-xu-lin-about.html

Redden, E., 2014. *Chicago to Close Confucius Institute*. Available from: www.insidehighered.com/ news/2014/09/26/chicago-severs-ties-chinese-government-funded-confucius-institute

Sahlins, M., 2014. Confucius Institutes: Academic Malware, *Asia-Pacific Journal: Japan Focus*, 12 (46). Available from: http://apjjf.org/2014/12/46/Marshall-Sahlins/4220.html

Shim, D., 2008. The Growth of Korean Cultural Industries and the Korean Wave. *In*: C.B. Huat and K. Iwabuchi, eds. *East Asian Pop Culture: Analysing the Korean Wave*. Hong Kong: Hong Kong University Press.

Stiglitz, J., 2015. The Chinese Century, *Vanity Fair*. Available from: www.vanityfair.com/news/ 2015/01/china-worlds-largest-economy

Sudworth, J., 2014. Confucius Institute: The Hard Side of China's Soft Power, *BBC News*, 22 December.

Tsai, T., Hung, M., and Liu, T., 2011. China's Foreign Policy in Southeast Asia: Harmonious Worldview and Its Impact on Good Neighbor Diplomacy, *Journal of Contemporary Eastern Asia*, 10 (1), 25–42.

UNCTAD, 2014. *FDI Overview: China*. Available from: http://unctad.org/sections/dite_dir/docs/ wir2014/wir14_fs_cn_en.pdf

Wang, Y., 2009. Confucius Institutes and International Promotion of the Chinese Language. *In*: D. Yang, ed. *The China Educational Development Yearbook, Volume 1*. Leiden: Brill.

Weber, C., 2014. *IR Theory: A Critical Introduction*. London: Routledge.

WTO Statistics Database (Trade Profiles: China), 2011. Available from: http://stat.wto.org/ CountryProfile/WSDBCountryPFView.aspx?Language=E&Country=CN

Wyszomirski, M., Burgess, C. and Peila, C., 2003. *International Cultural Relations: A Multi-Country Comparison*. Ohio: Center for Arts and Culture.

Zheng, B., 2005. China's 'Peaceful Rise' to Great-Power Status, *Foreign Affairs*, (September/October). Available from: www.foreignaffairs.com/articles/asia/2005-09-01/chinas-peaceful-rise-great- power-status

16

From arts desert to global cultural metropolis

The (re)branding of Shanghai and Hong Kong

Kristina Karvelyte

Introduction

Since the late 1990s, an urban policy model of culture-led development has become increasingly "fashionable" (Kong 2009) and an influential trend in many cities around the world. A vast number of rapidly developing East Asian cities, irrespective of their political systems, sizes or locations, have also suddenly rediscovered their cultural resources and one after another started to pursue the titles of 'creative city', 'cultural capital', or 'cultural and creative metropolis' (Yeoh 2005; Kong *et al.* 2006; Pang 2012).

In broad terms, the policy script of cultural/creative city[1] is developed, mobilized and globalized on behalf of neoliberal rationalities and capitalist interests (Harvey 1989; Pratt 2009; Peck 2011b). It is commonly aimed at tackling a growing inter-city competition, boosting consumption and powering up the economy. Nevertheless, considering different political and economic settings of each city, it is evident that the primary objectives for the application of the creative city policy script, as well as the meanings attached to the script, vary from place to place. In other words, one model cannot fit all and certain adjustments always "need to be made in order for it to work elsewhere" (McCann and Ward 2010, p. 176; see also Peck 2011a).

To gain a better understanding of how the 'imported' discourse of the cultural and creative city is translated and adopted in different urban spaces, this chapter examines the rationale behind the 'cultural turn' of two Chinese cities, Shanghai and Hong Kong, where cultural development, until very recently, has been largely neglected and underfunded by governments. It is argued that the objectives and meanings behind the notion of cultural/creative city are continually re-adjusted to fit the dominant ideologies and political as well as business interests of a specific place. This chapter thus suggests that the concept of the creative city should be viewed as a floating signifier, which transforms in line with local politico-institutional specifications as it travels from one place to another.

The main reason for selecting Hong Kong and Shanghai for this study was a unique combination of the cultural and ethnic affinities that bind these two cities together and the historical and political differences that divide them. Both cities are predominantly Chinese and seem to share similar cultural roots and social practices. This means that cultural differences

247

should have a minimal impact on their understanding and interpretation of the 'cultural turn'. On the other hand, due to the historical and political divergences, the two cities have developed different civic identities and distinct approaches to urban policymaking, thus providing an excellent ground for comparative research.

The study was based on the concurrent analysis of local policy documents and semi-structured elite interviews. A diverse range of documents, including annual policy statements, government reports, policy guidelines and research papers that deal with government research or policies directly related to the cultural affairs or cultural/creative city discourse were selected for analysis. In addition, a total of 21 interviews, including five written responses, were carried out between September 2014 and January 2015. The interviews were conducted with the key members of the institutions responsible for (or involved in) planning and supervision of cultural and creative development in Shanghai and Hong Kong, including government officials, policy advisors, academics and industry practitioners.

Globalizing discourse of the cultural and creative city

The idea of the cultural/creative city is centred on the utilization of cultural and creative resources in urban planning and management, which are argued to make a city more attractive for investors, businesses, skilled workers and visitors (Landry and Bianchini 1995; Landry 2000; Florida 2002; Cochrane 2007; Mommaas 2009).

The concept of the 'creative city' was first coined in relation to the application of culture and the arts for urban regeneration purposes (Landry and Bianchini 1995). However, due to the rapid technological advancement of and increasingly market-oriented approach to urban restructuring, the cultural realm was soon merged with the creative sector that entails more commercially appealing industries, such as design or advertising. As a result, today the dominant narratives linked to the creative city discourse include cultural as well as creative industries and initiatives (Landry 2000; Florida 2002; Comunian 2011).

Along with the expanding scope of the notion, the expectations attached to the concept of the creative city have also increased. Today, it is commonly associated with four major policy objectives. First, as noted before, the notion of the 'creative city' is used to attract and retain a talented and skilled workforce (Florida 2002; Sassen 2006; Grodach and Silver 2013). Second, it is employed to lure foreign investment and businesses (Zukin 1995; Mommaas 2009). Third, it serves to boost and sustain cultural production and consumption (Landry 2000; Mommaas 2009; Pratt 2009). Fourth, it is applied to differentiate the city in a global marketplace (Landry 2000; Florida 2002; Leslie 2005). An overarching role attached to the policy model of the 'creative city' that encapsulates all four objectives stated above is that of enhancing the image and reputation of the city (Zukin 1995; Yeoh 2005; Mommaas 2009; Pang 2012; Grodach and Silver 2013). This role, as will be shown further in this chapter, can emerge from both market-centred and state/city-centred considerations.

The idea of setting the city apart from others by promoting its cultural and creative properties has captivated the interest of many urban policymakers across the world, leading to the emergence of a vast number of self-proclaimed 'creative cities', all aspiring to "differentiate themselves, and to sell themselves as centers of culture" (Leslie 2005, p. 403; see also Gibson and Klocker 2004). Undoubtedly, one part of the success formula behind a global appeal and transferability of the cultural/creative city policy script rests on the unique competitive advantage it was believed to offer (Landry 2000; Florida 2002). However, the major reason for the contagiousness of this policy model was its conformity to the dominant neoliberal or 'entrepreneurial' approach to urban planning and development (Harvey 1989; Peck 2007).

Since the late 1970s, rapid deindustrialization coupled with a growing mobility of capital and labour has brought an intense inter-urban competition. In order to strengthen and boost their appeal in a global marketplace, cities were forced to engage in a number of entrepreneurial practices, including urban restructuring projects and place marketing campaigns (Harvey 1989; Hubbard 2006; Comunian 2011).[2] This does not mean, however, that cities became better places for *everyone* to live, because the primary focus of the entrepreneurial city has always been to serve the interests of global businesses and investors (Harvey 1989; Pacione 2009). Thus, only certain forms of urban experience that conform with expectations and resources of the middle or upper-middle class are encouraged in entrepreneurial cities. In this sense, as Harvey (2008) rightly observes, the quality of urban life, just like cities themselves, has been turned into a commodity for those with money.

The concept of the cultural/creative city not only complements the framework of urban entrepreneurialism (Peck 2005; Pratt 2008); it is, in fact, a product of it. Peck (2007) accurately depicts some of the major crossing points between the urban entrepreneurialism and creative cities:

> whereas the entrepreneurial cities chased jobs, the creative cities pursue talent workers; the entrepreneurial cities craved investment, now the creative cities yearn for buzz; while entrepreneurial cities boasted of their postfordist flexibility, the creative cities trade on the cultural distinction of *cool*.
>
> *(par. 28)*

This shows that a distinguishing characteristic between the entrepreneurial and creative cities is a strategy, not an ultimate objective. In a sense, being a creative city can be viewed as a strategy in itself, because ultimately, it assists in the efforts of becoming a more successful entrepreneurial city. As noted before, cultural policies and creative development are argued to differentiate the city in a global marketplace, to attract and retain certain groups of skilled labour and capital, to boost consumption and to improve the reputation of the place. In other words, like entrepreneurial cities, creative cities are focused on sustaining the power of capital and serving the interests of the middle class and elites. Furthermore, in a pursuit of displaying the attractive side of the urban core, like entrepreneurial cities, they tend to neglect vulnerable social groups "that do not fit this narrative of economic development" (Grodach and Silver 2013, p. 4), such as migrant populations, the urban poor and, ironically, artists whose work does conform to the envisioned format of the cultural and creative city. In other words, it is evident that there is nothing "revolutionary" (Peck 2005) about the policy script of the cultural/creative city: it does not challenge an existing policy framework and does not require any significant structural changes in urban governance models, provided a city is 'entrepreneurial'.

Another important characteristic that strengthens a universal appeal of the 'creative city' is the assumption that a positive impact of culture and creativity on the city *can* be proved in numbers. A tendency to overly rely on what is perceived to be 'solid' quantitative data has emerged as a result of increasingly 'evidence-based' policymaking (Belfiore 2004; Peck and Theodore 2010; Prince 2014). Richard Florida's Creativity Index (2002), which rests on the assessment of talent, technology and tolerance (3Ts), could be viewed as one of many examples of a commonly adapted practice to render the value of creativity and/or culture in quantitative terms. Although the methodology behind this index, particularly the direct connection between the 3Ts and economic growth, has been severely questioned in the literature (see Markusen 2006; Malanga 2004),[3] a number of cities have embraced Florida's measurement criteria to enact and promote their cultural and creative turn. This has also enabled the cities to see where they stand in terms of their 'creativity' (that is, in fact, Florida's version of 'creativity') in relation to other cities. However, rather than providing them with an assumed competitive advantage (Cochrane 2007), the ability to compare and contrast has only thrown the cities deeper into a vicious circle of more aggressive, zero-sum competition (Peck 2005).

Besides Florida's Creativity Index, there are plenty of scales and ranking systems designed to measure the cultural and creative potential of the city, each with its own criteria and methodologies. Some notable examples include the Creative City Index developed by Landry and Hyams (2012) or the criteria laid out for the UNESCO Creative Cities Network. The absence of a singular framework for the cultural/creative city implies that each city can adopt somewhat different descriptions of what 'creative city' means. This enables urban policymakers to reinvent and manipulate the meanings, roles and focal points of the creative city in accordance with their policy goals and objectives.

Hong Kong's attempt to transform from the 'arts desert' to cultural and creative global city

Since the late 1990s, urban policy models linked to culture and creativity have been gradually integrated into Hong Kong's policy trajectories (Kong *et al.* 2006; Chu 2012). This section examines specific historical, political and socio–economic conditions that prompted, shaped and defined Hong Kong's cultural and creative restructuring.

Historically, Hong Kong was often referred to as "an excellent current example" (Friedman 1981, p. 34) and a success story of *laissez-faire* capitalism (see also Rabushka 1979). The British colonial government in Hong Kong was praised for embracing a policy of non-interventionism that has transformed a small fishing village into a vibrant commercial centre (see Friedman 1981).

It should be acknowledged, however, that the presence of the government's 'non-interventionism' has been repeatedly questioned in the academic literature. A number of scholars identified a vast number of policy areas, where the colonial regime appeared to be involved in the economic and social development processes of Hong Kong (see, for example, Youngson 1982; Ngo 1999; Ngok 2007). In other words, it is now evident that an allegedly 'non-interventionist' model of governance was (and continues to be) based on a selective interventionism, which is a common practice in neoliberal states (see Peck 2004; Purcell 2009). Through selective interventionism, the government is not only able to "facilitate the accumulation of capital" (Purcell 2009, p. 142), but it can also neglect those fields or areas that are deemed unprofitable or considered a poor fit for the policy agenda of the state. Take, for example, industrial development in Hong Kong that for many years was perceived as a potential threat to the interests of the British manufacturers (Ngo 1999; Ngok 2007). The non-interventionist model enabled British colonial rule to conveniently refrain from intervening in selected industrial sectors thereby delaying Hong Kong's industrial development until the 1950s (Ngo 1999; Lee and Yue 2001).

A similar logic was applied to the cultural sector. Until the 1970s, despite the relative economic prosperity of Hong Kong, the cultural realm together with other non-trade related public services was largely neglected by the government (Ooi 1995). Chinese intellectuals who visited Hong Kong during the 1920s and 1930s have severely criticized the city's 'cultural backwardness', characterizing Hong Kong as a 'cultural desert' (*wenhua shamo*, Lu 1985 cited in Luk 1991, p. 660). Their impressions were undoubtedly influenced by strong anti-Western and anti-capitalist stances and reflected elitist views of culture (Fu 2003). At that time, Hong Kong had a very small number of public cultural venues. Traditional forms of Chinese culture were neither supported nor encouraged by the colonial government, and its tertiary education was underdeveloped (Ooi 1995; Ngok 2007). However, a lack of public cultural amenities or the absence of certain forms of culture does not make a city less 'cultural', and most certainly does not make it a 'cultural desert'. Instead, this merely shows that the city's cultural development occurs through other means or forms of culture. In the case of Hong Kong, for many years it was defined through the realms of popular culture, particularly film, cartoons and comics (*manhua*), popular music and martial arts (see Fonoroff 1988; Wong 2002).

In post-1997 Hong Kong, the notion of the 'cultural desert' has been strategically rejected as the remnant of the colonial past. First, this has served to re-shape the post-colonial identity of the city (Raco and Gilliam 2012). Second, this has helped to justify the contrasting image of *new* 'cultural' Hong Kong and to firmly place it within a broader framework of the neoliberal urban restructuring agenda. In the Policy Address 1999, Tung Chee-Hwa, then Chief Executive of Hong Kong Special Administrative Region Government (HKSARG), clearly echoes the rhetoric of culture-led urban development practices:

> Hong Kong's future development is not just a matter of pushing forward with physical construction. What we also need is a favourable and flourishing cultural environment that is conducive to encouraging innovation and creativity in our citizens. (...) I have proposed to develop Hong Kong into an international centre for cultural exchanges. This will help to strengthen our identity as a world-class city.
>
> *(HKSARG 1999, par. 164)*

This quote serves as one of many examples indicating that by the early 2000s, Hong Kong had embraced a global trend, a seemingly 'new' urban philosophy, where cultural development is perceived as an important part of a 'model' global city. It should be noted that this 'new' urban development agenda was, in fact, not new to Hong Kong – similar ideas had already been spotted in the (see Ooi 1995). Creating the effect of newness, whilst "not being new at all" (Lawton *et al.* 2014, p. 193) is a common feature of 'creative urbanism' (Peck 2011b) practices. Coupled with what appears a 'universal character' (Prince 2014, p. 91) of the cultural/creative city model, it allows for culture and creativity to be neatly placed within a broader framework of urban restructuring projects (Peck 2005; Lawton *et al.* 2014).

Similarly, in many interviews and policy documents the adoption of cultural and creative urban development practices was often framed and perceived as a *natural* 'way forward' (industry practitioner A, personal communication, 15 Oct 2014). This is how the former Chief Executive of Hong Kong, Donald Tsang, describes the emergence of the cultural and creative industries discourse:

> Globalization has brought about the rise of various cultural and creative industries. The markets for leisure goods, advertising, film, television, tourism, design, architecture and art are flourishing. These high value-added industries are environmentally friendly and compatible with the mode of economic development for global cities.
>
> *(HKSARG 2007, pp. 25–26)*

By framing the cultural/creative turn of Hong Kong as somewhat 'natural' and 'positive' outcome of globalization that could boost the economic development of Hong Kong, just like, as he suggests, it does in other global cities, Tsang escapes a deeper inquiry about the actual reasons behind Hong Kong's interest in the development of the cultural and creative sector. As shown below, it appears to be prompted by both global and context-specific factors.

The socio-economic impact of deindustrialization is among the most commonly acknowledged reasons behind the cultural turn of cities (see, for example, Hubbard 2006; Mommaas 2009; Communian 2011). Despite lacking support from the colonial government (Ngo 1999; Lee and Yue 2001), manufacturing industries in Hong Kong have been rapidly developing since the early 1950s. However, over the years, the economic prosperity and growth of the city led to rising labour costs, triggering a massive relocation of factories and industrial plants to China in the 1980s (Yeung 2002; Lee *et al.* 2013), forcing Hong Kong to reconsider its development strategies, or in Yeung's (2002) words, "to rediscover a new magic" (p. 5) for its growth. Like many other reindustrialising cities, Hong Kong has turned its focus from traditional manufacturing industries to the service sector, particularly financial services, trading and tourism (Yeung 2002; Ngok 2007). This transition required the government to increase public spending on education, social services and culture (Ngok 2007).

Until the 2000s, the value of culture and the arts in the city has been discussed primarily in relation to tourism. The tourism industry is one of four pillar industries in Hong Kong, accounting for 5 percent of Hong Kong's GDP (Census and Statistics Department 2013). Despite its rapid development in the 1980s, after the Asian financial crisis hit the city in 1997, the industry experienced a significant decline (Song *et al.* 2003). To boost the development of tourism, the government introduced a number of new civic 'boosterism' (Harvey 1989) strategies, including the promotion of Hong Kong as the "Asian centre of arts and culture":

> In order to enhance our appeal as a tourist destination, we will promote new attractions, which will complement our unique flavour and provide for a wider range of events in Hong Kong. Our broader vision is to cultivate Hong Kong's image as the Asian centre of arts and culture, and of entertainment and sporting events.
>
> *(HKSARG 1998, par. 45)*

Although since the late 1990s the cultural sector remains closely linked to tourism, it has been employed in a broader spectrum of policy programs. The 1997 Asian financial crisis, the SARS outbreak in 2003 and more recently, the global financial crisis have repeatedly threatened the economic stability of Hong Kong. Re-establishing the city as not merely a global centre of finance and business, but also as an 'International cultural metropolis' (Culture and Heritage Commission 2003) is now perceived as one of the means to maintain and strengthen the competitiveness of Hong Kong (see Lui 2008; Chu 2012). As stated in the Policy Recommendation Report issued by the Culture and Heritage Commission in 2003, should Hong Kong "neglect creative thinking and cultural education, it will lose its competitive edge, let alone become an international cultural metropolis" (p. 1). This quote clearly demonstrates how the culture-led urban development, as any form of urban entrepreneurialism, can lock cities in a zero-sum competition with one another. With a globalizing format of the 'cultural/creative city' impacting the policymaking processes in a growing number of cities, places that refuse to inject some cultural and creative 'vibes' in their policy agendas put themselves at risk of being viewed as losers in the competitive marketplace.

To what extent the cultural/creative city discourse can actually benefit the cultural life of a city is another question. Lui's (2008) study of the West Kowloon Cultural District project, which was launched by the government to pursue a vision of the 'international cultural metropolis', suggests that the production of cultural value has never been among the driving forces for this project. As Lui (2008) explains:

> [T]he emphasis was placed on competing with other global cities on the basis of building equally competitive infrastructure, rather than on a shared vision of Hong Kong's future cultural development.(…) *It was simply an attempt to be strategic in global competition.*
>
> *(p. 222, emphasis added)*

The last sentence could be easily applied to the whole policy model of cultural and creative urbanism in Hong Kong. Selective interventionism has enabled the government to support and facilitate primarily those cultural initiatives that are perceived as a good fit to the format of 'international cultural metropolis' and that are regarded as capable of standing out and competing in the global marketplace. For instance, interview data show that whilst the largest and the most reputable cultural events in the city, such as the Hong Kong Arts Festival or the Hong Kong International Film Festival, receive regular funding from the government, most other cultural groups and organizations are forced to compete with each other for one-off grants from the Arts Development Council (see also Lee *et al.* 2013). Moreover, until now, the Hong Kong government remains a chief landlord of cultural venues and facilities. This obstructs the development of private small-scale cultural initiatives (HKSARG official A, personal communication, 14 Oct 2014).

In neoliberal cities, the culture-led urban development agenda is often framed around a hyper-intense inter-urban competition and place marketing (Harvey 1989; Peck 2004). What makes Hong Kong's case different is that for Hong Kong, the narrative of cultural and creative development means a lot more than just keeping in line with the global economic competition. For Hong Kong, it is also a way of coping with the consequences of the 1997 political transition, when the city was handed back to China. The handover, or 'return', was marked by widespread anxiety and speculations regarding the possible decline of Hong Kong's global status and influence (Abbas 2000; Kong *et al.* 2006). An exposure to new political liabilities and the prospect of being placed alongside other Chinese cities threatened Hong Kong's position in the region (Abbas 1997, 2000; Yeung 2000; Chu 2012).

In response to these concerns, the government decided to invest in a new city branding campaign. In 2001, it established the Brand Hong Kong (BrandHK) office, a strategic communication agency responsible for promoting Hong Kong as 'Asia's world city'. This branding strategy is designed to serve a dual purpose, that is, to help the city keep up with global competition and most importantly, to differentiate Hong Kong from other Chinese cities. As stated on the BrandHK website:

> The idea of "branding" Hong Kong first emerged in 1997. At that time, much attention was focused on the return of Hong Kong to China, and there was concern in some quarters that Hong Kong might vanish from the international stage after reunification. Various strategies were considered, and the decision to develop Brand Hong Kong (BrandHK) was finally taken in 2000.
>
> *(BrandHK 2015a, par. 1)*

The branding slogan, 'Asia's world city', entails an overwhelming number of different catchphrases, including "international cultural metropolis", "creative hub of Asia" or "events capital of Asia". Clearly, it is all about the same candy wrapped in a different paper. Ultimately, they all reflect on the attempt to adopt a globalizing policy model of the cultural/creative city in order to create "a visionary unique identity" (BrandHK 2015b, p. 1) for Hong Kong. This aim has been further elaborated in the interviews with government officials in Hong Kong:

> If we say we are a world city, then we certainly have to have something distinct, something to be proud of, in terms of cultu...in the cultural sense".
>
> *(HKSARG official B, personal communication, 5 Sep 2014)*

> As a global city, you *need* now to have your sort of cultural identity.
>
> *(HKSARG official C, personal communication, 5 Sep 2014, emphasis added)*

On the one hand, this feeling of necessity and "no one can afford not to do it" (industry practitioner A, personal communication, 15 Oct 2014) attitude stems from the global pressure to compete. On the other hand, however, it also reflects on a fear of being "merged and submerged into the national" (Abbas 2000, p. 779; see also Chu 2012).

It could be debated whether labelling the city the 'international cultural metropolis' or 'creative hub of Asia' is really intended to help to facilitate a 'unique identity' of Hong Kong or blend it with other global cities. Borrowing from Abbas (1997), these tags serve as representations of Hong Kong's culture as a "culture of disappearance" (p. 7). In this sense, 'disappearance', as Abbas (1997) further explains, "is not a matter of effacement but of replacement and substitution, where the perceived danger is recontained through representations that are familiar and plausible" (p. 7). A portrayal of Hong Kong as an 'international cultural metropolis' could be viewed as one of many representations of that sort. Instead of creating a unique identity of Hong Kong, it conforms to what is generally perceived as a 'global' or 'universal' format of the cultural/creative global city. Thus, with other large Chinese cities, such as Shanghai, Beijing and Taipei adopting very similar policy scripts and formats, the cultural turn, rather than making Hong Kong 'reappear', seems to be directed at its 'disappearance'.

Re-establishing the past in the present: Shanghai's path towards global cultural metropolis

Contrary to the culture-led urban development in the Global North or some Asian cities, where urban re-industrialization was among the major factors driving the development of culture and the arts, a decline in manufacturing industries has never played a primary role in Shanghai's cultural turn (see O'Connor 2012; Gu 2012). Being an emerging metropolis in the midst of a real estate boom, Shanghai has enthusiastically embraced the process of deindustrialization as an opportunity for expansion (Zhang 2003). Empty industrial sites in the outskirts of and within the city were quickly demolished and replaced with modern office and apartment buildings. In other words, the Shanghai Municipal People's Government (SMPG) did not need to establish cultural and creative quarters to boost a real estate sector. Therefore, as Gu (2012) argues, a cultural economy in Shanghai "was never intended to be part of the plan for the new economy of the inner city" (p. 195).

Yet, by the end of 2010, the city had 15 cultural quarters and 80 creative clusters (SMPG 2011a) established in line with a newly proclaimed vision of 'International cultural metropolis' (*Guoji wenhua da dushi*, SMPG 2010). In 2008, the city also submitted a bid to UNESCO

Creative Cities Network and after two years was awarded a title of UNESCO City of Design. If deindustrialization was not a primary reason for culture-led urban development initiatives to unfold in Shanghai, what provoked a sudden interest in the cultural/creative city policy script? This section explores some of the major political and socio-economic factors that contributed to the 'cultural-turn' of Shanghai.

It is important to note that Shanghai's path towards modern and global cultural metropolis is strongly linked to its past. From the late 1920s to the early 1940s, when Chinese state power was in turmoil, the city occupied a very special position in the world. This period is commonly labeled Shanghai's 'golden age', because of economic prosperity, booming international trade and cosmopolitan culture that co-existed with the emerging modern Chinese culture in this semi-colonial city at the time. Back then, Shanghai was largely disconnected from the rest of China and was openly criticized and condemned by both the Chinese Nationalist Party and the Communist Party for being too 'foreign' (Bergère 1981, p. 3).

After Mao took over the rule of China in 1949, the affluent cosmopolitan cultural life of the city was discarded as "bourgeois and decadent" (Abbas 2000, p. 776) debris of the past. In a few years, from a thriving international metropolis Shanghai was turned into the center of domestic industrial production, where its main role was to "finance the modernization of the rest of the country" (Abbas 2000, p. 776; see also Wu 2000; Gamble 2003). Although accounting for only one percent of the population, the city became a major contributor to the state's budget, supplying around a sixth of the national revenue (Zhang 2002). Therefore, even after the launch of fiscal decentralisation reform in 1978, the Party was hesitant to cut off its major source of income and delayed the economic restructuring of Shanghai for more than a decade (Wu 2000; Zhang 2002).

The reforms finally took off in the early 1990s. In order to become an equal player in the world's economy, China had to reposition its major cities from domestic to global players and to develop them into global nodes of agglomeration for international services and firms (see Sassen 2006). This meant it could no longer ignore the "infrastructure upgrading needs" (Zhang 2002, p. 482) of Shanghai. The city's government was allowed to keep 25 percent of the tax revenue, to directly approve foreign investment, to issue and trade stocks, and to open foreign stores in Pudong New Area (Gamble 2003; Zhang 2002).

Since the 1990s, the official approach to the past of the city has also radically changed. Today the history of 1930s Shanghai is presented as a badge of honor and serves as a benchmark or a base for *re-establishing* the brand of modern, cultural and cosmopolitan Shanghai, capable of competing with other global cities in the region and beyond. As one respondent explains,

> Now, we seek to embrace this glorious history, embrace this as a resource (…) we dream of revoking the glory of those years. Of course, it is impossible to completely go back, but Shanghai is always under… Other cities [in China] do not experience such pressure (…) [whereas] Shanghai has these high expectations. (…) On the one hand, the glory of the past, provides the city with a base and capital, on the other hand, however, it puts Shanghai under immense pressure.
>
> *(academic, personal communication, 17 Nov 2014, translated from Chinese)*

This quote clearly demonstrates how much importance is now attached to Shanghai's pursuit of its 'glorious past' in its attempt to build new imaginaries of the future. However, in this "city of remake" (Abbas 2000, p. 778), the ultimate goal is not to revoke the past, but rather to reinvent the past anew in the light of the present objectives of the Party (O'Connor

2012). Through the selective "demolition and preservation" (O'Connor 2012, p. 25) of the city's 'golden age', the government chooses to retain only those elements that conform to the Party's narratives of 'Socialist modern international metropolis' (*Shehuizhuyi xiandaihua guoji chengshi*, SMPG 1991). Global fame and recognition of 1930s Shanghai, its cosmopolitanism, economic prosperity and cultural maturity, all serve to reassert 'internationalization' and 'modernisation' of the 'new' Shanghai. At the same time, the government conveniently dismisses the other side of the city's past. The city used to be known for its strained and distant relationship with the central government, politically active middle class and somewhat revolutionary ideas that circulated among local "intellectuals on the loose" (Bergère 1981, p. 3). Such fragmented re-modernization of Shanghai seems to be set to integrate the elements of both an 'entrepreneurial' and 'socialist' city. This seemingly unlikely combination manifests the dominant ideology of contemporary China that Harvey (2005) once defined as "neoliberalism 'with Chinese characteristics'" (p. 120).

Economic reforms in Shanghai boosted the growth of the city but proved insufficient in keeping up with increasing inter-urban competition. To bring Shanghai and other Chinese cities "in line with international practice" (Wu 2000, p. 1365), local authorities were impelled to adopt 'entrepreneurial' models of urban management. In an attempt to appeal to foreign businesses and investors, cities have started to actively invest in the infrastructure, local amenities, cultural facilities and city branding campaigns (Zou 1996; Wu 2000). In this context, the argument that in the past Shanghai used to be a 'global cultural metropolis' is evoked to reassert a unique experience and capabilities of the city, particularly in relation to other Chinese cities.

With other cities within China, Shanghai competes primarily for foreign capital and tourist inflows. However, outside China, at regional and global levels, its major goals and objectives extend far beyond the economic dimension. As a state-centered world city (Hill and Kim 2000), Shanghai does not fit into the conventional template of the 'world' or 'global city', where the city, and not the state, is recognized as a key node of command and control (see Friedmann 1986; Sassen 2006). Instead, Shanghai's growth and development is largely guided by the nation-state and shaped by national rather than urban policy agendas. A state-led developmentalism adds a political dimension to the cultural turn in Shanghai. Therefore, the cultural/creative city discourse in this context should be examined not only as an entrepreneurial urban practice, but also as part of a broader national project.

Today China is recognized as the most likely world power to challenge the hegemony of the United States (Layne 2009). A rapid accumulation of economic capital has already helped the nation to achieve a leader status in the world's economy. This position, however, does not guarantee global recognition and respect or, borrowing from Bourdieu (1977), 'symbolic power', which reflects on "a major dimension of political power" – the "power to impose the principles of construction of reality" (p. 164). As Bourdieu (1989) elsewhere explains, only "those who have obtained sufficient recognition", and thereby, 'symbolic capital', are "in a position to *impose* recognition" (p. 23, emphasis added). It is evident, that China still struggles to 'impose recognition' in many areas of social life. Human rights violations, environmental issues, corruption and censorship seem especially to hamper the reputation of China (Ding 2007; Wang 2011; Creemers 2015). Therefore, despite rapidly growing economic might, China's image in the Global North is still largely negative (Wang 2011). Subsequently, its 'symbolic power' remains relatively weak.

In its quest for alternative sources of influence, the Chinese government has discovered Joseph Nye's (2004) notion of 'soft power', defined as "the ability to shape the preferences of others" (p. 5) through the power of attraction. Peck and Theodore (2010) observe that policies and policy programs tend to travel as "selective discourses" rather than as "complete 'packages'" (p. 170). The notion of 'soft power' has also reached China as the 'selective discourse', and it has been greatly altered in line with political realities and imaginaries of the state. Nye (2004) based his concept of 'soft power' on the power of seduction and ability to attract, arguing that it is inherently relational and is not interchangeable with influence. However, in Mainland China, a subtle seductive aspect of 'soft power' is increasingly "eschewed in favor of a communications stance that seems passive-aggressive" (Creemers 2015, p. 12) with the word 'influence' (*yingxiangli*) time and again reiterated in the policy narratives of the ruling elites. As a result, in addition to Nye's (2004) three major sources of soft power that entail culture, political values and foreign policy, the Chinese version of soft power accommodates a number of other deeply politicized practices that include global propaganda-oriented media production, membership in multilateral organizations, and even overseas aid programmes (Kurlantzick 2007; Li 2008; Creemers 2015). In other words, the Chinese model of soft power clearly departs from the original concept and rests on a perceived ability to accumulate influence and to gain "'power *over*' rather than 'power *with*' others" (Nye 2011, p. 90, emphasis added).

Culture, particularly in a form of traditional Chinese culture and values, is commonly singled out as a major ingredient of Chinese soft power (Li 2008; Creemers 2015). Not a surprising choice, given that the Chinese culture generally receives a high degree of respect and admiration from the foreign audience (Wang 2011). In 2007, the Chinese government officially instated the development of 'cultural soft power' (*wenhua ruanshili*) as one of the key national initiatives in a pursuit of making China "more *influential* politically (*yingxiangli*), more *competitive* economically (*jingzhengli*), more *appealing* in its image (*qingheli*), and more *inspiring* morally (*ganzhaoli*)" (Wang 2011, p. 8).

Following on the 'cultural soft power' policy strategy, many cities in China, including Shanghai, have actively started to promote their cultural properties. In the 12th Five-Year Plan (2011–2015), Shanghai outlines its aspiration to enhance the international influence and soft power of the city through its cultural and creative advancement. The plan strategically places the narrative of the 'international cultural metropolis' within the ultimate vision for 2020, which is, to turn Shanghai into the "International centre of economy, finance, trade and shipping" (*Guoji jingji, jinrong, maoyi, hangyun zhongxin*, SMPG 2011b). With culture now recognized as a 'symbolic capital' of Shanghai (Gu 2015), it is increasingly utilized to gain respect, recognition and, ultimately, influence in the global city networks. In this sense, the policy script of the creative city is transformed into one of the Chinese soft power strategies, where an ultimate goal is political influence rather than economic success. Accordingly, the cultural and creative development strategy of the city is strongly linked to the Party's ambition for Shanghai to gain access to the elite group of 'model' global cities, specifically to reach and surpass two of the highest integrated world-cities, London and New York (GaWC 2012). The Shanghai Municipal Government sends numerous delegations to leading cities around the world, to learn what they consider best cultural policy practices and to determine ways to compete with them. As a senior government official from the Shanghai Municipal Administration of Culture, Radio, Film and TV indicates:

> We aim to become one of the front-ranking cities in the world. World-class city. Particularly in the field of culture. In the field of culture, we are now learning from some other foreign… Some international world-class cultural metropolises serve as… as models [for us]. For instance, now our focus lies on studying London, also New York. In Asia, it's Tokyo. These [cities] serve as certain benchmarks for us.
>
> *(personal communication, 19 Nov 2014, translated from Chinese)*

Clearly, the adoption of the 'best practices' from the developed cities in the Global North, which seem to be accepted as flawless and impeccable policy models, is viewed as a major contributing factor in Shanghai's efforts to catch up with other world cities. As the same official further maintains:

> We can't claim that Shanghai and England's London are the same now, that Shanghai has reached those standards yet. We have not reached those high standards yet. We have not reached that level yet. However, we are working hard to learn from the UK, to learn from London, [we] strive to turn Shanghai into the 'creative city'.
>
> *(personal communication, 19 Nov 2014)*

For Shanghai, reaching 'those high standards' equals acceptance into the elite global community. For China, this equals more power and influence. Therefore, in this context, the 'influence', encompassed by both 'international influence' (*guoji yingxiangli*) and 'reputational influence' (*zhiming yingxiangli*) becomes a crucial indicator in assessing the value of cultural activities in 'globalizing' Shanghai. Research data suggest that opting for 'the best', 'world-class' performances and generating influence through their presence is a key reason for the large-scale cultural events in Shanghai. As one respondent explains in relation to the Shanghai International Arts Festival:

> This is so important for Shanghai to make a statement. The outer appearance, the surface is very important to Shanghai. (....) What is important to them, the number of performances that they have, the number of high level artists that are in. Again, it's the report that they put together to send to [the] Ministry of Culture. It's a major, major focus for the [Arts] Festival. Because this is how they are judged, this is how they are evaluated.
>
> *(industry practitioner B, personal communication, 17 Nov 2014)*

A desire to generate more international influence also resonates with another clear tendency in the cultural turn of Shanghai, that is, an increasing 'internationalisation' of the events content, where local Chinese culture and cultural production is accommodated and adapted to what is perceived as 'foreign taste'. As a staff member from the Shanghai International Arts Festival indicates, "Chinese elements need to be expressed using the world's language" (industry practitioner C, personal communication, 23 Jan 2015, translated from Chinese). Such 'staged authenticity' (MacCannell 1973) assists in creating a 'global' identity of the events that subsequently conforms to the image of 'globalizing' Shanghai. Local artists as well as audience, on the other hand, tend to be largely discounted from cultural display sites because gaining 'local influence' (*difangxing yingxiangli*) is deemed of a little value for the international image of the city (industry practitioner B, personal communication, 17 Nov 2014).

In sum, it is evident that the cultural turn in Shanghai's urban development satisfies the needs and objectives of both the state and the market. It is perceived to reflect on the advancement and re-modernization of the city, to connect it with other cities through a global model of a cultural/creative city and to stimulate the middle class consumption and investment demand. However, similar to Hong Kong, it appears that this strategy is adopted to assimilate Shanghai with other global cities rather than to assist in the emergence of a unique model of modern socialist metropolis.

Discussion: tracing connections and disconnections between cities

This chapter sought to demonstrate how globalizing policy patterns of culture-led urban development pervade the policy agenda of cities, and how cities translate and alter the meanings of these patterns in accordance with their historical, political and socio-economic settings.

Both the colonial government in Hong Kong and the communist government under Mao in Shanghai did little to encourage cultural development in the cities. This by no means indicates the absence of cultural or creative practices; certain forms of culture and the arts have always been there. However, the cultural realm has never before been utilized to address such major political and economic issues as it is today. By adopting very similar, at times identical, narratives of cultural and creative development, both cities adhere to a neoliberal framework of a 'new' urban development. Their 'cultural turn' is undoubtedly influenced and powered by inter-urban competition for talents, investment and tourist inflows that, as a global trend, is commonly associated with neoliberal or market-oriented practice.

Nevertheless, it appears that the adoption of the same policy narrative does not necessarily derive from the same policy objectives. Due to the different governance models and policy interests of the cities, the 'creative city' script is deeply contextualized and continuously reframed to pursue specific policy agendas. For instance, in Shanghai, it reflects the attempt to enhance global influence and power of the state, whereas Hong Kong's 'cultural turn' has been directed at boosting tourism industry and assisting in the city's efforts to maintain its 'global city' identity. In other words, the notion of the cultural/creative city seems to be approached as a currency or a floating signifier, disconnected from any specific signification and imbued with meaning by contextualized policy discourses.

Clearly, political systems and governance models have a huge impact on the way cities attend to their cultural and creative development. Under state-led developmentalism, local authorities in Shanghai have very limited decision-making power. Therefore, the city's 'cultural turn' is shaped predominantly by national interests. The narrative of the 'international cultural metropolis' has also been established to, first and foremost, fulfill the ambitions of the Party rather than to assist in Shanghai's re-industrialization efforts. In this context, cultural development is perceived as Shanghai's ticket to the elite group of global cities. As a result, the government gives preference to large-scale cultural groups or initiatives that are perceived as more likely to generate a global impact.

In Hong Kong, policymaking is deeply rooted in neoliberal 'non-interventionist' ideology. Its 'cultural turn' was launched in relation to the commonly acknowledged market-development needs of the post-industrial city resulting from growing global competition and the rise of service industries, specifically tourism. Hong Kong's handover to China has not only accelerated the pace of the culture-led urban development but has also altered its scope and direction. A growing concern about being "merged and submerged into the national" (Abbas 2000, p. 779) has prompted the government to embrace a global policy script of the cultural and creative city as an opportunity of 'display' (Williams 1984). As a result, it has been incorporated into the broader branding strategy, designed to maintain a 'world-city' status for Hong Kong. In this context, the title of the cultural and creative city once again entails more than just economic interests. In Hong Kong, it is also about preserving an *international* identity of the city.

A number of crossing points between the two case studies pinpoint four important implications. First, this comparative study demonstrates that the adoption of cultural/creative urbanism practices is not optional: every city that seeks to be part of a global network has to fit in the frames of what is broadly defined as a cultural/creative city. Originally, the notions of 'world' and 'global' city were coined and discussed in relation to the world economy and international division of labor (see Friedmann 1986; Sassen 2006). However, it seems that in the last decade, a new, cultural/creative dimension has been added to this concept (see Krätke 2006). Framed along neoliberal lines of economic restructuring, inter-urban competition and a commodified notion of 'quality of life' (Harvey 2008), the narrative of cultural development is now perceived as a necessary component for any city aspiring to fit in a format of the global city. Hong Kong has been labelled a 'cultural desert' since the 1920s, and yet this has never stopped it from being very successful on a global stage of finance and trade. However, with an increased pressure to compete for investment, skilled workers and tourists coupled with an arguably weakened position after the handover, Hong Kong was forced to take the 'cultural turn' in urban development and to seek for the recognition as 'international cultural metropolis'. Shanghai, on the other hand, is a re-emerging global city and simultaneously a re-emerging 'international cultural metropolis'. Thus, it has lot to prove, as both a global and a socialist city. The ultimate goal for Shanghai is to access the elite group of the two highest integrated world cities, London and New York. To assimilate with those and other cities in the global city network, Shanghai is now also impelled to follow and emulate their strategies of culture-led development.

This brings us to the second major implication. It appears that in a non-western context, the policy script of the cultural/creative city is adopted as a tool for *convergence* rather than divergence. With a rapidly expanding number of international cultural metropolises around the world, the narrative of the cultural/creative city is no longer a novelty, but a common characteristic. It has clearly lost the scent of uniqueness that was originally used to promise a competitive advantage for cities (see Landry 2000; Florida 2002). Ironically, the 'commonness' of the script is now part of its appeal for many marginalized cities. It is approached as a guarantee of a certain status at the international stage and reflects on the "belonging to a particular type of global city" (Pang 2012, p. 136). As noted above, the policymakers that guide the 'global city making' process in Shanghai and Hong Kong seem to share the same belief that in order for their city to become (or remain) a 'global city', it must be established as not only the central hub for finance and trade, but also as a cultural and creative city.

Third, it is evident that a globalizing policy model of the cultural/creative city escalates the pace of the inter-urban competition. Although it often leads to a zero-sum game (Harvey 1989), cities cannot escape the somewhat vicious cycle of continuous monitoring, assessment, comparison and at times imitation of their counterparts. In a sense, they all seem to be playing a classical "Simon Says" game, where one inaccurate move or failure to repeat the actions of the leading player leads to an immediate defeat.

Fourth, it is important to acknowledge that the 'cultural turn' in the cities seems to benefit only *selected* cultural groups and organizations. The distribution of funds is unbalanced and correlates with the perceived advantage rather than with the actual need. In order to be recognized as cultural and creative cities, municipal governments throw large amounts of money in the development of 'flagship' cultural and creative industries, cultural landmarks and large-scale events. As several interviewees have suggested, the policymakers in Shanghai and Hong Kong often fail to provide a platform for local artists and smaller-scale cultural initiatives that cannot guarantee international impact or commercial success (see also Lui 2008; Chu 2012; O'Connor 2012; Lee *et al.* 2013). This, in effect, further increases the segregation between larger and more influential cultural groups and those smaller, locally based organizations.

This study only begins to reveal the role of the 'cultural turn' in Shanghai and Hong Kong. Considering that it has focused predominantly on the policymakers' approach to cultural/creative city 'making' as well as the major rationales behind it, further studies are needed to determine the full spectrum of implications of this process, particularly in relation to local citizens and individual artists. Future research could shed some light on this question by examining the perceptions of local artists and/or citizens about the 'cultural turn' in their cities. How do they feel about it? How are they included in and excluded from this process? What opportunities and challenges, if any, does the 'cultural turn' bring to them? Such and similar studies would help to link the context with the actual experience. Overall, it seems that there are more connections than disconnections between the cultural and creative trajectories of Shanghai and Hong Kong. Culture-led urban development has now become a vital part of the brand for both cities. Nevertheless, different adoption patterns and contextualized objectives indicate that this trend is not uniform and cannot be generalized. Therefore, another important task for future research could be to investigate the rationales for the 'cultural turn' in cities in the region. Such studies would help to refine and further elaborate on the findings of this research by providing a more definite view of what being a cultural/creative city in East Asia now really signifies.

Notes

1 In this chapter, the terms 'creative city', 'cultural city', 'cultural and creative city' and 'cultural/ creative city' will be used interchangeably.
2 Although urban entrepreneurialism has originated in the Global North, in the last two decades, it has also been widely adopted in many developing cities across East Asia (see Yeoh 2005; Pratt 2009).
3 Recently, the author himself has also recognized some limitations in his methodology (see Florida *et al.* 2015).

References

Abbas, A., 1997. *Hong Kong: culture and the politics of disappearance*. Minneapolis, MN: University of Minnesota Press.
Abbas, A., 2000. Cosmopolitan de-scriptions: Shanghai and Hong Kong. *Public Culture*, 12 (3), 769–786.
Belfiore, E., 2004. Auditing culture: the subsidised cultural sector in the New Public Management. *International Journal of Cultural Policy*, 10 (2), 183–202.
Bergère, M.C., 1981. 'The other China': Shanghai from 1919 to 1949. *In*: C. Howe, ed. *Shanghai: revolution and development in an Asian metropolis*. Cambridge, UK: Cambridge University Press, 1–34.
Bourdieu, P., 1977. *Outline of a theory of practice*. Cambridge, UK: Cambridge University Press.
Bourdieu, P., 1989. Social space and symbolic power. *Sociological Theory*, 7 (1), 14–25.
BrandHK, 2015a. *Evolution of Brand Hong Kong*. Hong Kong, Hong Kong Special Administrative Region Government. Available from: www.brandhk.gov.hk/en/#/en/about/development/launch. html [Accessed 1 October 2015].
BrandHK, 2015b. *Factsheet: BrandHK*. Hong Kong, Hong Kong Special Administrative Region Government. Available from: www.brandhk.gov.hk/pdf/factSheets/en/14_brandhk.pdf [Accessed 1 October 2015].
Census and Statistics Department, 2013. *The four key industries and other selected industries*. Hong Kong, Hong Kong Special Administrative Region Government. Available from: www.censtatd.gov.hk/hk-stat/sub/sp80.jsp?subjectID=80&tableID=189&ID=0&productType=8 [Accessed 1 October 2015].
Chu, S., 2012. Brand Hong Kong: Asia's World City as method? *In*: K. Chan, ed. *Hybrid Hong Kong*. Oxon: Routledge, 95–107.
Cochrane, A., 2007. *Understanding urban policy: a critical approach*. Oxford: Blackwell Publishing.

Comunian, R., 2011. Rethinking the creative city: the role of complexity, networks and interaction in the urban creative economy. *Urban Studies*, 48 (6), 1157–1179.

Creemers, R., 2015. Never the twain shall meet? Rethinking China's public diplomacy policy. *Chinese Journal of Communication*, 8 (3), 306–322.

Culture and Heritage Commission, 2003. *Culture and Heritage Commission: Policy Recommendation Report*. Hong Kong, Hong Kong Special Administrative Region Government. Available from: www.hkaaa.org.hk/uploads/hkaaa/201209/20120921_184528_6NwFjGItud_f.pdf [Accessed 1 October 2015].

Ding, S., 2007. Digital diaspora and national image building: a new perspective on Chinese diaspora study in the age of China's rise. *Pacific Affairs*, 80 (4), 627–648.

Florida, R., 2002. *The rise of the creative class: and how it's transforming work, leisure, community and everyday life*. New York: Basic Books.

Florida, R., Mellander, C., and Adler, P., 2015. Creativity in the city. *In*: C. Jones, M. Lorenzen and J. Sapsed, eds. *The Oxford handbook of creative industries*. Oxford: Oxford University Press, 96–117.

Fonoroff, P., 1988. A brief history of Hong Kong cinema. *Renditions*, 29/30, 293–308.

Friedman, M., 1981. *Free to choose*. Harmondsworth: Penguin Books.

Friedmann, J., 1986. The world city hypothesis. *Development and Change*, 17 (1), 69–83.

Fu, P., 2003. *Between Shanghai and Hong Kong: the politics of Chinese cinema*. Stanford: Stanford University Press.

Gamble, J., 2003. *Shanghai in transition: changing perspectives and social contours of a Chinese metropolis*. New York: Routledge.

GaWC, 2012. *The world according to GaWC 2012*. Available from: www.lboro.ac.uk/gawc/world2012t.html [Accessed 1 October 2015].

Gibson, C. and Klocker, N., 2004. Academic publishing as 'creative' industry, and recent discourses of 'creative economies': some critical reflections. *Area*, 36 (4), 423–434.

Grodach, C. and Silver, D., eds., 2013. *The politics of urban cultural policy: global perspectives*. Oxon: Routledge.

Gu, X., 2012. The art of re–industrialisation in Shanghai. *Culture Unbound*, 4 (1), 193–211.

Gu, X., 2015. Cultural economy and urban development in Shanghai. *In*: K. Oakley and J. O'Connor, eds. *The Routledge companion to the cultural industries*. New York: Routledge, 246–256.

Harvey, D., 1989. From manageralism to entrepreneurialism: the transformation in urban governance in late capitalism. *Geografiska Annaler*, 71 B (1), 3–17.

Harvey, D., 2005. *A brief history of neoliberalism*. New York: Oxford University Press.

Harvey, D., 2008. The right to the city. *New Left Review*, 53, 23–40.

Hill, R. and Kim, J.W., 2000. Global cities and developmental states: New York, Tokyo and Seoul. *Urban Studies*, 37 (12), 2167–2195.

Hong Kong Special Administrative Region Government (HKSARG), 1998. *The 1998 Policy Address: from adversity to opportunity*. Hong Kong, Hong Kong Special Administrative Region Government. Available from: www.policyaddress.gov.hk/pa98/english/index.htm [Accessed 1 October 2015].

Hong Kong Special Administrative Region Government (HKSARG), 1999. *The 1999 Policy Address. Quality people quality home: positioning Hong Kong for the 21st century*. Hong Kong, Hong Kong Special Administrative Region Government. Available from: www.policyaddress.gov.hk/pa99/eindex.htm [Accessed 1 October 2015].

Hong Kong Special Administrative Region Government (HKSARG), 2007. *The 2007–08 Policy Address: a new direction for Hong Kong*. Hong Kong, Hong Kong Special Administrative Region Government. Available from: www.policyaddress.gov.hk/07-08/eng/docs/policy.pdf [Accessed 1 October 2015].

Hubbard, P., 2006. *City*. London: Routledge.

Kong, L., 2009. Making sustainable creative/cultural space in Shanghai and Singapore. *Geographical Review*, 91 (1), 1–22.

Kong, L., Gibson, C. and Khoo, L., 2006. Knowledges of the creative economy: towards a relational geography of diffusion and adaptation in Asia. *Asia Pacific Viewpoint*, 47 (2), 173–194.

Krätke, S., 2006. 'Global media cities': major nodes of globalizing culture and media industries. *In*: N. Brenner and R. Keil, eds. *The global cities reader*. New York: Routledge, 325–332.

Kurlantzick, J., 2007. *Charm offensive: how China's soft power is transforming the world*. New York: Yale University Press.

Landry, C., 2000. *The creative city: A toolkit for urban innovators*. London: Earthscan.

Landry, C. and Bianchini, F., 1995. *The creative city*. London: Demos.

Landry, C. and Hyams, J., 2012. *The creative city index: measuring the pulse of the city*. Gloucestershire: Comedia.

Lawton, P., Murthy, E. and Redmond, D., 2014. Neoliberalising the city 'creative-class' style. *In:* A. MacLaran and S. Kelly, eds. *Neoliberal urban policy and the transformation of the city: reshaping Dublin.* New York: Palgrave Macmillan, 189–202.

Layne, C., 2009. The waning of U.S. hegemony—myth or reality? A review essay. *International Security,* 34 (1), 147–172.

Lee, E., *et al.,* 2013. *Public policymaking in Hong Kong: civic engagement and state-society relations in a semi-democracy.* Oxon: Routledge.

Lee, K. and Yue, J.W., 2001. A prolegomenon to the study of the role of rhetoric in the garbage-can policy process: the case of Hong Kong's positive non-interventionism. *International Journal of Public Administration,* 24 (9), 887–907.

Leslie, D., 2005. Creative cities? *Geoforum,* 36 (4), 403–405.

Li, M., 2008. China debates soft power. *Chinese Journal of International Politics,* 2 (2), 287–308.

Lui, T., 2008. City-branding without content: Hong Kong's aborted West Kowloon mega-project 1998–2006. *International Development Planning Review,* 3 (30), 215–226.

Luk, H.K., 1991. Chinese culture and the Hong Kong curriculum: heritage and colonialism. *Comparative Education Review,* 35 (4), 650–668.

MacCannell, D., 1973. Staged authenticity: arrangements of social space in tourist settings. *American Journal of Sociology,* 79 (3), 589–603.

Malanga, S., 2004. The curse of the creative class. *City Journal,* 14 (1), 36–45.

Markusen, A., 2006. Urban development and the politics of a creative class: evidence from the study of artists. *Environment and Planning A,* 38 (10), 1921–1940.

McCann, E. and Ward, K., 2010. Relationality/territoriality: toward a conceptualization of cities in the world. *Geoforum,* 41 (2), 175–184.

Mommaas, H., 2009. Spaces of culture and economy: mapping the cultural-creative cluster landscape. *In:* L. Kong and J. O'Connor, eds. *Creative economies, creative cities: Asian-European perspectives,* GeoJournal Library 98. New York: Springer, 45–59.

Ngo, T.W., 1999. Colonialism in Hong Kong revisited. *In:* T.W. Ngo, ed. *Hong Kong's history: State and society under colonial rule.* London: Routledge, 1–12.

Ngok, M., 2007. *Political development in Hong Kong: state, political society, and civil society.* Hong Kong: Hong Kong University Press.

Nye, J., 2004. *Soft power: the means to success in world politics.* New York: Public Affairs.

Nye, J., 2011. *The future of power.* New York: Public Affairs.

O'Connor, J., 2012. Shanghai modern: replaying futures past. *Culture Unbound: Journal of Current Cultural Research,* 4 (1), 15–34.

Ooi, V., 1995. The best cultural policy is no cultural policy: cultural policy in Hong Kong. *Cultural Policy,* 1 (2), 273–287.

Pacione, M., 2009. *Urban geography: a global perspective.* 3rd ed. Oxon: Routledge.

Pang, L., 2012. *Creativity and its discontents: China's creative industries and intellectual property rights offenses.* Durham: Duke University Press.

Peck, J., 2004. Geography and public policy: constructions of neoliberalism. *Progress in Human Geography,* 28 (3), 392–405.

Peck, J., 2005. Struggling with the creative class. *International Journal of Urban and Regional Research,* 29 (4), 740–770.

Peck, J., 2007. Creativity fix. *Fronesis 24.* Available from: www.eurozine.com/articles/2007-06-28-peck-en.html [Accessed 1 October 2015]

Peck, J., 2011a. Geographies of policy: from transfer-diffusion to mobility-mutation. *Progress in Human Geography,* 35 (6), 773–797.

Peck, J., 2011b. Creative moments: working culture, through municipal socialism and neoliberal urbanism. *In:* E. McCann and K. Ward, eds. *Mobile urbanism: cities and policymaking in the global age.* Minneapolis, MN: University of Minnesota Press, 41–71.

Peck, J. and Theodore, N., 2010. Mobilizing policy: models, methods, and mutations. *Geoforum,* 41 (2), 169–174.

Pratt, A.C., 2008. Creative cities: the cultural industries and the creative class. *Geografiska Annaler: Series B, Human Geography,* 90 (2), 107–117.

Pratt, A.C., 2009. Policy transfer and the field of the cultural and creative industries: what can be learned from Europe? *In:* L. Kong and J. O'Connor, eds. *Creative economies, creative cities: Asian-European perspectives.* GeoJournal Library 98. New York: Springer, 9–24.

Prince, R., 2014. Consultants and the global assemblage of culture and creativity. *Transactions of the Institute of British Geographers*, 39 (1), 90–101.

Purcell, M., 2009. Resisting neoliberalization: communicative planning or counter-hegemonic movements? *Planning Theory*, 8 (2), 140–165.

Rabushka, A., 1979. *Hong Kong: a study in economic freedom.* Chicago: Chicago University Press.

Raco, M. and Gilliam, K., 2012. Geographies of abstraction, urban entrepreneurialism, and the production of new cultural spaces: the West Kowloon Cultural District, Hong Kong. *Environment and Planning A*, 44 (6), 1425–1442.

Sassen, S., 2006. *Cities in a world economy.* 3rd ed. Thousand Oaks, CA: Pine Forge Press.

Shanghai Municipal People's Government (SMPG), 1991. *Dibage wunian jihua (1991–1995)* [The eighth five-year plan (1991–1995)]. Shanghai: Shanghai Municipal People's Government. Available from: http://shtong.gov.cn/node2/node2245/node72907/node72913/node72984/index.html [Accessed 1 October 2015].

Shanghai Municipal People's Government (SMPG), 2010. *Shanghai shi renmin zhengfu gongzuo baogao* [Shanghai Municipal People's Government's work report]. Shanghai: Shanghai Municipal People's Government.

Shanghai Municipal People's Government (SMPG), 2011a. *Shanghai shi wenhua chuangyi chanye fazhan 'shierwu' guihua* [The 12th five-year plan for the development of Shanghai's cultural and creative industries]. Shanghai, Shanghai Municipal People's Government. Available from: http://wenku.baidu.com/view/9acf3425192e45361066f5f5.html [Accessed 1 October 2015].

Shanghai Municipal People's Government (SMPG), 2011b. *Shanghai shi guomin jingji he shehui fazhan di shierge wunian guihua gangyao* [An outline of the Shanghai's 12th five-year plan for national economic and social development]. Shanghai: Shanghai Municipal People's Government. Available from: www.shanghai.gov.cn/shanghai/12wgh.pdf [Accessed 1 October 2015].

Song, H., Wong, K. and Chon, K., 2003. Modelling and forecasting the demand for Hong Kong tourism. *International Journal of Hospitality Management*, 22 (4), 435–451.

Wang, J., ed., 2011. *Soft power in China: public diplomacy through communication.* New York: Palgrave Macmillan.

Williams, R., 1984. State culture and beyond. *In:* L. Appignanesi, ed. *Culture and the state.* London: Institute of Contemporary Art, 3–5.

Wong, W.S., 2002. Manhua: the evolution of Hong Kong cartoons and comics. *Journal of Popular Culture*, 35 (4), 25–47.

Wu, F., 2000. The global and local dimensions of a place–making: remaking Shanghai as a world city. *Urban Studies*, 37 (8), 1359–1377.

Yeoh, B., 2005. The global cultural city? Spatial imagineering and politics in the (multi) cultural marketplaces of South–east Asia. *Urban Studies*, 42 (5/6), 945–958.

Yeung, Y., ed., 2002. *New challenges for development and modernization: Hong Kong and the Asia-Pacific region in the new millennium.* Hong Kong: Chinese University Press.

Youngson, A.J., 1982. *Hong Kong: economic growth and policy.* Hong Kong: Oxford University Press.

Zhang, L., 2003. Economic development in Shanghai and the role of the state. *Urban Studies*, 40 (8), 1549–1572.

Zhang, T., 2002. Urban development and a socialist pro-growth coalition in Shanghai. *Urban Affairs Review*, 37 (4), 475–499.

Zou, D., 1996. The open door policy and urban development in China. *Habitat International*, 20 (4), 525–529.

Zukin, S., 1995. *The cultures of cities.* Oxford: Blackwell Publishers.

17

Making cultural work visible in cultural policy

Roberta Comunian and Bridget Conor

Introduction

Cultural work, also referred to as creative labour (McKinlay and Smith 2009), has recently received more attention in academic journals and literature. This is in clear contrast with economic and cultural policy interventions in the last two decades that, while increasingly highlighting the role of culture and creativity in the economy and society, have failed to consider the centrality of cultural work and its practices and specificity (Banks and Hesmondhalgh 2009; Oakley 2013). Taking further the argument of Banks and Hesmondhalgh (2009) that cultural work has been mostly invisible in cultural and social policy, this chapter argues that there have been critical moments in recent years where cultural work has become more visible, contextualised and contested. We use a selection of these moments to highlight the need for a more sustained engagement with what Banks (2007) calls the politics of cultural work. Using these moments, we illustrate that the politics of cultural work become visible when a specific critical point is reached in which questions of its value, sustainability or ethics are raised. Furthermore, we highlight the role of academic engagement and research in this area and its potential impact. This is at the centre of recent UK-based projects focused on key issues in the field of cultural work studies. For example, recent AHRC-funded projects on cultural value and 'improving cultural work' have contributed to an increasing focus on examining inequalities in cultural and creative industries, a hitherto unspoken but pervasive problem in this sector. This kind of research, which seeks to connect academics with policymakers, union representatives, external stakeholders and practitioners, highlights the need to reflect and reconnect research with policy and practice to enable cultural work to become consistently visible and understandable.

In the chapter, we focus on three critical but different moments in the last decade that have made cultural work more visible and have facilitated interventions from policymakers, mass media and academia. First, we consider the emergence of new critical debates around the value of creative education and cultural work that have followed the introduction of full fees for UK students. This event has specially questioned the role of education in the sector as well as how higher education policy interconnects and shapes the future of cultural work (Comunian and Faggian 2014). Second, we consider the implementation of sector-based research and policy. Here we take the case of the recent role played by Creative Skillset in evidencing and implementing policy to promote diversity and gender equality in creative and cultural industries (CCIs). We highlight the importance of data but also the temporality of the actions and concerns around equality as well as how visible issues often return to invisibility (Gill and Pratt 2008). Following our discussion of temporality, we finally take the case of a union-led protest against working conditions of film workers in New Zealand to consider how specific industrial disputes in cultural sectors make the role of unions and workers momentarily visible in the creative and cultural industries (Conor 2015). All three moments make visible the politics of cultural work, the contestations that characterise them – in relation to access and inequality in particular – and the policymaking and legislative practices that shape them. The conclusion highlights other possible bottom-up responses to the invisible nature of creative and cultural work and the absence of it in current cultural policy.

Cultural work: definition, patterns and criticalities

The importance of cultural work is often understated and hidden behind its metonym: cultural and creative industries. However, while the creative and cultural industries are celebrated globally for their contribution to economies and to societies (UNESCO 2013), very little is acknowledged about the role of cultural work within them and/or about the everyday experiences of cultural workers. This is an important contradiction both in qualitative and quantitative terms. In relation to qualifying the importance of cultural work, all the literature (and the very first definition of creative industries in 1998 by the UK's Department of Culture, Media and Sport (DCMS)) points towards the fact that these industries rely heavily (sometimes exclusively) on talent (i.e. on skilled or 'creative' individuals). In relation to quantifying the role of cultural work, it is also widely acknowledged that most of these individuals are sole-traders, freelancers or contractors or are working in the context of small and medium size enterprises – again highlighting that cultural workers and cultural industries are often the same thing (Comunian 2009). Therefore, this chapter first considers the key contradictions that surround cultural work. On the one hand, there is a tendency to celebrate and promote the role of the creative economy and the cultural industries at local, national and international levels, and central to this tendency is the celebratory valuing of these industries via neoliberal milestones of economic growth, exports and 'success' (DCMS 2015a). On the other, we see a growing literature highlighting the unstable careers (Menger 2006), inequalities (Conor, Gill, and Taylor 2015) and fluctuating salaries (Comunian, Faggian, and Li 2010) offered to workers in creative and cultural occupations, suggesting the wider issue of a 'creative under-class' in these same economies (Morgan and Ren 2012).

Many of the issues faced by cultural workers seem to be placed within the pre-existing frameworks and business models of the CCI and their production systems and thus policymakers consider these challenges as endemic to the system and prefer to support its self-regulation.[1] This often leads to further inequalities and forms of exclusion as specific sections of the society are not able to adapt to the most challenging conditions of the sector. For example, the exclusivity of arts education favours the presence of certain classes within the arts and ensures that only the most privileged students can undertake the free or unpaid labour (via internships for example) that is now considered to be 'essential' to securing paid employment in the CCIs (Banks and Oakley 2016). While the working dynamics of the creative and cultural industries favour risk-sharing business models and unstable contract conditions, these are not the only industries that rely heavily on intellectual property and have to manage high levels of risk. For example, the science & technology and pharmaceutical industries operate via similarly high-risk business models. However, what is perhaps unique to work undertaken in the CCIs is that the majority of the weight, risks and costs are individualised, placed on the individual worker, and this is now the modus operandi of these industries. Interestingly, the individualisation of work and the structural imposition of precarity as a business model have been expanding beyond the CCIs and are now reaching other sectors (higher education, for example). Neilson and Coté (2014) confirm the continuous expansion of precarity beyond cultural work, and Ivancheva specifically highlights the increasing pressure of "self-exploitation, impoverishment and insecurity" (p. 40) within academia. Furthermore, with new professions emerging linking the creative economy with higher education, and new external impact agendas, there is also an increasing demand on new researchers to be freelancing or engaging in short-term contracts that lie somewhere between university work and external creative work (Comunian and Gilmore 2015).

In the sections that follow, we focus on three specific and divergent issues that often make work invisible within the CCIs and are particularly related to these dynamics of individualisation and precarity. Part of this invisibility is connected to the individualised nature of cultural work in many industries, but some of it we argue has been created also by a tendency of policy circles, at local, national and international levels, to promote the creative economy as the new answer to economic development without questioning or investigating its inner workings. The first is training and education. There is broader acknowledgement that creative and cultural industries workers are amongst the most highly qualified across a range of sectors; more than half (58.8%) of jobs in the Creative Economy in 2014 were filled by people who had at least a degree or equivalent qualification, compared to 31.8 percent of all UK jobs (DCMS 2015b). However, there is also a recognition that compared with other highly qualified individuals, they do not enjoy the same level of salary and economic stability (Comunian, Faggian and Jewell 2011). It is also important to recognise that cultural workers are often required to invest in continuous training and professional development (which often needs to be self-funded, as they are freelance or employed part time). In respect to training and education, we see a tendency towards it being seen as a personal investment, and in this chapter we question how this has stretched to also include debates within the provision of higher education and its funding models.

The second issue is diversity and access to cultural work. Oakley and O'Brien have recently highlighted what they term "unprecedented media interest in questions of representation and inequality in cultural production" (2015, p. 19). Their examples highlight the preponderance of recent headlines about the lack of gender and minority ethnic representation in the UK and US in, for example, Academy Award nomination lists or art school graduates. This is relatively new and novel, however, because as Conor, Gill and Taylor have also recently written, there has been a distinct *lack* of attention to inequalities in these fields in policymaking and cultural analysis and, as we noted above, this "is particularly striking and dissonant given the prominence attached both to 'creativity' in general, and the CCIs [cultural and creative industries] in particular, in national policies across the world" (2015, p. 1). While the CCIs benefit from a positive image as being open, flexible and anti-hierarchical, it is easy to present supporting evidence of the lack of diversity in the sector, in relation to gender (Conor, Gill, and Taylor 2015) ethnicity (Freeman 2007) and social class (Hesmondhalgh and Baker 2013).

The third is the role of unions and collective action in the field of cultural work. The unionisation of cultural workers such as actors, advertisers or visual effects workers is often viewed as rare, irrelevant or unnecessary in highly individualised, flexible and mobile industries. Unions or guilds are not routinely visible in cultural policymaking and the overall policy agenda, in the UK at least, has become "increasingly linked to educational and employment policy, but under the sign of economics rather than social reform or cultural equity" (Banks and Hesmondhalgh 2009, p. 428). Unions in the CCIs are at the frontlines when it comes limiting the adverse effects of insecure or unsustainable working conditions, and they also face significant challenges in representing their freelance and precarious members. There are crucial and isolated moments at which cultural workers become visible; these are times of disagreement, when collective action by actors, screenwriters or journalists makes cultural workers visible. The final section of our chapter focuses on one particular and highly visible dispute.

Problematising the relationship between higher education and cultural work

Arts degrees become the preserve of the wealthy

The Guardian, 26th September 2010

Don't stifle creativity with more cuts to arts education, say experts

The Guardian, 8th May 2015

As these headlines highlight, one of the debates that has made cultural work visible concerns its relation with creative (higher) education. More specifically, in the last three years – from the introduction of full fees for UK students to attain higher education – concerns have grown about the value of creative education per se and in relation to the opportunities to work in the CCIs. Of course, the introduction of full fees following the Browne Review in 2009 has opened up a debate around the value of education in general across all subjects (Wilkins, Shams and Huisman 2013). However, while most subject areas can demonstrate an economic return on salary for graduates attending those courses (Blundell et al. 2000), arts subjects have struggled to make the same arguments (Comunian, Faggian, and Li 2010). Even more, 40.82 percent of graduates from creative disciplines themselves in the longitudinal Higher Education Statistical Agency (HESA) data collection suggested that "the qualification was 'not required' at all" for their job (Abreu et al. 2012, p. 317). This is not only a short-term outcome but persistent in the long term (three and a half years after graduation). So aspiring creatives might risk investing more than £30,000 in a degree that would result in a job they could have secured without any tertiary degree (Comunian, Faggian, and Jewell 2015).

The literature on the poor economic rewards and unstable careers of cultural workers is extensive. However, only recently has the focus of this debate moved to embracing education, and this is partially in response to these policy changes (Oakley 2007; Banks and Oakley 2016; Comunian, Gilmore and Jacobi 2015). On one side of this debate of course rests a serious concern that higher education should not be only or primarily understood in terms of economic value and that the value of undertaking a university degree in a creative or arts & humanities-based discipline should rest in its cultural value and its ability to develop students into mature members of society with the ability to think critically (Belfiore and Upchurch 2013; O'Brien 2014). However, these arguments have been undermined by the market-driven approach adopted by many higher education institutions as well as by considerations that this kind of education might have become a luxury that only certain sectors of the population might be able to afford (Oakley and O'Brien 2015), as suggested by the first *The Guardian* headline at the opening of this section. Furthermore, it might lead to class-based stratification in the selection of degree courses students are accessing or attracted to (see Born and Devine 2015 for their recent work on music education).

In this brief account of new visibility in the role of education in cultural work, we focus on two key issues. The first is the role of the providers (higher education institutions) and cultural policy in shaping and connecting with opportunities and (existing or non-existing) demand in the sector; the second is about the true value of creative education beyond the creative industries as well as how cultural work could play a broader role in the economy and society.

In the academic literature, the lower economic rewards of cultural work have been strongly linked to issues of oversupply (Towse 2001; Abbing 2002). The same has not been explored by policy and higher education providers. In fact, the main argument explaining a considerable expansion of creative courses in higher education needs to be more focused on a new market-driven and neoliberal approach to education (Comunian, Gilmore and Jacobi 2015). This expansion is undeniable; however, it seems to be led by the demand and attractiveness of these courses to students, rather than by a growth in jobs and employment opportunities. From the early 2000s, HESA (2009) highlights the steady growth of creative subject areas. Between 2003/2004 and 2007/2008 Creative Arts and Design have shown a 14.2 percent increase, while Mass Communication and Documentation has shown a 7.3 percent increase. This compares to an overall growth across all subjects of 4.8 percent. A similar growth seems to extend until 2011 (Table 17.1, from HESA 2015) when there is a sudden drop in enrolment in these subjects (but also overall).

A similar accelerated positive trend seems to characterise staff numbers in these subjects until the fees introduction. Between 2004/2005 and 2011/2012 a Universities UK report highlights that two creative areas exhibited the highest level of expansion in percentage terms across all subjects in Architecture & Planning (+ 29.3%) and Design, Creative & Performing Arts (+ 24.0%) (Universities UK 2013). The same data published late in 2015 (Universities UK 2015) sees the same subjects towards the bottom of the list for growth; between 2012/2013 and 2013/2014, Design, Creative & Performing Arts (+ 8.5%) and Architecture & Planning (+ 2.0%).

We argue that cultural policy – and specifically New Labour's cultural policy agenda (Hesmondhalgh et al. 2015) has played a strong role in making the sector attractive and appealing both to prospective students and to higher education institutions aiming to expand their course offerings. As Heartfield (2005) highlights, many universities have expanded their

Table 17.1 Data extracted from HESA (2015) to highlight specific trends for creative disciplines

First year first degree enrolments by subject area 2007/2008 to 2013/2014

Subject area	2007/8	2008/9	2009/10	2010/11	2011/12	2012/13	2013/14	7 year % change
(E) Mass communications & documentation	13,400	14,360	15,090	14,470	15,550	13,010	14,050	5%
(H) Creative arts & design	46,725	48,490	51,600	50,685	53,775	46,545	48,880	5%
Total	460,240	493,650	518,850	518,280	552,240	495,275	521,990	13%

provision in these fields without questioning the real opportunities available to graduates. Overall, this strategy has promoted the creative industries and creative work as a whole, but in fact the data shows that few of these sectors are able to deliver sustainable career paths and a healthy job market for students graduating in creative disciplines (Comunian, Faggian and Jewell 2011). Furthermore, Buckingham and Jones (2010) critically point out "there is a danger that 'creativity' and 'culture' will come to be seen as magic ingredients that will automatically transform education" (p. 13). Cultural policy has translated, in higher education provision, into a belief that creativity and creative courses would automatically translate to employability and high economic competiveness, under the banner of the greater economic and social contribution of creative activities in our national economy. The introduction of full fees for higher education studies has exposed further issues of access to education for aspiring cultural workers. The introduction of fees has led to the perception that in a market-driven higher education system – where it is important to evidence returns on significant financial investments – arts degrees are not as 'valuable'. This connects also with further issues of the exclusivity of creative careers (O'Brien et al. 2016), which make arts degrees unaffordable for many students. These changes have also led to increased public debate and new advocacy groups – such as Arts Emergency[2] – that argue for the value of arts and humanities education in the face of ongoing funding cuts. However, in opposition to the arguments that led to the introduction of full fees for higher education, there has been limited debate about the 're-payment' problem and its long-term economic sustainability. In the long term, arts degrees might become cross-subsidised if employment opportunities do not grant for the repayment necessary – which seems more likely to happen from science and business courses[3].

Another key issue, connected to the educational infrastructure surrounding cultural work and highlighted by the limited benefit of creative education in relation to employability and salary satisfaction, relates to the ability of both graduates and higher education institutions to articulate the value of creative education beyond the creative industries and its broader role in the economy and society. Alper and Wassall (2006) tend to justify this poor return on investment in higher education by saying that artists are 'risk-takers' in their career choices and are aware that they are trying to maximize their opportunities and earnings in the long term. However, they do point out that the return on investment in education is low and that this does not tend to significantly increase their artistic earnings (but has a positive effect on their non-artistic earnings (Alper and Wassall 2006)). So interestingly while education might not make a difference to an individual's success as an artist, it possibly gives one a better opportunity to engage with other sectors of the economy. If we look beyond the creative industries to gain a broader understanding of the impact of creative knowledge and talent in the economy, it seems clear that creative graduates are undervalued in the labour market, especially when they do *not* enter a creative occupation (Faggian, Comunian and Li 2014; Comunian, Faggian, and Jewell 2015). This raises questions about the value of the education they receive in relation to the overall economy. Specifically, we can articulate two difficulties: first, there is a difficulty for the graduates themselves in articulating the value of their skills and training, possibly because during their education they have not been exposed or asked to think about how their knowledge and skills could apply more broadly across a range of careers and occupations. Second, there is a difficulty in terms of the economy: to place a value (and therefore offer a reasonable salary) on the contribution that creativity and artistic skills can add to a variety of sectors, not just the cultural economy.

Partially, it can be argued that the excessive emphasis of governments on the creative and cultural industries has limited understandings and applications of creativity to a narrow area of economic potential rather than supporting a broader understanding of the creative and cultural dimension of each economic activity (Hartley 2004; Mato 2009). This is partially confirmed by the data on digital graduates, because although there has been great emphasis on the role of digital technologies in cultural and creative industries and their convergence (Deuze 2007), there is little evidence of the embedding of these skills in the broader cultural and creative industries (Comunian, Faggian and Jewell 2015). Higher education institutions have the positions and the leverage to increase the visibility of creative education and cultural work in society more broadly, rather than silo'ing them within a few sectors of the economy; avoiding narrowly defined artistic career pathways would help creative graduates to position themselves more successfully within the wider economy (Oakley 2009). Overall, this section suggests that the strong emphasis on creative and cultural industries rather than on cultural work has contributed to the continued invisibility of cultural work. Recent work from NESTA (Bakhshi and Windsor 2015) highlights how half of creative occupations are now outside the creative industries and despite different 'creative intensity' across sectors, this should be made more visible. The creative skills of graduates in these disciplines are not visible enough in the labour market while the hype surrounding the creative industries has created an 'economic bubble' that has further expanded the provision of those skills without sustainable corresponding opportunities.

Making gender and diversity visible: policy work and interventions

Women successful yet sidelined in film writing and directing
The Guardian, 26th November 2013

UK's creative industries 'must back regional and ethnic diversity'
The Guardian, 24th February 2014

In this second section, we highlight the role of sector-based research and policy in providing evidence, as well as tracking changes, in relation to cultural work. In particular, we take the case of the recent role played by Creative Skillset in evidencing and implementing policy to promote diversity and gender equality in creative and cultural industries. We highlight the importance of data but also the temporality of the actions and concerns around equality; we are concerned here with how 'visible' issues can often return to invisibility (Gill and Pratt 2008).

Every year, the DCMS publishes data on employment in the UK's creative industries. For the past year the growth and success of the creative industries have made headlines as the total employment continues to show growth: "between 1997 and 2013, employment in the Creative Economy has increased from 1.81m jobs to 2.62m jobs. This was equivalent to a rise of 2.3 percent each year, around four times greater than the 0.6 percent increase each year in the number of jobs in the UK Economy" (DCMS 2015b, p. 7). However, in 2015, for the first time the DCMS published data to consider also the role that gender, ethnicity and class play in determining rates of employment, workforce entry and workforce retention in these industries. In relation to gender, the report highlights that women accounted for 36.7 percent of jobs in the Creative Industries (compared with 47.2 percent in the whole UK Economy). In relation to ethnicity, 11.0 percent of the jobs in Creative Industries were undertaken by Black, Asian and minority ethnic (BAME) workers "an increase of 8.0 percent between 2013 and 2014 (34.3% since 2011)" (DCMS 2015b, p. 21). However, in relation to class the 'more advantaged groups' (which usually make up 66 percent of the UK workforce) make up 92.1 percent of occupations in the Creative Industries. This is highlighted as a growing trend as 'more advantaged groups' have benefitted from a 17 percent employment growth since 2011 in the sector, in contrast with a 2 percent growth for the 'less advantaged group' (DCMS 2015b). However, the report does not attempt to link this information and consider how class might intersect with ethnicity and gender. Recent work from O'Brien et al. (2016) does highlight how class plays a role not only in creating barriers to entry in the creative industries but also – for the people who are employed in creative fields – remains a factor connected with lower career achievements and salaries. This is crucial as Oakley and O'Brien (2015) also note that there is hugely varying information about inequality, and some categories of disadvantage are more visible than others. We know quite a bit about gender inequality, something about inequalities of ethnicity and age, but relatively little about inequalities of class, sexuality, disability and region or place. We certainly know that patterns of inequality in relation to gender and ethnicity often replicate from industry to industry. But there are real gaps in our knowledge about how these inequalities intersect in any particular industry and then how these inequalities link up across regional, national or supra-national boundaries.

We discussed above how this also interconnects with the role played here by higher education as the level of entry in these sectors is high and degree qualification is a common trend. The greatly reduced opportunities for entrants from less advantaged or BAME backgrounds to successfully access higher education might be an initial barrier to future employment in the CCIs (Faggian et al. 2013). While in every sector there is a degree of difference across the range of sectors included within the creative industries, we are interested here to highlight some of the policy work and campaigns that particularly focused on the film and television sector to consider their role in making cultural work and its issues more visible.

In relation to the importance of diversity and its analysis, we argue that this increased attention is a result of a previous 'crisis' usefully highlighted in media and policy circles with the publication of the Creative Skillset Labour Force Survey in 2012, which then led to an increased emphasis and policy attention towards the level of diversity in cultural work. We explore this through two specific campaigns and media interventions; one is the Directors UK and BBC partnership "to improve work opportunities for women directors", the other is the establishment of the Creative Diversity Network as an umbrella body to support and monitor diversity in the sector.

In 2013, following and deepening early data provided by Creative Skillset, Directors UK commissioned a report specifically on the presence of women directors in UK screen production. The report highlighted "a worrying decrease in employment for women directors in the most recent two years analysed (i.e. 2011 and 2012), specifically in drama, entertainment and comedy" (2014, p. 2). While this is not only an issue in the UK (Walters 2015), it explored key barriers and dynamics in the sector, which created barriers for women's progression though the industry and more general access to opportunities. Others such as Wreyford (2015) have more recently highlighted the struggle of women in film to reconcile unstable working conditions with motherhood and personal life. Wing-Fai, Gill and Randle (2015) use the term career 'scramblers' to describe the gendered nature of freelancing in the UK film industry. They also highlight the ways in which motherhood is a key theme in sexist discourse in these industries, discourse that ensures that the challenges of juggling parenting or care work with work in this industry are relegated to 'women's problems'. The advocacy of sector associations like Women in Film and Television UK (WFTVUK) as well as policy bodies like Creative Skillset, and the added attention of mainstream media (Criado 2014), has allowed new visibility for these issues. As well as visibility, interventions and support initiatives, a number of career guidance documents have been published such as the *'Why her? Report'* (Skillset and Women in Film and Television UK 2009) investigating key factors that have influenced the careers of successful women working in film and TV – these paved the way for further conversations and possible policy interventions.

Similar to the gender gap recognised in the previous paragraph, Skillset work has also given visibility to the continued lack of BAME cultural workers. The 2012 Skillset Census revealed a steady decline of their contribution from 12,250 in 2009 to 10,300 in 2012 (BAME people represented 7.4 percent of the total workforce in 2006, compared to 6.7 percent in 2009 and 5.4 percent in 2012). Again, the data and report have made an issue secretly acknowledged widely visible. This has triggered further media headlines (Wiseman 2015) and even media patrons to the cause with actor and comedian Lenny Henry (Jackson 2015) taking a leading role. However, the debate and interventions seem to have specifically targeted the media and television sectors, with many key players in this sector contributing to a new umbrella forum called The Creative Diversity Network and a new industry-wide diversity monitoring system (Diamond) being launched in 2016 to facilitate monitoring of diversity across activities and organisations.

However, the same campaign seems to have received less visibility in other areas of cultural work despite an attempt from the Creative Industries Federation (2015) to map initiatives across a range of sectors. The invisibility of diversity is here explored both in current trends and business opportunities but also in relation to barriers and possible facilitators. In particular, and linking across our previous reflection on the role of higher education, access to education for BAME students seems to represent an initial hurdle often too high to overcome (O'Brien 2015).

Union-led protest and collective action in cultural work

> An October 2010 amendment to the New Zealand Employment Relations Act 2000, to exclude from the statutory definition of "employee" all those engaged in film production work, thereby removing employment-based rights and protections.
>
> *(International Labour Organisation 2014, p. 2)*

Following our discussion of inequalities and their visibility or lack of it, in the CCIs, we finally take the specific case of a union-led protest against working conditions of film workers in New Zealand to consider how specific industrial disputes in cultural sectors make the role of unions and workers momentarily visible in the creative and cultural industries (Conor 2015). As the above quote indicates, in a recent 'issues paper' on 'employment relationships in the media and culture industries', the International Labour Organisation highlighted a change to New Zealand employment legislation as one that signalled the increasing erosion of labour rights for cultural workers. This threatened or actual erosion is often visible at moments of crisis: particularly during disputes, strikes or other moments of collective action. A prominent example here would be the 2007–2008 screenwriters' strikes in which the relatively robust US Writers Guilds were able to mobilise their members to strike against producers in a collective action to secure future revenue from digital circulation of their work. Screenwriters are a good example of the individualised freelance cultural workers we discussed above – those who move from project to project and often have no guarantee of long-term job security. But where unions exist and can exercise some power in a particular industry, they ensure that their members can bargain collectively and thus secure minimum pay rates, benefits and due credit for their work. A less prominent and more worrisome example is the one signalled above by the ILO.

To briefly summarise, a dispute developed in New Zealand among New Zealand Actors Equity (NZAE, representing around 400 local actors), the Australian actors' guild (the Media Entertainment and Arts Alliance, MEAA) and the producers of *The Hobbit* films, concerning the use of non-unionised actors in the production. In New Zealand, film workers unions (such as the NZAE or the New Zealand Film and Video Technician's Guild, NZF&VTG) are voluntary organisations who work with two agreements (The Pink and Blue Books) as guidelines for film industry working conditions, both negotiated with the Screen Producers and Directors Association of New Zealand (SPADA), which covers best practice in the engagement of screen cast and crew (SPADA 2016). These best practices cover a range of issues from contracts and residuals to harassment and discrimination. These are guidelines only and not legally binding. Producers can offer their own contracts to engage cast and crew in New Zealand and can incorporate all or none of the Pink and Blue Book recommendations. As Kelly (2011) highlights, there had been ongoing concerns that New Zealand film workers had experienced 'deteriorating' conditions in the industry, with both local and international producers 'reducing conditions' and not complying with various aspects of the Pink and Blue Books.

In October 2010, International Federation of Actors (FIA) issued a 'do not work' order to its members and affiliates because the producers of *The Hobbit* films were offering non-union contracts with no minimum payments and conditions of work. When these New Zealand cultural workers raised concerns about their labour conditions, the producers of the films including the director Peter Jackson refused to offer union contracts and threatened that the production would "go east" (to Eastern Europe) if the dispute was not quickly resolved. Over the proceeding days, New Zealand union representatives met with the producers, but the dispute was also recast in the New Zealand media as a 'boycott', and this led to street protests, both by other local film workers concerned about their job security and members of the public.

The resolution to the dispute came after the widespread vilification of the NZAE and its members.Very quickly, the NZAE and MEAA had reached a resolution, in discussion with the New Zealand Council of Trade Unions (CTU), Warner Brothers, the principal Hollywood financers of the films and New Zealand government ministers. But in the mainstream New Zealand media, writer/producers Fran Walsh and Philippa Boyens characterised the New Zealand creative economy as inherently 'risky' and precarious as a result of the union action (Kelly 2011). In this context, Warner Brothers' executives flew to New Zealand to negotiate a settlement directly with the New Zealand government. Generous tax breaks and forms of marketing subsidisation were offered by the New Zealand government and willingly accepted by Warner Brothers, and these totalled nearly $NZ100 million (McAndrew and Martin Risak 2012, p. 71). But more than simply subsidisation, the agreement detailed 'emergency' overnight changes to New Zealand employment legislation that ensured that New Zealand film workers would never be legally considered employees in this industry in the future. They will always and by default be temporary contract workers. As McAndrew and Risak characterise it, such legislation is "effectively 'immunizing' the New Zealand film industry against union activity and legislated employment regulation" (Ibid., p. 57). But it is also another very interesting example of cultural policymaking (and law-making) used to shore up the model of the individualised and fully 'independent' cultural worker. McAndrew and Risak go on to note in their analysis that this specific legislative change can now be extended to other workers or workplaces in New Zealand, a "textbook example of an effective strategy to keep a workplace, an industry or even a national labour market union-free and unregulated" (Ibid., p. 74).

To connect this very distinctive case to the other critical moments we have presented in this chapter, it is important to highlight that this resolution is arguably an inevitable outcome of trends in cultural policymaking in New Zealand that have consistently side-lined or directly undermined issues of access and equality as they are understood within collective employment rights. This case represents a modest attempt by a small group of cultural workers to bargain collectively in order to secure those employment rights on a high-profile international film production; it was designed to enable exposure and visibility for these workers and their current and future conditions of work. The extreme and remarkable response by the New Zealand government, the further stripping out of those basic rights, also enabled visibility for this cultural work; in this case, it illuminated the lengths to which employment policy and legislation can be pushed in favour of cultural employers and producers as opposed to employees and workers. As Conor (2015) has discussed elsewhere, this case actually represents the latest episode in a long history of the dismantling of collective employment legislation and policy that would otherwise ensure that workers have recourse to voice and representation when it comes to issues such as workplace discrimination.

This is crucial because the New Zealand film industry replicates the patterns of inequality visible in many other cultural industries as we outlined above. In contrast to the UK, however, diversity statistics have not been routinely collected by organisations such as the New Zealand Film Commission although this has very recently changed (see New Zealand Film Commission 2014). Studies from Handy and Rowlands (2014) and Jones and Pringle (2015) have illustrated the 'inequality regime' in which New Zealand film workers operate. But as this case study indicates, cultural policymaking in New Zealand has been entirely geared to workforce 'flexibility', encouraging individually negotiated employment contracts determined by employers as opposed to workers. This sits within a wider policymaking context concerned with securing New Zealand's long-term position as a competitive service provider for international productions. For example, a Screen Advisory Board that was announced in 2014 will consult over issues such as gender equality but will primarily be focused on ensuring "the New Zealand screen sector create the skills and connections to be able to generate their own intellectual property, compete internationally and attract overseas finance" (Joyce and Finlayson 2014). Members of this Board include Peter Jackson and James Cameron, who has announced he will film his next three *Avatar* films in New Zealand (Trevett 2013) with unprecedented tax rebates, another cornerstone of New Zealand's film policy agenda.

After the resolution to *The Hobbit* dispute, a new SPADA/NZAE Individual Performance Agreement was introduced. This is an individual agreement only, to be negotiated between individual workers and producers and as NZAE describes it: "SPADA will be responsible for issuing the Agreements to producers on a production-by-production basis, and Equity New Zealand members will be able to access the Agreements for review" (New Zealand Actors Equity 2014). But the NZAE considers this to be an improvement over the unenforceable Pink Book and they have seen an increase in membership since *The Hobbit* dispute, from 438 members in 2012 to 613 in 2013 to 725 in 2014 (New Zealand Companies House 2016). Thus, this 'bottom-up' action has increased the visibility of the NZAE. The emergency legislative changes have also starkly illuminated the everyday working conditions of New Zealand cultural workers and the lengths to which both international and local producers and policymakers will go to ensure a cultural industry and its workers are framed as 'risk free' and 'open for business'.

Conclusions

In this chapter, we have tried to highlight some key issues surrounding cultural work and its understanding in academic, policy and media literature. We acknowledged the lack of visibility of cultural work within policy as highlighted also by Banks and Hesmondhalgh (2009). We also posed that this invisibility has been a barrier for cultural workers themselves to engage in debates about their working conditions as well as for durable and lasting policy interventions to take place. However, we also presented three very different examples of key critical moments where academic work, policymaking and media coverage have led to broader debates and interventions within this field. We argue that while these critical moments have been useful in framing the issues and making them visible, long-term change will happen only through continuous and sustainable bottom-up responses from cultural workers and their organisations. These responses may be newly influential in terms of policymaking and legislation. Our New Zealand case study above represents an extreme example of top-down legislative change having deleterious effects on cultural workers, but the case also indicates that local cultural workers can very effectively make visible the politics of their work and potentially the inequalities therein. We sketch here some further possible interventions that represent opportunities for cultural work to become more central to the general debates about working conditions and highlight some relevant areas for future research.

First, we would highlight the importance of sustained advocacy campaigns that engage workers – as well as the companies they work for – to critically reflect on access, opportunities and ethical practice. An interesting example of this has been the campaigns run by Carrotworkers' Collective and others (such as Intern Aware) focused on the established practice of unpaid internships in cultural work. These interlinked campaigns have been successful in arguing that alongside making an ethical case for the importance of *paid* labour in the creative and cultural industries, it is important to empower workers – in this case future workers entering the sector – as to the value of their work. The Carrotworkers have published and circulated a 'Counter Internship Guide in London' (Carrotworkers' Collective 2009) for example, and they are now working on curriculum guides for HEI courses in the CCIs. The Arts Council England followed suit, publishing its own guide for internships directed at arts organisations in 2011. Thus advocacy groups are explicitly engaged in a critical dialogue with policymakers as well as higher education practitioners and students in the full-fees era we outlined in section one. They are again focused on raising awareness and increasing the long-term visibility of the other issues we have discussed here: inequalities, exclusions and the potentialities of collective, grassroots action. We would also urge further research in this area, the documenting of grassroots or bottom-up initiatives and disputes (whether successful or not) led by cultural workers. An understanding of how cultural workers can directly effect change in policy and employment legislation will enable us to link up these otherwise disparate and potentially (still) invisible campaigns and actions.

Second and relatedly, we would highlight the importance of platforms and opportunities for cultural workers to come together and 'organise' in traditional and perhaps, new ways. The fragmented, freelance and project-based nature of cultural work seems to be geared towards individualisation and competitive behaviours as much of the CCIs and cultural work literature has documented. However, as the work of de Peuter and Cohen (2015) and their research network Cultural Workers Organise shows, there is evidence of an international emergence of groups, collectives and platforms trying to make visible the political and social insecurities of cultural work. It is crucial that popular and academic research, some of which we have highlighted in this chapter, continues to extend this visibility across industries, regions and places.

Finally, while it is important to make cultural work visible, we think it is also important to make it visible within and across sectors and alongside broader economic trends and issues. This could give rise to further cross-sector alliances, for example on issues of precarity, insecurity and visibility that go well beyond cultural work and have become a feature of our knowledge-driven society (as the International Labour Organisation 2014, has highlighted). If these common issues were addressed but also contextualised it would help unite cultural workers with other workers, for example in education and higher education, as well as in the rapidly expanding service sectors in which precarious, insecure and unequal experiences of employment are also the new norm. In fact, analysing the politics of cultural work across a range of sectors and disciplines is crucial, we believe, to understand, as Ross puts it "how it is that contemporary media, or the so-called creative industries, have emerged as an optimum field for realising the long-standing capitalist dream of stripping labour costs to the bone" (2008, p. 37). This also could open up to new research that tries to map the expansion of these dynamics beyond the cultural sector, for example, with recent literature emerging in relation to precarity in research and academia (Cupples and Pawson 2012; Ivancheva 2015).

Overall, this chapter has made the argument that the invisibility of cultural work should not be justified or accepted as endemic to the nature of the sector and its fragmentation or 'risky' business models. The invisibility of cultural work and its deleterious conditions are desirable and necessary for the continued exploitation of that labour and/or for the ongoing erosion of labour rights in a context of widespread precarity and uncertainty. Cultural labour, whether in film production, the music industry or the art market, is a process fraught with complex mobilities, temporalities and asymmetries. These should be openly discussed, questioned and challenged in order to empower those workers and illuminate those experiences that we do not otherwise see.

Notes

1 It is relevant here to reference David Cameron's speech after his visit to the Silicon Roundabout in East London (Geere 2010) where he highlighted that the government should play a minimal role in the sector by, in his words "giving power away and trusting in the creativity of the British people".
2 For more information visit www.arts-emergency.org/about-us/arts-humanities-matter/ (last accessed 23 March 2016).
3 For more details see McGettigan, A. (2015).

References

Abbing, H. 2002. *Why are artists poor? The exceptional economy of the arts.* Amsterdam: Amsterdam University Press.

Abreu, M.; A. Faggian; R. Comunian; and P. McCann. 2012. "Life is short, art is long": the persistent wage gap between Bohemian and non-Bohemian graduates. *The Annals of Regional Science* 49: 305–321.

Alper, N.O. and G.H. Wassall. 2006. Artists' careers and their labor markets. In *Handbook of the Economics of Art and Culture*, ed. G. Victor and T. David. Amsterdam: Elsevier, 814–864.

Arts Council England. 2011. Internships in the arts: a guide for arts organisations. Available at: www.artscouncil.org.uk/media/uploads/internships_in_the_arts_final.pdf.

Bakhshi, H. and G. Windsor. 2015. *The creative economy and the future of employment.* London: NESTA.

Banks, M. 2007. *The Politics of Cultural Work.* London: Palgrave Macmillan.

Banks, M. and D. Hesmondhalgh. 2009. Looking for work in the creative industries policy. *International Journal of Cultural Policy* 15: 415–430.

Banks, M. and K. Oakley. 2016. The dance goes on forever? Art schools, class and UK higher education. *International Journal of Cultural Policy* 22(1): 41–57.

Belfiore, E. and A. Upchurch. 2013. *Humanities in the twenty-first century: beyond utility and markets.* London: Palgrave Macmillan.

Blundell, R.; L. Dearden; A. Goodman; and H. Reed. 2000. The returns to higher education in Britain: evidence from a British cohort. *The Economic Journal* 110: 82–99.

Born, G. and K. Devine. 2015. Music technology, gender, and class: digitization, educational and social change in Britain. *Twentieth-Century Music* 12: 135–172.

Buckingham, D. and K. Jones. 2010. New Labour's cultural turn: some tension in contemporary educational and cultural policy. *Journal of Education Policy* 16: 1–14.

Carrotworkers' Collective. 2009. Counter Internship Guide. Available at: https://carrotworkers. wordpress.com/counter-internship-guide/.

Comunian, R. 2009. Questioning creative work as driver of economic development: the case of Newcastle-Gateshead. *Creative Industries Journal* 2: 57–71.

Comunian, R. and A. Gilmore. 2015. *Beyond the creative campus: reflections on the evolving relationship between higher education and the creative economy.* London: King's College London. Available at www. creative-campus.org.uk.

Comunian, R. and A. Faggian. 2014. Creative Graduates and Creative Cities: Exploring the Geography of Creative Education in the UK, International Journal of Cultural and Creative Industries 1:2, 18–34.

Comunian, R.; A. Faggian; and S. Jewell. 2011. Winning and losing in the creative industries: an analysis of creative graduates' career opportunities across creative disciplines. *Cultural Trends* 20: 291–308.

Comunian, R.; A. Faggian; and S. Jewell. 2015. Digital technology and creative arts career patterns in the UK creative economy. *Journal of Education and Work* 28: 346–368.

Comunian, R.; A. Faggian; and Q.C. Li. 2010. Unrewarded careers in the creative class: the strange case of bohemian graduates. *Papers in Regional Science* 89: 389–410.

Comunian, R.; A. Gilmore; and S. Jacobi. 2015. Higher education and the creative economy: creative graduates, knowledge transfer and regional impact debates. *Geography Compass* 9: 371–383.

Conor, B. 2015. The Hobbit law: precarity and inequality and market citizenship in cultural production. *Asia Pacific Journal of Cultural and Arts Management* 12: 25–36.

Conor, B.; R. Gill; and S. Taylor. 2015. Gender and creative labour. *The Sociological Review* 63: 1–22.

Creative Industries Federation. 2015. *Creative diversity – the state of diversity in the UK's creative industries and what we can do about it.* London: Creative Industries Federation.

Criado, E. 2014. Women directors in British TV: underrepresented and losing ground. *The Independent,* May 15th, last accessed 23 March 2016 www.independent.co.uk/news/media/fewer-women-directors-than-ever-in-british-tv-9380816.html

Cupples, J. and E. Pawson. 2012. Giving an account of oneself: the PBRF and the neoliberal university. *New Zealand Geographer* 68(1): 14–23.

DCMS. 2015a. *Boom in employment and exports for the UK's creative industries.* London: DCMS.

———. 2015b. *Creative industries economic estimates.* London: DCMS.

de Peuter, G. and S. Cohen. 2015. Emerging labour politics in creative industries. In *The Routledge Companion to the Cultural Industries,* ed. K. Oakley and J. O'Connor, 305–318. New York: Routledge.

Deuze, M. 2007. Convergence culture in the creative industries. *International Journal of Cultural Studies* 10: 243–263.

Directors UK. 2014. *Women directors – who's calling the shots? Women directors in British television production.* London: Directors UK.

Faggian, A.; R. Comunian; S. Jewell; and U. Kelly. 2013. Bohemian graduates in the UK: disciplines and location determinants of creative careers. *Regional Studies* 47(2): 183–200.

Faggian, A.; R. Comunian; and Q.C. Li. 2014. Interregional migration of human creative capital: the case of "Bohemian graduates". *Geoforum* 55: 33–42.

Freeman, A. 2007. *London's creative sector.* London: GLA.

Geere, D. 2010. Transcript: David Cameron sets out Britain's hi-tech future, *Wired* 4 November 2010. Archived at https://decherney.files.wordpress.com/2016/05/2010-11-04-cameron-roundabout-speech.pdf

Gill, R. and A. Pratt. 2008. In the Social Factory? Immaterial labour, precariousness and cultural work, *Theory, Culture and Society* 25: 7–8, 1–30.

Handy, J. and L. Rowlands. 2014. Gendered inequality regimes and labour market disadvantage within the New Zealand film industry. *Women's Studies Journal* 28: 2, 24–38.

Hartley, J. 2004. The 'value chain of meaning' and the new economy. *International Journal of Cultural Studies* 7: 129–141.

Heartfield, J. 2005. *The creativity gap*. London: Blueprint, ETP Ltd.

HESA. 2009. *Press release 141-science and medicine studies see five year growth*. Cheltenham: HESA.

HESA. 2015. *Students in Higher Education 2015/16* Last accessed 14 May 2017 www.hesa.ac.uk/data-and-analysis/publications/students-2015-16

Hesmondhalgh, D. and S. Baker. 2013. *Creative labour: media work in three cultural industries*. London: Routledge.

Hesmondhalgh, D.; M. Nisbett; K. Oakley; and D. Lee. 2015. Were new labour's cultural policies neo-liberal? *International Journal of Cultural Policy* 21: 97–114.

International Labour Organisation. 2014. Employment relationships in the media and culture industries. In *Issues paper for the Global Dialogue Forum on employment relationships in the media and culture sector, 14–15 May*.

Ivancheva, Mariya P. "The age of precarity and the new challenges to the academic profession" 2015. *Studia Universitatis Babes-Bolyai. Studia Europaea* 60(1): 39.

Jackson, J. 2015. Lenny Henry: ringfenced funding is needed to boost diversity in TV (Tuesday 25 August 2015). *The Guardian*.

Jones, D. and J. Pringle. 2015. Unmanageable inequalities: sexism in the film industry. *The Sociological Review* 63: 1, 37–49.

Joyce, S. and C. Finlayson. 2014. Screen Advisory Board announced, Press release last accessed 13 May 2017 www.beehive.govt.nz/release/screen-advisory-board-members-announced

Kelly, H. 2011. 'The Hobbit dispute', 12 April. Scoop News last accessed May 14 2017 www.scoop.co.nz/stories/HL1104/S00081/helen-kelly-the-hobbit-dispute.htm

Mato, D. 2009. All industries are cultural. *Cultural Studies* 23: 70–87.

McAndrew, I. and M. Martin Risak. 2012. Shakedown in the shaky Isles: union bashing in New Zealand. *Labour Studies Journal* 37: 56–80.

McGettigan, A. (2015). The accounting and budgeting of student loans. Higher Education Policy Institute. Report 75. Last accessed 23 March 2016 www.hepi.ac.uk/2015/05/21/accounting-budgeting-student-loans/.

McKinlay, A. and C. Smith. 2009. Creative Labour: working in the creative industries. In *Critical perspectives on work and employment*. Basingstoke: Palgrave MacMillan.

Menger, P.-M. 2006. Artistic labor markets: contingent work, excess supply and occupational risk management. In *Handbook of the economics of art and culture*, ed. V.A. Ginsburgh and D. Throsby, Elsevier: Amsterdam 765–811.

Morgan, G. and X. Ren. 2012. The creative underclass: culture, subculture, and urban renewal. *Journal of Urban Affairs* 34: 127–130.

Neilson, B. and M. Coté. 2014. Introduction: are we all cultural workers now? *Journal of Cultural Economy* 7 (1): 2–11.

New Zealand Actors Equity. 2014. SPADA and Equity New Zealand reach new actors' agreement. Available at: www.actorsequity.org.nz/in-the-news/spada-and-equity-new-zealand-reach-new-actors-agreement.

New Zealand Companies House. 2016. Annual return membership reports' 2012–2014. Available at: www.societies.govt.nz/cms/registered-unions/annual-return-membership-reports.

New Zealand Film Commission. 2014. NZFC feature film development funding information on gender 2009–2014. Available at: www.nzfilm.co.nz/sites/nzfc/files/NZFC_Gender_22-September-2014_website_1.pdf.

Oakley, K. 2007. *Educating for the creative workforce: rethinking arts and education*. ARC Centre of Excellence. Last accessed May 15 2017 www.ampag.com.au/wapap/campaign/2-education-educatingforthecreativeworkforce.pdf

———. 2009. From Bohemian to Britart-art students over 50 years. *Cultural Trends* 18: 281–294.

———. 2013. Absentee workers: representation and participation in the cultural industries. In *Theorizing cultural work*, ed. M. Banks, R. Gill, and S. Taylor, 56–68. London: Routledge.

Oakley, K. and D. O'Brien. 2015. *Cultural value and inequality: a critical literature review*. Swindon: AHRC: Arts & Humanities Research Council.

O'Brien, D. 2014. Cultural value, measurement and policy making. *Arts and Humanities in Higher Education* 14(1): 79–94.

———. 2015. The class problem in British acting: talking at Camden People's Theatre. Last accessed May 15 2017 https://stratificationandculture.wordpress.com/2015/04/27/the-class-problem-in-british-acting-talking-at-camden-peoples-theatre/

O'Brien, D.; Laurison, D.; Miles, A.; and Friedman, S. 2016. Are the creative industries meritocratic? An analysis of the 2014 British Labour Force Survey. *Cultural Trends* 25(2): 116–131.

Ross, A. 2008. The new geography of work: power to the precarious? *Theory, Culture and Society* 25: 31–49.

Sherer, K. 2010. 'The Big Picture' *New Zealand Herald* 3 December Last accessed 23 March 2016 www.nzherald.co.nz/business/news/article.cfm?c_id=3&objectid=10691502

Skillset and Women in Film and Television UK. 2009. Why her? Report: factors that have influenced successful women in Film and TV.

SPADA (Screen Producers and Directors Association New Zealand). 2016. Codes of Practice/Industry Resources. Available at: www.spada.co.nz/resources/codes-of-practiceindustry-resources/.

The New Zealand Herald Editorial. 2010. Price to keep Hobbit in NZ is extortionate. Available at: www.nzherald.co.nz/nz/news/article.cfm?c_id=1&objectid=10683762.

Trevett, C. 2013. 'Three new Avatar films to be made in NZ'. *The New Zealand Herald* 16 December. Available at: www.nzherald.co.nz/entertainment/news/article.cfm?c_id=1501119&objectid=11173287.

Towse, R. 2001. Partly for the money: rewards and incentives to artists. *KYKLOS* 54: 473–490.

UNESCO, U. 2013. Creative Economy Report: widening Local Development Pathways. New York & Paris: United Nations Development Programme (UNDP) and the United Nations Educational, Scientific and Cultural Organization (UNESCO).

Universities UK. 2013. *Patterns and trends in UK higher education 2013*. London: Universities UK.

———. 2015. *Patterns and trends in UK higher education 2015*. London: Universities UK.

Walters, J. 2015. Hollywood sexism is ingrained and should be investigated, ACLU says (Tuesday 12 May 2015). *The Guardian*.

Wilkins, S.; F. Shams; and J. Huisman. 2013. The decision-making and changing behavioural dynamics of potential higher education students: the impacts of increasing tuition fees in England. *Educational Studies* 39: 125–141.

Wing-Fai, L.; R. Gill; and K. Randle. 2015. Getting in, getting on, getting out? Women as career scramblers in the UK film and television industries. *The Sociological Review* 63: 50–65.

Wiseman, A. 2015. BBC Films boss: diversity increasingly on our agenda (26 March 2015). *Screen Daily*.

Wreyford, N. 2015. The real cost of childcare: motherhood and flexible creative labour in the UK film industry-review essay. *Studies in the Maternal* 5: 1–22.

18

Fringe to famous

Enabling and popularising cultural innovation in Australia

Mark Gibson, Tony Moore and Maura Edmond

Introduction

If there is any general question that cuts across different national contexts for the development of cultural policy it is the appropriate relation between government and commercial cultural industries. This question has guided most comparative work in cultural policy studies, allowing us, for example, to compare 'American' models of film production, broadcasting or the visual arts and 'European' models, with their stronger emphasis on active government involvement and state patronage. It also often provides the framework for historical analysis, such as the voluminous work on the implications for cultural policy of 'neoliberalism' or the relative withdrawal of government as an active player in the cultural domain, in many countries over the past 30 years.

In this chapter, we take a position on this question in the Australian context. We argue in general terms for a recognition of the essential role that commercial processes and models can play in cultural development while refusing suggestions that commerce and culture will always be harmoniously aligned. This may appear an unremarkable position to take, perhaps even so obvious that it hardly needs an elaborate defence. As we will outline, however, there has been a sharp polarisation in Australia in recent years between 'pro-' and 'anti-' market positions in relation to culture, which has made the moderate or 'compromise' position sometimes difficult to sustain. This situation is not entirely representative of longer-term patterns in Australia, which can be seen in international terms as something of a model for mixed approaches to cultural policy – giving considerable ground to commercial models while also seeing a place for countervailing forces. The best-known example is probably the 'hybrid' television system developed, between the 1950s and 1970s, pragmatically combining many of the best aspects of American and European broadcasting systems of the latter half of the twentieth century. However, some work is now required to recover this tradition.

There may be a particular tendency to polarisation in Australian work on culture, policy and economy. The debates occasioned over the last decade by the emergence of a strong pro-commercial position on culture have certain echoes, in form if not in content, of a debate during the 1990s around the so-called 'policy' position in Australian cultural studies – and indeed some of the protagonists have been the same. Then, as now, the provocations taken in these debates have often been seen internationally as somewhat extreme, distilling tendencies found elsewhere only in more qualified forms (Jameson 1993; McGuigan 2004). There is, however, some value in the chiaroscuro quality of Australian debates. They have produced abstract diagrams that can be used to clarify stakes that are otherwise difficult to discern. They have their closest relation internationally with debates in the United Kingdom, but can also be translated to many other contexts.

Fringe to Famous

The reflections in the chapter emerge more specifically from a three-year research project, 'Fringe to Famous', examining the conditions in Australia for crossover of fringe, independent and *avant garde* cultural production and mainstream cultural industries. The project started from the observation of a long tradition of circulation between small-scale experimental initiatives in art and culture and the mainstream publishing, design, film, broadcasting industries, as well as other cultural industries. This exchange between what Pierre Bourdieu (1996) called the markets of 'limited' and 'extensive' production has been particularly fertile since the 1980s and has been an important factor in cultural development and the growth of Australian cultural industries. The key research questions of the project have been: What are the factors that have facilitated or inhibited crossover of fringe/independent/ alternative arts practice and mainstream cultural industries in Australia since the 1980s? What are the policy settings that might affect such crossover? Understanding this process allows us to ask questions of government interventions – how has government assisted in (or hindered) the crossover between alternative and mainstream cultural production in this context?

The project is centred on five case histories covering: the evolution of Australian independent music scenes; the transformation of iconic local surfwear label Mambo into a successful consumer brand; the establishment of a lucrative, aesthetically playful and internationally oriented 'indie' gaming sector in Melbourne; the rise (and recent fall) of global short film franchise Tropfest; and the significance of independent production companies for Australian television comedy. The case histories have been developed through a combination of archival research and interviews with creative practitioners, cultural businesses, media entrepreneurs, curators, journalists, policy-makers and institutional management. The research is still in its mid-stages, so the following chapter reports on some of the findings emerging from the initial round of interviews, focusing in particular on the example of innovation in Australian television comedy.

'Fringe to Famous' has been concerned both with cultural and economic development. Most of the examples considered in the case histories have made substantial contributions to Australian cultural life. In the area of music, Nick Cave and Paul Kelly are generally considered to be among the most important figures to have arisen from contemporary Australian music over the last 30 years. A more recent generation of musicians to emerge from Australia's cultural fringes – Tame Impala, Royal Headache, Courtney Barnett – have had enthusiastic critical reception at home and abroad. The artists who designed for surfwear label Mambo gave a distinctive expression to a certain surreal eschatology to be found in Australian suburbia. The 'indie' computer game *Antichamber* – developed in Melbourne by a local digital media student – was celebrated for its complex and compelling gameplay and dubbed a 'first-person Escher' by reviewers. The television comedy producers who are discussed in more detail later in the chapter – Steve Vizard, Paul Fenech, Mark Conway and Mike Nayna – reflect and satirise diverse aspects of contemporary Australian life.

But at the same time, these examples have contributed to the development of important cultural *industries*. Despite the well-documented decline in total sales of recorded music, the dollar value of wholesale sales from recorded music in Australia in 2014 was still over AUD$317 million (ARIA 2014). Meanwhile ticket sales for live performances of contemporary music are growing, with total revenue estimated at over AUD$628 million (ACA 2014). The combined total is not far short of AUD$1 billion – not at the level perhaps of iron ore (AUD$66.7 billion – Reuters 2013), which was, until recently, at stratospheric heights as a result of the boom in infrastructure development in China, but certainly in the same league as other major Australian industries such as wheat (AUD$4.8 billion), wool (AUD$1.9 billion) or cotton (AUD$754 million) (all figures ABS 2012).

The other case studies offer their own examples of economic value. The video-game *Antichamber* became a global best-seller, achieving more than a 100,000 sales in its first two months on the specialist online store Steam (McElroy 2013). The game currently retails for USD$19.95, putting a 'back of the envelope' total retail figure for the game at nearly USD$2 million, after just two months of sales. For all its surreal designs and tongue-in-cheek company branding, Mambo Graphics also has an important business dimension. Following the 2000 Sydney Olympics, where Mambo was the official designer of the Australian team's outfits, the company was sold by its founders for over AUD$20 million (Carson 2008). Tropfest was both a screen industry institution and, for a long time, a highly successful generator of economic value and a significant player in what Mark Shiel and Tony Fitzmaurice (2008) have called the 'international film festival economy'. In a confidential audit done on behalf of Steve Vizard's production house Artist Services in 1994, it was estimated that the company's successful comedy television programs had generated tens of millions in advertising revenue for the Seven Network. Vizard later sold the company in 2000 for AUD$25 million (Bedwell 2007, p. 261).

How then should we understand the relation between culture and economy? One of the starting points for 'Fringe to Famous' was a frustration with a continuing tendency to dismiss the movement from the 'fringe' or 'independent' to the 'mainstream' or 'commercial' as 'selling out', 'appropriation' or 'watering down' of artistic integrity. Since the outset, we have been interested in the much more complex lived experience of creative practitioners transitioning between the two production markets. In finding support for this perspective, the project has drawn on work over the past decade, both in Australia and internationally, that has focused attention on productive links between cultural and economic development (Caves 2000; Hartley 2005; Cunningham 2006; Howkins 2007; Anderson and Oakley 2008; Flew 2012). This emphasis departs from more established approaches to cultural policy that have tended to see cultural and economic value as divergent, such that attention to one will generally be at the expense of the other. The Australian work of David Throsby is a good example here. Throsby (2001, 2006, 2010) has been a pioneer in reviving the field of cultural economics, and his work is remarkable in attempting to bridge economic and cultural analysis. His perspective, however, is generally 'preservationist', calling on governments to resist or moderate the influence of markets to ensure the maintenance of cultural value.

Throsby's argument is not a naïve one. He is by no means a simple opponent of the global expansion of capitalist market relations: 'There is no doubt that [this expansion] has brought enormous benefits to many, in terms of improved consumption choices, employment prospects, lifestyle patterns and so on' (Throsby 2001, p. 156). Throsby also accepts that there are areas of culture that could be seen as provided for by the market: there is a profit-making domain in supply of the arts, which 'embraces popular entertainments and cultural forms where demand is strong' (2001, p. 116). It is nevertheless clear that the function of cultural policy, for Throsby, is to offer a countervailing influence to the dominance of economic priorities in government decision-making. This means that his focus remains very much on the subsidised arts. The profit-making areas of the cultural industries fall outside his policy vision. They are classified as 'media and entertainment' and implicitly distinguished from culture proper.

Beyond preservationism

The starting point for 'Fringe to Famous', by contrast, was an interest in areas of consistency or complementarity between commerce and culture. An important point of reference for the project has been the perspectives that emerged from a particular moment in cultural studies and cultural policy in Britain in the 1980s. A major influence on the project has been Simon Frith and Howard Horne's (1987) classic *Art into Pop* on the role of art schools in the explosion of popular music styles in Britain from the 1960s. Frith and Horne's study exemplifies the open and reflective representation of the relation between culture and the market to be found in the best work of the period. It shows a depth of appreciation for the cultural qualities of the art and popular music that emerged in the 1960s, 1970s and 1980s, from the pop art of Richard Hamilton to the Sex Pistols and David Bowie. The culture is viewed as having important things to say about image, identity and style, youth, sex, capital, institutions and organisations – as much more, in short, than a simple economic commodity. At the same time, Frith and Horne are sensitive to the ways in which much of this culture was born on the currents of capitalist market relations. It had a fluidity and dynamism that would not have been possible within state-funded institutions and to which policy programmes merely of 'preserving' culture would not be attuned.

The approach can be seen as carrying forward the tradition of work in cultural studies of taking seriously, as culture, the products of commercial media and entertainment systems. In its original formation in Britain in the 1960s and 1970s, this tradition developed as a counterpoint to the then dominant form of cultural preservationism in Leavisite literary criticism. The Leavisites were trenchantly opposed, in particular, to popular commercial fiction, which they saw as offering cheap 'compensations' and 'distractions' luring all but a committed minority from the 'great tradition' of serious English literature (Leavis and Thompson 1933; Leavis 1939). British cultural studies reacted first against the elitism of this perspective, drawing attention to the patterns and structures that gave meaning to the everyday lives of ordinary people, particularly the working class (Hoggart 1957; Williams 1958). But as the field developed, it increasingly found cultural value not only in 'folk' traditions and everyday life, but also in popular media and commercial cultural forms that were expanding rapidly in the latter half of the twentieth century (Hall and Whannel 1964; Fiske and Hartley 1978; Hebdige 1979).

The clearest expression of this perspective at a policy level was the cultural industries policy of the Greater London Council in the mid-1980s. The key aspect of this policy, and the reason for its subsequent influence, was its attempt to embrace the commercial cultural industries – the sector produced the culture that the majority of the population actually consumed (Bianchini 1987; Garnham 2005; O'Connor 2009). It was not that it was *opposed* to the more established models of the subsidised arts; it was rather that it attempted to break down the boundaries between state-funded and commercial culture, seeing them both, together, as part of a complex ecology of cultural provision. It is a sad irony that the policy was never in fact implemented, as the GLC was disbanded by the Thatcher government in 1986, but it left a substantial legacy nonetheless, with a number of its ideas being taken up in other local governments in the United Kingdom and eventually in national policies, both within the country and abroad.

Australia has a parallel history around these questions, one that is by no means simply derivative. The first national cultural policy fully to embrace the commercial sector was in fact in Australia. While the most *influential* example has been the Creative Industries initiative of the Blair government in Britain in the late 1990s (DCMS 1998), the latter was preceded by Creative Nation, launched by the Keating government in 1994:

> This cultural policy is also an economic policy. ... Culture adds value. ... It is a valuable export in itself and an essential accompaniment to export and other commodities. It attracts tourists and students. It is essential to our economic success.
>
> *(DCA 1994, p. 7)*

More recently, this approach interweaving cultural and economic value was updated for the digital age in Creative Australia, the national cultural policy of the Gillard Federal Labor Government unveiled in 2013 just before it lost office. On the one hand the policy explicitly recognised, 'our culture defines us and we're unique in the richness of our Australian identity'; on the other, we should also recognise an economic dividend: 'A creative nation is a productive nation' (Crean 2013). Australia has also had its own cultural studies tradition, giving serious attention to the cultural significance of popular commercial forms (see for example, Fiske et al. 1987; Morris 1988; Martin 1994; Wark 1998). In both policy and cultural studies, there has been a complex series of exchanges between Australian and British developments. There are resources in both for a cultural policy framework sympathetic to commercial culture and moving beyond the perspective of cultural preservation or conservation.

The conception for 'Fringe to Famous' came initially from work by Moore (2012) on the history of Australian bohemian traditions. Drawing inspiration from the British work of Frith and Horne, but also on lessons from Australian cultural history, Moore draws attention to numerous points of intersection between cultural development in Australia and the development of commercial cultural industries. The case is made particularly in relation to the 1960s and 1970s. Many of the major figures to emerge during this period in experimental work in avant-garde theatre, satire, literature and underground film were profoundly influenced by mass media forms such as Hollywood film noir, gangster and western movies, television and of course rock 'n' roll – not just as a negative 'other' to be resisted, but as a positive creative inspiration. They also fed back into these forms in their creative practice, moving between more esoteric work for small audiences or readerships and roles as journalists, publishers, television broadcasters, filmmakers, advertisers and music industry entrepreneurs.

A further input into these arguments has been the work of Pierre Bourdieu, – not so much his analysis of taste in *Distinction* as his sociology of literary and artistic production in *The Rules of Art* (1996) and *The Field of Cultural Production* (1993). 'Fringe to Famous' takes from Bourdieu a scepticism about claims for the 'autonomy' of art from surrounding fields of material interests. It is not that such claims should be entirely dismissed: writers, artists and other cultural producers often make sacrifices, taking risks and foregoing immediate and obvious material rewards for their art. It is rather that the relation between artistic autonomy and art is a dynamic one. Autonomy, once achieved, acquires a material value. Precisely at the point where it appears to transcend the ordinary sphere of material relations it becomes an object of desire and is drawn into the sphere of economic calculation. This means that any attempt to 'preserve' culture from the market is inherently paradoxical. The attempt itself can often serve only to promote its market value.

Australian culture as an innovation system?

If this sets a general background, 'Fringe to Famous' has also been formed by an encounter with a more rigorous and theorised account of the relation between culture and economics around the idea of 'innovation systems'. The main proponents of this in Australia have been associated with the Centre of Excellence for Creative Industries and Innovation (CCI), which was funded by the Australian Research Council from 2005–2013 and centred at the Queensland University of Technology (Cunningham 2006; Hartley 2008; Potts 2008, 2011). In its early development, many believed the CCI was only taking forward the general trajectory of a cultural policy 'beyond preservationism', which we have sketched above. It was also quite catholic in reach, involving a range of figures who had been part of the broad histories of cultural studies and 'post GLC' policy development. Significant examples here included Kate Oakley, Graeme Turner and Justin O'Connor. In the later phase of the CCI, however, it developed a sharper, more refined, theoretical position. This has been highly controversial and has seen a significant breakdown of an earlier consensus on general directions for progressive cultural policy.

At the centre of this development has been the adoption of Schumpeterian economics and a reframing of creative industries around its capacity or otherwise to contribute economically through 'innovation'. This has opened up interesting lines of dialogue with management and economic theory on processes of industrial development, particularly around the ideas of 'open' or 'distributed' innovation (Chesborough 2003; von Hippel 2009). As the CCI authors have pointed out, there are a number of ways in which cultural or creative industries might be seen as exemplifying conditions that increasingly affect all areas of industrial production – the difficulty of maintaining proprietary control over intellectual inputs to innovation; the role of consumers in the creation of value; the volatile 'network' character of the field in which regimes of value are disrupted by high levels of feedback. This opens a heady prospect for the creative industries not only of gaining a place at the table of industry and economic policy, but of *leading* the conversations that might occur there.

There have also been costs, however, and the innovation systems perspective has attracted substantial criticism (see for example, Miller 2004; Oakley 2009; O'Connor 2009; Turner 2011). It has been more radically and uncompromisingly opposed to the preservationist assumptions of traditional approaches to cultural policy than the earlier departures from these assumptions sketched above. A future-facing, market-oriented approach is no longer proposed merely as a *complement* to established policy positions such as those represented by David Throsby. It appears rather as a comprehensive framework in which alternative approaches are systematically displaced. Value within the framework is associated, following Schumpeter, with disruption and change, so that the 'heritage' aspect of culture comes to be seen as merely residual, contributing to the present only as 'infrastructure'. More importantly, the framework appears to cede the possibility of a discourse around cultural value, as distinct from economic value, of the kind that can be found in older work in cultural studies such as Frith and Horne. As Justin O'Connor (2009, p. 389) has argued, the model is one of a seamless integration of the market and culture: the two converge as a single complex mechanism for generating novelty and economic growth.

Our response in 'Fringe to Famous' to the innovation systems perspective has been frankly conflicted. If approached in a piecemeal fashion, it can be appreciated as generating some interesting and productive ways of deepening an analysis of the economic dimensions of culture. A notable example is the attention it has brought to the role of audiences, readers or consumers in processes of creative development. In each of the case studies for the project, this appears from our initial research to have been an important factor: small, dedicated followings, in particular, have played a significant role in providing feedback and contributing to the growth of creative concepts or ideas. This is one area where the model of 'social network markets' is an illuminating one in understanding the dynamics of contemporary culture.

The provocative, activist character of the innovations systems perspective also holds some attractions in disrupting tired or complacent assumptions, which often take form around a view of culture merely as something to be preserved. It is relevant, for example, to our engagement in 'Fringe to Famous' with Australia's public service broadcaster, the Australian Broadcasting Commission (ABC). Our starting position in relation to the organisation is sympathetic: we believe from long observation – and indeed, for one of the project team, from a previous career within the organisation – that it has often played a fundamental role in nurturing emerging talent and allowing it to find broader audiences. We are critical, however, of a frequent tendency – exemplified, for example, by the citizen's lobby, *Friends of the ABC* – to adopt a reactive position in which market-based processes are simply cast as the enemy. Some of the most important and adventurous programming by the ABC over the last 20 years has resulted from the organisation's embrace of a complex hybrid economy, including the outsourcing of production, co-productions and other forms of partnership with commercial players, especially small scale emerging cultural cottage startups that form around artists and projects.

It is difficult, however, to disagree with critics of the innovation systems perspective about the costs of following it systematically to its logical conclusions. Kate Oakley (2009, p. 413) lists these costs acerbically as 'a thin notion of cultural value, declining cultural sectors and a crude version of innovation, which conflates it with novelty.' 'As such', she argues, 'it seems a fairly high price'. The members of the project team have all had long investments in cultural creation and/or appreciation and are not about to renounce aesthetic discourses for a purely economic point of view. One has been a long-time director of an art museum, another has been a television program-maker and all have had a longstanding interest in the specifically cultural qualities to be found in music, art, film, television, literature and other media.

Going to the empirical

'Fringe to Famous' might best be described, therefore, as adopting a 'soft' innovation perspective. There is, admittedly, a pragmatic aspect to our approach. 'Innovation' is a term that currently opens doors with government, enabling advocates for culture and the arts at least to get a hearing. In Australia's case, the Federal Government conceives of its research and development program as developing a 'National Innovation System'. Similarly, Prime Minister Malcolm Turnbull made his vision for an innovative Australia an essential part of his pitch for leadership of the Liberal Party.

In his first press conference after a successful leadership challenge in September 2015, Turnbull stressed, "The Australia of the future has to be a nation that is agile, that is innovative, that is creative" (Turnbull 2015). These are terms that provide opportunities for the cultural sector. As Tom O'Regan pointed out in the course of an earlier debate over directions for cultural policy in Australia, policy frameworks are always in part rhetorical. While their authors may imagine them to have pure origins, such purity is rarely maintained at the level of implementation. It is not necessary to use the language of innovation to subscribe to a fully theorised position from which it may appear to be authorised. This is not to say that 'Fringe to Famous' is merely cynical in its use of this language. The project is serious in attempting to identify areas of innovation, in an ordinary sense of the word, in Australia's cultural and media systems.

From the perspective of the project, the recent polarisation around creative industries and innovation systems theory has been unfortunate. The general program of seeking to understand and support cultural development in hybrid commercial and state-funded systems remains, in our view, as important now as when it emerged in the 1980s. But it is a program that has become increasingly difficult to sustain. On one side of the argument over creative industries and innovation, the innovation systems perspective has become increasingly abstract, theoretical and focused on arguments at the level of high economic policy, losing touch with the lived circumstances of cultural practitioners and organisations. Its proponents have sometimes voiced frustration that their efforts are not more appreciated. As Stuart Cunningham (2008, p. 3) has lamented, those in the cultural sphere have been their 'own worst enemy in many ways', showing little interest in the innovation agenda and foregoing the opportunity to make claims over resources available for R&D. As Cunningham wistfully remarks, it is as if they existed in 'parallel universes'.

On the other side of the argument, there has been a significant loss of the earlier hard-won openness to commercial processes in the cultural domain. In seeking to puncture the blithe optimism of the 'win win' proposition of the innovation systems perspective – in which, as Jason Potts (2011, p. 21) puts it, 'culture and economy co-evolve' – the critics have been driven to produce evidence of contradiction and divergence. A good example is the theme of 'precarity' of employment in the cultural and creative industries – the reality for many artists and cultural practitioners of exploitation, stress, overwork and financial insecurity (see for example, Hesmondhalgh and Baker 2001; Murray and Gollmitzer 2012). The literature that has developed around this theme has certainly succeeded in highlighting negative aspects of employment conditions in the cultural, media and communication fields. There is also a serious purpose in documenting these aspects in highlighting the exploitation of cultural workers and promoting policies to foster greater equality (Hesmondhalgh et al. 2015; McRobbie 2015; Oakley and O'Brien 2016). But it sometimes seems that the motivation is to rain on the parade of the innovation systems boosters and cheerleaders (as they would be seen by the critics).

From the perspective of the earlier, more nuanced, work on the commercial infrastructure for popular culture, the basic proposition in the literature on precarity would have been taken for granted. Most of those involved in developing this work had backgrounds in Marxism and socialist politics; the idea that there is much about employment relations under capitalism that is less than perfect would have appeared as obvious. However, the object in view for Frith and Horne, for the architects of the cultural industries policy in the Greater London Council, for many of those involved in cultural studies and in progressive cultural policy in the 1980s and 1990s, was larger than simply critique. It was to understand the ways in which cultural forms – or more particularly cultural forms that *matter* – can emerge and develop within complex market-oriented economies and to find ways to support them. Many would have preferred *not* to have found that commercial processes were an important medium for culture, but restrained their critical reflexes in recognition of the reality. It is this openness that risks being lost in the recent critical turn in debates around the relation between economics and culture. And it is this openness and complexity to which we seek to return by 'going to the empirical', the early results of which are recounted below.

The research team has so far conducted more than 50 in-depth interviews with leading Australian creative practitioners, cultural entrepreneurs, cultural policy-makers, commissioning editors, content producers and institutional staff. What we have discovered so far is a diversity of attitudes and approaches to the relationship between economic forces and cultural ones. Few of the interviewees occupy positions as polarised or entrenched as those expressed by recent scholarship on creative industries and innovation systems. Instead, the interviewees share an active and often self-conscious negotiation of market conditions, even while many remain deeply wary, cynical or critical of the possible impacts of commercial processes on creative work.

In this final section of the chapter, we focus on the emerging findings from the case history on Australian television comedy, highlighting in particular the work of Steve Vizard, Paul Fenech, Mark Conway and Mike Nayna. Spanning a period from the late 1980s to 2015, these comedians reflect a variety of approaches to Australian comedy, each in his own way responsible for ushering in culturally significant 'soft innovations' in the format of screen satire. They also reflect a diversity of approaches to the value of commercial processes and 'mainstreaming', from Vizard's enthusiastic embrace of the challenge of 'smuggling' progressive content into the living rooms of everyday Australians to Fenech's much more pragmatic, yet overtly transgressive sensibility in which fast, guerrilla filmmaking is a financial decision put to aesthetic and comedic ends.

Like all the interviewees in the project, the examples discussed here began in the market of limited production: Vizard in university revues and Melbourne's theatre restaurants; Fenech via entries in Sydney's then small-scale Tropicana Short Film Festival, while working as a jobbing trainee in the Indigenous Unit of the ABC; and Fancy Boy working in Melbourne's live comedy performance rooms. The project's focus has been on cultural producers who have crossed over from small-scale to popular markets, or are on the cusp of doing so – and in this sense has looked mainly at those who might be seen as 'successful'. This is not to minimise the difficulties of many in making a living in the fringe. Indeed, most of our interviewees have experienced significant setbacks at various stages in their careers and empathise strongly with those who have struggled to establish and maintain their careers. But this is tempered by a sense of the opportunities that have been made available for cultural practitioners at different times, such as outreach and encouragement of experimentation by mainstream public and commercial broadcasters, or potential for audience reach afforded by online digital platforms. Unless otherwise stated, all quotes are taken from the transcripts of 'Fringe to Famous' research interviews conducted in 2014 and 2015.

Steve Vizard – smuggling the avant garde into the mainstream

Steve Vizard was a successful IP and patents lawyer by trade but began his comedy career performing while an undergraduate in university student revues and later working Melbourne's inner city cabaret venues in the late 1970s and early 1980s, before transitioning to television sketch comedy. He is best known for the shows he produced (and often wrote for and starred in) for the commercial Channel Seven network during the late 1980s and 1990s. Australia's free to air television landscape consists of three commercial networks, and public broadcasters the ABC and the multicultural Special Broadcasting Service. In 1988 Vizard was commissioned by Channel Seven to come up with competition to *The Comedy Company*, a character-driven sketch show skewering the Australian suburbs, which was a huge ratings success for Channel 10 and had made stars out of many of Vizard's fellow Melbourne comedy circuit colleagues.

The result was *Fast Forward*, a fast-paced sketch comedy that tackled contemporary media, lampooning not just local media personalities and the media profiles of Australian politicians, but also the structure, formats and consumer habits associated with 1980s television (most memorably in the show's use of channel surfing, abrupt changes, fast-forwarding and re-winding). Initial reviews were positive, often pointing out that *Fast Forward* seemed like the first Australian television comedy show that was not carrying over old approaches from theatre or stand-up; it was made entirely for television and by a generation raised on televi-sion, re-inventing sketch comedy around what Raymond Williams discerned as the inherent 'flow' of the medium. The ratings for *Fast Forward* started solidly and grew impressively over the first season's eight-week run, and its popularity helped to launch the careers of Australian comedians such as Magda Szubanski, Gina Riley and Jane Turner (of *Kath and Kim* fame), colleagues of Vizard from student revue and the inner-city comedy fringe.

On the back of the success of *Fast Forward*, Channel Seven offered Steve Vizard a lucra-tive role hosting and producing *Tonight Live*, a David Letterman-style late-night variety show. Steve Vizard and Andrew Knight's company, Artist Services, became one of the largest production houses in Australia and went on to develop *Full Frontal,* which helped advance the careers of its stars Eric Bana, Shaun Micallef and Kitty Flanagan. It also pro-duced successful television shows like *SeaChange* and *Big Girl's Blouse* and later experimen-tal content for the Comedy Channel on subscription television (introduced in 1995) and feature drama films.

As mentioned briefly in the opening paragraphs of this chapter, there is also an import-ant economic dimension to Vizard's oeuvre. The initial comedy and variety programs, *Fast Forward, Tonight Live, Full Frontal,* were some of the highest rating comedy television shows in the history of Australian TV. In 1994, Artist Services hired a media analyst to estimate the value of the shows they were producing for the Seven Network. According to those reports, in 1989 through 1994 the advertising revenue created for Seven Network by Artist Services programs *Fast Forward* and *Tonight Live* was quoted at "between approximately $130 million and $140 million over a five year period, yielding a surplus to the network of between $65 million and $75 million" (Bedwell 2007, p. 173). Steve Vizard later sold the company to British production house Granada in 2000 for AUD$25 million (Bedwell 2007, p. 261).

For Vizard, there is little contradiction between culture and commerce. All artists, whether they are aware of it or not, are engaged, in his view, in negotiating both creative and business decisions. As he put it in the interview for 'Fringe to Famous', "I don't understand what it is that people are talking about when they say, 'I'm doing art' – 'I'm only doing art'... We talk about art and commerce – it's convenient – but actually you're talking about art and life, and commerce – money – is just a part of life". Art and commerce are inseparable, and so for Vizard the real measure of creative success is how well you can translate a new or challenging idea for a broad audience, that is, how well you can transition from a sphere of 'limited' to 'extensive' production. It is not as exciting, for Vizard, to make culture solely for an audience of likeminded peers, to "play to an audience that is already receptive to risk, and to a certain cultural framework":

> If I take an audience that were already largely there, and I leave them largely where they were, that's an interesting exercise ... but to me it's not nearly as valuable as taking that audience – a bigger audience – and saying, "have you thought about looking at things this way?" [...] What is the internal structure between the familiar and the challenging? Between mainstream and fringe? ... this is why I reject the idea of the polarities as being offerings that should exist at one end or the other ... I'm interested in places that woo people in and challenge them – blur all that.

This he believed could be accomplished on a commercial network, which in Australia has much larger working class and suburban audiences than the more highly educated loyal ABC audience. For Vizard it is harder and ultimately much more satisfying to "smuggle in some more challenging ideas" into the mainstream (a skill and a creative drive he honed early on, working Melbourne's cabaret scene where the audiences were a mix of inner-city bohemian types and couples in from the suburbs for a night out on the town). By gradually introducing audiences to what might have been *avant-garde*, or cutting edge concepts, bit by bit Vizard says "I can... actually inoculate people, as to what might have been contentious, by the end of a season, becoming mainstream. I can educate an audience".

Paul Fenech – 'Wogsploitation' and Guerrilla television

In stark contrast to Vizard's efforts to gradually 'woo' mainstream audiences, Paul Fenech's comedy of the 2000s and 2010s is loud, lewd and wilfully offensive. Fenech is the CEO of his own production company, and the creator and star of several popular and long-running 'ethnic' and 'bogan' comedies ('bogan' being Australian pejorative slang for the Anglo-Celtic proletariat and underclass). Fenech hails from a working-class and mixed Maltese and Indigenous background and got his start in the television industry as a stagehand, sweeping the floors at the Australian Broadcasting Commission, before securing a place with their Indigenous training program, an innovative initiative of the late 1980s. Ultimately Fenech says he found the ABC too staid, too bureaucratic, too middle class and subsequently found a platform for his fast-paced, bad-taste, ethno-comedy at the Special Broadcasting Corporation (SBS), keen to find local variants of their successful US import South Park.

SBS television was inaugurated as an ethnic broadcaster, governed by a charter to provide multilingual and multicultural programming, but over the past 20 years, its art house reputation and government permission to take advertising has seen it transformed into a cutting edge network, similar in style to Channel 4 in the UK. SBS local production was turbo-charged by the Keating Government's Creative Nation cultural policy, which provided funds for the establishment of SBS Independent, charged with commissioning and developing diverse innovative projects from independent producers. SBSI operated as an autonomous unit within the broadcaster from 1994 to 2007, providing opportunities for a new generation of comedy, documentary and feature filmmakers.

Fenech's comedies for SBS – most notably *Pizza*, centred on the employees of a greasy pizzeria and *Housos*, about the residents of a fictional Sydney public housing estate – are politically incorrect, vulgar, sexually explicit and often downright silly. Fenech rejects what he sees as a British cerebral comedy tradition of languid talk in favour of the fast-paced action and slapstick violence of vaudeville acts in the tradition of 'The Three Stooges'. His mission is to make fun of authority, notably the regulation, control and misrepresentation of marginalised people by state, media and the well meaning on both sides of politics.

Like the UK drama *Shameless*, Fenech's comedy challenges the middle-class representation of social housing tenants and immigrants as disadvantaged or victims, presenting them as entrepreneurial, artful dodgers. Shows like *Pizza* and *Housos* also reflect the ethnic diversity of Sydney's working-class western suburbs; a space where those in precarious employment and from Non-English-Speaking Backgrounds collide (sometimes literally) with each other and with marginalised, long-term unemployed, Ango-celtic Australians. The comedies depict a spectrum of 'brown' ethnicities spanning Indigenous Australians, Polynesians, Lebanese and Mediterraneans, which Fenech collectively refers to as 'chockos' and with which he himself identifies. *Pizza* in particular is often located in the subgenre of 'wogsploitation' comedy

(Speed 2005) and is routinely criticised for revelling in ethnic stereotypes, but Fenech's vision of 'ethnic diversity' is more complex than this easy critique. Fenech's ethnicised outer suburbia is an important counter to the lingering whiteness of most Australian television, especially prime time. Moreover, it is an innovative riposte to what Ghassan Hage (1998) calls 'governmental' multiculturalism – a strategy for managing ethnic difference that denies the complexity, vibrancy and hybridity of the 'multicultural real'.

Paul Fenech's background has necessitated a much more pragmatic approach to the interplay of market forces and creative ambition. Describing his work ethic in the interview for 'Fringe to Famous', Fenech says "I never had the luxury of just being able to be arty for the sake of it. In any job that I ever had, film or not, I had to survive by working hard". He explains that he is very willing to take creative risks but not financial ones. His comedy is frequently transgressive and offensive, but it is made very cheaply: "...that's just my philosophy on surviving as a producer. If we're going to make edgy stuff, you can't expect people to really pay top dollar, because if it's a failure, whoever has supported you is really going to cop it". His approach is to do much of the work himself (write, direct, produce, star), to keep production budgets low, to keep the overheads of the production company low and to keep the shoot as fast and fuss free as possible. The last part is made possible in part by Fenech's rapport with communities in western Sydney where, he says, the locals are much more relaxed about an impromptu film shoot. This fast, cheap, 'guerrilla' model of production in turn informs much of the look and feel of *Pizza* and *Housos*, especially their appropriation of documentary techniques, breakneck pacing and on-location shooting.

In many ways Fenech's approach resembles older traditions of exploitation filmmaking-niche content made for as little as possible finding wider appeal by trafficking in outrage and titillation, but here it has been applied to a multicultural television franchise (*Pizza* spans several spin-off television programs, films and hundreds of live revue shows). Leveraging the popularity of the original television series, the feature film *Fat Pizza* (2003) was made for a tiny budget of AUD $400,000 and took in AUD $3.6 million at the Australian box office, making it one the top 100 highest grossing Australian films of all time (SA 2015). A similar spinoff feature film, *Housos vs Authority* (2012), was made for even less, AUD $200,000, and made almost AUD $1.4 million at the box office. Not all titles have been as successful, but with such a small initial outlay the return on investment for many of Fenech's comedies would be the envy of any local production company, exploitation or otherwise.

Notwithstanding his success at combining audience appeal with innovation within the comedy form, Fenech is yet to be embraced by the Australian screen establishment, perhaps because of the overtly working-class and permissive tone of his work. In the interview for 'Fringe to Famous', he was critical of the precarious nature of current employment in the television sector and the diminution of training opportunities he had enjoyed at the ABC. However, in an environment where most comedy content commissioned by public broadcasters is produced by outsourced entities, Fenech sees his own independent productions providing opportunities for emerging talent to hone their skills and ideas working with more experienced hands, in a less bureaucratically constrained and more risk-taking environment than is available today in a large broadcaster. For example, *Pizza* was the first major comedic acting role for the then unknown Rebel Wilson, who has since gone on to develop a significant screen comedy career in the United States. He also provides employment for talent drawn from a diversity of ethnic and other marginalised groups, such as working class and disabled Australians, not ordinarily represented with this degree of agency on mainstream television.

Fancy Boy – finding creative autonomy in the cross-platform environment

Fancy Boy is a Melbourne comedy collective best known for a fast-paced, scatological and sexually explicit live variety show and short video sketches for YouTube. It is an entity that has developed across a range of platforms, including live club nights, YouTube and (recently) television following a successful submission to 'Fresh Blood' (an initiative jointly sponsored by the national screen funding body, Screen Australia and the national broadcaster, the Australian Broadcasting Corporation). As the name suggests, 'Fresh Blood' has been an experiment in 'unearthing' new comedy talent through a progressive competition. On the strength of the initial submission and previous success on YouTube, Fancy Boy was one of 25 emerging comedy acts chosen to produce sketches for distribution on the ABC's digital platform iView. It advanced to a second round of 'Fresh Blood', as one of five acts to receive funding to develop a 30-minute pilot, and eventually the team was commissioned to produce an entire *Fancy Boy* series for distribution on iView and ABC2.

Fancy Boy satirises pop culture and media, but it is a product of the 'post-South Park' generation, with an altogether darker and more perverse flavour of comedy than earlier sketch programs like Vizard's *Fast Forward* or *Full Frontal*. It is also a product of a post-YouTube era. *Fancy Boy*, along with other super low-budget, emerging Australian comedy acts like *Bondi Hipsters* or *Natalie Tran*, has found a substantial aggregate audience online (in the case of Natalie Tran's 1.7 million YouTube channel subscribers, these are audience numbers that would be considered 'mass' by Australian standards).

Although the *Fancy Boy* team has shown some entrepreneurial flair, the principal producers Mark Conway and Mike Nayna see commercial and creative processes as inconsistent. In their interview for 'Fringe to Famous', they go so far as to describe the two as 'mutually exclusive' (except, they acknowledge, in the United States where economies of scale ensure there is a viable audience for niche comedy). It is a view that we have seen echoed elsewhere in the cultural industries, in the contemporary independent music and games sectors in particular. For the Fancy Boy producers, wider audience reach and mainstream validation is important, at least in terms of developing a profile and opening up more opportunities for paid work, but not at the expense of 'creative fulfilment' and integrity. Success is not understood primarily as mainstream audiences or financial reward, but as freedom from the time-sapping tedium of chasing grants and the meddlesome oversight of funding bodies (of course achieved through some level of financial success and audience impact). As Mark Conway explains:

> So success to me would be not having to go through all these jumping hoops of funding, and justifying everything you're doing, and explaining step-by-step, and constantly having to check in. It would be that you've had enough success that – "Here's the money. Go do what you do and bring it back to us".

Of course that kind of freedom comes at a cost. Nayna and Conway began by setting up their own comedy club featuring performers they both liked. As Nayna explains this strategy, "I don't want to have to rely on someone else for the opportunities – I'd prefer to make it myself…. It's almost like artist/entrepreneur, and that's kind of how you have to be unless you want to be on the bottom rung of all this sort of stuff". Eventually they bought their own equipment and started a production company. Where at one time greater financial and creative independence might have been hard won through a record of past success, here it is acquired through a smart, prudential approach to business sustainability.

Although the *Fancy Boy* producers frame what they do in the new millennial language of start-up culture, being entrepreneurial and seizing opportunities, it can also be understood as the latest expression of DIY culture, which has always involved a dynamic interplay between economic and cultural value. The *Fancy Boy* franchise might seem worlds away from the multi-million dollar comedy empire that Steve Vizard built during the heyday of network television in the late 1980s and 1990s, but their more modest success across a range of platforms is evidence of a similar creative and business verve. The key difference is that in an era where even mainstream success is no guarantee of a financial windfall, Conway and Nayna are aware that lean operations and creative integrity are essential to doing good business in the long term.

Conclusion

These examples highlight some of the problems with the tendency to polarisation that has characterised a number of recent debates around cultural policy and economy. It is impossible to understand them without recognising the complex interconnection between commerce and culture. A 'preservationist' perspective that understands the two as opposites simply does not reflect the lived experiences or creative philosophies of most of the practitioners we have spoken to in the course of our research. The relation between creative development and business has many different forms. In the case of Australian screen comedy, Steve Vizard set out to 'woo' mainstream audiences. He introduced calculated doses of subversive satire, political critique, media analysis and formal experimentation within a popular, commercial television format. Meanwhile Paul Fenech has won a broad popular audience with a raucous, low-brow, low-budget brand of comedy and in doing so challenged the pervasive middle-brow whiteness of prime-time Australian television. In both cases, there is a close connection between aesthetic and business development.

This is not to say, however, that one can simply be reduced to the other. Contrary to the full-blown innovation systems perspective discussed earlier in the chapter, there are important moments of tension and divergence. Many creative practitioners we have talked to, especially those from a younger generation, place a high value on creative freedom and maintain a restless search for ways to prevent its subordination, either to business imperatives or the bureaucratic requirements of attracting government support. In keeping with a long tradition of 'indie' and DIY culture, producers like Mark Conway and Mike Nayna from *Fancy Boy* look continually for ways to gain some creative autonomy. While they are, in many ways, 'entrepreneurial', always on the lookout for new opportunities in the new cross-platform environment, business development is more a necessity than an end in itself. Like many creatives, they are seeking no more than to find a sustainable economic base for their practice.

There have been moments in Australian cultural policy where a certain balance has been found. The twin focus on culture and economy that was embraced in the 1994 Creative Nation policy was briefly revived under the 2013 Creative Australia policy introduced by the Federal Labour government (Crean 2013). At other times, however, policy directions have oscillated between extremes. In the two years following the defeat of Labor in late 2013, there was a marked return to preservationist policies under the conservative leadership of Tony Abbott. Although Creative Australia was not officially revoked by the Abbott Government, its pro-market liberalism was trumped by an instinct to subsidise the high arts and reintroduce state paternalism under a rubric of 'excellence'. Behind a romantic rhetoric critical of the alleged philistine utilitarianism of Creative Australia was an elitist return to older notions of arts patronage (involving, most controversially, a transfer of funds away from the 'arms-length' peer review process of the Australia Council to the 'hand-picked' control of the Arts Minister).

With the recent toppling of Abbott from within his own Liberal Party by the small 'l' liberal Malcolm Turnbull – a former media lawyer, merchant banker, tech entrepreneur and Communications Minister – there has been a return to a rhetoric of innovation and entrepreneurship. In the area of cultural policy this has seen the creation of a new funding program dubbed 'Catalyst', which "aims to support innovative ideas from arts and cultural organisations that may find it difficult to access funding" from traditional sources (Fifield 2015). It remains to be seen how this will play out. Many arts workers and cultural commentators are wary, wondering whether there is any functional difference between the Abbott and Turnbull policies, with each mention of 'excellence' merely being replaced with 'innovation' (Croggon 2015). What our research suggests is that there are dangers, in a complex market economy, of purifying cultural policy around either of these terms. Making a totem of 'excellence' by itself risks a static notion of culture that fails to register the real circumstances in which it is largely produced. To place the emphasis entirely on 'innovation', however, risks reducing creativity in the cultural arena merely to a business function, one that is unsympathetic to the actual motivations of the majority of creative practitioners.

'Fringe to Famous' suggests a number of further areas for research. If, as we have argued, the relation between commerce and culture should be seen as contingent rather than necessary, questions arise about the conditions under which they complement and reinforce each other and the conditions under which they diverge. Why is it, for example, that little antagonism was felt by Steve Vizard in the 1980s between aesthetic innovation and working in the heart of commercial television? Why is it that for younger creatives today, such as the Fancy Boy producers, the two appear contradictory? The crisis of business models in commercial media is probably a significant factor here. As the general profitability of the sector has declined, it has lost what might be called its 'margin of generosity' in which figures such as Vizard thrived. As the business dimension becomes tougher, less forgiving, it is perhaps more often experienced as fundamentally hostile to cultural aspirations.

This raises a larger set of questions about the implications for our argument of the emergence of digital media. How have digital media altered the relation between 'fringe' and 'famous'? The digital turn has led to vastly improved access to low-cost production and distribution and opportunities for self-curation. It is less clear, however, that it has actually delivered a diversity dividend. The collapse of mass media business models has made it increasingly difficult to make a living in creative practice, particularly in the early stages of a career. This often means that the field is left to those with independent means or alternative sources of income. Public broadcasters can perform some of the function of introducing new voices, such as in the case of the ABC's Fresh Blood initiative. However, they too are under pressure and cannot provide, by themselves, the conduit for popularisation and distribution that have been provided in the past by market processes. There are important questions for further investigation here.

There are finally questions about the prospects for the tradition in cultural policy of attempting to balance commercial and cultural imperatives. As we have outlined above, this tradition, which had an early provenance in Australia with policy settings under the Keating Labor Government, has had genuine successes, such as SBS Independent, connecting new and diverse work and talent with audiences. It saw a brief revival in 2013 with the release of *Creative Australia*, but its future is now uncertain. Internationally, policy approaches that take a positive interest in the commercial cultural industries have been strongly associated with the 'Creative Industries' paradigm developed in the United Kingdom under the Blair government during the late 1990s and early 2000s. Within the UK itself, the approach has largely died along with the fortunes of the Blairite 'third way' program of which it was part. While it has been taken up elsewhere, most notably in Asia, it has tended to have a harder economic edge than its original formulation; it is now widely regarded as subordinating culture almost entirely to the status of an economic resource. There remains scope, however, for recovering the older, more balanced approach – perhaps best represented, at the national level, in the Australian case. There are significant opportunities for further work here.

Interviews

Mark Conway and Mike Nayna. Interview conducted 01 November 2015, Melbourne.
Paul Fenech. Interview conducted 30 October 2014, Sydney.
Steve Vizard. Interview conducted 02 December 2014, Melbourne.

References

ABS (Australian Bureau of Statistics), 2012. Industry. *Year book Australia, 2012.* Canberra: Commonwealth of Australia. Available from: www.abs.gov.au/ausstats/abs@.nsf/Lookup/by%20 Subject/1301.0~2012~Main%20Features~Industry~8 (Accessed 2 March 2016).

ACA (Australia Council for the Arts), 2014. *ArtFacts: music concert ticket sales reached $1 billion in 2013.* Surry Hills, NSW. Available from: http://artfacts.australiacouncil.gov.au/music/industry-8/music-concert-ticket-sales-reached-almost-1-billion-in-2011-with-11-million-attendances-nationally/ [Accessed 2 March 2016].

Anderson, L., and Oakley, K. eds., 2008. *Making meaning, making money: directions for the arts and cultural industries in the creative age.* Newcastle Upon Tyne: Cambridge Scholars Publishing.

ARIA (Australian Recording Industry Association), 2014. *ARIA yearly statistics.* Sydney. Available from: www.aria.com.au/pages/documents/2014ARIAYearlyStatistics.pdf (Accessed 2 March 2016).

Australian Government, 2015. *National innovation and science agenda.* Canberra Available from:www.innovation.gov.au/theme/taking-leap [Accessed 9 March 2016].

Bedwell, S., 2007. *Vizard uncut: the full story.* Melbourne: Melbourne University Publishing.

Bianchini, F., 1987. GLC R.I.P. – Cultural policies in London, 1981–1986. *New Formations*, 1 (Spring), 103–117.

Bourdieu, P., 1993. *The field of cultural production.* Cambridge: Polity Press.

Bourdieu, P., 1996. *The rules of art – genesis and structure of the literary field.* Cambridge: Polity Press.

Carson, V., 2008. Mambo sold to privateers. *Sydney morning herald*, 30 January. Available from: www.smh.com.au/business/mambo-sold-to-privateers-20080129-1ovy.html [Accessed 2 March 2016].

Caves, R., 2000. *Creative industries: contracts between art and commerce.* Harvard: Harvard University Press.

Chesborough, H. W., 2003. The era of open innovation. *MIT Sloan Management Review*, 44 (3), 35–41.

Crean, S., 2013. Arts minister's introduction. *In: Creative Australia.* Canberra: Commonwealth of Australia.

Croggon, A., 2015. Catalyst: new arts policy name, same old story. *ABC Arts*, 25 November. Available from: www.abc.net.au/news/2015-11-23/new-arts-policy-same-old-story/6966910 [Accessed 2 March 2016].

Cunningham, S., 2006. *What price a creative economy?* Strawberry Hills, NSW: Currency House.

Cunningham, S., 2008. Creative destruction: lessons for science and innovation policy from the rise of the creative industries. *Cultural Science*, 1 (1). Available from: http://cultural-science.org/journal/index.php/culturalscience/article/view/7/17 [Accessed 2 March 2016].

DCA (Department of Communication and the Arts), 1994. *Creative nation – Commonwealth cultural policy.* Canberra: Commonwealth of Australia.

DCMS (Department of Culture, Media and Sport), 1998. *Creative industries mapping document.* London: HMSO.

Fifield, M., 2015. Guideline for new arts fund [press release, 18 November]. Minister for Communication and Minister for the Arts. Available from: www.minister.communications.gov.au/mitch_fifield/news/guidelines_released_for_new_arts_fund#.Vl0n33YrK71 [Accessed 2 March 2016].

Fiske, J., and Hartley, J., 1978. *Reading television*. London: Methuen.

Fiske, J., Hodge, B., and Turner, G., 1987. *Myths of Oz – reading Australian popular culture*. Sydney: Allen & Unwin.

Flew, T., 2012. *The creative industries – culture and policy*. Los Angeles: Sage.

Frith, S., and Horne, H., 1987. *Art into pop*. London: Methuen.

Garnham, N., 2005. From cultural to creative industries: an analysis of the implications of the 'creative industries' approach to arts and media policy making in the United Kingdom. *International Journal of Cultural Policy*. 11 (1), 15–29.

Hage, G., 1998. *White nation*. Sydney: Pluto Press.

Hall, S., and Whannel, P., 1964. *The popular arts*. London: Hutchinson Educational.

Hartley, J., ed., 2005. *Creative industries*. Malden, MA: Blackwell.

Hartley, J., 2008. From the consciousness industry to creative industries: consumer-created content, social network markets and the growth of knowledge. *In*: J. Holt and A. Perren, eds. *Media industries: history, theory and methods*. Oxford: Blackwell, 231–244.

Hebdige, D., 1979. *Subculture: the meaning of style*. London: Methuen.

Hesmondhalgh, D., and Baker, S., 2011. *Creative labour – media work in three cultural industries*. Abingdon: Routledge.

Hesmondhalgh, D., Oakley, K., Lee, D., Nisbett, M. 2015. *Culture, Economy and Politics: The Case of New Labour*. New Directions in Cultural Policy. Basingstoke: Palgrave Macmillan.

Hoggart, R., 1957. *The uses of literacy*. London: Chatto & Windus.

Howkins, J., 2007. *The creative economy – how people make money from ideas*. 2nd Edn. London: Penguin.

Jameson, F., 1993. On 'cultural studies'. *Social Text* (34), 17–52.

Leavis, Q.D., 1939. *Fiction and the reading public*. London: Chatto and Windus.

Leavis, F.R., and Thompson, D., 1933. *Culture and environment*. London: Chatto and Windus.

Martin, A., 1994. *Phantasms*. Ringwood, VIC: McPhee Gribble.

McElroy, G., 2013. Antichamber passes 100K sales mark on Steam. *Polygon*, 20 March. Available from: www.polygon.com/2013/3/20/4124946/antichamber-passes-100k-sales-mark-on-steam [Accessed 2 March 2016].

McGuigan, J., 2004. *Rethinking cultural policy*. Maidenhead: Open University Press.

McRobbie, A., 2015. *Be creative: making a living in the new culture industries*. Cambridge: Polity Press.

Miller, T., 2004. A view from a fossil: the new economy, creativity and consumption – two or three things I don't believe in. *International Journal of Cultural Studies*, 7 (1), 55–65.

Moore, T., 2012. *Dancing with empty pockets: Australia's bohemians since 1860*. Millers Point, NSW: Pier 9.

Morris, M., 1988. *The pirate's fiancée: feminism, reading, postmodernism*. London: Verso.

Murray, C., and Gollmitzer, M., 2012. Escaping the precarity trap: a call for creative labour policy. *International Journal of Cultural Policy*, 18 (4), 419–438.

Oakley, K., 2009. The disappearing arts: creativity and innovation after the creative industries. *International Journal of Cultural Policy*, 15 (4), 403–413.

Oakley, K., O'Brien, D., 2016. Learning to labour unequally: understanding the relationship between cultural production, cultural consumption and inequality. *Social Identities*, 22 (5), 471–486.

O'Connor, J., 2009. Creative industries: a new direction? *International Journal of Cultural Policy*, 15 (4), 387–404.

Potts, J., 2008. Social network markets: a new definition of creative industries. *Journal of Cultural Economics* 32 (3), 167–185.

Potts, J., 2011. *Creative industries and economic evolution*. Cheltenham, UK: Edward Elgar.

Reuters., 2013. Australia upgrades iron ore export forecast. *Sydney Morning Herald*, 26 June. Available from: www.smh.com.au/business/mining-and-resources/australia-upgrades-iron-ore-export-forecast-20130626-2ow3k.html [Accessed 2 March 2016].

Screen Australia (SA), 2015. *Top 100 Australian feature films of all time, ranked by total reported gross Australian box office as at February 2015*. Ultimo, NSW. Available from: www.screenaustralia.gov.au/research/statistics/cinematopfilmsalltime.aspx [Accessed 2 March 2016]

Shiel, M., and Fitzmaurice, T., 2008. *Cinema and the city: film and urban societies in a global context*. Oxford: Blackwell Publishers.

Speed, L., 2005. Life as a pizza: the comic traditions of Wogsploitation films. *Metro*, (146/147), 136–144.

Throsby, D., 2001. *Economics and culture*. Cambridge: Cambridge University Press.

Throsby, D., 2006. *Does Australia need a cultural policy?*. Strawberry Hills, NSW: Currency House.

Throsby, D., 2010. *The economics of cultural policy*. Cambridge: Cambridge University Press.

Turnbull, M., 2015. *Transcript: Vote on the Liberal Party Leadership*, 14 September. Available from: www. malcolmturnbull.com.au/media/transcript-vote-on-the-liberal-party-leadership [Accessed 2 March 2016].

Turner, G., 2011. Surrendering the space – convergence culture, cultural studies and the curriculum. *Cultural Studies*, 25 (4–5), 685–699.

von Hippel, E., 2009. Democratizing innovation – the emerging phenomenon of user innovation. *International Journal of Innovation Science*, 1 (1), 29–40.

Wark, M., 1998. *Celebrities, culture and cyberspace: the light on the hill in a postmodern world*. Sydney: Pluto Press.

Williams, R., 1958. Culture is ordinary. *In*: N. MacKenzie, ed. *Conviction*. London: MacGibbon & Kee.

19

Inside out

The role of 'audience research' in cultural policies in the United States

Jennifer L. Novak-Leonard

Introduction

"Cultural policy" in the US is not what it is elsewhere in the world. Uniquely, the recognized arts-related policies in the US have largely evolved from opportunities created within US tax code and the influence and financial support of philanthropic entities. This chapter discusses the evolution of arts policy-making since the mid-twentieth century in the US and the role of audience research in policy-making over this time. While audience research stemmed from a policy paradigm focused on supporting the nonprofit cultural infrastructure in the US, this chapter argues that social and policy contexts in the US and advancements made to audience and arts participation research over the past 10 years are calling for policy-makers to focus on expanding the view of arts and culture and deepening the role of arts and culture in democratic life.

"Cultural policy" in the United States[1]

While many countries have an identified policy-making body, such as a cultural ministry, for matters related to arts and culture and/or hold a membership in the United Nations Educational, Scientific and Cultural Organization (UNESCO), the US has neither (Rubin 2013). The US does not have a formal cultural policy, at least not in the tradition of many other countries. An integral part of the nation's fundamental beliefs is the freedom of expression, which is evoked as an aspect of policies related to culture in the US and is lawfully protected under the US Constitution (Kreidler 2013). Akin to other countries, the US has laws to protect intellectual property rights and to oversee exports. However, while the US does have regulations and allowances like many other countries, they are predominantly applied to market-driven commercial art and culture and are more commonly understood and handled as issues of trade as opposed to issues of "cultural policy" (Balassa 2008; Ivey 2008).

In the absence of a formal cultural policy or an official cultural policy-making body, prominent governmental and non-governmental institutions and vocal actors all shape policies about arts and culture in the US. A particularly powerful influence that has shaped cultural, or at least arts-related, policies in the US since the early twentieth century is the federal tax code. The tax code grants charitable organizations, which include arts and cultural organizations, tax exemption and qualifies these organizations as "nonprofit" and eligible for philanthropic support (Peters and Cherbo 1998; Mulcahy 2006; Woronkowicz et al. 2012; Kreidler 2013). Mulcahy (2006) succinctly describes how policy-making is affected by the structure of the tax code:

> To an extent unknown elsewhere, the American government through its tax code has delegated broad policy-making powers to private institutions in the pursuit of various eleemosynary goals.
>
> *(Mulcahy 2006, p. 328)*

Evolution of the nonprofit arts infrastructure and its information needs

Since the 1960s, providing direct funding to nonprofit arts organizations has been a primary policy intervention used by both non-government and government entities in an effort to fuel the arts in the US. Kreidler (1996, 2013) has chronicled the establishment of the nonprofit arts infrastructure in the US, which provides an important historical context for considering the current state of cultural policies in the US. In the late 1950s, major foundations whose endowments came from wealth accumulated during the Industrial Revolution worked together to examine the state of performing arts organizations. A product of these efforts was the landmark work of Baumol and Bowen (1966), which led to the principal conclusion that arts organizations faced structural financial challenges that the authors coined as "cost disease." The implication of this phenomenon was that the arts required financial subsidies to survive. At this time, there was also a general "cultural inferiority complex" in the US that reinforced the conclusion that arts organizations would require substantial subsidies because there was a desire to not only have the arts survive, but to have them thrive (Kreidler 1996, 2013). Kreidler (2013) characterizes this strategy as "supply side pump priming," the basic underlying theory being that subsidies would ultimately improve and expand the work of the organizations, reaching more audiences and attracting more sources of revenues for the organizations. Influenced by much of the same thinking, other philanthropic entities adopted this strategy, and in 1965 the National Endowment for the Arts (NEA) was founded (Kreidler 2013; Wyszomirski 2013). Wyszomirski (2013) describes financial sustainability as one of the agency's three fundamental, underlying policy aims, the other two being to support artistic vitality and, vitally important as a public agency, acknowledging the value of arts for the US public at large, originally referred to as "public access to the arts" in enabling legislation.

Given this supply-side focused environment, in the late 1960s and early 1970s the number of nonprofit arts organizations in the US exploded, establishing a notable and vocal constituency reliant on the direct and indirect benefits of philanthropic and public funding (Kreidler 1996). As Toepler (2013, p. 167–168) explains, this era placed the NEA "at the core of an implicit policy paradigm that kept most policy actors focused on the funding and support needs of the nonprofit cultural infrastructure." The NEA and philanthropic organizations supporting this system served as key policy-makers in the US, even if not formally designated as such.

Inside organizations: research on existing audiences

Alongside the increased number of nonprofit arts organizations in the 1960s and 1970s came a penchant for research on the audiences of these organizations. This early research focused almost exclusively on the relationships between the organizations and the audiences who came through their doors (DiMaggio et al. 1978; Pettit 2000). The surveys tended to include topics such as satisfaction with facilities and with the program attended. However, the primary stakeholders for this research, by and large, did not have a clear sense of its purpose. In their landmark review of 270 audience surveys, DiMaggio, Useem and Brown (1978, p. 4) concluded that two of the chief motives for nonprofit arts organizations undertaking audience research were (1) political leverage and (2) "a vague sense of concern for more information of some sort." DiMaggio et al. also identified the variable and overall low technical quality of the surveys as a key concern. The state of audience research made it difficult to draw inferences from the disparate studies to inform systems-level policy conversations.

After establishing a research division in 1975, the NEA took active interest in coordinating conversations and research about the arts at the national level. The NEA's Research Division worked to address concerns raised by the decentralized and inconsistent nature and quality of audience research and, importantly, the goal of having data to address the government's own objective of equitable access to arts (Tepper and Gao 2008, p. 25). The most significant effort was establishing the *Survey of Public Participation in the Arts* (SPPA), which was first implemented in 1982 and remains the primary source of national data about arts participation in the US.

In December 1977, the NEA convened the Conference on the Policy Related Studies of the National Endowment for the Arts. The creation of a national survey on arts participation was discussed at this conference and the competing priorities for arts research were articulated—study either what the public does or rather what select, high arts organizations offer (Orend 1978). The establishment of the SPPA was the initial milestone that bridged *audience research* into *arts participation research*. However, despite the fact that the fundamental idea for a national survey was "a concern about democracy and equitable access" (Tepper and Gao 2008, p. 25), another original driving force for establishing a national survey was to help monitor the health of nonprofit arts organizations by capturing data on arts attendance (AMS Planning and Research Corp 1995; Tepper and Gao 2008).

The earliest analyses using SPPA data largely focused on the differential rates at which members of different racial and ethnic groups reported participation in the arts (Keegan 1987; Robinson et al. 1987; DiMaggio and Ostrower 1992). Examining the SPPA by race and ethnicity, as well as other key demographic variables, has continued as a key analysis to inform discourse about "access" (National Endowment for the Arts 1999; Nichols 2003; Welch and Kim 2010; Silber and Triplett 2015). Early on, however, it was apparent that the pump-priming hypothesis was not effective at attracting a wider and more diverse audience, or at least not at attracting an adequately larger and more diverse audience (Kreidler 2013). So, even though the focus on supply-side investments continued to shape arts policy in the US, the tactics designed to bring audiences "into" the organizations evolved.

While the 1960s and early 1970s were generally a flourishing time for nonprofit arts organizations, the subsequent decades stood in sharp contrast, and the nonprofit arts sector assumed a defensive posture. In the 1980s and 1990s, the NEA faced a great deal of controversy, which ultimately resulted in significant funding cuts and staff reductions at the agency (National Endowment for the Arts 2009b). However, for the particular matter of policy-making, a critical impact of these resource reductions is the re-disbursement of influence on arts policy-making. The NEA and philanthropic organizations supporting this system, even if not formally designated, serve as key cultural policy-makers in the US. Therefore, declining financial support for the NEA meant that the influence on discourse for arts policies began to disperse from the centralized, influential voice and created the opportunity for more perspectives on what policies related to the arts could be. Yet at the start of what Toepler (2013) refers to as the "post-NEA era," there remained historical inertia favoring a centralized supply-side focused paradigm for arts policy. While most research had been focused on understanding differences between those attending and those not attending the arts, informing the policy structures in place, the 1980s and early 1990s brought about a need for research to justify and demonstrate the instrumental value of arts organizations and their work.

Efforts to bring audiences "in": research on potential audiences

In the late 1990s and 2000s, there was a shift in focus away from discussing access to arts organizations based on current audiences and toward audiences and participants seemingly willing to come "into" arts organizations. The general discourse within arts policy shifted from "access" to "outreach" and "audience development." It was during this time that the NEA launched initiatives to bring arts into more rural and underserved communities across different states as a quantifiable means to conclusively demonstrate public value (Wyszomirski 2013).

Several seminal pieces of research were produced, not under the auspices of the NEA, but sponsored by major foundations during this time. Foundations were also helping to establish arts research centers in policy schools at major research universities during this time,[2] signaling their desire and aims to contribute policy relevant research (Schuster 2002). The Wallace Foundation (at the time known as the Wallace-Reader's Digest Fund) sponsored seminal research conducted by McCarthy and Jinnett (2001), which gave rise to the now commonly used mantra amongst US-based nonprofit arts administrators—broaden, deepen and diversify arts audiences. One of the key recommendations stemming from McCarthy and Jinnett's research was that arts organizations should seek to learn about existing and potential audiences, which the authors referred to as "inclined" individuals, on the basis of their behaviors and attitudes, as opposed to solely on the basis of their demographics (2001, p. 36). This research informed a decade of funding investments made by the Wallace Foundation and others to support arts. Much of the research focused on marketing, messaging, ticketing and how to make audiences feel welcomed in a theater or museum.

Research on the value of and for audiences

The late 1990s and early 2000s also saw a greater focus on the economic impact of the arts as a means to demonstrate the instrumental value of arts organizations. Multiple researchers have raised important questions about the methodologies used for assessing economic impact. Some researchers fundamentally argued against the very premise of using economic impact as a metric for evaluating whether activities merit public subsidization on the basis that the less tangible, intrinsic values of art could not be enumerated by the approach (Cultural Policy Center 2004). This brought about a widespread debate within the nonprofit arts sector about instrumental and intrinsic arguments for evaluating and demonstrating the impact of arts on individuals and the role of both arguments in communications with legislators and other authoring stakeholders. *Gifts of the Muse: Reframing the Debate about the Benefits of the Arts* (McCarthy et al. 2004) proposed a language and conceptual framework for evaluating the arts, which integrated both instrumental and intrinsic perspectives. It took a good deal of time, debate and translation for the research first put forth in McCarthy et al. (2004) to be accepted by arts organizations (Brown 2006). Even after the concept of intrinsic impact achieved resonance, capturing and communicating intrinsic impact required the development of new analytical methods and systematic understanding, as done in Brown and Novak (2007), Radbourne et al. (2010), Brown and Novak-Leonard (2013) and Lord (2012).

Evaluating intrinsic impact represents a return to audience research in a more traditional sense of acquiring information about those who attend an arts event. The research emphasizes documenting how arts experiences can affect individuals, for example in how they can be emotionally moved or intellectually engaged. This measurement system currently remains in an early phase of focusing on relationships between organizations and audiences, but developing this line of research has been identified as a priority for research over the next 10 years (Markusen 2014). A specific question to be addressed is whether the data on how individuals are affected can be aggregated and interpreted in a meaningfully way for the purpose of informing policy-making.

Dispersion of the nonprofit arts infrastructure and its information needs

While major social changes were underway throughout the latter half of the twentieth century, by the late 2000s and early 2010s, these changes had risen to the fore of arts policy research. Prominent trends include expanded technology usage, shifts toward an increasingly racially and ethnically diverse population and a growing participatory cultural ethos (Novak-Leonard and Brown 2011; Novak-Leonard et al. 2014; Novak-Leonard et al. 2015b). Speaking generally, these societal shifts were welcomed as opportunities by some, but posed further challenges to other nonprofit arts organizations. Additionally, national indicators of arts participation, stemming from the SPPA, continued to indicate that smaller portions of the US adult population were attending arts events and that disparities between racial and ethnicity groups persisted (National Endowment for the Arts 2009a). Some *de facto* arts policy-makers recognized, as Kreidler (2013, p. 152) describes, the "diminishing returns" of the supply-side focused policy paradigm.

In recent years, the inertia behind the singular supply-side arts policy paradigm started to fade as policy-makers sought alternative policy paradigms, with a key alternative being demand-side policies (Zakaras and Lowell 2008; Kreidler 2013). Such approaches look at the ways individuals learn about, become familiar with and create arts outside of professional arts settings. The basic theory underlying demand-side policies is that investment in people's arts activities outside of professional arts settings could develop demand for the professional arts offered by nonprofit arts organizations. However, arts policy discourse also reflects a growing recognition that investing in demand is highly valuable in and of itself. With this realization has come an expanded sense of what aesthetic forms are considered "art," are meaningful to people in the US and should be part of an expanded arts policy discourse (Ivey 2008; Novak-Leonard et al. 2014). In a sense, this expanded view represents a return to a nineteenth century arts policy paradigm more focused on democratic ideals. Other scholars have written poignantly on the deeply rooted participatory spirit of democracy in the US and the role that arts participation plays within that spirit, as well as the historical role of democratic participation in the arts (DiMaggio et al. 1978; Tepper and Gao 2008; Conner 2013; Clark et al. 2014). This raises a critical question that is currently shaping this time of change in arts policies in the US—how, or whether, the current deeply rooted infrastructure surrounding nonprofit arts organizations can serve as bridges to achieving real equity/diversity of art forms and means of engagement.

Readiness for research

Just in recent years within the US, advances have been made in measuring and studying a broader range of "arts participation," not exclusively defined by attendance at nonprofit arts organizations. It is important to note that since its first wave in 1982, the SPPA has included measures of activities besides attendance, but the historical body of research using SPPA data overwhelmingly focused on attendance. While some earlier studies examined participation in acts of making art, such as Peters and Cherbo (1996) and Ostrower (2005), it was not until a few years ago that research looking at arts participation indicators other than those of attendance garnered attention amongst policy-makers and nonprofit arts organizations. Arguably, the confluence of social forces and a continued decline in the national rates of arts attendance prompted attention to such research.

Using the 2008 SPPA, *Beyond Attendance: A multi-modal understanding of arts participation* (Novak-Leonard and Brown 2011) fully leveraged the indicators available to analyze how patterns of individuals' arts participation varied across attendance behaviors, engaging in art making and consuming arts through various technology-based means. Even though the analyses presented in Novak-Leonard and Brown (2011) considered art-related behaviors beyond those typically connected to nonprofit arts organizations, the subsequent discussion of these research findings has largely focused on implications for nonprofit arts organizations, and such discussion is essentially still written in a manner that focuses on the health of arts organizations. Following this increased attention, major substantive changes were made for the next wave of SPPA in 2012 in an effort to collect more data on arts-related behaviors, generally, rather than focusing only on those behaviors specifically associated with traditional ways of engaging with nonprofit arts organizations. At the same time, international calls were issued for research tools "elaborated in the last century" to be revisited in order to better reflect contemporary life and "the rise of new cultural paradigms and behavior" (UNESCO Institute for Statistics 2012, p. 12). For example, the 2012 SPPA asked where people attended performing arts events and how they used digital devices to create different forms of art. However, balancing the inclusion of innovative questions in this survey instrument while preserving valuable, long-standing measurements is a challenge, and ultimately the emphasis on evaluating attendance remained (Novak-Leonard et al. 2015c).

More recent survey efforts focus on collecting data on arts attendance balanced with data on arts-making, arts-learning and other modes of arts participation. The Benchmark to Basic new Annual Arts Benchmark Survey (AABS) helps to adjust this imbalance. Starting in 2013, the AABS' two alternating questionnaires are to be used in the years between the SPPA, which is fielded every 5 years. The AABS includes much-abbreviated versions of the SPPA questionnaire, with a greater emphasis on arts making and learning in balance with attending events.[3] Additionally, the AABS questions pertaining to attendance are broad and not genre-specific, which reflects a response to the critique that the SPPA genre-specific questions comprise indicators left over from the survey's earliest days and are reflective of mid-twentieth century policy approaches (Novak-Leonard et al. 2015b). Such shifts are also reflected in some innovative regional surveys. The *California Survey of Arts & Cultural Participation* is a new instrument crafted to measure participation using each individual's own definitions of art, aesthetics and creative expression (Novak-Leonard et al. 2015a; Novak-Leonard et al. 2015b).[4] Sponsored by the James Irvine Foundation in California, this survey also represents the aforementioned trend in which major foundations are seeking to reassert their role in shaping policy at precisely the same time that the activity of arts research centers founded in the late 1990s/early 2000s is waning.

It remains unclear whether foundation-sponsored research is positioned to innovate at a large scale. It is clear that substantial innovations have been made in survey design and that some policy-makers are indeed considering activities well outside traditional nonprofit arts organizations activities. However, as Toepler (2013) explains:

there are no strong indications that the foundation field at large pursues innovation at a significant scale. Rather the data suggest a fairly high degree of continuity of foundation funding priorities over 25 years despite the major public policy upheavals of the 1990s.

(2013, p. 178)

Indeed, the NEA-sponsored Arts & Culture modules of the 2012 and 2016 waves of the General Social Survey (GSS), one of the most highly regarded and frequently utilized sources of data on adults' attitudes and opinions in the US, focused on measuring individuals' motivations for, and barriers to, attending live performing arts events and art exhibits (Blume-Kohout et al. 2015). This data collection effort mirrors its predecessors by focusing on informing the supply-side policy paradigm addressing issues of access.

The competing priorities for research for policy-making purposes are teetering between a continued sense of wanting to serve nonprofit organizations, in their traditional sense, and the need to inform policy that takes a broader purview. At the time of writing this chapter, the NEA is finalizing the design for the next wave of its SPPA, which will be fielded in July 2017 (National Endowment for the Arts 2016). In contrast to the GSS, the draft 2017 SPPA instrument used for pilot testing strikes a balance between the competing priorities for research. The draft instrument maintains the questions used for trend analyses, which are highly valued by the nonprofit arts sector, and includes updated and new questions. The revised questions aim to be inclusive of a broad range of artistic forms and activities and to document more detail about how people engage in art, including where and why they participate. While the term "arts participation" for many years was synonymous with arts audiences, the updates included in the 2017 SPPA pilot test questionnaire demonstrate greater parity of measurement among creating art, consuming and making art via and with technology and arts attendance. The broader range and greater balance of measures offer the possibility of informing a broader range of "arts policies" discourse.

Conclusion

"Cultural policy" in the US is in a period of great flux. This flux largely stems from reckoning a deeply rooted support and infrastructure system with contemporary society, including incorporating data and research into policy- and decision-making. Research focusing on arts audiences and the manners in which people engage with art has evolved over the past 10 years and continues to evolve. Whereas in the early days of audience research it was difficult to draw inferences from disparate studies to inform systems-level policy conversations, a current challenge arises from disparate nonprofit arts organizations' efforts to reconcile the findings of systems-level research within the context of their own work. Research is needed to elucidate how to develop sound, systemically comparable, yet organizationally specific, capacity and means to enable disparate organizations to document their own audiences and participants. Specifically, there is a growing desire among arts organizations to document the demographic composition and behaviors of their own audiences and to explore the degree to which the organizations' programs are relevant to their lives. As understanding of how people engage with art and artistic endeavors evolves, research is needed to understand whether and how the roles of artists are changing. Particularly as the modalities with which people engage with artistic endeavors touches on broader aspects of civic life, research is needed to help understand how and whether perceptions are changing as to who is considered an artist and the role that person plays within local communities.

Whereas in earlier decades, interest in audience and audience-related research stemmed from an established supply-focused policy paradigm, currently research is helping to inform the next policy paradigm, yet to be firmly shaped (Toepler 2013). Bennett (2004) discusses two factions of cultural policy research, one serving as formative and informative for the practical development of cultural policies, and the other reflective and critical of cultural policies. In a sense, this chapter can be understood as discussing how audience research began as the former and evolved into the latter, with developments in "audience research" over the past decade providing critical commentary on the relative narrowness of what has been the arts policy paradigm in the US. In the near future, understanding gained through this recent and ongoing research just might help drive the next cultural policy paradigm to take shape in the US.

Notes

1 The purpose of this chapter section is not to fully address what "cultural policy" is, either in a conceptual or operational sense, within the US context or as it relates to international cultural diplomacy efforts. Rather, the purpose is to describe a dominant and unique aspect of "policies" related to art or culture—meaning forms of aesthetic and artistic expression as opposed to a full anthropological approach to culture, for example that would include language—in the US.
2 The Center for Arts and Cultural Policy Studies (founded in 1994) at Princeton University and the Cultural Policy Center (founded in 1999) at the University of Chicago, and later The Curb Center for Art, Enterprise & Public Policy (founded in 2003) at Vanderbilt University.
3 At the time of writing this chapter AABS data had not yet been publicly released so I cannot provide commentary on the effectiveness of the AABS or its results.
4 Additional efforts had been made in recent years to measure 'arts participation' with broader or different definitional frameworks than the SPPA. Examples of such efforts include Brown, Novak and Kitchener (2008), Klineberg, Wu and Aldape (2012) and LaPlaca Cohen (2014).

References

AMS Planning and Research Corp, 1995. *A practical guide to arts participation research*. Washington, DC: National Endowment for the Arts.

Balassa, C., 2008. *America's image abroad: the UNESCO cultural diversity convention and U.S. motion picture exports*. Nashville, TN: The Curb Center for Art, Enterprise & Public Policy.

Baumol, W. J. and Bowen, W. G., 1966. *Performing arts, the economic dilemma: a study of problems common to theater, opera, music, and dance*. New York: Twentieth Century Fund.

Bennett, O., 2004. The torn halves of cultural policy research. *International Journal of Cultural Policy*, 10(2), 237–248.

Blume-Kohout, M. E., Leonard, S. R. and Novak-Leonard, J. L., 2015. *When going gets tough: barriers and motivations affecting arts attendance*. Washington, DC: National Endowment for the Arts.

Brown, A., 2006. An architecture of value. *Grantmakers in the Arts*, (Winter), 18–25.

Brown, A. S. and Novak, J. L., 2007. *Assessing the intrinsic impacts of a live performance*. San Francisco, CA: WolfBrown.

Brown, A. S. and Novak-Leonard, J. L., 2013. Measuring the intrinsic impacts of arts attendance. *Cultural Trends*, 22(3–4), 223–233.

Brown, A. S., Novak, J. L. and Kitchener, A., 2008. *Cultural engagement in California's Inland regions*. San Francisco, CA: WolfBrown.

Clark, T. N., et al., 2014. *Can Tocqueville karaoke? Global contrasts of citizen participation, the arts and development*. Bingley, UK: Emerald Group Publishing.

Conner, L., 2013. *Audience engagement and the role of arts talk in the digital era*. New York: Palgrave Macmillan.

Cultural Policy Center, 2004. Lasting effects: assessing the future of economic impact analysis of the arts. Lasting *Effects: Economic Impact Analysis Conference May* 2004 Rockefeller Brothers Fund Pocantico Conference Center. Chicago: Cultural Policy Center.

DiMaggio, P., Useem, M. and Brown, P., 1978. *Audience studies of the performing arts and museums.* Washington, DC: National Endowment for the Arts.

Ivey, B., 2008. *Arts, inc.: how greed and neglect have destroyed our cultural rights.* Berkeley, CA: University of California Press.

Keegan, C., 1987. *Public participation in classical ballet: a special analysis of the ballet data collected in the 1982 and 1985 Survey of Public Participation in the Arts.* Washington, DC: National Endowment for the Arts.

Klineberg, S. L., Wu, J. and Aldape, C. L., 2012. *The Houston Arts Survey: participation, perceptions and prospects.* Houston, TX: Kinder Institute for Urban Research.

Kreidler, J., 1996. Leverage lost: The nonprofit arts in the post-Ford era. *Journal of Arts Management, Law & Society*, 26(2), 79.

Kreidler, J., 2013. Modeling the future of US arts policy: beyond supply-side pump-priming. *Cultural Trends*, 22(3–4), 145–155.

LaPlaca Cohen, 2014. *CultureTrack.* LaPlaca Cohen: New York.

Lord, C., ed., 2012. *Counting new beans: intrinsic impact and the value of art.* San Francisco, CA: Theatre Bay Area.

Markusen, A., 2014. Creative cities: a 10-year research agenda. *Journal of Urban Affairs*, 36(s2), 567–589.

McCarthy, K. F. and Jinnett, K., 2001. *A new framework for building arts participation.* Santa Monica, CA: RAND.

McCarthy, K. F., et al., 2004. *Gifts of the muse: reframing the debate about the benefits of the arts.* Santa Monica, CA: RAND.

Mulcahy, K. V., 2006. Cultural policy: definitions and theoretical approaches. *Journal of Arts Management, Law & Society*, 35(4), 319–330.

National Endowment for the Arts, 1999. *Demographic characteristics of arts attendance: 1997.* Washington, DC: National Endowment for the Arts.

National Endowment for the Arts, 2009a. *2008 Survey of Public Participation in the Arts.* Washington, DC: National Endowment for the Arts.

National Endowment for the Arts, 2009b. *National Endowment for the Arts: a history 1965–2008.* Washington, DC: National Endowment for the Arts.

National Endowment for the Arts, 2016. *2017 Survey of Public Participation in the Arts.* Washington, DC: Office of Management and Budget. Available from: www.reginfo.gov/public/do/PRAViewDocument?ref_nbr=201601-3135-002 [Accessed 24 May 2016].

Nichols, B., 2003. *Demographic characteristics of arts attendance: 2002.* Washington, DC: National Endowment for the Arts.

Novak-Leonard, J. L. and Brown, A., 2011. *Beyond attendance: a multi-modal understanding of arts participation.* Washington, DC: National Endowment for the Arts.

Novak-Leonard, J., et al., 2014. *The changing landscape of arts participation: a synthesis of literature and expert interviews.* Chicago: NORC.

Novak-Leonard, J., et al., 2015a. *California Survey of Arts & Cultural Participation: technical report.* Chicago, IL: NORC.

Novak-Leonard, J. L., et al., 2015b. *The cultural lives of Californians: insights from the California Survey of Arts & Cultural Participation.* Chicago, IL: NORC.

Novak-Leonard, J. L., Wong, J. and English, N., 2015c. *A closer look at arts engagement in California: insights from the NEA's Survey of Public Participation in the Arts.* Chicago, IL: NORC.

Orend, R.J., 1978. Developing research on the arts consumer. In: D. Cwi, ed. *Research in the Arts: Proceedings of the Conference on Policy Related Studies of the National Endowment for the Arts*, 7–9 December 1977 The Walters Art Museum. Washington, DC: National Endowment for the Arts, 10–12.

Ostrower, F., 2005. *The diversity of cultural participation: findings from a national survey.* Washington, DC: The Urban Institute.

Peters, M. and Cherbo, J., 1996. *America's personal participation in the arts: 1992.* Washington, DC: National Endowment for the Arts.

Peters, M. and Cherbo, J., 1998. The missing sector: the unincorporated arts. *Journal of Arts Management, Law & Society*, 28(2), 115–129.

Pettit, B., 2000. Resources for studying public participation in and attitudes towards the arts. *Poetics*, 27(5–6), 351–395.

Radbourne, J., Glow, H. and Johanson, K., 2010. Measuring the intrinsic benefits of arts attendance. *Cultural Trends*, 19(4), 307–324.

Robinson, J. P., et al., 1987. *Survey of Public Participation in the Arts: project report.* Washington, DC: National Endowment for the Arts.

Rubin, A. J., 2013. U.S. loses voting rights at UNESCO. *The New York Times,* November 9, 2013, p. A4.

Schuster, M. J., 2002. *Informing cultural policy: the research and information infrastructure.* New Brunswick, NJ: Center for Urban Policy Research.

Silber, B. and Triplett, T., 2015. *A decade of arts engagement: findings from the Survey of Public Participation in the Arts, 2002–2012.* Washington, DC: National Endowment for the Arts.

Tepper, S. and Gao, Y., 2008. Engaging art: what counts? *In:* Tepper, S. J. and Ivey, B. eds. *Engaging Art.* New York: Routledge, 17–48.

Toepler, S., 2013. Shifting cultural policy landscapes in the USA: what role for philanthropic foundations? *Cultural Trends,* 22(3–4), 167–179.

UNESCO Institute for Statistics, 2012. *Measuring cultural participation.* Montreal: UIS.

Welch, V. and Kim, Y., 2010. *Race/ethnicity and arts participation: findings from the Survey of Public Participation in the Arts.* Chicago, IL: NORC.

Woronkowicz, J., Nichols, B. and Iyengar, S., 2012. *How the United States funds the arts.* Washington, DC: National Endowment for the Arts.

Wyszomirski, M. J., 2013. Shaping a triple-bottom line for nonprofit arts organizations: micro-, macro-, and meta-policy influences. *Cultural Trends,* 22(3–4), 156–166.

Zakaras, L. and Lowell, J. F., 2008. *Cultivating demand for the arts: arts learning, arts engagement, and state arts policy.* Santa Monica, CA: RAND.

20

Considering the second-order health effects of arts engagement in relation to cultural policy

Rebecca Gordon-Nesbitt

Introduction

In recent decades, there has been increased willingness to consider the social determinants of health in general and the impact of arts engagement in particular. At the same time, the shift towards evidence-based policy-making has been well documented, and the prevailing narrative in certain circles is that we lack evidence around the long-term relationship between health and engagement in arts activities beyond the clinical environment. In March 2014, Arts Council England (ACE) published an evidence review that attempted to account for the value of culture to people and society. While this review referenced large-scale Nordic research showing the positive impact of longitudinal cultural engagement, it ultimately deferred to the UK to conclude that 'there is no evidence that these improvements are sustained in the long term, and the majority of studies have been small scale and unable to do more than report a correlation between the intervention and these benefits' (ACE, 2014: 26).

Five months before the ACE evidence review was published, the Arts and Humanities Research Council put out a targeted call under the auspices of the Cultural Value Project, which noted that 'A number of research studies in recent years (most prominently drawing on long-term cohort study data from the Nordic countries) have suggested a positive correlation between engagement in cultural activities and long-term physical and psychological health after adjusting for a range of income, educational and social variables' (AHRC, 2013: 9). In response to this call, a research programme was designed that sought to build an evidence base around the longitudinal health impacts of engaging in arts activities in non-clinical settings. This suggests that engagement in the arts leads to longer lives better lived, prompting an urgent reassessment of the ways in which culture is valued and distributed within society. What follows is an account of this research programme and a consideration of its implications for cultural policy.

Context

The research outlined in this chapter took place against the backdrop of two largely unreconciled imperatives – first, that the arts should evidence their impact and, second, that we should engage with the arts for the good of our health.

On the one hand, the era of Cool Britannia witnessed the shift from a 'something for nothing' to a 'something for something' approach to the arts and their funding (Davies and Ford, 2000: 30). The nineteenth century paradigm of art for art's sake – which was not without its critics – was deemed inadequate, and, as in other forms of public culture (notably education), the arts were compelled to prove their extrinsic worth. The two main types of impact that the arts have been expected to demonstrate are economic and social. Economic impact is inextricably bound up with the elision of the arts and creative industries, the designation of creative cities and the dream of inward investment. Expectations of social impact are discernible in the social inclusion policies beloved by New Labour and the demand that the arts justify their worth in relation to a number of societal metrics (Matarasso, 1997). A backlash against consideration of (particularly social) impact, and an attempt to debunk evidence-based policy, was spearheaded by the centre right think tank, Policy Exchange, in favour of a libertarian, anti-statist narrative (Mirza, 2006). However, a glimpse at the Culture White Paper, published by the Conservative Government in March 2016, reveals the persistence of the drive towards impact, with intrinsic, social and economic value recognised separately and, perhaps disingenuously, in that order (Department for Culture, Media & Sport, 2016).

On the other hand, there has been a groundswell of initiatives making the connection between arts engagement and health. At one end of the diverse arts and health spectrum, professionally accredited therapists administer arts activities targeted at a range of clinical outcomes. At the opposite end of the spectrum, in a continuation of the late 1960s community arts ethos,[1] thousands of organisations offer participatory arts activities throughout the UK, generally to those at a low ebb. While the former area of practice can be framed primarily in health terms and its impact measured accordingly, the latter varies widely in its approach to health impacts, and evaluation remains patchy. Nonetheless, all those working in the health-orientated community arts movement affirm the benefits of arts-based approaches.[2]

The field of health in the developed world is undergoing a transformation from a biomedical to psychosocial model and from a focus on cure to an emphasis on prevention. This implies that the vast majority of communicable diseases have been eradicated and that the major challenges for current and future generations are long-term health conditions such as cancer, cardiovascular disease, dementia and obesity. The inextricability of physical and mental health is also readily acknowledged, as is consideration of the broader socioeconomic factors determining health.

Between 2005 and 2008, Professor Sir Michael Marmot chaired the World Health Organization Commission on the Social Determinants of Health, which found that:

> Social inequalities in health arise because of inequalities in the conditions of daily life and the fundamental drivers that give rise to them: inequities in power, money and resources. These social and economic inequalities underpin the determinants of health: the range of interacting factors that shape health and well-being. These include: material circumstances, the social environment, psychosocial factors, behaviours, and biological factors. In turn, these factors are influenced by social position, itself shaped by education, occupation, income, gender, city and race. All these influences are affected by the socio-political and cultural and social context in which they sit.
>
> *(Marmot et al., 2010: 16)*

Despite this acute analysis, the arts – which might usefully be thought of as psychosocial factors interacting with health and wellbeing – were conspicuous by their absence from the published thoughts of the Commission (Clift et al., 2010).

While the Commission on the Social Determinants of Health was mid-way through its work, the Chief Executive of the NHS commissioned Harry Cayton, National Director for Patients and the Public, to review the role of the Department of Health (DH) in advancing the arts and health. Cayton set up a working group, which reported that the arts were integral to health and health services and should be recognised as such. Simultaneously, DH and ACE collaborated on a prospectus for arts and health, outlining many examples of best practice and research-based evidence (Arts Council England, 2007). But, by the time the ACE strategic framework, *Achieving Great Art and Culture for Everyone*, was published in 2010, consideration of the health value of the arts had receded into the background.

Despite periodic recognition of the relationship between the arts and health, the quality of the evidence base is often cited as a reason for the arts being overlooked when health and its social determinants are discussed. Much progress is being made in this area, with a range of mixed methods approaches being used to capture the health impacts of arts activities. The research described here makes a tangential contribution to the field by taking a further step away from targeted impacts to consider the inadvertent health effects of engaging with the arts in galleries, museums, theatres and concert halls.

Methods

Literature search and study selection

A search was initially undertaken of the MEDLINE (using PubMed) and EMBASE (using Ovid SP) databases, beginning with such terms as 'art', 'culture', 'health', 'longitudinal'. However, as these words are ubiquitous within the literature – with 'culture' frequently appearing in relation to the cultivation of cells and 'art' regularly occurring in phrases such as 'state-of-the-art' and serving as an acronym for Atraumatic Restorative Treatment, Anti Retroviral Treatment and Assisted Reproductive Technologies – this generated an excess of 10,000 results when using Ovid. Sorting the results by relevance (five stars) failed to isolate three terms together. The use of truncated versions of the search terms – such as 'long' (306 results when searched with 'art' and 'survival' in Medline) – and Boolean operators – e.g. 'NOT HIV' (216 results in Medline) – reduced the quantity of results but came no closer to isolating even those studies that were known at the outset. That these known studies used little common language ultimately precluded the use of generic search terms. The review also sought to take account of grey literature in the field, but a search of Open Grey produced 11 irrelevant studies, reinforcing the need for other methods.

In light of the above, it was decided to conduct a hand search of material, beginning with the nucleus of known studies – specifically those undertaken by a team based in Sweden, led by Lars Olov Bygren and first published in the *British Medical Journal* in 1996 (Bygren et al., 1996) and its Finnish equivalent, led by Markku T. Hyyppä (Hyyppä et al., 2006). From there, the review radiated outwards, taking account of subsequent research published by these two teams and the studies to which they referred. This scoping process was complemented by the use of web-based search engines and facilitated by dialogues with the main researchers in the field, either by email or in person during a week-long trip to the Nordic region. Additionally, reports issued by policy-making bodies at Westminster and Holyrood were scrutinised, and civil servants in the Department for Culture, Media and Sport (DCMS) were consulted.

The longitudinal focus of the review precluded cross-sectional studies. All known physical and mental health conditions were included, as were subjective measures, such as self-rated health. Similarly, cultural engagement was considered across the art forms, taking account of attendance at arts events and (to a lesser extent) participation in creative activity. As arts engagement was understood to be a voluntary part of participants' lives, rather than an 'intervention', studies considering the therapeutic nature of creative engagement upon existing health conditions and those relying on randomised controlled trials were excluded from consideration.

As several of the studies only mentioned arts engagement as an incidental element of socio-cultural interaction, the ultimate criterion for inclusion became the consideration of two or more discrete cultural activities. The scoping process generated an initial long list of studies from which the eventual evidence base was culled. Data on study characteristics were extracted – including country of origin, authors, publication year, dataset, population sample size, age of respondents, outcome measure, cultural activities, confounders and results – are tabulated at the end of this report.

Results

The scoping review yielded an initial 14 key studies. A digital evidence base was compiled online (longitudinalhealthbenefits.wordpress.com), containing a précis of each study and links to the original research articles where copyright clearance was possible to secure. The online evidence base also includes a consideration of the main strengths and weaknesses of each study and a hint about the mechanisms thought to underlie any of the positive associations that were observed between the two main variables of arts engagement and health.

The evidence base was launched at the annual conference of the Faculty of Public Health of the Royal College of Physicians on 3 July 2014 and widely publicised among colleagues in the arts and health, research and policy-making fields. Since then, the scoping review has continued, and a further study has been added to the evidence base (Agahi and Parker, 2008). As of April 2016, the online repository had received 5,150 views from more than 30 different countries, including Brazil, Japan and South Africa. As this site solicits details of any omissions, the evidence base has the possibility to evolve, through attention being drawn to extant work in this area and new studies being carried out.

As suspected at the outset, the evidence base is largely centred on the Nordic region, specifically Sweden, Finland and Norway. In these countries, research teams benefit from population data collated over time, with the inbuilt possibility of linkage (through unique personal identification numbers) to registers detailing morbidity and mortality. The studies rely either on longitudinal panel surveys or on one-off questioning of a large cohort, subsequently followed up in relation to a given outcome measure. As discussed at greater length below, outcome measures range from general and cause-specific mortality to specific morbidities such as dementia and obesity, with a wide variety of potential confounders being considered. Numbers of participants range from 463 to 12,675, aged between 11 and 99. The majority of studies perform *a posteriori* analysis, with the researchers having no input into the formulation of questions and respondents inevitably being blinded to the purpose of such retroactive studies. The evidence base is variously grounded in social epidemiology, gerontology and occupational health; an interpretation of the findings of the studies in the evidence base is attempted here.

Mortality and chronic morbidity

Given the ready availability of data pertaining to date and cause of death in the Nordic countries, it is, perhaps, inevitable that several of the research teams have focused upon mortality or survival as their main outcome measure. Ten of the studies in the evidence base adopt such an approach to assess the impact of a range of socio-cultural factors upon longevity. Of these, five consider all-cause mortality (Bygren et al., 1996; Konlaan et al., 2000; Lennartsson and Silverstein, 2001; Hyyppä et al., 2006; Agahi and Parker, 2008), four introduce some differentiation among causes of death – through cancer (Welin et al., 1992; Bygren et al., 2009), cardiovascular disease (Hyyppä et al., 2007), external and other causes (Väänänen et al., 2009) – and one examines coronary heart disease mortality and morbidity together (Sundquist et al., 2004).

The first study in the evidence base is unable to find a link between socio-cultural activities and cancer-related mortality (Welin et al., 1992), while another assessment of all-cause mortality from a similar perspective detects a negligible effect upon survival from socio-cultural engagement (Lennartsson and Silverstein, 2001). The main Finnish team finds that leisure social participation mildly predicts all-cause mortality (Hyyppä et al., 2006), while having no discernible effect upon cardiovascular mortality (Hyyppä et al., 2007). Another Finnish team finds an association between external causes of mortality (such as accident and suicide) and (particularly socially orientated) cultural participation (Väänänen et al., 2009). While these results are ambiguous, more fruitful avenues of enquiry are opened up when longevity is approached in social and cultural terms.

Emphasising the social over the cultural

Social epidemiology presumes a 'category of environmental factors capable of producing profound effects on host susceptibility to environmental disease agents' (Cassel, 1976: 108). In this context, environmental factors are taken to include 'the presence of other members of the same species, or more generally, certain aspects of the social environment' (Ibid). In turn, consideration of the psychosocial determinants of health posits that social isolation increases the risk of all-cause mortality (Berkman and Syme, 1979), with social support thought to guard against a range of chronic diseases (House et al., 1982; Schoenbach et al., 1986; Kaplan et al., 1988) and self-reported symptoms, both physical and psychological (Berkman, 1995; Seeman, 1996). Accordingly, more than half of studies in the evidence base adopt what might be described as a social capital perspective, which takes close account of the individual's place within society.

While social capital is a multi-faceted and mutable construct that is notoriously difficult to define and measure, Hyyppä et al. have sought to demonstrate a relationship between social capital and health. The first of two studies showed leisure social participation to be a predictor of survival in middle-aged Finnish men (Hyyppä et al., 2006), while the second only just replicated this finding in relation to all-cause mortality but not to deaths from cardio-vascular causes (Hyyppä et al., 2007).

Marmot argues that 'living in supportive, cohesive social groups can be protective' of health (2015: 10), changing hormonal profiles and potentially lowering the risk of heart attacks, whereas being marginal in society can increase the risk of disease. Engagement in cultural activity in the public sphere is thought to increase the sense of community cohesion and confer a health-protective effect. However, this body of work suggests that the artistic specificities of engagement are subordinate to the social milieu in which engagement occurs. In order to ascertain cultural value, this approach needs to be inverted.

Isolating the cultural from the social

A social capital approach to arts engagement permits a multiplicity of diverse leisure-time activities to be bunched together in the analysis, obviating differentiation between art forms. In distinguishing cultural from social engagement, the team comprised of Bygren, Johansson and Konlaan has led the field. In the aforementioned *BMJ* study, which formed the basis of many subsequent research programmes, Bygren et al. initially acknowledged that the social element of cultural participation might be an important determinant of survival, suggesting that 'Perhaps cultural behaviour is so intermingled with life as a whole that it is impossible to discern its influence' (1996: 1578).[2] At the same time, they discovered possession of a social network to be a slight threat to male longevity and showed low (compared to regular) attendance at cultural events to significantly increase the likelihood of death. Four years later, the same team found social ties to have a negligible effect as a confounder, irrespective of their strength or quality (Konlaan et al., 2000). They also began to address the lack of differentiation between art forms – which had typified their own earlier studies and those of other research teams – to demonstrate a positive association between survival and attendance at the cinema, concerts and exhibitions. The same team's 2001 study shows a positive association between self-rated health and attendance at exhibitions, dance performances, films, popular music concerts and theatre plays, as well as establishing a directly proportional relationship between self-rated health and the number of cultural activities attended (Johansson et al., 2001).

Transferring this approach to a US context, Bygren would later collaborate on a cross-sectional study that tested this premise (Wilkinson et al., 2007). Rare cultural attendees were seen to be suffering from greater rates of cancer-related mortality than their high-attending counterparts in urban areas. Significantly, this study claims that cultural attendance evinces a potentially preventative effect, making it akin to physical activity and smoking as a predictor of cancer-related mortality, irrespective of health and socio-economic status.

Departing from the Bygren team to reconsider cultural engagement as a factor in social participation, Sundquist et al. (2004) drew up a participation index with 18 variables. It is noteworthy that those variables with the greatest significance were found to be the five forms of cultural attendance included in the index: cinema, theatre, concerts, art exhibitions and museums. These combined findings suggest that the intrinsic cultural experience has a part to play in militating against life-threatening conditions. The possible reasons for this will be discussed shortly.

Successful ageing

Another area in which the long-term relationship between arts engagement and health has been studied is that of successful ageing (Adams et al., 2011). Three of the studies in the evidence base focus on populations over the age of 65, with two focusing on survival (Lennartsson and Silverstein, 2001; Agahi and Parker, 2008) and one on the onset of dementia (Wang et al., 2002). All three consider participation in creative activity in addition to attendance at cultural events. On the understanding that 'The act of making [is] cognitively demanding and [requires] skills in planning, evaluation, counting, measurement and problem solving' (Liddle et al., 2013: 332), several of the studies in the evidence base acknowledge the mental component of arts engagement (Lennartsson and Silverstein, 2001; Wang et al., 2002; Bygren et al., 2009; Väänänen et al., 2009; Cuypers et al., 2012). In relation to dementia, attendance at cultural events has been categorised as social while participation in creative activity (such as drawing or painting) is defined as mental, with both types of activity found to exhibit a positive association with dementia prevention (Wang et al., 2002).

Weight management

With obesity looming as a major public health issue, a further area of research has centred on the relationship between socio-cultural engagement and weight gain. Focusing on the social aspects of participation, one study alluded to arts engagement increasing the likelihood of adolescent boys becoming overweight (Lajunen et al., 2009). Yet, while another study found no association between social participation and waistline measurement in adult women, it observed a greater likelihood of maintaining weight within the recommended range for adult men (Kouvonen et al., 2012). In the same year, a third study found that, as compared to social participation, cultural participation was negatively associated with obesity in teenage girls (Cuypers et al., 2012). This finding fits with research that has discovered an element of social communicability in relation to obesity (Christakis and Fowler, 2007) and consolidates the positive effects of cultural engagement observed elsewhere.

Gender

Work carried out around both successful ageing and obesity elaborates on the gendered nature of health effects. One paper in the evidence base takes gender as its main focus, drawing on a study population as it migrates from the Swedish Level of Living Survey to the Swedish Panel Study of Living Conditions of the Oldest Old. It is here that we encounter the most direct claims of causality, with a dose-response relationship between social participation and survival being reported in women. When differentiating a range of social activities, it is found that 'participation in cultural activities was the only activity that was significantly related to survival in both men and women' (Agahi and Parker, 2008: 865).

Discussion

Reviewing the studies in the evidence base suggests that there is a growing body of literature surrounding the longitudinal relationship between arts engagement and health. Largely centred on the Nordic countries, the evidence base suggests that engagement in the arts – primarily as an audience member but also as a practitioner – generally has a positive impact upon life expectancy, disease resistance, mental acuity and weight maintenance, through a variety of possible means.

Common to the majority of studies is the tentative nature of their claims, speaking of association (or correlation) rather than causation. In a similarly tentative way, arts engagement is assumed to have a preventative, rather than remedial, effect. Interestingly, the potentially detrimental effects of arts engagement have also been acknowledged from the outset, with Bygren et al. speculating that 'Negative effects of cultural activities could be that people lose their sense of reality and identify with asocial models of behaviour and are themselves encouraged towards asocial behaviour' (1996: 1578). This is echoed by Hyyppä, with the sentiment that 'It is highly probable that not all cultural activities are beneficial for health and survival; some can even be detrimental to health' (2010: 51). Further work is needed to establish the existence and direction of any causal relationship between the two main variables, and it is rightly argued that 'More prospective studies on large populations are needed to answer questions on causality' (Cuypers et al., 2011: 22).

The two greatest obstacles to attributing causality are the possibility of reverse causation and the likelihood of residual confounders. In the first case, it is generally assumed that people with poor health tend not to take part in cultural activities (or surveys), thereby skewing the results. Researchers on the HUNT Study in Norway, which provided data for the most recent study in the evidence base (Cuypers et al., 2012), have elsewhere given consideration to the biases that may arise through non-participation, finding not only disease but also socio-economic status to be the main reasons for non-response (Langhammer et al., 2012). A report published by the Scottish Government asserts that 'cultural engagement levels are highest in the highest household income groups in Scotland and decline to be lowest in the lowest household income groups' (Leadbetter and O'Connor, 2013: 7). At the same time, Taking Part data consistently demonstrate that white adults from higher socio-economic groups are the main beneficiaries of Arts Council England's strategy of 'great art and culture for everyone'.

In the second case, 'there is the unavoidable problem of possible unknown or latent confounders' (Hyyppä, 2010: ix). Table 20.1 at the end of this report shows the range of possible confounders that have been included in the evidence base; longitudinal research must continue to take account of individual and social factors that have an impact upon health irrespective of arts engagement.

In their seminal paper, Bygren et al. (1996) suggested that cultural participation might underlie the different survival rates observed across social classes. Low income, identified by Welin et al. (1992) as a residual confounder, was seen to be significant with respect to mortality. When subsequently considering the association between cancer-related mortality and cultural attendance, the *BMJ* team asserted that cultural attendance might serve as a 'proxy variable for other cancer preventive factors' (Bygren et al., 2009: 71). As the association between cancer-related mortality and cultural attendance could only be determined in urban locations, the researchers concluded that arts participation might be part of a healthy and active lifestyle and signal better access to information and health services. In much the same way, Hyyppä et al. found that 'economic status slightly modified the effect of leisure participation in men, thus emerging as a tentative mediator between social capital and health' (2007: 594). If we are to fully explain these observations, attention needs to be paid to the relationship between socio-economic factors (across multiple indicators) and levels of access to both health and cultural resources. Many of the datasets underlying the international evidence base are available for re-examination, and scope exists to draw upon UK-based datasets. Beyond the analysis of extant data, there is scope for intervention into the questions making up the surveys, and researchers at both DCMS and the HUNT Study indicated their willingness to consider this.

In the surveys underlying the evidence base, questions pertaining to arts engagement tend to be centred on frequency. Yet, many of the studies in the evidence base acknowledge that the qualitative, rather than quantitative, properties of arts engagement might be determining factors. If we are to unravel the association between arts engagement and health, much greater attention needs to be paid to the particular experience of engaging with art, film, music and theatre.

As the name suggests, cultural value was the starting point for the umbrella project under which this research was conducted. The Cultural Value Project sought to 'reposition first-hand, individual experience of arts and culture at the heart of enquiry' (Crossick and Kaszynska, 2016: 7). A primary focus on cultural value – in advance of considering any second-order health and wellbeing benefits – has the welcome side effect of adding lucidity to the debate around social capital.

One of the most interesting aspects of this study comprises the mechanisms that are speculated upon in cases where a positive relationship between arts engagement and health is observed, with the most compelling being psychoneuroimmunological and epigenetic in nature. In the case of psychoneuroimmunology, the nervous, immune and endocrine systems are implicated in psychosomatic mechanisms, stimulated by cognitive interactions (such as arts engagement) and mediated by cortisol, the stress hormone. As we have seen, social epidemiology admits that environmental factors can enhance susceptibility to disease. In considering the social determinants of health, it is increasingly accepted that the converse is also true, and an enriched environment can have health-protective effects. Bygren et al.

argue that arts engagement, as a form of environmental enrichment, can contribute to lowering stress, thus engendering a range of physical and mental health benefits.

This brings us to the emerging field of epigenetics, which suggests that environmental alterations bring about changes in the non-coding part of the genome that determines which genes are switched on or off at a given time. It has recently been discovered that epigenetic shifts are communicable through the generations, meaning that positive or negative environmental effects could be passed from parents to their children (Bygren, 2013). This has clear implications in relation to the social determinants of health and their persistence through the generations while also signalling a role for arts engagement as a form of environmental enrichment. Let us turn now to a consideration of the ways in which cultural policy could respond.

Implications

However tentatively the findings of individual studies in the evidence base are reported, the sense emerges that the relationship between arts engagement and health carries important public health implications, which have consequences for cultural (and health) policy.

The aforementioned Culture White Paper makes intrinsic value synonymous with well-being and life satisfaction, and it cites health as a social benefit, on the basis that 'There is considerable evidence of the beneficial effects of the arts on both physical and mental health. This includes improvements such as positive physiological and psychological changes in clinical outcomes; decreasing the amount of time spent in hospital; and improving mental health' (Department for Culture, Media & Sport, 2016: 15). This medley of positive health impacts seems to encompass a consideration of arts therapies and health-orientated community arts, with art in hospitals in between. When multifarious health impacts are hybridised in this way, it is impossible to determine whether international longitudinal studies and/or attendance at non-health-orientated arts events have been taken into account, but the accompanying bibliography and case studies (all of which are drawn from the UK) suggest not.

The significance of the finding that arts engagement is generally beneficial for health is two-fold, carrying implications for cultural venues and health-orientated community arts initiatives. In the case of cultural venues, the positive effects of arts engagement provide arguments for the continued funding of arts activities, in and of themselves. This might serve to convince evidence-based policy-makers of the continued necessity of supporting the arts in a non-clinical environment. Added to this, the fact that research has been carried out at a large scale – across whole populations and extended periods of time – potentially exempts individual organisations from continually having to justify their value to the public purse. That the individual, qualitative experience of arts engagement is taken to be paramount in manifesting health effects may ultimately serve to focus attention away from quantitative measurements of cultural value.

Notwithstanding the positive implications of this research for cultural venues, the fact that these health benefits are only being accessed by an already privileged part of the population remains a source of concern. It is here that health-orientated community arts organisations come into their own, consistently reaching those experiencing mild to moderate mental health issues, often in combination with physical conditions and often as a result of multiple deprivation. In their insistence upon process over product, such organisations tend to be weighted towards 'everyone' rather than asking who and what defines 'great'. The recommendation in the Culture White Paper that clinical commissioning groups and local authorities mount a concerted effort to support this work is a welcome one, offering a potential route for democratising access to arts engagement as a form of environmental enrichment and a psychosocial determinant of health.

Table 20.1 Comparative table of studies in the evidence base

Authors, year, country	Dataset, population sample size, age	Outcome measure	Confounders	Cultural activities	Results
Welin et al., 1992, Sweden	Men born in Gothenburg in 1913 (selected in 1963 and 1973), n = 769 60-year-olds; 220 50-year-olds	Mortality from cardio-vascular diseases, cancer and other causes to 1985	Smoking, alcohol consumption, previous stroke or heart attack, marital status, household size, income	Reading, cinema, theatre, concerts, museums/ galleries,	Middle-aged men with a good 'social network' may be partly protected against non-cancer mortality.
Bygren, Konlaan and Johansson, 1996, Sweden	Swedish Survey of Living Conditions 1982–3, n = 15, 198 (12,675) participants aged 16–74 years	Survival to 31 December 1991	Age, gender, education level, income, long-term disease, social network, smoking, physical exercise	Cinema, theatre, concerts, live music, art/other exhibitions, museums, reading, music-making, singing in a choir	Attending cultural events at least once a week has a positive effect upon survival.
Konlaan, Bygren and Johansson, 2000, Sweden	Swedish Survey of Living Conditions 1982–3, n = 10, 609 aged 25–74	Survival to 31 December 1996	Age, gender, cash buffer, educational level, long-term disease, smoking, physical exercise	Cinema, theatre, concerts, live music, art exhibitions, museums, music-making, reading	'Attendance at cultural events may have a beneficial effect on longevity' (p. 174).
Johansson, Konlaan and Bygren, 2001, Sweden	Swedish Survey of Living Conditions 1982–3 and 1990–1, n = 3, 793 aged 25–74	Self-reported health	Baseline health status, type of residence, geographical region of domicile, socio-economic status (level of education)	Cinema, theatre, concerts, live music, art exhibitions, museums, music-making, reading	'Those who became culturally less active between the first and second occasion, or those who were culturally inactive on both occasions, ran a 65% excess risk of impaired perceived health compared with those who were culturally active on both occasions' (p. 229).

Study	Sample	Outcome	Covariates	Cultural activities	Findings
Bygren et al., 2009, Sweden	Swedish Survey of Living Conditions 1990–1, n = 9, 011 aged 25–74	Cancer incidence in Swedish public death register to 31 December 2003	Age, gender, chronic conditions, disposable income, educational attainment, smoking status, leisure time physical activity, urban/non-urban residency	Cinema, theatre, live music, art gallery, museum	Rare and moderate cultural attendees were 3.23 and 2.92 (respectively) times more likely to die of cancer than regular attendees in urban areas.
Lennartsson and Silverstein, 2001, Sweden	Swedish Panel Study of Living Conditions of the Oldest Old 1992 n = 537 (463 non-institutionalised) aged 75+	Survival to 1996	Age, gender, educational level, functional impairment, presence of heart or circulatory problems, tobacco use	Cinema, cultural events, reading books or newspapers, hobbies	Solitary–active participation (e.g. gardening, hobbies) reduce mortality risk, particularly in men.
Wang et al., 2002, Sweden	Kungsholmen Project 1987–9, n = 1, 810 aged 75+	Onset of dementia between first follow-up (1991–3), and second follow-up (1994–6)	Age, gender, education, cognitive functioning, comorbidity, depressive symptoms, physical functioning at baseline	Theatre, concerts, art exhibitions (social), painting, drawing (mental), sewing, knitting, crocheting, weaving (productive)	'Engagement in mental, social, or productive activities was inversely related to dementia incidence' (p. 1081)'.
Sundquist et al., 2004, Sweden	Swedish Annual Level-of-Living Survey 1990–1, n = 6, 861, 35–74 years	Coronary heart disease morbidity or mortality to 31 December 2000	Socio-economic and educational status, housing tenure, smoking, age, gender, marital status, geographical region	Cinema, theatre, concerts, art exhibitions and museums, choir	An association found between low social participation and increased incidence of coronary heart disease morbidity and mortality. Attendance at the cinema, theatre, concerts, art exhibitions and museums had (by far, in most cases) the most significance within the social participation index.

(Continued)

Table 20.1 (Continued)

Authors, year, country	Dataset, population sample size, age	Outcome measure	Confounders	Cultural activities	Results
Hyyppä, Mäki, Impivaara and Aromaa, 2006, Finland	Mini-Finland Health Survey 1978–80, n = 5, 087, 30–59 years	Survival during 20 years of follow-up (first three years excluded)	Residential stability, socio-economic status, marital status and relations, trusting relationships, alcohol consumption, smoking; mental health, self-reported chronic diseases or disabilities, self-rated overall health	Theatre, cinema, concerts, art exhibitions, reading, listening to music, drama, singing, photography, painting and handicraft	'Leisure participation predicts survival in middle-aged Finnish men and its effect is independent of demographic features, of health status and of several other health-related factors' (p. 5).
Hyyppä, Mäki, Impivaara and Aromaa, 2007, Finland	Mini-Finland Health Survey 1978–80, n = 7, 217, 30–99 years	Survival during 24 years of follow-up (first five excluded) with attention to all-cause and cardiovascular mortality (including strokes) up to November 2004	Residential stability, socio-economic status, marital status and relations, trusting relationships, alcohol consumption, smoking; mental health, self-reported chronic diseases or disabilities, self-rated overall health	Theatre, cinema, concerts, art exhibitions, reading, listening to music, drama, singing, photography, painting and handicraft	Leisure participation is associated with reduced all-cause mortality in women and men (related to economic status in the latter case).
Agahi and Parker, 2008	Swedish Annual Level-of-Living Survey 1990–1 and Swedish Panel Study of Living Conditions of the Oldest Old 1992, n = 1, 246 men and women aged 65 to 95	Survival to 31 December 2003	A range of symptoms and diseases, functional status, age, gender, educational level (as a measure of socio-economic position), smoking, alcohol, body mass index.	Reading books, hobby activities (e.g. knitting, sewing, carpentry or painting), cultural activities (going to the cinema, theatre, concerts, museums or exhibitions), dancing, playing musical instruments, and choir singing.	Women demonstrated a dose-response relationship between overall participation and survival; men did not. 'Gender-specific analyses revealed that participation in cultural activities was the only activity that was significantly related to survival in both men and women' (p. 865).

Lajunen et al., 2009, Finland	FinnTwin12 study all twins born in Finland 1983–7, $n = 5, 184$ twins aged 11–12 years	Becoming overweight during follow-up at 14 and 17 years	Pubertal timing, socio-economic status of family	Television and video viewing, computer games, listening to music, playing musical instruments, reading, arts (drawing or painting, handicrafts, woodwork, building scale models)	Engagement in the arts in boys was detrimental to the maintenance of recommended weights. Among girls, few individual leisure activities predicted becoming overweight. However, the 'passive and solitary' cluster carried the greatest risk of becoming overweight in late adolescence.
Väänänen et al., 2009, Finland	Still Working survey (conducted by Finnish Institute of Occupational Health) 1986, $n = 7, 922$, working age	Survival 1986–2004	Socio-demographic factors, socio-economic status, work stress, social characteristics, diabetes, hypertension		High cultural engagement independently associated with decreased all-cause mortality and external causes of death (with solitary activities related to the former and socially shared cultural activities to the latter).

(*Continued*)

Table 20.1 (Continued)

Authors, year, country	Dataset, population sample size, age	Outcome measure	Confounders	Cultural activities	Results
Kouvonen et al., 2012, UK	English Longitudinal Study of Ageing waves 2 and 4, n = 4, 280 age 50+	Waist circumference at follow-up	Gender, age, ethnicity, marital status, total wealth, longstanding limiting illness, depressive symptoms, smoking status and physical activity	Arts or music group	No association was found between social participation and waistline measurement in women. Men with an initial waist measurement in the recommended range who participated in education, arts or music groups or in charitable associations were more likely to maintain their waist circumference.
Cuypers et al., 2012, Norway	HUNT Study 1995–7, n = 8, 408 13–19 years, followed up 2006–8, n = 1, 450 24–30 years	Obesity (body mass index, waist circumference, waist-hip ratio and natural development of the body over the life course)	Physical activity, socio-economic status, pubertal timing and genetic proclivity to obesity	Reading a book, listening to or playing music, doing homework, watching television	Participation in cultural activities guarded girls against being overweight. This was amplified when considering those who were at the recommended weight at baseline and when television was excluded as an activity

Notes

1 It is interesting to note that, in seeking to detach the participatory arts from ideology while advocating social impact, François Matarasso asserted that 'participation is not a euphemism for community arts' (1997: 4).
2 An example of best practice is to be found in Salford, where the organisation Start (founded in 1993) has purchased a building and installed specialist studios for woodwork and ceramics. To watch a film about some of the benefits accrued by service users, visit www.youtube.com/watch?v=wbyVL0MrOy0.
3 Asterisk in References indicates inclusion in the evidence base.

References[3]

Adams KB, Leibbrandt S and Moon H, A Critical Review of the Literature on Social and Leisure Activity and Wellbeing in Later Life. *Ageing Society*, 31, 2011, pp. 683–712.
*Agahi N and Parker MG, Leisure Activities and Mortality: Does Gender Matter? *Journal of Aging and Health*, 20, 2008, pp. 855–71.
All Party Parliamentary Group on Arts and Health, Inaugural Meeting, 15 January 2014.
Arts and Humanities Research Council, *Cultural Value Project: Targeted Call for Critical Reviews and Research Development Awards*, October 2013.
Arts Council England, *A Prospectus for Arts and Health* (London: Department of Health and Arts Council England, 2007).
Arts Council England, *The Value of Arts and Culture to People and Society: An Evidence Review* (London: Arts Council England, 2014).
Berkman LF, The Role of Social Relations in Health Promotion. *Psychosomatic Medicine*, 57, 1995, pp. 245–54.
Berkman LF and Syme SL, Social Networks, Host Resistance and Mortality: A Nine-Year Follow-Up of Alameda County Residents. *American Journal of Epidemiology*, 109, 1979, pp. 186–204.
Bygren LO, Intergenerational Health Responses to Adverse and Enriched Environments. *Annual Review of Public Health*, 34, 2013, pp. 49–60.
*Bygren LO, Johansson SE, Konlaan BB, et al., Attending Cultural Events and Cancer Mortality: A Swedish Cohort Study. *Arts and Health*, 1, 2009, pp. 64–73.
*Bygren, LO, Konlaan BB and Johansson SE, Attendance at Cultural Events, Reading Books or Periodicals, and Making Music or Singing in a Choir as Determinants for Survival: Swedish Interview Survey of Living Conditions. *British Medical Journal*, 313, 1996, pp. 1577–80.
Cassel J, The Contribution of the Social Environment to Host Resistance. *American Journal of Epidemiology*, 104, 1976, pp. 107–23.
Cayton H, *Report of the Review of Arts and Health Working Group* (London: Department of Health, 2007).
Christakis NA and Fowler JH, The Spread of Obesity in a Large Social Network over 32 Years. *New England Journal of Medicine*, 357, 2007, pp. 370–9.
Clift S, Camic P and Daykin N, The Arts and Global Health Inequities. *Arts & Health* 2(1), 2010, pp. 3–7.
Crossick G and Kaszynska P, *Understanding the Value of Arts and Culture: The AHRC Cultural Value Project* (Swindon: Arts and Humanities Research Council, 2016).
*Cuypers K, De Ridder K, Kvaløy K, et al., Leisure Time Activities in Adolescence in the Presence of Susceptibility Genes for Obesity: Risk or Resilience against Overweight in Adulthood? The HUNT Study. *BMC Public Health*, 12, 2012, p. 820.
Cuypers KF, Knudtsen MS, Sandgrenc M, et al., Cultural Activities and Public Health: Research in Norway and Sweden: An Overview. *Arts and Health*, 3, 2011, pp. 6–26.
Davies A and Ford S, Culture Clubs, *Mute*, 1 (18), 2000, pp. 28–35.
Department for Culture, Media & Sport, Culture White Paper (London: Department for Culture, Media & Sport, 2016).
House JS, Robbins C and Metzner HL, The Association of Social Relationships and Activities with Mortality: Prospective Evidence from the Tecumseh Community Health Study. *American Journal of Epidemiology*, 116, 1982, pp. 123–40.
Hyyppa, M. *Healthy Ties: Social Capital, Population Health and Survival* (London: Springer, 2010).

*Hyyppä MT, Mäki J, Impivaara O, et al., Leisure-Based Participation Predicts Survival: A Population-Based Study in Finland. *Health Promotion International*, 21, 2006, pp. 5–12.

*Hyyppä MT, Mäki J, Impivaara O, et al., Individual-Level Measures of Social Capital as Predictors of All-Cause and Cardiovascular Mortality: A Population-Based Prospective Study of Men and Women in Finland. *European Journal of Epidemiology*, 22, 2007, pp. 589–97.

*Johansson SE, Konlaan BB and Bygren LO, Sustaining Habits of Attending Cultural Events and Maintenance of Health. *Health Promotion International*, 16, 2001, pp. 229–34.

Kaplan GA, Salonen JT, Cohen RD, et al., Social Connections and Mortality from all Causes and from Cardiovascular Disease: Prospective Evidence from Eastern Finland. *American Journal of Epidemiology*, 128, 1988, pp. 370–80.

*Konlaan, BB, Bygren LO and Johansson SE, Visiting the Cinema, Concerts, Museums or Art Exhibitions as Determinant of Survival: A Swedish Fourteen-Year Cohort Follow-Up. *Scandinavian Journal of Social Medicine*, 28, 2000, pp. 174–78.

*Kouvonen A, Swift JA, Stafford M, et al., Social Participation and Maintaining Recommended Waist Circumference: Prospective Evidence From the English Longitudinal Study of Aging. *Journal of Aging Health*, 24, 2012, pp. 250–68.

*Lajunen HR, Keski-Rahkonen A, Pulkkinen L, et al., Leisure Activity Patterns and Their Associations with Overweight: A Prospective Study among Adolescents. *Journal of Adolescence*, 32, 2009, pp. 1089–1103.

Langhammer A, Krokstad S, Romundstad P, et al., The HUNT Study: Participation is Associated with Survival and Depends on Socioeconomic Status, Diseases and Symptoms. *BMC Medical Research Methodology*, 12, 2012, p. 143.

Leadbetter C and O'Connor N, *Healthy Attendance? The Impact of Cultural Engagement and Sports Participation on Health and Satisfaction with Life in Scotland* (Edinburgh: Scottish Government, 2013).

*Lennartsson C and Silverstein M, Does Engagement With Life Enhance Survival of Elderly People in Sweden? The Role of Social and Leisure Activities. *The Journals of Gerontology Series B: Psychological Sciences and Social Sciences*, 56, 2001, pp. S335–S342.

Liddle JLM, Parkinson L and Sibbritt DW, Purpose and Pleasure in Late Life: Conceptualising Older Women's Participation in Art and Craft Activities. *Journal of Aging Studies*, 27, 2013, pp. 332.

Marmot M, *The Health Gap: The Challenge of an Unequal World* (London: Bloomsbury, 2015).

Marmot M, Allen J, Goldblatt P, et al., *Fair Society, Healthy Lives: Strategic Review of Health Inequalities in England Post-2010* (London: The Marmot Review, 2010).

Matarasso F, *Use or Ornament? The Social Impact of Participation in the Arts* (London: Comedia, 1997).

Mirza, M, *Culture Vultures Is UK Arts Policy Damaging the Arts?* (London: Policy Exchange, 2006).

Schoenbach VJ, Fredman L and Kleinbaum DG, Social Ties and Mortality in Evans County, Georgia, *American Journal of Epidemiology*, 123, 1986, pp. 577–91.

Seeman, TE, Social Ties and Health: The Benefits of Social Integration. *Annals of Epidemiology*, 6, 1996, pp. 442–51.

*Sundquist K, Lindström M, Malmström M, et al., Social Participation and Coronary Heart Disease: A Follow-up Study of 6900 Women and Men in Sweden. *Social Science and Medicine*, 58, 2004, pp. 615–22.

*Väänänen A, Murray M, Koskinen A, et al., Engagement in Cultural Activities and Cause-Specific Mortality: Prospective Cohort Study. *Preventive Medicine*, 49, 2009, pp. 142–47.

*Wang HX, Karp A, Winblad B, et al., Late-Life Engagement in Social and Leisure Activities Is Associated with a Decreased Risk of Dementia: A Longitudinal Study from the Kungsholmen Project. *American Journal of Epidemiology*, 155, 2002, pp. 1081–87.

*Welin L, Larsson B, Svardsudd K, et al., Social Network and Activities in Relation to Mortality from Cardiovascular Diseases, Cancer and Other Causes: A 12 Year Follow up of the Study of Men Born in 1913 and 1923. *Journal of Epidemiology and Community Health*, 46, 1992, pp. 127–32.

Wilkinson AV, Waters AJ, Bygren LO, et al., Are Variations in Rates of Attending Cultural Activities Associated with Population Health in the United States? *BMC Public Health*, 7, 2007, p. 226.

Part V
Global issues, regional cultural policy

21

Inequalities

When culture becomes a capital

Laurie Hanquinet

Introduction

Since Bourdieu's famous 'Distinction' (1984), much has been written across society on the unequal distribution of cultural resources or 'cultural capital' and its role in the production and reproduction of social inequalities. As we will see, by unravelling the mechanisms behind the acquisition of a taste for the arts and culture, Bourdieu's theory revealed the extent to which apparently personal and innate cultural preferences are influenced by people's social origin and position. They are hence – to some degree at least – class-based mechanisms. His findings provided essential insights to re-think policies in favour of cultural democratization and a wider access to culture.

However, Bourdieu's views were most famously challenged by the figure of the 'omnivore' (Peterson & Simkus 1992; Peterson & Kern 1996; Peterson 2005). The omnivores would be characterized by a diversity of tastes and cultural activities and not only by an appetite for high culture. By crossing long-established boundaries between high and popular culture, the omnivores could arguably be the sign that society would have achieved cultural democracy through policies supporting a variety of cultural forms, which would be perceived as of equal value. We will see that such a thesis does not hold, as the omnivore does not signify anything like the end of social divisions and tensions based on unequal distribution of cultural resources. This reinforces the need to look at the composition of cultural capital. I will particularly outline 'emerging' forms of cultural distinction and their relationships with divisions of class and age. This chapter concludes by discussing possible areas for future research that would take seriously into account the reconfigurations of cultural capital and their implications for cultural policies.

Bourdieu and cultural capital

The notion of cultural capital has arguably been most often associated with Bourdieu's 'Distinction' (1984). Yet, the notion already appears in his earlier contributions to the field of the sociology of education. In 'The Inheritors' (1979), Bourdieu with his colleague Passeron sought to unveil the role of school in the reproduction of inequalities and of structures of power. They demonstrated the importance of cultural skills and knowledge acquired through familial transmission for the pupils' educational achievements, and in doing this they emphasized the role of cultural differences in social stratification. Schools were supposed to be meritocratic institutions in which everyone's own merit and abilities would be rewarded; yet, the two scholars showed instead that schools were, for the members of the dominant classes, a more comfortable place to develop oneself, as these institutions were built on principles these classes valued and disseminated.

The exact definition given to cultural capital in 'The Inheritors' and later 'Reproduction' (1970), two key joint works with Passeron, is rather vague. As Robbins (2005) points out, the concept of 'cultural capital' does not appear in the original – French – version of 'The Inheritors'. The authors used the terms '*capital linguistique*', which was translated into 'cultural capital'. I would add that, in the French version, Bourdieu and Passeron extensively referred to the idea of 'cultural heritage' ('*héritage culturel*'), which acts as a capital (the word is used) composed of knowledge, skills and savoir-faire transmitted by the parents to their privileged children. Sullivan discussed how '[f]orms of cultural capital such as a high level of linguistic fluency, broad cultural knowledge, and a knowledge of the "rules of the game" of academic assessments are an important part of what we mean by "academic ability"' (2007, p. 9) whose development is particularly promoted by certain groups of socially privileged parents.

In Bourdieu's writings on the relationships between cultural consumption and social stratification, the role of embodied cultural capital and of a taste for highbrow culture was further discussed and examined. Similarly, the implications of the concept of cultural capital for cultural policies became clearer. In his book written with Darbel (*L'Amour de l'Art* 1969), he exposed a paradox. Art museums are open to everyone; they have opened their doors to the whole society but remain mainly visited by the upper and middle classes. Far from being (only) an economic issue, he interpreted this paradox as illustrating the differential impact of cultural capital that refers first to the cultural knowledge inherited from the family and then to the level of education. Both lead to an individual propensity or *disposition* to consume cultural goods. Those who have been initiated to highbrow culture (and its institutions) by their families early in their lives develop a stronger need for cultural participation. A culturally favourable familial environment provides a set of skills useful to the educational trajectory and hardly delivered by the school. Hence, those who can be seen as 'initiated' can count on a 'cultivated disposition' thanks to the prime education by their parents.

This reveals that Bourdieu differentiated the level of education and embodied dispositions, such as the aesthetic disposition. The latter is ability 'to "decode" the formal [aesthetic] structure of the cultural work' (Lizardo 2008, p. 2). To be more specific, he distinguished there three different forms of capital, embodied ('*incorporé*'), objectified ('*objectivé*') and institutionalized ('*institutionnalisé*') (1979). The objectified forms of cultural capital refer to material supports in which cultural capital can be expressed and transmitted, such as cultural goods (writings, paintings, etc.) or monuments. These objectified forms require the embodied capital to be fully decoded and appreciated (symbolic appropriation). It also necessitates economic capital or resources to be bought or accessed (material appropriation). Institutionalized forms of cultural capital mean degrees and diplomas, which act as some sort of autonomous (legal) validation or evidence of embodied cultural capital. We can see that these two forms of cultural capital are intrinsically related with embodied capital, which is eventually '*le nerf de la guerre*' (i.e. the key issue) between the different definitions of cultural capital. In his text, he discussed the role of these embodied dispositions that act – in a disguised way – to enable their owners to decipher, interpret or, in more Bourdieusian terms, symbolically appropriate goods: they help, for instance, to 'consume a painting' ('*consommer un tableau*', 1979, p. 5).

His book on museum attendance offered a strategy to achieve a greater level of cultural democratization that outlined a clear link between cultural and education policies. 'The objective of cultural democratization is the aesthetic enlightenment, enhanced dignity, and educational development of the general citizenry' (Mulcahy 2006, p. 324). Dubois summarized what he perceived as Bourdieu's main policy recommendations from his book as follows:

1. Since the act of visiting museums (and by extension any cultural institution, and by extension again, access to culture) is determined by previously acquired dispositions that render such a visit thinkable or not, an efficient democratization policy should target these social dispositions.

2. Since the ability to understand and appreciate art is not innate but based on codes that enable understanding and appreciation, a democratization policy should aim at providing these codes to the social groups who have not acquired them.

3. Reciprocally, since the meaning of art is not necessarily given in the content of works of art, pedagogic support is required through explanatory panels or guides in the cultural venues themselves.

4. Since the sacralization of culture leaves out 'profane' agents, a cultural democratization policy should de-sacralize and humanize cultural institutions in order not to intimidate the visitors and to make them feel at ease. (Dubois 2011, p. 498)

Bourdieu here questioned the belief in the universal value of art that most cultural institutions, but also cultural policy-makers shared at that time (Dubois 2011), i.e. that art could touch anyone without any form of mediation. One just needed to put people in contact with culture in order to make it accessible. Bourdieu denounced that 'myth of the innocent eye' (Goodman 2001, p. 74) and quasi-religious visions of culture. He showed how this view participated in the reproduction of inequalities and the maintaining of the social hierarchies. The most privileged classes appear naturally refined and 'gifted' and then *superior* to the other classes while they have acquired the skills and codes to appreciate art and culture very early in their lives through their parents. The educational system simply reinforces this unequal distribution of cultural resources instead of counterbalancing it.

It should however be noted that Bourdieu advocated for a wider accessibility to the keys and codes at play within high culture and, even though he actively demonstrated its role in power struggles and hence its social nature, he hardly ever sought its complete dissolution. Instead, he had an 'ambivalent attitude to legitimate cultural content' (Ahearne 2004, p. 22). In a way it could be argued that Bourdieu helped de-mystify high culture as something sacred but never pleaded for cultural relativization (Chaumier 2011). In many places in his writings, high culture was still perceived as a tool for emancipation and enlightenment (Chaumier 2010); similarly, he did not want to get rid of cultural classifications (i.e. he does not seek to argue that all cultures are equal) as his emphasis on the role of autonomy in the cultural field showed (Ahearne 2004, p. 71). This is also somewhat supported by his description of popular aesthetics, which appears, as argued elsewhere, as an 'anti-aesthetic' (Shusterman 1991; Bennett et al. 2009).

Yet, his denunciations of the role high culture played in social domination resonated with a much more radical critique of high culture from artists and scholars, which became perceived mainly if not only as Bourgeois and as a source of alienation. The universal status of high culture was questioned as other forms of culture, especially popular forms, were valorised. High culture, as the Bourgeois and elitist culture, was increasingly seen as one culture among a plurality of other cultural expressions that could not be ordered. Note that Bourdieu was also critical of the 'populist' approaches of culture that emerged in the aftermath of May 68 (Ahearne 2004; Dubois 2011) and that he conceived as illusionary eventually springing from conditions of domination and exploitation (Ahearne 2004, p. 22). This process I have very succinctly described here had an important impact on high culture, which gradually diminished in importance (on this subject, see Chaumier 2010), without ever being completely disregarded. But it certainly enabled other issues to gradually come to the fore and to influence public policies in the cultural field. The development of the notion of 'cultural democracy', as the recognition of non-elite cultures previously ignored, is a key illustration of that. I will come back to that point in the next section.

In 'Distinction' (1984), Bourdieu continued his demonstration of the social nature of tastes and discussed how tastes could not only reflect people's natural inclinations but also act as social markers. Bourdieu's theory gives a quite complex picture of the – French – class society showing how social position is built upon different forms of resources, economic, cultural, social and, eventually, symbolic (i.e. social prestige). He particularly underlined the importance of cultural capital and its different forms in the production and maintenance of social stratification and inequalities. Those brought up in a culturally rich milieu are more likely to develop aesthetic dispositions and to acquire cultural skills through the 'habitus' that enable them to secure more easily potentially advantageous degrees. The habitus is an unconscious and systematic mechanism that converts social position into a set of dispositions, skills and attitudes but also affective response to cultural objects, which inform people's tastes and cultural consumption.

Economic, cultural and social capitals give a certain symbolic value – positive or negative – to individuals in society and contribute to the establishment of their lifestyle, as a set of attitudes, preferences, practices and behaviours that can be classified and that classify people. The different lifestyle dimensions are signals or markers that enable people to evaluate their positions as well as others' in a symbolic space. Bourdieu puts forward a homology principle in which the lifestyle space is one-to-one related to social space. In that respect, highbrow culture is linked to the upper classes (divided themselves into class fractions), who are the richest in terms of economic and cultural capital. The upper classes seek to distinguish themselves from the middle classes and their associated middlebrow tastes and, overall, from the popular classes who are defined by the 'choice of the necessary', which means that their social and economic conditions prevent them from having more refined tastes.

Following Bourdieu's work, many scholars have used his notion of cultural capital in so many ways (for an example of review, see Lamont & Lareau 1988) that it may have become a 'catch all' concept with a fluctuant meaning. This may be due to the fact that Bourdieu himself defined it in various ways across his writings. Yet, with his essay on this very concept in 1979 and other key works that developed his social theory of the game of position-taking according to diverse capitals, such as 'Distinction', the concept took a clearer shape. Cultural capital in its embodied forms, which is the most difficult to grasp, refers to a set of internalized dispositions that enable people to appreciate artistic and cultural items but also to develop 'good manners' in the way they dress, talk and more generally behave. People with high cultural capital appear to have naturally good taste, which gives them a greater social value and helps them find a better position in the social space. In other words, people with high cultural capital can decode the social world more effectively than those with low cultural capital can. High cultural capital helps those who possess it to secure more advantageous positions in society. Hence, cultural capital has a key role in power struggles between social groups and even more so that it helps to hide structural conditions of inequalities by making the dominated believe that others are naturally more equipped (in terms of intelligence, taste, etc.) to achieve better positions in life. This is what Bourdieu has called 'symbolic violence' (Bourdieu & Wacquant 1992).

Although Bourdieu's approach has kept a central place in cultural sociology and cultural policy, more recent perspectives have questioned the force of the distinction between high and popular culture.

The omnivore in an era of cultural democracy

For a long time in many Western countries, the focus of debate about cultural policies has been on cultural democratization, aimed at widening access to high culture. The latter was seen as intrinsically beneficial for all and therefore should be promoted in all the social strata. This objective has never disappeared and is still a central concern of political and research agendas.

However, this is 'a top-down approach that essentially privileges certain forms of cultural programming that are deemed to be a public good' (Mulcahy 2006, p. 234). As already discussed, it has unsurprisingly been accused of cultural elitism and of neglecting other forms of culture. In addition, repeated findings by cultural participation surveys on the 'elitist' nature of cultural audiences have *de facto* cast some doubt about the real impact of democratization efforts. In this context, the idea of cultural democracy became very important in the '70s and has had a durable impact on the reflections of what should be funded and whom culture belongs to by embracing the idea of cultural diversity. It represents a more active and more participatory dimension of cultural policies than the notion of democratization. As a result, the centrality of high culture in public policies itself has progressively decreased (on this subject, see Chaumier 2010) but has never vanished. This is in line with the promotion of popular and minorities cultures, which has been sustained by the cultural studies movement for instance.

According to this bottom-up perspective, what matters is that people be 'culturally active on their own terms': 'this shift involves a broad interpretation of cultural activities that comprises popular entertainment, folk festival, amateur sports, choral societies, and dancing schools' (Mulcahy 2006, p. 234). Such ideas move the debate away from any distinction between high and popular culture. Some have feared this shift because it would arguably leave the door open to a soulless, overriding, commercial culture controlled by the cultural industries (Chaumier 2010) in a society where cultural standards were becoming vague.

Interestingly, this principle of cultural democracy has resonated well with the development of a new notion in sociological research at the end of the '90s, the 'omnivore'. This notion was quickly to become a real challenger for Bourdieu's perspective but also helped re-define the ways scholars should perceive cultural inequalities. In the '90s Peterson and his colleagues observed that a growing part of the population, although mainly from the middle and upper classes, tended to appreciate both high and low forms of culture (Peterson & Simkus 1992; Peterson & Kern 1996). The idea is simple: the distinction that opposes high culture to popular culture has been progressively losing its relevance in favour of one between omnivores and univores. The very principle of homology is weakened by the fact that while upper social groups have more chances of liking high culture they also enjoy more popular cultural forms. The lower social groups are thus considered 'univores', characterized by a narrower range of activities and tastes. This movement from snob to omnivore could be interpreted as the progressive disappearance of a certain kind of univore, defined by a disposition towards high culture. The rise of the omnivore is due, according to Peterson (2005), to social structural and cultural changes, such as social mobility (see van Eijck 1999; Friedman 2012) or the aestheticization of popular culture (notably by the media).

331

The idea of omnivorousness has received a lot of attention in the sociological literature. While, at first sight, omnivorousness may have been the sign of some sort of cultural democracy, most studies revealed that it does not actually question the pertinence of mechanisms of cultural distinction put forward by Bourdieu. Instead, it revises how they operate (on which values). In what follows I have summarized what I conceive to be the three main lines of argument.

Omnivorous: a socially distinctive status

Research has shown the extent to which omnivorousness is a socially stratified phenomenon. It constitutes a 'boundary-drawing mechanism' (Lizardo & Skiles 2013) differentiating both horizontally and vertically social groups and their cultural referents. Omnivorousness has been defined as a feature of younger highly educated people (Peterson & Kern 1996; López-Sintas & Garcia-Álvarez 2002). However, the nature of the relation between omnivorousness and age appears more complex than the straightforward one with education. Peterson more recently revealed that younger cohorts were nowadays less likely to enjoy high culture (Peterson 2005; Rossman & Peterson 2005; Peterson & Rossman 2008), suggesting a sort of de-intellectualization or a popularization of cultural referents. Drawing on the terminology of Warde and Gayo-Cal (2009), younger cohorts are arguably increasingly more likely to be omnivores by volume (in the number of tastes and activities favoured) than by composition (a variety of tastes and practices characterized by diverse legitimacy). Warde and Gayo-Cal (2009) indicated that it was not necessarily younger people who were the most omnivorous but the middle-aged ones. This is supported by Donnat (2004) who identified a group in middle age characterized by broad cultural resources. These 'Branchés' (which could be translated as 'connected') have had greater exposure to diverse social contexts and have taken on board a greater diversity of cultural referents.

It has also been argued that there are various ways of being 'open to diversity' to paraphrase Ollivier (2008) and Bellavance (2008). Fridman and Ollivier (2004) even spoke of 'an ostentatious openness to diversity', suggesting that political, social and cultural tolerance was shown off by socially privileged people with a wide range of social, economic and cultural resources. Omnivorousness is then more than a wide range of tastes but also as a 'discriminating attitude' reflecting an ability to assess and value a diversity of cultural genres and products (Warde et al. 2008). It re-affirms the link between omnivorousness and cultural capital and distinction (Bryson 1996).

Omnivorousness is essentially related to social divisions and inequalities: the distinctive value of omnivorousness comes from the fact that the omnivores have the skills to draw boundaries between themselves and others based on the wide range of resources they can mobilize and have access to. More importantly, they achieve their special status by actually picking into the cultural referents of other lower social groups and mixing them with their own in a very specific way. Clearly, it is now more socially advantageous to look open and tolerant to a variety of cultural genres, objects, forms than to only be appreciative of high culture. Put in Bourdieu's terms, those with the highest cultural capital have a more eclectic repertoire of tastes, which selectively draws on distinctions between high and popular culture, as well as between younger and older forms of culture, rather than destroying these distinctions (see Bellavance 2008).

A more inclusive highbrow culture?

Omnivorousness requires the maintenance of cultural hierarchies, but these hierarchies may change over time. A few studies have envisaged that the *content* of highbrow culture could have changed over time and become more open to a diversity of cultural referents. Different authors have indeed discussed the extent to which the aesthetic criteria we rely on are the product of a historical moment (DiMaggio 1982; Levine 1990; Hanquinet et al. 2014).

In addition to this, some cultural forms that were traditionally seen as belonging to popular culture are now integrated in apparently more eclectic patterns of taste. Yet, they are also somewhat 'transformed' or reified in the process so that they could arguably be perceived as new forms of 'highbrow' culture. This consequently creates a hierarchy *within* cultural genres between the 'good' or refined disinterested popular culture versus the 'bad' or unsophisticated and commercial popular culture. Johnston and Baumann (2007) sought, for instance, to understand why specific working-class dishes, such as hamburgers, became appraised by specialist food magazines and food critics. They argued that some originally popular food items have been transformed in such a way that people now need economic and cultural capital to be able to afford and appreciate them. The burger becomes the 'gourmet' burger cooked with Kobe beef or beef from small local farmers that has enjoyed a healthy outdoor lifestyle. This distinction within food items, here the hamburger, or more generally cultural genres requires cultural knowledge and even, they put forward, a specific aesthetic disposition to be made. This aesthetic disposition transformed food into works of art (p. 198), capable to extract but also inject aesthetic values into traditionally popular items.

The culture of the upper classes may then have changed and appeared more inclusive, in order to reflect historical changes in the field of cultural production (such as the valorisation of popular traits in art, e.g. pop art). The upper classes may appear more omnivorous and tolerant towards cultural expressions, from the lower classes for instance, but their selective attitude and the way they consume these forms hardly reflect the emergence of cultural democracy; rather, it shows new ways in which the upper classes can distinguish themselves from the others.

Distinctive ways to be omnivorous

As we have just seen, omnivorous patterns of consumption rely on the appreciation of 'highbrow by-products' of popular culture (such as the *gourmet* burger). Survey research is not very well equipped to detect variations of taste within cultural genres. Therefore, omnivores can appear at first sight more diverse in their consumption because surveys have identified groups of people who declare to like 'pop music' or 'rock music' but haven't been able most of the time to investigate cultural hierarchies within 'pop' or 'rock' music (usually because of a lack of space) and to differentiate 'good' from bad pop and rock music.

In addition, and this is connected to what precedes, the justifications for liking specific artists or cultural items are crucial for understanding what being omnivorous means. Qualitative research indeed showed clearly that there are many ways to be culturally omnivorous and to justify this orientation (Bellavance 2008; Ollivier 2008). In the study of British comedy undertaken at the Fringe Festival in Edinburgh, Friedman (2011) declared that, when it came to comedy preferences, *what* people liked mattered less than *how* they appreciated it (on this see also Holt 1998). He showed that the same cultural product (here a show) could be enjoyed by people with very different sets of cultural resources and may appear quite undistinctive that way. However, people differ not by their *objectified* cultural capital (i.e. their reported tastes) but by their *embodied* cultural capital (i.e. their 'styles of appreciation'). This embodied cultural capital equips people with different – aesthetic-dispositions or ways to appreciate, decode and interpret cultural products or performances. For culturally privileged people, comedy cannot just be funny; it has to be clever, experimental; it has to make you think. For the less culturally privileged, there is a real pleasure in simply laughing and feeling good; comedy shows can be very familiar and rely on elements of everyday life. High cultural capital can therefore not only rely on an appreciation of traditional highbrow culture but include resources to appreciate emerging forms of culture in a socially valued way. This difference between what to consume and how to consume also enables us to understand how the upwardly socially mobile may develop omnivorous profiles but actually feel 'culturally homeless': they do not master the keys to a fully informed taste for traditional highbrow culture, yet, they know too well the low social value of popular and mass culture (Friedman 2012).

Emerging cultural capital

In what precedes, I have discussed the extent to which omnivorousness should not be considered as evidence for the irrelevance of Bourdieu's theory of cultural distinction (on this see also Coulangeon & Lemel 2007; Lizardo & Skiles 2016). I have argued more specifically that omnivorousness has actually never challenged the existence of a high culture, but rather reflects the fact that high culture has become more inclusive. Therefore what is socially and aesthetically valorized by those with high cultural capital has been updated to reflect wider cultural and social changes. Omnivorousness should not be perceived as the sign of a developing cultural democracy.

Yet, this sociological research in the context of an apparent growing eclecticism has had a consequence on surveys of cultural participation in Europe and in the US, which have rightly approached culture in a broad and encompassing way and included more and more 'ordinary' activities (such as shopping, going out, food consumption, etc.). Two new key findings have emerged from these broader surveys. First, one of their recurrent and worrying observations is that a rather large group of the population in various European countries is socially isolated since they do not participate in ordinary activities such as going to a bar or to a park, going out to see friends and family or to surf the Internet. In the French-speaking part of Belgium, almost a third of the population could be conceived as culturally 'disengaged', which means that they have a low cultural participation, whether be in terms of out-of-home or at-home activities (e.g. reading or listening to music, crafts), but also that they tend to be less engaged in everyday social activities. Elders and people with low educational achievements are overrepresented in this group (see Callier & Hanquinet 2012).

Although these surveys never include all activities people are involved in and are in a way always flawed, these results outline that the main cultural division in most European countries is between those who are culturally and socially active, whatever their activities are, and those who are much less, rather than between those appreciative of high culture and the amateurs of popular culture. This also shows a clear link between a low cultural participation and a risk of social isolation and exclusion. In a way, the debate about the kind of culture—elitist or popular—that should receive policy makers' attention has started to appear outdated when the increase of eclecticism suggests that what matters for well-being is to participate and to culturally engage (Miles & Sullivan 2010).

Second, broadening the scope of cultural participation surveys has also enabled researchers to observe the emergence of new forms of distinction based on the adhesion to new or, maybe more accurately, previously scorned values by the upper and middle classes, such as tolerance, fun, inclusion, but also associated cultural products (such as comedy, comic books, popular music, etc.). Related to this, a new body of literature on the notion of 'emerging cultural capital' has recently been developed (Prieur & Savage 2013). Prieur and Savage re-affirmed a long-forgotten key aspect of Bourdieu's theory: its relationality. For them, cultural capital should not be seen as 'fixed' but as 'floating' as it mirrors transformations of the cultural field. And to illustrate this argument, they both reflected on Prieur's research in Aalborg for and on the UK's *Cultural Capital and Social Exclusion Project*. The two research projects present striking similarities. They both show an opposition between those who are widely culturally engaged across a range of specific tastes and practices and those who appear to be much less engaged from a cultural point of view (similar findings have also been put forward by the BBC's Great British Class Survey (Savage 2015)). They argued that this new configuration around the tension between engagement versus disengagement results – among other things—from the decline of traditional highbrow culture but not its disappearance nor the decline of its association with the highly educated. Yet, it has to compete with new socially valued cultural references coming from non-Western cultures, mass culture when reflexively appropriated but also a scientific culture.

Of course, the widening of people's cultural tastes and activities is dependent on resources unevenly distributed among people according to their education and social class but also by other characteristics such as their ethnic origin and their age. Savage et al. (2013) have shown how both highbrow (classical music, attending stately homes, museums, art galleries, jazz, theatre and French restaurants) and emerging cultural capital (video games, social network sites, the Internet, playing sports, watching sports, spending time with friends, going to the gym, going to gigs and preferences for rap and rock) play a role in the formation of social class in the UK. For instance, the established middle class, the second most advantaged, shows high scores on both, and even the elite, although more invested in (traditional) highbrow culture, have a moderate knowledge of emerging cultural forms. This reveals that the two most advantaged social classes in the UK are able to competently draw on very diverse cultural forms when needed, which gives them more flexibility in the social world. Savage et al. (2015) subsequently argued that 'emerging cultural capital is […] not about liking popular culture per se, but rather demonstrating one's skill in manoeuvring between the choices on the menu, and displaying one's careful selection of particular popular artists; through one's ability to pick, choose and combine the "very best" of popular culture' (p. 115). What is put forward here is the ability of socially privileged individuals to justify their tastes of less socially sanctified cultural forms in a very intellectual and distinctive fashion. This in itself set them apart from others. In addition to that, those people have wider resources to adapt to a greater number of socially diverse situations, which represents a non-negligible asset. Moreover, good or high emerging cultural capital also appears key in the constitution of some specific classes of the typology used by Savage et al., such as the 'new affluent workers' and the 'emergent service workers'. While the first possesses more economic resources than the other, they both tend to include a high proportion of young people, which highlights once again the role of age.

Age has become essential in the understanding of the development of new forms of distinction[1] as these emerging forms of cultural capital tend to be more strongly associated with younger generations. A most telling example is the rise of the 'new screens' (computers, game consoles, smart phones, tablets, etc.) (Donnat 2016). The Internet, the World Wide Web and associated social networking sites, blogs and groups have abolished to some extent the boundaries between cultural producers, intermediaries and consumers. We now live in a connected world, and this has transformed our lifestyle, identities and sense of belonging. This, nonetheless, creates gaps between diverse social classes but also between generations since social media or other blogs, just to name one aspect, provide ways to be heard and to be influential for those who have the skills to use them. Donnat shows the extent to which these new screens are the domain of the young, urban and educated, which are nonetheless culturally active outside the home, while television attracts older and less-educated people to a greater extent. More positively, the Internet also offers new (maybe more accessible) means to reach and communicate with young populations and to tease their cultural appetite. It can also create new spaces to discuss and debate; cultural institutions can use these to give a more active role to young and less young citizens in the shaping of their cultural programmes and in the making of culture as a public good.

These considerations on the influence of age on emerging cultural capital could also incite us to consider that high culture is renewing itself as it progressively includes new items and aesthetic criteria. Bellavance (2008), for instance, designed a 'theoretical space of cultural items' based on two dimensions, an opposition between high and low culture and another one differentiating new and old. This creates four key theoretical configurations of tastes, contemporary (high/new), classic (high/old), pop (low/new) and folk (low/old). It has become problematic to see high culture as being simply embodied in traditional forms of culture (e.g. disposition to appreciate opera or classical music). An increasing enthusiasm shown to more contemporary, cosmopolitan forms of culture—in line with the postmodernist tendency—participates in the reconfiguration of cultural capital (DiMaggio & Mukhtar 2004). Yet, in order to deepen our understanding of these shifts in the structures and content of cultural capital, refined empirical analysis able to differentiate process of age, cohort or period effects must be further developed (a good example is Reeves 2016).

In conclusion, my exploration of the content of cultural capital also indicates that, as important as the question of cultural engagement is for the issues of social isolation and exclusion, it would be also erroneous to conclude that the tension between high and popular cultural forms has nowadays become irrelevant for policy makers. It cannot simply be assumed that high culture is in decline and is not useful anymore to consider issues of social stratification, as the position of those Savage et al. called the 'Elite' shows. It is still perceived with a very high social value because it is the one privileged by the educational system, and the state in the allocations of resources (Savage 2015) and most established cultural institutions. Yet, if older forms of distinction persist, new ones emerge, and those sociologists have labelled 'omnivores' are often those who master both forms of distinction. These omnivores, who could be perceived as 'engaged', do not like 'everything indiscriminantly' (Peterson & Kern 1996, p. 904) and (maybe not consciously but) carefully 'pick and mix' what can be socially advantageous for gaining a better position in the social game. They draw on a wide range of cultural items, including those traditionally defined as popular but do not consume them as such: either they create their own classifications with popular genres applying their own vision of what is good or bad, or they justify their appreciation of rather common genres in a more highbrow manner. New cultural distinctions are particularly interesting as they embrace at first sight authentic, playful or even open and cosmopolitan values and are sometimes built in opposition to serious, snobbish and pretentious cultural forms (Johnston and Baumann showed this very well with the gourmet cuisine); they are nevertheless sources of divisions and require resources unevenly distributed across society.

Possible areas for future research

In this chapter, I have attempted to show that the concept of omnivorousness never really challenged Bourdieu's social theory. Empirical research has shown that omnivorous patterns are entangled in new forms of distinction. Cultural refinement might no longer take the form of elitist cultural snobbishness, but rather that of a cosmopolitan openness;

it still represents a way to operate symbolic violence on those—usually from a lower social background—who are defined by a lack of cultural tolerance.

Moreover, and maybe more importantly, omnivorousness was actually never really developed as a theory (Gayo 2016). It simply coined an empirical manifestation of some changes in the structuration of cultural capital, but it was certainly not the sign that we have now achieved cultural democracy in which each culture would be seen as of equal value. As any form of capital, cultural capital is characterized by the amount of resources ('the volume') and the types of resources ('the composition') one has. Bourdieu saw the world in relational terms and could very well envisage that his theory would have to be updated. As Robbins reminded us, 'Cultural capital does not possess absolute value which is quantifiable. It only possesses value in exchange and the exchange is a social struggle as much as a struggle of cultural value judgment' (2005, p. 23).

On this point, the contribution of those working on 'emerging forms of cultural capital' has been essential: they showed that new cultural items have progressively become valorised in the society while being not symbolically accessible to everyone. These new resources, I have argued, have not seriously questioned the link between cultural capital and high culture, but their close examination would actually indicate that there might now be different high cultures, which can for instance take a more classic or contemporary outlook. This can complicate the task of those who advocate for cultural democratization, as new cultural forms have emerged, such as the new screen cultures, and have brought new challenges in terms of accessibility and of an even distribution of resources.

This outlines that one of the key areas for future research concerns the structure of cultural capital and how new cultural forms may become new resources involved in mechanisms of social stratification. This includes identifying these cultural forms but also the strategies of distinction in which they are involved and assessing the actual social and symbolic value these cultural forms give to people who draw on them. This is essential to evaluate the extent to which taking part in new activities or developing a taste for new cultural genres can actually be perceived as 'capital' that forms an essential asset in the competitive social field. Keeping track of these constant changes in the formation of cultural capital is essential as it can directly affect the ways culture is and should be defined, measured and valued by decision-makers.

Another area for future research concerns the link between place and culture. The study of this link has already received a great deal of attention. Research has pointed to the ambivalent role of culture in driving new urban dynamics (Zukin 1987). Florida's controversial theory of the 'creative' class (2002) has influenced policies to support the development of a cultural, educational and recreational infrastructure (Mulcahy 2006) in the hopes of attracting these creative 'trendy' people who carry cultural and economic capital useful to the development of cities. This thesis eventually perceives culture through the economic benefits it could bring (Gilmore 2014) and disregards potential negative aspects in terms of displacement and gentrification (see Peck's 2007 critique), while it has been established that gentrification is not a neutral process and should be critically considered (Slater 2006). Yet, less has been said about the importance of urban cultures in the re-configuration of cultural capital and the development of new forms of distinction and inequalities. It is likely that some forms of emerging cultural capital would hold an urban dimension. The 'emergent service workers' are, for instance, young urbanites (Savage et al. 2013). Similarly, in a recent article, I show that art museum visitors mainly come from areas with high and moderate density and that the socio-demographic but also urban characteristics of their place of residence can be related to the way visitors' cultural capital is composed (Hanquinet 2016). This reveals a possible fracture between (semi-) urban areas and rural areas when it comes to cultural participation.

Finally, in his work, Bourdieu has repeatedly shown the importance of the educational level in cultural participation and in the development of a highbrow taste. This has been confirmed by the omnivorous thesis as well. However, we know little about the reasons for such a link (for a notable exception, Reeves and de Vries 2016) and this should be further examined as the outcomes of this research would be essential to build education and cultural policies that work hand-in-hand. Cultural policies for a wider accessibility to culture should complement and not supplement a clearer insertion of arts training (whether it be knowledge in arts or active art practices) in the educational programmes, which would show openness to diversity in the cultures they promote.

Note

1 See the special issue in *Poetics* called 'Cultural sociology and new forms of distinction' edited by Friedman et al. (2015).

References

Ahearne, J., 2004. Between Cultural Theory and Policy: The Cultural Policy Thinking of Pierre Bourdieu, Michel de Certeau and Régis Debray. Centre for Cultural Policy Studies, University of Warwick, Research Papers, no. 7.

Bellavance, G., 2008. Where's High? Who's Low? What's New? Classification and Stratification Inside Cultural "Repertoires". *Poetics*, 36(2–3), pp. 189–216.

Bennett, T., Savage, M., Silva, E., Warde, A., Gayo-Cal, M. & Wright, D., 2009. *Culture, Class, Distinction*. London: Routledge.

Bourdieu, P., 1979. Les trois états du capital culturel. *Actes de la recherche en sciences sociales*, 30, pp. 3–6.

Bourdieu, P., 1984. *Distinction: A Social Critique of the Judgement of Taste*. Cambridge, MA: Harvard University Press.

Bourdieu, P. & Darbel, A., 1969. *L'amour de l'art. Les musées d'art européens et leur public*, 2nd edition. Paris: Editions de Minuit.

Bourdieu, P. & Passeron, J.-C., 1977 [1970]. *Reproduction in Education, Society and Culture*. Beverly Hills, CA: Sage.

Bourdieu, P. & Passeron, J.-C., 1979 [1964]. *The Inheritors: French Students and Their Relation to Culture*. Chicago, IL: University of Chicago Press.

Bourdieu, P. & Wacquant, L., 1992. *An Invitation to Reflexive Sociology*. Chicago, IL: The University of Chicago Press.

Bryson, B., 1996. " Anything But Heavy Metal": Symbolic Exclusion and Musical Dislikes. *American Sociological Review*, 61(5), pp. 884–899.

Callier, L. & Hanquinet, L., 2012. Étude approfondie des pratiques et consommation culturelles de la population en Fédération Wallonie-Bruxelles. *Observatoire des Politiques Culturelles-Etudes*, 1.

Chaumier, S., 2010. *L'inculture pour tous. La nouvelle utopie des politiques culturelles*, Paris: L'Harmattan.

Chaumier, S., 2011. Education. In A. Desvallées & F. Mairesse, eds. *Dictionnaire encyclopédique de muséologie*. Paris: Armand Colin, pp. 87–120.

Coulangeon, P. & Lemel, Y., 2007. Is "Distinction" Really Outdated? Questioning the Meaning of the Omnivorization of Musical Taste in Contemporary France. *Poetics*, 35(2–3), pp. 93–111.

DiMaggio, P., 1982. Cultural Entrepreneur-Ship in Nineteenth-Century Boston. *Media, Culture & Society*, 4, pp. 33–50.

DiMaggio, P. & Mukhtar, T., 2004. Arts Participation as Cultural Capital in the United States, 1982–2002: Signs of Decline? *Poetics*, 32(2), pp. 169–194.

Donnat, O., 2004. Les univers culturels des Français. *Sociologie et sociétés*, 36(1), pp. 87–103.

Donnat, O., 2016. The rising power of screens: Changing cultural practices in France from 1973 to 2008. In L. Hanquinet & M. Savage, eds. *Routledge International Handbook of the Sociology of Art and Culture*. Abingdon: Routledge, pp. 396–408.

Dubois, V., 2011. Cultural Capital Theory vs. Cultural Policy Beliefs: How Pierre Bourdieu Could Have Become a Cultural Policy Advisor and Why He Did Not. *Poetics*, 39(6), pp. 491–506.

Florida, R., 2002. *The Rise of the Creative Class: And How It's Transforming Work, Leisure, Community, & Everyday Life*. New York: Basic Books.

Fridman, V. & Ollivier, M., 2004. Ouverture ostentatoire à la diversité et cosmopolitisme. *Sociologie et sociétés*, 36(1), pp. 105–126.

Friedman, S., 2011. The Cultural Currency of a "Good" Sense of Humour: British Comedy and New Forms of Distinction. *The British Journal of Sociology*, 62(2), pp. 347–370.

Friedman, S., 2012. Cultural Omnivores or Culturally Homeless? Exploring the Shifting Cultural Identities of the Upwardly Mobile. *Poetics*, 40(5), pp. 467–489.

Friedman, S., Savage, M., Hanquinet, L. & Miles, A., 2015. Cultural Sociology and New Forms of Distinction. *Poetics*, 53, pp. 1–8.

Gayo, M., 2016. A Critique of the Omnivore: From the Origin of the Idea of Omnivorousness to the Latin American Experience. In L. Hanquinet & M. Savage, eds. *Routledge International Handbook of the Sociology of Art and Culture*. Abingdon: Routledge, pp. 104–115.

Gilmore, A., 2014. *Policy Paper: Raising Our Quality of Life: The Importance of Investment in Arts and Culture*. CLASS (Centre for Labour and Social Studies): London, available at: http://classonline.org.uk/docs/2014_Policy_Paper_-_investment_in_the_arts_-_Abi_Gilmore.pdf, retrieved on 15/05/17.

Goodman, N., 2001. La fin du Musée ? In N. Goodman & C. Elgin, eds. *Esthétique et Connaissance pour changer de sujet*. Combas: L'Eclat, pp. 68–81.

Hanquinet, L., 2016. Place and Cultural Capital : Art Museum Visitors across Space. *Museum and Society*, 14(1), pp. 65–81.

Hanquinet, L., Roose, H. & Savage, M., 2014. The Eyes of the Beholder: Aesthetic Preferences and the Remaking of Cultural Capital. *Sociology*, 48(1), pp. 111–132.

Holt, D., 1998. Does Cultural Capital Structure American Consumption? *Journal of Consumer Research*, 25(1), pp. 1–25.

Johnston, J. & Baumann, S., 2007. Democracy versus Distinction: A Study of Omnivorousness in Gourmet Food Writing. *American Journal of Sociology*, 113(1), pp. 165–204.

Lamont, M. & Lareau, A., 1988. Cultural Capital: Allusions, Gaps and Glissandos in Recent Theoretical Developments. *Sociological Theory*, 6(2), pp. 153–168.

Levine, L., 1990. *Highbrow/Lowbrow. The Emergence of Cultural Hierarchy in America*, Cambridge, MA: Harvard University Press.

Lizardo, O., 2008. The Question of Culture Consumption and Stratification Revisited. *Sociologica*, pp. 1–32.

Lizardo, O. & Skiles, S., 2016. After Omnivorousness: Is Bourdieu Still Relevant? In L. Hanquinet & M. Savage, eds. *Routledge International Handbook of the Sociology of Art and Culture*. Abingdon: Routledge, pp. 90–103.

Lizardo, O. & Skiles, S., 2013. Reconceptualizing and Theorizing "Omnivorousness": Genetic and Relational Mechanisms. *Sociological Theory*, 30(4), pp. 263–282.

López-Sintas, J. & Garcia-Álvarez, E., 2002. Omnivores Show up Again. The Segmentation of Cultural Consumers in Spanish Social Space. *European Sociological Review*, 18(3), pp. 353–368.

Miles, A. & Sullivan, A., 2010. *Understanding the Relationship between Taste*, Department of Culture, Media and Sport.

Mulcahy, K., 2006. Cultural Policy: Definitions and Theoretical Approaches. *The Journal of Arts Management, Law, and Society*, 35(4), pp. 319–330.

Ollivier, M., 2008. Modes of Openness to Cultural Diversity: Humanist, Populist, Practical, and Indifferent. *Poetics*, 36(2–3), pp. 120–147.

Peck, J., 2007. The Creativity Fix. *Fronesis*, 24 , available at www.eurozine.com/the-creativity-fix/, retrieved on 15/05/17.

Peterson, R., 2005. Problems in Comparative Research: The Example of Omnivorousness. *Poetics*, 33(5–6), pp. 257–282.

Peterson, R. & Kern, R., 1996. Changing Highbrow Taste: From Snob to Omnivore. *American Sociological Review*, 61(5), pp. 900–907.

Peterson, R. & Rossman, G., 2008. Changing Arts Audience: Capitalizing on Omnivorousness. In W. Ivey & S. Tepper, eds. *Engaging Art: the Next Great Transformation of American Cultural Life*. New York: Routledge, pp. 307–342.

Peterson, R. & Simkus, A., 1992. How Musical Tastes Mark Occupational Status Groups. In M.F.M. Lamont, ed. *Cultivating Differences. Symbolic Boundaries and the Making of Inequality*. Chicago, IL: The University of Chicago Press, pp. 152–187.

Prieur, A. & Savage, M., 2013. Emerging Forms of Cultural Capital. *European Societies*, 15(2), pp. 246–267.

Reeves, A., 2016. Age-Period-Cohort and Cultural Engagement. In L. Hanquinet & M. Savage, eds. *Routledge International Handbook of the Sociology of Art and Culture*. Abingdon: Routledge, pp. 116–131.

Reeves, A. & de Vries, R. (2016). The Social Gradient in Cultural Consumption and the Information-Processing Hypothesis. *The Sociological Review*, 64(3), 550–574.

Robbins, D., 2005. The Origins, Early Development and Status of Bourdieu's Concept of "Cultural Capital". *The British Journal of Sociology*, 56(1), pp. 13–30.

Rossman, G. & Peterson, R., 2005. The Instability of Omnivorous Cultural Tastes over Time. Paper Presented at the Annual Meetings of the American Sociological Association, Philadelphia, August 13.

Savage, M., Cunningham, N., Devine, F., Friedman, S., Laurison, D., Mckenzie, L., Miles, A., Snee, H. and Wakeling, P., 2015. *Social Class in the 21st Century*. London: Penguin Books.

Savage, M., Devine, F., Cunningham, N., Taylor, M., Li, Y., Hjellbrekke, J., Le Roux, B., Friedman, S. & Miles, A., 2013. A New Model of Social Class? Findings from the BBC's Great British Class Survey Experiment. *Sociology*, 47(2), pp. 219–250.

Shusterman, R., 1991. Form and Funk: The Aesthetic Challenge of Popular Art. *The British Journal of Aesthetics*, 31(3), pp. 213–213.

Slater, T., 2006. The Eviction of Critical Perspectives from Gentrification Research. *International Journal of Urban and Regional Research*, 30(4), pp. 737–757.

Sullivan, A., 2007. Cultural Capital, Cultural Knowledge and Ability. *Sociological Research Online*, 12(6), pp. 1–14.

van Eijck, K., 1999. Socialization, Education, and Lifestyle: How Social Mobility Increases the Cultural Heterogeneity of Status Groups. *Poetics*, 26, pp. 309–328.

Warde, A. & Gayo-Cal, M., 2009. The Anatomy of Cultural Omnivorousness: The Case of the United Kingdom. *Poetics*, 37(2), pp. 119–145.

Warde, A., Wright, D. & Gayo-Cal, M., 2008. The Omnivorous Orientation in the UK. *Poetics*, 36(2–3), pp. 148–165.

Zukin, S., 1987. Gentrification: Culture and Capital in the Urban Core. *Annual Review of Sociology*, 13, pp. 129–147.

22

Cultural policy and creative industries

Susan Luckman

This chapter examines the complex and often fraught scholarly relationship between cultural policy and the emergence of what has come to be identified as the creative industries. It charts the ascendency of creative industries' agendas out of the academy and into national policy, especially via the high profile and highly influential British creative industries model championed in the early 2000s by the Blair government's Department for Media, Culture and Sport, which was itself a further development of the short-lived Australian *Creative Nation* framework. It will explore how creative industries approaches have settled down through the lens of two key sites for action and concern. First, the rise of creative place making including, following Florida, the policy fetish for urban redevelopment focused upon attracting creative workers. Second, drilling down to the employment coalface of creative industries, it draws attention to the exclusions of the contemporary creative workforce (particularly those of gender) as but one means to examine what has been lost in the shift from cultural policy to creative industries, namely, the focus on socio-cultural inclusion. It argues that the adoption within creative industries policy and scholarly approaches of the US urban policy-driven 'creative class' ideas of economist Richard Florida represents a significant de-coupling of creative industries from cultural policy. Coupled with an emphasis on the utopian expansive possibilities of digital technology, this served to consolidate the creative industries as a commercially focussed championing of entrepreneurial creativity, at the expense of arts and cultural policy as social goods with value beyond that which can be economically defined.

From 'cultural' to 'creative' industries

In keeping with the global focus of this collection, the shift from cultural policy/cultural industries to creative industries has itself been something of a highly mobile feast, albeit one heavily though not exclusively concentrated until recently within the English-speaking world. As is well documented, the transition is not a benign one with much being, and remaining, at stake. It has also never been a clean break but rather is the result of a confluence of scholarly and policy ideas around, and institutional responses to, multiple global pressures. Key among them are the economic restructurings of the 1970s onwards that saw manufacturing shift from the Global North to cheaper labour cultures elsewhere, leading to a concurrent pressure on governments to find jobs through the development of new knowledge-intensive sectors. Within universities too, business models were changing and becoming more entrepreneurial and focussed upon making an economic case for the personal and community value of both degrees and research. However cultural policy as it initially emerged in the mid-twentieth century was largely focussed upon arts funding—what should be funded and how?—and was primarily concerned with this in relation to relatively elite art forms: opera, orchestras, theatre and the fine arts, galleries and museums, as well as the role of national broadcasting corporations as flagships of national identity. This more traditional and aesthetic gatekeeping role for cultural policy came under critique from those concerned with not only the extension of access to so-called 'high culture' as part of a larger social-democratic civilising agenda for the arts and culture, but also in light of wider social and academic movements in the 1960s and 1970s that challenged existing definitions of 'acceptable' culture. Strongly influenced by the rise of British cultural studies approaches to culture, which following the work of Raymond Williams have defined culture more broadly as a 'whole way of life', cultural policy then came to mean more than betterment defined in terms of access to subsidised elite art forms and free access for all to museums. Instead, more profound questions regarding diversity and whose culture counts came to the fore. Tony Bennett's work later extended this approach, applying a Foucauldian understanding of governmentality to develop a more expansive model of cultural policy out of cultural studies (O'Brien 2014; O'Regan 1993; Turner 2015).

It is also from within this context further enabled by a post-1960s shift in political focus towards a greater emphasis on 'do it yourself' practices, social inclusion and alternative economies that O'Connor, drawing upon ground-breaking policy engagements by Garnham and Bianchini, locates the emergence of a progressive cultural industries agenda extending out of a concern for arts policy beyond the rarefied worlds of establishment institutions. This particular incarnation of cultural policy as cultural industries was embodied in the short-lived but influential industrial regeneration activities of the Greater London Council (GLC) between 1979 and 1986 (Hesmondhalgh and Pratt 2005; McGuigan 2004; O'Brien 2014; O'Connor 2010, p. 27; Pratt 2005). Unafraid of the linking of 'art' and 'market', the socio-economic inclusion via micro-enterprise policies of the GLC provided a model for creativity as a driver of urban renewal and place-making and cultural employment as a valuable tool for socio-economic inclusion. Subsequently this social enterprise focus grew into a wider, more economically focussed policy agenda emphasising the development of small, local creative businesses and capacity, especially as the answer to stalled growth in areas hard hit by a decline in traditional industries, notably manufacturing (O'Connor 2010, p. 31). Moving forward into the 1990s, it was the particular confluence of the politico-economic context of post-Fordist manufacturing decline, neo-liberal policies of winding back state support and funding (and with it a shift to more individualised and entrepreneurial responses to social-cultural issues, iconically represented by political leaders such as Thatcher in the UK and Reagan in the UK), the game-changing production and consumption practices of Computer-Mediated Communication (CMC), and what came to be identified variously as the 'information', 'knowledge' or 'immaterial' economy, which gave rise to the emergence of the idea of the creative industries.

The 'New Labour' UK government of Prime Minister Tony Blair set in the early days of their office an agenda that quickly became an international model for the championing of the economic significance of what had been previously identified as cultural industries, or simply the 'arts sector'. The full flowering of the UK's creative industries agenda was achieved through the rising to greater policy power the then newly configured Department of Culture, Media and Sport (DCMS), which was formerly the more conservative (literally) historically focussed Department of National Heritage. However the coupling of creativity with the affordances of digital technology and IP championed by the Blair government had a slightly earlier public policy life in the short-lived but significant Australian government policy statement *Creative Nation: Commonwealth Cultural Policy*. Released in the dying days of the Australian Labor Party government of Paul Keating, the Department of Communication and the Arts' 1994 *Creative Nation* document foreshadowed that a culture-driven economy was an ideal model for approaching 'the information revolution and the new media not with fear and loathing, but with imagination and wit. We have to see the extraordinary opportunities for enjoyment and creativity it contains' (Department of Communication and the Arts 1994). Moving beyond a traditional cultural emphasis on the arts and formal cultural institutions, in language now familiar within creative industries discourse, it firmly established this cultural policy as 'also an economic policy':

> Culture creates wealth. … Culture employs. … Culture adds value, it makes an essential contribution to innovation, marketing and design. It is a badge of our industry. The level of our creativity substantially determines our ability to adapt to new economic imperatives. It is a valuable export in itself and an essential accompaniment to the export of other commodities. It attracts tourists and students. It is essential to our economic success.
> *(Department of Communication and the Arts 1994, no page)*

The release of *Creative Nation* occurred at a time when cultural policy in Australia was also developing a strong academic presence with Tony Bennett at Griffith University forming the Institute for Cultural Policy Studies in 1987. This was to eventually provide the basis for the Australian Key Centre for Cultural and Media Policy established in 1996 under the Directorship of Tony Bennett then Tom O'Regan, and influenced by Ian Hunter along with Jeffrey Minson, David Saunders and Dugald Williamson. The Key Centre brought together scholars from across Brisbane's three universities including Colin Mercer, Jennifer Craik, Stuart Cunningham, Terry Flew, Gillian Swanson, Peter Anderson, Julian Thomas, Patricia Wise, Brad Sherman, Denise Meredyth and Graeme Turner. Its members explored critical cultural policy studies in areas such as cultural citizenship and education; museum policy and cultural heritage; early attempts to engage with digital transformations, especially in relation to IP; and Indigenous media and cultural policy.

Aligning with broader trends around cultural policy, especially as informed by political economy perspectives such as those of Nicholas Garnham, Graham Murdock and James Curran, the Key Centre also had as a core focus a concern common to much mid-twentieth century cultural policy, namely, the maintenance of a diversity of voices and the protection of local and/or minority cultures in the face of globalised cultural industries, especially the dominance of American film, television and music (Cunningham 1992; O'Regan 1993). Against the broader backdrop in the 1980s and 1990s of increased market deregulation, broadcasting policy emerged as a core cultural policy focus at this time representing a commitment to providing a corrective to the commercial market and instead reflecting a faith that "demand should not just cater to existing tastes" (Oakley 2004, p. 25). Therefore just as the rise of national broadcasters such as the BBC (British Broadcasting Corporation), ABC (Australian Broadcasting Corporation), CBC (Canadian Broadcasting Corporation) and other similar organisations in the mid-twentieth century represented the desire to guarantee access to a diversity of local voices and minority tastes including for high cultural products as part of a 'civilising' impetus, amid the liberalisation of global media and the rise of multi-national free trade agreements in the late 1980s and beyond, the issue of media diversity and ownership emerged as a key cultural policy arena in Australia and elsewhere. But the vision of *Creative Nation* was never to be realised in its home nation with the election in Australia of the conservative Howard Liberal government in March 1996 signalling an end to the kind of approaches it advocated. However the ideas were shortly to rise phoenix-like from these ashes following the election in May 1997 of Tony Blair's Labour Party in the UK, which saw in its championing of the creative industries the realisation of the post-'subsidised arts' approach to intellectual property-driven cultural economic development outlined in *Creative Nation*.

What counts in the shift from 'culture' to 'creative'

Definitions of the *cultural* industries have long emphasised that their defining quality is the production of 'aesthetic' or 'symbolic' goods or services, and thus the basis for cultural policy around them had focussed on inclusion and contestations over the breadth of what counts as 'cultural'. The key break represented by the shift to the discourse and framing of *creative* industries is an emphasis on their being those segments of the *economy* concerned with the generation of *intellectual property* (Banks 2007; Flew and Cunningham 2010; Garnham 2005; Hartley 2004, 2005; Hesmondhalgh 2002; Pratt 2005); that is, of a shift in emphasis from aesthetic to economic goods and value. On account of the high profile of creative industries development as a key platform of the Blair government discussed above, the Department of Media, Culture and Sport (DCMS) definition of the sector is illustrative and remains influential. Their listing of the fields of the creative industries comprises: advertising; architecture; the art and antiques markets; crafts; design; designer fashion; film, video and photography; software, computer games and electronic publishing; music and the visual and performing arts; publishing; television; and radio (DCMS 2006). The inclusion of high volume software and digital content industries here is particularly illustrative of this focus on intellectual property as a marker of creative industries.

With the shift to a united 'industry' identity came the strategic capacity for claims to be made as to the sector's size and significance as a contributor to GDP and hence assertions of its value can be made in the dominant economic terms of the day. Within the framing of creative industries, the arts are reinvented as a driver of innovation and economic growth, rather than sector in need of public funding. The inclusion of software here is emblematic of what is at stake in the shift from cultural policy to creative industries. While arguably the "least cultural of [creative industries] activities", the inclusion of 'software' in measurement data on the economic performance of creative industries in the UK, and elsewhere, is "single-handedly" responsible for providing the economic basis upon which claims to the value of the creative industries are based (Campbell 2014, p. 999). Such a focus on value determined primarily in economic terms has in turn led to a policy focus on developing a statistical picture of the sector's size, scale and contribution to national economies and the emergence out of academia of new tools for doing so. One of the most influential models for this once again represented a transfer of ideas from Brisbane to London. Established in 2005, the Queensland University of Technology's ARC Centre of Excellence for Creative Industries and Innovation (CCI) brought together a number of the key figures involved in the latter iteration of the Australian Key Centre for Cultural and Media Policy alongside expertise from other disciplines, notably economics. The Centre for Excellence is itself the embodiment of global flows of cultural workers and creative industries' policy development as its members have been important players in the economic mapping and understanding of creative industries globally. For example, this Australian expertise has contributed directly to policy development in the United Kingdom (Flew and Cunningham 2010; Higgs, Cunningham and Bakhshi 2008; Potts and Cunningham 2008), and to some extent in Asia, especially China where creative industries discourses have been enthusiastically adopted by city and regional governments (Keane 2009, 2013).

The shift in emphasis from cultural policy to creative industries continues to come in for criticism. Artists themselves have often been at the forefront of critiques of the shift, principally on account of the economically rationalist way it enables the measurement and qualification of the value of a creative practice in largely, if not purely, economic terms. What is at stake here—especially in terms of the shift from creative work being defined and valued no longer in terms of its cultural or aesthetic contribution but rather its economic—is exemplified by the case of the craft sector, which in 2013 in the United Kingdom experienced an attempt to distance the larger, more 'big end of town'–friendly, contemporary and more easily scalable digital intellectual property generation and distribution (software) businesses from its own statistically messier, smaller scale, frequently individualised and often part-time (and hence dismissed as amateur or naïve) creative production. A battle over craft's official status as a British government-recognised creative industry erupted following the release of a DCMS consultation paper that explosively floated the idea that given that craft businesses tend to be sole trader operations (88 per cent according to a 2012 United Kingdom Crafts Council–commissioned study: BOP Consulting 2012, p. 4), and are frequently thus "too small to identify in business survey data" (DCMS 2013, p. 14), data on the sector should no longer be collected (DCMS 2013). Such an action would have had all sorts of flow-on ramifications in terms of support and recognition. Difficulties with obtaining accurate data on craft employment are not unique to the UK, and certainly the sector continues to present ongoing challenges in this regard. However and despite these difficulties, in no small part as a result of strong lobbying led by the highly organised UK Crafts Council, the DCMS backed down from the mooted possibility. Thus the DCMS continues to gather figures for 'crafts' alongside its other recognised creative sectors.

But what is clear here is that the presence of crafts disrupted the 'economic imaginary' that is the creative industries according to the DCMS model; unlike the naturalised presence of software industries, which enables the central and unquestioned narrative of creativity as an increasingly important driver of contemporary economic growth without any questioning of its 'culturally creative content' (Campbell 2014, p. 999). All this occurred ironically at a time of huge growth for the design craft sector and renewed consumer interest in the artisanal, handmade and bespoke, with small-scale manufacturing also being championed by various governments as a potential way to stem the loss of industries to cheaper labour markets offshore (Luckman 2015a). Moreover, and while they may be statistically difficult to track, self-employment and sole trader businesses are on the rise across the creative sector and beyond; a development often encouraged in government policy yet masking considerable un-and under-employment in the creative sector. Patently the creative industries as a policy framing has been particularly attractive to, and hence influential in, governmental policy circles precisely on account of its hardwiring of creativity to innovation and economic growth within knowledge economies. Since the 1980s, a giant shift in the commercial landscape has seen creative entrepreneurial cultural production shoot to centre stage of government and corporate planning, research and development, and nowhere has this been more evident than in the uptake of creativity as a driver of place-based renewal.

From cultural policy to creative places

For several decades now as part of the larger focus on the economic potential of creativity that underlies the shift from cultural to creative industries, there has been a parallel emphasis upon creativity-led urban regeneration strategies, which have become established mainstays of governmental cultural policy around the world. As indicated above, the shift from cultural to creative industries was, in its iconic emergence in the UK at least, in many ways a national-level manifestation of the pioneering small, local economic development of the GLC, and then later work in Manchester led by scholars at the Manchester Institute of Popular Culture (MIPC). Place-based cultural policy agendas for economic development and population management have been reinvigorated by such thinking. The need to innovate, and renovate, in this way has been felt especially strongly in cities, regions and suburbs hit hard by the move of manufacturing to offshore locations in search of cheaper labour and laxer regulation.

A number of different approaches to creativity-led urban renewal have become so iconic they are deployed—with varying degrees of success—around the world. One of the earliest, which arose out of the confluence of new ideas around urban planning as well as arts, creativity and cultural policy, is the Baltimore or Boston model of waterfront/docklands redevelopment, which turns post-industrial wastelands into waterside consumption-based leisure and residential playgrounds. Often such development catalysed around an iconic cultural institution as an 'anchor tenant', such as the Tate in Liverpool or Guggenheim in Bilbao. In this latter case, often referred to as the 'Guggenheim' Model or 'the Bilbao Effect', increased visitor numbers drive ancillary creative and tourism industries as a springboard for economic renewal. The creative industries are a factor here for not only, inherently, are such spaces sites for architectural innovation, in many instances artists and creative start-ups have led the way, seeking out such sites on account of their affordability prior to redevelopment. After renewal, creative businesses are often invited by policy-makers to cluster in such spaces (if they can afford the now-inflated rents) to facilitate cool and distinctive creative clusters, feeding into the lifestyle goods and experiences on offer, the general feel of the place, as well as the local night-time economy. Waterfront redevelopment has now become a mainstay of the creative consultant or city council urban activation toolkit, and examples can be found around the globe: the initial Baltimore and Boston revitalizations were soon followed by similar developments in cities as widely spread as London, Melbourne, Toronto, Singapore (Clarke Quay), Sydney, Salford (with the BBC northern headquarters as its centrepiece) and Liverpool (Tate Gallery). Such approaches are grounded in attracting desirable visitors and their disposable income; this latter approach in particular is heavily dependent upon tourism and the deliberate locating of a desirable cultural institution in what is otherwise seen as a highly undesirable or under-developed visitor location. Global competition for such institutions is intense; there are only so many Tates and Guggenheims to go around, though other independent philanthropic developments can serve a similar purpose such as the privately funded MONA (Museum of Old and New Art) in Hobart, Australia, where the 'MONA effect' has proven successful in re-energising local tourism and attracting new and often quite wealthy visitors from around the world. There's a strong sense across all these creativity-driven policy engagements of place-making as a subtle interacting of the social and the material; of an Actor-Network Theory sensibility or a more-than-human catalysation of place and people, that is, one that "acknowledges the profound and multiple significances of non-humans [including the agency of the affordances of the materiality of place] in social life" (Nimmo 2011, p. 109). The creative industries in this context are variously mobilised precisely because of not only their economic but their cultural role in society. Beyond simply building locales physically, creativity is seen as the key driver that will populate them culturally, socially and economically; it will create the 'vibe'. We can consider this variously: as an ecology in terms of Landry's 'soft infrastructure' (2006); culturally in terms of Williams' 'structures of feeling' (1973; also see Banks 2007, p. 148); or more sceptically, though no less accurately, in terms of "Alfred Marshall's (1890) notion of the 'atmosphere' of a place giving it a competitive advantage" (O'Connor 2010, p. 43).

With US commercial cultural products already a powerful IP-driven sector of the economy with global reach, it is in this incarnation—creativity as driver of urban policy—that, as Andrew Ross has written, we can see the 'turn to creativity' in the US (Ross 2007, p. 27). The particular hardwiring of place and creativity championed within US-driven approaches to urban planning intersected with creative industries-style approaches in other parts of the globe, on the back of the high-profile writing and consultancy work of American economist Richard Florida. Florida's 2003 bestseller *The Rise of the Creative Class* initiated a wave of interest globally among city officials and urban planners in attracting and keeping the knowledge workers seen as essential to economic growth in the new economy. Thus, much of the focus around creative industries in the first decade of the twenty-first century came to be concerned with the competition between cities for an idealised highly mobile global pool of creative talent. Effectively bringing together decades of leading North American scholarship on creativity and urban planning with the more British-driven focus on the creative industries—at least the profitable IP-producing parts of them—as key drivers of the contemporary knowledge economy, it established digital technology-driven entrepreneurship as the chief driver of creative economic growth. With this sector comes a workforce that he identifies as demanding the ongoing presence of *some* select aspects of the cultural industries as taken for granted lifestyle affordances. In this way, the market easily replaces cultural policy as the enabler of the small 'c' culture that creatives 'demand' of their community. Florida's influential and highly criticised definition of the creative class went even further than the DCMS's emphasis on IP/copyright-producing industries such as software development and games. In his rather expansive inner 'Super-Creative Core' he includes: scientists and engineers, university professors, poets and novelists, artists, entertainers, actors, designers and architects, as well as the thought leadership of modern society: nonfiction writers, editors, cultural figures, think-tank researchers, analysts and other opinion-makers (Florida 2003, p. 69). This group is further supported by a second group of "creative professionals" beyond this core whom he also identifies as part of his Creative Class on account of their work across a "wide range of knowledge-intensive industries such as high-tech sectors, financial services, the legal and health care professions, and business management" (Florida 2003, p. 69).

Florida's creative-class argument has fed directly into an earlier creative-city dialogue that included the aforementioned place-based policies of renewal (Markusen 2006, p. 1937). Originally focussed on the arts and creativity as drivers of urban economies and renewal, this wave of interest, assisted by Florida, morphed into an emphasis on the provision of unique yet somehow globally accepted lifestyle affordances as a baseline attractor of desirable knowledge workers. Florida's (presumed to be young and possibly single) creatives are stereotypically constructed as desiring café strips, openness and tolerance, diversity, a dynamic artistic and cultural environment, high-tech toys and mountain-biking trails. Consequently, in urban planning informed by these ideas there has been an emphasis on coffee shops, energised—'activated'—street life, serendipitous face-to-face meetings, clusters and densities, to the exclusion of other attractors and experiences. Florida's work effectively turns urban gentrification into a governmental creativity-driven cultural policy positive. As such, it too is illustrative of what exactly is at stake in the shift from 'cultural' to 'creative' industries. No longer is cultural policy deployed to enable access to and diversity within the cultural sector, within the creative class/industries framework, governmental emphasis and funding is often put towards local development projects, and questions of access left to market forces that may very well displace local artists and other low-paid or otherwise economically precarious creative practitioners, in favour of those (digital) creative class members able to afford to live in desirable, cosmopolitan urban communities (Luckman, Gibson and Lea 2009; Oakley 2004).

As a result of this perfect policy confluence of creativity and private sector-friendly urban revitalisation, cities have remained a focus for creative industries development, at the expense of greater attention to non-urban cultural or creative policy intervention. With a few notable exceptions, mostly arising from within cultural geography, the non-urban, non-city experience also remains under-explored in scholarly studies of cultural work and creative industries. For a complex set of reasons that includes such capacities as: the long-standing place of cities as enablers of innovation and exploration, attracting people willing to explore new ideas; economies of scale, clusters, expertise and labour availability; the emphasis in European cultural policy on 'Cities of Culture', and elsewhere the role of local governments as drivers of innovative cultural policies around creativity, starting as we saw with the influential GLC model, cities have been and remain privileged sites for the growth of cultural and creative industries. Approaches to the analysis of how creative milieus work or what they need to flourish have followed this emphasis on the kind of clustering most possible in cities. Thus the importance of clustering, and the economies of scale and synergies associated with it, has long been recognised as a significant driver of creative innovation and the development of local industries. Consequently, most existing creative industries' thinking and research has focused on how to facilitate creativity in macro settings such as the large city, at the expense of considering more geographically inclusive socio-economic strategies.

But as Waitt reminds us, "smallness itself would not appear to work against the creativity of people" (2006, p. 169). Indeed any quick look at recent history reveals that the emphasis in creative industries discourse especially in the 1990s and early 2000s on creativity and the city was not always the case. The western European Romantic movement, which emerged in the eighteenth century and gained strength in the face of the Industrial Revolution, is one key case in point. After them came those cultural and artistic champions of the Victorian era, Britons such as John Ruskin, William Morris and the wider Arts and Crafts Movement, who generated their own models for the realisation of 'good' cultural work (Hesmondhalgh and Baker 2011). In particular, in looking back to the medieval era for its idealised model of craft practice as a part of the fabric of a community, they favoured small workshops and enterprises, and out of this they championed quality handmade production organised on egalitarian and cooperative grounds such that "each talent might contribute to the whole" (Cullinan 1984, p. 51). Those inspired by their writings often sought out the countryside in which to realise this idealised vision of creative work (Luckman 2012). One of the most significant contributions to research into creative industries beyond the city is the work of David Bell and Mark Jayne who offer an important overview of the limited recognition creative industries' policy writings have given to creative work beyond urban sites and the concurrent absence of dialogue between rural and cultural policy (Bell and Jayne 2010). In wanting to embrace alternative forms of economic development to augment or replace traditional industries in the post-productivist countryside (Wilson 2001; see also Halfacree 1997), Bell and Jayne lament the habit of transferring assumptions based on urban case studies to rural cultural policy practice. Countryside creative industries are thereby presumed to have, and work with, the same kind of structures, forms and functions as "'best practice' examples in metropolitan centres" (Bell and Jayne 2010, p. 212). Further, in this vacuum created by the rural creative industries research deficiency and given the hegemony of ideas of rural idyll in the eyes of many decision makers, traditional rural practices such as crafts, art and antiques take precedence in rural policy, at the expense of newer (digital) creative industries. More recently, the upswing in agrarian food-based consumption practices has lent itself to the development at the local council level of tourism-based cultural policy focussing on arts trails, as well as crafts and antiques, reflecting the DCMS articulation of these and reinforcing traditional strengths, but also stereotypes, of the rural creative economy.

The exclusions of creative industries

Further important implications of the break from cultural policy with its emphasis on social inclusion are all too evident in the employment practices, and exclusions, of the creative industries. There is increasing awareness that the frequently unclear, informal and network-based work practices underpinning much employment in the creative, especially media, advertising and publishing industries, are effectively operating as a barrier to gender, ethnic, class and wider social inclusion in the creative economy resulting in profound impacts upon the content of cultural production.[1] So while social inclusion agendas may have been a focus of cultural policy, especially in communities seen as marginal or 'at risk' or in terms of a commitment to diversity, plurality and national broadcasting organisations, creative industries' employment practices tend to implicitly reinforce hegemonic hiring practices. While evidence indicates women "fare better in settings in which there is both greater formality to the hiring process and greater transparency" (Conor, Gill and Taylor 2015, p. 11), the informal networks through which contracts are secured in the creative industries reinforce social preferences to associate with people like yourself, that is people who hang out at the same places, look like you, work the same hours, like the same things and operate in similar cultural milieus:

> Informal recruitment practices dominate. While an up-to-date résumé is vital and film and television are increasingly graduate entry industries, a résumé and a degree are necessary but not sufficient. These are 'reputation economies' in which people are hired on the soft judgements of insiders about whether they are trustworthy, reliable and good to work with. Networks and contacts are the main means of gaining employment, which forms a barrier for fresh and diverse talent from under-represented groups, as many may not have access to social events and opportunities. … The spaces for networking – particularly pubs – could also form challenging environments for women, and the requirement for 'compulsory sociality' (Gregg 2006) after already long working days posed problems for everyone with caring responsibilities.
>
> *(Leung, Gill and Randle 2015, pp. 56–57)*

Creative labour markets are defined by such processes of 'network sociality' (Wittel 2001): "In such 'reputation economies' wherever you go, whoever you meet, represents a work opportunity. 'Life is a pitch', as one of Gill's (2010) interviewees put it pithily" (Conor, Gill and Taylor 2015, p. 10). As other authors in the Conor, Gill and Taylor collection note, while reputation economies—working almost exclusively with those you know or who are vouched for by people you know—may be seen as an essential means by which to mitigate risk in a sector where returns are rarely guaranteed, this homosocial reproduction or homophily (Ibarra 1992; Leung, Gill and Randle 2015; Wreyford 2015) importantly still means that "members of the dominant group replicate themselves" by seeing "people like themselves as the most trustworthy and competent" (Jones and Pringle 2015, p. 39). Thus perpetuating the exclusion of other social networks and groups from this important sphere of creative production.

This is significant not just at the level of workplace equity; it has profound implications for the kinds of cultural outputs produced by the creative industries sector. Such exclusionary practices are especially strong in media industries, including and notably film and television (Conor, Gill and Taylor 2015; Hesmondhalgh and Baker 2011), with clear implications for a lack of diversity of stories and voices even within strong state-supported broadcasting. Much of the research driving contemporary awareness of creative industries' exclusions arises out of the United Kingdom where existing class frameworks are reinforced when family ties remain key to securing even unpaid internships in desirable creative organisations. Homophily, 'bulimic' work patterns, and after-hours sociality all serve to exclude even relatively privileged educated middle-class women, especially those with care-giving responsibilities, who are at the forefront of the growth of home-based self-employment, including setting up a micro-enterprise in the absence of other employment options (Adkins 2012; Banks and Milestone 2011; McRobbie 2007). Arguably even more economically precarious than working irregularly for someone else, a line can be drawn between the growth of this 'magical solution' to the gendered exclusions of creative work (Luckman 2015b) and the shift from an emphasis from 'policy' to 'industry' around cultural production exemplified by the creative industries. These trends have led some to suggest that the contemporary creative economy produces a retraditionalization of gender roles (Morgan and Nelligan 2015, p. 66, drawing upon Adkins, Banks and Milestone 2011; Gill 2002, 2009). Certainly, the growth of home-based creative self-employment needs to be at least partly accounted for in terms of inequalities within contemporary creative workplaces, especially when it comes to accommodating creative industries employment alongside care-giving responsibilities.

The cultural marketplace post-cultural policy: the rise of the Hipster economy and entrepreneurial arts

Cultural theorist Jim McGuigan defines 'cool capitalism' as "the incorporation of disaffection into capitalism itself" (2009, p. 1); through processes of diffusion and defusion, it is more than capable of not only bringing resistance under its umbrella but in so doing actually strengthening its own hegemony. This is what, he argues, occurred in response to the countercultures of the 1960s that putatively sought to challenge "the dominant culture at its very heart. Yet, in truth, he argues the counter-cultural challenge effectively – and ironically – refreshed the culture and political economy of corporate America, thereby contributing to its survival and flourishing" (McGuigan 2009, p. 6). Today he identifies the creative industries as key enablers of capitalist innovation. A similarly powerful critique is offered by Luc Boltanski and Eve Chiapello in *The New Spirit of Capitalism*:

> To maintain its powers of attraction, capitalism therefore has to draw upon resources external to it, beliefs which, at a given point in time, possess considerable powers of persuasion, striking ideologies, even when they are hostile to it, inscribed in the cultural context in which it is developing. The spirit sustaining the accumulation process at a given point in history is thus imbued with cultural products that are contemporaneous with it and which, for the most part, have been generated to quite different ends than justifying capitalism.
>
> *(2007, p. 20)*

We can locate the rise of the creative industries within these larger trends. Underpinning all the interest in creative industries over the last couple of decades is a growing recognition of the place of creativity—and the 'creative' in place—as a key driver of economic growth in the new economy, with its associated appetite for content and lifestyle goods. This shift reflects wider trends around the aestheticisation of everyday life, the rise of recreational and lifestyle sectors of the economy, of copyright industries as drivers of global market share and an explosion in the number of people operating on a freelance, casual, contract or self-employed basis or in micro-, small- or medium-sized enterprises. This is not to mention a broader confluence of historical, cultural and economic circumstances logically enabling what we might call grassroots desires for creative entrepreneurialism motivated by progressive social agendas that also happen to elide neatly with post-Fordist capitalism's entrepreneurial imperative. Alongside this economic mainstreaming of creativity has come the marketing of 'cool' individuality as a commodity to be purchased, often together with a self-realising career as a creative professional; this dream in large part is driving the explosion of the creative sector and sustaining people despite the precariousness of work in the creative industries. For these reasons too, the idea of the creative industries has appealed to both university leaders and undergraduate students increasingly focussed upon vocational outcomes from degrees in the arts and humanities.

However, while it is important to acknowledge that the creative industries framework has been widely adopted and persists as discursively powerful, it is also far from all-consuming as witnessed by the ongoing use of the acronym 'CCIs' (cultural and creative industries), especially in the UK. As already asserted the shift from cultural policy to creative industries is strongly critiqued and, as we saw in the case of craft in the UK, capable of challenge (though as a central part of its campaign the Crafts Council did need to gather statistics on the sector's economic size, income and levels of educational attainment to make a case that also had strong and wide emotional support). Alternative definitional approaches to the cultural/arts/creative sector persist and are actively employed in policy, funding, organisational and/or academic contexts (see for example: KEA 2006; Throsby 2015; United Nations/ UNDP/UNESCO 2013; Work Foundation 2007). Certainly, the shift continues to be the source of ongoing debate over many fundamental aspects of culture and value, including the importance of arts and cultural industries as possessing a much longer and richer history of intrinsically contributing to society in non-economic ways. Thus a key challenge in the wake of the break marked by the shift from cultural policy to creative industries is to develop new ways to strongly and affectively articulate the value of cultural and creative activities to a wider (voting) public beyond the sector, however it may be defined.

Acknowledgements

Thank you to Terry Flew, Denise Meredyth and Julian Thomas for their insights into the formative days of cultural policy research in Australia.

Note

1 See for example Banks (2007), Banks and Milestone (2011), Conor, Gill and Taylor (2015), Eikhof and Warhurst (2013), Gill (2002, 2007, 2011), Gill and Pratt (2008), Grugulis and Stoyanova (2012), Hesmondhalgh and Baker (2011), McRobbie (2002, 2004, 2007), and Milestone (2016).

References

Adkins, L. (2012). 'Out of Work or Out of Time? Rethinking Labor after the Financial Crisis'. *The South Atlantic Quarterly*, *111*(4), 621–641.

Bain, A. (2013). *Creative Margins: Cultural Production in Canadian Suburbs*, Toronto: University of Toronto Press.

Banks, M. (2007). *The Politics of Cultural Work*. Basingstoke and New York: Palgrave Macmillan

Banks, M. and K. Milestone (2011). 'Individualization, Gender and Cultural Work'. *Gender, Work and Organization*, *18*(1), 73–89.

Bell, D. and M. Jayne (2010). 'The Creative Countryside: Policy and Practice in the UK Rural Cultural Economy'. *Journal of Rural Studies*, *26*, 209–218.

Bianchini, F. (1995). 'Night Cultures, Night Economies'. *Planning Practice and Research*, *10*(2), 121–126.

BOP Consulting (2012). *Craft in an Age of Change*, Commissioned by Crafts Council, Creative Scotland, Arts Council of Wales, and Craft Northern Island. London: BOP Consulting.

Campbell, P. (2014). 'Imaginary Success?—The Contentious Ascendance of Creativity'. *European Planning Studies*, *22*(5), 995–1009.

Conor, B., R. Gill and S. Taylor eds. (2015). *Gender and Creative Labour*. Chichester: Wiley Blackwell/ The Sociological Review.

Cullinan, E. (1984), 'Morris, Architecture & Art'. In ICA (Ed.), *William Morris Today*. London: Institute for Contemporary Art, 51–53.

Cunningham, S. (1992), *Framing Culture: Criticism and Policy in Australia*, North Sydney: Allen and Unwin.

Department of Communication and the Arts (1994). *Creative Nation: Commonwealth Cultural Policy*. Canberra: Commonwealth of Australia.

Department of Media, Culture and Sport (1998). *Creative Industries Mapping Document*. London: DCMS. Revised 2001.

Department of Media, Culture and Sport (2001). *Cultural Industries Mapping Document*. London: DCMS.

Department of Media, Culture and Sport (2006), *Creative Industries Statistical Estimates Statistical Bulletin*, London: DCMS.

Department of Media, Culture and Sport (2008). *Creative Britain: New Talents for the New Economy*. London: DCMS.

Department of Media, Culture and Sport (2013). *Classifying and Measuring the Creative Industries: Consultation on Proposed Changes*. London: DCMS.

Eikhof, D. R. and C. Warhurst (2013). 'The Promised Land? Why Social Inequalities are Systemic in the Creative Industries'. *Employee Relations*, *35*(5), 495–508.

Flew, T. and S. Cunningham (2010). 'Creative Industries after the First Decade'. *The Information Society*, *26*(2), 113–123.

Florida, R. (2003). *The Rise of the Creative Class: And How It's Transforming Work, Leisure, Community, and Everyday Life*. North Melbourne: Pluto Press Australia.

Garnham, N. (2005) 'From Cultural to Creative Industries: An Analysis of the Implications of the 'Creative Industries' Approach to Arts and Media Policy Making in the United Kingdom'. *International Journal of Cultural Policy*, *11*(1), 15–29.

Gill, R. (2002). 'Cool, Creative and Egalitarian? Exploring Gender in Project-Based New Media Work in Europe'. *Information, Communication & Society*, *5*(1), 70–89.

Gill, R. (2007). *Technobohemians of the New Cybertariat? New Media Work in Amsterdam A Decade after the Web*. Amsterdam: Institute of Network Cultures.

Gill, R. (2009). 'Creative Biographies in New Media: Social Innovation in Web Work'. In A.C. Pratt and P. Jeffcutt (Eds), *Creativity, Innovation and the Cultural Economy*. London: Routledge, 161–178.

Gill, R. (2010). 'Life Is a Pitch: Managing the Self in New Media Work'. In M. Deuze (Ed.), *Managing Media Work*. London: Sage, 249–262.

Gill, R. (2011). 'Sexism Reloaded, or 'It's Time to Get Angry Again'. *Feminist Media Studies*, *11*(1), 61–71.

Gill, R. and A. Pratt (2008). 'In the Social Factory? Immaterial Labour, Precariousness and Cultural Work'. *Theory, Culture & Society*, *25*(7–8), 1–30.

Gregg, M. (2006), 'On Friday night drinks: neoliberalism's compulsory friends', paper presented at the UnAustralia Conference of the Cultural Studies Association of Australasia.

Grugulis, I. and D. Stoyanova (2012). 'Social Capital and Networks in Film and TV: Jobs for the Boys?' *Organization Studies*, *33*(10), 1311–1331.

Halfacree, K. (1997). 'Contrasting Roles for the Post-productivist Countryside: A Postmodern Perspective on Counterurbanisation'. In P. Cloke and J. Little (Eds), *Contested Countryside Cultures: Otherness, Marginalisation and Rurality*. London: Routledge, 70–93.

Hartley, J. (2004). 'The 'Value Chain of Meaning' and the New Economy'. *International Journal of Cultural Studies*, 7(1), 129–141.

Hartley, J. (2005). 'Creative Industries'. In J. Hartley (Ed.) *Creative Industries*. Oxford: Blackwell, 1–40.

Hesmondhalgh, D. (2002). *Cultural Industries*. London, Thousand Oaks, and New Delhi: Sage.

Hesmondhalgh, D. and S. Baker (2011). *Creative Labour: Media Work in Three Cultural Industries*. London and New York: Routledge.

Hesmondhalgh, D. and A. Pratt (2005). 'Cultural Industries and Cultural Policy'. *International Journal of Cultural Policy*, 11(1), 1–13.

Higgs, P., S. Cunningham and H. Bakhshi (2008). *Beyond the Creative Industries: Mapping the Creative Economy in the United Kingdom*. London: NESTA.

Ibarra, H. (1992). 'Homophily and Differential Returns: Sex Differences in Network Structure and Access in an Advertising Firm'. *Administrative Science Quarterly*, 37(3), 422–447.

Jones, D. and J. K. Pringle (2015). 'Unmanageable Inequalities: Sexism in the Film Industry'. In B. Conor, R. Gill and S. Taylor (Eds), *Gender and Creative Labour*. Chichester: Wiley Blackwell/The Sociological Review, 37–49.

KEA (2006). *The Economy of Culture in Europe*. Report prepared for the European Commission, Directorate-General for Education and Culture. Brussels: KEA European Affairs. ec.europa.eu/culture/library/studies/cultural-economy_en.pdf

Keane, M. (2009).'Creative Industries in China: Four Perspectives on Social Transformation'. *International Journal of Cultural Policy*, 15, 431–434.

Keane, M. (2013). *Creative Industries in China: Art, Design and Media*. Cambridge and Malden: Wiley (Polity Press).

Landry, C. (2006). *The Art of City-Making*. London and Sterling, VA: Earthscan.

Leadbeater, C. (2000). *Living on Thin Air: The New Economy*. London: Penguin.

Leung, W.-F., R. Gill and K. Randle (2015). 'Getting In, Getting On, Getting Out? Women as Career Scramblers in the UK Film and Television Industries'. In B. Conor, R. Gill and S. Taylor (Eds), *Gender and Creative Labour*. Chichester: Wiley Blackwell/The Sociological Review, 50–65.

Luckman, S. (2012). *Locating Cultural Work: The Politics and Poetics of Rural, Regional and Remote Creativity*. Basingstoke and New York: Palgrave Macmillan.

Luckman, S. (2015a). *Craft and the Creative Economy*. London and New York: Palgrave Macmillan.

Luckman, S. (2015b). 'Women's Micro-Entrepreneurial Home-Working: A 'Magical Solution' to the Work-Life Relationship?' *Australian Feminist Studies*, 30(84), 146–160.

Luckman, S., C. Gibson and T. Lea (2009). 'Mosquitoes in the Mix: Just How Transferable Is Creative City Thinking?' *Singapore Journal of Tropical Geography*, 30(1), 47–63.

Markusen, A. (2006). 'Urban Development and the Politics of a Creative Class: Evidence from a Study of Artists'. *Environment and Planning A*, 38(10), 1921–1940.

Matarasso, F. and C. Landry (1999). *Balancing Act: Twenty-One Strategic Dilemmas in Cultural Policy* (Policy Note No. 4). Belgium: Council of Europe.

McGuigan, J. (2004). *Rethinking Cultural Policy*. Maidenhead: Open University Press.

McGuigan, J. (2009). 'Doing a Florida Thing: The Creative Class Thesis and Cultural Policy'. *International Journal of Cultural Policy*, 15(3), 297–300.

McRobbie, A. (2002). 'Clubs to Companies: Notes on the Decline of Political Culture in Speeded Up Creative Worlds'. *Cultural Studies*, 16(4), 516–553.

McRobbie, A. (2004). 'Making a Living in London's Small-scale Creative Sector'. In D. Power and A.J. Scott (Ed.), *Cultural Industries and the Production of Culture*. London and New York: Routledge, 130–143.

McRobbie, A. (2007). 'Top Girls?' *Cultural Studies*, 21(4–5), 718–737.

Milestone, K. (2016). ''Northernness', Gender and Manchester's Creative Industries'. *Journal for Cultural Research*, 20, 45–59. doi:10.1080/14797585.2015.1134059.

Morgan, G. and P. Nelligan (2015). 'Labile Labour-Gender, Flexibility and Creative Work'. In B. Conor, R. Gill and S. Taylor (Eds), *Gender and Creative Labour*. Chichester: Wiley Blackwell/The Sociological Review, 66–83.

Nimmo, R. (2011). 'Actor-Network Theory and Methodology: Social Research in a More-Than-Human World'. *Methodological Innovations Online*, 6(3), 108–119.

Oakley, K. (2004). 'Not So Cool Britannia: The Role of Creative Industries in Economic Development'. *International Journal of Cultural Studies*, 7(1), 67–77.

O'Brien, D. (2014). *Cultural Policy: Management, Value and Modernity in the Creative Industries*. Abingdon and New York: Routledge.

O'Connor, J. (2010). *The Cultural and Creative Industries: A Literature Review*. Newcastle upon Tyne: Creativity, Culture and Education. www.creativitycultureeducation.org/wp-content/uploads/CCE-lit-review-creative-cultural-industries-257.pdf.

O'Regan, T. (1993). '(Mis)taking Policy: Notes on the Cultural Policy Debate'. In E.J. Frow and M. Morris (Eds), *Australian Cultural Studies*. St Leonards: Allen and Unwin, 192–206.

Potts, J. and S. Cunningham (2008). 'Four Models of the Creative Industries'. *International Journal of Cultural Policy*, 14(3), 233–247.

Pratt, A. C. (2005). 'Cultural Industries and Public Policy'. *International Journal of Cultural Policy*, 11(1), 31–44.

Ross, A. (2007). 'Nice work if you can get it: The mercurial career of creative industries policy'. In G. Lovink and N. Rossiter (Ed.), *My Creativity Reader: A Critique of Creative Industries*. Amsterdam: Institute of Network Cultures, 19–41.

Throsby, D. (2015). 'The Cultural Industries as a Sector of the Economy'. In K. Oakley and J. O'Connor (Eds) *The Routledge Companion to the Cultural Industries*. Abingdon and New York: Routledge, 56–69.

Turner, G. (2015). 'Culture, Politics and the Cultural Industries: Reviving a Critical Agenda'. In K. Oakley and J. O'Connor (Eds) *The Routledge Companion to the Cultural Industries*. Abingdon and New York: Routledge, 535–544.

United Nations/UNDP/UNESCO (2013). *United Nations Creative Economy Report 2013 Special Edition*, New York: United Nations Development Programme (UNDP), www.unesco.org/new/en/culture/themes/creativity/creative-economy-report-2013-special-edition/.

Waitt, G. (2006). 'Creative Small Cities: Cityscapes, Power and the Arts'. In D. Bell and M. Jayne (Eds), *Small Cities: Urban Experience beyond the Metropolis*. Abingdon and New York: Routledge, 169–183.

Waitt, G. and C. Gibson (2009). 'Creative Small Cities: Rethinking the Creative Economy in Place'. *Urban Studies*, 46(5&6), 1223–1246.

Williams, R. (1989). *Resources of Hope: Culture, Democracy, Socialism*. London: Verso.

Williams, R. (1973). *The Country and the City*. New York: Oxford University Press.

Wilson, G.A. (2001). 'From Productivism to Post-productivism … and Back Again? Exploring the (Un)changed Natural and Mental Landscapes of European Agriculture'. *Transactions of the Institute of British Geographers*, 26, 77–102.

Wittel, A. (2001), 'Towards a Network Sociality', *Theory, Culture & Society*, 18(6), 51–76.

Work Foundation (2007). *Staying Ahead. The Economic Performance of the UK's Creative Industries*. London: The Work Foundation

Wreyford, N. (2015). 'Birds of a Feather: Informal Recruitment Practices and Gendered Outcomes for Screenwriting Work in the UK Film Industry'. In B. Conor, R. Gill and S. Taylor (Eds), *Gender and Creative Labour*. Chichester: Wiley Blackwell/The Sociological Review, 84–96.

23

Too-explicit cultural policy

Rethinking cultural and creative industry policies in Hong Kong

Louis Ho

Introduction

This chapter presents a study of the articulation and implementation of Hong Kong's cultural and creative industries policies. The observations are as follows: First, against the backdrop of economic transformation, cultural and creative industry policies in Hong Kong are biased towards macroeconomic, industrial and hardware infrastructure and structural formation, neglecting the individual "units" of Hong Kong's cultural and industrial industries, i.e. creative labour, both artistic and craft labour (Banks 2010). Second, under the global discourse of "creativity", especially that of Richard Florida (2002) and Charles Landry (2000), cultural and creative industry policies in Hong Kong are based on the vague concept of "creativity" as a panacea. It is also assumed that "creativity" is a singular concept, as if there is an absence of any diversity and complexity concerning the concept. This results in such policies neglecting the different requirements, usage and expression of "creativity" by different cultural and creative sectors. Therefore, such cultural and creative industry policies neglect the status and needs of cultural and artistic workers, such as writers or visual artists. The chapter takes each of these observations in turn, following a brief discussion of the historical context for the development of cultural and creative industry policies in Hong Kong.

Background

Since the 1990s, the development of Hong Kong's economy has been dictated by the goal of becoming an international financial hub. The government claimed that it would take a laissez-faire approach and uphold a capitalistic free market.[1] In 2014's Global Financial Centres Index, Hong Kong was ranked fifth, with only New York, London, Tokyo and Singapore ranking higher. From the economic boom in the 1960s until it was known as one of the "Four Asian Tigers" in the 1980s, Hong Kong became a player on the international stage due to its economic prowess with finance, trade and the service industries as its pillars. However, as an international metropolis, Hong Kong's cultural development has always been subject to criticism, even gaining the title of being a "cultural desert". Although the validity of this title remains debatable (Chen 2008), it is apparent that Hong Kong's cultural policy lacks an all-encompassing design.

After WWII, the colonial government enjoyed the long-term benefits of economic growth while facing the looming expiry of Hong Kong's lease. According to Chen's (2008) historical account of cultural policy development in Hong Kong, the government chose to implement "cultural policies" that were bureaucratically viable and met the short-term needs of the residents. This resulted in a disparate set of cultural policies for the region. Different departments implemented cultural, art and leisure-related policies with different methods and conceptualizations of "culture". Needless to say, the concept of cultural governance was virtually non-existent. After the handover in 1997, however, it seemed that "cultural and creative industries" became a prominent lead for Hong Kong's public policy concerning art and culture.

In Hong Kong, the "creative industry" concept was first raised by the Hong Kong Arts Development Council in 1999. Although it generated media interest at that time, it was not until 2002 that the Hong Kong Trade Development Council released its first report on Hong Kong's creative industries. In 2005, the Hong Kong Special Administrative Region (SAR) government recognised the importance of "cultural and creative industries", defining the 11 sectors of "Hong Kong's cultural and creative industries" as advertising; amusement services; architecture; art, antiques and crafts; cultural education and library, archive and museum services; design; film, video and music; performing arts; publishing; software, computer games and interactive media; television and radio. This definition developed the "creative industry" framework established in 2003 in accordance with the *Baseline Study on Hong Kong's Creative Industries* (2003) commissioned by the Central Policy Unit. In the same year, the government established CreateHK, a dedicated agency set up under the Commerce and Economic Development Bureau. The agency is responsible for "nurturing of local talent; supporting the development of start-up companies; developing local market; expanding overseas and Mainland China market; developing creative clusters; enhancing the atmosphere to promote creative industries in the community; and supporting the organization of mega events to promote Hong Kong's development as the creative capital in Asia" (Commerce and Economic Development Bureau 2009).

Currently, policies regarding the cultural and creative industries can mainly be classified into two development categories: The first is according to the "current growth model", which emphasises the possible economic development resulting from cultural and creative industries; the second is recognising "culture" as the core of cultural and creative policies and accepting the (inherent) restrictions of policy (Bell and Oakley 2015:34). Hong Kong's cultural and creative industries (as one of the six major industries selected by the government for intensive development) belong to the first category. Examining the overall implementation of Hong Kong's cultural and creative industry policies, however, raises doubt as to whether the policies are able to achieve results under the "current growth model", i.e. growth in the cultural sector (production and consumption) driving overall economic growth.

Overly macroscopic cultural and creative industry policies in Hong Kong

In recent years, various governments and academic institutes have grown increasingly concerned about the development of creative industries. This was mainly attributable to the decline of traditional economic industries, while the economic value of "culture and creativity" gained recognition – giving rise to the idea that symbolic value is more profitable than physical value. Since 2000, creative industries have developed at a quicker pace than traditional economic industries in most western economies (Murray and Gollmitzer 2012). The creative industries, however, were inevitably affected by the 2008 economic crisis.

Some critics also pointed out that creative industries are especially vulnerable to the impact of fluctuations in the external economy (Murray and Gollmitzer 2012). Despite this, governments all over the world seem to remain fixated on the idea of enhancing economic vitality and making cities more vibrant through the development of creative industries.

In Hong Kong, according to the *Baseline Study on Hong Kong's Creative Industries* (2003) commissioned by the Central Policy Unit and undertaken by the Centre for Cultural Policy Research of the University of Hong Kong, "creative industries" refer to "a group of economic activities that exploit and deploy creativity, skill and intellectual property to produce and distribute products and services of social and cultural meaning, which can become a system for creating wealth and employment".[2] From this definition, we can acknowledge that in the concept of "creative industry", "industry" is the main component of an economic production system, while "creative" describes the nature of the series of economic activities. The scope of "cultural and creative industries" subsequently listed by the SAR government mostly covered a range of private cultural and creative production activities, while leaving out public cultural and creative activities provided by the government such as public libraries and museums.[3]

In 2005, the SAR government renamed "creative industries" as "cultural and creative industries". In the policy address (The Government of the Hong Kong Special Administrative Region, 2005), the government proposed to "establish, as soon as possible, a consultative framework for cultural and creative industries, so that relevant representatives from these industries including outstanding personalities from outside Hong Kong can participate. Working together to study the vision for development, direction, and organizational structure to see how we may deploy our advantages, consolidate resources and pursue key areas" (Ho 2005).[4] The 11 sectors of Hong Kong's "cultural and creative industries" was generated from the "creative industry" framework. In 2009, the government proposed the idea of the "six priority industries of Hong Kong" and listed "cultural and creative industries" as one of them.[5] As a result, the overall policies of Hong Kong's cultural and creative industries are implemented by different government departments, namely Home Affairs Bureau, Commerce, Industry and Technology Bureau (CITB), Education Bureau, and CreateHK. The question is: why have cultural and creative industries been given such an important role in the overall economy of Hong Kong?

This question was also asked by Hesmondhalgh and Pratt (2005), who explore how and why the cultural industries became such a vital idea in cultural policy when those industries were largely absent in "traditional (arts-and heritage-based) policy" (2005:2). Hesmondhalgh and Pratt note that "the 1990s and early 2000s have been a boom time in cultural policy under the sign of the cultural and creative industries as a result of industrial and cultural changes that have themselves been influenced by broader "cultural" policy decisions" and "a great attraction of cultural industries policy, at the urban, regional and national levels, for many politicians and advisors, was that cultural policy, previously on the margins in many areas of government, could be seen to be economically relevant in an era when policy was judged primarily in terms of its fiscal rewards" (2005:5). Based on these inquires and observations, we may further ask: in what ways does the idea of cultural and creative industries, as a marginal policy agenda, embed and integrate itself into different policy models and frameworks?

Since the handover in 1997, Hong Kong has faced a series of economic crises: the burst of the property and stock market bubbles at the end of 1997 and in early 1998; the Asian financial crisis that impacted the Hong Kong dollar, the futures market and stock market; the burst of Hong Kong's dot-com bubbles, which was caused by the tech fever in the US in 1999; the outbreak of SARS in March 2003, which devastated the tourism industry; and the financial crisis in 2008, which affected the world and ended the five-year economic recovery of Hong Kong. The end of the economic recovery that began in July 2003 caused the stock and property market to plummet and caused a series of layoffs and business closures. Since then, "economic transformation", "moving towards a knowledge-based economy", and "development of high value-added, high-tech emerging industries" became buzzwords of the SAR government's economic policies. Cultural and creative industry policies thereafter became part of the policy structure of the knowledge-based economic transformation.

In Hong Kong, cultural and creative industry policies are mainly industry policies, and the implementation of such policies leans towards production and industry structure. The government promotes cultural and creative industry measures mainly in three areas. The first area is the legal framework. The SAR government promulgated the Intellectual Property Copyright Agreement in 1998 (which aimed to modernise Hong Kong's copyright law and provide greater protection for copyright owners). The government also stated that it recognised major international intellectual property regulations, including the Paris Convention for the Protection of Industrial Property; the Berne Convention for the Protection of Literary and Artistic Works; the Universal Copyright Convention; the Nice Agreement Concerning the International Classification of Goods and Services for the Purposes of the Registration of Marks; the Geneva Convention, which protects producers of recorded works from their products being recorded without authorisation; the Patent Cooperation Treaty; the Convention Establishing the World Intellectual Property Organization; the World Intellectual Property Organization Treaty; and the WIPO Performances and Phonograms Treaty.

The second area is the establishment of platforms for financing. The government supports the development of cultural and creative industries through different funds and subsidy programmes. For example, the Trade and Industry Department has subsidy plans (e.g. the SME Loan Guarantee Scheme, the SME Export Marketing Fund, the SME Training Fund and the SME Development Fund[6]), while the Innovation and Technology Fund also has subsidy programmes (e.g. the Innovation and Technology Support Programme, the General Support Programme, the University-Industry Collaboration Programme and the Small Entrepreneur Research Assistance Programme[7]). In addition, the government provides credit guarantees that allow financiers to obtain funding through traditional channels. For instance, the Hong Kong Export Credit Insurance Corporation provides export credit insurance and film loan guarantees. Using film as an example, the aforementioned policies are primarily handled by the CITB. The CITB assists the Hong Kong film industry in penetrating the Mainland China market through the Mainland and Hong Kong Closer Economic Partnership Arrangement (CEPA) to develop the possibility of making films jointly produced by Hong Kong and Mainland China. Besides, a Film Loan Insurance Fund was established to support mid- to low-budget film productions. In 2001, the Film Development Fund financed ten movies, allowing four directors and one producer to make their first attempts at producing drama films. According to the 2015 Policy Address (The Government of the Hong Kong Special Administrative Region, 2015), the government will continue to inject capital into the Film Development Fund with a recommended amount of HKD 200 million.

The third area is large-scale construction projects. This is the area, within the cultural and creative industries, in which the government has invested the largest amount of money, albeit via the construction industry. This area generates controversy in wondering if "Hong Kong culture" is used as spectacle for cultural tourism and urban rejuvenation. This approach of using "culture and creative" in policymaking is "significantly" influenced by the work of Charles Landry (2000) and Richard Florida (2002). Landry and Bianchini's (1995) model of the "creative city" introduces a discussion on the role of culture in dealing with social problems of a city and boosting economic growth. Charles Landry (2000) further promotes the idea of "creative city" by asserting the importance of creativity as a more reflexive process of thinking about the city in cultural planning. Landry (2000) thereby proposes the need to integrate cultural and creative thinking into all aspects of the urban policymaking process, namely, from public health to traditional arts-related policy. Since then, the idea of "creative city" has been widely used in discussions of urban policy that it has become a "shorthand term" in policy discourse for contemporary ideas about culture and the city. As Bell and Oakley (2015:88) remark, though this discourse may always refer to one "conventional creative city script" (Gibson 2013), there have been different versions of interpreting and implementing the creative city idea (Pratt 2012). What then is the exact version of the creative city idea for Hong Kong? It is a version related to a pseudo-Floridian approach of working in culture and creativity.

If we examine the details of the *Baseline Study on Hong Kong's Creative Industries* (2003) that signifies as the start of developing cultural and creative industry policies in Hong Kong, the influence of Florida's ideas can hardly be overlooked. Drawing upon the insights of urbanists and "new growth theorists" about the value of skilled labour, who he terms the "creative class", in urban and economic development (Bell and Oakley 2015:91), Florida (2002) argues that the mobility of the creative class is highly related to the qualities of the city's (or region's) culture and lifestyle options, which are referred to by his well-known ideas of "Bohemian index" and "Gay index". With the idea of the "creative class", Florida has become associated with the discourse of creative cities more generally. But his strategy for economic development is built around talent attraction, not the growth of the cultural industries.

One of the heaviest criticisms for Floridian urban strategy is its potential implication of legitimising urban gentrification and its lack of significant attention to various social inequalities (Bell and Oakley 2015:92). Despite these criticisms, Florida's (2002) work can be viewed as an example of the approach in working on the "street level" for cultural attractions in cultural urban planning (Bell and Oakley 2015:91). As we have seen, in Hong Kong the strategy for using culture for economic development is built around large-scale construction projects. It seems that Hong Kong has adopted a pseudo-Floridian approach in developing the "creative city", which absorbs the potential problems of the approach without developing the "good side" of developing the liveability of the city at the micro level.

The large-scale construction projects related to cultural and creative industries include the Digital Media Center (2003), Cyberport Information Center (2003–2004), Science and Technology Parks (2001), Disneyland (2005) and the West Kowloon Cultural Development Program (2005).[8] These large-scale construction projects typically start off as "creative" projects, but ultimately become large-scale real estate (luxury housing) projects or theme parks. In addition, CreateHK has assisted with two restoration projects of historical buildings, namely Comix Home Base[9] and PMQ.[10] Both projects have been criticised for being overly commercialised (especially the latter). This has given rise to the "cultural bulldozer" theory, in which old urban areas are being gentrified in the name of culture and creativity when in fact the land is utilised as high-priced real estate. As a matter of fact, such reasonable scepticism and criticism can be traced back to the vague definition and framework of "creativity" situated in Hong Kong's cultural and creative industry policies.

In the name of culture and creativity

It is generally agreed that the concept of "creative industry" began to have an impact on government policy and academic research after 1997 when the "New Labour Party" won the general election in the UK and implemented creative industry policies (Banks and

Hesmondhalgh 2009; Banks and O'Connor 2009). The Department of Culture, Media and Sport in the UK advocated the idea of creative industries with the definition "those industries which have their origin in individual creativity, skill and talent and which have a potential for wealth and job creation through the generation and exploitation of intellectual property" (Creative Industries Task Force 2001). This broad definition of the creative industries includes cultural and art-related industries such as television, film and music and involves industries such as software design, construction and design. This unspecific but surprisingly influential definition attempted to avoid the criticism of the concept of "culture industry" from the Frankfurt school by focusing on the importance of "creativity". The "diversified" definition was also a continuation of the heydays of "Cool Britannia", which began in 1997 (Banks and Hesmondhalgh 2009) and indirectly spread the idea of "creative industry" to other parts of the world, including Hong Kong.

When the Hong Kong Trade Development Council released the first report regarding Hong Kong's creative industries in 2002, there were an estimated 90,000 (approx.) people working in creative industries, and the output of creative industries accounted for approximately 2% of the local GDP. In 2003, the government defined the 11 sectors of creative industries and estimated that the output of Hong Kong's creative industries accounted for 4% of the local GDP between 2001 and 2002, with 170,011 persons involved in the industries. How did Hong Kong's cultural and creative industries achieve such a substantial and sustained amount of growth? It is probably the result of the expansion of the components of Hong Kong's cultural and creative industries under the general meaning of "culture and creativity". In 2013, 207,490 persons were employed within cultural and creative industries, of which, the category employing the most persons was "software, computer games and interactive media". Job functions include "publication and distribution of software and computer games; information technology services (i.e. computer games, software, design and development of websites and network systems); Internet and other telecommunications activities; entry-level website management; data processing, filing and related activities". There were 52,600 persons in this category, and they accounted for 25.4% of the total workforce within cultural and creative industries. The category in the second place was "publication". Job functions include "printing, publishing, wholesale and retail of books, newspapers and periodicals" and "news agency and other information service activities". There were 43,900 persons in this category, and they accounted for 21.2% of the total workforce within cultural and creative industries. This was followed by the "advertising" category. Job functions include "advertising and market research; conference and goods services; and manufacturing of commercial billboards". There were 18,510 persons in this category, and they accounted for 8.9% of the total workforce within cultural and creative industries (see Census and Statistics Department of HKSAR 2015).

The reason for stating the above statistics is to demonstrate that the most active component of Hong Kong's "cultural and creative industries" differs from the public perception of "conventional" cultural and artistic workers such as writers and artists who only account for a small proportion of the "performing arts" sector (the smallest sector among the 11 sectors). Another point worth noting is that the increasing number of people working within cultural and creative industries is related to the vague definition of creativity spreading to the educational sector.

According to official sources,[11] the "first" task of CreateHK (created in 2009) was to "cultivate local creative talent". CreateHK has started numerous "training" programmes, such as subsidising Hong Kong artists in international competitions and arranging paid internships in cultural and creative industry enterprises.[12] CreateHK has also established the CreateSmart

Initiative (CSI) and the graduate intern support programme, which is further divided into the "Hong Kong Digital Entertainment Industry New Graduate Support Scheme", which focuses on the training of talent in animation, comics, digital games, post production and visual effects, and the "Hong Kong Digital Advertising Industry Fresh Graduate Support Scheme".[13] CSI also provides subsidies for young designers to participate in exchange programmes overseas. Since 2009, CreateHK has granted subsidies totalling HKD 55 million under the "Hong Kong Digital Entertainment Industry New Graduate Support Scheme". In 2013, the government injected HKD 300 million into CSI (from HKD 300 million in 2009 to HKD 600 million in 2013) to support the development of young creative artists.

In terms of the number of Hong Kong's cultural and creative artists nourished and cultivated, universities and higher education institutes also play significant roles.[14] Different universities and higher education institutes have offered various culture- and creativity-related courses, such as the course of "Creative Media" in City University of Hong Kong, the course of "Design" in the Hong Kong Polytechnic University, and the design, multimedia and innovative technology courses offered by the Vocational Training Council. There are currently over 500 product- and digital design-related courses in Hong Kong, and over 200 are related to creative industries (Figures 23.1 and 23.2).

Here, it is insightful to juxtapose two sets of data: On the one hand, during the decade from 2003 to 2013, the number of participants of cultural and entertainment activities organised by the Leisure and Cultural Services Department increased at a rate of approximately 10%, and the number of participants in 2013 grew by 17% when compared with 2003. On the other hand, students enrolled in humanities, art, design and performing arts rose from 3,816 in 2003 to 6,238 in 2013, representing a growth rate of 63%. These two sets of statistics are compared side by side to raise the question: when comparing the proportion of cultural and creative industry producers trained in Hong Kong (number of students) to the consumption market (number of participants in cultural and entertainment

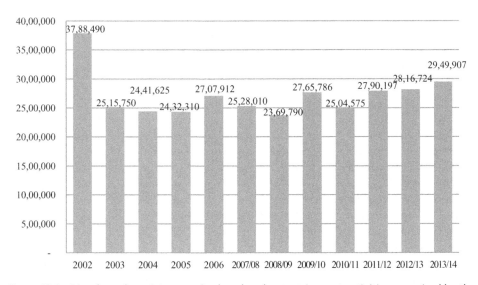

Figure 23.1 Number of participants of cultural and entertainment activities organised by the Leisure and Cultural Services Department (2002–2014)

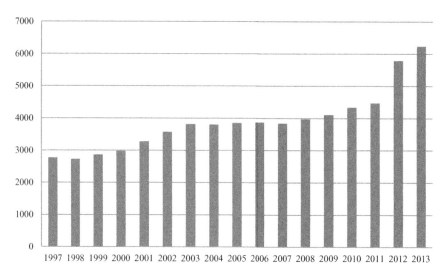

Figure 23.2 Number of students enrolled in humanities, art, design and performing arts (1997–2013)

activities), are Hong Kong's cultural and creative industries neglecting *de facto* demand of the creative labour market and "nurturing" too many cultural and creative artists? The answer to this question may need further empirical analysis, but this issue is brought up herein to reveal the overemphasis of public policies on "creativity" as a panacea and the excessive focus on the macro, production and supply aspects of cultural and creative industries, oblivious to the individuals that underpin the industry and the specific conditions and needs of creative labour.

Cultural and creative industry policies cannot replace cultural and art policies

Conventionally, and practically, cultural policy is considered the sum of a government's activities with respect to the arts, humanities and heritage. Thus, cultural policy encompasses a much broader range of activities than what is traditionally associated with an arts policy. In cultural policy studies, Jeremy Ahearne (2009) and David Throsby (2009) argue that there is a distinction between "explicit" cultural policies that are manifestly labelled as "cultural" and "implicit" cultural policies that are not nominally labelled as "cultural" but that work to shape cultural experiences. Indeed, the framework of "explicit" and "implicit" cultural policy is useful to recognise different kinds of policy aims and impacts in the complex networks of public policies. However, how does such a framework address practically the fluidity of various policies between the implicit and explicit boundary. Also, how does the framework understand the more theoretical problem of the boundary between the cultural and the non-cultural?

In Hong Kong, due to its history of (and the myth of) "laissez-faire" policies, cultural and creative industry policies, as shown above, remain on certain macroscopic levels: establishing symbolic platforms (law, connection), infrastructure construction (financing, construction), and training and education. This has caused numerous issues for Hong Kong's cultural and creative industry policies. First, policies are biased towards the "industries" and neglect the needs of individual workers. The policies have failed to address the needs of the "labour force" of Hong Kong's cultural and creative industries, i.e. the role and rights of creative labour. Needless to say, the possibility and implementation of a "cultural and creative labour policy" is nowhere near fruition. Second, the definition and scope of "creativity" in policies is too broad, ranging from performing arts to jewellery and theme parks, which cannot effectively reflect the true requirements of different creative activities; this made managing such activities even more difficult. Third, due to the vague definitions mentioned above, the policies are unable to pinpoint the needs of creative labour, especially the traditional cultural and art workers. As such, Hong Kong cultural and creative industry policies have to define "creativity" more precisely, so that creative labour in various cultural and creative jobs have access to cultural and creative industrial policies that can better suit their needs and expectations.

Notes

1 Milton Friedman, a Nobel Prize winner in Economics, therefore described Hong Kong as "a prime example of a laissez-faire" economy. However, the government announced in September 2006 that the "positive non-interventionism" system pioneered by Hong Kong was no longer applicable.
2 Commission on Strategic Development, Committee on Economic Development and Economic Cooperation with the Mainland: Promoting the Development of Creative Industries, 2006.
3 Feature Article in *Hong Kong Monthly Digest of Statistics*: The Cultural and Creative Industries in Hong Kong, March 2014.
4 Jin Yuanpu, The Rise of Modern Cultural and Creative Industries, www.cnci.net.cn/, 2008.
5 The six priority industries include testing and certification, medical services, innovation and technology, cultural and creative industries, environmental industry and educational services.
6 From 2001 to 30 April 2007, 132,405 items have been approved for a total subsidy of approximately HKD 10 billion, benefiting 48,300 SMEs. LegCo document no. CB(1)1849/06-07(03), SME Subsidy Program of the Panel on Commerce and Industry of LegCo, Commerce, Industry and Technology Bureau, Trade and Industry Department, June 2007.
7 As of 31 January 2015, the Fund has approved 1,356 items, granting a total subsidy of HKD 88.941 million. Innovation and Technology Fund – Statistics of Approved Projects, www.itf.gov.hk/l-tc/StatView101.asp.
8 According to the government, the West Kowloon Cultural Development Programme aims to amass a series of world-class cultural, art, trends, consumption and mass entertainment events in a comprehensive cultural venue that includes opera houses, museums, performance areas, theatres and plazas. This would enhance Hong Kong's cultural standards and global reputation, which would propel the development of Hong Kong's cultural and creative industries.
9 Located between Burrows Street and Mallory Street in Wan Chai, Comix Home Base was a pre-war building that was revitalised to become a "creative community based on animation and comics". The venue hosts regular workshops, exhibitions, seminars and also houses archives.
10 PMQ was formerly the Hollywood Road Police Married Quarters. It has now been developed into a "creative industry landmark focused on design, providing approximately 130 workshops for designers and members of the creative community to create and display their creative works".
11 Website of CreateHK. www.createhk.gov.hk/en/service_createsmart.htm Assessed on 29 January 2016.
12 From 2009 to 2011, CreateHK provided aid and support for approximately 140 events held by the industries, attracting over 2.7 million participants in Hong Kong and over 50 countries.
13 A full year of full-time work and on-the-job training is provided to up to 120 graduates each year.
14 The Education Bureau also plays a role in cultural and creative educational activities. Since 2001, the government has listed "creativity" as one of the three main common abilities after the reforms of secondary and primary school curriculums.

References

Ahearne, J. 2009. "Cultural Policy Explicit and Implicit: A Distinction and Some Uses." *International Journal of Cultural Policy*. 15(2): 141–153.

Banks, M. 2010. "Craft Labour and Creative Industries." *International Journal of Cultural Policy*. 16(30): 305–321.

Banks, M. and O'Connor, J. 2009. "Introduction: After the Creative Industries." *International Journal of Cultural Policy*. 15(4): 365–373.

Banks, M. and Hesmondhalgh, D. 2009. "Looking for Work in Creative Industries Policy." *International Journal of Cultural Policy*. 15(4): 415–430.

Bell, D. and Oakley, K. 2015. *Cultural Policy*. London and New York: Routledge.

Census and Statistics Department of HKSAR. 2015. "Feature Articles: The Cultural and Creative Industries in Hong Kong." Hong Kong Monthly Digest of Statistics. www.statistics.gov.hk/pub/B10100022015MM06B0100.pdf [Accessed on 29 January 2016].

Central Policy Unit of HKSAR. 2003. Baseline Study of Hong Kong's Creative Industries. Hong Kong: The University of Hong Kong: Centre for Cultural Policy Research. www.cpu.gov.hk/doc/en/research_reports/baseline%20study(eng).pdf [Accessed on 29 January 2016].

Chen, W. 2008. Xiang Gang You Wen Hua—Xiang Gang De Wen Hua Zheng Ce (Hong Kong Has Culture – Hong Kong Cultural Policy). Hong Kong: Arcadia Press Limited.

Creative Industries Task Force. 2001. Creative Industries Mapping Document 2001. London: Department for Culture, Media and Sport.

Commerce and Economic Development Bureau of HKSAR. 2009. Progress Report on the Motion on "Promoting the development of local creative industries" Passed by the Legislative Council on 4 February 2009. www.legco.gov.hk/yr08-09/english/counmtg/motion/cm0204-m3-prpt-e.pdf [Accessed on 29 January 2016].

Florida, R. 2002. *The Rise of the Creative Class*. New York: Basic Books.

Gibson, C. 2013. "Widening Development Pathways." The Creative Economy Report: Widening Local Development Pathways. New York: UNESCO.

Hesmondhalgh, D. and Pratt, A. 2005. "Cultural Industries and Cultural Policy." *International Journal of Cultural Policy*. 11 (1): 31–44.

Ho, P. 2005. Promoting the development of cultural and creative industries. www.hab.gov.hk/file_manager/en/documents/publications_and_press_releases/20050525other_lcq17_e.pdf [Accessed on 12 December 2016]

Hong Kong Trade Development Council of HKSAR. 2002. Annual Report 2001/2002. http://info.hktdc.com/annualreport2002//index.htm [Accessed on 29 January 2016].

Landry, C. 2000. *The Creative City: A Toolkit for Urban Innovators*. London: Earthscan.

Landry, C. and Bianchini, F. 1995. *The Creative City*. London: Demos.

Murray, C. and Gollmitzer, M. 2012. "Escaping the Precarity Trap: A Call for Creative Labour Policy." *International Journal of Cultural Policy*. 18(4): 419–438.

Pratt, A. 2012. 'A world turned upside down: The creative economy, cities and the new austerity' in *Smart, Creative, Sustainable, Inclusive: Territorial Development Strategies in the Age of Austerity*. London: Regional Studies Association. www.andycpratt.info/andy_c_pratt/Research_Writing__Downloads_files/A%20world%20turned%20upside%20down.pdf [Accessed on 18 May 2017].

The Government of the Hong Kong Special Administrative Region. 2005. Chief Executive's Policy Address 2005. www.policyaddress.gov.hk/2005/eng/ [Accessed on 29 January 2016].

The Government of the Hong Kong Special Administrative Region. 2015. Chief Executive's Policy Address 2015. www.policyaddress.gov.hk/2015/eng/ [Accessed on 29 January 2016].

Throsby, D. 2009. "Explicit and Implicit Cultural Policy: Some Economic Aspects." *International Journal of Cultural Policy*. 15(2): 179–185.

24

Cultural policy and mega-events

Beatriz Garcia

The notion of 'mega-events' has attracted considerable academic attention since the late 1990s. It first attracted scholars within leisure and tourism-related disciplines, but interest progressively expanded into sociology, geography and communication studies to name just a few of the other most dominant disciplines. This chapter considers the mega-event debate from a cultural policy perspective, touching on key issues such as the interdependence between local and global agendas, the reliance on global media conglomerates to project (as well as finance) event narratives, the importance of myth-building and the production of collective cultural meanings to frame what is often articulated as a 'once-in-a-lifetime' opportunity to tell stories of place and community that can resonate across the world.

The chapter focuses on examples from what is considered the largest 'mega-event' of all the Olympic Games and notes the way in which cultural policy issues have been viewed (or ignored) by its umbrella organisation, the International Olympic Committee, during most of its 100 year history. In particular, it discusses the contrast between the strong relevance of a cultural agenda for local event stakeholders and its low priority amongst the event global stakeholders.

Mega events as platforms for global cultural policy

Major events such as the Olympic Games and Football World Cup Finals have become dominant cultural actors at a global level due to their ability to attract the attention of international media, the large financial contributions of multinational corporations they involve, and the extensive use they make of global marketing and promotional campaigns (see Getz 2008; Gold and Gold 2012; Hall 1989; Roche 2000). Major events are thus shaped by their global stakeholders, but they are also shaped by the locations where they occur, in particular, by the leading stakeholders within the chosen host-city. This is so because local event stakeholders view the opportunity to attract worldwide attention over a concentrated period of time as a key platform to secure ongoing legacies at a local level. The contrast between the time and place-specific aspirations of local host stakeholders and the long-term international agenda of the event's global partners pose important questions from a cultural policy point of view that merit detailed interrogation. First, however, it is critical to understand what we mean by 'mega-event' and how this type of intervention differs from many other forms of cultural policy implementation.

What is a mega-event?

The term mega-event has been rapidly generalised since it first made an appearance and became popular in practitioner as well as academic circles during the late 1980s and 1990s. The term followed in the footsteps of previous denominations for staged national or international event interventions such as 'special events', 'planned tourist events' and 'hallmark events' (Getz 1991; Hall 1989). By the 1990s, it was common for policy agencies to have a formal 'special event' definition so that such interventions and their outcomes could be regularly monitored and documented. In Canada, for instance, special events were defined as a type of event that is:

> open to the public…; its main purpose is the celebration or display of a specific theme; it takes place once a year or less frequently; it has predetermined opening and closing dates; it does not own a permanent structure; its programme may consist of separate activities; all activities take place in the same local area or region.
>
> *(National Task Force on Data in Canada, cited in Haxton 1999, p. 13)*

This definition and approximate variations have been applied to a rapidly growing number of itinerant events since the 1990s. In this context, the notion of a 'mega-event' was considered a necessary addition to identify the largest scale and less frequent types of special events that, typically, involve considerably larger and more internationally diverse numbers of participants, audiences and media coverage.

In 2008, Getz mapped the main types of special events by considering the levels of demand and 'value' they generate from a tourism strategy point of view (see Figure 24.1).

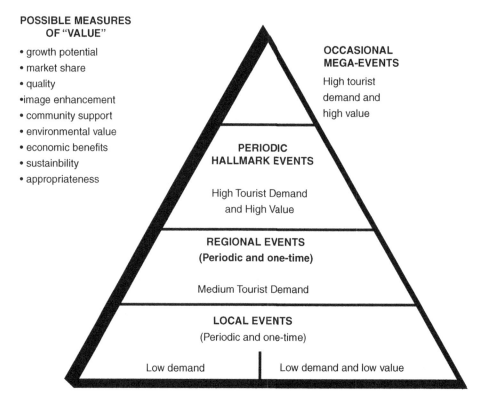

Figure 24.1 Types of special event from a tourism point of view

The above diagram followed on previous classifications, including a first attempt at indicating specific volume suggestions to mark the scale of mega-events, as indicated in Box 1:

Mega-event figures

- *number of participants:* 'over 100,000' and 'usually more international than local'
- *number of spectators:* 'from approximately 100,000 to one million or more'. 'They are mainly domestic but a large international contingent move to the place because of the event'
- *media coverage and live demand:* 'very high levels of international coverage and exposure. Very high demand of live coverage. Rights for extended media coverage typically require bidding to an international governing body'. (Adapted from: Getz 1991)

Beyond the above markers, mega-events are also characterised by the diversity of nation-states represented (e.g. more than 200 nations compete at the Olympic Games and are involved in the World Cup preliminaries); the volume of simultaneous broadcast audiences they attract (e.g. organisers claim that the Olympic Games Opening Ceremony regularly attracts billions of viewers worldwide – see IOC 2012). Although the veracity of the most spectacular metrics is regularly questioned (see Harris 2012), it is broadly accepted that mega-events regularly secure record broadcast viewing figures (see Laflin et al. 2012).

The Olympic Games and FIFA World Cup were rapidly identified as the two leading mega-events of the last three decades. Other events, such as the Universal Expo, were categorised as mega-events in the 1990s due to their historical trajectory up to that time and the diversity of nations involved (Roche 2000); however, they have failed to meet some of the 'scale' requirements listed above since the turn of the millennium. In particular, the Universal Expo has failed to keep up with its sporting event counterparts in terms of media coverage and, most noticeably, it has failed to secure simultaneous and high-profile live coverage across all participant nations.

The capacity to guarantee worldwide live media coverage is key to create 'global moments' (Giulianotti and Robertson 2009) and thus, despite some contestation (see Rowe 2003), live coverage has become the most determinant factor in achieving mega-event status. As discussed by Moragas et al. (1995), mega-events become so due to being media-events in their own right, that is, events designed to maximise mediatisation where all key components are perfectly attuned to address media and, specifically, broadcasters' needs (see also Dayan and Katz 1994). This dependence of the mega-event on (as well as influence over) global media stakeholders has important implications for cultural policy, as discussed in the next section.

What counts as cultural policy within a mega-event?

As just noted, a mega-event is defined by its international media dimensions. As such, event activities are planned, staged and narrated to address media requirements. From venue design (set up to accommodate, first and foremost, professional camera needs); to timing schedules (set up to meet the prime-time live television requirements of the most dominant stakeholder country),[1] these are all event components that have evolved from varied origins into an increasingly standardised form, dictated by the latest technological advancements and journalistic trends. At heart, thus, over the last few decades, mega events have been designed to *look good on TV.*

As I have discussed previously (Garcia 2014), the consequence of such a media imperative is that part of the live experience may be sacrificed (e.g. from the need to reserve the best seats to the cameras, to the push towards hard-to-access but spectacular – iconic – locations). However, over the last 25 years, the increasing loss of a collective festival atmosphere has been broadly accepted by leading event stakeholders as a necessary compromise to fulfil broadcaster needs and secure maximal audience ratings worldwide. As a result, mega-events have often risked their festival feel and become best experienced away from the collective live action, in the comforts of private living rooms.

Of course, much of what is being noted above was characteristic of a television-dominated area, where event feeds were mainly distributed by mainstream broadcasters at a given time and consumed by people around the world via fixed screens inside their homes. The advent of on-demand digital media and social media has opened other avenues for event consumption and created other types of demands in event staging and event narration (Rivenburgh 2002). Regardless, a series of core characteristics remain unchanged and retain similar implications for cultural policy-making in a global context:

- first, mega-event cultural policy must relate to and be informed by broader communication media policies;
- second, mega-event cultural policies should be understood primarily as image strategies;
- third, event narratives and image strategies are framed by an ongoing tension between local and global stakeholder needs and expectations.

Each of these characteristics is discussed in turn, below.

Culture, media and communication policies

The global media and communications framework so characteristic of all mega-events is important as it gives a marked focus to what counts as 'culture' within the event staging process. In my monograph, *The Olympic Games and Cultural Policy*, I dedicate a chapter to cultural policy in the context of globalisation, revisiting the early discussions that dominated institutional discourse as led by the United Nations Education, Science and Culture Organisation (UNESCO) between the 1960s and 1990s. A key turning point in the discussion, which coincided with the emergence of mega-events as a distinct phenomenon, was the pressing need to understand the interdependence between cultural and communication policies.

In the 1960s and 1970s, UNESCO pioneered international cultural policy debates by highlighting the notion of cultural democracy as a substitute for the principle of 'cultural democratisation' so popular in the 1950s (Garcia 2012, p. 5). This was a stepping stone to establish broader notions of policy-worthy cultural practices, e.g. grassroots (as opposed to institutional) culture (Kelly 1984) and led to formalising the debate around popular culture as well as interrogating traditional distinctions between high and low culture (Gans 1974). However, by the 1980s, such discussions were overshadowed by the need to understand the effect of an increasingly active and pervasive private sector within local and international cultural production and consumption trends. By this point in time, it became evident that cultural matters were of interest to private corporations and would, increasingly, be funded and promoted independently from public administration (Kong

2000). This process was termed '*privatisation of culture*' and motivated dedicated research programmes in institutions such as New York University, under the guidance of Toby Miller and George Yúdice (see Goldstein 1998 and early cultural policy monographs by Lewis and Miller 2003; Miller and Yúdice 2002). The work of García Canclini is central to these studies as it argues that the process of privatisation is a direct effect of the movement towards globalisation (Goldstein 1998: Contexts and Conditions of the Support of Culture, paragraph 3).

Discussion around the 'privatisation of culture' came along the re-emergence of the concept of 'cultural industries', first coined by Horkheimer and Adorno (1944) but taking a new meaning within cultural policy circles in the 1990s that has extended up to today. This heralded a new era in international (though Western dominated) cultural policy discourse, this time led not only by the likes of UNESCO but myriad academic institutions as well as policy think tanks and so-called 'cultural observatories' (Garcia 2012, p. 6). Key to the discussion was the realisation that global media networks were a leading cultural and creative industry with ever-expanding influence on cultural production and consumption patterns. Cultural policy, thus, needed to be understood in the context of broader media and communication policies. In other words, communication media were discovered as key to understand global cultural trends, and communication policy was argued by many to be a serious influencer on cultural policy – if not, as noted by Mirrlees (p. 108), as essentially the same thing.[2] In this context, media events can be seen as the ultimate example of global cultural policy merging with global communication policy.

Returning to the starting point for this section, understanding mega-events as fully dependent on their media and communication framework helps explain what counts as 'culture' within the event staging process. Cultural activity that does not occupy a clear media stage – and thus, enters the 'global' event viewers arena – can play no significant role within the event narrative during its staging nor, most significantly, throughout its aftermath. This, in turn, means that cultural policy-making in the context of mega-events tends to operate, primarily, as a platform for image-building and image projection.

Cultural policy as an image strategy

The use of cultural policy as an image strategy for cities and nations has been a common focus for debate, with discussions and analysis developing parallel to those around special and mega-events over the last three decades. My research demonstrates that image-making is one of the most dominant legacy aspirations within event-led regeneration plans (see Garcia 2004), and 'image-renaissance' is one of the most frequent references utilised to back up success claims post-event (see Garcia and Cox 2013). In 1993, Bianchini listed a few typical characteristics of cultural policy understood as a form of image strategy:

> Prestigious cultural projects acted as *symbols of rebirth*, renewed confidence and dynamism in declining cities like Glasgow, Sheffield and Bilbao… Cultural policies were used *as symbols of modernity and innovation* in cities like Montpellier, Nimes, Grenoble, Rennes, Hamburg, Cologne, Barcelona and Bologna, that wished to develop sectors of the economy such as fashion, crafts and design based manufacturing and high-tech industry….[C]ultural flagships like the Burrell collection in Glasgow…[and] the 160 new public squares created in Barcelona in the build up to the 1992 Olympics all became powerful physical *symbols of urban renaissance*.
>
> *(1993, pp. 15–16, emphasis added)*

This aspiration, considered new a few decades ago, has become so dominant in contemporary event rhetoric that it may feel unnecessary to discuss it as a distinct characteristic. However, in the context of events aspiring to reach out to a global audience, the use cultural policy as a catalyst for image projection takes on expanded connotations: rather than subtle images, the kinds of images to be projected need to be bold and simplified so that they can be easily recognised by media audiences with little understanding of the local host environment. They are thus closer to a form of contemporary myth-building exercise, relying as they do on established (often tokenistic) international place associations and mainstreamed historical imagery.

In this context, cultural policy focuses on providing tools for the identification and projection of iconic imagery that stands out and can be understood across widely diverse cultural contexts. It is about condensing broadly known characteristics and mixing them with a few contemporary twists that can work well across media platforms and – with social media increasingly dictating tone and focus – can be shared easily.

Given these pressures towards 'packaging' cultural narrative and maximising external projection, another underlying ambition of cultural policy frameworks within global events becomes the provision of background information and guidelines so that stakeholders can negotiate local sensitivities and the choice of projected images is not totally rejected at home. In this sense, a key task of mega-event cultural policy is to build bridges between local and global interests.

The local and the global in a mega-event

The final distinctive characteristic of mega-event cultural policy is the need to respond to and merge local and global stakeholder interests. Although it is often claimed that mega-events require different layers of cultural programming, with some activities aimed at a local audience and others aimed at national or international followers, decades of trial and error prove that the most broadly revered event editions have been those able to produce iconic imagery that works simultaneously across local and global communities of interest. One of the best-known examples is that of competing divers at the Barcelona 1992 Games: the divers plunged into the pool with the city skyline, dominated by the recognisable towers of the Sagrada Familia, as background.[3] This became the most iconic image of the 1992 Games and projected Barcelona as a globally desirable cultural centre. It was the result of an architectural decision: a roofless Olympic diving pool set on top of the Montjuic hill, a well-known and locally appreciated location that also hosted the main stadium. The outcome was the production of powerful city images fully integrated into the competitions broadcast to exemplify the idea that the city was a key protagonist within the sporting mega-event.

Other iconic images bridging local or national symbols with global spectacle include the 'Rocket Man' that protagonised the Los Angeles 1984 Olympic Opening Ceremony, epitomising the dominance of Hollywood as the home of 'show business' and the role of the USA landing on the moon or the use of bold op-art graphic design inspired by early Mexican cultures and folk-art as the unifying (i.e. global avant-garde as well as indigenous heritage) look for the Mexico 1968 Games.

The pressure towards iconic and spectacular imagery poses important questions about the depth and authenticity of event cultural narratives. Ultimately, it also suggests that there is a thirst for collectively owned statements, 'collective moments' or 'collective memories' that people from the most diverse backgrounds can feel an attachment to (see Nas 2011). I contend here that mega-events grounded on globally informed cultural policy frameworks have the capacity to create and project such statements.

Given its consistent standing as the largest global media event over the last three decades (with media coverage regularly reaching out to over 200 countries), the chapter now turns to the Olympic Games as a key example of global cultural policy-making in action.

The Olympic Games and cultural policy

The Olympic Games have always been framed, implicitly, by cultural policy, with broad requirements for the inclusion of official cultural programmes dating back to 1912 and the expectation that cities should host 'Olympic art competitions' extending between 1912 and 1948 (see Garcia 2008). However, culture has not been part of an active IOC-led strategy until 2014, with the creation of the first executive department dedicated to Culture and Olympic Heritage. This has been largely because, ever since the transformation of the Games into a global media event phenomenon in the 1980s, there has been a marked divide in the value given to culture by local as opposed to global stakeholders.

At a transnational level, while extensively detailed international marketing guidelines have existed since 1980 (e.g. the IOC 'Olympic Marketing Fact File', which is updated annually), the first explicit 'Olympic cultural policy' paper was not produced until 2000 (IOC 2000). Further, while media operations toolkits have always been part of the Games hosting process (especially since the advent of international broadcasts, pioneered at the Rome 1960 edition), formal statements on the centrality of culture as part of the 'Host City Candidature File' have not been apparent until 2008 (IOC 2008) and the first operational guideline on how to deliver cultural activity alongside the Games was not produced until 2011 (IOC 2011).

In contrast, locally, the importance of a strong cultural framework has been in the radar of host cities for decades, with the Berlin 1936 and Mexico 1968 editions as pioneering exemplars (see Garcia 2008) and more generalised interest by all Games organisers since the Barcelona 1992 edition. Barcelona showed the value of using a sporting mega-event as a platform for cultural identity projection and city representation, going as far as designing sports venues so that athletic competition media shots included the city skyline (see Figure 24.2). Subsequently, local stakeholders have become more strategic in their attempts to ensure that the city has some protagonism in Games coverage.

The latter trend has run parallel to the broader trend towards 'culture-led regeneration' as a dominant policy strategy in post-industrial cities (Garcia 2004). However, without the official backing and encouragement of global partners (i.e. sponsors and broadcasters) many attempts at Olympic cultural policy-making have remained invisible to international audiences, thus incapable of transferring from one Games edition to the next.

Prior to discussing how the interests of international stakeholders differ from those of local groups, it is worth reflecting on the key sources of cultural value and/or platforms for cultural production within an Olympic Games. I have discussed the merits and potentials of each of these areas in previous studies (see Garcia 2011). This chapter will provide a quick overview first (see Box 2), followed by some examples of their application within specific Games editions.

Figure 24.2   Iconic images: bridging local and global narratives in Mexico 1968

Box 2: Sources of Olympic cultural production

The main sources of Olympic cultural production could be summarised as:

1. *The symbols of the Games and the Olympic Movement*: These include the logo and emblem of each Games, the official Olympic posters, the mascots, all merchandising materials and commercial applications of Games symbols (e.g. accessories, clothing, decoration) and traditional collectables such as Olympic stamps and coins.
2. *Olympic ceremonies and rituals*: These include both the opening and closing ceremonies, which are considered the peak events of the Games in terms of public awareness and claim to be the most widely live-broadcast event in the world, and the torch relay, which is aimed at maximising direct public participation and community interest by taking place throughout the host country.
3. *The promotional strategy for the Games and 'brand image' of the host-city*: This includes the use of distinctive graphic design features to 'dress the city' (i.e. the so-called 'look of the Games' programme, involving building-wraps, flags, crowd sign-posting etc.), as well as staff uniforms, stationery, publications and venue design. Olympic slogans are also part of this category.
4. *The cultural activities programme or Cultural Olympiad*: This refers to the organisation of special cultural and arts events prior to and during the two weeks of Olympic competition. This is the least regulated of all the areas listed here and is becoming the strongest area of opportunity for the implementation of distinct cultural policies. (Adapted from: Garcia 2011, pp. 154–155)

While, traditionally, the International Olympic Committee (IOC) has focused on setting the rules and providing guidance towards the first two areas and overviewing the (increasingly dominant) role of the third area, the cultural activities programme has remained separate from the rest and has lacked a clear direction. In the following two sections, I discuss how host city stakeholders have tried to appropriate the least regulated sources of cultural narrative within the Olympic Games to fulfil local agendas, while global partners have limited their expectations to narrow heritage representations and/or standardised commercial interpretations.

Local framework

Olympic host cities have always shown an interest in exploiting the cultural policy possibilities presented by hosting the Games and attracting global attention. Most cities have focused on the opportunities for image projection, but there are some relevant examples of Games editions being used to advance broader economic, social and creative agendas through their Olympic cultural programming. In many cases, the pressures emerging out of operating within an outward-facing context, with national – or indeed, global –audiences and stakeholders in mind, have played a defining role to push new (or more ambitious) cultural policy frameworks than those in place pre-event.

Since the 1960s (the time when Olympic cities started to feel more empowered to develop a cultural narrative) the most dominant local agendas behind Olympic cultural programming can be summarised as:

1. 'Politics and identity'
2. 'Economics and regeneration'
3. 'Entertainment, look and feel'
4. 'Cultural and social change' (Garcia 2016)

The first, 'politics and identity', occurs when the official cultural narrative intends to grow or reignite national pride. This was the most frequent priority for Games editions during the Cold War era in the period from the 1960s to 1980s. Recognisable examples are the Moscow 1980 Games, which presented a large cultural programme celebrating Russian folklore as well as high culture icons in the areas of classical music and dance, and the Los Angeles 1984 response, which focused on a celebration of the USA 'way of life' through the lenses of postmodernism and popular culture as represented by the Hollywood film industry. Other editions with a strong political angle include those taking place in cities aiming to project minority cultures or to showcase a cultural identity distinct from larger nation states: Montreal in 1976 and Barcelona in 1992 used the Games cultural programme to present Quebecoise and Catalan culture and explain their differences in the context of Canada and Spain respectively (Garcia 2016).

Economic impact and city regeneration became the most noticeable agenda in the 1990s, with Barcelona and Sydney being two outstanding cases. Their cultural programme was linked to a larger tourism positioning strategy that saw the promotion of urban centres in opposition to outdated views of their host countries as loci for 'beach tourism' 'cheap food' and 'good weather' exclusively. The Cultural Olympiad thus emphasised activity that could highlight the most recognisable city skyline and iconic venues: la Sagrada Familia and Las Ramblas featured strongly in Barcelona, while the Sydney Opera House was the sole performing arts venue for the Olympic Arts Festival in 2000 (Garcia 2012).

A broader emphasis on 'entertainment, look and feel' has been common in Games editions where organisers understand cultural programming mainly as a tool to assist with crowd management and expand public engagement during Games time. Games editions prioritising this over any other agendas have often relied on a generalist type of cultural offer, favouring standardised entertainment practices and design motifs that have done little to present a distinct view of the local host and advance autochthonous cultural policies. However, there are examples of innovative and internationally influential approaches in the 1960s and 1970s, when the Games showcased avant-garde trends in graphic design and advertising. Mexico 1968 and Munich 1972 are two of the best examples (Garcia 2016).

Finally, 'cultural and social change' can be interpreted as the most ambitious and recent policy agenda, an area gaining prominence particularly after 2000. Sydney 2000 was ambitious in its plea to bring contemporary Aboriginal art troupes to the mainstream, and its dedicated Aboriginal Olympic arts festival ('Festival of the Dreaming') was pivotal in bringing Aboriginal work to the Sydney Opera House for the first time, as well as generating the expectation that emerging Aboriginal art should be showcased regularly within high profile festivals (Garcia 2012). Similarly, London 2012 contributed to the repositioning of disabled artists as world-class performers and creators through its nationwide programme 'Unlimited', which was supported by the British Council to inform work at the Rio 2016 Olympics (see Rodenhurst 2013, pp. 9–27). The London 2012 Cultural Olympiad also placed a strong emphasis on advancing the role of young people as producers – not only consumers – of art and culture and made this ambition manifest through its approach to programing design and production (Rodenhurst 2013).

All in all, there are many examples of progressive cultural policy being applied in the context of the Games and resulting in local, national and, at times, international advancements to position and expand the role of previously ignored or minority cultural causes and actors. However, few of these examples have benefited from the Games as a global communication platform. International media stakeholders have consistently failed to report on the Cultural Olympiad as a Games component, and official sponsors have provided no funding or promotional support for official cultural programming other than the (far less flexible or locally rooted) ceremonies and torch relay (see Garcia 2012). The final section analyses the key reasons and notes possible routes for change over the coming years.

International framework

Despite more than a century of aspirational rhetoric regarding the cultural foundations of the Olympic Games as the expression of a 'movement' aiming to 'blend sport with culture and education' in order to 'inspire the youth of the world' (IOC 2015), the opportunities to advance a global cultural policy framework adaptable to the 200 plus participant nation states officially involved in the Games have been limited. This is partly because, traditionally, Olympic culture has been defined through the narrow and (often) nostalgic interpretation of the ideals articulated by the Modern Games founder, Pierre de Coubertin, back in 1906 (see Muller 2000).

The International Olympic Committee established a Culture and Education Commission in 1968 in order to provide guidelines for these two named areas and their manifestation during Games time. The role of this group, however lengthy in time, has remained ambiguous and has focused predominantly on the preservation of early customs: from the value of documenting and promoting Olympic collectables such as coins and stamps, to the protection of protocol within the official Games pageant and the dissemination of pedagogic ideals as conveyed by de Coubertin at the start of the twentieth century. This focus on a vision around Olympic heritage as a (fixed) nineteenth century concept, has diminished (and, often, prevented) the IOC cultural leads' engagement with the discussions most common in international cultural policy circles from the 1980s onwards – including, paradoxically, engagement in the debate around the 'privatisation of culture' process, as heralded by the Olympics in that very period. As a result, Olympic cultural and educational policies have remained largely separate from the rapid evolution and transformation of Olympic communication policies and event management operations. However, with the advent of 'legacy' and 'sustainability' as essential keywords for the future of Olympic Games hosting (Moragas et al. 2003), the value and need for a more clearly defined (and contemporary) Olympic cultural policy has become increasingly apparent.

The way to address this need has been for the IOC to create, for the first time, a department dedicated to overseeing cultural matters with an explicit focus on 'International cultural relations' and a capacity to take on executive actions rather than just provide advice on an annual basis, as was the case with the Culture and Education Commission. One of the first actions by the new Department for Culture and Heritage has been to develop an 'IOC Cultural Action Plan' that can link to specific Games editions, while operating on an ongoing basis and retaining a transnational focus. This Action Plan is defined as a combination of 'networking/public relations' initiatives with cultural actors worldwide (e.g. a collaboration has started with the Victoria and Albert Museum in the UK); 'international programmes and diffusion' (e.g. artists in residence programme during the Rio 2016 Games, travelling exhibitions launched from Olympic Museum in Lausanne); and formal 'partnerships' with key Olympic stakeholders (e.g. proposing creation of 'cultural attaché' role within National Olympic Committees, International Sport Federations, sponsors) (Jamolli 2015).

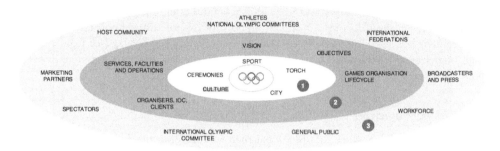

Figure 24.3   Visual representation of 'Olympic Experience' components

In order to best assist in the implementation of this Plan, the role and scope of the advisory Commission has also changed. For the first time since 1968, education matters are being handled by a separate Commission, while a new Culture and Olympic Heritage Commission has been formed to include not only champions of Olympic Movement historical accounts and traditions, but also expert representatives of contemporary cultural and creative industries sectors – an area never before fully considered part of the IOC definition of culture. Further, the definition of the official Games cultural programme or Cultural Olympiad is evolving and for the first time in 2008 was expressed as central to the 'Olympic experience' alongside the broader host city context. This was visualised in the following diagram to inform the candidature proposals of cities aiming to host the 2016 Games edition (see Figure 24.3)

Explicit reference to the Cultural Olympiad has also emerged within the IOC White Paper 'Olympic Agenda 2020', which offers a strategic roadmap for Olympic stakeholders over the next four years. This document includes three recommendations that have direct implications for cultural programming and offer a focus for the Action Plan:

> Recommendation num. 26: 'Further blend sport and culture' both 'during Games time' and 'between Games'.
>
> *(IOC 2014, p. 15)*

The Action Plan has responded to this recommendation by proposing the creation of an 'Olympic Laurel' award, to be offered to an outstanding artist or intellectual during a high profile Games moment from a media point of view. The first award was presented to Kipchoge Keino, the retired Kenyan distance runner, during the Opening Ceremony at Rio 2016. Other proposals include the aforementioned 'Artists in Residence' and 'Olympic Museum on the Move' programmes and the development of an Olympic House to showcase Olympic Movement heritage parallel to the well-established ' National Houses', which focus instead on providing an athletes' meeting point as well as entertainment and promotional opportunities for each of the national delegations participating at the Games.

> Recommendation num. 33: 'Further involve sponsors in the Olympism in Action programme'.
>
> *(IOC 2014, p. 17)*

This recommendation has not translated yet into a specific programme of actions, but in 2015 for the first time, the IOC – through its Culture and Heritage Department – was involved in conversations to encourage global Olympic partners (i.e. the sponsors holding exclusive rights of association with the Games worldwide) to become official presenters of cultural activity in Rio 2016 and thus maximise promotional opportunities and Olympic brand associations with culture.

> Recommendation num. 36: 'Extend access to the Olympic Brand for non-commercial use'.
> *(IOC 2014, p. 18)*

Access to the 'Olympic Brand' is the area that requires more detailed attention from a legal point of view and did not result in specific actions on time for the Rio 2016 Games edition. It builds on decades of debate around the existing barriers for grassroots cultural programming to be directly associated with the Olympics. Given the stipulation that the official Olympic partners have exclusive rights over the use of the Olympic symbol (the five rings) and the prohibition for the use of the word 'Olympic' in connection with any activity not led or funded by an official Olympic partner, few cultural organisations have ever been allowed to promote their work as Olympics related (see Garcia 2001, 2008, 2012). This lack of explicit association has resulted in the paradoxical situation that the most advanced, socially relevant, transformative and/or locally meaningful cultural programmes and activities taking place in the context of the Games have rarely (if ever) been promoted as 'Olympic' or seen as related in any way to the Games by their immediate communities of interest. This situation applies to many of the examples presented in the previous section, best examples of programming oriented towards 'cultural and social change' such as the 'Festival of the Dreaming' in Sydney.

Discussion over the need to establish a non-lucrative extension of the Olympic brand gained prominence in the lead to London 2012 and resulted in a one-off concession by the IOC in the form of the 'Inspired by 2012' logo. The 'Inspired by 2012' programme, which encompassed a broad range of grassroots cultural and educational activities throughout the UK, used the same visual identity markers as the rest of official London 2012 programming but excluded the use of the Olympic rings (see detailed discussion in Garcia 2015, and Figure 24.4, below).

The existence of an 'Inspired by' programme was, however, articulated as an 'exception' and was not delivered under IOC leadership. The Agenda 2020 recommendation noted above could enable other, similar practices to become embedded in the Olympic

Figure 24.4 'Inspired by 2012' as a referent for non-commercial Olympic branding
Source: London 2012 Olympic and Paralympic Games Organising Committee (courtesy of the IOC).

hosting process so that non-lucrative Olympic branding associations that can be implemented by cultural organisations in future host cities as well as by other interested parties between Games.

All of these factors combined suggest the emergence of a more clearly defined global cultural policy for the Olympic Games. It remains to be seen how the interests and pressures of leading commercial stakeholders (exclusive media rights broadcasters and sponsors, in particular) may shape the official IOC-sanctioned cultural narrative, but it is expected that, if nothing else, expectations around Games cultural programming will be raised, awareness of the possibilities and challenges of an Olympic cultural showcase relevant to audiences worldwide will grow and demand for the programme to take place and gain prominence will become more explicit.

Mega-*cultural policy-making*

Iconic vision, global moments, once-in-a-life time opportunities, larger-than-life experiences. ... The rhetoric and modus-operandi surrounding mega-events has traditionally led to unapologetic or grandiose takes on cultural statements. In this context, cultural policy becomes a tool to condense time and place into spectacular images and phrases that can reinvent (as well as dictate) the official rhetoric behind a given urban centre and its cultural representation for decades to come.

In the wake of the 1968 Games, Mexico City became largely associated with a black and white op-art indigenous look; since 1992, the imagery of Barcelona has been dominated by variations of what could be termed eccentric *modernisme* by the beach. It is hard to imagine the same levels of local community support towards such niche reimaginings outside the context of a mega-event. This is hard to imagine because, even though mega-events, and the Olympics in particular, are also attractors of opposition movements, highly organised activism and contestation,[4] their capacity to generate consensus and buy-in towards a collective image or shared cultural narrative is largely unrivalled.

The implications of such capacity to attain buy-in for cultural policy are vast but come with a warning: the rhetoric behind 'once-in-a-life-time' opportunities is believable only if it remains so, that is, if it is only resorted to in exceptional circumstances. Reversely, expecting cultural policy to deliver recurrent or continuous hype and euphoria as a measure of success is problematic and doomed to fail (see Waitt 2008).

Cities that choose festivalisation as their leading cultural strategy or, more drastically, cities that choose to focus on hallmark and mega-event bidding as their core cultural vision, tend to observe diminishing returns and/or a progressive lack of credibility. As an example, Barcelona, globally celebrated as a 'model' of urban regeneration and event hosting, failed to generate local enthusiasm and international interest for its Universal Forum of Cultures in 2004, a (new, self-awarded) mega-event that claimed to address the most pressing 'universal' issues of the day, from peace to diversity and sustainability (see Degen and Garcia 2012; Garcia 2004). Alternatively, Manchester, host of the 2002 Commonwealth Games, did not generate the same level of international attention but delivered a carefully conceived cultural programme (Garcia 2003) that provided the basis for its now well-established Manchester International Festival. The main difference between these two examples lies in the tone and approach of the cities' respective cultural policies in the aftermath of hosting a mega-event: while Barcelona basked in its success and resisted lowering the tone more than a decade after being in the global spotlight, Manchester progressively built its cultural narrative. Barcelona aimed to become the go-to place for cultural mega-events post 1992 (e.g. the city leaders placed bids to host the Universal Expo as well as the European Capital of Culture title, failing in both instances) so it focused on grand narratives and itinerant one-off events rather than prioritising smaller scale but more locally rooted cultural initiatives. Alternatively, Manchester decided to focus on the creation of a regular, city-owned, arts festival with a clear niche and grow it from edition to edition.

By 2016, the mega-event cultural policy legacy of each city is considerably different. In Manchester, we find a solidly defined and increasingly respected arts festival, supported by a comprehensive cultural and creative industries strategy that built on an 'event themed' rather than 'event led' legacy plan in the wake of its Commonwealth Games experience (see Smith and Fox 2007). Barcelona has developed a very strong and competitive global image as an urban tourism hub – with shopping and gastronomy as growing calling cards – but has a mixed record in its event hosting strategy and is generating increasing social contestation towards its perceived focus on external image projection over community inclusion decades after its Olympic hosting experience (Degen and Garcia 2012).

Overall, the mega-event phenomenon seems to be here to stay, with emerging economies keen to build on the models that dominated the 1990s and early 2000s in the Western world. Acceptance that cultural policy should be an essential part of mega-event planning in order to ensure post-event sustainability is a relatively new trend, with few fully successful referents over the last two decades. Despite many good examples of valuable local cultural policy implementation, the lack of coherent and sustained global frameworks suggests an ad-hoc approach dominated by time and place-specific interests but very limited knowledge-transfer or capacity for adaptation in subsequent event editions. The international bodies behind contemporary mega-events have thus a critical role to play shaping future definitions of cultural policy, this time with a global outlook and the aspiration to fully build on the most established strength of a mega-event process: i.e. its transnational media dimension. As proven by decades of trial and error, such approach to cultural policy-making can have a noticeable impact on the imaging and reimaging of event host cities through the construction of collective moments and the illusion of a shared, collective identity that 'looks good on TV' while also helping advance broader social and economic causes. Equally, as also proven by the observable aftermaths of many a 'model' host city, it is essential to ensure that this global-outlook-led approach to cultural policy-making is complemented by other, non-event-driven or internationally oriented, cultural policy foundations. This is so because, no matter its global outreach and external image success, for cultural policy to be sustainable, it needs to address the many fragmented, contested and difficult to 'translate' (or *iconicise*) cultural needs and aspirations of respective host communities.

Notes

1 In the case of the Olympic Games, the most dominant broadcasting nation is the United States.
2 Mirrlees argues that 'the emergence of horizontally and vertically integrated media firms and convergent culture industry, media industry and telecommunication markets has rendered the distinction between media policy and cultural policy problematic, if not irrelevant' (p. 108).
3 See examples of the image online: http://images.sports.cn/Image/2013/07/23/1106506039.jpg.
4 A long-standing example is the 'Bread not Circuses' coalition that emerged in opposition to the Toronto 2008 Olympic bid in the late 1990s and continued operating over a number of years and produced a wide range of publications (see: Bread Not Circuses (2001) *Stop playing games with Toronto: The people's anti-Olympic bid book*. Toronto: Authors).

References

Bianchini, F. (1993) 'Culture, conflict and cities: issues and prospects for the 1990s', in: Bianchini F. & Parkinson, M. (Eds), *Cultural Policy and Urban Regeneration: The West European Experience*. Manchester: Manchester University Press, (pp. 199–213).

Dayan, D., & Katz, E. (1994) *Media Events: The Live Broadcasting of History*. London: Harvard University Press.

Degen, M., & García, M. (2012) The Transformation of the "Barcelona Model": An Analysis of Culture, Urban Regeneration and Governance. *International Journal of Urban and Regional Research*, *36*(5) (pp. 2022–38)

Gans, H. J. (1974) *Popular Culture and High Culture. An Analysis and Evaluation of Taste*. New York: HarperCollins.

Garcia, B. (2016) 'Cultural Olympiads', in: Gold, J.R. & Gold, M.M. (Eds) *Olympic Cities: Urban planning, city agendas and the World's Games, 1896 to the present* (3rd Edition). London: Routledge.

Garcia, B. (2015) 'Placing culture at the heart of the games. Achievements and challenges within the London 2012 Cultural Olympiad', *The London Olympics and Urban Development: The Mega-Event City. London:* Routledge, (pp. 255–270).

Garcia, B. (2014) 'Reclaiming street festivities as a key to the local sustainability of global mega-events', *Streets as Public Spaces and Drivers or Urban Prosperity.* Stockholm: Ax:son Johnson Foundation, (pp. 45–58).

Garcia, B. (2012) *The Olympic Games and Cultural Policy.* New York: Routledge.

Garcia, B. (2011) 'The cultural dimension of olympic games: ceremonies and Cultural Olympiads as platforms for sustainable cultural policy', in: Fernández Peña, E. (Ed.) *An Olympic Mosaic: Multidisciplinary Research and Dissemination of Olympic Studies*. Barcelona: Centre d'Estudis Olímpics; Ajuntament de Barcelona, (pp. 153–164).

Garcia, B. (2008) 'One Hundred Years of Cultural Programming within the Olympic Games. (1912–2012): Origins, Evolution and Projections'. *International Journal of Cultural Policy, 14*(4), (pp. 361–376).

Garcia, B. (2004) 'Urban Regeneration, Arts Programming and Major Events: Glasgow 1990, Sydney 2000 and Barcelona 2004'. *International Journal of Cultural Policy, 10*(1), (pp. 103–118)

Garcia, B. (2003) *Evaluation of Cultureshock: North West Cultural Programme for the Manchester 2002 Commonwealth Games.* Manchester: Arts Council England North West.

Garcia, B. (2001) 'Enhancing Sports Marketing through Cultural and Arts Programmes. Lessons from the Sydney 2000 Olympic Arts Festivals', *Sports Management Review, 4*(2), (pp. 193–220).

Garcia, B. & Cox, T. (2013) *European Capitals of Culture*, Brussels: European Parliament

Getz, D. (2008) 'Event tourism: Definition, evolution, and research'. *Tourism Management, 29*, (pp. 403–428)

Getz, D. (1991) *Festivals, Special Events and Tourism*, New York: Van Nostrand Reinhold.

Giulianotti, R., & Robertson, R. (2009) *Globalization and Football*, London: SAGE.

Gold, J. R., & Gold, M. M. (2012) *Olympic Cities. Urban Planning, City Agendas and the World's Games, 1896 to present*. London: Routledge.

Goldstein, A. (1998) 'Conference Summary', *New Directions in Cultural Policy Conference. Privatization of Culture Project*, New York: New York University.

Hall, C. M. (1989) 'The Definition and Analysis of Hallmark Tourist Events'. *GeoJournal, 19*(3), (pp. 263–268)

Harris, N. (2012) London 2012: Beware Billions Bollocks. Ceremony to be huge TV hit, but not that huge. *Sport Intelligence.* www.sportintelligence.com

Haxton, P. (1999) Community participation in the mega-event hosting process: The case of the Olympic Games, PhD thesis, University of Technology, Sydney.

Horkheimer, M. and Adorno, T. (1944) 'The culture industry: Enlightenment and Mass deception'. In Szeman, I. & Kaposy, T. (eds) (2010) *Cultural Theory. An Anthology.* Wiley-Blackwell.

IOC (2015) *Olympic Charter*. Lausanne: IOC.

IOC (2014) *Olympic Agenda 2020. 20+20 Recommendations*. Lausanne: IOC.

IOC (2012) *London 2012 Olympic Games. Global Broadcast Report*. Lausanne: IOC www.olympic.org/ Documents/IOC_Marketing/Broadcasting/London_2012_Global_%20Broadcast_Report.pdf

IOC (2011) *Guide on the Cultural Olympiad (Post Vancouver 2010 Winter Games)*. Lausanne: IOC.

IOC (2008) *Candidature Acceptance Procedure. Games of the XXXI Olympiad in 2016*. Lausanne: IOC.

IOC (2000) *Forum on the IOC and its Cultural Policy*. Lausanne: IOC.

Jamolli, F. (2015) 'The Olympic Foundation for Culture and Heritage', in: *Communicating The Museum 2015: Differentiation Strategies. Cultural Partnerships.* Istanbul: Agenda http://agendacom.com/files/6716eaf3ff15e3f359134d8e9539d37e.pdf

Laflin, M., Rest, J. & Davis, R. (2012) 'Will London 2012 Be the Biggest Sporting Event Ever Staged?' *Sportcal, 26,* (pp. 10–13).

Lewis, J. and Miller, T. (2003) *Critical Cultural Policy Studies: A Reader.* London: Wiley.

Kelly, O. (1984) *Community, Art and the State: Storming the Citadels,* London: Comedia.

Kong, L. (2000) 'Culture, Economy, Policy: Trends and Developments'. *Geoforum, 31*(4), (pp. 385–390).

Mirrlees, T. (2013) *Global Entertainment Media: Between Cultural Imperialism and Cultural Globalization.* Routledge.

Moragas i Spà, M. Kennet, C. Puig, N. (2003) *The Legacy of the Olympic Games 1984–2000: International Symposium,* Lausanne: IOC.

Moragas, M. de, Rivenburgh, N. K., & Larson, J. F. (1995) *Television in the Olympics.* London: John Libbey.

Muller, N. (Ed.) (2000) *Pierre de Coubertin. Olympism (Selected Writings).* Lausanne: IOC.

Nas, P. (2011) *Cities full of Symbols.* Leiden: Leiden University Press.

Rivenburgh, N. K. (2002) 'The Olympic Games: Twenty-First Century Challenges as a Global Media Event'. *Culture, Sport, Society, 5*(3), (pp. 32–50).

Roche, M. (2000) *Mega-Events Modernity. Olympics and Expos in the Growth of Global Culture.* London: Routledge.

Rodenhurst, K. (2013) 'Case Studies'. Garcia, B. (Ed.) *London 2012 Cultural Olympiad Evaluation.* London: Arts Council England.

Rowe, D. (2003) 'Sport and the Repudiation of the Global'. *International Review for the Sociology of Sport, 38*(3), (pp. 281–294).

Smith, A., & Fox, T. (2007) 'From 'Event-led' to 'Event-themed' Regeneration: The 2002 Commonwealth Games Legacy Programme'. *Urban Studies, 44* (5–6), 1125–1143.

Waitt, G. (2008) 'Urban Festivals: Geographies of Hype, Helplessness and Hope'. *Geography Compass, 2*(2), (pp. 513–537).

25

The challenges of the new media scene for public policies[1]

George Yúdice

Introduction

The new ICT – especially social networks and new ways of distributing entertainment by mega-corporations – are radically transforming the media landscape around the world. On the one hand, it is a scenario in which promises are made to deliver totally diverse content, including those created by users, to satisfy any preference, and, on the other hand, to provide increasing digital access to the entire population of the world. Those who make that promise are not governments but the new Internet mega-platforms like Google and Facebook. Latin American governments are ill prepared both legally and in their ability to provide support to domestic enterprises, which in turn contribute to tax revenues. At the same time, the question arises as to who should provide a seemingly public service, such as the Internet, which is the equivalent of electricity, telephony and water in the 20th century: the public sector (government) or the private sector (corporations)? Or are there other alternatives? What effect does this all have on users? How are public policies designed for this new scenario?

> These children inhabit the virtual. The cognitive sciences have shown us that using the Internet, reading or writing messages (with one's thumb), or consulting Wikipedia or Facebook does not stimulate the same neurons or the same cortical zones as does the use of a book, a chalkboard, or a notebook. They can manipulate several forms of information at the same time, yet they neither understand it, nor integrate it, nor synthesize it as do we, their ancestors.
>
> They no longer have the same head. With their cell phone, they have access to all people; with GPS, to all places; with the Internet, to all knowledge. They inhabit a topological space of neighborhoods, whereas we lived in a metric space, coordinated by distances. They no longer inhabit the same space.
>
> *(Serres 2013: 6–7)*

In his defense of the youth culture, developed in the heat of the new media, Michel Serres argues that another way of thinking ("they do not have the same head") has emerged, more connected to digital technology and the new practices this technology makes possible. These would be the digital natives, but there are also older, well-assimilated digital migrants. One has to recognize that Serres is talking about French youth, who live in a rich country with good connectivity. That is why they have a high number – more than 85 percent – who access the Internet, especially through mobile telephony (Freier 2015; Global Internet Report 2015).

One might think that due to the marked inequality in "emerging" or "developing" countries, the new habitus would be radically different. According to Internet World Stats for February 2, 2016, Internet has 3.3 billion users worldwide,[2] 1.3 billion more than 5 years ago. This is more or less 45 percent of the 7.4 billion inhabitants of the earth.[3] Although access is growing rapidly, it is clear that there is much inequality between the richer (North America has 88 percent coverage) and poorer regions (Africa has 29 percent) (Kemp 2015; Pew Research Center 2015). Latin America is in the middle with 56 percent, but in this vast region there is also much inequality between and within countries.

Even so, the near future will see more access to the Internet, especially through mobile telephony. As researchers at the Pew Research Center found, young people in "emerging" or "developing" countries access the Internet much more than the older generations. The average age gap in the 32 countries studied is 15 percentage points, but in all the Latin American countries included in the study – Argentina, Brazil, Chile, Colombia, El Salvador, Mexico, Nicaragua, Peru and Venezuela – the gap is 30 or more percentage points, a fact that is also explained by differences in levels of education, incomes and knowledge of English (Pew 2015). In Brazil, for example, 72 percent of 18 to 43 year olds access the Internet or have a smartphone, in contrast to 35 percent of those aged 35 or older. According to the research department of the Groupe Mobile Sociale Association, or GSMA Intelligence, there are currently 7.7 billion mobile connections in the world and 3.8 billion unique subscribers of mobile accounts.[4]

These data are also confirmed when we look at peak numbers of users achieved worldwide by Facebook and Whatsapp at the end of 2015: 1.59 billion and 1 billion respectively. These platforms are mostly accessed by mobile (Martí 2016), 90.6 percent according to Facebook statistics.[5] In Latin America, Whatsapp has a subscribership of 93 percent and 84 percent of mobile Internet users in Brazil and Argentina respectively (Smith 2016). Of course, Facebook foresaw the rapid growth of Whatsapp when it paid $19 billion USD for the application in 2014 although it had only generated revenues of $20 million in 2013. Increasingly, these companies and others are expanding their functions, not only chat and links but also transmission of photos and live real-time videos between friends since December 2015 (Lavrusik 2016). These functions, delivered free of charge to users (or to be exact, in exchange for data collection), provide something like a simulacrum of public service, enabling these platforms to negotiate and compete with nation-states, as we shall see shortly.

The most popular uses of mobile Internet in "emerging" or "developing" countries are communication with family and friends, the use of social networks, and in second place, the search for information (Pew Research Center 2015). Access to media and entertainment via mobile telephony are growing rapidly (eMarketer 2016). Even live cultural events, such as concerts and theater, are accompanied by specialized applications such as Shazam, which recognizes any song and provides detailed information about the artist, the lyrics, when the next concert will take place in the vicinity of the user and online ticket sales (López 2015). Mobile applications not only deliver music, video, texts and user-created content but also provide a set of tools that enable users to access whatever they want (BuddeComm 2015). This choice gives advantages to mobile technologies and social networks. An analysis of media, cultural activities and cultural management in this new digital landscape cannot focus only on the habits and customs of users; the political economy of this scenario is even more important. Both users and enterprises/technologies co-construct this landscape.

This accelerated growth of social media is co-produced by large platforms that respond to users' interests. It is not the 20th century-style consumer society, explained and criticized by sociologists and political scientists from Veblen to Benjamin Barber, although consumerism remains very strong. The desire – some would say the need – to communicate and establish solidarity or ties of affection, as in Facebook, prompts the creation of new applications, which are monetized in different ways and not only oriented toward the consumption of goods. All kinds of causes and issues are enhanced by these forms of communication, including alternatives to hegemonic capitalism, such as the crowdfunding platforms Kickstarter and Catarse, which have pages on Facebook. Nevertheless, vast data streams are generated through these platforms, which are put to various uses and not only for the sale of products. Smart cities, the so-called Internet of Things, data on health and other social interests, as well as government or business espionage take advantage of this avalanche of information.

Thinkers like Michel Serres, cited above, and Jesús Martín-Barbero characterize this new scenario as a paradigmatic social change, in which a crisis ensues, a tremendous hubbub comprised by the chats and conversations of users. As Martín-Barbero writes: "The chats are not composed only of language but narrations, images, music, experiences communicated by people and very diverse cultures, saying things about life to each other' (Rincón and Yúdice, 2016). This noise is an expression not only of the failure of state institutions and society, but also of the desire for other arrangements, as seen in the expressions of outrage (indignation) throughout the world. But this social media landscape is also the apogee of new enclosures comprised of private clouds where data are stored and processed. The complexity is found in the simultaneity of enthusiasm for communication that seems not to be managed or governed and the lack of understanding about how communication, which now involves all life (as in the Internet of Things), is managed, analyzed and used by huge corporations that increasingly challenge governments over this new way of managing what is public, although the concept of the public loses robustness in this age of the user.

Citizen, public, audience, spectator, reader, consumer… lose their vitality (but they do not disappear) as epistemic and practical concepts together with the institutions that have sustained these categories. Both public service (including education) and the media weaken confronted by communication and knowledge among all (Martin-Barbero).[6] Information is no longer emitted from a center to an expanding circumference; users intervene in what is produced and emitted. This poses a challenge for cultural management, accustomed to researching and knowing audiences to whom culture is delivered. What does research into publics mean in an age of usership and producership?

On this issue, the transformation of the music industry is revealing. In streaming services, which show increasing growth as the purchase or download of phonograms wanes (IFPI 2015), it is use itself – registered in databases and processed by recommendation software – that guides the creation of repertoires for users. It is a form of curatorship, which today is one of the most valuable services, in which media provider and experience designer converge. These providers compete to create memorable sensations that ensue not from spectacle but from experience (Mulligan 2014). One could sum up the phenomenon by invoking the concept of affect, which is increasingly used to characterize value in the new era of access and use. New digital ventures, especially those associated with brands, seek to absorb the expression of affect to attract ever more users.

It is not by chance, therefore, that large telephone companies offer free streaming services (for a limited time) to attract users. For example, Deezer has partnered with the telephone companies Tim and Vivo, which offer Vivo Music. In an ad for this service, they express one of the major principles of the new media landscape: "The music you want, when and wherever you may be."[7] And there is always the possibility to access YouTube for free music and video streaming. The combination of mobile telephony and streaming services makes it possible to transform cultural enjoyment by "freeing" the user not only from the place where he or she enjoys but also from the traditional platforms of television, which dictate what programs can be seen, in what order and at what time. Breaking out of this rigid framework explains in part the rapid growth of Netflix, the film and television streaming service. Called the Uber of TV (IDGNow 2015), Netflix, which recently achieved availability in 190 countries (Chacón Jiménez 2016), also produces its own series, such as 3 percent in Brazil, using the information it collects on the habits and preferences of users. An example is the detection of when users get hooked to a series (Spangler 2015). In my travels throughout Latin America I have had a few Marxist friends, who are very critical of the political economy of the media, talk about being glued to the television or tablet watching 50 episodes of a show on a weekend.

While the television networks offer programs that not every viewer wants to see, and therefore need to develop strategies to keep the attention of these viewers throughout the night so as to achieve good ratings and therefore advertisers, the new streaming services and OTT (over-the-top content, or content transmitted without the intervention of an operator) offer what viewers want to see, when they want to and without advertising. That's why Amazon Prime created Amazon Studios, to produce their own series using data from user preferences.[8] For Amazon Prime, a well-varied offering based on preferences ensures that people will sign onto their service (Miller 2016).

In what follows, I raise these topics for debate: (1) changes in cultural enjoyment; (2) the biopolitics implied in these changes; (3) the political economy of the new media scenario.

Changes in cultural enjoyment

In the first place, we need to recognize that there has been a fundamental shift in attitude toward intellectual and cultural property. In the first moment of transition to the digital world, file sharing prevailed (a practice called piracy by the media industry in post-Napster times). Industry failed to convince users that file sharing is a crime. In a second moment, ad-supported streaming services appeared, as in various music and video services (e.g., YouTube and the first iterations of Last.fm, Spotify, Pandora and Deezer), thus converting sharing into a business. Even if a third moment – the transition to paid streaming subscriptions – never consolidates as a significant enterprise, streaming is nevertheless growing in number of users and profitability. What is interesting about these new services is that users are no longer interested in being collectors. As Martín-Barbero says, knowledge takes place among all and therefore should generate another attitude regarding property. In the new political economy of networks, there is much talk of the commons (Gutiérrez 2016). I will return to this topic, but here I would like to emphasize attitudes toward access and sharing, according to which it is not necessary to own anything. These attitudes intervene in practices of collecting culture: recordings, books, films.

There are several theories of collectionism, among them those where discernment, knowledge and expertise prevail, others where taste and passion excel and yet others that emphasize fetishism. For Benjamin, who wrote much about collectionism, passion and fetishism are fundamental qualities: it's a matter of an intimate relationship with objects (1968: 67). In contrast to the Renaissance collector, who was public and staged his high status, the modern collector emerges in anonymity and the privacy of inner life. The modern collector struggles, additionally, with a contradiction inherent in modern art: on the one hand, the fetishization of the object and on the other the refusal of commodification of the object in order to transform it into art. This makes art a mere object of contemplation. In this way, art is only a function of taste, which in turn masks the collector's lack of expertise and limited experience, which is invested in the objects of the collection. Ackbar Abbas points out that for Baudelaire, this lack of experience is tantamount to the inability to assimilate the experience of modernity, that is, the "inhospitable and blinding age of big-scale industrialism" (Benjamin 1973: 111, cit. 227).

Benjamin also contrasts the way in which the writer and the collector come to their experience. The latter removes the objects from circulation by inserting them into the frame where they "turn to stone" (1999: 305). Objects enter a closed loop. The Internet users are more like Benjamin's writer; in their practices, information opens up to rhizomatic connections, sharing and the establishment of the commons. Abbas stresses the writer's experience in Benjamin, referring to tactics of acquisition against grain, which include borrowing books and not returning them or systematically failing to read them or inheriting them. Even the most obvious way to acquire them – to buy them – has its tactics, which differ depending on whether books are bought in bookstores or catalogs or auctions. But "the 'most praiseworthy' method of acquiring books is 'writing them oneself'" (Abbas 1988: 230). In this analysis, Benjamin seems to anticipate the modus operandi of the Internet, where property parameters are questioned and other forms of acquiring and experimenting with production and symbolic exchange are practiced without becoming a proprietor. It could be said that the collector of the 19th and 20th centuries becomes a disseminatory user in the new media scene, although property laws and conventional profit strategies limit this trend.

To understand the transformation of collecting in our time, we would have to do the same as Benjamin did: insert collecting into the political economy of symbolic production, which has some features different from the 19th and 20th industrial mode of production and the mid-20th century mode of consumerism. In the new economy-of-information-experience-and-affect the content of the products – which are exchanges, services, communications, etc. – is intangible, which is what circulates and links subjectivities and bodies. This is to say that the affect previously invested in objects finds other circuits of cathexis; this intangible content becomes more valuable than physical things used to produce these exchanges, services and communications. It is not by chance that in the new digital age, we deal with texts, images, sounds, communications, that is, everything that can be recombined and not appropriated but supplemented and put into circulation again. The value given by users to these items is definitely a use value and at the same time a circulation value, but not necessarily an exchange value. In any case, at present we see a tension between the desire for the commons that many users assume to exist in their practices and the tendency of companies to monetize any action and turn it into property. The fuel for the production of value in the Internet economy is the very action of users, which in most cases they do not even realize they provide.[9]

The biopolitics of the new media scene

Benjamin's insights would support the idea that users of social networks manifest an agency, not only in directly political actions such as the movements of outrage around the world,[9] but also in media consumption, as argued by Simone Pereira de Sá (2016), from another theoretical perspective, with respect to fans in social networks. Yet the very use of social networks has biopolitical repercussions. You only have to think about the mining of data generated by users. It is significant that in this biopolitics users want to use the platforms that profit from the information that they hand over. They are not subjected or oppressed. This harvesting of value is not experienced as exploitation. The vast majority do not even read the terms of use and simply accept them in order to get access to the platforms on which they express themselves and connect to others. This imperative to express themselves predominates in social networks that are necessary for the experience-and-affect economy. At a time when less profit is generated by the sale or licensing of cultural products, new companies have developed technologies to facilitate the expression of affect, which is a means of business and also control. The affective turn in cultural studies in the new millennium tends not to have a critical view of the technologies that facilitate the generation of affect. The analysis of the data generated by recognition software in streaming services, of the preferences in the new curatorship of music and audiovisual texts and of new forms of co-creation, as in Jorge Drexler's *aplicanciones* (Jorge Drexler[n]) are some examples of the use of affect. Biopolitics takes advantage of what we have understood to be the most profound materiality of human being: affect.

It could be said that affect is the intermediary solvent in which subjectivities, bodies and cybernetic machines are cathected. Affect theorists Patricia Clough et al. argue that in the current stage of capitalism, "the distinction between organic and non-organic matter is dissolving in relation to information," with the result that matter itself emerges as informational (2007: 62). This reflection leads them to postulate that "science and capital are engaged in efforts to directly modulate the pre-individual or the potentiality of the indeterminate, the emergent creativity of affect-itself," thus requiring critical thinkers to pay attention to the tension between control (the topic of Deleuze's (1992) frequently cited essay on control societies) and the indeterminate emergence or potency in the Spinozian terms of Hardt and Negri (2005). This tension "constitutes the problematic at the heart of a radical neoliberal governance of productivity" (Clough et al. 2007: 63).

The Internet of Things (IoT) or the Internet of Everything, this galactic network of interconnection and communication of things, processes and people through sensors and databases, is already becoming an everyday experience in the linking of culture, cities, transportation, health, agriculture, industry, housing, etc. in a "smart" environment. In the early stages of this network, one of the most cited affect theorists characterized ubiquitous computing as an immersive and interactive web suggestive of the IoT, which:

> seamlessly and continuously relay digitally coded impulses into and out of the body through multiple, superposable sense connections, eventually developing into an encompassing network of infinitely reversible analog-digital circuiting on a planetary scale.
>
> *(Massumi 2002: 142)*

In fact, Massumi was talking about the potentiality of affect. In relation to affect, the cultural and creative industries in the digital age play an important role in the changes that are taking place in society and economy because they are quite apt as the means to insert people in immersive environments. As we have seen in the case of streaming, people are increasingly connected to music and video, and this traffic of contents stimulates the extension of the so-called cloud, which is nothing more than centers where all data is stored and processed. According to a 2014 report, "2/3rds of digital universe content is consumed or created by consumers... video watching, social media usage, image sharing" (Meeker 2014: 65), thus playing a key role in the growth of IoT. According to estimates, the IoT will reach 50 billion connected objects and a value of $14.4 trillion USD in just 4 years, which would today equal the second economy in the world, between the United States and China (Edwards 2015).

Data mining and analysis, which will increase exponentially with the IoT, has a beneficial side in terms of the administration of public services, support to business enterprises, health monitoring, empowerment of people with disabilities, etc. However, security, which is one of the chief uses of IoT, is a more complex issue. Everyone needs security, not only in terms of defense against crime or natural contingencies, but IoT facilitates the invasion of privacy. In a world saturated with "smart" appliances everything will be known, or already is known. With an arsenal of analytical tools, and using technologies developed in cognitive psychology and neuromarketing, not only are attention, perception, behavior, preferences and feelings measured, but so also is the unconscious. The objective of these measurements is to go beyond the thinking brain to understand what lies at the most material level of affect where "motivation begins... With a series of brain chemical triggers rooted in primal neural circuits that evolved to help humans make decisions" (Crowe 2013).

Given the enormity of the IoT, it is evident that only the richest states or the world's largest platforms/companies can make the investments required to create and manage this new phenomenon. And this gives them the opportunity to harness information and the profit or the "intelligence" for surveillance that derives from that information. For example, it is for such a purpose that Google paid $3.2 billion USD to acquire Nest Labs, a manufacturer of thermostats and high-tech smoke detectors. The thermostat regulates the ambient temperature in relation to users' preferences; in this way, the device learns over time. These devices operate with algorithms that allow all of a user's devices to communicate with each other, creating user profiles to anticipate their needs (Trefis Team 2014). Thus, Google increases the reach of the cloud where the data is stored and creates a system of rhizomatic communication among users, devices and the media.

Political economy of the new media scene

It is true that more than half of the world's population is excluded from the web, although more and more are connecting through mobile phones. In relation to that gap, companies like Facebook and Google have strategies to connect to the disconnected. To achieve this, Facebook bought a fleet of drones that will continuously fly for months or years thanks to solar energy, emitting laser broadband signals in areas with low connectivity in Asia, Africa and Latin America (Wakefield 2014). Yael Maguire, engineering director of Facebook Connectivity Lab, designed an intermediate backbone between satellites and land terminals that will receive at all times signals from drones flying at 20 km altitude, above other aircraft and even the weather, but sufficiently close to the earth for signals to be strong, approximating the quality of optical fiber (Internet.org 2014).

Likewise, in 2013 Google began Project Loon, which will send helium balloons 20 kilometers high to transmit Internet signals to disconnected or poorly connected areas. Google also bought Titan Aerospace, a company that makes drones, for an undisclosed amount to complement the balloons of the Loon project. It also acquired Skybox Imaging for $1 billion USD, a company that has its own satellite network and specializes in data mining and analysis and the production of detailed videos and images of the earth, extending Google Earth's ability to capture images of the planet in real time, thus linking profiles and location (Inam 2014).

Of course, it is naive to think that Facebook and Google are providing a humanitarian public service that governments do not provide, although it is true that there will be more connectivity and that the poor may have cheaper access to such operations as digital bank transfers or receiving remittances via cell phone, among others. The Gates Foundation, in partnership with the World Bank, has a project to integrate billions of people into the banking system by means of mobile telephony and digital money. Google does not need to profit directly from these transactions; people will use their platform with the endorsement of an intergovernmental public institution (Bill & Melinda Gates Foundation 2015), and it's this added value that matters. To facilitate the use of its platform, Google has introduced a cheap smartphone in Africa where 95 percent of Internet access takes place via mobile telephony. The phone prioritizes two Google properties: the Android operating system and use of YouTube (owned by Google), specially tailored for offline use (Sengupta 2015). The development of cheap smartphones by other companies – Mozilla ($33 USD), Huawei ($80 USD), etc. – is facilitating an increase in the number of users and the triumph of the Android platform.[10]

These giant companies emerged in the new millennium to combine the packaging of web pages, e-mail, text messages, audiovisual texts and music file transferred via FTP, financial services, etc., which were offered separately on the Internet by the end of the 1990s (van der Velden and Kruk 2012–2013). This bundling takes place on these companies' own platforms, to which the metaphor of the cloud was applied, but which are rooted in a very costly and polluting materiality. As reported by Glanz (2012), global data centers "use about 30 billion watts of electricity, roughly equivalent to the output of 30 nuclear power plants...", but video occupies more and more space on the web. According to Cisco Systems (2014) global IP video traffic will be 79 percent of all Internet consumer traffic by 2018, up from 66 percent in 2013. This does not include video exchanged via peer-to-peer (P2P) file sharing. The sum of all forms of video (TV, video on demand [VOD], Internet and P2P) will be in the range of 80 to 90 percent of global consumer traffic by 2018. All of the six largest companies that build cloud infrastructure – Amazon, Microsoft, IBM, Google, Oracle, Rackspace – are American and provide services to other companies (Netflix and other streaming providers) and governments (e.g. the US Central Intelligence Agency) (Weinberger 2015).

In the next section I comment on Internet.org, Facebook's foundation, which seeks to establish agreements with governments to provide Internet access to those without connections. This attempt by Facebook is part of its political economy; by simulating a public service it intends to exponentially increase its market value. Precisely in terms of the increase in the number of users on their platforms, especially via mobile telephony, that Facebook, Google and other companies are valued in the market. On February 2, 2106, the newly created Alphabet, Google's parent company, overtook Apple as the most valued company in the world. Five of the nine most valued companies in the world are Alphabet ($ 554.8 billion USD), Apple ($ 529.3 billion USD), Microsoft ($ 425 billion USD), Facebook ($ 334 billion USD) and Amazon ($ 264 billion USD). At the beginning of February, these five companies had a combined value of $ 2.1 trillion (Krantz 2016), which is equivalent to India's GDP, the 7th largest economy in the world, overtaking the GDP of Italy, Brazil and Canada (Statistics Times 2016).

It is not surprising, therefore, as Benjamin Bratton (2014) writes, that platforms increasingly exercise transnational and global sovereignty, and some nations adapt to the form of the platform (e.g. the National Security Agency NSA, new Chinese initiatives such as the microblogging site Sina Weibo, etc.). The issue of sovereignty is crucial, since the big platforms run the Internet of Things, which, as we have seen, aims to manage everyday life through the connection of appliances and other devices, media, objects, cities and human behaviors.

The power and size of these companies make it easier for them to compete and negotiate with governments. The conflict between China and Google is well known. China aims to replace Western platforms (Gibbs 2014), which in turn – as in the case of Google – behave as if they were protecting a global sovereignty and not just their business. In turn, China refers to Chinese Internet sovereignty (Information Office 2010), although some analysts see such sovereignty claims as informational authoritarianism and censorship (Jiang 2010).

Latin America

Following the scandal of privacy violations revealed by Edward Snowden, the Brazilian government accelerated the process of consultation and design of the Civil Internet Framework that President Rousseff sanctioned in April 2014 (Estarque 2014). In anticipation of the new law, Google, which has collaborated with the NSA spying on communications from heads of state around the world (IBN Live 2013), moved its DNS service from Brazil to the USA, which permitted making visible use of its service on the Internet. Internet analyst Doug Madory (2013) argued that this move affected the service –delaying the time of data transmission – because, in its efforts to avoid the monitoring of its operations by the Brazilian government, operations were now carried out in the US.

Another example of the conflict and negotiation of platforms and states was seen at the Summit of the Americas in Panama in April 2015, when the presidents of Argentina, Brazil, Panama and Peru met with the Facebook Chief Executive, Mark Zuckerberg, who sought to establish agreements for its foundation Internet.org with those countries, adding them to the agreements it had already brokered with Colombia, Guatemala and Paraguay, the latter where the beta version of Facebook Livre was tested. The debate in Brazil is an example of the complexity and danger of the promise of free Internet for the poor, at least according to the Internet.org model. Zuckerberg and President Rousseff signed an agreement that would appear to be in conflict with the Civil Internet Framework. One of the problems is that Facebook Livre provides only a subset of Internet services for the poorest, thus creating unequal access. Another problem is that the practice of Zero Rating seems to violate the principle of net neutrality since "operators… and some technology companies… allow free access, or do not charge for mobile data traffic for some online services, such as social networking apps and messages" (Ribeiro 2015).

Carolina Botero, executive director of the Karisma Foundation in Colombia, and one of the most important activists on equal access to the media and Internet, criticized Internet. org and the governments that support it:

> We have serious concerns that Internet.org is presented as a public policy strategy for universal access to the Internet. This initiative compromises everyones' rights and blurs the government's obligation to reduce the digital divide for its citizens for compromised access to certain applications. No matter how interesting they are, these services are associated with the commercial interest of a multinational which the state is directly supporting.
>
> *(Cited in Bogado and Rodríguez 2015)*

By the end of 2015, this apparent contradiction, which is in violation of the principle of neutrality that is underpinned by the Civil Internet Framework, had not yet been resolved. In the process of recommending to the president for the preparation of the Draft of the Presidential Decree that will regulate the Civil Code, the Task Force on Internet Management was able to "reach an agreement, without mentioning zero-rating" (Aquino 2015).

Conclusion

What has all this – globalized platforms, sovereignty, Internet of Things, etc. – to do with cultural management? In my view, a lot. Public policies – including the lack of policies, which is a policy in itself – have a double effect: on the one hand, they can facilitate or hinder new undertakings and practices, not only for making culture but also circulating and sharing it; on the other hand, they contribute to or regulate biopolitical intervention and the growth of huge Internet platforms, which in turn exercise sovereignty.

Latin America is a very coveted region for many reasons (Téllez 2015). It is the region where users spend more time connected to the Internet (Mander 2015). According to the Internet analytics company Com.Score, five of the ten most active countries in social network use are in Latin America: Brazil, Argentina, Peru, Mexico and Chile. Latin America as a region has almost double the world average of user connection hours in social networks; and Brazil stands out with 240 percent above the world average (ComScore 2013: 21). But as in the rest of the world, American platforms such as Facebook, Google, YouTube and Twitter (Vaughn-Nichols 2013) dominate, and they want not only to maintain their dominance but to increase it. Facebook is the leading publisher in the two largest media markets, Mexico and Brazil (ComScore 2013: 49). And Google/YouTube is the largest video provider in the region (52).

This information is crucial for Latin America, especially if we think about how to access the media. As for connections to Internet, Latin America is the third region in the world after North America and Europe, with 10.2 percent of global connections for a world population share of 8.6 percent.[11] In terms of the online market, Latin America is the second fastest growing market in the world, after China, and much of this growth is due to mobile telephony (eMarketer 2015b). As for mobile accounts, in 2014 penetration was 65.2 percent, with 395.5 million unique accounts. Mobile Internet access accounts will grow from 55.4 percent in 2015 to 72.6 percent in 2019 (Statista 2016). As for smartphones, in 2012 there was a penetration of 20 percent, estimated at about 48 percent in 2017, a number that will grow rapidly in 2020, when it is estimated there will be 245.7 million smartphones or a penetration of 57 percent (eMarketer 2015a). To be sure, mobile Internet connections outnumber fixed-line connections throughout the region (GSMA 2014: 16). These data require incorporating the use of mobile phones into any inquiry into the enjoyment of music, video and text, but also the consequences in terms of the uses to which the information collected from users is put.

Culture is transversal, necessarily intertwined with technology, media, enterprise, politics, etc. It is also globalized. The United States and its allies in cognitive-experience-and-affect capitalism seek to establish and strengthen world trade laws through the intergovernmental institutions they dominate (WTO, WIPO, etc.). Latin America is a very unequal region in cultural commerce: according to PriceWaterhouseCoopers (2012), the media and entertainment market for 2015 was estimated at 6 percent of the world market. But that does not mean that Latin American ventures exported this percentage. That's the size of what dominant companies can take advantage of. The export market would be more similar to the percentage of Latin American companies included in the Forbes list of the world's largest companies, which is more or less 3 percent (Wright and Pasquali 2015). Of course, the most important criteria to be taken into consideration in assessing Latin America's market share, from a cultural viewpoint, are the cultural offerings, in the broadest sense of what might be meant by culture, and this has not been measured in these reports on cultural industries or media and entertainment. But even when the measure shows that the market is larger, the arguments I offer in this essay suggest that the platforms on which the cultural sector is developed are very important, and these platforms have the ability to monitor and guide development, as in the example given above of telephone operators that offer streaming services. In addition to thinking about small local markets in the region, which is fundamental, one must think about the regional macro-market, since the dominant companies aim to capture it precisely in these terms, as a region.

This is why although national policies are necessary (e.g. the Civilian Internet Framework) they are not sufficiently effective; regional agreements are needed with other countries seeking to level the playing field. In this sense, I comment very briefly on a promising initiative, but it should include a serious and actionable reflection on the new media scene, both in terms of its effects on culture and its techno-economic policy, which are two sides of the same coin.

I refer to MICSUR, the South American Cultural Industries Market, whose first edition was held in Mar del Plata, Argentina, in May 2014 and second in Bogotá, Colombia, in October 2016. Its importance has to do with the regional alliance necessary to address inequalities in Latin American cultural trade. As we already know, the sources and strategies of public financing for cultural enterprises are quite weak in all Latin American countries. The creation of a general market aims to increase imports from neighboring countries, thus generating income that remains in the region and does not migrate to the United States or Europe. To do this, other ministries and undertakings from other sectors – telephone operators, the law, banking, engineering, etc. – should be included in addition to those that are mentioned (education and tourism) in cultural meetings. Moreover, these Latin American cultural summits should reflect on policies that support a commons, not just a cultural one but one in which diverse cultural practices and forms of circulation interact with other sectors. This goal requires a set of strategies debated and linked between governments, enterprises, the legal sector, civil society and social networks.

Notes

1 First appeared, in Portuguese, in Revista Observatório, 20 (2016): 87–112. http://www.itaucultural.org.br/revista/91827/

2 The number of users in real time can be found at: www.internetlivestats.com/internet-users/. 2/2/16.

3 The world population in real time can be found at: www.worldometers.info/world-population/. 2/2/16.

4 GSMA Intelligence statistics in real time can be found at: https://gsmaintelligence.com/. 2/4/16, 20:17 -6 time zone.

5 http://newsroom.fb.com/company-info/. 1/28/16.

6 The reference to what is "known among all" requires at least mention of various adaptations of the concept of General Intellect proposed by Marx in the *Grundrisse*. There he suggests that starting with a particular point of capital development the real generation of wealth will depend not only on labor time but also on scientific expertise and organization. The main factor of production will be the general productive forces of the social brain (Marx 1973). Marx anticipates information theory and the knowledge economy, or cognitive capitalism, which for some heralds the potential for neo-communist transformation of the world by the constituent power of the multitude (Virno, Hardt and Negri) and for others constitutes the necessary development for salvaging the neoliberal world order, which foments greater inequality, for example, information systems that make possible outsourcing and transnational subcontracting that lead to greater precarity (Dean 2005; Žižek 2009).

7 Vivo Música, www.vivo.com.br/VivoMusica. 7/21/15.

8 In Hollywood, there are several companies specializing in sentiment analysis for the purpose of fine tuning screenplays and audiovisual soundtracks (Barnes 2013).

9 There is an interesting debate about the concept of value in relation to the actions of users in this new digital scene. On the one hand, there are those like Christian Fuchs (2013: 11) for whom the prosumer [a neologism resulting from the combination of producer + consumer or professional + consumer] creates value that is voluntarily yielded in use. Assuming a more orthodox Marxist position, Rabosto (2014: 40) argues that what is productive is exclusively labor that "is objectified as a use value for consumption by others, in platforms, networks, contents, etc." That other labor "which transforms data and information into advertising profiles to facilitate the transformation of goods into money" is unproductive. Those who produce the data are not the users but the engineers who design the software that enables the transformation of use of networks and data (2. 3).

10 In early February 2016, Mozilla's board of directors declared that the company would no longer offer a good mobile experience, which suggests that it failed in its attempt to compete with Google's (Android's) dominance in the mobile market (Heilman 2016).

11 Statistics taken from: www.internetlivestats.com/internetusers/, for the number of users in real time, and www.worldometers.info/world-population/#region for the population of Latin America in January 2016.

References

Abbas, Ackbar. 1988. "Walter Benjamin's Collector: The Fate of Modern Experience". *New Literary History*, 20:1 (Autumn, 1988): 217–237.

Aquino, Miriam. 2015. "Comitê Gestor da Internet Fecha Texto Para Regulação do Marco Civil". Tele Síntese, 10 de novembro. www.telesintese.com.br/comite-gestor-internet-fecha-texto-para-regulacao-marco-civil/. January 28, 2016.

Barnes, Brooks. 2013. "Solving Equation of a Hit Film Script, with Data". *New York Times*, 5 de maio. www.nytimes.com/2013/05/06/business/media/solving-equation-of-a-hit-film-script-with-data.html. January 28, 2016.

Benjamin, Walter. 1968. "Unpacking My Library". Em *Illuminations*. Trad. Harry Zohn. New York: Schocken Books.

Benjamin, Walter. 1973. *Charles Baudelaire: A Lyric Poet in the Era of High Capitalism*. Trad. Harry Zohn. London: Verso 1973.

Benjamin, Walter. 1999. "The Collector", em The Arcades Project. Cambridge: Harvard University Press, 203–211.

Bill & Melinda Gates Foundation. 2015. "Our Big Bet for the Future: 2015 Gates Annual Letter". https://al2015.gatesnotesazure.com/assets/media/documents/2015_Gates_Annual_Letter_EN.pdf January 28, 2016.

Bogado, David e Katitza Rodríguez. 2015. "Does Internet.org Leave Latin Americans Without A Real Internet? Electronic Frontier Foundation, 20 de abril. www.eff.org/deeplinks/2015/04/does-internetorg-deprive-latin-americans-real-internet. January 28, 2016.

Bratton, Benjamin. 2014. "The Black Stack", *e-Flux Journal*, 53. www.e-flux.com/journal/53/59883/the-black-stack/, 8 de noviembre de 2016.

BuddeComm. 2015. "Global Digital Media-The Unstoppable Video Streaming, TV and Entertainment Industries". 24 de junho. www.budde.com.au/Research/Global-Digital-Media-The-Unstoppable-Video-Streaming-TV-and-Entertainment-Industries.html. Acessado 28 de janeiro de 2016.

Chacón Jiménez, Krisia. 2016. "Netflix se expande a 130 nuevos países". *El Financiero*, 6 de janeiro. www.elfinancierocr.com/tecnologia/Netflix-expande-nuevos-paises_0_879512043.html. Acessado 28 de janeiro de 2016.

Cisco Systems. 2014. "Cisco Visual Networking Index: Forecast and Methodology, 2013–2018". 10 de junho. www.cisco.com/c/en/us/solutions/collateral/service-provider/ip-ngn-ip-next-generation-network/white_paper_c11-481360.html. Acessado 28 de janeiro de 2016.

Clough, Patricia Ticineto, Greg Goldberg, Rachel Schiff, Aaron Weeks e Craig Willse. 2007. "Notes Toward a Theory of Affect Itself". *ephemera* 7(1): 60–77.

Com.Score. 2013. Futuro Digial 2013: El Estado Actual de la Industria Digital y las Tendencias que Están Modelando el Futuro. Mayo. www.comscore.com/content/download/20841/1065191/file/Futuro_Digital_Latinoamerica_2013_Informe.pdf. Acessado 28 de janeiro de 2016.

Crowe, Kelly. 2013. "Marketers Exploiting Secrets of the Living Brain". CBC News, 1° de janeiro. www.cbc.ca/news/health/marketers-exploiting-secrets-of-the-living-brain-1.1273976. Acessado 28 de janeiro de 2016.

Dean, Jodi. 2005. "Communicative Capitalism: Circulation and the Foreclosure of Politics". *Cultural Politics* 1(1): 51–74. https://commonconf.files.wordpress.com/2010/09/proofs-of-tech-fetish.pdf. Acessado 28 de janeiro de 2016.

Deleuze, Gilles. 1992 "Poscript on the Societies of Control." *October,* 59 (Winter): 3–7. January 28, 2016.

Drexler, Jorge. s/f. Aplicanciones: una nueva manera de experimentar la música de autor, en la que el usuario interviene en la composición. Disponível em: http://wakeapp.com/app/jorge-drexler. January 28,2016.

Edwards, John. 2015. "The Internet of Things Generates Trillions in Revenue by Connecting Billions of Devices". Forbes, 17 de março. www.forbes.com/sites/teradata/2015/03/17/the-internet-of-things-generates-trillions-in-revenue-by-connecting-billions-of-devices/print/. January 28, 2016.

eMarketer. 2015a. Global Media Intelligence Report 2015. www.emarketer.com/public_media/docs/GMI-2015-ExecutiveSummary.pdf. January 12, 2016.

eMarketer. 2015b. "Latin America Is Home to a Robust Mobile Market". 15 de setembro. www.emarketer.com/Article/Latin-America-Home-Robust-Mobile-Market/1012985. January 28, 2016.

eMarketer. 2016. "Internet of Things Is Changing How Media and Entertainment Companies Operate". 4 de fevereiro. www.emarketer.com/Article/Internet-of-Things-Changing-How-Media-Entertainment-Companies-Operate/1013545?ecid=NL1001. February 4, 2016.

Estarque, Marina. 2014. "Dilma sanciona Marco Civil e critica espionagem em evento em SP". DW, 23 de abril. www.dw.com/pt/dilma-sanciona-marco-civil-e-critica-espionagem-em-evento-em-sp/a-17588584. January 28, 2016.

"Facebook busca ampliar el acceso a Internet en el país". El Universal, 5 de setembro de 2014. http://periodicocorreo.com.mx/anuncia-pena-nieto-colaboracion-con-facebook/. January 28, 2016.

Freier, Anne. 2015. "Which Social Media and Messaging Apps Do Teenagers Prefer?" Business of Apps, 16 de setembro. www.businessofapps.com/which-social-media-and-messaging-apps-do-teenagers-prefer/. January 28, 2016.

Fuchs, Christian. 2013. "Class and Exploitation on the Internet. Digital labor". Em *The Internet as playground and factory.* Ed. Trebor Scholz. London: Routledge, 211–224.

Gibbs, Samuel. 2014. "China plans to oust Microsoft, Apple and Android with own software". *The Guardian*, 26 de agosto. www.theguardian.com/technology/2014/aug/26/china-microsoft-apple-android-state-software. January 28, 2016.

Glanz, James. 2012. "Power, Pollution, and the Internet". *The New York Times,* 22 de setembro. www.nytimes.com/2012/09/23/technology/data-centers-waste-vast-amounts-of-energy-belying-industry-image.html?pagewanted=all&_r=0. January 28, 2016.

GSMA. 2014. Economía Móvil América Latina 2014. http://latam.gsmamobileeconomy.com/GSMA_ME_LatinAmerica_2014_ES.pdf. January 28, 2016.

Gutiérrez, Bernardo. 2016. "Do comum às redes". *Revista Observatório Itaú Cultural*, 20 (enero–junio): págs. 127–140. www.itaucultural.org.br/revista/91827/. November 8, 2016.

Hardt, Michael and Antonio Negri. 2000. *Empire.* Cambridge: Harvard University Press.

Heilman, Dan. 2016. "Mozilla to Shut Down Firefox Mobile OS". News Factor, 5 de fevereiro. www.newsfactor.com/news/Mozilla-Shuts-Down-Firefox-Mobile-OS/story.xhtml. February 6, 2016.

IBN Live. 2013. "Snowden says Google, Facebook, Apple gave direct access to NSA". 9 de julho. www.ibnlive.com/videos/india/snowden-latest-snowden-byte-2-622417.html. January 28, 2016.

Idgnow. 2015. "Netflix fatura R$500 milhões no Brasil e é chamado de 'Uber da TV'". 10 de agosto. http://idgnow.com.br/internet/2015/08/10/netflix-fatura-r-500-milhoes-no-brasil-e-e-chamado-de-uber-da-tv/. January 28, 2016.

IFPI. 2015. "IFPI Digital Music Report 2015". www.ifpi.org/downloads/Digital-Music-Report-2015.pdf. January 28, 2016.

Inam, Adeel. 2014. "Google to acquire Skybox for $1 billion". Triple Tremelo, 27 de maio. www.tripletremelo.com/google-to-acquire-skybox-for-1-billion/. January 28, 2016.

Information Office of the People's Republic of China. 2010. "The Internet in China". 10 de junho. www.china.org.cn/government/whitepaper/node_7093508.htm. January 28, 2016.

Internet.Org. Inventing the Future of Creativity. Youtube, 27 de março. www.youtube.com/watch?v=pxX6r-xDgG4. January 28, 2016.

Internet Society 2015 Global Internet Report 2015. Mobile evolution and development of the Internet. Reston: Internet Society. www.internetsociety.org/globalinternetreport/assets/download/IS_web.pdf. January 28, 2016.

Jiang, Min. 2010. "Informational Authoritarianism: China's Approach to Internet Sovereignty". *SAIS Review of International Affairs*, 30(2) (Summer-Fall): 71–89.

Kemp, Simon. 2015. Digital, Social & Mobile in 2015. We Are Social. Janeiro. www.slideshare.net/wearesocialsg/digital-social-mobile-in-2015. January 28, 2016.

Krantz, Mark. 2016. "USA rules! The 10 most valuable companies". USA Today, 2 de fevereiro. www.usatoday.com/story/money/markets/2016/02/02/usa-rules-10-most-valuable-companies/79698014/. February 32016.

Lavrusik, Vadim. 2016. "Expanding Live Video to More People". Facebook Newsroom, 28 de janeiro. http://newsroom.fb.com/news/2016/01/expanding-live-video/. January 28, 2016.

López, Ignacio. 2015. "¿Qué es Shazam y cómo funciona?" Vinagre Asesino, 7 de abril. www.vinagreasesino.com/que-es-shazam-y-como-funciona/. January 28, 2016.

Madory, Doug. 2013. "Google DNS Departs Brazil Ahead of New Law". Dyn Research, 22 de novembro. http://research.dyn.com/2013/10/google-dns-departs-brazil-ahead-new-law/#!prettyPhoto. January 28, 2013.

Mander, Jason. 2015. "Internet users in LatAm spend the most time online". 16 de Janeiro. www.globalwebindex.net/blog/internet-users-in-latam-spend-the-most-time-online. January 26, 2015.

Martí, Anna. 2016. "WhatsApp reafirma su trono llegando a los 1.000 millones de usuarios". 28 de janeiro. www.xatakamovil.com/aplicaciones/whatsapp-reafirma-su-trono-llegando-a-los-1-000-millones-de-usuarios. January 29, 2016.

Marx, Karl. 1973. *Grundrisse*. Harmondsworth: Penguin.

Massumi, Brian. 2002. *Parables for the Virtual: Movement, Affect, Sensation*. Durham: Duke University Press.

Meeker, Mary. 2014. *Internet Trends 2014 – Code Conference*, Kleiner Perkins Caufield & Byers KPCB, 28 de mayo. www.kpcb.com/file/kpcb-internet-trends-2014. January 28, 2016.

Miller, Toby. 2016. "Amazon Studios". 14 de janeiro. http://cstonline.tv/amazon-studios?print=true. January 14, 2016.

Mulligan, Mark. 2014. "Digital Ascendancy: The Future Music Forum Keynote". Music Industry Blog, 24 de setiembre. https://musicindustryblog.wordpress.com/2014/09/29/digital-ascendency-the-future-music-forum-keynote/. January 28, 2016.

Pew Research Center. 2015. "Internet Seen as Positive Influence on Education but Negative on Morality in Emerging and Developing Nations". 19 de março. www.pewglobal.org/files/2015/03/Pew-Research-Center-Technology-Report-FINAL-March-19-20151.pdf. January 28, 2016.

PriceWaterhouseCoopers PWC. 2012. *Global Entertainment and Media Outlook 2012–2016*. www.careercatalysts.com/pdf/PwCOutlook2012-Industry%20overview%20%283%29.pdf. January 28, 2016.

Rabosto, Andrés N. 2014. "Apuntes para una crítica de los etudios de Internet". http://sedici.unlp.edu.ar/bitstream/handle/10915/50455/Documento_completo.pdf?sequence=1

Ribeiro, Gabriel. 2015. "O que é Zero Rating? Entenda polêmica que envolve Facebook e operadoras". Tech Tudo, 25 de maio. www.techtudo.com.br/noticias/noticia/2015/05/o-que-e-zero-rating-entenda-polemica-que-envolve-facebook-e-operadoras.html. January 28, 2016.

Rincón, Omar y George Yúdice. 2016. Entrevista a Jesús Martín Barbero. *Revista Observatório Itaú Cultural*, 20 (enero-junio): págs. 237–255. www.itaucultural.org.br/revista/91827/. November 8, 2016.

Sá, Simone Pereira de. 2016. "Afetos, Performance de Gosto e Ativismo de Fãs nos Sites de Redes Sociais". *Revista Observatório*, 20: 172–183. www.itaucultural.org.br/revista/91827/. November 8, 2016.

Sengupta, Caesar. 2015. "A Step Toward Better Mobile Experiences in Africa". Android Official Blog, 18 de agosto. http://officialandroid.blogspot.com/2015/08/a-step-toward-better-mobile-experiences.html. January 28, 2016.

Serres, Michel. 2013. *A polegarzinha: uma nova forma de viver em harmonia e pensar as instituições, de ser e de saber*. Rio de Janeiro: Bertrand Brasil.

Smith, Craig. 2016. 50 Amazing WhatsApp Statistics. DMR, 22 de janeiro. http://expandedramblings.com/index.php/downloads/whatsapp-statistic-report/. January 28, 2016.

Spangler, Todd. 2015. "Netflix Data Reveals Exactly When TV Shows Hook Viewers – and It's Not the Pilot". *Variety*, 23 de setembro. http://variety.com/2015/digital/news/netflix-tv-show-data-viewer-episode-study-1201600746/. January 28, 2016.

Statista. 2016. "Mobile phone internet user penetration in Latin America from 2013 to 2019". www.statista.com/statistics/284209/latin-america-mobile-phone-internet-user-penetration/. January 28, 2016.

Statistics Times. 2016. "Projected GDP Ranking (2015–2020)". 7 de fevereiro. http://statisticstimes.com/economy/projected-world-gdp-ranking.php. February 7, 2016.

Téllez, Omar. 2015. "Understanding Tech Penetration in Latin America". Tech Crunch, 7 de abril. http://techcrunch.com/2015/04/07/understanding-tech-penetration-in-latam/. January 28, 2016.

Trefis Team. 2014. "Google's Strategy Behind The $3.2 Billion Acquisition Of Nest Labs". *Forbes*, 17 de janeiro. www.forbes.com/sites/greatspeculations/2014/01/17/googles-strategy-behind-the-3-2-billion-acquisition-of-nest-labs/. January 28, 2016.

van der Velden, Daniel e Vinca Kruk (Metahaven). 2012–2013. "Captives of the Cloud", partes 1 a 3. e-flux. www.e-flux.com/journal/captives-of-the-cloud-part-i/, www.e-flux.com/journal/captives-of-the-cloud-part-ii/ y www.e-flux.com/journal/captives-of-the-cloud-part-iii-all-tomorrows-clouds/. January 28, 2016.

Vaughn-Nichols, Steven. 2013. "Facebook remains top social network, Google+, YouTube battle for second". ZDNet, 14 de maio. www.zdnet.com/article/facebook-remains-top-social-network-google-youtube-battle-for-second/. January 28, 2016.

Virno, Paolo. 1996. "Notes on the General Intellect". Em Marxism Beyond Marxism, ed. Saree Makdisi, Cesare Casarino e Rebecca E. Karl. Londres: Routledge.

Wakefield, Jane. 2014. "Facebook Drones to Offer Low-Cost Net Access". *BBC*. 28 de março. 2014. www.bbc.com/news/technology-26784438. January 28, 2016.

Weinberger, Matt. 2015. "The cloud wars explained: Why nobody can catch up with Amazon". Business Insider, 7 de novembro. www.businessinsider.com/why-amazon-is-so-hard-to-topple-in-the-cloud-and-where-everybody-else-falls-2015-10. January 28, 2016.

Wright, Gilly e Valentina Pasquali. 2015. "World's Largest Companies". 19 de novembro. www.gfmag.com/global-data/economic-data/largest-companies. January 28, 2016.

Žižek, Slavoj. 2009. "Privatization of the General Intellect". Žižek-in-cite, 16 de outubro. http://vanishingmediator.blogspot.com/2009/10/privatization-of-general-intellect.html. January 28, 2016.

26

Uniting the nations of Europe?

Exploring the European Union's cultural policy agenda

Kate Mattocks

Introduction

> No one wants to see a technocratic Europe. European Union must be experienced by
> the citizen in his everyday life.
>
> *(Tindemans Report on European Union, 1975, p. 12)*

Where does culture fit in in the 'experience' of the European Union? This chapter explores
the European Union's involvement in the field of cultural policy. A formal part of a European treaty since 1992, culture is seen as a rather limited but symbolically powerful policy
area.[1] Over the past few decades, culture has become a more developed policy area in the
EU. Despite this, questions surrounding its EU cultural policy governance often remain on
the periphery of both cultural policy studies and EU studies. What kind of cultural programmes does the EU operate? What legal powers does it have, and who is responsible for
making decisions about cultural policy? These questions are important ones, not only for the
discussion of cultural policy in a supranational and global context, but also for deepening the
understanding of the EU in cultural terms. As Kathleen McNamara states, "we have spent
much less time examining the cultural underpinnings of the EU's governance" (2015, p. 22),
in favour of primarily economic and political paradigms.

What exactly do we mean by 'EU cultural policy'? The 2007 Agenda for Culture, the
EU's current framework for cultural action, does not explicitly define culture, but refers to
its many possible meanings and says that "it plays a fundamental role in human development
and in the complex fabric of the identities and habits of individuals and communities" (CEC,
2007, p. 3). Culture is a 'functional' policy area in the European Union, meaning that the EU
has a narrow and specific remit (Versluis et al., 2011), which can be divided into three basic
powers: (1) encouraging and facilitating cooperation between Member States; (2) promoting
the incorporation of culture into other areas of EU jurisdiction; and (3) cooperating with
Member States on cultural action. Much of EU cultural policy is based on voluntary cooperation, restricted by the principle of subsidiarity,[2] as "[l]egally speaking, it is not for the EU
to take the lead or to control" in this sector (Sandell, 1996, p. 271).

Thinking about 'culture' and 'the European Union' brings to mind innumerable topics, from questions on European identity and citizenship to narrower questions concerning specific cultural programmes. It also challenges us to think beyond the nation-state, traditionally the most common 'level of analysis' associated with cultural policy (Sassatelli, 2006). This is in part due to cultural policy's symbolic association with legitimacy, nation-building, stability, and boundary-marking (in both a literal and metaphorical sense), which can be traced to the relationship of culture, cultural identity, and political legitimacy. The cultural foundations of modern citizenship are civic responsibility and social trust (Kalberg, 1993, in Shore, 2001); both of these, in turn, "depend upon the sense people have of belonging to a political community" (Shore, 2001, p. 108). Cultural policy thus plays a role in nation-states' identity formation and perpetuation. In fact, for these same reasons the EU introduced a cultural programme, in an attempt to emphasise a shared cultural heritage and sense of cultural identity in order to garner more popular support for European integration.

The existing literature on EU cultural policy encompasses a broad variety of themes. A holistic picture of cultural governance is difficult to find (though, see Psychogiopoulou's (2015a) recent edited volume), although scholars have been interested in many different areas pertaining to culture and the EU: questions concerning the European Union's basis for legitimacy (Delanty, 1995; Shore, 2000); issues of agenda setting, framing, and historical progression of the cultural competence (Forrest, 1994; Sandell, 1996; Littoz-Monnet, 2007, 2012, 2015); legal perspectives, including the role of the European Court of Justice in cultural matters and 'cultural mainstreaming' – the incorporation of culture into other EU policy areas (see Craufurd Smith, 2004a; Psychogiopoulou, 2006; Isar, 2015); specific cultural programmes and actions (see sources in the list below); and finally European cultural identity and heritage (see Shore, 2000, 2001, 2006; Sassatelli, 2002, 2006, 2009; Eder, 2009; Vidmar-Horvat, 2012; Calligaro, 2013a).[3] Much of this work interprets 'culture' broadly, and thus it is often difficult to delineate where cultural policy begins and ends, a challenge facing cultural policy researchers in general (Ahearne, 2009).

The chapter investigates EU cultural policy from a governance perspective (Kohler-Koch and Rittberger, 2006), reflecting a more general view that the study of cultural policy can benefit from more institutionally rigorous analysis. A governance perspective asks questions about everyday processes, actors, and institutions in policy-making.[4] Its focus is not the substantive content of policy but how it is made and how the EU functions on a day-to-day basis.[5] In order to understand how changes in sovereignty due to Europeanization and integration have affected governance within the EU, the chapter draws on the concept of multi-level governance (MLG) (Marks, 1993). MLG refers to the changing nature of boundaries between different levels of government and the changes and challenges to sovereignty this brings about. It has three main premises (Hooghe and Marks, 2001). First, decision-making in the EU is more than bargaining amongst national governments – supranational institutions such as the European Commission and Parliament also exert their own influence. Second, this "involves a significant loss of control for individual national governments" (*Ibid.*, p. 4). The final premise is that actors operate in subnational, national, and supranational arenas and so are not nested but interconnected. MLG therefore provides a framework for researchers to address the complexities of diffused competences as well as the interactions between various levels of government (Littoz-Monnet, 2007).

The chapter is framed around three key themes that run throughout the discussion; these are the multi-level nature of EU cultural governance, the institutional fragmentation and complexity of EU cultural policy, and the role of culture in European integration. These themes also form the basis of the discussion later in the chapter. The EU is a multi-layered organisation, with negotiations and decision-making taking place within Member States, between Member States and the EU, and between EU institutions. With cultural policy transcending all levels, this makes for an intricate set of actors and negotiations, all with their own ideas of what the EU's involvement in the field should be. This makes the field of EU cultural policy a complex and fragmented one, due to both the nature of EU policy-making in general and the specific challenges that culture presents as a 'limited' and controversial policy field. Some scholars even suggest that complexity is the defining feature of EU governance (Zahariadis, 2013). It is not that other political systems are not *also* complex, but rather that "the complexity of the EU renders policy-making difficult to understand" (*Ibid.*, p. 810).[6] In addition, culture is a policy area in which:

> diversities between member states are particularly obvious – not only are peoples' cultures, in an anthropological sense, very different, but institutional forms of managing this area are also specific to each country – and anchored in national cultural styles.
>
> *(Littoz-Monnet, 2007, p. 2)*

This means that there are competing institutional positions on the nature of what the EU's involvement in culture should be. The chapter will show that while the EU does a great deal in the field of culture, particularly regarding funding in its current programme, Creative Europe, this does not translate into a coherent narrative on the bigger question of culture's role in EU integration.

The chapter proceeds as follows. I first turn to a brief historical overview of the European Union and its involvement in cultural policy. I then give an overview of the EU's current programmes and policies before discussing the main actors in EU cultural policy and their roles within the complex EU policy-making process. The chapter concludes with a discussion that brings the three main themes together.

The European Union and cultural policy: a historical overview[7]

What is now known as the European Union has its origins in the European Coal and Steel Community, created in 1951 with the signing of the Treaty of Paris by France, West Germany, Italy, Belgium, Luxembourg, and the Netherlands (see Rittberger, 2012). The ECSC brought these countries together to safeguard economic and geopolitical stability. Perhaps unsurprisingly, early Community treaties contained only "fleeting" references to culture (Sandell, 1996, p. 268), such as article 36 of the 1957 Treaty of Rome, which concerns the protection of national treasures with "artistic, historic or archaeological value." However, in the decades prior to Maastricht, the European Community had some involvement in the cultural sector. This was mostly accomplished through the European Commission's framing of culture in economic terms (Craufurd Smith, 2004b; Littoz-Monnet, 2007). This activity actually took place without legal grounding. The focus at this time was economic and industrial aspects of cultural production and consumption, such as training, working conditions, and the distribution of cultural goods. This framing of intervention on economic terms was a "successful agenda-setting exercise," which led to "extending the reach of its competence to the cultural sector when its formal powers were limited to the economic sphere" (Littoz-Monnet, 2007, pp. 43–44).

In the early 1980s, EU cultural ministers began meeting, first informally and then formally. Early cultural programmes, including the European Youth Orchestra and the European City (now Capital) of Culture were created, respectively, in 1976 and 1985. While these have been deemed "cautious and largely symbolic" initiatives, they represent Community action before any formal competence (Craufurd Smith, 2004b, p. 22) and thus a coming-together of the Member States. At the same time, the European Court of Justice throughout the 1970s and 1980s made judgements on subjects such as copyright and book trade (Littoz-Monnet, 2007).

Sentiments expressed in a series of high-profile reports throughout the 1970s and 1980s encouraged a deepening of cultural action in the Community in order to boost popular support for European integration. Leo Tindemans, in his 1975 Report on European Union, outlined several ideas for implementing a 'Citizen's Europe,' such as fundamental rights and consumer rights. Similarly, the Committee on a People's Europe (Adonnino report) in 1985 recommended various developments concerning television, an Academy of Science, Technology, and Art, a Euro-lottery ("to make Europe come alive for the Europeans"), and access to museums and cultural events. The report argued that culture and communication can contribute to "support for the advancement of Europe," which "can and must be sought" (p. 21) in order to "strengthen and promote [European Community] identity and its image both for its citizens and for the rest of the world" (p. 5).

While most of the intergovernmental cultural initiatives of the 1970s and 1980s were modest and symbolic, these initiatives paved the way for culture's more formal introduction in the early 1990s. The EC's legitimacy regarding cultural matters had increased, and 'European identity' and 'European culture' were becoming mainstream discourses within the EU's institutions (Sassatelli, 2009). Policy framing thus began to go beyond the economic argument in an attempt to develop a sense of community identity – "a crucial necessity for integration, which hitherto had barely been touched upon" (Urwin, 1996, p. 9). In the 1987 Communication *A Fresh Boost for Culture in the European Community*, the Commission argued for a deepening in cultural cooperation in advance of the Maastricht Treaty, arguing that "…it is this sense of being part of a European culture which is one of the prerequisites for the solidarity which is vital if the advent of the large market … is to secure the popular support it needs" (CEC, 1987, p. 5).

A cultural remit was thus first formally introduced in the Treaty on European Union (TEU, also known as the Maastricht Treaty), which was signed in 1992 and came into effect in 1993. Maastricht created the European Union – a "new social-political framework within an accelerated economic and monetary union" (Nectoux, 1996, p. 31). Article 128 of the TEU (now 167 in the Treaty on the Functioning of the European Union) stated that,

1. The Union shall contribute to the flowering of the cultures of the Member States, while respecting their national and regional diversity and at the same time bringing the common cultural heritage to the fore.
2. Action by the Union shall be aimed at encouraging cooperation between Member States and, if necessary, supporting and supplementing their action in the following areas:

    -improvement of the knowledge and dissemination of the culture and history of the European peoples,
    -conservation and safeguarding of cultural heritage of European significance,
    -non-commercial cultural exchanges,
    -artistic and literary creation, including in the audiovisual sector.

3. The Union and the Member States shall foster cooperation with third countries and the competent international organisations in the sphere of culture, in particular the Council of Europe.
4. The Union shall take cultural aspects into account in its action under other provisions of the Treaties, in particular in order to respect and to promote the diversity of its cultures.[8]

The article both legitimised the EU's prior activities in the field and paved the way for new ones (Shore, 2001). It was a compromise, reflecting the contentious nature of supranational cultural policy:

> While the broader and historically more significant principle of culture being a legitimate area of Community competence was secured by the countries which took a maximalist approach, the minimalist countries built into the drafting various restraining, defensive elements. ...
>
> *(Sandell, 1996, p. 270)*

This inclusion, along with other competences in social policy, was a turning point, with the added social and cultural dimension representing an 'ever-closer union' – an attempt, argue many, by political elite to increase political support for deeper European integration (Delanty, 1995; Shore, 2006). The rise of the cultural agenda must be therefore seen as a part of the grander European integration project (Barnett, 2001), an attempt to reduce the 'cultural deficit' (Shore, 2006) and garner more popular support. It is from this point that we can begin to analyse the EU's current involvement as it has developed since culture's formal treaty introduction. I now turn to an overview of the policies and programmes that the EU currently operates.

Policies and programmes

As indicated above, Member States maintain full autonomy over their own cultural policies: the introduction of a cultural competence was "not to establish a 'common' cultural policy but to bring to the forefront Community efforts rooted in the protection and promotion of Member States' diverse cultural systems" (Psychogiopoulou, 2006, p. 583). The main document that sets out the EU's overarching cultural priorities is the 2007 *Agenda for Culture*. This document outlines the three main strategic objectives around which the EU bases its cultural activities:

1. Promotion of cultural diversity and intercultural dialogue;
2. Promotion of culture as a catalyst for creativity in the framework of the Lisbon Strategy for growth and jobs;[9]
3. Promotion of culture as a vital element in the Union's international relations (CEC, 2007).

The EU's activities in the cultural field encompass a wide variety of actions. Notably, the word 'policy' itself is rarely used to describe action in the field – rather, less binding-sounding terms such as 'programmes' and 'actions' are favoured. In the European Commission's own words,

> [the] work done by the EU complements that and adds a different dimension. Information gathered from the EU as a whole can be used to support national policy decisions or provide examples of best practice that others can share. Programmes run across the EU can have a greater overall impact than those just run on national grounds, and policies put in place throughout the EU can help further national goals.
>
> *(CEC, 2013, p. 3)*

The EU's current programmes are outlined below, separated into supporting, coordination and communicative, and supplementary measures. These programmes have all developed at varying times and have different historical trajectories; they thus should not necessarily be seen as a congruent set of initiatives but rather co-existing. Where possible, I have included further sources on these programmes. This list focuses on 'explicit' actions within the Directorate-General for Education and Culture (see below); cultural aspects of other programmes in different fields such as cohesion and education policy have largely been left out here.

Supporting measures

- *Creative Europe* – Creative Europe (CE) is the EU's current cultural funding programme. Between 2014 and 2020 it will award €1.46 billion within its two strands, MEDIA and Culture. This funding is used to support cooperation projects that involve three or more Member States. For more on CE, see Kandyla (2015).
- *EU prizes* – Administered by the Commission, the EU has several annual prizes in the fields of literature, music, heritage, and contemporary architecture.
- *European heritage including annual heritage days and the heritage label* – Heritage has been an increasingly important area for the European Union. The EU's role is "to assist and complement the actions of the Member States in preserving and promoting Europe's cultural heritage" (CEC, 2015). It has its own heritage label[10] and promotes, along with the Council of Europe, annual heritage days.[11] For more on heritage see Calligaro (2013a) and Lähdesmäki (2014).

Policy coordination and communication measures

- *Open Method of Coordination (OMC)* – The OMC is a voluntary policy coordination process that brings together Member States in a series of working groups in order to share best practices on themes that have been agreed upon in the Council of Ministers' triennial Work Plans for Culture. Used in other policy areas as well, the OMC seeks to "put the EU Member States on a path towards achieving common objectives, while respecting different underlying values and arrangements" (de la Porte, 2002, p. 39). On the culture OMC, see Psychogiopoulou (2015b) and Mattocks (2017).
- *Structured Dialogue* – Structured Dialogue exists to foster exchange between the cultural sector and the EU via a series of transnational platforms and a biennial Culture Forum. The platforms and Forum bring together stakeholders, cultural sector representatives, and policy-makers to debate and discuss key issues in the field (see Ecorys, 2013; Littoz-Monnet, 2015).
- *Expertise* – As part of its dialogue with the sector, the EU supports a transnational network of experts, the European Expert Network on Culture (EENC). According to its website, the group "contributes to the improvement of policy development in culture in Europe, through the provision of advice and support to the European Commission in the analysis of cultural policies and their implications at national, regional and European levels."
- *Information provision and cooperation* – the Commission has undertaken or commissioned a large number of studies about various issues relating to the cultural sector. It also cooperates with other European networks on information dissemination and networking.

Supplementary measures

- *European Capital of Culture programme* – Perhaps the most well known of all of the EU's cultural programmes, the ECoC started in 1985 and has been held in 53 cities since. The programme aims to increase arts and cultural programmes within the city but also strengthen and project its 'European dimension' (see Palmer-Rae Associates, 2004; Sassatelli, 2009; Garcia et al., 2013; Patel, 2013).
- *Audiovisual policy* – Television without Frontiers was established in 1989 and amended in 2007 to the 'audiovisual media services directive' (DIRECTIVE 2010/13/EU). This policy makes it easier to access audiovisual material from other European countries and sets out a number of minimum requirements with regards to digital access. It is a binding agreement with flexibility to the Member States as to how to implement it. Requirements include the accessibility for people with disabilities, measures for the promotion of European works, some requirements for commercial communications, and rules concerning sponsorship and product placement. On audiovisual and media policy, see Collins (1994), Wheeler (2004), Harcourt (2006), Sarikakis (2007a), and Erickson and Dewey (2011).
- *Mainstreaming culture* – The Commission works with other EU and external organisations to incorporate culture into other policy areas where possible, such as external relations and European Neighbourhood Policy.[12] For more on this see Craufurd Smith (2004b) and Psychogiopoulou (2006).

Key actors

One of the difficulties in studying EU policy-making is grappling with the sheer number of actors involved as well as their interconnectedness. As Dewey (2008, p. 100) comments, "few people know how to navigate the complicated maze of laws, institutions, policy actors, and affiliated organizations in this field."[13] This section unpacks the complexity of EU governance and offers a brief description of the main actors in EU cultural policy as well as their roles. It demonstrates the competing positions of various institutions, reflecting the necessity of consensus and inter-institutional bargaining in EU governance.

European Commission

The main EU institution involved in cultural policy is the European Commission, the EU's executive institution. In 'national' terms, the Commission can be considered the equivalent of an executive branch of government, whereas legislative power is shared by the Council and Parliament. The Commission is the guardian of the treaties (and therefore takes subsidiarity seriously) and in general has power of policy initiation.

The Commission is composed of a core appointed College of Commissioners as well as an administrative bureaucracy of Directorate-Generals (DGs). Culture is part of the Directorate-General for Education and Culture, known informally as DG-EAC. The DG's remit in terms of culture is encompassed in "culture and audiovisual."[14] The administration and management of most of the programmes listed above are shared by two units in DG-EAC, called 'Cultural Diversity and Innovation' and 'Creative Europe programme,' and the Commission's Education, Audiovisual and Culture Executive Agency.[15]

Historically, the Commission has played a rather important role in the development of EU action in this field. The work of Annabelle Littoz-Monnet (2007, 2012), for example, shows how the DG has taken an active stance in advancing further cultural cooperation by framing intervention in terms of culture's potential to foster economic growth and competitiveness, bringing it in line with competition and economic policy of the Lisbon Strategy (European Council, 2000). The DG also has a history of collaboration and networking with other DGs, such as DG Regional Policy and DG Internal Market, as well as external actors (Sassatelli, 2006; Littoz-Monnet, 2012). Littoz-Monnet (2012, p. 516) argues that "by extending the traditional realm of participants to the policy formulation process, DG Culture can more effectively promote the strategic role of culture as a potential solution to broader economic challenges." In line with this argument, Sassatelli (2006) maintains that networking and collaboration, primarily with NGOs and cultural networks, have given creed to the DG's policies. In other words, despite its limited remit, the Commission has done all it can to maximise cultural collaboration in the EU and has been a key driver of further cooperation in the field since 1992.

Although DG-EAC is the main DG for culture, other DGs' remits fall into the cultural realm as well, reinforcing both the fragmented nature of organisation and the often-controversial question of where 'culture' begins and ends. For example, DG Internal Market is responsible for copyright issues, and DG Regional Policy can, with substantial budgeting privileges, grant funding to regions for cultural projects via the structural funds (see Delgado-Moreira, 2000).

European Parliament

The European Parliament (EP), which shares legislative power with the Council of the European Union, is composed of 751 directly elected representatives from the 28 Member States. Members of the European Parliament represent their constituency and sit in one of seven political groups. Legislation is brought to the EP and is then sent to one of 22 parliamentary standing committees, where it is evaluated. The decision-making system in the EP operates entirely on negotiation and consensus-building because by design there is not a majority political party: to achieve anything, compromises must be made (Versluis, van Keulen, and Stephenson, 2011).

Culture is represented in the standing committee on Culture and Education, composed of 31 Members of the European Parliament (MEPs). The committee outlines its priorities as such:

> the cultural aspects of the European Union, and in particular: (a) improving the knowledge and dissemination of culture, (b) the protection and promotion of cultural and linguistic diversity, (c) the conservation and safeguarding of cultural heritage, cultural exchanges and artistic creation.
>
> *(European Parliament, 2014, p. 144)*

Unfortunately, there is little work dedicated to the role of the EP in cultural policy-making, although consensus is that the Culture and Education Committee has in general advocated for an increased role for the EU in this field (Forrest, 1994; European Parliament, 2001; Littoz-Monnet, 2007; Staiger, 2013), carving out a distinct role for itself in advocating for a firmer stance on culture's role in integration (aligning with the Committee of the Regions but opposed to the more restrained position of the Council – see below). Much of the Parliament's work on culture argues that EU cultural action must go beyond a symbolic role and gives credit to the "specificity of culture and the need for special laws" to govern it (Littoz-Monnet, 2007, p. 34). The EP has often focused on specific problems, such as labour market issues for artists in Europe (Gordon and Adams, 2007). Barnett's (2001) findings also indicate that the EP has tried over the years to expand the cultural programme but has not met with much success. His findings are supported by Gordon and Adams (2007), who argue that more robust proposals from both the Parliament and Commission are often stymied by the Council of Ministers and in particular the larger Member States.

Council of the European Union (Council of Ministers)

The Council of the European Union, also known as the Council of Ministers (to avoid confusion with the European Council), is the body that represents the interests of Member States. It is composed of current ministers from Member States' national governments. The Council shares legislative power with the European Parliament. Broadly, its role is to evaluate legislation from the point of view of perceived benefits or losses to citizens in their Member State. The Council's Presidency also rotates every six months, allowing limited agenda-setting power for that particular Member State. The Council is split into ten groups, or formations. What this means is that '*the* Council' is actually several policy sector-specific 'Councils.'

Cultural policy is the responsibility of the Education, Youth, Culture, and Sport Council (EYCS). The EYCS Council is composed of national ministers of culture and meet several times a year to debate relevant issues. Most legislation in the field is non-binding and does not legally require national Parliaments to adopt it. According to the official Council website,

> The policy areas covered by the EYCS Council are the responsibility of member states. The EU's role in areas of education, youth, culture and sport is therefore to provide *a framework for cooperation between member states*, for exchange of information and experience on areas of common interest.
>
> *(Council of the European Union, 2015; emphasis added)*

Until November 2014, decisions on cultural policy matters were taken by unanimity. This changed with the introduction of Qualified Majority Voting (QMV) as a part of the 2009 Treaty of Lisbon. However, outside of the meetings of the culture ministers for the EU-28, an extensive system of work is done by permanent representatives in both ad hoc and permanent committees and workings parties. The Cultural Affairs Committee (CAC), composed of seconded representatives from the Member States, prepares the work of EU ministers for culture, and a high percentage of decisions are 'settled' at the level of permanent representatives, rather than by the EU-28 Culture Ministers themselves (Versluis et al., 2011). This reflects the multi-level nature of the Council's work and the fact that boundaries are no longer able to be neatly drawn between various levels of subnational, national, and supranational government as seconded representatives in the Council in Brussels are often working with two hats on.

Historically, the Council has played, perhaps a bit surprisingly, a role in the development of some of the first cultural activity at the intergovernmental level. In 1985, the European City of Culture programme was initiated in the Council by then Greek Minister for Culture Melina Mercouri. The founding principles were based on culture as a vehicle of cohesion, along with the special role of cities as locales of cultural exchange. However, in general, the Council's role to act in the interests of the Member States has meant that as an institution it is highly respectful of subsidiarity and therefore cannot be considered an agenda-setter in the field.

Other actors

COMMITTEE OF THE REGIONS (COR)

The Committee of the Regions is an advisory body composed of 350 members who are regionally and locally elected in Member States. Its role is to represent regional interests at the European level and to provide a local viewpoint on relevant legislation that affects regions, to bring regional and local perspectives into EU policy-making. For a competence like cultural policy, this is important, as culture is a subnational competence in some EU Member States. The CoR is consulted on all cultural policy proposals.

The CoR is divided into six 'Commissions,' one of which is Education, Youth, Culture, and Research (EDUC). The body has, since its inception in 1992, argued for an enhanced role for local and regional actors in the design of cultural policy (Barnett, 2001). Barnett maintains that the CoR has had some influence in helping strengthen networking systems within the cultural field through increased dialogue. The body has questioned the meaning of subsidiarity and argued that cultural action is not necessarily the responsibility of the Member States (since this incorrectly assumes homogenous national cultures within them) and that culture is best handled at the subnational level. Despite this, as the CoR is an advisory body and not a decision-making one, its overall influence has been relatively limited (Gordon, 2010; Versluis et al., 2011).

LOBBY GROUPS AND CIVIL SOCIETY PLATFORMS

Brussels is the second most lobbied city in the world after Washington (Versluis et al., 2011). and lobbying has been the subject of a large amount of research on the role it plays in agenda setting and policy-making, particularly within the European Parliament. The role and influence of lobbying is better understood in other sectors because it has been the subject of more scrutiny. However, it is often difficult to determine the precise role that lobby groups play, particularly as politicians may be reluctant to admit how much they are influenced by them. There is even less known about the relatively smaller lobbying presence of cultural groups and organisations and the amount that they may or may not influence decision-making, though the Commission is committed to dialogue with the sector. Historically, professional cultural networks in Europe have been critical of the sector's slow development and fragmented funding schemes within the EU (Barnett, 2001). This gave rise to the mobilisation of arts and cultural advocacy organisations, particularly after the inclusion of the competence in the Treaty of Maastricht, who have generally advocated for a greater role for culture in European integration.[16] However, while they have participated in a great deal of dialogue and cooperation concerning cultural matters, more work needs to be done to trace the precise impact this has had in EU decision-making.

Discussion

So far in this chapter we have discussed the historical trajectory of EU cultural policy, the main programmes and policies that it operates, and the main political actors involved in creating and managing these. It is now time to bring these areas together and address the overarching themes that run throughout the discussion.

The first theme running throughout the chapter concerns the *multi-level nature* of EU cultural governance. Thinking back to Hooghe and Marks' three premises of multi-level governance, culture conforms, to varying degrees, to all three of them. First, supranational institutions such as the European Commission exert their own influence when it comes to EU cultural policy. Consensus is that Commission has been the institution responsible for advancing further cooperation in the field, at least since Maastricht, and plays a crucial role in setting the supranational cultural policy agenda; Commission officers try to do what they can within the legal limitations of the competence (Mattocks, 2017). This results in a loss of control for individual Member State governments in that they must compromise to achieve agreement. Bargaining, particularly in the Parliament and the Council of Ministers, is important. The EU's institutional procedures are designed to allow consensus to be achieved, which sometimes presents difficulties in a controversial competence such as culture where certain Member States and EU institutions would like to see a more robust programme and others would not.

Multi-level governance also means that a plethora of actors operate in interconnected relationships involving local, regional, national, and supranational levels of government, not to mention the complicated influences of public-private partnerships, lobby groups, civil society platforms, and non-government organisations in cultural matters. These relationships are present in the EU institutions themselves – the Commission, Parliament, and Council of Ministers – as well as the Committee of the Regions and formal and informal cultural networks. Individuals within these institutions operate within a complex system of interconnectedness: complex domestic relationships also extend to the supranational level, meaning that there are always questions regarding the exact nature of cultural policy, its jurisdiction (particularly in those Member States where culture is a regional competence), and the extent to which the EU should be involved in it.

The second theme is the *complex and fragmented nature of EU cultural policy and governance.* Community involvement in the cultural field pre-Maastricht, argues Craufurd Smith (2004b, p. 49) was "at best fragmented, at worst inconsistent or distorted." What can we say about it now, more than 20 years later? There are two linked points to develop here, the first the nature of the policies themselves and second the fragmentation of EU governance more generally. First of all, the EU's involvement in the cultural field has grown since Maastricht, with more programmes, actions, and initiatives now than ever before. However, while made somewhat clearer in documents such as the *Agenda for Culture*, EU cultural policy is still highly fragmented: there is no one place to turn to for an overall picture of what the EU does in this field, nor the impacts it has. Nor is there an overarching narrative about culture's overall 'role' within the European Union. From the literature on public policy, we know that governments rarely make single decisions for any given policy issue; rather, sets of cumulative decisions add up to outcomes (Howlett et al., 2009). In addition, policy is rarely systemic or easily traceable. This indeed what we see within EU cultural policy. Programmes are piecemeal and fragmented, having been developed at different times throughout history, reflecting bargaining and consensus-seeking, various justifications for EU interventions, and different goals.

Another reason for this fragmentation has to do with the political sensitivity of culture. As Patel (2013) outlines, EU cultural action is marked by a paradox: it is desired in order to further European integration and unity, but its development is constrained by subsidiarity and Member States' wishes to keep culture a national competence. In their book on analysing the EU policy process, Versluis et al. (2011) designate culture as a policy area in which 'the EU' (perhaps left vague for a reason) would like to have more involvement but is met by resistance from Member States, who still see culture as best handled at the national or subnational level. Similarly, Littoz-Monnet (2007, p. 2), argues that culture has been an area that Member States have been "particularly disinclined" to transfer competence to the EU. Simply put,

Because it is of minor importance and yet ideologically highly charged at the same time, culture is considered a controversial issue – especially when it comes to discussing the division of competencies between the EU and its member states.

(Kaufmann and Raunig, 2002, n.p.)

Part of the issue of this fragmentation is to do with the complexity of EU governance and not only the number of actors involved in decision-making but their competing positions. This complexity makes studying the European Union challenging because of the high number of actors, the diversity of their interactions, and the multitude of different ways or 'modes' that policy is made.[17] In addition, culture is a competence that "entered the arena of EU jurisdiction under complex and contradictory conditions" (Sarikakis, 2007b, p. 14). Quite simply, there are debates between those actors who wish to extend the competence and those who do not (Barnett, 2001). As the EU does not have the competences to override, but only supplement, Member States on cultural policy, action in the field requires constant justification. This means that it is difficult to create and operate robust cultural programmes and policies at the European level. This has led McNamara (2015) to argue that the European cultural space is so focused on not eroding 'the national' that cultural governance is additive and piecemeal.[18]

This leads onto the third overarching theme, which is the *role of culture in European integration*. Cultural policies in the EU "cannot be understood outside of the wider context of the political project for European integration" (Shore, 2001, p. 107). After all, the continued integration of a supranational European polity, from European Community to Union, has been a project of economics rather than a cultural or social one, these traditionally being policy areas that Member States prefer to keep in the domestic domain. Where does culture fit in in the 'ever-closer' union? Ultimately, the EU lacks an overall narrative about what culture is and what the nature of its intervention in the field should be. Clive Barnett (2001, p. 412) has argued that culture has become "a multi-dimensional sector" that can be co-opted for a number of policy pursuits, be they employment, social cohesion, or urban regeneration. It is more difficult, if nigh on impossible, to operate a fuller cultural programme for *cultural* purposes due to a lack of political will: the EU does not have the legal power to harmonise cultural policy, and Member States agreeing to a supranational legally binding cultural policy is not viable: a "consensual approach to European culture...is simply unreachable" (Calligaro, 2013b, p. 29). This is in part emblematic of the particular difficulties of culture as a contested policy field, as well as the restricted legal conditions under which it operates.

Because of the 'soft' and supplementary nature of EU governance, the EU's cultural programmes have had rather modest and uneven impacts in the Member States (Gray, 2000). The Creative Europe programme is somewhat unique among the EU's actions, as it represents direct funding to Member States. The EU's efforts at cooperation, networking, and promotion initiatives such as Heritage Days and the European Capital for Culture can also be said to have many positive benefits, particularly in raising the profiles of artists and helping cross-border mobility and visibility (Bell and Oakley, 2015). Policy coordination via the OMC has also shown to produce limited policy transfer and convergence, though it represents an opportunity for intergovernmental exchange and learning (Mattocks, 2017). However, in general, most of the policies and programmes do not have a significant impact within national policies or programmes, nor have they been shown to substantively further deepen a sense of shared European identity (Shore, 2000; Palmer-Rae Associates, 2004; Sassatelli, 2008, Garcia et al., 2013).

Conclusion

This chapter has demonstrated the complex relationship between the European Union and cultural policy. The development of EU cultural policies has been a process of legitimation since the 1970s, with the 1992 Maastricht Treaty representing a turning point in terms of a legal grounding and a move towards the deepening of the European project. However, the chapter has shown that despite a place in the treaty, cultural action is subject to restraints and contradictions, making a robust programme at the European level difficult to achieve. Development in this policy field is constrained by the principle of subsidiarity as well as some Member States (such as the United Kingdom, Germany, and Nordic countries) who do not desire further cooperation in the field. Member States retain control of their own cultural policies. Turning back to earlier in this chapter, a close reading of article 167 shows just how restricted the legal base of the cultural competence is: paragraph 2 lays out the areas that the Community may become involved in, "if necessary," and paragraph 5 restricts the Union from any policy harmonisation. EU cultural governance is thus mostly accomplished through voluntary cooperation, resulting in a series of programmes that typically have uneven impacts at the national and subnational levels.

Policy-making in the European Union is a fragmented process best characterised as a multiplicity of 'processes' rather than a single, linear progression. As the chapter has shown, there are multilevel interactions among subnational, national, and supranational actors in all of the key EU institutions in cultural policy – the European Commission, Parliament, Council of Ministers, and Committee of the Regions. This multitude of actors participates in an ongoing dialogue with respect to the appropriate scale and measures that the EU should be involved in. The most important institution is the European Commission, which has been shown to be an agenda-setter in the field acting where possible within its remit to foster cooperation between Member States.[19] However, the domain of cultural policy still rests with the nation-state, a scenario that is unlikely to change.

To end, it is worthwhile thinking back to the beginning – the history of European cultural involvement, which developed in an effort to forge popular support for European integration and foster a sense of common European identity. Culture is still emphasised as an important part of this.[20] However, there is a disconnect between what is presented in policy documents and what happens in practice. Indeed, despite these efforts, "there has been no corresponding shift in popular sentiment or political loyalty" (Shore, 2000, p. 18). The narrative of culture's 'place' in the European Union has been a subject of controversy from the beginning and, while the EU has made important strides in its funding, networking, and cooperation projects in particular, the reality of European cultural policy is still rather at odds with the view that Europe needs a robust, imaginative cultural programme in order to tackle the current and future challenges facing the continent.

Notes

1 As a supranational body, the European Union has 'competences' in specific fields. These competences are set out in the various European treaties, which are signed by all Member State governments. In general, there are four categories of competence: exclusive, shared, supporting, and special. Culture belongs to the 'supporting' category.

2 Subsidiarity, outlined in article 5(3) of Maastricht (TEU) is a principle of EU law. It says that the EU will only become involved in a policy area if it is deemed the best 'level' of government to do so, i.e. Member States acting on their own is insufficient.

3 This list is not exhaustive but rather aims to show the key areas of the literature to date.

4 By 'everyday' I mean not the 'high politics' of the Heads of State and EU leaders, but the policy officers and managers, legislators, and civil servants responsible for creating and implementing programmes.

5 For more on the content of EU cultural policy, see the references to individual programmes below, as well as Littoz-Monnet (2015).

6 Versluis, van Keulen, and Stephenson's (2011) volume is a good introduction for those wanting to know more about EU governance more generally.

7 Due to space restraints, this is a shortened and condensed version. For more detail, see, for example, CEC (1992), Shore (2000), Craufurd Smith (2004a), and Sassatelli (2009). In addition, the Council of Europe – an entirely separate supranational institution – had been involved in the cultural field since just after the Second World War. The development of EU cultural policy should be seen in conjunction with the CoE's development (see Sassatelli, 2009).

8 Article 167 also contains a fifth paragraph referring to legal and policy-making procedures, which explicitly excludes any policy harmonisation between Member States in the field of culture.

9 The Lisbon Strategy (2000–2010) has been replaced by Europe 2020 (2010–2020), focusing on "smart, sustainable, and inclusive growth."

10 http://ec.europa.eu/programmes/creative-europe/actions/heritage-label/discover_en.htm.

11 www.europeanheritagedays.com/.

12 http://cultureinexternalrelations.eu/.

13 For an example of how EU cultural policy is made step-by-step, see Dewey (2008) on the 2007 Agenda for Culture.

14 Obuljen (2004) notes that in most EU countries, culture and audiovisual would not be separated out as such, but be both considered a part of cultural policy and be subsumed within the Ministry of Culture (or equivalent). Audiovisual policy has a different history within the EU, as it has been more easily framed around economic and free trade objectives.

15 The European executive agencies perform largely management and administrative roles.

16 According to the website of one of the main lobby groups in the arts and cultural sectors, Culture Action Europe, created in 1992, their aim is to "be the leading platform for representing the diverse interests of the sector with a coherent and clear message."

17 Wallace and Wallace (2007) identify five different modes of policy-making in the EU, each with its own processes and treaty bases.

18 For McNamara, culture is "a process of meaning making, shared among some particular group of people" (p. 27), so much more in line with broader customs and habits than a narrower definition of artistic practices.

19 A fruitful topic for future research is investigating in more detail the role of non-institutional bodies such as the Committee of the Regions and professional cultural networks and lobby groups located in Brussels.

20 To take one example, at the opening of the Culture Forum in November 2013, Past President of the European Commission Jose Manuel Barroso said that "Culture is, and always has been, the cement that binds Europe together. It is an essential part of the very foundations of our European project and must remain firmly entrenched in our ideals if we are to succeed in achieving a more united, a stronger and open Europe."

References

Adonnino, P. 1985. A People's Europe. Report from the Ad Hoc Committee. *Bulletin of the European Communities*, Supplement, 7/85.

Ahearne, J. 2009. Cultural policy explicit and implicit: a distinction and some uses. *International Journal of Cultural Policy*, 15(2), 141–153.

Barnett, C. 2001. Culture, policy and subsidiarity in the European Union: from symbolic identity to the governmentalisation of culture. *Political Geography*, 20(4), 405–426.

Bell, D. and K. Oakley. 2015. *Cultural Policy.* London: Routledge.

Calligaro, O. 2013a. *Negotiating Europe: The EU Promotion of Europeanness since the 1950s.* New York: Palgrave Macmillan.

Calligaro, O. 2013b. "From 'European Cultural Heritage' to 'Cultural Diversity': The Changing Core Values of European Cultural Policy", 10th General Conference of the ECPR (European Consortium for Political Research), Bordeaux, France.

Commission of the European Communities (CEC). 1987. A Fresh Boost for Culture in the European Community. Commission Communication to the Council and Parliament. December 1987 (COM 87 603 final). *Bulletin of the European Communities*, Supplement, 4/87.

CEC. 1992. *Communication from the Commission to the Council, the European Parliament and the Economic and Social Committee. New prospects for Community cultural action.* COM (92) 149 final.

CEC. 2007. *Communication from the Commission to the European Parliament, the Council, the European Economic and Social Committee and the Committee of the Regions. Communication on a European agenda for culture in a globalizing world.* COM (2007) 242 final.

CEC. 2013. Culture and audiovisual. The European Union explained series. Available online at: http://europa.eu/pol/pdf/flipbook/en/culture_audiovisual_en.pdf (accessed 31 October 2015). Brussels: European Commission.

CEC. 2015. Supporting cultural heritage. Available online at: http://ec.europa.eu/culture/policy/culture-policies/cultural-heritage_en.htm (accessed 31 October 2015).

Collins, R. 1994. *Broadcasting and Audio-Visual Policy in the European Single Market.* London: John Libbey.

Council of the European Union. 2015. Education, Youth, Culture and Sport Council configuration (EYCS). Available online at: www.consilium.europa.eu/en/council-eu/configurations/eycs/ (accessed 31 October 2015).

Craufurd Smith, R. ed. 2004a. *Culture and European Union Law.* Oxford: Oxford University Press.

Craufurd Smith, R. 2004b. Community intervention in the cultural field: continuity or change? In R. Craufurd Smith (ed.) *Culture and European Union Law.* Oxford: Oxford University Press, pp. 19–78.

Delanty, G. 1995. *Inventing Europe: Ideas, Identity, Reality.* Basingstoke: Macmillan Press Ltd.

De la Porte, C. 2002. Is the open method of coordination appropriate for organising activities at European level in sensitive policy areas? *European Law Journal*, 8(1), 38–58.

Delgado-Moreira, J.M. 2000. Cohesion and citizenship in EU cultural policy. *Journal of Common Market Studies*, 38(3), 449–470.

Dewey, P. 2008. Transnational Cultural Policy-Making in the European Union. *The Journal of Arts Management, Law and Society*, 38(2), 99–118.

Ecorys. 2013. Evaluation of the open method of coordination and the structured dialogue, as the Agenda for culture's implementing tools at European Union level: final report for the European Commission Directorate-General for Culture and Education.

Eder, K. 2009. A theory of collective identity. Making sense of the debate on a "European identity". *European Journal of Social Theory*, 12(4), 1–21.

Erickson, M. and P. Dewey. 2011. EU media policy and/as cultural policy: economic and cultural tensions in MEDIA 2007. *International Journal of Cultural Policy*, 17(5), 490–509.

European Council. 2000. Presidency Conclusions. Lisbon European Council of 23 and 24 March 2000.

European Parliament. 2001. Report on cultural cooperation in the European Union. 2000/2323(INI).

European Parliament. 2014. Rules of Procedure, 8th parliamentary term. Available online at: www.europarl.europa.eu/sipade/rulesleg8/Rulesleg8.EN.pdf (accessed 18 May 2017).

Forrest, A. 1994. A new start for cultural action in the European Community. Genesis and implications of article 128 of the treaty on European Union. *International Journal of Cultural Policy*, 1(2), 11–20.

Garcia, B., et al. (2013) *European Capitals of Culture. Success Strategies and Long Term effects.* Brussels: European Parliament.

Gordon, C. 2010. Great expectations – the European Union and cultural policy: fact or fiction? *International Journal of Cultural Policy*, 16(2), 101–120.

Gordon, C. and T. Adams. 2007 The European Union and Cultural Policy – Chimera, Camel or Chrysalis? Consultative draft paper prepared for the European Cultural Foundation.

Gray, C. 2000. *The Politics of the Arts in Britain.* Basingstoke: Macmillan.

Harcourt, A. 2006.*European Union and the Regulation of Media Markets.* Manchester: Manchester University Press.

Hooghe, L. and G. Marks. 2001. *Multi-level Governance and European Integration.* Lanham: Rowman and Littlefield.

Howlett, M., M. Ramesh, and A. Perl. 2009. *Studying Public Policy: Policy Cycles and Policy Subsystems.* Don Mills, Canada: Oxford University Press.

Isar, Y.R. 2015. Culture in EU external relations: an idea whose time has come? *International Journal of Cultural Policy*, 21(4), 494–508.

411

Kalberg, S. 1993. Cultural foundations of modern citizenship. In B.S. Turner (ed.) *Citizenship and Social Theory*. London: Sage Publications, pp. 91–114.

Kandyla, A. 2015. The Creative Europe Programme: policy-making dynamics and outcomes. In E. Psychogiopoulou (ed.) *Cultural Governance and the European Union: Protecting and Promoting Cultural Diversity in Europe*. Basingstoke: Palgrave Macmillan, pp. 49–60.

Kaufmann, T. and G. Raunig. 2002. Anticipating European Cultural Policies. European Institute for Progressive Cultural Policies. Available online at: http://eipcp.net/policies/aecp/kaufmannraunig/en (accessed 12 October 2015).

Kohler-Koch, B. and B. Rittberger. 2006. Review article: the 'governance turn' in EU studies. *Journal of Common Market Studies*, 44(s1), 27–49.

Lähdesmäki, T. 2014. The EU's implicit and explicit heritage politics. *International Journal of Cultural Policy*, 16(3), 401–421.

Littoz-Monnet, A. 2007. *The European Union and Culture: Between Economic Regulation and Cultural Policy*. Manchester: Manchester University Press.

Littoz-Monnet, A. 2012. Agenda setting Dynamics at EU Level: the case of the EU's cultural policy. *Journal of European Integration*, 34(7), 505–522.

Littoz-Monnet, A. 2015. Encapsulating EU cultural policy into the EU's growth and competiveness agenda: explaining the success of a paradigmatic shift in Brussels. In E. Psychogiopoulou (ed.) *Cultural Governance and the European Union: Protecting and Promoting Cultural Diversity in Europe*. Basingstoke: Palgrave Macmillan, pp. 25–36.

Marks, G. 1993. Structural policy and multilevel governance in the EC. In A. Cafruny and G. Rosenthal (eds.) *The State of the European Community vol. 2: The Maastricht Debates*. Boulder, CO: Lynne Riener and Harlow: Longman, pp. 391–410.

Mattocks, K. 2017. *Intergovernmental coordination in European Union cultural policy: the Open Method of Coordination and the 2011–2014 Work Plan for Culture*. PhD thesis, City, University of London.

McNamara, K. 2015. JCMS Annual Review Lecture: Imagining Europe: The Cultural Foundations of EU Governance. *Journal of Common Market Studies*, 35, 22–39.

Nectoux, F. 1996. The politics of European integration after Maastricht. In P. Barbour (ed.) *The European Union Handbook*. Chicago: Fitzroy Dearborn Publishers, pp. 31–43.

Obuljen, N. 2004. *Why we need European cultural policies. The impact of EU enlargement on cultural policies in transition countries*. CPRA version. Available online at: www.encatc.org/pages/uploads/media/2004_cpra_publication.pdf (accessed 31 October 2015).

Palmer-Rae Associates. 2004. *European Cities and Capitals of Culture: Study Prepared for the European Commission*. Brussels: Palmer-Rae Associates.

Patel, K.K. 2013. *The Cultural Politics of Europe: European Capitals of Culture and European Union since the 1980s*. London: Routledge.

Psychogiopoulou, E. 2006. The cultural mainstreaming clause of Article 151(4) EC: Protection and promotion of cultural diversity or hidden cultural agenda? *European Law Journal*, 12, 575–592.

Psychogiopoulou, E. ed. 2015a. *Cultural Governance and the European Union: Protecting and Promoting Cultural Diversity in Europe*. Basingstoke: Palgrave Macmillan.

Psychogiopoulou, E. 2015b. The cultural open method of coordination. In E. Psychogiopoulou (ed.) *Cultural Governance and the European Union: Protecting and Promoting Cultural Diversity in Europe*. Basingstoke: Palgrave Macmillan, pp. 37–48.

Rittberger, B. 2012. The treaties of Paris. In E. Jones, A. Menon and S. Weatherill (eds.) *The Oxford Handbook of the European Union*. Oxford: Oxford University Press, pp. 79–94.

Sandell, T. 1996. Cultural issues, debate, and programmes. In P. Barbour (ed.) *The European Union Handbook*. Chicago and London: Fitzroy Dearborn, pp. 268–278.

Sarikakis, K. ed. 2007a. *Media and Cultural Policy in the European Union*. Amsterdam and New York: Rodopi.

Sarikakis, K. ed. 2007b. The place of media and cultural policy in the EU. In K. Sarikakis (ed.) *Media and Cultural Policy in the European Union*. Amsterdam and New York: Rodopi.

Sassatelli, M. 2002. Imagined Europe: the shaping of a European cultural identity through EU cultural policy. *European Journal of Social Theory*, 5(4), 435–451.

Sassatelli, M. 2006. The logic of Europeanizing cultural policy. In U.H. Meinhof & A. Triandafyllidou (eds.) *Transcultural Europe: Cultural Policy in a Changing Europe*. Basingstoke: Palgrave Macmillan, pp. 24–42.

Sassatelli, M. 2008. The European cultural space in the European cities of culture: Europeanization and cultural policy. *European Societies*, 10(2), 225–245.

Sassatelli, M. 2009. *Becoming Europeans: Cultural Identity and Cultural Policies*. Basingstoke: Palgrave Macmillan.

Shore, C. 2000. *Building Europe: The Cultural Politics of European Integration*. London and New York: Routledge.

Shore, C. 2001. The cultural policies of the European Union and cultural diversity. In T. Bennett (ed.) *Differing Diversities: Cultural Policy and Cultural Diversity*. Strasbourg: Council of Europe Publishing, pp. 107–121.

Shore, C. 2006. "In uno plures" (?) EU cultural policy and the governance of Europe. *Cultural Analysis*, 5, 7–26.

Staiger, U. 2013. The European Capitals of Culture in context: cultural policy and the European integration process. In K.K. Patel (ed.) *The Cultural Politics of Europe. European Capitals of Culture and European Union since the 1980s*. London: Routledge, pp. 19–38.

Tindemans, L. 1975. European Union. Report by Mr. Leo Tindemans, Prime Minister of Belgium, to the European Council. *Bulletin of the European Communities, Supplement*, 1/76.

Urwin, D.W. 1996. From a Europe of states to a state of Europe? An historical overview of the uniting of western Europe. In P. Barbour (ed.) *The European Union Handbook*. Chicago: Fitzroy Dearborn Publishers, pp. 3–14.

Versluis, E., M. Van Keulen, and P. Stephenson. 2011. *Analyzing the European Union Policy Process*. Basingstoke: Palgrave Macmillan.

Vidmar-Horvat, K. 2012. The predicament of intercultural dialogue: reconsidering the politics of culture and identity in the EU. *Cultural Sociology*, 6(1), 27–44.

Wallace, H. and W. Wallace. 2007. Overview: the European Union, politics and policy-making. In K.E. Jørgensen, M. Pollack, and B. Rosamond (eds.) *The Handbook of European Union Politics*. London: Sage, pp. 339–358.

Wheeler, M. 2004. Supranational regulation: television and the European Union (Review). *European Journal of Communication*, 19(3), 349–369.

Zahariadis, N. 2013. Building better theoretical frameworks of the EU's policy process. *Journal of European Public Policy*, 20(6), 807–816.

Part VI
Development and cultural policy

27

The international politics of the nexus 'culture and development'

Four policy agendas for whom and for what?

Antonios Vlassis

Culture and development are both ubiquitous and highly contested terms in social sciences. By paraphrasing Joseph Nye's quote on power and love (Nye 1990, p. 177), I should perhaps acknowledge two things: whereas culture, like love, is easier to experience than to define or measure, development seems to be the reverse; it's easier to define or measure than to experience. Of course, in recent years, there has been a proliferation of international norms and mechanisms dealing with the 'culture and development' nexus, and multiple actors have demonstrated a willingness to promote a specific set of ideas on the nexus. At the same time, the main question asked by an increasingly academic form of research is from which point of view to address the links among culture, cultural policies, and development (Stupples and Teaiwa 2016): sociological, economic, anthropological, institutional, or legal?

The chapter that follows is more empirical and analytical than theoretical. It does not aim to highlight if the increased attention has necessarily improved our understanding on the interactions between culture, cultural policies, and development. By contrast, it explores these interactions by contextualizing the dynamics of international policy agenda setting for this issue and by dealing with four main questions: who seeks to set an international policy agenda on the 'culture-development' nexus, for what reasons, under which conditions, and with which outcomes.

Here, I attempt to see how the relationship between culture and development has been defined and used by multiple actors in international relations, thereby demonstrating its importance for world politics. To address these questions, the chapter primarily discusses the initial political pathways through which the nexus travelled onto the international stage. It focuses, furthermore, on four policy agendas that have emerged within international arenas since the early 1990s: the free trade-focused approach, the policy agenda based on the diversity of cultural expressions, the creative economy perspective, and the policy agenda based on the intangible cultural heritage. In the end, I examine how the post-2015 development agenda and the arrival of digital age could produce new insights into the links among culture, cultural policies, and development.

'Culture and development' in the multilateral arenas: first steps

Since the 1970s, UNESCO – as the sole UN agency with a cultural mandate – has sought to feed the multilateral debate on the links between culture and development (De Beukelaer 2015, pp. 50–55; Garner 2016, pp. 71–102; Vlassis 2016a). In the wake of decolonization of the 1950s and 1960s, UNESCO was faced with the needs and expectations of a number of newly independent States, and with an approach that saw culture as 'a marker of identity' (UNESCO 2007, p. 76). In 1970, the organization took the initiative to organize the Intergovernmental Conference on the Institutional, Administrative and Financial Aspects of Culture in Venice, which acknowledged the responsibilities of national governments with respect to the cultural life of the nation (UNESCO 1970, pp. 7–11). Following this, in 1974, the 18e UNESCO General Conference established the International Fund for the Promotion of Culture, the first intergovernmental Fund dealing with the public support to cultural development. At the same time, UNESCO adopted in 1972 the World Heritage Convention, the first standard-setting instrument recognizing the importance of culture in international cultural policies. Additionally, UNESCO organized the World Conference on Cultural Policies (Mondiacult), held in Mexico in 1982 and attended by 960 participants from 126 States. The Mondiacult Declaration argued for strengthening the links between development and culture in the broadest sense, and it called for 'humanizing development' (UNESCO 1982).

Alongside such developments, UNESCO went through an unprecedented institutional and financial crisis. The political controversy for establishing a New World Information and Communication Order (NWICO) advanced under the leadership of the Non-Aligned movement led to the United States (US) and United Kingdom (UK) withdrawing from the organization in 1984. In fact, the 'Third World' countries denounced the dominance of information and cultural products from the Western media industries as bringing about a cultural imperialism and called on UNESCO to pay special attention to maintaining national cultures and political independence for the development of the global South. In 1980, UNESCO published the report *Many Voices, One World*, prepared by the International Commission for the Study of Communication Problems chaired by Irish Nobel Prize winner Sean MacBride. The report stressed that the implementation of the free flow principle had resulted in an imbalance in international information exchanges, and it called for a more equitable circulation of information and cultural products. By contrast, the main US arguments for their withdrawal focused on two points: (i) an international debate threatening the 'free flow information' and 'free trade' principles in media industries; (ii) a harsh critique of the politicization of the UNESCO, and of a lack of efficiency, relevance and pragmatism on the part of the organization (Imber 1989).

Despite financial and institutional challenges during the 1980s and 1990s,[1] UNESCO launched the World Decade for Cultural Development (1988–1997), the most tangible result of the Mondiacult conference, which aimed to place culture at the heart of development. As part of that Decade, in 1991, UNESCO established the World Commission on Culture and Development, chaired by former UN Secretary-General Javier Pérez de Cuéllar. In 1996, the Commission presented the report *Our Creative Diversity*. As argued in the report, "is culture an aspect or a means of 'development', the latter understood as material progress, or is culture the end and aim of 'development', the latter understood as the flourishing of human existence in its forms and as a whole?" (World Commission on Culture and Development 1996, p. 13). In the same vein, the Stockholm Intergovernmental Conference on Cultural Policies for Development was held in 1998, again aiming to embed cultural policy as a key component of development strategy (objective 1 of the Action Plan on Cultural Policies for Development) and to make more human and financial resources available for cultural development (objective 5 of the Action Plan on Cultural Policies for Development). Yet all these initiatives did not advance far enough towards more prescriptive actions. The debates were thus limited to broad moral commitments, without establishing institutional mechanisms and standard-setting instruments.

Lastly, it's worth pointing out that these initiatives were based on the UN debates with reference to an alternative approach of development, beyond its economic aspects. The last two decades of the twentieth century saw the flourishing of new conceptions questioning economic and material criteria as hegemonic policy principles of development: the adoption of the Declaration on the Right to Development in 1986, the publication of the Brundtland Report 'Our Common Future' prepared by the United Nations Commission on Environment and Development in 1987, and the first publication of the Human Development Report in 1990 commissioned by the United Nations Development Program (UNDP) and based on Amartya Sen's philosophical ideas. Such initiatives paid attention to the non-economic dimensions of development and considered development as a multifaceted problem. That is, growth is not an end in itself but needs to have a positive impact on human well-being. Moreover, it was argued that development should be measured by a broad spectrum of data, including political rights, economic and social freedoms, nutrition, governance structures, gender policies, the health system, and environmental and educational policies (Rist 2007, pp. 345–416).

Four policy agendas on the 'culture-development' nexus

As Risse (1994) said, "ideas do not float freely" on the international stage, but they are linked to actors and institutions. With this in mind, the agenda setting as regards the 'culture-development' nexus is closely attached to interests and resources of a wide variety of actors who exercise power across borders, mobilize multiple strategies, and promote their own specific set of ideas. In this respect, this section explores the political dynamics of the setting of four policy agendas on the nexus, highlighting how the nexus is defined, which issues are created, and which norms and programs are established.

A free trade-focused approach on development

Since the early 1990s, the deregulation of cultural markets and the elimination of regulatory and financial measures in the cultural sector, as prominent conditions of development for the sector, have been a major priority of the US diplomacy as well as a stumbling block in the process of the international and regional economic integration (Vlassis 2015a). As Miller and Yúdice (2002, p. 174) note, "The US motivation was obvious: replacing national societies of culture with a global society of alleged efficiency". The goal of the US administration, followed mainly by several powerful industrial associations such as the Motion Picture Association of America, was to include cultural goods and services within the agenda of international trade negotiations, including the last period of negotiations on the General Agreement on Trade in Services (GATS) of the World Trade Organization (WTO) in 1993; the negotiations on the Multilateral Agreement on Investment within the Organization for Economic Cooperation and Development; and the negotiations around free trade agreement (FTA) between the US and Canada brought into force in 1989, as well as on the North American Free Trade Agreement among US, Canada, and Mexico entered into force in 1994.

The US position was largely associated with the Washington consensus in development policies, which has gained ascension since the end of the Cold War and the collapse of the bipolar world order. The consensus asserts that global welfare would be maximized by the liberalization of trade, finance, and investment, and by restructuring national economies to provide an enabling environment for capital (Rist 2007). Consequently, the Washington consensus called for governments to focus on macroeconomic criteria and to open up their economies to market forces. In this regard, by the 1990s, as neoliberalism emerged triumphant, the assumption was cultural policies should admit an underlying principle that "human well-being can best be advanced by liberating individual entrepreneurial freedoms and skills within an institutional framework characterized by strong private property rights, free markets, and free trade" (Harvey 2005, p. 2).

Even though a coalition of actors, driven by France and Canada, defended the term 'cultural exception' (*exception culturelle*) in order to protect cultural policies and to exclude cultural goods and services from the agenda of the trade negotiations, the WTO does have a competence for trade of cultural services, and the latter are not permanently excluded from WTO negotiations (Pauwels and Loisen 2003). As of February 2016, 36 WTO members have agreed to make some commitments in the audiovisual services sector.[2] Interestingly, whereas 18 governments[3] of 134 founding members of the WTO took commitments in 1995, during the period from 1996 to 2016, 18 governments[4] of the 27 new WTO members agreed to be subject to certain restrictions in the audiovisual sector. This reveals not only the strong US pressures – mostly to the economically developing countries – in order to push the liberalization of their audiovisual sector forward, but also the fact that a government negotiates its accession to the WTO without being able to build political coalitions favoring the protection of cultural policies.

Likewise, the US sought to judicialize its trade disputes in terms of cultural services through the WTO Dispute Settlement Body. In 2009, following a complaint lodged by the US administration in 2007, the WTO condemned China for its trade practices within the cultural sector and especially for its strict regulatory policies on audiovisual services, such as the annual quota of 20 foreign films to be distributed, and revenue sharing (Neuwirth 2010; Vlassis 2016b). As a result, the US and China signed a 'Memorandum of Understanding on WTO Related Problems in the Film Industry', which provides that China allows the importation of 14 more Hollywood movies and increased the percentage of sharing revenues to the foreign operators from 13 percent to 25 percent.

However, since 2001 (the Doha Round), the WTO has struggled to conclude a round of trade negotiations among its members, illustrating an institutional crisis of its multilateral model. The US administration, therefore, has opted for the bilateral pathway, concluding FTAs with several countries. During bilateral negotiations, the lack of human resources and of expertise, the lack of pressure from culture professional organizations – often loosely organized and representing poorly developed industries, as well as the ability of other more powerful sectors to influence the decision-making process, often lead developing countries to give in to the demands of trading partners, such as the US, and to not preserve the cultural field (Vlassis and Richieri Hanania 2014; Gagné 2016). Conversely, the bilateral nature of negotiations offers a power asymmetry to the benefit of the US administration, whereby the negotiating countries cannot hide behind alliances in favor of cultural policies and the recognition of cultural specificity. That is, seven countries – Oman, Panama, Bahrain, Guatemala, Honduras, Nicaragua, and El Salvador – inscribed few reservations within their bilateral agreements with the US regarding the cultural sector; therefore, they have significantly limited their capacity to implement public policies in that sector.

Diversity of cultural expressions: recognizing cultural industries in development policies

Rapid financial globalization, international and regional economic integration, and the liberalization of trade exchanges raised major concerns for several actors over the implications for cultural policies, flows of cultural goods and services, and cultural diversity. By the end of the 1990s, an alliance of actors including national governments, such as Canada and France; intergovernmental organizations, such as *Organisation internationale de la Francophonie* and Council of Europe; sub-national governments (Quebec and Catalonia); and non-governmental organizations (National Coalitions for Cultural Diversity[5]) has mobilized in favor of 'the diversity of cultural expressions' and the establishment of an international policy tool on this principle (Musitelli 2005; Vlassis 2015a).

Just as during the debate on the NWICO, several countries made a strong plea for balanced and equitable flows of cultural goods and services around the world, whereas the US administration called for two policy principles: free trade and free flow of information and images. Following hard negotiations on a number of issues such as the link between trade agreements and culture, the appropriate cultural policies for the protection and promotion of diversity of cultural expressions, or the type of contributions for a fund for cultural diversity, a new standard-setting instrument – the Convention on the Protection and the Promotion of Diversity of Cultural Expressions (hereafter CDCE) – was adopted by UNESCO in 2005. As of December 2016, it has received the support of 144 Member States and of the European Union (EU). Instead, the US – fierce opponent of the CDCE – Russia, Japan, Turkey, Pakistan, as well as several Southeast Asian (Malaysia, Myanmar, Philippines, Singapore, Thailand) and Middle Eastern (Iran, Israel, Lebanon, Saudi Arabia, Syria) countries have not yet ratified the CDCE.

The object of the CDCE does not refer to cultural diversity in the broadest sense of the term, but to a specific aspect of the latter with reference to the cultural goods and services created, produced and distributed by cultural industries. The CDCE recognizes the specificity of cultural goods and services and the importance of cultural policies for the protection and promotion of the diversity of cultural expressions. Furthermore, even though the main interest of CDCE's promoters was to offer an international culture-driven response towards the international trade regime, the CDCE included also concrete provisions to the link 'culture and development'. These provisions are the result of a request by several developing countries and independent experts that did not want to make the CDCE a normative tool serving only the interests of developed countries (Vlassis 2011, p. 498).

The CDCE stipulates the integration of cultural industries in sustainable development (Article 13), and it aims to strengthen international cultural cooperation through various tools, such as the expert and information exchange among the Parties (Articles 9 and 19), the collaborative arrangements (Article 15), and the preferential treatment for developing countries (Article 16) as well as the setting up of the International Fund for Cultural Diversity (IFCD), a multi-donor voluntary fund established under Article 18 (Albornoz 2016; Vlassis 2014). As of March 2017, the IFCD has supported 84 projects in 49 developing countries, and the total contributions received reach 8.8 million USD. More than 75 percent of the projects are either in Africa or in Latin America and the Caribbean. Yet the contributions are increasingly disparate. On the one hand, the combined contributions of France, Finland and Norway reach more than 3.8 million USD,[6] and those of three new international powers, namely, Brazil, China, and Mexico, are so far regular and dynamic, reaching more than 1.1

million USD. On the other hand, the UK, the Netherlands, Republic of Korea and Italy, very developed countries in terms of cultural goods and services, have not yet contributed to the IFCD resources.

In addition, throughout 2011–2015, UNESCO established an expert facility project, funded by the EU in order to implement the CDCE through the strengthening of the system of governance for cultural industries in developing countries. Besides, the expert facility activities for 2015–2017 are funded with the support of Swedish Agency for International Development Cooperation, which also gave resources for the elaboration of the 2005 Convention Global Report published in 2015. In this respect, during the period of 2011–2017, the project has allocated in total €3.7 million for creating a pool of 57 experts in public policies for cultural industries. Twenty-five technical assistance missions have been put in place in order to transfer knowledge and know-how towards countries in Africa (Burkina Faso, Democratic Republic of the Congo, Kenya, Malawi, Mauritius, Morocco, Niger, Rwanda, Seychelles, Senegal, Tunisia, Zimbabwe), Latin America (Argentina, Colombia, Honduras), Asia (Cambodia, Indonesia, Vietnam), and the Caribbean (Barbados, Cuba, Haiti).

In a similar vein, the Protocol on Cultural Cooperation is a new policy instrument elaborated by the European Commission in order to promote the CDCE's implementation through trade agreements, and especially Article 16 regarding the 'Preferential treatment for developing countries' (Loisen and De Ville 2011; Vlassis 2016c). Since 2008, the Commission has introduced in total four protocols, with the Caribbean States (Cariforum) signed in 2008, with the Republic of Korea concluded in 2009, with Central America signed in 2010, and with Peru/Colombia concluded in 2011.

Creative economy: linking 'culture and development' to informational society

Since the early 2000s, the United Nations Conference on Trade and Development (UNCTAD), an international organization traditionally "reflecting the aspirations and needs of least developed countries" (Davies and Woodward 2014, p. 348), has elaborated a new approach on the nexus 'culture and development', based on the concept of 'creative economy', which is seen as a "feasible development option" (UNCTAD 2010). Under the leadership of the UNCTAD Secretary-General from 1995 and 2004, Rubens Ricupero, former Brazilian minister of finance, and the support of Brazilian culture minister Gilberto Gil, the UNCTAD XI Conference held in Brazil in 2004 introduced the creative industries into the international economic and development agenda (Isar 2008). The Sao Paulo Consensus, adopted by 153 Member States, stressed, "The international community should support national efforts of developing countries to increase their participation in and benefit from dynamic sectors and to foster, protect and promote their creative industries" (UNCTAD 2004, p. 19). In this context, a UN multi-agency Partnership for Technical Assistance for Enhancing the Creative Economy in Developing Countries has established at a 'UN Global South-South Creative Economy Symposium' held in Shanghai (China) in December 2005. This partnership was mobilized for the preparation of the first Creative Economy report, launched during the UNCTAD XII Conference in Ghana in 2008.

The aim of this policy-oriented report was to make an intellectual contribution of UN agencies to the discussions of creative economy with a view to assist governments in formulating policies and to reshape the development agenda with creative industries in mind. The report gives a central role in the linkage among creativity, intellectual property, knowledge, and access to information. It sees the creative industries as a key new growth sector of the global economy and as contributors to wealth creation, employment growth, and export performance for developing countries, giving a potential to diversify their economies.

> "The creative economy has become an even stronger driver of development: world trade of creative goods and services totaled a record 624 billion USD in 2011, more than doubling between 2002 and 2011. The average annual growth rate of the sector during that period was 8.8 percent, and the exports of creative goods were even stronger in developing countries, averaging 12.1 percent in growth annually over the same period".
>
> *(UNCTAD 2013, p. 153)*

In fact, the UNCTAD classification of creative industries seems to "integrate and assimilate the cultural industries" (Tremblay 2008, p. 67), and it is divided into four broad categories: cultural heritage, arts, media, and functional creations (design, architecture, advertising, research and development, computer services, etc.). UNCTAD and UNDP took the lead in preparing the 2008 and 2010 reports,[7] whereas the 2013 report was notably executed by UNESCO and UNDP. The reports brought contributions from UNCTAD, UNDP, UNESCO, World Intellectual Property Organization (WIPO), and International Trade Centre. Moreover, the last few years have seen a boom in interest in the idea of 'creative industries'. That is, the creative economy policy strategy was manifested in initiatives across several Latin American, Caribbean, and Asian countries, such as Peru, Colombia, Barbados, Jamaica, Singapore, Thailand, Taiwan, or even in EU, whose new program for the cultural and creative sectors (2014–2020, budget €1.46 billion) is called *Creative Europe* (Littoz-Monnet 2012).

Noteworthy is that the concept 'Creative industries' first has been elaborated in Anglo-Saxon countries (Garnham 2005; Cunningham 2009). It has emerged in Australia with the Labour government's 'Creative nation' initiative of 1994. It was given wider exposure with the election of 'New Labour' in the UK in 1997 when the Blair government set up the Creative Industries Task Force as a central activity of its new Department of Culture, Media and Sport. Hence, it established the creative industries "as a plank of the UK's 'post-industrial' economy", strongly linked to policy agendas surrounding technological convergence, innovation policy, and information society and going beyond the traditional ideas of the subsidized arts (Flew and Cunningham 2010, p. 113).

As Galloway and Dunlop (2007, p. 18) argued, culture was abandoned as elitist and exclusive, whereas 'creativity' was embraced as democratic and inclusive. In the early 2000s, policy consultant and journalist John Howkins (2001) claimed in an influential and widely read book that creative economy would be the dominant economic form in the twenty-first century. In the meantime, the US academic and policy consultant Richard Florida (2002) popularized the idea that creativity is central to new economies, leading to a change in the class system itself, with the rise of a 'new creative class' (Hesmondhalgh 2008, pp. 560–561). In this context, in 2008, the document *Creative Britain* "sets out an ambitious agenda which sought to reiterate the significance of the creative industries to the UK's economic future" (Banks and O'Connor 2009, p. 365). Nevertheless, several countries that made a strong plea for the cultural exception (see above) appeared reluctant to the new concept, insofar as the amalgamation of cultural industries and creative economy harbors a real danger: "that of watering down the specificity of cultural industries and the weakening of arguments in favor of the intervention of public authority" (Tremblay 2008, p. 83).

Intangible cultural heritage: deconstructing the Western development paradigm?

At a diplomatic level, the building of the Convention for the Safeguarding of the Intangible Cultural Heritage (hereafter CSICH) is mainly based on the political support of non-Western countries, such as Japan – the first country that recognized the 'intangible cultural properties' in 1950 – Republic of Korea, China, Turkey, Peru, and Colombia. The objective was to rebalance the global political economy of the cultural heritage and to put on the international cultural policy agenda an issue-area of their choice.

The first international legal instrument dealing with the preservation of the intangible cultural heritage was the Recommendation on the Safeguarding of Traditional Culture and Folklore adopted by UNESCO in 1989. Subsequently, several initiatives have affirmed the necessity for a convention that would address the protection of intangible cultural heritage: the establishment of the UNESCO-Japan Funds-in-Trust for the Preservation and Promotion of the Intangible Cultural Heritage in 1993; the program 'Living Human Treasures' proposed by the Republic of Korea in 1993, identifying persons who possess to a high degree the knowledge and skills for performing or recreating specific elements of the intangible cultural heritage; and the program titled 'Proclamation of Masterpieces of Oral and Intangible Cultural Heritage of Humanity' in 1997 (Kozymka 2014). At the end of 1990s, several governments were already committed to safeguard intangible cultural heritage as their national heritage, revealing the bottom-up character of the Convention: according to UNESCO's 2000 World Cultural Report, 57 States adopted national cultural policies related to intangible cultural heritage and 80 States provided moral or economic support to individuals and institutions promoting intangible heritage (UNESCO 2000, p. 175).

The political process to the adoption in 2003 of the CSICH has also been facilitated by two factors. First, the international debate on intangible heritage met the cultural turn in development questioning Western ethnocentrism. At the end of 1990s, several multilateral institutions such as World Bank, Inter-American Development Bank and UNDP began to focus on 'culturally appropriate development' (Stupples 2014) or 'culturally sensitive approaches' (Sims 2015, p. 6)[8]. Second, the intangible cultural heritage took part of the main mandate's priorities of the UNESCO's Director-General, Kōichirō Matsuura, a Japanese career diplomat, elected in 1999.

The CSICH recognizes a new type of heritage as an expression of the cultural identity of peoples and communities, thereby questioning the Western and monumental approach on heritage, depending on the 1972 World Heritage Convention and based on a sacralization of the object rather than on the practices. In turn, the CSICH deals with the safeguarding of intangible cultural heritage, meaning the practices, representations, expressions, knowledge, and skills that communities, groups, and, in some cases, individuals recognize as part of their cultural heritage. It proposes five broad domains in which intangible cultural heritage is manifested: oral traditions and expressions; performing arts; social practices, rituals, and festive events; knowledge and practices concerning nature and the universe; and traditional craftsmanship. The Convention thus stresses the importance of international cooperation for development and provides for the establishment of the Fund for the Safeguarding of the Intangible Cultural Heritage. "The intangible cultural heritage is the mainspring of cultural diversity and a guarantee of sustainable development" (UNESCO 2007, p. 133).[9]

Clearly, the World Heritage List, inspired by movable cultural property and material cultural expressions, which are specifically Western concepts, favors European monuments and buildings, and is unbalanced in terms of regional distribution (Frey and Steiner 2011). As of

December 2016, 52.5 percent of all cultural sites 'of outstanding universal value' are to be found in Europe and North America – 426 out of 814 cultural sites.

On the one hand, accompanied by fears of global cultural homogenization and hegemony by the West, the CSICH questions "Western ethnocentrism as the implicit culture of developmentalism" as well as the paradigm 'modernization/westernization'. In this respect, it illustrates "the retreat from structural and macro approaches in development practices in favor of micro and actor-oriented approaches" (Nederveen Pieterse 1995, p. 176). Consequently, it strongly challenges the Eurocentricity of the World Heritage List. As of December 2016, 40 percent of all the elements within the List of Intangible Cultural Heritage are to be found in 11 non-Western countries (171 out of 430 inscribed elements): China (39), Japan (21), Republic of Korea (19), Turkey (15), Mongolia (13), India (13), Iran (12), Vietnam (11), Peru (10), Colombia (9), and Mexico (9). Obviously, "the West is no longer a privileged interlocutor in the age of polycentrism" (Nederveen Pieterse 1995, p. 176).

On the other hand, CSICH Article 15 recognizes the communities as a main actor for creating, maintaining, and transmitting intangible cultural heritage. This has led several Western countries to wonder about the risks from a political use of the CSICH and to express reluctance about the promotion of the 'intangible cultural heritage' on the international development agenda. In this sense, five Anglo-Saxon countries with strong communitarian traditions, namely the US, Canada, Australia, New Zealand, and the UK, have not yet ratified the CSICH. They particularly worried either about the manipulation of the CSICH by the country's communities or the exploitation by the central national government of the communities' heritage (Maguet 2011). Last but not least, note too that Finland, Sweden, Denmark, and the Netherlands, parties to the CSICH, have not proposed any element for inscription within the List of the Intangible Cultural Heritage.

Conclusion: beyond the four policy agendas?

Today, the interactions among culture, cultural policies, and development could be defined in new ways by the rising of two major issues: the post-2015 UN development agenda and the arrival of digital age, which have spurred additional calls for new norms and new responsibilities for the actors involved.

On the one hand, throughout 2012–2015, several actors were advocating that culture be explicitly integrated within the post-2015 agenda on the Sustainable Development Goals, replacing the Millennium Development Goals. UNESCO, followed by many Latin American, African, and Asian countries, intergovernmental organizations (UNCTAD, UNDP), and NGOs on cultural affairs, stressed that culture should play an essential role in the social, environmental, and economic development pillars of sustainable development agenda. Yet the political strategy of these actors was a broad and potentially contradictory mixture of components from three of the policy agendas examined above: diversity of cultural expressions, intangible cultural heritage, and creative economy. Unsurprisingly perhaps, it included ambivalent policy principles relating to crucial issues: the role of government policy in the cultural sector, the importance of marketization and of private entrepreneurship in the domain of culture, and the impact of indigenous peoples and local communities in maintaining and promoting traditional cultural expressions. Thus, references to culture in the final version of the agenda are minor. Notably, international mobilization for the inclusion of culture in the post-2015 development agenda faced the reluctance of developed countries, based on two main arguments. One, culture is broad, abstract, and has no quantifiable domain, complicated by developed countries seeking to rationalize the objectives and economic resources of the future UN development agenda and emphasizing an operationalized agenda dealing with measurable targets and indicators. Two, culture is a controversial concept, raising the risks of cultural relativism. In other words, culture could justify policy practices that would be the reverse of the previous national commitments to key priorities of the agenda, such as human rights, status of women, or environmental protection (Vlassis 2015b, pp. 1655–1657).

On the other hand, the reality of the dematerialization of cultural content, of technological convergence, and of the deterritorialisation of cultural offerings raises enormous challenges for the *raison d'être* of cultural policies. New powerful digital actors such as content aggregators (iTunes), video sharing websites (YouTube), video on demand services (Netflix), social networking services (Facebook), electronic commerce companies (Amazon) have unequalled capacities to disseminate cultural expressions and "exercise considerable influence over whether and how cultural expressions can be accessed, in turn controlling much of the cultural offerings and influencing the evolution of the diversity of cultural expressions" (Guèvremont 2015, p. 149). Besides, as the European Digital Agenda highlighted, the free trade approach and the creative economy brand become increasingly attractive for the formulation of cultural policies. This suggests laying emphasis on economic competitiveness, innovation, and free flow of cultural contents. This would be superficially effective, insofar as regulatory measures seem to be obsolete at the digital age and the great multiplication of cultural offers and the remarkable facilitation of access give the illusion of balanced flow of cultural contents.

However, at the end of the day, it should be acknowledged that the arrival of the digital age turns upside down the components of the four policy agendas discussed above, and it poses five significant opportunities and risks for the interactions among culture, cultural policies, and development (Rioux et al. 2015, p. 10): One, the greater affordability of cultural products and the possibility to reach dispersed and far away publics, but decreasing financial means because of piracy, free sharing, and the marginalization of certain populations because of this digital fracture. Two, the establishment of new forms of financing (participative financing), but the emergence of new powerful actors playing a decisive role in access to cultural content. Three, the increasing accessibility of content on the web, but institutional and economic uncertainties. Four, hyper-multiplication of cultural contents, but the amplification of a process of concentration in Internet economic powers controlling data and networks. Five, the potential strengthening of international cultural exchanges, but major problems of effectiveness of national cultural policies regarding regulations, fiscal systems, and property rights regimes.

Notes

1 The UK and the US returned to UNESCO in 1997 and in 2003, respectively.
2 According to the WTO, the audiovisual sector includes motion picture and videotape production and distribution services, motion picture projection services, radio and television services, and sound recording.
3 Central African Republic, Dominican Republic, El Salvador, Hong Kong, India, Israel, Japan, Kenya, Republic of Korea, Lesotho, Malaysia, Mexico, New Zeeland, Nicaragua, Singapore, Thailand, US, and Vietnam.
4 Armenia, Cape Verde, China, Gambia, Georgia, Jordan, Kyrgyzstan, Oman, Panama, Russia, Samoa, Saudi Arabia, Seychelles, Taiwan, Tajikistan, Tonga, Vanuatu, and Yemen.
5 In September 2007, the International Federation of the Coalitions for Cultural Diversity was created by 42 national coalitions for cultural diversity grouping in the aggregate more than 600 cultural professional organizations representing creators, artists, independent producers, distributors,

broadcasters, and editors in the publishing, motion picture, television, music, performing arts, and visual art fields. The Federation is incorporated in Canada and has its Secretariat in Montreal.

6 It's worth noting that many countries seek to favor more the development aid by bilateral or plurilateral channels perhaps more efficient than the multilateral institutions. For instance, it's important to mention two policy instruments towards the film cooperation: the French financial aid *Aides aux cinemas du monde,* with an annual budget of €6 million and the program IBERMEDIA, including Spain, Portugal, and several countries in Latin America, to which Spain has contributed 36 million USD in the period of 1998–2014.

7 The 2008 and 2010 Creative Economy Reports have been coordinated by Edna dos Santos (Brazil), a development economist working as Chief of the UNCTAD Creative Economy and Industries Program and Francisco Simplicio (Brazil), Chief of the Division for Knowledge Management and Operations of the UNDP Special Unit for South-South Cooperation, with the strong support of Yiping Zhou, former senior trade official for the Chinese government and Director of the UNDP Special Unit for South-South Cooperation.

8 The World Bank, under the leadership of its former Egyptian vice president Ismaïl Serageldin (1992–2000), made a plea for the contribution of culture and identity of peoples to economic development. In 1998, the organization hosted, with UNESCO's sponsorship, the international conference 'Culture and development at the Millennium: the Challenge and the Response' in Washington DC, and in 1999, it published the report *Culture and Sustainable Development: A Framework for Action.*

9 It's worth mentioning that in 2000, the WIPO members established an Intergovernmental Committee on Intellectual Property and Genetic Resources, Traditional Knowledge and Folklore. In 2009, they tasked the Committee to undertake negotiations for the development of an international standard-setting instrument that would give traditional knowledge, genetic resources, and traditional cultural expressions effective protection.

References

Albornoz, L., 2016. The International Fund for Cultural Diversity: a new tool for cooperation in the audiovisual field. *International Journal of Cultural Policy,* 22(4), 553–573.

Banks, M. and O'Connor, J., 2009. After the creative industries. *International Journal of Cultural Policy,* 15(4), 365–373.

Cunningham, S., 2009. Trojan horse or Rorschach blot? Creative industries discourse around the world. *International Journal of Cultural Policy,* 15(4), 375–386.

Davies, M. and Woodward, R., 2014. *International Organizations: A Companion.* Cheltenham: Edward Elgar.

De Beukelaer, C., 2015. *Developing Cultural Industries: Learning from the Palimpsest of Practice.* Amsterdam: European Cultural Foundation.

Flew, T. and Cunningham, S., 2010. Creative industries after the first decade of debate. *The Information Society,* 26(2), 113–123.

Florida, R., 2002. *The Rise of the Creative Class.* New York: Basic Books.

Frey, B. and Steiner, L., 2011. World Heritage List: does it make sense? *International Journal of Cultural Policy,* 17(5), 555–573.

Gagné, G., 2016. *The Trade and Culture Debate: Evidence from US Trade Agreements.* Lanham: Lexington Books.

Galloway, S. and Dunlop, S., 2007. A Critique of Definitions of the Cultural and Creative Industries In Public Policy. *International Journal of Cultural Policy,* 13(1), 17–31.

Garner, B., 2016. *The Politics of Cultural Development. Trade, Cultural Policy and the UNESCO Convention on Cultural Diversity.* London: Routledge.

Garnham, N., 2005. From cultural to creative industries. *International Journal of Cultural Policy,* 11(1), 15–29.

Guèvremont, V., 2015. The 2005 convention in the digital age. In C. De Beukelaer, M. Pyykkönen, J. P. Singh (eds.), *Globalization, Culture, and Development.* New York: Palgrave MacMillan, 147–159.

Harvey, D., 2005. *A Brief History of Neoliberalism.* Oxford: Oxford University Press.

Hesmondhalgh, D., 2008. Cultural and creative industries. In T. Bennett and J. Frow (eds.), *The Sage Handbook of Cultural Analysis.* London: Sage Publications, 552–569.

Howkins, J., 2001. *The Creative Economy: How People Make Money from Ideas.* London: Penguin Books.

Imber, M., 1989. *The USA, ILO, UNESCO, and IAEA. Politicization and Withdrawal in the Specialized Agencies.* New York: St Martin's Press.

Isar, Y. R., 2008. The intergovernmental policy actors. In H. K. Anheier and Y. R. Isar (eds.), *The Cultural Economy.* London: Sage Publications, 108–120.

Kozymka, I., 2014. *The Diplomacy of Culture. The Role of UNESCO in Sustaining Cultural Diversity.* London: Palgrave Macmillan.

Littoz-Monnet, A., 2012. Agenda-setting dynamics at the EU level: the case of the EU cultural policy. *European Integration,* 34(5), 505–522.

Loisen, J. and De Ville, F., 2011. The EU-Korea protocol on cultural cooperation: toward cultural diversity or cultural deficit? *International Journal of Communication,* 5, 254–271.

Maguet, F., 2011. L'image des communautés dans l'espace public. In C. Bortolotto (ed.), *Le patrimoine culturel immatériel. Enjeux d'une nouvelle catégorie.* Paris: Éditions de la Maison des sciences de l'homme.

Miller, T. and Yúdice, G., 2002. *Cultural Policy.* London: Sage Publications.

Musitelli, J., 2005. L'invention de la diversité culturelle. *Annuaire français de droit International,* 51, 512–523.

Nederveen Pieterse, J., 1995. The cultural turn in development: questions of power. *The European Journal of Development Research,* 7(1), 176–192.

Neuwirth, R. J., 2010. The 'Culture and Trade Debate' Continues: the UNESCO Convention in Light of the WTO Reports in *China – Publications and Audiovisual Products*: Between Amnesia or *Déjà Vu? Journal of World Trade,* 44(6), 1333–1356.

Nye, S. J., 1990. The changing nature of world power. *Political Studies Quarterly,* 105(2), 177–192.

Pauwels, C. and Loisen, J., 2003. The WTO and the audiovisual sector. Economic free trade vs cultural horse trading? *European Journal of Communication,* 18(3), 291–313.

Rioux, M., Deblock, C., Gagné, G., Tchéhouali, D., Fontaine-Skronski K., Vlassis, A., 2015. *For a Diversified Networked Culture. Bringing the Convention on the Protection and Promotion of the Diversity of Cultural Expressions in the Digital Age.* Montreal: Centre d'études sur l'intégration et la mondialisation.

Risse, T., 1994. Ideas do not float freely: transnational coalitions, domestic structure and the end of the cold war. *International Organization,* 48(2), 185–214.

Rist, G., 2007. *Le développement, histoire d'une croyance occidentale.* 3rd edition. Paris: Presses de SciencesPo.

Sims, K., 2015. Culture, community-oriented learning and the post-2015 development agenda: a view from Laos. *Third World Quarterly,* 36(10), 1922–1943.

Stupples, P., 2014. Creative contributions: the role of the arts and the cultural sector in development. *Progress in Development Studies,* 14(2), 115–130.

Stupples P. and Teaiwa, K., eds, 2016. *Contemporary perspectives on Art and International Development.* London: Routledge.

Tremblay, G., 2008. Industries culturelles, économie créative et société de l'information. *Global Media Journal – Edition canadienne,* 1(1), 65–88.

UNCTAD, 2004. *Sao Paulo Consensus,* TD/410, UNCTAD, 25 June.

UNCTAD, 2010. *Creative Economy Report: A Feasible Development Option.* New York: UNDP-UNCTAD.

UNESCO, 1970. *Rapport final: Conférence intergouvernementale sur les aspects institutionnels, administratifs et financiers des politiques culturelles.* Venice: UNESCO.

UNESCO, 1982. *Mexico City Declaration on Cultural Policies.* Mexico: UNESCO.

UNESCO, 2000. *World Culture Report 2000: Cultural Diversity, Conflict and Pluralism.* Paris: UNESCO.

UNESCO, 2007. *UNESCO and the Question of Cultural Diversity, 1946–2007: Review and Strategies.* Paris: UNESCO.

UNESCO-UNDP, 2013. *Creative Economy Report 2013.* New York, Paris: UNESCO/UNDP.

Vlassis, A., 2011. La mise en œuvre de la Convention sur la diversité des expressions culturelles: portée et enjeux de l'interface 'commerce-culture'. *Études internationales,* 42(4), 493–510.

Vlassis, A., 2014. Cultural development and technical and financial assistance on the basis of the CDCE. In L. Richieri Hanania (ed.), *Cultural Diversity in International Law: Effectiveness and Normativity of the 2005 Convention on Diversity of Cultural Expressions.* London: Routledge, 167–180.

Vlassis, A., 2015a. *Gouvernance mondiale et culture: de l'exception à la diversité.* Liège: Presses de l'Université de Liège.

Vlassis, A., 2015b. Culture in the post-2015 development agenda: the anatomy of an international mobilization. *Third World Quarterly*, 36(9), 1649–1662.

Vlassis, A., 2016a. UNESCO, cultural industries and the international development agenda: between modest recognition and reluctance. In P. Stupples and K. Teaiwa (eds.), *Contemporary Perspectives on Art and International Development*. London: Routledge, 48–63.

Vlassis, A., 2016b. Soft power, global governance of cultural industries and rising powers: the case of China. *International Journal of Cultural Policy*, 22(4), 481–496.

Vlassis, A., 2016c. European Commission, trade agreements and diversity of cultural expressions: between autonomy and influence. *European Journal of Communication*, 31(4), 446–461.

Vlassis, A. and Richieri-Hanania, L., 2014. Effects of the Convention on trade negotiations. In L. Richieri Hanania (ed.), *Cultural Diversity in International Law: Effectiveness and Normativity of the 2005 Convention on Diversity of Cultural Expressions*. London: Routledge, 25–39.

World Commission on Culture and Development, 1996. *Our Creative Diversity*. Paris: UNESCO.

28

Reimagining development in times of crises

Cultural policies, social imagination, and the creative economy in Puerto Rico

Mareia Quintero Rivera and Javier J. Hernández Acosta

Introduction

This essay intends to articulate a situated reflection based on the authors' direct involvement in the developing of cultural policies through participatory methodologies, in the recent experience of the Commission for Cultural Development (CODECU). Puerto Rico represents a singular case, with historical and cultural parallels with Latin America, but subject to the legal, political, and trade framework of the United States. We propose to understand cultural policies not as an instrument for the advancement of given development agendas, but as a vital arena for discussing and re-imagining development strategies. Debates on culture in Puerto Rico are generally subordinated to political or economic issues. In the face of an unparalleled economic and financial crisis, cultural policies tend to be seen as irrelevant. But they can also wake up passions for its connotations in controversies over the colonial question and political status. We argue that culture is crucial for facing present dilemmas in Puerto Rican society and that its place in public policy should be urgently redefined.

Once seen as a showcase of democracy and development, Puerto Rico is now submerged in a multidimensional crisis. After a decade of economic recession, a heavily indebted government with no political powers to decide how to manage its financial emergency, critical structural problems in its economy, a significant presence of drug trafficking with its detrimental social consequences, and growing citizenship distrust in public institutions and the political process, no signs of hope are detected on the nearby horizon. Within this context, the Commission for Cultural Development (CODECU), created in 2013, faced the challenge of thinking about the role cultural policies could perform in helping the island to move ahead. Named by the former governor as an independent and non-remunerated body, CODECU counted on a small amount of public resources to put forward a participatory process aimed at proposing a cultural policy. In June 2015, the Commission presented its final report, together with a study of the cultural ecosystem in Puerto Rico, developed as part of its research process.

To set the basis for a reflection of our experience in CODECU, we start by addressing current debates around culture and development, stressing the importance of public policies committed to enabling citizens' social agency and autonomy in the face of hegemonic values. Second, we present a historical synthesis of the evolution of cultural policies in Puerto Rico, pointing to the particularities of the island's cultural dynamics, as a consequence of colonial subjection to the United States, and tracing the development of the main public cultural institutions.

CODECU's initial proposal was based on two main ideas: first that a cultural policy should arise from an open and active public discussion and second that it must incorporate a research process to generate a radiography of cultural dynamics in the island. The third section of this article details the participatory process that was put forward, as well as the components of a study of the cultural ecosystem. Finally the latter sections address CODECU's main findings and proposals, which include: (1) a shift from an idea of culture as a sector to an understanding of culture as a transversal and fundamental dimension of public policy; (2) a need to re-design the institutional framework of cultural policies, based on principles such as horizontality, participation, articulation of different agents, and cultural rights; (3) the strengthening of an eco-system that promotes cultural initiatives and entrepreneurship, based on a paradigm of sustainability; (4) a space to problematize and rethink our values and modes of social interaction, including challenging all forms of discrimination, exclusion and cultural hierarchies.

Special attention is given to the emergence of the creative economy as a new field of action for cultural policies. Stepping away from an uncritical notion that praises the creative industries as a panacea for jumping the economy, we stress on the importance of contextualizing the discourses that surround it. The development of frameworks and strategies for the creative economy require, among other things, the creation of cultural information systems, which should play a fundamental role as a support for decision-making. In order to broaden the discussion of the creative industries' impact, we proposed a sustainable creative economy index. Our experience as academics and cultural agents in the collective process put forward by CODECU strengthened our belief in building sustainable collaborations between academic research and public policy.

Cultural agency and social imagination

In times of multiple crises, governments, international organizations, the private sector and citizen's movements have turned to culture as a resource for fostering economic growth, social inclusion and wellbeing (Yúdice, 2003). This general approach has brought about an innumerable array of policies, projects and initiatives in very different contexts, often with dissimilar methodologies and variable effects. It has also produced different kinds of discourses about cultural instrumentalization, from the entirely functional to neoliberalism, to the utterly critical that invoke culture as a space to question hegemonies and incite social transformation. Paradoxically, objections to viewing culture as a resource also come from a very broad ideological spectrum, from a conservative claim for culture's autonomy, to a criticism of cultural policies as governing tools.

At the heart of these debates lies the relationship between culture and development: an affair with a long history of tensions, attractions and contradictions (Arizpe, 2004). Even though much has been written and discussed about culture as a constitutive dimension of development (Sen, 2004), public agenda tends to be culture-blind in many ways. On the other extreme, when invoked as a resource, culture is frequently seen as a magic wand, as a recently found gold mine ready to be exploited for immediate profit. Between these poles, culture's potentialities of actively having a role in personal and collective strategies to deal with

431

everyday challenges, and build resilient and transformative practices, can be overshadowed. What kind of expediency is expected from culture? Who is supposed to capitalize on it?

Doris Sommer (2006, 2014) refers to *cultural agency*-in a Gramscian sense, as a "room for maneuver", as the "small shifts in perspective and practice" that put forward collective change. Exploring the ways in which culture enables agency demands a careful consideration of a broad range of concrete experiences where cultural practices engage with community and social processes. In Latin America, there is a long history of social practice deeply sensible to culture as a key element of intervention in emancipation processes. As noted by Ochoa (2002), this involvement is rooted in the legacy of endogenous practices – such as the ones developed by Paulo Freire, Orlando Fals Borda and others – and not solely in discourses around culture and development promoted by international organizations, such as UNESCO. An understanding of these legacies in their specific contexts, and with their particular dilemmas, might help us move from the mining metaphor (with all its potential collateral damage) to a more sustainable perspective based on mobilizing agency.

But how could cultural policies contribute to enable citizen's agency? We suggest seeing cultural policies as a potential alley for expanding social imagination about the present and the future, a job that artists and cultural agents are continually involved with. Following institutionalism theories, economist Franscico Catalá (2007) has described the incapacity of successive Puerto Rican government administrations to put forward new paths for economic development, as a product of a "ceremonial encapsulation", or blind faith in the instruments that once made growth possible. Instead of a mere tool for development, culture should be seen as the arena for rethinking development; for demystifying old strategies and opening up emergent and more sustainable values and practices. Instrumentalizing culture, without interrogating development strategies in an integral way, will only reproduce and accentuate social inequalities.

To challenge prevailing ideologies of progress in Puerto Rico requires a thorough working with the collective social imagination. When a high-level public servant justified the exclusion of poor people from a projected development plan by affirming, in a public hearing with the community in 2009, that "not everyone has been born with the same luck", and "such is life", it became clear that we are living in a society where inequalities are seen by many people – including government representatives – as a natural phenomenon. Fortunately, the community responded. And responded through cultural agency. The discussion had to do with a plan for the gorgeous terrains of Roosevelt Roads Naval Station on the eastern coast of Puerto Rico, closed in 2004. The government's plan included the construction of a marina for luxury yachts, casinos, hotel facilities and "world class" boutiques, all activities for elite consumption. According to the then-director of the Port Authority, low-income people could amuse themselves by watching the rich consumers walking around and having a very popular kind of artisan ice cream that we call "limber". A few days after such unfortunate declarations, the community was celebrating a "Limber" Festival, paying tribute to this long-lasting tradition of self-generating income, proclaiming their dignity and defending another development model: one based on citizens' participation, on local commerce instead of foreign investment, on community enjoyment, instead of exclusive elite consumption. The phrase "such is life" became a popular way to refer, with irony, to the increasing social polarization of Puerto Rican society, as well as to the invisible alliances between the political and economic powers. The festival became an annual celebration that serves as a reminder of how community culture can mobilize social imagination.

According to Grimson (2014), culture is "a condition, a medium, and an end of development" [translation by the authors]. If economic justice and political participation are essential requirements to build democratic societies with high levels of human development, it is also critical to direct policies towards cultural justice, which implies "to increase the autonomy of the citizens against the historically instituted common senses" [translation by the authors] (Grimson, 2014, p. 11). Rao and Walton (2004) suggest that considering the centrality of culture in the development process involves moving the emphasis from "equal opportunities" to "equality of agency". Before discussing CODECU's strategies to develop policies committed to opening roads for an equality of cultural agency, the next section contextualizes the role culture and cultural policies have played in Puerto Rico until the present.

Cultural policies in Puerto Rico

A former Spanish colony, Puerto Rico became a US territory in 1898 and since 1952 holds commonwealth status. The "Associated Free State of Puerto Rico", as it was named, enabled self-government, but it is subject to the plenary powers of the United States Congress and Federal Constitution. The country's cultural dilemmas burst from this double colonial experience whose imprints can be traced in many dimensions of Puerto Rican society, from the way social hierarchies and inequalities have been embedded to the dynamics of interrelations between individuals, the colonial state and the imperial power.

After a military invasion of the island, as part of the Spanish-Cuban-American War, the United States imposed a colonial regime with scarce participation of Puerto Ricans in government. Based on the idea of a "civilizing tutelage", an assimilation policy was implemented through the creation of a public education system. English was imposed as the official language to a Spanish-speaking population, and US symbols were disseminated in schools, through rituals such as the pledge of alliance, civic parades to commemorate US holidays, patriotic songs and images of the founding fathers, maps and landscapes unfamiliar to the Island's children (Flores Collazo, 2004; Quintero, 2013).

The legislative arena provided a small space of maneuver for opposing colonial cultural policy. During the first four decades of US rule, some approved legislation intended to affirm national identity and Spanish heritage. These included the reinstatement of several local holidays, the establishment of the Historical Archive of Puerto Rico, the appointment of a Historian of Puerto Rico, the construction of public libraries, the erection of monuments in honor of illustrious local figures and the conservation of Spanish colonial architecture (Rodríguez Cancel, 2007). The acceptance of these measures can also be understood as part of the United States' strategy to gain popular consent and avoid uprisings in the colony. The imposition of US citizenship to the population in 1917, even though controversial at the time, was a key factor in the consolidation of a hegemonic power (Rivera Ramos, 2001). On the other hand, the extension of labor rights to workers in Puerto Rico generated support for annexation movements as a means of expanding democratic rights.

The progressive expansion of Puerto Rican's self-governing powers during the 1940s, culminating in the establishment of the Commonwealth in 1952, enabled the foundations for a cultural policy of a greater scope. Efforts were directed to mitigate the cultural impact of fast-paced modernization. Through the so-called "Operation Serenity", cultural policies aimed at strengthening the link between the state apparatus and the citizenship, particularly the rural population, as exemplified by the creation of the Division for Community Education (DIVEDCO) under the Education Department. Some of the most distinguished artists of the time were recruited to create educational materials in the form of posters, films and booklets that would spread basic lessons of citizenship for democracy (Marsh Kennerley, 2009). In 1949, together with the establishment of the DIVEDCO, Spanish was reinstalled in the public education system, after decades of resistance to the imposition of a foreign language. The Education Department was also the home of the first educational radio station, created in 1950, and since 1958 of the public television station (WIPR-TV).

The decade of the 1950s observed the foundation of long-standing public cultural institutions. The Institute of Puerto Rican Culture (ICP) was created in 1955 with a focus on the preservation and dissemination of cultural heritage. The Casals Festival, the Puerto Rican Symphonic Orchestra and the Conservatory of Music were created between 1957 and 1959, under the influence of Pablo Casals, who was residing in the island. The advancement of classical music was consonant with a civilizing agenda of locating Puerto Rico within modernity (Quintero, 2009). The institutions created by Casals were part of the Industrial Development Company and had a role in the strategy promoting the island as a destiny for manufacturing industries and tourism. Ever since the foundation of these two cultural policy fronts, a contentious relationship was generated between the cultural nationalism represented by the ICP and the promotion of high culture as part of a modernizing development strategy.

Under the direction of anthropologist Ricardo E. Alegría, the ICP worked towards the preservation and dissemination of cultural expressions and traditions that, until that time, did not benefit from government support. In a short period of time, the institution gained social legitimacy and international recognition for its intensive program of cultural initiatives. Some of these included: the revival of autochthonous music instruments and of traditional crafts, through research, workshops and the establishment of itinerary markets; the foundation of a Visual Arts School; the assembly of a national art collection and the creation of the San Juan Print Biennial; the organization of a national archive; a program for historic site's preservation; the foundation of theater festivals and promotion of dance groups; and the formation of local cultural centers throughout the island. The ICP was designed as a public semi-autonomous corporation, governed by a board of directors appointed by the governor, in some cases with the recommendation of cultural organizations. The policies advanced by DIVEDCO and the ICP consolidated a domain for the advancement of a national culture dissociated from the political status and seemingly protected from political and social ruptures, which divide Puerto Rican society (Flores Collazo, 2000; Marsh Kennerley, 2009).

According to Lydia Milagros González (1990), the growing sense of national identity affirmation, promoted by the ICP, also emanated from community cultural engagement. González observes a shift from political activism and workers' organizations to the cultural sphere, in search for more democratic spaces of participation (not provided by traditional parties) and of broader popular support, based on culture's unifying strength in Puerto Rican society during the decade of the 1970s. These grassroots movements' appeal to culture – in defense of environmental causes, and other social issues – converged with the adoption of cultural traditions and symbols by advertising campaigns (González, 1990; Dávila, 1997). Political parties would also reformulate their discourses towards national identity, assuming – with subtle differences – a rhetoric defense of Puerto Rican culture.

Beyond this apparent discursive consensus, political and ideological disputes have persistently affected the management of cultural public institutions and the development of coherent cultural policies, particularly after the Popular Democratic Party (PPD) lost its hegemony at the end of the 1960s with the rise of the statehood movement and its political instrument, the New Progressive Party (PNP). A dispersed institutional apparatus with no clear policies and increasing lack of social legitimacy has been, partly, a consequence of political alternation between the PPD and the PNP, which represent the two main electoral forces in the island. Under PNP administrations, there has been a tendency to limit the ICP's range of action. For example, the creation of a State Historic Preservation Office in 1983, transfer from the ICP to this new agency the responsibilities of overviewing the compliance with the federal National Historic Preservation Act of 1966, even though the ICP still has local responsibility over historical and archeological patrimony. The current situation is characterized by an inefficient duplicity of duties with zones of ambiguous jurisdiction over patrimony. Another example of this dispersing politics was the relocation of resources to promote the artisan sector from the ICP to the Department of Economic Development.

Neoliberal policies of the last decades have focused on promoting tourism and investing in building monumental facilities – a convention center and a coliseum arena, among others – as a strategy to insert the island in global circuits of the entertainment industry. The creation of new governmental cultural dependencies in the last decade has favored culture's economic potential, as exemplified by the Program for the Development of the Film Industry and the Division of the Creative Industries, both attached to the Department of Economic Development. The emphasis on promoting the island as location for the international film industry, instead of strengthening national film production, has been subject of criticism and debate. On the other hand, public financing of cultural institutions has been in steady decline for more than one decade. From 2005 to 2015, the budget of cultural public instrumentalities decreased by 24% (CODECU, 2015b, pp. 61–62).

The public cultural sector is comprised today of seven governmental entities of the executive branch and four programs that are part of the Economic Development Department. These are: the Institute of Puerto Rican Culture; the Corporation for Public Broadcasting; the Corporation for the Musical Arts; the Luis A. Ferré Performing Arts Center; the Conservatory of Music of Puerto Rico; the School of Visual Arts; the State Historic Preservation Office; the Program for the Development of the Film Industry; the Division for Crafts Promotion; the Division of the Creative Industries, and the Convention Center District Authority. Aside from these entities, a group of non-governmental organizations depends heavily on public allocations, such as the main museums, and some performing ensembles, among others (CODECU, 2015b).

An arena for public debate

In 1979, after serving a three-year term as member of the Arts Council in Great Britain, cultural theorist Raymond Williams wrote a brief article analyzing the core challenges of the Council and outlining a few proposals for its reformation (Williams, 1989). The central principle of his proposal was democratization in structure and modes. This could only be achieved, in his opinion, with a wider, complex discussion, allowing "vigorous public argument" around the Council and within it. Debates on cultural policies have moved from the conception of State-based interventions to the recognition of different agents' involvement and the importance of citizen participation in policy-making. According to Ochoa (2003), cultural policy can be defined as "the mobilization of culture carried out by different actors-the State, social movements, cultural industries, institutions, such as museums or tourist organizations and associations of artists-for the purpose of aesthetic, organizational, political, economic and/or social transformation" [translation by the authors] (Ochoa, 2003, p. 20). Furthermore, as recognized by Vich (2006), it is not only important to understand the interests that move each of these actors, his or her strategies and aims, but it also becomes crucial to consider the intersections among them and their possible spaces of coincidence. A strategic articulation of different actors could enable cultural policies that work towards the transformation of social relationships (Vich, 2006, p. 47).

The Commission for Cultural Development was not the first attempt to reform cultural public institutions in Puerto Rico through a process of evaluation and analysis. However, its extensive call for citizen participation, with the interest in enabling a social dialogue, had no precedent in our context. In 2002 and 2005, two different governmental efforts were carried out aiming at developing a coherent cultural policy. The first one was launched by the Senate's Commission on Culture, Science, and Education and the second one by a cultural policy committee designed by the governor (Comisión de Educación, Ciencia y Cultura del Senado de Puerto Rico, 2005; Junta de Política Cultural, 2005). The 2002 Senate report on public cultural institutions was based on public hearings with the participation of 20 deponents, individual and group meetings with leaders in the cultural field and analysis of legislation, reports and the existing bibliography about cultural activities in the country. It introduced international discussions on culture and development to the local context and made a valuable diagnosis of some of the state's cultural institutions. It identified contentious zones in cultural legislation, particularly regarding heritage preservation, and the obstacles to implement coherent policies that respond at the same time to the federal and local legal dispositions (Comisión de Educación, Ciencia y Cultura del Senado de Puerto Rico, 2005). However, the report does not address the private and non-profit cultural sector or the municipal sphere of action. In this sense, it presents only a partial scope of the cultural ecosystem.

The special committee named by the governor in 2005 made a call for presentations and received 89 papers in a short period of time, making evident a very high interest in the process from the cultural sector. However, the papers were not presented in public hearing or made available with the report, which was not published (Junta de Política Cultural, 2005). This situation severely limited the possibility of generating a broader social dialogue on the subject. The report introduces the concept of a "culture of high performance", understood as an emblematic symbolic production that should receive priority for its economic, humanizing and normative potential. Both reports highlighted the importance of restructuring the cultural agencies. However, they do not elaborate on a new architecture for cultural institutions, aside from some imprecise suggestions. They also coincide in underlining the need for greater government's funds allocation. In both cases, very few of the recommendations were implemented.

After more than a decade of failed attempts to revise cultural policies, CODECU was created with the task to recommend a remodeling of public cultural institutions and providing a roadmap for the development of cultural entrepreneurship and self-initiative. Diverse actors in the cultural sector have been demanding governmental action, particularly in the face of a continuous reduction in budget allocations. However, there seem to be profound disagreements in the public opinion, concerning the performance of public cultural institutions, as well as the government's role with regards to culture. In this sense, CODECU understood that a space for vigorous public argument was needed. While the cited attempts to develop a cultural policy incorporated participatory mechanisms, these consisted basically of audience hearings. CODECU decided to go a step further, proposing a dialogical methodology. The challenge was to open ears to the others' experiences, ideas and world-views, and finding common ground without obliterating differences. This is a process that takes time, which may trouble those who are accustomed to making decisions unilaterally but cultivates what Martha Nussbaum (2010) defines as our "inner eye", our ability to think from the place of the other.

In addition to the participatory character, a second element that has internationally proven vital to the development of democratic cultural policies is interdisciplinary research and accessibility to data sources that can inform public policy decisions. Thus, together with the participatory dialogues, CODECU elaborated a comprehensive study of the cultural ecosystem in Puerto Rico, which serves as the basis for the future establishment of a cultural information system. In sum, CODECU's methodology comprised four key perspectives: The *socio-analytical perspective* encompassed the participatory dialogues with different sectors and the collection of empirical data through a study of the cultural ecosystem. The *interpretative perspective* included an extensive literature review in the field of cultural policies, research on the historical background of the local cultural scene, including the main institutions and agents that have built each of the arts and cultural sectors and conversations with local and international experts. The *practical perspective* included designing institutional mechanisms that could respond to the strengths and needs of the cultural sector, provide cohesion and vitality and assure the understanding of culture as a transversal element of all public policies. Specific proposals were elaborated as well for the cultural and creative industries, the arts and heritage and cross-cutting topics, such as internationalization of the Puerto Rican culture, ties and cooperation with the diaspora, diversity and equity. Finally, the *documentary perspective* consisted of making available the outcomes of dialogues and research experiences, throughout the whole process, as a tool to amplify the scope and further democratize the discussion and elaboration of alternatives.

Thematically, CODECU structured its work plan from a multi-level perspective, grouping the different subject matters into the following three categories: *creative sectors* (music, theater, dance, visual arts, crafts, cinema and audiovisual, literature, design, gastronomy, criticism and research); *cultural infrastructure* (public administration, private sector, museums, archives, libraries, performing spaces, festivals, digital media, etc.); and a *transversal approach* (cultural rights, heritage and memory, entrepreneurship and cultural industries, education, racism, social capital and community, internationalization, culture and environment, etc.). Various formats for the collection of ideas, experiences and proposals were developed. Four multi-sectorial meetings were held on different regions of the island, promoting the inclusion of populations outside the metropolitan area. Additionally, a meeting with the Puerto Rican diaspora was held in New York. Sectorial and thematic discussions took the form of participatory table dialogues, forums, chats, conferences, focus groups and surveys, among others. The intention was to guarantee a balance between the inclusion of all interested individuals and groups, and the space for discussion and analysis with specialized agents. Overall, 29 public discussion activities were held in a one-year period. The attendance lists collected the signature of 1, 283 participants, 26% of whom represented organizations (approximately 260); 18.5% being artists; 17.7% linked to the Academy and 14% to government entities. Some arts sectors and other interest groups organized themselves independently to develop recommendations and presented them to CODECU to be incorporated into the analysis.

To complement the data collection, the study on the cultural ecosystem included an economic impact analysis, a survey for cultural agents, a survey on cultural consumption and participation and interviews with key informants linked to the academia, government, foundations, non-profits, private sector and the cultural sector. Existing data were systematized to provide a picture of the dynamics of production and employment in the cultural sectors and their relationship with the rest of the Puerto Rican economy. A survey of 164 artists, businesses and cultural organizations presented a profile of their operation, including aspects such as voluntary work, unpaid work, intellectual property and management. Finally, a representative survey of 800 people around the country provided a picture of the patterns of consumption and participation in a broad array of cultural activities, including the arts, heritage, media, new technologies and social imaginaries. It enabled an audience profile of each sector and pinpointed differences in access and cultural participation according to socio-economic and geographic variables, among others.

Transversal and participatory policies

Cultural policies need to be particularly sensitive to specific socio-political conditions. CODECU's participatory process included an effort to understand the ideas about culture that circulate in our context, aiming to make visible the hierarchies and power relations that prevail in the cultural ecosystem, its dynamics of exclusion and inclusion as well as identifying emergent practices. When asked about the notions of culture that inform their practice, participants of the meetings came up with a very broad array of references. From arts to science and technology, from tradition to experimentation, from identity and heritage to creative freedom and a global reach, from education to empowerment and entrepreneurship, from personal transformation to social justice, the participatory process revealed that culture is seen and practiced by cultural agents in a very transversal and interrelated way.

These outcomes strengthen the idea that proposals for cultural policies should assert the importance of a transversal approach to culture in public policy. They also validate the idea that cultural policies need to question some of its most foundational notions, such as "arts" and "heritage". In some contexts, cultural policies have been restricted to arts policies. However, several authors have recognized at least two dimensions in cultural policies: one that has to do with the ways of life of a society, its conceptions of history, its ideas of the future, its values, among other element related to culture in an anthropological sense, and another one that refers to the socially organized symbolic production, including the arts, traditions, heritage and cultural industries (Brunner, 1998; Miller & Yúdice, 2002; Garretón, 2008). Policies regarding the first dimension are often "invisible", while the State's cultural institutions usually have to do with the second dimension. Grimson (2011) suggests that there is a theoretical and political need to transcend the idea of culture as a distinct sphere separated from economy or politics. For the author, cultural policies, in a broad sense, are the ones "that intend to explicitly have an impact in signification processes" [translation by the authors] (Grimson, 2014, p. 10). In this line, Vich (2013) proposes to *deculturalize culture*, a move in cultural policies towards intervening in the social imagination.

Based on the belief that the State is an essential actor in the fulfillment of cultural rights, rethinking public institutions was at the core of CODECU's task. However, the Commission was highly conscious that institutions don't work in a vacuum. Thus, one of its main challenges was to design a way to connect different actors and promote an articulation of their agendas. Cultural institutions in their form and content respond to the ways culture and the arts are seen in society. At the same time, as Douglas (1986) has noted, the role of institutions is fundamental in the forging of these imaginaries. In the Puerto Rican context, this dynamic is very complex, because of our political subjection to the U.S. and the contrasting visions towards culture in both societies. Developing a proposal for a new cultural policy in Puerto Rico requires addressing the conflicts with the public policy framework of the United States. Following the four cultural policy approaches developed by Hillman and McCaughey (1989), the United States represents one of the scenarios of less direct intervention in cultural policy, which could be defined in the category of *facilitator*. In this case, the federal government uses the mechanism of the National Endowment for the Arts for direct support, and indirect support is supplied through tax credits to private contributions.

Cultural institutions founded in the decade of the '50s in Puerto Rico responded to a vision much more in tune with the Latin American context than the US model. However,

Puerto Rican public policies in general and cultural institution in particular have been increasingly influenced by federal policies. This situation has forged a sort of hybrid model, creating various contentious zones and instances where significant clashes occur. CODECU's proposal tried to respond to the very specific characteristics of the Puerto Rican context, understanding that some areas – such as media policies – are determined by federal law, leaving little room to maneuver at the local level. A group of fundamental principles was articulated to serve as a guide in the entire cultural policy design process. These include: autonomy from the political parties and their influence in the public service; creative independence; determination to fight inequalities, prejudices and social violence; endorsing diversity in all its dimensions; acknowledgment of the State's role as a coordinator, facilitator and generator of infrastructure; promoting access and participation of every person in cultural life; transversal approach to cultural policies; and strengthening entrepreneurship and nongovernmental cultural organizations.

In addressing the institutional challenge, CODECU took into consideration emerging models of governance, as well the organizing models that sprout from the experience of artists and cultural agents. Cultural networking, for example, is a phenomenon on the rise, as "open organizational forms, flexible and contingent [that] work as complement to more stable institutions of the State, the market and civil society" [translation by the authors] (Yúdice, 2003b). Networks are not only a product of the growing interest in participation, but enable "different logics" of organization of cultural work (Nivón et al., 2012). A revalorization of reciprocity, the channeling of collective efforts to increase the political influence of cultural agents and the generation of spaces for exchanging experiences and information, are some of the characteristics of contemporary cultural networks. Beyond the cultural field, networks have emerged as new figures of public policies, capable of producing new kinds of articulation between different actors in public and private organizations. They have been recognized also as a factor of innovation of the governmental apparatus (Considine & Lewis, 2007).

Several initiatives in Latin America have generated significant changes in the relations between the state and civil society, focusing on the principle of participation as a human right. On the one hand, there has been a growing process of organization of non-governmental associations and national networks, establishing common agendas and alliances, and, on the other, in some contexts public policies have institutionalized participation processes. Within this frame of reference, CODECU proposed an institutional redesign based on participation, autonomy and horizontality, through the creation of a National Network of Culture (ReNaC or Red Nacional de Cultura), an organism that would combine decision-making functions exercised in an horizontal and participatory manner through a multi-sectorial board and advisory and coordinating functions exercised by specialists in cultural policies, information systems, finance and strategic planning. Its governing board will be comprised of a majority of cultural agents, elected by their peers, and with regional representation and participation of the Puerto Rican diaspora, representatives of the academia, of the general citizens through the cultural centers and governmental appointees as liaison with the Institute of Puerto Rican Culture, the Education Department, Tourism, the Department of Economic Development, and Municipal Governments. Its mission will be to create bridges between state cultural agencies, other governmental dependences, universities, municipalities, the non-profit and private sectors, artists, educators and other professionals of culture as well as the general citizenship, in order to generate and periodically review culture plans, which would establish common priorities and serve as a framework for the internal work plan of each of the agents that participate in the network.

The articulation of a network such as the one proposed by CODECU is based on the need to develop a transversal approach to cultural policy, where culture becomes an integral dimension to be considered in any kind of public policy. Culture has an extremely dynamic and changing dimension, with the continuous emergence of new practices and emerging actors. In terms of strengthening its capacity of articulation and efficiency, it is our belief that institutions must have the flexibility to respond to these changes and maintain their relevance. They must be porous to social dynamics and incorporate mechanisms for an ongoing review of programs and processes, becoming incubators of social and cultural innovation. Finally, public institutions of culture must exist according to the fulfillment of the cultural rights of the population. Their social penetration should be a high-priority objective. Cultural institutions should avoid, at all costs, becoming strongholds of particular sectors. To reach different sectors of the population requires differentiated strategies and an attitude of permanent social dialogue.

Creative economy as a new dimension of cultural policies

Most of the discourse around the creative economy has been grounded in the approach of culture as a resource (Yúdice, 2003a). This has been evidenced by an increase in research on the direct and indirect impacts of cultural and creative industries. Some of the main aspects include its impact on international trade (UNCTAD, 2010) and the effect of the creative economy in local development (Florida, 2002). However, these arguments have met strong criticism because of the lack of empirical evidence to support this impact. They have raised concerns based on the dangers of generalizing strategies, with the creative economy as a development engine (De Beukelaer, 2014), the role of creative industries in urban development (Markusen, 2006), working conditions of cultural workers (McRobbie, 2016) and the lack of causality concerning the development of large cultural infrastructures' impact in cities and international designation, such as the European Capital of Culture (Campbell, 2014; Miles, 2015). For this reason, it is important to stress that creative economy strategies and dynamics should respond to cultural policies, since the production of symbolic content remains their main impact, and this has major implications beyond economics.

The creative economy is one of the new fields of action of cultural policies. There are big debates about what the main focus should be for the development of the economic dimension of cultural activity. Often, it is argued that cultural industries must respond only to the economic logic of production, employment and exports. However, it is also important that these dynamics respond to cultural policies, since the production of symbolic content remains their main impact, and this has major implications beyond economics.

How can we develop strategies for cultural and creative industries to maximize their economic potential while guaranteeing and advancing cultural policy objectives? An important premise is that a key segment of creative activity is generated outside the market dynamics. Precisely this characteristic makes it innovative and attractive to multiple markets. Then, ensuring creative freedom, diversity, access and participation is necessary to develop and strengthen a sustainable cultural and creative ecosystem.

Definitions for the creative industries have been a constant challenge for countries, considering that broad definitions may be the result of the interest in overestimating the economic impact and not necessarily the development of cultural policies (Hesmondhalgh & Pratt, 2005). Sometimes, the concept of creative industries has complemented the cultural sector by incorporating activities related to creative services and technology. However, it

440

is important to establish that many of these new activities are actually support elements for cultural activities and incorporate cultural content into their business models. Therefore, a broad definition of creative industries is recommended, ranging from heritage to creative services, allowing the collaboration and cross-fertilization that promote innovation and added value. In the case of Puerto Rico, in addition to the traditional sectors, activities such as gastronomy and cultural tourism, as well as interactive media, design and creative services were included.

The pyramid of the cultural ecosystem

In the process of developing new frameworks to promote sustainability in the creative sector, we propose understanding the cultural ecosystem as a priority of creative industries policies. The ecosystem concept is very relevant to the cultural sector. It could be described as a set of interdependent organisms that share a habitat, which is precisely the way in which cultural activity works. Unlike other industries, it is necessary to establish that economic activity is not generated in isolation. It is an environment in which each agent has its role, and altering that system has negative results.

All cultural agents have a role in the creative economy, and the responsibility of public policy is to recognize that role and enhance their development. Indeed, the main benefit is that some ventures nurture others with talent, by providing research and development (R&D) of artistic and creative practices, promoting education that translates into audience development, promoting diversity and covering certain gaps in their value chains. Therefore, it is important to establish that cultural organizations and businesses also have a responsibility to understand their role in the ecosystem and incorporate strategic actions to strengthen it.

A strategy for the development of cultural and creative industries should be designed primarily to strengthen the ecosystem and not only incentivize individual companies and start-ups. The first approach ensures the latter, but not the opposite way. Sometimes, the development of high-impact ventures requires supporting and subsidizing projects and organizations whose main contribution is not a direct economic impact, but audience and talent development and innovation.

A pyramid schematic with three levels is proposed as a framework to understand a cultural ecosystem. In the pyramid, the highest levels will produce a higher direct economic impact. However, as expected in a pyramid structure, their presence depends on a broad and solid base. In between, there is a segment of market-oriented businesses and organizations with a better balance between economic and cultural value (Figure 28.1).

- **Input Firms** – This level is composed mainly of individual artists and organizations in the segments of training, creation and conservation in the value chain of the cultural sector. Usually, their main focus is to produce or preserve artistic and cultural goods and expressions. In many cases, their activities are based on traditional or highly innovative and experimental cultural expressions, so their scope, mainly, is not market oriented. These sectors often work on a project basis and are financed through incentives, grants or subsidies. In many cases, financial sustainability is their main challenge because of the lack of formal structures and continuity. Yet, this also could represent their greatest contribution. Operating outside the market (supply and demand logic) ensures both ends of the value chain: ensuring the preservation of traditional cultural expressions or serving as innovation agents that alter the established order in artistic and cultural production.

- **Competitive Firms** – This level is composed of organizations or companies operating in a market-oriented dynamic. In many cases, companies operate under a sector, such as traditional arts, media, entertainment and other creative industries. In many cases, these organizations compete in a free market economy and receive their main income streams from services to private companies or through the sale of goods and services to final consumers. Sometimes, they access government funds to develop specific projects, although it is not usual to sustain their operations through subsidies.
- **High-Impact Firms** – This level is composed of ventures that have a direct economic impact through the sale of cultural goods and services for local and international markets. These cultural and creative projects sometimes have a direct impact through revenues and employment and promoting local and international recognition. Some of them are sometimes supported by multinational companies and benefit from digital business models.

There are several key assumptions in this model. The nature of the pyramid suggests that if the base is weak, the emergence of high-impact projects will be more difficult. Similarly, the pyramid does not mean that companies will level up. Although some companies may show a sustained growth, the logic of the ecosystem recognizes the role of each component in the macro analysis of the ecosystem. Therefore, it is a mistake to think that it is necessary to focus on the higher levels and avoid those companies that require subsidies to survive. CODECU decided to use this model as a framework for its cultural and creative industries strategy. The initial efforts to promote the creative economy in Puerto Rico based success indicators on variables such as revenues and employment. However, because the cultural and creative ecosystem is at a very early stage, it is important to be inclusive in the policy approach, assuming that many grassroots projects do not generate a high direct economic impact but are responsible for generating cultural innovation, which subsequently results in economic development. A strategy that impacts different firm levels will allow greater diversity in the creative economy in Puerto Rico.

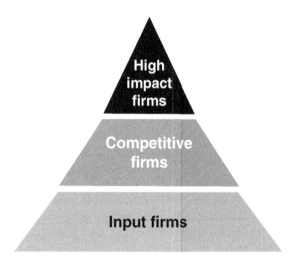

Figure 28.1 The cultural ecosystem pyramid

Source: This image is reproduced with the permission of the International Journal of Arts Management.

A strategy for the creative industries

Countries and local governments should be able to develop strategies beyond formal institutions. These strategies should be based on a combination of methodologies as described earlier. In the case of Puerto Rico, the analysis was based on macro level data, benchmark analysis and a survey on the production side, including artists, cultural agents, nonprofit organizations and businesses. Also, the analysis includes meetings and interviews with key informants. Based on diagnosis, summarized through a SWOT analysis, four key problems were identified. These problems were translated into strategic actions that included the creation of cultural businesses; access to financing; access to markets and the development of cultural information systems. Each of the strategic actions includes objectives, actions, timeframe and agents responsible for its implementation (Figure 28.2).

Cultural information systems

Cultural information systems have become an important tool to support decision-making in cultural policy. In recent years, countries like Brazil, Argentina, Spain, Colombia and Mexico, among many others, have emphasized these processes (Ministerio de Cultura de Colombia, 2010; Ministerio de Educación, Cultura y Deporte, 2012; Instituto Nacional de

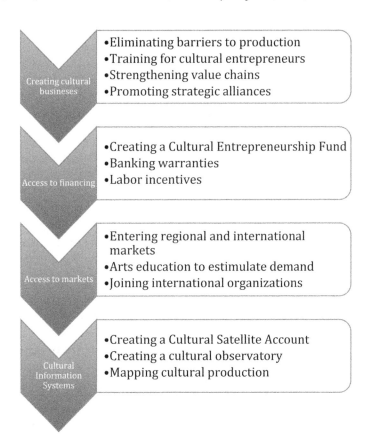

Figure 28.2 A strategy for the creative industries

Estadística y Geografía, 2014). In many cases, it has been a coordinated effort among government, academia, the private sector and the cultural sector. Generally, governments are responsible for gathering information and keeping updated statistics on national accounts. Similarly, academia mainly provides support in the stages of design and data analysis.

Toward a sustainable creative economy index

There is a need to build bridges between cultural information systems and a new discourse on the development of cultural and creative industries. One proposal is the creation of a *Sustainable Creative Economy Index*. These indices always have the challenge of simplifying complex dynamics surrounding social, economic and cultural aspects. However, the use of adequate indicators could precisely suggest that complexity and its multidisciplinary dynamics. Until now, indicators such as production, employment and exports lead the discussion. As stated by being under the scope of cultural policies, other objectives and indicators should get into the discussion. The proposed index has four major components: the economic, the creative ecosystem, education and cultural consumption. Each of these components integrates several indicators available through the national accounts and cultural information systems in different countries.

The first component integrates macroeconomic indicators such as production, employment and international trade. This in itself can be a sub-index, which must be analyzed considering the differences between creative sectors and levels of imports of goods and cultural services.

The second component, the creative ecosystem, raises the need for a diversified production. Beyond the direct impact at the macro level, it is necessary to ensure diversity in terms of creative activity and location. This may seem to contradict cluster theories based on activity and geographical agglomeration as an element of competitiveness. However, existing linkages between different creative sectors is more relevant to cultural industries. Therefore, a sustainable creative economy requires a balance of artistic production, media, design, creative services and heritage. Similarly, excess geographical agglomeration of cultural activity could represent barriers to cultural consumption, which arose repeatedly in the consultation process in Puerto Rico, related to the high concentration of cultural production and diffusion in the metropolitan area. Therefore, concentration indexes, such as the Herfindahl-Hirschman Index, could be used in the cultural industries as part of a measure of a sustainable creative economy. The Herfindahl-Hirschman Index allows determining the level of market concentration of firms in an industry at a geographical area (Alonso & Ríos, 2011).

The third component is still not present in the discourses of the creative economy but is key to achieving a balance between production and consumption. In many cases countries have a vast artistic and cultural production. However, almost all sectors face a limited demand. The *Survey on Cultural Consumption and Participation* of Puerto Rico establishes a direct relationship between arts education during childhood and adulthood and a higher level of cultural consumption (CODECU, 2015a). For this reason, indicators such as the ratio of arts teachers to students in primary and secondary school and the offering of courses in this area are proposed as indicators. Similarly, human capital is an important indicator, so the total number of graduates annually in the various creative professions is another key indicator.

Finally, we propose an indicator of cultural consumption. This sub-index should include elements such as diversity in cultural consumption (number of activities performed) by individuals, the demographic profile of consumers, always from a perspective of diversity and barriers to accessing cultural consumption, including variables such as geography, gender, income and education level.

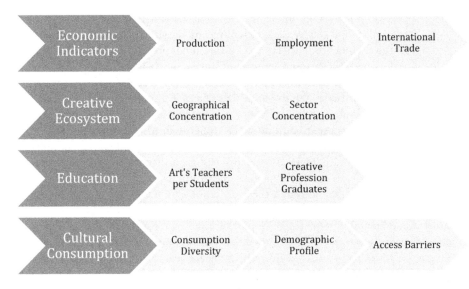

Figure 28.3   Sustainable creative economy index

The recommendations presented by the Commission for Cultural Development represent an effort to develop a comprehensive and coherent cultural policy for Puerto Rico. However, a proper implementation requires the development of a system of indicators that reflect the diversity of its impact. The proposal of a *sustainable creative economy index* represents an opportunity to place the creative economy as a component of cultural policy. Thus, the analysis is not limited to direct economic impact, but includes dimensions such as education, diversity, equity and access, elements that guided the cultural policy proposed by CODECU (Figure 28.3).

Cultural policies and development in question

The state's cultural policies in Puerto Rico, as well as in most Latin American countries, were forged around three basic areas: heritage preservation, arts promotion and cultural dissemination (Mejía, 2009). These notions, however, have been the subject of interrogation and reformulations, which are fundamental for rethinking contemporary cultural policies. The demarcations between "Art" with a capital letter and other practices of symbolic production have been problematized (Gaztambide-Fernández, 2013). Their boundaries are no longer seen as natural, but are the result of processes of distinction, elaboration of aesthetic and social hierarchies and complex symbolic systems of inclusion and exclusion. Arts and heritage have ceased to be considered "sacred objects" and are understood as practices in which meanings are embedded in the particular contexts in which they emerge. Thus, their significance and connotations are subjected to continuous transformation. The notion of cultural dissemination has also been questioned, because of its hidden assumptions, based on the cultural hierarchies mentioned before. Moreover, the development of cultural industries and technological innovations has induced major and ongoing changes in the modes of producing and circulating symbolic goods.

These transformations in the cultural sector, and in the critical approaches to understand its complex dynamics, constitute a fundamental arena for the emergence of new paradigms

445

in cultural policies. However, as we have discussed, cultural policies are been requested to broaden their scope and pay attention to the modes in which culture is embedded in social life. What role is culture playing in the questioning and restyling of national, ethnic, gender and sexual identities, among others? How is culture implicated in economic development? What has it to do with policies to promote environmental sustainability and consciousness? How are cultural agents involved in expanding democratic practices? To see culture as a tool is probably a reductive mistake, but to obliterate its participation in multiple social processes can hinder a complex understanding of reality, and the potentialities of cultural agency.

As the Puerto Rican context has illustrated, engaging in participatory processes for the development of cultural policies enables a space for a social dialogue and for collective imagination. However, cultural policies also require certain principles of political action. The government's invitation to artists, academics and cultural producers to lead a process of articulating a cultural policy, through the creation of CODECU, could be seen as a step towards the recognition of these agents as vital for the revision of current public policies. But the fact that one year after presenting its report, which was apparently well received by government officials, none of the main proposals has been put into practice is certainly a matter of concern. Of course, it is true that precisely in the last year, the country's fiscal emergency has worsened, and there seems to be no space in the public agenda to speak of anything else. Once again, and contrary to what CODECU's report tried to convey, culture is not understood as a basic need and is not taken into account in the process of conceiving alternatives to the island dead-end road.

When the government opens up spaces for citizens' participation and does not compromise with the outcomes, skepticism and distrust in public institutions increase. However, a rich occasion of exchange and conversation, a "vigorous public argument" in Williams' (1989) terms, is never lost time. Social dialogue is vital so that we may face our assumptions and find a lexicon to envision social and cultural transformations. Government's inaction in the cultural realm is confronted day after day with an array of individual and communal initiatives. CODECU's proposal makes a plea to different sectors, such as academia, cultural producers, artists, social movements and others, to engage in continuous exchange of ideas and practices, to strengthen their interconnections and capacity to collaborate.

Intense social dialogue, collective imagination and articulation, as well as a vindication of the public, are indispensable elements of addressing a much-needed rethinking of development strategies. In this endeavor, local processes could be tremendously enriched from an international critical conversation.

References

Alonso Cifuentes, Julio & Ríos Millán, Ana M. (2011). Concentración de la producción de las industrias culturales de Cali. *Estudios Gerenciales, 27* (119), 99–121.

Arizpe, Lourdes. (2004). The intellectual history of culture and development institutions. In Vijayendra Rao & Michael Walton (Eds.), *Culture and Public Action* (pp. 163–184). Stanford, CA: University of Stanford Press.

Brunner, José Joaquín. (1988). *Un espejo trizado: Ensayos sobre cultura y políticas culturales.* Santiago de Chile: Flacso.

Campbell, Peter. (2014). Imaginary success? The contentious ascendance of creativity. *European Planning Studies, 22* (5), 995–1009.

Catalá, Francisco. (2007). Desenvolvimiento económico de Puerto Rico: dependencia de senda y encapsulamiento ceremonial. *Revista de Ciencias Sociales 17.* San Juan: Centro de Investigaciones Sociales, Universidad de Puerto Rico, 58–77.

Comisión de Educación, Ciencia y Cultura del Senado de Puerto Rico. (2005). *Informe sobre las Instituciones Culturales en Puerto Rico*. San Juan: Instituto de Cultura Puertorriqueña.

Comisión para el Desarrollo Cultural. (2015a). *Estudio sobre el ecosistema cultural en Puerto Rico*. CODECU: San Juan. Retrieved from: https://es.scribd.com/doc/267486776/CODECU-Estudio-sobre-el-ecosistema-cultural.

Comisión para el Desarrollo Cultural. (2015b). *Hilando voluntades: Cultura para la equidad, la diversidad y el emprendimiento*. CODECU: San Juan. Retrieved from: https://es.scribd.com/doc/267489708/Informe-Final-de-la-Comision-para-el-Desarrollo-Cultural.

Considine, Mark & Lewis, Jenny M. (2007). Innovation and innovators inside government: from institutions to networks. *Governance: An International Journal of Policy, Administrations, and Institutions, 20* (4), 581–607.

Dávila, Arlene. (1997). *Sponsored Identities: Cultural Politics in Puerto Rico*. Philadelphia, PA: Temple University Press.

De Beukelaer, Christiaan. (2014). *Developing Cultural Industries: Learning from the Palimpsest of Practice*. Amsterdam: European Cultural Foundation.

Dos Santos, Edna. (2013). *Creative Economy Report 2010*. United Nations.

Douglas, Mary. (1986). *How Institutions Think*. London: Routledge & Kegan Paul.

Flores Collazo, María Margarita. (2000). La competencia por fijar y definir la identidad nacional: el debate en torno a la instauración del Instituto de Cultura Puertorriqueña, 1955. *Cuadernos del Ateneo*, San Juan, 66–81.

Flores Collazo, María Margarita. (2004). *25/4 julio. Conmemorar. Festejar. Consumir en Puerto Rico,* San Juan: Academia puertorriqueña de la historia/Centro de Investigaciones Históricas, Universidad de Puerto Rico.

Florida, Richard. (2002). *The Rise of the Creative Class*. New York: Basic Books.

Garretón, Manuel Antonio (2008). Las políticas culturales en los gobiernos democráticos en Chile. In Antonio Albino Canelas & Rubens Bayardo (Eds.), *Políticas Culturais na Ibero-América* (pp. 75–118). Salvador, Bahia: EDUFBA.

Gaztambide-Fernández, Rubén A. (2013). Why the Arts Don't Do Anything: Towards a New Vision for Cultural Production in Education. *Harvard Educational Review, 83* (1), 211–236.

González, Lydia Milagros. (1990). Cultura y grupos populares en la historia viva de Puerto Rico hoy. In Fernando Calderón y Mario R. dos Santos (Eds.), *¿Hacia un nuevo orden estatal en América Latina. Vol 8. Innovación cultural y actores socio-culturales* (pp. 323–342). Buenos Aires: CLACSO.

Grimson, Alejandro. (2011). *Los límites de la cultura. Crítica de las teorías de la identidad*. Buenos Aires: Siglo XXI.

Grimson, Alejandro. (2014). Introducción. Políticas para la justicia cultural. In Alejandro Grimson (Ed.), *Culturas políticas y políticas culturales*. (pp. 9–14). Buenos Aires: Fundación de Altos Estudios Sociales.

Harvey, David. (2005). *A Brief History of Neoliberalism*. New York: Oxford University Press.

Hernández, Javier. (2014). Understanding 'cultural return': spill-over management in the creative industries. In: Kooyman, R., Hagoort, G. & Schramme, A. (Eds.) *Beyond Frames: Dynamics between the Creative Industries, Knowledge Institutions and the Urban Context* (pp. 56–64). Utrecht: Eduron.

Hesmondhalgh, David and Pratt, Andy C. (2005). Cultural industries and cultural policy. *International Journal of Cultural Policy*, 11 (1), 1–14.

Hillman, Harry, and Claire McCaughey. (1989). The arm's length principle and the arts: an international perspective-past, present and future. In M. C. Cummings and J. M. D. Schuster (Eds.), *Who's to Pay for the Arts? The International Search for Models of Arts Support*. New York: Consejo Americano de las Artes.

Instituto Nacional de Estadística y Geografía. (2014). *Encuesta Nacional de Consumo Cultural de México 2012*. México: CONACULTA.

Junta de Política Cultural. (2005). *Pensar a Puerto Rico desde la cultura*. Unpublished Manuscript.

Markusen, Ann. (2006). The artistic dividend: urban artistic specialization and economic development implications. *Urban Studies, 43* (10), 1661–1686.

Marsh Kennerley, Catherine. (2009). *Negociaciones culturales. Los intelectuales y el proyectos pedagógico del estado muñocista*. San Juan: Ediciones Callejón.

McRobbie, Angela. (2016). *Be Creative*. Cambridge: Polity.

Mejía Arango, Juan Luis. (2009). Apuntes sobre las políticas culturales en América Latina, 1987–2009. In *Pensamiento Iberoamericano*, (0004), 105–129

Miles, Malcolm. (2015). *Limits of Culture: Urban Regeneration vs Dissident Art*. London: Pluto Press.

Miller, Toby & Yúdice, Georges. (2002). *Cultural Policy*. Thousand Oaks, CA: SAGE Publications.

Ministerio de Cultura de Colombia. (2010). *Compendio de Políticas Culturales*. Colombia: Ministerio de Cultura.

Ministerio de Educación, Cultura y Deporte. (2015). *Encuesta de hábitos y prácticas culturales en España 2014–2015*. España: Ministerio de Educación Cultura y Deporte.

Nussbaum, Martha C. (2010). *Sin fines de lucro. Por qué la democracia necesita de las humanidades*. Buenos Aires: Katz.

Nivón Bolán, Eduardo, Mesa Iturbide, Rafael, Pérez Camacho, Carmen, & López Ojeda, Andrés (2012). *Libro Verde para la institucionalización del Sistema de Fomento y Desarrollo Cultural de la Ciudad de México*. México: Secretaria de Cultura DF.

Ochoa, Ana María (2002). Políticas culturales, academia y sociedad. In Daniel Mato (Ed.), *Estudios y otras prácticas latinoamericanas en cultura y poder* (pp. 213–224). Caracas: Clacso/Ceap Faces, Universidad Central de Venezuela.

Ochoa, Ana María. (2003). *Entre los deseos y los derechos. Un ensayo crítico sobre políticas culturales*. Bogotá: Instituto Colombiano de Antropología e Historia.

Quintero Rivera, Mareia. (2009). La Universidad y la vida musical: una mirada a medio siglo de políticas culturales. In Pedro Reina Pérez (Ed.), *El Arco Prodigioso: Perspectivas de Pablo Casals y su legado en Puerto Rico* (pp. 97–116). San Juan: EMS Editores.

Quintero Rivera, Mareia (2013). Debates identitarios y capital simbólico: Políticas culturales en torno a la música tradicional puertorriqueña. *Latin American Research Review*, 48 (Special Issue), 30–49.

Rao, Vijayendra & Walton, Michael (2004). Culture and Public Action: Relationality, Equality of Agency, and Development. In Vijayendra Rao & Michael Walton (Eds.), *Culture and Public Action* (pp. 3–36). Redwood City, CA: Sanford University Press/ The International Bank for Reconstruction and Development / The World Bank.

Rivera Ramos, Efrén. (2001). *The Legal Construction of Identity. The Judicial and Social Legacy of American Colonialism in Puerto Rico*. Washington, DC: American Psychological Association.

Rodríguez Cancel, Jaime. (2007). *La Guerra fría y el sexenio de la puertorriqueñidad: Afirmación nacional y políticas culturales*. San Juan: Ediciones Puerto.

Sen, Amartya. (2004). How does culture matter? In Vijayendra Rao & Michael Walton (Eds.), *Culture and Public Action* (pp. 37–58). Redwood City, CA: Stanford University Press.

Sommer, Doris. (2006). *Cultural Agency in the Americas*. Durham, NC: Duke University Press.

Sommer, Doris. (2014). *The Work of Art in the World: Civic Agency and Public Humanities*. Durham, NC: Duke University Press.

UNCTAD. (2010). *Creative Economy Report*. Geneva: United Nations.

Vich, Víctor. (2006). Gestionar riesgos: agencia y maniobra en la política cultural. In Guillermo Cortés & Víctor Vich (Eds.), *Políticas culturales: ensayos críticos* (pp. 45–70). Lima: Instituto de Estudios Peruanos.

Vich, Víctor. (2013). Desculturalizar la cultura. La gestión cultural como forma de acción política. *Latin American Research Review*, 48 (Special Issue), 129–139.

Williams, Raymond. (1989). *Resources of Hope*. London and New York: Verso.

Yúdice, George. (2003a). *El recurso de la cultura: usos de la cultura en la era global*. Barcelona: Gedisa.

Yúdice, George. (2003b) Sistema y redes culturales: ¿cómo y para qué? Paper presented at the International Symposium *Políticas culturales urbanas: experiencias europeas y americanas*, Bogotá May 5–9, 2003. Retrieved from: www.brasiluniaoeuropeia.ufrj.br/es/pdfs/sistemas_y_redes_culturales_como_y_para_que.pdf.

29

Neoliberalised development of cultural policies in Taiwan and a case of the Taiwanese film industry in a creative industries model

Hui-Ju Tsai and Yu-Peng Lin

Introduction

The neoliberalised plan of creative industries has eroded the public value of culture and media policies and changed the cultural landscape. Neoliberal rhetoric has become pivotal to the successful 'common-sense' of recent decades (Harvey 2005, pp. 39–42; Hall 2011). It has not only infiltrated society but also penetrated the field of cultural policies. The British conception of creative industries, for example, was grafted onto a new cultural and creative industries project in Taiwan. The localisation of British policy discourses and the process of public acceptance—this common-sense that 'culture is a good business' of the same underlying neoliberal agenda—has occurred not only in Britain but also in the Taiwanese context.

This article analyses neoliberalised cultural industries policies in Taiwan, in particular, how its discourses shape the image of 'creative industries' and profoundly change the form of public subsidies. The research explores this issue across three dimensions: the adoption of the British creative industries model in Taiwan; the neoliberal subsidy system in creative industries policy; and the combination of a broadly neoliberal frame for cultural policy and emerging utilitarian agents.

First, creative industries policy was officially adopted in 2002 and accelerated the neoliberal development of culture and media policies in Taiwan. However, 2000 to 2002 was a crucial period for the dissemination of creative economies from Britain through the international creative economy conferences. The British Council and several independent cultural organisations invited creative industries experts from Britain as a stepping stone to developing an official creative industries policy statement and *Taiwan Cultural and Creative Industries Project* in 2002 (Executive Yuan 2002). Secondly, neoliberal creative industries policy accelerated a serious deterioration of the Taiwanese film production industry. For example, the film market structure was monopolised by chain cinemas and Hollywood film distributors in Taiwan (Crane 2014). Consequently, Taiwanese filmmakers face two structural dilemmas: first, neoliberalised public subsidy and investment policies in a creative industries model and, second, a Hollywood-dominated industry (i.e., movies, distributors, and domestic chain cinemas) that has maintained a high market share for decades.[1] This occurred as a result of competitive and cooperative situations, which inserted a neoliberalised creative industries model. The neoliberal rhetoric of creative industries policies discourse seeped almost imperceptibly into the film industry subsidy system, in particular, the National Development Fund (NDF), a new investment mechanism for supporting emerging industries such as creative industries since 2003. However, these projects for the revitalization of the film industry were not successful because they were too focused on short-term results, such as prioritising immediate profit over creating shared value rather than on long-term thinking. The government should mainly provide plentiful and planned public funds allowed for the cultivation of directing, camera and editing talents. It will also encourage companies to invest in equipment and training for domestic film production and screening. Finally, we explore how market-oriented film policymaking and the commercialised public subsidies system have changed the relationship between independent filmmaker and the public sector. Here the government and private corporations began to develop a new close relation through neoliberal discourse, arguing that the new public-private partnerships are more efficient than public investment (Von Rimscha 2011). These developments are explored through analysis of official records, documentary material, newspapers, previous studies, and surveys tracing the history of creative industries policymaking.

The diffusion and adaptation of creative industries policy

Welcoming the international creative industries experts between 2000 and 2002

Neoliberalism, global capitalism and the profitable growth of global cultural industries gradually penetrated the direction of cultural policy in Taiwan. Its first official cultural and creative industries project was proposed in 2002. The 'creative industries' concept had been discussed in the United Kingdom since 1997 and Australia since 1994 (Flew 2012). Here, the imbalance of priorities in cultural policies has been linked to the chronic short-termism of cultural governance. These discourses regard the creative industries as a feasible solution for transforming traditional industry and increasing employment and the value of production. However, as this economic role of cultural policy has intensified, it has created a new conflict between two values: market-oriented investment and public-service subsidies.

To several Asian countries such as Japan, Taiwan, Korea, and Singapore, this British creative industries policy appeared to be a successful paradigm since New Labour won the 1997 election. Several international conferences of 'creative industries' were held between 2000 and 2002, and the Taiwanese government implemented a creative industries policy in 2002. Therefore, the conceptions and practices of British creative industries were portrayed as a new strategy for both cultural policy and cultural economy in Taiwan.

These three conferences (2000–2002)[2] were key moments for disseminating discourses relating to creative economies from Britain to Taiwan; in particular, the British Council and several independent cultural institutions played a significant role in the process. The British Council was one of the most important intermediaries in the export of the idea of creative industries. Elledge (2012) analysed the British Council as an ambitious player, successfully introducing British culture and reputable education system to the global market. He said:

> The British Council, it's widely thought, is a thoroughly good thing. It is the epitome of soft power, a long-established arm of the Foreign Office that promotes British interests not with bombs and guns, but through culture and education.[...] The British Council isn't just a charity.
>
> *(Elledge 2012)*

Another study (Kong et al., 2006) goes even further, arguing that the creative industries discourse was disseminated from West Europe to Asia, especially in cities such as Hong Kong, Taipei, Tokyo, Seoul, and Singapore between 1999 and 2000. The adoption of creative industries policy discourse by the cultural policy planners, artists, and academics was derived from Western creative industries experts through various international conferences, procurement contracts and consultancy work. International conferences, workshops, and seminars held by the British Council and other local cultural organisations can be understood in the context of the needs of the new Asian cultural economy and its interests.

The first forum, entitled '2000 New Government and New Cultural Policy', consisted of two main sections (see Table 29.1). First, Dr Chris Bilton, who since 1997 had been a lecturer at Warwick University where he founded and acted as course director for a master's programme in creative and media enterprises, spoke about British cultural and creative policy, particularly the New Labour government's policies and the new relationship between government and small creative businesses. The second section of the seminar comprised a discussion. The main participants were two members of parliament, artists, representatives of local cultural organisations, art institutions, and Bilton. Some attendees worried that the protection of Taiwanese cultural industries may be insufficient in an era of globalisation (Shi 2000, p. 14). Bilton's speech was the main event and focused on cultural localisation and globalisation. The critique of high-cost cultural events was reported in national newspapers such as *United Daily News* and *Chinese Times* (Chen 2000, p. 11; Shi 2000, p. 14). Bilton (2000), in this first conference, pointed out the contradictions in cultural policymaking in Britain and expressed the belief that small creative businesses, local cultural organisations, and individuals were the hope of cultural policy. He asserted that the government should support them by building training infrastructure, providing opportunities, and coordinating different sectors through micro-policy (Bilton 2000; Chen 2000; Shi 2000). In response to the plight of New Labour's cultural policy, Bilton (2000) suggested that the government should more vigorously support the growth of local culture, such as small creative businesses. Furthermore, he demonstrated that the optimal development of the creative industries must not be driven by government. On the contrary, the role of the government should be that of a facilitator or promoter in the process.

Representing the localised approach, conference attendees—Taiwanese politicians, cultural organisations and scholars—responded by describing conflicts between globalised cultural industries and the subjectivity of Taiwanese culture (Chen 2000; Shi 2000). Accordingly, the practice of art education, the development of community culture and the preservation of cultural heritage were discussed in the second section of the seminar.

However, the problems relating to New Labour's creative industries policymaking were not unveiled until 2004 (Oakley 2004; Garnham 2005; McGuigan 2005a,b). Only a few critical academics writing about the UK addressed these issues during that period (McGuigan & Gilmore 2000; Volkerling 2001), even though certain dilemmas were mentioned at the conferences; for example, the overextended development of intellectual property rights legally sanctioned monopolistic practices, leaving enterprises free to set their own prices (Bilton 2001). At the same time, positive aspects, such as increasing employment, industrial transformation and freelancers in creative industries were magnified, rather than negative aspects.

In 2001, three experts from the UK participated in the second meeting, titled *2001 Creative Money: Culture Economy Seminar* (see Table 29.1). This was also the first time that the local government (Taipei City) supported this activity. Experts from academia, local cultural affairs, and government sectors contributed with further practical help and effective advice. *Creative Industries International Summit* was held in 2002 soon after the government announced the second national project. Five experts came from Britain, some of whom shared the successful British experience in terms of holding regional cultural festivals. Some worked in government sectors such as the Department for Culture, Media & Sport (DCMS) and local council, which shared the idea of 'Cool Britannia' and the Millennium Dome as an urban renewal project. However, New Labour adopted a neoliberal approach to practice its 'democratisation of culture' and Hewison (2014) analysed how New Labour's cultural policy was ornamented with fake democracy (p. 33). Hewison (2014) demonstrated that DCMS is a neoliberal project that combines all cultural aspects, including arts, broadcasting, creative industries, the national lottery, tourism, sport, and Olympics, and is 'creating an efficient and competitive market [which] is consistent with the neoliberal approach to culture' (p. 70). According to several studies (McGuigan 2004, 2016; Oakley 2004; Garnham 2005; Hewison 2011, 2014; Hesmondhalgh et al. 2015; Bell & Oakley 2015; Newsinger 2015), the problems of cultural policies in the UK during the post-Thatcherite period were different from those of the previous period. Under Thatcherism, the arts and culture were of little importance, perhaps no more worthwhile than other commodities in the marketplace.

Table 29.1 Creative industries seminars in 2000, 2001, and 2002

Date	Topic	International speakers/background		Organisers
17 April 2000	2000 New Government, New Cultural Policy	Chris Bilton	Director of MA in Creative and Media Enterprise, Centre for the Studies of Cultural Policy, School of Theatre Studies, University of Warwick, UK	Organised by 1. School of Continuing Education, Chinese Culture University 2. Culture Concern Association 3. British Council
18–19 August 2001	Creative Money: Culture Economy Seminar	Chris Bilton Phyllida Shaw Toby Hyam	Listed above Researcher in cultural policy and practice Chief Executive of The Huddersfield Media Centre	Advised by Department of Cultural Affairs, Taipei City Government, British Council, and Ministry of Economic Affairs. Organised by academic institutions and cultural foundations.
25–27 October 2002	Creativity Is Endless Resources: 2002 Creative Industries International Summit	Michael Seeney Phyllida Shaw Kathryn McDowell Alastair McDonald Jeremy Tyndall	Head of the creative industries division in the department for culture, media and sport Researcher in cultural policy and practice Director city of London Festival Director of the Highland Festival Head of Festivals, Cheltenham Borough Council	Organised by Council for Cultural Affairs, British Council, and other foundations

The second creative industries seminar (see Table 29.1) focused on a very different objective: exploring the economic value of creative industries. The title, *Creative Money: Culture Economy Seminar*, revealed the real intent of new cultural policymaking, and the seminar showed that the discourse of the creative industries was developing new keywords: turnover, size of employment, profit, loss and growth potential. At the seminar, the economic value of the creative industries was heavily emphasised. Some successful British experiences were embellished with statistical data to demonstrate that the creative industries worked economically in the UK. The introduction to the project declares its purpose: 'Great Britain brought in the Industrial Revolution in the 18th century, and now the British creative industries will again be crucial to a new wave of industrial revolution in the 21st century' (2001 Creative Money: Culture Economy Seminar 2001). It also asked a question: 'Do art and culture have weak performance compared to industry?' The aim of the programme implied that the creative industries should be combined with cultural activities to double their economic value in the industrialised economy. Three British experts were invited to the second conference: Bilton (2001), who spoke at the first conference; Phyllida Shaw (2001), a freelance researcher in cultural policy; and Toby Hyam (2001), who founded a successful creative business and advised the cultural sector in local government in developing creative industries (see Table 29.1). New ideas were discussed on this occasion, such as new cultural policymaking, increasing self-employment (freelance), and the new relationship between the government and enterprises. These ideas illustrated that these new creative industries require cooperation among the government, corporations, and creative individuals.

It can be argued that the increase in cultural and creative jobs has been a key employment trend in the knowledge economy and information society. Self-employment has not only meant creative freedom but has also entailed financial risk. In addition, young people who choose to engage with creative and cultural works usually deal with erratic incomes and low wages. However, the freedom to pursue a job that one likes may be the main reason that new entrants into the labour force manage to muster low wages without fighting for their economic rights or for reasonable treatment. In her speech, Shaw explained the meaning of 'self-employment' as creative freedom and financial risk. However, she also rationalised the structure of exploitation in the context of 'creative people with a saleable skill' (Shaw 2001). She opined: 'It would be quite wrong to imply that all self-employed people in the cultural sector are struggling financially. This is not so. For anyone who is offering a service that the market wants, there is a good living to be earned' (Shaw 2001). Nevertheless, except for those offering a marketable service or saleable skill, such as record producers, film actors, screen writers, and pop musicians, most freelancers are on the lower income scale in the creative industries. Regional cultural sector officials, local cultural institutions, and artists played a significant role in the second conference.

The invited Taiwanese artists and cultural organisations mainly discussed the protection of their livelihoods in the new creative industries in Taiwan. It can be argued that this was the moment the projected development of the creative industries began, since government representatives from the economic and cultural sectors were questioned by artists and cultural workers who had also been deployed along the front lines in this conference. Questions focused particularly on the new relationship among the government, private enterprises, and the individuals involved—artists, curators, cultural workers, and so on—in developing the creative industries environment.

The third conference—*Creativity Is Endless Resources: Creative Industries International Summit*—was held after the second national project in 2002. As the name suggests, the conference focused on the new creative industries programme for policy planners and the implementation of new creative enterprises. The list of international experts, which included the head of the Creative Industries Division of DCMS, three heads of regional cultural festivals, and Shaw focused more on effectiveness, for instance, economic benefits deriving from cultural festivals and the new commercial models of creative industries. These British representatives and professionals influenced the direction of and discourse about creative industries policy in the third conference, and the British experience was deemed a great success and an effective economic stimulus (Li 2001a,b; 2001 Creative Money: Culture Economy Seminar 2001).

The purpose and agenda did not categorically include cultural workers' viewpoints, which were presented in the second conference, and issues relating to the self-employed in creative industries was only briefly mentioned. The topics were in keeping with the general ambience of the increase in future wealth (Mcdonald 2002; Mcdowell 2002; Seeney 2002; Shaw 2002; Tyndall 2002). In particular, the economic effectiveness that may result from creative industries attracted mostly positive attention. A quotation from the British creative industries mapping document (Creative Industries Task Force 1998) illustrated that ambiguity is the essence of creative industries, a point also featured in the opening words of the conference.

> Those industries which have their origin in individual creativity, skill and talent and which have a potential for wealth and job creation through the generation and exploitation of intellectual property.
>
> *(2001 Creative Money: Culture Economy Seminar, 2001)*

Moreover, the discourse of the conference reflected the state of neoliberalised cultural policymaking, which involved the use of the resulting policy space to pursue a variety of short-term economic programmes for cultural policy.

In Table 29.1, we see the change in organisers for each year. Moreover, it is clear that the British Council acted as the intermediary between the British creative industries discourse, the experts and independent cultural organisations in Taiwan. It is very interesting to explore the meaning behind the selection of representative 'experts of creative industries'. Only one international expert was invited in the first year of the conference to introduce British cultural policy and creative industries. Consequently, the British experience of developing creative industries was theoretically and historically introduced by Bilton (2000, 2001). Further discourse during the conference reflected the state of new cultural policymaking, with the resulting policy space used to pursue a variety of economic short-term programmes for cultural policy. Advocates of this policy are still at a loss for what to expect from the public. The growing neoliberal consensus is also helping to shape the new cultural landscape by focusing on the profit-making production of culture. Neoliberal reform for cultural and creative policymaking in Taiwan has generally failed to promote public interest. The creative economy has heavily influenced the development of cultural policy discourse. The Taiwanese government embarked on a major cultural policy shift towards neoliberalism after concluding that its adoption of 'creative industries' policy from Britain in 2002 had failed to reform the structure of the media and cultural industries. As a trajectory of neoliberalisation in Taiwan, public expenditure on the expansion of the creative industries sector in the last decade illustrates that creative industry policymaking was embodied in a complete neoliberal transformation in the past decade.

Emphasising creative industries policy in the national development project

Before the release of the official creative industries policy in the national development project, Challenge 2008 Six-Year National Development Plan (Executive Yuan 2002), creative industries seminars that focused on the British experience were held by local cultural organisations, academics and the British Council in Taiwan in 2000 and 2001. The third seminar took place after the announcement of the creative industries policy and was held by cultural organisations and the government in 2002. Following the success of the British case and experiences, the official document directly emphasised the economic value of the creative industries. In addition, the 'creative industries project' was one of the most significant national plans in Challenge 2008: Six-Year National Development Plan (Executive Yuan 2002). This project was also the first national project that established the importance of cultural policy. This section thus introduces the creative industries programme, particularly the securely anchored principles for the primary development of the programme. This national project has served as a prominent symbol of the orientation towards an ambitious agenda for the creative industries.

It can be argued that the new creative industries project was of the highest importance in a post-Fordist period. Interestingly, while 'post-Fordism' was not mentioned as a category in the first project, it appeared in the background in descriptions of the plight of industrial development. It was claimed that the Taiwanese economy faced the new prospect of deindustrialisation; in particular, the superiority of large-scale manufacturing disappeared since neighbouring countries had a greater abundance of cheaper labour than Taiwan (Executive Yuan 2002). Moreover, two main approaches were more specific to Taiwan: (1) high-tech industries, developed as high-tech original equipment manufacturers (OEMs) in Taiwan over decades; (2) the launch of a new sustainability strategy for the knowledge economy, which set out a joint approach to sustainability. The government also indicated that the 'cultural and creative industries' had enabled Taiwan to secure substantial additional value in the 'knowledge economy' for the post-Fordist generation. Therefore, it asserted that the objectives of creative industries policy were to double employment, triple output value, and create a new leading position for Taiwanese creative industries in the Chinese-speaking world (Executive Yuan 2002, p. 37). To introduce the new cultural policy, the government even claimed that 'culture could be part of the economic policy; however, it has been ignored for a long time' (p. 37).

The government first coined the term 'cultural creative industries' in this national project by combining the concepts of cultural industries and creative industries. It attempted to develop Taiwanese 'cultural and creative industries' and had consulted international experts about possible policies, including related to a global vision and localised practice. The national project assumed that the flourishing creative industries and this new business model would facilitate a new form of manufacturing that integrated high-tech, aesthetic design with a high quality of production (Executive Yuan 2002, p. 43). Several ongoing sub-projects were presented, including an inter-ministerial group, an industrial general survey, a mapping document, annual reports, new environmental facilities (such as a creative industries park), various training programmes, intellectual property protection, new public subsidies and investment incentive policies. The inter-ministerial group consisted of representatives from four government departments: the Ministry of Economic Affairs, the Council for Cultural Affairs, the Ministry of Education, and the Council for Economic Planning and Development (Executive Yuan 2002, p. 37; Cultural and Creative Industries Promotion Team, Ministry of economic affairs 2004, 2005). Further, many domestic and foreign experts, professionals, and artists were invited to participate in the new group with the aim of implementing the new policy and drafting the law. There was special interest in concepts and experiences from Britain, Australia, New Zealand, and Hong Kong. There was an attempted localisation of British creative industries policy within the government's commercialised cultural policy reforms. This was done to encourage businesses to innovate practical solutions and policies in exchange for new public subsidies.

Over the next few years, new creative parks such as a pop music centre and design centre were constructed in abandoned city factories as part of the new urban renewal plan. For example, one of the most 'successful' and high-profit cases in the capital city of Taipei was Huashan1917 Creative Park, which was reconstructed from a former national brewery. In addition, many new creative businesses and companies were set up during the period. According to the online search system of the government, the Commerce Industrial Service Portal (Ministry of Economic Affairs 2016), the number of 'cultural and creative' company registrations illustrates that a swarm of emerging 'creative' businesses were thriving during the decade. There were 1265 'cultural and creative' enterprises founded after 2002. Forty-five companies had been set up by 2002.

The project made mention of the 'knowledge economy' in the context of the innovative economy and 'sustainable development' and 'the social function of culture' in the context of social justice. The fundamental contradiction of neoliberal ideology was embodied in the discourse of the knowledge economy, which focused on increasing employment after the decline of traditional manufacturing in Taiwan. Cultural policy, however, was not considered a policy tool for this sort of economic development. It was promised through a more results-oriented and efficient administration, such as the privatisation of national industries, instead of propping up the gradual decline of the manufacturing industry, which had been moving production overseas. Thus, the project aimed at a modern and innovative approach to promoting more 'efficient' management for industrial development.

Finally, the creative industries project encouraged the education system to set up more 'creative industries' departments for providing tailored training in relevant skills for the creative industries. As the second national project estimated, there was an increase in the number of people, especially younger people, working in such creative industries. At the same time, there were problems specifically related to job instability and low wages.

This section has dealt with the origin of creative industries policy development. In the next section, film industry policy is analysed, particularly the influence of creative industries policy in failing to revive this industry.

Neoliberal film industry policy in a new creative industries model (2002–2009)

Two main film industry projects—the *Film Industry Promotion Project* and *the Flagship Film Industry Development Project*—were announced in 2002 and 2009, respectively. These two film industry plans were sub-projects of the Cultural and Creative Industries Project. The NDF also supports film industry projects through a public-and-private investment system.

The two film industry policymaking projects became dangerously unbalanced, and the new mechanism of state subsidies and private investment changed the concept of public subsidy. *The Film Industry Promotion Project* was part of the first creative industries policy project, which was announced in 2002 (Executive Yuan 2002). The government claimed that the enormous efficiencies of the knowledge economy and digital and information technology would influence a variety of types of digital content and products: 'We must seize the initiative on the knowledge economy' (Executive Yuan 2002, p. 2). It was convinced that the increasing employment rate in the creative industries, the good reputation of the 'cultural and creative' industries, and the gradually recovering economy would solve the crisis of the relocation of traditional manufacturing industry. Here the case of British creative industries policy seemed to successfully present the idea that future prosperity depended on economic growth via New Labour's creative industries policy.

Therefore, the project suggested the Taiwanese film industry should integrate digital technology and information technology to grasp new business opportunities and a new market. This would be the only way to protect Taiwanese culture from being destroyed by other dominant cultures. The creative industries project was a point where the traditional audio and video industries, the high-technology industry, the digital software design industry, and creative talents could all converge. The potentially huge advantage of horizontal and vertical integration would continue to develop and move forward to the high-tech, high creativity, and high marketability of the film industry.

This project included three goals, and the total budget was almost £16 million in the first seven years (Executive Yuan 2002, p. 27). The short-term goal was increasing production, creating alternative channels for film screenings, and providing advice to the government on incentives for film investment. Different official departments such as the Industrial Development Bureau and the Council for Cultural Affairs and Government Information Office were told to cooperate and amend original film industrial policies, regulations, and laws to integrate talent, technology, production, marketing, and private investment as the medium-term goal of the project.

The Flagship Film Industry Development Project was the second project and was announced in 2009. Following this main project was *Creative Taiwan: Cultural and Creative Industries Development*, which was smaller and had three main objectives (CCA 2009). The first objective was assisting filmmakers to make good movies via a new market research sector, creative originality awards, and funding high-cost and high-risk film productions, as a means to making the films critically acclaimed box-office hits. The second objective was focusing on the Chinese film market, by which the government aimed to improve indigenous film marketing in both domestic and foreign markets. In addition, a plan for increasing Taiwanese film audiences was to be promoted through film education. Finally, the project would encourage international film productions to make films in Taiwan and improve technical exchange. The film industry talent and education plan was to be funded by the government (CCA 2009, p. 34).

In *Flagship Film Industry Development Project*, the government increasingly encouraged Taiwanese filmmakers to target the Chinese market. *The Cross-Strait Service Trade Agreement* aimed to develop new treaties between the film industries of Taiwan and China. According to the Chinese policy of deregulation, the Taiwanese government believed that a new co-production deal offered Taiwanese filmmakers the chance to grab a piece of China's booming but heavily censored movie industry. Thus, the Chinese market became a key project in 2009. The private enterprises that gained public sources of funding for investing in filmmaking also believed that film production should focus on the Chinese market, to recover investment and even improve profitability. However, such a strategy raised problems for production in Taiwan. For example, the Hong Kong film industry changed after the Closer Economic Partnership Arrangement (CEPA) was signed in 2003. Many studies (Kang 2012) have demonstrated that this arrangement brought more opportunities for producing Chinese movies; however, the production of indigenous Hong Kong films, with local culture, has dropped sharply in the past decade.

However, neither film industry project solved the problem; in particular, film policy-making did not develop stable growth in terms of production or at the box office, and film industry talent training required a long-term plan (see Table 29.2). Many public resources were aimed at the aspect of effective investment under the creative industries model. Avant-garde and innovative filmmakers fell by the wayside. It is perfectly understandable that some films are not funded by government subsidies if they are not potentially popular commodities. However, this was a secondary concern when political posturing and the neoliberal creative industries policy discourse attempted to accelerate the potential of film investment with little success in improving the film industry's environment.

For example, the amendment to the Film Act, which passed in 2015, extended the reduction to taxation rates. In particular, reduced tax rates were available to foreign motion picture production businesses in Taiwan. The long-term goal of the *Film Industry Promotion Project* was to develop both the global film market and international cooperation. As for policy coherence in the development of the Taiwanese film industry, policy discourse forms a common language that underlines the ideology of neoliberalism, where the government has shown a consistent commitment to developing a vibrant private investment market in Taiwan. The conception of tax relief originally encouraged private enterprises to invest in film production, especially to reduce their investment risk. Decreasing indigenous film production (and the box-office slump) was not realised by increasing private investment. Film production in Taiwan has faced challenges since the 1990s, with high-profile projects such as *Cape No. 7* (海角七號) biting the dust.

While Taiwan's filmmaking has ostensibly blossomed in recent years, global film distribution corporations still dominate most of the film market in Taiwan. The unbalanced distribution between indigenous films and foreign films has influenced Taiwanese film production and audiences for a long time (e.g., the Taipei film box office from 2006 to 2011) (see Table 29.3).

The wide disparity in box office numbers between indigenous and foreign films illustrates the dilemma of the Taiwanese film industry. Foreign films, especially those from Hollywood, accounted for almost 90% of box-office revenue from 2006 to 2011. According to reports (Ministry of Culture 2013c,d, 2014), Taiwanese film production has been increasing since the government promoted creative industry policy in 2002. Both film industry projects claim that the Taiwanese film industry bucked the trend during the economic

Table 29.2 Two film industry projects in creative industries model

Date	2002–2008	2009–2013
Title of the Plan (comes from) Sub program (comes from) Main Project	Film Industry Promotion Project Cultural and Creative Industries Development Plan Challenge 2008: Six-Year National Development Plan	Flagship Film Industry Project Six Flagship Plans Creative Taiwan: Cultural and Creative Industries Development
Main targets	• Short-term goal (2004–2007): increasing production and box-office growth (10%) • Medium-term goal (2008–2011): box-office growth (10%–20%) and international cooperation • Long-term goal (2012–2014): box-office growth (20%–40%) and more international cooperation	• Plan 1: Make movies that have great acclaim and are big box-office hits • Plan 2: Successful marketing and promotion in the Chinese film market • Plan 3: Develop an industrial base and emerging talent

Source: Combined by the author from *Film Industry Promotion Project* and *Flagship Film Industry Development Project* (CEPD 2008; CCA 2009).

Table 29.3 Domestic market shares of Taiwanese cinema in Taiwan (cumulative total of Taipei City box office) from 2006 to 2011

		Taiwanese cinema	*Hong Kong and Chinese film*	*Foreign films*	*Total*
2006	Quantity	19	30	277	326
	Percentage box office	1.62%	3.70%	94.68%	100%
2007	Quantity	22	19	309	350
	Percentage box office	7.38%	1.94%	90.68%	100%
2008	Quantity	29	29	320	378
	Percentage box office	12.09%	6.98%	80.93%	100%
2009	Quantity	31	32	316	379
	Percentage box office	2.13%	2.26%	95.61%	100%
2010	Quantity	38	38	352	428
	Percentage box office	7.31%	5.33%	87.36%	100%
2011	Quantity	36	38	406	480
	Percentage box office	18.65%	2.63%	78.71%	100%

Source: The Trend of Film and Television Industries Report (Ministry of Culture 2013e, p. 10).

downturn with a year of steady growth in revenue and attendance. However, the slogan 'The Taiwanese film industry is booming now' is not practical, particularly in terms of successful creative industries policy. The film industry projects were able to attract additional private investment via the NDF. The government believes that through this mechanism private investment can stimulate more domestic film production and innovation, which will enable Taiwan to retain what it has built, create what is yet to be built, and specifically, attract private capital investment to augment any public contribution. Private investment flows in, but the diversification of film production is limited. Furthermore, the relationship between the government (NDF), private capital (investors), and creative labourers (filmmakers) changed via the new investment and subsidy system.

Emerging utilitarian agents and marginalised agents in the new subsidy system

Since 1986, before Taiwanese film industry policy was changed to a creative industries model, it was part of an open market that emphasised the free trade of foreign films, particularly by movie distributors from Hollywood. It can be said that the production line of indigenous films gradually decayed during this period. Although the Government Information Office (GIO) has pushed a film subsidy grant policy since 1989, the film market has been monopolised by Hollywood movie distributors and local motion picture projections for a long time. The film subsidy grant mechanism has assisted several Taiwanese filmmakers in making films, some of which were global film festivals winners, but it cannot support an entire film industry. Many Taiwanese filmmakers are ridiculed, and are said to be like manual labourers with makeshift equipment, provisional settings and non-existent production lines. Before the creative industries project, a small part of the public allowance system was used to support individual cultural workers such as filmmakers, artists, and local cultural organisations. However, the cultural budget in the public sector is always very low, including the film subsidy grant mechanism. These public subsidies support cultural affairs and individuals directly without the intermediary of investment consulting firms.

Since 2003, the NDF has become an important public resource supporting *the Strengthening Investment in Cultural and Creative Industries Project*. Initially, the purpose of the NDF was to strengthen the implementation of industrial policies, particularly in high-risk industries, such as the petrochemical, semiconductor, and biotech sectors, which could become highly effective, core sources of meaning and strategic importance. An additional aim of the NDF was to foster an environment that encourages entrepreneurship, industrial upgrading, industry innovation and research, and the development and creation of Taiwanese brands. *The Plan for the Executive Yuan Development Fund* to Invest in Digital Content, Software and Cultural Creative Industries was drafted, while *the Challenge 2008: Six-Year National Development Plan* (Executive Yuan 2002) supported the creative industries project. Consequently, *the Plan to Invest in the Digital Content, Software and Cultural Creative Industries* (2005) was implemented following the principles of *the 2005 Plan to Strengthen Promotion of Digital Content Industry Development* (NDF 2007, 2008).

New cultural and creative enterprises and domestic investment consulting firms were the main targets of investment and subsidy. The NDF, which initially cultivated traditional and high-tech industries, vigorously promoted the creative industries project through financial support. The creative industries project was officially recognised as a key national development programme, while cultural policy has been approached as an economic tool since 2002. Public investment underwent neoliberalisation during the second period (see Table 29.4). Under this trend, the NDF increased funding, approving and allocating NT$10 billion for *the Executive Yuan National Development Fund Implementation Programme* for *Strengthening Investment in Cultural and Creative Industries*. In addition, a new public–private partnership involving the state, investment consulting companies, and creative professionals such as filmmakers and artists was established (NDF 2011, 2012, 2013).

Table 29.4 Transition of the public subsidy and investment system

Period	Title	Form
Before creative industries projects, there were several cultural subsidy policy	For example, Film subsidy grants Art Subsidy	Limited subsidies and small grants from the public sector
2002–2008 Stage 1 (DPP government)	Cultural & Creative Industries Development Project (from the Challenge 2008: Six-Year National Development Plan)	Retained the original grant system, but increased the public budget for investment in the digital content industry and creative industries
2009–2013 Stage 2 (KMT government)	Creative Taiwan: Cultural and Creative Industries Development	More investment via NDF was authorised

The Strengthening Investment in Cultural and Creative Industries Project seems to have broken the vicious circle of the marginalised status of the domestic film industry. In particular, the NDF's investment and loan projects were expected to increase film production. In addition, private investors were allowed to apply through the NDF to support creative industries. This investment option was especially attractive to professional investment consulting companies that could reduce their investment risk, provide effective financial management and safeguard profitability. It seemed a reasonable proposition that the investment consulting companies could provide professional management services for the effective application of public funds and private investments in the film industry. However, the pursuit of high return on investment (ROI) has not proven able to drive development of the Taiwanese film industry. Currently, filmmakers must not only navigate government bureaucracy but also negotiate with the professional investment-consulting firms when applying for subsidies and investment in film production. The criteria for funding approval may value box-office numbers and ROI above film content.

The Strengthening Investment in Cultural and Creative Industries project is the most recent, representative neoliberal policy. As mentioned, it allocated NT$10 billion to investment-consulting firms such as management consulting companies to invest in various cultural creative industries approved by the government. Twelve management-consulting companies qualified for this funding, but only five were established after establishment of the project. However, after the first stage of implementation, this policy failed to achieve its expected goals. The government distributed only NT$8.13 billion of the planned NT$40 billion in the first stage. In addition, contracts with four venture companies were terminated because they failed to accomplish key performance indicators required by the Ministry of Culture. The ministry then developed the second stage of the project and planned to distribute NT$20 billion to domestic and international companies, including non-cultural creative companies, to assist in the development of cultural industries. For indicative cultural-creative businesses, the government increased the investment ratio from 1:1 to 3:1 (Jiang 2015).

As the former Minister of Culture Lung In-Tai clearly stated, the NDF plays the role of an investor, not a subsidiser. This statement accurately describes the state's role in transferring funds in the film industry. For investments, loss or profit must be taken into consideration in each case, so the public sector applies corporate managerial standards to creative companies. These public–private cooperative ventures face constant criticism, especially due to excessive expectations. For example, *Ripples of Desire* (2012) received investment from the NDF, TC Cultural Fund (文創1號), and Chinese capitalists. The production costs totalled NT$150 million, blockbuster standards in the Taiwanese film industry, but the film was a box-office failure, earning approximately NT$3.5 million. Even in Chinese markets, it made only RMB2.14 million in the first ten days of screening. All sectors of society criticised this failure. The press reported that this film seemed to benefit the Chinese holder of the distribution rights, but the TC Cultural Fund and NDF carried a higher proportion of production costs than the Chinese distributor. The Ministry of Culture explained that it sold the copyright to the Chinese distributor, so it could make profits regardless of box-office losses or gains (Ministry of Culture 2013c).

Putting aside this controversial claim, this statement clearly illustrates the profit orientation of the creative industries project. As long as this investment system operates, earnings will be the most important criterion for judging creative projects. This policy does not lift constraints on companies, and its influence extends beyond the narrowly defined film industry. This design of the system indirectly contributes to many pressures on filmmakers who worry about box-office returns. In addition, companies tend to support only the most successful and conservative projects to avoid losing government investment. Companies working through the NDF do not favour new and alternative filmmakers. Funding is usually directed at the production costs of potential blockbusters to stimulate economic development, attract more investment capital, and create the appearance of major achievements. This system has only widened the gap between filmmakers rather than offering significant aid to the whole film industry.

The new film industry subsidy system and investment policy, one of the main projects of creative industries policy, was expected to change the structure of the Taiwanese film industry. Creative industries policy and new public investment from the NDF was focused on not only investing in the creative industries but also spurring investment consulting firms to 'expand the synergy to promote the encouragement of emerging industries through investments' (NDF 2014, p. 18). While it can be said that the new partnership between the state and private investment consulting firms is a process of cultural and creative industries policy outsourcing for a more 'efficient public-and-private cooperation', it is actually a classic neoliberal economic model. The investment consulting enterprises were encouraged to invest in emerging creative industries such as films and digital content production for a certain percentage of public investment where the public sector offers incentives and reduces risk. The government claimed that the profit motive has provided an incentive for the private sector to create a flourishing indigenous film industry, without putting pressure on taxpayers. However, the pursuit of profit and economic value now ranks far too highly as a corporate objective, and diversification and cultural value rank too low. This new subsidy and investment mechanism has changed the relationship of the state (cultural sector), filmmakers (creative workers), the investment consulting firms, and the new creative business entrepreneurs. The main contradiction today is that the subsidy and investment system indirectly encourages these agents to compete for public sources of funding rather than create culture.

The subsidy system progressively changed when the government embraced creative industries policy in 2002. Before the creative industries project, artists and filmmakers had access to several limited cultural subsidies, which were not sufficient to support and build the domestic Taiwanese film industry and market. In particular, the film subsidy was granted only to individual filmmakers for a single production and did not cover all production costs, forcing filmmakers to seek loans or private sponsorship. Sometimes, the box office decided whether filmmakers would receive more subsidies (see Figure 29.1). As mentioned, local theatres and Hollywood film distributors had monopolised the domestic film market for the previous 30 years.

Importantly, cultural and communication policy was another target of neoliberal influence. Cultural and communication policy underlines the popularity of public discourse on business sponsorship and artists' individual responsibility to secure funding. The new term 'creative industries' came to represent the neoliberal trend and the retreat from democratisation of the arts. Throughout the process of neoliberalisation, the relationship of the state, cultural policies, artists (cultural workers) in cultural industries, and the public (audiences) underwent a dynamic process of change.

Under the creative industries model, the new subsidy system revealed the imbalance among the public sector, private investment and cultural workers (see Figure 29.2). Professional investment advisor management was required in the process for 'effective investment', and cooperation between the government and private enterprises formed a new funding model for 'improving the common good of the industry'. The new measures severely restricted diversification and affected the film industry.

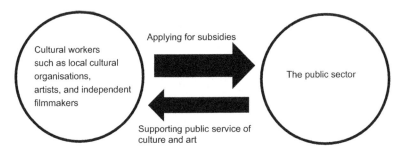

Figure 29.1   Model of public subsidy system before creative industries policy

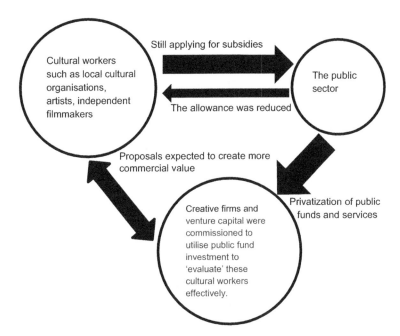

Figure 29.2   Model of public subsidy system after creative industries policy

Conclusion

This chapter studied the initial acceptance of British trajectories and the creative industry policies that were popular in cultural policymaking over a 10-year period in Taiwan. It then explored the impact of this acceptance, as public policy positioned the Taiwanese film industry at the core of creative industries development. Further, it demonstrated the urgent need to reassess creative industries policy, which represents a significant 'investment' by the government. For a long time, such investment has meant outsourcing to a few private capital players under a neoliberal model.

Many studies have pointed out that market-oriented cultural policies would injure the public value of culture, as well as common culture. In this case, the creative industries became the main focus of cultural policy, while at the same time they marginalised the core meaning of cultural policy. However, policy on creative industries should represent only a component of the cultural policies in Taiwan, and the perspective of public cultural policy provides a new opportunity to reorient the over-commercialised creative industries project. The recommendation is that the long-term development of arts and cultures and public service should be the core of the creative industries, as opposed to the quest for short-term profit in the film, TV and pop music industries. Training and media technology innovation, which plays a role in the integration of all resources relating to media content, will allow profit from policy to benefit the public rather than remaining in the hands of a few private capital players.

From the perspective of public cultural policy, film policy—under the framework of creative industries policy – should emphasise long-term development rather than short-term targets. Although the film industry entails the injection of private capital, this does not suggest that the public sector should act as a facilitator in pursuing the maximisation of profits. Hsiao-Hsien Hou, who won Best Director for *The Assassin* at the 68th Cannes Film Festival, made the following comment: 'Film which has both commercial and cultural traits should be supported via the governmental legislation. France defines that film is culture and Taiwan should do so.' In the creative industries model, film is more like a cultural commodity in relation to policymaking (Newsinger 2015).

In fact, the public sector should secure the existing system to directly assist filmmakers rather than only investment–consulting companies. For film industries, the most urgent issue the public sector can regulate is securing equitable distribution for each film, thereby avoiding imbalanced competition among Hollywood, chain distributions, and independent distributors. For example, a 2014 Taiwanese film, Elena, exhibited brilliant box-office performance during its run but had to withdraw from the market because no movie theatres were willing to provide this film with longer theatrical runs. Hollywood and strong local distributors dominate the film market channels in Taiwan. Therefore, this situation may be related to the idea of screen quotas, following the logic of 'cultural exception' from the late 1980s—although it is true that screen quotas have never been implemented, despite being mentioned several times.

The cultural exception could be an important conception against the head of the Motion Picture Association of America in Hollywood: Jack Valenti particularly despised European film directors for pleading with their governments to exclude cinema. South Korea is another role model, as it has had screen quotas in place since 1994. Initially, these quotas strictly mandated that Korean cinema had to be displayed at each movie theatre for 146 days each year; however, this was reduced to 73 days in 2007. During this period, Korean cinema gradually cultivated its niches and gained competitive power. Therefore, on one hand, screen quotas represent a new plan for the public cultural policy; on the other hand, they can replace neoliberal thinking in creative industries. This long-term-oriented cultural policy will be conducive to a more complete and robust industry.

Notes

1 Taiwan has been one of the most important international markets for Hollywood films for decades. Taiwan dropped film-import restrictions as it joined the World Trade Organisation (WTO) in 2001, and today, foreign movies take 97% of box office revenues (Jaffe 2011).

2 These three conferences are named: '*2000 New Government, New Cultural Policy Keynote Speech & Symposium*', '*2001 Creative Money: Culture Economy Seminar*' and '*2002 Creative Industries International Summit*'.

References

Bell, D. & Oakley, K. 2015. *Cultural Policy*. London: Routledge.

Bilton, C. 2000. *New government, new cultural policy*. Available from: http://w3.sce.pccu.edu.tw/creative/2000/ztyj.htm (Accessed 22 March 2014).

Bilton, C. 2001. *Funny money: the value of the creative industries*. Available from: http://w3.sce.pccu.edu.tw/creative/2001/M_default.htm (Accessed 22 March 2014).

Bilton, C. & Shaw, P. 2001. *The value of the creative industries*. Available from: http://w3.sce.pccu.edu.tw/creative/2001/M_default.htm (Accessed 22 March 2014).

Crane, D. 2014. Cultural globalization and the dominance of the American film industry: Cultural policies, national film industries, and transnational film. *International Journal of Cultural Policy*, 20(4), 365–382.

Creative Industries Task Force. 1998. *Creative industries: Mapping document, 1998*. London: Creative Industries, Department for Culture, Media and Sport.

Elledge, J. 2012. The British Council: friend or foe? *The Guardian*. Available from: www.theguardian.com/education/2012/oct/08/british-council-education-training (Accessed 4 September 2015).

Flew, T. 2012. *The Creative Industries Culture and Policy*. London: Sage.

Garnham, N. 2005. From cultural to creative industries: An analysis of the implications of the 'Creative Industries' approach to arts and media policy making in the United Kingdom. *International Journal of Cultural Policy*, 11(1), 15–29.

Hall, S. 2011. The neoliberal revolution. *Soundings*, 48(Summer), 9–27.

Harvey, D. 2005. *A Brief History of Neoliberalism*. Oxford: Oxford University Press.

Hesmondhalgh, D., et al. 2015. *Culture, economy and politics: the case of New Labour*. London: Palgrave Macmillan.

Hewison, R. 2011. "Creative Britain": Myth or monument? *Cultural Trends*, 20(3–4), 235–242.

Hewison, R. 2014. *Cultural capital: The rise and fall of creative Britain*. London: Verso.

Hyam, T. 2001. *Developing Networks of Artists and Creative Enterprises*. Available from: http://w3.sce.pccu.edu.tw/creative/2001/M_default.htm (Accessed 22 March 2014).

Jaffe, G. 2011. Will the great film quota wall of China come down? *The Guardian*. Available from: www.theguardian.com/business/2011/mar/24/china-film-quota.

Kong, L., Gibson, C., Khoo, L. & Semple, A. 2006. Knowledges of the creative economy: Towards a relational geography of diffusion and adaptation in Asia. *Asia Pacific Viewpoint*, 47(2), 173–194.

Lindsay McIntosh. 2009. Film-makers fear their industry is being ignored by Creative Scotland (News). *The Times* (London, England), p. 23.

Mcdonald, A. 2002. *The Highland Festival and Its Importance to the Culture and the Economy of the Highlands of Scotland*. Available from: http://w3.sce.pccu.edu.tw/creative/2002/info-e_4.htm (Accessed 22 March 2014).

Mcdowell, K. 2002. *The City of London Festival – Past, Present and Future*. Available from: http://w3.sce.pccu.edu.tw/creative/2002/info-e_3.htm (Accessed 22 March 2014).

McGuigan, J. 2004. *Rethinking Cultural Policy* (Issues in Cultural and Media Studies). Berkshire: McGraw-Hill Education.

McGuigan, J. 2005a. The cultural public sphere. *European Journal of Cultural Studies*, 8(4), 427–443.

McGuigan, J. 2005b. Neo-liberalism, culture and policy. *International Journal of Cultural Policy*, 11(3), 229–242.

McGuigan, J. 2016. *Neoliberal Culture*. Basingstoke: Palgrave Macmillan.

McGuigan, J. & Gilmore, A. 2000. Figuring out the dome. *Cultural Trends*, 10(39), 39–83.

NDF, 2007. *2006 Annual Report of Development Fund*. National Development Fund Management Committee, Executive Yuan. Available from: www.df.gov.tw/attachement/95%E5%B9%B4%E5%B9%B4%E5%A0%B1%E5%85%A7%E5%AE%B9.pdf (Accessed 15 January 2015).

NDF, 2008. *2007 Annual Report of Development Fund*. National Development Fund Management Committee, Executive Yuan. Available from: www.df.gov.tw/attachement/2007%E5%B9%B4%E5%A0%B1.pdf (Accessed 15 January 2015).

NDF, 2011. *2010 Annual Report of Development Fund*. National Development Fund Management Committee, Executive Yuan. Available from: www.df.gov.tw/attachement/%E5%9C%8B%E7%99%BC%E5%9F%BA%E9%87%9199%E5%B9%B4%E5%A0%B1%E5%85%A7%E9%A0%81.pdf (Accessed 15 January 2015).

NDF, 2012. *2011 Annual Report of Development Fund* National Development Fund Management Committee, Executive Yuan. Available from: www.df.gov.tw/attachement/100%E5%B9%B4%E5%A0% B1%E5%85%A7%E6%96%87.pdf (Accessed 15 January 2015).

NDF, 2013. *2012 Annual Report of Development Fund* National Development Fund Management Committee, Executive Yuan. Available from: www.df.gov.tw/attachement/101%E5%B9%B4%E5%A0% B1%E5%85%A7%E6%96%87.pdf (Accessed 15 January 2015).

NDF, 2014. *2013 Annual Report of Development Fund*. National Development Fund Management Committee, Executive Yuan. Available from: www.df.gov.tw/attachement/102%E5%B9%B4%E5%A0% B1%E5%85%A7%E6%96%87.pdf (Accessed 15 January 2015).

Newsinger, J. 2015. A cultural shock doctrine? Austerity, the neoliberal state and the creative industries discourse. *Media, Culture & Society*, 37(2), 302–313.

Oakley, K. 2004. Not so cool britannia: The role of the creative industries in economic development. *International Journal of Cultural Studies*, 7(1), 67–77.

Seeney, M. 2002. *Creative Industries: The UK Experience*. Available from: http://w3.sce.pccu.edu.tw/ creative/2002/info-e_1.htm (Accessed 22 March 2014).

Shaw, P. 2001. *Self-Employment in the Cultural Sector. The UK Experience*. Available from: http://w3.sce. pccu.edu.tw/creative/2001/M_default.htm (Accessed 22 March 2014).

Shaw, P. 2002. *A Profile of Arts Festivals in the UK*. Available from: http://w3.sce.pccu.edu.tw/ creative/2002/info-e_2.htm (Accessed 22 March 2014).

Tyndall, J. 2002. *The Cheltenham Festivals: One Town – Many Festivals*. Available from: http://w3.sce. pccu.edu.tw/creative/2002/info-e_5.htm (Accessed 22 March 2014).

Volkerling, M. 2001. From cool Britannia to hot nation: 'Creative industries' policies in Europe, Canada and New Zealand. *International Journal of Cultural Policy*, 7(3), 437–455.

Von Rimscha, M. 2011. Handling financial and creative risk in German film production. *Wide Screen*, 3(1), 1–19.

Chinese references

CCA. 2009. Creative Taiwan: cultural and creative industries development. Council for Cultural Affairs.

CEPD. 2008. The Challenge 2008 Six-Year National Development Plan: (2) The final report of cultural and creative industries developing project. Council for Economic Planning and Development, Executive Yuan.

Chen, S. L. 2000. New government, New Cultural policy, New Challenge. *China Times*, p. 11.

Creative Industries International Summit. 2002. http://w3.sce.pccu.edu.tw/creative/2002/ (Accessed 22 March 2014).

Creative Money: Culture Economy Seminar. 2001. http://w3.sce.pccu.edu.tw/creative/2001/ (Accessed 22 March 2014).

Executive Yuan. 2002. The Challenge 2008 Six-Year National Development Plan.

Jiang, Z. L. 2015. The second stage of the project invests on Culutral Creative industries NDF budget 2 Billion. *Radio Taiwan International*. Available from: http://www.rti.org.tw/m/news/detail/? recordId=205498 (Accessed 15 January 2015).

Kang, Yu Ping. 2012. *Going northward-the division of cultural labor in the movie co-production between China and Hong Kong: After the implement of CEPA*. Unpublished master's thesis, National Chengchi University, Taipei, Taiwan.

Li, Y. L. 2001a. Developing Culture and Art Business: Learn from England. *United Daily News*, 2001 August 8, p. 14.

Li, Y. L. 2001b. Culture Economy Seminar 'Creative Industries' Put Forward. *United Daily News*, 2001 August 20, p. 14.

Ministry of Culture. 2013a. *2012 Taiwan Cultural & Creative Industries Annual Report*. Available from: http://stat.moc.gov.tw/Research.aspx (Accessed 15 January 2015).

Ministry of Culture. 2013b. *2013 Taiwan Cultural & Creative Industries Annual Report*. Available from: http://stat.moc.gov.tw/Research.aspx (Accessed 15 January 2015).

Ministry of Culture. 2013c. *2014 Taiwan Cultural & Creative Industries Annual Report*. Available from: http://stat.moc.gov.tw/Research.aspx (Accessed 15 January 2015).

Ministry of Culture. 2013d. *Ripples of Desire enter into Chinese market by a turnkey and profit-sharing project, To Guarantee profits in Taiwan rather than line China's pockets.* Available from: www.moc.gov.tw/information_250_13942.html (Accessed 15 January 2015).

Ministry of Culture. 2013e. *2011 The Trend of Film and Television Industries Report.* Available from: http://stat.moc.gov.tw/Research.aspx (Accessed 15 January 2015).

Ministry of Culture. 2014. *2013 The Trend of Film and Television Industries Report.* Available from: http://stat.moc.gov.tw/Research.aspx (Accessed 10 April 2016).

Ministry of Economic Affairs. 2016. *Commerce Industrial Service Portal.* Ministry of Economic Affairs. Available from: http://gcis.nat.gov.tw/mainNew/subclassNAction.do?method=getFile&pk=23 (Accessed 15 January 2016).

New Government, New Cultural Policy Keynote Speech & Symposium. 2000. http://w3.sce.pccu.edu.tw/creative/2000/ (Accessed 22 March 2014).

Shi, M. H. 2000. New government, New Cultural policy The British Experts Offer Advices. *United Daily News*, p. 14.

The group of the creative industry promotion, Ministry of economic affairs. 2004. *2003 Taiwan Cultural & Creative Industries Annual Report.* Available from: http://stat.moc.gov.tw/Research.aspx (Accessed 28 September 2015).

The group of the creative industry promotion, Ministry of economic affairs. 2005. *2004 Taiwan Cultural & Creative Industries Annual Report.* Available from: http://stat.moc.gov.tw/Research.aspx (Accessed 28 September 2015).

30

Uneasy alliances

Popular music and cultural policy in the 'music city'

Catherine Strong, Shane Homan,
Seamus O'Hanlon and John Tebbutt

Introduction

Administrators and policy makers in a number of cities worldwide (for example, Austin, Berlin and Liverpool) are increasingly seeking to utilise local music to promote their cities' cultures and increase tourism and trade. Designation as a 'music city', 'sonic city' or indeed as a formally recognised UNESCO 'City of Music' is seen as a means of harnessing local music cultures for the purposes of city branding and economic development. The concept of the 'music city' clearly has utility for governments and policy makers; however, a critical understanding of its parameters and usage has yet to be developed. In this chapter, we draw on a range of disciplinary traditions to examine the concept of the 'music city' with a view to understanding how cultural policy is changing in relation to popular music and how in turn the process of formally recognising music as a driver of cultural policy may be changing the relationships of governments, those working in the music industry, musicians, and the wider community.

In concentrating on Melbourne, Australia, as a useful contemporary music city case study we will assess the role of popular music in the city's dual status as music and cultural capital of Australia. The chapter will address how localised cultural and media industries intersect with state and federal strategies and discourses of popular culture and heritage. Beyond local music economies, Melbourne has become part of global music city circuits, in terms of both promotional discourse and policy intervention. For example, in November 2015, the City of Melbourne Council hosted *We Can Get Together: Melbourne Music Symposium* with national and international academic, industry and government workers to discuss global music city policy issues. Melbourne leads global debates in noise complaint mechanisms for live venues.[1] Coupled with the recent Victorian state government[2] funding package for popular music, the city represents an intriguing case study where future industrial growth is dependent upon the reconciliation of stubborn local problems (especially urban planning issues) and the ability to more forcefully enter into global branding and trade networks.

After giving an overview of the development and use of the concept of the 'music city', we concentrate on three aspects of popular music in Melbourne: government policy, media (in the specific form of radio), and heritage, as a way of illustrating how Melbourne has staked its claims as a music city. We will demonstrate how this claim has developed in a haphazard and uneven way, with government policies never clearly mapping out a path in this direction. Indeed, even at the current moment when policies are clearly in support of promoting Melbourne as a music city there are contradictions in, and unintended consequences of, policy decisions that work against the city securing its position in this regard. In presenting this case study, we contribute to international debates about the role of the neoliberal city and state in protecting or supporting popular music making. We also interrogate the role of the broader community in the creation of the music city and question the extent to which the competing imperatives of the two are compatible. In discussing 'popular music', we are referring to music that traces its development back to the rock and roll of the 1950s, in terms of its musical structure, embeddedness in mass production processes (although not always mass produced) and cultural signifiers, particularly in relation to youth culture (see Regev 2013).

Framing the music city

As the most sophisticated configuration of human existence, the city enjoys obvious advantages, primarily density (of peoples, structures and networks). Particularly since the 1700s, the experience of city life has been layered with governmental, social and corporate developments that attest to modernity, incorporating an increasingly global interdependence in finance, trade, transport, communication and other systems of the 'modern' city. While the continuing implications of half the global population residing in cities cannot be discussed in depth in this chapter, it is clear that cities are in fierce competition with each other in ways that proceed well beyond specific economic impacts and incorporate concerns about the symbolic and cultural. This is evident, for example, in the various ways in which administrators seek to produce distinctive brands for their cities for national and international consumption (see, for example, Dinard 2015), which are then harnessed to attract workers, artists or tourists.

It has been argued that the contemporary city will anchor "increasingly global and mobile culture, with locative dynamics that secure culture's real-time, life embodiment" (Hartley et al. 2013, p. 44). This marks a distinct turn from previous understandings of the relationships between arts, culture and the city. The first tranche of work on this topic in media, cultural/urban studies examined how cities can exploit a mixture of arts and culture in order to position themselves as global leaders (e.g. Landry 1990; Landry and Bianchini 1995; Hall 1998). In this way, in specific historical periods, cities such as Berlin, London and Vienna defined themselves through distinctive mixtures of design, art, music or literature, which in turn added impetus to their existing strengths in cultural and other trade networks. This allowed us to conceive of the 'literature city', the 'information city', or the 'film city' (Hall 1998), where "flexible specialisation" (Scott 2006, p. 3) enabled regional and global advantage.

The second tranche of work took up the challenge of exploring the implications of this from cultural geography, economic geography, cultural studies and urban planning perspectives (e.g. Kong 2000). Much of this work has focused on the particular roles of culture and creativity in the new urban economy; the geo-spatial patterns of creative work (networks and clusters); the unique geography and infrastructure of successful cities; and the proper role for government (Scott 2006). It also paralleled a shift in urban planning studies, where a focus on 'quality of life' and the construction of the 'right' infrastructure to attract the creative workforce (Florida 2002) were emphasised as cities competed to build effective brands.

Ignoring many of the dubious claims in modelling and in relation to outcomes, 'creative' or 'cultural' city discourses have been adopted by local and national governments to an astonishing extent. This raises questions about the role of the state in promoting creativity and in establishing governance platforms that enhance cultural production and consumption, as well as about how individual cities – and cultural industries – literally find their place within larger national, regional and global networks.

Popular music is associated with a useful set of cultural industries and activities through which we can examine how artistic creativity operates in contemporary cities and whether music as creative practice offers anything more to city administrators than an instrument of employment and/or urban regeneration. The concept of the 'music city' has entered the cabinet rooms of all tiers of government in the last two decades. This represents more than an offshoot of creative industries discourse. Music has become a prominent vehicle for staking claims about how culture can construct unique civic, industrial and individual identities, evident in the histories (and current touristic myth-making) of cities such as Detroit, Liverpool, London, Nashville, New York, Manchester and Berlin. Some of these older music cities, foundational sites for particular genres and subcultures, remain "global music cities" (Watson 2008) yet are being challenged by others seeking their own industrial niche. For example, Seville, Glasgow, Bogota, Gent, Bologna, Brazzaville, Hamamatsu, Mannheim and Hannover have all been designated as 'Cities of Music' by UNESCO as part of its 'creative city' networks.

What does the music city mean within local and international contexts? Key UNESCO criteria include the visible promotion of festivals, music education, genres and the prominence and prevalence of the cities' music industries (UNESCO 2014). A recent report – which described itself as "a universal 'roadmap' to create and develop Music Cities anywhere in the world" – from the International Federation of Phonographic Industries (IFPI) and Music Canada argues that "a Music City, by its simplest definition, is a place with a growing music economy" (IFPI/Music Canada 2015, np). This includes "[a]rtists and musicians; a thriving music scene; access to spaces and places; a receptive and engaged audience; and record labels and other music-related businesses" (along with state support, infrastructure and education programs) (ibid. p. 13). Part reassurance about the need for music in healthy creative cities and part primer for emerging music cities, the *Mastering of a Music City* report makes recommendations for fostering a city's music strengths that include "music-friendly and musician-friendly policies; a Music Office or Officer; a Music Advisory Board; engaging the broader music community to get their buy-in and support; access to spaces and places; and audience development" (IFPI/Music Canada 2015, pp. 13–15). In making these suggestions, it is implied that governmental support will be repaid in various ways, including through an increase in employment, tourism, urban regeneration and technological innovation, as well as other less tangible benefits.

Unsurprisingly, industry calls to (re)direct governmental resources to music tend to gloss over the more complex implications and consequences. First, the discourse is often one of inevitability – that constructing the music city is a natural outcome of organic structures and the 'already there'. Yet rarely are competing cultural claims (why not the film city, or the literature city?) made or tested, while the benefits claimed for local and national economies remain a very inexact science. Second, including music in urban planning in the name of 'vibrancy' can produce very mixed outcomes. The mix of planning, zoning and heritage discourses has always been controversial in terms of live music venues (e.g. Chevigny 1993). The original Florida (2002) thesis (the creative class reinvigorating 'lapsed' cities in both lifestyle and economic terms) in some cases has worked too well. Gentrification in urban

CBD areas is now a common global problem for live music venues facing closure from noise complaints and rising land rent; and for musicians unable to afford to live near their live performance spaces. In this outcome, we see the positioning of the artist as "shiny prophet (evidence of new populations of middle class consumerism) or villain (evidence of new populations of middle class consumerism!)" (Homan 2016, np). Indeed, Florida has slightly revised his original thesis to acknowledge that "the benefits of highly skilled regions accrue mainly to knowledge, professional and creative workers"; the non-creative and non-professional classes are particularly affected by rising land and housing costs due to the more intensive clustering of talent within cities (Florida 2013).

Third, the global preoccupation with licensing, noise complaint mechanisms and land use planning attests to the fact that often a more correct label for music cities is 'live music cities'. Austin (the self-proclaimed 'live music capital of the world') remains the best example in terms of leveraging their collection of music bars, honky tonks and nightclubs as global markers of difference, reinforced by their annual South by SouthWest music industry gathering. However, a few cities are developing other specialisations, with Mannheim, Montreal and Groningen exploiting strong music education networks and high youth populations (de Rook and Nasra 2015; Rauch 2015). Berlin has also highlighted the role of music 'tech start-ups' within its Smart City Berlin initiatives (Zimmer 2015).

Fourth, even as music city policies are increasingly globalised, driven by the growing number of music city conferences, policy summits and inter-city visits by administrative leaders, local contingencies must still be taken into account. For example, the Chinese and Shanghai governments are determined to construct the city as an emerging music capital; yet the music capital's substantial advantages in education and high art performance venues are more than offset by highly restrictive state control of recording production and media exposure for local musicians. Finally, the music city is an interesting means by which to dissect cultural funding discourses. Its rise has proven to be an effective way for popular music industries to gain governmental attention and largesse within local and national budgets where classical music retains considerable privileges and funding. Continually mindful of the competing demands upon their annual budgets, state and city governments are often receptive to regulatory reform, but not to increasing financial allocations. These global trends all inform the way Melbourne has been framed as a music city, and we will now turn to a more in-depth consideration of the local conditions.

The historical context: deindustrialisation, urban crisis and the 'cultural turn' in Melbourne

As with many of the international cities that have sought to leverage their cultural and musical assets for economic advantage, in Melbourne the turn to culture as economic 'saviour' was a product of crisis rather than a grassroots evolutionary movement. In line with other would-be 'music cities' such as Liverpool, Manchester and Detroit, the end of the Fordist era of manufacturing production was not kind to Melbourne (O'Hanlon 2009). As in those other cities, Melbourne's postwar prosperity was based on manufacturing, especially of low-value added consumer goods. But in the face of reductions in tariff protection and the emergence of the new manufacturing economies of Asia and elsewhere, these industries – mostly inner city based – went into severe decline in the 1970s and 1980s. Concurrently, Melbourne's other major economic strength as a national business and financial centre came under strain as Sydney emerged as Australia's major gateway and regional financial centre. The relocation of a number of media and cultural organisations to Sydney in the 1980s saw

Melbourne struggle for a defining role in the nascent post-industrial global era. The world-wide recessions of the early 1980s and again in the early 1990s were felt particularly hard in Melbourne, especially the inner area, which had suffered significant job losses and population declines from the mid-1970s onwards (O'Hanlon 2009).

Again in line with international trends, local and state government responses to these crises involved both a commitment to free market, neo-liberal economic restructuring. Along with a withdrawal of financial support for declining manufacturing industries, there was, contradictorily, a mostly publicly funded policy of transforming the economic and cultural profile of the inner city through major programs of cultural and morphological change (O'Hanlon 2010). In Melbourne, first a social democratic government in the 1980s and then a more radical free market regime in the early 1990s oversaw major cultural projects designed to enhance the city's vitality and tourist appeal, including the construction of a new museum, a new concert hall and recital centre, new and refurbished art galleries, and the redevelopment of the State Library as a key locus of the city's and state's literary heritage. The library now hosts the Wheeler Centre, which since 2008 has been the headquarters of the city's UNESCO 'City of Literature' office. The early 2000s also saw the opening of Federation Square, a government-funded, architecturally striking arts, leisure and cultural hub adjacent to the city's main railway station (O'Hanlon 2012).

These same governments sought to revitalise the inner city's economy and 'vibe' by committing resources to the cultivation of an arts and creative industries agenda through the support of major official and more grassroots cultural activities and events. At a state level, official support involved among other things the inauguration of an annual writers' festival and sponsorship of an annual 'international festival of the arts'. At a grassroots level, funding was made available for a range of community festivals, mostly in local 'ethnic' shopping strips and neighbourhoods, mainly in the inner city (O'Hanlon 2009). The grassroots cultural policy also recognised and provided funding to more 'street-based' endeavours, including Melbourne's then-emerging national strength in stand-up comedy. The major outcome of this was the inauguration of an annual Comedy Festival in 1987 – now the third largest annual comedy festival in the world. Perhaps most importantly for the purposes of this chapter, various governments – although mostly at that stage at the municipal level – recognised and sought to capitalise on the importance of rock and pop music to the creative and night time economy of local streets and neighbourhoods. A series of street festivals celebrating local music scenes was inaugurated in a number of declining inner city areas.

The St Kilda Festival was once such early initiative, inaugurated by the local municipal council in 1980 in recognition of the musical and cultural vitality of a suburb that was home to musicians and a series of important local and national live music venues including the Crystal Ballroom, the Esplanade and Prince of Wales hotels, and the glamorous but fading 3000-seat Art Deco-era Palais Theatre (Upton 2001; Aizen 2004). In the three decades since, the St Kilda Festival has become one of the largest street gatherings in Australia, a week-long carnival that culminates in 'Festival Sunday', where more than 400,000 people regularly gather to watch bands and DJs perform on numerous public stages and multiple other venues around the neighbourhood (St Kilda Festival). Similarly, council-sponsored local festivals, such as the Darebin Music Feast, have become common across inner suburban and wider metropolitan areas, as we shall see below. As a consequence, gentrification and rising property values have priced musicians and other artists out of their old haunts in inner-city neighbourhoods such as St Kilda (Shaw 2013).

More recently, both conservative (the Liberal Party in Australian parlance) and social democratic (the Labor Party) state governments, as well as the formally politically unaligned

City of Melbourne municipal council have sought to recognise and harness the music industry for economic (and political) purposes. The City of Melbourne's Music Strategy 2014–17 was, for instance, developed in recognition that "Melbourne is a city where music matters" and where "music makes a huge contribution to the social, cultural and economic fabric of the city" (City of Melbourne 2014, p. 6). The strategy thus seeks to harness the city's music cultures and concomitant economic impact in order to "promote Melbourne's strengths as a music destination" that can "take its rightful place alongside some of the great music cities of the world including Austin, Berlin, Nashville and Toronto" (City of Melbourne 2014, p. 6).

In the state of Victoria, a long-term Labor government developed a policy called 'Victoria Rocks' in 2007, which provided support and grants for emerging and more established musicians 'to break into the industry to further their careers' (Creative Victoria 2007). The same policy sponsored the launch of the annual Melbourne Music Festival and the free 'Victoria Rocks' concert in October 2010, which was designed to showcase artists who had received funding through the program. The festival was held, however, in the lead-up to a state election campaign where the contrasts between these initiatives and the effect of other government policies on live music were becoming obvious. Melbourne's live music cultures appeared threatened as venues struggled to keep operating in the face of new liquor licensing and crowd control measures introduced by the state government in 2009. Those concerns were most vividly shown when 10,000–20,000 people attended a protest rally in the city centre in February 2010 in response to the imminent closure of a long-standing venue, The Tote, in inner urban Collingwood (Donovan 2010). SLAM (Save Live Australian Music), a lobby group that organised the rally along with Fair Go 4 Live Music (organised by venue owner Jon Perring), became an important driver of policy change. This has particularly been the case in relation to the introduction of 'agent of change' regulations by the state parliament. These regulations work to reduce the impact of noise complaints on venues by putting the onus on new developments to ensure their residents will not be affected by noise, rather than requiring pre-existing venues to change their practices or install expensive soundproofing. The fact that the government felt a need to respond to the concerns of musicians and fans is perhaps indicative of a growing political recognition of the importance of music to the culture and economy of Melbourne, especially for its inner region where constituents are increasingly voting for the more left-wing Greens political party rather than Labor.

Having lost the 2010 election, in the lead-up to the 2014 poll Victoria's then Labor Opposition Leader (now Premier) Daniel Andrews sought to present himself as a champion of Melbourne's music scenes by reintroducing the 'Victoria Rocks' program that had been defunded by the Liberal Party government. More specifically, in recognition of Melbourne's place as the 'music capital of Australia' Andrews promised to create a 'Music Market' as a 'one-stop-music hub for recording and distribution, open to artists, venues, managers and industry development organizations" (ALP Victoria 2014). The Music Market was also to be "the headquarters of a new Victorian Music Development Office, providing leadership on investment, grants, exports and music business development" (ALP Victoria 2014). More substantially, and perhaps harking back to older policies of combining grassroots funding for artists with a commitment to a spatial outcome, the Music Market was to provide "space for performances, skills development and recording assistance, and facilities for industry peak bodies, not-for-profit industry organisations and support the values of contemporary music". And perhaps most importantly it was to house a proposed Australian Rock and Roll Hall of Fame (ALP Victoria 2014). Most of these proposals were announced in mid-2015 as part of what has now become known as 'Music Works', a "$12.2 million investment in Victoria's contemporary music sector" (Creative Victoria 2015).

In Melbourne, as in other post-industrial cities internationally, the success of such government-sponsored cultural initiatives has been a dual-edged sword. Aside from the question of whether popular music should ever allow itself to become hostage to mainstream politics and politicians, there is also the question of whether there is a place for such music in the new, more wealthy and gentrified inner city of the post-industrial era. In Melbourne as elsewhere urban renewal and cultural industry policies have seen once-declining areas that were home to various waves of immigrants, working class people and students, or in the case of Central Business District (CBD), virtually resident-free, become increasingly economically prosperous and culturally vibrant – and very expensive. One result of this rapid uplift in land and residential value has been a major influx of new and wealthy residents; they move especially into thousands of new and highly visible apartment complexes that have been built inside of or instead of defunct former factories (O'Hanlon 2016). A result of this development is in the displacement of the creative communities that played a part in making these areas attractive (Shaw 2009). Additionally, as cultural planner Kate Shaw has extensively documented, many of these new developments are adjacent to existing live music venues, some decades old. As she notes, gentrification means formerly under-utilised spaces "are under pressure from the raft of issues … that affect gentrifying cities the world over", such as noise complaints or simply being located on increasingly valuable (and developable) land (Shaw 2013, p. 337). As will be seen again below in relation to music heritage, this highlights the contrast between Melbourne as a music city where culture is valued and Melbourne as part of a neoliberal, free market economy where the benefits that musicians bring to a community are not generally rewarded financially.

Community radio and the music city

While the previous section looked at the political aspects of how music policy relating to Melbourne has developed over time, including how it has been shaped by global economic trends, such top-down accounts can fail to take into account specific local forms of music making and dissemination. In Melbourne's case, we suggest community radio has been a crucial marker of the city's musical vitality and will use this as a way to unpack some of the specificities of Melbourne's music scene, thus adding depth to our analysis. Music of course is a critical global cultural product that has emerged with media technologies and the electronic packaging of entertainment. Given the almost symbiotic link between music and radio, it is surprising that this medium has often been overlooked when infrastructure is studied regarding the formation of music cultures in local areas. The 2015 IFPI/Music Canada *Mastering of a Music City* report found that "[s]trong community radio supporting local independent music" was often mentioned with regard to elements that support a music city's success; however, it was not ranked as 'essential' or 'important' (p. 17).

There are several reasons media and specifically radio are not factors in music city analysis. First, contemporary commercial radio has generally forgone badging content as 'local' in the search for larger audiences driven by demographic data. National markets can mean that radio interests are antithetical to city-based cultural industries. Further, music as a global industry prioritises 'band brand manufacturing' rather than growing a solid fan base through local audiences. Finally, the study of radio has always suffered from the suspicion that it is nothing more than a technical distribution method that has no role in the affective aggregation that underpins a fan base in music. More recently the introduction of a range of digital formats for music distribution – from on-demand access to 'celestial jukeboxes' to personalised Internet radio where a listener 'seeds' a service by providing a single artist or genre to develop a customisable online music stream – led many to foretell the imminent death of radio, particularly local radio. In not giving media serious consideration, however, many of these analyses were unable to address alternative forms of cultural contributions that sit outside the mainstream circulation of music. In doing so they contribute to legitimising particular forms of music as relevant to music city cultures only if they are commercially successful. With this, policies that address success in terms of playlists and audience numbers tend to support industrial forms of music distribution and contribute to the tensions between music cultures and corporate outcomes.

If death is a characteristic of radio, then the medium is the pre-eminent zombie media: always on the verge of extinction but never finally buried. While networked, commercial, formatted audio broadcasts may well have nothing 'live' about them, radio also provides the limit case of music for the development of paradigmatic city-based music scenes. Nashville was initially placed on the music map by its radio program *Grand Ole Opry*. In the early days of radio in the United States music that came to be known as 'country' was broadcast across the nation by the Nashville-based radio program. It was originally one of many programs based on American 'barn dance' formats, but *Grand Ole Opry* had the benefit of a powerful transmitter that provided a clear signal to listeners. The popularity of the program helped propel 'country music' into a nation-wide genre and facilitated the development of Nashville as an important music 'scene' (Florida 2002). Now Nashville ranks as one of the most successful operations in 'branding' a city through music (IFPI/Music Canada 2015, p. 86).

In Australia, the radio industry's role in promoting culture has been recognised in federal policy. The potential for national popular culture markets to be flooded by products from overseas, initially Europe and Britain and then from the 1950s America in particular, has motivated policy-makers to support Australian cultural production. Australia has legislated for locally composed music in radio broadcasts since the 1940s. The 1970s saw, as we noted earlier, pop music secure an increased importance for the recapitalisation of Australian urban cultural economies. This was reflected in cultural policies that led to the introduction of a performance quota for local music compositions that contributed to what the regulator described as an "efflorescence in Australian popular music" (ABT 1986, p. 9; Wilson 2013, pp. 102–103). Still, the larger cities of Sydney and Melbourne were the key to a successful local music industry even while significant music scenes were developing in other Australian cities (see Stafford 2004; Brabazon 2005).

The 1970s saw a rapid expansion in Australian radio. A reformist federal Labor government, elected in 1972, opened up the FM band to radio broadcasting for the first time and introduced a range of 'experimental' broadcasters including limited commercial stations in Sydney and Melbourne, specialist youth and multicultural broadcasters and not-for-profit public (later community) broadcasters. While a number of these experiments faltered (notably the limited commercial stations), others, such as the community broadcasting movement, grew, or in the case of the youth and multicultural broadcasters, were integrated into the government-funded public broadcasting system. The introduction of FM competitors to the commercial sector led to a significant shake out in the industry with a number of long-standing stations closing within 12 months of the new FM music broadcasters coming to air. While community broadcasters and the government-funded youth station drew on the burgeoning suburban and inner city live music scenes to engage new listeners and develop important relationships with urban subcultures, commercial broadcasters began to withdraw from the field.

By the early 1980s Melbourne community stations had achieved a significant grassroots base and strong links with the city's music scenes, in part because the government-funded youth station, 2JJ (Double J), only broadcast in Sydney. Whereas Melbourne community stations such as 3RRR and later 3PBS relied on subscribers and listener support for both capital and volunteer labour, Double J was able to secure salaried staff and access to public broadcasting equipment and technicians. It became the focus for a dynamic youth culture in Sydney while metropolitan-wide community stations focused on fine music and education. Meanwhile in Melbourne, without a government-funded youth broadcaster in the city the economically precarious community stations developed an extensive volunteer-based gift economy (including music give-aways and performance tickets) to support their operations. By the time Double J developed a national network in 1989 (as FM station triple j), RRR in Melbourne was so well established it held its own in audience share (Phillips 2006, pp. 214–17). Competition and consolidation in the commercial radio industry saw that sector move away from 'new music' (at this time largely punk, new wave and emerging hip-hop artists) into safer Gold and Adult Contemporary formats. Straitened economic times in the 1980s led to the commercial radio industry lobbying against the Australian music quota, which was eventually rolled into a self-regulatory system.

While commercial broadcasters can be crucial to the long-term sustainability of specific artists, commercial cultures, with their aversion to risk, often find it difficult to link with local, independent music cultures that do not necessarily rely on mainstream success. Melbourne community radio presents a special case for a music media that has a significant integration of artists, radio presenters, labels, promoters and programs. The city has one of the longest-standing continuous community sectors, with 2016 marking 40 years of licensed broadcasting. 3RRR was one of the first stations licensed and while ostensibly under an educational licence, the broadcasts adopted contemporary music and "quickly became identified with the punk/new wave sound" (Phillips 2006, p. 16). Soon after the first community licences were awarded the community-based Progressive Broadcasting Society (PBS) formed to broadcast "specialist, quality and unrepresented music" (Middlemast 2004). After gaining a licence in 1979, the cooperative that managed the station moved to a venue in St Kilda, the Prince of Wales Hotel, where they broadcast live concerts of local and touring bands for six years before moving to a cooperative-owned building in 1985. Along with 3CR, which began as a commercial broadcasting experiment in the early 1970s but was maintained as a federation of community organisations, and 'fine music' broadcaster 3MBS (also licensed in 1976), these community stations form an ecology of media that supports local cultural events and music broadcasts.

The commitment to new music in the case of 3RRR and under-represented music at 3PBS has in particular allowed these stations to develop loyal listeners, who provide a core subscriber base for ongoing financial support and volunteer labour. The stations developed close relationships with music promoters and venues, with RRR becoming an important Melbourne-based media partner for touring bands in the 1980 and 1990s. City music businesses and cultural institutions became important sponsors attracted by the station's youth base (Phillips 2006, p. 102). A number of local city-based musicians became program presenters on both of these stations. PBS attracted aficionados of various musical styles who tuned in to their specialist programs. Moreover, its arrangement with the Prince of Wales Hotel gave it access to a 300-seat theatre from which it broadcast live music under the title of PBS Radio Theatre. The cooperative formed an Outside Broadcast (OB) group that drew in technicians, sound engineers and music mixers who became crucial to the ongoing commitment to live music at the station (Paine 1989). The longevity of both stations demonstrates the value for music of media that incorporate active audience participation into their programming strategies. In this way, community radio, working within a 'gift economy' at the margins of mainstream cultural enterprises, was able to graft onto and reflect local music cultures of the city. The strength of RRR enhances Melbourne's claims to be a music city, and despite the station's independence from government structures it can still be deployed as part of arguments for the city's music city status. In this way, grassroots and community activity can align with policy objectives. However, as will be demonstrated in the following section, this is not always the case.

Laying claim to music heritage

One important way in which music comes to be seen as central to the identity of a place is through the way it can create a connection to the past. The idea that a city is a 'music city' will be strengthened through demonstrations that music is not only important to the city now, but has been for a long time and is central to how the identity of the city has been shaped (see Bennett 2010; Roberts 2014). Indeed, one of the recommendations made in the first report commissioned by the Melbourne City Council (MCC) when developing their music strategy highlighted "improv[ing] information relating to music heritage and tourism for city residents" as a key factor in supporting music (Homan and Newton 2010). This connection of heritage and tourism reflects the way music heritage is increasingly being used as a tourist drawcard around the world, as official processes replace or complement the fan-driven pilgrimages that had been taking place for decades. Unlike somewhere like Liverpool, where the music heritage of the city has been a main driver behind its designation as a 'music city' and key to many of its tourism successes, in Melbourne, on the local and state levels, this aspect of the music city agenda has been developing only slowly. However, there are ways in which Melbourne is moving towards the greater incorporation of popular music into heritage discourses, mainly due so far to the activities of members of the community rather than because of official actions.

The most notable development has been a move towards naming public places, particularly laneways, after (usually) deceased Australian musicians. To date there have been four such namings. AC/DC Lane in the CBD, dedicated in 2004, was the first of these and as such was the most controversial, with a long process and some community opposition leading up to its establishment (Frost 2008). Paul Hester Walk followed soon after in 2005. Hester was the drummer from Crowded House who committed suicide in that year, and the walkway named after him is near where he lived in the suburb of Elwood (under the auspices of Port Phillip Council). More recently, in 2015, Chrissy Amphlett (1959–2013), singer from the band The Divinyls, was commemorated with Amphlett Lane in the Melbourne CBD, and Rowland S. Howard Lane, situated in the seaside suburb of St. Kilda, was named after the late Birthday Party guitarist (1959–2009) (for an extended discussion of these namings, see Strong 2015). Given that street names are for the most part reserved for significant historical figures, this trend (also observed in other western cities) gives a clear indication of the growing importance of popular music in constructing the identity of a city or nation. Melbourne's laneways are also seen as being a unique aspect of the city's landscape, promoted as tourist destinations in ways that tie specific local music histories that also reinforce the centrality of music to the city.

The processes leading up to the naming of these lanes generated much publicity and eventually attracted political interest. In the 2014 Victorian state election campaign, Labor candidate Martin Foley became involved with the Rowland S. Howard Lane initiative. This was in the context of support for music being a key policy area for both major parties in this election (see Music Victoria 2014). The victory of the Labor Party saw considerable funding provided for other measures relating to music heritage. This included $400,000 for a project called 'Rocking the Laneways' that was about furthering the connection between music and public spaces not only in Melbourne but throughout Victoria. A further $1.3 million was earmarked for an Australian hall of fame (as mentioned above).

These limited moves towards celebrating Melbourne's popular music history put it somewhat behind, for example, Brisbane, which already has a music 'Walk of Fame' in its music precinct near the CBD, as well as much more prominent public spaces named after musicians such as the Go-Between Bridge and Bee Gees Way. The latter is perhaps an exemplar of how public spaces can go beyond simply being named after musicians, in that it incorporates a permanent display about the career of the band, as well as bronze statues of the musicians. Currently the Melbourne lanes have little in the way of drawcards in the laneways beyond the name itself. The question of the utilisation of the laneways, and particularly in ways that strengthens the music/Melbourne nexus they are designed to create, was not previously considered and is only now being researched further (see Strong et al., 2016).

Furthermore, it is noteworthy that until the Labor Party commitments, the heritage activities relating to popular music have been driven by the community, rather than being initiated by councils or state governments. All of the laneway namings have come about as a result of campaigning by fans or family members and friends of the musicians. This reflects the fact that until recently only fans were preserving popular music's past and are still working in huge numbers as unofficial archivers and curators (Baker and Huber 2013). Given the nature of popular music, it is considered vitally important that audiences and fans be taken seriously and be consulted (Leonard 2010). However, the fact that there has been no consideration of process in relation to the construction of heritage sites in Melbourne means there is a possibility that heritage-related activities are left in the hands of a small group of active members of the Melbourne music community, people who have particularly high levels of cultural capital in the city or who are adept at drawing attention to their causes. The campaigns for AC/DC Lane and Amphlett Lane, for example, were driven by people with strong connections to the media and to key figures in Melbourne's music scenes. This raises questions about how to ensure that, with the new schemes, community and audience input continues and in a way that incorporates as many different voices as possible. When music heritage is used as part of a story about a 'music city', there can be a tendency to emphasise certain types of music that suit an official narrative (see Cohen and Roberts 2014). The community-driven nature of the street namings may place Melbourne in a position to continue on this inclusive path, but more questions still need to be asked about how decisions are being made about music and heritage, and who makes them.

Such decisions need to be made in a context where heritage making is happening independently of official processes and where at times the idea of Melbourne as a music city can be deployed as a way of challenging decisions made by people in positions of power. The championing of music by the various councils and state government has also been used as a way of opposing decisions they make and drawing attention to ways in which governments are working against, rather than for, popular music-making. One example of this is the threatened demolition of the Palace Theatre, a mid-sized venue in the CBD. In 2012, it was sold to a property development company who planned to replace the building with a high-rise luxury hotel. This proposal met with vehement community opposition, and a 'Save the Palace' group was established to try to save the venue. This group has deployed a number of strategies, from vigils and demonstrations through to administrative appeals. A key defence has emphasised the heritage aspects of the building itself rather than its purpose as a venue. However, the group has also focused on the disjunction between the rhetoric of the 'music city' and the closure of key venues such as the Palace. In arguments put forward by Palace supporters at Melbourne City Council meetings where the fate of the venue was debated, the damage that the loss of the venue would do to Melbourne's international reputation as an important music hub was raised often, as was the apparent contrast between the Council's stated support for music and their willingness to let venues like this close. Although the final fate of the Palace has yet to be decided, this case shows how a commitment to building Melbourne's image as a 'music city' can be utilised – in conjunction with ideas about heritage – by community members with a stake in the local music scene to put pressure on governments to actually follow through on their statements about supporting music.

Conclusion

There are many important factors in considering what makes a music city, how it develops and how it is maintained. This chapter has only had space to consider how Melbourne was consciously developed as a cultural hub in the post-industrial era and how radio and heritage have been located within discourse around the concept of the 'music city' that has developed in the last decade or so. While limited in scope, these case studies are a way of demonstrating the role policy has played in framing Melbourne as a music city, but also how music-making at the grassroots and community levels in the city often exists separately from, and sometimes in opposition to, its positioning as an economic and branding good. As such, while current policy-makers at local and state levels clearly recognise the value of popular music in making the city economically competitive and culturally distinctive in a global marketplace, the intersections between policy and the development of a music city are far from clear-cut. While the infrastructure developments designed to reinvigorate Melbourne in the 1980s laid the groundwork for a focus on culture in the city, the way that an economically thriving city can be counter-productive to cultural activity, as demonstrated through the problems associated with the gentrification of the inner city, is still being grappled with by policy-makers. Melbourne's music city status is bolstered by the presence of stations like RRR, which, although originally created in response to government initiatives, have long been self-sustaining. The way that cities can benefit from the activities undertaken in communities and the extent to which those benefits are enjoyed by those who create them is a question that has rarely been considered to date (the position of musicians needs to be considered in this regard also). Popular music heritage is something that can be used by or against policy-makers and where the difference between the rhetoric and the reality of a music city can become apparent.

As Melbourne seeks to consolidate its position as a global music city in the late 2010s, and as popular music is increasingly on the radar of its policy-makers, we are presented with a unique opportunity to gain a greater understanding of how policy interacts with culture. While more partnerships are being forged between governments and those representing the music sector, it cannot be taken for granted that such outcomes will work to the advantage of music makers and audiences in the city. More research is required to understand how such alliances shape music-making in the city and the extent to which the community and musicians feel their voices are being fully heard in an environment where music is increasingly framed as an economic good rather than as a fundamental aspect of social life. Incorporating more information about how different aspects of Melbourne's music scene have helped to shape its identity as a music city – for example, venues, important bands, other types of media such as street press and so forth – will provide greater depth to our understanding and knowledge of the relationship of policy, actual music-making practices and the global image of the city. Similar detailed case studies of the experiences and practices of other music cities in different social and cultural contexts globally have clear potential for future research collaborations among scholars of the contemporary city.

Notes

1 Cities such as Edinburgh are examining Melbourne's recent Agent of Change noise law for possible local implementation (City of Edinburgh 2015, p. 13).
2 Australia has three levels of government: federal, state and local.

References

ABT (Australian Broadcasting Tribunal). 1986. *Australian Music on Radio*. Sydney: ABT.

Aizen, R. 2004. *Pots, Punks and Punters: A History of Hotels in St Kilda and South Melbourne*. Melbourne: St Kilda Historical Society.

Australian Labor Party, Victoria. 2014. Music works: Supporting local acts and jobs. *Media Release*, Melbourne, 3 November. Available from: www.viclabor.com.au/media-releases/music-works-supporting-local-acts-and-local-jobs (Accessed 13 November 2015).

Baker, S. and Huber, A. 2013. Saving "rubbish": preserving popular music's material culture in amateur archives and museums. *In*: S. Cohen, R. Knifton, M. Leonard and L. Roberts, eds. *Sites of Popular Music Heritage: Memories, Histories, Places*. New York: Routledge, 112–124.

Bennett, A. 2010. Popular music, cultural memory and everyday aesthetics. *In*: E. de la Fuente and P. Murphy, eds. *Philosophical and Cultural Theories of Music*. Boston: Leiden, 243–262.

Brabazon, T. (ed.) 2005. *Liverpool of the South Seas: Perth and Its Popular Music*. Perth: University of Western Australia Press.

Chevigny, P. 1993. *Gigs: Jazz and the Cabaret Laws in New York City (After the Law)*. New York and London: Routledge.

City of Edinburgh. 2015. *Desire Lines: A Call to Action from Edinburgh's Cultural Community*. Edinburgh: City of Edinburgh Council.

City of Melbourne. 2014. *City of Melbourne Music Strategy: Supporting and Growing the City's Music Industry 2014–2017*. Melbourne: City of Melbourne.

Cohen, S. and Roberts, L. 2014. Unveiling memory: blue plaques as in/tangible markers of popular music heritage. *In*: S. Cohen, R. Knifton, M. Leonard and L. Roberts, eds. *Sites of Popular Music Heritage: Memories, Histories, Places*. New York: Routledge, 221–238.

Creative Victoria. 2007. Victoria Rocks – New program to boost Victoria's contemporary music scene. *Media* Release, Melbourne, 25 July. Available from: http://archive.creative.vic.gov.au/News/News/Archive/Media_Releases/2007/Victoria_Rocks_-_New_Program_to_Boost_Victorias_Contemporary_Music_Scene

Creative Victoria. 2015. Budget provides $12.2m for Victoria's music future. *Media Release*, Melbourne, 11 May. Available from: http://archive.creative.vic.gov.au/News/News/2015/Budget_Provides_122m_For_Victoria%E2%80%99s_Music_Future (accessed 15.05.2017)

De Rook, P. and Nasra, S. 2015. 'How Groningen and Montreal are retaining skilled youth and creating growth and jobs through music industry policy', Music Cities Convention, 13 May, Brighton.

Dinard, C. 2015. Cities for sale: Contesting city branding and cultural policies in Buenos Aires. *Urban Studies*, 24 September, doi:10.1177/0042098015604079.

Donovan, P. 2010. They can't shut us down: thousands rally for live music. Melbourne: *Age*, February 23.

Florida, R. 2002. *The Rise of the Creative Class: and How It's Transforming Work, Leisure, Community, and Everyday Life*. New York: Basic Books.

Florida, R. 2013. More losers than winners in America's new economic geography. *The Atlantic*, CityLab section, 30 January. Available from: www.citylab.com/work/2013/01/more-losers-winners-americas-new-economic-geography/4465/.

Frost, W. 2008. Popular culture as a different type of heritage: The making of AC/DC Lane. *Journal of Heritage Tourism*, 3 (3), 176–184.

Hall, P. 1998. *Cities in Civilization*. Michigan: Pantheon.

Hartley, J., Potts, J., Cunningham, S., Flew, T., Keane, M. and Banks, J. 2013. *Key Concepts in Creative Industries*. London: Sage.

Homan, S. 2016. The music city. *In*: S. Brunt and G. Stahl, eds. *Made in Australia and New Zealand: Studies in Popular Music*. London: Routledge.

Homan, S. and Newton, D. 2010. *The Music Capital: City of Melbourne Music Strategy*. Melbourne: City of Melbourne.

IFPI/Music Canada. 2015. *The Mastering of a Music City: Key Elements, Effective Strategies and Why It's Worth Pursuing.* IFPI and Music Canada with MIDEM.

Kong, L. (ed). 2000. Special issue on culture, economy, policy. *Geoforum,* 31 (4), 385–600.

Landry, C. 1990. *Glasgow: The Creative City and its Cultural Economy.* Glasgow: Glasgow Development Agency.

Landry, C. and Bianchini, F. 1995. *The Creative City.* London: Demos.

Leonard, M. 2010. Exhibiting popular music: Museum audiences, inclusion and social history. *Journal of New Music Research,* 39 (2), 171–181.

Middlemast, A. 2004. *PBS History: 25 Years and Still Kicking Out the Jams!*Available from: www.pbsfm. org.au/PBS-25years (Accessed 16 November 2015).

Music Victoria. 2014. *2014 Victorian State Election Report Card.* Available from: www.musicvictoria. com.au/projects/election-report-cards (Accessed 20 July 2015).

O'Hanlon, S. 2009. The events city: Sport, culture, and the transformation of inner Melbourne, 1977–2006. *Urban History Review/Revue d'Histoire Urbaine,* 37 (2), 30–39.

O'Hanlon, S. 2012. *Federation Square Melbourne: The First Ten Years.* Melbourne: Monash University Publishing.

O'Hanlon, S. 2016, Selling "lifestyle": post-industrial urbanism and the marketing of inner-city apartments in Melbourne, c1990–2005. In S. High, L. MacKinnon and A. Perchard, eds. *The Deindustrialized World: Confronting Ruination in Postindustrial Places.* Vancouver: UBC Press (forthcoming 2017).

O'Hanlon, S. (with A.E. Dingle). 2010. *Melbourne Remade: The Inner City Since the Seventies.* Melbourne: Arcade Publications.

Paine, C. 1989. *PBS History: Ten Years of Live from Studio 2.* Available from: www.pbsfm.org.au/ tenyearslive (Accessed 16 November 2015).

Phillips, M. 2006. *Radio City, the First Thirty Years of 3RRR.* Melbourne: The Vulgar Press.

Rauch, M. 2015 'Property, development, creativity and space: How developers, planners and regulatory bodies support city strategies by supporting music businesses', Music Cities Convention, 13 May, Brighton.

Regev, M. 2013. *Pop-Rock Music: Aesthetic Cosmopolitanism in Late Modernity.* Cambridge: Polity Press.

Roberts, L. 2014. Talkin bout my generation: Popular music and the culture of heritage. *International Journal of Heritage Studies,* 20 (3), 262–280.

Scott, A.J. 2006. Creative cities: Conceptual issues and policy questions. *Journal of Urban Affairs,* 28 (1), 1–17.

Shaw, K. 2009. The Melbourne indie music scene and the inner city blues. *In:* L. Porter and K. Shaw, eds. *Whose Urban Renaissance?* London: Routledge, 366–385.

Shaw, K. 2013. Independent creative subcultures and why they matter. *International Journal of Cultural Policy,* 19 (3), 333–352.

Stafford, A. 2004. *Pig City: From the Saints to Savage Garden.* Brisbane: University of Queensland Press.

St Kilda Festival. 2015. Event Info. Available from: www.stkildafestival.com.au/festival-sunday/ event-info (accessed 15.05.2017)

Strong, C. 2015. Laneways of the dead: Memorialising musicians in Melbourne. *In:* C. Strong and B. Lebrun, eds. *Death and the Rock Star.* Aldershot: Ashgate.

Strong, C., I. Rogers and F. Cannizzo. 2016. *Melbourne's Music Laneways Report.* Melbourne: Creative Victoria, RMIT.

UNESCO. 2014. *Creative Cities Network – Music.* Available from: www.unesco.org/new/en/culture/ themes/creativity/creative-cities-network/music/ (Accessed 17 November 2015).

Upton, G. 2001. *The George: St Kilda Life and Times.* Melbourne: Venus Bay Books.

Watson, A. 2008. Global music city: Knowledge and geographical proximity in London's recorded music industry. *Area,* 40 (1), 12–23.

Wilson, C.K. 2013. Youth, radio and Australian popular music policy. *Perfect Beat,* 14 (2), 100–119.

Zimmer, N. 2015. 'Property, development, creativity and space: How developers, planners and regulatory bodies support city strategies by supporting music businesses', Music Cities Convention, 13 May, Brighton.

Part VII

The nation state and cultural policy

31

Cultural policy in India

An oxymoron?

Yudhishthir Raj Isar

Introduction

In India, cultural policy is not an academic discipline or congeries of disciplines. This is surprising, for the country's 1.25 billion inhabitants enjoy a flourishing and variegated cultural life. Their government(s) – the federal or 'central' government as well as those of the Indian Union's 29 States and 7 Union Territories – ostensibly subsidise the arts and heritage. Identity politics has always existed in India and has become increasingly vehement today, but the tensions play out in connection with religion, caste and class rather than ethnicity. Yet there is little scholarly exploration of these issues; analytical speculation of the sort long practiced in Western Europe (and increasingly nowadays in other regions, notably East and Southeast Asia), is practically non-existent. Nor has cultural policy in India become a favoured terrain of foreign researchers, as it has in East Asia.

Hence it is next to impossible in the Indian case to address one of the main overarching themes of this volume, namely issues that emerge from the ways in which cultural policy is dealt with by different academic disciplines. In India, there is no such relationship. Hence producing an informed analysis is not an easy task for an external observer, although the research on the Indian practice of international cultural relations carried out by the present author in 2013 has provided him with a small head start.[1] Infinitely more useful in filling the knowledge gap, however, was a substantive *Country Profile: India* published in 2013 – albeit not as the outcome of indigenous agency but as part of the *WorldCP-International Database of Cultural Policies*.[2] Were it not for this 188-page study, the short overview below of what different layers of government (as well as Indian non-state actors) envision and enact as cultural policy would have been impressionistic and impossible to verify.[3]

Despite the lack of an explicit strategy, the federal and state governments provide patronage and funding for selected arts and heritage activities that conform to an established high culture canon. This may be seen as a largely implicit cultural policy (Ahearne, 2009), of which many aspects are ripe for deeper analysis than can be provided here. In view of the comparative purposes of this volume, this chapter explores two Indian specificities: (i) the largely instrumental terms in which governmental patronage is critiqued by the Indian intelligentsia and (ii) the absence of the Western European 'creative economy' discourse that has become so hegemonic elsewhere, notably in East and Southeast Asia.

That the ends and purposes of state patronage have remained largely unquestioned reflects the consensual, 'settled' idea of how the elite envision 'Indian culture', at least so far. There has been scant consideration of cultural policy understood as 'the clash of ideas, institutional struggles and power relations in the production and circulation of symbolic meanings' (McGuigan, 1996, p. 1), in other words as the 'politics of culture'. In India today, while such clashes of ideas have become frequent, they are not seen within a category recognised as 'cultural policy'. As it is elsewhere, the terrain of contested meanings is bound up with ideas of the nation and its cultural selfhood. Rather more than elsewhere, however, there is a strong conflation between the 'arts and heritage' and 'ways of life' understandings of culture – which is hardly surprising, given that Hinduism is a diverse collection of orthopraxis rather than just a system of belief and observance. Out of this conflation, a good deal of journalistic and scholarly commentary has emerged.

This has occurred as the majoritarian vision of an essentially Hindu India (although 15 percent of the population is Muslim and there are 28 million Christians, as well as Sikhs, Jains and Parsees) is being championed by Bharatiya Janata Party (BJP) governments at the 'Centre' (i.e. the national government) and in many states. This stance seeks to displace the secularist, generally Leftist, yet liberal pluralism that has been the reigning ideology of the intellectual and cultural elite. The BJP's idea of India on the other hand is monist, in ways that stem from a 'semitization' of Hinduism – the reduction of plural Hindu belief systems to a single corpus (Thapar, 1993). This accompanies the belief system usually described as 'Hindu nationalism'. The term 'Hindu chauvinism' for such a view of 'true' Indian-ness purely in terms of Hindu religious values or *Hindutva* (or 'Hindu-ness', a term coined by one of the movement's founders) would be more appropriate, however, given the plural make-up of the country's population (Guha, 2014). In this context, the chapter takes up two issues that are salient today: (i) the challenges to the freedom of expression, notably freedom of artistic expression, posed by non-state actors driven by *Hindutva* ideology and (ii) the manner in which the ruling party is placing its loyalists in leading positions in the arts and heritage sector (and of course beyond). Before doing so, however, it would be opportune to explore the origins of the Indian upper caste urban elite's terms of engagement with a certain idea of the 'national culture' – an explicitly 'high culture' canon, accompanied by token gestures towards 'folk cultures'.

Culture: a special and reserved domain

The political theorist Partha Chatterjee argued many years ago that anti-colonialist nationalists in India produced their own domain of sovereignty within colonial society well before beginning their political struggle with the imperial power. While the material domain was that of the colonizer's sovereignty, the nineteenth-century nationalists staked a claim to the cultural in the broad sense of the term, including arts and heritage to be sure, but more prominently the spiritual sphere, represented by religion, institutions such as caste, family practice, the un-westernized peasantry, etc. Throughout the twentieth century and still today, Indian culture – that is, essentially Hindu culture – has been self-consciously articulated and invented as the privileged expression of this inner domain, often through processes of revival and reconstruction. While the outer, or material, world of public and political life, business, science and technology was dominated by the colonizing West, the Bengali middle class Hindus of the nineteenth century drew strength from a cultural world, a 'distinctive, and superior spiritual culture' (Chatterjee, 1993, p. 121) that could not be so annexed. These middle-class elites first imagined the nation into being via this spiritual dimension and then readied it for political contest.

The strength of subsequent Indian nationalism, Gandhi's in particular, was largely based on this process, while also drawing freely on western political and cultural ideas. Witness his often-quoted affirmations (1921, p. 170):

> I do not want my house to be walled in on all sides and my windows to be stuffed. I want the cultures of all lands to be blown about my house as freely as possible. But I refuse to be blown off my feet by any. I refuse to live in other people's houses as an interloper, a beggar or a slave.

This refusal, reaffirmed in the 1950s by the leaders of independent India, was accompanied by deep attachment to the flourishing of a particular construct of Indian-ness, as a way of life that also subsumed the arts and heritage. As Rajadhyaksha et al. put it (2013, p. 7),

> so pervasive is the representation of culture as national legacy, as both *sanskriti* (being cultured) and as *parampara* (tradition), that no corresponding practice or corresponding policy statement involving the Arts could exist without in some form incorporating (or at least adequately accounting for) prevailing definitions of *sanskriti*. This imbalance has been incarnated into the very substance of all prevalent arts & culture policy ever since this period and well into the present.

From the early twentieth century, during colonial rule, a range of arts institutions such as Tagore's *Shantiniketan* or Rukmini Devi's *Kalakshetra*, had paved the way for the subsequent adoption by the elites of independent India of a broadly modernist arts agenda in the service of Indian nationalism. As we shall see further on, this nationalist location of culture was and is broader than the arts and heritage. Yet the performance scholar Anita Cherian (one of very few academics whose work informs our topic), in her exploration of the fashioning of a national theatre in post-independence India, has noted how the arts and heritage 'were perceived to be a critical site reinforcing the idea of the nation' (Cherian, 2009, p. 33). The folding of them into the frameworks of development was an affirmation 'of the seemingly contradictory desire for both an authentic Indian aesthetic and a planned progression towards a post-colonial modernity'. Cherian has suggested therefore:

> that the braided histories of colonialism, nationalism, Independence and post-colonial state-formation are the conditions of possibility for a context wherein modernity is represented and performed through the institutions of the State, its acts of planning and, its multifarious forms of governance. Yet, the State's performances of modernity are based on an understanding of culture as both the locus of the traditional and, as the imagined foundation of a social solidarity that makes the modern State possible.
>
> *(pp. 33–34)*

Cherian also tracked the evolving rhetoric of culture understood as arts and heritage in India's Five Year Plans: in the First, identity was evoked to work and produce for the nation; the Second made provisions for institutionalisation; the Third opened up the discourse of retrieval and protection, 'its staging as a sign of the past' and as the site of the traditional (p. 37). As regards the performing arts, 'the idea of the classical allows the nation-state to acquire the aura of the sacred'. The state has constituted a classical canon by nationalising dance forms such as Bharata Natyam, Kathakali, Kathak and Manipuri, 'making these forms iconic of *its* cultural antiquity' (pp. 48–49) – a process that has played out as well in the federal states whose populations are entirely or largely made up of distinct ethnic groups. She pointed out, however, that also at stake was the 'revitalizing' of the folk arts, which added a dimension to the rhetoric of "unity in diversity", 'by drawing the marginalised, "folk" and/or tribal peoples into the nation's representational framework', completing an aesthetic paradigm founded on the recovery of 'elements thought to embody the traditional and the authentically Indian' (p. 51).

The arts and heritage: the engagement of the state and civil society

The absence of cultural policy as a theme of public debate is apparent from the lack of publications on the topic, apart from a 44-year-old monograph entitled *Some Aspects of Cultural Policy in India* written for UNESCO's 'Studies and documents on cultural policies' series by Kapila Vatsyayan, an accomplished Indian art historian and cultural bureaucrat. The UNESCO effort was far more an exercise in national representation than in objective analysis, however.[4] Vatsyayan's long, lyrical and conceptually dense introduction explores the exceptionality of Indian culture and civilization.[5] The tone is characteristic of the upper-caste Hindu elite vision mentioned earlier (another striking example is provided in Singh, 2009). While the structure of cultural institutions and mechanisms described in the monograph has not changed (although it has been considerably enriched) many other developments have taken place in the last few decades. These have been expertly reviewed in the *Country Profile: India* referred to above. The Indian film scholar Ashish Rajadhyaksha was the lead author of this profile; he was based at the time at the Centre for the Study of Culture and Society in Bangalore, which between 1998 and 2014 was the sole Indian entity wholly dedicated to cultural policy research but has since significantly reduced the scope of its activities.[6] Another publication, encouragingly entitled *Towards a Cultural Policy*, was published in 1975 as the proceedings of a seminar held at the Indian Institute of Advanced Study in 1972 at which an interdisciplinary group of scholars was asked to 'take stock of the cultural situation in the country', analyse emerging trends and try to 'evolve the broad outlines of a cultural policy for the country' (Saberwal, 1975, p. v). The volume disappoints, however, for it contributes little to our understanding. Most of the participants dealt with broad 'ways of life' issues such as inequality, language policy, social exclusion and the like in orthodox Marxist terms that appear simplistic and dated today. Besides, these issues are discussed far better by Rajadhyaksha et al. A notable exception was the contribution of the sociologist Rajni Kothari, which concluded with a plea for autonomy and dignity for the country's creative people but affirmed that while 'there is great need for the involvement of intellectuals and creative people in the general process of policy-making in economic, social and other matters, by the same token there is no room for a "cultural policy". For culture is not a matter of policy – except the policy of leaving it alone' (Kothari, 1975, pp. 30–31). This manner of throwing the baby out with the bathwater still characterises elite Indian thinking – it is of course also redolent of earlier attitudes in the UK and still current in the US: the arts are no business of government. Particularly ours, the Indian argument would go, which is inept, corrupt and managed by ignorant bureaucrats incapable of understanding or nurturing the ineffable. End of story. … A case in point was the judgement of a 2008 national level committee set up by the ministry of culture that in India's plural society any clearly enunciated policy would be exclusionary.[7]

Nevertheless, given the high degree of cultural self-awareness among the ruling elite, the central government ('the Centre') put in place between the early 1950s and the 1960s a range of institutions under the aegis of the Ministry of Culture to provide patronage and disburse funds. This configuration is duplicated at State level and in some cities. The central Ministry of Culture's mandate is for the protection and promotion of 'cultural diversity and heritage' seen as 'important pillars of inclusive national development'.[8] The mandate emphasises the right of all sections of Indian society to conserve their language and culture as the rich heritage of its composite culture. Its efforts mainly involve establishing museums, libraries and arts institutions and protecting ancient monuments and archaeological sites. The Ministry has numerous organisations under its jurisdiction, some of which had been created long before by the British colonial government. The 'Subordinate Offices' include the Anthropological Survey of India, the Central Reference Library, the National Gallery of Modern Art, the National Museum and the National Research Laboratory for Conservation of Cultural Property. The 'Attached Offices' include the Archaeological Survey of India (created in 1961), the Central Secretariat Library and the National Archives of India. 'Autonomous Bodies' include various Museums, Libraries, *Akademis*, Zonal Cultural Centres and Buddhist Institutions.

Through the 1950s and into the 1960s, the government of India founded institutions that provided the 'dominant paradigms for the "arts and culture" field as a whole' (Rajadhyaksha et al., 2013, p. 5; Isar, 2014). These were, in New Delhi, the Indian Council for Cultural Relations (1950); the *Sangeet Natak Akademi* or academy of the performing arts (1953); the National Museum, the *Sahitya Akademi* or academy of letters, the National Gallery of Modern Art and the *Lalit Kala Akademi* or academy of fine arts (all set up in 1954, following an initiative of India's first Prime Minister, Jawaharlal Nehru, and its first Education Minister, Maulana Azad) and the National School of Drama (1959). Then came the Film Institute of India (1959) in Pune and the National Institute of Design (1961) in Ahmedabad. Mirroring the central *Akademis* that are the apex arts bodies in New Delhi are state equivalents in the fields of literature, music and dance, sculpture, visual arts, folk arts, etc.

As in other countries, other ministries fund different dimensions of cultural life – and the slogan of 'joined up' policy making is as hard to apply here as it is elsewhere. The Ministry of Education deals with arts education and technical education relating to crafts, while the Ministry of Human Resource and Development deals with 153 educational and cultural institutions including notably the Indian Council for Historic Research (ICHR), the Indian Council of Social Science Research (ICSSR) and the National Council for Educational Research and Training (NCERT). The Ministry of Commerce and Industry runs the National Institute of Design (NID), and the Ministry of External Affairs oversees the Indian Council for Cultural Relations (ICCR). In addition, the Ministry of Tourism, the Ministry of Tribal Affairs, the Ministry of Minority Affairs and the Ministry of Youth Affairs & Sports deal with cultural issues. The country's 29 states and 7 Union Territories either have a department of culture or a department for culture, focusing understandably on local languages, 'folk cultures' and contemporary arts. As Rajadhyaksha et al. observe, all this does not constitute 'a coherent or unitary cultural policy. Instead, the policy has covered a range of complex, and often mutually contradictory, definitions. … These do not necessarily add up to a coherent "arm's length" policy, or even necessarily to a "federal" policy, but can sometimes resemble aspects of both' (p. 12).

It is no surprise, therefore, that only a tiny proportion of public funds goes to the arts and culture. In the central government's budget for 2016–2017, for example, the culture ministry's budget, which has gone up by 17.2 percent, comes to but 0.3 percent of total government outlay. Over 30 percent of the budget is allocated to the Archaeological Survey of India (ASI), the custodian of a limited number of protected monuments and sites around the country.[9] The ASI's principles of conservation and management are considered to be completely outdated by heritage professionals, notably members of INTACH (see below), while its functioning is as inefficient as that of all the other state-run cultural bodies. Rajadhyaksha et al. cite the 'tensions arising from the fact that the understanding of cultural heritage management is largely state-led with little or no…policy or legal provisions that help assert the rights of local communities in the management of heritage' (p. 66). In 1984, an Indian National Trust for Art and Cultural Heritage (INTACH) was created under the aegis of the Prime Minister Rajiv Gandhi as a non-profit membership organisation that would act as a counterweight. It has functioned in this capacity ever since with considerable official backing as well as active civil society participation.

In the judgement of the cross-section of representative civil society, stakeholders interviewed for the EU project mentioned above, the Indian State has done little more than dispense patronage to a small circle of practitioners favoured by the bureaucracy (Isar, 2014). In the view of some, the 'nationalistic model of patronage has created a plethora of inefficient institutions unable to adapt their vision, strategies, and activities to the major changes that have taken place in Indian society since the economic liberalisation of the 1990s or address the cultural needs of new generations of stakeholders. In the 1970s already, the rural-urban divide, for example, prompted the theatre director Habib Tanvir to state that:

> while the occasional dark areas in our rural cultural traditions can be overcome easily, to my mind the influence of the ultra-modern obscurantism of the urban elite is far more pernicious. To fight it we have to nurture our rural art forms. These would gain from exposure to the urban cultural milieu but, more important, the latter needs the revitalising influence of rural art forms. Their mutual interaction will give us the synthesis we need.
>
> *(Tanvir, 1974, p. 144)*

The country's high economic growth rate in recent years and growing urban affluence have in no ways increased governmental spending; in some instances outlays on culture have even declined. The rapid growth of an urban and globalized so-called 'middle class' (the term is a misnomer, since it refers to an extremely privileged class in socio-economic terms that by no means occupies the middle range of income distribution) has heightened demand for cultural provision. This demand is being met increasingly by civil society and private initiatives, making the arts and heritage scene today far denser and more diverse than previously.

Grant-giving private foundations are rare, however, although a few operating foundations have been created by and for wealthy benefactors, particularly in the visual arts. The best known of the independent foundations and the only one whose scale of operations is financially significant is the India Foundation for the Arts (IFA), which disbursed almost 2 million dollars in 2010–2011 in a range of arts disciplines (Rajadhyaksha et al., 2013). Others include the Sanskriti Foundation, founded in 1979 by a philanthropic former businessman, with its programme of international residencies for artists, and the Raza Foundation, set up in 2005 by the eminent painter Syed Haider Raza (which also provides grants).

By and large, the Indian corporate world conforms to the international norm of supporting the arts as an essentially promotional strategy. It therefore prioritises the visible, influential, safe and respectable, drawing on advertising budgets for *ad hoc*, one-off commitments to cultural presentations and products. As observed by a former head of the India Foundation for the Arts,

> even when the goals of corporate patronage and product promotion are aligned, support tends to go out to art that needs it the least … the arts are defined for corporate

leaders and marketing executives by the elite social circles in which they move. As long as product promotion remains their principal justification for supporting the arts, business houses will continue to give no attention to creative processes, constraints and innovation.[10]

Although recent legislation includes the arts and culture as a recognised category of 'Corporate Social Responsibility', it does not appear that arts and culture projects and programmes have been favoured recipients.

The interactions of Indian cultural operators with counterparts in the rest of the world have grown organically in recent years, despite many difficulties of funding, infrastructure and organisation. A noteworthy aspect of these interactions is the way in which the European national cultural institutes operating in India such as the British Council, the *Institut français* and the *Goethe-Institut*, have stepped in to encourage issues and/or engage in practice that neither the Indian government nor the private sector interest would support, e.g. new, experimental or hybrid forms.[11] This foreign intervention, in other words, compensates for official indifference to these dimensions. A key role has been played by myriad cultural sector 'movers and shakers', individuals as well as non-governmental organisations, many of them operating in smaller cities and towns, but generally with little or no municipal support.[12] Their efforts have made for better cultural provision and vivified relations with partners in other countries. Despite this vibrancy, the sector is fragmented and very precarious financially. It lacks professionalism, apart from a few exceptions that prove the rule. It is against this backdrop that cultural entrepreneurship has developed apace in both the not-for-profit and for-profit cultural sectors. The contemporary visual arts are thriving commercially, with many galleries in the major cities catering to the demands of an expanding new stratum of extremely affluent Indian patrons, as shall be taken up in more detail further on.

As is often the case elsewhere, media and communications policy is not generally seen as 'cultural policy' by Indian commentators. The governance of the media comes under the Ministry of Information and Broadcasting; matters concerning satellite communications and linked technologies under the Ministry of Science and Technology. The *Country Profile: India* foregrounds recent civil society resistance (sometimes successful) to IP legislation and/or regulation that could have had negative implications for copyright holders and/or freedom of expression. Also contested were governmental intentions to pre-screen user content of networking sites such as Yahoo, Facebook and Google, embodied in an IT Act of 2000, when a BJP-led coalition was in power. These measures were seen as 'draconian'; efforts to block passage of the new raft of regulations did not succeed, however.

Instrumental rather than deontological critique

Deontological issues such as access and participation, or choosing between democratization and democracy in the cultural realm, are rarely evoked in the grumblings of the Indian intelligentsia, some of whose more vocal members have stated categorically, echoing Kothari's judgement cited earlier, that there should be no official cultural policy because politicians and bureaucrats are too inept. In January 2014, the Ministry of Culture constituted a 'High-Powered Committee' (HPC) to examine the functioning of the cultural organisations operating under the aegis of the Ministry, to imagine pathways for synergies amongst them and to review their 'management problems, lack of clarity of vision and policies, unclear distribution of authority powers and responsibility, transparency, elitism, coordination and strategy' (Government of India, 2014, p. 5). In accordance with the customary Indian pattern, the group was made up of a recently retired senior civil servant, one serving bureaucrat (as secretary) and five members from the arts community. Strangely enough, no doubt in view of pending general elections (these swept the ruling alliance out of power in May 2014) the HPC was given only three months in which to submit its report. It appears to have thought deeply and in novel ways about the *performance* of these apex state-supported cultural bodies, in other words the *means*. It also appears to have consulted relatively widely with independent cultural actors (albeit all drawn from the same elite circles as the commissioners themselves). Yet nowhere in its report is there any reflection on *ends*, rhetorical references to 'vision' notwithstanding. The report's Preamble closes with the following acerbically critical paragraph:

> The representatives of Government often believe that theirs is the power and right to receive obeisance. On the other hand, our ambassadors of culture are sometimes so uncultured in their ways; some of them do not know the difference between self-actualisation and self-aggrandisement ... [T]hey must realize that they are answerable to the public, to the ordinary citizen; they are responsible for the honest utilization of the taxpayer's money. How does one then find a balance, in practical ways, between benign patronage and excessive control, between creativity and accountability, between a stolid bureaucracy and cultural freedom?
>
> *(Government of India, 2014, p. 3)*

The Report also notes that similar committees had been mandated in 1964, 1972 and 1990 but that no 'significant changes in the bureaucratic systems and the style of functioning of our institutions' had resulted (Government of India, 2014, p. 6). While the stress is on the absence of positive change, what is more significant is that such change is envisaged only in 'nuts and bolts' terms, related to 'basic issues of structure and processes' (p. 8). This is clearly a pattern in Indian thinking about arts policy. Thus the *Country Profile: India* identifies the key issues public debate as: the search for different models of arts funding, involving the creation of a series of 'zonal cultural centres' for the arts in order to surmount regional divides and the creation of a National Culture Fund, a trust that is a new avenue enabling institutions and individuals to partner with government to support arts projects. Related to this thrust is 'the perception that governmental interference often did more harm than good; and that the government should only make such infrastructure available to independent and credible not-for-profit agencies who would be better able to run it if left to themselves' (Rajadhyaksha et al., 2013, p. 137).

Policy and practice in the small state of Goa, home to just 1.3 million people, which belonged to the Portuguese overseas empire until 1961, appears to be an exception to this picture, however. The *Country Profile: India* does not examine state patronage of the sector in the country's federal states apart from making passing reference to the *Akademis* and other mechanisms of the southern state of Karnataka. Having spent the last few months in Goa, however, the author has observed a rather different picture there. A clear policy has been enunciated in *State Cultural Policy 2007*, which boldly asserts the intention to 'launch an experiment in Cultural Democracy in Goa' (Government of Goa, 2007, p. 1). Invoking Article 27 of the Universal Declaration of Human Rights, the document also sets out principles that would be familiar in Western Europe, such as the promotion of individual creativity, equality of access to cultural life, freedom of expression, cultural renewal and quality, 'to make it possible for culture to be a dynamic, independent and challenging force' (p. 1). It identifies the following key 'thrust areas': preservation; dissemination; research;

training, education and animation; empowerment and gender justice and even advocates an 'inter-sectoral approach' as regards cultural administration. The following sectors are to benefit from grants, job creation and the provision of facilities: folklore; dance and music; drama and theatre; languages and literature; arts and crafts; architecture and sculpture; fairs, festivals and markets; food and beverages; costumes, dress and fashion; journalism, television and radio; cultural industry, photography, films and popular media; IT and culture; event organisation; cultural heritage, tourism and museology; paintings and cultural education.

The crafts sector: more 'culture' than 'art'

The country's vast handicrafts sector has been an arena of intensive policy making over the years, initially framed in developmentalist terms, i.e. incomes and livelihoods, under the country's Five Year Plan process that began in 1951. The sector comes under the Ministry of Textiles, which runs the Export Promotion Council for Handicrafts (EPCH), the Handicrafts and Handlooms Export Corporation (HHEC), the National Institute of Fashion Technology (NIFT) and the National Handicrafts and Handlooms Museum. The Ministry of Micro, Small and Medium Enterprises runs the *Khadi* and Village Industries Commission. The condition of the artisan has been central in the nationalist location of culture (Rajadhyaksha et al., 2013). The nineteenth-century ruin of the Indian handicrafts sector (notably the spinning industry) at the hands of British colonial exploitation is a key theme in Indian economic history; it has moulded policy in this sector. Thus, the elaborate programmes that were developed in connection with an early 'development' vision may well be unique. Craftspeople were seen as a repository of 'true' Indian culture; they were integral to the nationalist project of identifying and protecting a 'national heritage', yet their economic importance gave their uplift great visibility, 'informing the most ambitious and difficult aspect of national development: the agenda of agrarian reform' (Rajadhyaksha et al., 2013, p. 8). At the same time, support to the artisan presented a real synergy with the nationalist goals of industrialisation and an emphasis on the development of science and technology.

Culture in the development project

Rajadhyaksha et al. lay great stock by the fact that the role of culture was foregrounded in India's first three 'Five Year Plans', during what they call the 'period of development' as regards the state's engagement with the cultural domain. Indeed language in those Plans prefigured the 'culture and development' discourses that were to emerge internationally only in the 1970s. By the Third Plan (1961–1966), a more specific claim was articulated for cultural values as resources for planning under a synthesis of tradition and modernity. Similar objectives were laid out for 'village industries', the reorganisation of village economies, the links between cottage industry with large-scale industrial production and research and marketing. The documents also stress helping the economically disadvantaged and the tribal people of India, who 'needed to be enabled to develop along the lines of their own genius, with genuine respect and support for their own traditional arts and culture and without pressure or imposition from outside' (Third Five Year Plan, cited on p. 19). In fact, however, while governmental support to the crafts has always been highly organised, subsidies to craftspeople have never been as great as is commonly believed (Dhamija, 2008). There has always been a considerable gap between Plan ambitions and their execution. The Plans have been largely discursive gestures, built into the nation's narrative strategies in Bhabha's sense (1994), both pedagogical and performative, long on rhetoric but short on implementation.

These authors also conclude that 'the role of the State in cultural terms today has credibility mainly in its ability to support those who cannot receive support otherwise: i.e. the truly disadvantaged: the poor, the economically marginalised...' (p. 24), yet curiously they fail to point out that in reality governmental provision does no such thing. There is a direct link here with the social and cultural capital, in Bourdieu's sense, accumulated by the Indian elite and the distance it has established vis à vis the peasantry and the lower castes, seen as ignorant and backward. The 'newly formed institutions explicitly acknowledged the reality of castes as part of the "given cultural material" with which the nation was constructed' (Schech and Haggis, 2000, pp. 134–135) and embodied Indian national culture as the culture of the new so-called 'middle class'. Hence Chatterjee's assertion that:

> the story of national emancipation is also a story of betrayal. Necessarily so. Because it could only confer freedom by imposing at the same time a whole set of new controls, it could only define a cultural identity for the nation by excluding many from its fold, and it could only grant the dignity of citizenship to some because the others always needed to be represented; they could not be allowed to speak for themselves.
>
> *(Chatterjee, 1992, p. 214)*

Indeed, many groups in India are excluded from the processes of inventing the national culture. While they cannot identify with this project, there are few signs yet of their frontally challenging it (Bhabha, 1994). Particularly as regards the aboriginal or 'tribal' people of India, formally known as the 'Scheduled Tribes' and officially included among the 'backward classes', the paternalistic upper-caste vision has re-appropriated a good deal from prior colonialist attitudes. Thus the Backward Classes Commission recommended in 1955 that 'we offer certain concessions and help to the Scheduled Tribes in their effort to come up to the general standard. While the state should help tribal people to modernize, it should also recognise that they have 'certain good things to offer to us – such as folk-dances, folk-songs and many customs' (cited by Schech and Haggis, 2000, p. 126). Yet there has been scant support for the 'welfare of the weak', notably in the light of development. Witness this recent comment on the ways in which environmental depletion and economic development have together disrupted the lifeworlds of the traditionally self-employed, notably craftspeople:

> Particularly badly hit are nomadic groups, their migratory routes disrupted, their lifestyles and cultures marginalized, misunderstood or denigrated, and their own younger generations turning away under myriad influences. The Anthropological Survey of India estimated that there were at least 276 non-pastoral nomadic occupations (hunter-gatherers and trappers, fishers, craftspersons, entertainers and story-tellers, healers, spiritual and religious performers or practitioners, traders and so on). Most of these are threatened, some already extinct or dying, and the people displaced from these livelihoods are either getting absorbed into the insecure, undignified, low-paid and exploitative sector of unorganized labour, or left simply unemployed.
>
> *(Shrivastava and Kothari, n.d., p. 10)*

No 'creative economy' discourse

The success of the 'global script' of the 'creative industries' in East and Southeast Asia is now widely acknowledged (see in particular Kong et al., 2006; Kong, 2010). In India, a different picture has emerged (UNESCO-UNDP, 2013).[13] A commercially triumphant private media

494

and entertainment industry serves a huge consumer market (as in China). The television market in India is the third largest in the world; other segments include a major print publishing and newspaper sector, television and radio, not forgetting a film industry that produces over 800 films annually, not just in Hindi, the language of Bollywood, but also in Bengali, Tamil, Telugu, Punjabi and Malayalam. PricewaterhouseCoopers brought out a series of annual reports, published initially in cooperation with the Federation of Indian Chambers of Commerce and Industry (FICCI), that have mapped this vast sector, mainly for the benefit of prospective private investors, both Indian and foreign. A 2006 report, entitled *The Indian Entertainment and Media Industry. Unravelling the Potential*, recognised the (limited) measures taken to liberalize foreign investment and resolve regulatory bottlenecks in certain segments of the industry. It held that 'with concerted efforts by industry players on deterrents such as piracy and other challenges, the E&M (entertainment and media) industry has the potential to evolve into a star performer of the Indian economy' (PricewaterhouseCoopers, 2006, p. 5). In like manner, Ernst & Young's 2012 *Film Industry in India. New Horizons* (produced in co-operation with the Los Angeles India Film Council) reviewed the flourishing of the broader media and entertainment industry, its potential for growth and for collaborations between Bollywood and Hollywood. None of these stakeholders use the creative economy terminology at all, nor does the government, which acts mainly as a facilitator by gradually introducing regulatory and fiscal reforms to encourage growth and enhance investment and export.

In 2005, UNESCO organised with much fanfare a regional symposium in Jodhpur, Rajasthan, expressly designed to promote the development of 'creative economy' policy. While there appears to have been some positive follow-up elsewhere in the Asia-Pacific region, in India itself the lessons of the symposium did not 'take'. Although the following year the Planning Commission did use classic British creative industries formulations in several of its documents, these references applied to the traditional arts and crafts sector that provides livelihoods to well over 10 million people – in other words the arguments were couched in craft-intensive rather than technology-intensive terms (Srinivas et al., 2009). The Commission's executive head wrote that 'a dynamic global business using creativity, traditional knowledge and intellectual property to produce products and services with social and cultural meaning, points to the next Big Idea' in the development-planning context, but his real emphasis was on livelihoods in the crafts sector, one that is 'self-organized and not unorganized' and whose importance lay in its 'critical human resource component'. Furthermore, he argued, this resource needs recognition and 'ground level support, similar to that given for IT and other empowered initiatives – not handouts' (Ahluwalia, 2006, p. 3). The task would be to turn cultural industries (traditional arts and crafts) into creative industries with the help of the 'design and media industry' and thus 'create original inroads into the global market' and produce 'distinctively Indian products and services... our own original contribution that can hold its own against the best the world has to offer'. As part of this process, the star designer Rajeev Sethi, named Vice-Chairperson of the Planning Commission's Task Force on Cultural and Creative Industries, proposed a shimmering scenario for the employment of vast numbers of currently unemployed/underemployed people, especially in rural areas. But practically nothing has come of these ideas.[14]

On the other hand, a contemporary visual art market flourishes. New Delhi's India Art Fair is a private initiative, organised under the aegis of the auction house Sotheby's since 2008; its 5th edition in 2013 presented the work of 104 galleries from 24 countries, including many in Europe. Till that year, it was estimated to have attracted over 300,000 visitors, from India, other Asian countries and the rest of the world. More recent figures are not available, but reports concur that its footfall and notoriety have increased significantly. Late 2012 also saw the launch of the country's first art biennial, the 'Kochi-Muziris Biennale 2012', whose two highly successful editions have been financed through a mix of public and private-sector support.[15] Aware of the potential of this field, the Federation of Indian Chambers of Commerce and Industry (FICCI) established a Committee on Art and Business of Art composed of artists, gallery owners, auctioneers, art historians, tax experts and policy makers so as to 'add momentum of the growth of the visual art sector in India… [and] to engage Indian corporates in bringing about holistic development in arts.' Its 2010 report, entitled *Art Industry in India: Policy Recommendations* assessed Indian legislation and taxation for the visual arts. In 2012, FICCI also published *Art and Corporate India*, whose principal focus was again the visual arts.

Other initiatives could be cited in other domains that would be labelled 'creative industry' in most other settings. For example, the DSC Jaipur Literature Festival produced by *Teamwork*, the leader among several private entertainment companies now operating in the country.[16] There is a growing number of private cultural businesses, notably in publishing and the book trade. The Oxford Book Store chain (with more than 30 stores across the country) has co-publishing and translation agreements with publishing houses in Europe; it has also created the Apeejay Kolkata Literary Festival, which introduces Indian readers to contemporary writing, both European and Indian.

'Creative economy' is not a term of choice used in relation to any of these initiatives. The 'creative' has not become the talismanic notion it has become elsewhere. Why is this so? The answer is no doubt to be found in a number of factors. Most importantly, perhaps, the Indian film industry – now known as Bollywood – developed largely as a commercially viable business, as did other pursuits such as book publishing. Somewhat as is the case in the USA, it is taken for granted in India that mass-produced cultural goods and services are commercially produced and do not require direct state support. Nor, being less noble than the high culture forms that embody tradition and identity, do they warrant it. A concrete contributing factor has been the scale of *informality*, in terms of both the number of enterprises and jobs; the informal economy has been estimated to contribute as much as half of total GDP and informal employment an even higher proportion of total employment. Hence, there has been no deliberate positioning of the cultural sector in 'creative industry' terms that was introduced in the UK in the late 1990s and adopted elsewhere (Isar, 2012). In the view of the present author, this is not itself a bad thing, given the tedious tendentiousness of so much of the reigning 'creative industry' or 'creative economy' discourses.

Threats to cultural freedom

We turn now to cultural politics. Threats against artistic freedom – and against freedom of expression in general – now occupy centre stage in public debate. While the threats concern arts policy, the societal anxieties and insecurities driving them have far broader purchase. Their principal agents are non-state actors: Hindu and Muslim fundamentalist movements who are introducing novel forms of 'cultural policing', i.e. 'all attempts at imposing ways of thinking and behaving on behalf of value systems pertaining to religion or morality that resort to symbolic or physical violence, blackmailing or any other form of constraint' (Gayer et al., 2010, p. 148).

Writers, painters and filmmakers are increasingly attacked for 'blasphemy and outraging religion' in their work or for tackling issues such as homosexuality and widow remarriage. This alarming trend was initiated by the Bajrang Dal, the armed wing of the Hindu right-wing Rashtriya Sevak Samaj (RSS), which has taken the latter from a policy of example to one of constraint.[17] Founded in 1925, the RSS has assigned itself the principal task of defending the Hindu community against Muslim threats, real or imagined. Hence its paramilitary overtones, which, however, went together for many years with a quietist attitude: the RSS hoped to spread its message through example, not constraint. Things changed in the 1990s with the rise of the Bajrang Dal. Artists, particularly when they were Muslim, were its first targets.

The emblematic case has been that of the celebrated painter M.F. Husain. In 1996, BD militants attacked a show of his works in Ahmedabad (Gujarat), destroying canvases and wall hangings in retaliation for a 1976 depiction of the goddess Saraswati – she was too scantily clad in their eyes. Two years later they ransacked the painter's Bombay apartment in protest against his canvas, 'Sita Rescued', that depicted the famous scene in the Ramayana epic where Sita is freed from the demon Ravana – again because she was scantily dressed. An exhibition of reproductions of Husain's works and photographs, organised to protest the artist's exclusion from the India Art Summit in August 2008, was vandalized by another right-wing group. As the mere presence of Husain's work in the public sphere seemed to invite a violent reaction from these quarters, he went into self-imposed exile soon afterwards and died abroad in 2011. The intolerance has extended to Hindu artists whose work is thought to 'hurt Hindu sentiments' as well as to obscure amateurs operating in purely local settings.

In the year 2000, Indian/Canadian director Deepa Mehta was shooting her film *Water* on the fraught lives of Hindu widows in Benares in the 1930s, condemned to celibacy, begging and prostitution. The screenplay envisaged an 'illicit' relationship between a Brahmin widow and an untouchable and the rape of another. A BJP dignitary declared that the film insulted 'ancient Indian culture and traditions' and threatened 'more violent protest' if Mehta tried to shoot in India.[18] She proceeded to do so nevertheless, after having secured all the necessary authorizations, but the set built on the banks of the Ganges was ransacked by Bajrang Dal militants and she was prevented by force from shooting elsewhere.

Some artists have even made the poignant decision to end their public lives because of attacks on their work. In January 2015, a well-known Tamil language writer announced on Facebook: 'Perumal Murugan, the writer, is dead. As he is no God, he is not going to resurrect himself. He has no faith in rebirth. As an ordinary teacher, he will live as P. Murugan. Leave him alone' (cited in Vari, 2015). His decision was prompted by virulent protests by Hindu and local caste-based groups against his novel, *Madhorubhagan*, which, they complained, denigrated Hindu deities and women. The protestors were mainly troubled by its critique of the caste system, particularly the inhumane treatment of the untouchables by caste Hindus. The same modus operandi is in force among Muslim fundamentalists, it must be said, although Indian Islamists have no coherent organisation like the RSS network. But this has not prevented them from launching recurrent campaigns against 'deviant' artists.[19] 'For a country that takes great pride in its democracy and history of free speech, the present situation is troubling, 'says Nilanjana Roy, a columnist and literary critic. 'Especially in the creative sphere, the last two decades have been progressively intolerant' (cited in Vari, 2015). Beyond the arts, fringe groups such as the *Sri Rama Sena* (army of Rama) in Karnataka, not all of which are formally associated with the RSS, have launched violent attacks on minorities and women.

Life on university campuses has also been affected, in large part through the exertions of the *Akhil Bharatiya Vidyarthi Parishad* (ABVP—Indian Students' Association), the country's largest student union in terms of membership, founded by the RSS in 1948, whose primary aim initially was to combat communist influence, but has now taken on the cause of *Hindutva* as well. Confrontations between ABVP militants and student leaders on the

Left have led recently to two high-profile dramas: the January 2016 suicide of Dalit student Rohith Vemula at Hyderabad University and the February 2016 arrest on charges of sedition for 'anti-national' statements of Kanhaiya Kumar, President of the Jawaharlal Nehru University Students' Union (and a leader of the All India Student Federation, the student wing of the Communist Party of India).

Towards counter-hegemony in the apex institutions?

Today, the question arises of whether and in what way BJP governments will begin policing cultural institutions directly. Will they applying Gramscian principles and strategies of hegemony? In 2013, the authors of the *Country Profile: India* noted the government's loss of credibility in the arts but detected attempts to overcome the crisis of credibility in the then Congress Party-led coalition's support for autonomous initiatives such as arm's length bodies, new cultural foundations, etc. Today, however, the very idea of autonomy is contested. Already in 1990, however, the Haksar Committee had found autonomy to be either nullified or rendered toothless by governmental interference that starved institutions of funds or delayed appointments. But content was by and large spared (the secularist and left of centre doxa was never challenged, it must be said).

Things changed when the BJP was in power earlier, between 1998 and 2004. The policy of the then minister for human resources and development, Murli Manohar Joshi, was entirely in tune with *Hindutva* leanings: he appointed personalities who had been close to the movement to key positions in the Indian Council of Historical Research (ICHR), the Indian Council of Social Science Research (ICSSR), as well as the National Council for Educational Research and Training (NCERT) and entrusted them with the task of designing a new school curriculum. For one of Joshi's priorities was to create new textbooks – including those dealing with Indian history – rewritten in line with Hindu chauvinist ideology (Jaffrelot, 2015).

These efforts went only so far. But today, they appear to have been revived and given even broader scope and depth. 'We will cleanse every area of public discourse that has been westernised and where Indian culture and civilisation need to be restored—be it the history we read, our cultural heritage or our institutes that have been polluted over years', the current Minister of State for Culture is quoted as saying.[20] This ambition goes well beyond the pattern that is familiar, not just in India, of new ruling parties placing their friends and followers in high places in a spirit of cronyism rather than of ideological command. In 2015, for example, students at the Film and Television Institute of India (FTII) were on strike for 139 days, protesting the appointment of an undistinguished series-B actor, Gajendra Chauhan, whom they saw as grossly unqualified, as the chairman of the institution. He was the BJP national convener for culture, responsible for promoting 'the party's ideology through cultural activities', as he put it in an interview with *The Indian Express* (cited in Bhattacharya, 2015). Equally troubling was the selection of other unqualified people to the FTII's governing council.

Conversely, in *The New York Review of Books*, the economist and Nobel laureate Amartya Sen described how the government had pressured him to step down as chancellor of the newly formed Nalanda University – most likely because of his criticism of Prime Minister Modi before the elections (Sen, 2015). Sen also listed the ways in which the government had interfered in the management of other academic institutions – the Tata Institute of Fundamental Research, IIT Delhi, IIT Bombay and the National Book

Trust. It had proposed a bill that would give it direct control of the 13 Indian Institutes of Management. 'The caliber of two recent appointments is also alarmingly questionable: Lokesh Chandra, the newly selected head of the Indian Council of Cultural Relations, has said Modi is an incarnation of God, and Yellapragada Sudershan Rao, the new head of the Indian Council of Historical Research, has praised the caste system' (Bhattacharya, 2015, accessed 20 April 2016).

In April, 2016, the Minister of Culture dissolved the board of the prestigious Indira Gandhi National Centre for the Arts in New Delhi (admittedly a grossly underperforming white elephant created by earlier Congress governments), removing several members before the end of their tenure and installing some of his own candidates. He appointed as president a veteran Hindi language journalist who had been the organising secretary of the ABVP during the 1974 Bihar movement led by Jayaprakash Narayan against governmental misrule and corruption. As the government places its loyalists at the head of the cultural institutions, and the process has continued with a variety of other recent appointments, those in the secularist/pluralist camp wonder how soon its pursuit of the larger agenda, which is a transformation of the very idea of Indian civilization, will be put in place.

Conclusions

This account has sought to reveal, in broad brushstrokes, how state patronage for the arts and heritage has been conceived in India and how it has unfolded, the institutions it has created for this purpose, as well the themes and registers it has privileged and ignored. All this is in the absence of any meaningful concern with expanding the capacities of the cultural sector or promoting cultural expression in a spirit of cultural democracy and inclusiveness. The patronage has been guided by and has in turn reinforced a sense of how Indian high culture can and should embody a certain national idea. Although it has been defined secularist and pluralist terms so far, this has nevertheless been an essentially elitist articulation, whose exclusionary nature has been largely unchallenged. Equally unquestioned have been its aims: critique focuses purely on the efficiency – or rather, the inefficiency – of the state-sponsored institutions. Today, non-state cultural sector actors are partially compensating for these inadequacies.

Recent years, however, have seen the secularist and pluralist idea of India challenged by the current ruling party and by civil society groups that support *Hindutva* ideology, often by means of symbolic and physical violence, notably on behalf of a version of Indian identity based exclusively on Hindu references. Cultural policing has become commonplace and the current administration clearly seeks to control the 'commanding heights' of the political economy of the culture sector, in a positively Gramscian deployment of power viewed as domination plus intellectual and moral leadership. But this kind of religion-based majoritarian thinking in a society where pluralism is a core value and a diversity of diversities is taken for granted by the majority will be difficult to impose across the board. It is likely, therefore, that as far as conceptions of India's 'cultural identity' is concerned, the coming years will see increasingly acute clashes of ideas, institutional struggles and contests for power, in other words an increasingly fractious politics of culture.

Acknowledgements

The author is grateful for constructive comments formulated by Galia Saouma and S.V. Srinivas.

Notes

1 Preparatory Action Culture in EU External Relations. http://cultureinexternalrelations.eu/.
2 Modelled on the *Compendium of Cultural Policies and Trends in Europe*, the profiles cover some 80 categories and indicators organised under 9 main chapters. For the full structure, see: www.worldcp.org/profiles-structure.php.
3 www.worldcp.org/profiles-download.php.
4 The 51 monographs were descriptive rather than analytical; at the time, however, they nevertheless provided the only information available to scholars.
5 The opening paragraph captures the complexity of the Indian cultural scene very adeptly:

> …it is essential to keep constantly in view the complex, intricate and multilayered, multidimensional cultural fabric of the country, both in time and space. Such a framework would be necessary for the study of any civilization but is imperative in a situation of incredible cultural continuity which has survived through 5,000 years of history marked by periods of unrest, invasions, wars, political subjugation, economic underdevelopment and one which has conditioned, guided and governed the value-system of a whole people, today numbering 531 million, spread over an area of 3,276,141 square kilometres comprising a bewildering multiplicity of races, castes, ethnic groups, sub-cultures and religious sects.
>
> *(Vatsyayan, 1972, p. 9)*

6 The CSCS website is still active: http://cscs.res.in/. The author had speculated that CSCS downsized in 2014 mainly for lack of funding, reflecting the limited interest in cultural policy as a field, but a founding member of the Centre, S.V. Srinivas, has explained in an oral communication that while funding was indeed always difficult, the Centre was more severely challenged by India's changing higher education environment, including the creation of private universities and the increased activity of government-sponsored research centres, which made it difficult for the CSCS to sustain its research and teaching.
7 See: http://timesofindia.indiatimes.com/india/Panel-members-against-one-cultural-policy/articleshow/3089531.cms (Accessed 10 May 2016).
8 As stated in the Citizen's/Client's Charter for Government of India (Ministry of Culture). http://indiaculture.nic.in/sites/default/files/citizen%20charter/mculture%20citizens%20charter.pdf (Accessed 20 April 2016).
9 Source: http://economictimes.indiatimes.com/news/news-by-industry/et-cetera/union-budget-2012-13-culture-ministry-gets-rs-67-crore/articleshow/12292630.cms.
10 Anmol Vellani, 'The Case for Independent Arts Philanthropy, website of the India Foundation for the Arts. www.indiaifa.org/index.php?option=com_content&view=article&id=20&Itemid=17 (Accessed 10 March 2012).
11 The approaches of the European cultural institutes contrast with those of countries such as China, Japan or South Korea, whose cultural centres focus on promoting their own cultural forms and agents.
12 In the Indian polity, municipalities are not empowered to function as autonomous cultural policy making or implementing entities.
13 This section borrows from my analysis in UNESCO/UNDP, 2013.
14 Some forward movement might emerge, however, from a workshop on 'Art and cinema industries in India: Norms, workers and territories', that was organised in May 2016 by Christine Iturbide, a researcher working with the French Centre for Social Sciences and Humanities (CSH) in New Delhi, on the basis of her earlier as well as ongoing research on the cultural industries in India.
15 www.kochimuzirisbiennale.org.
16 http://teamworkproductions.in/.
17 The word *bajrang*, meaning 'strong', is associated with the monkey god, Hanuman – sometimes also referred to as *Bajrang Bali* – who is generally depicted brandishing a club.
18 Quoted in *The Hindu*, 5 February 2000.
19 The first major episode of this recent history was the Rushdie affair: before taking on a transnational dimension in the wake of Ayatollah Khomeini's *fatwa*, the campaign against *The Satanic Verses* was actually launched in India.
20 Cited on www.firstpost.com/politics/culture-minister-mahesh-sharmas-strikes-again-bible-quran-not-central-to-soul-of-india-2438340.html (Accessed 18 April 2016).

References

Ahearne, J. 2009. Cultural policy explicit and implicit: a distinction and some uses. *International Journal of Cultural Policy*, 15(2), 141–153.

Ahluwalia, M.S. 2006. *Positioning the Big Idea-India: Creative and Cultural Industries as a Lead Sector*. New Delhi: Asian Heritage Foundation.

Bhabha, H. 1994. *Locations of Culture*. London: Routledge.

Bhattacharya, A. 2015. Narendra Modi's worrying push into India's cultural institutions. *Al Jazeera America*, 23 July 2015. http://america.aljazeera.com/opinions/2015/7/indian-governments-worrying-push-into-cultural-institutions.html (accessed 20 April 2016).

Chatterjee, P. 1992. Their own words? An essay for Edward Said. In M. Sprinkler (ed.), *Edward Said: A Critical Reader*. Cambridge, MA: Blackwell, 194–220.

Chatterjee, P. 1993. *The Nation and Its Fragments. Colonial and Postcolonial Histories*. Princeton: Princeton University Press.

Dhamija, J. 2008. Globalization and the Crafts in South Asia. In H. K. Anheier & Y.R. Isar (eds.), *The Cultural Economy. The Cultures and Globalization Series, 2*. London: Sage Publications.

Cherian, A. 2009. Institutional Maneuvers, nationalizing performance, delineating fenre: reading the Sangeet Natak Akademi Reports 1953–1959. *Third Frame: Literature, Culture and Society*, 2(3), 32–60.

Federation of Indian Chambers of Commerce and Industry (FICCI). 2010. *Art Industry in India: Policy Recommendations*. New Delhi: FICCI.

Gandhi, M.K. 1921. *Young India*. 1 June, 1921 (also available on www.mkgandhi.org/momgandhi/chap90.htm).

Gayer, L., Jaffrelot, C. and Maheshwari, M. 2010. Cultural policing in South Asia: an anti-Globalization Backlash against freedom of expression? In H. K. Anheier & Y.R. Isar (eds.), *Cultural Expressions, Creativity and Innovation. The Cultures and Globalization Series, 3*. London: Sage Publications.

Government of Goa. 2007. *State Cultural Policy 2007*. Panjim: Directorate of Art and Culture.

Government of India. 2014. *Report of the High-Powered Committee Appointed to Review the Constitution as Well as the Working of Akademies/Institutions under Ministry of Culture*. Delhi: Ministry of Culture.

Guha, R. 2014. The Fear of Fascism – India's democratic institutions are too strong to let Fascists win. *The Telegraph*. March 22, 2014. www.telegraphindia.com/1140322/jsp/opinion/story_18095590.jsp (accessed 25 April, 2016).

Isar, Y.R. 2012. Artists and the creative industries: problems with the paradigm. In I. Elam (ed.), *Artists and the Arts Industries*. Stockholm: The Swedish Arts Grants Committee.

Isar, Y.R. 2014. India Country Report. *Preparatory Action on Culture in EU External Relations*. www.cultureinexternalrelations.eu/cier-data/uploads/2016/08/India_report54.pdf

Jaffrelot, C. 2015. Introduction: the invention of an Ethnic Nationalism. In C. Jaffrelot (ed.), *Hindu Nationalism*. Princeton: Princeton University Press.

Kong, L. 2010. Creative economy, global city: globalizing discourses and the implications for local arts. In H. K. Anheier & Y.R. Isar (eds.), *Cultural Expressions, Creativity and Innovation. The Cultures and Globalization Series, 3*. London: Sage Publications.

Kong, L., Gibson, C., Khoo, L.M. and Semple, A.L. 2006. Knowledge of the creative economy: towards and relational geography of diffusion and adaptation in Asia. *Asia Pacific Viewpoint*, 47(2), 173–194.

Kothari, R. 1975. Policy and culture. In S. Saberwal (ed)., *Towards a Cultural Policy*. New Delhi: Vikas.

McGuigan, J. 1996. *Culture and the Public Sphere*. London and New York: Routledge.

PricewaterhouseCoopers. 2006. *The Indian Entertainment and Media Industry: Unravelling the Potential*. New Delhi: PricewaterhouseCoopers.

Rajadhyaksha, A., Radhika, P., Tenkalaya, R. 2013. *Country Profile: INDIA*. Sydney: IFACCA.

Saberwal, S. (ed.). 1975. *Towards a Cultural Policy*. New Delhi: Vikas.

Schech, S. and Haggis, J. 2000. *Culture and Development. A Critical Introduction*. Oxford: Blackwell.

Sen, A. 2015. The stormy revival of an international university. *The New York Review of Books*, 13 August 2015.

Singh, B.P. 2009. *India's Culture: The State, the Arts and Beyond*. New Delhi: Oxford University Press.

Srinivas, S.V., Radhika, P. and Rajadhyaksha, A. 2009. Creative Industries. The Way Forward. Bangalore: Centre for the Study of Culture and Society. Unpublished paper.

Tanvir, H. 1975. Cultural policy and the performing arts. In S. Saberwal (ed.), *Towards a Cultural Policy*. New Delhi: Vikas Publishing House.

Thapar, R. 1993. Interview: interpretations of Indian history. *India International Centre Quarterly*, 20(1–2), 115–135.

UNESCO/UNDP. 2013. *United Nations Creative Economy Report 2013. Special Edition. Widening Local Development Pathways*. New York and Paris: UNDP and UNESCO.

Vari, M. 2015. Creative and academic freedom under threat from religious intolerance in India. *The Conversation*. 1 July 2015. http://theconversation.com/creative-and-academic-freedom-under-threat-from-religious-intolerance-in-india-43743 (accessed 20 April 2016).

Vatsyayan, K.M. 1972. *Some Aspects of Cultural Policy in India*. Paris: UNESCO.

32

From Cultural Revolution to cultural engineering

Cultural policy in post-Revolutionary Iran

Ali Akbar Tajmazinani

Introduction

With the victory of an Islamic Revolution in 1979 in Iran, the cultural landscape of the country experienced a dramatic transformation both at the grassroots level and the formal structural levels. The most notable policy development with direct impact for cultural policy in this phase was the issuance of Ayatollah Khomeini's mandate to undertake a 'Cultural Revolution' in various aspects of society. The 'Supreme Council of Cultural Revolution' was established and activated. A complete revision in the educational system and other public spheres was one of the main features. The Council has remained as the main policymaking authority until now and has directly formulated policies, while influencing other policies adopted by various administrative and legislative institutions.

This chapter reviews policy documents adopted by various administrative and legislative bodies to map the evolution of Iran's cultural policy scene in the past four decades. It begins with a brief introduction of the country, followed by a section on cultural policy orientations in the pre-Revolution era to contextualize cultural policy in Revolutionary Iran. The chapter continues by elaborating the processes and features of Cultural Revolution and its impact on policymaking after the Revolution. It then deals with the most recent policy development, which has been the adoption of a 'Cultural Engineering' approach by the Council through which it seeks to ensure that all economic, social and political policies, programs and measures undertaken by various parts of the administrative bodies are in line with cultural orientations approved by the system. It will be argued that the new approach is mainly a change of rhetoric, which seeks to materialize the original goals of the Revolution within the new atmosphere, not a substantive shift of policy for which one could find grounds to envisage a notable success.

The chapter concludes with some theoretical and practical analysis of cultural policy in Iran and tries to locate the system within the main typology of cultural policy systems in the world. While having its unique features, the existing cultural policy model seems close to the engineer model (though with some main differences) as well as having some similarities with the nurturer model.

Iran: and overview of the context

Known mainly through the western media representation focusing largely on political issues, Iran is less familiar to the outside world, especially those in the west, from a socio-cultural perspective. This is partly because of a series of significant political events taking place in recent decades revolving around Iran. The overthrow of the pro-western king (*Shah*) of Iran and the establishment of a theocratic state (the Islamic Republic of Iran) in 1979 was the first in this series of events that heralded nearly four decades of considerable political upheavals in the region as well as at the international level. The capturing of the U.S. embassy in Tehran by university students and people who had strong anti-American sentiments was the second on the list; having roots mainly in vast interventions by the U.S. in Iran's domestic affairs (including the 1953 coup against the popular Prime Minister Mohammad Mosaddeq) the feelings peaked when the Shah entered the U.S. after fleeing the country in 1979.

The longest political crisis began when Saddam Hussein invaded Iran in 1980 in order to seize the opportunity of post-Revolutionary chaos to establish his position as the strongest regime in the region. The war, which lasted for eight years, was marked by strong support for Saddam by western powers (such as the U.S., the United Kingdom, France and Germany), eastern powers (mainly the former Soviet Union and the People's Republic of China) as well as Arab countries (including Saudi Arabia, Egypt and Kuwait) who considered Revolutionary Iran as a common threat to their interests (for various reasons). Iran's continuance of its nuclear energy plans (which is considered as a potential threat by western powers due to possibility of obtaining nuclear weapons) has provided western media with enough opportunities in recent years to maintain the same line of negative representations of the country.

It is beyond the scope of this study to discuss or challenge those representations. However, it is useful to have a brief introduction about some of the main features of the Iranian society for a better understanding of the socio-political context of its cultural policy. The first point with relevance to cultural policy is the contrast of pre- and post-Islamic history and heritage of the country that has inspired two contrasting lines of cultural policy in modern Iran before and after the Islamic Revolution.

Officially known as the 'Islamic Republic of Iran', the country was called Persia at the international level until 1935 (although it was referred to as Iran at the domestic level from ancient times). The current name is derived from the word 'Aryan', which means the 'land of Aryans' (noble people). Aryan refers to the Indo-European race; members inhabited this part of the world in ancient times and they are believed by some scholars to be the ancestors of the European peoples (Encyclopædia Britannica Inc., 2005a). Iran is home to one of the oldest civilisations in the world. Recorded history began with the Elamites c 3000 BC. The Medes flourished from c 728 BC but were overthrown (550 BC) by the Persians. Cyrus the Great (558–529 BC) is the most famous emperor during this era who appears in the Bible as the liberator of the Jews held captive in Babylon (Encyclopædia Britannica Inc., 2005b) and who is believed to have issued the 'first human rights charter' in the world (ICS, 2016a), the original version of which is kept in the British Museum.

Islam came to Iran in the 7th century when the Sāsānian dynasty (AD 224–651) was defeated by Muslim Arabs. However, the majority of Iranian Muslims were from the Sunni sect until the Safavid dynasty (1502–1736) established a dominant Shi'ite state. The last dynasty, which ruled Iran before the Islamic Revolution in 1979, was the Pahlavi dynasty (1926–1979). Its founder, Reza Shah, overthrew the Qājār dynasty (1794–1925) through a coup backed by the British Empire. He and his successor (his son, Mohammad Reza Shah) were known as pro-western, autocratic and anti-religious rulers and provided the ground for a vast and influential presence of western powers in the country, especially the United Kingdom (U.K.) and later the United States (Encyclopædia Britannica Inc., 2005b,c).

These orientations and their cultural, political, social and economic implications evoked dissatisfaction among various sectors of the society (left wing parties, religious leaders, nationalist movements, academic forums and the grass roots) and led to the victory of the Islamic Revolution in 1979. The Revolution had as its main slogans 'independence, freedom, Islamic Republic' and 'no to West, no to East, [yes to] Islamic Republic'. The establishment of the Islamic Republic of Iran under Ayatollah Khomeini, who passed away in 1989 and was replaced through the selection of Ayatollah Khamenei as Supreme Leader (1989-present) by the Assembly of Leadership Experts, began a new era in the history of the country, which brought about a series of serious changes to various aspects of the Iranian society, notably in the field of culture and cultural policy.

The second notable issue relates to demographic characteristics. With a population of 75,149,669, Iran enjoys a diverse society both in terms of language and ethnicity with languages being linked to ethnic groups. The main ethnic groups with their own unique languages are Fars or Persians 60% (including Persian sub-groups such as the Mazandaranis, Tats, and Gilakis), Azeris or Turks 20%, Kurds 7%, Lors 3%, Arabs 2%, Baloochis 2%, Turkmens 2%, Turkic tribal groups (e.g. Qashqai) 2%, and non-Persian, non-Turkic groups (e.g. Armenians, Assyrians and Georgians) 2% (Library of Congress, 2008). Unlike ethnicity and language, Iranian society is not a diverse one in terms of religion. Based on 2011 national census, more than 99.4% of the population are Muslim and the rest consists mainly of Christians, Jews and Zoroastrians (SCI, 2012).

A third issue related to the nature of cultural policy in Iran is its state-dominated economy. The majority of large-scale industries including the oil industry, broadcasting, telecommunication, banking, automobile manufacturing, insurance, roads and railroads, shipping and energy are under state ownership and control. Privatisation and economic adjustment has been a constant and often contradictory policy paradigm since the end of the Iraq-Iran war with subsequent governments following various approaches to this issue. The most recent development is the reinterpretation of Article 44 of the Constitution in a way that allows for the private sector to play a more active role (80% of the state assets should be privatised).

Last, the nature of the political system in Iran influences cultural policy to a great extent. Based on the 1979 Constitution[1] and its amendment in 1989, the political system of Iran is 'Islamic Republic' with Shi'a Islam being the official religion while officially recognising the other Islamic sect (Sunni) and other main religions, namely, Christianity, Zoroastrianism, and Judaism. The Supreme Leader (who must be a prominent religious figure) is the highest state authority and is elected by the Assembly of Leadership Experts (elected by direct public votes).

The President is the head of executive branch and the highest state authority after the Supreme Leader. He is elected by universal suffrage (for four years with a possibility of being elected for a second term) and is responsible for the implementation of the Constitution. Apart from the cabinet, he is also head of the Supreme Council of Cultural Revolution (explained below). The national Parliament (Majles) is composed of 290 members elected by people (at municipality levels) for four years and is the main legislative entity, although it has a so-called rival in the field of cultural legislation (Supreme Council of Cultural Revolution).

Cultural policy in the pre-Revolution era

To have a clear understanding of the motives and drivers of cultural policy after the Islamic Revolution and especially the necessity of a 'Cultural Revolution' from the perspective of its agents, there is a need to illustrate the cultural policy scene of pre-revolution era. It could be argued that integrated attempts towards modern cultural policy began with the establishment of Pahlavi dynasty as part of the overall modernisation agenda of the country. The period spans from 1925 until 1979 and includes the ruling of Reza Shah (1925–1944) and his son Mohammad Reza Shah (1944–1979). The dynasty was founded four years after a British-assisted coup (in 1921) when Reza shah overthrew Ahmad Shah Qajar, the last king or Shah of the Qajar dynasty.

Four main orientations could be identified in the cultural policy of Pahlavi era, namely ancientisation/archaism, westernisation, secularisation, and assimilation. Although these four elements are interrelated and overlapping, distinct features and policies could be traced for each component:

(A) Ancientisation/Archaism

The Pahlavi dynasty had a strong emphasis in its cultural policy on symbols and elements of ancient or pre-Islamic era legacy. Although this tendency began with Iranian intellectuals during Qajar dynasty (Ashna, 2009), it was only under Reza Shah that formal cultural practices were guided by this principle.

By ancientisation we mean authentication of a contemporary national identity by reference to Iranian ancient symbols and practices. First, Reza Shah labelled his dynasty 'Pahlavi', which refers to an ancient Iranian language. Second, the strengthening of archaeology, to discover and preserve the remains of ancient Iranian civilisation, was put on the agenda of cultural policy. Several archaeologist teams were invited from countries such as Germany, the United States of America and France to work alongside Iranian archaeologists and the *Museum of Ancient Iran* (currently National Museum of Iran) was established. Third, the national calendar was changed from Hijri Qamari (an Islamic lunar calendar beginning in AD 622, during which the emigration or *Hijrah* of Prophet Muhammad from Mecca to Medina to establish an Islamic state occurred) to a Persian Imperial Calendar (a solar calendar beginning with the birth of the Persian Empire founder, Cyrus the Great, in 559 BC). Fourth, a series of festivals was held in 1971 on the occasion of the 2,500th anniversary of the founding of the Iranian monarchy by Cyrus the Great (referred to as "The 2,500 Year Celebration of the Persian Empire"). Fifth, the international name of the country was changed from Persia to Iran to denote the nobility of Aryan or Indo-European race. Sixth, epic poems and epic poets were highly promoted especially *Ferdowsi* and his book *Shahnameh* (Book of Kings), which contains the longest epic poem of the Iran and Persian-speaking world and is characterised by pure Persian language, free from imported words from other languages especially the Arabic language (Fazeli, 2006; Ashna, 2009; Ohadi and Hajirajabali, 2016).

(B) Westernisation

Intentions of the Pahlavi dynasty for rapid modernisation based on western experience, values and principles led it to adopt several measures including in the field of culture. Although some of these cultural measures were basic in their nature, others were imitations of the most superficial aspects of western culture. Establishment of a modern schooling system throughout the country based on the western model, including mixed schools of girls and boys, was among the most notable measures. While these schools aimed to raise children who are loyal to the royal family and their homeland and serve the process of nation-state building, the curricular and extra-curricular content and activities clearly pursued the goal of westernisation and pro-moting the idea of western civilisation's superiority, towards which the country should ultimately move.

The establishment and expansion of universities, based on western models, was also a prominent measure in this era, although some institutions such as *Darolfonoon* were set up several years before (in 1851), inspired by western higher education institutions. Tehran University was established in 1934, and the number of univer-sities raised from four universities (with 14,500 students) in 1953 to 16 universities (with 154,315 students) in 1977 (Abrahamian, 1980). Alongside adopting educa-tional methods and contents (especially in humanities and social sciences), there were strong and extensive relationships between Iranian universities and their western counterparts.

Forced promotion of western-style dressing for women and men was another measure taken by Reza Shah. Unification of Iranian's Dressing Law was first adopted in 1929 for men and was followed by the banning of *Hijab* for women in 1935. It was believed that traditional dressing was a barrier for modernisation and participation of women in social life and that unification of dressing in line with western styles was a prerequisite for modernisation. Although forced application of the dressing codes was not followed by his successor Mohammad Reza Shah, western style dressing was still promoted and encouraged by all elements of the cultural apparatus including schools, universities and mass media.

A fourth aspect of this policy was the vast promotion of western style art in all fields especially cinema, theatre and music. 'Shiraz/Persepolis Festival of Arts' was the main annual event held at an international level for 11 years (from 1967 to 1977) in the city of Shiraz and Persepolis, although this festival also included Iranian classic arts.

Of notable importance with regard to the diffusion of western thought was the wide-spread translation of western literature in all fields. Comparing the list of compiled books in Farsi and those translated into Farsi, Ashna (2009) concludes the second group has dramatically outweighed the first category.

(C) Secularisation

Reza Shah used religious gestures as a tool to attract support from the clergy and the public during his first steps of serious political life, including throughout the initial years of his rule as king. However, he soon came into conflict with religious leaders and their followers by pursuing his modernisation agenda. In fact, all policies outlined under ancientisation and westernisation were considered by religious oppo-sition to be part of a broad de-Islamisation and secularisation agenda. Ancientisation policies were focusing on pre-Islamic history and elements and icons to marginalise Islamic symbols and thoughts. Westernisation policies were also used to modernise various aspects of social life based on western lifestyles and were strong drivers of change towards secularisation given the central position of secularism in contempo-rary western culture.

In addition to those policies, more direct measures were aimed at excluding reli-gion and religious manifestations from the public sphere. Forbidding or limiting some religious rituals exercised in public spaces, supporting secular intellectuals including through promotion of their ideas and products and controlling, limiting or oppressing religious figures who were opposing the secularisation agenda are more notable among these measures (Fazeli, 2006; Navakhti Moghadam and Anvarian Asl, 2010; Devos and Werner, 2014; Ohadi and Hajirajabali, 2016).

(D) Assimilation

As outlined above, the Iranian population consists of several ethnic groups with a rich diversity of languages and cultural heritages. The process of nation-state building in the Pahlavi era, especially under Reza Shah, included a cultural assimilation agenda as an integral part of modernisation. It was believed that a strong centralised state was needed to preserve the national integrity and solidarity, which in turn required the construction and promotion of a unified national identity (Ramezanzadeh, 1997: 246; Salehi Amiri, 2009, 285–288). Construction of this new identity took place through a plethora of measures *inter aila*:

- Promotion of Persian (Farsi) language as the official language including through formal education system for all ethnic groups, while trying to purify it from non-Persian elements, particularly Arabic and Turkish words, especially through the establishment of the Persian Academy (Ashna, 2009).
- An emphasis on the Aryan Race and trying to promote it as the superior race that should be preserved and purified (Fazeli, 2006; Navakhti Moghadam and Anvarian Asl, 2010).
- Trying to weaken local and ethnic cultural diversities including through the promotion of unified codes of dressing, oppression of ethnic movements, stabilising the residence of migrating tribes and nomads (including their forced displacement to Persian-speaking areas) and changing the local non-Persian names of places and tribes (Salehi Amiri, 2009; Vaez Shahrestani, 2009).

The Islamic Revolution and its Cultural Revolution agenda

Iran witnessed dramatic political upheavals in the last years of the 1970s, which ended up in the Islamic Revolution of 1979. Although groups from different schools of thought were engaged in fighting the Pahlavi regime for various reasons, the religious movement under the leadership of Ayatollah Khomeini was successful and came to dominate the socio-political movement. This was mainly due to the popularity of Islamic values and slogans among the majority of highly traditional and religious population of the country, as well as the ability of religious leaders to communicate effectively with the masses and to utilise religious teachings, symbols and institutions (thousands of mosques, *Hussainia,*[2] religious schools or *Hawzah,*[3] religious charities, etc. that were present in every neighbourhood of the country) in their struggle against the regime.

The main lines of socio-cultural oppositions of the religious movement were directed at the cultural policies pursued by the Pahlavi regime. Actually, all four main policy orientations discussed above were considered to be in contradiction with the religious identity of the Iranian population and the authority of religious leaders associated with it. Highlighting the Ancient and pre-Islamic history during the Pahlavi era was a sign, for the religious opposition, that Pahlavi cultural policy tried to denote the inferiority of the Islamic legacy by its portrayal as the main cause for the backwardness of the country. It was also employed in legitimising the monarchy and the superior status of the monarch against other sources of authority. The secularisation agenda was in sharp contrast with claims of religious leaders regarding the capacity and mission of Islam to provide solutions for social, political and economic questions and the needs of human beings in every time and place during the history and throughout the world; something that was only in their competence and capacity of the religious to materialise. Westernisation promoted a lifestyle and set of ideas that seriously challenged the virtue of Islamic morality, whilst codes of conduct and assimilation policies were mainly aimed to facilitate a model of rapid modernisation based on western values.

It was in this context that the Revolutionary forces tried to radically transform the cultural scene of the country after it was changed in the political arena. National Iranian Radio and Television (NIRT) underwent a radical change to align with the Revolution and purify itself from non-Islamic elements, including those products that promoted the western lifestyle. Its name was changed to Islamic Republic of Iran Broadcasting (IRIB) and it remained under state control with the monopoly of domestic radio and television services in the country. Cinema, theatre and music witnessed the same shift in content and went under strict scrutiny by the government, first through the Ministry of Culture and Higher Education and then through the Ministry of Culture and Islamic Guidance (MCIG). It was also the case for the publishing industry (newspapers, magazines, books, etc.) to experience state monitoring and control mainly through the MCIG.

Reforming the public culture was also on the top of the agenda of the Revolution. Islamic clothing (Hijab) became mandatory for women first in state-owned and controlled places and then in all public spaces. All kinds of trades and interactions related to alcohol production and consumption, gambling and prostitution were banned. In fact, all aspects of life in the public sphere were supposed to be in accordance with the Islamic cultural norms.

The most remarkable development was in the field of higher education. As was mentioned above, universities were developed in Iran based on western models in their form and content and were in contrast to traditional religious schools. After the Revolution, universities were the main platform for student branches of various political groups (including leftist parties and forces) to promote their ideas that were not in conformity with the dominant Islamic ideology. In 1980, Ayatollah Khomeini issued a mandate for a 'Cultural Revolution', which was mainly aimed at a radical revision in higher education. The main measures undertaken in this period were:

- Purging non-conformist lectures and students from universities (especially leftist forces),
- Purifying the contents of books and attempting to revise them or compile new texts in accordance with Islamic teachings (especially in the field of humanities and social sciences),
- Establishing a specific procedure for the selection and admission of lectures and students (to approve their political and religious eligibility in addition to academic qualifying),
- Attempting to unify (or at least make close) university education with the educational system in religious schools,
- Restricting and regulating aspects of informal student life including clothing codes, socialising mixed events, etc.

(Sobhe, 1982; Gheissari and Nasr, 2006; Keddie and Richard, 2006; Encyclopaedia Iranica, 2011)

The Cultural Revolution Headquarters was established in 1980 to pursue this agenda, but it was replaced with the Supreme Cultural Revolution Council, which holds more power and authority than its predecessor. The Council is headed by the President (with its membership comprising of individual and ex-officio members pertaining to cultural, educational and religious entities) and is now the main policymaking and monitoring body in the field of cultural policy in Iran.

Cultural policy has gone through various phases after the Revolution, with each phase having some distinguishing features (see Table 32.1). It has been mainly influenced by the dominant political discourse of the time and has been shaped by the socio-economic and political conditions of the country. However, Seddigh Sarvestani and Zaeri (2010) argue that two broad discourses could be identified in post-Revolutionary Iran: Traditional-Revolutionary Discourse (from 1979 to 1988 and from 2005 to 2013) and Liberal-Developmental Discourse (1989 to 2005). Keeping this in mind, one could identify the three phases of 'Early post-Revolution', 'Imposed War (Holy Defence)', and 'Principle-ism' with the Traditional-Revolutionary Discourse and the other three phases ('Reconstruction', 'Reforms', and 'Moderation') with the Liberal-Developmental Discourse. In fact, the first two phases were heavily influenced by the Revolutionary spirit, which favoured the resurgence of Islamic traditions in all aspects of life. This discourse was also dominant in Ahmadinejad's period with his prominent emphasis on 'back to Islamic principles and values', which were claimed to be weakened by non-Revolutionary orientations of Rafsanjani and Khatami administrations. In response to the hard-line cultural orientations of the 'Principle-ism' phase, which aimed to impose a traditionalist reading of the social

Table 32.1 Main cultural policy developments in post-Revolution era

Titles of the phases	Years and heads of administration	Main policy developments
Early post-Revolution	1979–1981 (multiple)	Cultural Revolution; launch of mandatory Hijab; banning and closure of alcohol production and consumption, gambling, and prostitution places
Imposed War (Holy Defence)	1981–1988 (Mousavi)	Domination of formal and public culture by the war; establishment of Islamic Azad University (non-governmental but public)
Reconstruction	1989–1997 (Hashemi Rafsanjani)	Structural adjustments and privatisation; Launch of private schools; promotion of consumptionist culture; expansion of cultural facilities
Reforms	1997–2005 (Khatami)	Civil society expansion; strengthening the role of NGOs in the field of culture; more open environment for publishers of newspapers, magazines and books (but tough reaction from the judicial system); international cultural cooperation; dialogue among civilisations
Principle-ism	2005–2013 (Ahmadinejad)	Cultural Engineering; more emphasis on religious aspects of culture; expansion of cultural facilities; more roles for Basij and mosques in delivering cultural policy
Moderation	2013-present (Rouhani)	More roles for NGOs representing members of culture and art community; more open to public culture; loosening scrutiny mechanisms on cultural products; cultural diplomacy

and cultural life through the new 'cultural engineering' agenda, voters elected moderate Rouhani, who was supported publicly by Khatami and Rafsanjani and promised to follow a more open cultural policy. As the head of Supreme Council for Cultural Revolution, Rouhani has decreased the level of activities and interventions of the Council in the overall design and delivery of cultural policy in favour of more authority for cultural bodies of his administration; he regularly faces criticisms and confrontations from religious figures as well as revolutionary entities outside the government. Banning or making disruptions in cultural activities like some pop music concerts, films, theatres and festivals approved by the Ministry of Culture (under Rouhani) on behalf of or by the above-mentioned figures and entities are examples of these confrontations that aim to disappoint voters and supporters and send a clear message to the public that the government cannot say the final word in the field of culture.

Cultural policy orientations in post-Revolutionary Iran

A plethora of cultural policy instruments have been adopted after the Islamic Revolution in Iran, and numerous cultural initiatives have been launched based on these instruments. Content analysis of these instruments shows a dramatic change in cultural policy orientations of the country in the past four decades. The main documents and instruments included in the analysis are: Constitution of the Islamic Republic of Iran; Five-Year Economic, Social, and Cultural Development Plans (first to fifth plans); Mega policies adopted by the Expediency Discernment Council of the System and policies adopted by the Supreme Cultural Revolution Council.

As it is evident from the main categories, as well as from the subcategories and themes extracted from the documents and instruments mentioned above, there is a sharp deviation from the policy orientations in pre-revolution cultural policy. Contrary to the Pahlavi era, cultural policy is bestowed with the sacred mission of Islamisation in all fields of social life. The ancient Iranian legacy and culture is marginalised or absent from these policies, and there is a strong caution about the so-called cultural invasion of the western world.

There are numerous instruments, institutions/bodies, budget allocations, etc. regarding each of the subcategories (listed under each main category) in the public administration of the country that are outside the range of this chapter, but below is a brief list of the main themes and subthemes:

Promotion and consolidation of religious and ethical doctrine

Given the nature of the political system established following the Islamic Revolution, it is not surprising that the most frequent theme appearing in all policy instruments revolves around its religious and ethical doctrine. It is clearly against the secularising agenda of the Pahlavi era and tries to bring religion into all fields of social life. As an example, promotion of Quranic culture is practiced through a variety of measures: provision of Quranic courses (recitation, memorising, meaning and interpretation, etc.) in cultural centres, schools, universities, neighbourhood houses of municipalities, cultural and arts centres of mosques, production of cultural items (films, books, TV series, etc.) with Quranic themes, decoration of public spaces with Quranic messages, organising Quranic competitions in various disciplines (recitation, memorising, meaning and commentary, etc.) at various levels by a variety of institutions including the above-mentioned bodies.

The main subthemes under the first category are as following:

- Emphasising the centrality of Islamic values and superiority of the monotheist perspective
- Promotion of moral virtues and ethical codes
- Confronting superstition and religious deviance and aberrance
- Promoting and implementing the 'Enjoining Good and Forbidding Wrong' principle
- Promotion of prayer and praying culture
- Promotion of Quranic culture
- Organising and enhancement of cultural aspects of religious rituals
- Promotion of chastity and Hijab culture
- Promotion of reasonable thrift, contentment and non-luxury lifestyle

Strengthening of Islamic Revolution values

While the first category of policy orientations seeks to ensure the religious character of the society, this second category deals with the preservation and strengthening of its Revolutionary characteristics. Again, it is a mandate for all public bodies to promote these values in their activities through various forms. A prominent element of this category is the 'diffusion of Basiji[4] Culture'. Established in November 1979 based on a mandate from the founder of the Islamic Republic, Basij is a paramilitary volunteer force subordinate to the 'Islamic Revolutionary Guard'. The full name of the force is *Nirou-ye Moqavemat-e Basij* (Mobilisation Resistance Force) or *Basij-e Mosta'afin* (Mobilisation of the Oppressed) with its main features and functions being deep loyalty to the supreme leader, providing voluntary public services, morals policing, engaging in internal security as a law enforcement auxiliary force and confronting dissident gatherings. The organisation has branches in nearly all mosques, neighbourhoods, schools, universities, factories, governmental and public bodies, etc. Given the key role of Basij in post-Revolution history with regard to defending the country as well as supporting the political system, extensive cultural activities have been commissioned to it, while other public bodies are also mandated or encouraged to promote Basiji culture.

The main subthemes under the second category are as following:

- Observation and consolidation of Islamic Revolution values
- Paying attention to Revolutionary values in allocation of resources
- Promoting and vitalising thoughts of Imam Khomeini and the Great Leader
- Diffusion of Basiji Culture
- Diffusion of self-sacrifice and martyrdom culture
- Deepening the spirit and insight of knowing and fighting enemies

Conservation and strengthening of Islamic-Iranian culture and identity

Unlike the pre-Revolution era, the Iranian identity (especially if linked with the pre-Islamic history) does not receive prominent status in cultural policy instruments; it is usually mentioned in conjunction with the Islamic identity. It means that only those elements of Iranian identity and culture are proper to be preserved and promoted that are compatible with Islam or at least are not contradicting it. Therefore, while, for example, very big cinema films and TV series dedicated to the introduction of national-Islamic heroes and scholars receive considerable support, there is almost no publicly funded cultural project dedicated to heroes, legendary figures and scholars from the pre-Islamic history of the country. The main sub-categories related to this theme are:

- Consolidation of national unity
- Strengthening of national identity
- Identification and preservation of cultural heritage
- Promotion of Persian language and literature

Consideration of cultural dimensions in other sectors

A main mission of cultural policy instruments is to envisage mechanisms and structures that ensure that policies, plans and measures in other fields (economy, politics, social) are in conformity with the Islamic, Revolutionary and Iranian culture. For example, it is believed that the Islamic-Iranian identity of cities in the country is weakened through the process of modernisation, and elements of non-Iranian culture are increasingly witnessed in urban landscapes. Therefore, there are regulations that aim to stop this trend and to promote domestic and indigenous elements of architecture. Other subthemes in this field include the following:

- Providing grounds for synergy of non-cultural sectors with cultural policies
- Land use based on cultural considerations
- Paying attention to Islamic-Iranian culture in architecture and city-building
- Observation of cultural aspects in privatisation

Respecting cultural diversity and cultural rights

Cultural diversity has received only marginal attention in cultural policy instruments, just as is the case for cultural rights. It seems that there has been a historical reluctance to acknowledge diversity since it is considered a threat to the presumably unified national-Islamic identity. Existing references to this category address the following items:

- Supporting cultural and religious diversity
- Supporting and safeguarding legitimate freedoms
- Protecting cultural rights

Active and influential cultural interactions

Another issue addressed in cultural policy documents is the necessity of cultural interactions with other nations as well as with cultural entities at the international level to have an influential presence while using the positive aspects of other cultures. However, more emphasis is on cultural influence on other nations and playing as an inspiring cultural role model for other Muslim societies. Subthemes include:

- Cultural communication and interaction (with other countries)
- Taking advantage of other cultures
- Cultural presence at the international level

Confronting cultural invasion

The cultural interaction explained in the previous section is limited by a very serious caution about the harmful aspects of other cultures, in particular the western culture represented by American culture (and exported through new mechanisms of cultural colonialism). Consumerism, lack of respect for traditional family forms and religion, sex, violence, drugs and alcohol, which are promoted in the cultural productions (including in cinema, TV, and fashion industry) of the west, especially the United States, are regarded as the main threats to Iranian-Islamic culture. With the end of the Iraq-Iran war and the beginning of the construction era, this theme began to be raised increasingly in the cultural policy instruments. Related subthemes include:

- Confronting cultural cringe (towards other cultures)
- Confronting grounds for cultural invasion
- Active promotion of alternative cultural models

Encouraging cultural participation and culture of participation

Participation is a key theme in nearly all policy instruments both as means and as an end. While a mission of cultural policy is to extend citizens' participation in cultural activities, it also should pave the way for a cultural participatory ethics in all aspects of social life. However, as will be discussed in the final section of this chapter, this is more related to democratisation of culture than devolving the control over cultural policy to the public through cultural democracy. Subthemes in this field include the following:

- Emphasising the right to participation
- Providing grounds for participation
- Strengthening and encouraging cultural participation
- Promoting a spirit of participation
- Encouraging the sense of responsibility

Enhancement of citizenship ethics and culture

Nurturing citizens who are aware of and dedicatedly practicing and observing their commitments in various aspects of social life is seen as a main item on the agenda of cultural policy. Therefore, various sorts of cultural productions and cultural activities are deemed to follow this agenda. Related subthemes include:

- Enhancement of work ethics and responsibility
- Expanding the culture of valuing work and production
- Strengthening a culture of law-abiding and discipline
- Strengthening a culture of environment protection

Consolidation of family institution and the status of women in society

The traditional family occupies a pivotal position as a sacred institution in the ideology of the Iranian political system. Therefore, in theory no cultural item should be produced or distributed that weakens this position. Even women's employment, which is usually regarded to be on the agenda of social and economic policies, has received special attention and dedicated policy instruments by the SCCR to ensure that they are compatible with the roles of women in the family. The main subthemes under this category are the following:

- Protecting the sacredness of the family institution
- Strengthening the family institution
- Policies regarding women's employment
- Socio-cultural policies regarding women's involvement in sports

Optimising the extent and way of state intervention in culture

Besides the above-mentioned categories that deal with the content and orientation of cultural policy, two other themes are related to the administrative aspects of cultural policy. With extensive state intervention in culture after the Revolution, a need was felt in the second and third decades to optimise this intervention by limiting it to the policymaking level and devolving executive functions to non-governmental public and private entities. Inspired by the post-war structural adjustment approach, this rhetoric has not been realised while the language of policy instruments in this regard is still very state-oriented. Subthemes in this field include the following:

- Necessity of government responsibility and accountability in the field of culture
- Centralisation of policymaking and decentralisation of implementation
- Supporting and enhancement of public/state media
- Developing the cultural economics
- Supporting public cultural activities
- Regulation of relations and interactions among stakeholders of the cultural sector
- Promotion of creativity and innovation

Establishment of an integrated system of strategic cultural management in the country

The Existence of multiple and parallel governmental and semi-governmental cultural institutions is a major issue in the design and delivery of cultural policy in Iran. Therefore, there is a need for an integrated system of cultural management under the supervision of SCCR. Various instruments have addressed the need for this including through the following subthemes:

- Taking advantage of cultural facilities of non-cultural bodies
- Systematic monitoring of cultural developments
- Increasing efficiency of cultural bodies
- Strengthening cultural research
- Development of human resources in the cultural sector
- Expansion of ICTs in the cultural sector

The above-mentioned categories and subcategories illustrate the main cultural policy orientations in Iran from 1979 to 2005 with the main agenda of launching a 'cultural revolution' in the country. However, it was felt after three decades that those policies had not been effective in producing the desired outcomes, while they are also not compatible with (and enough) for the contemporary era. Therefore, a new wave of cultural policy initiatives was launched under the 'Cultural Engineering' rhetoric that will be discussed below.

Cultural engineering: a new era?

The 'Cultural Engineering' concept was raised in 2005 by the Supreme Leader of Iran and was followed and promoted by various cultural bodies, resulting in the formulation and adoption of the 'Cultural Engineering Map' by the Supreme Council of Cultural Revolution in 2013 (SCCRS, 2013). This new rhetoric raised many questions and ambiguities (including in the first 'Conference on Cultural Engineering' in 2007) regarding such issues as: the relationship between the two concepts of 'cultural engineering' and 'engineering of culture', the status of religion in cultural engineering, the paradox between the concrete and highly standardised concept of 'engineering' and a completely different concept of 'culture', which may mean an overwhelming intervention by the political power (see e.g. Fouladi, 2009; Moeidfar, 2006). The long-time span from 2005 to 2013 between the time when the concept was first raised and the time it was adopted as an official instrument may point to some of these ambiguities.

It seems that the new cultural trends in the Iranian society that were accelerated by the end of the imposed war against Iran by Saddam Hussein played a key role in the adoption of this new approach. These trends included the gradual weakening of revolutionary and religious values, attitudes and behaviors after the war, cultural globalisation (Afshari Naderi, 2007) and the spread of western values and lifestyles including through new media, the growth of consumerism and a relatively moderate orientation in cultural policy during the Khatami administration. These trends combined with the ambition of the Iranian political system to establish a 'new Islamic civilization' (Masjedjameie, undated) using culture as a strong catalyser of development and progress as grounds for this new policy approach.

A review of the vision, principles, goals, strategies (13 mega and 104 national strategies) and measures (302 national measures) outlined in the 'Cultural Engineering Map' shows that this new instrument reflects nearly all the themes of previous cultural instruments adopted so far, while it addresses some new issues as well. It has a maximalist approach and covers nearly all areas of social life, even the issue of fertility and population growth rate. Given the current low population growth rate and an ageing population trend, this section is more elaborate than other sections, pointing to specific actions to promote a culture of valuing marriage and childbearing through various economic, social and welfare incentives.

As expected, the meaning of culture employed in this map is highly related to and overshadowed by religion and religious values, attitudes, behavior and symbols. There is a new emphasis on strengthening the soft power components of the system to confront the 'soft war' against the Revolution, alongside stressing the role of arts and new ICTs in pursuing the cultural goals of the system.

It could be argued that the main feature of this new instrument is its mandate and endeavor to establish an integrated national system of cultural policy under the supervision of the SCCR, which ensures that all kinds of policymaking (social, political, economic, cultural) are compatible with Islamic and Revolutionary characteristics. Moreover, there is an ambitious intention to purify, standardise and enrich the public culture to establish a new Islamic civilisation that could emerge as a role model and source of inspiration for all Muslim societies. It will be argued in the concluding section that it is hard to consider the adoption of this new approach as a fundamental change of policy and to envisage a notable success for it.

Concluding remarks

Cultural policy has an interesting history during the past half century and has witnessed considerable transformations and fluctuations especially due to the victory of the Islamic Revolution in Iran. However, it is also possible to trace instances of continuity alongside tremendous change. For example, despite very different points of emphasis, there is a similarity of policy intention between the pre- and post-Revolution periods with regard to the issue of cultural assimilation. While cultural policy in the Pahlavi era was following measures to assimilate various sections of the population in line with modern and western lifestyle (e.g. through forced codes of dressing), cultural policy during the Islamic Republic era has had the agenda of creating and nurturing a 'revolutionary and religious citizen' (including for example through mandatory Hijab). In fact, a common cultural policy assumption in both periods is that culture is a unique platform and a manipulable instrument for pursuing the main goals of the system, be it nation-state building and modernisation or Islamisation and building a new Islamic civilisation (in line with the notion of 'imagined communities' developed by Anderson, 1991). Therefore, cultural policy in Iran is of an 'instrumental' character (McGuigan, 2004), but ironically with little or no emphasis on economic instrumentality.

Another line of continuity in cultural policy in Iran (between the pre- and post-Revolution periods) could be found in terms of following a democratisation of culture agenda instead of a cultural democracy paradigm (Evrard, 1997). In both periods there have been measures to build public cultural facilities, promote access to and use of cultural facilities and services and popularising high culture and cultural knowledge (though with completely different value orientations), but there has been a lack of serious attention to cultural diversity, full and effective cultural representation and participation, as well as democratic control of cultural life. As an example, one can compare the approach of 'Youth Palaces' in the pre-Revolution era with 'Culture Centres' in the post-Revolution period. While young people in the former were exposed to a range of cultural activities in line with the four elements of Pahlavi cultural policy (especially the westernisation agenda), young people in the latter are exposed to different cultural activities that aim to nurture the ideal young people desired by the Islamic system (though with gradual loosening of this agenda during the last two decades). However, the approach and mechanisms are nearly the same and are far from the cultural democracy paradigm.

Cultural policy in Iran certainly falls under a 'stating discourse' in McGuigan's typology of cultural policy (2004) in which the state follows a maximalist intervention approach in culture. Reflecting on the typology of cultural policy models provided by Craik (2007) that identifies five models of state intervention in the fields of arts and culture (the patron model; the architect model; the engineer model; the facilitator model; elite nurturer model) it could be argued that the Iranian model is a mixture of the engineer and nurturer models. It is close to the engineer model because it prioritises culture as an objective of political education allied with the ideological cast of the state. However, there is a difference between the Iranian model and that of the former Eastern Bloc countries because the government does not own all the artistic means of production and creators are not employees of the government, although there are mechanisms to control or 'guide' them in line with the political agenda of the state. There are also similarities with the nurturer model because the state provides a small number of elite cultural entities (based on its own criteria) to receive budgets and generous subsidies, which protect them from having to compete with 'outsider' cultural organisations.

As a final remark it is noteworthy that Iranian society has a hybrid identity consisting of various ancient, Islamic and modern components (Amuzegar, 2014), and the Iranian people seem to be eager to exercise a bricolage of various components and are not ready to leave one in favour of the other. This is an issue that is beyond the scope of this chapter and needs further elaboration in other academic works. Therefore, it appears that strict cultural engineering policies and practices could not meet their full objectives.

Notes

1 The complete text of the Constitution in English containing detailed information about the following bodies, authorities and procedures cited in this section as well as some concise information about the Iranian political system is accessible, *inter alia,* at: www.iranchamber.com/government/government.php.
2 A congregation hall for Shia commemoration ceremonies.
3 A seminary where Shi'a Muslim clerics are trained.
4 Members of Basij Organization are called Basiji.

References

Abrahamian, E. (1980), Structural causes of the Iranian revolution, in MERIP Reports No. 87, *Iran's Revolution: The Rural Dimension* (May, 1980), pp. 21–26. Available at: http://islamicgroupatasu.wikispaces.com/file/view/Abrahamian.pdf.

Amuzegar, J. (2014), *The Islamic Republic of Iran: Reflections on an Emerging Economy (Europa Perspectives: Emerging Economies)*, New York: Routledge.

Anderson, B. (1991), *Imagined Communities: Reflections on the Origin and Spread of Nationalism*, London: Verso.

Ashna, H. (2009) *From Politics to Culture: Cultural Policies of the State in Iran (1925–1941)*, Tehran: Soroosh Publications.

Craik, J. (2007), *Re-visioning Arts and Cultural Policy: Current Impasses and Future Directions*, Canberra: ANU E Press.

Devos, B. and Werner, C. (2014), *Culture and Cultural Politics under Reza Shah: The Pahlavi State, New Bourgeoisie and the Creation of a Modern Society in Iran*, New York: Routledge.

Encyclopaedia Iranica (2011), Women's Education in the Pahlavi Period and after, *Encyclopaedia Iranica* Online. Available at: www.iranicaonline.org/articles/education-xxvi-womens-education-in-the-pahlavi-period-and-after (accessed January 9, 2016).

Evrard, Y. (1997), State intervention in culture: democratizing culture or cultural democracy?, The *Journal of Arts Management, Law, and Society*, 27(3), 167–175.

Fazeli, N. (2006), *Politics of Culture in Iran*, New York: Routledge.

Gheissari, A. and Nasr, V. (2006), *Democracy in Iran*, Oxford: Oxford University Press.

ICS (Iran Chamber Society) (2016a), *The Cyrus the Great Cylinder*. Available at: www.iranchamber.com/history/cyrus/cyrus_charter.php.

Keddie, N. and Richard, Y. (2006) *Modern Iran: Roots and Results of Revolution*, London: Yale University Press.

Library of Congress (2008) *Iran: A Country Study*. Library of Congress, Federal Research Division, Available at: http://cdn.loc.gov/master/frd/frdcstdy/ir/irancountrystudy00curt_0/irancountrystudy00curt_0.pdf.

McGuigan, J. (2004), *Rethinking Cultural Policy*, Berkshire: Open University Press.

Navakhti Moghadam, A. and Anvarian Asl, H. (2010), Ideological basis of cultural policies during the Pahlavi dynasty, *Islamic Revolution Studies*, 6 (19), 115–140.

Ohadi, P., and Hajirajabali, K. (2016), Dialogue contextualization in cultural policies of the 1st Pahlavi, *Political Quarterly*, 45(4), 859–876.

Ramezanzadeh, A. (1997), Development and ethnic challenges, in *Development and Public Security Conference Proceedings*, Tehran: Ministry of the Interior.

Salehi Amiri, R. (2009), *National Integrity and Cultural Diversity*, Tehran: Strategic Research Institute.

SCCRS (the Supreme Council of Cultural Revolution Secretariat) (2013), *The Cultural Engineering Map*. Available at: www.sccr.ir/Pages/?current=news&gid=11&Sel=640633.

SCI (2012) *National Census 2011: excerpt of results*. Available at: www.amar.org.ir/Portals/0/Files/abstract/1390/n_sarshomari90_2.pdf.

Seddigh Sarvestani, R. and Zaeri, Gh. (2010), A study of post-Revolutionary discourses and four trends affecting cultural policy in the Islamic republic of Iran, in Amirentekhabi, Sh. (2010), *Cultural Policy (54)*, Tehran: Centre for Strategic Research.

Sobhe, Kh. (1982) Education in revolution: is Iran duplicating the Chinese cultural revolution?, *Comparative Education*, 18(3), 271–280.

Vaez Shahrestani, N. (2009), Goals and processes of cultural policy regarding tribes and nomads during the first Phlavi, *History of Islam and Iran Journal*, 19(1), 131–159.

33

K-pop female idols

Culture industry, neoliberal social policy, and governmentality in Korea

Gooyong Kim

South Korea (hereafter, Korea) rapidly achieved its economic modernization in less than four decades (1960s–1980s), a phenomenon commonly known as the Miracle on the Han River. This dynamic development has brought about the recent global popularity of Korean popular culture such as film, TV dramas, popular music (K-pop), and live performances coined as *Hallyu* or the Korean Wave. For Katsiaficas (2012), along with democratic uprisings against military juntas in the '70s and the '80s, *Hallyu* has become a symbol for Korea's competent advancement to a more civil and sophisticated country. Historically, owing to the devastated economic, social, and political conditions after the Japanese colonial occupation and the Korean War, the state's cultural policies have been instrumental in helping realize the government's political, economic, social, and/ or ideological agendas (Yim 2002). For example, President Park Chung-hee, who seized power through a military coup in 1961, made full use of Confucian cultural policies that emphasized obedience, diligence, loyalty, frugality, and cooperation in order to implement export-oriented, labor-intensive industrialization, which provided the illicit political elite with a rationale for developmental-*dictatorship* in the poverty-trodden country.

Just as Park Chung-Hee led the Miracle by advancing its distinctly masculine, exploitative modernization project through mobilizing young, docile female workers in the labor-intensive manufacture industry from the '60s to the '70s, Park Geun-Hye, the daughter of dictator-President Park Chung-Hee and the country's ex-President, who was impeached for multiple criminal charges in December 2016, declared her intention to recreate it through *Hallyu* during her inaugural speech in February 2013. In this respect, regarding national development as a result of an active "incorporation of the actively residual [social, cultural, political, and economic traditions] – by reinterpretation, dilution, projection, discriminating inclusion and exclusion" (Williams 1977, p. 123), the author strives to critically examine the proliferation of K-pop within a continuum between Korea's residual legacy of developmentalism and post-IMF neoliberal state policies. Reconsidering the social, cultural and political, and economic backgrounds, the chapter provides an alternative approach to a recent, global popularity of K-pop, and in turn, criticizes the current, dominant academic literature, which does not pay due attention to those structural issues.

In this chapter, the author pays critical attention as to how Korean cultural industries became capable of producing marketable and profitable entertainment content in the context of the country's neoliberalization. It aims to investigate how the industry, which was comparatively under-developed, has achieved the state of art in its aesthetic, technological, and business features in a short period of time since the mid-1990s and competed against other already advanced foreign products and services in a jungle-like neoliberal market. To this end, the author argues the Korean government's neoliberal social policy assisted its culture industry to produce high-quality culture commodities, which in turn played an important role in helping *Hallyu* become successful. By examining the political economy of K-pop's success, the author reconsiders a continuity of Korea's developmentalism that largely relies on under-paid female workers as a docile, disposable labor force in K-pop's dominant modality of neoliberal, service-oriented market rationality. However, there is an important caveat to be discerned to correctly understand the neoliberal characteristics of the K-pop industry. K-pop idols "voluntarily" become prey of the K-pop industry's rampant profiteering, which capitalizes on their competitive spirits, perseverance, and physical strength in their dream of being financially successful and socially famous in the neoliberal show business, while under Park's developmental-dictatorship, female workers had to endure exploitative, inhumane working conditions to support themselves and their families as a matter of survival on sweatshop factory floors in the '60s and the '70s. In this regard, as a popular mode of governmentality, the idols as manufactured cultural commodities by the industry – highly visible, adored, and respected by the public – have an effective, hegemonic agency that normalizes and perpetuates neoliberal subjectivation and subjectification in one's everyday life, while the "industrial warriors" who largely paved the way for the Miracle were despised as "Kong-suni," or "Kong-dori"[1] and have still not received due recognition for their contribution to national development. In sum, this chapter sheds critical light on K-pop idols' political, economic, cultural, and social impact and implications for post-IMF Korean society in a nexus between the state's politico-ideological necessity and the market's economic imperatives.

In this political economy of development, the chapter argues the country's young, docile, disposable female bodies have continuously been manipulated and exploited in the name of national modernization and growth under different agendas and slogans throughout contemporary Korean history. Thus, it maintains that K-pop idols have been closely associated with the Korean government's neoliberal development policies, examining Girls' Generation (hereafter, SNSD) as the most successful K-pop female idol group. For this purpose, the author reviews Foucault's (2008) notion of governmentality as a means to analyze how, by their popularity and ubiquity, the idols have played an ideological state apparatus (Althusser 1971), which normalizes and perpetuates the neoliberal value system, and in turn, interpellates individuals to be neoliberal subjects. As such, the author examines how K-pop helps implement the government of others (subjectification: "how one is objectified as a subject through the exercise of power/ knowledge"), normalization of a neoliberal value system, and the government of one's self (subjectivation as a "relation of the person to him/herself") (Rosenberg and Milchman 2010, p. 66). In this respect, like Binkley (2006), this chapter argues that the recent popularity of K-pop is a micromechanism for individuals to naturalize neoliberal governmentality and become active, voluntary agents of neoliberalism. By doing so, it contributes to reconsidering a lingering legacy of state-developmentalism, the nature of development, and socio-economic roles in post-IMF Korea.

Political economy of K-pop: national development in neoliberal Korea

Considering that music is a product of larger structural conditions (Negus 1999), it is important to acknowledge that K-pop was incepted when Korea was in the middle of state-led aggressive globalization campaign (including hastily attaining membership of the OECD in 1996). As a response to the large socio-economic imperatives mandated by the state and emulating short-lived American idols, such as New Kids on the Block, the industry has mimicked European or American music and used English lyrics in an unnecessary excess. As an allegory of Korean economy that relies on export for its economic, political, and social development and maintenance, K-pop is mainly produced and/or played by Koreans for the purpose of product exportation in the context of the 1997 Asian financial crisis and the Korean economy's subsequent IMF bail-out (Oh and Park 2012; G. Park 2013b). From this perspective, K-pop's global popularity coincided with the government's aggressive neoliberal efforts to expand its economic territories by ratifying multiple Free Trade Agreements (FTA), especially with the US, in the mid-2000s.

In this regard, among *Hallyu* items like movies and dramas, K-pop is the most strategic cultural commodity, incepted through rigorous market research and experiments (Shin and Kim 2013). K-pop's main features consist of addictive, fast, and dynamic beats and sounds, garnished with a perfectly synchronized, mesmerizing choreography by attractive, physique male idols or appealing, delicate, and sexy female idols (C. Kim 2012). These signature characters of K-pop, which is aesthetically influenced by Western popular culture, have been made possible by the K-pop industry's aggressive replication of the traditional business strategies used by Korea's labor-intensive manufacture conglomerates that ushered in the Miracle in the '60s and the '70s. Likewise, the contemporary K-pop industry takes advantage of a hegemonic model that produces quickly profitable, homogenized, disposable commodities from a highly concentrated, hierarchal production system that integrates in-house procedures of artist recruiting, training, image-making, composing, management, contracting, and album production. As much as Korea's manufacture industry giants achieved their fortune by exploiting cheap, docile, and abundant workers from the '60s to '80s, the K-pop industry capitalizes on the competitive spirits, perseverance, and physical strength of young trainees and idols who dream of being successful and famous.

Thus, as the most salient example of *Hallyu*'s state of art, K-pop is a neoliberal industry that reflects how business demands have shifted from sweatshop manual workforce to service, immaterial labor since the 90s. Retaining Korea's traditional culture of Confucian sexism, female idols are employed to meet the growing demand of the service sector economy, and by doing so, they are effectively reinterpreting the traditional Confucian code of ethics by opening up a broader range of workplaces for women. While women strictly used to be confined to the domestic area, with changing economic and industrial needs, they are entitled to pursue professional careers in the public domain such as governmental offices and the mass media. In this respect, K-pop female idols can better be understood within a continuum between Korea's residual legacy of Confucianism and developmentalism. In other words, while the idols ostensibly promote female entitlement and empowerment in the public domain, they are still subject to dominant power relations of Confucian gender hierarchies, developmental capitalism, and neoliberalism. In this hegemonic structure, the idols convey the "political unconscious", exemplifying what is important, what to think, and how to govern oneself (Jameson 1981).

However, with a rapid rise of *Hallyu*, there are growing numbers of scholarly endeavors that investigate how it has been possible from mainly microscopic perspectives, attributing the success to Korean culture industry's technical and business innovations. For example, cultural hybridity allows Asian audiences to relate their sentiment to K-pop's glossy features (Ryoo 2009; Shim 2006); a cultural and historical proximity, which shares commonalities such as Confucianism and experiences of Japanese colonial occupations, makes K-pop palatable to the region's burgeoning tastes (Cho 2011; Iwabuchi 2001); K-pop's innovative production value, such as seamless choreography, catchy songs, fashionable outfits, and spectacular music videos (Park 2013a,b); K-pop industry leaders' strategic manufacturing and business planning led to a global success (Shin and Kim 2013); YouTube is a major factor in K-pop's global reach (Jung and Shim 2014; Oh and Lee 2013; Oh and Park 2012). In sum, the current academic literature is celebratory, merely focusing on microscopic analyses rather than larger socio-cultural and politico-economic contexts.

While there are a few scholars who have examined a contemporary liberalization of the media industry (Jin 2007; Shim 2002), their arguments are not successful in explaining how governmental interventions have been an integral part of *Hallyu*. For example, Shim (2008) believes liberalized global market conditions rather than the state's promotional policies to export the cultural commodities caused *Hallyu*'s international success. Although the author has no objection to this observation, there is a need for critical attention as to how Korean cultural industries became capable of producing marketable and profitable entertainment content, which can compete with state-of-art quality cultural commodities from foreign countries, in the context of the country's neoliberalization. In order to better understand how the Korean entertainment industry has become competitive in its aesthetic, technological, and business features in a short period of time, the author examines how the Korean government's neoliberal social policy assisted its culture industry in producing high-quality culture commodities, which in turn played an important role in helping *Hallyu* become successful.

Therefore, in order to better examine how seemingly contradictory systems of economic, political, and social governance, that is state-developmentalism, Confucianism, and neoliberalism, coexist and support each other in the K-pop industry, the author theoretically contends that, in the current *Hallyu* scholarship, there is a general misconception of neoliberalism. In other words, the dominant *Hallyu* scholarship maintains a myopic view of neoliberalism as a void role of government through a short-sighted opposition between state and market, which ignores the variegated, contradictory nature of neoliberal social formations and aims to debunk it. Since the market is configured within institutional frameworks and rules as its conditions of possibility (Foucault 2008; Harvey 2005), K-pop has been conditioned to prosper while the state is in charge of reconstructing its national economy to accommodate neoliberal challenges for economic development, which is stuck between technologically advanced economies such as the US and Japan and labor-intensive one like China. With a different set of roles and expectations, the state is an integral part of the neoliberal program via a construction of minimal social safety nets, while providing private sectors with industrial fundamentals like mandatory education, infrastructure, and legal frameworks (OECD 2000b; World Bank 2002). In other words, since the market itself is an effect of the state's policies and regulations (Yeung 2000), neoliberalism is internally combined with the developmental state to the extent that an emergent combination of neoliberalized economic management and authoritarian state, which guarantees a maximum capacity of the market economy and in turn, provides a political legitimacy for the regime (Harvey 2005; Peck and Tickell 2002). In this respect, since developmental states facilitate internal as well as external competition, free trade, and open export market practices, Harvey (2005) indicates that "Neoliberalization therefore opens up possibilities for developmental states to enhance their position in international competition by developing new structures of state intervention" (p. 72). The Korean government's strategic support and promotion for information and communication technologies (ICTs) and culture industry is a distinctive case in point. Practically, ICTs are not only a major arsenal for speculative global financial transactions but also a basis for commodification of the cultural. Thus, contrary to its rhetoric, neoliberalism works best in a strong regulatory state, especially in Korea's dirigiste mode of state-led capitalist development (OECD 2000a).

Subsequently, while Korea's culture industry has conflated the cultural and the economic and further legitimized a systematic commercialization of the previously un-marketed, such as female affects and sexualities in the name of national economic competitiveness, the state has associated the economic with the ideological so as to compensate for its weak political legitimacy since dictator-President Park.

Neoliberalism and governmentality in K-pop idols

As opposed to liberalism's mission to balance two distinctive spheres of state and market, public and private, and political and commercial, neoliberalism has blurred the boundaries, transplanting the market principles into the core functions of the state (Miller and Rose, 2008). With the notion of "*homo economicus,*" Foucault (2008) maintains that neoliberalism universalizes economic logic as the general matrix of people's daily behaviors in everything that human beings endeavor to realize based upon a meticulous calculation of cost for benefit. In other words, neoliberalism is an implementation of market-oriented techniques of government in the realm of the state and the personal and in turn constructs neoliberal subjects who are active, responsible, competitive and self-interested. In this active formation of subjectivity, a neoliberal agent is an "entrepreneur of himself, being for himself his own capital, being for himself his own producer, being for himself the source of his own earnings," in contrast to a classical liberal person of utilitarian exchange based upon his/her needs (p. 226). Furthermore, Foucault (2008) uses a notion of "human capital" as a neoliberal regime of truth and life that conditions individuals' behavioral rules and codes to pursue any activity, which increases their capacity to achieve their goals, create self-interest, and engage in competition. Thus, neoliberalism affects itself as a form of biopolitics that (re)produces neoliberal subjectivity and transforms society into a massive market (Foucault 2008; Hardt and Negri 1994). Privatization and deregulation are key tenets of neoliberal political strategy in order to govern individuals through a discursive invention of self-interest, investment and competition in all social spheres (Hardt and Negri 2001, 2004). Thus, neoliberalism should be regarded not only as the political economy of marketization in society, but also, more importantly, as a biopolitical subjectification of individuals (Foucault 1995) in an effort to internalize particular forms of responsibility produced by market practices (Nealon 2008).

In this respect, neoliberal governmentality simultaneously works through a macro-technological manner in state policies and a micro-technological level through individuals governing themselves by naturalizing neoliberal rationalities as the basis for their conducts (Binkley 2007; Lemke 2001; Rose et al. 2006). A major benefit of applying the notion of governmentality to K-pop idols is that it provides a better understanding of them as an extra-juridical institution that helps condition and govern individuals' thought and behavior in a nexus between power relations and subjectification processes. As a synecdoche or an ethos (Barry et al. 1996) of neoliberal Korea that implies particular mentalities and governing manners, which are realized and practiced in individuals' concrete thoughts, feeling, behaviors, habits and perceptions, the author believes K-pop idols are a form of everyday pedagogy that tells how people understand, articulate and argue about social values and practices through specific lexicons of media spectacles. Thus, the recent popularity of K-pop has played a role in naturalizing neoliberal governmentality. As a result, the next section examines how K-pop contributes to implementing a form of subjectification on the part of the government, making those involved in K-pop active, voluntary agents of neo-liberalism.

Female idols as the poster-child of neoliberal, culture industry

According to statistics on Korea's biggest music chart site, Melon, between 2005 and 2013, a total of 244 different K-pop idol groups have come and gone, (130 all-boy, 103 all-girl and 11 co-ed groups) (KpopStarz 2013). In 2013 alone there were 30 new idol groups, and it is difficult to find solo musicians on the chart, where 7–8 spots out of 10 were dominated by idols for the last 5 years. Starting with the female musical groups, SNSD and Wonder Girls, debuting in 2007, the numbers of all-girl idol groups have been growing, with at least 10 new groups per year (KpopStarz 2013). These figures do not include those not ranked on the chart, and the number would be even higher if we considered the total number of trainees. In sum, K-pop idols disclose that contemporary Korean society is conditioned to run on a limited number of socio-cultural pathways, ruling out anything that is not considered profitable or fashionable.

The contemporary proliferation of K-pop female idols symbolically represents the political, economic, social and cultural transformation of post-IMF Korea by a neoliberal replacement of a labor-intensive industry with a service one, which is a feminized sector in order to capitalize on the gendered-nature of production and consumption (Gonick 2006). The first K-pop female idol group, SM entertainment's S.E.S., marked the beginning of the systematic management of female singers and their imagery in 1997. This came as an effort to shore up the Korean culture industry and market to overseas audiences, since the local economy was devastated by the 1997 Asian financial crisis and Korea's subsequent bail-out by the IMF. This strategy is similar to the way in which the Korean popular music industry began in the post-Korean War era when local musicians performed at various clubs for US soldiers as economic as well as cultural endeavors *(Kim and Shin 2010)*.

Deploying various styles and feminine images from innocent and cute to sexy and mature, S.E.S. made an earnest effort to break into the Japanese market, but was not favored as much as in Korea. However, BoA, SM Entertainment's other female idol, saw success with her first Japanese album, *Listen to My Heart*, which was first ranked in Japan's Oricon Daily Chart and Oricon Weekly Chart in 2002. By teaming up with a major Japanese music label, Avex, BoA was successful in marketing and promoting her Japanese albums, such as *Listen to My Heart* (1.3 million copies in 2002), *Valenti* (1.3 million in 2003) and *No. 1*, (1.4 million in 2004) (BoA n.d.). This success prompted the Korean Culture and Information Service (KOCIS 2011), a government agency, to regard K-pop as a strong strategic item for export businesses accounting for US$ 180 million profit.

As the most sought-after, and globally well-known K-pop group today, SNSD debuted as a group of nine girls chosen by SM Entertainment in 2007, an event that coincided with the initiation of the negotiation of the Free Trade Agreement between Korea and the United States (KOR-US FTA). As a product of years of conditioning during rigorous traineeship periods of 5 to 7 years, the girls each have her own "talent" and attractive appearance, whether her face, body or image: With SM Entertainment's complete direction, everything from the girls' outfits, hairstyles, makeup, dance moves, gestures and romantic relationships are completely planned out to gain the audience's favor. The phenomenal success of their song, 'Gee,' with its addictive, catchy hooks and fast beats decorated by amicable 'crab dance' choreography, brought the group to international popularity in January 2009 and subsequently motivated SM Entertainment to aggressively deploy SNSD to market to overseas audiences. The song topped all of Korea's major music charts within two days, and the music video gathered one million views on YouTube in less than a day. SNSD followed up with more award-winning, instant hits with catchy, easy-to-follow tunes, rhythms and dance moves.

A distinctive characteristic of K-pop idols is that they are expected to be not just singers, but celebrities, who act, endorse, model and advertise. Likewise, SNSD's appearances in various media platforms made them media enterprise figures who demonstrate global popularity and appeal by appearing in multiple commercial endorsements in Asia, and their success is scrutinized in terms of an effective Korean business model like Samsung and Hyundai. As a main media promotion strategy, SNSD has appeared on the country's major variety TV shows like *Infinite Challenge* to promote new songs or album releases and to showcase each member's personality, character, interest and so on. Individual members also have their own media practices; for example, Tae-Yeon is a radio music show DJ, Yoon-Ah is a well-known drama actress and Jessica and Tiffany are musical performers. Furthermore, as a total promotion operation, SNSD has hosted its own variety TV shows, such as *Girls Go to School, Right Now: It's Girls Generation, Factory Girl, Girls Generation and the Dangerous Boys,* and *SNSD behind the Story.* There is a double feedback loop between SNSD's initial media exposure as performers and the publicity the group amasses from advertisements, which again feeds positively into their celebrity reputation. In this respect, SNSD has successfully publicized itself as a singular cultural commodity, (re)defining what it means to be a successful K-pop idol.

SNSD has been deployed in the state's official events and ceremonies as the nation's representative cultural icon. For example, Korea Tourism Organization (KTO), a governmental agency to promote Korea's tourism overseas, hypes SNSD as exemplary of Korea's popular culture that sets "global standard for girl idol groups" (KTO n.d, n.p.). In November 2010, the government hosted the 2010 G20 Seoul Summit, an international forum where 20 major world economies' governments and central banks gathered to discuss the global financial system and the world economy. SNSD was extensively mobilized as a part of the state's PR practices, including being a member of the G20 Star Supporters and Talking to the G20 Leaders (Chun 2010). More extensively, SNSD assumed numerous endorsement duties for the state, like Ambassador for Gangnam District Office in 2012, Honorary Ambassadors for 2010–2012 Visit Korea in 2011, Ambassador for Incheon Airport Customs in 2010, Ambassador for the Incheon World Ceramics Festival in 2009, Volunteer Ambassador for the Seoul City Government in 2007. In turn, as a token of the state's recognition, SNSD is the only K-pop group who received the Prime Minister's Award at the 2011 Korean Popular Culture and Arts Awards, organized by the Korea Creative Content Agency (KOCCA), a state government agency, for its successful overseas publicity and popularity as a means of PR practice for Korea.

Recently, SNSD's 2012 American debut marked another significant coincidence with Korea's aggressive neoliberalization, that is, Korean President Lee Myung-Bak's (2008–2013) visit to the White House to nudge President Obama to sign the KOR-US FTA. SNSD's strategic debut on CBS's *Late Show with David Letterman* on January 31 and ABC's *Live! With Kelly Ripa* on February 1 played a significant role in distracting attention from serious issues with the KOR-US FTA. Claiming that Koreans should be more competitive and aggressive in the global marketplace, the mainstream Korean media celebrated that SNSD explored and "conquered" a new, uncharted marketplace that would bring Korea economic fortunes. Thus, more than a global cultural commodity, the group became an Althusserian ideological apparatus to justify and perpetuate the myth of competition as the sole source of international success to rebut the danger of the FTA.

Theoretically, Debord's (1967) society of spectacle captures how K-pop has been an integral part of Korea's increasing neoliberalization, characterized with the production and consumption of images, staged media events and consumerism. Via K-pop's glossy sexualized spectacles, everyday experiences are mediated and conditioned to the extent that the spectacle constitutes social relationships based on and mediated by images, and it is integral to capitalist imperatives that cultivate the cultural mechanism of consumption and entertainment. Textually, equipped with highly crafted spectacles as a manifestation of ideal beauty and propriety (S. Lee 2012), K-pop is a neoliberal ideology of positive thinking filled with color, play, camaraderie and love, which forces the audience to focus on a positive, rosy future of society. In this respect, considering that a capitalist economy is dependent upon a seamless continuation of consumption, K-pop idols are cultural linchpins that teach and provide cues to utilizing commodities as a means of self-transformation into someone better. By doing so, they help mobilize individuals to be a steady force of neoliberal consumerism, while invoking an asocial fantasy of evading established rules and the romanticism of narcissistic pleasure as cultural amnesia. K-pop's relentless repetition of fantasy enforces a feedback loop upon its audiences that entraps them in the eternal return of always wanting more. Thus, the overwhelmingly visual nature of K-pop is an example of Wolf's (2004) "entertainment economy," which transforms Korean soundscape into a subcategory of neoliberal service economy.

Therefore, K-pop's spectacular entertainment is a major allegory of neoliberal Korea where its economy, politics, cultural forms, modes of everyday experiences and social relations are increasingly re-configured by media spectacles. With fast beats and salient rhythms K-pop is an episteme of neoliberalism, which overwhelms people not just by its neck-breaking speed of transforming society into a miniature of the market but, more importantly, with its simple ideological pitch that instigates people's desire to be rich and successful. In other words, just as neoliberalism has mesmerized people with an unrealistic valorization of market logic, K-pop has captivated audiences by seamless breath-taking choreography and appealing, sexy appearances of K-pop performers.

K-pop as neoliberal social policy

As discussed above, neoliberalism is far from a retreat of central governments; rather it is market-driven state reform in order to guarantee a maximum functionality of market principles and a commodification of social life at large (Moran 2003). The neoliberal social policy seeks to fend off any possible anti-competitive dimensions, by forcing individuals to confront and endure socio-economic risks personally, as opposed to Keynesianism that aims to compensate, nullify, or absorb possible negative effects of economic liberalization. However, since state policies do not automatically guarantee economic competitiveness in the global economy, the bio-political aspect of neoliberalism plays an important role in shaping subjects as competitive agents in the international regime of capitalism. Thus, neoliberalization works not only by political imperatives to restructure the national economic system, but procures its legitimacy and necessity through civil society's voluntary, bottom-up support for the reforms as indispensable social, economic and even ethical responsibilities (Lim and Jang 2006).

The commercialization of culture has been a tenet of neoliberal knowledge/information-based economy, and a commodification of K-pop came to play an important role in shoring up Korea's national economy. Given the fact that the commodification of culture has existed since the Renaissance (Cowen 1998), what is special in the recent popularity of K-pop comes from the state's integral role in intensifying its scope and power in the name of post-IMF national competitiveness and economic development. Moreover, the state's neoliberal policy is characterized by the formal boundary between culture and economics, and art and commerce becoming obscure, if not obsolete (Hesmondhalgh and Pratt 2005). Moreover, this border crossing establishes culture as a mere marketing strategy to promote the state and to host foreign capital as soft power (Gibson and Kong 2005; Jang and Paik 2012; Lee 2009; Nye 2009; Nye and Kim 2013). In this respect, K-pop is regarded as a culture technology (CT) economy for revitalizing Korea's post-industrial, service-oriented neoliberal economy along with the four strategic technologies: ICT, bio-technology, nano-technology and environmental technology (Shin 2009). In this respect, Soo-man Lee, CEO of SM Entertainment is boastful of his CT manual that mandates components

> necessary to popularize K-pop artists in different Asian countries … [like] what chord progressions to use in what country; the precise color of eyeshadow a performer should wear in a particular country; the exact hand gestures he or she should make; and the camera angles to be used in the videos.
>
> *(Seabrook 2012, n.p.)*

In sum, K-pop subsumes culture as a mere instrument for economic profits and strengthening the country's international competitiveness (Jin 2006; Nam 2013). The K-pop industry has systematically been promoted through the government's methodological interventions (Cloonan 1999; Sassen 2001). As a major governmental body, the Ministry of Culture, Sports, and Tourism (MCST 2011) has taken charge of constructing *Hallyu* as the nation's strategic, new economic growth engine. The MCST has promoted the "Cultural Content Industry through cooperation among government agencies," systematically funding media production for global audiences, training "creative professionals through planning and marketing, project-linked" programs, and educating students with "renowned educational institutes in other countries" (p. 17). Specifically, based on the Framework Act on Cultural Industry Promotion, the Korea Creative Content Agency (KOCCA) was established on May 7, 2009, in order to aggressively develop and promote profitable cultural commodities in the global market. As a collective of various state institutions and agencies like Korea Broadcasting Institute, Korea Culture and Content Agency, Korea Game Industry Agency, Cultural Contents Center and Digital Contents Business Group of Korea IT Industry Promotion Agency, KOCCA commands a comprehensive strategy from developing human resources to supporting a "development of specialized culture technologies from design to production, the commercialization of contents, and the promotion of various overseas expansion projects to develop the content industry into an export industry" (n.d., n.p). The 'Content Industry Promotion Act' of 2010 deploys a more assertive administrative support to emphasize monetary benefits of cultural "content" enterprises like online game development. Furthermore, the government has provided the industry with financial supports such as tax breaks and loans (Ministry of Strategy and Finance 2012). Those governmental measures indicate how much K-pop's recent success has benefited from a continuity of Korea's decade-long state developmentalism.

As was the case during its dynamic industrialization period from the '60s to the '80s, the Korean government has actively treated *Hallyu* as an export item to keep its national economy floating. Institutionally, the *Hallyu* Culture Promotion Organization and the Korea Foundation for International Culture Exchange (KOFICE) were founded to further facilitate overseas promotions and exports of *Hallyu* products in 2012. Practically, the Korean Wave Index, created by the MCST in 2010, quantifies how Korean culture has been consumed and favored so that the industry can modify export portfolios and strategies to cater to each country's selling points and perspectives. In turn, with theses state initiatives, in 2011, K-pop achieved a revenue of $3.4 billion, and its exports reached $180 million with 112 percent increase compared to 2010 with almost 80 percent annual growth since 2007 (Naidu-Ghelani 2012). Establishing the Priority Sectors criterion to support new economic growth engine sectors, the Export-Import Bank of Korea announced that it would provide loans and credit guarantees worth of US$917 million to help spread K-pop and other *Hallyu*-related products (Na 2013). For example, a sizeable part of the government's fund for '2013 Popular Music Production Support Project,' designed originally to assist independent musicians in promoting diversity, went to several K-pop idols such as Girls' Day and Hyorin of Sistar who have been manufactured and marketed by major K-pop industry leaders (*MoneyToday* 2014). KOCCA, the fund administrator, maintains that the decision was necessary in order to facilitate an overseas promotion of K-pop, since Korea's economy became heavily dependent on export after the 1997 IMF crisis (Crotty and Lee 2006). Amongst 17 fund recipients, seven went to major K-pop management companies, claiming approximately $500,000 from $888,000 and negating the *raison d'etre* of the governmental policy.

More than just an export item, K-pop became a comprehensive marketing tool to help raise overseas market recognition of Korean brands. In order to conflate K-pop's global popularity with Korean manufactured goods' quality, the Korea Trade Promotion Agency with another governmental agency, the Korea Trade Insurance Corporation, signed a memorandum of understanding to assist small companies with less than an annual export revenue of $50,000 by giving "free marketing and financial consulting to the companies, as well as insurance discounts" (J. Kim 2014, n.p.).

Furthermore, K-pop has been deployed as an item of destination tourism in Korea as a neoliberal economy strategy. Through private-state partnership with uses of various governmental venues, the state government has hosted several international K-pop events like the annual K-pop World Festival. Though the Festival is planned and organized by multiple government bodies, such as the MCST, the Ministry of Foreign Affairs and Trade, the KOFICE and the Presidential Council on Nation Branding, the media publicize it, conglomerates like Samsung fund and engage in PR and the municipal governments recruit tourists for the event. In this regard, K-pop has been a center of strategic relations among state, society and market as neoliberal service economy has counted on the culture industry. Thus, emphasizing the role of intellectual property and creativity and reducing any cost of production and logistics, K-pop is a new economic model that procures a faster, higher profit margin than the traditional manufacturing industry, like automobiles, as a "distinct spatiotemporal configuration" of post-IMF Korean economy: "The sharper the differentiation between these two temporalities grows (with dematerialization/digitalization), the more abundant the business opportunities become" (Sassen 2001, p. 268).

As reviewed earlier, dictator-President Park deemed his administration's cultural policy a social intervention to support the state's industrialization projects. In the same way, confronting the IMF's structural adjustment programs, President Kim Dae-Jung's democratic administration (1998–2003) implemented an industrial model of cultural policy, which highlighted the economic potential and value of culture as an important source of national wealth. As a benchmark for Park's industrialization projects, in the '60s and '70s, the Kim administration enforced the "five-year plan for the development of cultural industries [in 1999], the vision 21 for cultural industries [in 2000] and the vision 21 for cultural industries in a digital society" in 2001 (Yim 2002, p. 41). It is in this context of the Korean government's utilization of cultural policies as a subcategory of political and economic imperatives that K-pop idols have been produced and consumed in Korea.

In this political economy context, SNSD is a cultural commodity that emerged from a nexus of Confucian patriarchism, neoliberalism and state developmentalism. Perpetuating a commodified model of female sexuality constructed by the industry with a "positive" twist, which is "girl power" or "female sexual empowerment" (Frost 2005; Gill 2008; Gill and Scharff 2011; McRobbie 2009), K-pop female idols have become a unique socio-cultural phenomenon that facilitates economic profiteering. In this respect, unfortunately, K-pop has been turned into an economic stunt by the K-pop industry and the government's neoliberal policy as a means to regain national economic competitiveness and confidence. Actually, K-pop contributes to raising the confidence of Korea's neoliberal service industries such as popularizing private dance and singing academies, and supplying tourist-driven shopping malls with fashion items (Mahr 2012). Therefore, with K-pop's economic success, the Korean government is both omnipresent and minimal: universally engaged to naturalize the neoliberal principles and maximally disengaged by having private talent agencies enact its policies.

In sum, K-pop should be recognized in Pratt's (2005) notion of neoliberal social policy: As a popular form of social inclusion based upon the individual's desire to be successful and rich within the existing global economy structure, K-pop contains socially dissatisfied, alienated, yet musically talented youths, encouraging them to stick with the neoliberal mantra of self-endurance, self-discipline and self-development as the key factors for success. By preaching a possibility of social mobility based on their musical talent rather than conventional means such as studying and hard work, the post-IMF neoliberal society encourages and mobilizes artistically talented or interested young people. These aspiring young people then form a large pool of potential talents for the culture industry, which (re)produces a concentrated and hierarchal structure of Korea's previous manufacture industry conglomerates, thus, channeling young people's social energy to the competitive market economy and in turn achieving social-inclusion goals (Scott 2011).

K-pop female idols: regime of truth and life in neoliberal subjectification

In tandem with the Korean government's supports, the K-pop industry has implemented its private, economic goals as a public agenda of national development, exercising Foucauldian biopolitics that (re)produces and proliferates neoliberal subjects. A concept of discipline, especially docility-utility (Foucault 1995) is permeated in K-pop idols who have been conditioned through years of training, and audiences who internalize and glorify their favorite K-pop stars. Broadcasting seemingly raw video footages that show how the idols undergo military boot camp style training procedures plays an important role in normalizing the brutal conditions of competition, self-development, multi-tasking, and flexibility as a general social environment that fans themselves have to overcome. In this respect, as a mundane, popular mechanism for penetrating a neoliberal self-government of the populace, reality TV shows, such as *Real Wonder Girls*, *2NE1 TV* and *Big Bang TV*, provides an experimental training ground for the government of the neoliberal enterprising self (Ouellette and Hay 2008).

This process functions as a method of controlling and subordinating the idols' individuality and characters to the industry's entrepreneurial goals and principles on the one hand and permeates and intensifies a neoliberal government of successful self-managers in the fabric of individuals' daily lives on the other. For example, in the 7th episode of *One Day*, a reality program that covered JYP Entertainment's 13-member-idol-group project, which begat two separate groups, 2AM and 2 PM, JYP's CEO delivered a speech establishing that the K-pop industry and its training processes are a form of popular pedagogy to anyone who wants to equip a survival technique as a condition of one's citizenship in neoliberal society:

> it might have been tough [to get to here], but this training is so much easier than the road you are about to walk on. You guys, as singers, will be heading toward the direction of world stars. But it will be psychologically and mentally 10 times or 100 times harder than this. (n.p.)

The nation-wide popularity of K-pop audition TV programs such as *Super Star K*, *K-pop Star*, *Great Birth*, and *Korea's Got Talent* and the surge in applications for the programs indicate how the neoliberal governmentality of competition and success is widespread in Korea. For example, there were cumulatively over 2 million applicants for *Super State K*, Season 4 (August 17–November 23, 2012). In this respect, K-pop idols, who are important role models for fans, are an effective tool for conditioning thoughts and behaviors, producing auto-regulated or auto-correcting selves who are free yet fulfil neoliberal ideals of rational and self-responsible individuals, competitive and flexible workers and self-calculating consumers. Thus, K-pop helps create docile social subjects who endure political and economic instabilities and risks.

As neoliberalism has marketized what was thought to be non-marketable, such as emotions, care, feelings and sentiments, K-pop female idols are successful in intensively expanding economic profiteering into the previously unexplored or under-explored manipulation of female sexualities by images of girlish cuteness, innocence and delicate sexuality. As such, SNSD's massive fan base includes *sam-chon* fans. These middle-aged male fans indicate how the group has deftly exploited Korea's gendered virtue of *aegyo,* which is a complex quality of ideal female coquettishness with decency, humor, submissive sexuality and affective readiness for male counterparts. Although *aegyo* has been practiced by Korean women to serve male counterparts for ages, it has been confined to private, domestic relationships between couples. Moreover, there was not a case of systematic mass production, marketing and distribution of *aegyo* as an affective commodity prior to K-pop female idols like SNSD. Recently, as its members get older, SNSD has aggressively expanded its collective image from girlish cuteness to more explicit, eroticized sexiness since their American debut in 2012.

Politically and economically speaking, just as with the 1996 Telecommunication Act, a neoliberal deregulation of media ownership directly caused the proliferation of aggravating pornographic media representations on female pop stars in the US (Levande 2008), there is a skyrocketing intensification of sexually explicit portrayals of K-pop female idols as a cultural symptom of Korea's growing neoliberalization. As Korea's neoliberalization intensifies and the number of K-pop female idols multiplies, the idols' escalating competition to grasp audiences' attention has led to images of women becoming increasingly more suggestive. Differently put, the mere fact that there is a growing number of K-pop female idols does not mean that they have successfully achieved and exerted autonomous (sexual) agency; however, they perform a seemingly positive role of the active female (sexual) subject rather than embody and enact it. In other words, increasing numbers of female idols face a double bind as they are presented as active subjects while being re-objectified and in turn lead female audiences to believe they too can commend active (sexual) subjectivity. However, this process does not change the existing patriarchal gender hierarchy.

As an indicator of the idols' double gender bind, SNSD's human capital lies in their attractive appearances and charming behaviors that beget teenage followers. Considering that consumers automatically become producers or carriers of the neoliberal ethics of self-development and self-competitiveness (Foucault 2008), SNSD's appealing, sexualized visual images and lifestyle have conditioned Korean women to imitate or emulate them by purchasing the same or similar commodities. To show how K-pop idols are seamlessly weaved into other neoliberal industries like fashion and beauty industries, there are numerous online shops and communities where SNSD's fashion items are introduced, promoted and sold globally. Among others, www.style.soshified.com, a subsection of www.soshified.com, the most popular, authoritative, largest SNSD fan community with well over 200,000 active members and 176 staff, stands out since it has a monthly average of 1 million visitors and 10 million page views internationally. Claiming to provide a complete list of "what Girls' Generation wore or what items they were seen with" (n.p.), the online site is an extensive advertising outlet where virtually all walks of SNSD's everyday lives are commodified and promoted, integrating SNSD into the neoliberal consumer economy. Basically, it teaches audiences what to buy and how to use lifestyle commodities so that they can express pseudo individualities, and in turn shape their identities as an outcome of stylistic self-fashioning and improvisation in the neoliberal consumer culture of seductive images and sensations. What is noteworthy is that there is a tutorial category where users, as self-reliant everyday experts, post seemingly self-help know-how to follow or emulate the idols' fashion styles on "Get This Look," "Hair Tutorial," "Make-Up Tutorial," "Outfit of the Week," "Reviews" and so on. By acquiring, customizing and personalizing commodities promoted by SNSD, the vernacular experts to keep up with a current, trending consumer lifestyle are actively enacting governmentality in which self-development, self-realization, self-glamorization and personal well-being are an on-going neoliberal life project. In other words, hosting a participatory genre of peer tutorials in styling issues, the site encourages fans to exercise their free, capable agency in neoliberal self-fashioning and self-renovation opportunities and requirements and in turn, governs them by teaching how to govern themselves as neoliberal, self-reliant lifestyle subjects.

SNSD's influences on fans' life-style choices and self-promotion strategies go beyond unobtrusive measures to the extent that fans pursue plastic surgery. For example, K-pop Combo, that is a common, or sometime mandatory, plastic surgery for double eye-lids and a higher, pointy nose amongst the idols, is an easy, rampant measure for the fans to look cute and amicable, associated with an ideal *aegyo* quality (K-pop Surgery 2014). More specifically, SNSD Plastic Surgery stands for "some of the best and carefully done plastic surgical procedures of the world" by its capability to maintain "natural looks" (SNSD Plastic Surgery n.d., n.p.). Not to mention numerous non-surgical procedures like a Botox injections, skyrocketing rates of plastic surgery amongst Korean females proves the idols' biopolitical power that revolves around a sensual image of an "ideal new feminine subject demanded by neoliberalism" (Francis 2013; Gonick 2006, p. 11).

Considering the first plastic surgery was done on a Korean prostitute who wanted to appeal to American soldiers in 1961 (Stone 2013), plastic surgery in Korea is socio-economically instrumental in order to get a better job or a raise. Due to bleak job-market prospects coupled with the proliferation of K-pop and beauty industries in the daunting post-IMF economy, an ever increasing number of Koreans accept and are willing to transform their bodies in a hope of being successful (Chung 2015; Ho 2012; Lim 1993). Though individuals ostensibly exercise their 'free choices,' personal accountability, and self-empowerment as ethics of neoliberal citizenship, this neoliberal logic of human capital has increasingly made the population subject into a mere object of profiteering, and furthermore, auto-regulating and auto-correcting consumers who are confirmative to the *status-quo* (T. Kim 2003). By consuming various beauty commodities and services, female audiences, who are the main engine of neoliberal consumerism, try to change their appearances and images as a means to accumulate human capital, which ultimately confines them to rapacious commercialism. By doing so, they become active agents of neoliberal governmentality, which preaches personal responsibility, self-development and self-enterprise as ethics of 'good' citizens who comply with a pre-determined, gendered pathways and to be obedient consumer-workers in society. In this respect, SNSD is a popular, effective form of neoliberal biopolitics that employs "technologies of subjectivity ... to induce self-animation and self-government so citizens optimize choice, efficiency, and competitiveness" (Ong 2006, p. 5).

Girls' generation not in their own terms: from factories to performance stages

Manufactured and marketed by SM Entertainment, SNSD as the most successful K-pop idol girl group is not an exemplar of girl power since it is an exemplar of how women are objectified and commodified as a subordinate class (Radin and Sunder 2005). As a neoliberal social policy that is more concerned with the state's economic competitiveness and growth than its deterioration of living standards, K-pop is one of the most successful models of Korea's dirigisme mode of capitalist development through exploiting a cheap, docile, abundant, willing workforce (Escobar 1995). Thus, it is Korea's signature neoliberal service economy that provides the state with global competition as a political legitimation and universalizes governmentality by its conditioning of "the human body [with docility-utility], human body parts [for sexuality], and human behavior [of competition and enterprise] as commodities" (J. Lee 2010, p. 12). As an automated embodiment of governmentality, K-pop idols are the most salient example of alienation, who are adored, celebrated and respected as a role-model of neoliberal economy.

In the working process of the Miracle on the Han River, the rhetoric of self-empowerment, self-responsibility and voluntarism was effectively deployed to legitimize Park Chung-Hee's developmental dictatorship (1961–1979). As the nation's ethos, the socio-cultural rhetoric ceaselessly and effectively mobilized rural, unwed women to work as an obedient, docile, cheap, disposable workforce on the sweatshop floors of textile factories. Now, the same ethos is spectacularly and sensationally deployed in post-IMF neoliberal Korea through the K-pop industry. Consequently, since "[p]olitics (in the broad sense of relations, assumptions, and contests pertaining to power) is what links value and exchange in the social life of commodities" (Appadurai 2005, p. 42, emphasis original), it is no coincidence that current President Park Geun-Hye, daughter of dictator-President Park Chung-Hee, declared that the Second Miracle on the Han River would be realized through Korea's popular culture.

In closing, the author suggests some possible research directions for future studies. Based on this chapter's arguments on K-pop idols as a popular mode of neoliberal governmentality, further empirical studies need to specifically delineate how K-pop idols interpellate audiences to become an agent of certain commercial, ideological and possibly political interests.

In turn, further ethnographic studies should substantiate how K-pop idols are an effective tool to (re) shape individuals' value, behavior and decision-making in their everyday lives. Moreover, as equally important and popular as female idols, K-pop male idols must be examined in terms of their different modalities of perpetuating governmentality. By doing so, further research needs to investigate whether or how they are sexualized like female idols, if not, then how male idols are commercialized and commodified in Korea's neoliberal economy. In sum, extensive empirical, ethnographic research should address varied practical ramifications of K-pop's governmentality in neoliberal Korea.

Note

1 Derogatory terms that indicate "factory girl" and "factory boy" respectively. See, Shin, K. 2002. The Discourse on Women in Korea: Episodes, Continuity, and Change. *The Review of Korean Studies*, 5, 7–27.

References

Althusser, L., 1971. *Lenin and Philosophy and Other Essays*. New York: Monthly Review Press.

Appadurai, A., 2005. Commodities and the Politics of Value. *In*: M.M. Martha and J.C. Williams, eds. *Rethinking Commodification: Cases and Readings in Law and Culture*. New York and London: New York University Press, 34–43.

Barry, A., Osborne, T., and Rose, N.S., eds. 1996. *Foucault and Political Reason: Liberalism, Neo-liberalism and Rationalities of Government*. Chicago: The University of Chicago Press.

Binkley, S., 2006. The Perilous Freedoms of Consumption: Toward a Theory of the Conduct of Consumer Conduct. *Journal for Cultural Research*, 10, 343–362.

Binkley, S., 2007. Governmentality and Lifestyle Studies. *Sociology Compass*, 1, 111–126.

BoA (n.d.). Profile. http://boa.smtown.com/.

Cho, Y., 2011. Desperately Seeking East Asia amidst the Popularity of South Korean Pop Culture in Asia. *Cultural Studies*, 25, 383–404.

Chun, S., 2010. "Nation Abuzz with Support for G20 Summit." *The Korea Herald*, 7 November. Available from: www.koreaherald.com/common_prog/newsprint.php?ud=20101107000164&dt=2.

Chung, H. 2015. Jobseekers get plastic surgery for palm lines, voice. *The Korea Times*, 2 October. Available from: www.koreatimes.co.kr/www/news/nation/2015/10/116_187872.html.

Cloonan, M., 1999. Pop and the Nation-State: Towards a Theorisation. *Popular Music*, 18, 193–207.

Cowen, T., 1998. *In Praise of Commercial Culture*. Cambridge, MA: Harvard University Press.

Crotty, J., and Lee, K.-K., 2006. The Effects of Neoliberal 'Reforms' on the Post-crisis Korean Economy. *Review of Radical Political Economics*, 38, 669–675.

Debord, G., 1967/1994. *The Society of the Spectacle*. New York: Zone Books.

Escobar, A., 1995. *Encountering Development: The Making and Unmaking of the Third World*. Princeton, NJ: Princeton University Press.

Foucault, M., 1995. *Discipline and Punishment: The Birth of the Prison*. New York: Vintage Books.

Foucault, M., 2008. *The Birth of Biopolitics: Lectures at the Collège de France, 1978–1979*. New York: Palgrave Macmillan.

Francis, J., 2013. "The K-pop Effect: South Korea's Obsession with Beauty." *SBS Dateline*, 19 March. Available from: www.sbs.com.au/news/article/1748046/The-K-Pop-effect-South-Koreas-obsession-with-beaut (accessed on March 21, 2013).

Frost, L., 2005. Theorizing the Young Women in the Body. *Body and Society*, 11, 63–85.

Gibson, C., and Kong, L., 2005. Cultural Economy: A Critical Review. *Progress in Human Geography*, 29, 541–561.

Gill, R., 2008. Empowerment/Sexism: Figuring Female Sexual Agency in Contemporary Advertising. *Feminism & Psychology*, 18, 35–60.

Gill, R., and Scharff, C., eds. 2011. *New Femininities: Postfeminism, Neoliberalism and Subjectivity*. Houndmills, Basingstoke, Hampshire: Palgrave Macmillan.

Gonick, M., 2006. Between 'Girl Power' and 'Reviving Ophelia': Constituting the Neoliberal Girl Subject. *NWSA Journal*, 18, 1–23.

Hardt, M., and Negri, A., 1994. *The Labor of Dionysus: A Critique of the State Form*. Minneapolis: University of Minnesota.

Hardt, M., and Negri, A., 2001. *Empire*. Cambridge, MA: Harvard University Press.

Hardt, M., and Negri, A., 2004. *Multitude: War and Democracy in the Age of Empire*. New York: The Penguin Press.

Harvey, D., 2005. *A Brief History of Neo-Liberalism*. Oxford: Oxford University Press.

Hesmondhalgh, D., and Pratt. A-C., 2005. Cultural Industries and Cultural Policy. *International Journal of Cultural Policy*, 11, 1–13.

Ho, S.L., 2012. Fuel for South Korea's "Global Dreams Factory": The Desires of Parents Whose Children Dream of Becoming K-pop Stars. *Korea Observer*, *43*(3), 471–502.

'Hyorin/ Girls' Day Album Received $99,000 respectively … "Balanced Promotion of Popular Music"?' *MoneyToday*, 10 July 2014. Available from: http://news.mt.co.kr/mtview.php?no=2014071009167618223&type=1 (accessed July 11, 2014).

Iwabuchi, K., 2001. Becoming 'Culturally Proximate': The A/scent of Japanese Idol Dramas in Taiwan. *In*: Moeran, B., ed. *Asian Media Productions*. Surrey: Curzon, 54–74.

Jameson, F. 1981. *The Political Unconscious: Narrative as a Socially Symbolic Act*. Ithaca, NY: Cornell University Press.

Jang, G. and Paik, W.K., 2012. Korean Wave as Tool for Korea's New Cultural Diplomacy. *Advances in Applied Sociology*, 2(3), p. 196–202.

Jin, D.-Y., 2006. Cultural Politics in Korea's Contemporary Films under Neoliberal Globalization. *Media, Culture & Society*, 28, 5–23.

Jin, D-Y., 2007. Reinterpretation of Cultural Imperialism: Emerging Domestic Market vs. Continuing US Dominance. *Media, Culture & Society*, 29, 753–771.

Jung, S., and Shim, D., 2014. Social Distribution: K-pop Fan Practices in Indonesia and the "Gangnam Style" Phenomenon. *International Journal of Cultural Studies*, 17, 485–501.

Katsiaficas, G., 2012. *Asia's Unknown Uprisings: South Korean Social Movements in the 20th Century*. Oakland, CA: PM Press.

Kim, T., 2003. Neo-Confucian Body Techniques: Women's Bodies in Korea's Consumer Society. *Body & Society*, 9, 97–113.

Kim, C-N., 2012. *K-pop: Roots and Blossoming of Korean Popular Music*. Seoul: Hollym Corp Press.

Kim, J.-Y., 2014. 'Overseas Companies Get K-pop Help.' *The Korea Joong Ang Daily*, 31 July. Available from: http://koreajoongangdaily.joins.com/news/article/Article.aspx?aid=2992786.

Kim, P.-H. and Shin, H., 2010. The Birth of 'Rok': Cultural Imperialism, Nationalism, and Glocalization of Rock Music in South Korea, 1964–1975. *Positions: East Asia Cultures Critique*, 18, 199–230.

Korea Creative Content Agency (KOCCA). n.d. *Introduction*. http://eng.kocca.kr/en/contents.do?menuNo=201433.

Korea Culture and Information Service (KOCIS). 2011. *K-pop: A New Force in Pop Music*. Seoul: Ministry of Culture, Sports and Tourism.

Korea Tourism Organization (KTO). n.d. *K-pop*. http://english.visitkorea.or.kr/enu/CU/CU_EN_8_7_1_17.jsp.

KpopStarz, 2013. 244 Idol Groups Debuted in the Last 9 Years?! How Many Can You Name? 18 September. www.kpopstarz.com/articles/41923/20130918/244-idol-groups-debuted-last-nine-years.htm (accessed Nov. 15, 2013).

K-pop Surgery, 2014. Plastic Surgery Meter: Jessica, Girls' Generation (SNSD). www.kpopsurgery.com/nose-job/plastic-surgery-meter-jessica-girls-generation-snsd/ (accessed July 20, 2014)

Lee, G., 2009. A soft power approach to the "Korean wave". *The Review of Korean Studies*, 12(2), 123–137.

Lee, J-K., 2010. *Service Economies: Militarism, Sex Work, and Migrant Labor in South Korea*. Minnesota: University of Minnesota Press.

Lee, S., 2012. The Structure of the Appeal of Korean Wave Texts. *Korea Observer*, 43, 447–469.

Lemke, T., 2001. 'The Birth of Bio-Politics': Michel Foucault's Lecture at the Collège de France on Neo-liberal Governmentality. *Economy and Society*, 30, 190–207.

Levande, M., 2008. Women, Pop Music, and Pornography. *Meridians: Feminism, Race, Transnationalism*, 8 (1), 293–321.

Lim, Y. 1993. Plastic Surgery a Career Tool in Korea. *The Los Angeles Times*, 21 March. Available from: http://articles.latimes.com/1993-03-21/news/mn-13642_1_cosmetic-surgery.

Lim, H.-C., and Jang, J.-H., 2006. Neo-liberalism in Post-crisis South Korea: Social Conditions and Outcomes. *Journal of Contemporary Asia*, 36, 442–463.

Mahr, K., 2012. 'South Korea's Greatest Export: How K-pop's Rocking the World.' *Time Magazine*, 7 March. Available from: http://world.time.com/2012/03/07/south-koreas-greatest-export-how-k-pops-rocking-the-world/print/.

McRobbie, A., 2009. *The Aftermath of Feminism: Gender, Culture and Social Change.* London: Sage.

Miller, P., and Rose, N., 2008. *Governing the Present.* Malden, MA: Polity Press.

Ministry of Culture, Sports, and Tourism. 2011. *Culture Enjoyed by Everyone: Happy Republic of Korea.* Seoul.

Ministry of Strategy and Finance. 2012. *Plan for Relieving Discrimination for Service Industry… Strengthening Tax Support.* 7 September.

Moran, M., 2003. *The British Regulatory State: High Modernism and Hyper-Innovation.* Oxford: Oxford University Press.

Na, J. 2013. 'Eximbank to Finance "Hallyu" Business.' *The Korea Times*, 6 February. Available from: http://koreatimes.co.kr/www/news/biz/2013/02/602_130133.html.

Naidu-Ghelani, R. 2012. 'Move over Bieber—Korean Pop Music Goes Global.' *CNBC*, 16 July. Available from: www.cnbc.com/id/48157880#.

Nam, S. 2013. The Cultural Political Economy of the Korean Wave in East Asia: Implications for Cultural Globalization Theories. *Asian Perspective*, 37, 209–231.

Nealon, J.T., 2008. *Foucault beyond Foucault: Power and Its Intensifications since 1984.* Stanford: Stanford University Press.

Negus, K., 1999. *Music Genres and Corporate Cultures.* London and New York: Routledge.

Nye, J.S., 2009. South Korea's Growing Soft Power. *Project Syndicate,* 10 November. Available from: http://belfercenter.hks.harvard.edu/publication/19694/south_koreas_growing_soft_power.html.

Nye, J.S. and Kim, Y., 2013. Soft Power and the Korean Wave. *In:* Y. Kim, ed. *The Korean Wave: Korean Media Go Global.* New York: Routledge, 31–42.

Oh, I., and Lee, H.-J., 2013. Mass Media Technologies and Popular Music. *Korea Journal*, 53 (4), 34–58.

Oh, I., and Park, G.-S., 2012. From B2C to B2B: Selling Korean Pop Music in the Age of New Social Media. *Korea Observer*, 43, 365–397.

Ong, A., (2006). *Neoliberalism as Exception: Mutations in Citizenship and Sovereignty.* Durham, NC and London: Duke University Press.

Organisation for Economic Co-operation and Development. 2000a. *Korea and the Knowledge-Based Economy: Makin the Transition.* Paris: OECD Publications

Organisation for Economic Co-operation and Development. 2000b. *Pushing Ahead with Reform in Korea: Labour Market and Social Safety-Net Policies.* www.oecd.org/korea/36868635.pdf.

Ouellette, L., and Hay, J., 2008. *Better Living through Reality TV: Television and Post-welfare Citizenship.* Malden, MA: Wiley-Blackwell.

Park, G.-S., 2013a. From Fragile Cosmopolitanism to Sustainable Multicultural Vigor. *Korea Journal*, 53 (4), 5–13.

Park, G.-S., 2013b. Manufacturing Creativity: Production, Performance, and Dissemination of K-pop. *Korea Journal*, 53 (4), 14–33.

Peck, J., and Tickell, A. 2002. Neoliberalizing Space. *In:* Brenner, N., and Theodore, N., eds. *Spaces of Neoliberalism: Urban Restructuring in North America and Western Europe.* Oxford: Blackwell, 33–57.

Pratt, A.C., 2005. Cultural Industries and Public Policy: An Oxymoron? *International Journal of Cultural Policy*, 11, 31–44.

Radin, M.J. and Sunder, M., 2005. Introduction: The Subject and Object of Commodification. *In:* Ertman, M.M., and Williams, J.C., eds. *Rethinking Commodification: Cases and Readings in Law and Culture.* New York and London: New York University Press, 8–29.

Rose, N., O'Malley, P., and Valverde, M. 2006. Governmentality. *Annual Review of Law and Social Science*, 2, 83–104.

Rosenberg, A., and Milchman, A. 2010. The Final Foucault: Government of Others and Government of Oneself. *In:* Binkley, S., and Capetillo-Ponce, J., eds. *A Foucault for the 21st Century: Governmentality, Biopolitics and Discipline in the New Millennium.* Newcastle upon Tyne: Cambridge Scholars Publishing, 62–71.

Ryoo, W., 2009. Globalization, or the Logic of Cultural Hybridization: The Case of the Korean Wave. *Asian Journal of Communication,* 19, 137–151.

Sassen, S., 2001. Spatialities and Temporalities of the Global: Elements for a Theorization. *In:* Appadurai, A., ed. *Globalization.* Durham, NC: Duke University Press, 260 278.

Scott, M., 2011. Popular Music as Social Policy: Hybrid Hierarchies and Social Inclusion through New Zealand's Pop Renaissance. *Journal of Sociology,* 48, 304–322.

Seabrook, J. 2012. Factory Girls: Cultural Technology and the Making of K-pop. *The New Yorker,* 88–97. Available from: www.newyorker.com/reporting/2012/10/08/121008fa_fact_seabrook?currentPage=all (March 15, 2013).

Shim, D. 2002. South Korean Media Industry in the 1990s and the Economic Crisis. *Prometheus: Critical Studies in Innovation,* 20, 337–350.

Shim, D. 2006. Hybridity and the Rise of Korean Popular Culture in Asia. *Media, Culture & Society,* 28, 25–44.

Shim, D. 2008. The Growth of Korean Culture Industries and the Korean Wave. *In:* Huat, C.B and Iwabuchi, K., eds. *East Asian Pop Culture: Analyzing the Korean Wave.* Hong Kong: Hong Kong University Press, 15–32.

Shin, K. 2002. The Discourse on Women in Korea: Episodes, Continuity, and Change. *The Review of Korean Studies,* 5, 7–27.

Shin, H., 2009. Have You Ever Seen the Rain? And Who'll Stop the Rain? The Globalizing Project of Korean Pop (K-pop). *Inter-Asia Cultural Studies,* 10, 507–523.

Shin, S., and Kim, L., 2013. Organizing K-pop: Emergence and Market Making of Large Korean Entertainment Houses, 1980–2010. *East Asia,* 30 (4), 255–272.

SNSD Plastic Surgery. n.d. One of the Best Plastic Surgery Examples

Stone, Z., 2013. The K-pop Plastic Surgery Obsession. *The Atlantic,* 24 May. Available from: www.theatlantic.com/health/archive/2013/05/the-k-pop-plastic-surgery-obsession/276215/.

Williams, R., 1977. *Marxism and Literature.* Oxford and New York: Oxford University Press.

Wolf, M.J. 2004. *The Entertainment Economy: How Mega-Media Forces Are Transforming Our Lives.* New York: Three Rives Press

World Bank. 2002. *World Development Report 2002: Building Institutions for Markets.* Oxford: Oxford University Press.

Yeung, H.W.C. 2000. State Intervention and Neoliberalism in the Globalizing World Economy: Lessons from Singapore's Regionalization Programme. *The Pacific Review* 13 (1), 133–162.

Yim, H., 2002. Cultural Identity and Cultural Policy in South Korea. *International Journal of Cultural Policy,* 8, 37–48.

34

'Regeneration' in Britain

Measuring the outcomes of cultural activity in the 21st century

Peter Campbell and Tamsin Cox

Introduction

This chapter offers a case study of practices of evidence-gathering relating to regeneration and culture in Great Britain. It reviews literature from the last decade to explore the 'regenerative' outcomes sought from cultural interventions, the types of proposition that underlie these outcomes, and the types of evidence produced to support these propositions. This offers an analytical framework that elucidates key aspects of the policy discourse relating to culture (i.e. what activities are funded and what claims are made for them) and the approaches to 'evidencing' the claims made within that discourse. In doing so, we reflect upon the nature of this evidence base and upon some of the common methodological challenges encountered in the production of evidence.

'British cultural policy' and 'regeneration'

In some regards, it is difficult to assess 'British cultural policy'. First, Britain contains the major part of three distinct countries, with certain policy domains delegated to national assemblies, including cultural policy. Britain thus contains a range of national cultural policies (Allin 2015, p. 15). Second, substantive 'cultural policy' itself can be difficult to locate (Selwood 2015, p. 1) and has remained marginal, being administered by the smallest of government departments – the 'Department for Culture, Media and Sport' (DCMS) (Gordon *et al.* 2015, p. 51), with local government budgets shrinking year on year in recent times. These challenges, though, are not exclusively British. Despite these challenges, what can clearly be seen across Britain (and also far beyond), is a focus on the *outcomes* of policy (cultural or otherwise), with a particular emphasis on *economic* outcomes, and the production of *evidence* with regards to these outcomes (e.g. Gordon *et al.* 2015, p. 52; Hesmondhalgh *et al.* 2015, p. 38; Stevenson 2014, p. 134).

The conceptual linking of cultural activity and an outcome of urban 'regeneration' of some form achieved a particular prominence in Britain from the late 20th century, and so can be seen as an exemplar of broader international trends. Whilst the apex of both policy discourse and practice that refers to this linkage may have been reached (see e.g. Hesmondhalgh *et al.* 2015, p. 139; O'Brien and Matthews 2015), not only do major regeneration funding streams such as the Single Regeneration Budget, European Regional Development Fund and Housing Market Renewal Scheme maintain a position for cultural activity (cf. ACAVA 2014; DCLG 2013; European Commission 2013; NFASP 2010), but 'regeneration' remains a clear part of the argument made by government and non-governmental funding bodies to justify investment in culture (ACE 2014; DCMS 2013, 2016). This chapter seeks to contribute to our understanding of practices and discourses that link cultural activity and regeneration by demonstrating the practical steps taken to constitute a body of 'evidence' on this topic, identifying where common claims arise and understanding the approaches taken in justifying these.

Method

This chapter takes as its base a literature review of the 'evidence' that has been produced in making the case for the regenerative impact of culture in Britain, focusing on examples from the last decade. This was done as part of the wider 'Cultural Value' project funded by the UK's 'Arts and Humanities Research Council' considering the means by which the range of cultural values might best be captured (Campbell *et al.* 2016; Crossick and Kaszynska 2016). This project builds upon previous reviews but uses a particular analytical framework to explore what arguments are made within the discourse constituted by these sources and what evidence is produced to support these. Our approach is to ask:

1   What 'regeneration' is supposed to result from cultural activity? ('Outcome')
2   What propositions support these outcomes? ('Proposition')
3   What evidence is produced to support these propositions, and how? ('Evidence')

Identifying relevant material is made difficult by the nebulous nature (or at least usage) of the idea of 'regeneration'. In order to assess relevant evidence, the activity discussed below is that which explicitly articulates, however loosely, some kind of proposition for how, or why, regeneration will occur as a result of a cultural intervention. The associated evidence is then presented to establish this proposition. A full account of the evidence-gathering process can be found in Campbell *et al.* (2016), but briefly, academic and grey literature and national evidence databases (e.g. the CASE (Culture and Sport Evidence) programme led by DCMS) were reviewed, in addition to consultation with arts funding bodies and organisations. We do not claim here to provide a comprehensive record of *all* evidence in existence, but to provide a clear typology of the evidence produced in practice in Britain. It should also be noted that as this chapter draws from a larger study, it does not reflect all sources upon which the study is based. As such, individual sources are in many cases *examples* of types of intervention, types of methods for evidence production and types of impact.

In the remainder of the chapter, results are discussed, with each of the 'outcomes' identified as being commonly referred to across a number of activity/evidence examples described in turn, followed by associated 'propositions' and then the methods commonly used to produce evidence in each area.

OUTCOME 1: Regeneration via sector development of cultural and creative industries

In their assessment of the rationale for much activity seeking to achieve 'regeneration', Böhm and Land (2009, p. 93) summarise the situation thus: "the arts are seen as central to the development of social entrepreneurs whose creative energies will revitalise both the local culture and economy", and account for this position as follows:

> The assumption seems to be that 'creativity' is a transferable skill, and that developing the population's artistic creativity will deliver creativity and innovation in other sectors.

> *(2009, p. 80)*

Arts provision is thus seen as leading to regeneration via the development of 'creative' skills, which can be used in many sectors, or in industries related specifically to cultural activity, resulting in increased employment. Statements regarding the UK's most recent staging of the European Capital of Culture (ECoC) programme, for instance, can be seen to reflect this position:

> Creativity has a lot to offer industry and business and we need to make sure that all employees, employers and business people understand that. Winning European Capital of Culture shows how key creativity is to Merseyside; to its people, to its economy and to its future.

> *(Jones 2008)*

This position has clear links to the influential 'creative class' thesis, wherein differing forms of 'creativity', be they cultural, economic or technological, are seen as "interlinked and inseparable" (Florida 2004, p. 8). From such a position, any activity conceived as 'creative', including cultural activity, is vital for achieving success, even if cultural activity only acts as "an instrumental sideshow that in turn attracts the workers, which attracts the hi-tech investors" (Pratt 2008, p. 108). The idea that culture is part of an overarching system of creativity, generating income and employment as part of a move to a 'creative economy', as well as having a social role to play can be seen to have maintained some dominance in recent years, both at an international level (e.g. European Commission 2010, p. 2; Lähdesmäki 2014, p. 490) and within Britain at national (ACE *et al.* 2010, p. 1; DCMS *et al.* 2008, p. 7), and local levels (e.g. Liverpool City Council 2012, 2013).

Below, we consider the activities undertaken and evidence produced to substantiate these links between cultural activity and increased/diversified economic activity and what propositions are (or can be) used to make this link. Evidence will be considered in relation to **three** propositions.

Proposition 1: Cultural activity stimulates the creative industries, leading to:

- Economic growth, diversification and competitiveness
- A change in industrial profile, supporting wider investment

Evidence generated: Volume of 'creative' individuals/firms, level of economic activity & trends in these
From: Secondary datasets, stakeholder surveys

Some have sought to establish the role culture may play as an attractive force in decision-making processes around migration from primary survey data (Biddle *et al.* 2006). Others, such as Clifton (2008), have attempted specifically to locate Florida's 'creative class' using national datasets such as the census and Labour Force Survey (p. 66). Evidence regarding the number of 'creative industries' in a location is also often derived from national datasets such as the ONS (Office for National Statistics) 'Annual Business Inquiry' (Impacts 08 2010a, p. 37). Such datasets provide the data that underlie statements such as this:

> Investment in the arts and heritage can be put to work to help economic recovery. The sector covered by the Department for Culture, Media and Sport accounts for 10% of GDP.
>
> *(ACE et al. 2010, p. 5)*

Concern with the overall size and contribution of the 'high growth' creative sector is also clear in Local Enterprise Partnerships and local authority plans (e.g. D2N2 LEP 2012, p. 12; GBS LEP 2014, p. 65). Such strategies do not necessarily link creative industries *directly* to cultural interventions, however, and may associate the sector with tourism, 'digital'/ IT activities, biological and life sciences or advanced manufacturing. Typically, documents supporting sector development include assessments of the size and spread of business units (e.g. The Economic Strategy Research Bureau 2011) and employment (e.g. Morris and Jones 2009). This kind of mapping of secondary data is, however, specifically drawn on in more recent cultural interventions. The 'UK City of Culture' competition requires applicant cities to supply an assessment of the "current nature and strength of the cultural and creative sectors" in their area, as well as an assessment of how the UK City of Culture programme will "help to boost these sectors" (DCMS 2013, p. 19). The most recent winning bid for this competition specifies a target to increase employment in the creative industries by 10% by 2017 (Hull City Council 2014), suggesting that changes in the size of the sector will continue to be seen as key indicators of successfully regenerative cultural interventions, and these indicators will likely continue to rely on data from ONS and local directories to substantiate the level of change.

Relatedly, some (e.g. Bailey 2006, p. 2) give evidence of high levels of new business in the creative sector and attribute this to the impact of cultural regeneration, thus drawing links among cultural activity, new business activity and the potentially high economic rewards that can be drawn from this activity. Similar datasets are used to establish the impact of developments in cultural infrastructure (New Economy 2013). Some research also uses more anecdotal data to establish whether stakeholders express the view that creative activity has increased (General Public Agency 2008, pp. 21–22), or whether survey results demonstrate a belief that job opportunities are being provided (Biddle *et al.* 2006), rather than seeking more 'hard' data.

Proposition 2: Cultural activity stimulates the development of creative skills/approaches, leading to:

- The development of new creative workers (in both subsidised and unsubsidised environments), addressing employment issues

Evidence generated: Qualitative data on perceptions, quantitative data on programmes, individuals involved, artist employment

From: Interviews, focus groups, surveys, monitoring data

Roger Tym and Partners (2011, pp. 45–47) used structured interviews with economic development and arts development organisations, revealing opinions on the extent to which cultural institutions influence business-location decisions and the attraction and retention of skilled workers, whereas Biddle *et al.* (2006) undertook a general survey of the population of Newcastle-Gateshead, finding that over 90% agreed with the proposition that the Quays were providing opportunities for young people to develop artistic talent. A preponderance of more anecdotal evidence in this area, however, may reflect a relative lack of activity within flagship cultural projects to directly promote or engage with creative industries (Comunian and Mould 2014).

At a policy level, 'Creative and Cultural Skills' and the 'National Skills Academy for Creative and Cultural' specifically run workforce development programmes, including activities for young people. The Backstage Centre, a "technical training and rehearsal facility", works with young people to support the development of skills related to the creative industries. The facility is described as being "at the heart of a cultural industries business zone [...] and is part of a major *regeneration* project" (CCS 2014a, emphasis added). The Centre won the RICS' East of England award for Regeneration and was described by CCS as being developed "to encourage local talent to stay in the area and aspire for the best jobs" (CCS 2014b). Similarly, a programme hosted by Tate Modern entitled 'START' looked to engage unemployed south London residents through cultural organisations providing training and workplace experiences in jobs as gallery and retail assistants (Hyslop 2012). Whilst evidence of the *existence* of such interventions is clear, however, evidence of their efficacy in terms of 'regeneration' is less easy to establish. Nevertheless, writers such as Holden (2007, p. 26) argue that schemes that promote involvement with the arts (such as the UK government's 'Creative Partnerships') help "build the creative individuals of the future".

Proposition 3: Prominent cultural interventions (e.g. mega-events) result in:

- Higher profile, and conditions conducive to the operation of cultural and creative industries
- Subsidised cultural organisations and individuals being more ambitious, collaborative, innovative, networking, etc.

Evidence generated: Sector perceptions of the success, and indirect benefits, of regeneration initiatives, sector experiences and direct impacts of regeneration initiatives
From: Surveys, interviews, focus groups, monitoring data

Some have gathered evidence regarding creative workers' views of the impacts of cultural programmes on their practice. An evaluation of an empty shops scheme in Lancashire (Green 2011) that aimed to develop local creative industries, for instance, provided data on the value of reported sales and reported potential future clients, evidence of new audiences for participating artists and creative businesses through artist-reported estimates and evidence of new networks and contacts through interviews with participants. Similar lines of enquiry have been followed using interview and survey techniques around programmes such as the ECoC (Campbell 2011) and other flagship cultural projects (e.g. Comunian and Mould 2014). Views elicited are, at best, mixed regarding the results of such interventions and the direct impact such a programme can make on commercial creative practice, with British examples to some extent reinforcing the findings of Palmer-Rae Associates' historic analysis of the ECoC programme, which found that, when consulted, "very few cities submitted evidence of following through in any meaningful way on genuine economic targets" (2004, p. 103).

More generally, in providing evidence of what activity has been achieved, many evaluations report basic quantitative indicators such as the volume of artists involved, often broken down by, for example, levels of local artists, international artists, etc., and discussions of approaches taken to provide artists with opportunities to develop their work (cf. García and

Cox 2013). Again, however, data on what activity has *taken place* does not necessarily enable us to establish the *effects* of this activity.

OUTCOME 2: Regeneration via interventions that promote public profiles and levels of engagement

When considering the means by which culture can achieve regeneration, analyses of the economic 'impact' of tourism and related spending have proved consistently popular in Britain (and beyond); they proliferate in press reports of the effects of cultural programmes (e.g. Owens 2013; Young 2013). Tourism is often specifically linked to particular infrastructural developments, via the so-called 'Bilbao effect' of attractive, 'iconic' cultural centres but also via the association of cultural festivals with wider physical change. These physical developments can also 'regenerate' an area as part of a broader set of interventions.

Arts projects on a small scale are also sometimes used as a means to regenerate the physical fabric of urban areas. A relatively recent phenomenon is the 'empty shops' movement in a number of towns and cities. Whilst some earlier interventions are independent of any form of wider funding (e.g. 'Empty Shop' Durham, founded in 2008 (Empty Shop 2014)), there is a rising pattern of support from local authorities and similar bodies in response to declining levels of retail unit occupancy and a desire to reinvigorate empty high streets using art installations and cultural enterprises (Burchill 2011; Empty Shops Network 2014).

As well as new cultural *practice*, some interventions seek to utilise the arts to render wider processes of physical regeneration more 'creative' in some way. The Commission for Architecture and the Built Environment (CABE 2008, pp. 3–4), for instance, discuss "join[ing] forces with Arts & Business and Public Art South West […] to inject creativity into development" and to "include artists in determining the future look and feel of our towns and cities" (p. 6).

This association of culture with some transformation of physical space is often broadened to include a transformation of the *meanings* associated with that space, with cultural activity positioned as a key driver to achieve positive media coverage or image change (García 2010), which in addition to being valuable in and of itself can also attract a range of audiences.

This section highlights the emphasis placed upon interventions, which introduce new content to a locale, be this a physical asset or cultural programme of activity. In some cases, the intervention is specifically temporary or a 'one-off' (for example, in the case of 'City of Culture' programmes). In this section, evidence will be considered in relation to **six** propositions.

Proposition 4: Cultural interventions involving a change in the built environment will:

- Provide new, or improve existing, cultural facilities for residents
- Improve the look/feel of areas and residents' experiences of them
- Support more usage/reuse of stock/urban areas, reducing problems associated with disuse

Evidence generated: Data on physical changes/additions, changes in land values
From: Secondary data sets (on physical investment), land-use maps, photographs, resident surveys, stakeholder interviews, monitoring data

Secondary data regarding physical investment offers basic information on the process of physical change, such as levels of investment (e.g. Bailey 2006, p. 6) and the range of facilities created or improved (e.g. Barnardo's 2005; Liverpool Culture Company 2008). For example, for many of the 'empty shops' projects, data on levels of reoccupation of vacant retail units are suggested as one indicator of success (e.g. Newport City Council 2011). Such data are commonly reported either as a stand-alone indicator of physical change or as one component in a wider set of indicators. Some studies, however, have relied solely on other sources of evidence, such as stakeholder interviews (General Public Agency 2008).

Other studies have employed multiple and mixed methods. The 'Townscape Heritage Initiative' sought regeneration by funding a range of conservation activities relating to heritage, including repairing the fabric of heritage assets, restoring original details and materials, securing continued use or bringing vacant space into use and supporting public realm works. In addition to using data on physical investment and conducting surveys and interviews with residents and stakeholders, the longitudinal review of the Townscape Heritage Initiative used a 'townscape survey' involving land use maps and the observation of "30 to 50 different views of the streetscapes of each THI site" (THRU 2013, p. 11) against 25 measures, in order to map overall changes in the physical environment of the case studies.

The manner in which space is used by the public is seen by some studies as an important measure of the regenerative impact of culture. For 'empty shops' projects, local authorities are naturally keen, for instance, to use attendance figures as a basic indicator of the extent to which these cultural interventions are re-animating space (Burchill 2011; Green 2011). Qualitative data from interviews with artists, visitors and participants (Green 2011) are also used to provide evidence of the effects of such schemes. In the case of the longitudinal review of the Townscape Heritage Initiative (2013, p. 16), public usage and traffic flow was analysed in quantitative terms, with higher levels of usage of public space – as observed by the research team and reported by local residents and stakeholders – being interpreted as a positive indicator of regeneration. For other studies, observation of how 'regenerated' public space is actually used is an opportunity to record the experiences of those who might otherwise be overlooked or excluded from formal evaluation processes, using both repeated survey data and more ethnographic methods (Sharp 2007, p. 282). In the Barnardo's (2005, pp. 32–34) review 'Art of Regeneration', researchers use insights from stakeholder interviews (community workers, activists, young people) to form an impression of how renovated space is used, by whom, and for what purposes.

Proposition 5: A cultural programme of activity improves usage of space by:

- Providing new opportunities, engaging local residents in different ways, supporting social inclusion/civic pride
- Providing a focal point/shared narrative for actors from different agencies
- Animating spaces

Evidence generated: Volume and type of activity involved in programming, volume and types of public engagement

From: Monitoring data, audience surveys

As noted above, a common method of providing evidence on the effect of cultural programming is simply to give data regarding the number of events that were held, the number of opportunities there were to participate or the number of people that engaged with events in some way, be it through passive or active forms of engagement (Burchill 2011; New Economy 2013). Sometimes there is particular emphasis by evaluators on *new* events or festivals created by a cultural intervention, particularly in cases where this new activity is sustained in the long term (García and Cox 2013, p. 116; New Economy 2013, p. 11). In either case, implicit in such evidence is the assumption that the very existence of cultural events is, in and of itself, of benefit, and that more/new equals better. In any case, the mere *existence* of cultural activity in a location is often taken to be evidence of improved usage of that location.

Proposition 6: Cultural intervention involving a change in the built environment (through new/changed assets) will benefit the surrounding area by:

- Improving the value and use of land and property

Evidence generated: Increase in land/property prices and/or usage as a result of new cultural assets

From: Land Registry House Price Index combined with data on physical location of cultural institutions and other variables, stakeholder interviews, resident surveys, 'townscape surveys'

Some studies equate a revived local property market with regeneration and therefore seek to explore the relationship between cultural interventions and indicators such as greater demand for property, increasing property prices and changing patterns of property use. A report by the Centre for Economics & Business Research (CEBR 2013), for example, attempts to evidence a positive relationship between 'cultural density' (the number of cultural institutions within a particular area) and house prices. Similarly, Hyslop (2012, p. 158) attributes a role for the opening of Tate Modern in the increasing property prices.

The review of the Townscape Heritage Initiative (2013, pp. 15–16) also considered the capital and rental value of property in case study areas but, in addition, monitored shifts in the *patterns* of usage for local land and retail space, through a combination of local and national data sources, physical observation and interviews and questionnaires with local people. Although few studies have the capacity to employ such a resource-intensive approach, others have also looked at trends in local land and property use, with an evaluation of Salford's Lowry, for instance, pointing to an increase in the number of households during the period 2001–2011 as evidence of wider regeneration of which the venue is part (New Economy 2013, p. 23).

Proposition 7: Cultural activities and interventions involving a change in the built environment (through new/changed assets) will benefit the surrounding area by:

- Attracting visitors and increasing levels of tourism

Evidence generated: Data on tourism and associated spend

From: Secondary data sets (e.g. STEAM, bed nights and hotel occupation), primary data surveys of visitors/attendees

Surveys to ascertain levels of tourism and associated retail spending have been used as evidence for economic regeneration for some time (cf. Reeves 2002, p. 8) and continue to have a prominent role in establishing the value of cultural interventions (cf. Arts Council England 2014; Sacco and Blessi 2007). Evidence on the economic benefits of tourism associated with new or refurbished cultural facilities generally involve counts of a number of indicators, including the level of visitors, overnight stays, 'bed nights' sold, employment in hotels (or in the service sector more broadly) and spending (ACE *et al.* 2010; LGA 2013). These raw indicators are often supplemented with additional analysis detailing the proportion of visitors that were explicitly motivated to visit due to the draw of the attraction being evaluated (FiveLines 2012, p. 17; Impacts 08 2010a), visiting from outside the area of interest (LGA 2013, p. 13) or visiting during the 'low season' for local tourism (FiveLines 2012, p. 16). Banardo's (2005, p. 30) used box office data to look at what proportion of the Albany's audience came from further afield than the immediate boroughs.

Proposition 8: Cultural activities and interventions involving a change in the built environment (through new/changed assets) will benefit the surrounding area by:

- Creating economic value through direct employment and associated indirect and induced benefits
- Creating economic value through direct supply chain spending and associated indirect and induced benefits
- Creating economic value through direct tourism spending and associated indirect and induced benefits

Evidence generated: Calculations/indicators of economic impact or size
From: Economic impact analysis, visitor surveys, government statistics, organisational accounts/ management information, pre-existing input/output models/multipliers (usually from the tourism sector)

There is no shortage of studies linking cultural activity specifically to *economic* regeneration, with evidence in this area having been generated in quite large quantities for a number of years (Madden 2001). Most comprise analysis of 'economic impact' and share the same basic premise, albeit with considerable methodological variations in execution (e.g. FiveLines 2012; GHK 2009; Hyslop 2012). Typical approaches include attempts to assess the economic value of employment and spending in the supply chain created by an activity or organisation or the building of a new physical asset. Approaches may also include attempts to ascertain the proportion of visitors brought into an area along with the associated spending and potential effects of that spending. In some cases, efforts are made to consider 'additionality' – i.e. the additional effects of a particular activity, above those that might have taken place in any case. Considerations of a detailed counterfactual case are rarely included.

Many reports calculate a single figure for 'economic impact'. For instance, a recent report by the Local Government Association notes that,

> The 500,000 visitors to the Hepworth Wakefield during its first year contributed an estimated £10 million to the local economy in Wakefield and a recent economic impact of the Yorkshire Sculpture Park estimated its annual contribution to the local economy to be £5 million.
>
> *(LGA 2013, p. 6)*

Similarly, the economic impact of the fourth edition of the AV Festival – a biennial contemporary art, music and film festival held in North East England – was evaluated using the Impact Evaluation Framework (IEF) based on the UK Treasury's 'Green Book', which gives guidance on methods of evaluation and data relating to organiser and visitor expenditure derived from festival accounts and visitor surveys respectively. Using this approach, the net economic impact of the 2012 festival was estimated to be £1,091,435, with a return of £2.88 for every £1 of public funding the festival received (BOP Consulting 2012, p. 7).

Figures regarding the economic 'size' of an event or institution, whether in terms of the jobs it 'supports' or in terms of its gross overall revenue or share of gross domestic product, are frequently used as evidence of the regenerative potential of culture. In a study of the economic impacts of the Lowry on the area surrounding it, the authors point to the fact that the "Quays area accounted for almost 75% of new employment opportunities in Salford between 2003 and 2008" (New Economy 2013, p. 23). Results such as these are also available relating to the economic impact of Turner Contemporary in Margate (FiveLines 2012). Such analyses can also be found relating to objects other than single programmes or new buildings – the regular activities of the group of major cultural institutions in Liverpool grouped under the 'Liverpool Arts Regeneration Consortium' banner, for instance, are also the object of an economic impact assessment (Roger Tym and Partners 2011, p. 27).

Some studies report more general economic statistics for the area under consideration, either to support or refute the proposition that a cultural intervention has altered an area's economic prosperity. Jones (2013, p. 57), for instance, uses the ONS' Business Structure Database to show that the area surrounding the landmark development of Newcastle-Gateshead Quayside suffered private sector job losses, compared to private sector jobs growth in the city of Newcastle as a whole. This example is helpful in highlighting the way in which evidence is often presented for interventions selectively and without any significant articulation of the potential relationship between an intervention and wider economic changes and factors. Other studies, meanwhile, refer to the effect that funding for cultural activity has on leveraging additional funding (General Public Agency 2008, p. 21) or combine data from various different sources to create composite measures of wider economic 'vitality'. The longitudinal evaluation of the Townscape Heritage Initiative (THRU 2013, p. 16), for example, used surveys and interviews with residents and local business people, observations of physical change and statistical data to arrive at a judgement of 'business vitality', defined by the study as a situation where there are few vacant properties and the cultural intervention is bound up with, or triggers, further investment. In this instance, what is being offered as evidence is the *perception* of economic benefit.

Proposition 9: Cultural activities and interventions involving a change in the built environment (through new/changed assets) will benefit the surrounding area by:

- Changing the image of the area, internally and externally

Evidence generated: Changes/improvements in perceptions and media coverage
From: Media analysis, stakeholder interviews, surveys of tourists/non-residents and residents, business surveys, city ranking systems, 'expert' opinion, other indicators of 'profile'

Higher profile and image improvement are among the most frequently claimed benefits of cultural activity and typically occupy a key role in 'regeneration' narratives. These purported benefits are supported by a range of evidence, the most common of which include indicators derived from traditional or social media analysis, such as the total volume of media coverage associated with an intervention, the attitudes expressed by this coverage and its 'equivalent advertising value' (FiveLines 2012; LGA 2013; THRU 2013, p. 16), indicators derived from the perceptions of those based *inside* the immediate area of interest, including residents and local stakeholders (Biddle *et al.* 2006; General Public Agency 2008, p. 22), indicators derived from the perceptions of those based *outside* the immediate area of interest, such as tourists, non-residents and non-local businesses (Impacts 08 2010a, pp. 31, 46), the views of 'experts' or 'peers' in the arts and tourism sectors (Impacts 08 2010a, p. 35), and the judgments of city ranking systems or 'league tables' (García and Cox 2013, p. 131). It is worth noting that both ranking systems and monetary valuations of media coverage are often widely used without methodological explanations, making them difficult to analyse or understand in terms of validity.

Whilst various ECoCs have tracked local perceptions of the host city, with a range of positive effects claimed, the extent to which reported improvements are sustained in the long term is not clear, as surveys are typically undertaken soon after the end of the event year itself (García and Cox 2013, pp. 128–129). In the British case of Liverpool, neighbourhood surveys and workshops that explored residents' perceptions of the city, among other things, found that perceptions improved between 2007 and 2009 (Impacts 08 2010b). Biddle *et al.* (2006) found agreement concerning pride as a result of cultural capital developments in a local population survey. Bailey (2006) also discusses a population survey revealing that, "the vast majority (93%) agreed that the North East is a creative region". Beyond these indicators, the value of cultural interventions is sometimes evidenced through the awards that such interventions attract, e.g. Gateshead Council's (2006) listing of the various awards that the Angel of the North has received or a similar listing for the Dream sculpture in St Helens (Dream St Helens 2010), demonstrating a heightened profile for an area, and a (new) positive association with cultural activity.

OUTCOME 3: Regeneration via improved social circumstances

In addition to urban regeneration being achieved via broader economic outcomes, the particularly *social* impacts of cultural activity continue to be emphasised, with cultural engagement being seen as having the potential not just to alleviate economic deprivation but also to transform a social, or perhaps even spiritual, poverty (cf. O'Brien 2013, p. 41). Böhm and Land (2009, p. 77) date this increasing attention to the "less tangible benefits" of cultural activity as a later development in the discourse around culture and regeneration. In 2002, for example, Belfiore (p. 97) identifies Matarasso's 1997 work as being "so far the only" to attempt to evaluate such benefits and notes some of the assumed areas in which cultural activity is positioned as having an effect:

> The arts and culture could increase social inclusion and community cohesion, reduce crime and deviance, and increase health and mental wellbeing.

Activity discussed in previous sections included interventions that sought to improve facilities for resident communities, or (in the broadest sense) engage these communities, as well as interventions with vaguer propositions that some would argue have an implicit social benefit, via a general economic benefit. One report reviewed suggests that the social and the economic may link in a two-stage process thus:

> Community development: Engagement of disadvantaged populations in activities which promote participation, personal and community empowerment and the skills required to be involved in the regeneration process
>
> Community regeneration: The development of new forms of economic participation, engagement with the labour market and improved take up of training opportunities leading to economic recovery.
>
> *(Adamson* et al. *p. 2)*

Here it is the eventual economic impact that determines activity as specifically *regenerative*. More broadly, this is worth considering in the context of the adoption of methods by

CASE for monetising well-being, using the ONS British Household Panel Survey (CASE 2011), where economic benefit is understood primarily in individual, rather than broader social terms.

This section considers activities that specifically seek to engage with communities in order to create a positive social outcome. This includes programmes or activities to connect communities to, for instance, physical developments, major events and festivals and wider regeneration activity. On the whole, the propositions made for potential social outcomes are amongst the least clearly defined we have come across in this review process. As Colomb (2011, p. 81) notes, "the evidence base on the 'social' impacts of cultural regeneration remains relatively thin".

Indeed, *evidence* of these outcomes is arguably even more difficult to establish than those areas considered up to now. Nevertheless, a range of research activity is regularly carried out in this area, including, for example, surveys and interviews with audience members and programme participants to determine the effects of cultural activity. In some cases, it is difficult to relate outcomes directly to cultural interventions. Due to the perceived potential impact of cultural programmes, however, wider 'indicators' such as crime statistics, household income, health statistics and general population data for a given location are also often included in research (e.g. Ela Palmer Heritage 2008; Impacts 08 2010a; THRU 2013).

In this section, evidence will be considered in relation to **three** propositions.

Proposition 10: Cultural projects provide opportunities to engage in cultural 'work' or activity, in order to:

- Develop the (potentially) transferable skills and confidence of a participating group
- Address issues of education/life attainment indirectly, through positive cultural experiences

Evidence generated: Skills development, educational attainment, personal development
From: Volunteer and participant surveys, resident surveys, education statistics

There are examples of cultural activity that aspires to have a positive impact on the skills, personal development and educational attainment of those involved, whether as audience members, volunteers or members of the general public, with these impacts frequently linked, more or less directly, with 'regeneration' narratives. This view is echoed by ACE *et al.* (2010, p. 1), who argue that the arts and heritage can assist "with jobs, training, skills, experience, hope". In the case of Matarasso and Moriarty (2011), impacts on self-confidence and self-esteem were evidenced with extracts from interviews with project participants. Surveys of festival volunteers routinely uncover evidence of increased communication skills, teamwork skills, decision-making ability and leadership skills, as a result of the volunteering experience (BOP Consulting 2012, p. 24; Impacts 08 2010a, p. 22), whilst some studies see engagement with volunteering opportunities around cultural organisations as evidence of positive social impact (New Economy 2013, p. 28). In terms of direct impacts on young participants in particular, Holden (2007) cites an analysis of the DCMS 'Creative Partnerships' programme, which found that engagement with arts practice "enhanced motivation" and "encouraged high aspirations" amongst young people, evidenced via their reporting of such states. Oakley *et al.* (2013) qualify their view of the same programme as follows:

As might be expected, the evaluation of initiatives such as Creative Partnerships tends to find mixed results (McLellan *et al.* 2012). Common findings are that pupils' confidence and self-esteem are improved, with the implication that this improves efficacy and sense of well-being.

Similarly, an evaluation of the 'Music for Life' project in Liverpool, funded as part of Kensington's New Deal for Communities regeneration programme, reports "improved pupil behaviour, raising self-confidence and self-esteem" (BaseLine 2007, p. 4). In this particular instance, the project is praised for the integration of the intervention and the school curriculum (the project was delivered predominantly through music sessions in schools).

On the whole, what is unclear in these examples is the degree to which positive experiences genuinely alter future prospects. Ennis and Douglass (2011, pp. 9–10) state that,

> there is evidence that arts programmes in schools can increase self-confidence but there is no strong evidence demonstrating that this leads to improved economic outcomes for the participant. In a similar vein, there is evidence that cultural programmes can boost the self-confidence of offenders leaving prison, but there is no evidence that this leads to a decrease in the reoffending rate.

What this seems to suggest is an absence of 'follow-up' evaluation, as well as an absence of focus on causality.

For the review of the Townscape Heritage Initiative (THRU 2013, p. 14), by contrast, the investigators looked at overall levels of educational attainment in the area surrounding each heritage zone, as well as surveying local people to explore their perceptions of the employment situation, whilst comparing local employment and occupational statistics against broader regional trends. Whilst the data in this instance makes a clear case for the possible 'need' of a community in terms of low educational attainment, it is less clear that this particular project proposed to respond to this need or how it anticipated causality between the intervention and any positive change that might be demonstrated.

Proposition 11: Cultural projects and activities engage communities in order to:

- Ensure social inclusion in wider cultural programmes
- Support community cohesion and empowerment
- Contribute to other elements of community life, such as crime prevention

Evidence generated: Civic and community pride levels, engagement in new activities, new participants in activity, communities presenting their own creative outputs, perceptions of community vibrancy, engagement and safety
From: Audit of community organisations/assets, audience/participant/volunteer surveys and interviews, stakeholder interviews, contextual area statistics, direct observations, monitoring data

A goal of some cultural activity is to develop 'social capital', either by bringing communities together, empowering groups seen as disempowered, including groups that do not typically participate, or raising the overall level of civic activity within a particular area. Evidence relating to these objectives is generated using a number of methods. One common approach is to survey or interview volunteers, audience members or participants for a particular project, to see whether, in their opinion, the project or event led to new or strengthened interpersonal relationships, including with people from communities that the respondent may previously have been unfamiliar with or hostile to. Matarasso and

Moriarty (2011) quoted from interviews with participants to argue that cultural activity in North Liverpool had led to a greater sense of community, less loneliness, more friends and more civic activity. The project also went beyond 'softer' outcomes, to suggest that participants had become more mentally and physically active. Similarly, volunteers with the Liverpool Capital of Culture reported that the experience of volunteering allowed them to "reach out to others and make connections and friendships" (Impacts 08 2010a, p. 22).

Adopting a different approach, the review of the Townscape Heritage Initiative (THRU 2013, p. 14) looked to audits of community organisations to determine the extent to which the initiative succeeded in boosting social inclusion in case study areas, with the proposition that lower levels of community organisations would reflect "a low sense of cohesion, community and vitality". A majority of volunteers surveyed for the AV 2012 Festival reported that the experience either 'greatly' or 'slightly' increased their confidence and self-esteem (BOP Consulting 2012, p. 24).

Some studies have attempted to explore the link between cultural interventions and measures of crime or the fear of crime, albeit with varying degrees of methodological sophistication. For example, whilst General Public Agency (2008, p. 31), in their review of 'Art at the Centre' (an Arts Council South East initiative), use stakeholder interviews alone to gauge whether work on the Isle of Wight had had any effect on anti-social behaviour, the review of the Townscape Heritage Initiative (THRU 2013, p. 15) combines crime statistics, physical observation and the perceptions of local people (as captured by surveys and interviews), to determine the extent to which the condition of each area changed over time. Neighbourhood research by Impacts 08 (2010b) also explored perceptions of crime and anti-social behaviour and feelings of personal safety, and how these changed before and after Liverpool's year as ECoC in 2008, through the use of neighbourhood surveys.

Whilst some activities may target particular communities with the sole intention of positive social outcomes, others are part of wider cultural programmes where communities may be targeted or engaged with to ensure that they do not 'miss out', or to ensure that a project can be said to be inclusive. Typical evidence of such activities may simply include basic assessments of activity run for/with local communities and levels of engagement. Liverpool's ECoC programme included a dedicated "Creative Communities" strand, some of which is enumerated in the end-of-year publication (Liverpool City Council 2009) and evaluation of the Dream sculpture in St Helens recorded "people involved in educational workshops, events, art projects and study visits" as evidence of levels of social inclusion (Dream St Helens 2010).

Evidence on the potential social impacts of cultural activity often comes by measuring the number of events, the size and social characteristics of the audience (e.g. the extent to which the activity succeeded in attracting a local audience or one drawn from particular social groups) or the size and social characteristics of the volunteer base (e.g. García and Cox 2013; Impacts 08 2010a; Liverpool Culture Company 2008). Demographic information about audiences/visitors/participants/volunteers is often patchy, making it difficult to understand if major events and other activities are reaching groups who might not normally be reached. There are examples of mixed methods being used, including box office data, surveys and general observation (e.g. Barnardo's 2005), which suggests that there remains an issue (potentially of cost/resources) in undertaking sufficient and robust fieldwork in order to ascertain *who* is actually engaging with cultural activities and the effects of this engagement.

By way of context for much of this activity seeking to engage new groups, it is perhaps worth noting the effects of the removal of entrance fees for national museums:

> Research shows that when the national museums in England dropped their entrance fees in 2001, this did not broaden the audience for museums but rather meant that the existing primarily middle class audience went more often.
>
> *(ESRC 2009, p. 7)*

Proposition 12: Cultural interventions that take place in the context of wider regeneration programmes can:

- Emphasise the role of culture, thereby engaging people in a different manner, adding value to existing programmes or in some cases ameliorating some of the negative effects of regeneration
- Provide an 'alternative' (perhaps even a resistance) to regeneration activity

Evidence generated: Levels of engagement between communities and regeneration planning processes, alternative responses to regeneration programmes
From: Interviews, case studies of activities

The evaluation of 'Art at the Centre' used interviews with artists and local politicians, as well as residents, in order to analyse the extent to which programme activity was successful in engaging the community with the development process around regeneration activities. The range of activities included explicitly cultural interventions and attempts to use cultural personnel or methods to engage the community in broader regeneration processes. In one example, the evaluators note that the absence of the arts strategy (which was developed through the project) in the area's overall published masterplan was seen as reflecting a "lack of commitment to the arts", and the evaluators suggest that "better parity should be sought with regeneration processes" (General Public Agency 2008, p. 27).

Similarly, the evaluation of the Music for Life project in the Kensington area of Liverpool suggested that, in order to have a greater effect within the local community and to ensure that it was not seen as competing with the wider regeneration programme that funded it (New Deal for Communities), it should,

> attempt to move towards a fuller integration with environmental, social and economic policies in Kensington. For example, a review of the management arrangements may be required […] the inclusion of a broad spectrum of community leaders is encouraged. These local voices should be tasked with selling and promoting the value of the project and re-assuring residents that the project […] represents best value for the local communities [and] is not simply siphoning away money from spending on 'concrete developments' in the local area.
>
> *(Baseline 2007, p. 4)*

In both these instances, cultural projects are seen as needing to fight for a place within broader regeneration programmes.

Qualitative data is also available to demonstrate positive attitudes towards the value of schemes involving artists in processes of planning. A report produced by the Commission for Architecture and the Built Environment (CABE 2008) provides information on case studies and interviews with architects, for instance, to demonstrate that artist involvement was seen as valuable:

> Both architects acknowledged that [the artist's] work had allowed them to develop a much deeper understanding of staff requirements and the needs of day centre users [...] and that the process had validated the need for Public Arts programmes to be run at both health centres. (p. 8)

Others report the potential of arts practice to "facilitate community involvement" (p. 16) in the process of redevelopment. All evaluation of this project rested on eliciting the opinions of stakeholders in the project.

It is also worth noting examples of activities that seek to resist or offer alternatives to the 'agreed' narrative around regeneration programmes. The Liverpool Biennial project 2Up 2Down/Homebaked brought an artist to work with a community in an area that had been subject to a Housing Marketing Renewal programme. The programme has sought to re-establish a community bakery in a building previously used as a bakery and to support the community to engage in and determine the future development of their own neighbourhood (2Up 2Down 2012). In national press coverage, the project is framed as a response to what is perceived to be failed regeneration practice, particularly the HMR programme (e.g. Hanley 2012; Moore 2012) and an empowerment of the local community in the response to large, structural programmes that fail to recognise the needs of those communities.

Conclusion

This chapter has sought to demonstrate the range of practices that have been used to offer evidence for the regenerative role of culture over recent years in Britain. In many ways, these practices reflect those found in earlier reviews of the nature of regeneration and evidence gathering (e.g. Evans and Shaw 2004; Reeves 2002; Vickery 2007). Whilst we do not therefore claim that our findings regarding the key areas on which evidence gathering focuses or the ways in which this evidence gathering is done are brand new, to confirm that key patterns persist 10 or more years is important. This is all the more important due to the apparent lack of progress in dealing with the 'gaps' or problems with this body of evidence.

Considering in detail the kinds of data in use in the studies above reveals a reliance on secondary data and proxies from beyond the cultural sector, on research seeking perceptions of cultural activity from convenience samples, on data treating the very existence of cultural activity as sufficient to demonstrate beneficial outcomes and on relatively short-term research projects. We consider possible explanations for this in more detail elsewhere (Campbell et al. 2016), but it must be noted that whilst culture continues to be seen as having a regenerative role to play, there is typically little or no discussion of the role of culture in relation to overall findings of major regeneration programmes (e.g. Audit Commission 2011; DCLG 2010). As such, we return to noting the relatively minor position of cultural policy, which leads to limited resources not just for interventions themselves, but for their evaluation. Short term projects, convenience samples, and a focus on secondary data are understandable given such resources, but this leads to a continued situation wherein there is a relative absence of robust, longitudinal, or historical data for the cultural sector; for instance, no reliable economic input-output model for subsidised activity in the sector, limited longitudinal audience and engagement data, and so on. It is perhaps inevitable that secondary data tends to come from outside the sector as there is so little standardised or comparative data freely available within the sector.

Given the wider policy climate emphasising the importance of economic outcomes, it is also perhaps of little surprise that we see such an emphasis on the production of a range of evidence relating to such outcomes, even though its ultimate usefulness may well be questioned. What is, perhaps, less understandable, however, is the lack of clarity within research itself of what propositions are being made. Those highlighted above are usually those seemingly implicit within research but seldom explicitly articulated. Indeed, what we have sought to achieve here is to ask 'what is this evidence *for*?' Any research that does not have a clear question risks unclear answers, especially when (as is often the case in this body of evidence) methods themselves remain opaque.

We do not suggest, then, that the body of evidence above is in any way ideal, but that its nature is instructive of the wider policy climate and that its shortcomings can be understood in the context of this climate. We also suggest that improving this body of evidence is not merely a matter of resource but of considering the outcomes proposed and the mechanisms being examined to question the emergence of this outcome. It is thus hoped this case study raises useful questions for the British case and beyond.

References

2Up 2Down (2012) *About 2Up 2Down*. www.2up2down.org.uk/about/.

ACAVA (2014) *Regeneration Archive*. www.acava.org/regeneration/regeneration-archive.

Adamson, D., Fyfe, H. and Byrne, P. (2008) *Hand in Hand. Arts-based Activities and Regeneration*. Cardiff: Arts Council Wales.

Allin, P. (2015) 'English Cultural Policy: Is Well-Being the Goal?' *Cultural Trends*, 24(1), 15–20.

Arts Council England (2014) *The Value of Arts and Culture to People and Society*. Manchester: Arts Council England.

Arts Council England, Association of Independent Museums, Cultural Learning Alliance, English Heritage, The Heritage Alliance, Heritage Lottery Fund, Local Government Association, Museums Association, Museums Libraries and Archives Council, National Campaign for the Arts, National Heritage Memorial Fund, National Museum Directors' Conference, Society of Archivists, Society of Chief Librarians, The Art Fund, The National Archives, and Visit England (2010) *Cultural Capital – A Manifesto for the Future*. www.artscouncil.org.uk/media/uploads/publications/Cultural_Capital_Manifesto.pdf.

Audit Commission (2011) *Housing Market Renewal: Housing, Programme Review*. http://archive.audit-commission.gov.uk/auditcommission/SiteCollectionDocuments/Downloads/201103HMR programmereview.pdf.

Bailey, C. (2006) *Cultural Values and Culture Led Regeneration – The Case of Newcastle-Gateshead*. www.fokus.or.at/fileadmin/fokus/user/downloads/acei_paper/Bailey.doc.

Barnardo's (2005) *Art of Regeneration: Evaluating the Impact of the Arts in a Disadvantaged Community*. www.dmss.co.uk/wp-content/uploads/2013/06/art_of_regeneration_report.pdf.

Baseline (2007) *Evaluation of the Music for Life Project*, Liverpool: LJMU.

Belfiore, E. (2002) 'Art as a Means of Alleviating Social Exclusion: Does It Really Work? A Critique of Instrumental Cultural Policies and Social Impact Studies in the UK', *International Journal of Cultural Policy*, 8(1), 91–106.

Biddle, P., Archer, A. and Lowther, H. (2006) *CISIR Report on Research Findings 2006*, Northumbria University.

Böhm, S. and Land, C. (2009) 'No Measure for Culture? Value in the New Economy', *Capital and Class*, 33(1), 75–98.

BOP Consulting (2012) *Evaluation of AV Festival 12*. www.avfestival.co.uk/documents/_view/5294b6847cbb88d61d000cf4.

Burchill, A. (2011) *Art and Empty Shops*. http://misachievement.wordpress.com/curatorial/empty-shops/.

CABE (2008) *Artists & Places: Engaging Creative Minds in Regeneration.* www.liminal.org.uk/uploads/9/warwick_bar_masterplan_Artist_and_Places_2008-pdf/.

Campbell, P. (2011) 'Creative Industries in a European Capital of Culture', *International Journal of Cultural Policy*, 7(5), 510–522.

Campbell, P., Cox, T., Crone, S. and Wilks-Heeg, S. (2016) *Evidence of Things that Appear Not – A Critical Review of the Role of Arts and Culture in the Regeneration of Urban Places and Urban Communities.* http://repository.liv.ac.uk/2035440/.

CASE (2011) The Art of the Possible - Using Secondary Data to Detect Social and Economic Impacts From Investments in Culture and Sport: A Feasibility Study. www.gov.uk/government/uploads/system/uploads/attachment_data/file/77608/CASE_The_Art_of_the_possible_2.pdf.

CCS (2014a) *Who We Are and What We Do.* http://ccskills.org.uk/about.

CCS (2014b) *The Backstage Centre Scoops Prestigious Royal Institute of Chartered Surveyors Award.* http://ccskills.org.uk/downloads/The_Backstage_Centre_scoops_prestigious_Royal_Institute_of_Chartered_Surveyors_award1.pdf.

Centre for Economics and Business Research (2013) *The Contribution of the Arts and Culture to the National Economy.* www.artscouncil.org.uk/media/uploads/pdf/CEBR_economic_report_web_version_0513.pdf.

Clifton, N. (2008) 'The "Creative Class" in the UK: An Initial Analysis', *Geografiska Annaler B*, 90(1), 63–82.

Colomb, C. (2011) 'Culture *In* the City, Culture *For* the City? The Political Construction of the Trickle-Down in Cultural Regeneration Strategies in Roubaix, France', *Town Planning Review*, 81(1), 77–98.

Comunian, R. and Mould, O. (2014) 'The Weakest Link: Creative Industries, Flagship Cultural Projects and Regeneration', *City, Culture and Society*, 5, 65–74.

Crossick, G. and Kaszynska, P. (2016) *Understanding the Value of Arts & Culture – The AHRC Cultural Value Project.* www.ahrc.ac.uk/documents/publications/cultural-value-project-final-report/.

D2N2 LEP (2012) *Strategy for Growth 2013–2023.* www.d2n2lep.org/write/Audio/D2N2_Strategy_for_Growth_2013-23_LR_05.07.13.pdf.

DCLG (2010) *The New Deal for Communities Experience: A Final Assessment – The New Deal for Communities Evaluation: Final Report – Volume 7.* http://extra.shu.ac.uk/ndc/downloads/general/A%20final%20assessment.pdf.

DCLG (2013) *Investing in Your Future: Case Study Booklet-East Midlands European Regional Development Fund Programme, 2007–2013.* www.gov.uk/government/uploads/system/uploads/attachment_data/file/147821/East_Midlands_ERDF_Case_Study_Booklet_Edition_1.pdf.

DCMS (2013) *UK City of Culture 2017. Guidance for Bidding Cities.* www.gov.uk/government/uploads/system/uploads/attachment_data/file/89369/UK_City_of_Culture_2017_Guidance_and_Criteria.pdf.

DCMS (2016) *The Culture White Paper.* www.gov.uk/government/uploads/system/uploads/attachment_data/file/510798/DCMS_The_Culture_White_Paper_3_.pdf.

DCMS, BERR and DIUS (2008) *Creative Britain: New Talents for the New Economy*, London: DCMS.

Dream St Helens (2010) *Coverage and Outputs.* www.dreamsthelens.com/dream-facts-figures/coverage-outputs/.Ela Palmer Heritage (2008) *The Social Impacts of Heritage-Led Regeneration.* www.ahfund.org.uk/docs/Report%20Social%20Impacts%20of%20Heritage-led%20Regeneration.pdf.

The Economic Strategy Research Bureau (2011) Report 3: The D2N2 Economy. www.d2n2lep.org/write/Documents/Board%20Mins/Report_3_-_D2N2_Economy_FINAL_Dec_2011.pdf.

Empty Shop (2014) *Everything You Need to Know.* http://emptyshop.org/about/.

Empty Shops Network (2014) *Empty Shops Network.* http://emptyshops.wordpress.com/.

Ennis, N. and Douglass, G. (2011) *Culture and Regeneration – What Evidence Is There of a Link and How Can It Be Measured?*, London: GLA.

ESRC (2009) *Not Only… But Also: Capturing the Value of Culture, Media and Sport.* http://centrallobby.politicshome.com/fileadmin/epolitix/stakeholders/Not_Only…But_Also__Capturing_the_Value_of_Culture__Media_and_Sport_Publication.pdf.

European Commission (2010) *Unlocking the Potential of Cultural and Creative Industries* http://ec.europa.eu/culture/our-policy-development/doc/GreenPaper_creative_industries_en.pdf.

European Commission (2013) *Housing Investments Supported by the European Regional Development Fund 2007–2013: Housing in Sustainable Urban Regeneration* http://ec.europa.eu/regional_policy/sources/docgener/studies/pdf/housing/2013_housing_study.pdf.

Evans, G. and Shaw, P. (2004) *The Contribution of Culture to Regeneration in the UK: A Review of Evidence,* London: DCMS.

FiveLines (2012) *Turner Contemporary – Year 1 Economic Impact Assessment Report,* [no publisher].

Florida, R. (2004) *The Rise of the Creative Class,* New York: Basic Books.

García, B. (2010) *Media Impact Assessment (part II): Evolving Press and Broadcast Narratives on Liverpool from 1996 to 2009.* www.liv.ac.uk/impacts08/Publications/Media_Impact_Assessment_Part2.pdf.

García, B. and Cox, T. (2013) *European Capitals of Culture: Success Strategies and Long-Term Effects.* www.europarl.europa.eu/RegData/etudes/etudes/join/2013/513985/IPOL-CULT_ET%282013%29513985_EN.pdf.

Gateshead Council (2006) *The Angel of the North.* www.gateshead.gov.uk/DocumentLibrary/Leisure/Angel/Angel%20Pack%20large.doc.

GBS LEP (2014) *Greater Birmingham and Solihull Strategic Economic Plan.* http://centreofenterprise.com/wp-content/uploads/2014/03/GBS-Strategic-Economic-Plan-Final-with-links1.pdf.

General Public Agency (2008) *Art at the Centre Phase II – Final Evaluation Report 2005–2008,* London: General Public Agency.

GHK (2009) *Economic Impact of HLF Projects, Volume 1 – Main Report.* www.hlf.org.uk/aboutus/howwework/Documents/Economic_impact_HFprojects2009_Finalreport.pdf.

Gordon, C., Powell, D. and Stark, P. (2015) 'The Coalition Government 2010–2015: Lessons for Future Cultural Policy', *Cultural Trends,* 24(1), 51–55.

Green, L. (2011) *Turning Empty Spaces into Creative Places: Empty Shops Evaluation Report for Pennine Lancashire.* www.creativityworks.info/images/uploads/pdfs/let-evaluation-report-final.pdf.

Hanley, L. (2012) *This Is How We Can Solve the Housing Crisis – One Home at a Time.* www.theguardian.com/commentisfree/2012/aug/13/solve-the-housing-crisis.

Hesmondhalgh, D., Oakley, K., Lee, D. and Nisbett, M. (2015) *Culture, Economy and Politics – The Case of New Labour,* Hampshire: Palgrave Macmillan.

Holden, J. (2007) *Publicly-Funded Culture and the Creative Industries,* London: Demos.

Hull City Council (2014) *The Countdown Has Begun.* http://2017-hull.co.uk/uploads/files/Hull_Countdown_to_2017_web.pdf.

Hyslop, D. (2012) 'Culture, Regeneration and Community: Reinventing the City', *Gateways: International Journal of Community Research and Engagement,* 5, 152–165.

Impacts 08 (2010a) *Creating an Impact: Liverpool's Experience as European Capital of Culture.* www.liv.ac.uk/impacts08/Papers/Creating_an_Impact_-_web.pdf.

Impacts 08 (2010b) *Neighbourhood Impacts: A Longitudinal Research Study into the Impact of the Liverpool European Capital of Culture on Local Residents.* www.liv.ac.uk/impacts08/Publications/Neighbourhood_Impacts.pdf.

Jones, C. (2008) *Capital of Culture: People's Opening.* www.liverpoolecho.co.uk/news/liverpool-news/capital-of-culture-peoples-opening-3494050.

Jones, A. (2013) *City Arts Strategies in a Cold Climate' in RSA and Arts Council England's Towards Plan A: A New Political Economy for Arts and Culture.* www.artscouncil.org.uk/media/uploads/pdf/RSA-Arts-Towards-Plan-A.pdf.

Lähdesmäki, T. (2014) 'European Capital of Culture Designation as an Initiator of Urban Transformation in the Post-Socialist Countries', *European Planning Studies,* 22(3), 481–497.

Liverpool City Council (2009) *Liverpool '08 European Capital of Culture. The Impacts of a Year Like No Other.* www.liverpool08.com/Images/End%20of%20Year%2008%20brochure%20COMPLETE%20FINAL_tcm146-147580.pdf.

Liverpool City Council (2012) *Liverpool Knowledge Festival.* http://liverpool.gov.uk/mayor/messages-from-the-mayor/speeches/liverpool-knowledge-festival/.

Liverpool City Council (2013) *Cultural Action Plan and Cultural Investment Framework,* Liverpool: Liverpool City Council.

Liverpool Culture Company (2008) *Liverpool Culture Company Final Report 2003–2008,* Liverpool: Liverpool Culture Company.

Local Government Association (2013) *Driving Growth through Local Government Investment in the Arts,* London: LGA.

Madden, C. (2001) 'Using 'Economic' Impact Studies in Arts and Cultural Advocacy: A Cautionary Note', *Media International Australia incorporating Culture and Policy,* 98, 161–178.

Matarasso, F. and Moriarty, G. (2011) *Telling Stories: The Arts and Wellbeing in North Liverpool.* www.larc.uk.com/wp-content/uploads/2011/05/LARCTellingstorieswebjob.pdf.

McLellan, R., Galton, A., Steward, S., and Page, C. (2012) *The Impact of Creative Initiatives on Wellbeing: A Literature Review.* London: Arts Council England.

Moore, R. (2012) *Liverpool Biennial – Review.* www.theguardian.com/artanddesign/2012/sep/23/liverpool-biennial-review-hmr-anfield.

Morris, K. and Jones, A. (2009) *Innovation and the Future Leeds City Region Economy.* www.leedscityregion.gov.uk/LCR-Corporate/media/Media/Research%20and%20publications/business%20innovation%20and%20growth/Innovation-in-LCR-Final-Report.pdf?ext=.pdf.

National Federation of Artists' Studio Providers (2010) *Developing Affordable Artists' Studios in a Housing Market Renewal Area.* http://artspace.org.uk/download-file/downloads/Manor-Oaks-CS.pdf.

New Economy (2013) *Beyond the Arts: Economic and Wider Impacts of the Lowry and Its Programmes.* www.thelowry.com/Downloads/reports/The_Lowry_Beyond_the_Arts.pdf.

Newport City Council (2011) *URBAN: Using Retail Buildings for Arts in Newport.* www.newport.gov.uk/stellent/groups/public/documents/leaflets_and_brochures/cont609142.pdf.

Oakley, K., O'Brien, D. and Lee, D. (2013) 'Happy Now? Well-Being and Cultural Policy', *Philosophy and Public Policy Quarterly,* 31(2), 18–26.

O'Brien, D. (2013) *Cultural Policy: Management, Value and Modernity in the Creative Industries,* New York: Routledge.

O'Brien, D. and Matthews, P. (2015) *After Urban Regeneration: Communities, Policy and Place,* Bristol: Policy Press.

Owens, M. (2013) *City of Culture Win Would Impact Dundee Now.* www.eveningtelegraph.co.uk/news/local/city-of-culture-win-would-impact-dundee-now-1.127211.

Palmer-Rae Associates (2004) *European Cities and Capitals of Culture,* Brussels: Palmer-Rae.

Pratt, A.C. (2008) 'Creative Cities: The Cultural Industries and the Creative Class', *Geografiska Annaler: Series B, Human Geography,* 90(2), 107–117.

Reeves, M. (2002) *Measuring the Economic and Social Impact of the Arts: A Review,* London: Arts Council England.

Roger Tym and Partners (2011) *Economic Impact of the Liverpool Arts Regeneration Consortium.* www.larc.uk.com/wp-content/uploads/2011/10/LARC-Economic-Impact-Final-Report.pdf.

Sacco, P.L. and Blessi, G.T. (2007) 'European Culture Capitals and Local Development Strategies: Comparing the Genoa and Lille 2004 Cases', *Homo Oeconomicus,* 24(1), 111–141.

Selwood, S. (2015) 'Cultural Trends Election Special', *Cultural Trends,* 24(1), 1–5.

Sharp, J. (2007) 'The Life and Death of Five Spaces: Public Art and Community Regeneration in Glasgow', *Cultural Geographies,* 14(2), 274–292.

Stevenson, D. (2014) 'Scottish Cultural Policy', *Cultural Trends,* 23(3), 133–135.

Townscape Heritage Research Unit (2013) *Townscape Heritage Initiative Schemes Evaluation – Ten Year Review Report,* Oxford: Townscape Heritage Research Unit, Oxford Brookes University.

Vickery, J. (2007) *The Emergence of Culture-Led Regeneration: A Policy Concept and Its Discontents,* Warwick: Centre for Cultural Policy Studies.

Young, A. (2013) *Feelgood Freedom Festival Injects Extra £2m into Hull's Economy.* www.hulldailymail.co.uk/Feelgood-Freedom-Festival-injects-extra-pound-2m/story-20006454-detail/story.html.

35

Japanese cultural policy, nation branding and the creative city

Tomoko Tamari

Introduction

This chapter briefly outlines how Japanese cultural policy has developed in response to changing political and economic circumstances from the early 20th century to the present. It also focuses on contemporary Japanese cultural policy and pays particularly attention to two recent phases. Firstly, the Cool Japan initiative, arguably one of the most prominent nation branding strategies. Secondly, the Tokyo-based new creative city project. Both could be seen as attempts to open up new horizons for cultural policy in Japan.

Although Japanese cultural policy, as we will see, became fully institutionalized in the late 20th century, cultural policy in general has a long pre-history, which can be traced back to the international expositions of the mid 19th century. International expositions provided displays of the latest industrial, military and communication technologies along with art, crafts, folk cultured exotica from Western nations and their colonies. Japan quickly saw the importance of using the international expositions not only to learn about western civilization, but also as an opportunity to display and legitimate a particular image of Japan to the rest of the world,[1] especially as it had been long closed off from the West in the Tokugawa Era (1603–1868). More importantly, to avoid the threat of Western invasion and keep its independence, the new Japanese government after the Meiji Restoration of 1868 decided that rather than attempting a military defence, a cleverer strategy could be to become seen as a civilized nation-state by the West that was worthy of equal treatment. This was because 'the best defence against the Western nation-state was the construction of a modern, legal state of its own' (Najita and Harootunian 1990: 716). It must be noted that to follow the Western nation-state model also involved colonialism; hence, Japan developed a policy of endorsing its civilizational credentials by showing its national power and colonial ambitions to the rest of East Asia.

Prior to the emergence of the 20th century mass media and the revolutions in communication technology, which are powerful devices to influence not only people's view of everyday life, but also public opinion, some of the most effective political devices to bolster a nation's image, in order to enhance its political influence, were international expositions. This is what we would now call public diplomacy: a political strategy entailing cultural practices/activities framed by the desire to win 'hearts and minds' and establish mutual trust.

It is implemented by establishing 'a selected national image by exporting appealing *cultural products*' (Iwabuchi 2015: 419, emphasis added).

These cultural products are usually categorized as 'soft power' (Nye 2004), a term that has frequently been used in the context of 'Cool Japan'.[2] In the Japanese context, soft power has often been equated with Japanese popular culture, such as manga, anime, video games and fashion. Following Nye's concept, we can understand that soft power works in creating 'more receptive to Japan's positions through the dissemination of the country's cultures and values' (Iwabuchi 2015: 419–420). The growing consciousness of the significance of cultural power in the context of contemporary cultural diplomacy, and the potential of Cool Japan as a new cultural policy, can be seen as a strategy that developed since the year 2000, in order to draw attention from consumers around the world and make Japanese popular culture not only a globally successful popular culture for revitalizing the economy, but also an effective vehicle for soft power and cultural diplomacy. The idea of creating a positive image of the nation so as to sustain or improve its privilege or advantageous position in the global national ranking can be seen as closely bound to that of nation branding. Whereas conventional public diplomacy targeted the creation of amicable international relations between nation-states, the new cultural policy and nation branding via soft power sought to appeal to both ordinary people who were their own national citizens and people in other countries.

Although nation branding aims to cultivate a better image of Japan among Japanese people, initiatives such as Cool Japan are not necessarily the most successful ways to cultivate the sense of national belonging. Rather, global mega-events such as the Olympics and International Expositions could well stimulate more positive images of one's own nation and nationalistic sentiments. Tokyo, the capital city of Japan, has been elected as the host city for the Olympic and Paralympic 2020 Games. There has been considerable concern in Tokyo about how best to present and stage itself to promote a positive image of contemporary Japan, one that should be significantly different from that of the 1964 Tokyo Olympics. The image of Tokyo inevitably stands for the national image of Japan. In this sense, Tokyo can serve as the most effective cultural diplomatic device. The device could also work to cultivate Japanese people's positive self-esteem, as well as heighten other counties' perception of Japan.

The idea of the city as a 'cultural powerhouse' (Yeoh 2005: 945) has been discussed in debates about creative cities (Kong 2014). Although Tokyo has been widely acknowledged as a huge economic and political centre and mature consumer city, it is far behind in becoming a world-class creative city. To improve the current situation, a new cultural urban plan was proposed in 2014. Contrasting the dominant image of cultural richness in south central Tokyo (e.g. Aoyama, Roppoingi and Ginza), the proposal highlights the rich traditional cultural resources of north central Tokyo (e.g. Ueno, Hongo, Akihabara, Kanda, Jinbocho and Yushima). Through an attempt to re-activate, re-discover and re-connect with traditional cultural assets in these regions, the new cultural urban plan, 'the Tokyo Cultural Resources District Vision' proposes to create 'a cultural unit'. This idea could be expanded to apply to all regions throughout Tokyo. Each cultural unit can be seen as composed of diversified local/regional cultural assets. Then eventually all cultural units of the various communities/locals/regions could transform Tokyo into a 'cultural museum' (Yoshimi 2016).

This chapter, then, focuses on the formation of Japanese cultural policy from the early 20th century onwards. This can illuminate the complex relationship between the political objectives of public diplomacy and various practices of cultural policy. Focusing on contemporary cultural policy in Japan, the paper also examines the Cool Japan initiative and the ways in which it has been expected to be a vital cultural device for creating a new image of Japan as a pioneer of soft power, and a political device for improving Japan's self-esteem and reputation for other countries. In this light, the Cool Japan initiative can also be closely related to the principle of nation branding.

Since Japan has been elected as the host city of the next 2020 Olympics, the paper also locates the effort of nation branding within the context of creative city policy in Japan, drawing on an on-going city project, the Tokyo Cultural Resources District Vision. The chapter argues that this can be seen as a new type of urban reform to challenge conventional mega-scale city planning and creative city policy. By proposing the re-connection of cultural assets to enhance cultural value, and connectivity of people to pick up as many voices as possible, the Tokyo Cultural Resources District Vision emphases the importance of creating networking not only as top-down cultural resources used at the regional level, but also among cultural specialists, local communities, NGO, the government institutions and various civic groups. In this light, the paper asserts that the Cultural Resources District Vision can be viewed as a good speculative case to suggest that crucial elements of the lived cultural policy can be brought together to work as a practice of re-vitalization of cultural values and a consensus-making process to enhance mutual understanding, collaboration and active participation.

The backgrounds of Japanese cultural policy

The concern with the promotion of cultural value, its positive reception by both domestic and foreign audiences and its enhanced national image have become pivotal components for contemporary cultural policy. Although today's Japanese cultural policy is highly institutionalized, the field of cultural policy was neither systematic nor regulated until the late 1980s (Kawashima 2012: 296). The early steps of the development of Japanese cultural policy can be traced back to Japan's greater involvement in the emerging international community of nations, which gained momentum after World War I.

Important impetus was proceeded by the needs of many countries to observe U.S. President Woodrow Wilson's diplomatic communications about the need to stabilize the international order after World War I. This eventually led to the formation of the League of Nations, the interwar forerunner to the United Nations. Another key experience for the Japanese was the eloquent Chinese delegation against Japanese expansionism in China at the Paris Peace Conference supported by systematic anti-Japanese sentiment on the part of Chinese intellectuals. This prompted a Japanese reaction with the Ministry of Foreign Affair (MOFA) establishing the Department of Information in April 1920 and a new policy of cultural exchange with China.

In 1934, the Society for International Cultural Relations was established (incidentally, the British Council was also established the same year). This was the time 'Japan became the first and only non-Western nation to establish a modern international cultural exchange organization' (Ozawa 2009: 273). Such imitations had to be suspended with the invasion of Manchuria and the China War after 1931, followed by the Second World War in 1939.

After World War II, Japan as a defeated country was under the unconditional occupation of the Allied Forces and effectively under the control of the United States. Japan was required to abandon its state-controlled cultural policies and needed to transform itself from its self-image as a militaristic, semi-feudalistic and authoritarian state to a peaceful democratic and liberal state by creating a new vision guided by cultural related policy. Hence 'Prime Minister Tetsu Katayama, in an important speech, advocated the "construction of a culture state" in order to restore national pride and international credibility' (Ozawa 2009: 274). The Korean War (1950–1953) proved to be a key event in the reconstitution of the Japanese economy and gradual rehabilitation and reintroduction into international affairs.

The 1964 Tokyo Olympics and the 1970 Osaka Expo were global mega events that helped Japan to deliver evidence of its full recovery from the devastation of the war, as well as demonstrating its potential to become a world-class economic power with advanced science and technology. Yet there was still considerable ambivalence. On the one hand, Japanese economic success drew attention from the West with books like Vogel's *Japan as Number One* (1979), showing how the United States could benefit from the lessons of Japan, such as meritocratic practices, corporate organisations, basic education, welfare and so on (see Sugimoto 2014: 201). On the other hand, Japanese businessmen were still negatively called 'economic animals' and seemed seriously over-dedicated, over-loyal and dutiful to their own companies. One of the consequences was the establishment of the Agency for Cultural Affairs in 1968. Reflecting the anti-Japanese sentiments and increasing attention to economic success and 'suffering from Japan-U.S. frictions over trade imbalances and the Nixon Shocks',[3] the Japanese diplomatic community began to see combating misunderstandings about Japanese culture and behaviour as an urgent diplomatic goal (Ozawa 2009: 275).

The Foreign Minister Takeo Fukuda also took an initiative to establish an international cultural exchange organization that initially focused on relations with the United States. This plan led to the setting up the Japan Foundation, which operated under the supervision of the cultural division of MOFA (Ministry of Foreign Affairs) in Japan in October 1972. The foundation dealt with the exchange of leading academic and cultural personnel, the promotion of Japanese studies overseas and Japanese language education and the organization of workshops and seminars to introduce Japanese culture. The objective of the foundation today is the promotion of international cultural exchange through a comprehensive range of programmes in all regions of the world. The foundation's global network consists of its Tokyo headquarters, the Kyoto Office, two Japanese-language institutes and 24 overseas offices in 23 countries (The Japan Foundation official home page). The foundation became an independent administrative institution in October 2003.

Prime Minister Noboru Takeshita spoke of his 'international cooperation initiative' in London in May 1988. The plan consisted of three major themes: cooperation for peace, enhancement of ODA (official development assistance) and strengthening international cultural exchange. At this point, cultural exchanges became the first priority issue in Japanese diplomatic strategies. After this speech, the Advisory Group on International Cultural Exchange was set up. The period between the late 1980s and early 1990s was one in which Japanese global economic power became more salient. This economic success drew much criticism in the United States, regarding the huge trade imbalances and substantially closed market conditions in Japan. After the Soviet Union collapsed, the sense of irritation and fear of the United States towards Japan helped 'Japan bashing' to grow. Reflecting on this condition in 1991, the advisory group emphasized Japan's greater contributions to the international community and established the Japan Foundation Centre for Global Partnership (日米センター literally in Japanese, the Centre for Japan and U.S. Partnership). The mission of the Centre was

> to promote collaboration between Japan and the United States with the goal of fulfilling shared global responsibilities and contributing to improvement in the world's welfare and to enhance dialogue and interchange between Japanese and U.S. citizens on a wide range of issues, thereby improving bilateral relations.
>
> *(Ozawa 2009: 277)*

The 1990s was also the time when other East Asian countries began to be acknowledged as global economic powers, which started to generate a sense of regionalism and created a new identity: 'We Asians' (Ozawa 2009: 277). Under the changing Asian communities, the second report of the Conference for the Promotion of International Cultural Exchange in 1994 underscored the importance of fostering a sense of the Asian communities' spirit for the future. This was the time; the new cultural diplomatic strategies shifted from the conventional idea of introducing Japanese traditional culture and value to responding to the need for Asian identity formation.

Yet in the 2000s, the actual diplomatic situation between Japan and the rest of East Asia, especially Korea and China, had begun to deteriorate with events such as the controversies of the Yasukuni Shrine[4] and the Japanese school history textbook problem.[5]

In response to the criticism, the Council for the Promotion of Cultural Diplomacy was launched by Prime Minister Koizumi in December 2004. The council suggested that it was important to promote a better understanding of Japan and an improvement of Japan's image (inside and outside Japan) and that '(better) understanding of Japan by the public of foreign countries may be the most influential factor for the government of that country in deciding policies and actions towards Japan' (Ozawa 2009: 278). This improvement of the nation's image through appealing to the wider public (people) both inside and outside the nation can be understood as a new initiative of cultural diplomacy in which is the now so-called 'nation branding' became a central strategy for cultural policy. To explore Japanese nation branding policy, which has resulted from governmental political and cultural initiatives, I now turn to the discussion of the specific case of 'Cool Japan.'

Cool Japan and nation branding

The Japanese government has been promoting nation branding with the slogan 'Cool Japan' since the beginning of the present century. This new initiative sought to capitalize upon Japanese popular culture such as manga, anime, video games and fashion, which have drawn the attention of consumers around the world and has become a globally popular culture. The aim of 'Cool Japan' is not only to expand the creative industry market to the global level, but also to replace the dominant 'uncool' images of Japan as a highly regulated society with rigid hierarchal working practices. This was influenced by the American journalist Douglas McGray's report (2002), in which he coined the term 'Gross National Cool' to express the increasing popularity of Japanese popular culture as the Cool Japan phenomenon.[6] Such international endorsement of valid Japanese cultural presence created the hope and expectation that Japan could recover from the prolonged economic stagnation since the late 1990s, often called 'the lost decade'. Interestingly, the high esteem for Japanese popular culture was not only the result of diplomatic efforts on the part of the Japanese government. Here a number of factors can be identified: the culture-related industries sought overseas markets because of the stagnating domestic economy; the Internet and other information technologies helped create a greater receptivity for other cultures, including Japan; there were visibly more economic, educational and cultural exchanges in what became termed the 'Asian Union' (Gresser 2004 cited in Sugiura 2008: 137).

It is often suggested that the idea of Cool Japan came from 'Cool Britannia', which was associated with Prime Minister Tony Blair's New Labour's political campaign in the 1990s. The aim of the campaign was to promote national pride, enhance cultural industries and improve the national reputation and image, through supporting and embracing British popular culture. Even though the campaign had a mixed reception, 'the Cool Britannia campaign was studied closely by the Japanese actors involved in nation branding' (Valaskivi 2013: 492). With a need for greater competitiveness in 'the age of the global economy', nation branding became a powerful strategy to enhance the nation's global economic power through highlighting its innovative, creative, aesthetic and authentic characteristics. Hence, nation branding became an important issue.

Yet, nation branding has been always already exercised in the context of public diplomacy, since the very aim of public diplomacy is to improve national image in order to create or sustain privileged or advantageous national status in the global ranking. But this was generally mobilized by the governmental apparatus delivering diplomatic messages and was largely conducted at the inter-state relations level in order to maintain smooth international relationships. But as mentioned earlier, contemporary nation branding seeks to create a positive national identity both for its own national citizens and for those in other countries (see Fan 2010). Furthermore, given the situation of the expanding networks and links between civil societies, the growing influence of non-governmental actors/agents and the increasing visibility of diverse individuals through social media, nation branding as components of cultural diplomacy carry more weight. In the new phase of global network communication, Cool Japan, therefore, became a more significant strategy of nation branding.

In the speech of the Foreign Minister Aso (who become Prime Minister 2008 to 2009) in 2006, he expressed his views about the attractiveness of the image of Cool Japan and its role as a key element in Japanese cultural diplomacy (see Iwabuchi 2015: 424). He also emphasized the effectiveness of popular culture and its capacity to increasingly influence ordinary people.[7]

> What we have now is an era in which diplomacy at the national level is affected dramatically by the climate of opinion arising from the average person. And that is exactly why we want pop culture, which is so effective in penetrating throughout the general public, to be our ally in diplomacy. To put this another way, one part of diplomacy lies in having a competitive brand image, so to speak. Now more than ever, it is impossible for this to stay entirely within the realm of the work of diplomats. It is necessary for us to draw on assistance from a broad spectrum of people who are involved in Japanese culture.
>
> *(Aso, 2006 at Digital Hollywood University 'A New Look at Cultural Diplomacy: A Call to Japan's Cultural Practitioners')*

In the wake of the rising competitiveness of Japanese popular culture, the Japanese government made sustained efforts to bring it into the sphere of cultural diplomacy. It became firmly institutionalized under Prime Minister Junichiro Koizumi (2001–2006). He actively planned to improve Japan's attractive image and soft power by encouraging the development of the cultural industries. This initiative led to the establishment of various committees and councils since the beginning of the 2000s, such as the Division of Culture and Information Related Industries (2001), the Headquarters for Intellectual Property Strategy (2003), the Japan National Tourism Organisation (2003) and the Research Committee for Content Business (2005) (see Iwabuchi 2015: 423). Although the Cool Japan policy took place in different ways through the strategies of a numbers of relevant ministries, offices, local governments and other organizations, following the Proposal by the Cool Japan Advisory Council in May 2011, the Ministry of Economy, Trade and Industry (METI) took charge of directing the 'Cool Japan/Creative Industries Policy' initiative (METI official webpage).[8] The goal of the policy is to 'promote overseas advancement of an internationally appreciated "Cool Japan" brand, cultivation of creative industries, promotion of these industries in Japan and abroad and other related initiatives from cross-industry and cross-government standpoints' (METI office web page).[9]

The Cabinet Secretariat started the 'Cool Japan Promotion Council' in 2013. In his speech in the first meeting of the "Cool Japan" Promotion Council at the Prime Minister

Shinzo Abe's Office, he stated that 50 billion yen would be submitted to the Diet for promoting 'Cool Japan'.

He remarked:

> It [Cool Japan] is one of the important policy issues for the Abe Cabinet to break through the stagnation that hangs over Japan and to develop the country further from now on, *have the Japanese people feel confident of the greatness of Japan* including its tradition and culture, and make all people realize that *things from Japan are great,* which will also lead to the burgeoning of a sense of respect for Japan.
>
> *(Abe, 2013, Prime Minister of Japan and His Cabinet*
> *official home page, emphasizes added)*[10]

Cool Japan's internal and external projection

Abe's political intention in the speech is clear: Cool Japan was understood not only as nation branding to boost Japan to a higher position in the Nations Brands Index but also as a domestic political device to reinforce positive self-esteem for Japanese citizens. Drawing on Simon Anholt's theory of branding in the context of marketing (2007: 6), Valaskivi correctly points out that establishing a strong internal culture sharing the same values and 'the spirit of the organization' is a crucial factor for building a powerful reputation. A successful nation brand needs a good perception of itself. Since 'branding is nevertheless first and foremost directed inward, towards the nation itself, aimed at creating a stronger, more coherent sense of the national "self" and building self-esteem' (Valaskivi 2013: 490). The Cool Japan initiative, with its various governmental activities, could help fashion a new narrative of the nation to reinforce the sense of national belonging. Such self-internalization of the nation's brand image could be constructed by the process of re-discovering Japan, re-valuing cultural heritage and tradition and re-articulating the 'taken-for-granted' social and cultural values and meanings, at the same time recognizing 'new' Japan by using carefully chosen symbols of politically invented new narratives and meanings.

However, how far the Cool Japan nation branding actually affected Japanese citizens' perception of Japan and nurtured national pride remains an open question. According to the report of the public opinion survey on social awareness conducted by the Government Public Relations Office in the Cabinet Office in 2016, to the question of what you can be most proud of in Japan and the Japanese people, the highest percentage of answers were from those who thought that Japan had 'good public safety (a high security society)' (56.6%). The second highest percentage group was those who were proud of 'beautiful nature' (55.4%) and the third highest group was those who were proud of 'excellent culture and arts' (49.9%). The 'excellent culture and arts' group has not been the leading category for more than 23 years (Overview of the Public Opinion Survey on Social Awareness 2016: 13).[11]

The supplemental public opinion survey, conducted in 2009, further detailed people's opinions about Japanese culture. To answer the question of what are you most proud of in 'Japanese culture and the arts' towards the rest of the world, the answer with the highest percentage was traditional art (64.7%); the second highest was a group who was proud of historical architecture and spots/remains/ruins (56.4%), and the third highest was those who a proud of Japanese food culture (31.5%).[12] What these statistics illuminate is that Japanese citizens think that both culture in general and contemporary popular culture involved in Cool Japan in particular are not necessarily the things one can be the most proud of. This is to say that the Cool Japan initiative along with the other new narratives and images of

Japan driven by political imperatives, failed to adequately reinforce Japanese identity and national pride.

There is a belief in 'culture' as a means to help nurture Japanese pride though embracing Japanese traditional and contemporary culture.[13] However, it seems that 'culture' can only work to create 'imaginary' Cool Japan or the rhetorical power to create an 'imaginary' Japan. Since Noriko Aso claims that, '[I]n Japan, when the going gets tough – too much international scrutiny, failure to achieve domestic political goals, loss of confidence in political economic institutions – a common response is to bring up "culture"' (McVeigh 2004: 198; see also Aso 2002 cited in Daliot-Bul 2009: 260–261). Daliot-Bul concludes that 'culture' (*bunka*) is thus often positioned at the rhetorical core of national renovation projects' in the context of Japanese politics. Daliot-Bul also elaborates on the national renovation project, Cool Japan. No matter how 'culture' can help to reinforce a sense of national identity, the Cool Japan initiative can be seen as a political attempt to re-discover 'Japan's national cultural power and a reflection of the requisites of disseminating influential message for creating national identity, which formed "national pride"' (see Daliot-Bul 2009: 259).

In the Intellectual Property Strategic Programs in 2005,

> [t]he authors encourage the Japanese people to sufficiently 'utilize [their] *outstanding capabilities in inventing and creating*' (Nihonjin no mottmo sugureta sozoryoku sosakuryoku) and on contributing to the development of the world's futures and civilizations with the inventions and creations of Japanese people, aspiring for Japan to '*uphold an honoured position in the world*'.
>
> *(Intellectual Property Strategic Program 2005: 2 cited in Daliot-Bul 2009: 260 emphasis added)*

This suggests that there are 'recurrent self-congratulatory and ethnocentric assertions embedded in it' (Daliot-Bul, 2009:260). Daliot-Bul concludes that 'the Japan Brand Strategy is thus also seen as a means to revitalize patriotic pride and recruit those patriotic feelings for national ends'. Hence, it can be viewed as a rhetorical imaginary of Japan in the domestic political context. So far there is, however, no clear evidence indicating that the Japan Brand Strategy, in other words, Japan's nation branding equipped with the Cool Japan initiative, has helped to revitalize patriotic pride or a sense of love for the country. The question of Japanese identity for ordinary Japanese people cannot always be seen as an imminent issue in everyday contexts, since such consciousness often arises in non-ordinariness, including cases of encountering situations that make Japanese people feel alienated or disorientated through the unfamiliar (e.g. going abroad or being in a non-Japanese community). Such feelings can always be seen as dependent on particular contexts. Amongst those that centrally emphasize national identity and belonging are global mega events, such as an the Olympic Games or International Expositions. There are situations that place nations in 'the same time and place' as they are invited to compare and compete with each other. Joining in such politicized games, means that nations are required to win in the sporting game, as well as in the political and economic game among nations.

Here, it is worth noting that there is an interesting public opinion survey on patriotic sentiment/spirits conducted by the Cabinet Office Minister's Secretariat Government Public Relations Office. This annual survey shows that Japanese people's social awareness includes a question about the feeling of love for one's country, by asking people to respond in terms of whether their feelings are: 'strong/do not know/weak'. In the period of more than three and half decades when the surveys were conducted, the highest percentage (58%) is for the group of those who answered that they have much stronger/relatively stronger feeling of love for the nation than other people do; this occurred February 2013 (Overview of the Public Opinion Survey on Social Awareness, 2016: 1).[14]

The campaign to host the Tokyo Olympics and Paralympics had started a few years before the survey. Many committees and organizations had been established, such as the committee to campaign to host the Olympics in 2011, and it had been taken over by the Tokyo Organizing Committee of the Olympic and Paralympic Games since 2014. The Japanese Olympic Committee (JOC) organized a series of campaign activities, such as a parade of the 71 London Olympic medallists at Tokyo Ginza Street in August 2012, which attracted a crowd of more than 500,000 people (Japanese Olympic Committee official webpage).[15] These campaigns did not just aim to appeal to the IOC, but also to create excitement amongst Japanese people. They also helped to develop an atmosphere conducive to supporting the national project and generate patriotic pride. Accordingly, Tokyo as the Olympic city has become an important platform for Japan to create a new image. In the next section, I investigate how global cities, such as Tokyo, have the potential to become creative cities, which could play a key role in engendering favourable national images.

The city as a cultural imaginary device

Today the city can be seen as a main cultural powerhouse often discussed in the context of growing Asian cities in the age of globalization (see Yeoh, 1999, 2005) and seen as one of the most important components of cultural policy (Lim 2012: 261). Cities, then, should not be seen as just vital places for the concentration of financial and political power, but also vibrant spaces for the display of cultural capital and emblematic spaces for nation branding. The idea of city as a 'cultural powerhouse' (Yeoh 2005: 945) engendered "'Asian mega projects' such as Tokyo's Teleport Town (*Toukyo rinkai fukutoshin keikaku*) and Yokohama Minato Mirai 21 Project' (Yeoh 2005: 947). Both can be seen as creative city projects that were part of 'a new strategic urban planning method to reinvent the city as a vibrant hub of creative industries with the potential to improve the "quality of life" for citizens' (Landry 2008 cited in Kim 2015: 1) and to enhance the national image.

According to the report of Policy of Cultural Affairs in Japan, Fiscal 2015, the Creative City Network of Japan was established in January 2013 so as to improve and enhance the network of creative cities all over Japan. 'The Agency of Cultural Affairs supports this network in order to promote the Cultural and Artistic Creative City throughout Japan' (Agency for Cultural Affair 2015: 33).[16] The purpose is 'to be a foundation to construct a peaceful and symbiotic *Asian creative city network* as well as to contribute to the reconstruction and regeneration of Japanese society by spreading and developing creative cities in our country' (Creative City Network Japan English homepage, emphasizes added).[17]

Similar statements, targeting 'the development of a cultural and artistic creative city' throughout Japanese cities in order to create a network with Asian cities, can be found in 'the Creative Tokyo Proposal' announced by the Ministry of Economy, Trade and Industry' in 2012. The proposal manifests a vital role of the capital city, Tokyo. The proposal has a subtitle saying 'Moving towards Creative Tokyo-Transforming Tokyo into a Creative Hub', which expresses that Japan today should build a new society through the combined power of its industries, economy and culture and that Tokyo should become 'the most prominent creative hub in Asia' by fostering the development and diversity of Japan's creative industries (The Creative Tokyo Proposal homepage).[18]

One of the major tasks is,

> With the support of Tokyo districts, *Japanese creativity will be conveyed across both internationally and domestically*. Through this, we will seek to bring in talented human resources, relevant information and funds from all around the world. We will also aim to establish Tokyo as a leading creative hub.
>
> (The Creative Tokyo Proposal, emphasis added)[19]

In this light, Tokyo is the main platform for expanding Japanese creativity both externally and internally and is expected to be become the leading creative city in Asia. This can be seen as a reflection of Japan's concerns about losing its prominent position and its presence in Asia, since the rapidly growing Chinese economy and expanding Korean cultural industries, generated fears of being overtaken and threatening Japan's pride in Cool Japan. Such concerns for revitalization of Tokyo's brand competitiveness had already been expressed in the Creating a New Japan Proposal (*Atarashii nihon no kozo*) produced by the Cool Japan Advisory Council in May 2011. More precisely, the council proposed that one way to enhance the creative industries and the content industry was to collaborate with the tourist campaign in order to increase Japan's presence and attractiveness. It also suggested that making links between the Aoyama, Roppongi, Ginza and Sumida regions (where 'the Skytree' was built) would help to create a diversified Tokyo brand ('Creating New Japan' 2011: 10). Except for the Sumida region, Tokyo's southwest city districts, Aoyama, Roppongi and Ginza have been internationally well acknowledged as 'innovative', 'creative', 'fashionable', 'trendy' and 'sophisticated urbane modern' city areas. Yet there is currently a new type of creative city plan being developed, which could draw our attention to various innovative and practical efforts to produce a new city landscape.

Cultural resources in the central Tokyo North (CTN)

To challenge the current dominant image of cultural richness of south-central Tokyo, (Aoyama, Roppoingi, Ginza etc.), the new urban cultural plan (proposed in 2014 and currently being implemented), has re-discovered the rich cultural resources of north-central and eastern Tokyo (Ueno, Hongo, Akihabara, Kanda, Jinbocho and Yushima). The districts have been characterized as follows,

> This area is composed of Ueno, home of Japan's largest concentration of history and art museums, as well as the Tokyo University of the Arts; Hongo, a centre of academic learning home to the University of Tokyo; Yanesen, a popular spot among foreign tourists filled with old shops, alleys, row houses, and temples; Yushima, a neighbourhood of religious and culinary culture entered on the axis stretching from Yushima Seido, a Confucian Temple, and Kanda Shrine to Yushima Tenjin Shrine; Jimbocho, the birthplace of modern learning in Japan once familiar to Sun Yat-sen, Lu xun, Zhou Enlai, and other young leaders of Aisa, and Today a district of private universities, publishers, and bookstores; and Akihabara, known today across the world not only as an electronics town, but also as a mecca of manga, anime and game culture.
>
> (The Report of the Tokyo Cultural Resources District Vision 2016: 2)[20]

This project has been driven by the Tokyo Cultural Resources Alliance, which was founded as a result of preliminary discussions by the Tokyo Cultural Resources District Vision in

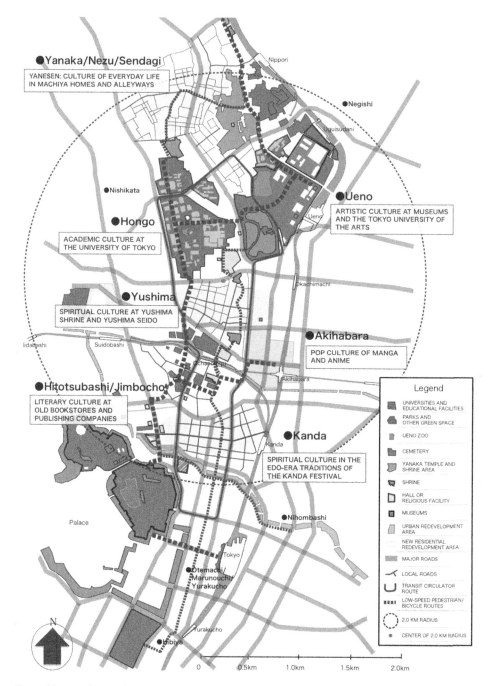

Figure 35.1   Tokyo Cultural Resources District Vision
Source: Tokyo Cultural Resources District Vision Homepage.

June 2014.[21] The participants consist of 'practitioners and specialists belonging to the cabinet, Ministry of Land, Infrastructure, and Transport, Cultural Agency, universities, private research organizations and companies' (Tokyo Cultural resources District Vision Homepage: 3).[22]

The Tokyo Cultural Resources District Vision emphasizes the importance of Tokyo's historical tradition of cultural and intellectual creativity in order to increase competitiveness in the global nation brand market and enhance Japan's presence in the world. They postulate that although Tokyo has enormous potential to develop its rich cultural resources, it has remained far behind in its efforts to become a world-class creative city. Since the Edo period (1603–1868), the north-central and eastern areas of Tokyo, which were the main commoner neighbourhoods, did not become subjected to large-scale redevelopment and so *survived* relatively intact the past half century of prioritization of motorway construction and high-rise buildings. This city planning phase is epitomized by the 1964 Olympic Games Metropolitan Expressway, Aoyama Boulevard and Olympic facilities, such as the Yoyogi National Gymnasium and Komazawa Olympic Park Stadium. After that, many high-rise buildings in West Shinjuku were increasingly constructed in the 1970s. Since the 1980s, Roppongi, Ebisu, Shingagwa and Shiodome in south-central Tokyo have become the main areas to create a fashionable cultural centre relying on large-scale city planning (see Tokyo Cultural Resources District Vision Report 2016: 1).[23]

The central Tokyo North's cultural resources and an idea of 'tradition'

The Tokyo Cultural Resources Alliance declared that the 2020 Tokyo Olympics should not repeat the same scale of city planning as the 1964 Tokyo Olympics. The Alliance emphasizes that large-scale redevelopments and the 'scrap and rebuild' format are dated principles. The Tokyo Cultural Resources Alliance also argued that Tokyo's distinctiveness is not because of its huge population, economic power, political centre, advanced technology or mature consumer culture. The Alliance explained that looking back to the 17th century, Edo, as Tokyo was known until 1868, was already the world's largest city and the place that prompted Japanese modernization. In fact, Edo was a multicultural metropolis that was created by the *Sankin Kotai* system (the feudal lords with their retainers were required to spend every other year in residence in Edo. The system created chances to bring many local cultures from all over Japan to Edo and took Edo culture back to their regions). Accordingly, Edo was a cultural powerhouse, which developed with a flourishing cosmopolitan culture among commoners, such as *Kabuki* theatre, *ukiyo-e* prints, *haiku* poetry and Dutch learning. Following the Meiji Period (1868–1912), many other cultural fields, such as architecture, literature, painting and film were also largely cultivated in Tokyo. Hence, The Alliance concluded that Tokyo had always already been a city encompassing a huge cultural heritage with clear world competitive value (see Tokyo Cultural Resources District Vision Report 2016: 1–2).[24]

It is worth noting that a good deal of the traditional cultural assets cultivated over the last several centuries in Tokyo, as explained earlier, are still to be found in the Central Tokyo North (CTN) district, the areas the Tokyo Cultural Resources Alliance wants to revitalize. This focuses on the discourse of Japanese tradition as an unchangeable authentic cultural asset, has also been used in expressing the Tokyo Cultural Resources District Vision's of the 2020 Tokyo Olympics. In its report, the Tokyo Cultural Resources Alliance claimed that 'with 2020 Tokyo Olympics in mind, Tokyo should improve its attractiveness by promoting the uncontested value of Central North Tokyo, which has long been cultivated through Edo and Meiji's culture and life (Tokyo Cultural Resources District Vision Report 2016: 4).

The discourse of 'Japanese tradition' portrays 'a historical Japanese national character that is radically different from anything else and is expressed in a diversified range of symbolic forms, old and new' (see Moeran 1996 cited in Daliot-Bul 2009: 253). This is why Japanese tradition has often been used and re-used as an effective means to create an ahistorical image of Japan.

One of the core members of The Tokyo Cultural Resources Alliance, a professor at the University of Tokyo, Shunya Yoshimi, advocates that Japan as the 2020 Olympic host country should pursue new values and social perspectives, which should be different from those of the 1964 Tokyo Olympics. Rather than executing a large-scale city infrastructure and prioritizing motor car culture (which were central to the plans for the 1964 Tokyo Olympics), Japan today should pay more attention to revitalizing and recreating something that has been damaged, destroyed and 'disconnected' due to the urbanizing process in Tokyo. Cultural assets in the Central Tokyo North districts are mostly survivors, irreplaceable cultural resources created in the past-Japanese tradition. Hence, Yoshimi's proposal further emphasizes the importance of the revitalization and sustainability of 'tradition' as the main vision of the Alliance.

Tokyo as a cultural device for nation branding

Recently, Central Tokyo North has been also acknowledged as an ideal place to realize the Tokyo Metropolitan Government's Tokyo Vision for Arts and Culture. It outlines the idea of 'Tokyo as a city of individuality and diversity, born of the coexistence and fusion of traditional and modern culture' (Tokyo Cultural Resources District Vision Report 2016: 2).[25] Both Japanese traditional culture and contemporary popular culture lie in the Central Tokyo North area. The Alliance believed that this principle is congruent with a fundamental idea of the creative cities movement that cities 'must be rooted in cultural tradition, creative talent and tolerance of diversity' (Tokyo Cultural Resources District Vision Report 2016: 2).[26] In line with this definition, the Alliance asserts that 21st century leading cities will be those cities that respect cultural tradition with open-mindedness to diversity. These cities can also attract gifted creative people from around the world.

Therefore, there is the need to reassess and revitalize the cultural resources a city has accumulated over its history. The Alliance emphasized the significance of 'restoring the unity of the Tokyo Cultural Resources District in Central Tokyo North in order to renovate the region as an epicentre for culture, arts, and science' district through 'connecting' Ueno (arts culture), Yanasen (community culture), Hongo (intellectual culture), Yushima (religious and spiritual culture), Jimbocho (publishing culture) and Akihabara (popular culture). This can 'produce the space where people enjoy walking, dwelling and living. This will be a vital strategy to create Tokyo's "legacy" in the world' (Tokyo Cultural Resources District Vision Report 2016: 4). This view can also resonate with the International Olympic Committee (IOC)'s principle for the Olympic Games in the 21st century, 'sustainable legacies'. Hence, the Tokyo Cultural Resources Alliance concludes that '(all these processes) will promote not only the 2020 Olympic city, Tokyo's cultural presence, but rather Japan's cultural presence in the world' (Tokyo Cultural Resources District Vision Report 2016: 3).[27]

Here, we can see Tokyo has been cast as a nation-branding device. There are many attractive spots, which can be 'connected' to each other in various ways to create Tokyo Central North as a cultural unit. An artist, art producer and professor of the Arts at Tokyo University, Katsuhiko Hibino, observes that 'Tokyo is constituted of various different regionalities/localities.' (*Asahi Newspaper*, evening, 6 January: 4). This suggests that each community and region in Tokyo could possibly become 'a cultural unit'. This is what Yoshimi calls 'community as a cultural museum'. This means that each region contains various cultural entities, which can be represented as unknown/forgotten narratives and should be revitalized by rediscovering traditional cultural connectivities and networks that existed in the past. This idea can also be further stretched to the whole of Tokyo. Accordingly, the attractive 'cultural units' throughout Tokyo can be connected to each other to create a wider cultural constellation. Eventually Tokyo as a creative city and a device of national branding, could become an influential world class cultural centre, Tokyo as a cultural museum, which is therefore able to represent and enhance the distinctiveness of Japan's cultural presence in the world.

Concluding remarks

The Tokyo Cultural Resources District Vision says that 'The 2020 Tokyo Olympics will take place roughly 150 years after the Meiji Restoration (1868). The first half of this period encompassed the 75 years of modernization and militarization, and the second half was the 75 years of recovery, high growth, and maturation of society' (The Tokyo Cultural Resources District Vision official homepage: 6).[28] In the second 75 years, Japan had to develop its cultural diplomacy for the promotion of its international presence in order to make a better economic and political relationship with the west and the rest of Asia. With the increasingly concern for cultural diplomacy, cultural policy gradually became a central and firmly institutionalized issue. Promoting the various culture exchange programmes was seen as an effective way to further mutual understanding between Japan and the United States, as well as the rest of Asia (especially Korea and China). In the 2000s under the Prime Minister Junichiro Koizumi, cultural policy was firmly institutionalized along with a new initiative, 'Cool Japan'. The increasing global popularity of Japanese pop culture, such as manga, anime and TV games, the so-called soft power, became tightly incorporated into nation branding. The Cool Japan Brand Strategy became carefully embedded into the broader political message and diplomatic rhetoric, not only to improve Japan's image, but also to reinforce a sense of national belonging and patriotic pride for Japanese people.

Although there is no clear evidence that Japan's nation brand strategy worked to create a new image of Japan and reinforce the sense of national identity, some evidence indicates that the 2020 Tokyo Olympics campaigns seem to have stimulated Japanese people's awareness of 'Japan in the world' and of being Japanese. In this light, Tokyo as a creative city is now expected to play a vital role in promoting Japan's nation branding with a new image of contemporary Japan. In 2014, the launch of the Tokyo Cultural Resources Alliance drew not only on people who came from the government, but also those from universities, private research organizations and companies. These groups were involved in taking the initiative to revitalize the regional cultural assets, which have survived and enhanced Japanese cultural distinctiveness over radical urbanization, which had been taking place since the 1964 Tokyo Olympics. The areas of Ueno, Hongo, Yanesen, Yushima, Jimbocho and Akihabara, consumption and production zones of 'cultural capital' (Bourdieu and Passeron 1977) with the cultural differences and values, used to be connected in the past but are now disconnected.[29] The Tokyo Cultural Resources Alliance seeks to re-connect these areas to create a walkable and accessible concentrated 'cultural capital' zone, which can empower and increase the attractiveness not only of the local communities, but also of Tokyo as a whole.[30] All their various suggestions entail the re-discovery of traditional local stories and the creation of new cultural narratives with the intention of offering new urban experiences.

These practices are often carried out by cultural specialists. They are able to extract new values from existing information, knowledge and experiences along with new ways of interpretations and meanings. Cultural specialists are usually people who work in creative occupations, such as artists, cultural practitioners and cultural entrepreneurs. This links to the debate on the two sides of their socio-cultural influence. On the one hand, 'artists and cultural producers, often called the "creative class" (Florida 2002), are seen as triggering gentrification processes, since their presence attracts affluent consumers and dwellers who are supposed to share aesthetic value and lifestyle with the "creative class" (see Gainza 2016: 2). The subsequent environmental changes can eventually lead to the evacuation of the lower-class original inhabitants. On the other hand, they have the capacity to revitalize forgotten cultural capital in communities in order to stimulate economic value and improve the habitants' quality of life. The debate is still oscillating between cultural innovation for people and its negative effects in terms of gentrification (see Gainza 2016: 2).

Yet, public institutions with their rigid regulations and often highly hierarchically structures tend to fail to fully deal with vital points of city life in terms of the people's lived everyday practices, such as the capacity for old people to walk easily to shops, for children and mothers to walk safely to nursery and for inhabitants to live in a good secure environment. Cultural specialists with extensive webs across various local sectors could make crucial links between cultural practices and lived experience with community-based networks and collaborative projects and participatory initiatives. Hence, with more self-governing administrative structure, their activities can offer practical and realistic solutions for many problems.

Here, we can see that the most important component for creative cities is collaboration among cultural specialists, local communities, the private sectors, Non-Profit Organizations, governmental institutions and various civic groups. With this in mind, all the practices of the Tokyo Cultural Resources District Vision should not be univocal but should endeavour to pick up as many voices as possible and incorporate their various visions and practices. This resonates with Japanese cultural policy scholar Yasuo Ito's definition of cultural policy. He asserts '(Cultural policy) serves to clarify a consensus building system which sustains the activities of various cultural entities (the government, local communities, artists, art practitioners, corporations and citizens) .... It also helps people to share the same assumptions [value] in the outcome/product of cultural activities in order to pass them on to the next generation' (2008 author translation). Hence, this definition can echo with the practices of the Tokyo Cultural Resources District Vision, since the Alliance seeks a wider network of business, government, universities and the private sectors, by emphasizing the importance of collaborative and participative cultural practices in order to produce a 'new version' of creative Tokyo.

In the 2000s, Japanese cultural policy had become weighed down and subjected to the state's policy by the keyword, 'creativity' (see Valaskivi 2013: 495). The *Creating a New Japan* proposal in 2011 by the Cool Japan Advisory Council suggested 'Creative Tokyo', which is the idea of branding Tokyo by combining several areas to orchestrate different pieces of pre-existing cultural assets. In this context, creativity can be understood not as a principle to seek something new, but rather a strategy to extract value from the existing, the original, or traditional, to create new narratives. Thus, the Tokyo Cultural Resources District Vision can be seen as strong evidence for the potential to explore and experiment with 'creativity': how to extricate values and meanings from existing (traditional) cultural assets; in what way to re-construct cultural practices with and for people; how different people's voices are in play; how these re-discovered cultural assets can create a new image and enhance cultural presence for Tokyo; and how all these re-constructive processes can help to promote the Japan brand. In line with this, it can be conceived that some of the oft-cited critical factors for nation branding and cultural policy (often characterized by keywords, such as: attractiveness, distinctiveness and competitiveness), can only be realized through interactive, participatory, incorporative and self-governing activities with both the public and the private sectors over time. For a deeper and more nuanced understanding of the range of meanings incorporated in the term cultural policy, a fuller range of historical, political, social and cultural dimensions of Japanese society need to be carefully examined. Innovative initiatives such as the Tokyo Cultural Resources District Vision, then, can provide the stimulus for widening our frame of reference and opening up new horizons for future cultural policy.

Notes

1 In fact, Japan was one of the first to present itself to the world with a national pavilion at the 1867 Paris Exposition. This was followed by the participation of the new Japanese Meiji nation-state at the 1873 Vienna International Exposition.

2 Soft power – The term, soft power was coined by Joseph Nye (1990) reflecting on the Cold War; it was believed that 'cultural diplomacy may well be a more appropriate weapon than warfare' (Anholt 2015:194). This development was further fuelled by the Bush Administration's response to the September 11 terrorist attack in 2001. It must note that Cool Japan was prompted not only by nation branding but also by the spreading 'soft power paradigm' (see Fan, Y 2008).

3 U.S president Richard Nixon stopped the direct convertibility of the U.S. dollar to gold in 1971 ('dollar shock') and cancelled the Bretton Woods system in 1973. Nixon also terminated the U.S. confrontational policy toward China without consultation with Japan, in 1972. 'These shocking experiences reminded the Japanese leaders of their catastrophic isolation in the 1930s and 1940s' (Ozawa 2009:274).

4 Prime Minister Junichiro Koizumi visited the shrine for those who died in the service of Japan. Among the 2.4 million souls of dead soldiers enshrined, some were, however, World War II war criminals. The visit of the prime minister was seen as violating the principle of a pacific nation and provoked memories of Japan's military/fascist past. This is the reason the prime minister was strongly criticized by China and South Korea.

5 The problem was the recognition of the historical past by the Japanese government. There are strong discrepancies in the war history between Japan and countries that were occupied by Japan during wartime, such as China and Korea. This has led to a long debate since the 1950s, yet it became more serious at the time of Prime Minister Koizumi's government.

6 It should be noted that Japan has proved to be attractive to the West with the forms of Japonism appearing in the Western imagination several times in the past. In the 19th century, the French Impressionists were influenced by Japanese art, and Japanese pottery and ornaments also become popular consumer goods in the United Kingdom. In the 1980s, the global success of Japanese business organizational systems and marketing strategies also drew much attention from the world. 'Tentatively, it appears that "Japan" has been either admired or feared and hated in "the West"' (Valaskivi 2013, 501; see Sugimoto 2014, Napier 2007 and Sugiura 2008).

7 See Hirai (2015) and Huang (2011) for a detailed account of the reception of Japanese popular culture in East Asia.

8 www.meti.go.jp/english/policy/mono_info_service/creative_industries/creative_industries.html (accessed 20 Sep 2016).

9 www.meti.go.jp/english/policy/mono_info_service/creative_industries/creative_industries.html (Accessed 20 Sep 2016).

10 http://japan.kantei.go.jp/96_abe/actions/201303/04cooljpn_e.html (accessed 20 Sep 2016).

11 www.gov-online.go.jp/eng/pdf/summarys15.pdf (Accessed 24 Sep 2016). The survey was conducted in the period 28 January - 14 February 2016. It covered more than 10,000 individuals (comprised of adults over 20 years old) from all over Japan, and the response rate was 58.8% (5,877 individuals). Multiple answers were allowed.

12 http://survey.gov-online.go.jp/h21/h21-bunka/2-5.html (Accessed 24 Sep 2016). The survey was conducted by the by the Government Public Relations Office in the Cabinet Office in the period

5–15 November 2009. It covered more than 3,000 individuals (comprised of adults over 20 years old) from all over Japan, and the response rate was 61.8% (1,853 individuals). Multiple answers were allowed.

13 The concept of culture (*bunka,* 文化) in Japan has been transformed in relation to the process of nation-state formation. Although the term, *bunka* was not very widely used before the 20th century, it has often been associated with governmental strategies that include not only public diplomacy but also political devices; it is based on the totality of the practices, beliefs and values that are held to unify society. A more nuanced understanding of the range of meanings in the term *bunka* would require the examination of the range of other strands in the social terrain that relate to the process of modern state formation and consumer society. In this chapter, the focus will be confined to the political strategic perspective on culture.

14 www.gov-online.go.jp/eng/pdf/summarys15.pdf (Accessed 24 Sep 2016).

15 https://tokyo2020.jp/en/news/bid/20120820-01.html (Accessed 24 Sep 2016).

16 www.bunka.go.jp/english/about_us/policy_of_cultural_affairs/pdf/2015_policy.pdf (Accessed 24 Sep 2016). The Agency of Cultural Affairs also established 'the Office for Promotion of the Creative City, the Agency for Cultural Affairs in April 2014, which provides advice to local government in order to promote the creation of the Cultural and Artistic Creative City' (Agency for Cultural Affair, *The Policy of Cultural Affairs in Japan, Fiscal 2015:* 33).

17 http://ccn-j.net/english/ (Accessed 20 Sep 2016).

18 www.meti.go.jp/policy/mono_info_service/mono/creative/creative_tokyo/about/sengen_en.html (Accessed 20 Sep 2016).

19 www.meti.go.jp/policy/mono_info_service/mono/creative/creative_tokyo/about/sengen_en.html (Accessed 20 Sep 2016).

20 http://tohbun.jp/wp-content/uploads/Homepage-Tokyo-Cultural-Resources-District-Vision.pdf (Accessed 20 Sep 2016).

21 'The Tokyo Cultural Resources Alliance and the Tokyo Cultural Resources District Promotion Committee (tentative name), a public-private-academic-industry organization envisioned to be established in 2018, will take the lead in realizing the Tokyo Cultural Resources District vision' (the Report of the Tokyo Cultural Resources District Vision 2016:23). see http://tohbun.jp/wp-content/uploads/Homepage-Tokyo-Cultural-Resources-District-Vision.pdf (Accessed 20 Sep 2016).

22 http://tohbun.jp/wp-content/uploads/Homepage-Tokyo-Cultural-Resources-District-Vision.pdf (Accessed 24 Sep 2016).

23 http://tohbun.jp/wp-content/uploads/Homepage-Tokyo-Cultural-Resources-District-Vision.pdf (Accessed 24 Sep 2016).

24 http://tohbun.jp/wp-content/uploads/Homepage-Tokyo-Cultural-Resources-District-Vision.pdf (Accessed 24 Sep 2016).

25 http://tohbun.jp/wp-content/uploads/Homepage-Tokyo-Cultural-Resources-District-Vision.pdf (Accessed 24 Sep 2016).

26 http://tohbun.jp/wp-content/uploads/Homepage-Tokyo-Cultural-Resources-District-Vision.pdf (Accessed 24 Sep 2016).

27 http://tohbun.jp/wp-content/uploads/Homepage-Tokyo-Cultural-Resources-District-Vision.pdf (Accessed 24 Sep 2016).

28 http://tohbun.jp/wp-content/uploads/Homepage-Tokyo-Cultural-Resources-District-Vision.pdf (Accessed 24 Sep 2016).

29 Today it is hard to see the inter-connectivities between regional/local cultures that once were more interwoven. Yet, in the past, there existed a walking route from Hongo to Ueno, Yanaka, Yushima, Akihabara and Jimbocho. There was a daily walking route for Ogai Mori who is one of the most famous novelist in the Meiji and Taisho periods. He walked around entire areas of Central Tokyo North, which houses the academic, literary and spiritual legacies of Edo culture (see Tokyo Cultural Resources District Vision Report 2016:14). This suggests that there might be invisible paths that could possibly be made visible again. The district also has a notable concentration of traditional buildings from the Meiji period and earlier. Some of them are registered as cultural heritage properties. Part of the planned cultural programme of the Tokyo Cultural Resources Alliance is to preserve them and re-activate and re-use them for communal cultural practices (Tokyo Cultural Resources District Vision Report 2016: 29). The preference for conservation of local vernacular styles through the reactivation of traditional buildings also helps to create new urban

designscapes. These buildings provide distinctive aesthetics to reinforce local identities and attract both cultural consumers and producers. A good example is the contemporary art gallery, SCAI Bathhouse in Yanaka, which was a public bath in the past.

30 This process can also create new channels for flows of information, knowledge and experiences in Tokyo. In the past, cities were often seen in terms of organic metaphors (See Tamari 2014), and many have argued that '[h]istorically the city grew organically' (Landry 2000:58). The city has never developed in a linear way but is continuously changing and transforming to adjust to ever-changing environments.

References

Agency for Cultural Affair, *The Policy of Cultural Affairs in Japan, Fiscal 2015.*

Andy, C (2000) *The Creative City, A Toolkit for Urban Innovators*, London: Routledge.

Anholt, A (2015) Public Diplomacy and Competitive Identity: Where's the Link?, in: Golan, G.J., Yang, S.-U. and Kinsey, D.F. (ed.) *International Public Relations and Public Diplomacy, Communication and Engagement*, p. 4. New York: Peter Lang Publishing.

Asahi Newspaper (2016), evening paper, 6 January: 4, '*Let's find out alternative values for 2020 Tokyo Olympic*' discussions with Shunya Yoshimi and Katsuhiko Hibino.

Aso, N (2002) Sumptuous Re-past: The 1964 Tokyo Olympic Arts Festival, *Positions* 10 (1): 7–38.

Aso, T (2006) '*A New Look at Cultural Diplomacy: A Call to Japan's Cultural Practitioners*' The official web-page of Ministry of Foreign Affairs of Japan, www.mofa.go.jp/announce/fm/aso/speech0604-2.html (Accessed 22 Sep 2016).

Bourdieu, P and Passeron J C (1977) *Reproduction in Education, Society and Culture*, London: Sage Publications.

Brienza, C (2013) Did Manga Conquer America? Implications for the Cultural Policy of 'Cool Japan', *International Journal of Cultural Policy* 20 (4): 383–398.

Creative City Network Japan English Homepage, http://ccn-j.net/english/ (Accessed 22 Sep 2016).

The Creative Tokyo Proposal, www.meti.go.jp/policy/mono_info_service/mono/creative/creative_tokyo/about/sengen_en.html.

Daliot-Bul, M (2009) Japan Brand Strategy: The Taming of 'Cool Japan' and the Challenges of Cultural Planning in a Postmodern Age, *Social Science Japan Journal* 12 (2): 247–266.

Fan, Y (2008) Soft Power: Power of Attraction or Confusion? *Place Branding and Public Diplomacy* 4(2): 147–158.

Fan, Y (2010) Branding the Nation: Towards a Better Understanding, *Place Branding and Public Diplomacy* 6 (2): 97–103.

Florida, R.L. (2002) *The Rise of the Creative Class: And How It's Transforming Work, Leisure, Community and Everyday Life*, New York: Basic Books.

Gresser, E (2004) The Emerging Asian Union?, *Policy Report* (May), http://altbib.com/bak/dox/1856.html (accessed 22 May 2017).

Hirai, T (2015) The Reception of Japanese Animation and Its Determinants in Taiwan, South Korea and China, *Animation: An Interdisciplinary Journal* 10 (2): 154–169.

Huang, S (2011) Nation-Branding and Transnational Consumption: Japan-Mania and the Korean Wave in Taiwan, *Media, Culture & Society* 33 (1): 3–18.

Ito, Y (2008) Net Tam: What Is Cultural Policy in Toyota Art Management, www.nettam.jp/course/cultural-policy/3/ (Accessed 22 Sep 2016).

Iwabuchi, K (2015) 'Pop-Culture Diplomacy in Japan: Soft Power, Nation Branding and the Question of "International Cultural Exchange"', *International Journal of Cultural Policy* 21 (4): 419–432.

The Japan Foundation official home page, www.jpf.go.jp/e/about/index.html.

Kawashima, N (2012) Corporate Support for the Arts in Japan: Beyond Emulation of the Western Models, *International Journal of Cultural Policy* 18 (3): 295–307.

Kim, C (2015) Locating Creative City Policy in East Asia: Neoliberalism, Developmental State and Assemblage of East Asian Cities, *International Journal of Cultural Policy*, 23: 312–330. doi:10.1080/10286632.2015.1048242.

Kong, L (2014) Transnational Mobilities and the Making of Creative Cities, *Theory Culture & Society* 31 (7–8): 273–289.

Landry, C (2008) *The Art of City Making*, London, Sterling, VA: Earthscan.

Lim, L (2012) Introduction for Special Issue on Cultural Policy in Asia, *International Journal of Cultural Policy* 18 (3): 261–264.

Roche, M (1998) Mega-Events, Culture and Modernity: Expos and the Origins of Public Culture, *International Journal of Cultural Policy* 5 (1): 1–31.

McVeigh, B.J. (2004) *Nationalism of Japan: Managing and Mystifying Identity*, Oxford: Rowman and Littlefield.

The Ministry of Economy, Trade and Industry (METI) Official Webpage, www.meti.go.jp/english/policy/mono_info_service/creative_industries/creative_industries.html.

Moeran, B (1996) The Orient Strikes Back: Advertising and Imagining Japan, *Theory Culture & Society* 13(3): 77–112.

Najita, T and Harootunian, HD (1990) Japanese Revolt against the West: Political and Cultural Criticism in the Twentieth Century, in: *The Cambridge History of Japan Volume 6: The Twentieth Century*, pp. 711–744. Cambridge: Cambridge University Press.

Napier, S (2007) *From Impressionism to Anime: Japan as Fantasy and Fan Cult in the Mind of the West*. New York: Palgrave Macmillan.

Nye, J (1990) *Bound to Lead: The Changing Nature of American Power*, New York: Basic Books.

Nye, J (2004) *Soft Power: The Means to Success in World Politics,* New York: Public Affairs.

Overview of the Public Opinion Survey on Social Awarenesss, 2016 www.gov-online.go.jp/eng/pdf/summarys15.pdf.

Ozawa, T (2009) Origin and Development of Japan's Public Diplomacy, in: Snow, N. and Taylor, P.M (eds.) *Routledge Hand book of Public Diplomacy.* New York and London: Rutledge.

The Policy of Cultural Affairs in Japan, Fiscal 2015 www.bunka.go.jp/english/about_us/policy_of_cultural_affairs/ (Accessed 21 Sep 2016).

Prime Minister of Japan and His Cabinet, http://japan.kantei.go.jp/96_abe/actions/201303/04 cooljpn_e.html.

The Report of the Tokyo Cultural Resources District Vision, 2016.

Sugimoto, Y (2014) Japanese Society: Inside Out and Outside in, *International Sociology* 29 (3): 191–208.

Sugiura, T (2008) Japan's Creative Industries, Culture as a Source of Soft Power in the Industrial Sector, in: Watanabe, Y., and McConnell, D.L. (ed.) *Soft Power Super Powers, Cultural and National Assets of Japan and the United States*, pp. 128–153. New York: Routledge.

Tamari, T (2014) Metabolism: Utopian Urbanism and the Japanese Modern Architecture Movement' in Special Section on Global Public Life, *Theory Culture & Society* 31 (7–8): 201–225.

Valaskivi, K (2013) A Brand New Future? Cool Japan and the Social Imaginary of the Branded Nation, *Japan Forum* 25 (4): 485–504.

Yeoh, BSA (1999) Global/Globalizing Cities, *Progress in Human Geography,* 23: 6–7–616.

Yeoh, BSA (2005) The Global Cultural City? Spatial Imagineering and Politics in the (Multi) Cultural Marketplaces of South-east Asia, *Urban Studies* 42 (5/6): 945–958.

Yoshimi, S (2016) *Asahi Evening Newspaper*, 6th January, page 4.

36

Cultural policy and the power of place, South Africa

Rike Sitas

Introduction

South Africa is often lauded as having a sophisticated policy landscape. Nevertheless, the terrain is still hotly contested, and many disjunctures between policy and implementation exist. It is therefore unsurprising that cultural policy debates are marked by disputes and dissensus. Post-apartheid cultural policy in South Africa is based on the 1996 White Paper on Arts Culture and Heritage, with a draft Revised White Paper circulating unsuccessfully since 2013. Although there are numerous consultative processes drawing in perspectives from different interests, little consensus has been reached, which has a direct impact on implementation.

This chapter is particularly interested in the relationship between cultural policy and urban public life in South Africa. As cultural and urban policy increasingly coalesce, there is a profound effect on the way cities are structured. South African cities are rapidly urbanising, but urban–rural linkages are not as binarised as is often assumed. Although cultural policy agendas are mandated nationally, implementation largely happens at a local scale, and resources tend to flow generally towards urban centres and dominant cultural institutions. This chapter starts by giving an overview of post-apartheid cultural policy, drawing out some of the key ideological assumptions and contestations that underpin the sector. In addition to exploring shifting local priorities, implicit in this discussion is examining global policy mobility, specifically unpacking how UNESCO and African Union ideals have travelled into South African policy.

One of the biggest challenges is that despite the best intentions of these global policy instruments, the way they land can be problematic. The chapter therefore goes on to explore three terrains where cultural and urban policy logics coalesce and collide related to: policy, implementation and governance; creative cities, creative economies and culture-led development; and history, heritage and nationalist agendas. These sections explore how cultural policy largely foreground an inequitable cultural economy, which perpetuates a cultural elite that remains disproportionally White; second, they run the risk of essentialising, fixing and preserving simplistic notions of cultural tradition and heritage; preserving colonial architecture and artefacts; and supporting new, often very expensive, nationalist agendas.

The framing of cultural and urban policy has left some significant gaps, especially related to the public life of many ordinary South Africans. Despite these challenges, a wide range of projects and initiatives have emerged that could better inform more contextually relevant policy. This chapter will draw on the example of the African Centre for Cities' project entitled *Public Art and the Power of Place*: a public-facing art project that aims to explore the significance of place in Cape Town's townships. Through an open call for proposals, five projects were given R50,000 grants (±$3600), and two projects R25,000 (±$1800) grants to develop projects at the intersection of public space and urban enquiry in order to challenge dominant representations in and of Cape Town's townships. The chapter concludes by drawing on what projects such as *Public Art and the Power of Place* can offer cultural and urban policy in and for South Africa and the global South.

Ultimately the chapter argues that in order to ground cultural and urban policy imperatives and implementation, four shifts are helpful: first, re-thinking the centrality of global policy mobilities and focusing on contextually relevant and localised cultural policy priorities; second, recognising that the formal and informal economies are inextricably interlinked and recasting the creative economy to reflect this will offer new renderings of how cultural industries emerge and sustain; thirdly, based on this knowledge re-thinking funding and support streams that appropriately draw on cultural and urban policy coalitions; and finally, by recognising the fluidity of art, culture and heritage as always in the making can challenge problematic tangible-intangible heritage boundaries and mitigate against inherent contradictions that perpetuate a problematic status quo.

Post-apartheid cultural policy and influential instruments

The optimism that marked the transition to democracy in South Africa in 1994 permeated many policy considerations including the development of the 1996 White Paper on Arts, Culture and Heritage (DAC, 1996). Given the history of socio-economic inequality entrenched through colonialism and apartheid, the policy was premised on redress and socio-economic transformation in the interest of what Nelson Mandela in his inaugural address claimed as: 'a rainbow nation at peace with itself and the world'. Art, culture and heritage were viewed as essential in the process of national healing and reconciliation. The purpose of the Department of Arts and Culture (DAC) was to 'realise the full potential of arts, culture, science and technology in social and economic development, nurture creativity and innovation, and promote the diverse heritage of our nation' (DAC, 1996). The mandate prioritised art, culture, heritage, diversity (including linguistic), literature and equitable support for diverse cultural experiences, heritage and symbols. The policy was intrinsically linked to the values espoused in the Bill of Rights of the Constitution. In addition, legislative instruments such as the 1999 National Heritage Resources Act and the 2009 National Policy on South African Living Heritage (draft) have emerged as mechanisms to govern art, culture and heritage.

An important component of the policy was to enable dissemination of resources that had historically been funnelled towards urban centres supporting predominantly White[1] creative practitioners and industries. Twenty years after the development of the 1996 White Paper, concerns about the adequate implementation of the policy abound. Although there has been some transformation of the arts and culture sector, the mainstream art economy is still dominated disproportionally by White practitioners. In addition, there is unequal provision of art at schools, which has an impact on university intakes of students as there is a tendency that only more affluent urban ex-Model C[2] and private schools have well-established arts curriculum, resources and facilities. Another increasing concern for arts-based civic organisations is that much of the public funding for arts and culture serves to support large institutions such as the state theatre instead of smaller neighbourhood-based organisations.

With shifting regional, local and global cultural policy imperatives, the 1996 White Paper was revisited in the form of the 2013 Draft Revised White Paper on Art, Culture and Heritage. This document saw a move from the 1996 version from cultural expression to creative industries and economies. According to (then) Minister Mashatile '[t]he new vision of arts and culture goes beyond social cohesion and nourishing the soul of the nation. We believe that arts, culture and heritage play a pivotal role in the economic empowerment and skills development of people'. This conception of the economic instrumentality of art, culture and heritage was supported by development of the manifesto for the Mzansi Golden Economy, which was designed as a way to imagine the 'Contribution of the Arts, Culture and Heritage Sector to the New Growth Path' (DAC, 2013). The purpose of the New Growth Path was to 'place jobs and decent work at the centre of economic policy' with a target of creating 5 million new jobs by 2020. It therefore became the imperative of each ministry to plan how sectors would contribute to this goal.

Since its drafting, the Revised White Paper has been used as the basis for a wide range of multi-stakeholder engagements and has been subject to various layers of critiques and dissensus as competing interests and generational perspectives[3] intersect. Many of the older generation of cultural activists, who had been instrumental in drafting the 1996 version, are concerned that economising the arts and culture industry can run the risk of compromising artistic integrity. Younger generations seem less concerned about normative understanding of the creative economy and are interested in exploring other ways of thinking of economies, but many are also committed to the radical or subversive role of art that may not be adequately represented in the policy.

Alongside the developmental shifts within South Africa over the last 20 years, there have been two influential global sets of processes: the development of the African Union's (AU) Charter for African Cultural Renaissance (2006) and Agenda 2063 and the concurrent development of UNESCO Conventions linked to culture and heritage. The premise of the UA's charter is that 'any human community is necessarily governed by rules and principles based on culture; and that culture should be regarded as the set of distinct linguistic, spiritual, material, intellectual and emotional features of the society or a social group, and that it encompasses, in addition to art and literature, lifestyles, ways of living together, value systems, traditions and beliefs' (African Union, 2006). The concept of the African Renaissance is based on culture being the basis for renewal on the continent and was envisioned as a way of setting post-colonial intellectual agendas of and for the African continent. Previous South African President Mbeki championed the idea and although critiqued, it still maintains prominence in many cultural circles in South Africa.

Simultaneously, UNESCO was consolidating its Convention for the Safeguarding of the Intangible Heritage (2003) and Convention on the Protection and Promotion of the Diversity of Cultural Expressions (2005). These two instruments have had wide impact on cultural policy across the continent, and elements are evident both in the Revised White Paper and in policy discussions. The Conventions also involved consultation with South African policy experts, and the underpinning ideologies reflect a sensitisation to contexts in the global South. Another influential UNESCO initiative is reported in the Creative Economy Report (2013).

The simultaneity of different scales of policy development can be seen in contemporary explorations of the relationship between cultural and urban policy as '...cultural policy issues have been thrust into the center of urban politics' (Grodach & Silver, 2013, p. 1). Although decentralisation has been the rallying call of global cultural and urban policy and governance advocates, this remains complex where many states only have national or provincial cultural ministries or departments with a direct mandate for arts, culture and heritage (Birabi, 2007; Olowu & Wunsch, 2004; Resnick, 2012).

Competing cultural policy logics

Despite the best intentions of policy instruments, the reality of how they land can be more complicated. This section of the chapter explores three ways the logics of cultural policy interact by looking at ideological critiques at a glance; policy, implementation and governance; assumptions about creative economies, creative industries and culture-based development; and preserving cultural heritage. Particular focus is given to the ways in which cultural policy manifests in cities and thereby impacts on the public life of residents.

Policy, implementation and governance

One of the biggest challenges across the African continent is the disjuncture between policy and implementation. Even South Africa – that has some of the most well-developed infrastructure, relatively reliable funding streams and robust policy realms – struggles with equitable and wide spread implementation of cultural policy. Although there are still some nations that do not have separate cultural policies such as Cameroon, Congo, DRC and Tanzania who claim to have integrated cultural imperatives into other policies, many states do have national policy plans and frameworks. The process of cultural policy development has been supported by UNESCO, and the language of cultural diversity and heritage espoused in the Conventions is evident (Ndoro & Pwiti, 2001, 2009). While this has meant a more comprehensive policy landscape on paper, the realities of implementation are less convincing, particularly on a local scale (Birabi, 2007; Chirikure, 2013). The trend, barring a few exceptions, in Africa remains that policy is developed nationally and implemented locally, but the reality of cities, especially large, rapidly growing ones, is that they take control of implementation even if not within formal governance structures. Cities in Africa are growing at such a rapid pace that decentralisation is inevitable in order to meet city-specific challenges, but this has been largely under-explored in the context of culture and heritage in Sub-Saharan Africa (Tidjani & Noorderhave, 2001). Where these instruments do exist, such as the City of Cape Town's Art Culture and Heritage Framework, they are not accompanied with appropriate budgets. Although ambitious and technically in line with UNESCO imperatives, many policies have not been adequately funded, and therefore there is no solid fiscal base for implementation. This is particularly evident at the local scale, as very few regions or cities have specific frameworks, mandates or governance structures to support implementation.

Funding is largely disseminated nationally through institutions such as the National Arts Council, the National Lotteries Commission and a range of European funders such as the Goethe-Institut (German), Alliance Francaise (French) and Pro Helvetia (Swiss). These kinds of organisations have offices that tend to be located in Johannesburg, and national dissemination is largely based in the urban centres such as Durban and Cape Town. Although policy development is modelled on international norms, largely those set by UNESCO, the reality of how money circulates is important to consider. To put this in perspective, South Africa, which has one of the biggest arts and culture budgets in Africa, has a population of

±55 million people, and the National Arts Council spends an average of around $7.5 million annually. England has a similar population of ±53 million people, and their Arts Council has an annual budget of around $450 million. The difference in resources is astounding and has a critical impact on the possibilities of implementing local, regional or global objectives such as UNESCO Conventions. With a global downturn in cultural funding, new financing models have yet to be adequately explored, particularly in the context of cultural policy implementation at the city scale in the global South.

Well-established cultural institutions such as national museums and theatres have been in a better position to leverage cultural policy to ensure financial support from a variety of public and private actors than smaller community-based organisations. In South Africa these have been successful in part due to two seemingly incongruous, but mutually beneficial, processes: the colonial heritage and entrenchment of the institutions in the cultural milieu, and partly because they were seen as priority spaces for transformation à la African Renaissance. There has been some transformation of these institutions with growing audiences predominantly in Johannesburg, but they remain expensive to run and have been receiving increasing critique, particularly from emerging youth movements such as #FeesMustFall and #RhodesMustFall who feel their relevance as public priorities need to be re-examines as part of a bigger cultural decolonisation and transformation project.[4]

Creative economies, creative industries and culture-led development

The importance of creative economies, cultural industries and culture-led development has become a global fixation and an increasingly dominant development priority in cities. Although this has not been enabled through cultural policy alone, new articulations of cultural policy priorities have made it easier for developmental policies at the city scale to operationalise arts, culture and heritage for social, economic and spatial development (Bell & Oakley, 2015).

Dominant thinking about the creative economy is underpinned by the idea that 'there is an urgent need to find new development pathways that encourage creativity and innovation in the pursuit of inclusive, equitable and sustainable growth and development' and creative industries are in a good position to contribute to this (UNESCO, 2013, p. 2). Through this, the creative city has become the means to achieve 'world-class' city status. Although limited, there is growing evidence that creative economies can contribute to some forms of economic growth (CIDA). In South Africa, the film and craft industries have been pegged as yielding opportunities according to the Department of Labour's (2008) report entitled 'The Creative Industries in South Africa' even though the document admits that there is limited data to work from. Despite limited data, there is a 'reframing of traditional progressive policy goals like diversity, inclusion, quality of life, and sustainability as facets of growth' (Grodach & Silver, 2013, p. 5). This has also been fuelled by place branding and marketing through cultural means, seen most explicitly in the Creative Cities Networks (Dovey, 2014).

Growing creative industries have been leveraged beyond the sectors themselves and have become the basis for urban development, as cultural precincts have gained traction throughout the world. Some are privately led with property developers at the helm: in South Africa the most prominent neighbourhoods are Maboneng in Johannesburg spearheaded by property company Propertuity (Walsh, 2013) and Woodstock in Cape Town that has largely been enabled through Indigo Properties (Wenz, 2012). Others have been publicly driven, such as the development of museum precincts like The Red Location Museum precinct in Port Elizabeth and the Hector Petersen Museum in Soweto.

Culture-led urban renewal, often through the vehicle of boosting creative industries, has been both lauded and vilified: having been critiqued for 'softening the blow' of development that favours affluent urban elites (Grodach & Silver, 2013; Miles, 2005; Peck, 2005; Zukin, 1995). On the one hand it is seen as an essential driver for economic development and place branding for cities (Florida, 2002; Landry, 2007), and on the other it is critiqued for compromising urban heritage, gentrifying neighbourhoods and marginalising the urban poor. It is within culture-based development that the logics of the property market and the imperatives of social and spatial justice can collide as cultural production shifts towards cultural consumption in the double displacement often referred to as part and parcel of many culture-based gentrification processes. It is not always the case as the Row Houses project suggests and therefore not as simple to binarise in reality (Thompson, 2012). In South Africa new cultural clusters of activity have emerged that service the social and leisure time of urban youth who are not universally affluent, as Braamfontein and Maboneng in Johannesburg attest (Gregory, 2015). They have also bred resistance as the Woodstock middle class residents' support for the eviction of poor by private developers demonstrates. Although there are clear challenges with shifting values in cities that favour the affluent, binarising the critique may not be helpful in unravelling the potential for culture-based development in culture and urban policy development and implementation. According to Markusen and Gadwa (2010, p. 380), it is important to 'clarify the impacts, risks, and opportunity costs of various strategies and the investments and revenue and expenditure patterns associated with each, so that communities and governments avoid squandering "creative city" opportunities'. Clarifying these opportunities is an important step in re-casting creative cities as drivers of social and spatial justice.

History, heritage and nationalist agendas

Heritage is often the most well articulated and implemented aspect of cultural policy but is also highly contested, where 'cultural heritage is valued in a number of ways and driven by different motives, principally, economic, political, cultural, social, spiritual and aesthetic. Each of these values has varied ideals, ethics and epistemologies. As a result, different ways of valuing have led to different approaches to preserving heritage' (Ndoro & Pwiti, 2009). Although historians have explored the challenges of fixing history through heritage processes, these questions have not trickled down into cultural policy spaces adequately, especially in relation to urban sustainability. New urban conservation paradigms propose a more fluid approach when recognising cities are in constant flux (Jigyasu & Bandarin, 2014).

While the UNESCO Conventions intend to balance the importance of tangible and intangible heritage, this is not necessarily how the policy manifests in reality. Although gains have been made in the conservation of historic cities in Africa, these policy imperatives have also been leveraged to protect colonial architecture and institutions and point to the conundrum of urban development and growth in relation to historic preservation (Araoz, 2011; Elong Mbassi, 2002). As there are strong architectural heritage protection lobby groups that are generally well networked and resourced, critical transformation in these areas can often be stymied. Although most people in principle believe in fostering more equitable and integrated cities, in practice NIMBYism (Not in My Back Yard) is rife. NIMBYism is one of the barriers to social and spatial integration in South Africa, and culture and heritage are often used as ways to mask resistance to change. For example, the preservation of heritage of neighbourhoods with colonial buildings can be used by rates payers associations who leverage claims on heritage to protect property prices.

Heritage management is also caught up either in colonial institutions (such as national museums) or in new nationalist agendas such as Freedom Park in South Africa (Birabi, 2007; Marschall, 2005, 2010; Meskell, 2012). These tend to be expensive projects that do not necessarily yield adequate audiences – especially amongst the youth who feel alienated from the discourses and forms of expressions. Preserving intangible cultural heritage can run the risk of essentialising culture in the interest of cultural tourism (McGregor & Schumaker, 2006). In South Africa, these can manifest in cultural villages creating spectacles of traditional cultures for foreign audiences. In addition, there is still a primary emphasis on tangible heritage. Although intangible heritage is foregrounded in many of the policy documents, the implementation of intangible heritage projects has been limited, largely because of the ephemerality of the intangible. In addition, it has been argued that separating tangible and intangible heritage is problematic and '[o]n the contrary, the system of material and intangible heritage, intended to redress past inequalities, seems to create new – and perpetuates existing – dichotomies and inequalities between North and South' (Leimgruber, 2010, p. 167).

Art, culture, heritage and public life in post-apartheid cities

The previous section drew out some of the policy contradictions. This section starts by looking at how culture and urban policy coalesce in post-apartheid cities, paying particular attention to Cape Town, before providing some examples that offer other practices that may have progressive policy implications.

Culture and urban policy in Cape Town

The 'cultural turn' in planning has had a profound impact on the urban fabric in cities around the world, which has spawned a wide range of political and politicised responses. Cultural and urban policy have been drawn closer together in unprecedented ways. Culture has been increasingly leveraged as vital in urban development and policy instruments have emerged to harness this. This has involved a range of different actors engaging with policy such as municipal departments including art, culture, tourism, planning and urban design, social development and parks; elected and employed officials such as mayors and civil servants; non-governmental organisations focusing on arts, culture and heritage; private entities such as property developers; and ordinary citizens (Markusen & Gadwa, 2010). With these coalitions come a range of different interests and politics.

Grodach and Silver (2013, pp. 14–15) explore these complexities through a range of cases across the globe that address 'urban cultural policy as an object of governance'; provide examples of cities that are 'rewriting the creative city script'; unpack the 'implications of urban cultural policy agendas for creative production'; and explore 'coalition networks, alliances and identify framing'. Although the politics of cultural policy has been widely explored (Bradford, Gary, & Wallach, 2000; Clark & Hoffman-Martinot, 1998; Miller & Yudice, 2002), this volume attempts to locate the debate within the realm of the urban. There has been a push for decentralisation of governance, and it is therefore unsurprising that cultural policies would also find new urban articulations (Arterial Network, 2011; Olowu & Wunsch, 2004; Ribot, 2002).

Cape Town has explicitly embraced building its identity as a creative city, through Creative Cape Town that 'communicates, supports and facilitates the development of the creative and knowledge economy in the Central City of Cape Town' in order to 'make the central city into a leading centre for knowledge, innovation, creativity and culture in

Africa and the South' (Creative Cape Town, 2016). This move has shaped place-branding and cultural priorities of the city. Although Landry's (2007, 2008) notion of the creative city focuses on creativity as a planning imperative in the interest of more equitable and liveable cities through creative economies, Creative Cape Town is more focused on the development and promotion of cultural industries in the CBD. The creative city concept has been a largely successful driver of certain creative industries and in particular in relation to design. In 2013, Cape Town was awarded the World Design Capital status. Although the impact of the award has been contested, it has been a driver of development of the growing design district around Woodstock – a historically low-income residential neighbourhood and one of the few affordable places to live close to the CBD. In recent years gentrification has intensified, and disputes around dislocation of local residents abound (Booyens, 2012; Wenz, 2012).

Unlike some other cities, culture-led development in neighbourhoods like Woodstock is not a state-led initiative: it is largely driven by private developers. Rare in African cities, Cape Town has an Arts, Culture and Creative Industries Policy that focuses on social cohesion, positions the city for global cultural tourism, protects heritage, supports artists and beautifies 'damaged' neighbourhoods (City of Cape Town, 2014). Although the policy instrument exists, as argued earlier, cultural funding is limited, and therefore cultural development is often market driven along the same logics as the formal economy.

South Africa has a long history of radical public art, where cultural activism was inextricably connected to the anti-apartheid struggle. Dollar Brand's, a Cape Town jazz legend, wrote a song called 'Mannenberg Is Where It's Happening' which became an unofficial anthem for the struggle. In addition, Cape Town's townships have been the hotbed of radical hip hop (Haupt, 2001), and a wide range of community arts projects (Grunebaum & Maurice, 2012). The transition to democracy in 1994 saw a shift in focus explained by Makhubu and Simbao (2013, p. 300): 'the official phasing out of "ideological driven" artist collectives through defunding and governmentalization seemed to steer art practices into commercialized private-sector initiatives. Furthermore, the rampant pressures to commercialize increased emphasis on idolized individual artists and curators'.

Cape Town has a plethora of high-profile mainstream galleries and Michaelis, a globally prestigious art school. Given the socio-economic and spatial inequalities stemming from colonialism and entrenched during apartheid, Cape Town remains stubbornly divided, and the bulk of arts, culture and heritage funding circulates within the CBD and through affluent, predominantly White creative practitioner circles. Nevertheless, there are hundreds of small art affiliations working in the townships of Cape Town that fall out of the mainstream networks of resources.

The intersection of urban and cultural policy has a profound impact on the public life of cities. In South Africa, there is a long history of public spaces heavily regulated according to race; this meant that many spaces were transitory – it was illegal to gather, and therefore people tended to move through spaces instead of linger. Despite the fact that finding more vibrant public spaces is on the planning agenda, the reality is that many open spaces are defunct and unsafe for women and children. Given township planning and housing typologies, few public spaces for engagement exist, and this legacy has prevailed. Unlike many other African cities, South Africa does not have a widespread active social public life. Public life tends to happen in interstitial spaces between public and private, and therefore these binarising categories may not be the most helpful. This chapter is particularly interested in how cultural and urban policy has coalesced to shape specific kinds of public life and proposes some possible ways to localise policy development and implementation.

Public art and the power of place

In response, in 2015, the African Centre for Cities, with the support of the National Lotteries Commission, initiated *Public Art and the Power of Place* – 'a public-facing art project aimed at exploring the significance of place in Cape Town's townships'. The project built on a growing practice of creating public-facing art projects in the interest of sustained engagement with socio-spatial issues, such as the Visual Arts Network South Africa's *Two Thousand and Ten Reasons to Live in a Small Town* (2012), *2013 ways of doing public art*, and *2014 Ways of Being here*; the work of the Joubert Park Project in Johannesburg, Public Eye and Gugulective in Cape Town and dala in Durban and in the spirit of socially engaged art.

Socially engaged public art in South Africa has followed similar trajectories and is imbued with similar tensions as is reflected in the literature from the global North (Bishop, 2012; Bourriaud, 2002; Deutsche, 1998; Kester, 2004; Lacy, 1995; Sharp, Pollock, & Paddison, 2005). Despite these challenges, socially engaged art processes have demonstrated an ability to enable alternative forms of political enrolment; enrich cultural citizenship; and create new spaces for urban learning (Miles, 1997; Minty, 2006; Pinder, 2005, 2008; Sitas & Pieterse, 2013). According to Minty (2006, p. 438) these kinds of projects have 'opened a whole set of new narratives linked to previously marginalised stories and histories and to imaginings for a better future'. At the core, it is 'not simply art placed outside... (it) is art which has at its goal a desire to engage with its audiences and to create spaces – whether material, virtual, or imagined – within which people can identify themselves, perhaps by creating a renewed reflection on community, on the uses of public spaces or on our behaviour within them' (Sharp et al., 2005, p. 1004).

With the upsurge in student politics there has been an expanding socially, politically and spatially engaged arts world in Cape Town. With the interest of supporting this swelling cohort of artists, *Public Art and the Power of Place* focused on supporting predominantly Black[5] artists living in Cape Town's townships interested in engaging the significance of space. The project involved providing financial support to seven projects in and around Cape Town.

'Amasokolari' was a collective of stand-up comedians interested in simultaneously using comedy as a means to explore more serious issues and developing comedy audiences in the vernacular (isiXhosa) in Khayelitsha.[6] In addition to performing in both formal (community theatres and restaurants) and informal spaces (shebeens[7]), 'Amasokolari' experimented with stand-up comedy in public spaces along transport routes – such as minibus taxis, trains and train and bus stations. 'Artfricraft' is a network of artists and performers in Delft. The project used a series of events and performances to draw South Africans and foreign nationals together to challenge xenophobia. 'Fast Forward Here' used film workshops with youth to explore alternative urban futures. Taking turns to film, direct, interview and edit, the project unpacked different ways to address social and spatial inequality in Cape Town.

'Ghetto Trek' developed a street festival on gang street corners in the Cape Flats. The purpose was to reclaim ordinarily dangerous spaces through cultural and performative action. The Harare Academy of Inspiration developed a month-long programme of events, clustered as a 'semester', as a way to experiment with culture and learning in Khayelitsha. Theatre in the Backyard extended the existing practice of site-specific theatre-making by developing a production emerging out of, and performed in, backyards in Nyanga. 'Township Boys' are a group of high school learners who worked with a local NGO to develop a large-scale mural for the local soccer stadium.

Rethinking place, culture and policy imperatives

This section draws on three examples from the project to draw out some suggestions on how to strengthen cultural and urban policy in the interest of more fair and equitable policies and industries (Figure 36.1).

Heritage in its most formal sense in the Western Cape remains dominated by colonial museums and naval and war artefacts and is protected by older and predominantly White custodians. The role of heritage tends to be split between the preservation of – primarily problematic – pasts and the interests of foreign tourism. *Public Art and the Power of Place* was interested in supporting projects working with other kinds of heritage practices and processes. 'Theatre in the Backyard' is one example where historical injustices are explored theatrically through contemporary realities. Fundamental to the process is producing the theatre pieces in the backyards of private houses, weaving everyday realities with astute socio-historical critique. In the context of this project, the backyards were identified in Nyanga, one of the poorest and most violent townships in Cape Town, the neighbourhood in which the director lives.

The director worked with professional performers to construct stories that relate directly to the social, spatial and historical context. For the most part, audiences were made up of local residents. The purpose was to take theatre out of formal institutions and the CBD in order to build audiences, but also to generate dialogue about more complex spatially situated urban issues. In addition, collaboration between the projector and cultural organisation, Coffeebeans Routes, has explored ways to promote the theatre pieces as alternative tourist destinations. Tourists pay for the performance and dinner in the homeowner's backyard. 'Theatre in the Backyard' has become an alternative mechanism for weaving 'storytelling, social and cultural capital, and social and spatial justice' (Interview, 2016).

The 'Harare Academy of Inspiration' was a collective of three women who drew together a month-long programme of events within a 'semester' of cultural activities (see Figure 36.2 for the programme).[8] The sessions were led by a combination of community-based organisations and practitioners and well-connected cultural professionals and were held at emerging arts and culture venue Moholo LiveHouse in the township of Harare. The programme emerged out of workshops with locals to gauge appropriate content. The purpose of the programme was to re-think the role of arts and culture as and in education. This was timely, as it was implemented in the wake of national #rhodesmustfall and #feesmustfall protests

Figure 36.1 Theatre in the Backyard. Image c/o Laura Wenz

Figure 36.2 Harare Academy of Inspiration Programme

that initiated a renewed engagement with decolonising and transforming universities specifically and education more generally. The artists felt that alternative learning academies
are vital for new ways to address social, cultural and spatial injustices. The artists felt this
was an experiment of alternative, collective and public pedagogies à la Freire (Freire, 1970;
Sandlin, Schultc, & Burdick, 2010). The programme mixed lectures (on different kinds of
art practices), seminars (on topics such as the politics of public art and public space), performances (from well-known and lesser-known musicians and performers) and exhibitions
(generated as part of the process, and sourced from major galleries in Cape Town). 'Learners'
were made up largely of unemployed youth, but included cultural activists and elites alike.
Collective reflection was built into the process and therefore ongoing analysis of the project
was enabled.

Although the Harare Academy of Inspiration has not managed to raise funding for another academy, the popularity of the programme has helped to generate a committed following to ongoing events at the Moholo LiveHouse, which has a unique business model.
Initiator Brenda Skelenge gained access to a building that had been designated as a tavern and
created an entertainment venue that brings food, music and performance to local residents.
The venue is on a square opposite the public library and in the same precinct as both retail
and municipal services. The popularity of the venue has also started attracting CBD-based
elites, enticing them out of the urban centre and into a township historically seen as a dangerous no-go zone in the popular imagination of the affluent. It thereby offers new in roads
for re-spatialising the city. It has also become a cultural precinct of sorts.

Whereas the other projects were working in familiar registers, 'Amasokolari' attempted to
popularise a less familiar form of performance. Stand-up comedy in South Africa has tended

towards being centred on big performances in theatres in the urban centres, where performers largely delivered content in English, until recently where there has been an increasing attempt to broaden audiences through the support of new talent. Prior to 'Amasokolari', this was largely in Johannesburg and Durban. The purpose of the project was threefold: to develop new performances and audiences in isiXhosa in Cape Town; to experiment with alternative and public performance spaces as a mechanism to do this; and to use comedy as a way to explore more serious urban issues.

The performers quickly realised that some public spaces were more amenable than others. Performing on public transport to captured audiences meant being able to actively entertain and recruit new talent to stand-up workshops. Public transport terminals were more problematic because people are usually in transit. Shebeens were not as successful as township-based restaurants, as shebeens could run the risk of an alcohol-induced lack of sense of humour, whereas restaurants tended to be more sober spaces. For the performers, the most important focus in developing stand up is through storytelling that reflects the experiences of audiences in the vernacular and that can tap into 'bitter-sweet' everyday realities. 'Amasokolari' produced a promotional DVD as part of the project, and through the project's amplified marketing, Siya Seya has become a nationally renowned comedian who works between the mainstream and townships circuits across the country, demonstrating the traction of engaging the significance of space through novel registers.

These examples demonstrate three things: they explore alternative avenues and mechanisms for arts, culture and heritage production and learning; they re-think creative economies and culture-based development; and they hint at a case for alternative scales for policy production and implementation.

Although these kinds of socially and spatially engaged art projects are not new globally, they were novel in post-apartheid South Africa, where these kinds of projects have largely been driven by well-resourced and well-networked arts organisations and led by predominantly affluent artists who have come through the art academy. Many projects have been set up in vulnerable or marginalised neighbourhoods, but leading artists have rarely stemmed from the areas themselves, running the risk of the alterity Foster (1996) warned about. These projects were driven by artists working outside of mainstream cultural industries, in their own neighbourhoods, and reflected a contextual sensitivity that was able to be dextrous in the face of contested social and spatial issues. All three also experimented with art, culture and heritage practices that fall outside or on the periphery of normative assumptions espoused in policy documents: 'Theatre in the Backyard' in its sitedness; 'Harare Academy of Inspiration' in its pedagogical explorations; and 'Amasokolari' in using a type of artistic expression not usually associated with 'high' or 'popular' culture.[9]

Falling outside of the dominant norms of art and culture in South Africa as imagined by cultural policy can also work to stretch the notions of art, culture and heritage. They can challenge the binaries of tangible and intangible heritage and work to spatialise cultural preservation within more temporal frames. 'Theatre in the Backyard' demonstrates the importance of apartheid housing typologies in the construction of social realities. Although it is questionable whether these tangible sites should be preserved, their material entanglements with contemporary history and heritage need to be recognised as an important part of South African's historical picture and may be more accessible than monumental museums to which ordinary residents may never have access. All three projects also offer alternative cultural actors to the cultural elites that dominate critiques of creative economies and culture-led development discourses. These artists are savvy and networked in ways that these critiques are unable to recognise. The networked social and cultural capital necessary to supplement the modest budgets to realise such ambitious projects suggests the need to rework the criteria that usually focus on economic capital. In addition to re-thinking the notion of cultural actors, these projects also challenge the role of finance in these projects. Although big national cultural institutions such as theatres, ballets, operas and museums regularly use ticket sales, it is often assumed that smaller organisations in the service of 'communities' should not use them, as they carry a stigma that could be seen as antithetical to community development. In this case, each project was able to leverage the project work towards more financially sustainable objectives, by mobilising informal networks as well as following similar strategies to their bigger counterparts. 'Theatre in the Backyard' and 'Amasokolari' used modest and affordable ticket sales. They felt that this was essential as part of audience development as people felt they were investing in something worthwhile, giving them power as opposed to being passive recipients of culture. When interviewed, all three projects reported the intricate webs of informal creative economies that were tapped into – systems of favours and skills bartering that have been the bedrock of marginalised creative communities. Systematic research of the formal–informal creative economies in South Africa, and indeed the global South are sorely missing from the academic record.

In addition, the close link between the 'Harare Academy of Inspiration' and Moholo Livehouse revealed an alternative way to think of culture-led development that is not adequately represented in cultural and urban policy. State-led solutions have historically involved delivering award-winning architectural community centres that tend to end up largely defunct (Sitas, 2015), and property development initiatives often result in displacement and exclusion of the urban poor. This example demonstrates a much simpler approach to a culture-led precinct that is both socially and spatially responsive to specific contexts.

These three examples were also chosen because although they may respond broadly to policy imperatives of supporting emerging art, culture and heritage initiatives, they fall outside or on the outskirts of funding chains. In South Africa, organisations generally need to be registered as non-profit organisations in order to be eligible for funding. None of these projects was officially registered as an entity, which immediately alienates it from most funding opportunities. In some instances, the criteria for funding – such as for the Lottery Distribution Commission – also include being able to provide 2 years' worth of audited financial statements and have the ability to keep meticulous financial records. The reality of much of the cultural industry is that it operates between and across the formal and informal sectors. Artists travel by minibus taxis and support a range of informal businesses, many of which do not provide receipts, making budgets hard to track. Artists are also not able to commence work without funds and cannot complete projects without receiving the full budget as quickly as possible. Because the African Centre for Cities is a non-profit organisation linked to a university, it was able to by-pass these requirements and pay artists directly without the stringent criteria.

This requires a re-thinking of how policy is developed, implemented and governed at the local scale. One of the critiques levelled at cultural and urban policy and governance by project participants and echoed through interviews with other cultural practitioners is that cultural policy thinkers are out of touch with the desires of a predominantly Black and youthful population of cultural producers. Youth feel alienated from policy documents as much as their imperatives, as they find it difficult to recognise themselves or their practices in the documents.

In addition, because budgets are managed nationally, there are challenges to ensure adequate devolution of funds. Although some decentralisation has occurred with cities like Cape Town having its own policy instruments, these have not been adequately funded and are therefore difficult to implement. Finding ways to assert different forms of creative expression and production and to leverage alternative creative economies and actors may enable more relevant policy discourses, mechanisms for implementation and governance at the local scale. In the absence of budgets, perhaps cultural and urban policy imperatives can create new funding coalitions to ensure the enabling of additional, similar projects.

Conclusion

This chapter started by giving an overview of the South African and global policyscape before unpacking how cultural and urban policy has coalesced in Cape Town. This situated the African Centre for Cities' *Public Art and the Power of Place* project within the policy discourses, as well as within a broader engagement of art in the interest of critically engaged public life in Cape Town. Drawing on three examples from the project, the previous section argued that there may be alternative ways to ground culture and urban policy coalitions in the interest of more socially and spatially equitable societies in South Africa. The chapter concludes by inserting these reflections into global debates about cultural policy.

Critiques of contemporary cultural policy have often concentrated on the neoliberal creep into policy instruments and governance. Concerns are largely levelled at the instrumentalisation of art, culture and heritage as a means for elite-centric developments. Although neoliberal traces can be found when global and local policy instruments and implementation align, neoliberal critiques alone may not be sufficient to understand the South African situation. South African policy instruments stem from socialist and developmentalist policy imperatives that inform the transition to democracy. They are comparably robust and distribute a large amount of money to select institutions on an annual basis, but these still tend to have an affluent urban skew. Although it would be easy to argue that this is part of global neoliberal inequalities, this does not give an accurate picture in its entirety. Despite the urge to sway South African cultural policy towards more neoliberal and economised ends, the failure of the Revised White Paper to gain traction suggests that the developmentalist ideals of the 1996 version espoused by older generations invested in an ANC-led post-apartheid semi-socialist and cohesive reality, coupled with the radical tendencies of youth movements committed to decolonisation and transformation is still holding neoliberalism to account to some degree. Although there are pressures to financialise the arts and culture industry, the Mzansi Golden Economy (DAC, 2013) sees cultural industries as drivers of job creation as opposed to being solely vehicles to enable profit-driven ends. A neoliberal takeover also implies a certain degree of organisation that cannot be facilitated in governance systems that have not adequately decentralised. This is not to argue that neoliberalism does not play a role. It is more complicated ideologically to cast art, culture and heritage projects and policy squarely at one end of the socialist-neoliberal pendulum. The reality in South Africa is messier.

Many of the critiques argue that working with the state or in relation to capitalist industries will always result in being complicit in replicating the problematic and neoliberal status quo (Bishop, 2012; Miles, 2005; Sharp et al., 2005). In contexts with staggering rates of youth unemployment, livelihoods are at stake. There are no national arts culture and heritage stipends. Creative practitioners on the margins are often cultural entrepreneurs seeking ways to monetise cultural practice but not in the predictable ways that formal art and culture markets produce.

It may be more useful to see cultural policy and its urban manifestations through a different lens. Recognising the gaps and disjuncture between policy and implementation may mean looking inwards in addition to outwards and towards global policy instruments such as UNESCO Conventions. The majority of cultural practitioners are carving out a living on the margins of the formal economy in interesting ways that may be able to provide more contextually relevant lessons for cultural policy. The urban articulation of culture, although the current source of anxiety, can also be an important opportunity if culture and urban policy can be more closely drawn together to recognise the strength of formal and informal entanglements that may better reflect and support the interests of urban youth and in turn more socially and spatially diverse urban futures that recognise art, culture and heritage as transient and constantly in the making.

Notes

1 Although racial categories are problematic constructs, they remain important socio-economic and political determinants in a South African context.
2 Model C schools historically served White students and were only integrated post 1994. Given the ongoing race-based spatial segregation in many South African cities, these schools still tend to serve the interest of affluent urban communities.
3 These perceptions have been tracked through interviews with creative practitioners. For more details see Sitas (forthcoming).
4 In 2015, student movements coalesced nationally around the call for equitable access to education and a call for fair fees at tertiary institutions. This has intensified non-partisan youth politics that are working towards new conceptions of the decolonized intellectual project. 2016 has seen a renewed bout of student political activity and activism.
5 'Black' in the context of this chapter is seen as a social and political construct that has vital economic implications. It is used as an encompassing term to include Black African, Coloured, Indian and mixed race as per the South African racial categories.
6 Stand-up comedy is not a common form of creative practice in poorer neighbourhoods and in the vernacular.
7 Shebeens are informal and often illegal bars largely found in South African townships.
8 Documentation of the project can be found at www.facebook.com/harareacademy/.
9 I use inverted commas as these concepts are contested and problematic binaries often used to prop up inequalities within creative industries.

References

African Union. (2006). *Charter for African Cultural Renaissance*. Addis Ababa, Ethiopia: African Union.
Araoz, G. (2011). Preserving heritage places under a new paradigm. *Journal of Cultural Heritage Management and Sustainable Development*, 1(1), 55–60.
Arterial Network. (2011). *Decentralisation*. Arterial Network, www.arterialnetwork.org/ckeditor_assets/attachments/504/africalia_decentralised_booklet_-_fa_lores.pdf.
Bell, D., & Oakley, K. (2015). *Cultural Policy*. New York: Routledge.
Birabi, A. (2007). International urban conservation charters catalytic of passive tools of urban conservation practices among developing countries? *City & Time*, 3(2), 4.
Bishop, C. (2012). *Artificial Hells: Participatory Art and the Politics of Spectatorship*. London: Verso.
Booyens, I. (2012). Creative industries, inequality and social development: Developments, impacts and challenges in Cape Town. *Urban Forum*, 23 (1), 43–60.
Bourriaud, N. (2002). *Relational Aesthetics*. Dijon: Les presses du reel.
Bradford, G., Gary, M., & Wallach, G. (2000). *The Politics of Culture*. New York: The New Press.
Chirikure, S. (2013). Heritage conservation in Africa: The good, the bad, and the challenges. *South African Journal of Science*, 109(1/2), 1–3.
City of Cape Town. (2014). *Arts, Culture, and Creative Industries Policy (Policy Number 29892)*.
Clark, T., & Hoffman-Martinot, V. (1998). *The New Political Culture*. Boulder, CO: Westview Press.
Creative Cape Town. (2016). www.creativecapetown.com/.
Department of Arts and Culture. (1996). *White Paper on Arts, Culture and Heritage*. Pretoria: DAC.

Department of Arts and Culture. (2013). *Mzansi Golden Economy*. Retrieved from www.dac.gov.za/taxonomy/term/379.

Deutsche, R. (1998). *Evictions: Art and Spatial Politics*. Cambridge, MA: MIT Press.

Dovey, K. (2014). Planning and place identity. In G. Young et al. (Eds.), *The Ashgate Research Companion to Culture and Planning* (pp. 257–271). Farnham: Ashgate Publishing Company.

Elong Mbassi, J. (2002). *Decentralization, Assistance, Investments & Future of the Historic Centres of Africa. Partnerships for World Heritage Cities: Culture as a Vector for Sustainable Urban Development*. Paris: UNESCO.

Florida, R. (2002). *The Rise of the Creative Class*. New York: Basic Books.

Foster, H. (1996). The artist as ethnographer. In H. Foster (Ed.), *The Return of the Real*. Cambridge, MA: MIT Press.

Freire, P. (1970). *Pedagogy of the Oppressed*. New York: Continuum.

Gregory, J. (2015). Creative industries and urban regeneration – The Maboneng precinct, Johannesburg in *Local Economy: The Journal of the Local Economy Policy Unit*. Vol 31(1–2)

Grodach, C., & Silver, D. (2013). *The Politics of Urban Cultural Policy: Global Perspectives*. New York: Routledge.

Grunebaum, H., & Maurice, E. (2012). *Uncontained: Opening the Community Arts Project archive*. Cape Town: Centre for Humanities Research.

Haupt, A. (2001). Black thing: Hip-hop nationalism, "race" and gender in Prophets of da City and Brasse vannie Kaap. In Z. Erasmus (Ed.), *Coloured by History, Shaped by Place. New Perspectives on Coloured Identities in Cape Town*. Cape Town: Kwela Books.

Jigyasu, R., & Bandarin, F. (2014). The intangible dimension of urban heritage. In F. Bandarin & R. van Oers (Eds.), *Reconnecting the City: The Historic Urban Landscape Approach and the Future of Urban Heritage*. Oxford: Wiley-Blackwell.

Kester, G. (2004). *Conversation Pieces: Community and Communication in Modern Art*. Berkeley: University of California Press.

Lacy, S. (1995). *Mapping the Terrain: New Genre Public Art*. Seattle, WA: Bay Press, Incorporated.

Landry, C. (2007). *The Art of City Making*. London: Earthscan.

Landry, C. (2008). *The Creative City: A Toolkit for Urban Innovators*. London: Earthscan.

Leimgruber, W. (2010). Switzerland and the UNESCO convention on intangible cultural heritage. *Journal of Folklore Research*, 47(1–2), 161–196.

Makhubu, N., & Simbao, R. (2013). The art of change: Perspectives on transformation in South Africa: Editorial. *Third Text*, 27(3), 299–302.

Markusen, A., & Gadwa, A. (2010). Arts and culture in urban or regional planning: A review and research agenda. *Journal of Planning Education and Research*, 29(3), 379–391.

Marschall, S. (2005). Forging national identity: Institutionalizing foundation myths through monuments. *SA Journal of Cultural History*, 19(1), 18–35.

Marschall, S. (2010). Articulating cultural pluralism through public art as heritage in South Africa. *Visual Anthropology*, 23(2), 77–97.

McGregor, J., & Schumaker, L. (2006). Heritage in Southern Africa: Imagining and marketing public culture and history. *Journal of Southern African Studies*, 32(4), 649–665.

Meskell, L. (2012). *The Nature of Heritage in the New South Africa*. Chichester: Wiley-Blackwell.

Miles, M. (1997). *Art, Space and the City: Public Art and Urban Futures*. London: Routledge.

Miles, M. (2005). Interruptions: Testing the rhetoric of culture led urban development. *Urban Studies*, 42(5), 889–911.

Miller, T., & Yudice, G. (2002). *Cultural Policy*. Thousand Oaks, CA: SAGE.

Minty, Z. (2006). Post-apartheid public art in Cape Town: Symbolic reparations and public space. *Urban Studies*, 43(2), 421–440.

Ndoro, W., & Pwiti, G. (2001). Heritage management in southern Africa: Local, national and international discourse. *Public Archaeology*, 2(1), 21–34.

Ndoro, W., & Pwiti, G. (Eds.). (2009). *Legal Frameworks for the Protection of Immovable Cultural Heritage in Africa*. Rome: International Centre for the Study of the Preservation and Restoration of Cultural Property.

Olowu, D., & Wunsch, J. (2004). *The Challenges of Democratic Decentralization*. London: Lynne Reinner Publishers.

Peck, J. (2005). Struggling with the creative class. *International Journal of Urban and Regional Research*, 29(4), 740–770.

Pinder, D. (2005). Arts of urban exploration. *Cultural Geographies*, *12*, 383–411. doi:10.1191/1474474005eu347oa.

Pinder, D. (2008). Urban interventions: Art, politics and pedagogy. *International Journal of Urban and Regional Research*, *32*(3), 730–736.

Resnick, D. (2012). Decentralization and service delivery in African cities. Retrieved August 15, 2015, from http://unu.edu/publications/articles/decentralization-and-service-delivery-in-african-cities.html.

Ribot, J. (2002). *African Decentralization: Local Actors, Powers and Accountability*. Geneva: UNRISD.

Sandlin, J., Schultc, B., & Burdick, J. (2010). *Handbook of Public Pedagogy: Education and Learning Beyond Schooling*. London & New York: Routledge.

Sharp, J., Pollock, V., & Paddison, R. (2005). Just art for a just city: Public art and social inclusion in urban regeneration. *Urban Studies*, *42*(5), 1001–1023.

Sitas, R. (2015). Community centres in crisis: The story of the Tsoga Environmental Resource Centre. In M. Brown-Luthango (Ed.), *State/Society Synergy*. Cape Town: African Centre for Cities.

Sitas, R., & Pieterse, E. (2013). Democratic renovations and affective political imaginaries. *Third Text*, *27*(3), 327–342.

Thompson, N. (2012). Socially Engaged Art Is a Mess Worth Making in *Architect*. Aug2012 p86–87

Tidjani, B., & Noorderhave, N. (2001). Culture, governance and economic performance: An explorative study with a special focus on Africa. *Journal of Cross-Cultural Management*, *1*(1), 31–52.

UNESCO. (2013). *Creative Economy Report 2013: Special Edition*. Paris.

VANSA. (2012). *2010 Reasons to Live in a Small Town*. Johannesburg: VANSA.

Walsh, S. (2013). 'We won't move': The suburbs take back the center in Johannesburg. *City: Analysis of Urban Trends, Culture, Theory, Policy, Action*, *7*(3), 400–408.

Wenz, L. (2012). Changing tune in Woodstock. *Gateways: International Journal of Community Research & Engagement*, *5*, 16–34.

Zukin, S. (1995). *The Cultures of Cities*. Cambridge, MA: Wiley.

Part VIII
Conclusions

37

The light touch

The Nigerian movie industry in a low policy environment

Jade L. Miller

What is successful cultural policy? Cultural policy research catalogues a broad spectrum of efforts national and local governments have taken to spur and support sustainable creative industries, from the national Indian government granting industry status to the film industry in order to spur investment, to South Korean initiatives to send its future producers and pop stars abroad to internationalise markets, to more local efforts to create walkable arts districts à la Richard Florida's platonic ideal of a creative city (2002). Initiatives like these have served to support the transformation of burgeoning artistic production into sustainable creative industries (or, in other cases, may have represented ill-considered governmental expenditures with little to show for it).

Nigeria's prolific English language movie industry, known popularly as Nollywood,[1] emerges from a policy environment that was not designed to be supportive to the formation of cultural industries. The types of policy that form the infrastructure of many formal cultural industries around the world exist nominally at best in Nollywood: neither copyright enforcement, contract enforcement, governmental training initiatives, nor government grants to burgeoning filmmakers are reliable institutions, and those controlling the industry generally attempt to evade governmental attention as much as possible. The only reliable governmental intervention in the industry has come through the Censor's Board, which has at times expanded its focus well past censoring content and has looked (unsuccessfully) towards restructuring power dynamics in the industry.

This chapter first outlines the existent regimes of copyright, contract enforcement, and other government initiatives that have proven to be quite weak, with the exception of censorship functions. It then discusses the industry's self-made alternative structuring institutions that circumvent governmental oversight or intervention, marked by the strength of the industry's informal guilds and the strength of personal and ethnic ties in the industry. The chapter concludes with reflections on the relevance of Nigeria's cultural policy environment to studies of other cultural production globally.

Background

The history of Nigeria's English language movie industry has been told many times now (see Adesanya 2000; Haynes & Okome 2000), and I will only outline the most relevant pieces of Nollywood history to the themes of this chapter. Popular press reports in particular tell the story of Nollywood history as a story of creating something out of "nothing" with little external support or encouragement. Of course, the industry didn't actually emerge from "nothing." Most academic accounts tell the story of the rise of the industry as a response to a reduction in audiovisual distribution avenues in the 1990s and the rise of new distribution channels in Nigeria's open-air marketplaces.

The industry emerged in the early 1990s partly in response to a series of pressures on Nigerian popular culture at the time. As oil prices tumbled, the Nigerian currency went into freefall, and government corruption led to a sharp uptick in street crime, discouraging people from leaving home to pursue entertainment options (or anything else) after dark. Two of the more popular arts venues at the time were experiencing crises: the government broadcaster cut funding and opportunities for popular domestic soap opera production, switching over in some cases to inexpensive foreign syndicated programming instead, while the nation's popular private travelling theatre troupes were having problems funding their productions. At the same time, entrepreneurs running the grey market electronics stalls in networks of open-air markets across Nigeria came into a surplus of VHS products, as first generation VHS technologies began to age in their primary markets.

Kenneth Nnebue, one of these electronics traders, famously tied these pieces together in a moment of "entrepreneurial clarity" (Miller 2016a). Hiring underemployed theatre troupe actors and soap opera directors and crew, Nnebue created the first of what came to be known as "Nollywood" movies. These movies were shot directly on video and circulated in video (VHS) format primarily through the network of open-air electronics markets that already circulated imported home entertainment equipment and pirated foreign movies (Larkin 2007).

Nnebue both funded and distributed his early movies, and this model has persisted. As other electronics traders saw the potential to make money by selling VHS copies of entertainment content that they themselves had produced, an industry emerged, fuelled by sales of hard copies of VHS, exchanged at the open-air markets where the industry's executive producers already controlled distribution networks of open-air stalls. These executive producers became known as marketers. Despite the power involved in their roles as distributors and executive producers, they are still referred to as "marketers" in the industry, and I will use the same term here.

Twenty-five years later, the marketers still control the majority of the industry's executive production and distribution. Recently, a new sector of the industry has emerged, known as "New Nollywood," featuring high budget titles with more cinematic aims (sometimes shot on film and shown in cinemas) and controlled by an elite contingent of renowned directors with access to more diverse potential funding and distribution avenues. However, the marketers' portion of the industry produces the lion's share of titles. While New Nollywood movies are popular, neither the consumption appetite of Nollywood fans nor the ledgers of Nollywood distribution outlets can be sustained on these titles alone. Both fans and distributors rely on the marketers' productions for the bulk of their titles, despite the preference some might have for "New Nollywood."

Government agencies

Nigerian Film Corporation

Given the industry's roots in informal little-regulated open-air marketplaces, the industry has traditionally had little interaction with government agencies. The cultural ambitions of

Nigeria's oil-rich government in the 1970s foresaw a different relationship with a national movie industry. In 1972, the national government set up quotas for foreign films (in the nation's cinemas, still functional at the time, two decades before rising crime kept people at home and shuttered many entertainment venues) and put limits on foreign ownership of cinema houses via the Nigerian Enterprises Promotion Decree (Okome 1995). Seven years later, in 1979, the government inaugurated the Nigerian Film Corporation, meant to support domestic film production with production and post-production facilities, cinema-building and training initiatives, amongst other goals.

None of these initiatives ever came to fruition, but the government agency remained and still exists today. It is located in Jos, a city in central Nigeria far from Nollywood's hubs in Lagos and Onitsha. While Nigeria's prolific video industry is centred in the nation's economic capital (Lagos), the Nigerian Film Corporation, or NFC, was formed with an eye towards celluloid film production. With a limited budget, the agency's achievements have been limited to a film archive, a film school (also in Jos) and sometimes booths at various international film festivals meant to showcase high-end larger budget Nigerian movies. The film school, the National Film Institute, is well regarded but is largely disconnected from the Nigerian video industry that functions thousands of miles away and recruits new talent without recourse to evidence of government-sponsored training.

Nigerian Copyright Commission

Though not directly aimed at supporting a movie industry (which was virtually non-existent at the time), Nigeria's adoption of copyright law in 1988 – and signing of the international standard Berne Convention in 1993 – had the potential to create a cultural industry policy environment based on copyright. However, the Nigerian Copyright Council (inaugurated in 1989 and upgraded to the Nigerian Copyright Commission, or NCC, in 1993) has never had any resources to execute its goals, and enforcement has remained unfunded.

While Nigeria has signed onto the Berne Convention, few in the Nigerian creative industries are aware of the parameters of these copyright rules, which automatically assign copyright to the main resource provider with no need for registration. Most functional global copyright regimes assign enforcement to police or other specialised enforcement agencies. In Nigeria, the NCC was given enforcement rights (and duties) in 1992 but no increase in funding. This means that the NCC, an agency made up of lawyers and administrators, has no ability to order or run raids. Any copyright raids that do occur in Nigeria tend to be financed by foreign governments or corporations looking to protect their own copyright interests and involve a special payment to the police force in return for the raid they carry out.

The NCC's only direct intervention in copyright enforcement is to prosecute criminal cases using information brought to them by aggrieved parties. However, court cases usually drag on for years, due to the pace of the Nigerian legal system. The slow pace of the system is driven by the lack of specialised copyright judges, the need to begin trials over when a judge is transferred and the four to six year appeals process tacked onto the initial case (NCC lawyer 1 2009). Because of this, most cases will be resolved by a civil agreement between the two parties years before the NCC prosecution can be expected to culminate, and the agreement usually involves the complainant dropping out of the criminal case in return for an agreed-upon fee (ibid). During my research at the NCC, there were no pending cases regarding the movie industry at all; according to lawyers at the NCC, the NCC prosecutions that do occur most frequently regard the book publishing industry (ibid).

National Film and Video Censors Board

Unlike the above government agencies with a charge to support Nigeria's movie industry, the National Film and Video Censors Board, or NFVCB, has been effective in pursuing its primary mission: censorship of movies released in Nigeria. While the NCC and NFC seemed ignorant of the nascent video industry in its early years, the federal Nigerian government created the NFVCB in 1993, the very first year that domestic video films began to populate the electronics markets of Nigeria. By 1994, submitting one's video to the NFVCB for approval was an unavoidable step in the movie production and distribution process in Nigeria and continues to be so today.

It may seem surprising that a new Nigerian industry, informal in funding and distribution, would feel compelled to submit movies to the national censorship board prior to release. One explanation is the robust nature of censorship in what was at the time a military regime. The NFVCB and the NFC alike were both housed in the Ministry of Information as opposed to the Ministry of Culture, reflecting governmental attitudes about the importance of the power of mass media to relay information and influence opinion, overshadowing its power to contribute to the nation's cultural profile. Though November 2015 saw, under new president Muhammadu Buhari, the merger of what was at that point called the Ministry of Culture and Tourism with the Ministry of Information, neither the NFVCB nor the NFC, the agencies with direct charge to interact with the movie industry, were linked with the nation's cultural aims until that bureaucratic merger.

More practically, the NFVCB has been afforded the resources to pursue non-conforming filmmakers. Despite the unregulated nature of the exchange of physical copies of Nigerian movies, each movie comes with the contact information of its main initial distributor printed on the packaging, and those distributors would be fined and harassed if they were to release a title that hadn't pursued and received NFVCB approval. That said, NFVCB guidelines generally serve as preventative as opposed to punitive. The agency's standards discourage explicit sexual content and amoral consequences, but violations of the code are rare. Nigerian popular movies tend to pass through the Censors Board without issue, arriving already without potentially offending content.

While demands for re-edits are rare at the NFVCB, the agency has flexed its muscles in the past decade with an ambitious heavy-handed initiative meant to restructure distribution in the industry. Going outside its stated aims to control content in the industry, the NFVCB spent years attempting to implement a licensing scheme for distributors (see Bud 2014, for an in-depth examination of this project) in an effort to chip away at the marketers' dispersed power in favour of a more easily regulated industrial structure. Begun in 2006 at the behest of ambitious then-director Emeka Mba, the Framework dictated that all distributors must register with the NFVCB as national, regional or local. The goals of the Framework were to encourage the emergence of a small number of large visible national distributors.

The philosophy guiding this endeavour was a drive to transform the vast sea of opaque financing and distribution opportunities offered by marketers into a scenario in which the industry would be controlled by a small number of large companies that were more easily regulated and taxed by the government, more accountable and more attractive to outside investors looking for reliable record-keeping and transparent ledgers. The agency's incursions into structuring the industry were controversial but, by 2009, after much rancour and struggle, nearly every distributor in Nigeria had complied and acquired a license. The marketers, however, circumvented the scheme's goals as distributors of all capacities registered for the national distributor classification, a category initially intended to only have about a dozen registrants, with the other distribution categories attracting very few. After years of struggle, the NFVCB's most ambitious policy attempt to structure the industry had little effect, and the framework is generally considered to have failed in its end-goals, even as it succeeded in forcing a registration process upon the marketers (Bud 2014).

Federal grant funds

While Nigerian moviemakers are free to apply for international grants for making movies, it is rare for them to do so, given the tendency of such grants to go to art cinema, while Nolly-wood epitomises popular cinema. Until recently, there has been little in the way of domestic grant funds to pursue. At times, however, federal announcements regarding funds to support the movie industry have been used as political tools. Sometimes these funds materialise, while, at other, the funds fall through.

Former president Goodluck Jonathan, for instance, announced a series of well-financed initiatives to support the movie industry during his last year in office, including a $9.5 million (3 billion naira) grant-making and training fund for the industry and a $11 million invest-ment by the Nigeria Bank of Industry to a single powerful producer, Gabriel Okoye (known as Gabosky) to duplicate the marketers' national distribution infrastructure with a 'privately owned national distribution system' named G-Media, likely meant as a second shot at dis-rupting the marketers after the NFVCB's failure (Bud 2014). Two years later, allegations circulated that the 3 billion naira fund has been squandered and distributed along clientelist lines (*The Punch* 2016), and the fund's future is in question (Husseini 2016), while Gabosky's distribution scheme, like that of the NFVCB, has failed to disrupt existent distribution net-works. Governmental grants, like the NFC and the NCC, have never become a reliable resource; instead, we can see NFVCB censorship as the only functional government inter-vention in the industry.

Institutions and alternatives

While the Nigerian movie industry has grown in an environment without reliable copyright or contract enforcement, with little to no reliance on government grant-making or train-ing initiatives, the industry is, in fact, highly structured, and its entrepreneurial executive producers – the marketers – continue to fund and produce new titles that are distributed widely. The absence of state-provided structure does not mean that this is an industry in chaos. In every place where one could imagine cultural policy stepping in, the Nigerian movie industry has an alternative, created and maintained by those that run the industry. Much of this is structured by the industry's guilds, a system of nationally elected representa-tives that constitute the elite of the industry and govern many industry norms. Other struc-ture comes from the strength of trust-based and kin-based relationships that gird an industry based on the norm of repeat collaboration. In this section, I will examine two institutions and their guild-formed alternatives to government structure: labour agreements and the protection of intellectual property.

Contract enforcement, guilds and trust

While labour contracts exist across industries, theorists on the creative industries have high-lighted the importance of contracts in industries that rely on freelance labour as opposed to salaried employment (see Caves 2000). Creative industries are more likely to rely on such labour than other sectors, and film production the world over tends to be particularly reliant on freelance labour, reformulating teams for each new shoot and offering employment on a per-job basis[2] (ibid.). The Nigerian industry represents an extreme example of team reformulation, due to the sheer number of shoots onto which regular industry workers must be hired in order to make ends meet. The rapidity of filming and large number of titles the industry releases per year combines with the modest per-title pay offered workers to create a system in which those working in the industry are often lining up jobs one after another in quick succession. The rapidity and frequency of team formation mean that good relationships with potential co-workers and employers, important in any industry, are particularly necessary here (Miller 2016b).

Just as the lengthy trials and appeals in the Nigerian court system undermine potential copyright enforcement, official legal contract enforcement for freelance labour in Nigeria is virtually non-existent. This is not to say that there is no recourse in Nollywood's labour disputes, however. Rather than relying on government infrastructure to mediate conflict, the Nigerian movie industry is structured by business relationships built on informal "memorandums of understanding" and even more on trust, respect, clout and handshakes. Labour disputes are meant to be resolved through the guild system that structures the industry. Nearly every worker in the industry is a member of a guild, ranging from a guild for make-up artists to the highly powerful guild representing the marketers, FVPMAN (Film and Video Producers and Marketers Association of Nigeria). Each guild is national and governed by elected representatives, usually made up of the most well-connected and well-known in each respective profession. Elections can be fraught with conflict, as leaders have access to member funds, wield power, and, perhaps most importantly, are accorded a degree of reverence and respect as a result, both in the industry and outside of it.

Guilds generally cooperate with one another, and the elite in the leadership of each guild tend to be friendly with one another. Large-scale auditions, for instance, are meant to have representatives of the major guilds present over-seeing procedure. The frequency of such events as well as the consistent parade of premieres and banquets that mark the social life of the industry's elite in Lagos means that the leadership of each guild will often be travelling in one another's social circles and seeing each other frequently.

When disputes arise, guilds are supposed to represent their members in a quest for a solution. If, for instance, a crew member and producer have dispute over payments or working conditions, the guild of the party deemed to be in the wrong is meant to discipline the transgressor or otherwise ameliorate the situation. For those without clout in the offender's guild, workers are meant to contact their own guild representative who will represent them in discussions or negotiations with a representative from the other guild.

While this system works well in theory, it can fall short in addressing the concerns of unpopular or non-powerful complainants. Many working in the industry believe the guilds serve the interests of the elite that run them as opposed to their constituents. If their concerns are not resolved via the guild system's dispute resolution process, they have no recourse save for maligning the name of the offending party. This is not as minor as it may seem, however; given many workers' reliance on rapid-fire repeat freelance employment, lining up job after job, the threat of one's name losing cache can be significant. Public complaint and gossip can be a particularly powerful tool in an industry governed heavily by interpersonal relationships and incentivised by the potential for repeat employment.

Copyright enforcement and pricing

As mentioned earlier, Nigeria lacks a funded enforcement force to carry out copyright violation raids, and copyright violations are rarely pursued within the Nigerian legal system, due to the length of resolution of such court cases in the Nigerian courts. This is coupled with a normalisation of piracy (which I will refer to here as unauthorised distribution, in order to remain value neutral) as a means of distribution within Nigerian society (see Larkin 2007) to produce an environment in which profiting from intellectual property is particularly challenging. Goods in Nigeria, from foreign movies (Hollywood, Bollywood, etc.) to electronics, often arrive via black and grey markets rather than official authorised distribution channels. Hollywood studios, for instance, make virtually no effort to distribute their titles in Nigeria for theatrical or home screening; the low returns anticipated there make it a blank area in global distribution plans. This means that nearly every time a Hollywood film is viewed in Nigeria, it has arrived via unauthorised distribution networks (with the exception of films screened at the nation's small handful of upscale multiplexes in Lagos and Abuja, which arrive via a South African corporation (Silverbird) which has licensed African theatrical rights from Hollywood studios). There are few social constraints against purchasing unauthorised access to copyrighted materials in a place where such access is the only possible access. In my interviews with foreign consulate workers in Lagos, the US consulate employee in charge of copyright enforcement there told me she routinely purchased unauthorised copies of Hollywood films on the streets of Lagos for her own personal use, as it was the only place to find them.

In his influential work on Northern Nigerian film, Brian Larkin has illustrated the ways in which the distribution networks for unauthorised foreign movies, snaking through Nigeria's electronics markets, are the very same networks distributing authorised copies of domestic Nollywood movies through the nation, as well as funding their production (2007). The lines between authorised and unauthorised can become quite murky in this context. The marketers responsible for executive producing Nollywood movies are moving their products through the same businesses that are also often accused of engaging in unauthorised distribution of Nollywood and foreign movies alike. In a nation where there is little differentiation between authorised and unauthorised products (and, indeed, they often are identical in both appearance and price), "piracy" of domestic content proliferates.

While directors and producers of Nigerian movies often publicly complain about copyright violations, they have banded together via their guilds to safeguard their content themselves, as opposed to putting energy into lobbying the government for reliable copyright enforcement. Guilds have, for instance, engaged in campaigns to educate consumers about copyright, encouraging everyday consumers to reject pirated content and support Nigerian talent via billboards and other signage in Lagos, though the impact of this campaign cannot be measured. The best defence the industry's executive producers have against loss of sales due to unauthorised distribution is via the lightning-fast market adjustments achieved by the cohesiveness of the marketer's guild, FVPMAN. Nearly every innovation made by unauthorised distributors has been met by a response from the marketers, linked collectively by their guild as well as kinship networks.[3]

One way to describe pricing in the domestic Nigerian market is that movies wholesale in VCD (video compact disc, the preferred format in Nigeria for the past decade) form for around 350–400 naira (around $1 USD) per full movie, and that this has been a steady price for years. While this is true, the pricing system has morphed considerably over the years to compete with unauthorised distributors on a price basis. For years, it was common for a movie to be released in two parts, with each part wholesaling for 150–200 naira (about 50 US cents), adding up to 300–400 naira for the whole story at wholesale prices. In recent years, this trend has multiplied, with some movies being split into eight parts in extreme cases, selling for 43 naira (about 14 US cents) wholesale per copy (Njoku 2013).

To be clear on how drastic this pricing is, this means a wholesale price of 43 naira (14 US cents) for a brand new title in its initial release in its original packaging. The cost of production of a VCD has been estimated at 26 naira per copy leaving 17 naira (6 US cents) per copy gross profit, a remarkable rate for intellectual property that challenges the profit margins of unauthorised distributors. Since buyers purchasing Part 1 will also likely buy Parts 2 through 8, overall revenue for the movie might actually be the same as if the movie were sold in just two parts, leaving prices static for consumers. The cost of VCD replication, however, could crunch the profit margins of producers, authorised and unauthorised alike. To be clear, this is just one extreme in pricing. Most movies are still sold in less than eight parts – more like two, three, or four. In either instance, this reflects a marketer trend towards cutting prices and extending the number of 'parts' to better compete with unlicensed distribution.

Another strategy the marketers have pursued in their battle with unauthorised distribution is an extreme windowing system: three weeks after a movie's release, the price of a given movie will sink to just 50 naira retail, or 16 US cents. Similar to windowing in cinema-based film industries, this is known as the movie's secondary market. A well-connected producer spelled out what this could mean financially for a hypothetical very popular movie: a movie selling 100,000 copies in the domestic market in the first three weeks of its release could garner 10 million naira ($32,000 USD). This same title might sell an additional 200,000–300,000 copies in the secondary market, once the first three weeks had passed, garnering a possible 2 million naira ($6,300 USD) in wholesale secondary domestic sales. To be clear, this is $6,300 gathered from intellectual property sold at an astounding 10 naira, or 3 US cents per copy (these would be sold in the markets for 50 naira, or 16 US cents retail). Making over $6,300 on intellectual property sold at 3 US cents per title is a powerful challenge to unlicensed distribution, and one that could give pause to unlicensed distributors. To be clear, the figures cited here describe a remarkably popular movie, and average movies in the industry will not sell at this scale. That said, these strategies are used on movies across the spectrum of Nigerian offerings. And the potential to take profits on intellectual property sold at such low rates serves as a profound challenge to unauthorised distribution, not through the threat of legal prosecution, but through squeezing legitimate profits enough to actually compete on *price* with "pirates" who did not need to also pay for the production budget. The reason these strategies have been able to take hold is largely the cohesiveness of the marketers in FVPMAN. This large number of small to medium scale executive producers and distributors will generally follow one another's lead, linked together by ethnic ties and led by their elected guild leader.

Discussion

The Nigerian movie industry began without any government intervention, and was, in effect, governed only by the censorship board in its growth years. Significant governmental attention to the video industry took at least ten years to come about, and attempts by the government to interact with the industry after this time have generally fallen flat. Today, governmental institutions providing for film development funds, filmmaker training, grant-making, contract enforcement, and copyright protection in Nigeria are nominal at best. While three government agencies exist with a direct charge to support the movie industry (the NFC, the NCC, and the NFVCB), only one can truly be said to have been an effectual regulator over the years: the censorship authority (though, in recent years, even this agency has lost its influence). While many in the industry lament the lack of structure and demand specific government interventions (particularly directors without the resources to fund or distribute their own movies, frustrated at their dependence on the marketers and looking for structural change), many others (particularly those currently profiting from and running the industry: the marketers) complain that the government has little justification to interfere in something developed without its support. Can government – particularly in a state such as Nigeria, ineffectual in many of its initiatives – structure an already self-formed largely informal industry? Can structure through governmental intervention be laid on top of an industry born largely outside of any formal governmental rules or policies? While the answers to these questions cannot be known directly, as the industry is still developing and the story is far from over, we can take note of the failure of specific policy and governmental oversight initiatives that the government made two decades into the birth of a dynamic informal creative industry. Both state-financed initiatives to restructure power and distribution in the industry – the NFVCB and G-Media initiatives – have failed, and any further attempts seem likely to meet the same fate.

This policy environment, though distinct from the many examples of intentional cultural policy worldwide, is by no means rare. Indeed, much cultural production on a global level emerges from contexts in which institutions like contracts and copyright are weak. The global fame the Nigerian movie industry has garnered in the two past decades makes the industry one of the more *visible* examples of a cultural industry functioning in a light policy environment, but far from unique.

Studying the Nigerian movie industry in the context of cultural policy allows us to consider the potentials for the development of sustainable cultural industries in an environment absent of significant government intervention. With no functioning copyright enforcement mechanism and with current distribution channels largely outside of possible governmental intervention or even attention, Nollywood stands as a model for industrial development in the context of a particularly low level of cultural policy – or simply a model for what a sustainable cultural industry can look like without the governmental institutions often thought of as supportive of industrialised cultural production. The answer here is an industry full of small-scale entrepreneurs, funding their own productions out of the profits they make from personally overseeing distribution, structured by personal ties and guilds and with consistent resourceful responses to challenges like unauthorised distribution.

As technological and financial barriers to entry to various production and distribution avenues become lowered on a global scale, one could expect to see sustainable creative production develop in a diversity of policy environments, particularly those that do not fit the parameters of traditional thought on the ideal role of cultural policy. Future policymakers would do well to consider the limitations involved in supporting and regulating cultural production largely created and circulated via venues outside of their control. Researchers, in turn, would do well to consider alternatives to governmental policy as possibilities for structuring sustainable creative production and could look to the Nigerian experience for guidance. As online and mobile phone distribution venues begin to make incursions in the Nigerian mediascape, those researching Nollywood will need to assess whether the possibility of increased transparency in distribution opens doors for government intervention, or if the accompanying unauthorised distribution venues leave the Nigerian movie industry as separate as ever from governmental oversight and infrastructure.

Notes

1 While there are many issues with using the name "Nollywood" as a stand-in for Nigeria's multi-faceted movie industry (see Haynes 2007; Adejunmobi 2015), I use it in this chapter as shorthand for ease of reference, though acknowledging its drawbacks.
2 Though this looks quite different in film industries operating on a "studio system" framework, employing salaried cast and crew. The studio system, though once structuring both American and Indian film production, no longer structures any of the world's prominent film industries.
3 FVPMAN is the guild for marketers from the Igbo ethnicity. Other marketer guilds for other ethnicities do exist, but the industry is largely run by the Igbo marketers making up FVPMAN.

References

Adejunmobi, M., 2015. African film's televisual turn. *Cinema Journal*, *54*(2), 120–125.

Adesanya, A., 2000. From film to video. In J. Haynes (ed.) *Nigerian video films* (pp. 37–50). Athens: Ohio University Center for International Studies: Research in International Studies Africa Series No. 73.

Bud, A., 2014. The end of Nollywood's guilded age? Marketers, the state and the struggle for distribution. *Critical African Studies*, *6*(1), 91–121.

Caves, R., 2000. *Creative industries: Contracts between art and commerce*. Cambridge: Harvard University Press.

Florida, R., 2002. *The rise of the creative class: And how it's transforming work, leisure, and every day life*. New York: Basic Books.

Haynes, J., 2007. Nollywood: What is in a name? *Film International*, *5*(4), 106–108.

Haynes, J. & Okome, O., 2000. Evolving popular media: Nigerian video films. In J. Haynes (ed.) *Nigerian video films* (pp. 51–88). Athens: Ohio University Center for International Studies: Research in International Studies Africa Series No. 73.

Husseini, S., 17 July 2016. Buhari sings a different tune for Project ACT Nollywood. *The Guardian* [online]. Available from: http://guardian.ng/art/buhari-sings-a-different-tune-for-project-act-nollywood/.

Larkin, B., 2007. *Signal and noise: Media, infrastructure, and urban culture in Nigeria*. Durham, NC: Duke University Press.

Miller, J., 2016a. *Nollywood central*. London: BFI.

Miller, J., 2016b. Labor in Lagos: Alternative global networks. In M. Curtin and K. Sanson (eds.) *Precarious creativity: Global media, local labor* (pp. 146–158). Berkeley: University of California Press.

NCC lawyer 1, 2009. Personal communication with the author, July 30.

Njoku, J., 13 Dec 2013. Alabanomics: Yesterday, today, and the future of Nollywood. *Just Me: Jason Njoku: Blog* [online]. Available from: www.jason.com.ng/post/70277008903/alabanomics-yesterday-today-and-the-future-of.

Okome, O., 1995. Film policy and the development of the African cinema. *Glendora Review: African Quarterly on the Arts*, *1*(2), 46–53.

The Punch, 11 Oct 2016. Nollywood: Emeka Ike seeks probe of N3bn intervention fund [online]. Available from: http://punchng.com/nollywood-emeka-ike-seeks-probe-n3bn-intervention-fund/.

38

The political career of the culture concept

Tony Bennett

My concerns in this chapter are with the discursive coordinates that shaped a distinctive episode in the political career of the cultural concept: that comprised by the role it played in the development of assimilationist conceptions of multiculturalism in the inter-war period through to the early post-war period. The key developments here focus on the successive elaborations of Franz Boas's interpretation of the culture concept – briefly, the conception of culture as an ordered way of life – that informed the trajectories of American anthropology during a period when it was both intellectually dominated by Boasians and, somewhat contrary to Boas's own inclinations, entering into increasingly close forms of collaboration with a range of governmental agencies (Mandler 2013; Price 2008). By focusing on this episode in the political career of the culture concept, I also aim to throw some fresh light on a later moment in its history when, in the founding years of British cultural studies, it was annexed to a conception of class politics in which the ways of life of working-class cultures were constituted as potential sources of resistance to dominant class formations. This interpretation of the concept departed from its inter-war history in being fashioned as a source for counter-conducts rather than as a governmental actor and, as an aspect of this, the way in which its relations to aesthetic conceptions of culture were interpreted also changed. I shall show how its earlier history as a policy actor in the United States rested on a particular governmental mobilisation of formalist aesthetics that informed the conception of ways of life as being endowed with a particular shape or pattern derived from the creativity of the people concerned. The initial phases of its use in British cultural studies detached it from the coordinates of race and ethnicity that informed its earlier American anthropological career, coordinates to which the concept has been re-attached in its later career in cultural studies in the light of its re-reading by Stuart Hall and others. While this later episode in the political career of the culture concept goes beyond the historical remit of my concerns in this chapter, it nonetheless informs my engagement with its earlier moments.

The order of discussion will be as follows. I look first at the definitional issues associated with the concept of culture as a way of life across its relations between anthropology and cultural studies. I then look more closely at the Boasian and post-Boasian interpretations of the concept within American anthropology, focusing particularly on its aesthetic properties and the differential interpretation of these across its application to the cultures of

Native Americans, Caucasians, African-Americans and European migrants. This prepares the ground for a closer examination of the deployment of the concept in the early years of the development of American assimilationist policies and particularly the political logics informing the exclusions effected by these policies. I conclude by reflecting on current critical re-engagements with the relations between the Boasian culture concept and the category of race.

From universal hierarchy to patterned differences

In his classic *Beyond Nature and Culture*, Philippe Descola insists that it was only with Boas 'that there emerged the idea that each people constitutes a unique and coherent configuration of material and intellectual features sanctioned by tradition, that tradition being typical of a certain mode of life, rooted in the specific categories of a language and responsible for the specificity of the individual and collective behaviour of its members' (2013: 73). As such, its significance consisted in replacing the grading of peoples in evolutionary terms 'by a synchronic table in which all cultures are equally valid' (73). It was further, Descola argues, through his acquaintance with Boas that Claude Lévi-Strauss, in subscribing to 'the idea that nothing justified setting up a hierarchy of cultures in accordance with either a moral scale or a diachronic series' (75), contributed to the production of culture as a new surface for the management of differences, ostensibly replacing both race and earlier aesthetic hierarchies, that informed the debates leading to UNESCO's post-war statements on race. There were, of course, other intellectual currents running into UNESCO's founding documents than the Boasian one: Lévi-Strauss's relativism arguably owed as much to his association with Paul Rivet at the Musée de l'Homme as to his acquaintance with Boas (Laurière 2008), and the reworking of the legacy of early twentieth century anthropology effected by Mass Observation also fed into UNESCO's early adjudications of the relations between race and culture (Kushner 2004). These qualifications to one side, however, there can be little doubt regarding the long-term impact of UNESCO's formulations in producing culture as a policy actor for the regulation of differences that have shaped a variety of its programmes – running up to, in the 1990s, *Our Creative Diversity* (1996) and, more recently, its *Convention on the Protection and Promotion of the Diversity of Cultural Expressions* (2005) – with significant consequences for the development of a wide range of national cultural policies.

I am more immediately interested here, however, in Descola's disputation of those accounts that attribute a continuous history to the culture concept as running uninterruptedly from Edward Burnett Tylor's 1871 formulation of culture as 'that complex whole which includes knowledge, belief, art, morals, law, custom, and any other capabilities and habits acquired by man as a member of society' (1). He has particularly in mind the influential codification of the history of the culture concept effected by two of Boas's students, Alfred Kroeber and Clyde Kluckhohn, in their *Culture: A Critical Review of Concepts and Definitions*. In presenting Tylor and Boas as the two key figures on the road leading toward the science of culture they wished to establish, Kroeber and Kluckhohn overlooked what Descola highlights as the crucial difference between them: Tylor's commitment to an evolutionary and hierarchical ordering of the relations between different cultures as calibrated by the degree of their approximation to Euro-American norms of civilisation. This long-standing criticism of Tylor within the anthropological literature has been accompanied by another that, again, accentuates the differences between Tylor and Boas. Whereas Boas viewed culture as a creatively ordered whole in which the elements that comprise it are configured into a distinctively patterned way of life, Tylor's conception of culture amounted to no more than 'a list of traits, with the consequence that culture might be inventoried but never analysed' (Kuper 2000: 57).

Williams who, in his *Keywords* entry on Culture (1976), relies a good deal on Kroeber and Kluckhohn's text, nonetheless registers his unease at their attempt to draw a clear line of demarcation between a scientific, anthropological approach to culture and its aesthetic conception – a distinction that, it should be added, is given a nationalist inflection in Kroeber and Kluckhohn's interpretation of the former as an American approach developed in opposition to European humanistic traditions (Gilkeson 2010). This is evident, for example, in their comments on T.S. Eliot who, while being congratulated for speaking of culture 'in the quite concrete denotation of certain anthropologists' as exemplified by his famous characterisation of the activities that go together to make up the English way of life (Eliot 1962), is chastised for attempting to reconcile 'the humanistic and social science views' of culture as a misuse of the American anthropological tradition on which he drew (Kroeber and Kluckhohn 1952: 32–33). Williams (1965), while failing to acknowledge the differences between them, draws more on the aesthetically inflected registers of the culture concept articulated by Ruth Benedict's conception of the distinctive patterning of the relations between the elements comprising a whole way of life than on Tylor's listing of cultural traits. The same was true of Richard Hoggart who, Richard Handler (2005) has suggested, was influenced by the modernist inflection that was given to the culture concept in the 'culture and personality' school, most notably represented by Edward Sapir, whose contrast between 'genuine' and 'spurious' culture (Sapir 1924) provided a model for Hoggart's analysis of the relations between working class and mass culture (Hoggart 1969). It is the distinctive aesthetically patterned form that it acquires from the situated creativity of the working classes, Hoggart argues, that imbues working-class culture with its resilience – its capacity to resist the synthetic orderings of commercial mass culture. At the same time, if, as Handler puts it, this account rests on 'the assumption (standard in anthropological theory) that the pattern of working-class culture is alive – adaptive, resistant, persistent – precisely because its "bearers," the "natives," hold to it unconsciously' (Handler 2005: 163–164), this failure to attain a critical self-consciousness also entails its devaluation from the modernist perspective that informs Hoggart's work: it might survive but can never become a general model. Williams similarly, Handler argues, universalise a modernist conception of creativity in attributing the dynamism of culture to the general interplay between inherited cultural forms and the creativity of groups or individuals, while nonetheless retaining, in his conception of culture as ordinary, a modernist distinction between 'the most ordinary common meanings and the finest individual meanings' (Williams 1989: 4).

I make these points by way of noting how the influence of the American culture concept on the founding texts of British cultural studies was largely filtered through the later, more explicitly high modernist interpretations of that concept by Eliot and Sapir with neither Hoggart nor Williams looking much beyond these to the earlier history of the concept or its political articulations. This was even more true of the subsequent development of the concept in British cultural studies where, in being switched initially from the axes of race in being attached to those of class, the 'anthropological concept of culture', as it came to be known, was typically endorsed for its value-neutral, levelling qualities in asserting the equal value of all forms of cultural creativity irrespective of the place accorded them within official cultural hierarchies. This was an aspect of its early history in post-war Britain, evident, for example, in Williams's role in contributing to a limited shift in the Arts Council's priorities from an initial exclusive focus on high culture to a broader conception of the range and kinds of cultural practice that might merit government support. We need, however, to look to the earlier history of the culture concept and its relations to the fieldwork tradition in American anthropology, to appreciate how its aesthetic properties were initially acquired and how these came to be fused with its operations as a policy actor. It's a history in which the idea of culture as a patterned articulation of the relations between elements in a way of life became attached to assimilationist programs within a hierarchical ordering of racial categories.

The aesthetic ordering and differentiation of cultures

From its inception in the work of Tylor, the culture concept has been shaped by the relations between the practices of collecting materials from subordinate cultures and ordering the relations between these and dominant cultures, in ways that have informed practices of governing. While the limitations of ruptural interpretations of the development of the fieldwork phase in anthropology in the late nineteenth and early twentieth centuries have been widely canvassed (Fabian 2000), the place accorded fieldwork within the Boasian tradition did significantly shift, while not entirely displacing, the place accorded 'primitive cultures' within the earlier paradigm of evolutionary anthropology. Key here was the transition from the style of armchair anthropology practiced by Tylor and the evolutionary assumptions underlying the typological method of museum displays that informed his collecting practices. Objects culled from diverse locations – by missionaries, traders, policemen or looters – were brought together in evolutionary sequences in testimony to a universal path of human development (Bennett 2004). This lack of concern with the configurational ordering of relations between traits comprising a particular culture has often been assessed as a limitation from the perspective of the later Boasian development of the concept. In fact, though, it constituted a different principle of ordering that was shaped by a political program that, in identifying those traits that represented what Georges Didi-Huberman (2002) characterises as a 'spectral time' – a legacy of the past that is disconnected from the present that has superseded it – also identified those aspects of 'primitive cultures' that were to be surgically removed by colonial governance. Tylor was perfectly clear about this implication of his doctrine of survivals that was not, he argued, to be understood as a 'mere abstract truth, barren of all practical importance' but, to the contrary, as a means of identifying those 'streams of folly' that, persisting from the past, have to be eliminated in order to integrate 'the savage' into the culture of the higher races (Tylor 1867: 93).

Although Boas cut his anthropological teeth in projects directed by Tylor, the problem space that he went on to develop was, George Stocking (1968) contends, a quite different one in which the interpretation of fieldwork evidence made the specific patterns produced by the intermixing of the traits comprising any specific culture a particular historical problem that was not susceptible to any general laws of an evolutionary kind. Susan Hegeman develops this line of argument further seeing the Boasian fieldwork problematic as a key moment in the development of a new form of anthropological authority based on the anthropologist's unique ability to decipher the distinguishing qualities of other cultures. In place of a commitment to the collection of objects that could be put on display for all to see as evidence of a universal narrative of humanity, the Boasian paradigm substituted the more abstract object of 'cultures'. This required special methods of collection alert to the interrelations of objects, myths, rituals, language, etc., within a specific way of life accessible only to the trained anthropologist immersed in the culture in question (Hegeman 1999). Each culture, as Boas put it, 'can be understood only as an historical growth determined by the social and geographical environment in which each people is placed and by the way in which it develops the cultural material that comes into its possession from the outside or through its own creativeness' (2010: 4). Ruth Benedict registered the shift that this involved in chastising the earlier generation of armchair anthropologists for the undue emphasis they had placed on the collection of material culture:

> Strictly speaking, material culture is not really culture at all. ... Behind every artefact are the patterns of culture that give form to the idea for the artefact and the techniques of shaping and using it. ... The use and meaning of any object depends almost wholly on non-material behaviour patterns, and the objects derive their true significance from such patterns.
>
> *(Benedict 1947: 1)*

This form-giving capacity was subject to different formulations at different moments in the development of the culture concept. Boas was notably reticent on the subject, implicitly drawing on the Germanic tradition to impute the creativity of a people to their unique genius, a capacity he sometime interpreted in terms of Herder's categories, sometimes in terms of those provided by Humboldt and sometimes in Kantian terms (Bunzl 1996; Stocking 1968). As subsequently developed by his various students, however, the distinctive shape of a culture was re-interpreted in more explicitly modernist terms (Hegeman 1999) as the result of a form-giving activity modelled on the work of art that, whether performed by individual or collective social agents, broke through inherited patterns of thought and behaviour to crystallise new social tendencies. This is evident, for example, in Benedict's concept of the pattern of culture that, drawing on Wilhelm Worringer's conception of abstract form (Worringer 1997), she interprets as 'the result of a unique arrangement and interrelation of the parts that has brought about a new entity,' a process she compares to that 'by which a style in art comes into being and persists' (Benedict 2005: 47). Melville Herskovits, like Benedict one of Boas's students, took the analogy further arguing that it 'it is necessary to know the "style" of a culture—which is merely another way of saying that we must know its patterning—in precisely the same way that the student of art must know the styles that characterise the various periods of art-history in order to cope with the individual variations that are exemplified in the works of artists of a given epoch' (Herskovits 1938: 22).

It was, then, this conception of a configurational order arising out of the form-giving principles that expressed the inner necessities of group life – of culture as 'an integrated spiritual totality which somehow conditioned the form of its elements' (Stocking 1968: 21) – that differentiated the Boasian culture concept from Malinowski's functional conception of the social whole as an amalgamation of the pragmatic functions performed by different traits. The anthropologist's attention was redirected accordingly: 'The anthropologist,' as Margaret Mead put it, 'is trained to see form where other people see concrete details' (1942: 4–5). At the same time that it was advanced as a general theory of culture, however, the culture concept also distinguished between cultures – and it did so along lines derived from the principles of aesthetic modernism. This was clear in Boas's *Primitive Art*, his most extended treatment of the subject in which he explicitly disputed the various grounds on which earlier generations of anthropologists had either denied colonised peoples any capacity for aesthetic creativity or acknowledged it only in a diminished form. The conception of a universally valid sequence for the development of art forms; the contention that the mental capacities of 'primitives' are inferior to those of 'civilised' peoples; the denial of any capacity for aesthetic innovation to 'primitive people' as a consequence of the force of habit in inhibiting the development of originality: all of these are given short shrift. Like their modern counterparts, Boas argues that primitives differed from one another in the degree to which their aesthetic capacities are developed: 'intense among a few, slight among the mass' (Boas 2010: 356).

There are, however, still differences between moderns and primitives – relative rather than absolute, and accounted for in sociological rather than biological terms – but differences nonetheless:

> What distinguishes modern aesthetic feeling from that of primitive people is the manifold character of its manifestations. We are not so much bound by a fixed style. The complexity of our social structure and our more varied interests allow us to see beauties that are closed to the senses of people living in a narrower culture. It is the quality of their experience, not a difference in mental make-up that determines the difference between modern and primitive art production and art appreciation.
>
> *(Boas 2010: 356)*

It was, however, a hallmark of the Boasian tradition that the closure of primitive cultures was always presented in relative rather than absolute terms. Its unity, accordingly, was always conceived as incomplete and provisional. If the unity of a culture is derived from the aesthetic form-like properties that give a distinctive shape to the elements comprising a way of life, that unity, Benedict argued, is always a fractured one. Why? Because most of the traits that comprise the building blocks of a culture come from sources that 'are diverse and unlike' (Benedict 1947: 1), thus constituting contradictory elements that either cancel each other out or are brought together in a new form of synthesis. It is in the processes through which such new syntheses are produced that the aesthetic and the spatial aspects of the culture concept – most fully expressed in the concept of culture area – are brought together. For the Boasians, culture was always both territorially grounded and subject to disruption from the trans-territorial flows of cultural traits carried by the histories of peoples in movement. It is to these matters that I now turn as a prelude to considering how the aesthetic and spatial registers of the culture concept combined in shaping its qualities as a policy actor.

Mutable spatialisations of cultures in movement

Let me go back to Williams. In opening his essay 'Culture is ordinary', Williams first looks to connections between place and way of life to convey a sense of culture's ordinariness. 'To grow up in that country,' he says, 'was to see the shape of a culture, and its modes of change' (1989: 4). The country in question – the Border Country between England and Wales – is richly evoked by recounting a bus journey from Hereford to the Black Mountains. Orchards, meadows, hillside bracken, early iron works, Norman castles, steel mills, pitheads, the railway, scattered farms, town terraces – this is the regional scene that Williams starts with before populating it by describing his own working-class affiliations to it through his father and grandfather. But it is the sense of a wider spatially defined culture that comes first, and class second. The complex interplay between these regional and class co-ordinates also spills over into questions of Englishness as, with T.S. Eliot in his sights, he insists that working-class culture – and not the petty niceties of the English ruling class – gives English culture, understood as a way of life, its distinctive coherence. Welsh culture too, of course; however, in this essay, it is Englishness that most concerns Williams in pinning his colours to the principles of 'a distinct working-class way of life … with its emphases of neighbourhood, mutual obligation, and common betterment as … the best basis for any future English society' (8). Ways of life are thus defined spatially as well socially; they are regionally embedded, and the relations between them are nationally defining.

In highlighting the relations between place and way of life, Williams followed in the footsteps of T.S. Eliot who included among the three main conditions for culture 'the necessity that a culture should be analysable, geographically, into local cultures' (Eliot 1962, Kindle loc. 70). He acknowledges his debt to the American school of anthropology in this regard: 'By "culture", then, I mean first of all what the anthropologists mean: the way of life of a particular people living together in one place' (loc 1687; see further Manganaro 2002). Although these connections between culture and place were, in the Boasian tradition, fluid and mutable, they have often been read as binding different ways of life, people and territories into essentialist relations to one another. There are several reasons for this. Some have to do with the interpretation of the culture concept in the context of American assimilationist policies in the late 1920s and 1930s in which the conception of America as a melting pot defined an emerging American national self-consciousness that was differentiated from European nationalisms (Gilkeson 2010; Mandler 2013) – and I shall have more to say on this shortly. Others derive from the territorialisation of the culture concept during the 1939–1945 war and the post-war period when it was revised to refer to a field of national differences that were to be made commensurable with one another through the new geopolitical-diplomatic order of the United Nations (Price 2008).

Some of Boas's early work also echoed Herder's conception of culture as the expression of a geographically delimited people. Later, however, he rejected any sense that regional environments might be regarded as having a determining influence on cultures. 'It is sufficient,' he wrote in 1932, 'to see the fundamental differences of culture that thrive one after the other in the same environment, to make us understand the limitations of environmental influence', adding, as a pointed contrast, that the 'aborigines of Australia live in the same environment in which the White invaders live' (Boas 1932: 256). The key questions here bear on Boasian conceptions of the relations between processes of cultural diffusion and the organisation of cultural areas. These questions have been revisited in a substantial body of recent work that argues that the Boasian construction of these relations anticipates contemporary accounts of the relations between trans-border cultural flows and migration in breaking with the modern order of nation states. It was, Ira Bashkow argues, 'axiomatic to the Boasians that cultural boundaries were porous and permeable', citing Robert Lowie's contention that any given culture is 'a "planless hodgepodge," a "thing of shreds and patches"' as economically summarising the view that any particular culture 'develops not according to a fixed law or design but out of a vast set of contingent external influences' (Bashkow 2004: 445). These are brought into historically contingent, impermanent and unstable fusions with one another in particularly territorially marked culture areas, only to be later disaggregated in the context of different relations of cross-cultural contact and population migrations. Brad Evans similarly interprets Boas's significance as consisting not in his pluralisation of the culture concept – something that Herder had already done – but in his conception of the 'detachability' of the texts and objects that comprise the elements of a culture from any organic association with any particular spatial or historical culture so that they might serve as 'vehicles for the articulation and disarticulation of meaning across discontinuous geographies and temporalities' (Evans 2005: 15). Recounting Boas's role in the reconceptualisation of folklore studies under the influence of turn-of-the-century developments in philology, Evans argues that these undermined earlier romantic and nationalist conceptions of an inherent connection between a particular people and a particular culture by reconceptualising cultures as being, like languages, 'public objects' formed by processes of historical interaction and migration beyond the control of individual speakers or speech communities.

The pattern of a culture, then, is not expressive of an essential set of relations of a people, place and way life but is a conjunctural and pliable articulation of those relations that derives its distinctive qualities from the creative, form-giving capacity of the people concerned. As cultural traits are diffused across cultural areas, their meaning is transformed: 'The nature of the trait,' as Benedict put it, 'will be quite different in the different areas according to the elements with which it has been combined' (2005: 37). In turning now to consider how these spatial and aesthetic aspects of the culture concept informed the governmental rationalities that characterised the development of the relations between earlier 'settlers' and more recent immigrants and between both of these and Native Americans and African Americans, I engage with recent re-evaluations of the relations between the culture concept and racial categories.

The culture concept, race and assimilation

While the reappraisals of the Boasian tradition that I have drawn on above accentuate those aspects of the culture concept that resonate with contemporary accounts of processes of cultural hybridisation, they are also careful to stress the differences. Moreover, many of the other qualities conventionally attributed to the culture concept – its rebuttal of hierarchical orderings of the relations between different cultures and its critique of racial categories – do not withstand scrutiny. Although Boas contested the conception of 'primitive cultures' as having had no history ('even a primitive people has a long history behind it' [1909: 68]) the distinction between primitive and civilized peoples was never entirely jettisoned. As we have seen, it informed Boas's account of the difference between 'modern aesthetic feeling' (2010: 356) and that of the primitive. Perhaps more crucially, however, this relative generosity toward the primitive was not matched by a corresponding assessment of the cultural creativity of contemporary African or Native Americans. These exclusions were constitutive of the culture concept during this period. When Boas wrote about the 'creative genius' of Africans, it was always only with reference to their traditional culture in Africa. He took no account of the consequences of the Middle Passage or the contemporary cultural creativity of African Americans, even though he produced his most important work at the University of Columbia at the time of the Harlem Renaissance (Lamothe 2008; Zumwait 2008). When discussing African Americans his attention focuses on 'the backwardness, inertia, and lack of initiative of the great masses in the South', contrasting this with the 'active life that the same people led before the baneful influence of the whites made itself' as the slave trade separated the Negro from 'the culture that he has developed in his natural surroundings'.[1] While, courtesy of the anthropological fieldworker, the cultures of Native Americans provided a defamiliarising device that highlighted the distinctive qualities of American culture (Hegeman 1999), there was never any sense – in Boas, in Benedict or in Mead – that they might be counted a part of that culture. As Steven Conn (2004) has shown, Boasian anthropology played a key role in detaching Native Americans from the realms of American history and painting and assigning them to a timeless anthropological present that was in America, but not of it.

This bears on the third limitation of the culture concept: its relations to a set of biological race categories that excluded African Americans and Native Americans from the machineries of assimilation that the concept established. This is not to discount the significance of Boas's persistent probing of racial accounts of human difference. 'It has not been possible,' he wrote in 1920, 'to discover in the races of man any kind of fundamental biological differences that would outweigh the influence of culture' (Boas 1920: 35). This was, however, never a matter that he entirely put to rest. Throughout his career, and paralleling his 'fieldwork' among the Kwakiutal, the public school provided Boas with another context for collecting – not, though, stories, myths or languages, but anthropometric data relating to changes in the body types of second, relative to first, generation immigrants (Baker 2010: 137–146). Boas conceived this work as a critical engagement with the problem space of anthropometry: 'we have to consider the investigation of the instability of the body under varying environmental conditions as one of the most fundamental subjects to be considered in an anthropometric study of our population' (Boas 1922: 59). However, while demonstrating the plasticity of bodily types in ways that suggested that immigrants might be just as malleable in their physiognomies as in their ways of life, Boas – and his followers – retained a distinction among 'Caucasoid', 'Mongoloid' and 'Negroid' as biologically differentiated stocks of humanity. Although not organising the relations between them in hierarchical terms, these categorisations led Boas to place the Negro in a different position from the immigrant with regard to processes of assimilation. He interpreted this as not just a cultural process but as a physio-anatomical one that would likely depend on the disappearance of the Negro as a distinct physical type through miscegenation. Arguing that this would lead to a progressive whitening of the black population, he concluded that the continued persistence of 'the pure negro type is practically impossible' (Boas 1909: 330).

The situation with regard to Native Americans was different but scarcely more auspicious. On the one hand, in racial terms, they hardly mattered. The degree of intermarriage between Indians and settlers, Boas argued, had not been sufficient in 'any populous part of the United States to be considered as an important element in our population' (1909: 319). Nicely distanced from the urban centre of metropolitan America, Native Americans were not a part of the mix from which the future of America's population stock or its culture was to be forged. The 'skeleton in the closet' of Boasian anthropology, William Willis has argued, consists in the fact that, when applied across the colour line separating Caucasian from other populations, its lessons regarding the plasticity and conjunctural mutability of inherited cultures was translated into the one-way enculturation of coloured people into white culture. 'The transmission of culture from coloured peoples to white people was largely ignored,' he argued, 'especially when studying North American Indians' (1999: 139). Either that or, in Ruth Benedict's conception, the cultures of the Indian and of white Americans had – after an initial period of interaction – come to face each other as two impermeable wholes, each unable to find any space for the values of the other within its own. 'The Indians of the United States,' as she put it, 'have most of them become simply men without a cultural country. They are unable to locate anything in the white man's way of life which is sufficiently congenial to their old culture' (1974: 1) and were thus located outside the melting pot of an emerging American culture.

My account here draws on the work of Mark Anderson (2013), Kamala Visweswaran (2010) and, more particularly, Matthew Jacobson (1998) who interpret the significance of the culture concept in terms of the role it played, alongside changing conceptions of whiteness, in adjudicating capacities for citizenship against the backdrop of the longer history of American republicanism. Jacobson focuses particularly on the 1924 Johnson-Reed Act as prompting a pivotal revision of the category of whiteness. Whereas whiteness and citizenship were linked in a 1790 Act of Congress according to a 'nativist' concept limiting citizenship to free white persons with rights of residence, the period from 1840 to 1924 witnessed a strategic redefinition of whiteness designed to address the dilemmas of American white nativism faced with new waves of immigration from diverse sources. This produced new racialised divisions within the earlier undifferentiated category of whiteness, disbarring some 'white' groups from the liberal criteria defining fitness for self-government by producing new shades of darkness that differentiated groups like the Poles and the Irish from Anglo-Saxons, the privileged representatives of white nativism. The 1924 Act constituted a new articulation of this tendency in differentiating desirable European migrants (defined as 'Nordic', a wider category than Anglo-Saxon in that it also included German and Scandinavian migrants) from 'Alpines' and 'Mediterraneans' (who had been the main sources of new immigrants since the 1880s, and whose numbers were curtailed by this measure). The logic governing the revision of the category of whiteness after 1924, when the tensions around immigration from southern Europe lessened somewhat as a consequence of the reduction in their numbers, was, Jacobson, argues, 'one in which the civic story of assimilation (the process by which the Irish, Russian Jews, Poles, and Greeks became Americans) is inseparable from the cultural story of racial alchemy (the process by which Celts, Hebrews, Slavs, and Mediterraneans became Caucasians' (1998: 8).

This conception of a project of assimilation organised around a newly homogenised category of the Caucasian defined against the categories of the Mongolian and the Negro provided the political rationality informing the governmental mobilisation of the culture concept. I have argued elsewhere the need to attend to the relations between the processes of 'making culture' and 'changing society', arguing that the cultural disciplines have played a key role in organising distinctive 'working surfaces on the social' through which governmental practices are brought to bear on the conduct of conduct (Bennett 2013). The trajectory of the Boasian culture concept is a case in point. From the late 1920s through the 1930s and into the 1940s, the relations between the aesthetic conception of the pattern of culture, its spatial coordinates, and its malleability came to inform a program in which cultural planners, guided by anthropologists, were to regulate the conditions in which American society would creatively transform itself by absorbing immigrant cultures in an assimilationist logic that focused exclusively on the relations between different periods of European migration. The culture concept was, Anderson argues, integral to 'the larger processes whereby stigmatized European immigrant populations were "whitened" and rendered assimilable into the "American" mainstream' (Anderson 2013: 5). The key reference point for this governmental rationality was that of the 'third generation'. In applying the culture concept to ask what were the uniquely defining characteristics of the American character, Mead argued that Americans establish their ties with one another by finding common points on the road that they are all expected to travel 'after their forebears came from Europe one or two or three generations ago' (Mead 1942: 28). It is a road defined by the forging of new ties and by a dialectic of 'remembrance and purposeful forgetting of European ancestry' and an initial clinging to European ways of life in Little Italies followed by a scattering 'to the suburbs and the small towns, to an "American" way of life' (Mead 1942: 29). It was in this sense, she argued, that 'however many generations we may actually boast of in this country, however real our lack of ties in the old world may be, we are all third generation' (31). Negroes, Native Americans and, in some formulations, Jews were special cases to be dealt with differently.

Anthropology, Willis argued, was the discipline that, in one way or another, made non-white people into different human beings from white people. Whereas this had earlier been done by explicit racist ideologies, the Boasians achieved the same end through the concepts of culture and cultural relativism – sleights of hand, he suggests, which avoided black outrage at white dominance while retaining the status of non-whites as objects to be manipulated in a 'laboratory' setting, be it that of the field, the Indian reserve, or the public school. These were, however, more than just sleights of hand. They constituted, albeit partially and problematically, a displacement of race but also, as John

Dewey (1939) recognised, a displacement of the primacy hitherto accorded individuals in liberal forms of rule as cultures, and the relations between them, came to be conceived as providing the working surfaces on the social through which the relations between the populations constituting a multicultural polity were to be managed. This was, however, a polity with its own constitutive exclusions.

Conclusion

I want, in concluding, to look more closely at the position from which these exclusions were organised, and at the distinctive form of aesthetic ordering they embodied. It will be instructive to go back to Tylor whose ordering, constructed from the vantage point of a generalised European cultural superiority, effected an equally generalised devaluation of the primitive as representing a generalised level of backwardness that was abstracted from any particular national or colonial history: the ordering of cultures was always that of their relative placement on a universal sequence of development. In being cut to the cloth of American assimilationism, the forms of governmental action effected by the culture concept were significantly transformed albeit in ways that also differed from the abstracted forms of relativism and universalism that were attributed to the concept in the founding texts of UNESCO's post-war cultural programmes. For the ordering principles of the 'third generation' were those of a diversity of traits, brought together from diverse sources, that were to be woven into a distinctively American 'cultural pattern' whose political logic arose from a fusion of white nativist and European perspectives into which, once they had shed their differentiating racial characteristic, African Americans and Native Americans would eventually be melded. Benedict articulated this political logic clearly when, in asking why public schools, in arranging assembly programmes 'where the Negro children sing their spirituals and the Balkan children dress in their native costumes and wonder why they don't like it,' she answers:

> In Eastern Europe such programs would be realistic-each group is proud of its traditional customs and they have perpetuated them generation after generation. In America each generation wants to be more and more American. It is the barriers we native born set up against their learning how which hinders them. They have the will to be Americans until we prevent it. Each new generation is ashamed of its hang-overs. Those who are working to promote race relations should take advantage of this if they would, and watch for occasions where the aliens could work shoulder to shoulders with the native born of the ward or the village or the city for better city administration, better schools, better housing-occasions when they would be working as citizens of America and not as a group singled out and labelled for their differences from other citizens.
>
> *(Benedict 1941: 4)*

It is significant in this regard that the most influential interpreters of the culture concept – Boas and his students – shared two characteristics. First, they were either white nativists – like Benedict and Mead – or they were first- or second-generation European migrants, like Boas himself, Sapir and Kroeber. Second, they were all, in their family backgrounds, schooling and early intellectual careers, steeped in European aesthetic traditions – the influence of Kantian conceptions of Bildung on Boas is well-covered territory (Cole 1999) while both Benedict and Mead had backgrounds in literary education prior to their acquaintance with anthropology, particularly Benedict during her years at Vassar College (Banner 2004). It is, however, notable that none of the other participants in the Boasian fieldwork tradition played any significant role in the development of the culture concept. It was not something that George Hunt, Boas's Native American 'informant' at Fort Ruppert, contributed to (Briggs and Bauman 1999). Nor was it an aspect of Boas's work that significantly engaged Zora Neale Hurston. An African American woman who had studied with Boas, Hurston's *Mules and Men* (1986) brought Boasian methods to bear on the collection of African-American folk tales in a significant departure from the black folklore collecting practices that had earlier been developed in association with the 'uplift' programmes of the Hampton Folklore Society. However, her affiliations were much more strongly with the Harlem Renaissance – which also recruited Melville Herskovits's interests (Jackson, 1986) – rather than with the practical applications of anthropology developed by Boas's white American and European students.

If the culture concept did not cross the line separating white nativists and European immigrants from Native Americans, nor did it travel across the colour line. Rather, it was rebutted in favour of a politically inflected early nineteenth-century 'raciocultural' paradigm – most influentially articulated by Hippolyte Taine (Evans 2005) – in which race is interpreted not according to the biological template derived from later evolutionary paradigms but as 'accumulated racial differences carried somehow in the blood' (Visweswaran 2010: 56). It was on the basis of such conceptions, Visweswaran argues, that W.E.B Dubois maintained his distance from the culture concept. Yet Dubois, like Boas, was profoundly influenced by the post-Kantian history of Bildung, albeit interpreting it differently in his concern to harness that 'striving in the souls of black folk' to be co-workers in the 'kingdom of culture' (DuBois 1994: 3, 7) to a theologically inflected political program in which African Americans would take the lead in mobilising the capacity of culture to overcome the schisms of a divided humanity.

There is not space to pursue this line of argument further here. My purpose in ending on this note, however, is to underscore the continuing, unresolved tension between the roles performed by the categories of culture and race in the field of differences.

Acknowledgements

This chapter draws on research conducted as a part of the project *Museum, Field, Metropolis, Colony: Practices of Social Governance* (DP110103776) funded by the Australian Research Council (ARC). I gratefully acknowledge the ARC's support, as I do that of my partners in this project: Fiona Cameron, Nélia Dias, Ben Dibley, Rodney Harrison, Ira Jacknis and Conal McCarthy. I am especially grateful to Ira Jacknis for what I have learned about the history of American anthropology from both his publications and my conversations with him during the course of this project. The chapter draws on other publications from this project, particularly Bennett (2014, 2015), the formulations informing Bennett et al. (2016) and chapter 10 of Bennett (2017). I am also grateful to Meaghan Morris for alerting me to the significance of Zora Neale Hurston's work.

Note

1 Taken from an undated paper in the Boas Papers held by the American Philosophical Society in Philadelphia.

References

Anderson, M. 2013 'Ruth Benedict, Boasian anthropology and the problem of the colour line'. *History and Anthropology*, 25 (3), 395–414.

Baker, L. D. 2010. *Anthropology and the Racial Politics of Culture*. Durham and London: Duke University Press.

Banner, L. W. 2004. *Intertwined Lives: Margaret Mead, Ruth Benedict, and Their Circle*. New York: Vintage Books.

Bashkow, I. 2004. 'A Neo-Boasian conception of cultural boundaries'. *American Anthropologist*, New Series, 106 (3), 443–458.

Benedict, R. 1941. 'Anthropology and some modern alarmists'. Anna Howard Shaw Lecture, no. 5, 10 March. Ruth Fulton Benedict Papers, Vassar College, Folder 58.6.

Benedict, R. 1947. 'The growth of culture'. Unpublished paper, Ruth Fulton Benedict Papers, Vassar College, Folder 54.7.

Benedict, R. 2005 [1934]. *Patterns of Culture*. Boston and New York: Mariner Books.

Bennett, T. 2004. *Pasts beyond Memory: Evolution, Museums, Colonialism*. London and New York: Routledge.

Bennett, T. 2013. *Making Culture, Changing Society*. London and New York: Routledge.

Bennett, T. 2014. 'Liberal government and the practical history of anthropology'. *History and Anthropology*, 25 (2), 150–170.

Bennett, T. 2015. 'Cultural studies and the culture concept'. *Cultural Studies*, 29 (4), 546–568.

Bennett, T. (2017) *Museums, Power, Knowledge*. London: Routledge.

Bennett, T., F. Cameron, N. Dias, B. Dibley, R. Harrison, I. Jacknis and C. McCarthy. 2016. *Collecting, Ordering, Governing: Anthropology, Museums and Liberal Government*. Durham and London: Duke University Press.

Boas, F. 1909. 'Race problems in America'. *Science*, 29 (752), 839–849.

Boas, F. 1920. *Race and Democratic Society*. New York: J.J. Augustin.

Boas, F. 1922. 'Report on an anthropometric investigation of the population of the United States'. *Journal of the American Statistical Association*, 18 (138), 181–209.

Boas, F. 1932. 'The aims of anthropological research'. In Boas, 1982. *Race, Language and Culture*. Chicago and London: University of Chicago Press, 243–259.

Boas, F. 2010 [1927]. *Primitive Art*. New York: Dover Publications.

Briggs, C. and R. Bauman. 1999. '"The foundation of all future researches": Franz Boas, George Hunt, Native American texts, and the construction of modernity'. *American Quarterly*, 51 (3), 479–528.

Bunzl, M. 1996. 'Franz Boas and the Humboldtian Tradition: from *Volksgeist* and *NationalCharakter* to an anthropological concept of culture'. In *Volksgeist as Method and Ethic: Essays on Boasian Anthropology and the German Anthropological Tradition*, edited by G. Stocking Jr. Madison: University of Wisconsin Press.

Cole, D. 1999. *Franz Boas: The Early Years, 1858–1906*. Seattle: University of Washington Press.

Conn, S. 2004. *History's Shadow: Native Americans and Historical Consciousness in the Nineteenth Century*. Chicago and London: University of Chicago Press.

Descola, P. 2013. *Beyond Nature and Culture*. Chicago and London: University of Chicago Press.

Dewey, J. 1939. *Freedom and Culture*. New York: G.P. Putnam's Sons.

Didi-Huberman, G. 2002. 'The surviving image: Amy Warburg's Taylorian anthropology'. *Oxford Art Journal*, 25 (1), 59–70.

Du Bois, W. E. B. 1994 [1903]. *The Souls of Black Folk*. New York: Dover Publications

Eliot, T. S. 1962. *Notes towards the Definition of Culture*. London: Faber and Faber.

Evans, B. 2005. *Before Culture: The Ethnographic Imagination in American Literature. 1865–1920*. Chicago, IL: University of Chicago Press.

Fabian, F. 2000. *Out of Our Minds. Reason and Madness in the Exploration of Central Africa*. Berkeley, Los Angeles, London: University of California Press.

Gilkeson, J. 2010. *Anthropologists and the Discovery of America*. Cambridge: Cambridge University Press.

Handler, R. 2005. *Critics against Culture: Anthropological Observers of Mass Society*. Madison: University of Wisconsin Press.

Hegeman, S. 1999. *Patterns for America: Modernism and the Concept of Culture*. Princeton, NJ: Princeton University Press.

Herskovits, Melville J. 1938. *Acculturation: The Study of Culture Contact*. New York: J.J. Augustin Publisher.

Hoggart, R. 1969. *The Uses of Literacy*. Harmondsworth: Penguin.

Hurston, Z. N. 1986. *Mules and Men*. Bloomington: Indiana University Press.

Jackson, W. 1986. 'Melville Herskovits and the search for Afro-American culture' in George Stocking Jr (ed) *Malinowski, Rivers, Benedict and Others. Essays on Culure and Personality*. Madison: University of Wisconsin Press.

Jacobson, M. F. 1998. *Whiteness of a Different Color: European Immigrants and the Alchemy of Race*. Cambridge, MA: Harvard University Press.

Kroeber, A. L. and C. Kluckhohn. 1952. *Culture: A Critical Review of Concepts and Definitions*. Cambridge, MA: Papers of the Peabody Museum of American Archaeology and Ethnology, Harvard University.

Kuper, A. 2000. *Culture: The Anthropologists' Account*. Cambridge, MA: Harvard University Press.

Kushner, T. 2004. *We Europeans? Mass-Observation, 'Race' and British Identity in the Twentieth Century*. London: Ashgate.

Lamothe, D. 2008. *Inventing the New Negro: Narrative, Culture and Ethnography*. Philadelphia: University of Pennsylvania Press.

Laurière, C. 2008. *Paul Rivet le savant et le politique*. Paris: Muséum national d'Histoire naturelle.

Mandler, P. 2013. *Return from the Natives: How Margaret Mead won the Second World War and Lost the Cold War*. New Haven and London: Yale University Press.

Manganaro, M. 2002. *Culture, 1922: The Emergence of a Concept*. Princeton, NJ: Princeton University Press.

Mead, M. 1942. *And Keep Your Powder Dry: An Anthropologist Looks at America*. New York: William Morrow and Company.

Price, D. H. 2008. *Anthropological Intelligence: The Deployment and Neglect of American Anthropology in the Second World War*. Durham and London: Duke University Press.

Sapir, E. 1924. 'Culture, genuine and spurious'. *American Journal of Sociology*, 29, 401–429.

Stocking, G. W. Jr. 1968. 'Franz Boas and the culture concept in historical perspective'. In *Race, Culture, and Evolution: Essays in the History of Anthropology*, edited by G. Stocking Jr. Chicago: University of Chicago Press.

Tylor, E. B. 1867. 'On traces of the early mental condition of man'. *Notices of the Proceedings at the Meetings of the Royal Institution of Great Britain*, 5, 83–93.

Tylor, E. B. 1871. *Primitive Culture: Researches into the Development of Mythology, Philosophy, Religion, Language, Art and Custom*. London: J. Murray.

UNESCO. 1996. *Our Creative Diversity. Report of the World Commission on Culture and Development*. Paris: UNESCO.

UNESCO. 2005. *Convention on the Protection and Promotion of the Diversity of Cultural Expressions*. Paris: UNESCO.

Visweswaran, K. 2010. *Un/common Cultures: Racism and the Rearticulation of Cultural Difference*. Durham and London: Duke University Press.

Williams, R. 1965. *The Long Revolution*. Harmondsworth: Penguin.

Williams, R. 1976. *Keywords: A Vocabulary of Culture and Society*, London: Fontana/Croom Helm.

Williams, R. 1989 [1958]. 'Culture is ordinary'. In *Resources of Hope: Culture, Democracy, Socialism*, edited by R. Williams. London: Verso.

Willis, W. S. Jr. (1999). 'Skeletons in the anthropological closet'. In *Reinventing Anthropology*, edited by D. Hymes. Ann Arbor: University of Michigan Press.

Worringer, W. 1997 [1908]. *Abstraction and Empathy: A Contribution to the Psychology of Style*. Chicago, IL: Ivan R. Dee. Inc.

Zumwait, R. L. (2008). *Franz Boas and W.E.B. Du Bois at Atlanta University, 1906*. Philadelphia, PA: American Philosophical Society.

Index